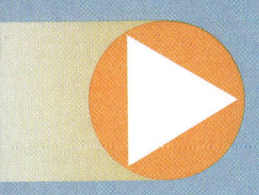

THERAPYED'S

National Occupational Therapy Assistant Certification Exam Review & Study Guide

4th Edition

RITA P. FLEMING-CASTALDY, PhD, OTL, FAOTA
Professor Emeritus
University of Scranton
Scranton, PA

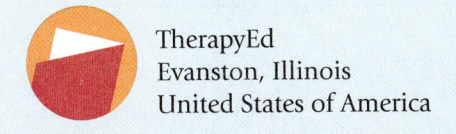

TherapyEd
Evanston, Illinois
United States of America

Copyright © 2020, 2017, 2015, 2010, 2005 by TherapyEd, Ltd.

"TherapyEd" is a service and trademark of TherapyEd, Ltd.

ISBN: 978-1-7338477-2-8

"NBCOT®", COTA®, and "OTR®" are registered service and trademarks of the National Board for Certification in Occupational Therapy, Inc. at each appearance in the text. TherapyEd is not affiliated with the NBCOT®. "AOTA®" is a service and trademark of the American Occupational Therapy Association, Inc. at each appearance in the text.

All marks are registered in the United States of America.

Printed in the United States of America. All rights reserved. No portion of this book or accompanying software may be reproduced, stored in a data base retrieval system or transmitted electronically or in any other way without written permission from the publisher.

The authors and contributors have made a faithful attempt to include relevant summaries of current occupational therapy practice and other information at the time of publication. It is recognized that recommended practices, drug therapies, equipment, devices, governmental regulations, administrative procedures and other protocols and factors may change or be open to other interpretations. Therapists should take responsibility for being aware of technological advances, new information or conclusions available through research, new governmental regulations and/or revised ethical guidelines.

The publisher disclaims any liability or loss incurred as a result of direct or indirect use of this book. Use of this book does not guarantee successful passage of the examination for occupational therapy assistants.

Copies of this book and software may be obtained from:
TherapyEd
500 Davis Street, Suite 512
Evanston, IL 60201
Telephone (847) 328-5361
Fax (847) 328-5049
www.TherapyEd.com

Preface

Purpose of This Text

Currently, all states in the United States (U.S.) and most U.S. jurisdictions (e.g., District of Columbia, Puerto Rico) require a passing grade on the National Board for Certification in Occupational Therapy (NBCOT®) exam for occupational therapy assistants (OTAs) as a qualifying criterion for initial licensure, registration, and/or certification. Thus, to legally practice as an OTA in the U.S., future practitioners must pass the NBCOT®'s COTA® exam. A passing score on the certification exam is required to earn the professional credential of certified occupational therapy assistant (COTA®).

This fourth edition of the TherapyEd *National Occupational Therapy Assistant Certification Exam Review & Study Guide* is designed to assist graduates of accredited occupational therapy assistant (OTA) education programs effectively prepare for the high-stakes NBCOT® examination for COTA®s. This text provides a comprehensive overview of the depth and breadth of current OTA practice according to the field's seminal textbooks, the American Occupational Therapy Association's (AOTA's) Practice Framework, Guide to Occupational Therapy Practice, and Standards of Practice. Since the *Review and Study Guide's* first edition in 2005, many have reported that it has served as an invaluable resource during their academic coursework and clinical affiliations. This text can also be helpful to practitioners who are new to the field, changing practice areas, and/or initiating a new role (e.g., fieldwork supervisor).

The text chapters cover all of the practice domains established by the NBCOT®'s most current exam outline. While the text contributors did not have access to an actual COTA® exam or to specific exam items, all chapter content and the online exams are based on the editor's and authors' critical review of the NBCOT®'s most recent publications and the textbooks that the NBCOT® identifies as foundational to the COTA® exam. Because the COTA® exam items cover the entirety of the OT profession, information that is foundational to entry-level OT practice (i.e., anatomy, theoretical models, OT tools of practice, clinical conditions, and practice standards) is provided. This solid foundation is required to clinically reason through exam items and ensure that you acquire the "knowledge necessary to perform tasks critical for safe and competent practice as an entry-level occupational therapy assistant practicing under U.S. jurisdiction" (NBCOT®, 2018, p. 4). Throughout the text, the relationship of chapter content to the NBCOT®'s COTA® exam is described in boxes labeled "exam hints." The following describes the content of these boxes.

> **EXAM HINT:** Key chapter content is placed into the context of the COTA® exam outline that identifies the domains, tasks, and knowledge that are essential for competent and safe OTA practice. The percentage of COTA®s identified in the NBCOT® practice analysis as providing services to persons with specific diagnoses is also provided to highlight the likelihood that prevalent disorders may be on the NBCOT®'s COTA® exam (NBCOT®, 2018).

Specific methods of evaluation and intervention are provided in chapters organized according to clinical approaches, rather than according to diagnosis. This holistic, integrative approach allows for in-depth coverage while eliminating redundancy and reductionism. It also makes this text compatible with a multitude of OTA curriculum designs. For example, the section on cognitive-perceptual approaches includes evaluation and intervention methods for cognitive-perceptual dysfunction that are relevant to many psychiatric, neurocognitive, and neurological disorders.

Because maintaining client safety is a primary ethical responsibility of OTAs and a fundamental expectation of state regulatory boards (SRBs), the text chapters contain boxes that highlight important safety considerations. These are described as follows.

CAUTION: Intervention precautions, contraindications, and risk factors that can result in potential harm and actions that do not reflect best practice are provided in these boxes.

RED FLAG: Unsafe actions, contraindications, and serious risk factors that are known to cause harm and situations that require an immediate response to ensure a person's safety and well-being are identified in these boxes.

Each chapter in this *Review & Study Guide* is presented in an outline format that is easy to read and provides a helpful guide for organizing your study plan. Upon reviewing each chapter's outline, you will be able to assess your level of comfort with, and mastery of, each content area. The identification of areas of strength and weakness can bolster your confidence and help focus your studying in an efficient and effective manner. The text is not a substitute for primary resources, such as classroom lectures and course textbooks. However, by first using this text, you will not spend time extensively studying information already known. Rather, specific areas in which further knowledge is required will be identified and needed study time can be planned. References for sources that served as the foundation for text content are presented at the end of each chapter.

Strategies for effective exam preparation and successful test-taking and 600 opportunities to practice their use via this text's three online exams are provided. Completion of the simulated exams will help you evaluate your preparedness for your certification exam. Consistent with the COTA® exam format, this text's exam items are designed to test mastery of professional knowledge by asking you to apply this knowledge to practice situations. Guidelines for the effective use of the online exams that accompany this *Review and Study Guide* are discussed at the end of this text. Detailed explanations of answer rationales are provided to help you understand why one answer is considered the best response and the others are incorrect. Your critical analysis of this information can be used to identify content areas requiring further study. The critical reasoning skills used to determine the correct responses to the simulated exam items are also analyzed to provide you with additional information that can guide your successful examination preparation.

References

National Board for Certification in Occupational Therapy (NBCOT®). (2018). Practice analysis of the certified occupational therapy assistant: Executive summary [PDF file]. Retrieved from https://www.nbcot.org/-/media/NBCOT/PDFs/2017-Practice-Analysis-Executive-

Table of Contents

Section I: Introductory Information

Chapter 1: Certification of the Occupational Therapy Assistant 1
Chapter 2: Principles of Effective Examination Preparation 17

Section II: Foundational Knowledge for Occupational Therapy Practice

Chapter 3: The Process of Occupational Therapy 31
Chapter 4: Professional Standards and Responsibilities 63
Chapter 5: Human Development Across the Lifespan: Considerations for Occupational Therapy Practice 115

Section III: Clinical Conditions in Occupational Therapy Practice

Chapter 6: Musculoskeletal System Disorders 157
Chapter 7: Neurological System Disorders 187
Chapter 8: Cardiovascular and Pulmonary System Disorders 223
Chapter 9: Gastrointestinal, Renal-Genitourinary, Endocrine, Immunological, and Integumentary Systems Disorders 257
Chapter 10: Psychiatric and Cognitive Disorders 283

Section IV: Evaluation and Intervention Approaches for Occupational Therapy Practice

Chapter 11: Biomechanical Approaches: Evaluation and Intervention 319

Chapter 12: Neurological and Cognitive-Perceptual Approaches: Evaluation and Intervention 337

Chapter 13: Psychosocial Approaches: Evaluation and Intervention 359

Chapter 14: Evaluation and Intervention for Performance in Areas of Occupation 385

Chapter 15: Mastery of the Environment: Evaluation and Intervention 407

Epilogue

Professional Development After Initial Certification 443

Appendices

Appendix 1: Selected Prefixes and Suffixes 445

Appendix 2: State Occupational Therapy Regulatory Board and State OT Association Contact Information 448

Appendix 3: Review Questions and Answers 458

Guidelines for Effective Use of Online Practice Examinations 489

Examination A Answer Rationales 492

Examination B Answer Rationales 614

Examination C Answer Rationales 736

Index 861

Contributors[1]

Marge E. Moffett Boyd, PhD, OTR/L
Retired, Pearl River, New York
Former Assistant Professor
Coordinator of Graduate Academics and Community/
Dominican College
Orangeburg, New York

Ann Burkhardt, OTD, OTR/L, FAOTA
Professor and Program Director
Occupational Therapy Doctorate Program
College of Health and Wellness
Johnson and Wales University
Providence, Rhode Island

Donna M. Costa, DHS, OTR/L, FAOTA
Program Director and Associate Professor
Occupational Therapy Program
University of Nevada, Las Vegas
Las Vegas, Nevada

Jan G. Garbarini, PhD, OTR/L
Former Program Director, Assistant Professor, and
 Research Coordinator
Occupational Therapy Department
Dominican College
Orangeburg, New York

Christina Gavalas, MS, OTR/L
Occupational Therapist
Northwell Health–Transitions of Long Island
Manhasset, New York

Glen Gillen, EdD, OTR, FAOTA
Professor and Director, Programs in Occupational
 Therapy
Vice Chair, Department of Rehabilitation and
 Regenerative Medicine
Assistant Dean, Vagelos College of Physicians
 and Surgeons
Columbia University Medical Center
New York, New York

Kari Inda, PhD, OTR
Professor and Chairperson
Occupational Therapy Department
Mount Mary University
Milwaukee, Wisconsin

William L. Lambert, MS, OTR/L
Faculty Specialist
Department of Occupational Therapy
The University of Scranton
Scranton, Pennsylvania

Regina M. Lehman, MS, OTR/L
Associate Professor and Program Director
Faculty Co-Director of Assessment and Institutional
 Learning
Occupational Therapy Assistant Program
LaGuardia Community College
Long Island City, New York

---

[1] Contributors to prior editions of this text who provided foundational information for this fourth edition include Josephine Dolera, Linda Kahn-D'Angelo, Colleen McCaul De Riitis, Janice Romeo, Susan C. Robertson, Julie Ann Starr, and Toni Thompson.

Colleen Maher, OTD, OTR/L, CHT
Assistant Professor and Program Director of the Post-
 baccalaureate MOT Program
Department of Occupational Therapy
University of Sciences
Samson College of Health Sciences
Philadelphia, Pennsylvania

Marlene Joy Morgan, EdD, OTR/L
Associate Professor
Department of Occupational Therapy
The University of Scranton
Scranton, Pennsylvania

Rochelle J. Mendonca, PhD, OTR/L
Associate Professor
Department of Rehabilitation Sciences Occupational
 Therapy Program
Temple University
Philadelphia, Pennsylvania

Susan B. O'Sullivan, PT, EdD
Professor Emerita
Department of Physical Therapy
School of Health and Environment
University of Massachusetts Lowell
Lowell, Massachusetts

Todd C. Sander, PT, PhD, SCS, ATC
Associate Professor
Doctoral Program in Physical Therapy
Army-Baylor University
JBSA-Fort Sam Houston, Texas

Thomas Sutlive, PT, PhD
Professor
Doctoral Program in Physical Therapy
Army-Baylor University
Joint Base San Antonio
Fort Sam Houston, Texas

Mackenzie Thompson, MS, OTR/L
Occupational Therapist
New York City Department of Education
Brooklyn, New York

Patricia Wisniewski, MS, OTR/L, CPRP
Faculty Specialist
Department of Occupational and Physical Therapy
The University of Scranton
Scranton, Pennsylvania

Acknowledgments

Organizing the depth and breadth of occupational therapy assistant education and practice into a comprehensive review book and study guide can be a daunting task. The completion of this text and prior editions was greatly aided by the capable assistance of many. I thank Christina Gavalas and Arianna Velcich (former University of Scranton students), for their help in revising this text. Past editions of this text benefited from the excellent production and editorial assistance of Melissa Teresco, Kristin Leccese, Jenna Osborn, and John Patro (former University of Scranton graduate assistants); Allison Blake, Katherine Regimbal, Mariah Vellek, Samantha Zarro, and Stephanie Freije (former University of Scranton work-study employees); Sue Ward (former secretary for TherapyEd); Kathleen Smyth (former personal administrative assistant); and Raymond Siegelman, President of TherapyEd.

1

Certification of the Occupational Therapy Assistant

RITA P. FLEMING-CASTALDY

Chapter Outline

- Credentialing Agencies, 2
- Certification Examination Content and Format, 2
- Certification Examination Procedures, 4
- The Examination Day, 8
- After the Examination, 12
- References, 15

Credentialing Agencies

National Board for Certification in Occupational Therapy (NBCOT®)

1. NBCOT® is currently the only national independent credentialing agency for occupational therapy assistants (OTAs) and occupational therapists.
2. NBCOT® develops and implements all policies related to occupational therapy (OT) professional certification, including the national certification examinations and the certification renewal program.
   a. NBCOT® holds the copyright to the designations Certified Occupational Therapy Assistant (COTA®) and Occupational Therapist, Registered (OTR®).
      (1) Individuals not certified by NBCOT® cannot use these credentials.
   b. NBCOT® certification is not equivalent to state certification, licensure, or registration.
   c. NBCOT® certification is initially granted for three years. Certification must be renewed every three years according to the procedures of the NBCOT® Certification Renewal Program.
3. NBCOT®'s official website (www.nbcot.org) contains all current information about the NBCOT® certification process.
   a. As an independent organization, NBCOT® can change its certification requirements and procedures *at any time*; therefore, this website should be consulted on a regular basis by exam candidates.

State Regulatory Boards (SRBs)

1. SRBs are public bodies created by legislation to define and regulate the qualifications a professional must have to practice within their state.
   a. OTA practice is now regulated by all 50 states and most United States jurisdictions (e.g., District of Columbia, Puerto Rico). See text's Appendix 2 for contact information for each state.
2. State regulation may take the form of certification, registration, or licensure.
   a. Definitions of, and requirements for, state certification, registration, or licensure vary from state to state.
   b. The terms 'certification,' 'registration,' and 'licensure' are often used interchangeably even though they are different types of regulations.
   c. Each state regulation should be carefully reviewed to ensure understanding of its requirements and provisions.

RED FLAG: It is against the law to practice OT without meeting state requirements for certification, registration, or licensure.

3. Currently, all states, the District of Columbia, Puerto Rico, and Guam require a passing grade on the NBCOT® certification exam as one qualifying criterion for initial state licensure, registration, and/or certification.
   a. If you want your NBCOT® certification exam score to be sent to an SRB, you must indicate this on your application and pay a fee in accordance with NBCOT®'s guidelines.
      (1) A passing NBCOT® score does not ensure attainment of licensure.
   b. States vary in the additional criteria they require to attain licensure, registration, and/or certification.
4. Some states grant temporary licenses to individuals eligible to become licensed in their state.
5. SRBs should be contacted directly to obtain their regulations and an application. Most states do not have reciprocal agreements, so one must meet the requirements of every state in which one intends to practice.
6. Some states require OT practitioners who allow their state licensure, registration, or certification to lapse for several years to re-take and pass the NBCOT® exam to renew their state credentials.

Certification Examination Content and Format

Background Information

1. Practice analysis.
   a. To guide the development of items for the exam, the NBCOT® conducts periodic (every 5–7 years) surveys of OT practitioners to "identify the domains, tasks, and knowledge required for occupational therapy practice relative to the respective credential" (NBCOT, 2019a, p. 2).
   b. The analysis of these survey results is used to construct the exam outline, create test specifications, and guide the writing of test items (NBCOT®, 2019a).

c. The exam outline implemented in January 2019 was derived from the outcomes of a practice analysis study completed in 2017 (NBCOT®, 2018).
   (1) This *Review and Study Guide* presents the most current information available at the time of its publication about the COTA® exam content, format, administration, and scoring.
2. Item development.
   a. Exam items are developed by subject matter experts who represent a diversity of practice settings, geographic regions, and demographics, and who have completed an item writing training program.
   b. Items are designed to differentiate the presence of inadequate from adequate entry-level practice knowledge and skills.
   c. All exam items are reviewed for appropriateness in measuring the knowledge and skills needed for entry-level OTA practice according to the exam specifications developed from the practice analysis.
   d. All exam items are also reviewed to ensure that the language, context, terminology, descriptions, and content are unbiased, inoffensive, and appropriate to all population groups.

Examination Content

1. The COTA® exam tests three domains of OTA practice, with each domain comprising a set percentage of the exam. As of January 2019, these domains and percentages are as follows:
   a. "Domain 01 Collaborating and Gathering Information: Assist the OTR® to acquire information regarding factors that influence occupational performance throughout the occupational therapy process: 28%.
   b. Domain 02 Selecting and Implementing Interventions: Implement interventions in accordance with the intervention plan and under the supervision of the OTR® to support client participation in areas of occupation throughout the occupational therapy process: 55%.
   c. Domain 03 Upholding Professional Standards and Responsibilities: Uphold professional standards and responsibilities to promote quality in practice: 17%" (NBCOT®, 2018, p. 18).
2. Specific task and knowledge statements for each domain are provided in the 2018 *Practice Analysis of the Occupational Therapy Assistant: Executive Summary*, which is available on the NBCOT®'s website (NBCOT®, 2018).

3. Exam content reflects language typically used in practice and is not solely based on any practice framework model.
   a. Certain aspects of a given practice framework (e.g., American Occupational Therapy Association's [AOTA's]) may be integrated into exam content if they represent test specifications as determined by an NBCOT® practice analysis.
4. A large item bank is maintained so that each exam will be composed of a unique combination of items drawn from this bank.
   a. Different forms of the exam are offered simultaneously.
   b. Items are selected according to the weightings of exam domains and content areas to ensure each exam contains consistent percentages of each domain and content area.

Examination Format

1. The exam has 200 multiple choice (MC) items, which include single-response MC items and multi-select MC items.
2. All exam items have a stem that contains basic information (e.g., a diagnosis and practice setting) followed by a question or statement that addresses a specific aspect of OT practice (e.g., the best activity to use for intervention).
3. The single-response MC items require you to select *one* correct response from *three or four* answer options.
   a. Some of the single-response MC items are grouped into a scenario in which the item's stem is followed by several related questions (e.g., the most effective intervention goal, the best treatment method, the recommended discharge plan).
      (1) Each of the questions in the MC scenario items are presented in the same format as the 'stand-alone' MC items.

> **EXAM HINT:** Your response to one question in the MC scenario item does not influence the next question in the item.

4. Multi-select items will have *six* answer options after the stem.
   a. You are required to select the *three* best responses from the six choices.

> **EXAM HINT:** No answers in the three- or four-option single-response MC items or the six-option multi-select MC items are provided in a combination format (e.g., "A and C", "all" or "none of the above").

5. Each administered exam contains items that the NBCOT® is field testing for future exams.
   a. The field test items are not considered operational and they are not scored.
   b. The field test items are intermixed with the items that are scored. The scored items have been pre-equated by the NBCOT® and deemed operational.
   c. Field test items that perform well statistically will become part of the operational pre-equated item bank used for future exams.

> **EXAM HINT:** There are no identifying characteristics to distinguish unscored field test items from the scored operational items.

Certification Examination Procedures

Eligibility Requirements for the NBCOT® Certification Examination

1. General requirements.
   a. Information submitted on the application must be accurate and truthful.
   b. Candidates submitting misleading or inaccurate information will be prohibited from taking the certification exam.
   c. Information related to felonies must be provided by all candidates.
   d. The NBCOT® conducts background checks on all exam applicants.
      (1) There is no additional application cost for the background check.

   > **CAUTION:** If after taking the exam it is determined that a candidate was ineligible to take the exam (or that eligibility was questionable), NBCOT® will either hold or void the exam.
   > If a candidate was certified and later found to be ineligible for the exam, certification will be revoked.

   e. The NBCOT®'s Disciplinary Action Committee reviews cases of questionable eligibility to determine if any disciplinary action is warranted and if the candidate will or will not be permitted to take the exam at a future date.
2. Specific requirements.
   a. Must be a graduate of an OT assistant education program accredited by the Accreditation Council for Occupational Therapy Education (ACOTE).
   b. Must have completed all full-time Level II fieldwork requirements of the education program. Optional additional fieldwork affiliations must be completed before a candidate is eligible to take the exam if these affiliations are also needed to fulfil degree requirements.
   c. Completion of the above two criteria must be accomplished on or before specific deadlines as set forth in the NBCOT® *Certification Exam Handbook* (NBCOT®, 2019a).
   d. Candidates not seeking NBCOT® certification may take the exam to meet state regulatory requirements.
      (1) The NBCOT® should be contacted directly to obtain information about licensure only application procedures.
      (2) Applications for state credentialing must be submitted to the SRB, not the NBCOT®.
3. Exam eligibility limit.
   a. There is no limit to the number of times a candidate is eligible to take the exam.
   b. A candidate can continue to take the exam until they successfully pass.
      (1) Candidates who do not pass the certification exam within five years of their graduation date are now required to demonstrate their continued exam eligibility if they graduated during or after 2016.
      (2) These candidates may be required to complete additional coursework to show that they meet the exam standards that are in effect when they apply for their exam.
   c. Candidates should consult the SRB of the state in which they seek to obtain a license to determine the state's standards regarding limits on the number of times and/or the length of time post-graduation the exam can be taken to obtain licensure.

Examination Application Process

1. The NBCOT® *Certification Exam Handbook* contains all required forms for the exam application and provides specific instructions for completion of the application (NBCOT®, 2019a).
   a. The *Exam Handbook* and its application forms are available at www.nbcot.org.
      (1) All information from this website can be printed out.

(2) The exam application can be completed, submitted, and processed online or via post-mail.
      (a) The NBCOT® encourages online applications for this process.
      (b) When completing an online application, be certain to set up only one account because the NBCOT® will charge a fee if a duplicate account is created.
      (c) It is faster and more efficient to check application status online.
2. Application directions and procedures must be adhered to strictly.
   a. Applications that are incomplete, inaccurate, and/or do not follow instructions will be rejected and returned to the applicant.
      (1) If you make any changes or corrections, other than updating contact/address information after your initial application submission, the NBCOT® will charge a fee to process these.
   b. Applications are also returned if there are any problems with the fee payment.
   c. Applications returned to candidates can be resubmitted with the fee payment, but this reapplication will delay examination administration.
   d. Review and proof your application carefully before submitting it.
      (1) If you make any changes or corrections, other than updating contact/address information after your initial application submission, the NBCOT® will charge a fee to process these.
3. Only one application is required. Do not complete both an online and a paper post-mailed application.
4. When completing the application, be sure to use your first and last names as they appear on the two forms of identification that you will bring to the testing center.
   a. The names you provide on your application will be those that will be printed on the letter that will authorize you to take the COTA® exam, so they must match the forms of identification that you will present at the exam administration site; middle names do not count.
      (1) If your name changes after your application has been submitted to the NBCOT® and/or your Authorization to Test (ATT) letter has been generated, you must follow NBCOT® guidelines for processing a name change.
5. After submitting your application and payment, you must have your college or university verify your exam eligibility by directly sending your official final transcript or an Academic Credential Verification Form (ACVF) to the NBCOT®.
   a. This procedure has been in effect for many years, so college registrars are familiar with this requirement.
   b. Do not ask your school to submit your transcript or an ACVF before you have completed your application.
      (1) Transcripts and ACVFs received before an exam application is submitted are destroyed by the NBCOT® 30 days after receipt.
6. Within three days of the NBCOT® approving a completed application, candidates will receive an Authorization to Test (ATT) letter via email from the NBCOT®.
   a. This ATT letter gives the candidate permission to contact Prometric Testing Centers to schedule an exam administration date.
   b. The ATT letter is valid for 90 days.

> **EXAM HINT:** If you realize that your ATT letter will expire before you are able to take your exam, you can submit a request to reissue an ATT letter. If you had scheduled an exam with Prometric, you must cancel this prior to making your request. This ATT reissue request "*must occur while the original ATT letter and exam application are still valid*" (NBCOT 2019a, p. 14).

   c. Carefully review your name as it appears on the ATT letter.
      (1) It must match exactly the forms of identification that you will present on the exam day.
      (2) To correct any errors on the ATT letter, follow the NBCOT® published guidelines.
   d. The ATT letter is required for entry into the test administration area.
7. Applications are valid 90 days.
   a. If an application expires, an exam candidate must submit a new application and pay the full application fee.

Testing Accommodations

1. Candidates with disabilities can receive accommodations that can support their success on the COTA® exam.

> **EXAM HINT:** We strongly urge all eligible students to apply for *any and all* accommodations for which they are eligible.

2. The NBCOT® uses the definition of disability set forth in the Americans with Disabilities Act (ADA) to determine eligibility for TA.
   a. Candidates must have a documented disability, which can include a mental or physical impairment (e.g., learning, cognitive, or psychological

disability; hearing, visual, speech or orthopedic impairment) that substantially limits a major life activity.
3. Exam candidates seeking testing accommodations (TA) should download the *Testing Accommodations Handbook* from the NBCOT® website.
   a. All of the steps outlined for requesting TA in this handbook should be strictly followed (NBCOT®, 2019b).
4. The application for TA must be filled out accurately with all documentation completed according to the instructions.
   a. Incomplete applications or applications with insufficient documentation will not be considered by the NBCOT® and TA will not be made for a candidate.
   b. Documentation completed by a qualified professional must establish a *current* need for TA.
      (1) The submission of a detailed, comprehensive, written report completed and dated *within seven years* of the exam application is required.
      (2) The receipt of accommodations during an OTA education program does not guarantee that accommodations will be provided for the COTA® exam.
      (3) If there is no prior accommodation history in educational and/or testing experiences, the submitted documentation needs to explain why no accommodations were needed in the past and justify why accommodations are needed for the COTA® exam.
      (4) All required documentation must be received by the NBCOT® before the review of TA application can begin.

> **EXAM HINT:** Candidates who have multiple disabilities that warrant TA must submit separate documentation for each disability to support each accommodation that is being requested.

5. Candidates who have medical or health conditions (e.g., diabetes) that may require them to have a snack or water and/or take medicine or restroom breaks should contact the NBCOT® for information about how to obtain TA based on medical necessity.
   a. If a pregnancy results in a medical complication, TA may be considered due to medical necessity; however, these are not automatically granted since pregnancy is not defined as a disability in the ADA.
6. Candidates with temporary conditions that do not meet the ADA definition of disability (e.g., fractures) but who may need TAs (e.g., wheelchair access) should contact NBCOT® for information about how to obtain special testing arrangements.
   a. If a temporary disability warrants TAs after you have an ATT letter and a scheduled exam, you will need to have a new ATT letter re-issued by the NBCOT® and may have to reschedule your exam.
7. English as a second language is not considered a disability; therefore, the use of a dictionary and/or extra time to complete the exam due to language difficulty are not permitted for individuals for whom English is not the primary language.
8. Text anxiety and technophobia are not defined as disabilities in the ADA; consequently, TAs will not be considered for these conditions.
9. TA recommendations made by professionals are considered and reviewed by the NBCOT® but are not automatically granted.
   a. Denials of requests for TA can be appealed according to procedures provided in the *Testing Accommodations Handbook*.
10. The NBCOT® adheres to ADA's guidelines for accommodations.
    a. Table 1-1 lists potential TA which, if approved by the NBCOT®, can be provided by Prometric and identifies several Prometric pre-approved personal items that do not require a request for NBCOT® TAs.
       (1) A complete list of pre-approved personal items is available on the Prometric website.
11. All information about a candidate's disability and request for TA is confidential.
    a. The NBCOT® and its testing agency communicate only with the candidate; the candidate's authorized, verified representative; and/or, with the candidate's permission, a professional knowledgeable about the candidate's disability.
    b. No information about the candidate's application or request for TA is released by the NBCOT® or its testing agency without the written authorization of the candidate.
12. All TAs must be approved by the NBCOT® prior to the exam date.
    a. No requests for TAs will be approved at the test site.
    b. After taking the exam, a candidate cannot retroactively declare a disability.
13. There are no additional fees required to request or receive TAs.
14. The NBCOT® will not issue an ATT letter until after TA decisions have been made.

Examination Administration and Scheduling

1. Test centers.
   a. The Prometric Test Centers are the only locations at which the COTA® exam can be administered.

Table 1-1

Prometric Testing Accommodations (TA) for the COTA® Examination

PRE-APPROVED PERSONAL ITEMS: NO TA REQUIRED	POTENTIALLY AVAILABLE TAS: TA APPLICATION REQUIRED

• Medicine and medical devices
  – Earplugs (foam, no strings or wires)
  – Bandages, braces, casts, arm/shoulder slings, walking boot casts, surgical face masks, and cervical collars
  – Eyeglasses, eye patches, and eye drops
  – Handheld magnifying glass (nonelectric)
  – Glucose monitor and tablets
  – EpiPen or inhaler
• Medical devices attached to body
  – Catheter or colostomy bag
  – Oxygen tank
  – Insulin pump
• Communication aids
  – Hearing aid/cochlear implant
• Mobility devices
  – Cane, crutches, wheelchair, walker
	• Architecturally accessible test centers or alternative site arrangements.
	• Auxiliary aids and services.
	• Extra exam administration time.
	• A quiet, private room.
	• Ergonomic equipment, such as adjustable height tables and ergonomic keyboards.
	• Screen magnifiers and/or anti-glare screens.
	• Other TAs based on documented need.

(1) There are more than thousands of Prometric Test Centers located in more than 160 countries throughout the world.
b. Test center and scheduling information is located at www.prometric.com.
c. Exam scheduling should be completed online by candidates who are not receiving TA.
  (1) Candidates with approved TA must schedule their exam by directly calling Prometric at 1-800-967-1139.
    (a) Not all Prometric sites are able to provide approved TA.

> **EXAM HINT:** Prometric will assign an advocate to assist a candidate with the scheduling and administration of the COTA® exam and ensure approved TAs are implemented.

  d. Any desired change in location must be handled directly by the candidate and the Prometric staff.
2. Administration schedule.
  a. Exams are offered on a continuous, on-demand basis and can be scheduled by a candidate throughout the year.
  b. Exams can be scheduled Monday through Saturday for a morning or afternoon administration.

> **EXAM HINT:** It is wise to try to schedule your exam for the time of day that you are at your best. Do not schedule a morning exam if you are still bleary eyed at 11am or an afternoon exam if you fade after lunch. Respect your natural rhythms. Your COTA® exam administration is *not* the time to ignore your internal clock.

  c. Some Prometric Centers schedule afternoon sessions only after all morning appointments are filled.
    (1) If afternoons are your peak performance time of day, take the time and make the effort to obtain an afternoon exam administration.
  d. The NBCOT® requires exam candidates to schedule their exam at least 48 hours before the selected administration date.
    (1) Because COTA® exam candidates are competing with all other test-takers who use Prometric services, it is best to schedule your exam shortly after you receive your ATT letter to ensure that you are able to obtain your preferred exam date.
    (2) A delay in scheduling an exam administration can result in the need to take the exam at a less-preferred day and/or site.
    (3) Prior exam candidates have advised that Saturday exams can be difficult to schedule so it is best to schedule a Saturday exam a minimum of six weeks in advance; weekday exams can be scheduled two to four weeks in advance.
  e. Candidates who experience a personal or medical emergency that will prevent them from taking a scheduled exam must notify the NBCOT® and request a rescheduled exam in writing.
    (1) Supporting documentation and payment of a fee must accompany this notification and request.

The Examination Day

Pre-Preparation Plans

1. Be prepared physically.
   a. Get a good night's sleep.
   b. Eat a well-balanced high protein meal to sustain you.
   c. Avoid too much caffeine.
   d. Wear clothing that can be comfortable in a warm or cold room and adjusted if the room temperature changes (e.g., a long-sleeve cotton knit shirt with sleeves that you can roll up or down).
      (1) A light sweater or a jacket may be worn into the testing area.
         (a) You can doff or don the sweater or jacket throughout your exam as needed.
      (2) Head coverings worn for religious reasons (e.g., turbans, yarmulkes, scarves) can be worn into the testing area; they must remain in place during the exam.
         (a) Head coverings will be visually inspected before you enter the testing area; any adjustments to a head covering must be made in the waiting area.
         (b) The donning of a jacket or sweater hood to cover one's head is not allowed in the testing area.
         (c) If you must wear a head covering due to a health reason, you must have received pre-approval from the NBCOT® for this accommodation.
      (3) Your exam administration time will not be extended to accommodate for any clothing adjustments made in the waiting area (e.g., adjusting a head scarf) nor for the time needed to check out of and then check back into the testing area.

   CAUTION: Do not wear clothing that can raise unnecessary security concerns (e.g., hoodies, jackets with pockets, and cargo shorts or pants with deep pockets).

   e. Do not wear a watch or any jewelry other than a wedding or engagement ring. If you do wear a watch and/or additional jewelry, you will be required to doff them and place them in your assigned locker.

   CAUTION: It is wise to check with the staff at your Prometric administration site about their current clothing and jewelry requirements and enforcement procedures; these can change at any time due to new security concerns.

   f. Go to the restroom before checking in.

2. Be prepared emotionally.

   EXAM HINT: Remind yourself of past achievements (e.g., completing a rigorous OTA education program) and adopt the attitude that passing the COTA® exam is one more accomplishment to be added to this list.

   a. Plan to arrive earlier than required to eliminate the anxiety of being late.

   CAUTION: If you have never travelled to the test site, do a trial run before your exam date on the same day of the week that you are planning to take the exam. Exam day is not the time to discover that mass transportation or traffic patterns are different from those with which you are familiar.

3. If you are late for your exam or need to cancel or reschedule it, you must follow the procedures and pay the fees that are outlined in the *Certification Exam Handbook* (NBCOT®, 2019a).

Test Center Procedures

1. You should plan to be at the test center up to 5 hours and 15 minutes.
   a. This time frame includes registration, four hours to take the exam, and time to complete two tutorials (if desired), a survey, and other administrative requirements.
2. You *must* arrive 30 minutes before your scheduled exam.
   a. It is best to arrive earlier to allow sufficient time to *calmly* check in.

   RED FLAG: No one is admitted without an ATT letter.

3. Two forms of identification, including two forms of primary identification (valid government-issued photo ID with legal name and signature (e.g., passport, driver's license, green card or permanent resident card, military identification card), or one primary identification and one secondary identification (e.g., credit card, ATM card, employee identification card, voter registration card or letter, or student identification) must be presented at the test center.
   a. Social security cards are not accepted.
   b. Copies of identification are not acceptable.
   c. The first and last names on the identifications you present must match the name on your ATT letter exactly.

d. Both forms of identification must have signatures that match exactly.

> **RED FLAG:** No one is admitted without required identification.

   e. If the identifications you present do not match the name on your ATT letter, you will not be allowed to take the exam and your ATT letter will be voided.
      (1) You will be required to request a new ATT letter and pay a reactivation fee.
   f. No name changes can be made on-site at a Prometric enter; however, on-site address changes can be made.
4. Enhanced security procedures include being scanned with a hand-held metal detector.
   a. A video describing the Prometric check-in process can be accessed at https://www.youtube.com/watch?v=j0UEaKn3W70.
5. Upon check-in, if you applied for and obtained TAs, verify that these TAs are available for you.
6. Only a wet board, marker, and pre-approved personal items are allowed into the test administration area. See Table 1-1.
   a. All personal items will be visually inspected by the Prometric staff.
   b. Adjustments to medical devices must be made in the waiting area.
   c. Headphones and the wet marker board must be obtained from Prometric personnel; you can bring your own earplugs, but they cannot be attached to any wires or strings.
7. Electronic devices (i.e., cell phones, Google glasses, digital/smart watches, and cameras) are not allowed in *any* part of the testing facility.
8. Water and snacks can be stored and accessed in the waiting area.
   a. Some Prometric centers allow small 'comfort' items (e.g., tissues, cough drops) to be brought to the test area. Others do not.
   b. All items are carefully checked.
   c. It is wise to check with the staff at your Prometric administration site about their current procedures for storing and accessing items in the waiting area and allowing 'comfort' items into the test area.
9. A locker is provided to store all other personal possessions (e.g., jacket, wallet, purse, watch, jewelry).
   a. This locker is not accessible until the conclusion of the exam.
10. Food and drink are not allowed in the test area. Food and drink can be consumed in the waiting area.

> **EXAM HINT:** Be judicious about your food and drink consumption prior to the exam and during the exam to decrease the need for bathroom breaks.

11. A brief tutorial on how to use the computer and complete the exam is available prior to commencement of the exam.
    a. Candidates who have not taken an exam preparation course and/or completed practice exams are strongly advised to take this tutorial.
    b. The time spent on the tutorial before the exam does not count toward the 4-hour administration time, so you can use this time to get physically comfortable (e.g., move the computer screen to decrease glare, adjust the chair, take a bathroom break).
    c. You are not allowed to take notes during the tutorial or at any time before you start your exam.

> **EXAM HINT:** Notes can be taken *after* the exam clock has started counting down.

12. The Prometric personnel can also provide an orientation to the exam.
    a. They are available prior to the exam's start to answer questions and clarify the exam procedures.
13. If you are assigned an exam location that is dissatisfying for any reason (i.e., poor lighting, computer screen glare, poor ventilation, unacceptable noise level), request a change to another computer cubicle *before* the exam begins.

> **CAUTION:** You *cannot* change locations once you have begun the exam.

14. The Prometric centers do not dedicate times just for NBCOT® test-takers. Many individuals taking a variety of exams may be coming, going, or receiving orientation during your exam.
    a. Some individuals find the use of earplugs or headphones helpful in decreasing these auditory distractions.
       (1) If you anticipate using earplugs or headphones during your exam administration, you should use these when you complete the online exams that accompany this text.
          (a) These practice sessions can help you determine if the use of earplugs or headphones enhances or hinders your ability to concentrate.
15. There are no scheduled breaks during the exam unless pre-arranged as a TA for a disability or medical necessity.
    a. Restroom breaks are allowed during the exam; however, the exam's clock does keep running.
       (1) At the beginning of a break you will need to check out with the Prometric staff, and after

the break you will need to check in with the Prometric staff.
   (a) This may require waiting while other people check in for their exams.
16. All areas that are accessible to candidates are videotaped, and these tapes are reviewed by Prometric personnel.
17. You are not allowed to talk or read aloud during the exam.
18. If you take a break and are observed using a banned electronic device (e.g., a cell phone, iPad), your exam will be terminated.
   a. The Prometric testing center administrator (TCA) will file a Candidate Proctor Report (CPR) with NBCOT®, which will detail your infraction.
   b. Your eligibility to take a future COTA® exam will be determined by the NBCOT® after a review of the CPR.

Examination Time and Time Keeping

1. Four hours are allowed to complete the exam.
   a. You must personally monitor your time to ensure that you complete the exam within the allotted four hours.
2. Additional time is not provided for any reason other than as a pre-approved TA for a disability.
3. There are no scheduled breaks during the exam.
   a. Restroom breaks are allowed during the exam; however, the exam's clock does keep running unless you received breaks as a TA.

> **EXAM HINT:** It is recommended that you spend an *average* of 45 seconds to complete each three-option single-choice item, 1 minute to complete each four-option single-choice item, and 1 minute 30 seconds to complete each six-option multi-select item. This pace will enable you to complete an average of 50 items in an hour, providing you with a bank of approximately 40 minutes that you can use to review and answer more challenging exam items.

4. A running clock on the computer will indicate the time remaining, and a counter will indicate the number of questions left to answer so you can readily see if you are progressing at the needed pace.
   a. Periodically check the clock and/or counter to be sure that you are on track with your timing.
      (1) Avoid spending too much time checking this clock and counter.
   b. If you are ahead of schedule, take a brief breather and congratulate yourself; then maintain this pace, for you can use this additional time later during the exam to review more challenging questions.
   c. If you are behind schedule, your pace is too slow and you will need to speed up to complete the exam.
   d. Do not belabor difficult questions. Move on to other questions.
5. Some students report feeling listless as the exam progresses, and they have found a brief break re-energized them and enabled them to resume the exam at a revitalized pace.

Test-Taking Strategies

1. Decrease your anxiety level before you begin by taking the tutorial and asking any and all questions.
2. Do not panic. OTA programs are challenging, yet you passed your coursework and fieldwork to get to this point, so you must have done something right! Remember this and give yourself credit.
3. Pace yourself. Use the timing advice provided above.
4. Select the best answer(s).
   a. Think logically and eliminate obviously wrong answers.
   b. Jot down notes on the dry erase board that Prometric staff will provide you upon request.
      (1) Often, visualizing the remaining options of a familiar list (e.g., Allen's Cognitive Levels) will jog one's memory and make it easier to arrive at a correct answer.
   c. Narrow your choices to the best possible answers and use your knowledge of the clinical condition and OT standards of practice to clinically reason and determine the best answer.
   d. Do not read extra information into the question; just consider what is stated in the question.
      (1) Decide what the question is basically about by looking for key words (e.g., initial intervention, discharge).
   e. Avoid thinking "but" and "what if." Often, your first instincts are accurate, so decrease second-guessing.
   f. Do not think about people you know with this condition or practices you have seen in the clinic; think of and apply basic OT principles (i.e., what the book says, not what you saw during fieldwork).
   g. It may help to read the answer choices before you read the exam item scenario and question. Then you will be able to focus your reading of the item scenario and question on issues directly related to the answer choices.
      (1) It may also help to try to answer the question without reading the answer choices. However, Be certain to read *all* answer choices before making your final choice.

h. The answer should be grammatically consistent with the question.
   (1) After you have selected an option, read the question, then your choice. Does it flow? If not, review other options.
   (2) Save this hint for questions you're not sure of. (Who said APA wouldn't come in handy?!)
   (3) If English is your second language, you must remember to 'think' in English when reading and answering questions.
      (a) Noting past versus present tense in an item is particularly important.

> **EXAM HINT:** Use the test-taking strategies provided in Tables 1-2 and 1-3 to develop the skills you need to effectively and correctly answer COTA® exam items.

Table 1-2

General Strategies for Answering COTA® Exam Items

- Read the exam item carefully before selecting a response to the question posed.
- Employ relevant clinical experience.
  - Remember trends and consistent cases in your experience.
  - Do not call on unusual cases or atypical presentations.
- Read the exam item for key words that set a priority (e.g., pain, disorientation).
- Identify the stage of the OT process (e.g., screening, evaluation, initial intervention, discharge) and the practice setting (e.g., acute care, school, skilled nursing facility).
- Correct answers must be consistent with established practice standards for the OT stage and setting.
- Apply clinical reasoning skills to determine the relevance of item information (i.e., diagnosis, stage of the OT process, setting, intervention methods, and theoretical principles). See Chapter 2.
- Use your knowledge of medical terminology to decipher unknown terms by applying the meanings of known prefixes, suffixes, and root words. See Appendix 1.
- Select responses that most closely reflect the fundamental tenets of OT (e.g., ethical actions, the use of meaningful occupations and purposeful activities).
- Choose client-centered, person-directed actions.
- Identify choices that focus on the emotional well-being of the person.
- Use your clinical judgment to support the best answer.
- Check your answer to see if it is:
  - theoretically consistent with the exam item scenario (e.g., the use of a biomechanical approach for a person with a musculoskeletal condition).
  - diagnostically consistent with the exam item scenario (e.g., the recommended interventions for persons with different levels of TBI according to the Rancho Scale).
  - developmentally consistent with the exam item scenario (e.g., the selection of play activities that match a child's cognitive level according to Piaget).
- Eliminate choices that contain contraindications, as these must be incorrect.
- Consider eliminating options that state "always," "never," "all," or "only," as there are few absolutes in OT practice.
- Eliminate unsafe options.
- Choose answers that reflect entry-level COTA® practice.
- Remember the COTA® exam is not a specialty certification exam.

Table 1-3

Specific Strategies for Answering Multiple Choice Exam Items

- Identify the theme of the item. Ask yourself, "What is the question posed *really* asking?"
- Avoid 'reading into' the item. Read the question asked and nothing but the question.
- Identify choices that seem similar or equally plausible.
  - If two choices basically say the same thing or use synonyms in their answers, both cannot be right; therefore, both can be eliminated.
- Carefully consider choices that are opposites of one another. If you cannot eliminate both opposites right away, one may be the correct answer.
- Determine the best answer using strategies identified in Table 1-1.
  - For the three- or four-option single-response MC items, you must choose the option that is *most* correct.
  - For the six-option multi-select MC items, *three* answers will be correct.
- Select positive, active choices rather than passive, negative ones.
- Before changing an answer, make sure that you have a good reason to eliminate your original choice and a good reason to make your new choice.
  - Good reasons include realizing that you misunderstood the item's theme (e.g., discharge), missed a key word (e.g., screening) in the exam item, and/or you gained a clue from a subsequent exam item (e.g., SCI levels).
- Do not let second-guessing talk you out of the correct answer.

Completion of the Examination

1. Answers can be recorded by using keystrokes or the mouse.
2. Do not skip any exam item.
   a. Although every item is not scored, there is no way to know which items are operational; therefore, you must answer all exam items to the best of your abilities using the strategies described above and in Tables 1-2 and 1-3.
3. If you are uncertain of an answer, mark the question by using the mark/unmark button.
   a. You can return to a marked item to review and change the answer (if desired) at any time *before* you end your exam.
4. Change the answer only if you have a good reason.

> **EXAM HINT:** Solid reasons for changing an answer include the following.
> - You missed an important key word like "pain," "disorientation," "initial," or "best."
> - Your original answer was not consistent with the stage of the OT process (e.g., screening, evaluation, intervention, discharge).
> - You obtained a solid hint from a subsequent exam item (e.g., TBI levels).
>
> Before you change your answer, you should feel as if a brilliant lightbulb has been turned on in your brain to illuminate the correct answer. If you do not experience a 'lightbulb' moment, *do not* change your answer.

5. If you remain unsure of an answer, make a logical guess based on the test-taking strategies outlined in Tables 1-2 and 1-3. Because there is no penalty for an incorrect answer, it is worth guessing; you may guess correctly and add to your exam score.
6. Do not communicate with anyone other than Prometric personnel while completing the exam.
    a. An innocent passing remark to another person can be mistaken for an attempt to cheat.
7. Keep your eyes on your own computer screen and do not look at other screens if you take a break.
    a. A fleeting glance at another computer screen can be interpreted as an attempt to cheat.
8. Do not panic if you are stumped by some exam item questions.
    a. Focus on what you know, because it is likely you know a lot.
    b. We often tend to remember our 'failures' and not our 'successes.' Be kind to yourself.
9. If you are running out of time and have not completed the exam, pick a letter (i.e., A, B, or C) and mark all remaining answers in the three- and four-option single-response MC items using that one letter choice.
    a. Laws of probability will enable you to get some right.
    b. After clicking on your chosen letter for all remaining items, use the time you have left to calmly and thoughtfully revisit your answers to determine if your selected answer was correct or not.
    (1) If you determine that your answer was incorrect, use all of the strategies identified in this chapter to determine the best answer and change your response.
    (2) If you determine that your answer was correct, say a silent "YES!" to yourself and continue your review of these items until your exam administration time runs out.

> **EXAM HINT:** There is no penalty for incorrect answers, so it does not make sense to leave any answer blank. If you narrow your answer choices in the single-response three- or four-option MC items between two items, you have a 50% change of choosing the correct answer; if you have three options, you have a 33% change of choosing the correct answer. These are better odds than a zero chance, which will occur if you do not answer these items.

10. Once you have exited the exam you cannot return to it.
    a. You are able to review the entire exam and make changes prior to exiting the exam.
    (1) Again, only change an answer if there is a strong 'lightbulb' reason to do so.
11. Congratulate yourself for what you knew and for making educated guesses on what you did not know. Remember, you do not need to answer 100%, 90%, or even 80% of the questions correctly in order to pass the exam.

After the Examination

Examination Administration Complaints

1. Only complaints regarding an administrative or technical problem with the exam are accepted (e.g., the computer screen freezes).
    a. The Prometric centers are in the business of providing optimal environments for test taking, so administrative and technical problems are rare.
    b. Time spent to remedy a technical malfunction will not count against your exam time.
    c. If a technical problem cannot be resolved within 30 minutes, you have the right to reschedule the exam for another day within your eligible time period (NBCOT®, 2019a).
2. If you do experience a problem, *immediately* after you complete your exam file an on-site complaint with the Prometric staff.
    a. Be very specific about the nature of your complaint, the rationale for the complaint, and any actions that were taken to try to deal with the complaint on-site.
    b. Request a customer care card for your complaint.
    (1) Depending on the nature of your complaint you may or may not be given a 'ticket number.'
    c. You must email the NBCOT® *within 24 hours* to provide them with a summary of your complaint and its assigned number, if applicable.
    d. You must follow-up with Prometric *within 24 hours* of the incident.

> **CAUTION:** Be certain to adhere to the complaint guidelines in the NBCOT® *Certification Exam Handbook*. There are no exceptions.

  e. Complaints are investigated by the NBCOT® and the testing agency, and written responses are sent to the candidate within 21 days of the complaint

Examination Scoring and Reporting

1. Item analysis.
   a. All exams use items that have been analyzed as performing well on previous exams.
   b. All scored items are pre-equated and determined to have sound statistical attributes.
2. Equating.
   a. The passing score for each exam is statistically adjusted to compensate for differences in the difficulty level of each exam.
   b. This equating aims to ensure that candidates with equivalent abilities will be equally likely to pass the exam.
   c. From the NBCOT®'s and their testing agency's points of view, all examination candidates have a fair and equal chance to pass the exam, regardless of the administration date.
3. Scoring processes.
   a. Only the pre-equated operational items are scored.
      (1) The pre-operational items that are being field tested are not scored.
   b. For the three- and four-option single-response MC items, a score is awarded for the selection of a correct response.
      (1) *No score* is deducted if an incorrect answer is chosen or if the answer is left blank.
   c. For the six-option multi-select MC items, a score is awarded *only* when all *three* correct responses are chosen.
      (1) There is no partial score awarded for the selection of one or two of the three correct options.
   d. Statistical procedures convert candidates' raw scores (number of correct items) into 'scaled scores,' which are then comparable for all exams based upon the equating process.
   e. The exam results are reported on a scale from 300 to 600 points.
   f. A scaled score of at least 450 is needed to pass the exam.
   g. This passing score of 450 remains the same for all exam administration dates. There are no adjustments made after the score is determined by the equating process.
4. Scoring schedule and score reporting.
   a. Several steps are followed by the testing agency to produce accurate exam reports in as timely a manner as possible.
      (1) Early score results are not given.
   b. Exams are scored several times a month.
      (1) The exam scoring schedule is posted on the NBCOT® website at www.nbcot.org.
      (2) Exam candidates can access their score report online by logging into their NBCOT® account.
         (a) Candidates must use their username and password to access this score information.
      (3) Candidates who submitted a transcript with their application can typically obtain an unofficial pass/fail score on the next business day after their exam was scored.
      (4) Candidates who submitted an ACVF with their application cannot obtain their unofficial pass/fail score until an official final transcript is received by the NBCOT®.
   c. Official score reports are mailed within four to six weeks of the exam administration date.
      (1) If a score report is not received after four weeks of taking the exam, you should contact the NBCOT®.
   d. Candidates who pass the exam receive a letter of congratulations, a report with their total score, and a wallet card designating their certification status.
   e. Candidates who fail the exam receive a report of their total score and information on their performance on each exam domain.
      (1) This score report also identifies the regulatory agencies the NBCOT® has informed about the failing score.
   f. Score reports are only provided to exam candidates or their legally verified representative.
   g. Score reports can be provided to SRBs and other regulatory agencies upon the written authorization of the exam candidate.
   h. Aggregate score reports are provided to the program directors of OT education programs for candidates who are graduates of their programs.

Waiting For and Receiving Examination Results

1. Accept that the exam is done, and move on to other enjoyable activities.
2. Focus on your successes. Congratulate yourself on questions you answered confidently.
3. Avoid focusing on exam difficulties. The exam was not solely about the two obscure diagnoses that you could not recall. Remember, not all items are scored.

Of the items that were scored, many were likely about content that you knew well.
4. Surround yourself with your 'fan club,' people who assure you of your competencies.

> **CAUTION:** Avoid and ignore individuals who continually question the exam's fairness and perseverate about their ability to pass. The COTA® exam may be challenging but it is constructed and graded fairly.

5. Ignore rumors about the exam's pass rate.
   a. No one knows this information until it is published by the NBCOT®.
   b. OTA educational programs do not receive this information before the students do.
   c. OTA educational programs do not receive information identifying the names of students who do not pass the exam.
6. If you passed, congratulate yourself and begin your lifelong pursuit of a rewarding career in occupational therapy.
7. If you did not pass, do not denigrate yourself; rather, make a plan to retake the exam and succeed.

Implications of Not Passing the Examination

1. The implications of not passing the exam vary from state to state. You must follow your SRB's procedures for notification of exam failure.
2. If you are currently employed as an OTA or you have specific plans to begin employment, you must notify your employer immediately.
3. Depending on the state, you may be able to continue employment under an extension of a temporary license or have your position reconfigured as a rehabilitation aide/associate, with a corresponding decrease in responsibility and salary.

Retaking the Examination

1. A new and complete application must be submitted to retake the exam.
2. The NBCOT® requires a waiting period after a failed exam administration date before you can take the exam again. Use this time to:
   a. Obtain support to handle your legitimate disappointment.
   b. Review exam results to identify and analyze areas of strength and weakness; do not agonize over exact percentages in your score report.
   c. Reflect on your exam experience to identify behaviors that may have hindered success. Common mistakes include:
      (1) Taking too much time to answer difficult questions.
      (2) Becoming anxious or upset over a question that seemed to have no good answer (or two good answers).
      (3) Becoming distracted by other test takers.
      (4) Arriving in a rushed, harried manner.
      (5) Not seeking and obtaining TAs when qualified to receive these as a candidate with a disability.
3. Be realistic about the obstacles you can change and those you cannot. For example, if you were stressed due to a traffic jam, you can leave earlier or stay in a nearby hotel the night before your exam. On the other hand, you cannot change the fact that the test is on a computer even though you dislike this format.
4. Increase your comfort level with taking a computerized exam by using this text's exams.
   a. The text's online exams can be interrupted, returned to, and used repeatedly.
5. If you had received TAs for your previous exam, you need to notify the NBCOT® via accommodations@nbcot.org that you are requesting these accommodations again for your next exam.
6. If you are eligible for reasonable accommodations but did not previously request them, follow the NBCOT®'s guidelines and adhere to the deadline dates to attain needed TA.
   a. Since the COTA® exam requires four hours of computer work, carefully and realistically assess your cognitive, physical, and psychosocial abilities to complete this task and any limitations that may warrant TAs.
7. Develop a plan of action to ensure success.
   a. Review this text's Chapter 2 on exam preparation and critically evaluate what you did to prepare for your first exam.
   b. Take (or re-take) an exam preparatory course.
      (1) TherapyEd offers free re-takes of its two-day exam preparation course. Your first-hand exam experience can help you identify your test-taking strengths and weaknesses, make the strategies taught in the course for selecting the best answer more applicable, and make managing stress and time even more relevant.

> **CAUTION:** Do not rush to re-take the exam, for this may not allow you sufficient time to adequately prepare for the exam. It is better to delay the exam than rush your preparation and risk being underprepared.

8. Adopt the perspective that your first experience with the exam can be viewed positively, in that you can re-take the exam with a clear idea of what the experience is like.
   a. You are aware of your strong and weak points; therefore, your chances of passing the re-take are greater.
9. Recognize that there are many skilled and competent OTAs who did not pass the certification exam on their first (or even their second) attempt.
   a. You can join their ranks by honestly self-assessing your exam preparedness and taking concrete steps to remediate your difficulties and build upon your strengths.
   b. Being able to practice occupational therapy is well worth the effort.

References

Fleming-Castaldy, R. (2019). *Occupational therapy assistant course manual*. 4th ed. Evanston, IL: TherapyED.

Killen, E. (2017). Preparing to take the NBCOT exam. *OT Practice, 22*(11), 24–25.

National Board for Certification in Occupational Therapy (NBCOT®). (2019a). *Certification exam handbook* [PDF file]. Gaithersburg, MD: Author. Retrieved from https://www.nbcot.org/-/media/NBCOT/PDFs/Cert_Exam_Handbook.ashx

National Board for Certification in Occupational Therapy (NBCOT®). (2019b). *Testing accommodations handbook*. Gaithersburg, MD: NBCOT®.

National Board for Certification in Occupational Therapy (NBCOT®). (2018). *Practice analysis of the certified occupational therapy assistant: Executive summary* [PDF file]. Retrieved from https://www.nbcot.org/-/media/NBCOT/PDFs/2017-Practice-Analysis-Executive-COTA.ashx?la=en

Sides, M., & Korcheck, N. (Eds.). (1998). *Successful test-taking: Learning strategies for nurses*. Philadelphia: Lippincott.

2

Principles of Effective Examination Preparation

RITA P. FLEMING-CASTALDY AND KARI INDA

Chapter Outline

- Effective Examination Preparation, 18
- Critical Reasoning and NBCOT® Exam Performance, 23
- References, 29

Effective Examination Preparation

Overview and General Guidelines

1. The National Board for Certification in Occupational Therapy (NBCOT®) exam tests general knowledge and fundamentals of occupational therapy (OT) in an integrated manner.
   a. There are four main levels of objective exam questions.
      (1) Table 2-1 describes each question level and its relevance to the COTA® exam and provides related exam preparation strategies.

2. This chapter provides comprehensive information about effective exam preparation strategies, including an extensive discussion about the relationship between critical reasoning and COTA® exam performance.

> **EXAM HINT:** The effective application of clinical and critical reasoning skills is needed to correctly answer COTA® exam items. Using the information provided in Table 2-2 about the major types of clinical reasoning and their application to the COTA® exam can facilitate exam success.

Table 2-1

Levels of Exam Questions

QUESTION LEVEL AND DESCRIPTION	RELEVANCE TO COTA® EXAM	COTA® EXAM PREPARATION STRATEGY
1. Knowledge Recall of basic information. For example, DSM diagnoses, spinal cord levels, wheelchair measurements.	A solid knowledge foundation of *all* information related to entry-level OTA practice is required to answer COTA® exam items. It is likely that very few items on the OTA exam will be solely at this level.	A strong commitment to studying is needed to remember all the information acquired during your OTA education. Fortunately, this text provides extensive information in an outline format to ease your review. Memorization of this information is required to be able to readily recall it during the 200 multiple choice (MC) items on the OTA exam.
2. Comprehension Understanding of information to determine significance, consequences, or implications. For example, the impact of a tenodesis grasp on function.	The COTA® exam is not a matching column type of test; therefore, you cannot just recall information on the OTA exam. You must fully understand the content area to be able to understand the nuances of an exam item. All items will require comprehension, but only some will be solely at this level.	When studying the text to review basic content and acquire your foundational knowledge, ask yourself how and why this fundamental information is important. Studying with a peer or a study group can provide you with additional insights about the relevance, significance, consequences, and implications of the information. Do not enter the exam without strong comprehension of all major areas of OT practice.
3. Application Use of information and application of rules, procedures, or theories to new situations. For example, the classroom modifications that a therapist would make for a child with autism.	The COTA® exam requires you to use your knowledge and comprehension as described above, along with the competencies you developed during your clinical fieldwork, in a manner that best fits the specific practice scenario in an exam item. Many OTA exam items will likely be at this level, for a main goal of the COTA® exam is to assess your ability to respond competently to different situations.	Once you have acquired a solid knowledge base and good comprehension skills in all domains of OT as put forth in this text, you should take the computer-based simulated practice exams that accompany this text. These exams require you to apply your knowledge in a manner similar to the COTA® exam. Upon completion of these exams, you receive an analysis of your performance so that you can determine how well you are applying your knowledge.
4. Analysis Recognition of interrelationships between principles and interpretation or evaluation of data presented. For example, the most appropriate focus for discharge planning sessions for a parent with a traumatic brain injury.	The COTA® exam assumes that you have mastered and comprehended entry-level knowledge and that you can competently apply this information to diverse situations; therefore it may ask you to analyze and respond to ambiguous, not 'straight from the book' situations. Many OTA exam items are at this level, for the main objective of the exam is to determine your ability to be competent in complex practice situations.	Use the analyses of the text's practice exams to reflect on your reasoning mistakes. Critically review the extensive rationales provided in the text for the correct exam answers. Reflecting with a peer or study group can be helpful in determining your gaps in analysis of exam items. Review the text's section on critical reasoning skills and reflect on the questions provided in Table 2-5 to ascertain the actions you need to take to adequately prepare for the complexities of the COTA® exam.

Table 2-2

Clinical Reasoning Applied to COTA® Exam Items

TYPE OF REASONING	QUESTIONS TO CONSIDER	RELATIONSHIP TO EXAM SUCCESS
Procedural Reasoning Requires the systematic gathering and interpreting of data to identify problems, set goals, plan intervention, and implement treatment strategies. It is the 'doing' of practice.	What does the exam item tell/ask you about: Diagnosis? Symptoms? Prognosis? Assessment methods? Treatment protocols? Theories/practice frameworks to support procedures?	Correct answers on the COTA® exam will be consistent with the published evaluation standards and intervention protocols for a given clinical condition and congruent with established theories and relevant practice frameworks.
Interactive Reasoning Focuses on the client as a person and involves the therapeutic relationship between the practitioner, the individual, caregivers, and significant others.	What does the exam item tell/ask you about: Rapport building? Family/caregiver involvement? Therapeutic use of self? Teaching/learning styles? Successful collaboration?	Correct answers on the COTA® exam will have the OTA engaging with the person, family, caregivers, and others in an empathetic, caring, respectful, collaborative, and empowering manner.
Pragmatic Reasoning Considers the context(s) of service delivery including the person's situation and the practice environment to identify the real possibilities for a person in a given setting.	What does the exam item tell/ask you about: Person's client factors? Practice setting characteristics? Reimbursement issues? Legal parameters? Referral options?	Correct answers on the COTA® exam will be realistic given the person's assets and limitations, their environmental supports and barriers, and the practice setting's inherent opportunities and constraints.
Conditional Reasoning Represents an integration of procedural, interactive, and pragmatic reasoning in the context of the client's narrative.[1] Focuses on past, current and possible future social contexts.	What does the exam item tell/ask you about: The individual's unique roles, values, goals? Impact of illness on this person's function? How will the condition's course influence the person's future? Where the person will be able to live after discharge?	Correct answers on the COTA® exam will take into account all case information that is provided in the item scenario. COTA® exam items do not include extraneous details so carefully reflect on the relevance of the information provided in each item scenario to determine the best answer.

Reference: Fleming-Castaldy, R. (2010, November 8). The NBCOT® examination: Strategies for success. *OT Practice*. 7–10.

Note: [1]The application of narrative reasoning is not likely required during the NBCOT® exam since this type of reasoning deals with the individual's occupational story and uses critical imagination to help the person reach an imagined future. This important process is not readily measured by objective exam questions.

Psychological Outlook

1. When preparing for a professional certification exam, your psychological outlook is a critical aspect of effective exam preparation. See Table 2-3.
   a. Fears, doubts, and negative attitudes must be replaced with a positive 'I can' attitude.
      (1) Remember that to be eligible for the COTA® exam, you had to pass a rigorous occupational therapy assistant (OTA) education program and challenging fieldwork; thus, your academic and clinical educators have asserted that you possess the knowledge and skills needed for entry-level OTA practice by passing you.
   b. Because developing a positive attitude can be difficult to do alone, surround yourself with your 'fan club', people who know that you will be a terrific Certified Occupational Therapy Assistant (COTA®).
   c. Practice techniques to reduce anxiety during the exam while preparing for the exam.
      (1) Techniques of visual imagery, muscle relaxation, controlled diaphragmatic breathing, cognitive-behavioral strategies, meditation, positive self-talk, and/or exercise can be just as beneficial for you as the individuals with whom you will be working.
2. Keep your 'eye on the prize.'
   a. Write down two reasons why you want to be a COTA®.
      (1) Keep these statements where you will read them every day so that they help you to stay motivated.
   b. Write down two reasons why you *will* pass the exam. For instance, "I will pass the certification exam because I have developed a clear study plan

Table 2-3

Psychology of Successful Test Taking

CONCEPT	PRINCIPLE	ACTIONS
Control	Only you can determine your future.	• Take charge; determine exactly what is needed to succeed. • Set goals to meet these needs. • Develop and implement concrete plans to succeed.
Self-awareness	Knowing one's innate capabilities enables one to build on strengths and effectively deal with limitations.	• Critically analyze test-taking errors and content knowledge gaps. • Be honest about your test-taking and content knowledge, strengths and limitations. • Avoid self-defeatist behaviors.
Self-confidence	Your past accomplishments provide a solid foundation for future success.	• Review exam content prior to completing practice exams. • Use a diversity of learning methods to achieve mastery. • Recognize and celebrate your successes and achievements.
Self-fulfilling prophecy	Your self-expectations will influence the outcomes of your efforts.	• Expect success. • Use positive self-talk throughout exam preparation. • Continue to think positively during the exam administration.
Self-esteem	You are a person capable of excellence.	• Remember your personal and academic achievements. • OT academic course work and fieldwork are demanding; give yourself well-earned credit for your success.
Motivation	Your desire to succeed and a fear of failure can be channeled for success.	• Understand that the early stages of studying will have uncertain results. • Remind yourself of what initially motivated you to enter OT school. • Harness fear and establish a doable study plan.
Courage	Taking responsibility for one's failures is key to success.	• Honestly critique precipitators/reasons for an exam failure. • Do not make excuses. • Do not strive for perfection.
Perseverance	You can only succeed if you persevere.	• Re-establish goals. • Seek support for goal attainment. • Utilize multiple resources to stay on track.
Freedom	You can freely choose your attitude.	• View test taking as an opportunity. • Keep your 'eye on the prize'. • Exam success equates to achievement of your goal to become an OT practitioner.

Reference: Sides, M. (1998). Forming the psychology of test-taking success. In M. Sides and N. Korcheck. (Eds). *Successful test-taking: Learning strategies for nurses* (pp. 49–61). Philadelphia: Lippincott.

and will implement it." "I passed the hardest class in the world with the most difficult teacher ever."

3. If you have previously failed the exam, honestly critique what did not work for you in preparing for and taking this previous exam (e.g., did you not practice taking a complete exam during an uninterrupted four-hour period; did you ignore studying professional standards and responsibilities because you found your management class boring?).
   a. Develop and implement remediation strategies to effectively deal with these difficulties.
   b. Maintain a positive attitude, but be careful, and do not accept false reassurance from others.

Structuring a Review of Professional Education

1. Establish your knowledge and skill level.
   a. The COTA® exam tests general knowledge and fundamentals of OT in an integrated manner. See Chapter 3 for a review of the profession's tools of practice.
      (1) Your clinical reasoning skills and critical thinking skills will be vital to use because the COTA® exam emphasizes the application of knowledge.
         (a) Table 2-2 outlines the application of clinical reasoning to COTA® exam items.
   b. Critique your knowledge of the three NBCOT® OTA exam domains to identify your areas of strength and weakness to create a personal study plan. These domains are listed in Chapter 1.
   c. Review your academic history to clarify strengths and weaknesses. Honestly appraise which course topics you mastered and those with which you struggled.
   d. As you proceed through the chapters in this text, rate your knowledge of key content according to a scale of these categories: know very well, know adequately, know very little, know nothing.
      (1) Based on this critical self-assessment, make a personal "OT Knowledge Continuum" for yourself, listing topics from strongest to weakest.

(a) Your aim is to enter the exam with solid knowledge in all critical content areas.
2. Develop and implement an individualized study plan.
   a. Content areas that are rated as 'know nothing' or 'know very little' will become your 'Must Study' list.
   b. Content areas that are rated as 'know very well' or 'know adequately' will become your 'Review' list.
   c. Organize both your 'Must Study' list and 'Review' list into a logical schedule.
      (1) For example, if you are weak in your knowledge about biomechanical evaluation and intervention approaches, but have a good recall of clinical conditions, review the chapter on musculoskeletal conditions and then study the biomechanical chapter.
         (a) Studying these two chapters together will provide an integrative learning experience since diagnoses will be included in exam items testing your knowledge about evaluation and intervention approaches.
   d. Allocate study time according to your knowledge continuum, 'Must Study' list, and 'Review' list; begin with your weakest area first.
      (1) After you master a weak content area, reward yourself by reviewing a content area of strength.
      (2) Continue studying to progress along your knowledge continuum, alternating between your 'Must Study' list and 'Review' list. This will help prevent exam preparation fatigue and burnout.
   e. Plan to spend more time studying areas that compose a greater percent of the exam content, especially if these areas are on the low end of your 'OT Knowledge Continuum' and on your 'Must Study' list.
   f. Allow yourself sufficient time to study over a period of time, and set aside enough time to master your weakest areas and to review all areas in general.
      (1) Be realistic about your inherent capabilities (e.g., being a poor memorizer) and your external constraints (e.g., being a single parent who must rely on childcare) when planning the amount of study time needed to ensure success.

   > **CAUTION:** Studying in cram sessions can increase anxiety, result in knowledge gaps, and contribute to burnout.

   g. Critically assess the study habits you used throughout your OTA education to identify routines that worked most effectively for you.
   h. Establish a study schedule and routine and adhere to it strictly.
      (1) Study one major content area per study session.
      (2) Limit interruptions.
         (a) Turn your cell phone *OFF* so that you are not distracted by phone calls, text messages, e-mails, tweets, etc. (if needed, lock your cell phone in your car's glove compartment).
         (b) *Do NOT* study by a computer; the latest Facebook post, TravelZoo ad, and/or Pinterest post will be far more interesting than supervisory guidelines.
         (c) If you are a parent and/or caregiver, arrange for child, home health, and/or respite care.
      (3) If an unexpected event results in a loss of planned study time, immediately schedule time to make up for this loss.
3. *Do NOT* take the online practice exams that accompany this text until after you have implemented your study plan and gained mastery of your 'Must Study' list.
   a. Completing a practice exam *before* you have attained mastery of essential content will only reinforce that you have key gaps in your foundational knowledge.
      (1) This can diminish confidence, lower self-esteem, and make the prospect of studying more overwhelming.
   b. Completing a practice exam *after* the implementation of your study plan will provide you the opportunity to demonstrate your acquired knowledge.
      (1) This can increase confidence, boost self-esteem, and enable your subsequent studying to be more targeted on areas that you had initially not focused on in depth.
4. Complete the first online practice exam that accompanies this text using the test-taking strategies provided in Chapter 1.
   a. Reflect on the analysis of your exam performance that will be provided after you complete the exam.
      (1) This analysis will provide information about your content knowledge strengths and gaps and your critical reasoning abilities. Both are important for exam success.
      (2) You can use this analysis for ongoing review.
   b. Revise your study plan based on this analysis of your exam performance.
      (1) Implement this revised study plan to address identified content knowledge gaps.
   c. Review the analysis of your critical reasoning skills. This chapter provides in-depth information about the relevance and application of critical reasoning for exam success.
5. Complete the second online practice exam that accompanies. this text using the test-taking strategies provided in Chapter 1 that can most effectively address the errors you made on your first practice exam.
   a. Reflect on the analysis of your second exam performance that will be provided after you complete the exam and update your study plan to address remaining content knowledge gaps.
6. Repeat this process for the third online practice exam that accompanies this text.

Table 2-4

Personalities of Test Takers

PERSONALITY TYPE	CHARACTERISTICS	STRATEGIES
The Rusher	• Impatient. • Jumps to conclusions. • Skips key words. • Inadequate consideration of exam items.	• Take practice exams in a timed manner to establish a non-desperate pace and help realize that the time allotted for the exam is sufficient. • Use positive self-talk and relaxation techniques during exam. • Employ the strategies provided in Tables 1-2 and 1-3 in Chapter 1 to slow your pace and not make the errors that are endemic to rushing.
The Turtle	• Overly slow and methodical. • Over attention to extraneous detail. • Reads and re-reads exam item's details. • Misses theme of exam items.	• Take practice exams in a timed manner to establish a pace of completing 50 MC exam items in an hour. • Study in bullet format. • Use the strategies provided in Tables 1-2 and 1-3 in Chapter 1 to identify each item's focus and select the best answer, and then move on to the next item.
Philosopher	• Is a thoughtful, talented, intelligent, and disciplined student. • Excels in essay questions. • Over-analyzes and reads into exam items. • Wants to know everything and answer everything about the topic. • Over-applies clinical knowledge.	• Study in bullet, not paragraph form. • Focus only on the exam item. • Look for simple, straightforward answers. • Remind yourself that your 'job' on the exam is to select the best answer for the question posed, not to address all possible aspects of an item's scenario. • Apply the strategies provided in Tables 1-2 and 1-3 to stay focused on answering each item as it is presented.
Lawyer	• Is a thoughtful, talented, intelligent, and disciplined student. • Picks out some bit of information and builds a case on that. • Reads into an exam item to make a case for a preferred answer instead of determining what the question is asking.	• Focus on what the exam item is asking and only what the exam item is asking. • Remind yourself that your 'job' is to pass the COTA® exam, not prove a point. • Remember you can train to be an NBCOT® item writer and write 'better' exam items after you pass the exam.

Second-Guesser	• Often a philosopher who reads into an item.
	• Frequently looks at the exam item from every angle.
	• Keeps changing answers, increasing anxiety, thinking less clearly and then changing answers more rapidly.
		• Apply the 'lightbulb' strategy described in Chapter 1.
		  – Identify a good reason to reject your first answer (i.e., missing a key word).
		  – Identify a good reason to select a new answer (i.e., obtaining a solid hint from a subsequent exam item).
		• If you do not experience a 'lightbulb' moment, do not change your answer.

Squisher/ Procrastinator	• Puts things off. • Does not reschedule missed study time. • Mastery of exam content is not attained and major knowledge gaps remain.	• Focus on developing a step-by step study plan. • Dig in and get started. • Adopt a "no excuses" attitude. • Join a study group or work with a study partner to stay on track.

Reference: Korchek, N. (1998). Personalities of test-takers. In M. Sides and N. Korcheck. (Eds). *Successful test-taking: Learning strategies for nurses* (77–89). Philadelphia: Lippincott.

---

7. Answering exam items can also assist in identifying your test-taking personality. Acquiring knowledge about your test-taking personality is as important as identifying your content areas of strength and weakness.
   a. Table 2-4 outlines typical test-taking personalities, their corresponding characteristics, and effective behavior management strategies.
8. If you have trouble with a specific content category (e.g., neurological disorders and neurophysiological approaches), the on-line practice exams include an option that allows you to take content-specific mini-exams to focus on particular content areas.
9. Be certain to complete each online practice exam in its entirety during a continuous 4-hour period to increase comfort with the cognitive, visual, and ergonomic demands of the actual testing situation and help habituate effective test-taking skills.

> **EXAM HINT:** During your exam simulation, be sure to include a 10–15 minute break since it is highly likely that you will need to take a restroom break when you are taking your COTA® exam in real-time.

   a. This amount of break time is needed because Prometrics will require you to check out from the exam administration area to go to the restroom and check in to return to the exam administration area.

> **EXAM HINT:** Simulating the exam in its timed format can increase comfort with the format and pace of the COTA® exam; this ease can contribute to a less stressful experience when you are taking your actual exam. When you take each online exam that accompanies this text, practice using the test-taking strategies provided in Chapter 1 and the test-taking personality behavior management strategies provided in Table 2-4 to facilitate the habituation of these effective techniques. This habit training will help you be well prepared to use these strategies during your COTA® exam.

10. Do not memorize sample exam items.

> **CAUTION:** Similar items may be on the COTA® exam, and answer choices may even be the same, but a change of only one word (e.g., "initially") can significantly alter the focus of an exam item.

11. Understanding the rationale for the correct/incorrect answers is most relevant for exam preparation.
    a. This *Review and Study Guide* contains extensive rationales for the text's three online simulated exams.
12. Take a preparatory course.
    a. The style, format, quality, and price of courses will vary, so you will want to assess your learning style, your needs, and past participant reviews to select the best course for you.
       (1) The following section and the back inside cover of this text provide information about TherapyEd's highly regarded preparation course for the COTA® exam.

Key Exam Preparation Resources

1. Effective preparation for the COTA® exam requires the recognition that there are two components to exam success. They are adequate content knowledge and solid objective exam test-taking skills.
2. This *Review & Study Guide* has been designed to be a primary content knowledge resource for studying for the exam.
    a. Our chapter authors have used the major OT textbooks identified by NBCOT® as providing the foundation for exam items as their chapter references.
    b. If you are particularly weak in a certain area, additional OTA textbooks, course notes, and handouts can be helpful to supplement your study from this text.
3. Knowledge of exam content does not ensure success on the COTA® exam.
    a. Competent students with good histories of academic success and satisfactory fieldwork experiences have reported failing the COTA® exam because they have poor objective exam test-taking skills.
       (1) Entrenched test-taking personalities as described in Table 2-4 must also be effectively managed for exam success.
4. Exam preparatory courses can develop your ability to apply clinical reasoning and critical thinking skills to correctly answer MC items
    a. TherapyEd offers an intensive course that focuses on the self-assessment of exam content knowledge and test-taking abilities through the answering and discussion of practice exam items and their answer rationales.
       (1) The effective management of test-taking personalities and the development of an efficient exam preparation plan are emphasized.
       (2) Extensive participant feedback indicates that the TherapyEd preparatory course, is highly effective for achieving COTA® exam success.
       (3) If you purchased this *Review and Study Guide* from TherapyEd, your purchase price can be credited to the course registration fee.
       (4) See www.TherapyEd.com for further information about this exam preparation course and participant reviews.
5. Fellow exam candidates are a valuable resource, and many report taking a course and/or studying together as a group to be very beneficial.

Critical Reasoning and COTA® Exam Performance

Overview of Critical Reasoning

1. Critical reasoning is a decision-making process that utilizes a person's knowledge, skills, experience, and logic to draw conclusions about everyday situations.
2. Critical reasoning skills are the foundation for how we reason the situations we encounter in daily life.

3. They are the base from which people draw conclusions about their world and what they determine to be true.
4. When used judiciously, critical reasoning is undertaken with purpose, clarity, accuracy, and thoroughness.

Relationship to the COTA® Exam

1. Critical reasoning is vitally important for COTA® exam success.
   a. The COTA® exam does not merely test the ability to recall facts that are readily found in books.

   > **EXAM HINT:** Knowledge of facts is a vital foundation for COTA® exam success, but accurately answering the exam items requires more than the simple recall of knowledge. The COTA® exam integrates the different levels of objective questions (i.e., application and analysis) to measure the knowledge, skills, and behaviors needed for competent entry-level OTA practice.

   b. Most COTA® exam items focus on contextualized practice situations that test your ability to correctly reason and make prudent decisions about challenging clinical circumstances and/or complex practice situations.
   c. Factual information (e.g., a person's symptoms, diagnosis) must be applied to practice scenarios in which you will need to draw conclusions (e.g., most appropriate intervention, expected outcome).
2. Due to its daily use and intuitive nature, the relationship between critical reasoning and professional exam success is often not acknowledged. Therefore, the conscious and proactive use of critical reasoning skills is an important part of your exam preparation.
   a. The three online exams that accompany this *Review and Study Guide* provide multiple opportunities for you to demonstrate how well you can reason out challenging practice scenarios as you answer their 600 MC items.
      (1) Each exam item will require you to draw upon your knowledge, skills, and experiences to arrive at a correct conclusion.
         (a) This accurate determination is made through critical reasoning.
3. The development of critical reasoning skills is fostered during OTA academic coursework and fieldwork, so at this point you will have developed a solid repertoire of critical reasoning skills.
   a. Your achievement of this level of critical reasoning skills has enabled you to succeed in your pursuit of your OTA degree.

   b. These capabilities will serve you well in your preparation for the COTA® exam.
      (1) Increasing your awareness about how these critical reasoning skills are reflected in MC items will further enhance your exam success.
4. The following sections will make explicit important facets of critical reasoning skills and help you prepare to successfully complete the COTA® exam.

Five Subskills of Critical Reasoning

1. There are five subskills of critical reasoning that provide the foundation for good critical reasoning.
   a. They are described by Facione (1990a, 1990b, 2006) and are based on a consensus of many critical thinking experts about the skills used in reasoning out challenging circumstances.
   b. They include inductive, deductive, analytical, inferential, and evaluative reasoning.
2. These subskills and their relevance to the COTA® exam are described in the following sections.

Inductive Reasoning

1. The process of reasoning in which the assumptions of an argument are believed to endorse the conclusion, but do not guarantee it.
2. Starts with reasoning in specific situations and then moves to more generalized situations.
3. An important skill clinically because it helps us to look at all our possible options in a circumstance and determine which seems most reasonable.
4. Used in diagnostic thinking to form assumptions about what to expect from a diagnosis as it evolves and changes over time.
5. May start with observations in a specific situation and then lead to drawing conclusions about larger circumstances.
   a. This generalization process can lead to flawed reasoning.
      (1) For example, upon observing a person post-cerebral vascular accident (CVA) with dysarthria, an OTA concludes that all individuals post-CVA have dysarthria, which is untrue.
         (a) This false conclusion is reflective of a faulty reasoning process that applied an observation from a specific situation to a larger, more global assumption.
6. Inductive reasoning must be used cautiously when answering COTA® exam items because situation-specific knowledge is not an adequate foundation for making universal assumptions.

a. Recognizing the limitations of inductive reasoning is an important part of successful exam performance; additional critical reasoning skills are required to adequately analyze exam items.

> **EXAM HINT:** Be sure to not make hasty generalizations about an exam item practice scenario. Generalizations are needed in life and even during the COTA® exam, but you must be prudent in making such generalizations and not jump to conclusions when answering exam items.

7. To help you identify exam items that require the formation of assumptions, the analysis of your performance on this text's three practice exams will have a picture of binoculars next to inductive reasoning items.

Deductive Reasoning

1. The process of reasoning in which conclusions are drawn based on facts, laws, rules, or accepted principles.
2. The reverse thinking process of inductive reasoning.
3. Starts with information about larger circumstances, broader principles, and general theories and applies this knowledge to specific situations.
   a. For example, an OTA applies the OT ethical principle of veracity to conclude that a fellow therapist who falsely documents a treatment procedure to fraudulently bill Medicare is behaving in an unethical manner.
4. Provides important guidelines for OT practice by putting forth protocols (e.g., diagnostic-specific clinical pathways), procedures (e.g., range of motion [ROM], manual muscle test [MMT]), rules (e.g., OT code of ethics), and laws (e.g., Individuals with Disabilities Education Act [IDEA], Americans with Disabilities Act [ADA]) that can be applied to a specific practice scenario without necessitating independent judgment for the situation.
5. Deductive reasoning must be used cautiously when answering COTA® exam items because erroneous assumptions about the premises of a theory can be made and then mistakenly applied to a specific circumstance.
   a. For example, an OTA who staunchly adheres to the belief that all persons with disabilities want to be independent in all activities of daily living (ADL) would be wrong to apply this viewpoint to a person from a cultural background that views family-provided assistance as a sign of loving care. This OTA would be deducing from a flawed premise, which would lead to a faulty conclusion.

> **EXAM HINT:** Recognizing the limitations of deductive reasoning is an important part of successful exam performance; the soundness and trustworthiness of the applied procedures, theories, principles, and concepts must be thoughtfully critiqued before they are applied to a specific situation.

6. To help you identify COTA® exam items that require their correct answer to be based on facts, laws, rules, or accepted principles, the analysis of your performance on this text's three practice examinations will have a picture of a microscope next to deductive reasoning items.

Analytical Reasoning or Analysis

1. The process of interpreting the meaning of information, determining relationships within the information presented, and then making assumptions or judgments about that information.
   a. Helps to examine ideas and concepts and the relationships between them.
2. Information presented in the form of graphs, charts, tables, and pictures encourage analytical reasoning skills because one must interpret the information that is depicted and determine what it precisely means.
   a. Information can also be presented in a narrative manner that requires one to make a 'mental chart' of the information presented.
3. Used in OT practice to categorize information (e.g., define a symptom based on a behavioral description, or classify a condition based on a cluster of reported symptoms).
   a. Important in OT practice, because it helps the OTA determine the potential impact of a clinical condition on occupational performance.
4. Analysis is required to correctly answer many COTA® exam items.
   a. Analytical reasoning is used when some descriptors are included in an item stem (e.g., member characteristics of a mature-level group), but some key descriptors needed to answer the question are not provided (e.g., the leader's role in a mature group), leaving the test taker to make assumptions about what the best answer would be (e.g., the type of activity to use in the group) based on the partial information provided.

> **EXAM HINT:** Analysis exam items are often frustrating since limited information upon which an answer must be selected is provided; however, they accurately reflect the practice reality that OT practitioners rarely have complete information about a person or group.

5. To help you identify exam items that require the examination of ideas and concepts and the relationships between them, the analysis of your performance on this text's three practice exams will have a picture of a beaker next to analytical reasoning items.

Inferential Reasoning or Inference

1. The process of drawing conclusions or making logical judgments based on facts, concepts, and evidence rather than direct observations.
2. Used in practice situations when an OTA infers the symptoms to expect based on a diagnosis (e.g., a person with a left CVA will exhibit right hemiplegia and aphasia) or the likely progression of a disease or disorder (e.g., amyotrophic lateral sclerosis will steadily progress until death, while the course of multiple sclerosis is characterized by exacerbations and remissions).
   a. Inferences about the nature of a disease, all of its possible symptoms, and its sequelae are not guaranteed to be 100% accurate; therefore, skilled inference must be based on the OT practitioner's knowledge and experience.
3. Inferential reasoning is also utilized in practice situations when OTAs have to decide on a best course of action.
   a. Inferences about clinical courses of action are not guaranteed to be 100% accurate. For example, when treating an individual with a rotator cuff tear, an OTA cannot be 100% certain that the chosen intervention will result in the successful therapeutic outcome of improved occupational performance. Therefore, skilled inference must be based on the OT practitioner's knowledge and experience.
4. Inferential reasoning is regularly used by OT practitioners in their decision-making process, and this reality is precisely why the skill is important for successful COTA® exam performance.
5. Inference is required to correctly answer many COTA® exam items.
   a. Questions that ask the test taker to determine what is best, most important, or most likely to occur often require inferential reasoning.

EXAM HINT: Exam items of this nature can be difficult because they ask the test taker to determine what is believed to be true, even though there is no 100% assurance that the selected answer is correct; however, they accurately reflect the realistic uncertainties of OT practice.

6. Inferential reasoning must be used cautiously when answering COTA® exam items because inadequate consideration of the information presented in an exam item or the use of faulty or hasty logic to determine what may occur in certain situations can lead to the selection of an incorrect answer.
   a. For example, an OTA determines that it is most appropriate for a person with T12 paraplegia to focus on the upper trapezius and levator scapulae muscles in preparation for functional mobility with crutches, rather than the triceps and lower trapezius muscles. This decision is erroneous because it does not consider the nature of the task at hand (i.e., ambulation with crutches) or tie the muscle functions with the use of crutches for functional mobility.
7. Since quick decisions can lead to suboptimal intervention, the COTA® exam requires judicious use of inferential reasoning.
8. To help you identify COTA® exam items that require you to draw conclusions or make logical judgments based on facts, concepts, and evidence rather than direct observations, the analysis of your performance on this text's three practice examinations will have a picture of a lightbulb next to inferential reasoning items.

Evaluative Reasoning or Evaluation

1. The process by which the merits of an argument are weighed for their validity and the inherent value of the argument itself is critiqued.
   a. The determination that an argument 'holds water' or not.
   b. If the value is found in the argument itself, the assignment of a value to it.
2. People make judgments about the merits and value of the information they receive all the time and are often unconscious of the thought process that is involved.
3. In OT practice, evaluative reasoning must be conscious.
   a. A good evaluative thinker listens with a skeptical ear to determine the trustworthiness of information before assigning a value to it.
   b. Accepting information at face value can be a reasoning pitfall since there can be additional information needed to complete an accurate assessment of a situation.
4. Evaluative reasoning helps guide thinking about a correct course of action.
5. Evaluation is often used in OT practice when difficult decisions must be made in areas that have no clear-cut answers.
   a. Practice situations can be ambiguous and require the OTA to evaluate the situation, weigh the information presented, and determine a correct course of action, given their knowledge and experience.
   b. These dilemmas pose a challenge to practitioners since the correct course of action must be determined.

c. For example, during an intervention session, an OTA observes bruises on a resident in a skilled nursing facility and must determine if the correct course of action is immediately notifying the charge nurse, the physician, adult protective services, and/or the family; or asking the resident to explain the source of the bruises; or documenting the observation and continuing with the session as planned.
6. Pitfalls in evaluative reasoning lie in assigning great value to information that has little value to the situation, not assigning enough value to highly valuable information, and finally not utilizing principles and guidelines that are put into place to help guide one's thinking (e.g., OT Code of Ethics, treatment protocols).
   a. For example, an OTA working in home care with a patient who becomes short of breath must determine if they should immediately call 911, notify the occupational therapist, notify the physician, or continue with the treatment session.
      (1) It would help the OTA to know if the shortness of breath is an expected symptom given the patient's diagnosis, medical history, and past response to treatment. This information would guide the OTA's thinking about a correct course of action.
      (2) Evaluative reasoning is important in this clinical situation because the OTA could overreact to the situation and call 911 for expected shortness of breath that often accompanies chronic obstructive pulmonary disease or underreact and fail to call 911 when a person is also complaining of co-occurring severe unremitting substernal pain, which can be indicative of a myocardial infarction.

> **EXAM HINT:** Evaluative reasoning is often required during the COTA® exam to correctly answer exam items about ethical dilemmas.

7. To help you identify exam items that pose challenging practice situations and ethical dilemmas, the analysis of your performance on this text's three practice exams will have a picture of a cogwheel next to evaluative reasoning items.

Developing Critical Reasoning Skills for COTA® Exam Success

1. Since critical reasoning is not learned during a quick lesson or improved upon by simply reading the above basic descriptions of them, practice with items that test reasoning skills and provide feedback on your performance is essential.
   a. The good news is that this *Review and Study Guide* provides 600 opportunities to develop your reasoning skills.
      (1) Each MC item in this text's three online simulated practice exams has an accompanying rationale for the correct and incorrect answer choices and an explanation of its corresponding critical reasoning subskill and the knowledge or skill required to select the correct answer.
2. When reviewing the analysis of your exam performance on this text's three simulated practice exams, pay particular attention to the five types of critical reasoning that are listed with each MC item.
   a. The five symbols assigned to designate the different types of critical reasoning are:

      = Inductive Reasoning.

      = Deductive Reasoning.

      = Analytical Reasoning.

      = Inferential Reasoning.

      = Evaluative Reasoning.

3. Carefully review this feedback to identify any performance patterns that emerge.
   a. Is your exam performance weaker in a certain area of reasoning?
      (1) Since critical reasoning skills are based on knowledge and day-to-day experiences, it is not uncommon to be stronger in certain areas of reasoning than others.
4. If you have a weakness in a certain area(s) of reasoning, do not despair.
   a. Being aware of your gaps in reasoning is the first essential step in the development of a corrective plan of action.
5. As you review the rationales provided for the practice exam items in this *Review and Study Guide*, refer back to your incorrect responses and see if there is a pattern to the types of items you are answering incorrectly related to a subskill of critical reasoning.
   a. Do you notice that you have difficulty with certain types of questions?

Table 2-5

Critical Reasoning Self-Assessment Questions

OBSERVED EXAM DIFFICULTY	REASONING CHALLENGE	NBCOT® EXAM PREPARATION STRATEGY
Do you: – have difficulty with taking specific information and applying it to larger populations? – select incorrect answers because you cannot generalize your knowledge?	Inductive	When studying a specific content area, think about how the discrete information that you are reviewing can be applied to a diversity of situations. Use a reflective "what if" stance to think how this information may be generalized to a broader context. This can be a fun and effective study group activity.
Do you: – prefer to follow your instincts rather than the guidelines that a protocol may provide? – select incorrect answers because you are unfamiliar with established practice standards or major theoretical approaches?	Deductive	Be sure when you study that you master all major facts, laws, rules, and accepted principles that guide OT practice. Carefully review all of the frames of reference, practice models, and intervention protocols and procedures provided in Chapters 11–15 and the AOTA Code of Ethics and legislation information provided in Chapter 4.
Do you: – tend to misinterpret information provided and make poor judgments and apply inadequately conceived assumptions about it? – select incorrect answers because you misjudged the effects of a clinical condition on occupational performance?	Analytical	Be sure to obtain a solid knowledge of all major clinical conditions, their symptoms, diagnostic testing and criteria, anticipated sequelae, and expected outcomes. This information is extensively reviewed in Chapters 6–10 to help you make accurate judgments and correct assumptions about the potential impact of a clinical condition on occupational performance.
Do you: – have difficulty with thinking about how clinical conditions and practice situations may evolve over time? – assume information is valid when in fact it is not true? – select incorrect answers because you have difficulty deciding the best course of action in a practice scenario?	Inferential	When studying the clinical conditions in the chapters identified above, be sure to think about how the presentation of these conditions may sometimes vary from textbook descriptions. Use the knowledge and experience you acquired during your clinical fieldwork to assess the trustworthiness of your assumptions. Study the frames of reference and practice models presented in Chapters 11–13 to develop a solid foundation on how to decide the best course of action based on facts, concepts, and evidence.
Do you: – feel anxious when you have exam items that are ambiguous and you cannot find answers to them in a textbook? – rely on protocols and guidelines more than gut instinct? – select incorrect answers because you become overwhelmed by exam items that present ethical dilemmas?	Evaluative	When reviewing specific content, think about the practice ambiguities and ethical dilemmas you observed during your fieldwork related to these areas. Be sure to study the guidelines for ethical decision making that are provided in Chapter 4 to help you evaluate NBCOT® question scenarios, weigh the information presented, and determine a correct course action.

This table was adapted with permission from Kari Inda's research on critical reasoning and the OT certification exam.

6. Once you have identified a weakness in critical reasoning, take some time to reflect on why this is so.
   a. Ask yourself the questions identified in Table 2-5 and determine if they are reflective of your exam performance.
      (1) Questions answered affirmatively can help you identify critical reasoning skills that can be improved.
      (2) Implement the corresponding suggested exam preparation strategies to develop needed critical reasoning skills.

> **EXAM HINT:** An honest appraisal of your performance patterns and the thoughtful application of relevant exam preparation strategies will help build your knowledge of, and experience with, the effective application of critical reasoning skills.

7. This preparation will help you successfully meet the challenges of the COTA® exam.

References

Facione, P. (2006). *Critical thinking: What it is and why it counts.* Millbrae, CA: California Academic Press.

Facione, P. (1990a). *Critical thinking: A statement of expert consensus for purposes of educational assessment and instruction. Research findings and recommendations.* Newark, DE: American Psychological Association.

Facione, P. (1990b). *Critical thinking: A statement of expert consensus for purposes of educational assessment and instruction ("Executive summary: The Delphi report").* Millbrae, CA: California Academic Press.

Fleming-Castaldy, R. (2019). *Occupational therapy assistant course manual.* (6th ed.). Evanston, IL: TherapyED.

Sides, M., & Korcheck, N. (Eds.). (1998). *Successful test-taking: Learning strategies for nurses.* Philadelphia: Lippincott.

Sladyk, K., Gilmore, S., & Tufano, R. (2005). *OT exam review manual.* (4th ed.). Thorofare, NJ: Slack.

3

The Process of Occupational Therapy

RITA P. FLEMING-CASTALDY

Chapter Outline

- The Process of Occupational Therapy, 32
- Referral, Screening, and Evaluation, 32
- Intervention, 38
- Re-evaluation/Intervention Review, 43
- OT Tools of Practice, 44
- Appendix 3A, 57
- Appendix 3B, 60
- References, 60
- Review Questions, 62

The Process of Occupational Therapy

Overview

1. The occupational therapy (OT) process comprises three main aspects of service delivery: evaluation, intervention, and outcomes.
2. This process is client-centered, interactive, and dynamic.
3. Table 3-1 provides a summary of the OT process as put forth in the American Occupational Therapy Association (AOTA) Practice Framework.

> **EXAM HINT:** The National Board for Certification in Occupational Therapy (NBCOT®) exam for the Certified Occupational Therapy Assistant (COTA®) exam places a heavy emphasis on the OT process, with 92% of the exam focused on service delivery to the client; the remaining 8% is focused on professional standards and responsibilities.

Referral, Screening, and Evaluation

Referral

1. The basic request for OT services. This may also be termed an 'order' or a 'consultation.'
2. Sources include the individual, family or caregivers, physicians, social workers, physical therapists, nurse practitioners, allied health professionals, teachers, administrators, insurance companies, employers, state and local/public and private agencies.
3. The content and form of a referral/order varies among program types and practice areas and can range from the highly specific (e.g., a resting hand splint) to the very general (e.g., evaluate for developmental delay).
4. While anyone can refer themselves or others to OT services, the ability of the OT practitioner to act upon the referral is determined by state licensure laws and/or third-party reimbursers.
5. According to established practice standards, if an occupational therapy assistant (OTA) receives a referral, the OTA must give the referral to the supervising occupational therapist who is responsible for responding to the referral.

> **EXAM HINT:** While the legal standards for OT referrals can vary from state to state, the NBCOT® is a national certification exam so it will only ask questions about national standards (e.g., American Occupational Therapy Association [AOTA] standards for practice, Medicare guidelines).

Screening

1. The acquisition of information to determine the need for an in-depth evaluation and to obtain a preliminary understanding of the individual's needs, limitations, assets, and resources.
2. Screening procedures are usually brief and easy to administer since they must be applied to a large number of individuals (i.e., all persons who receive an OT referral need to be screened to determine the appropriateness of the referral).
3. The OTA contributes to the screening process.
   a. The OTA can collect screening data and report information with supervision from the occupational therapist.
   b. The amount of supervision required will depend upon the OTA's experience and the establishment of service competency.
4. Screening tools measure broad performance abilities and include chart/medical record review, checklists, structured observations, and/or brief interviews with the individual, family, and/or caregivers.
5. Data collected during screening will be analyzed by the occupational therapist to determine the areas of performance, performance components, and/or performance contexts that require further evaluation.

> **EXAM HINT:** If an exam item identifies screening as the current stage of the OT process, any answer choice that includes goal-setting, intervention planning, and/or implementing/managing intervention(s) would be incorrect because goals cannot be established or treatment implemented/managed until after an evaluation is completed.

Evaluation

1. "The comprehensive process of obtaining and interpreting the data necessary to understand the individual, system, or situation" (Hinojosa, Kramer, & Crist, 2005, p. 2).

Table 3-1

Operationalizing the Occupational Therapy Process

EVALUATION		INTERVENTION			TARGETING OF OUTCOMES
OCCUPATIONAL PROFILE	**ANALYSIS OF OCCUPATIONAL PERFORMANCE**	**INTERVENTION PLAN**	**INTERVENTION IMPLEMENTATION**	**INTERVENTION REVIEW**	**OUTCOMES**
• Identify the following: • Why is the client seeking service, and what are the client's current concerns relative to engaging in activities and occupations? • In what occupations does the client feel successful, and what barriers are affecting their success? • What aspects of the contexts or environments does the client see as supporting and as inhibiting engagement in desired occupations? • What is the client's occupational history? • What are the client's values and interests? • What are the client's daily life roles? • What are the client's patterns of engagement in occupations, and how have they changed over time? • What are the client's priorities and desired targeted outcomes related to occupational performance, prevention, participation, role competence, health and wellness, quality of life, well-being, and occupational justice?	• Synthesize information from the occupational profile to focus on specific occupations and contexts. • Observe the client's performance during activities relevant to desired occupations. • Select and use specific assessments to identify and measure contexts or environments, activity and occupational demands, client factors, and performance skills and patterns. • Select outcome measures. • Interpret assessment data to identify supports for and hindrances to performance. • Develop and refine hypotheses about the client's occupational performance strengths and limitations. • Create goals in collaboration with the client that address desired outcomes. • Determine procedures to measure the outcomes of intervention. • Delineate a potential intervention based on best practice and available evidence.	1. Develop the plan, which involves selecting the following: • Objective and measurable occupation-focused goals and related time frames; • Occupational therapy intervention approach or approaches, such as create or promote, establish or restore, maintain, modify, or prevent; and • Methods for service delivery, including who will provide the intervention, types of intervention, and service delivery models. 2. Consider potential discharge needs and plans. 3. Recommend or refer to other professionals as needed.	1. Determine and carry out occupational therapy intervention or interventions, which may include the following: • Therapeutic use of occupations and activities; • Preparatory methods and tasks; • Education and training; • Advocacy; and • Group interventions. 2. Monitor the client's response through ongoing evaluation and re-evaluation.	1. Re-evaluate the plan and implementation relative to achieving outcomes. 2. Modify the plan as needed. 3. Determine the need for continuation or discontinuation of occupational therapy services and for referral.	1. Early in the intervention process, select outcomes and measures that are: • Valid, reliable, sensitive to change, and consistent with outcomes; • Congruent with client goals; and • Based on their actual or purported ability to predict future outcomes. 2. Apply outcomes to measure progress and adjust goals and interventions. • Compare progress toward goal achievement to outcomes throughout the intervention process. • Assess outcome use and results to make decisions about the future direction of intervention.

←—— Continue to renegotiate intervention plans and targeted outcomes. ——→

←———— Ongoing interaction among evaluation, intervention, and outcomes throughout the process. ————→

Reference: American Occupational Therapy Association. (2014). Occupational therapy practice framework: Domain and process (3rd ed.). *American Journal of Occupational Therapy, 68*(Suppl. 1), S17. http://dx.doi.org/10.5014/ajot.2014.682006. Reprinted with permission.

2. The evaluation process includes obtaining the person's occupational profile and an analysis of their occupational performance. See Table 3-1.
3. The OTA contributes to the evaluation process.
   a. The OTA can assist with the collection of evaluation data once service competency is established with supervision from the occupational therapist.
   b. The level of supervision required depends upon the OTA's experience and established service competency.
4. If the individual and the OT practitioners do not share a common language, an interpreter must be used to ensure the validity of the information obtained.

> **EXAM HINT:** In the NBCOT® practice analysis of the COTA®, "more than 30% of respondents indicated that they communicated in languages other than English in their primary occupational therapy employment setting" (NBCOT®, 2018, p. 15). Due to this prevalence, it is likely that the exam will have items about a COTA® conducting an evaluation with a non-English-speaking person.

5. The supervising occupational therapist determines which assessment will attain information essential for setting goals and planning intervention.
   a. The OTA contributes to this determination process.
   b. Considerations in determining appropriate assessments.
      (1) Individual's baseline functional level, major concerns, and pressing needs as determined through the screening process.
      (2) The environmental context in which the assessment will be conducted.
         (a) The length of stay of the setting influences comprehensiveness of evaluation.
         (b) The primary focus of the setting (e.g., pre-vocational versus self-management).
         (c) Legislative guidelines and restrictions (e.g., in a school setting, assessments must focus on areas related to the child's educational needs).
         (d) The facility's resources of space, equipment, and supplies.
      (3) The environmental context of the individual's current and expected environment.
         (a) Sociocultural aspects including roles, values, norms, supports. For example, in some cultures home management is considered a valued role only for females, so there is no need to do a home management evaluation for a male of this cultural background.
         (b) Physical environment characteristics. For example, it would be essential to measure functional mobility and endurance for a person who lives in a third-floor walk-up apartment.
      (4) The temporal context of the individual and their disability.
         (a) Person's chronological and developmental age.
         (b) Anticipated duration of disability (e.g., short-term, long-term, permanent).
         (c) Recent occurrence of illness or exacerbation of a long-standing, chronic condition.
         (d) Stage of illness (e.g., acute stage versus terminal stage).
      (5) The evaluation tool's compatibility with the frame of reference selected to guide treatment planning.
      (6) The existing evidence to support evaluation's use.
6. If service competency is established, the OTA administers the assessment according to recommended guidelines, administration protocols, and/or standardized procedures with the supervision of the occupational therapist.

> **RED FLAG:** Standard precautions must be observed during *all* evaluation procedures, and transmission-based precautions must also be implemented as needed to prevent infection. See Appendix 3A and Appendix 3B.

7. The OTA and/or occupational therapist scores or rates assessment results according to published guidelines or standardized procedures.
8. The occupational therapist interprets the assessment results in relation to uniform terminology, the practice framework, and/or a specific frame of reference. The OTA collaborates with the occupational therapist to:
   a. Integrate referral, screening, and diagnostic information and data gathered from assessment.
   b. Relate all information to functional abilities and disabilities relevant to person's roles, occupational performance areas, and environmental contexts relevant to the individual.

> **CAUTION:** The interpretation of information based on a person's self-report or the results of a highly structured assessment may not reflect actual performance in their natural contexts.

   c. Identify functional strengths and deficits in occupational performance areas relevant to the individual.
   d. In school/educational settings, assessment information must be related to the multiple aspects of educational performance.
      (1) Academic.
      (2) Mobility.
      (3) Psychosocial.
      (4) Behavioral.
      (5) Self-care.

9. The occupational therapist and the OTA collaborate with the individual, family, caregivers, and other team members to obtain a broader picture of the person's situation and to put the OT assessment results into a larger context.
   a. In school/educational settings, medically necessary OT must be separated from educationally relevant OT.
      (1) Referrals to after-school, home care, and/or community-based OT services are indicated for noneducational OT.
10. The supervising occupational therapist prioritizes identified problems in collaboration with the OTA and the individual to develop an intervention plan.
11. Consider the ethical concerns of all parties that have an interest in the process and outcomes of an OT evaluation. Table 3-2 describes the ethical responsibilities of OT practitioners in the selection and use of OT assessments.

EXAM HINT: In the NBCOT® exam outline for the COTA®, Domain 01 "Assist the OTR to acquire information regarding factors that influence occupational performance on an ongoing basis throughout the occupational therapy process" comprises 28% of the COTA® exam (NBCOT®, 2018, p. 18). The application of knowledge about the above general evaluation guidelines and the following assessment methods and tools used in OT practice can help you determine correct answers for Domain 01 NBCOT® exam items.

Assessment Tools

1. The OTA can utilize a diversity of assessment tools with the supervision of the occupational therapist and the establishment of service competency.
2. Observation involves visual assessment of an individual, their behavior, and environmental contexts. An overview of the skills needed for accurate observations is provided in the following section.
3. Interviews involve the practitioner asking the individual specific questions. An overview of interviewing techniques is provided in a subsequent section.
4. Self-report requires the individual to disclose personal information in an organized manner, e.g., through the completion of a questionnaire.
5. Checklists require the use of a predetermined listing of items against which a person's performance is checked to determine the presence or absence of these items.
6. Rating scales require the individual or occupational therapy practitioner to rate reactions, performance, or set criteria according to an established scale.
7. Goal attainment scaling (GAS) uses interviews and rating scales during initial sessions to facilitate clients' participation in the goal-setting process by identifying intervention outcomes that are personally relevant to them; used during posttreatment sessions to assess client progress toward desired goals.
8. Performance tests involve structured guidelines and/or standardized procedures for engaging the individual in performing an activity and for scoring this activity.
9. Norm-referenced assessments produce scores that compare the individual's performance to a set population's performance.
10. Criterion-referenced assessments provide scores that compare the individual's performance to a preestablished criterion.
11. The OTA can utilize assessment tools with the supervision of the occupational therapist and upon the establishment of service competency.
    a. State licensure laws, regulations, and statutes may limit the OTA's role in assessment, but this variability will not be tested on the NBCOT® examination.

Observation Skills

1. Observation of a person during actual occupational performance is critical.
2. Observation of performance must be done in different contexts and in structured and unstructured situations.
3. Observation of environmental contexts is also important to assess physical and sociocultural supports or barriers.
4. Use of a structured tool to note observations can increase reliability.
5. Observations must be ongoing to assess the nuances of performance and subtle changes in function.
6. The OTA must be aware of their own sociocultural background, as this is the lens through which they observes and it can influence the interpretation of observations (e.g., appropriateness of the individual's nonverbal behavior).
7. The OTA shares their observations with the supervising occupational therapist.
    a. Interpretation of these observations is made by the supervising occupational therapist in collaboration with the OTA.

CAUTION: All interpretations must be validated by the individual and/or caregiver.

Interviewing Guidelines

1. Establish the purpose of the interview.
    a. Questions asked and information sought should be consistent with stated purpose.
    b. Interviewee should feel each question is relevant and significant.

Table 3-2

Ethical Considerations for the Selection and Use of Occupational Therapy Assessments

OCCUPATIONAL THERAPIST COMPETENCIES

The occupational therapist must ensure they have the knowledge, skills, and attitudes to competently:

- determine assessment foci based on the needs and goals of the person being assessed
- select, administer, and interpret assessment results using established evaluation guidelines
- complete standardized assessments according to published protocols
- supervise other OT personnel in their collection of assessment data
- ensure all delegated assessment tasks are completed in a competent manner
- document the assessment in a manner that accurately describes its procedures and outcomes

OCCUPATIONAL THERAPY ASSISTANT COMPETENCIES

The OT assistant must ensure they have the knowledge, skills, and attitudes to competently:

- complete the assessment data collection that they are responsible to perform
- determine that their training and supervision is adequate to carry out assigned assessment procedures
- report the assessment data in an accurate manner
- contribute to the evaluation process

CLIENT/CONSUMER AND/OR THEIR CAREGIVER/GUARDIAN VESTED INTERESTS

The OT practitioner must ensure that the person being assessed and/or their caregiver/guardian:

- have provided input about their needs and goals to inform the assessment process
- have been fully informed about the purposes and administrative procedures of an assessment
- understand how the assessment results will be used to inform intervention
- have been provided the opportunity to decide if the assessment should be administered
- know how the assessment will be billed

EMPLOYER AND INTER-DISCIPLINARY TEAM MEMBERS VESTED INTERESTS

The OT practitioner must ensure that:

- the assessment is consistent with the mission of the setting and helps attain desired outcomes
- the assessment's findings, interpretation, and recommendations are effectively communicated to team members and meaningfully contribute to an inter-disciplinary intervention plan

PAYER VESTED INTERESTS

The OT practitioner must ensure that:

- the assessment is a necessary and billable service that is accurately documented for reimbursement
- if there is no third-party reimbursement, the person being assessed knows this and has given consent before the completion of an assessment
- payment is requested only for the services provided

PROFESSIONAL STANDARDS

The OT practitioner must ensure that:

- selected assessments are evidence-based (to the extent possible) and within OT's recognized scope of practice
- specific training and/or specialized credentials required to use an assessment have been completed by the assessment's administrator
- permission to use copyrighted assessments has been obtained, fees to use an assessment have been paid, and assessment use complies with the laws regulating their use
- the assessment does not hinder the fair and equitable distribution of OT services to all persons in a setting needing OT services

Adapted by Rita Fleming-Castaldy from Hansen, R.A. (1990). Lesson 10: Ethical considerations. In C.B. Royeen (Ed.), *AOTA self-study series: Assessing functions*, (p. 9). Bethesday, MD: American Occupational Therapy Association.

c. Irrelevant, spurious, and/or extraneous questions should not be asked.
2. Establish rapport with interviewee.
   a. Initial interview is often the beginning of a long-term therapeutic relationship.
   b. Set an atmosphere of trust by maintaining confidentiality.
   c. Set an atmosphere of respect by being on time, asking pertinent questions, and actively listening.
3. Ask questions in an organized, formalized manner.
   a. Interviews are not casual conversations.
   b. A haphazard approach will not obtain information needed to achieve the purpose of the interview.
   c. Numerous assessment tools are available to guide the interview.
      (1) The OTA can use these tools with the supervision of the occupational therapist and upon establishment of service competence.
4. Observe interviewee's nonverbal communications during the interview.
   a. What is not said during an interview can be as important as what is said.
      (1) Gaps in information presented.
      (2) Affect and mood.
      (3) Physical mannerisms.
      (4) Speech patterns and inflections.
   b. Interpret with the supervising occupational therapist the congruence or incongruence of nonverbal behaviors with actual verbalizations.
5. Listen before talking.
   a. Counteracts preconceived views of interviewee.
   b. Prevents premature recommendations.
6. Question and re-question, as needed, to obtain essential information.
   a. Follow-up questions should be specific.
   b. Open-ended, leading questions facilitate discussion.
   c. Questions that can be answered by yes or no should be avoided.
7. Comment in a limited manner and only when directly related to the stated purpose of the interview.
   a. Reassuring comments are used to facilitate interviewee's participation.
   b. Specific suggestions or advice should only be given if intervention is part of interview's purpose.
8. Answer personal questions directed to interviewer by interviewee in a direct and honest manner.
   a. Purposes of personal questions asked by interviewee.
      (1) To show a general polite interest in interviewer.
      (2) To move the therapeutic relationship to a closer level.
      (3) To indirectly introduce a personal concern of their own.
   b. Interviewer should immediately redirect interviewee to purpose of interview and to themself after providing a brief, truthful answer.
9. Lead and direct interview to achieve stated purpose.
10. Maintain confidentiality at all times.
11. The OTA shares interview results with the supervising occupational therapist.
    a. The supervising occupational therapist interprets verbalizations and nonverbal communications to formulate hypotheses about interviewee's situation.
12. The supervising occupational therapist develops a plan in collaboration with the OTA based on the information obtained from the interview and the hypotheses formulated about the person's situation.
    a. Plan can include the need for further evaluation and more information.
    b. The use of an interview to formulate a plan can prevent interviewing just for the sake of interviewing.
    c. Plans for intervention should be developed collaboratively with the individual using a client-centered approach.

> **EXAM HINT:** The NBCOT® exam outline for the COTA® identifies the task of acquiring "information by using available resources about a client's functional skills, roles, culture, performance context, and prioritized needs in order to contribute to the development and update of an occupational profile" (NBCOT®, 2018, p. 21) as essential for competent OTA practice. The application of knowledge about the above information gathering methods can help you effectively answer exam items about the COTA®'s role during the evaluation process.

Developmental Considerations in Evaluation

> **EXAM HINT:** The NBCOT® exam outline identifies the task of recognizing "the influence of development . . . on a client's occupational performance" (NBCOT®, 2018, p. 21) as essential for competent practice. The application of knowledge about the following developmental considerations can help you determine the correct answer for NBCOT® Domain 01 exam items.

1. With supervision from the occupational therapist, the COTA® can complete the following assessment tasks and contribute to the evaluation process.
   a. Conduct family/teacher interviews and home/classroom observations.
      (1) To explore environmental characteristics related to the child's development.
      (2) To identify family supports and community resources.

(3) To identify cultural values.
(4) To establish family-centered priorities.
b. Consider the child's developmental levels in selecting assessments, toys, and other evaluation media.
c. Observe symmetries/asymmetries, stability of trunk, pelvis, hips, and shoulders, at rest and during movement.
d. Observe transitional movement in and out of prone, supine, side-lying, quadruped, sitting, standing, kneeling, half-kneel, and in various sitting positions such as tailor, long, heel, or side-sitting.
e. Assess the quality of movement in and out of the above positions.
f. Assess fine motor coordination.
g. Consider proper positioning and adaptive equipment, seating, and technology needs.
h. Assess cognition in the context of play and other occupations.
i. Assess psychosocial skills (i.e., coping, emotional regulation, frustration tolerance, and social interaction skills).
j. Assess sensory processing. Refer to Chapter 12.
k. Consider visual and auditory status and aides.
2. Refer to Chapter 5 for more information about developmental assessment.

Intervention

Types of Intervention

1. Prevention: interventions designed to promote wellness, prevent disabilities and illnesses, and maintain health.
   a. Primary prevention: the reduction of the incidence or occurrence of a disease or disorder within a population that is currently well or considered to be potentially at risk (e.g., parenting skills classes for teen parents to prevent child neglect or abuse).
      (1) In the AOTA practice framework, primary prevention is termed "create/promote" and "health promotion."
         (a) Interventions focus on providing enrichment experiences to enhance person's occupational performance in their natural contexts.
   b. Secondary prevention: the early detection of problems in a population at risk to reduce the duration of a disorder/disease and/or minimize its effects through early detection/diagnosis, early appropriate referral, and early/effective intervention (e.g., the screening of infants born prematurely for developmental delays and the immediate implementation of intervention for identified delays).
   c. Tertiary prevention: the elimination or reduction of the impact of dysfunction on an individual (e.g., the provision of rehabilitation services to maximize community integration).
   d. In the AOTA practice framework, the term "disability prevention" is used to designate interventions that address the needs of persons with or without disabilities who are considered at risk for problems with their occupational performance.
      (1) Interventions focus on preventing the occurrence or minimizing the effects of barriers to occupational performance.
2. Meeting health needs: interventions designed to satisfy inherent, universal human needs. These needs are not automatically met, and they include:
   a. Psychophysical: the need for adequate shelter, food, material goods, sensory stimulation, physical activity, and rest (e.g., institutionalized orphans confined to cribs require sensorimotor interventions to counter environmental deprivation).
   b. Temporal balance and regularity: the need for a satisfying balance between work/productive activities, leisure/play, and rest (e.g., forced leisure due to involuntary unemployment requires intervention to achieve temporal balance).
   c. Safety: the need to be in an environment free from hazards or threats (e.g., living in a chaotic, abusive home does not meet this need, and interventions are needed to ensure safety).
   d. Love and acceptance: the need to be accepted and loved for one's personal attributes and uniqueness, not for one's accomplishments (e.g., the barriers caused by aphasia and ataxia can hinder meeting this need; therefore, supportive interventions are indicated).
   e. Group association: the need to feel a connection to others who share similar interests and goals (e.g., the stigma and symptoms of mental illness can prevent regular interactions with a group; therefore, interventions to develop social interaction skills and provide community supports are indicated).
   f. Mastery: the need to successfully complete an activity or meet a goal because it is interesting and challenging (e.g., deficits in performance components

can hinder successful performance and block mastery; therefore interventions to develop performance skills and/or adapt activities are needed).
- g. Esteem: the need to be recognized for one's accomplishments (e.g., a lack of opportunity to do activities perceived as worthwhile by others requires interventions to facilitate recognized contributions).
- h. Sexual: the need for recognition of one's sexuality and the satisfaction of sexual drives (e.g., institutional rules against adult consensual sex prohibit meeting this need and require review and revision). Also, physical impediments to sexuality may require activity adaptations and environmental modifications.
- i. Pleasure: the need to do things just for fun (e.g., the child on an intensive school and home physical rehabilitation program needs an intervention plan supportive of spontaneous play).
- j. Self-actualization: the need to engage in activities just for oneself and for personal satisfaction (e.g., the person who writes poetry through an augmentative communication device for the joy of free expression).

3. The change process: interventions designed to achieve behavioral changes and functional outcomes.
   a. This type of intervention is the most commonly used in OT practice and is the most reimbursable.
   b. This process is often the only form of intervention discussed or documented.
   c. Guidelines for intervention planning and intervention implementation relate directly to this process.
   d. In the AOTA practice framework, the terms "establish/restore/remediation/restoration" are used to distinguish interventions that change a person in some manner.
      (1) Interventions focus on establishing a skill or ability that a person had never developed and/or restoring a skill or ability that the person had lost due to impairment.

4. Management: interventions designed to reduce or minimize disruptive or undesirable behavior that interfere with therapeutic activities or procedures needed to change areas of dysfunction that are the main focus of intervention (e.g., an individual becomes excessively anxious during their first use of a wheelchair in an environment outside of the hospital. Supportive interventions are needed to decrease anxiety, thereby enabling the person to work on essential community mobility skills).
   a. In the AOTA practice framework, the terms "modify/compensation/adaptation" are used to distinguish interventions that alter the context or demands of an activity to reduce distracting features.
      (1) Compensation and adaptation techniques are also used to alter the context or demands of an activity to support the person's ability to engage in areas of occupation (e.g., the provision of cues).

5. Maintenance: interventions designed to support and preserve the individual's current functional level (e.g., a reminiscence group to maintain the cognitive and social skills of individuals with early to mid-stage neurocognitive disorders).
   a. No improvement in function is planned due to the chronicity of the disorder or the progression of the disease.
   b. A decline in function is prevented, as much and for as long as possible.
   c. Maintenance programs include familial, environmental, and social supports and consistent and regularly scheduled follow-ups.
   d. While maintenance is not often reimbursed by third-party payers, it is a major type of OT intervention because OT practitioners often work with people who have chronic and/or progressive disorders.
      (1) The Centers for Medicare and Medicaid Services (CMS) has recognized that OT services to prevent or slow deterioration and maintain a person at their highest possible functional level are skilled and covered if these services are reasonable and necessary. See Chapter 4.
   e. In the AOTA practice framework, the term "maintain" is used to designate these interventions.

Intervention Planning

1. The formulation of the plan for intervention based upon an analysis of evaluation results according to selected frame(s) of reference.
2. The supervising occupational therapist is responsible for the intervention plan.
   a. The OTA contributes to this plan in a collaborative process.
3. Collaboration with the individual, family, significant others, and/or caregivers is essential to establish a relevant, meaningful plan that will be followed.

> **CAUTION:** If the OTA does not share a common language with the individual, family, significant others, and/or caregivers, an interpreter must be used to ensure that their perspectives are obtained to inform and guide the development of an intervention plan.

4. Prioritization of problem areas to be addressed in intervention.
   a. Values, interests, and needs of the individual, family, significant others, and caregivers.
   b. Individual's current and expected roles and environmental contexts.

c. The treatment setting's characteristics, resources, and limitations (e.g., length of stay).
d. The likelihood that the problem will respond to intervention within the given setting.
  (1) Concrete and specific problems are more likely to be effectively resolved than abstract global ones.
  (2) Services must be available within the setting to effectively address the problem; otherwise a referral is indicated.
5. Formats of written intervention plans can vary from setting to setting.
6. Intervention plan content.
  a. Long-term goals (LTGs): the change in activity limitations and participation restriction that will occur, prior to the termination of intervention, in order to achieve the desired functional occupational performance outcome.
  b. Short-term goals (STGs) or objectives: the component subskills that are to be achieved over shorter time frames, leading to the attainment of the long-term goal.
    (1) STGs must be directly related to the LTG.
    (2) Due to the reality of very brief lengths of stay (LOS) in some settings, only STGs may be accomplished prior to the termination of intervention.
    (3) Referrals to other settings with longer LOS or home care services may be required for intervention to attain LTGs.
  c. Intervention methods.
    (1) The meaningful occupations and purposeful activities and their associated tasks, techniques, procedures, and modalities that are used to achieve goals.
    (2) Methods of intervention must be clearly related to, and theoretically consistent with, the established goals.
    (3) Home programs and/or family caregiver training may be included.
    (4) Adaptive/assistive equipment, orthotics, prosthetics, and/or environmental modifications to meet individual's needs are specified.
  d. Duration, frequency, and number and type of intervention sessions planned to attain goals are specified (e.g., 10 community mobility groups, meeting for 1 hour, three times per week).
  e. Recommendations for additional OT services and referrals, if needed, to other professionals are provided.
  f. The design of all intervention plans must actively use clinical reasoning to ensure that each plan's primary focus is on the individual's engagement in occupation and participation in their chosen contexts. See this chapter's section on clinical reasoning.
  g. The existing evidence to support potential interventions must be reviewed and used to guide the intervention plan.

> **EXAM HINT:** In the NBCOT® exam outline for the COTA®, "Domain 02 Implement interventions under the supervision of the OTR in accordance with the intervention plan and level of service competence to support client participation in areas of occupation throughout the occupational therapy process" (NBCOT®, 2018, p. 24) comprises 55% of the exam. The application of knowledge about the above intervention planning guidelines and the following intervention implementation standards can help you determine correct answers for Domain 02 NBCOT® exam items.

Intervention Implementation

1. Fundamental OT principles are used to guide OT interventions. See Table 3-3, "Principles of Occupations."
2. The OTA is responsible for intervention implementation with supervision of the occupational therapist.
  a. Clinical reasoning is used to guide the implementation of intervention. See this chapter's section on clinical reasoning.
  b. State licensure laws, regulations, and statutes may limit the OTA's role in the implementation of intervention, but this variability will not be tested on the NBCOT® examination.
3. Overview of OT intervention methods.
  a. Individual, group, or population interventions may be used.
    (1) Refer to Table 3-4 for a comparison of indications for individual vs. group interventions.

> **EXAM HINT:** The NBCOT® exam outline for the COTA® identifies knowledge of the "factors related to determining the context and type of individual and group activities for effectively supporting intervention goals and objectives" (NBCOT®, 2018, p. 23) as essential for competent practice. Knowing the information provided in Table 3-4 can help you determine the correct answer for NBCOT® about determining when to use individual versus group interventions.

  b. Purposeful activities and meaningful occupations are used therapeutically.
  c. Environmental modifications and adaptations are provided to enhance function.
  d. Promotion of engagement in valued occupations is used to foster health and wellness.

Table 3-3

Principles of Occupations That Support Their Value and Use in Intervention

PRINCIPLE	EXPLANATION	EXAMPLE
Occupations and activities act as a therapeutic change agent to *remediate* or *restore*.	People have the potential to improve performance skills, patterns (habits, routines, and rituals), and body functions.	A homemaker who has impairments and problems in motor skills resulting from a stroke benefits more from working in the actual occupation of preparing meals in conjunction with exercises to increase her ROM, muscle strength, and coordination as opposed to solely using exercise equipment and objects stimulating the motor actions of the activity (Gasser-Wieland & Rice, 2002).
The use of new occupations as interventions provides the means for *establishing* performance skills and for developing habits.	The features of the context and environment may have changed and thus may demand the use of new performance skills and habits for the client to perform successfully.	Women with developmental delays and psychiatric conditions had a reduced rate of inappropriate behaviors and increased rate of socially appropriate behaviors in a new community living arrangement when given positive reinforcement in perusing everyday occupations (Holm, Santangelo, Fromuth, Brown, & Walter, 2000).
Valued occupations are *inherently motivating*.	Chosen occupations often are a reflection of what people value and enjoy and thus are more likely to be satisfying.	Older adults were motivated to resume engagement in occupations because of opportunities to reestablish relationships with others during engagement in valued occupations (Chan & Spencer, 2004).
Occupations promote the identification of *values and interests*.	Values influence occupational choice. When active in occupations, one experiences pleasure and satisfaction, thus generating interests (Kielhofner, 2002).	Older adults living within their communities related the three most important activities required for them to remain in their communities as using the telephone, using transportation, and reading; health professionals' list consisted of using the telephone, managing medications, and preparing snacks (Fricke & Unsworth, 2001).
Occupations create opportunities to *practice* performance skills and to *reinforce* performance.	The client must have the opportunity to develop patterns that include the remediated skill in routine daily tasks (Holm, Rogers, & Stone, 2003, p. 477).	Elementary students with learning disabilities and handwriting problems who practiced keyboarding in a training program improved written communication skills for performance at school (Handley-More, Deitz, Billingsley, & Coggins, 2003).
Active engagement in occupations produces *feedback*.	Corrective feedback regarding performance helps the client modify behavior.	A computer system was modified for a person with a head injury to provide an auditory prompt to mark the commencement of each planned activity. "I was just sitting there on the sofa doing something like reading a newspaper, and had completely forgotten the swimming bath, the computer started to bleep; oh, what had I forgotten now?" (Erikson, Karlsson, Soderstrom, & Tham, 2004, p. 267).
Engagement in occupations facilitates *mastery* or *competence* in performing daily activities.	Successes motivate further change and continued use and practice of newly learned performance skills during engagement in occupations.	People with severe mental illness developed skills and competence in work and social activities while participating in a supported work setting (Gahnstrom-Strandqvist, Liukko, & Tham, 2003).
Selected occupations promote *participation* with individuals or groups.	Interventions designed to eliminate physical and social barriers increase opportunities for social interaction, leading to increased interaction and sense of control in context and environment.	Children with impaired performance skills used an adapted powered-mobility riding toy, which increased opportunities for participation with other children and adults during the occupation of play (Deitz, Swinth, & White, 2002).
Through engagement in occupations, people learn to *assume responsibility for their own health and wellness*.	Interventions that focus on improving a client's ability to self-direct change in lifestyle choices can lead to a sense of control.	People with chronic disorders who participated in community-based group services developed responsibility for their own health by empowerment of the group members (Taylor, Braveman, & Hammel, 2004).
Occupations exert a positive influence on *health* and *well-being* (Law, 2002b).	Regardless of the presence of impairments, a person may remain active and engaged in healthy occupations.	People with fibromyalgia who successfully used activity modification strategies to complete daily activities reported positive quality of life and health (Lindberg & Schkade, 2001).

(Continued)

Table 3-3

Principles of Occupations That Support Their Value and Use in Intervention (Continued)

PRINCIPLE	EXPLANATION	EXAMPLE
Occupations provide the means for people to *adapt* to changing needs and conditions.	A person's capacity for performance is affected by the status of body structures and functions. Permanent loss of capacity necessitates modification of the context and environment and of activity demands.	Patients who had hip fractures demonstrated more efficiency and greater satisfaction in recovering performance skills in daily occupations when modified activity procedures were emphasized (Jackson & Schkade, 2001).
Occupations contribute to the creation and maintenance of *identity* (AOTA, 2002; Christiansen, 1999).	Discovering identity is related to what a person does and to those people with whom they come in contact during daily occupations and activities.	People with injuries to the hand resumed occupations that facilitated resumption of their identity (Chan & Spencer, 2004).
Successful performance in occupation can positively affect *psychological* functioning.	A person's evaluation of performance in occupations and activities influences perceptions about himself or herself.	People recovering from a stroke demonstrated positive views and acceptance of the need for a wheelchair, described opportunities for continuity of previous life activities, maintenance of mobility, and decreased burden on the caregiver (Barker, Reid, & Cott, 2004).
Occupations have unique *meaning* and *purpose* for each person, which influences the quality of performance (AOTA, 2002).	The meaning of occupations refers to the subjective experience one has when engaging in activities.	People recovering from a stroke stood longer when performing personally meaningful tasks (Dolecheck & Schkade, 1999).
Engagement in occupations gives a sense of *satisfaction* and *fulfillment* (AOTA, 2002).	Performance of valued occupations provides for achievement of personal goals in a variety of roles.	Satisfaction through occupations was found when older adults maintained daily routines and engaged in fulfilling occupations (Bontje, Kinebanian, Josephsson, & Tamura, 2004). Goldberg, Brintell, and Golberg (2002) found a correlation between engagement in meaningful activities and life satisfaction.
Occupations influence how people spend time and *make decisions* (AOTA, 2002).	People occupy time through engagement in activity.	In a study of time use, older people spent most of their time completing activities that were meaningful for them and not necessarily the activities that were necessary for them to remain in the community (Fricke & Unsworth, 2001).

From: Moyers, P.A., & Dale, L. (2007). *The guide to occupational therapy practice* (2nd ed., pp. 45–46). Copyright 2007 by the American Occupational Therapy Association. Reprinted with permission.

---

e. Adaptive equipment, assistive technology, and orthotic devices are designed, fabricated, and applied to facilitate function.
f. Adaptive equipment, assistive technology, orthotics, and prosthetic use training are provided to promote independence.
g. Physical agent modalities are used to prepare for, or as an adjunct to, engagement in therapeutic functional activities.
h. Ergonomic principles are applied to the performance of meaningful occupations.
i. Standard precautions are observed.
  (1) Standard precautions are the primary strategy for control of nosocomial infection and are used in the care of all persons (Appendix 3A).
j. Transmission-based precautions are used for persons with known or suspected infections of highly transmissible or epidemiologically important pathogens.
  (1) Includes airborne precautions, droplet precautions, and contact precautions (Appendix 3B).

RED FLAG: Standard precautions must be observed during *all* interventional procedures, and transmission-based precautions must also be implemented as needed to prevent infection.

EXAM HINT: The COTA® exam outline identifies knowledge of "standard infection control procedures and universal precautions for reducing transmission of contaminants" (NBCOT®, 2018, p. 29) as essential for competent and safe practice. Knowing the standard and transmission-based precautions that are outlined in Appendix 3A and Appendix 3B can help you determine the correct answer for COTA® exam items about the task of incorporating "risk management techniques at an individual and practice-setting level" (NBCOT®, 2018, p. 29).

Table 3-4

Individual vs. Group Intervention

Individual	Learning capacity of the person
	Amount of attention and skill required from the occupational therapy practitioner owing to body structure and function impairments
	Need for privacy
	Need for greater control over the context and environment
	Difficulty or complexity of occupation and activity demands, performance skills and performance patterns
	Inappropriate or dangerous behavior of the person
Group	Developing interpersonal skills
	Engaging in socialization
	Receiving feedback from people experiencing similar conditions
	Being motivated by peer role models
	Learning from other people
	Placing one's own condition into perspective
	Developing group normative behavior for successful performance in shared occupations (e.g., work, study, and leisure groups)

From: Moyers, P.A., & Dale, L. (2007). *The guide to occupational therapy practice* (2nd ed., p. 47). Copyright 2007 by the American Occupational Therapy Association. Reprinted with permission.

Developmental Considerations in Intervention

> **EXAM HINT:** The NBCOT® exam outline for the COTA® identifies knowledge of the "collaborative processes and procedures for prioritizing intervention goals and activities based on client . . . developmental skills" (NBCOT®, 2018, p. 22) and "clinical decision-making for implementing modifications to the intervention plan and prioritization of goals under the supervision of the OTR in response to . . . developmental needs of the client" (NBCOT®, 2018, p. 23) as essential for competent and safe practice. The application of knowledge about the following developmental considerations in intervention can help you determine the correct answer for NBCOT® Domain 01 exam items.

1. When collaborating with the OTR to plan intervention and when implementing intervention with supervision, the COTA® should:
   a. Consider and respect the family's cultural background.
   b. Ensure all activities, toys, and other intervention media are appropriate to the child's developmental level.
   c. Use play activities as the primary occupation intervention.
   d. Recognize that family education is essential.
      (1) Identify environmental characteristics that facilitate the child's development.
      (2) Provide advocacy training to link families to community.
      (3) Identify psychosocial factors that promote the child's development.
      (4) Teach avoidance of triggers that precipitate behaviors that may interfere with learning and occupational engagement.
      (5) Train in the use of effective behavior management strategies that enable participation.
   e. Provide consultation or direct treatment to facilitate school performance and achieve educational goals. See Chapter 4.
   f. Provide treatment to facilitate sensorimotor, cognitive, and psychosocial development.
   g. Fabricate or requisition positioning equipment and technological aides for home and/or school. See Chapters 14 and 15.
   h. Ensure that the visual and auditory aides used during treatment sessions can be easily understood and accessed by the family members/caregivers. See subsequent section on teaching-learning principles and methods.
   i. Review the pediatric and developmental clinical condition information provided in the Clinical Conditions chapters (6–10) about diagnostic-specific interventions.

Re-evaluation/Intervention Review

Overview

1. The process of determining whether the individual's occupational performance has improved, declined, or remained the same after intervention.
2. Frequent monitoring of an individual's response to intervention is an integral part of all OT interventions.
3. Effective interventions resulting in the individual's progress require intervention plan modification and an upgrading of goals, as long as there is a reasonable

expectation that the individual can improve functional performance.
4. If the individual is not progressing according to plan, different intervention methods, referral(s) to experts in the field or other professions or to another level of care, and/or discharge from intervention may be indicated.

The Role of the OTA

1. The supervising occupational therapist is responsible for the review of intervention and re-evaluation process.
   a. The OTA contributes to this process in a collaborative manner.
2. The OTA shares all observations regarding an individual's response to intervention and any other information that may affect intervention and intervention plans.
   a. The supervising occupational therapist is responsible for intervention plan modification.
   b. The OTA contributes to this process.

Discharge Planning

1. The process for planning for discontinuation of services.
2. The supervising occupational therapist is responsible for this process.
   a. The OTA contributes to this process in a collaborative manner.
3. Reasons for discharge.
   a. The individual's goals have been met.
   b. The individual has reached a functional plateau.
   c. The individual does not require skilled services, for maximum benefit has been achieved.
   d. An exacerbation of an illness or a medical crisis requires discharge to a higher level of care.
   e. The person's allotted length of stay in the setting has expired, and extension of LOS is not possible.
4. General principles.
   a. Discharge planning begins with the initial evaluation and is an inherent part of the intervention planning process. All interventions should be planned with consideration of the expected, planned discharge environment.
   b. Collaboration with the individual, family, significant others, caregivers, other professionals on the team, employers, and reimbursers is required for an effective and realistic discharge plan.
   c. Discharge may include transfer to a long-term care setting (e.g., a skilled nursing or assistive living facility), to an intermediate care facility (e.g., a halfway house), or to a home setting.
      (1) A predischarge home evaluation must be completed to ensure the individual will be safe and to identify needed home adaptations or supports (e.g., bathroom modifications, home health aide).
         (a) If an on-site evaluation is not possible, alternative assessment methods must be used to obtain needed information (e.g., having a family member/caregiver complete a home safety checklist and photograph and/or video record the home environment).
   d. A well-planned discharge facilitates community participation and maintenance of functional gains.
5. Follow-up referrals for further OT intervention and/or other supportive services must be made.
   a. Home programs.
      (1) Recommendations to the individual, family, significant others, and caregivers on techniques and procedures to maintain and/or improve functional status.
      (2) Training should be provided prior to discharge.
      (3) Information on additional supports should be provided.
   b. Community resources.
      (1) Recommendations and referrals to specific services in the community that can support function and quality of life (e.g., Alcoholics Anonymous, a psychosocial clubhouse, adult day treatment, Meals on Wheels).

OT Tools of Practice

Definition

1. The established, legitimate means by which the practitioners of a profession achieve the profession's goals and meet society's needs.

Occupation

1. Definition: goal-directed pursuits that typically extend over time.
   a. They have purpose, value, and meaning to the performer and involve multiple tasks.

b. They are the ordinary and familiar things that people do every day.
2. Basic concepts of occupation.
   a. Every individual has multiple occupations that are meaningful (e.g., self-care, home management, work, and leisure) and needed to function in roles (e.g., parent, worker, student, hobbyist).
   b. Humans are innately occupational beings and are driven by an inherent need for mastery, self-actualization, self-identity, competence, and social acceptance.
   c. Occupations have social, cultural, physical, and temporal contextual dimensions because they involve activities within specific settings and extend over time.
   d. Occupations have symbolic and spiritual dimensions, as individuals infuse individualized meanings into occupations.
   e. Occupations are interdependent (e.g., one must work to pay for leisure; one must have leisure to sustain and renew oneself for work).
   f. Health is attained when the dynamic balance between occupations and rest is appropriate and meets the needs of the individual.
   g. Occupation can be viewed and used as a 'means' or a method to change an individual's performance (e.g., playing a board game to increase motor skills).
   h. Occupation can also be viewed and used as an 'end' or desired outcome (e.g., playing a board game to improve the ability to engage in age-appropriate social play).
   i. Engagement in occupation to support the individual's participation in environment(s) of choice is the overriding desired outcome of occupational therapy.
3. Areas of occupation.
   a. Activities of daily living (ADL): activities that involve care of self; often called personal activities of daily living (PADL) or basic activities of daily living (BADL).
   b. Instrumental activities of daily living (IADL): activities that involve environmental interaction; they are more complex than self-care and can be optional (e.g., home maintenance, care of others, and community mobility activities).
   c. Work: all productive activities that contribute services, goods, or commodities to society, whether financially compensated or not (i.e., a volunteer is working).
   d. Education: activities that involve the student role and participation in an educational environment.
   e. Play/leisure: all activities engaged in for pleasure, relaxation, amusement, and/or self-fulfillment.
   f. Social participation: activities involving interaction with community, family, and peers/friends.
   g. Rest and sleep: quiet and relaxing activities and daily routines that enable participation in sufficient rest and sleep that are needed to support health and occupational engagement.

EXAM HINT: In the NBCOT® exam outline for the COTA®, "Domain 02 Implement interventions under the supervision of the OTR in accordance with the intervention plan and level of service competence to support client participation in areas of occupation throughout the occupational therapy process" (NBCOT®, 2018, p. 24) comprises 55% of the exam (NBCOT®, 2018, p. 18). The application of knowledge about the above and following OT tools of practice can help you effectively determine the best possible answer to Domain 02 exam items that address intervention approaches.

Purposeful Activities

1. Definition.
   a. Doing processes that are directed toward a desired and intended outcome and require energy and thought to engage in and complete.
   b. The goal-directed tasks and/or behaviors that make up occupations.
2. Characteristics of purposeful activities.
   a. Universally, people participate in purposeful activities, although there are personal and sociocultural differences in the manner in which activities are performed (e.g., dressing).
   b. Fundamental to the development and acquisition of performance component skills is active participation in purposeful activities (e.g., the development of eye-hand coordination through play).
   c. Fundamental to occupational performance areas is the performance of purposeful activities (e.g., to work involves completion of multiple tasks).
   d. Purposeful activities are composed of identifiable parts that can be analyzed.
   e. Purposeful activities are holistic.
   f. Purposeful activities can be manipulated and adapted to be appropriate to, and/or therapeutic for, the individual.
   g. Purposeful activities can be graded along many dimensions to meet the needs of an individual.
   h. Determination of the individual's differential responses to purposeful activities can provide information for the selection of appropriate activities for use in evaluation and intervention.
   i. Verbal and nonverbal communication is facilitated through engagement in purposeful activities.

j. Organization and ability to focus are enhanced, because purposeful activities provide concrete structure.
k. Doing is emphasized.
l. Involvement in, and with, the nonhuman environment is enhanced.
m. Purposeful activities can vary on a continuum from conscious to not conscious/unconscious.
n. Purposeful activities vary on a continuum from real to symbolic.
o. Purposeful activities vary on a continuum from simulated in a clinical setting to real in the individual's natural environment.

Task/Activity Analysis and Synthesis

> **EXAM HINT:** The NBCOT® exam outline for the COTA® identifies knowledge of "task analysis in relation to a client's performance skills, the occupational profile, practice setting, stage of occupational therapy process, areas of occupation, and activity demands" (NBCOT®, 2018, p. 22) as essential for competent and safe practice. The application of knowledge about the following task/activity analysis methods can help you determine the correct answer for NBCOT® Domain 01 exam items.

1. Task/activity analysis
   a. The breaking down and identification of the component parts of a task/activity.
   b. Determination of the abilities needed to effectively perform and successfully complete the task/activity.
   c. Determination if the task/activity has therapeutic value.
   d. Methods of task/activity analysis.
      (1) Specify the exact task/activity to be analyzed (i.e., not just 'dressing' but 'donning a sweatshirt').
      (2) Identify and know the procedures, materials, and tools needed to complete the specific task/activity.
      (3) Analyze the task/activity as it is typically performed under ordinary circumstances.
      (4) Analyze the task/activity to be certain that all client factors, performance skills, and activity and occupational demands, task performance components and performance contexts are considered.
      (5) Select a frame of reference to determine which aspects of the task/activity are to be emphasized in the analysis.
2. Activity synthesis.
   a. The process of designing an activity for OT evaluation or intervention.
   b. Combines information obtained from the activity analysis with assessment information about the individual to ensure that a suitable match is made between the activity requirements and the person's needs and abilities.
   c. Effective activity synthesis often requires the adaptation and/or gradation of the selected activity.
3. Purposes and methods of activity analysis and synthesis.
   a. Teaching an activity.
      (1) Analyze the nature and sequence of the subtasks within the activity.
      (2) Synthesize to determine the best way to present the activity as a learning experience.
   b. Determining whether an individual can perform an activity.
      (1) Analyze the performance component requirements of the activity.
      (2) Synthesize by comparing the activity requirements with the individual's functional level.
   c. Adapting an activity.
      (1) Evaluate the individual's functional capabilities.
      (2) Analyze what parts of the activity can be changed.
      (3) Identify what functional aids can be used to allow the individual to successfully perform the activity.
   d. Grading an activity.
      (1) Determine what aspects can be changed along a continuum of performance.
      (2) Identify the individual's performance deficit(s) and/or client factors requiring intervention.
      (3) Synthesize to upgrade or downgrade complexity or difficulty level of the activity to meet the needs of the individual.

> **EXAM HINT:** The NBCOT® exam outline identifies knowledge of the "methods for grading an activity, task, or technique based on level of development, client status, response to intervention, and client needs" (NBCOT®, 2018, p. 25) as essential for competent and safe practice. The application of knowledge about the principles identified above for grading activities can help you determine the correct answer for NBCOT® Domain 02 exam items about the implementation of occupation-based interventions.

The Teaching-Learning Process

1. Definition: the process by which the OT practitioner designs experiences to facilitate the individual's acquisition of the knowledge and skills needed for living.
2. Principles of learning.
   a. Learning is influenced by the individual's interests, age, sex, sociocultural factors, and current assets and limitations.

b. Attention to the learning experience and perception of the situation influence learning.
c. The learner's sources of motivation must be identified and used for engagement in learning experiences.
d. Learning goals made by the individual are more likely to be met than goals determined by others.
e. Learning is enhanced when the individual understands the reason for and purpose of the learning activity.
f. Learning is increased when it recognizes the individual's current functional level and is initiated within the person's capabilities (i.e., not too high or too low).
g. Learning is enhanced when activities and experiences proceed at a rate that is comfortable for the individual.
h. Individuals who actively participate in the learning process learn more, for experiential learning is more effective than didactic learning.
i. Reinforcement and feedback on the individual's behavior and/or task performance are important parts of the learning experience and can be used to support desired behaviors and extinguish undesirable behaviors.
j. Learning can be enhanced through trial and error, shaping, and imitation of models.
k. Frequent repetition and practice in different situations facilitate learning and encourages generalization.
l. Planned movement from simplified wholes to more complex wholes facilitates integration of what is to be learned.
m. Inventive solutions to problems (as well as more useful or typical solutions) should be encouraged.
n. The environment of the learning experience can strongly influence the success of that experience.
o. Individual differences in the way anxiety affects the individual's learning must be considered.
p. Conflicts and frustrations, inevitably present in the learning situation, must be recognized and provisions made for their resolution or accommodation.
q. Continuity between the planned therapeutic learning experiences and the real-life situations for which the individual needs to be prepared facilitates the effective transfer of learning and the generalization of knowledge and skills.

3. Teaching methods.
   a. Definition: ways to present information and/or a task to an individual on a one-to-one basis or in a group.
   b. Demonstration and performance.
      (1) The OT practitioner performs the task, and the individual imitates the OT practitioner's performance.
      (2) For example, the OT practitioner demonstrates one-handed cooking techniques and the use of adaptive equipment; the individual with a unilateral upper extremity amputation imitates therapist's task performance.
   c. Exploration and discovery.
      (1) A diversity of activities is made available, and the individual is permitted to choose any activity and try it without specific instructions or directions.
      (2) For example, in an expressive arts group, members can select from a diversity of media and create individual works.
   d. Explanation and discussion.
      (1) A verbal explanation of the task and a discussion of the activity components to either plan an activity or to review what occurred during the activity are provided by the therapist.
      (2) For example, in a vocational group, the steps for applying for a job are reviewed prior to clients submitting job applications and what happened during a job interview and what happened during a job interview is reviewed after the interview is completed.
   e. Role play.
      (1) The OT practitioner and/or individual(s) assume roles and act out scenarios to practice behaviors prior to doing the behavior in a real situation.
      (2) For example, the OT practitioner plays the interviewer and the individual plays the job applicant.
   f. Simulation.
      (1) The individual acts out an activity performance using simulated tasks and/or objects.
      (2) For example, the individual uses a driving simulator prior to driving in a car on a roadway.
   g. Problem solving.
      (1) The process of teaching a person to analyze a situation, define the problem, outline potential solutions, select the solution that appears to be most viable, implement the solution, evaluate the outcome to determine if problem is resolved, and retry a new solution, if needed.
      (2) For example, working with an individual living in a supportive apartment who has a roommate who does not do household tasks to develop and use strategies for engaging the roommate in home maintenance tasks (e.g., the use of a weekly chore list).
   h. Audiovisual aids.
      (1) The use of slides, videos, and/or audio cassettes to teach material with or without the presence of a therapist.

(2) For example, an individual with anxiety is provided with relaxation tapes to use at home.
i. Repetition and practice.
(1) The repetitious engagement in a task to increase accuracy and speed.
(2) For example, repeatedly closing the fasteners on clothing to decrease the time needed to get ready for work in the morning.
j. Behavioral management.
(1) The identification of behaviors that require development (e.g., appropriate social skills) and/or require extinction (e.g., hitting people).
(2) The implementation of a structured program to facilitate the desired behavioral change.
(3) For example, interactions that are consistent with societal norms are rewarded with praise; whereas, aggressive acts are addressed with time-out periods.
k. Consumer/family/caregiver education.
(1) An organized, systematic approach to formally present information to increase knowledge.
(2) The nature of the illness or disease, including etiology, signs and symptoms, functional implications, prognosis, and intervention are explained.
(3) The maintenance of roles and occupational performance is emphasized.
(4) Methods for the prevention of secondary problems (e.g., decubiti), are provided.
(5) Community resources and supportive services are explored with appropriate referrals made.

EXAM HINT: The NBCOT® exam outline for the COTA® identifies knowledge of the "fundamental strategies used for addressing health literacy to enhance nonverbal and verbal interactions with a client and relevant others in order to promote positive health behaviors, enable informed decisions, maximize safety of care delivery, and promote carry-over of the intervention to support positive intervention outcomes" (NBCOT®, 2018, p. 22) as essential for competent and safe practice. The application of knowledge about the previously mentioned learning principles and teaching methods can help you determine the correct answer for NBCOT® Domain 01 exam items about health literacy.

Clinical Reasoning

1. Definition: the complex mental processes the therapist uses when thinking about the individual, the disability, and the personal, social, and cultural meanings the individual gives to the disability, the uniqueness of the situation, and himself/herself.

2. Value for OTAs in practice.
a. Improves clinical decision making by giving OTAs tools for self-conscious reflection on their decisions.
b. Improves ability to explain the rationales behind OTAs' decisions to consumers, family members, team members, and medical finance agencies (e.g., insurers).
c. Improves job satisfaction by making OTAs more aware of the complexity of their work, the value of their practice.
3. Types of clinical reasoning.
a. Procedural reasoning/scientific reasoning.
(1) Involves identifying problems related to OT's domain of concern, goal setting, and treatment planning.
(2) Involves implementing treatment strategies via systematic gathering and interpreting of client data.
(3) The actual technical 'doing' of practice.
(4) The reasoning that is documented the most for reimbursement purposes.
b. Interactive reasoning.
(1) Deals with how the disability or disease affects the person; focuses on the client as a person.
(2) Involves the therapeutic relationship between the OTA, the individual, and caregivers.
(3) Facilitates effective treatment, as it focuses on the personal meaning of illness and disability which can influence how a person engages in treatment (i.e., how motivational issues affect a client's performance).
(4) Congruent with the profession's philosophy and heritage of caring.
c. Narrative reasoning.
(1) Deals with the individual's occupational story and focuses on the process of change needed to reach an imagined future.
(2) Identifies what activities and roles were important to the person prior to illness/injury.
(3) Analyzes what valued activities and roles the individual can perform now.
(4) Explores what valued activities and roles are possible in the future, given the person's disability.
(5) Asks what valued activities and roles the individual would choose as priorities for the future.
(6) Neglects larger practice area issues in which the client/practitioner interaction is occurring (e.g., pragmatic constraints imposed by reimbursement, equipment, and/or organizational culture).
d. Pragmatic reasoning.
(1) Considers the context in which the OT practitioner's thinking occurs.

(2) States that mental activities are shaped by the situation (i.e., is a setting long term or acute?).
(3) Considers the treatment environment and OT practitioner's values, knowledge, abilities, and experiences.
(4) Focuses on the treatment possibilities within a given treatment setting.
(5) Reframes understanding of the influence of personal and practical constraints on OT practice.
(6) The most effective OT practitioners are able to negotiate pragmatic contextual issues in favor of quality care.
e. Conditional reasoning.
(1) Involves an ongoing revision of treatment.
(2) Focuses on current and possible future social contexts.
(3) Represents an integration of interactive, procedural, and pragmatic reasoning in the context of the client's narrative.
(4) Requires multidimensional thinking.

EXAM HINT: In the NBCOT® exam outline for the COTA®, the task of monitoring "the intervention plan and progress toward goals in collaboration with the OTR by using clinical reasoning (and) therapeutic use of self" (NBCOT®, 2018, p. 23) is identified as essential for competent practice. The application of knowledge about the types of clinical reasoning described above and the following information about the therapeutic use of self can help you determine the correct answer for NBCOT® Domain 01 exam items.

Therapeutic Use of Self

1. Definition: the practitioner's conscious, planned interaction with the individual, family members, significant others, and/or caregivers.
   a. The conscious, planned use of one's personality, unique characteristics, perceptions and insights during the therapeutic process.
2. Purposes of therapeutic use of self.
   a. Provide reassurance and/or information.
   b. Give advice.
   c. Alleviate anxiety and/or fear.
   d. Obtain needed information.
   e. Improve and maintain function.
   f. Promote growth and development.
   g. Increase coping skills.
3. Essential characteristics of therapeutic use of self.
   a. Perception of the individuality and uniqueness of each person.
   b. Respect for the dignity and rights of each individual regardless of past or present situation or possible future potential.
   c. Empathy to enter and share the experiences of an individual while maintaining one's own sense of self.
   d. Compassion to be kind and want to alleviate pain and suffering.
   e. Humility to recognize one's own limitations.
   f. Unconditional positive regard to be nonjudgmental and accept, respect, and show concern and liking for each individual as a human being, regardless of presenting behaviors.
   g. Honesty to be truthful and straightforward.
   h. A relaxed manner to leave other concerns aside and schedule sufficient time to be with the person so that external issues do not impede the relationship.
   i. Flexibility to modify behavior to meet the needs of each individual and deal with circumstances as they arise or change.
   j. Self-awareness to accurately know one's assets and limitations and to be able to make changes as needed to interact more effectively in therapeutic relationships.
   k. Humor to appropriately recognize and/or use what is amusing and comical.
4. Common issues and responses that can affect therapeutic relationships.
   a. Negative attitudes, fear, or hostility toward individuals who are different and/or toward the unknown.
   b. Resistance to establishing a rapport due to past rejections and/or fear of future rejection.
   c. Communication difficulties.
      (1) Incongruence between verbal and nonverbal communications (when spoken words do not match a person's facial expression, tone of voice, gestures, or postures), resulting in confusion.
      (2) Language difficulties.
         (a) Psychiatric symptoms such as blocking, circumstantiality, flight of ideas, confabulation, grandiosity, articulated delusions, loosening of association, and/or poverty of content can hinder effective communication.
         (b) Cultural, class, educational, and/or regional differences can result in misunderstandings or lack of comprehension between individuals.
         (c) Misinterpretations can occur due to differences in primary language.
   d. Dependency that is excessive and hinders the individual's growth toward interdependence and/or independence.
   e. Transference and countertransference.
      (1) Transference is an unconscious response to an individual that is similar to the way one has responded to a significant person (e.g., the practitioner is responded to as a parent).

(2) Countertransference is an unconscious response to transference in which the individual responds in a manner that is expected and desired by the person who has transference towards them (e.g., the practitioner assumes a parental role towards a client).
  f. Difficulty in expressing feelings due to personal reticence or cultural background.
  g. Overinvolvement that results in a loss of objectivity or a fear of involvement that leads to detachment.
  h. Difficulty with developing an individual therapeutic style that is a comfortable 'fit.'
5. Supervision and support.
  a. Develops the ability to use oneself therapeutically.
  b. Assists with the common issues and responses noted in prior section.
  c. Increases effectiveness in applying therapeutic principles in daily practice.

Group Process, Therapeutic Groups, and Activity Groups

EXAM HINT: The NBCOT® exam outline for the COTA® exam identifies knowledge of the "methods for facilitating individual and group participation in shared tasks or activities consistent with the type, function, format, context, goals, and stage of the group" (NBCOT®, 2018, p. 25) as essential for competent and safe practice. Knowing the following information about group process and therapeutic groups can help you determine the correct answer for NBCOT® exam items about group interventions.

1. Overview of group dynamics.
  a. Group dynamics are the forces that influence the nature of small groups, the interrelationships of their members, the events that typically occur in small groups, and ultimately, the outcome(s) of these groups.
  b. Group dynamics can be examined according to the group's structure, content, and process.
2. Group development: the stages groups typically go through from their initial beginnings to their termination.
  a. Origin phase involves the leader composing the group protocol and planning for the group (e.g., size of the group, member characteristics, location of meetings).
  b. Orientation phase involves members learning what the group is about, making a preliminary commitment to the group, and developing initial connections with other members.
  c. Intermediate phase involves members developing interpersonal bonds, group norms, and specialized member roles through involvement in goal-directed activities and clarification of group's purpose.
  d. Conflict phase involves members challenging the group's structure, purposes, and/or processes and is characterized by dissension and disagreements among members.
    (1) Successful resolution of this phase results in modifications to the group that are acceptable to members, enabling the group to proceed to the next phase of development.

CAUTION: Unsuccessful resolution of this phase results in dissolution of the group.

  e. Cohesion phase involves members regrouping after the conflict with a clearer sense of purpose and a reaffirmation of group norms and values, leading to group stability.
  f. Maturation phase involves members using their energies and skills to be productive and to achieve group's goals.
  g. Termination phase involves dissolution of the group due to members' goal attainment, accomplishment of desired task(s), lack of member engagement, inability to resolve conflict, and/or administrative constraints (e.g., only four sessions allotted for a discharge planning group), goal attainment, or task accomplishment.
3. Group roles: describe the patterns of behavior that are typical within groups.
  a. Instrumental roles are functional and assumed to help the group select, plan, and complete the group's task (e.g., initiator, organizer).
  b. Expressive roles are functional and are assumed to support and maintain the overall group and to meet members' needs (e.g., encourager, compromiser).

CAUTION: Individual roles are dysfunctional and contrary to group roles, for they serve an individual purpose and interfere with successful group functioning (e.g., aggressor, blocker).

4. Group norms: the standards of behavior and attitudes that are considered appropriate and acceptable to the group.
  a. Behavior that falls outside of the group's range of acceptable behavior is considered deviant and is often negatively sanctioned.
  b. Norms can be explicit and clearly verbalized (e.g., confidentiality is maintained by all group members, aggression is not tolerated).
  c. Norms can be nonexplicit and not verbalized (e.g., discussion topics that are taboo).
  d. Norms can vary in different groups and can change as a group develops and/or membership changes.

e. Therapeutic norms.
      (1) Encourage self-reflection, self-disclosure, and interaction among members.
      (2) Reinforce the value and importance of the group by being on time and well prepared.
      (3) Establish an atmosphere of support and safety.
      (4) Maintain confidentiality and respect.
      (5) Regard group members as effective agents of change by not placing the group leader in the expert role.

> **EXAM HINT:** Knowledge of the above therapeutic group norms can help you determine the best answer for COTA® exam items about effective group interventions. Correct answers will include adherence to these norms; incorrect answers will violate these norms.

5. Group goals: the desired outcomes of the group that are shared by a sufficient number of the group's members.
   a. The group's effort is mostly aimed at attaining these goals.
   b. Group goals provide focus for the group and guidelines for group activities and interactions.
   c. Group goals are not a compilation of individual member goals. Members may have diverse goals, but attainment of the group goal will facilitate personal goal achievement.
   d. Benefits of member participation in group goal setting.
      (1) A match between members' goals and group's goal(s).
      (2) Increased understanding of the requirements for achievement of the goal(s).
      (3) Increased appreciation of each member's contribution to achieving group's desired outcomes.
6. Group communication: the process of giving, receiving, and interpreting information through verbal and nonverbal expression.
   a. Effective group communication is a prerequisite to, and a requirement for, all group functioning.
   b. Effective communication occurs in a group when a member sends a message and the message is interpreted by the other group members receiving the message in the manner that the sender intended.
   c. Sending and receiving messages often takes place simultaneously due to the dynamic process of verbal and nonverbal communication.
   d. Communication can take many forms, including monologue, criticism, orders, questions and answers, and open give-and-take.
   e. Group communication that is adaptive may include clarifying goals and the sharing of ideas, experiences, and feelings.

> **CAUTION:** Maladaptive group communication can include seeking to control the group by controlling the channels of communication and/or avoiding specific issues or persons.

7. Group cohesiveness: the degree to which members are committed to a group and the extent of members' liking for the group (i.e., the sense of 'we-ness').
   a. Factors that contribute to cohesiveness.
      (1) Extensive interaction between members.
      (2) Similarity or complementariness in member characteristics.
      (3) Perception of relevance of group to individual needs.
      (4) Members' expectation of goal attainment and successful group outcome.
      (5) Democratic leadership and member cooperation.
8. Group decision making: the process of agreeing on a resolution to a problem. The solution may be obtained through different processes.
   a. Unanimous decision in which all group members agree.
   b. Consensus in which members agree to the majority's decision but retain the right to reconsider their decision.
   c. Majority rule in which the majority's decision is accepted with no reevaluation of the decision by members.
   d. Compromise in which a combination of different points of view results in a decision that is different from each distinct point of view.
9. Group leadership styles and membership roles.
   a. Directive leadership takes place when the OT practitioner is responsible for the planning and structuring of much of what takes place in the group.
      (1) This style is needed when the members' cognitive, social, and verbal skills, as well as engagement, are limited (e.g., parallel or project/associative level groups).
      (2) Directive leaders select the activities to be used in the group.
      (3) They provide clear verbal and demonstrated instruction to complete tasks.
      (4) Group maintenance roles and feedback is predominately provided by the directive leader.
      (5) The directive leader's goal is task accomplishment.
   b. Facilitative leadership occurs when the OT practitioner shares responsibility for the group and for group process with the members.
      (1) This style is advised when members' skill levels and engagement are moderate (e.g., egocentric-cooperative/basic cooperative or cooperative/supportive cooperative).

(2) Facilitative leaders collaborate with group members to select the activities to be used in a group.
(3) Members and leaders share instruction throughout the group's process.
(4) Group maintenance roles and feedback are provided by members with the leader facilitating the process.
(5) The facilitative leader's goal is to have members acquire skills through experience.

c. Advisory leadership takes place when the OT practitioner functions as a resource to the members who set the agenda and structure the group's functioning.
(1) This style is assumed when members' skills and engagement are high (e.g., cooperative/supportive cooperative, mature groups).
(2) Members select and complete the group's activity with leader's advice, if needed.
(3) Group maintenance roles are independently assumed by group members.
(4) Feedback occurs as a natural part of the group's self-directed process.
(5) The advisory leader's goal is to have members understand and self-direct the process.

d. Refer to Table 3-5 for Medicare guidelines for group therapy member selection and Table 3-6 for Medicare guidelines for group leadership responsibility.

> **EXAM HINT:** Medicare guidelines for group interventions are relevant and helpful standards that can apply to exam items about group interventions, regardless of practice setting or service payer.

Table 3-5

Medicare Indicators for Group Membership

THE INDIVIDUAL IS ABLE TO:
- engage willingly in group
- attend to group guidelines/procedures
- actively participate in group process
- benefit from group leadership input
- benefit from group membership/peer input
- respond appropriately throughout group process
- incorporate feedback
- complete activities toward goal attainment
- attain greater benefit from the group intervention than from 1:1 intervention

Reference: Adapted from United States Government Printing Office. *Code of Federal Regulations*, Title 42, Volume 3. Retrieved from http://www.cms.gov. December 21, 2003.

Table 3-6

Medicare Criteria for Group Leadership

THE LEADER:
- provides active leadership
- instructs members as a group
- monitors and documents individual's participation and response to intervention
- provides individualized guidance and feedback
- documents person's progress toward goals defined in the individual intervention plan in objective, measurable, functional terms

Reference: Adapted from United States Government Printing Office. *Code of Federal Regulations*, Title 42, Volume 3. Retrieved from http://www.cms.gov. December 21, 2003.

10. Co-leadership: occurs when there is sharing of group leadership between two or more therapists and/or OTAs.
    a. Advantages.
       (1) Each leader can assume different leadership roles, tasks, and styles.
       (2) Both leaders can provide and obtain mutual support.
       (3) Observations and objectivity can increase.
       (4) Co-leaders can share knowledge and skills.
       (5) Co-leaders can model effective behaviors.

> **CAUTION:** Challenges to co-leadership may arise. These can include:
> - splitting by group member(s) of one leader against the other.
> - excessive competition among coleaders.
> - unequal responsibilities resulting in an unbalanced workload among coleaders.
>
> These challenges must be dealt with in a proactive manner to ensure effective co-leadership.

11. Curative factors of groups as defined by Yalom.
    a. Altruism is the giving of oneself to help others.
    b. Catharsis is the relieving of emotions by expressing one's feelings.
    c. Universality comes from recognizing shared feelings and that one's problems are not unique.
    d. Existential factors address accepting the fact that the responsibility for change comes from within oneself.
    e. Self-understanding (insight) involves discovering and accepting the unknown parts of oneself.
    f. Family re-enactment leads to understanding what it was like growing up in one's family through the group experience.
    g. Guidance comes from accepting advice from other group members.

h. Identification involves benefiting from imitation of the positive behaviors of other group members.
i. Instillation of hope is experiencing optimism through observing the improvement of others in the group.
j. Interpersonal learning occurs when receiving feedback from group members regarding one's behavior (input).
k. Interpersonal learning also occurs by learning successful ways of relating to group members (output).

> **EXAM HINT:** Knowledge of the above curative factors of groups can help you determine the best answer for COTA® exam items about effective group interventions. Correct answers will maximize these curative factors; incorrect answers will ignore these factors.

12. Taxonomy of activity groups:
    a. Mosey (1996) provided a standard classification to identify major types of activity groups.
    b. Evaluation group.
        (1) Purpose/focus: to enable the client and the OT practitioner to assess the client's skills, assets, and limitations regarding group interaction.
        (2) Assumption: to accurately evaluate an individual's functional abilities, one must observe the person in a setting where the skills can be demonstrated.
        (3) Type of client: all individuals who will be involved in groups or who lack group interaction skills.
        (4) Role of the OTA group leader.
            (a) Orients clients to group's purpose.
            (b) Provides needed supplies for activities that were selected in collaboration with the supervising occupational therapist for their interactive aspects.
            (c) Does not participate or intervene in group (except to maintain safety, if needed), but observes and reports members' interaction and functional skill level to the supervising occupational therapist.
            (d) Closes group by sharing general observations with members.
            (e) Asks for clients' input and reports feedback to the supervising occupational therapist.
        (5) Suitable activities: tasks that can be completed in one session and require interaction to complete.
    c. Thematic group.
        (1) Purpose/focus: to assist members in acquiring the knowledge, skills, and/or attitudes needed to perform a specific activity.
        (2) Assumptions.
            (a) Improvement of ability to engage in activities outside of group can result from teaching of these activities within group.
            (b) Learning is facilitated by practicing and experiencing needed behaviors, with reinforcement of appropriate behaviors given.
        (3) Type of client.
            (a) Determined by the specific goals of the group.
            (b) Members' needs, concerns, and goals must match the objectives of the group.
            (c) Members must have a minimal group interaction skill level equal to a parallel group skill level.
        (4) Role of the OTA group leader.
            (a) Contributes to the selection, structuring, and gradation of suitable activities to teach needed skills.
            (b) Interventions vary according to group's level, needs, and goals.
            (c) May range on a continuum from a highly structured, supportive director to a resource advisor.
            (d) Reinforces skill development.
            (e) Attention is not paid to intra- and interpersonal conflicts unless they interfere with or are directly related to the activity.
        (5) Suitable activities.
            (a) Simulated, clearly defined, structured activities that enable members to practice and learn needed skills, attitudes, and knowledge within the group.
            (b) Activities selected are directly related to the skills needed to perform the activity outside of the group (e.g., a cooking group to learn how to cook).
    d. Topical group.
        (1) Purpose/focus: to discuss specific activities that members are engaged in outside of group to enable them to engage in the activities in a more effective, need-satisfying manner.
            (a) Concurrent topical groups are concerned with activities already engaged in outside of group (e.g., a parenting skills group for parents of children with developmental disabilities).
            (b) Anticipatory topical groups are concerned with activities that are expected to be done in the future (e.g., a parenting skills group for persons with disabilities who are expecting a child).
        (2) Assumptions.
            (a) Improvement of ability to engage in specific activities outside of group results from discussion of these activities.

(b) Discussion of problem areas and potential solutions, reinforcement of effective behaviors, and experiential learning facilitate skill acquisition.
    (3) Type of client.
        (a) Individuals who share similar current or anticipatory problems in functioning.
        (b) Members must be at least at an egocentric-cooperative/basic cooperative group skill level.
        (c) Sufficient verbal and cognitive skills to engage in discussion and to problem solve are present.
    (4) Role of the OTA group leader.
        (a) Facilitates group discussion while maintaining focus on the circumscribed activity.
        (b) Helps members problem solve, gives feedback and support, reinforces skill acquisition.
        (c) Shares leadership with members; acts as a role model.
    (5) Suitable activities.
        (a) Group activity is a verbal discussion on a circumscribed activity that members are engaged in (concurrent) or will be engaged in (anticipatory) outside of group (e.g., parenting, home maintenance, discharge from hospital, work, and leisure).
        (b) Discussion may include members' current or anticipated fears and problems, potential solutions, and coping mechanisms.
        (c) Role play and homework may be utilized.
e. Task-oriented group.
    (1) Purpose/focus.
        (a) To increase clients' awareness of their needs, values, ideas, feelings, and behaviors as they engage in a group task.
        (b) To improve intra- and inter-psychic functioning by focusing on problems that emerge in the process of choosing, planning, and implementing a group activity.
    (2) Assumptions.
        (a) Activities elicit feelings, thoughts, and behaviors.
        (b) Activities are the means by which members can explore and experience these thoughts, feelings, and actions.
        (c) Through activities, members can increase their self-awareness and practice new behaviors.
    (3) Type of client.
        (a) Individuals whose primary dysfunction is in the cognitive and socioemotional areas due to psychological or physical trauma.
        (b) Clients with fair verbal skills who can interact with others.
    (4) Role of the OTA group leader.
        (a) Initially, very active; defines group goals and structure.
        (b) Assists with activity selection, offers guidelines and suggestions.
        (c) Facilitates discussion among members.
        (d) Gives feedback and support.
        (e) Assists members in exploring relationships between thoughts, feelings, and actions.
        (f) Encourages members to experiment with new behavior patterns.
        (g) As the group develops, the leader is less active, helps members give more feedback and input; however, the OT practitioner remains the leader and ensures that the task is a means to the end, not the end itself.
    (5) Suitable activities.
        (a) Activities that are chosen by members and will create an end product or demonstrable service for the group itself or for persons outside the group.
        (b) Activities are selected, planned, and carried out by members with the understanding that the task is a means to study, understand, and practice behavior.
f. Developmental group.

> **EXAM HINT:** Because developmental groups are on a continuum, some group levels will be more common in certain practice settings than others. For example, inpatient units will typically have more groups at the parallel and/or project/associative group level due to clients' acute symptoms and their short lengths of stay. Community-based settings with stable populations and extended (or unlimited) lengths of stay will typically have more groups at the cooperative/supportive cooperative and/or mature level. The application of knowledge about the purposes of each group level, their leadership roles, and suitable activities can help you determine the best answer for COTA® exam items about effective group interventions in diverse practice settings.

    (1) A continuum of groups consisting of parallel, project/associative, egocentric-cooperative/basic cooperative, cooperative/supportive cooperative, and mature groups.
    (2) Purpose/focus is to teach and develop members' group interaction skills.
        (a) Parallel.
            • To enable members to perform individual tasks in the presence of others.

- To minimally interact verbally and non-verbally with others even though task does not require interaction for successful completion.
- To develop a basic level of awareness, trust, and comfort with others in group.
  (b) Project/associative.
    - To develop the ability to perform a shared, short-term activity with another member in a comfortable, cooperative manner.
    - To develop interactions beyond those that the activity requires.
    - To enable members to give and seek assistance.
  (c) Egocentric-cooperative/basic cooperative.
    - To enable members to select and implement a long-range activity that requires group interaction to complete.
    - To develop an understanding of group goals and group interaction norms.
    - To enable members to identify and meet the needs of themselves and others (e.g., safety, esteem).
  (d) Cooperative/supportive cooperative.
    - To enable members to engage in a group activity that facilitates free expression of ideas and feelings.
    - To develop sense of trust, love and belonging, and cohesion.
    - To enable members to identify and meet socioemotional needs.
  (e) Mature group.
    - To enable members to assume all functional socioemotional and task roles within a group.
    - To enable members to reinforce behaviors that result in need satisfaction and task completion.
(3) Assumptions.
  (a) Learning principles are the basis. They are utilized throughout the five developmental levels.
  (b) Members are made aware of and helped to engage in effective group behavior.
  (c) Feedback and reinforcement are utilized. Learning of needed behaviors occurs when adaptive behaviors are reinforced and when maladaptive behaviors are not.
  (d) Maladaptive behaviors result from deviations, lags, or insufficiencies in development. These developmental deficiencies can be treated by participating in groups that are similar to the ones in which the skills would have been developed.
  (e) Subskills fundamental to mature group function must be acquired in a sequential manner.
(4) Type of clients: individuals with decreased group interaction skills.
(5) Role of the OTA group leader.
  (a) Contributes to the assessment process and the placement of individuals in the appropriate group in collaboration with the supervising occupational therapist.
  (b) Orients all members to group's goals, structure, and norms.
  (c) The OTA provides group leadership with supervision from the supervising occupational therapist.
    - Lower level groups require more active, direct leadership.
    - As group matures and attains a higher level of group interaction, leadership is shared among members.
(6) Parallel group leadership role.
  (a) Provide unconditional positive regard to develop trust.
  (b) Actively fill all leadership functions and meet all members' needs.
  (c) Reinforce all behaviors appropriate to group, no matter how small.
  (d) Provide structure.
  (e) Facilitate interaction.
(7) Project/associative group leadership role.
  (a) Select and structure activities that can be shared by two or more members.
  (b) Fulfill all of members' needs while encouraging members to give and seek assistance and interact beyond activity requirements.
  (c) Reinforce cooperation, mild competition, trial-and-error learning, sharing, and interactions.
(8) Egocentric-cooperative/basic cooperative group leadership role.
  (a) Less of an active, direct leader.
  (b) Facilitate and allow members to fulfill functional leadership roles to function independently.
  (c) Provide guidelines and assistance as needed.
  (d) Reinforce members' meeting needs of self and others.
  (e) Serve as a role model.
(9) Cooperative/supportive cooperative group leadership role.

(a) Act as a nonauthoritarian advisor, not as a direct leader.
(b) Leader and members are mutually responsible for giving feedback, identifying and meeting needs, and reinforcing behavior.

(10) Mature group leadership role.
(a) Acts as a peer, an equal, a group member.
(b) Members assume all roles, with the OT group leader filling in only if and when needed to maintain group.
(c) All members satisfy needs and reinforce behavior while maintaining a balance between need satisfaction and task completion.

(11) Suitable activities.
(a) Parallel.
- Members perform activities independently of others but in the presence of others.
- Interactions are not required to successfully complete activity.
- Activities should be similar or utilize common tools or materials to facilitate interaction and sharing.
- Activities should be relevant to a person's ability, age, gender, and interest so they are more able to interact with and about it.

(b) Project/associative.
- Task is short-term and requires the participation of two or more people.
- Task is shareable and requires interaction to successfully complete.
- Group interaction, not project completion, is emphasized.

(c) Egocentric-cooperative/basic cooperative.
- Activity allows 5–10 people to work together.
- It is selected and implemented by members.
- It is longer-term, requiring more than two meetings to complete.

(d) Cooperative/supportive cooperative.
- Activities facilitate and allow for free expression of ideas and feelings.
- Activity is secondary to need fulfillment and may not produce an end product.

(e) Mature.
- Activity requires a number of people to work together.
- It requires an end product or has an inherent time limit for completion.

- During group, activity may be stopped for members to explore what is going on within the group.

g. Instrumental group.
(1) Purpose/focus.
(a) To help members function at their highest possible level for as long as possible.
(b) To meet mental health needs.
(2) Assumption.
(a) Individuals are functioning at their highest possible level and cannot change or progress.
(b) A supportive, structured environment that provides appropriate activities can prevent regression, maintain function, and meet mental health needs.
(3) Type of client.
(a) Individuals who have demonstrated in treatment an inability to change or progress.
(b) Individuals who cannot independently meet their mental health needs and/or need assistance to maintain function due to cognitive, psychological, neurocognitive, perceptual-motor, and/or social deficits.
(4) Role of OTA group leader.
(a) Provide unconditional positive regard, support, and structure to create a comfortable, safe environment for patients.
(b) Select and design activities in collaboration with the supervising occupational therapist that will meet member's health needs and maintain highest possible level of function.
(c) Assist members with activity as needed.
(d) Make no attempt to change client.
(5) Suitable activities.
(a) Members can successfully complete activities with structure and assistance of therapist as needed.
(b) Nonthreatening and nondemanding.
(c) Interesting, enjoyable, and attractive to members.
(d) Meet mental health needs of patient by enabling him/her to experience pleasure, have fun, socialize with others, etc.
(e) Maintain function by providing sensory, cognitive, perceptual-motor, and social input.

h. Role of the OTA in group work.
(1) The OTA in collaboration with a supervising OTR® is active in all aspects of group work.
(2) Refer to Chapter 13 for additional group information and Chapter 4 for more information about the role of the COTA®.

Appendix 3A

Standard Precautions

OVERVIEW

Standard Precautions combine the major features of Universal Precautions (UP) and Body Substance Isolation (BSI) and are based on the principle that all blood, body fluids, secretions, excretions except sweat, nonintact skin, and mucous membranes may contain transmissible infectious agents. Standard Precautions include a group of infection prevention practices that apply to all patients, regardless of suspected or confirmed infection status, in any setting in which health care is delivered. These include hand hygiene; use of gloves, gown, mask, eye protection, or face shield, depending on the anticipated exposure; and safe injection practices. Also, equipment or items in the patient environment likely to have been contaminated with infectious body fluids must be handled in a manner to prevent transmission of infectious agents (e.g., wear gloves for direct contact, contain heavily soiled equipment, properly clean and disinfect or sterilize reusable equipment before use on another patient). The application of Standard Precautions during patient care is determined by the nature of the health-care worker (HCW)–patient interaction and the extent of anticipated blood, body fluid, or pathogen exposure. Standard Precautions are also intended to protect patients by ensuring that health-care personnel do not carry infectious agents to patients on their hands or via equipment used during patient care.

Assume that every person is potentially infected or colonized with an organism that could be transmitted in the health-care setting and apply the following infection control practices during the delivery of health care.

HAND HYGIENE

1. During the delivery of health care, avoid unnecessary touching of surfaces in close proximity to the patient to prevent both contamination of clean hand from environmental surfaces and transmission of pathogens from contaminated hands to surfaces.
2. When hands are visibly dirty, contaminated with proteinaceous material, or visibly soiled with blood or body fluids, wash hands with either a nonantimicrobial soap and water or an antimicrobial soap and water.
3. If hands are not visibly soiled, or after removing visible material with nonantimicrobial soap and water, decontaminate hands in the clinical situations described in a–f as follows. The preferred method of hand decontamination is with an alcohol-based hand rub. Alternatively, hands may be washed with an antimicrobial soap and water. Frequent use of an alcohol-based hand rub immediately following hand washing with nonantimicrobial soap may increase the frequency of dermatitis. Perform hand hygiene:
    a. Before having direct contact with patients.
    b. After contact with blood, body fluids or excretions, mucous membranes, nonintact skin, or wound dressings.
    c. After contact with a patient's intact skin (e.g., when taking a pulse or blood pressure or lifting a patient).
    d. If hands will be moving from a contaminated body site to a clean body site during patient care.
    e. After contact with inanimate objects (including medical equipment) in the immediate vicinity of the patient.
    f. After removing gloves.
4. Wash hands with nonantimicrobial soap and water or with antimicrobial soap and water if contact with spores (e.g., *Clostridium difficile* or *Bacillus anthracis*) is likely to have occurred. The physical action of washing and rinsing hands under such circumstances is recommended because alcohols, chlorhexidine, iodophors, and other antiseptic agents have poor activity against spores.
5. Do not wear artificial fingernails or extenders if duties include direct contact with patients at high risk for infection and associated adverse outcomes (e.g., those in intensive care units [ICUs] or operating rooms).
    a. Develop an organizational policy on the wearing of nonnatural nails by health-care personnel who have direct contact with patients outside of the groups as previously specified.

PERSONAL PROTECTIVE EQUIPMENT (PPE)

1. Observe the following principles of use:
    a. Wear PPE, as described in 2–4 as follows, when the nature of the anticipated patient interaction indicates that contact with blood or body fluids may occur.
    b. Prevent contamination of clothing and skin during the process of removing PPE.
    c. Before leaving the patient's room or cubicle, remove and discard PPE.
2. Gloves.
    a. Wear gloves when it can be reasonably anticipated that contact with blood or other potentially infectious materials, mucous membranes, nonintact skin, or potentially contaminated intact skin (e.g., of a patient incontinent of stool or urine) could occur.

(Continued)

Standard Precautions (*Continued*)

  b. Wear gloves with fit and durability appropriate to the task.
   (1) Wear disposable medical examination gloves for providing direct patient care.
   (2) Wear disposable medical examination gloves or reusable utility gloves for cleaning the environment or medical equipment.
  c. Remove gloves after contact with a patient and/or the surrounding environment (including medical equipment) using proper technique to prevent hand contamination.
   (1) Do not wear the same pair of gloves for the care of more than one patient. Do not wash gloves for the purpose of reuse since this practice has been associated with transmission of pathogens.
  d. Change gloves during patient care if the hands will move from a contaminated body site (e.g., perineal area) to a clean body site (e.g., face).
3. Gowns.
  a. Wear a gown that is appropriate to the task to protect skin and prevent soiling or contamination of clothing during procedures and patient-care activities when contact with blood, body fluids, secretions, or excretions is anticipated.
   (1) Wear a gown for direct patient contact if the patient has uncontained secretions or excretions.
   (2) Remove gown and perform hand hygiene before leaving the patient's environment.
  b. Do not reuse gowns, even for repeated contacts with the same patient.
  c. Routine donning of gowns upon entrance into a high-risk unit (e.g., ICU, neonatal intensive care unit [NICU], hematopoietic stem cell transplantation [HSCT] unit) is not indicated.
4. Mouth, nose, eye protection.
  a. Use PPE to protect the mucous membranes of the eyes, nose, and mouth during procedures and patient-care activities that are likely to generate splashes or sprays of blood, body fluids, secretions, and excretions. Select masks, goggles, face shields, and combinations of each according to the need anticipated by the task performed.
5. During aerosol-generating procedures (e.g., bronchoscopy, suctioning of the respiratory tract [if not using in-line suction catheters], endotracheal intubation) in patients who are not suspected of being infected with an agent for which respiratory protection is otherwise recommended (e.g., M. tuberculosis, SARS, orhemorrhagic fever viruses), wear one of the following: a face shield that fully covers the front and sides of the face, a mask with attached shield, or a mask and goggles (in addition to gloves and gown).

RESPIRATORY HYGIENE/COUGH ETIQUETTE

1. Educate health-care personnel on the importance of source control measures to contain respiratory secretions to prevent droplet and fomite transmission of respiratory pathogens, especially during seasonal outbreaks of viral respiratory tract infections (e.g., influenza, respiratory syncytial virus [RSV], adenovirus, parainfluenza virus) in communities.
2. Implement the following measures to contain respiratory secretions in patients and accompanying individuals who have signs and symptoms of a respiratory infection, beginning at the point of initial encounter in a health-care setting (e.g., triage, reception and waiting areas in emergency departments, outpatient clinics, and physician offices).
  a. Post signs at entrances and in strategic places (e.g., elevators, cafeterias) within ambulatory and inpatient settings with instructions to patients and other persons with symptoms of a respiratory infection to cover their mouths/noses when coughing or sneezing, use and dispose of tissues, and perform hand hygiene after hands have been in contact with respiratory secretions.
  b. Provide tissues and no-touch receptacles (e.g., foot pedal–operated lid or open, plastic-lined waste basket) for disposal of tissues.
  c. Provide resources and instructions for performing hand hygiene in or near waiting areas in ambulatory and inpatient settings; provide conveniently located dispensers of alcohol-based hand rubs and, where sinks are available, supplies for hand washing.
  d. During periods of increased prevalence of respiratory infections in the community (e.g., as indicated by increased school absenteeism, increased number of patients seeking care for a respiratory infection), offer masks to coughing patients and other symptomatic persons (e.g., persons who accompany ill patients) upon entry into the facility or medical office and encourage them to maintain special separation, ideally a distance of at least 3 feet, from others in common waiting areas.
   (1) Some facilities may find it logistically easier to institute this recommendation year-round as a standard of practice.

PATIENT PLACEMENT

1. Include the potential for transmission of infectious agents in patient placement decisions.
  a. Place patients who pose a risk for transmission to others (e.g., uncontained secretions, excretions or wound drainage, infants with suspected viral respiratory or gasrointestinal infections) in a single-patient room when available.
2. Determine patient placement based on the following principles:
  a. Route(s) of transmission of the known or suspected infectious agent.
  b. Risk factors for transmission in the infected patient.

Standard Precautions (*Continued*)

    c. Risk factors for adverse outcomes resulting from a hospital-acquired infection (HAI) in other patients in the area or room being considered for patient placement.

    d. Availability of single-patient rooms.

    e. Patient options for room sharing (e.g., cohorting patients with the same infection).

PATIENT-CARE EQUIPMENT AND INSTRUMENTS/DEVICES

1. Establish policies and procedures for containing, transporting, and handling patient-care equipment and instruments/devices that may be contaminated with blood or body fluids.

2. Remove organic material from critical and semicritical instrument/devices, using recommended cleaning agents before high-level disinfection and sterilization to enable effective disinfection and sterilization processes.

3. Wear PPE (e.g., gloves, gown), according to the level of anticipated contamination, when handling patient-care equipment and instruments/devices that are visibly soiled or may have been in contact with blood or body fluids.

CARE OF THE ENVIRONMENT

1. Establish policies and procedures for routine and targeted cleaning of environmental surfaces as indicated by the level of patient contact and degree of soiling.

2. Clean and disinfect surfaces that are likely to be contaminated with pathogens, including those that are in close proximity to the patient (e.g., bed rails, over bed tables) and frequently touched surfaces in the patient-care environment (e.g., door knobs, surfaces in and surrounding toilets in patients' rooms) on a more frequent schedule compared to that for other surfaces (e.g., horizontal surfaces in waiting rooms).

3. Use Environmental Protection Agency (EPA)–registered disinfectants that have microbiocidal (i.e., killing) activity against the pathogens most likely to contaminate the patient-care environment. Use in accordance with manufacturer's instructions.

    a. Review the efficacy of in-use disinfectants when evidence of continuing transmission of an infectious agent (e.g., rotavirus, C. difficile, norovirus) may indicate resistance to the in-use product and change to a more effective disinfectant as indicated.

4. In facilities that provide health care to pediatric patients or have waiting areas with child play toys (e.g., obstetric/gynecology offices and clinics), establish policies and procedures for cleaning and disinfecting toys at regular intervals.

    a. Use the following principles in developing this policy and procedures:

        (1) Select play toys that can be easily cleaned and disinfected.

        (2) Do not permit use of stuffed furry toys if they will be shared.

        (3) Clean and disinfect large stationary toys (e.g., climbing equipment) at least weekly and whenever visibly soiled.

        (4) If toys are likely to be mouthed, rinse with water after disinfection; alternatively wash in a dishwasher.

        (5) When a toy requires cleaning and disinfection, do so immediately or store in a designated labeled container separate from toys that are clean and ready for use.

5. Include multiuse electronic equipment in policies and procedures for preventing contamination and for cleaning and disinfection, especially those items that are used by patients, those used during delivery of patient care, and mobile devices that are moved in and out of patient rooms frequently (e.g., daily).

    a. No recommendations are provided for use of removable protective covers or washable keyboards. This is an unresolved issue.

TEXTILES AND LAUNDRY

1. Handle used textiles and fabrics with minimum agitation to avoid contamination of air, surfaces, and persons.

2. If laundry are used, ensure that they are properly designed, maintained, and used in a manner to minimize dispersion of aerosols from contaminated laundry.

SAFE INJECTION PRACTICES

These are not included here since OT practitioners do not give injections. See CDC website.

WORKER SAFETY

Adhere to federal and state requirements for protection of health-care personnel from exposure to bloodborne pathogens.

Reference: Centers for Disease Control and Prevention. (2007). *Guideline for isolation precautions: Preventing transmission of infectious agents in healthcare settings.* Retrieved March 9, 2010 from http://www.cdc.gov/ncidod/dhqp/gl_isolation_standard.html

Appendix 3B

Transmission-based Precautions

There are three categories of Transmission-Based Precautions: Contact Precautions, Droplet Precautions, and Airborne Precautions. Transmission-Based Precautions are used when the route(s) of transmission is (are) not completely interrupted using Standard Precautions alone. For some diseases that have multiple routes of transmission (e.g., SARS), more than one Transmission-Based Precautions category may be used. When used either singly or in combination, they are always used in addition to Standard Precautions. When Transmission-Based Precautions are indicated, efforts must be made to counteract possible adverse effects on patients (i.e., anxiety, depression and other mood disturbances, perceptions of stigma, reduced contact with clinical staff, and increases in preventable adverse events) in order to improve acceptance by the patients and adherence by health-care workers.

AIRBORNE PRECAUTIONS

In addition to Standard Precautions, use Airborne Precautions, or the equivalent, for patients known or suspected to be infected with serious illness transmitted by airborne droplet nuclei (small-particle residue) that remain suspended in the air and that can be dispersed widely by air currents within a room or over a long distance (for example, Mycobacterium tuberculosis, measles virus, chickenpox virus).

1. Respiratory isolation room.
2. Wear respiratory protection (mask) when entering room.
3. Limit movement and transport of patient to essential purposes only. Mask patient when transporting out of area.

DROPLET PRECAUTIONS

In addition to Standard Precautions, use Droplet Precautions, or the equivalent, for patients known or suspected to be infected with serious illness microorganisms transmitted by large particle droplets that can be generated by the patient during coughing, sneezing, talking, or the performance of procedures (for example, mumps, rubella, pertussis, influenza).

1. Isolation room.
2. Wear respiratory protection (mask) when entering room.
3. Limit movement and transport of patient to essential purposes only. Mask patient when transporting out of area.

CONTACT PRECAUTIONS

In addition to Standard Precautions, use Contact Precautions, or the equivalent, for specified patients known or suspected to be infected or colonized with serious illness transmitted by direct patient contact (hand or skin-to-skin contact) or contact with items in patient environment.

1. Isolation room.
2. Wear gloves when entering room; change gloves after having contact with infective material; remove gloves before leaving patient's room; wash hands immediately with an antimicrobial agent or waterless antiseptic agent. After glove removal and handwashing, ensure that hands do not touch contaminated environmental items.
3. Wear a gown when entering room if you anticipate your clothing will have substantial contact with the patient, environmental surfaces, or items in the patient's room, or if the patient is incontinent or has diarrhea, ileostomy, colostomy, or wound drainage not contained by dressing. Remove gown before leaving patient's room; after gown removal, ensure that clothing does not contact potentially contaminated environmental surfaces.
4. Single-patient-use equipment.
5. Limit movement and transport of patient to essential purposes only. Use precautions when transporting patient to minimize risk of transmission of microorganisms to other patients and contamination of environmental surfaces or equipment.

Reference: Centers for Disease Control and Prevention. (2007). *Guideline for isolation precautions: Preventing transmission of infectious agents in healthcare settings.* Retrieved March 9, 2010 from http://www.cdc.gov/ncidod/dhqp/gl_isolation_standard.html

References

American Occupational Therapy Association. (2010). Standards of practice for occupational therapy. *American Journal of Occupational Therapy, 64* (Suppl. 6), S106–S110.

American Occupational Therapy Association. (2014). Occupational therapy practice framework: Domain and process (3rd ed.). *American Journal of Occupational Therapy, 68* (Suppl. 1), S1–S48.

American Occupational Therapy Association. (2015). Standards of practice for occupational therapy. *American Journal of Occupational Therapy, 69* (Suppl. 3), http://dx.doi.org/10.5014/ajot.2015.696S06.

American Occupational Therapy Association. (2017). AOTA's societal statement on health literacy. *American Journal of Occupational Therapy, 71*(Suppl. 2), 7112410065. https://doi.org/10.5014/ajot.2017.716S14

American Occupational Therapy Association. (2018). *Reference manual of the official documents of the American Occupational Therapy Association (23th ed.).* Bethesda, MD: Author.

Asher, I. E. (2007). *An annotated index of occupational therapy evaluation tools.* (3rd ed.). Bethesda, MD: AOTA Press.

Braveman, B. (2016). *Leading and managing occupational therapy services: An evidence-based approach,* 2nd ed. Philadelphia: F.A. Davis.

Case-Smith, J., & O'Brien, J. C. (Eds.). (2015). *Occupational therapy for children and adolescents,* 7th ed. St. Louis, MO: Elsevier Mosby.

Cole, M., & Donohue, M. (2011). *Social participation in occupational contexts: In schools, clinics, and communities.* Thorofare, NJ: Slack.

Hansen, R. A. (1990). Lesson 10: Ethical considerations. In C. B. Royeen (Ed.), *AOTA self-study series. Assessing function.* Bethesda, MD: American Occupational Therapy Association.

Hemphill-Pearson, B. J. (1999). *Assessments in occupational therapy mental health: An integrative approach.* Thorofare, NJ: Slack.

Hinojosa. J., & Kramer, P. (2014). *Evaluation in occupational therapy: Obtaining and interpreting data,* 4th ed. Bethesda, MD: AOTA Press.

Hopkins, H., & Smith, H. (Eds.). (2003). *Willard and Spackman's occupational therapy,* 10th ed. Philadelphia: J.B. Lippincott.

Hussey, S., Sabonis-Chafee, B., & Clifford-O'Brien, J. (2011). *Introduction to occupational therapy* (4th ed.). St. Louis, MO: Elsevier Mosby.

Jimmo v. Sebelius settlement agreement fact sheet. (2013). Retrieved from http://www.cms.gov/Medicare/Medicare-Fee-for-Service-Payment/SNFPPS/Downloads/Jimmo-Fact Sheet.pdf

Mailloux, Z., May-Benson, T. A., Summers, C. A., Miller, L. J., Brett-Green, B., Burke, J. P., et al. (2007). The issue is—Goal attainment scaling as a measure of meaningful outcomes for children with sensory integration disorders. *American Journal of Occupational Therapy, 61,* 254–259.

McCormack, G., Jaffe, E., Goodman-Lavey, M. (Eds.). (2003). *The occupational therapy manager.* (4th ed.). Bethesda, MD: American Occupational Therapy Association.

Mosey, A. C. (1996). *Psychosocial components of occupational therapy.* New York: Raven Press.

Moyers, P., & Dale, L. (2007). *The guide to occupational therapy practice.* Bethesda, MD: American Occupational Therapy Association.

National Board for Certification in Occupational Therapy (NBCOT®). (2018). *Practice analysis of the certified occupational therapy assistant: Executive summary* [PDF file]. Retrieved from https://www.nbcot.org/-/media/NBCOT/PDFs/2017-Practice-Analysis-Executive-COTA.ashx?la=en

Ottenbacher, K. J., & Cusick, A. (1990). Goal attainment scaling as a method of clinical service evaluation. *American Journal of Occupational Therapy, 44,* 519–525.

Ryan, S., & Sladyk, K. (2005). *Ryan's occupational therapy assistant: Principles, practice issues, and techniques.* (4th ed.). Thorofare, NJ: Slack.

United States Government Printing Office. (2003). *Code of Federal Regulations, Title 42, Volume 3.* Retrieved December 21, 2003, from http://www.cms.gov.

Review Questions

The Process of Occupational Therapy

Following are five questions about key content covered in this chapter. These questions are not inclusive of the entirety of content about the occupational therapy process that you must know for success on the COTA® exam. These questions are provided to help you jump-start the thought processes you will need to apply your studying of content to the answering of COTA® exam items. Thus, they are not in the exam format. Exam items in the COTA® format, which cover the depth and breadth of content you will need to know to pass the exam, are provided on this text's computer-based exams. The answers to the questions below are provided in Appendix 3.

1. An OTA is collaborating with an occupational therapist in preparation for the evaluation of a client. What contextual considerations should the OTA and supervising occupational therapist take into account when determining the assessments that will be appropriate to use with the client?

2. An OTA provides services to preschool children with developmental, intellectual, and physical disabilities. When should the OTA use standard precautions? What policies and procedures should the OTA use to guide the use of standard precautions in this preschool practice setting?

3. An OTA provides services in a community-based setting that offers individual and group interventions. What factors should the OTA discuss with the supervising occupational therapist when determining if it is best to use an individual intervention or a group intervention with each client?

4. An OTA working in a long-term care facility is asked by the supervising occupational therapist to co-lead a discharge planning group with a social worker. What are the advantages to this co-leadership? What issues may arise to impede effective co-leadership that the OTA should discuss with the supervising occupational therapist and the social worker prior to the initiation of this group?

5. An OTA provides services to a group of parents of infants and toddlers who each recently incurred a disability. The OTA collaborates with the supervising occupational therapist to plan a thematic and a topical group to address goals related to the clients' parental role. What would be appropriate foci and relevant activities for these groups?

4
Professional Standards and Responsibilities

RITA P. FLEMING-CASTALDY

Chapter Outline

- Professional Ethics, 64
- Ethical Jurisdiction of Occupational Therapy, 68
- OT Practitioner Roles, 70
- Supervisory Guidelines for OT Personnel, 71
- Team Roles and Principles of Collaboration, 74
- The U.S. Health-Care System, 79
- Payment for Occupational Therapy Services, 81
- Occupational Therapy Documentation Guidelines, 86
- Federal Legislation Related to Occupational Therapy, 91
- Service Delivery Models and Practice Settings, 98
- Service Management, 107
- References, 111
- Review Questions, 113

Professional Ethics

Code of Ethics Overview

1. Developed by the American Occupational Therapy Association (AOTA) as a statement to the public to identify the values and principles used to promote and maintain high standards for the behavior of occupational therapy (OT) practitioners.
2. A set of principles that apply to all levels of OT personnel.
3. Actions that are in violation of the purpose and spirit of the AOTA's Code of Ethics are considered unethical by the AOTA (2015a).
4. All OT practitioners are obligated to uphold these standards for themselves and their colleagues.
5. The *Occupational Therapy Code of Ethics and Ethics Standards* (AOTA, 2015) are written to address the ethical concerns that most typically arise in OT education, research, and practice.
6. This ethical code has two main purposes. These are to:
   a. Provide "aspirational Core Values that guide members toward ethical courses of action in professional and volunteer roles" (AOTA, 2015b, p. 1).
   b. Delineate "enforceable Principles and Standards of Conduct that apply to AOTA members" (AOTA, 2015b, p. 1).

EXAM HINT: The NBCOT® exam outline for the COTA® identifies knowledge of the "application of ethical decision-making and professional behaviors guided by the NBCOT® standards of practice and Code of Conduct" (NBCOT®, 2018, p. 28) as essential for competent and safe practice. Knowing how the AOTA Code of Ethics is used to guide OT practice can help you determine the correct answer for NBCOT® Domain 03 Upholding Professional Standards and Responsibilities exam items related to ethical practice.

Occupational Therapy Code of Ethics

1. "Beneficence. Principle 1. Occupational therapy personnel shall demonstrate a concern for the safety and well-being of the recipients of their services.... Occupational therapy personnel shall:
   a. Provide appropriate evaluation and a plan of intervention for all recipients of occupational therapy services specific to their needs.
   b. Re-evaluate and reassess recipients of service in a timely manner to determine whether goals are being achieved and whether intervention plans should be revised.
   c. Use, to the extent possible, evaluation, planning, intervention techniques, and therapeutic equipment that are evidence-based and within the recognized scope of occupational therapy practice.
   d. Ensure that all duties delegated to other occupational therapy personnel are congruent with credentials, qualifications, experience, competency, and scope of practice with respect to service delivery, supervision, fieldwork education, and research.
   e. Provide occupational therapy services, including education and training, that are within each practitioner's level of competence and scope of practice.
   f. Take steps (e.g., continuing education, research, supervision, training) to ensure proficiency, use careful judgment to ensure their own competence, and weigh potential for harm when generally recognized standards do not exist in emerging technology or areas of practice.
   g. Maintain competency by ongoing participation in education relevant to one's practice area.
   h. Terminate occupational therapy services in collaboration with the service recipient or responsible party when services are no longer beneficial.
   i. Refer to other providers when indicated by the needs of the client.
   j. Conduct and disseminate research in accordance with currently accepted ethical guidelines and standards for the protection of research participants, including determination of potential risks and benefits.
2. Nonmaleficence. Principle 2. Occupational therapy personnel shall intentionally refrain from actions that cause harm.... Occupational therapy personnel shall:
   a. Avoid inflicting harm or injury to recipients of occupational therapy services, students, research participants, or employees.
   b. Avoid abandoning the service recipient by facilitating appropriate transitions when unable to provide services for any reason.
   c. Recognize and take appropriate action to remedy personal problems and limitations that might cause harm to recipients of service, colleagues, students, research participants, or others.

d. Avoid any undue influences that may impair practice and compromise the ability to safely and competently provide occupational therapy services, education, or research.
   e. Address impaired practice and when necessary report to the appropriate authorities.
   f. Avoid dual relationships, conflicts of interest, and situations in which a practitioner, educator, student, researcher, or employer is unable to maintain clear professional boundaries or objectivity.
   g. Avoid engaging in sexual activity with a recipient of service, including the client's family or significant other, student, research participant, or employee, while a professional relationship exists.
   h. Avoid compromising the rights or well-being of others based on arbitrary directives (e.g., unrealistic productivity expectations, falsification of documentation, inaccurate coding) by exercising professional judgment and critical analysis.
   i. Avoid exploiting any relationship established as an occupational therapist or occupational therapy assistant to further one's own physical, emotional, financial, political, or business interests at the expense of recipients of services, students, research participants, employees, or colleagues.
   j. Avoid bartering for service when there is the potential for exploitation and conflict of interest.
3. Autonomy. Principle 3. Occupational therapy personnel shall respect the right of the individual to self-determination, privacy, confidentiality, and consent. . . . Occupational therapy personnel shall:
   a. Respect and honor the expressed wishes of recipients of service.
   b. Fully disclose the benefits, risks, and potential outcomes of any intervention; the personnel who will be providing the intervention; and any reasonable alternatives to the proposed intervention.
   c. Obtain consent after disclosing appropriate information and answering any questions posed by the recipient of service or research participant to ensure voluntariness.
   d. Establish a collaborative relationship with recipients of service and relevant stakeholders to promote shared decision making.
   e. Respect the client's right to refuse occupational therapy services temporarily or permanently even when that refusal has potential to result in poor outcomes.
   f. Refrain from threatening, coercing, or deceiving clients to promote compliance with occupational therapy recommendations.
   g. Respect research participant's right to withdraw from a research study without penalty.
   h. Maintain the confidentiality of all verbal, written, electronic, augmentative, and nonverbal communications, in compliance with applicable laws, including all aspects of privacy laws and exceptions thereto (e.g., Health Insurance Portability and Accountability Act [Pub. L. 104-191], Family Education Rights and Privacy Act [Pub. L. 93-380]).
   i. Display responsible conduct and discretion when engaging in social networking, including but not limited to refraining from posting protected health information.
   j. Facilitate comprehension and address barriers to communication (e.g., aphasia; differences in language, literacy, culture) with the recipient of service (or responsible party), student, or research participant.
4. Justice. Principle 4. Occupational therapy personnel shall promote fairness and objectivity in the provision of occupational therapy services. . . . Occupational therapy personnel shall:
   a. Respond to requests for occupational therapy services (e.g., a referral) in a timely manner as determined by law, regulation, or policy.
   b. Assist those in need of occupational therapy services in securing access through available means.
   c. Address barriers in access to occupational therapy services by offering or referring clients to financial aid, charity care, or pro bono services within the parameters of organizational policies.
   d. Advocate for changes to systems and policies that are discriminatory, unfairly limit, or prevent access to occupational therapy services.
   e. Maintain awareness of current laws, AOTA policies, and official documents that apply to the profession of occupational therapy.
   f. Inform employers, employees, colleagues, students, and researchers of applicable policies, laws, and official documents.
   g. Hold requisite credentials for the occupational therapy services they provide in academic, research, physical, or virtual work settings.
   h. Provide appropriate supervision in accordance with AOTA official documents and relevant laws, regulations, policies, procedures, standards, and guidelines.
   i. Obtain all necessary approvals prior to initiating research activities.
   j. Refrain from accepting gifts that would unduly influence the therapeutic relationship or have the potential to blur professional boundaries and adhere to employer policies when offered gifts.
   k. Report to appropriate authorities any acts in practice, education, and research that are unethical or illegal.
   l. Collaborate with employers to formulate policies and procedures in compliance with legal, regulatory, and ethical standards and work to resolve any conflicts or inconsistencies.

m. Bill and collect fees legally and justly in a manner that is fair, reasonable, and commensurate with services delivered.
n. Ensure compliance with relevant laws and promote transparency when participating in a business arrangement as owner, stockholder, partner, or employee.
o. Ensure that documentation for reimbursement purposes is done in accordance with applicable laws, guidelines, and regulations.
p. Refrain from participating in any action resulting in unauthorized access to educational content or exams (including but not limited to sharing test questions, unauthorized use of or access to content or codes, or selling access or authorization codes).

5. Veracity. Principle 5. Occupational therapy personnel shall provide comprehensive, accurate, and objective information when representing the profession. . . . Occupational therapy personnel shall:
   a. Represent the credentials, qualifications, education, experience, training, roles, duties, competence, views, contributions, and findings accurately in all forms of communication.
   b. Refrain from using or participating in the use of any form of communication that contains false, fraudulent, deceptive, misleading, or unfair statements or claims.
   c. Record and report in an accurate and timely manner, and in accordance with applicable regulations, all information related to professional or academic documentation and activities.
   d. Identify and fully disclose to all appropriate persons errors or adverse events that compromise the safety of service recipients.
   e. Ensure that all marketing and advertising are truthful, accurate, and carefully presented to avoid misleading recipients of service, students, research participants, or the public.
   f. Describe the type and duration of occupational therapy services accurately in professional contracts, including the duties and responsibilities of all involved parties.
   g. Be honest, fair, accurate, respectful, and timely in gathering and reporting fact-based information regarding employee job performance and student performance.
   h. Give credit and recognition when using the work of others in written, oral, or electronic media (i.e., do not plagiarize).
   i. Provide students with access to accurate information regarding educational requirements and academic policies and procedures relative to the occupational therapy program or educational institution.
   j. Maintain privacy and truthfulness when using telecommunication in the delivery of occupational therapy services.

6. Fidelity. Principle 6. Occupational therapy personnel shall treat clients, colleagues and other professionals with respect, fairness, discretion, and integrity. . . . Occupational therapy personnel shall:
   a. Preserve, respect, and safeguard private information about employees, colleagues, and students unless otherwise mandated or permitted by relevant laws.
   b. Address incompetent, disruptive, unethical, illegal, or impaired practice that jeopardizes the safety or well-being of others and team effectiveness.
   c. Avoid conflicts of interest or conflicts of commitment in employment, volunteer roles, or research.
   d. Avoid using one's position (employee or volunteer) or knowledge gained from that position in such a manner as to give rise to real or perceived conflict of interest among the person, the employer, other AOTA members, or other organizations.
   e. Be diligent stewards of human, financial, and material resources of their employers, and refrain from exploiting these resources for personal gain.
   f. Refrain from verbal, physical, emotional, or sexual harassment of peers or colleagues.
   g. Refrain from communication that is derogatory, intimidating, or disrespectful and that unduly discourages others from participating in professional dialogue.
   h. Promote collaborative actions and communication as a member of interprofessional teams to facilitate quality care and safety for clients.
   i. Respect that practices, competencies, roles, and responsibilities of their own and other professions to promote a collaborative environment reflective of interprofessional teams.
   j. Use conflict resolution and internal and alternative dispute resolution resources as needed to resolve organizational and interpersonal conflicts, as well as perceived institutional ethical violations.
   k. Abide by policies, procedures, and protocols when serving or acting on behalf of a professional organization or employer to fully and accurately represent the organization's official and authorized positions.
   l. Refrain from actions that reduce the public's trust in occupational therapy.
   m. Self-identify when personal, cultural, or religious values preclude, or are anticipated to negatively affect, the professional relationship or provision of services, while adhering to organizational policies when requesting an exemption from service to an individual or group on the basis of conflict of conscience" (AOTA, 2015b, pp. 2–8).

Ethics in Practice

1. Ethics guide the behavior and decision-making of OT practitioners to help them determine the morally right course of action.
2. Occupational therapy assistants (OTAs) often are faced with issues and events that challenge their values and beliefs and professional ethics.
3. NBCOT® exam questions may include practice scenarios that reflect ethical distress or ethical dilemmas.
   a. Ethical distress.
      (1) When a practitioner knows the correct action to take but an existing barrier prevents the practitioner from taking this course of action.
         (a) For example, when an admissions policy to a day treatment program excludes persons with substance abuse histories, yet this program would provide appropriate intervention for a client who has mental illness and is chemically addicted.
   b. Ethical dilemmas.
      (1) When there are two or more potentially morally correct ways to solve a problem. However, these solutions are exclusive; therefore, choosing one course of action prohibits acting on the other choices.
         (a) For example, a group of OT private practitioners has the opportunity to bid on a lucrative contract for the provision of OT services in a school system. However, none of the currently employed OTAs have pediatric experience and the practice relies on OTAs to implement treatment. The options in this case may include not bidding on the contract or bidding on the contract, and if the contract is won, incurring the expense of hiring pediatric-trained OTAs to implement treatment.
4. Decisions about what are the right or wrong courses of action to take to resolve ethical distress or dilemmas are based on the profession's Code of Ethics.
   a. COTA® exam items require the application of the AOTA Code of Ethics.

Patient/Client Abuse and Neglect

1. Definition of abuse.
   a. Abuse is defined as deliberately hurting a person physically, mentally, or emotionally.
   b. Neglect is defined as deliberately withholding services that are necessary to maintain an individual's physical, mental, and emotional health.
   c. Definitions may vary from state to state.
2. Facts and figures.
   a. All ages are at risk for abuse.
      (1) Refer to Chapter 5 for specific information on child and elder abuse.
   b. Facts and figures for patient/client abuse are subsumed into institutional elder abuse and abuse of the mentally ill.
3. Signs of patient/client abuse.
   a. Individual's report of abuse and/or neglect.
   b. Frequent unexplained injuries or complaints of pain without obvious injury.
   c. Burns or bruises suggesting the use of instruments, cigarettes, etc.
   d. Passive, withdrawn, and emotionless behavior.
   e. Lack of reaction to pain.
   f. Sexually transmitted diseases or injury to the genital area.
   g. Unexplained difficulty in sitting or walking.
   h. Fear of being alone with caretakers.
   i. Obvious malnutrition.
   j. Lack of personal cleanliness.
   k. Habitually dressed in torn or dirty clothes.
   l. Obvious fatigue and listlessness.
   m. Begs for food, water, or assistance (especially in regard to toileting).
   n. In need of medical or dental care.
   o. Left unattended for long periods.
   p. Bedsores and skin lesions.

> **EXAM HINT:** The OT Code of Ethics requires "occupational therapy personnel to "demonstrate a concern for the safety and well-being of the recipients of their services" (AOTA, 2015b, p. 2); thus, it is likely that the COTA® exam will include items about the OTA's role in identifying and responding to patient/client abuse. The application of knowledge about the signs of patient/client abuse described above and the following information about the role of OT practitioners can help you determine the correct answer to items about patient/client abuse.

4. Role of OT practitioners.
   a. It is an ethical responsibility of all OT practitioners to report any observed or suspected incidents of patient/client abuse or neglect.
      (1) The party to whom reporting is required varies from state to state, as do the penalties for not reporting.
         (a) Minimum reporting standards require reporting to one's immediate supervisor.
   b. OT practitioners should also provide interventions to victims of abuse and/or neglect. These can include:
      (1) Treatment for physical and emotional injuries.
      (2) Development of a trusting relationship.
      (3) Provision of support to family and loved ones.

(4) Referral to appropriate disciplines and agencies.
(5) Contribute to staff training programs to prevent abuse.

Ethical Decision-Making

> **EXAM HINT:** The application of knowledge about the following guidelines for ethical decision-making can help you determine the correct answer for NBCOT® Domain 03 Upholding Professional Standards and Responsibilities exam items related to ethical practice.

1. Identify the ethical issues and potential dilemmas.
2. Gather relevant information.
   a. Identify all individuals affected by the issue.
   b. Determine prior history of the issue.
   c. Analyze the dynamics and culture of the setting(s).
   d. Ask open-ended questions to obtain descriptive data.
3. Determine conflicting values and areas of agreement.
   a. A commitment to patient autonomy versus the principles of beneficence and nonmaleficence may need to be considered.
4. Identify as many relevant alternative courses of action as possible.
   a. Consider who would take these actions and when these actions would need to occur.
5. Determine all possible positive and negative outcomes for each possible action.
   a. Include outcomes for all participants in the dilemma. An ethical dilemma never involves just one person.
   b. It can take time and thought to identify all those who may possibly have a 'stake' or will be touched by a specific decision.
6. Weigh, with care, the consequences of each outcome.
   a. This step includes the process of reordering or rearranging parts of different decisions to arrive at a new alternative, which may be the best possible course of action.
7. Seek input from others (i.e., rehabilitation director, OT supervisor).
   a. Provide information in an anonymous fashion that enables the individual to give advice in a more objective manner and to provide recommendations that cannot be construed to be biased or prejudicial.
8. Apply best professional judgment to choose the action(s) to recommend.
9. Contact any and all agencies that have jurisdiction over a practitioner if there are questions about potential ethical violations that could cause harm or have the potential to cause harm to a person.
10. Determine desired and/or potential outcome of filing an ethical complaint.

Ethical Jurisdiction of Occupational Therapy

American Occupational Therapy Association (AOTA)

1. The profession's official membership organization that develops, publishes, and disseminates the field's ethical code.
2. The AOTA's Code of Ethics is a statement to the public that identifies the values and principles used to develop, endorse, and sustain high standards of behavior for OT practitioners.
3. These ethical standards are often the guide by which other bodies judge professional behaviors to determine if malpractice has occurred.
4. As a voluntary membership organization, the AOTA has no direct authority over practitioners (occupational therapists and OTAs) who are not members and no direct legal mechanism for preventing non-members who are incompetent, unethical, or unqualified from practicing.
5. Ethics Commission.
   a. The component of the AOTA that is responsible for the Code of Ethics, and the Standards of Practice of the profession.
   b. The Ethics Commission is responsible for informing and educating members about current ethical issues, upholding the practice and education standards of the profession, monitoring the behavior of members, and reviewing allegations of unethical conduct.
      (1) Ethical complaints filed with the Ethics Commission initiate an extensive, confidential review process according to the AOTA's established enforcement procedures for the OT Code of Ethics.

National Board for Certification in Occupational Therapy (NBCOT®)

1. The national credentialing agency for OT practitioners.
   a. Certifies qualified persons as certified occupational therapy assistants (COTA®s) and occupational therapists, registered (OTR®s), initially through a written exam for entry-level practitioners.
   b. The NBCOT® also maintains COTA® and OTR® certification through a voluntary certification renewal program.
   c. Jurisdiction is over all NBCOT® certified OT practitioners as well as those eligible for NBCOT® certification.
2. As a voluntary credentialing agency, NBCOT® has no direct authority over practitioners (occupational therapists and OTAs) who are not certified by NBCOT®, and no direct legal mechanism for preventing uncertified practitioners who are incompetent, unethical, or unqualified from practicing.
3. NBCOT® has developed investigatory and disciplinary action procedures for NBCOT® certified practitioners whose practices raise concern due to incompetence, unethical behavior, and/or impairment.

State Regulatory Boards (SRBs)

1. Public bodies created by state legislatures to assure the health and safety of the citizens of that state.
   a. Their specific responsibility is to protect the public from potential harm that might be caused by incompetent or unqualified practitioners.
   b. State regulation may be in the form of licensure, registration or certification. Refer to Appendix 2.
   c. Each state has legal guidelines that usually specify the scope of practice of the profession, and the qualifications that must be met to practice in that state.
2. Ethical jurisdiction.
   a. SRBs usually provide a description of ethical behavior. In many instances, SRBs have adopted the AOTA's Code of Ethics for this purpose.
   b. By the very nature of their limited jurisdiction (i.e., only over therapists and assistants practicing in their state), SRBs can monitor a profession closely.
   c. SRBs have the authority by law to discipline members of a profession if the public is determined to be at risk due to malpractice.
   d. SRBs also intervene in situations where the individual has been convicted of an illegal act that is directly connected with professional practice (i.e., fraud or misappropriation of funds through false billing practices).
   e. Since SRBs are primarily concerned with the protection of the public from harm, they will typically limit their review of complaints to those involving such a threat.

Disciplinary Actions for Ethical Violations and Professional Misconduct

1. When the AOTA, the NBCOT®, and/or a SRB determine that a person has violated their standards for ethical practice, different actions can be used as a disciplinary measure.
   a. These actions are based on agency internal investigations to determine the severity of an infraction and can include:
      (1) Reprimand: the private communication of the respective agency's disapproval of a practitioner's conduct.
      (2) Censure: a public statement of the respective agency's disapproval of a practitioner's conduct.
      (3) Ineligibility: the removal of eligibility for membership, certification, or licensure by the respective agency for an indefinite or specific time period.
      (4) Probation: the requirement that a practitioner meet certain conditions (e.g., further education, extensive supervision, individual counseling, participation in a substance abuse rehabilitation program) to retain membership, certification, or licensure by the respective agency.
      (5) Suspension: the loss of membership, certification, or licensure for a specific time period.
      (6) Revocation: the permanent loss of membership, certification, or licensure.
2. All of these actions (except for reprimand) are made public by the respective agencies.
   a. Disciplinary actions that are made public by one agency (e.g., the NBCOT®) can trigger an investigation into a practitioner's professional conduct by other practice jurisdictions (e.g., SRBs).

Common Law Related to Ethical Violations and Malpractice

1. Common law evolves from legal decisions and can impact occupational therapists and OTAs.
   a. Malpractice suits can be filed by individuals and/or their caregivers if the OTA is viewed to be personally responsible for negligence or other acts that resulted in harm to a client.

(1) Negligence.
  (a) Failure to do what other reasonable practitioners would have done under similar circumstances.
  (b) Doing what other reasonable practitioners would not have done under similar circumstances.
  (c) The end result was harm to the individual.
  (d) Every individual (OTA, occupational therapist, student OTA, or student occupational therapist) is liable for their own negligence.
b. Supervisors or superiors may also assume the liability of their workers if they provided faulty supervision or inappropriately delegated responsibilities.
c. The institution usually assumes liability if an individual was harmed as a result of an environmental problem.
  (1) Falls resulting from slippery floors, poorly lit areas, lack of grab bars.
d. The institution is also liable if an employee was incompetent or not properly licensed.
e. Personal malpractice insurance is advisable for all levels of OT practitioners.

OT Practitioner Roles

General Information

1. OT practitioners include occupational therapy assistants (OTAs) and occupational therapists.
2. Due to the implementation of the voluntary NBCOT® certification renewal program, all OTAs may not be COTA®s and all occupational therapists may not be OTR®s.
3. OT aides have an important role but are not considered OT practitioners.
4. OT practitioners can assume a variety of roles including entry to advanced level practitioner, peer and/or consumer educator, clinical/fieldwork educator, supervisor, administrator, consultant, academic clinical/fieldwork coordinator, faculty member, academic program director, researcher/scholar, and/or entrepreneur.
5. Role development and advancement depends on practitioner's experience, education, practice skills, and professional development activities (i.e., self-study, continuing education, advanced degrees).

COTA®/OTA Information

1. COTA®s/OTAs are graduates of Accreditation Council for Occupational Therapy Education (ACOTE) accredited technical educational programs, which are generally two years in duration, resulting in an Associate degree or a Certificate.
   a. COTA®s are certified by the NBCOT® and participate in the NBCOT® certification renewal program. OTAs are not certified by the NBCOT®.
2. COTA®'s/OTA's primary role is to implement treatment.
   a. COTA®s/OTAs can contribute to the evaluation process but they cannot independently evaluate or initiate treatment prior to the occupational therapist's evaluation.
   b. COTA®s/OTAs can contribute to development and implementation of the intervention plan and the monitoring and documenting of the individual's response to intervention with the occupational therapist's supervision.
3. COTA®s/OTAs can expand their role by establishing service competency.
   a. Service competency is the ability to complete the specified task in a safe, effective, and reliable manner, (i.e., the COTA®/OTA and occupational therapist can perform the same or equivalent procedure and obtain the same results).
   b. COTA®s/OTAs who establish service competency do not become independent; they continue to work with the occupational therapist's supervision.

> **EXAM HINT:** The application of knowledge about the standards for service competence can help you determine the correct answer for exam items about a COTA®'s ability to perform a task that is beyond entry-level COTA® practice. If the exam item does not provide information establishing the COTA®'s service competence, the correct answer cannot have the COTA® performing the given task.

4. COTA®s/OTAs can be activities directors in skilled nursing facilities (SNFs) and can supervise OT aides.

5. The AOTA supports the independent practice of COTA®s/OTAs with advanced-level skills who work for independent living centers.
   a. State licensure laws and scope of practice legislation may supersede this recommendation.

OT Aide Roles

1. Although OT aides are not considered OT practitioners, the use of OT aides has increased in response to changes in the health-care system (i.e., pressures to control costs have resulted in the delegation of non-skilled tasks to aides).
2. OT aides can be trained by COTA®s/OTAs or occupational therapists to perform specific non-skilled tasks.
3. The occupational therapist is responsible for the determination and delegation of the client and non-client tasks an aide performs and the outcome of these activities.
   a. Non-skilled, non-client tasks aides may perform include routine maintenance and clerical activities (e.g., preparation of clinic area for intervention, organizing supplies).
   b. Non-skilled client tasks (e.g., contact guarding a client during transfers) can only be delegated to an OT aide after the occupational therapist has determined that the following conditions have been met.
      (1) The anticipated result of the delegated task is known.
      (2) The performance of the delegated task is clearly established, predictable, and will not require the aide to make any interpretations, adaptations, and/or judgment calls.
      (3) The patient's situation and the practice environment are stable and will not require the aide to make any interpretations, adaptations, and/or judgment calls.
      (4) The patient has previously demonstrated some capabilities in performing the task.
      (5) The aide has been appropriately trained in the competent performance of the task and is able to demonstrate service competency in task performance.
      (6) The aide has received specific instructions on task implementation relevant to the specific client with whom the aide will be performing the delegated task.
      (7) The aide knows the precautions of the designated task and patient signs and symptoms that could indicate the need to seek assistance from the COTA® or occupational therapist.
4. Tasks performed by OT aides must be supervised by a COTA®/OTA or an occupational therapist, and this supervision must be documented.

> **EXAM HINT:** The delegation of a nonskilled client-related task to an OT aide that adheres to the previously described conditions will be the correct answer for a COTA® multiple-choice exam item. Incorrect answers would be options that include delegating a skilled task to an OT aide.

Supervisory Guidelines for OT Personnel

General Supervision Information

1. Supervision is the process in which two or more individuals collaborate to establish, maintain, promote, or enhance a level of performance and quality of service.
2. It is a mutually respectful joint effort between supervisor and supervisee.
3. It promotes professional growth and development and facilitates mentoring.
4. It ensures appropriate training, education, and use of resources for safe and effective service provision.
5. Supervision facilitates innovation, supports creativity, and provides encouragement, guidance, and support while working toward attainment of a shared goal.
6. Only OT practitioners can supervise OT practice; OT aides cannot supervise OT practice.
7. Occupational therapists are responsible and accountable for all aspects of OT service delivery.
   a. COTA®s/OTAs must be supervised by occupational therapists for any and all aspects of the OT service delivery process (AOTA, 2014).
8. To develop best practice competencies and foster professional growth, COTA®s/OTAs and occupational therapists should all use supervision and mentorship.
   a. The method, degree, amount, and pattern of supervision required can vary. For example, a novice COTA®/OTA requires frequent and direct supervision while an COTA®/OTA with 15 years of experience may require monthly minimal supervision. See following sections.

Methods of Supervision

1. Direct: face-to-face contact between supervisor and supervisee.
   a. Includes co-treatment, observation, instruction, modeling, and discussion.
2. Indirect: no face-to-face contact between supervisor and supervisee.
   a. Includes electronic, written, and telephone communications.

The Supervision Continuum

1. Supervision occurs along a continuum that includes close, routine, general, and minimum.
   a. Close: daily, direct contact at the site of work.
   b. Routine: direct contact at least every two weeks at the site of work, with interim supervision occurring by other methods such as telephone or written communication (e.g., email).
   c. General: at least monthly direct contact with supervision available as needed by other methods.
   d. Minimal: provided only on a needed basis and may be less than monthly.
2. Formal supervision can be supplemented by functional supervision, which is the provision of information and feedback to co-workers (a sharing of expertise).
3. The degree, amount, and pattern of supervision required can vary depending on the:
   a. Practitioner's knowledge and skills.
   b. Complexities of client needs and caseload characteristics and demands.
   c. State laws, licensure requirements, and other regulatory mandates.
   d. Practice setting type and facility procedures.

> **EXAM HINT:** Know that the supervising occupational therapist is the one who determines the appropriate level of supervision, not the supervisee, administrator, or employer.

4. Ethically, the OT supervisor must ensure that the type, amount, and pattern of supervision match the supervisee's level of role performance. See Table 4-1.
5. OT aide supervision may be intermittent or continuous depending on the task being performed.
   a. Intermittent supervision is sufficient for non-client-related tasks. It requires periodic discussion, demonstration, or contact between the supervisor and aide on at least a monthly basis.
   b. Continuous supervision is required for client-related tasks. A supervisory COTA®/OTA or occupational therapist must be within auditory and/or visual contact in the immediate area of the aide during the aide's task performance.

Specific OT Roles and Supervisory Guidelines

1. Occupational therapist.
   a. Functions to provide quality OT services (i.e., assessment, intervention, program planning and implementation, discharge planning, related documentation, and communication).
   b. Can be direct, indirect, or consultative in nature, and can range from entry-level to advanced-level, depending on experience, education, and practice skills.
   c. The occupational therapist has ultimate responsibility for service provision.
   d. Occupational therapists that do not have access to formal supervision are advised to seek mentoring to facilitate professional growth and develop best practice skills.
2. Certified occupational therapy assistant (COTA®)/occupational therapy assistant (OTA).
   a. Functions to provide quality OT services to assigned individuals under the supervision of an occupational therapist.
   b. Can range from entry-level to advanced-level depending on experience, education, and practice skills.
   c. Development from entry-level to advanced-level is dependent upon demonstration of service competency.
   d. OTAs who are certified by the NBCOT® and participate in the NBCOT® certification renewal program use the designation of COTA®.
3. Educator (consumer, peer).
   a. Functions to develop and provide training or educational offerings related to OT's domain of concern to consumer, peer, and community groups or individuals.
   b. Can be an occupational therapist or a COTA®/OTA with appropriate supervision.
4. Clinical/fieldwork educator.
   a. Functions as the manager of Level I and/or II fieldwork in a practice setting, providing students with opportunities to practice and implement practitioner competence.
      (1) Entry-level COTA®s/OTAs and occupational therapists may supervise Level I fieldwork students.[1]

---

[1] According to ACOTE standards, currently licensed and professionally credentialed personnel may supervise Level I fieldwork students. This standard includes occupational therapists, OTAs, and non-OT personnel such as nurses, nurse practitioners, psychologists, vocational counselors, physician assistants, recreation therapists, music therapists, teachers, speech therapists, social workers, and physical therapists.

Supervisory Guidelines for OT Personnel

Table 4-1

Guide for Supervision of Occupational Therapy Personnel

OCCUPATIONAL THERAPY PERSONNEL	SUPERVISION	SUPERVISES
Entry-level OT* (working on initial skill development or entering new practice) (AOTA, 1993a, p. 1088)	Not required. Close supervision by an intermediate-level or an advanced-level OT recommended.	Aides, technicians, all levels of OTAs, volunteers, Level I fieldwork students.
Intermediate-level OT* (working on increased skill development and mastery of basic role functions, and demonstrates ability to respond to situations based on previous experience) (AOTA, 1993a, p. 1088)	Not required. Routine or general supervision by an advanced-level OT recommended.	Aides, technicians, all levels of OTAs, Level I and Level II fieldwork students, entry-level OTs.
Advanced-level OT* (refining specialized skills with the ability to understand complex issues affecting role functions) (AOTA, 1993a, p. 1088)	Not required. Minimal supervision by an advanced-level OT is recommended.	Aides, technicians, all levels of OTAs, Level I and Level II fieldwork students, entry-level and intermediate-level OTs.
Entry-level OTA* (working on initial skill development or entering new practice) (AOTA, 1993a, p. 1088)	Close supervision by all levels of OTs, or an intermediate or an advanced-level OTA who is under the supervision of an OT.	Aides, technicians, volunteers.
Intermediate-level OTA* (working on increased skill development and mastery of basic role functions, and demonstrates ability to respond to situations based on previous experience) (AOTA, 1993a, p. 1088)	Routine or general supervision by all levels of OTs, or an advanced-level OTA, who is under the supervision of an OT.	Aides, technicians, entry-level OTAs, volunteers, Level I OT fieldwork students, Levels I and II OTA fieldwork students.
Advanced-level OTA** (refining specialized skills with the ability to understand complex issues affecting role functions) (AOTA, 1993a, p. 1088)	General supervision by all levels of OTs, or an advanced-level OTA, who is under the supervision of an OT.	Aides, technicians, entry-level and intermediate-level OTAs, volunteers, Level I OT fieldwork students, Level I and Level II OTA fieldwork students.
Personnel other than occupational therapy practitioners assisting in occupational therapy service (aides, paraprofessionals, technicians, volunteers)*** (AOTA, 1993a, p. 1088)	For non-client-related tasks, supervision is determined by the supervising practitioner. For client-related tasks, continuous supervision is provided by all levels of practitioners.	No supervisory capacity.

*Refer to the *Occupational Therapy Roles* document for descriptions of entry-level, intermediate-level, and advanced-level OTs and OTAs (AOTA, 1993a).
**Although specific state regulations may dictate the parameters of certified occupational therapy assistant practice, the American Occupational Therapy Association supports the autonomous practice of the certified occupational therapy assistant practitioner in the independent living setting (AOTA, 1993b, p. 1079). (*Note*. Removed from active files and placed in archives April 1999).
***Students are not addressed in this category. The student role as a supervisor is addressed in the *Essentials and Guidelines for an Accredited Educational Program for the Occupational Therapist* (AOTA, 1991a) and *Essentials and Guidelines for an Accredited Educational Program for the Occupational Therapy Assistant* (AOTA, 1991b).
From: Guide for supervision of occupational therapy. *American Journal of Occupational Therapy, 53* (p. 594) by the American Occupational Therapy Association Commission on Practice. Copyright 1999 by the American Occupational Therapy Association. Reprinted with permission.

---

(2) Occupational therapists with one year of practice-based experience may supervise Level II OT students.

(3) COTA®'s/OTA's with one year of practice experience may supervise OTA Level II fieldwork students.

(4) Three years of experience are recommended for individuals supervising programs with multiple students and multiple supervisors.

5. Supervisor.
   a. Functions as the manager of the overall daily operation of OT services in defined practice area(s).
   b. Can be a COTA®/OTA or an occupational therapist.
   c. Experienced COTA®'s/OTA's may supervise other OTAs administratively as long as service protocols and documentation are supervised by an occupational therapist.

6. Administrator.
   a. Functions to manage department, program, services, or agency providing OT services.
   b. Can be an occupational therapist with a graduate degree or continuing education relevant to management and experience appropriate to the size and scope of department and program(s), (i.e., a minimum of three to five years of experience).

7. Consultant.
   a. Functions to provide OT consultation to individuals, groups, or organizations.
   b. Can be a COTA®/OTA or an occupational therapist at the intermediate or advanced practice level.

c. The COTA®/OTA and occupational therapist are responsible for obtaining the appropriate level of supervision to meet regulatory and professional standards.
8. Academic clinical educator/fieldwork coordinator.
   a. Functions to manage fieldwork within the OT academic setting.
   b. Can be a COTA®/OTA or an occupational therapist with a recommended three years of practice experience and experience in supervising fieldwork students.
   c. General supervision by the OT academic program director is recommended.
   d. Close supervision to routine supervision is recommended for new faculty.
9. Faculty.
   a. Functions to provide formal academic education to OT students.
   b. Can be a COTA®/OTA or an occupational therapist with an appropriate advanced professional degree and intermediate to advanced skills in teaching.
   c. General supervision is recommended by academic program director.
   d. Close supervision to routine supervision for new, adjunct, and part-time faculty by program director.
10. Program director (academic setting).
    a. Functions to manage the occupational therapist or OTA education program with an appropriate advanced professional degree, experience as a faculty member, and experience or continuing education in academic management.
    b. General to minimal administrative supervision from designated administrative officer (e.g., Academic Dean).
11. Researcher/scholar.
    a. Functions to perform scholarly work of the profession; i.e., examining, developing, refining, and/or evaluating the profession's theoretical base, philosophical foundations, body of knowledge, and service outcomes.
    b. Can be an occupational therapist or a COTA®/OTA with additional self-study, continuing education, experience, and formal education related to research and scholarly activities.
    c. Additional academic qualifications are needed for COTA®s/OTAs to be principal investigators.
    d. COTA®s/OTAs without additional education can contribute to the research process.
    e. Supervision needs range from close to minimal depending on the skills of the researcher/scholar and the scope of the project.
12. Entrepreneur.
    a. Functions as a partially or fully self-employed individual who provides OT services.
    b. Can be a COTA®/OTA or an occupational therapist who meets state regulatory requirements.
    c. COTA®s/OTAs who provide direct service have the responsibility to obtain appropriate supervision from an occupational therapist.

Team Roles and Principles of Collaboration

Overview

1. A team is a group of equally important individuals with common interests collaborating to develop shared goals and build trusting relationships to achieve these shared goals.
2. Members of the team include the service recipient, their family, significant others, and/or caregivers; health care professionals; and the reimbursing agencies' gatekeepers.
   a. Service recipients are typically called patients in medical model settings (e.g., hospitals), *clients* in community-based settings (e.g., outpatient clinics), consumers in recovery-oriented programs (e.g., clubhouses), and residents in residential settings (e.g., group homes, SNFs).
3. Professional members on a team will vary according to practice setting.
4. The service recipient, family, significant other, and/or caregiver role on the team has become increasingly important. Collaboration with these individuals is even mandated by law (e.g., Omnibus Budget Reconciliation Act [OBRA], Individuals with Disabilities Education Act [IDEA]; see this chapter's section on legislation).

Principles of Collaboration

1. Factors that influence effective team functioning.
   a. Member skill and knowledge.
   b. Membership stability.
   c. Commitment to team goals.
   d. Good communication.
   e. Membership composition.
   f. A common language.
   g. Effective leadership.

2. Recognize that all members of the team are equally important.
   a. No one's opinion or area of competence takes precedence over the other.
      (1) Facility chain of command guidelines will determine who is ultimately responsible for the team's decision.
3. Understand principles of team collaboration and that correct exam answers will adhere to these principles.
4. Know the different types of teams and their respective limits and benefits for team efficacy.
5. Know all potential team members and their respective role responsibilities. NBCOT® exam items can ask questions that require an answer that includes a referral to another team member.
6. Recognize that OT practitioners are competent in many domains of concern, but our scope of practice does have its limits.
   a. Be prepared to recognize these limits.

> **EXAM HINT:** To test knowledge about the scope of OT practice and the scope of other professions, the COTA® exam may include items for which a correct answer includes a referral to another team member. For example, the correct answer for an exam item in which a distraught parent of a child with a progressive neuromuscular disease angrily questions the meaning of life and the relevance of their faith during an OT session would have the OTA collaborating with the occupational therapist to refer the parent to pastoral care.

Types of Teams

1. Intradisciplinary.
   a. One or more members of one discipline evaluate, plan, and implement treatment of the individual.
   b. Other disciplines are not involved; communication is limited, thereby limiting perspectives on the case.
   c. This 'team' is at risk due to potential narrowness of perspective.
   d. Comprehensive, holistic care can be questionable.
2. Multidisciplinary.
   a. A number of professionals from different disciplines conduct assessments and interventions independent from one another.
   b. Members' primary allegiance is to their discipline. Some formal communications occur between team members.
   c. Limited communication may result in lack of understanding of different perspectives.
   d. Resources and responsibilities are individually allocated between disciplines; therefore, competition among team members may develop.
3. Interprofessional.
   a. All professional disciplines relevant to the case at hand agree to collaborate for decision-making.
   b. Evaluation and intervention are still conducted independently within defined areas of each profession's expertise. However, there is a greater understanding of each profession's perspective.
   c. Members are directed toward a common goal and not bound by discipline-specific roles and functions.
   d. Members tend to use group process skills effectively (e.g., during team treatment planning meetings).
   e. The exchange of information, prioritization of needs, and allocation of resources and responsibilities are based on members' expertise and skills, not on 'turf' issues.
4. Transdisciplinary.
   a. Characteristics of interdisciplinary teams are maintained and expanded upon.
   b. Members support and enhance the activities and programs of other disciplines to provide quality, efficient, cost-effective service.
   c. Members are committed to ongoing communication, collaboration, and shared decision-making for the patient/client's benefit.
   d. Evaluations and interventions are planned cooperatively, yet one member may take on multiple responsibilities. Role blurring is accepted.
   e. Ongoing training, support, supervision, cooperation, and consultation among disciplines are important to this model, ensuring that professional integrity and quality of care are maintained.
5. Team efficacy.
   a. Interprofessional and transdisciplinary teams are the most common and considered the most effective in today's health care system.

Lay Team Members and Role Responsibilities

1. Service recipient.
   a. The most important and primary member of the treatment team.
   b. The service recipient's occupations, values, interests, and goals must be determined and used in all treatment planning.

> **CAUTION:** If the service recipient and the COTA®/OTA do not share a common language, an interpreter must be used.

2. Family/primary caregiver.
   a. Family's sociocultural background, socioeconomic status, and caregiving tasks, needs, and skills must be considered as they can impact the outcome of intervention.

> **CAUTION:** If the family and the COTA®/OTA do not share a common language, an interpreter must be used.

Paraprofessional Team Members and Role Responsibilities

1. Personal Care Assistants (PCAs)/Home Health Aides (HHAs).
   a. Individuals who provide primary care to enable a person with a disability to remain in his or her own home.
   b. Most states require some minimum training and certification as a PCA/HHA. Standards and educational requirements can vary greatly from state to state.
   c. Responsibilities.
      (1) Personal care such as bathing, grooming, dressing, and feeding.
      (2) Home management such as shopping, cleaning, and cooking.
      (3) Supervision of home programs as directed by a health-care professional (e.g., therapist, nurse).
   d. Due to the tremendous importance this role has in maintaining a person with a disability in their own home, OT practitioner collaboration with PCAs/HHAs is critical.
   e. OT practitioners can educate and train service recipients and/or their family members/caregivers on the hiring, training, and supervision of PCAs/HHAs.

Professional Team Members and Role Responsibilities

> **EXAM HINT:** The NBCOT® exam outline for the COTA® identifies knowledge of the "characteristics and functions of interprofessional teams for coordinating client care and providing efficient and effective programs and services consistent with specific core competencies, expertise, unique contributions, team roles, and context of the organization" (NBCOT®, 2018, p. 22) as essential for competent and safe practice. The application of knowledge about the role responsibilities of the professional team members described as follows can help you determine the correct answer for NBCOT® Domain 01 exam items about interprofessional collaboration.

1. Alternative practitioners.
   a. May include massage therapists, acupuncturists, Reiki practitioners, and others.
   b. Training and licensure requirements vary greatly.
   c. The roles and tasks of alternative practitioners will be determined by state practice regulations and reimbursing agencies' guidelines.
2. Athletic trainer.
   a. An allied health professional.
   b. Assesses athletes' risk for injury, conducts injury prevention programs, and provides treatment and rehabilitation under the supervision of a physician when athletic trauma occurs.
3. Audiologist.
   a. A professional who is a graduate of an educational program in audiology.
   b. Administers assessments to determine an individual's auditory acuity, level of hearing impairment, and damage site(s) in the auditory system.
   c. Provides recommendations for assistive devices (e.g., hearing aids) and/or special training to enhance residual hearing and/or adapt to hearing loss.
4. Biomedical engineer.
   a. A graduate of an engineering program who specializes in the biomedical application of engineering theory and technology.
   b. Serves as a technical expert to recommend commercial products, adapt available devices, and/or modify existing environments.
   c. Develops, designs, and fabricates customized equipment, devices, and techniques.
5. Certified orthotist.
   a. Evaluates the need for orthotic equipment (splints, braces).
   b. Designs, fabricates, and fits orthoses for individuals to prevent or correct deformities and/or support body parts weakened by injury, disease, or congenital deformity.
   c. Educates the client on the purpose of orthoses, recommended care, and wearing schedule.
   d. May be an occupational therapist, a physical therapist, or an individual with specialized training.
6. Certified prosthetist.
   a. Evaluates the need for a prosthesis.
   b. Designs, fabricates, and fits prosthesis for an individual to ensure proper fit and to promote functional abilities.
   c. Educates client and/or caregiver(s) about the use and care of the prosthesis.
   d. Works directly with occupational therapy practitioners, physical therapists, and physicians.
7. Chiropractor.
   a. A professional who is a graduate of an educational program in chiropractic who is usually licensed by state boards.
   b. Assesses the individual's spinal column and intervenes to restore and maintain health and decrease or eliminate pain.

8. Dietician/clinical nutritionist.
   a. A licensed professional who is a graduate of an accredited educational program and who passed a national registration examination.
      (1) Practitioners who pass this registration examination are credentialed as Registered Dietician (RD) or Dietician Technician, Registered (DTR), depending on level of education.
   b. Evaluates individuals' nutritional status and dietary needs.
   c. Provides nutrition therapy for diseases such as diabetes and preventive counseling for issues such as obesity.
9. Expressive/creative arts therapist.
   a. Professionals who are graduates of specialized education programs.
   b. Depending on the state, they may or may not be licensed or registered.
   c. Includes art, dance/movement, music, horticulture, and poetry therapists.
   d. Conducts individual and/or group interventions that use select expressive modalities to facilitate self-expression, self-awareness, social skills, symptom reduction, and management.
10. Job coach.
    a. Provides on-site, one-on-one training to employees with disabilities to help them learn to perform their jobs accurately, efficiently, and safely, and acclimate to the work environment.
    b. Performs job analyses at work sites to match people with optimal positions.
    c. Conducts assessments, develops jobs, and provides counseling, travel and mobility training, and other services required to retain employment.
    d. The job coach's degree of involvement with the employee decreases over time as the employee masters the job with follow-up services provided as needed.
11. Nurse practitioner (NP).
    a. An advanced practice nurse who has completed post-professional graduate education to obtain a master's or a doctoral degree in nursing.
    b. NPs are nationally certified in specific areas of specialty (e.g., pediatrics, geriatrics, family practice, acute care).
    c. Depending on a state's scope of practice act, NPs can serve as primary care providers, prescribe medications, and complete referrals for OT and other rehabilitative services.
    d. Diagnoses, treats, and manages acute and chronic medical conditions.
12. Registered nurse (RN).
    a. A licensed professional who is a graduate of an accredited nursing education program.
    b. Serves as the primary liaison between the individual and physician.
       (1) Often serves as the primary case manager.
    c. Monitors vital signs, symptoms, and behaviors.
    d. Dispenses medications and assists the physician with the titration of medications.
    e. Performs or supervises bedside care and assists with activities of daily living (ADL) in collaboration with occupational therapy practitioners.
    f. Conducts group and individual interventions related to wellness and prevention and disease and symptom management (e.g., medication education).
    g. Performs patient, family, and caregiver education to facilitate recovery and maximize quality of life.
    h. Supervises and is assisted by licensed practical nurses (LPNs), certified nursing assistants (CNAs), and aides.
       (1) Due to the major role LPNs, CNAs, and aides have in providing direct care to individuals, OT collaboration with these team members is essential.
13. Optometrist/vision specialist.
    a. A professional who is a graduate of an educational program in optometry.
    b. Examines the eye to determine visual acuity, level of visual impairments, and damage to or disease in the visual system.
    c. Prescribes assistive devices (e.g., corrective lenses) and recommends other appropriate treatment (e.g., visual-motor training).
    d. Optometrists can refer individuals to outpatient OT.
14. Pastoral care.
    a. Serves as the spiritual advisor to the individual, their family, caregivers, and the team.
    b. Provides individual, couple, and family counseling in a non-denominational manner.
15. Physiatrist.
    a. A physician who specializes in physical medicine and rehabilitation and is certified by the American Board of Physical Medicine and Rehabilitation.
    b. Leads the rehabilitation team and works directly with occupational, speech, and physical therapists and others to maximize rehabilitation outcomes for persons with physical disorders.
    c. Diagnoses and medically treats individuals with musculoskeletal, neurological, cardiovascular, pulmonary, and/or other body systems disorders.
16. Physical therapist.
    a. A licensed professional who is a graduate of an accredited physical therapy (PT) education program at a baccalaureate, graduate, or doctoral level.
    b. Evaluates clients' physical motor skills.

c. Develops a plan of care and administers or supervises treatment to develop, improve and/or maintain client's physical motor skills, to alleviate pain, and to correct or minimize physical deformity.
d. Delegates portions of treatment program to supportive personnel, e.g., physical therapist assistant (PTA).
e. Supervises and directs supportive staff (assistants, aides) in designated tasks.
f. Re-evaluates and adjusts plan of care as appropriate.
g. Performs and documents final evaluation and establishes discharge and follow-up plans.

17. Physical therapist assistant (PTA).
    a. A skilled allied health-care technologist, usually with a two-year associate's degree.
    b. Must work under the supervision of a physical therapist.
       (1) If the supervisor is off-site, delegated responsibilities must be safe and legal practice, with ready access to the supervisor.
       (2) In home health, required periodic joint on-site visits or treatments with physical therapist.
    c. Able to adjust treatment procedure in accordance with the patient's status.
    d. May not evaluate, develop, or change plan of care, or write discharge plan or summary.

18. Physician's assistant.
    a. A professional who is a graduate of an accredited physician's assistant educational program and who has passed a national certification examination.
    b. Performs routine diagnostic, therapeutic, preventative, and health maintenance services.
    c. Specializations can include family medicine, geriatrics, pediatrics, obstetrics, orthopedics, psychiatry, and emergency care.
    d. Must work under the direction of, and be supervised by, a physician.

19. Primary care physician (PCP).
    a. A physician who serves as the "gatekeeper" for service recipients in managed health-care systems.
    b. Provides primary health care services and manages routine medical care.
    c. Makes referrals, as needed, to other health care providers and services including specialty tests and examinations, rehabilitation services, and OT.
    d. PCPs can be a doctor of medicine (MD) or a doctor of osteopathic medicine (DO).
       (1) DOs undergo a similar education as MDs with the addition of specific training in osteopathic medicine techniques.

20. Psychiatrist.
    a. A physician who specializes in mental health and psychiatric rehabilitation.
    b. Leads the rehabilitation team and works directly with occupational therapy practitioners, psychologists, social workers, and others to maximize rehabilitation outcomes for persons with psychiatric disorders.
    c. Diagnoses and medically treats individuals with psychiatric disorders.
    d. Responsible for ordering transfers to long-term care settings and for determining competence and the need for involuntary treatment.

21. Psychologist.
    a. A professional with a PhD in psychology.
    b. Evaluates psychological and cognitive status with standardized and non-standardized assessments.
    c. Provides individual, couple, family, and group supportive therapy, cognitive retraining, and behavior modification.

22. Recreational therapist/therapeutic recreation specialist.
    a. A professional who is a graduate of a baccalaureate or graduate-level recreation therapy education program.
    b. Conducts individual and/or group interventions to develop leisure interests and skills; to facilitate community, social, and recreational integration; to manage stress and symptoms; and to adjust to disability.
    c. May be called an activities therapist, but the two positions are not synonymous; activities therapists may only have on-the-job training.

23. Respiratory therapy technician, certified.
    a. A technically trained professional with an associate's degree who has passed a national certification examination.
    b. Administers respiratory therapy as prescribed and supervised by a physician.
    c. Performs pulmonary function tests and inter-venes through oxygen delivery, aerosols, and nebulizers.

24. Social worker.
    a. A licensed/registered professional who is a graduate of an accredited educational social work program at a baccalaureate level (BSW) or at a graduate level (MSW).
    b. Upon passing a national certification examination, a social worker is eligible to use the credentials Certified Social Worker (CSW).
       (1) In states with licensure requirements, a social worker may have the credential of licensed clinical social worker (LCSW).
    c. Assesses client's social history and psychosocial functioning via clinical interviews and structured assessments.
    d. Assists clients, families, and caregivers with accessing social support services (e.g., home care, support groups) and obtaining needed reimbursement/funding (e.g., Medicaid, food stamps) through the completion of required application processes and through active advocacy.

e. Provides individual, couple, and family counseling.
  f. Serves as a primary care manager, enabling individuals to function optimally and maintain quality of life.
  g. Provides crisis intervention and recommendations for additional services.
  h. Contributes to discharge plan and completes tasks needed for implementation of discharge orders (e.g., application to a SNF).
  i. Supervises and is assisted by social work assistants.
25. Special educator/teacher.
    a. A professional teacher certified to provide education to children with special needs.
       (1) Visual and/or hearing impairments.
       (2) Emotional and psychosocial disabilities.
       (3) Physical and sensorimotor disabilities.
       (4) Developmental disabilities.
       (5) Learning and cognitive disabilities.
    b. Assesses and monitors student learning, plans and implements instructional activities, and addresses the special developmental and educational needs of each student.
    c. Advanced training in instructional methods for teaching children with special needs to develop to their fullest educational potential is required.
    d. Additional training in teaching children with multiple disabilities is often needed.
    e. May be assisted by teacher aides who provide direct care and 'hands-on' support to students in the classroom.
       (1) Collaboration with aides is required for effective follow-through of OT programming in school settings.
26. Speech-language pathologist (SLP) or speech therapist (ST).
    a. A professional who is a graduate of an accredited educational program in speech-language pathology.
    b. Assesses language and speech abilities and impairments.
    c. Develops and conducts intervention programs to restore, improve, or augment the communication of persons with speech and/or language impairments.
    d. May receive advanced training and specialize in oral-motor functioning (e.g., the evaluation and treatment of dysphagia).
27. Substance abuse counselor.
    a. A professional who may come from a diversity of educational backgrounds (psychology, social work, OT) who has completed a specialized training program.
    b. Provides individual and/or group intervention.
    c. Certified Alcohol Counselor (CAC) and Certified Alcohol and Drug Counselor (CADC) are the two main credentials designating this specialized role.
28. Vocational rehabilitation counselor.
    a. A professional who is a graduate of an educational program in vocational rehabilitation.
    b. If certified, the counselor is able to use the credential of Certified Rehabilitation Counselor (CRC).
    c. Evaluates prevocational skills and vocational interests and abilities via standardized and non-standardized assessments to determine an individual's employability.
    d. Provides counseling to maximize the individual's vocational potential.
    e. Refers individual to appropriate vocational programming and/or job placement.
    f. Serves as liaison between the individual and state educational and vocational departments for persons with disabilities to obtain funding for needed services.

The U.S. Health-Care System

Overview

1. A group of decentralized subsystems serving different populations.
2. Health care in the United States is overwhelmingly insured and delivered by privately owned companies.
3. The Patient Protection and Affordable Care Act (ACA), signed into law in 2010, with implementation into 2016, sought to expand access to health insurance for all Americans and improve the quality of health care provided in the United States.[2]

---

[2] At the time of publication of this publication, the future of the benefits afforded by the ACA (e.g., expansion of Medicaid, mandated coverage for pre-existing conditions) or its health care service initiatives (e.g., Affordable Care Organizations, Patient-Centered Medical Homes) is unclear.

4. Relatively small federal and state governmental programs work in conjunction with a large private sector; however, the government pays for a large portion of these private sector services through Medicare and Medicaid reimbursement.
5. Decentralization results in overlap in some areas and competition in others; therefore, health care is primarily a market driven business.
    a. Patients are viewed as consumers due to this economic focus.
    b. Cost containment while maintaining quality of service is a delicate balancing act that is not always achieved.
6. Primary care physicians have increased significance as the first line for evaluation and intervention, as well as being the referral source for specialized and/or ancillary services.

Health Care Regulations

1. Health care is a highly regulated industry with most established practice mandated by federal and state law.

> **EXAM HINT:** Due to the great variance in state laws and regulations, the COTA® exam will likely only contain exam items that require knowledge of federal laws and regulations.

2. The Centers for Medicare and Medicaid Services (CMS), a division of the U.S. Department of Health and Human Services (HHS), is the federal agency that develops rules and regulations pertaining to federal laws governing the Medicare and Medicaid programs.
    a. Facilities that participate in Medicare and/or Medicaid programs are monitored regularly for compliance with CMS guidelines by federal and state surveyors.
    b. Facilities that repeatedly fail to meet CMS guidelines lose their Medicare and/or Medicaid certification(s).
    c. Long-term settings (i.e., SNFs) are strongly influenced by CMS regulations since Medicare and/or Medicaid pays for all or most of the expense of long-term care.
3. Standards related to safety are set forth and enforced by the Occupational Safety and Health Administration (OSHA), a division of the U.S. Department of Labor.
    a. Structural standards and building codes are established and enforced by OSHA to ensure the safety of structures.
    b. The safety of employees and consumers is regulated by OSHA standards for handling infectious materials and blood products, controlling bloodborne pathogens, operating machinery, and handling hazardous substances.
4. State accreditation to obtain licensure for a health care facility is mandatory. Individual states develop their own requirements, with state agencies enforcing these regulations.
5. Local city or county entities also develop regulations pertaining to health care institutions (e.g., physical plant safety features such as fire, elevator, and boiler regulations).

> **EXAM HINT:** The NBCOT® exam outline for the COTA® identifies the task of providing "occupational therapy services in accordance with . . . accreditation guidelines in order to protect consumers and meet applicable reimbursement requirements in relation to the service delivery setting" and knowledge of "methods for identifying, locating, and integrating federal regulations, facility policies, and accreditation guidelines related to service delivery across occupational therapy practice settings" (NBCOT®, 2018, p. 29) as essential for competent and safe practice. The application of knowledge about the following accreditation information may help you determine the correct answer for NBCOT® Domain 03 Upholding Professional Standards and Responsibilities exam items.

Voluntary Accreditation

1. Voluntary accreditation and self-imposed compliance with established standards is sought by most health care organizations; for example, hospitals, SNFs, home health agencies, preferred provider organizations (PPOs), rehabilitation centers, health maintenance organizations (HMOs), behavioral health (including mental health and chemical dependency) facilities, physicians' networks, hospice care, long-term care facilities, and others.
2. Accreditation is a status awarded for compliance with established standards.
3. Accreditation ensures the public that a health care facility is adequately equipped, meets high standards for patient care, and employs qualified professionals and competent staff.
4. Accreditation affirms the competence of practitioners and the quality of health care facilities and organizations.
5. Accreditation through an accrediting agency is voluntary; however, it is mandatory to receive third-party reimbursement and to be eligible for federal government grants and contracts.
6. CMS and many states accept certain national accreditations as meeting their respective requirements for participation in the Medicare and Medicaid programs and for a license to operate.
7. Voluntary accrediting agencies include the Joint Commission (JCAHO), Healthcare Facilities Accreditation Program, Commission on Accreditation of Rehabilitation Facilities (CARF), the Accreditation Council for Services for Mentally Retarded and Other Developmentally Disabled Persons (AC-MRDD), and others.

The Accreditation Process

1. Accreditation is initiated by the organization applying for review or survey by the accrediting agency.
2. A self-study or self-assessment is conducted to examine the organization based on the accrediting agency's standards.
3. An on-site review is conducted by an individual reviewer, surveyor, or team visiting the organization.
4. The accreditation and the re-accreditation processes involve all staff. Tasks include document preparation, hosting the site visit team, and interviews with accreditors.
5. Once accredited, the organization undergoes periodic review, typically every three years.

Value of Accreditation to Occupational Therapy

1. Self-study and self-assessment can be an opportunity to identify areas of strength, validate competence, and promote excellence.
2. Areas needing improvement can be identified (i.e., procedures can be streamlined, additional resources can be obtained, team communication can be enhanced).
3. Program goals are clarified.
4. Practice is defined and documented.
5. Accreditors can share information regarding best practices.
6. An increased recognition of the OT practitioners' contributions to the agency and identification of functional outcomes can result in increased visibility for OT and increased referrals.

Payment for Occupational Therapy Services

Key Terms

1. Beneficiary: a person receiving services.
2. Capitation.
   a. Payment system under which the provider is paid prospectively (i.e., on a monthly basis) a set fee for each member of a specific population (i.e., health plan members) regardless if no covered health care is delivered or if extensive care is delivered.
   b. Payment is typically determined in terms of per member per month (PMPM).
   c. The healthier the enrollees (and the fewer services used), the more the provider retains of the total PMPM payment.
3. Coinsurance: the monetary amount to be paid by a patient, usually expressed as a percentage of total charge.
4. Clinical/critical pathway: a standardized recommended intervention protocol for a specific diagnosis.
5. Deductible: the amount a patient must pay to a provider before the insurance benefits will pay; usually expressed as an annual dollar amount.
6. Denial: the refusal by a payer to reimburse a provider for services rendered. Reasons for denial include benefits exhausted, duplication of services, and services not indicated.
7. Diagnosis code: a code that describes a patient's medical reason or condition that requires health service.
8. Diagnostic related groups (DRGs): the descriptive categories established by CMS that determine the level of payment at a per case rate.
9. Fee for service: the payment system under which the provider is paid the same type of rate per unit of service. Traditionally, payer pays 80% and patient or provider is responsible for the remaining 20%.
10. Health insurance marketplace: established by the ACA to allow consumers to compare the cost of insurance plans in their area.
    a. Also known as health-care exchanges.[3]
11. Health maintenance organization (HMO): a common form of managed care. Maintains control over services by requiring enrollees to see only doctors within the HMO network and to obtain referrals before seeking specialty or ancillary care.
12. Managed care: a method of maintaining some control over costs and utilization of services while providing quality health care. Managed care organizations (MCOs) include HMOs and PPOs.
13. Per diem: a negotiated, per day fee for service. Typically used for inpatient hospital stays and SNFs.
14. Preferred provider organization (PPO): a form of managed care that is similar to an HMO but usually offers a greater choice of providers. However, as choices increase, percentage of payment decreases.
15. Private payment: the individual receiving services is responsible for payment.
16. Procedure codes: codes that describe specific services performed by health professionals.

---

[3] At the time of this publication, the future status of these programs is unknown.

17. Prospective payment system (PPS): the nationwide payment schedule that determines the Medicare payment for each inpatient stay of a Medicare beneficiary based on DRGs.
18. Provider: the entity responsible for the delivery and quality of services. Providers bill Medicare, HMOs, and PPOs for services rendered.
19. Third-party payers: agencies and companies who are the primary sources of reimbursement for health care in the U.S. (e.g., Blue Cross). HMOs and PPOs are also third-party payers.
20. Treatment authorization request (TAR): the Medicaid form a primary care provider must complete to document the need for requested medically necessary covered services with a supporting rationale.
21. Usual and customary rate (UCR): the average cost of specific health care procedures in a geographic area. This is the maximum amount the insurer will pay for a service and covered expense.
22. Vendor/supplier: the entity that supplies services.

Private Insurance and Managed Care Plans

1. Largest source of insurance payment in U.S.
   a. These plans can be managed by for profit or not-for-profit companies, organizations, and/or networks.
   b. There are broad variations among plans and plan options.
2. Many private insurers contract with Medicare to handle the day-to-day operations of Medicare. They are called intermediaries.
3. Insurers (e.g., Blue Cross/Blue Shield, Aetna, MetLife, and Prudential) offer many insurance products, including PPOs, HMOs, and MCOs.
4. Coverage cannot be assumed based on the name of plan alone.
   a. Coinsurance, deductibles, and co-payments are common.
   b. Most plans cover OT in hospitals.
   c. Outpatient coverage varies greatly.
   d. Total number of visits and/or type and amount of services per diagnosis are limited.
5. Historically, private insurers have not been federally regulated.
6. Under the ACA, federal regulations were established for private insurance coverage.[4] Key ones include the following:
   a. Insurers must provide essential benefits to participants in their plans; these include mental health, substance abuse, and behavioral health treatment; rehabilitative, habilitative, and chronic disease management services and devices; and preventative and wellness services.
   b. Insurers could no longer refuse coverage to persons with preexisting conditions.
   c. Insurers could not raise insurance premiums based on a person's occupation, gender, preexisting condition, health status, or claim history.
   d. Insurers must allow young adults until their 26th birthday to be covered under their parents' plans, if these plans cover dependents.
   e. Insurers could not set caps on annual and lifetime coverage.
7. States can set their own requirements and regulations for insurers who operate within their borders.

EXAM HINT: As a national examination, the COTA® exam will not test state-specific requirements or regulations.

8. Cost-controlling payment strategies such as case management, precertification or preauthorization, mandatory second opinions, and preferred provider networks are often implemented.
9. OT practitioners can join health care provider panels and/or a preferred provider network.

EXAM HINT: The NBCOT® exam outline for the COTA® identifies knowledge of the "influence of reimbursement policies and guidelines related to skilled and medically necessary occupational therapy service delivery" (NBCOT®, 2018, p. 29) as essential for competent and safe practice. Because the NBCOT® exam is a national exam, it will not ask specific questions about private insurance; however, the application of knowledge about the industry trends as previously described can help you determine the correct answer for NBCOT® Domain 03 exam items. Since Medicare is a federal program and the major national payer for OT services, specifics about Medicare will likely be tested on the NBCOT® exam. The application of knowledge about the following Medicare information will be required to determine the correct answer to COTA® exam questions about reimbursement.

Medicare

1. General information.
   a. Largest single payer for OT services.
   b. Administered by CMS.
   c. Intermediaries determine if services provided are within Medicare guidelines.
   d. Persons eligible for Medicare medical coverage for health care services.
      (1) Persons 65 years or older.

---
[4] At the time of this publication, the status of these provisions is unclear.

(2) Individuals of all ages with end-stage renal disease/permanent kidney failure that may require dialysis treatment or a kidney transplant.
(3) Persons with a long-term disability (e.g., amyotrophic lateral sclerosis [ALS], multiple sclerosis [MS]) who have received government-funded disability benefits for 24 months may be eligible.
(4) Retired railroad workers.
2. Part A: pays for services provided by inpatient hospitals, SNFs, home health agencies, rehabilitation facilities, and hospices.
   a. Part A is automatically provided to all who are covered by the Social Security System that meet the above coverage criteria.
   b. Services provided in acute care hospitals receive a prospective, predetermined rate based on DRGs.
      (1) The DRG per case rate covers all services including OT.
      (2) It is a fixed dollar amount for patient care for each diagnosis regardless of length of stay (LOS) or number of services provided.
      (3) Treatment supplies (i.e., adaptive equipment, splints) are included in this per case rate.
      (4) Individual hospitals determine the combination of services a patient will receive.
   c. Part A covered services have specific time limits and also require deductible and coinsurance payments by the beneficiary.
      (1) Annual deductible fees must be paid by patient.
      (2) Twenty percent of home health care must be paid by the patient.
3. Part B: pays for physician services, hospital outpatient services, durable medical equipment, orthotics, prosthetics, supplies, and other professional services including OT services provided by independent practitioners.
   a. Part B is considered a Supplemental Medical Insurance Program and therefore must be purchased by the beneficiary, usually as a monthly premium.
   b. Part B services have no specific time limit and require 20% co-payment.
4. Criteria for coverage of OT services.
   a. Prescribed by a physician or furnished according to a physician-approved plan of care.
   b. Performed by a qualified occupational therapist or a COTA®/OTA with the general supervision of an occupational therapist.
   c. Service is reasonable and necessary for treatment of individual's injury or illness.
   d. Diagnosis can be physical, psychiatric, or both. There are no diagnostic restrictions for coverage.
5. The primary difference between Part A and Part B is the frequency in which the individual receives services. Inpatient Part A coverage requires services for a minimum of five days per week services. Part B typically covers three days per week outpatient services.
6. Medicare does not cover most chronic illnesses, long-term supportive care, or all medical expenses incurred when ill.
7. Medicare does cover a therapist's design of a maintenance plan and the occasional re-evaluation of this plan's effectiveness.
   a. Reimbursement is not provided for a therapist to carry out a maintenance plan that does not provide skilled services.
   b. In 2013, existing Medicare policy about reimbursable skilled therapy to maintain a person's functional status and quality of life was clarified.
      (1) The restorative potential of a person was determined to *not* be the sole payment criteria for skilled therapy services.
      (2) Therapy services to prevent or slow deterioration and maintain a person at their highest possible functional level was recognized as skilled and covered if these services are reasonable and necessary.
         (a) If maintenance services can be performed safely and effectively by unskilled personnel, coverage for skilled therapy services is not mandated.
   c. Evaluation and training of caregivers are considered part of the design and re-evaluation of a maintenance plan.
   d. The competence of caregivers to carry out the maintenance plan must be documented prior to discharge from OT.
8. OT in SNFs is covered if the patient requires skilled nursing or skilled rehabilitation (i.e., OT, PT, ST).
   a. The Resource Utilization Groups (RUGs) reimbursement system has been used since 1998 to pay for therapy services provided in SNFs.
   b. As of October 2019, the Patient Driven Payment Model (PDPM) is replacing the RUGs system.
      (1) This is a substantial change in payment for OT services.
      (2) Under RUGs, the provision of more services (including OT) resulted in a higher reimbursement rate to the SNF.
         (a) This payment system resulted in a press to provide more services to clients and at times unrealistic productivity standards.
      (3) Under PDPM, the reimbursement paid to SNFs will no longer be based on the service provision.
         (a) Payment to SNFs will be based on the client's characteristics regardless of the amount *or type* of provided services.
         (b) To be reimbursed under PDPM, OT practitioners will need "to clearly articulate the value of their services" (Amini & Furniss, 2018, p. CE-2).

> **EXAM HINT:** Because the current COTA® exam content is based on a practice analysis that was completed in 2017 and published in 2018, it is unlikely that details of the PDPM will be tested on the exam. However, the practice impact of the RUGs system ending and the PDPM system beginning may be reflected in COTA® exam items. As the implementation of the PDPM progresses, COTA® exam items about reimbursement will likely focus on service quality, not service quantity.

9. OT in home care is covered if the individual is homebound and needs intermittent skilled nursing care, PT, or ST before OT began. OT services can continue after need for skilled nursing, PT, or ST has ended.
   a. Homebound status criteria.
      (1) The person is typically not able to leave the home; i.e., is "confined" to the home.
         (a) "Confinement" may be due to the need for the aid of ambulatory devices, the assistance of others, or special transportation.
         (b) It considers medical, physical, cognitive, and psychiatric conditions.
      (2) If the person leaves the home it requires considerable effort (CMS, n.d.).
      (3) A person may leave their home for medical appointments (e.g., kidney dialysis) and nonmedical short-term and infrequent appointments or events (e.g., to get a haircut, attending a wedding).
      (4) The need for adult day care and attendance at religious services does not preclude a person from receiving home health services.
   b. Home health agencies are reimbursed under a prospective payment system.
      (1) This rate per episode of care reimbursement system applies to all home health services including all forms of therapy and medical supplies.
      (2) Durable medical equipment is excluded.
      (3) A classification system called Home Health Resource Groups (HHRGs) is used to determine an episode payment rate.
      (4) An episode is defined as a 60-day period beginning with the first billable visit and ending 60 days after the start of care.
   c. An initial assessment visit and a comprehensive assessment using the Outcome and Assessment Information Set (OASIS) must be completed to verify the person's eligibility for Medicare home health benefits, to verify the continuing need for home care, and to plan for the person's nursing, medical, social, rehabilitative, and discharge needs.
      (1) Occupational therapists can complete the initial OASIS if the need for OT establishes program eligibility.
      (2) The initial assessment must be completed within 48 hours of referral or within 48 hours of the person's return home.
      (3) Occupational therapists can conduct follow-up, transfer, and discharge evaluations.
   d. The AOTA is actively working to change federal legislation to have OT identified as an initial qualifying service for home health care, so barriers to OT home health services may be removed in the future.
10. OT in hospice care is provided to persons who are certified as terminally ill (medical prognosis of fewer than six months to live).
    a. OT services are provided to enable a patient to maintain functional skills, and ADL performance and/or to control symptoms.
11. OT is covered as an outpatient service when provided by or under arrangements with any Medicare-certified provider (i.e., hospital, SNF, home health agency, rehabilitation agency, a clinic) or when provided as part of comprehensive outpatient rehabilitation facility (CORF) services.
12. OT services can also be covered if provided by a Medicare-certified occupational therapist in independent practice (OTIP) when services are provided in the therapist's office or in the patient's home.
    a. Payment is according to the fee schedule entitled the resource-based relative value scale (RBRVS).
13. Criteria for coverage of OT services rendered in a physician's office or in a physician-directed clinic.
    a. The occupational therapist or COTA®/OTA is employed by the physician or clinic.
    b. The service is furnished under physician's direct supervision, and the services are directly related to the condition for which the physician is treating the patient.
    c. OT service fees are included on the physician's bill to Medicare.
14. Criteria for coverage of Partial Hospitalization Program (PHP) services affiliated with a hospital or a community mental health psychiatric day program.
    a. The beneficiary would otherwise have required inpatient psychiatric care.
    b. OT services are covered under general Medicare guidelines (i.e., MD's prescription, reasonable and necessary, function expected to improve).
    c. Active treatment incorporating an individualized multidisciplinary intervention plan to attain measurable, time-limited, medically necessary, functional goals directly related to the reason for admission must be provided.
       (1) Psychosocial programs that provide structured diversional, social, and/or recreational services or vocational rehabilitation do not meet the criteria for active treatment in a PHP and are not reimbursable under Medicare.

15. All of these standards can change when and if new federal legislative guidelines are passed for Medicare.

Medicare Coverage of Durable Medical Equipment, Prostheses, and Orthoses

1. Rental or purchase expenses for durable medical equipment (DME) are covered if used in beneficiary's home and if necessary and reasonable to treat an illness or injury or to improve functioning.
2. A physician's prescription is needed and must include diagnosis, prognosis, and reason for DME need.
3. Criteria for DME.
    a. Repeated use can be withstood.
    b. Primarily and customarily used for a medical purpose (e.g., a wheelchair or walker).
    c. Generally not useful to a person in the absence of injury or illness.
4. Self-help items, bathtub grab bars, and raised toilet seats are not reimbursable DME because other people can use them and they are not considered medically necessary.

> **EXAM HINT:** The NBCOT® exam outline for the COTA® identifies the task of integrating "durable medical equipment into the intervention . . . to enable participation in meaningful occupation" (NBCOT®, 2018, p. 27) and knowledge of the "influence of reimbursement policies and guidelines on occupational therapy service delivery" (NBCOT®, 2018, p. 29) as essential for competent practice. The application of knowledge about the Medicare DME reimbursement criteria described above can help you determine a correct answer to COTA® exam items about service recipients who rely on Medicare to pay for their medical expenses. For example, a three-in-one commode would be the correct answer for an exam item that identifies a client's need for equipment to safely and independently toilet; whereas, a raised toilet seat and/or grab bars would be an incorrect answer. The former will be covered by Medicare because a three-in-one commode is not considered useful to persons without an illness or disability; the latter would not be covered by Medicare since a raised toilet seat and grab bars are considered useful to persons without an illness or disability and are not medically necessary.

Medicaid

1. General information.
    a. A state/federal health insurance program for persons who have an income that is below an established threshold and/or have a disability.
    b. States administer the program but receive at least 50% of their funding from the federal government.
       (1) Under the ACA, states receive increased federal contributions to expand their Medicaid programs.[5]
    c. Includes federally mandated services and state optional services.
    d. Mandated services must be provided if a state receives federal funds.
    e. Coverage of optional services varies greatly from state to state.
       (1) As a result, questions about state specific Medicaid coverage should not be on the NBCOT® exam.
2. Mandated Medicaid services.
    a. Inpatient and hospital services.
    b. Outpatient (e.g., laboratory work, x-rays, skilled nursing) and physicians' services.
    c. Home health (level and amount of care can vary).
    d. Early periodic screening diagnosis and treatment services (EPSDT) for persons 21 years old and younger.
    e. Services identified as needed to treat a condition during EPSDT (including OT) must be provided.
    f. SNFs receiving Medicaid must provide skilled rehabilitation services (including OT) to residents who require them.
3. Optional Medicaid services.
    a. OT, PT, speech-language therapy.
    b. Durable medical equipment.
    c. Services provided by independently practicing licensed professionals including psychologists, psychiatric social workers, and other mental health professionals.
    d. Targeted case management.
    e. Prescription medication.
    f. Dental care, eyeglasses.
    g. Crisis response services.
    h. Transportation.
    i. Psychiatric inpatient services for persons aged under 21 or over 65.
    j. Related services (including OT) provided by school systems to children with disabilities. (Note: This provision overlaps with Individuals with Disabilities Education Act (IDEA) legislation and has led to questioning as to whether services to individual children should be funded as an educational or a health care service).
4. Under the ACA, Medicaid must provide the same minimum essential benefits that are provided in the insurance exchanges established by the ACA.
    a. States were not required to expand their Medicaid programs, and the current status of ACA provisions

---

[5] At the time of this publication, several states have reversed their Medicaid expansion programs, and the future status of Medicaid expansion on a national level is unknown.

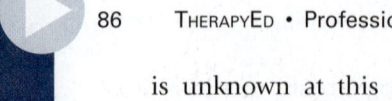

is unknown at this time; thus, questions about state-specific Medicaid coverage should not be on the NBCOT® exam.
  b. See prior information on the ACA.
5. Medicaid reform.
  a. Due to rapidly rising costs, there is an increased press for cost containment.
  b. States are examining ways to reformulate Medicaid benefits.
  c. Reform options may include placing caps or other limitations on types and length of therapy, reducing or eliminating optional benefits, and/or developing and implementing managed care approaches.
  d. Individual states can apply to the federal government for a waiver that gives the state flexibility in the types of services and delivery systems they provide under Medicaid.

Worker's Compensation

1. Designed to compensate employees who have job-related illness or injuries.
2. Funded jointly by individual employers or groups of employers and state governments.
3. Each state has a Workers' Compensation Commission board that determines regulations for employer participation, benefit provision, employee coverage, and insurance administration.
4. Administration can be through contract with private insurance companies or through individual employers or groups of employers who administer their own programs. This is known as self-insuring.
5. Coverage varies from state to state, with many states initiating cost-containment measures including limits on choice of providers, use of set fee schedules, utilization review, and managed care.
6. Workers' compensation programs include cash benefits and medical benefits. OT may be included.
7. Rehabilitation and disability management to return the person to gainful employment is a primary focus. See Chapter 14 for information on work evaluation and intervention.

Personal Payment, 'Pro Bono,' Philanthropic Care, and Grants

1. Individuals whose health insurance has discontinued coverage of OT services may elect to pay for these services personally, providing that benefit can be derived from continued services.
2. Individuals without health insurance or with no coverage for rehabilitative services may also pay for OT personally.
3. OT services provided in nonmedical settings (e.g., wellness and prevention programs) are generally not covered by insurers, so their clients must pay privately.
4. 'Pro bono' or free or reduced-rate care may be supported by the individual practitioner's personal donation of services or through philanthropic donations.
5. Grants and/or philanthropic donations can be used to support programs not typically covered by insurance (e.g., an adaptive Yoga program for persons with disabilities, a lifestyle redesign program for persons aging in place).

Occupational Therapy Documentation Guidelines

Purpose of Documentation

1. Provides a legal, serial record of client's condition, evaluation and re-evaluation results, course of therapeutic intervention, and response to intervention from referral to discharge.
2. Justifies the necessity of skilled services to payers by providing a rationale for service provision.
3. Serves as an information resource for client care, can be used by a covering occupational therapist/COTA/OTA in absence of primary occupational therapist/COTA/OTA.
4. Enhances communication among health-care or educational team members.
5. Provides data for use in intervention, program evaluation, research, and education.
6. Electronic medical records (EMRs)/electronic health records (EHRs) provide digital versions of paper charts.

COTA®/OTA Documentation Guidelines

1. COTA®s/OTAs are qualified to write notes in medical charts and other documentation formats.
2. COTA®/OTA notes are not required to be co-signed by an occupational therapist by the AOTA, but state and federal governments may mandate co-signing

as a tangible way to demonstrate compliance with COTA®/OTA supervisory laws and regulations.
3. The AOTA recommends COTA®/OTA notes that will be included in medical charts, Individualized Education Plans (IEPs), and other legal documents be co-signed by an occupational therapist.
   a. As official documents, these records may be subject to subpoena.

General Documentation Standards

1. Legible handwriting must be used for handwritten documentation.
   a. Illegible notes may result in denial of reimbursement.
2. Documentation for an EMR/EHR must adhere to all established documentation standards.
3. Correct grammar and spelling are required.
   a. Errors detract from a professional presentation.
4. Concise but complete information should be recorded.
   a. If it is not recorded, it does not exist and never happened.
   b. Nonimportant, extraneous details (i.e., color of clothing) should be left out.
5. Objective statements, with clear distinctions between facts and behavioral data and opinions and interpretations, are required.
6. All documentation must be relevant, current, and accurate.
7. Institution and/or program guidelines, as well as reimbursing agencies'/third-party payers' guidelines must be followed.
   a. Documentation should explicitly justify the need for billable services.
   b. Noncompliance with established guidelines can result in services and/or payment being denied.
8. Standard, well-recognized abbreviations (e.g., ROM, MMT) should be the only ones used.
   a. Avoid alphabet soup.
   b. Write in functional terms using uniform terminology consistent with the AOTA's Standards of Practice and state practice acts.
9. Person-first language should be used at all times (e.g., "a parent with schizophrenia," or "the student with an intellectual disability").
10. Client's name and ID number should be on every page.
11. The blocking out or deletion of information is unacceptable.
    a. In handwritten notes, errors must be crossed out with one line, initialed, and dated. Black or blue ink is used at all times.
12. The complete date (i.e., day, month, and year) must be provided.
13. The type of documentation (i.e., initial note, progress note, discharge plan) should be identified.
14. Compliance with confidentiality standards is mandated (i.e., do not put other clients' names in a note).
15. Informed consent for treatment can be given only by a competent adult.
    a. Minors or adults determined to be incompetent must have written consent provided by a parent, legal guardian, person with power of attorney, or proxy.
16. A full signature (first and last name with professional designations) should directly follow documentation content with no space left between content and signature.
17. Co-signature by an occupational therapist on documentation written by a COTA®/OTA or a student if required by law or the facility.
18. OT notes and records are legal documents; thus, all documentation may be subject to subpoena.
    a. Adherence to documentation standards is a must.

Content of Documentation

1. Identification and background information.
   a. Name, age, sex, date of admission, treatment diagnosis, and case number if one exists.
   b. Referral source, reason for referral, chief complaint relevant to OT's domain of concern.
   c. Pertinent history that indicates prior levels of function and support systems, including applicable developmental, educational, vocational, socioeconomic, and medical history. This can be brief.
   d. Secondary problems or pre-existing conditions that may affect function or treatment outcomes.
   e. Precautions, risk factors and contraindications, medications, surgery dates.
2. Evaluation and re-evaluation documentation.
   a. Assessments administered and the results included.
   b. Summary and analysis of assessment findings in measurable, functional terms.
      (1) Sufficient baseline objective data.
      (2) In re-evaluation, compare findings to initial findings.
      (3) Indicate change, if any.
   c. References to other pertinent reports and information including relevant psychological, social, and environmental data.
   d. OT problem list, specific and sufficient to develop intervention plan.
   e. Recommendations for OT services (can include recommendation that no OT services are indicated).

f. Client's understanding of current status and problems, and client's subjective complaints.
  g. Client's interest and desire to participate in therapy.
3. Intervention plan documentation.
  a. A prioritized problem list.
  b. Goals related to problem list and indicating potential for function and improvement.
  c. The structure of a goal statement.
    (1) The person who will exhibit the skill, almost always written as "the patient/client will." However, the caregiver, family member, and/or teacher may be the focus of the goal.
    (2) The desired functional behavior that is to be demonstrated or increased as the outcome of intervention.
    (3) The underlying factors (e.g., performance skill deficits, client factors) that must be remediated to achieve functional outcome.
    (4) The circumstances under which the behavior must be performed or the conditions necessary for the behavior (e.g., independent, with cueing, with assistance).
    (5) The degree at which the behavior is exhibited (e.g., three out of four times, minimum number of repetitions).
  d. Short- and long-term goals written in a SMART manner.
    (1) Specific. For example, not "increase self-care skills"; rather, "develop ability to button shirt using nondominant hand."
    (2) Measurable, as to number of times or a percent.
    (3) Attainable, as to what can be realistically achieved. For example, 100% return is unlikely.
    (4) Relevant, to roles and expected environment.
    (5) Time-limited, anticipated time to achieve goals.
      (a) Time allotted for goal attainment must be relevant to setting's LOS (e.g., in acute care, goals are measured in days, whereas in long-term care, weekly or monthly goals are acceptable).
    (6) The acronym RUMBA is similarly used to guide documentation (R = realistic/relevant, U = understandable, M = measurable, B = behavioral, A = attainable/achievable).

> **EXAM HINT:** The acronyms SMART and RUMBA are helpful standards to determine if the answer to a COTA® exam item about documentation is correct. Answer choices that are not "SMART enough to RUMBA" are likely incorrect.

  e. Long-term goals must indicate the final desired functional outcome before discharge, regardless of LOS.
    (1) A clear reason for skilled therapeutic intervention.
    (2) Statement of potential functional outcome that is clearly related to goal.
  f. Activities and/or treatment procedures and methods related to stated goals and problems.
  g. Type, amount, duration, and frequency of treatment needed to accomplish goals.
  h. Explanation of treatment plan to client and a provision of statement of goals in client's words.
4. Intervention implementation documentation.
  a. Activities, procedures, and modalities used.
  b. Client's response to treatment and the progress toward goal attainment as related to problem list.
  c. Goal modification when indicated by the response to treatment. Rationale for changes in goals needed.
  d. Change in anticipated time to achieve goals with rationale for change and new time frame specified.
  e. Attendance and participation with treatment plan (attendance can be a check format).
  f. Statement of reason for individual missing treatment.
  g. Assistive/adaptive equipment, orthoses, and prostheses if issued or fabricated, and specific instructions for the application and/or use of the item, including wearing schedule and care.
  h. Patient-related conferences and communication with physicians, third-party payers, case manager, team members, etc.
  i. Home programs developed and taught to client and/or caregiver(s).
  j. Client's and/or caregiver's compliance with home program.
5. Discharge plan documentation.
  a. Summary of evaluation and intervention.
  b. Compare initial and discharge status.
  c. Specify number of sessions, goals achieved, and functional outcome.
  d. Reason for discharge.
    (1) Goals attained.
    (2) Client no longer making functional gains.
    (3) Client refuses or does not follow the intervention plan.
    (4) Client moves to another location.
    (5) Setting does not match the individual's needs.
  e. Home programs to be followed after discharge.
  f. Client and family education.
  g. Equipment provided and/or ordered.
  h. Follow-up plans/recommendations with rationales.
  i. Referral(s) to other health care providers and community agencies.

Specific Documentation Formats

1. Problem Oriented Medical Record (POMR): a system of providing structure for progress note writing that is based on a list of problems based on assessment.
  a. SOAP notes.

(1) Subjective: information reported by the client, family, or significant other.
(2) Objective: diagnosis, medical information and history, and measurable, observable data obtained through formal assessments.
(3) Assessment: therapist's interpretation and clinical reasoning based on objective data includes analysis of client's status and goals and a prioritized problem list.
(4) Plan: the specific OT plan of intervention to resolve identified problems and meet stated goals.
2. Consultation reports: meetings and/or phone conversations with team members, other professionals, the individual client, and their caregivers.
3. Critical incident reports: significant, out of the norm events that may occur during OT evaluation or intervention (e.g., the individual slips during a transfer).
4. All of these must comply with general documentation standards and contain all fundamental components of documentation.

Documentation for Reimbursement

1. Refer to the preceding sections on documentation standards, guidelines, and content.
   a. Documentation must include essential content and adhere to established documentation standards and guidelines to receive payment for services.

> **EXAM HINT:** Recent federal legislation and CMS policy decisions have shifted health care reimbursement from a focus on the quantity of services provided to a focus on the quality of service outcomes. As this paradigm shift becomes embedded in practice, it will likely be reflected in the COTA® exam. Thus, correct answers to exam items about documentation for reimbursement should substantiate the distinct value of OT and the efficacy of OT outcomes.

2. Coding and billing for services.
   a. To be reimbursed, OT services must be properly coded and billed, as required by payers.
   b. Practitioners must represent their services in terms of diagnosis and procedure codes.
   c. Diagnosis codes describe a person's condition or medical reason for requiring services.
      (1) The *International Classification of Diseases (ICD)* is the most frequently used diagnosis-coding system in the U.S.
         (a) Each service, procedure, supply, or piece of equipment must be related to a current *ICD* code.
      (2) In 2014, the *ICD-10 Clinical Modification (ICD-10-CM)* replaced the *ICD-9-CM*.
      (3) Because the *ICD* is regularly updated, the COTA® exam should not include specific codes.
   d. Procedure codes describe the specific services provided by health care professionals.
      (1) HCFA Common Procedure Coding System (HCPCS) is most widely used.
      (2) HCPCS includes the Physician's Current Procedural Terminology (CPT).
      (3) The most current HCPCS and CPT codes must be used in practice. However, because they are updated often, the COTA® exam should not include specific codes.
      (4) Specific codes that most closely describe the service(s) provided should be used. Each procedure, modality, and/or treatment should be coded.
   e. Specific billing forms are used by institutional providers (i.e., hospitals and home health agencies) and by physicians and OT practitioners in independent practice for Medicare, Medicaid, and most states' workers' compensation programs. Form numbers may change, so NBCOT® should not ask questions about specific forms.
   f. Outpatient OT services provided under Medicare Part B must report functional data on their claims in the form of G-codes.
      (1) G-codes identify the primary issue being addressed by therapy; modifiers are used to report the person's impairment/limitation/restriction.
         (a) All G-codes are available to be used by all therapy disciplines (i.e., OT practitioners can use the codes for mobility, memory, swallowing, and cognition).
      (2) G-codes will be used to track patient outcomes over time.

> **EXAM HINT:** As of January 2019, outpatient occupational therapists with private practices can opt into the Merit-Based Incentive Payments System (MIPS). RUGs are not used in this system. Because the current COTA® exam content is based on a practice analysis that was completed in 2017 and published in 2018, it is likely that the MIPS will not be on the exam until this system is well-integrated into OT practice on a national level.

   g. COTA®s/OTAs are generally not eligible for direct payment because they require supervision and do not perform evaluations without supervision.
3. Documentation "red flags."
   a. The use of certain words, terms, and/or physician's errors can result in delay, denial, and/or discharge from services.
   b. Avoid these in all documentation, unless they are true and accurate representations of a client's status.

c. If a client has met their goals and/or is no longer making significant functional gains, this must be documented and the client must be discharged from services.
d. Words to carefully consider, for they do not reflect progress.
　(1) Chronic.
　(2) Status quo, no change in status.
　(3) Maintaining.
　(4) Little change.
　(5) Plateau.
　(6) Making slow progress.
　(7) Stable or stabilizing.
e. Words to carefully consider, for they do not reflect potential for improvement.
　(1) Same as.
　(2) Uncooperative, noncompliant.
　(3) Dislikes therapy.
　(4) Confused/disoriented.
　(5) Inability to follow directions.
　(6) Custodial care needed.
　(7) Treatment repeated.
　(8) Repeated instruction.
　(9) Unmotivated.
　(10) Extreme depression.
　(11) Fair to poor potential.
　(12) Chronic/long-term condition.
　(13) General weakness.
f. Errors in physician's orders, for they can result in denial or delay of payment for OT services.
　(1) Incomplete or nonspecific orders.
　(2) Orders with a span of frequency over the duration of intervention (e.g., two to three times/week for four to six weeks).
　(3) Orders that do not state a specific type of intervention (e.g., activities, splint or equipment, as needed).
　(4) Orders that cover only evaluation, but intervention has been initiated.
　(5) Order is specific to a certain type of treatment, but the treatment plan does not include it.
　(6) Order does not include duration of treatment.
　(7) The plan changes mid-month, but the order is not updated to meet the new plan change.
　(8) There is no discharge order or there is no order immediately after treatment ends.

Documentation for Medicare Reimbursement

1. Overview.
　a. Many private reimbursing agencies and state Medicaid programs follow federal Medicare guidelines, so if documentation meets Medicare standards, it will generally be acceptable to other insurers.
　b. It is advisable to get copies of state and individual insurers' guidelines for OT services, as adherence to these guidelines will be critical for reimbursement.

> **EXAM HINT:** Due to the potential wide variance in these guidelines, the COTA® exam should not test information beyond the established federal Medicare guidelines.

　c. Previously stated standards and guidelines for documentation apply to reimbursement for Medicare.
2. Medicare prescription documentation.
　a. Required from a physician as defined by state practice acts.
　b. The certification could be:
　　(1) A signature on the bottom of the note.
　　(2) An MD or DO signed 700 or 701 form.
　　　(a) Some state licensure acts may not all allow a DO to prescribe OT.
　c. Make sure diagnoses are acute, not chronic.
　　(1) Rephrase the diagnosis for the physician if needed.
　　(2) Use onset dates of within 60 days of admission to services, if possible. For example: instead of rheumatoid arthritis [RA] × 10 years, use acute exacerbation of RA as of 1-15-19.
3. Intervention documentation.
　a. Content must indicate that the treatment shows a level of complexity and sophistication, or the condition of the person must be of a nature that requires the judgment, knowledge, and skills of a qualified practitioner. This statement is as per Medicare.
　b. Skilled rehabilitation intervention is mandatory.
　　(1) Delineate the specific skilled care rendered. This is the biggest cause for retroactive denial.
　　(2) Notes must reflect skilled therapeutic interventions. For example, documenting that an intervention session focused on helping a person dress does not indicate that skilled therapeutic interventions were provided. Documenting that an intervention session focused on decreasing extensor tone and/or increasing bilateral integration to enable independent dressing does indicate that skilled interventions were provided.
　c. Skilled care rendered must match the diagnosis and the physician's order.

> **CAUTION:** Services must be unique to OT and not sound like PT or SLP. Medicare does not pay for duplication of services.

　d. In home care, homebound status due to functional limitations must be clearly delineated.
　　(1) If the diagnosis may not render the individual homebound, explain why this particular person is homebound.

(2) Do not give a reviewer any doubt that this person does not meet Medicare homebound criteria (e.g., do not state client was not at home when you arrived. Rather, state there was no answer to a locked door).
e. Document honestly, but not over-optimistically. Medicare reviewers are interested in determining the need for continued intervention.
  (1) If a person has improved but can benefit from further intervention, document this need, rather than emphasizing the improvement.
    (a) Provide behavioral observations that substantiate need for further care.
f. Documentation must demonstrate that the person is making significant functional improvement in a reasonable and generally predictable period of time.
  (1) Improvement should be noted with a description of functional change(s).
  (2) If a person has improved but can benefit from further intervention, the OT practitioner should clearly document why continued treatment is medically necessary.
    (a) Provide behavioral observations and evaluation results that substantiate the need for further care.
  (3) If improvements are not observed and/or progress is slower than expected, the reason(s) for the lack of progress including extenuating circumstances and/or limiting factors (e.g., a secondary diagnosis) should be documented.
g. If improvement is not made or expected, justifiable interventions to prevent deterioration and maximize function are covered.
  (1) Occupational therapists are reimbursed for the documented design of a maintenance program performed by others (e.g., CNAs, HHAs, PCAs) and periodic evaluations of the program's effectiveness.
  (2) Occupational therapists can continue to provide OT services to persons not expected to improve if they adequately substantiate the need for skilled services.
  (3) Medicare no longer denies payment due to lack of improvement; coverage is denied due to inadequate documentation.
h. All documented service must be reasonable and necessary.
  (1) Was the service effective and completed in a timely fashion?
  (2) In long-term care, if the treatment does not lessen the amount of care needed by staff, what made the service worthwhile?
i. If there is no medical justification for continued treatment, the person should be discharged in a timely fashion.

Federal Legislation Related to Occupational Therapy

Overview

1. Historically, the opportunities available to and the roles afforded to persons with disabilities have been influenced by federal legislation.
2. Federal laws establish numerous standards and provide funding for health benefits, medical services, rehabilitation, early intervention, education, vocational programming, professional training, and research.
3. These laws directly affect the profession of OT by establishing practice guidelines and reimbursement standards.
4. Major social movements that have precipitated federal legislation and/or have resulted from federal legislation include deinstitutionalization, early intervention, mainstreaming, and full inclusion.
5. State laws also influence OT practice but, due to their variability, they would not be included in a national exam.

EXAM HINT: The NBCOT® exam outline for the COTA® identifies the task of providing "occupational therapy services in accordance with laws, [and] regulations . . . in order to protect consumers" (NBCOT®, 2018, p. 29) as essential for competent practice. To ensure best practice, the AOTA Code of Ethics states that practitioners have an ethical responsibility to "maintain awareness of current laws . . . that apply to the profession of occupational therapy" (AOTA, 2015b, p. 5). The application of knowledge about the following laws can help you determine the correct answer for NBCOT® Domain 03 Upholding Professional Standards and Responsibilities exam items.

Patient Protection and Affordable Care Act (ACA)[6]

1. Consisted of 10 separate legislative titles that sought to improve the accessibility, fairness, quality, efficiency, accountability, and affordability of health insurance coverage in the U.S.
2. See prior section on payment for OT services for ACA details.

Health Insurance Portability and Accountability Act (HIPAA)

1. Sets standards and safeguards to assure the individual's right to continuity in health care coverage and to ensure privacy and security of health care records.
2. All persons must be informed of the setting's privacy policies, and a good faith effort must be made to obtain written acknowledgement from each person about their attainment of this knowledge.
    a. If the person refuses to sign, the provider should document the efforts made; failure to obtain written acknowledgement is not a violation of the rule.
    b. Written consent must be obtained from a person before any personal health information is used or disclosed in the provision of treatment, obtainment of payment, or the carrying out of any health care related operations.
        (1) Exemptions to the written notification/acknowledgement are allowed if the attainment of this will prevent or delay timely care (i.e., emergency care). Written acknowledgement must be obtained as soon as possible.
        (2) If language barriers preclude signed acknowledgement, treatment can occur if the physician believes consent is implied.
3. Prior to discussing a person's status with a family member/significant other or other provider, the provider must obtain the person's permission or give the person the opportunity to object.
    a. Providers can use their clinical judgment to determine whether to discuss the person's case with others if the person cannot give permission or objects.
        (1) Documentation for this decision is essential (e.g., person is at risk of harming self due to lack of judgment; consultation with a specialist is essential to ensure quality of care).
    b. All information used or disclosed about a person's status must be limited to the minimum needed for the immediate purpose.
4. The HIPAA Privacy Rule requires that all providers protect patient confidentiality in all forms (i.e., oral, written, and electronic) and implement appropriate physical, technical, and administrative safeguards to assure this privacy.
    a. Settings must reduce the physical identifiability of patient information; that is, door tags and whiteboards can only list last names, no diagnoses or treatment procedures may be listed, sign-in sheets with names only are allowed.
    b. Charts and any documentation with patients' names or other identifiers must be stored out of public view and in secure locations.
    c. Opaque covers should be used for clipboards that contain paperwork with patient information.
    d. All computers that are used to record, document, or transmit patient information should be equipped with monitor privacy screens.
    e. All faxes must contain cover sheets noting confidentiality of accompanying information and be sent only to dedicated fax machines in secure locations.
    f. All e-mails must use password protection and encryption if going over the Internet.
    g. All faxes and computer printouts must be immediately destroyed or placed in the person's chart, as most appropriate.
    h. All conversations regarding a person's health status must be done in private areas, in low tones, and with minimal disclosure.
5. An individual has the right to access all of their records.
    a. Providers can charge reasonable copying costs and have 30–60 days to respond.
    b. Individuals have the right to request that information in their record be amended.
        (1) The provider can refuse the request, providing their rationale.
        (2) The provider can comply with the request by documenting the request and the reason for compliance. The original documentation should not be removed/excised.
6. HIPAA does not exclude treatment from occurring in group settings or open clinics.
    a. Discussion regarding treatment should be done quietly and, if possible, behind a screen/room divider.
7. HIPAA does not require a guarantee of 100% confidentiality; it does require reasonable and vigilant safeguards.
8. HIPAA guidelines for research are complex, but they are congruent with the established guidelines for human subject research and Institutional Review Board (IRB) standards.
    a. A limited data set that does not include any identifiable patient information can be used in research without patient approval (e.g., diagnosis, age, LOS).

---

[6] At the time of this publication, the future of the benefits afforded by the ACA is unknown.

9. The Administrative Simplification rules also provide standardization of codes and formats for medical data.
10. HIPAA does not override state laws that further restrict privacy and it defers to state laws governing minors.

Substance Use-Disorder Prevention that Promotes Optimal Recovery and Treatment (SUPPORT) for Patients and Communities Act (HR6)

1. Requires the CMS to develop acute care practice guidelines for non-pharmacological pain management and opioid use disorder prevention.
    a. These guidelines are to be developed with input from health care professionals, including OT practitioners.
2. Promotes Medicaid coverage for non-pharmacological therapies for the management of pain, including coverage of OT services.
3. Requires training programs about pain care for health professionals to include information about non-pharmacological alternatives for pain management.
4. Expands National Institutes of Health research on pain to include non-pharmacological interventions.
5. See Chapters 6 and 7 for more information about OT evaluation of and intervention for pain.

Key Legislation Related to Overall Disability Rights

1. Medicare Title 18-PL 89-97.
    a. Established Medicare and Supplemental Security Income (SSI).
    b. SSI enables persons with disabilities to receive a monthly income enabling them to live in the community. This was a major contributor to the deinstitutionalization movement.
2. Rehabilitation Act of 1973.
    a. Prohibits discrimination on the basis of disability in any program or activity that receives federal assistance.
    b. Required all federal agencies to develop action plans for the hiring, placement, and advancement of persons with disabilities.
    c. Required contractors who received federal contracts over a preset amount to take affirmative action to employ persons with disabilities.
3. Fair Housing Act.
    a. Prohibits discrimination on the bases of disability, religion, sex, color, race, national origin, and familial status.
    b. Required owners of housing to make reasonable exceptions to their standard tenant policies to allow individuals with disabilities equal housing opportunities (e.g., allowing a seeing eye or service dog in a "no-pets" apartment).
    c. Required that tenants with disabilities be allowed to make reasonable modifications to common use areas and to their private living space to enable access.
        (1) The housing owner is not required to fund these modifications.
    d. Required that newly constructed multi-family residences (four or more apartments) be built to meet established accessibility standards.
4. Omnibus Budget Reconciliation Act (OBRA) of 1981.
    a. Affirmed application of Section 504 of the Rehabilitation Act of 1973, which prohibits discrimination in federally funded programs to a diversity of services (i.e., Head Start programs, block grant programs, community development programs).
    b. Provided Medicaid financing for community-based services for people with developmental disabilities when services were demonstrated to be less expensive than institutional care.
5. Americans with Disabilities Act (ADA) of 1990.
    a. Prohibits discrimination against qualified persons with disabilities in employment, transportation, accommodations, telecommunications, and public services.
    b. Criteria for classifying an individual as disabled.
        (1) A person with a physical or mental impairment that substantially limits one or more major life activities.
        (2) A person having a record of such an impairment.
        (3) A person regarded as having such an impairment.
    c. Individuals who are actively abusing substances or compulsively gambling or persons who have kleptomania, pyromania, or sexual behavior disorders are not protected by ADA.
    d. Title I—Employment.
        (1) Prohibits employers from discriminating against persons with disabilities in any aspect or phase of employment including recruitment, hiring, working conditions, hours, promotion, training opportunities, termination, social activities, and other privileges of employment.
        (2) Allows questions about one's ability to perform a job but prohibits inquiries as to whether one has a disability.
        (3) Prohibits employment tests that tend to screen out people with disabilities.

(4) A "qualified individual with a disability" means a person with a disability who is able to perform the "essential functions" of a job (that is, the tasks fundamental to the position) with or without reasonable accommodations.
(5) "Reasonable accommodations" must be provided by businesses with 15 or more employees to persons with disabilities to enable them to perform essential job functions unless such accommodations would impose an "undue" hardship on the business.
  (a) Types of reasonable accommodations.
    - Acquisition or modification of equipment or devices.
    - Modifications or adjustments to examinations, training materials, or publications.
    - Provision of ancillary aids or services.
    - Modified or part-time work schedules, job restructuring, or re-assignment to a vacant position.
    - Improvement of existing facilities used by employees so they are usable by and accessible to persons with disabilities and/or other similar accommodations.
  (b) Types of auxiliary aids and services.
    - Taped texts, qualified readers, or other methods that can effectively make visually delivered materials accessible to persons with visual impairments.
    - Qualified interpreters or other methods that can effectively make aurally delivered materials accessible to persons with hearing impairments.
    - Modification or acquisition of devices or equipment.
    - Similar actions or services that increase accessibility.
  (c) Undue hardship is defined as action that would be significantly difficult or overly expensive given the financial resources of the employer, its size, and major functions.
(6) The U.S. Government, Indian tribes, and/or private tax-exempt membership clubs are exempt from ADA employer guidelines.
e. Title II—Public Services.
  (1) Mandates that state and local governments and their departments, agencies, and/or component parts may not discriminate against, exclude, or deny persons with disabilities participation in or benefit from the services, programs, or activities of these public entities.
    (a) This includes transportation, public education, employment, recreation, social services, health care, courts, town meetings, and voting.
f. Title III—Public Accommodations and Services Operated by Public Entities.
  (1) Mandates that places of public accommodation (i.e., hospitals, health care providers' offices, schools, day care centers, restaurants, theaters, and other places of accommodation) may not discriminate against persons with disabilities with respect to their participation in or ability to benefit from the service, goods, facility, use, or other programming aspects.
  (2) Public places operated by private entities must be designed, constructed, and altered to comply with accessibility standards.
    (a) All new construction of public accommodations must be accessible.
    (b) Physical barriers in existing facilities must be removed if removal is able to be carried out without much difficulty or expense.
    (c) The U.S. Government, Indian Tribes, religious organizations, and/or private tax-exempt membership clubs are exempt from ADA accessibility standards.
  (3) Private services that serve the public (e.g., restaurants, stores, and theaters) cannot discriminate in the provision of services.
  (4) Public transportation systems must be accessible.
  (5) Private transportation systems must be accessible and nondiscriminatory (e.g., livery services, taxis, tour bus companies).
g. Title IV—Telecommunications.
  (1) All televisions manufactured after 1993 must include closed captioning.
  (2) Telephone companies must provide telecommunications relay services (TRS) to persons with hearing or speech impairments 24 hours per day, seven days per week.
6. ADA Amendments Act (ADAAA) of 2008.
  a. Enacted to rectify the problems resulting from post-ADA Supreme Court decisions, which drastically narrowed the ADA definition of disability and substantially limited ADA protections.
  b. Reaffirmed that a disability is the actual presence of a disorder or condition that impairs participation in one or more major life activities, a record of a limiting impairment, or being regarded as having an impairment.
    (1) The use of "mitigating measures" (e.g., wheelchairs, hearing aids, taking insulin) to address a disability or the remediation of a condition (e.g., recovery from cancer, a repetitive stress disorder, or schizophrenia) does *not* negate the person's ability to be protected by the ADA.
  c. Redefined major life activities to include major body functions and organ operations, performing

basic and instrumental activities of daily living, completing physical movements and manual activities, sleeping, working, reading, learning, communicating and interacting, and thinking and concentrating.
   d. Broadened the interpretation of a "substantially limited" impairment to include the inability to perform one major life activity as it is typically performed by the general population.
7. Ticket to Work and Work Incentives Improvement Act (TWIIA).
   a. Strives to make it more realistic and easier for a person with a disability to work.
   b. Removes a major disincentive to work by allowing individuals with disabilities to maintain their Medicare or Medicaid health care benefits.
      (1) Allows an individual with a disability to keep Medicare benefits for an additional 54 months after starting work.
      (2) Eliminates limits on Medicaid "buy-in" options.
   c. Enables consumers to have a choice in their service provider beyond public assistance programs.
   d. Establishes community-based vocational planning and assistance programs.
   e. Increases consumer choices for accessing employment support services.
   f. All states can design their own program.
8. Work Investment Act (WIA).
   a. Established a federally sponsored national employment and vocational training.
   b. Established a "One-Stop" delivery system for all adults aged 18 or older seeking access to employment and training services. This means traditionally separate unemployment offices and vocational rehabilitation services are now available at a One-Stop Center.
      (1) Availability of all employment and training services at a One-Stop Center is aimed to allow for universal access for persons with disabilities—a core principle of WIA.
      (2) Categories of One-Stop services.
         (a) Core services, which include outreach, intake, and orientation; initial assessment; eligibility determination for services; assistance with job search and placement; job market information; and career counseling.
         (b) Intensive services for individuals who do not attain successful employment after receipt of core services. Services can include comprehensive assessments of service needs and skill level, development of individualized plans for employment, case management, and counseling.
         (c) Training services for individuals who do not attain successful employment after receipt of core and intensive services. These services are typically provided off-site from the One-Stop Center and can include adult education and literacy training, on-the-job training, and individualized vocational training.
      (3) The One-Stop system of services is provided through a network in each state. The names of these systems can vary from state to state.
   c. Persons determined to be eligible for WIA services receive an Individual Training Account (ITA), which is used to obtain services from any approved provider. Specific ITA procedures can vary from state to state.
   d. Services for youth (aged 14–21) with disabilities to successfully transition from school to work are also provided for in the WIA and TWIIA.

Select Legislation Specific to Technology

1. Assistive Technology (AT) Act of 2004.
   a. Improved access to and acquisition of AT by funding direct services to support individuals with all types of disabilities and all ages, in all environments including school, work, home, and leisure.
2. Technology Related Assistance for Individuals with Disabilities Act.
   a. Funded the development of technology and technologic aids for persons with disabilities to improve communication, mobility, self-care, transportation, and education.
3. Title IV—Telecommunications of the ADA. See prior ADA section.
4. Telecommunications Act of 1996.
   a. Required providers of telecommunications systems and manufacturers of telecommunications equipment to make services (e.g., caller ID, operator assistance) and equipment (e.g., cell phones) usable by and accessible to individuals with disabilities, if at all possible.

Legislation Specific to Children and Youth

1. Child Abuse Prevention and Treatment Act (CAPTA).
   a. Defines child abuse and neglect as mental or physical injury, negligent treatment, maltreatment, or sexual abuse of a child less than 18 years of age by a person responsible for the child's welfare under circumstances that indicate that a child's welfare or health is being threatened or harmed.

> **RED FLAG:** Health care and education professionals, including occupational therapy practitioners, are ethically bound and *legally mandated* to report any suspected abuse or neglect to law enforcement officials.

    b. OT practitioners were included in this list of mandated reporters.
    c. Direct OT intervention may be needed to remediate the emotional or physical disorders that result from abuse.
       (1) See Chapter 5 for further information about child abuse.
2. Early Intervention and Education Acts.
    a. Multiple acts have provided the foundation for current early intervention and education services. These include the following:
       (1) Mandates for free and appropriate education (FAPE) for all students regardless of ability or disability (aged 3–21), in the least restrictive environment.
          (a) Mainstreaming (i.e., integrating students with disabilities into classrooms) was the means to ensure education is provided in the least restrictive environment.
       (2) Requirements for public schools to provide OT to special education students if OT is needed for the student to benefit from the special education.
       (3) The designation of OT as a primary early intervention service.
       (4) Funding for family support services and programs to train professionals in early intervention.
       (5) Recommendations for states to develop infant and toddler programs (birth to three years).
          (a) Programs are voluntary and vary from state to state, but all states participate to some degree.
          (b) OT is considered a primary developmental service.
3. Reauthorization and Amendment of Individuals with Disabilities Education Act (IDEA).
    a. Emphasizes that the purpose of the IEP is to address each student's unique needs as related to their disability and decide how these needs can be served so that students with disabilities have full access to the general education curriculum and can participate in the general education classroom.
    b. Clarifies that the IEP can include consideration of assistive technology and behavioral interventions, strategies, and supports (an area in which OT can offer a great deal).
    c. States that the IEP planning team is open to related personnel at the request of the parent or school, in addition to the regular education teacher, if the student is in a regular education class.
    d. States that the education the student receives should prepare them for independent living and employment in adult life.
       (1) Transitional planning begins at the age of 14 (or younger if indicated) to help the student plan a course of study that will lead to post-school goals.
       (2) Transition services begin at the age of 16 (or younger if indicated) to provide student with a coordinated set of services to attain post-school goals.
          (a) These services can include community experience, specific instruction, and/or ADL and vocational assessment and intervention.
       (3) The student must be invited to attend IEP meetings that discuss their transition planning and services to allow for self-advocacy and self-determination.
       (4) This transition plan must be updated annually with appropriate service revision provided.
    e. Maintains the established definition of related services (including OT).
    f. Expands orientation and mobility services by broadly interpreting them to include all students with disabilities.
    g. Students with disabilities may be punished in the same manner as other students for serious offenses (i.e., carrying illicit drugs or a weapon). However, disciplinary prevention measures are stressed.
       (1) If disciplined students are removed to an alternative placement, they must still receive educational and related services.
    h. Clarifies early intervention services and systems.
       (1) Mandates an Individual Family Service Plan (IFSP) for children birth through two years of age.
       (2) OT is identified as a primary early intervention service.
4. Individuals with Disabilities Education Improvement Act.
    a. Directly addresses the student's functional performance along with academic performance.
       (1) Requires that evaluations for IDEA eligibility include relevant functional and developmental information, not just academic achievement data.
       (2) Expands the IEP's annual goals to include academic *and* functional goals.
       (3) Specifies that accommodations must be provided as needed to measure the functional performance and academic achievement of all students with disabilities.
       (4) Enables services to be provided to students as soon as learning needs become apparent via a Response to Intervention (RtI) approach.

(a) RtI provides evidence-based early intervention services to children who are having difficulty learning to prevent academic failure.
b. Provides for the piloting of a multi-year (not to exceed three years) IEP to allow for long-term planning and to coincide with a student's 'natural' transitions (e.g., pre-school to elementary school, middle school to high school).
   (1) Plan is optional for parents.
c. Provides for increased flexibility in IEP meetings.
   (1) Allows IEP team members to be excused from IEP meetings if their area of concern is not being addressed or modified at the meeting or if a written report is submitted prior to the meeting.
      (a) District and parental approval for a team member's absence is required.
      (b) Parental approval must be in writing.
   (2) Allows IEP revisions and/or amendments to be made by parents and districts after an annual IEP meeting.
      (a) Parents must be provided with a written copy of the revised/amended IEP.
   (3) Allows the use of technological alternatives to face-to-face IEP meetings (i.e., videoconferences, conference calls).
d. Requires that recommendations for early intervention, special education, related, and supplementary services and aids be made based on peer-reviewed research to the extent that this is practical.
   (1) This requirement raises concern that established intervention methods may be questioned due to a real or perceived lack of evidence supporting their efficacy.
   (2) This requirement may spur research on early intervention and school-based OT to support evidence-based practice.
e. Clarifies that a screening done by a specialist is not equivalent to an evaluation for eligibility for IDEA services.
   (1) OT practitioners can conduct informal classroom-based screenings and provide consultations for classroom modifications and other teaching strategies without completing a formal evaluation according to IDEA procedures. See prior section on RtI.
f. Requires that all students with disabilities be assessed in compliance with the Elementary and Secondary Education Act (ESEA), commonly known as No Child Left Behind Act.
   (1) The IEP team determines if the student should take an alternative assessment or the standard assessment with or without accommodations.
g. Provides for early coordinated intervening services for general education students from kindergarten through 12th grade who do not require special education services but who do need additional supports to succeed in school. See prior section on RtI.
h. Clarifies that the purpose of the IDEA is to prepare children with disabilities for further education, employment, and independent living.
i. Allows school personnel to individually consider each case of a student with a disability who violates the school's code of conduct.
   (1) Students with disabilities who are disciplined must:
      (a) Be provided with services to continue to progress toward achieving their IEP goals.
      (b) Receive appropriate functional behavioral assessments and interventions, and service modifications as needed to address their conduct violation(s).
j. Allows each state to define developmental delay criteria to determine if an infant or toddler is eligible for early intervention in that state.
   (1) Typically, states define developmental delays quantitatively (e.g., a percentage of delay according to a standardized developmental assessment).
k. Requires that an IFSP be completed to include:
   (1) The infant's or toddler's developmental level.
   (2) Family priorities, concerns, and resources.
   (3) The infant's or toddler's natural environments.
   (4) Measurable outcomes.
   (5) Projected, length, frequency, and duration of research-based services.
   (6) Transition plans to pre-school or other services, as appropriate.
l. Clarifies the role of the parent and IFSP team in determining the site for service provision.
   (1) Requires states to maximize the provision of early intervention services in the infant's or toddler's natural environments, as appropriate.
m. Requires states to establish procedures for the referral of infants and toddlers who are victims of abuse and/or neglect to early intervention services.
   (1) This provision was also included in the Keeping Children and Families Safe Act.
5. Every Student Succeeds Act (ESSA).
   a. Reauthorized the No Child Left Behind (NCLB) act, which was formerly called the Elementary and Secondary Education Act (ESEA).
   b. A general education law that emphasizes standards-based education with a focus on improving the educational opportunities and outcomes for children from lower-income families.
   c. Considers occupational therapy practitioners to be pupil services personnel and sets no requirements for OT services.

d. Requires schools to provide accommodations, if needed by students, for mandated tests.
   (1) OT practitioners can recommend testing alternatives and/or classroom accommodations.

Legislation Specific to Older Adults

1. Age Discrimination in Employment Act.
   a. Prohibits employment practices that discriminate or unfairly affect workers 40 years and older.
   b. Prohibits mandatory retirement of older workers. Employers cannot fix a retirement age.
2. Freedom to Work Act.
   a. Amended the Social Security Act to enable Americans receiving retirement Social Security (SS) benefits to be able to work without affecting their SS income.
      (1) There are no income restrictions in this amendment.
3. Omnibus Budget Reconciliation Act (OBRA) of 1990.
   a. Applied to all nursing homes that receive federal money for Medicare or Medicaid patients.
   b. Emphasized attending to resident rights, autonomy, and self-determination; providing quality of care; and enhancing quality of life within nursing homes.
   c. Mandated a comprehensive resident assessment system, the Minimal Data Set (MDS), which is administered upon admission and thereafter on an annual basis, unless there is a significant change in the resident's condition.
      (1) MDS is coordinated by an RN. OT practitioners can contribute information.
   d. Psychosocial well-being and activity pursuit patterns must be considered along with the resident's physical condition and cognitive abilities.
      (1) This has broadened OT's role in nursing homes.
   e. Mandated that the evaluation and treatment of conditions found during the MDS follow specific guidelines called the Resident Assessment Protocols (RAP).
      (1) The structured approach to assessment is called the Resident Assessment Instrument (RAI).
      (2) Individualized care plans must be established within specific time frames.
   f. The enhancement of quality of life through restraint reduction and the provision of restraint-free environments are strongly emphasized.
      (1) Nursing homes must show evidence of consultation by an occupational or physical therapy practitioner for consideration of interventions that are less restrictive than restraints.
      (2) OT practitioners are frequently consulted for ADL treatment, seating adaptations, positioning ideas, environmental modifications, psychosocial interventions, and activity programming.
   g. Aims to guarantee that residents have the right to choose how they want to receive care and live their lives.
      (1) Residents should have a choice in determining their ADL and community participation activities.
      (2) Residents should be able to function as independently as possible.
   h. Post-discharge plans must meet specific criteria including client or caregiver education.

Service Delivery Models and Practice Settings

Overview

1. A working knowledge of service delivery models and practice settings ensures that OT practitioners make educated decisions about their employment and competent referrals for their clients.
2. As a result of legislative initiatives and health care system changes, service delivery models and practice settings are evolving from medical-based models and settings to more community-based models and settings (e.g., IDEA has solidified schools as a practice setting).
3. Implications for OT practice.
   a. Fewer practitioners are working in hospitals and long-term care facilities.
   b. More practitioners are working in community- and home-based settings (e.g., primary care, day treatment, home care, school settings).

Models of Practice

1. Criteria for determining a model of practice.
   a. The type of setting.
   b. Philosophy and mission of the particular setting and department.
   c. The role the practitioner plays as a team member within that particular setting.

2. Medical model.
   a. Views the individual with a disability as a person who has incurred a physiological insult that has resulted in reduced functional capacity.
   b. Focus is placed on identifying the disease or dysfunction.
   c. Treatment addresses the disease, dysfunction, client factors, and/or performance component deficits contributing to decreased functional skills.
   d. OT frames of reference address the pathological process of the disease or dysfunctions (e.g., biomechanical, neurodevelopmental).
3. Education model.
   a. Views the individual with a disability as lacking knowledge or skills.
   b. Focus is placed on learning and making the behavioral changes needed to interact successfully in the environment.
   c. An individual's skill deficits are determined, and related goals are established, to promote learning to adequately perform within a particular environment.
   d. Behaviors are measured in terms of obtaining skills, knowledge, and competency to successfully meet the demands of the environment.
   e. OT frames of reference are based on learning theories to facilitate adaptation in the environment (e.g., role acquisition, cognitive remediation).
4. Community model.
   a. Views the individual with a disability as lacking the skills, resources, and supports needed for community participation.
   b. Focus is placed on identifying and developing the skills needed for one's expected environment.
   c. If skills cannot be developed, community resources and supports are identified and developed to enable participation within the person's chosen environment.
   d. OT frames of reference promote development of performance skills and/or engagement in desired occupational roles within the individual's unique performance contexts (e.g., life-style performance, occupation adaptation).
5. Telehealth model.
   a. A service delivery model that can include features of the previous models by providing medical, rehabilitative, and/or educational services to persons via telecommunications technologies.

Institutional Practice Settings

1. Acute care hospitals.
   a. Admission is for a medical or psychiatric diagnosis that cannot be treated on an outpatient basis.
      (1) Initial onset of a new illness or major health problem.
      (2) Acute exacerbation of a chronic illness.
      (3) In psychiatry, a person may be involuntarily admitted to an acute unit if they are considered to be a danger to self or others, or as having a grave disability.
   b. LOS is determined by diagnosis and presenting symptoms.
      (1) LOS can be limited to one to seven days.
      (2) Longer LOS requires significant documentation to justify need for further hospitalization.
      (3) Ongoing need for care frequently results in discharge to another setting.
   c. OT evaluation process focuses on quick and accurate screening of major difficulties impeding function (e.g., cognitive status, home safety skills).
   d. OT intervention focus.
      (1) Stabilization of client's status.
      (2) Engagement of the client in the therapeutic relationship and purposeful activities/meaningful occupations so that they can see that change is possible, thereby increasing motivation to pursue follow-up.
      (3) Discharge planning and after-care referrals.
      (4) Family, caregiver, and consumer education.
   e. The role of an acute care OT practitioner can be a generalist or a specialist (e.g., neonatology).

> **EXAM HINT:** The COTA® exam is designed to test entry-level OTA competencies, thus, specialized practice roles that require advanced knowledge and skills should not be evaluated on the COTA® exam.

2. Sub-acute care/intermediate-care facilities (ICFs).
   a. Admission is for a medical or psychiatric diagnosis that has progressed from an acute stage but has not stabilized sufficiently to be treated on an outpatient basis.
   b. LOS is determined by diagnosis and presenting symptoms.
      (1) LOS can range from 5–30 days.
      (2) Longer LOS requires significant documentation to justify need for further hospitalization.
      (3) Ongoing need for intervention or long-term care frequently results in discharge to another setting.
   c. OT evaluation can include more in-depth assessments and more thorough observations of client's functional performance.
   d. OT intervention focus.
      (1) Functional improvements in performance components and performance areas.
      (2) Active engagement of the client in the treatment planning, implementation, and re-evaluation process.
      (3) Discharge planning to expected environment.
   e. Sub-acute care and ICFs can be housed in hospitals or SNFs.

3. Long-term acute care hospital (LTAC).
   a. Admission is for chronic or catastrophic illnesses or disabilities that require extensive medical care and/or dependency on life support or ventilators.
      (1) Patients often have multiple diagnoses with major complications.
   b. The average LOS is greater than 25 days to maintain Medicare certification.
   c. OT evaluation and intervention are often limited by the population's severe and complex medical needs.
      (1) For all patients, evaluation and intervention are concerned with palliative care and the prevention and treatment of complications (e.g., positioning to prevent decubiti and contractures).
      (2) For individuals who are cognitively intact, the focus of evaluation and intervention is mastery of the environment and the attainment of client-centered goals.
4. Rehabilitation hospitals.
   a. Admission is for a disability that is medically stable but that has residual functional deficits requiring skilled rehabilitation services.
   b. LOS is determined by presenting deficits and rehabilitation potential.
      (1) LOS can range from a week to months.
      (2) Documentation requirements supporting the need for an extended LOS are dependent on institutional, state, and third-party payer guidelines.
      (3) LOS ends when coverage is expended. The client is then discharged to the appropriate environment.
         (a) A SNF.
         (b) A supportive community residence.
         (c) Home/independent living.
   c. OT evaluation can be extensive and focus on all areas of occupation, performance skills, and occupational roles that will be required in the expected environment.
      (1) Environmental assessment of the planned discharge environment must be completed.
   d. OT intervention focus.
      (1) Functional improvement in performance areas, performance skills, and occupational roles.
      (2) Development of compensatory strategies for residual deficits.
      (3) Provision of adaptive equipment and training in use of the equipment to promote independent function.
      (4) Modification of the discharge environment, as needed, to enhance function.
      (5) Education of the individual, family, and caregivers on abilities, limitations, compensatory techniques, and advocacy skills.
5. Long-term hospitals.
   a. Admission is for a medical or psychiatric diagnosis that is chronic with the presence of symptoms that cannot be treated on an outpatient basis.
   b. LOS is determined by diagnosis and presenting symptoms.
      (1) LOS can range from a month to years.
      (2) Documentation requirements supporting need for increased LOS are dependent upon institutional, third-party payer, and/or state guidelines.
      (3) LOS in private long-term hospitals is determined by insurance coverage. When coverage is expended, an alternative discharge environment is needed for the client.
         (a) A state-run long-term hospital.
         (b) A SNF.
         (c) Home or supportive residence.
   c. OT evaluation can be extensive due to increased LOS.
   d. OT intervention focus.
      (1) Functional improvements in performance skills and performance areas.
      (2) Development of compensatory strategies for residual deficits.
      (3) Maintenance of quality of life.
      (4) Development of skills for discharge to the least restrictive environment.
6. Skilled nursing facilities (SNFs)/extended care facilities (ECFs).
   a. Admission is for a medical or psychiatric diagnosis that is chronic and requires skilled care, but the individual's illness is stable with no acute symptoms.
   b. Due to managed care constraints on acute hospital stays, many individuals are being admitted to SNFs for medical care and rehabilitation.
   c. LOS can range from one month to the individual's lifetime. Several factors influence LOS.
      (1) The progression of the illness.
      (2) Availability of family and/or community supports.
      (3) Insurance coverage.
   d. OT evaluation and intervention are guided by Medicare standards.
      (1) For individuals with rehabilitation potential, the focus of evaluation and intervention is the same as identified under Rehabilitation Hospitals.
      (2) For individuals without rehabilitation potential, evaluation and intervention are more concerned with palliative care and the maintenance of quality of life.
7. Forensic settings.
   a. Admission is due to engagement in criminal activity by a person. The person can be remanded to a variety of settings depending on the nature of

the crime and if a psychiatric diagnosis has been made.
- (1) Jail: a city or county facility that is the individual's first entry into the criminal justice system and the placement for those convicted of crimes with sentences of less than a year.
- (2) Prison: a state or federal facility for individuals found guilty of crimes with sentences greater than a year.
- (3) Forensic psychiatric hospital or unit: a specialized hospital or unit within a hospital that provides inpatient psychiatric care for individuals convicted of a crime and found guilty but mentally ill or not guilty by reason of insanity.

b. LOS is determined by court-ordered directives and criminal sentences.

c. The availability and quality of services vary greatly from none in most jails to extensive in some forensic hospitals.

d. Due to serious gaps in mental health and social services, the incarceration rate of persons with mental illness has increased significantly (e.g., a homeless person with schizophrenia steals food due to hunger).

e. OT evaluation and intervention focus.
- (1) Determination of individual's competency to stand trial, in forensic psychiatry settings.
- (2) Areas similar to those described under rehabilitation hospitals to develop community living skills needed for successful community reintegration upon release.
- (3) Facilitation of skills and provision of structured programs to enable the person to function at their highest level within their current environment since discharge may be delayed or not possible, depending on the nature of the crime.
- (4) Restoration of competency to stand trial in forensic psychiatry settings.

8. Outpatient/ambulatory care.
   a. An individual who does not require hospitalization but has functional deficits requiring evaluation and intervention may receive OT services on an outpatient basis in private clinics, medical offices, and/or hospital satellite centers.
   b. Focus of outpatient care is diagnostic evaluations, interventions to increase functional performance, consumer education, and prevention.

Community-Based Practice Settings

1. Early intervention programs.
   a. Acceptance criteria for an early intervention evaluation are based on "at-risk" status of the infant or toddler who is under the age of three.
   - (1) Birth complications.
   - (2) Suspected delays in development.
   - (3) Failure to thrive.
   - (4) Maternal substance abuse during pregnancy.
   - (5) Birth to an adolescent/teen mother.
   - (6) Established disability/diagnosis.

   b. Acceptance criteria for early intervention services are based on the following criteria.
   - (1) The extent of the delay (typically a 33% delay in one area of development or a 25% delay in two areas).
   - (2) An established diagnosis/disability.

   c. Length of service provision.
   - (1) If the infant/child qualifies for services, an individualized family service plan (IFSP) is completed by the service coordinator after a review of all assessments and in collaboration with the family and early intervention team.
   - (2) Six-month reviews are submitted by all professionals to determine if services should continue.

   d. OT evaluation.
   - (1) Assessment of five developmental areas.
     - (a) Cognitive.
     - (b) Physical.
     - (c) Communication.
     - (d) Social-emotional.
     - (e) Adaptive.
   - (2) Determination of the effects of current development on the areas of play and activities of daily living.
   - (3) Evaluations need to be written in a strength-oriented manner.
   - (4) Functional goals must be written in family-friendly terms and include levels of functioning, unique needs, and recommended services.

   e. OT intervention process.
   - (1) Development of cognitive, psychosocial, and sensorimotor components.
   - (2) Development of play, self-care, and developmental skills.
   - (3) Provision of family education.
   - (4) Provision of advocacy and advocacy training.
   - (5) Transition planning from early intervention to pre-school is essential.

2. Schools.
   a. Acceptance criteria for OT services as a related service in an educational setting.
   - (1) The child requires special education services and OT will enable the child to benefit from special education.
   - (2) OT will facilitate the child's participation in educational activities and enhance the child's functional performance.
   - (3) Referrals are received from the previous agency that provided early intervention services, the child's teacher, and/or school's child study team.

(4) The school reviews the referral and, if indicated, recommends an OT evaluation.
  (a) If an OT evaluation has already been completed, the need for OT intervention services is discussed.
  (b) The frequency, length of sessions, and duration of the intervention are also determined.
b. Length of services is dependent on the impact of OT services on the child's abilities and prevention of loss of abilities.
  (1) If OT services can improve the child's ability to participate in education-related activities and allow full access to the general education curriculum, services can be continued.
  (2) A review of services and progress made toward the child's individualized education plan (IEP) is conducted on an annual basis.
c. OT evaluation.
  (1) Assess client factors, performance skills and patterns, and areas of occupation that impact the educational performance of the child within the school.
    (a) Findings are used to contribute to the IEP, in which goals and objectives are formulated to address the overall educational needs of the student.
  (2) Assess the child's functional and developmental level to contribute to the Functional Behavioral Analysis.
d. OT intervention focus.
  (1) Based on an educational model versus a medical model.
  (2) Addresses the student's functional performance along with academic performance.
  (3) Activities are utilized to address the goals and objectives documented in the IEP using both corrective and compensatory methods.
  (4) Assistive technology and transition services, in accordance with the regulations of IDEA, are provided.
  (5) Client factors and performance skill deficits (i.e., sensorimotor, cognitive, and psychosocial) are treated to improve the child's ability to participate in and perform education-related activities within a school setting.
  (6) Skills in the occupational performance areas of ADL, school, and play are developed to improve the child's ability to participate in and perform education-related activities within a school setting.
  (7) Skills for adult life after school are developed in accordance with the student's transition plan.
e. The OT practitioner needs to know the school district's and state's funding sources and regulations and interpretations of the federal laws regarding education (see this chapter's section on legislation).
f. The role of OT practitioners in school-based practice has expanded beyond IDEA-related services to include programs that address students' psychosocial needs and prevent school violence.
  (1) Behavioral Intervention Plans, which include Response to Intervention (RtI), Early Intervening Services (EIS), and Positive Behavioral Supports (PBS), may be a component of school-based OT service provision.
    (a) RtI is an evidence-based, structured intervention approach that uses EIS to address academic difficulties and PBS to address behavioral problems early in a child's education.
      - An RtI is designed to meet the needs of children who are having difficulty learning without requiring a full evaluation as required for an IEP.
      - The provision of classroom modifications (e.g., the use of a therapy ball as a seat instead of a standard desk chair) and the use of educational strategies (e.g., incorporating movement into class lessons) can positively impact children's ability to learn.
      - If the RtI approach is not effective, the occupational therapist can recommend the completion of a comprehensive evaluation and the development and implementation of an IEP.

3. Supported education programs.
  a. Participant criteria include adolescents or adults who require intervention to develop skills that are needed to succeed in secondary and/or postsecondary education.
    (1) The person may have never developed these skills or lost them due to a psychiatric disability or mental health problems.
  b. LOS is determined by agency's funding and person's attainment of goals.
    (1) Discharge is upon entry into, or completion of, an educational program or the attainment of a graduate equivalency degree (GED).
  c. OT evaluation is focused on the individual's client factors and performance skills and patterns that impact the occupational role of student.
  d. OT intervention focus.
    (1) Improvement in performance skills and patterns that are needed for the occupational role of student (e.g., time management and task prioritization).
    (2) Education and training in compensatory strategies to support academic performance (e.g., studying in a quiet room).

(3) Exploration of participant's educational interests and aptitudes to ensure self-determined engagement in a school, college, technical training program, or community-based adult-education class(es).
4. Prevocational programs.
   a. Participant criteria include adolescents or adults who require intervention to develop skills that are prerequisite to work.
      (1) The person may have never developed these skills due to developmental delays, environmental insufficiencies, illness, or disability.
      (2) The person may have lost these skills due to illness or disability.
   b. LOS is determined by agency's funding and person's attainment of goals.
      (1) Discharge is usually to a vocational program.
      (2) Discharge to a work setting can occur if sufficient abilities are developed.
   c. OT evaluation is focused on the individual's task skills, social interaction skills, work habits, interests, and aptitudes.
   d. OT intervention focus.
      (1) Improvement in task skills and social skills that are prerequisite to vocational training or work.
      (2) Development of work habits and abilities.
      (3) Exploration of work interests and aptitudes to ensure discharge to a relevant vocational training program, school, or work setting.
5. Vocational programs.
   a. Acceptance is for development of specific vocational skills.
      (1) Person has the prerequisite abilities to work (e.g., good task skills and work habits) but requires training for a specific job and/or ongoing structure, support, and/or supervision to maintain employment.
      (2) Person has to develop their work capacities to a level acceptable for competitive employment (e.g., strength and endurance).
   b. LOS is determined by agency's funding and attainment of goals.
      (1) In vocational rehabilitation workshops (formerly called sheltered workshops) and supportive employment programs, discharge is not always a goal.
         (a) Maintenance of the person in these specific work environments can be the desired objective for some individuals, while others will be discharged to other programs or to work.
      (2) Transitional employment programs (TEPs) are generally time limited (three to six months) with discharge to competitive employment, supportive employment, or rehabilitation workshops.
      (3) Employee Assistance Programs (EAPs) provide ongoing support, intervention, and referrals as needed to a company's employees to enable these individuals to maintain this employment.
   c. OT evaluation is focused on the individual's functional skills and deficits related to work in their current and expected vocational environment.
   d. OT intervention focus.
      (1) Remediation of underlying performance component deficits that affect the work performance area.
      (2) Development of general work abilities and specific job skills.
      (3) Consultation to and/or supervision of vocational direct care staff.
      (4) Identification and implementation of reasonable accommodations in accordance with ADA.
      (5) Referral to state offices of vocational and educational services (i.e., One-Stop Centers) for persons with disabilities for further evaluation, education, and training.
6. Residential programs.
   a. Admission is for a developmental, medical, or psychiatric condition that has resulted in functional deficits that impede independent living but are not severe enough to require hospitalization.
      (1) Residential programs are on a continuum from 24-hour supervised quarter way houses, halfway houses, or group homes, to supportive apartments with weekly or biweekly "check-in" supervision.
      (2) The degree of functional impairment determines the residential level of care needed.
   b. LOS for transitional living programs (e.g., quarter way and halfway house programs) is determined by agency's funding.
      (1) Long-term and permanent housing options (i.e., group homes and supportive apartments) are available and are funded through the individual's social service benefits.
   c. OT evaluation is focused on assessment of the individual's skills for living in the community and determination of the social and environmental resources and supports needed to maintain the individual in their current and expected living environment.
   d. OT intervention focus.
      (1) Consultation to and/or supervision of residential program staff.
      (2) Remediation of underlying client factors and performance skill deficits that affect independent living skills.
      (3) ADL training, activity adaptation, and environmental modifications to facilitate community living skills.

(4) Referral to appropriate residential services along the continuum of care as individual's functional level improves.
(5) Education about ADA, the Fair Housing Act, and Section 8 Housing.

7. Partial hospitalization/day hospital programs.
   a. Admission is for a medical or psychiatric condition that has been sufficiently stabilized to enable an individual to be discharged home or to a community residence (e.g., a halfway house or supported apartment); however, the individual still has symptoms remaining that require active treatment.
   b. Treatment is up to five days per week with multiple interventions scheduled each day.
   c. LOS is determined by diagnosis, presenting symptoms, and response to treatment.
      (1) LOS can vary from one week to six months.
      (2) Documentation requirements supporting the need for an extended LOS are dependent on institutional, state, and/or third-party payer guidelines.
      (3) Once LOS is expended, discharge is usually to a less intensive community day program and/or clubhouse.
   d. OT evaluation is focused on the individual's functional skills and deficits in their performance areas and the occupational roles that are required in their current and expected environment(s).
   e. OT intervention focus.
      (1) Functional improvement in performance areas and occupational role functioning.
      (2) Remediation of underlying performance skill deficits that affect functional performance.
      (3) Development of skills for community living and identification of community supports for community integration.

8. Clubhouse programs.
   a. Membership is open to adults and elders with a current mental illness or a history of mental illness.
      (1) All members have equal access to all clubhouse functions and opportunities regardless of functional level or diagnosis.
      (2) Individuals who pose a significant and direct threat to the safety of the clubhouse community are the only persons excluded.
   b. Services are provided by staff and members with the responsibilities of operating the clubhouse shared equally by staff and members under the oversight of a director.
      (1) Due to this role equality, it can be difficult to distinguish between members and paid staff.
      (2) Staff's main role is to engage membership and provide needed support and structure.
   c. Individual schedules will vary to meet each person's unique needs and interests.
      (1) Clubhouses are typically open at least five days per week. Many are open seven days per week.
      (2) The daily schedule is organized around the 'work-ordered' day, which parallels typical working hours to engage members and staff in the running of the clubhouse.
      (3) Evening and weekend schedules are focused on avocational interests and recreational pursuits.
      (4) Additional services that can be provided include literacy and education programs, transitional employment placements, independent employment assistance, community support and outreach services, housing programs, and legal and financial advisement.
   d. LOS is indefinite; members can exit and re-enter a clubhouse community at will.
   e. OT evaluation and intervention are not provided in a formalized manner.
      (1) The role of the OT practitioner is integrated into the clubhouse model, which has staff acting as generalists who contribute to the development and enrichment of members' abilities and the attainment of recovery.

9. Adult day care.
   a. Admission is for adults and elders with chronic physical and/or psychosocial impairments, and/or for individuals who are frail but semi-independent.
   b. Services are provided in a congregate or group setting.
   c. Individual schedules will vary.
      (1) Flexibility in scheduling is provided to address daily caregiver needs and allow for planned respite.
      (2) Schedules can range from one afternoon per week to five full days.
   d. LOS is indefinite.
      (1) Ongoing services are provided to individuals with chronic conditions who might otherwise be institutionalized or to individuals who are frail and need ongoing support (e.g., cooked meals, socialization opportunities).
   e. OT evaluation is focused on the individual's client factors, functional skills and deficits in the performance areas, their home environment, and the adult day center's environment.
   f. OT intervention focus.
      (1) Maintenance of the healthy, functional aspects of the individual and facilitation of adaptation to impairments.
      (2) Engagement in purposeful activities that provide appropriate stimulation, reflect lifelong interests, develop new interests, and foster a sense of community with other participants.

(3) Caregiver education, support groups, home visits, consultations, and referrals to community resources.
(4) Modifications to the day care center's environment and the individual's home environment to maximize the person's comfort in, and mastery and control of, these environments.

10. Outpatient/ambulatory care.
    a. Admission is for a medical or psychiatric condition that is not serious enough to warrant hospitalization or for a condition that has sufficiently stabilized to enable the individual to be discharged from a hospital, but remaining symptoms require active treatment.
    b. Treatment is usually provided in short 30- to 60-minute sessions once a day for up to five days a week.
    c. LOS is determined by diagnosis, presenting symptoms, response to treatment, and insurance coverage or ability to pay a fee for service.
    d. OT evaluation focused on the individual's functional assets and deficits in their performance skills, his/her areas of occupation, and their home, work, leisure, and social participation environments.
    e. OT intervention focus.
        (1) Active engagement of the client in the treatment planning, implementation, re-evaluation, and discharge process.
        (2) Remediation of underlying performance skill deficits that affect functional performance.
        (3) Functional improvements in occupational performance areas and occupational roles.
        (4) Compensatory strategies for remaining deficits.
        (5) Consumer, family, and caregiver education.

11. Home health care.
    a. Acceptance criteria for home health services.
        (1) Presence of a medical or psychiatric condition that is not serious enough to warrant hospitalization or for a condition that has sufficiently stabilized to enable the individual to be discharged from a hospital but that still has remaining symptoms requiring active treatment.
        (2) Reimbursing agencies can have strict and variable criteria for qualifying for home health care. See earlier section on Medicare and third-party reimbursement.
    b. Treatment is usually provided in 60-minute sessions, once a day for up to five days a week, as determined by insurance coverage.
    c. LOS is determined by diagnosis, presenting symptoms, response to treatment, insurance coverage, or ability to pay a fee for service.
    d. OT evaluation is focused on the individual's functional assets and deficits in their performance skills and patterns, areas of occupation, and the occupational roles that are required in the person's current and expected environment(s).
    e. OT intervention focus.
        (1) Active engagement of the client, family, and caregivers in the treatment planning and other places of accommodation, implementation, and re-evaluation processes.
        (2) Functional improvement in areas of occupation and occupational role functioning within the home.
        (3) Remediation of underlying performance skill deficits that affect functional performance within the home.
        (4) Education of the family, caregivers, and/or home health aides to provide appropriate care and/or assistance as needed.
        (5) Environmental modifications and activity adaptations that maintain optimal functioning and improve quality of life.
        (6) Increasing ability to resume occupational roles outside of the home.
        (7) Prevention of hospitalization and avoidance or delay of residential institutional placement.

12. Hospice.
    a. Acceptance criteria for hospice services.
        (1) Terminal illness that has a life expectancy of six months or less.
    b. Services are most often provided in the home with the type and quantity of services determined by the needs of the individual, their family, significant others, and caregivers.
        (1) Hospice services may also be provided in an independent facility or in a special unit of a SNF or a hospital.
    c. LOS is determined by the person's terminal outcome.
    d. OT evaluation is focused on determining the individual's occupational functioning and their physical, psychosocial, spiritual, and environmental needs that are most important to them.
    e. OT intervention focus.
        (1) Maintenance of the individual's control over their life.
        (2) Facilitation of engagement in meaningful occupations and purposeful activities that are consistent with the individual's roles, values, choices, interests, aspirations, abilities, and hopes and that contribute to a satisfactory quality of life.
        (3) Reduction or removal of distressing symptoms and pain.
        (4) Environmental modifications and activity adaptations that maintain optimal functioning and improve quality of life.

(5) Caregiver and family education and support to maintain optimal functioning and improve quality of life for all.
13. Case management programs.
    a. There are two different focuses to case management programs: one is clinical and one is administrative.
       (1) Clinical case management provides individualized support and intervention to a client with a serious illness that significantly limits their ability to access and/or engage in existing community services and/or therapeutic programs, ensuring that the person is able to remain in the community and not be re-hospitalized.
       (2) Administrative case management connects a person with a serious illness to the appropriate and needed community services and/or therapeutic programs, overseeing this service provision to ensure that quality of care in a cost-effective manner is achieved.
    b. Services can be provided in an office and/or in the individual's home and community.
    c. LOS is determined by the individual's ability to independently access needed services and by funding availability.
    d. OT evaluation is focused on the individual's functional assets and deficits in their performance skills, areas of occupation, and the occupational roles that are required in their current expected environment.
       (1) Assessment of the individual's supports and barriers for community integration is critical.
    e. Case management interventions can be purely referral-based in the administrative model or encompass the full range of interventions in the clinical model (e.g., one-on-one counseling, family education, ADL training, community re-entry, etc.).
       (1) Both models aim to prevent regression and re-hospitalization and promote optimal functioning and quality of life.
       (2) Both models actively engage the individual and family in the treatment planning, implementation, and re-evaluation processes.
       (3) Both models plan discharge, if appropriate, to an environment that will best serve an individual's needs.
14. Wellness and prevention programs.
    a. Acceptance is most often by individual's self-referral to meet a personal need or by an institution's provision of a program to its members or employees (e.g., a parenting skills class for pregnant teens in a school).
    b. Programs have been developed to serve populations considered at risk and are held in offices, individual's residences, and/or at community sites.
    c. LOS is determined by the individual. It is usually influenced by program's planned length (e.g., a six-week joint protection program) or by individual's achievement of a desired outcome (e.g., smoking cessation).
    d. OT evaluation focuses on risk factors for illnesses and disabilities and the individual's functional skills and deficits in the occupational roles that are required in their current and expected environment.
    e. OT intervention focus.
       (1) Disease prevention and health promotion.
       (2) Interventions can range from the traditional domain of OT (e.g., home safety and environmental modifications) to contemporary areas of concern (e.g., stress management, smoking cessation, life coaching).
       (3) Refer to Chapter 3 for definitions of and specific interventions for primary, secondary, and tertiary prevention.

> **EXAM HINT:** The NBCOT® exam outline for the COTA® identifies the tasks of providing "information regarding the influence of current conditions, contexts, and task demands on occupational performance in order to assist the OTR in planning interventions and monitoring progress as guided by the practice setting" (NBCOT®, 2018, p. 22) and engaging "in professional development and competency assessment activities by using evidence-based strategies and approaches to provide safe, effective, and efficient services relevant to the . . . practice setting" (NBCOT®, 2018, p. 28) as essential for competent and safe practice. The application of knowledge about the institutional practice settings and the community-based practice settings described in prior chapter sections can help you determine the correct answer for NBCOT® Domain 01 and Domain 03 exam items.

Private/Independent Practice

1. In any and all of the previously mentioned community and institutional settings, the OT practitioner can work in an entrepreneurial manner by negotiating a fee-for-service agreement and/or a long-term contract.
2. COTA®s/OTAs in private independent practice must receive supervision from an occupational therapist and abide by all state and federal regulations for OT practice.

Service Management

Management Principles, Functions, and Strategies

1. Managers who have a positive attitude about change and innovation foster best practice.
2. Successful management supports open communication, team building, decentralization of resources, and the sharing of power.
3. Management that utilizes strategic thinking in a systems model can respond proactively to market demands and changes.
4. The use of different management styles (i.e., the manager's characteristic way of performing management tasks) has a significant impact on productivity, change, and growth. See text's section on leadership styles in Chapter 3.
5. Management's understanding and application of theories of motivation and behavior facilitates appropriate and effective responses to situations, fosters program efficacy, and promotes employee satisfaction.
6. Administrative functions of management include program development, fiscal and personnel management, and program evaluation. See separate sections for specifics on each major function.
7. Management by Objective (MBO): a complete system of management based upon a core set of goals to be accomplished by a program.
   a. Mission and goals are established.
   b. Measurable objectives are quantified.
   c. Specific time frames for accomplishment of objectives are established.
   d. Staff training needs and deterrents to progress are identified.
   e. Program evaluation is instituted.

Program Development

1. Purposes of developing specific programs.
   a. To directly meet the needs of a specific population(s) or group(s).
   b. To clearly focus evaluation and intervention efforts and activities.
   c. To increase visibility and use of available services (e.g., offering an outpatient cardiac rehabilitation program is more visible than individual referrals, resulting in increased recognition and utilization of this service).
   d. To convert an idea into a practice reality.
2. Role of the COTA®/OTA.
   a. Collaborate with occupational therapist to assess needs, develop program plan, and implement evaluation program.
   b. Perform specific tasks with OT supervision.
   c. If employed as an activities director, a COTA®/OTA may be primarily responsible for all program development steps.
3. Four basic steps of program development.
   a. Needs assessment.
      (1) Describe the community; its physical, social, cultural, and economic factors; and populations at risk.
      (2) Describe the target population's demographics, disorder(s), functional level(s), and presenting problem(s).
      (3) Identify specific needs of target population.
         (a) Perceived needs of the population as reported by others (e.g., family, physicians, other professionals).
         (b) Felt needs as stated by the individual members of the target population.
         (c) Real needs, which are the actual disabilities and functional limitations of the target population.
      (4) Determine discrepancy between real, perceived, and felt needs.
      (5) Establish unmet needs according to priority.
      (6) Identify resources available for program implementation.
         (a) Formal or institutional resources such as staff, supplies, money, and space.
         (b) Informal resources such as family, friends, cultural or religious figures, and self-help/consumer groups.
      (7) Needs assessment methods.
         (a) Survey, interview, or self-report of target population. A representative sample is required.
         (b) Key informant, which involves the surveying of specific individuals who are knowledgeable about the target population needs.
         (c) Community forums to obtain information through public meetings or panels.
         (d) Service utilization review of records and reports.
         (e) Analysis of social indicators to identify social, cultural, environmental, and/or economic factors that can predict problems.

b. Program planning.
   (1) Define a focus for the program based on the needs assessment results.
       (a) Problem areas, functional limitations, and unmet needs that are relevant to the majority of the target population are the priority focus.
       (b) Program level of difficulty as determined by the range of population's functional levels and the level required by the current and expected environment.
   (2) Adopt a frame or frames of reference that are most likely to successfully address and meet the needs that are the program's focus.
   (3) Establish objectives and goals of the program specifically related to primary focus.
       (a) Individual goals that will be met by the program are set.
       (b) Programmatic goals that establish standards for program evaluation are determined.
   (4) Describe integration of program into existing system of care.
       (a) Establish realistic timetable for program implementation.
       (b) Define staff roles, responsibilities, and assignments.
       (c) Identify methods for professional collaboration.
       (d) Determine the physical setting and space requirements.
       (e) Consider potential barriers to program implementation.
       (f) Develop methods to effectively deal with identified obstacles before program implementation.
   (5) Develop a system of referral for entry into, completion of, and discharge from the program.
       (a) Evaluation protocols to standardize information to be obtained from each person referred to the program and to assess the type of program services needed.
       (b) Criteria for acceptance into the program and for movement through program levels.
       (c) Discharge criteria to determine when an individual has achieved maximum gain from the program, usually defined as the achievement of program goals.
   (6) Describe the fiscal implications of program plan.
       (a) Determine projected volume or service demand to estimate revenue.
       (b) Identify resource utilization and projected expenses to estimate costs.
       (c) Directly compare estimated revenue and estimated expenses to determine financial viability of program.

c. Program implementation.
   (1) Initiate program according to timetable and steps set forth in the program plan.
   (2) Document program activities, procedures, and use.
   (3) Communicate and coordinate with other programs within the system.
   (4) Promote program to ensure it reaches target population.
d. Program evaluation. See this chapter's section on program evaluation and quality improvement.

Personnel Management

1. The oversight of OT practitioners and support personnel and the services they provide.
2. Role of the COTA®/OTA.
   a. Collaborate with the occupational therapist and perform specific management tasks as delegated and supervised by an occupational therapist.
   b. If employed as an activities director, a COTA®/OTA may be primarily responsible for all aspects of personnel management for the activities department.
3. Purposes of personnel management.
   a. To serve as the link between the individuals working for an organization and the larger organizational structure.
   b. To attain best practice from personnel.
4. Major personnel management tasks.
   a. Design work roles and write job descriptions.
   b. Recruit, select, and orient personnel to perform the roles.
   c. Supervise and evaluate personnel to ensure adequate role performance and the attainment of organizational goals.
   d. Support personnel's ongoing professional development.
   e. Deal with difficult personnel issues as they arise.

Program Evaluation and Quality Improvement

EXAM HINT: The NBCOT® exam outline for the COTA® identifies knowledge of the "methods for contributing to continuous quality improvement processes and procedures related to occupational therapy service delivery" (NBCOT®, 2018, p. 28) as essential for competent and safe practice. The application of knowledge about the following purposes, types, and terms of program evaluation and quality improvement can help you determine the correct answer for NBCOT® Domain 03 exam items related to quality improvement.

1. The systematic review and analysis of care provided to determine if this care is at an acceptable level of quality.
2. Role of the COTA®/OTA.
   a. Collaborate with the occupational therapist and contribute to the process by performing specific tasks with supervision (e.g., the collection of outcome data).
   b. A COTA®/OTA may assume primary responsibility for this process if they are directly responsible for program outcomes (e.g., as the director of an activities program in a SNF).
3. Purposes of program evaluation.
   a. To measure the effectiveness of a program; that is, were program goals accomplished?
   b. To use information obtained in the evaluation to improve services and assure quality.
   c. To meet external accreditation standards (see this chapter's section on voluntary accreditation).
   d. To identify program problems/limitations and to resolve them.
4. Major types and terms.
   a. Continuous quality improvement (CQI): a system-oriented approach that views limitations and problems proactively as opportunities to increase quality.
      (1) Prevention is emphasized.
      (2) Blame is not attributed to persons; problems are related to organizational improvement needs.
      (3) A prospective viewpoint is used.
         (a) Current services are critically reviewed and improvements that can enhance the efficacy of future service delivery are identified and implemented.
   b. Total quality management (TQM): the creation of an organizational culture that enables all employees to contribute to an environment of continuous improvement to meet or exceed consumer needs.
   c. Performance assessment and improvement (PAI): a systematic method to evaluate the appropriateness and quality of services.
      (1) Utilization of an interdisciplinary systems focus.
      (2) A client-centered approach that focuses on the rights, assessment, care, and education of the person.
      (3) Organizational ethics, improved organizational performance, leadership, and management are emphasized.
5. Goal attainment scaling (GAS): an evaluation tool that attains clients' goals for intervention and measures goal attainment and intervention outcomes after a specified time period.

a. Utilization review (UR): a plan to review the use of resources within a facility.
   (1) Determination of medical necessity and cost efficiency.
   (2) Often a component of a CQI or PAI system.
b. Statistical utilization review: reimbursement claims data are analyzed to determine the most efficient and cost-effective care.
c. Peer review: a system in which the quality of work of a group of health professionals is reviewed by their peers.
d. Professional review organization (PRO): groups of peers who evaluate the appropriateness of services and quality of care under reimbursement and/or state licensure requirements.
e. Prospective review.
   (1) Evaluation of proposed intervention plan that specifies how and why care will be provided.
   (2) Used by third-party payers to approve proposed OT intervention program.
f. Concurrent review.
   (1) Evaluation of ongoing intervention program during hospitalization, outpatient, or home care treatment.
   (2) Method to ensure appropriate care is being delivered.
   (3) Often a component of a CQI or PAI system.
g. Retrospective review.
   (1) Audits of medical records after interventions were rendered.
   (2) Method to ensure appropriate care was given.
   (3) A UR tool for third-party payers that can be time consuming and costly.
h. Risk management: a process that identifies, evaluates, and takes corrective action against risk and plans, organizes, and controls the activities and resources of OT services to decrease actual or potential losses.
   (1) Potential risks are client or employee injury and property loss or damage with resulting liability and financial loss.
   (2) OT practitioners are responsible to ensure proper maintenance of equipment and a safe treatment environment.
   (3) Staff education and training (e.g., certification/recertification in CPR) is required.
   (4) Effective communication with consumers (e.g., informed consent) and with team members is required.
   (5) Risk management is an integral part of program evaluation.
   (6) If risk management fails and an incident occurs, completion of an incident report according to setting's standards is required.

> **EXAM HINT:** In the NBCOT® exam outline for the COTA®, the ability to "incorporate risk management techniques at an individual and service-setting level by using standard operating procedures, safety principles, best practice guidelines, and relevant compliance trainings to protect clients, self, staff, and others from injury or harm during interventions" (NBCOT®, 2018, p. 29) is identified as a key task of the COTA®. Knowledge of "precautions or contraindications associated with a client condition or stage of recovery," "standard infection control procedures and universal precautions for reducing transmission of contaminants," "basic first aid in response to minor injuries and adverse reactions," "essential safety procedures to integrate into intervention activities," and "preventive measures for minimizing risk in the intervention environment" (NBCOT®, 2018, p. 29) are identified as essential for effective and competent risk management. The following provides an overview of risk management in OT practice. Information about precautions, contraindications, and safety procedures are provided in Chapters 6–13. Universal and transmission-based precautions are provided in Chapter 3 and first aid procedures are provided in Chapter 8. The application of this specific knowledge and the general risk management information provided in this chapter can help you effectively determine the correct answers to NBCOT® Domain 03 exam items about risk management.

Fieldwork Education

1. A key service management function is to develop, implement, and support clinical fieldwork education for OTA and OT students.
   a. ACOTE guidelines for Level I and Level II fieldwork education are to be followed.
   b. Supervisory qualifications and guidelines for fieldwork educators are provided in this chapter's section on OT practitioner roles and supervision.
2. Fieldwork education managerial tasks.
   a. Collaboration with the academic education program to develop specific fieldwork learning objectives and activities consistent with facility's and school's philosophies and missions.
   b. Development of professional development plans and activities for the students' clinical supervisors to ensure adequate fieldwork supervision.
   c. Establishment of departmental policies and procedures for a student program and its supervision.
   d. Assurance of quality care provided by student(s) according to established program standards and professional ethics.
   e. Evaluation and supervision of students' performance and completion of ACOTE's evaluation tool.
   f. Completion of cost-benefit analysis to collect data for institutional support of clinical education.

Professional Development

> **EXAM HINT:** The NBCOT® exam outline for the COTA® identifies the task of engaging "in professional development and competency assessment activities by using evidence-based strategies and approaches to provide safe, effective, and efficient services relevant to the job role, practice setting, scope of practice, and professional certification standards" (NBCOT®, 2018, p. 28) and knowledge of the "methods for identifying, documenting, and monitoring service competency and professional development needs based on scope of practice and certification standards for occupational therapy" (NBCOT®, 2018, p. 28) as essential for competent and safe practice. The application of knowledge about the following professional development activities can help you determine the correct answer for NBCOT® Domain 03 Upholding Professional Standards and Responsibilities exam items.

1. All OT practitioners have an ethical responsibility to engage in professional development activities that maintain and enhance their competence and ability to provide client-centered, occupation-based, and evidence-based practice.
2. Professional development activities are required to develop advanced and specialized knowledge and skills beyond entry-level competencies.
3. Supervisory feedback, peer review, and active self-reflection should be used to identify professional development needs and establish professional development goals.
4. Practitioners should seek and participate in professional development activities that are relevant to their practice setting, client population, job responsibilities, and professional goals.
   a. Activities can include (but are not limited to) facility-based training, active professional association membership and conference participation, continuing education workshops and/or online courses, independent study, professional presentations and publications, and research.
5. Professional development tools (PDTs) are available to guide the self-assessment of professional development needs and interests and develop a professional development plan.
6. Most state regulatory boards (SRBs) and the NBCOT® require evidence of participation in professional

development activities to maintain licensure and certification, respectively.
a. The amount and nature of these requirements vary between different jurisdictions.
(1) It is the practitioner's responsibility to ensure that all professional development requirements are fulfilled within the required time frame (e.g., every two to three years) and that all documentation (e.g., proof of continuing education units [CEUs]/professional development units [PDUs] earned) is available for review upon request by an SRB or the NBCOT®.
(a) The use of a professional portfolio is an effective means to track and document professional development activities.

References

Alexander, T. C. (October 20, 2003). Capital briefing: Members want to know. *OT Practice*, 7.

American Dietetic Association. (2005). *Scope of dietetics practice framework*. Chicago, IL: American Dietetic Association.

American Occupational Therapy Association. (2003). *Professional development tool*. Bethesda, MD: Author. Retrieved from https://www.aota.org/Education-Careers/Advance-Career/PDT.aspx

American Occupational Therapy Association. (2006). *The new IDEA: Summary of the Individuals with Disabilities Education Improvement Act of 2004* (P.L. 108–446). Bethesda, MD: Author.

American Occupational Therapy Association. (2010). Standards of practice for occupational therapy. *American Journal of Occupational Therapy, 64*(Suppl. 6), S106–S110.

American Occupational Therapy Association. (2014). Guidelines for supervision, roles, and responsibilities during the delivery of occupational therapy services. *American Journal of Occupational Therapy, 68*, S16-S22.

American Occupational Therapy Association. (2015a). Enforcement procedures for occupational therapy code of ethics and ethics standards. *American Journal of Occupational Therapy, 69*(Suppl. 3), 69(Supplement_3):6913410012p1-6913410012p13. doi: 10.5014/ajot.2015.696S19

American Occupational Therapy Association. (2015b). Occupational therapy code of ethics and ethics standards. *American Journal of Occupational Therapy, 69*(Suppl. 3), S1–S8.

American Occupational Therapy Association. (2015c). Standards for continuing competence. *American Journal of Occupational Therapy, 69*, 6913410055p1–6913410055p3. doi:10.5014/ajot.2015.696S16.

American Occupational Therapy Association. (2018). *Occupational therapy included in new law to address opioid epidemic*. Retrieved from https://www.aota.org/publications-news/otp/archive/2018/support-act.aspx

Amini, D., & Furniss, J. (2018, October). The Occupational Therapy Practice Framework: A foundation for documentation. *OT Practice*, CE-1–CE-8.

Bausch, M. E., Mittler, J. E., Hasselbring, T. S., & Cross, D. P. (2005). The Assistive Technology Act of 2004: What does it say and what does it mean? *Physical Disabilities: Education and Related Services, 23*(2), 59–67.

Bogenrief, J. (2019, January). New patient-driven groupings model will change HH PPS payment. *OT Practice, 24*(1), 10–11.Boyt Schell, B. A., & Gillen G. (Eds.). (2018). *Willard and Spackman's occupational therapy* (13th ed.). Baltimore, MD: Wolters Kluwer.

Braveman, B. (2006). *Leading and managing occupational therapy services*. Bethesda, MD: AOTA Press.

Case-Smith, J., & O'Brien, J. C. (Eds.). (2015). *Occupational therapy for children* (7th ed.). St. Louis, MO: Elsevier Mosby.

Centers for Medicare and Medicaid Services (CMS). (2009). *Medicaid benefit policy manual*. Washington, DC: Author.

Centers for Medicare and Medicaid Services. (2017a). *Medicare and home health care*. Retrieved from https://www.medicare.gov/Pubs/pdf/10969-Medicare-and-Home-Health-Care.pdf

Centers for Medicare and Medicaid Services. (2017b). *Medicare and your mental health benefits*. Retrieved from https://www.medicare.gov/sites/default/files/2018-07/10184-medicare-mental-health-bene.pdf

Chandler, B. (2008, January 21). School system special interest section. *OT Practice*, 25.

Clark, G. (2008). The infants and toddlers with disabilities program (Part C of IDEA). *OT Practice, 13*(1), CE-1–CE-8.

Clifton, D. (2004). Workers' comp: A plethora of opportunities. *Rehab Management, 32*, 34–36.

Department of Health and Human Services, Office of Inspector General. (2001). *Nursing home resident assessment: Resource utilization groups* (OEI-02-99-00041). Retrieved from https://www.oig.hhs.gov/oei/reports/oei-02-99-00041.pdf

Department of Training. (2001). *Training manual*. Trenton, NJ: Department of Health and Human Services.

Gennerman, M. (2005, May 9). CPT coding: Defining our practice. *OT Practice, 10*(8), 19–23.

Grossman, J., & Bortone, J. (2000). Program development. In R. P. Cottrell (Ed.). *Proactive approaches in psychosocial occupational therapy* (pp. 39–45). Thorofare, NJ: Slack.

Hussey, S., Sabonis-Chafee, B., & O'Brien, J. (2007). *Introduction to occupational therapy* (3rd ed.). St. Louis, MO: Elsevier Mosby.

International Center for Clubhouse Development. (1994). *Standards for clubhouse programs*. New York, Author.

Jacobs, K. (2000). Innovation to action: Marketing occupational therapy. In R. P. Cottrell (Ed.). *Proactive approaches in psychosocial occupational therapy* (pp. 505–507). Thorofare, NJ: Slack.

Jacobs, K., & Logigan, M. K. (1999). *Functions of a manager in occupational therapy* (3rd ed.). Thorofare, NJ: Slack.

Jimmo vs Sebelius settlement agreement fact sheet. (2013). Retrieved September 21, 2013 from http://www.cms.gov/Medicare/Medicare-Fee-for-Service-Payment/SNFPPS/Downloads/Jimmo-FactSheet.pdf

Job Accommodation Network. (2009). *Accommodation and compliance series: The ADA Amendments Act of 2008*. Morgantown, WV: Author.

Johnson, K. V. (2000, September). Home health PPS: The new payment system. *OT Practice*, CE1–CE8.

Kornblau, B. (2015, May). The Americans with Disabilities Act in 2015: Implications for practice. *OT Practice*, CE1-CE4.

Kornblau, B., & Burkhardt, A. (2012). *Ethics in rehabilitation: A clinical perspective* (2nd ed.). Thorofare, NJ: Slack.

Kyler, P. (Ed.). (2005). *Reference guide to the occupational therapy code of ethics*. Bethesda, MD: American Occupational Therapy Association.

Leary, D., & Mardirossian, J. (2000, Sept. 11). Ethical knowledge = collaborative power. *OT Practice*, 19–22.

McCormack, G., Jaffe, E., & Goodman-Lavey, M. (Eds.). (2003). *The occupational therapy manager* (4th ed.). Bethesda, MD: American Occupational Therapy Association.

Medcom. (2003). *HIPAA: A guide for health care workers*. Cypress, CA: Author.

Moyers, P., & Dale, L. (2007). *The guide to occupational therapy practice*. Bethesda, MD: American Occupational Therapy Association.

Murer, C. (2007, October). Psychiatric partial hospitalization: An overview. *Rehabilitation Management*, 48–49.

National Board for Certification in Occupational Therapy (NBCOT®). (2007, Fall/Winter). *Report to the profession*. Gaithersburg, MD: Author.

National Board for Certification in Occupational Therapy (NBCOT®). (2008). *Qualifications and compliance review information*. Gaithersburg, MD: Author.

National Board for Certification in Occupational Therapy (NBCOT®). (2018). *Practice analysis of the certified occupational therapy assistant: Executive summary*. Gaithersburg, MD: Author. Retrieved from https://www.nbcot.org/-/media/NBCOT/PDFs/2017-Practice-Analysis-Executive-COTA.ashx?la=en

National Council on Disability and National Urban League. (2000). *A guide to disability rights laws*. Washington, DC: Author.

Opp, A. (2007, September 27). Reauthorizing No Child Left Behind: Opportunities for OT. *OT Practice, 12(17)*, 9–13.

Ottenbacher, K. J., & Cusick, A. (1990). Goal attainment scaling as a method of clinical service evaluation. *American Journal of Occupational Therapy, 44*, 519–525.

Ryan, S., & Sladyk, K. (2005). *Ryan's occupational therapy assistant: Principles, practice issues, and techniques* (4th ed.). Thorofare, NJ: Slack.

Scaffa, M., & Reitz, M. (2014). *Occupational therapy in community-based practice settings* (2nd ed.). Philadelphia, PA: F.A. Davis.

Schindler, V. P. (2000). Occupational therapy in forensic psychiatry. In R. P. Cottrell (Ed.), *Proactive approaches in psychosocial occupational therapy* (pp. 319–325). Thorofare, NJ: Slack.

U.S. Government Printing Office. (2011). *Code of Federal Regulations*, Title 42, Volume 5. Retrieved from https://www.govinfo.gov/content/pkg/CFR-2011-title42-vol5/pdf/CFR-2011-title42-vol5.pdf

Vance, K., McGuire, M. J., & Nanof, T. (2009, August). Medicare coverage of occupational therapy in the home and community. *OT Practice, 14*, CE-1–CE-8.

Wilmarth, C. (2009, November 9). Using aides to provide therapy. *OT Practice, 14(20)*, 8.

Review Questions

Professional Standards and Responsibilities

Below are five questions about key content covered in this chapter. These questions are not inclusive of the entirety of content on occupational therapy professional standards and responsibilities that you must know for success on the COTA® exam. These questions are provided to help you jump-start the thought processes you will need to apply your studying of content to the answering of exam questions; hence they are not in the COTA® exam format. Exam items in the COTA® format which cover the depth and breadth of content you will need to know to pass the exam are provided on this text's online exams. The answers to the questions below are provided in Appendix 4.

1. You are working in a skilled nursing facility. Your supervising occupational therapist is on vacation. An administrator asks you to actively treat a new resident who is very frail with multiple medical complications. Upon admission, the occupational therapist had evaluated the resident and determined that the resident would not be able to tolerate occupational therapy services. During the evaluation, the resident had stated that chronic pain made all activities very difficult. Pain relief and rest were the only things the resident identified as personally desired. How should you respond to the administrator's request? Which principles of the AOTA Code of Ethics should you use to guide your response? Explain how these principles relate to this situation.

2. A large regional health care system provides occupational therapy services across the continuum of care. Settings in which occupational therapy services are provided include an acute care hospital, an outpatient clinic, a subacute rehabilitation unit, a skilled nursing facility (SNF), a palliative care unit, and a home health agency. All settings employ occupational therapists and occupational therapy assistants (OTA). What factors should be considered when determining the level of supervision that the OTA should receive from the occupational therapists? What is a key determinant for deciding if an OTA can ethically be given more responsibility?

3. An OTA is collaborating with an occupational therapist to start a private occupational therapy practice. What procedures should the OTA and therapist implement to ensure full compliance with the Health Insurance and Portability Accountability Act (HIPAA)?

4. You are beginning a new job as an OTA for a Medicare-certified home health agency. Most of your clients will be dependent or have limited independence in basic activities of daily living. What are key Medicare guidelines for home-based occupational therapy you must consider when working with these individuals and their caregivers?

5. An OTA is employed by a school system to provide direct services to students with disabilities under the supervision of an occupational therapist. The OTA's caseload includes middle and high school students. Which federal legislative mandates can help guide the OTA's interventions with these students? Describe major regulations and their relationship to the provision of school-based OT services.

5

Human Development Across the Lifespan: Considerations for Occupational Therapy Practice

MARGE E. MOFFETT BOYD, JAN G. GARBARINI, RITA P. FLEMING CASTALDY, MARLENE MORGAN, CHRISTINA GAVALAS, LINDA KAHN D'ANGELO, AND SUSAN B. O'SULLIVAN

Chapter Outline

- Development, 116
- Sensorimotor Development, 116
- Psychosocial Development and Major Theorists, 127
- Cognitive Development, 128
- Development of Play, 131
- Self-Care Development, 131
- Lifespan and Occupational Therapy Developmental Theorists, 135
- Child Abuse, 138
- Aging, 140
- Nutrition and Older Adults, 150
- Elder and Vulnerable Adult Abuse, 151
- References, 152
- Review Questions, 155

Development

Definition

1. Sequential changes in the function of the individual.
   a. Qualitative or quantitative.
   b. Influenced by biologic determinants and biopsychosocial environmental experiences.

> **EXAM HINT:** The NBCOT® exam outline for the certified occupational therapy assistant (COTA®) identifies knowledge of the "impact of typical development and aging on occupational performance, health, and wellness across the lifespan" (NBCOT®, 2018, p. 21) as essential for competent and safe practice. The application of knowledge about the developmental information provided in this chapter is required to correctly answer COTA® exam items about working with persons of all ages throughout the occupational therapy (OT) process.

Sensorimotor Development

Fetal Sensorimotor Development

1. Gestational age: age of the fetus or newborn, in weeks, from first day of mother's last normal menstrual period.
   a. Normal gestational period 38–42 weeks.
   b. Gestational period divided into three trimesters.
2. Conceptual age: age of a fetus or newborn in weeks since conception.
3. Refer to Table 5-1.

Development of Sensorimotor Integration

1. Prenatal period.
   a. Responds first to tactile stimuli.
   b. Reflex development.
   c. Innate tactile, proprioceptive, and vestibular reactions.
2. Neonatal period.
   a. Tactile, proprioceptive, and vestibular inputs are critical from birth onward for the eventual development of body scheme.
   b. Vestibular system, although fully developed at birth, continues to be refined and impacts the infant's arousal level.
      (1) Helps the infant to feel more organized and content.
   c. Visual system develops as infant responds to human faces and items of high contrast placed approximately 10 inches from the face.
   d. Auditory system is immature at birth and develops as the infant orients to voices and other sounds.
3. First 6 months.
   a. Vestibular, proprioceptive, and visual systems become more integrated and lay the foundation for postural control, which facilitates a steady visual field.
   b. Tactile and proprioceptive systems continue to be refined, laying the foundation for development of somatosensory skills.
   c. Visual and tactile systems become more integrated as the child reaches out and grasps objects, laying the foundation for eye-hand coordination.
   d. Infant movement patterns progress from reflexive to voluntary and goal directed.
4. 6 to 12 months.
   a. Vestibular, visual, and somatosensory responses increase in quantity and quality as the infant becomes more mobile.
   b. Tactile and proprioceptive perceptions become more refined, allowing for development of fine motor and motor planning skills.
   c. Tactile and proprioceptive responses also lead to midline skills and eventual crossing of midline.
   d. Auditory, tactile, and proprioceptive perception are heightened, allowing for development of sounds for the purpose of communication.

Table 5-1

Fetal Sensorimotor Development

	FIRST TRIMESTER	SECOND TRIMESTER	THIRD TRIMESTER
Muscle spindle	Muscle starts to differentiate Tissue becomes specialized	Motor end plate forms Clonus response to stretch	Some muscles are mature and functional, others still maturing
Touch and tactile system	First sensory system to develop Response to tactile stimulus	Receptors differentiate	Touch functional Actual temperature discrimination at the end of the third trimester Most mature sensory system at birth
Vestibular system	Functioning at the end of the first trimester (not completely developed)		
Vision	Eyelids fused Optic nerve and cup being formed	Startle to light Visual processing occurs	Fixation occurs Able to focus (fixed focal length)
Auditory		Will turn to auditory sounds	Debris in middle ear, loss of hearing
Olfactory			Nasal plugs disappear, some olfactory perception
Taste	Taste buds develop		Can respond to different tastes (sweet, sour, bitter, salt)
Movement	Sucking, hiccuping Fetal breathing Quick generalized limb movement Positional changes 7½ weeks; bend neck and trunk away from perioral stroke	Quickening Sleep states Grasp reflex Reciprocal and symmetrical limb movements	28 weeks, primitive motor reflexes Rooting, suck, swallow Palmar grasp Plantar grasp MORO Crossed extension

O'Sullivan, S. B., & Siegelman, R. P. (2013). *National Physical Therapy Examination Review and Study Guide* (p. 285). Evanston, IL: TherapyEd.

---

e. Tactile, proprioceptive, gustatory, and olfactory perception are integrated, allowing for primitive self-feeding.

5. 13 to 24 months.
   a. Tactile perception becomes more precise allowing for discrimination and localization to further refinement of fine motor skills.
   b. Further integration of all systems promotes complexity of motor planning as the toddler's repertoire of movement patterns expands.
   c. Symbolic gesturing and vocalization promote ideation, indicating the toddler's ability to conceptualize.
   d. Motor planning abilities contribute to self-concept as the toddler begins to master the environment.

6. 2 to 3 years.
   a. This is a period of refinement as the vestibular, proprioceptive, and visual systems further develop, leading to improved balance and postural control.
   b. Further development of tactile discrimination and localization lead to improved fine motor skills.
   c. Motor planning and praxis ideation also progress during this period for more skillful occupational performance.

7. 3 to 7 years.
   a. Child is driven to challenge sensorimotor competencies through roughhouse play, playground activities, games, sports, music, dancing, arts and crafts, household chores, and school tasks.

(1) These activities provide opportunities to promote social development and self-esteem.

Reflex Development and Integration

1. Predictable motor response elicited by tactile, proprioceptive, or vestibular stimulation.
2. Primitive reflexes are present at or just after birth and typically integrate throughout the first year.
3. The persistence or re-emergence of these primitive reflexes are indicative of central nervous system (CNS) dysfunction that may interfere with motor milestone attainment, patterns of movement, musculoskeletal alignment, and function.
4. Refer to Tables 5-2 and 5-3 for reflex timetables, stimulus, response, and functional significance.
5. Refer to Figures 5-1 through 5-9 for pictures of some key reflexes.

EXAM HINT: The developmental sequence for sensorimotor integration and reflex development and integration described above and the following information about motor development provides foundational knowledge for answering COTA® exam items about working with children with typical and atypical sensorimotor development.

Table 5-2
Reflexes that Integrate During Typical Development

REFLEX	STIMULUS	RESPONSE	FUNCTIONAL SIGNIFICANCE	ONSET AGE	INTEGRATION AGE
Rooting	Stroke the corner of the mouth, upper lip, and lower lip	Movement of the tongue, mouth, and/or head during the stimulus	Helps the baby locate the feeding source to begin feeding	28 weeks' gestation	3 months
Suck-swallow	Place examiner's index finger inside infant's mouth with head in midline	Strong, rhythmical sucking	Facilitates nutritive sucking for the ingestion of liquid	28 weeks' gestation	2–5 months
Traction	Grasp infant's forearms and pull-to-sit	Complete flexion of upper extremities	Promotes momentary grasp to enable the child to hold onto mother when being pulled	28 weeks' gestation	2–5 months
Moro	Rapidly drop infant's head backward	First phase: arm extension/abduction, hand opening. Second phase: arm flexion and adduction	Protective response to 'stress;' helps develop extensor tone during a period when flexor tone is dominant	28 weeks' gestation	4–6 months
Plantar grasp	Apply pressure with thumb on the infant's ball of the foot	Toe flexion	Increases input to sole of foot; integration is associated with readiness for independent gait	28 weeks' gestation	9 months
Galant	Hold infant in prone suspension, gently scratch or tap alongside the spine with finger, from shoulders to buttocks	Lateral trunk flexion and wrinkling of the skin on the stimulated side	Enhances trunk stabilization by facilitating lateral trunk movement	32 weeks' gestation	2 months
Asymmetric tonic neck	Fully rotate infant's head and hold for 5 seconds	Extension of extremities on the face side, flexion of extremities on the skull side	Promotes visual attention to upper extremity; decreases incidence of rolling	37 weeks' gestation	4–6 months
Palmar grasp	Place a finger in infant's palm	Finger flexion; reflexive grasp	Increases palmar tactile input; prepares muscles for voluntary grasp	37 weeks' gestation	4–6 months
Tonic labyrinthine - Supine	Place infant in supine	Increased extensor tone	Facilitates full-body extensor tone; allows posture to adapt to that of the head	>37 weeks' gestation	6 months
Tonic labyrinthine - Prone	Place infant in prone	Increased flexor tone	Facilitates full-body flexor tone; allows posture to adapt to that of the head	>37 weeks' gestation	6 months
Landau	Hold infant in horizontal prone suspension	Complete extension of head, trunk, and extremities	Regulates tone; promotes prone extension to manage flexor tone	3–4 months	12–24 months
Symmetric tonic neck	Place infant in the crawling position and extend the head	Flexion of hips and knees	Facilitates quadruped position in preparation for crawling; breaks up total-body extension	4–6 months	8–12 months
Neck righting (on body) (NOB)	Place infant in supine and fully turn head to one side	Log rolling of the entire body to maintain alignment with the head	Facilitates rolling; maintains body orientation in response to cervical position changes	4–6 months	5 years
Body righting (on body) (BOB)	Place infant in supine, flex one hip and knee toward the chest and hold briefly	Segmental rolling of the upper trunk to maintain alignment	Promotes trunk and spinal rotation to facilitate sitting and quadruped positions	4–6 months	5 years

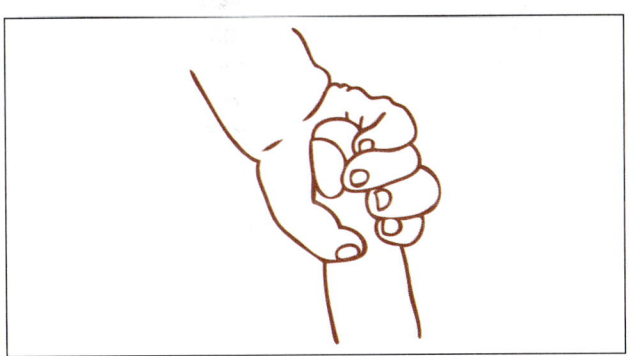

Sensorimotor Development 119

Figure 5-1 Palmar Grasp Reflex.
Groenweghe, Marisa with permission.

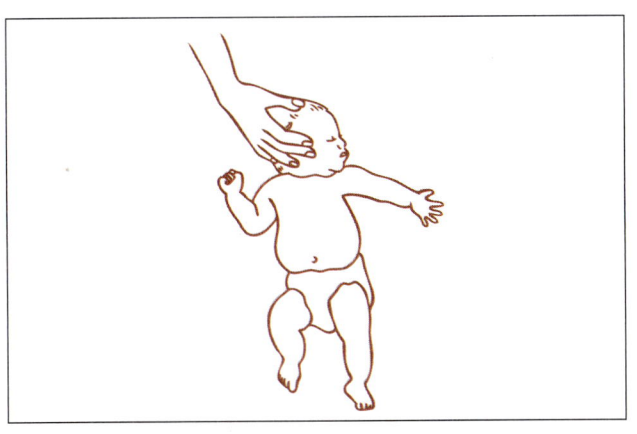

Figure 5-2 Asymmetric Tonic Neck Reflex (ATNR).
Groenweghe, Marisa with permission.

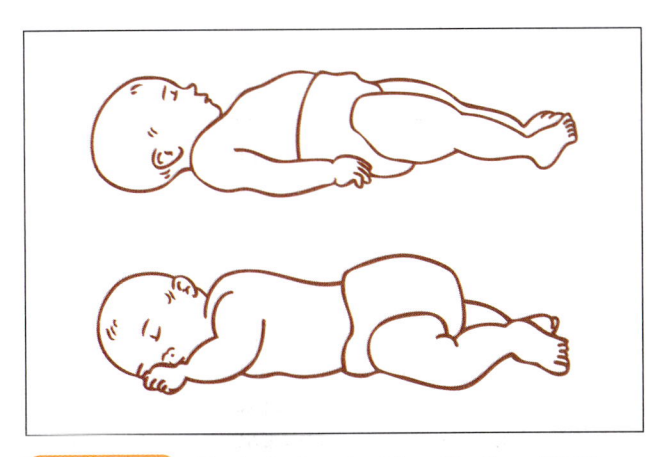

Figure 5-3 Tonic Labyrinthine Reflex (TLR).
Groenweghe, Marisa with permission.

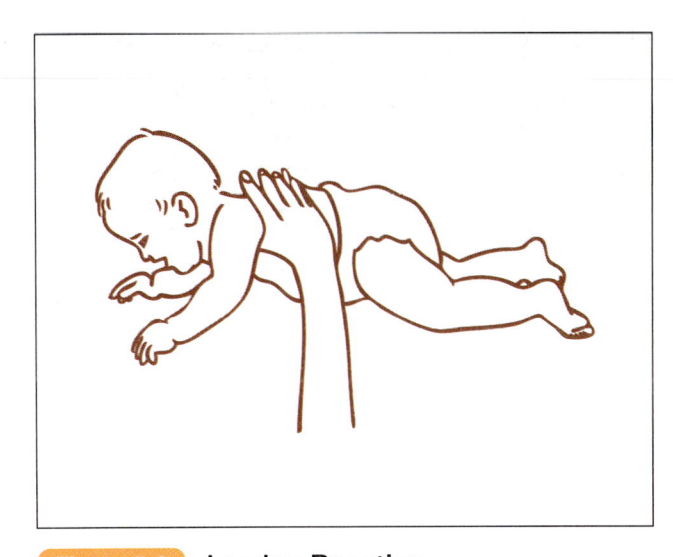

Figure 5-4 Landau Reaction.
Groenweghe, Marisa with permission.

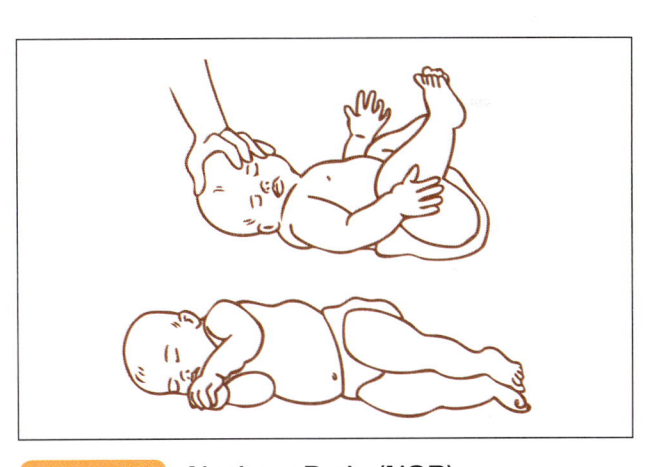

Figure 5-5 Neck on Body (NOB).
Groenweghe, Marisa with permission.

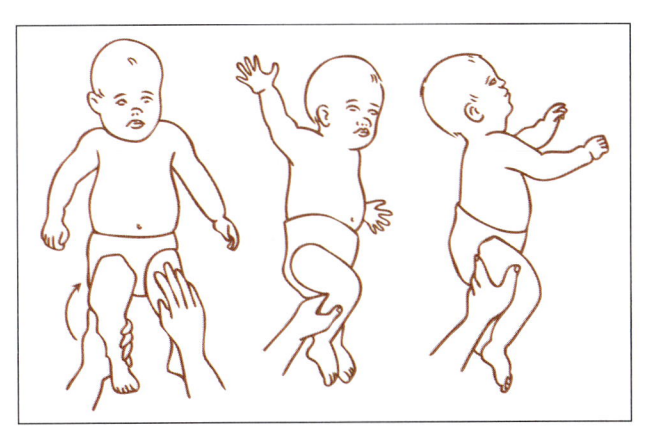

Figure 5-6 Body Righting Reaction on Body (BOB).
Groenweghe, Marisa with permission.

Table 5-3

Reflexes that Persist Throughout Life

REFLEX	STIMULUS	RESPONSE	FUNCTIONAL SIGNIFICANCE	ONSET AGE
Labyrinthine/optical (head) righting	Hold infant suspended vertically and tilt slowly (about 45°) to the side, forward, or backward	Upright positioning of the head	Basis for head management and postural stability; orients head in space vertically	Birth–2 months
Downward parachute (protective extension downward)	Rapidly lower infant toward supporting surface while suspended vertically	Extension of the lower extremities	Prepares lower extremities for surface contact (i.e., standing); breaks a fall	4 months
Forward parachute (protective extension forward)	Suddenly tip infant forward toward supporting surface while vertically suspended	Sudden extension of the upper extremities, hand opening, and neck extension	Places upper extremities in anticipation of surface contact to break a fall; supports prop sitting	6–9 months
Sideward parachute (protective extension sideward)	Quickly but firmly tip infant off-balance to the side while in the sitting position	Arm extension and abduction to the side	Unilaterally supports body for use of opposite arm; prevents falls	7 months
Backward parachute (protective extension backward)	Quickly but firmly tip infant off-balance backward	Backward arm extension or arm extension to one side spinal rotation	Protects from backwards falls	9–10 months
Prone tilting	After positioning infant in prone, slowly raise one side of the supporting surface	Curving of the spine toward the raised side (opposite to the pull of gravity); abduction/extension of arms and legs	Facilitates postural adjustments to maintain center of gravity	5 months
Supine tilting and Sitting tilting	After positioning infant in supine or sitting, slowly raise one side of the supporting surface	Curving of the spine toward the raised side (opposite to the pull of gravity); abduction/extension of arms and legs	Facilitates postural adjustments to maintain center of gravity; promotes sitting balance	7–8 months
Quadruped tilting	After positioning infant on all fours, slowly raise one side of the supporting surface	Curving of the spine toward the raised side (opposite to the pull of gravity); abduction/extension of arms and legs	Facilitates postural adjustments to maintain center of gravity and preserve positioning in quadruped	9–12 months
Standing tilting	After positioning infant in standing, slowly raise one side of the supporting surface	Curving of the spine toward the raised side (opposite to the pull of gravity); abduction/extension of arms and legs	Facilitates postural adjustments to maintain center of gravity and balance during standing and walking	12–21 months

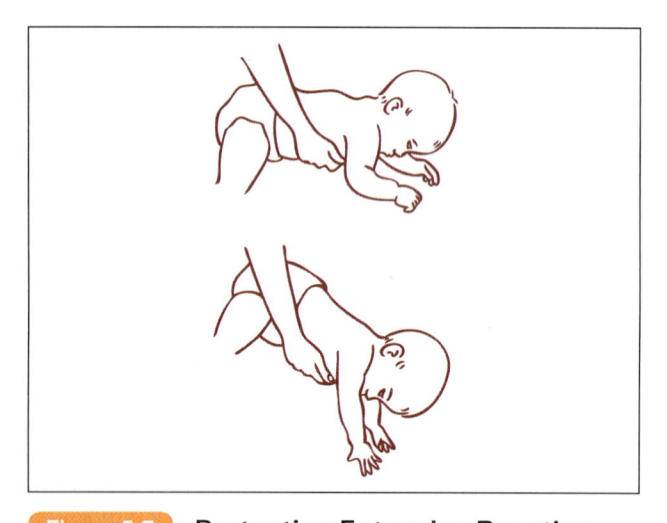

Figure 5-7 Protective Extension Reaction Forward.

Groenweghe, Marisa with permission.

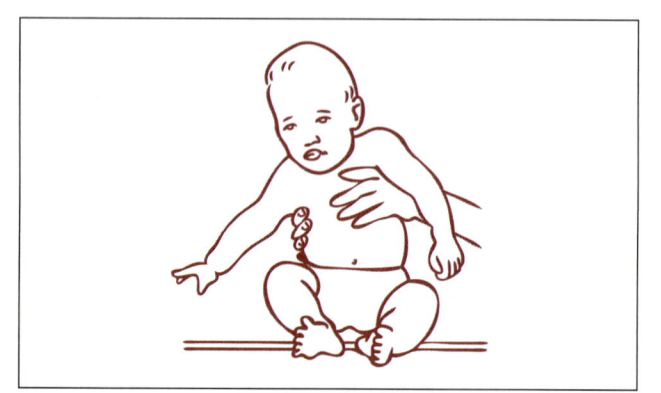

Figure 5-8 Protective Extension Reaction Sideward.

Groenweghe, Marisa with permission.

Figure 5-9 Protective Extension Reaction Backward.

Groeneweghe, Marisa with permission.

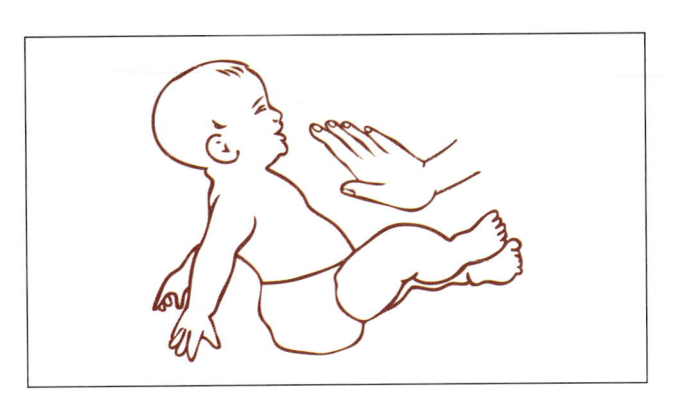

Motor Development

1. Performance of occupational roles can be enhanced or inhibited based on the reflex development and integration noted previously and in additional areas noted as follows.
   a. Crossing the midline: as the child becomes more mobile, movement against gravity and weight-shift increase, leading to eventual crossing of the midline, often in an attempt to reach for a toy, while weight bearing on the opposing upper extremity for balance (begins at 9–12 months).
   b. Laterality: hemispheric specialization for specific tasks varies with different individuals (e.g., handedness is considered to be stable by age 5; however, strong preferences can be seen much earlier).
   c. Bilateral integration: as the child experiments with movement, the nervous system is stimulated, and the resulting sensations help the child to coordinate the two sides of the body (begins at 9–12 months).
   d. Fine motor coordination and dexterity. (See subsequent section on development of hand skills.)
   e. Visual-motor integration is dependent upon the lower level skills of visual attention, visual memory, visual discrimination, kinesthesia, position in space, figure ground, form constancy, and spatial relations.
   f. Oral-motor control, which is developed in the area of feeding, provides the foundation for early oral communication and later language development.
2. General principles of motor development.
   a. Occurs in a cephalocaudal/proximal to distal direction.
   b. Progresses from gross to fine motor movement.
   c. Progresses from stability to controlled mobility.
   d. Occurs in a spiraling manner, with periods of equilibrium and disequilibrium.
   e. Sensitive periods occur when the infant/child is affected by environmental input.
3. Normal sensorimotor development in key positions. See Tables 5-4 and 5-5.
4. Important aspects in the development of upper extremity function.
   a. Head and trunk control.
   b. Eye/hand interaction/sensory-perceptual interaction.
   c. Shoulder-scapular stability/mobility.
   d. Humeral control.
   e. Elbow control.
   f. Forearm control.
   g. Wrist control.
   h. Thumb opposition and stability.
   i. Palmar arches of hand.
   j. Isolated finger control.
5. Important components in the development of hand skills.
   a. Reaching skills.
      (1) Visual regard accompanied by swiping/batting, with closed hand and abducted shoulder (newborn).
      (2) Hands come together at midline for bilateral reaching with shoulders abducted with partial internal rotation, forearm pronation, and full finger extension (4 months).
      (3) Increased dissociation of body sides allows for unilateral reaching with less abduction and internal rotation of the shoulder, and the hand is more open (6 months).
      (4) As trunk stability improves, shoulder flexion with slight external rotation, elbow extension, forearm supination, and slight wrist extension begin to emerge (9 months).
   b. Grasping skills according to Erhardt Prehension Developmental Levels.
      (1) Grasp of the pellet (prone or sitting).
         (a) No voluntary grasp or visual attention to the object (natal).
         (b) No attempt to grasp, but visually attends to the object (3 months).
         (c) Raking and contacting object (6 months).
         (d) Inferior-scissors grasp: raking object into palm with adducted totally flexed thumb and all flexed fingers, or two partially extended fingers (7 months).
         (e) Scissors grasp: between thumb and side of curled index finger, distal thumb joint slightly flexed, proximal thumb joint extended (8 months).
         (f) Inferior pincer grasp: between ventral surfaces of thumb and index finger, distal thumb joint extended, beginning of thumb opposition (9 months).

Table 5-4

Sensorimotor Development Mobility and Stability

AGE	GROSS MOTOR SKILL
Prone Position	
0–2 months	Turns head side to side Lifts head momentarily Bends hips with bottom in air Lifts head and sustains in midline Rotates head freely when up Able to bear weight on forearms Able to tuck chin and gaze at hands in forearm prop Attempts to shift weight on forearms, resulting in shoulder collapse
5–6 months	Shifts weight on forearms and reaches forward Bears weight and shifts weight on extended arms Legs are closer together and thighs roll inward toward natural alignment Hips are flat on surface Equilibrium reactions are present
5–8 months	Airplane posturing in prone position; chest and thighs lift off surface
7–8 months	Pivots in prone position Moves from prone position to sit
9 months	Begins to dislike prone position
Supine Position	
0–3 months	Head held to one side Able to turn head side to side
3–4 months	Holds head in midline Chin is tucked and neck lengthens in back Legs come together Lower back flattens against the floor
4–5 months	Head lag is gone when pulled to a sitting position Hands are together in space
5–6 months	Lifts head independently Brings feet to mouth Brings hands to feet Able to reach for toy with one or both hands Hands are predominantly open
7–8 months	Equilibrium reactions are present
Rolling	
3–4 months	Rolls from prone position to side accidentally because of poor control of weight shift Rolls from supine position to side
5–6 months	Rolls from prone to supine position Rolls from supine position to side with right and left leg performing independent movements Rolls from supine to prone position with right and left leg performing independent movements
6–14 months	Rolls segmentally with roll initiated by the head, shoulder, or hips

Table 5-4

Sensorimotor Development Mobility and Stability (Continued)

AGE	GROSS MOTOR SKILL
Creeping	
7 months	Crawls forward on belly
7–10 months	Reciprocal creep
10–11 months	Creeps on hands and feet
11–12 months	Creeps well
Sitting	
0–3 months (held in sitting)	Head bobs in sitting Back is rounded Hips are apart, turned out, and bent Head is steady Chin tucks; able to gaze at floor Sits with less support Hips are bent and shoulders are in front of hips
5–6 months (supports self in sitting)	Sits alone momentarily Increased extension in back Sits by propping forward on arms Wide base, legs are bent Periodic use of "high guard" position Protective responses present when falling to the front
5–10 months (sits alone)	Sits alone steadily, initially with wide base of support Able to play with toys in sitting position
6–11 months	Gets to sitting position from prone position
7–8 months	Equilibrium reactions are present Able to rotate upper body while lower body remains stationary Protective responses are present when falling to the side
8–10 months	Sits well without support Legs are closer; full upright position, knees straight Increased variety of sitting positions, including "w" sit and side sit Difficult fine motor tasks may prompt return to wide base of support
9–18 months	Rises from supine position by first rolling over to stomach then pushing up into four-point position
10–12 months	Protective extension backwards, first with bent elbows then straight elbows Able to move in and out of sitting position into other positions
11–12 months	Trunk control and equilibrium responses are fully developed in sitting position Further increase in variety of positions possible
11–24 months +	Rises from supine by first rolling to side then pushing up into sitting position

Table 5-4

Sensorimotor Development Mobility and Stability (Continued)

AGE	GROSS MOTOR SKILL
Standing	
0–3 months	When held in standing position, takes some weight on legs
2–3 months	When held in standing position, legs may give way
3–4 months	Bears some weight on legs, but must be held proximally Head is up in midline, no chin tuck Pelvis and hips are behind shoulders Legs are apart and turned outward
5–10 months	Stands while holding onto furniture
5–6 months	Increased capability to bear weight Decreased support needed; may be held by arms or hands Legs are still spread apart and turned outward Bounces in standing position
6–12 months	Pulls to standing position at furniture
8–9 months	Rotates the trunk over the lower extremities Lower extremities are more active in pulling to a standing position Pulls to a standing position by kneeling, then half-kneeling
9–13 months	Pulls to standing position with legs only, no longer needs arms Stands alone momentarily
12 months	Equilibrium reactions are present in standing
Walking	
8 months	Cruises sideways
8–18 months	Walks with two hands held
9–10 months	Cruises around furniture, turning slightly in intended direction
9–17 months	Takes independent steps, falls easily
10–14 months	Walking: stoops and recovers in play
11 months	Walks with one hand held Reaches for furniture out of reach when cruising Cruises in either direction, no hesitation
15 months	Able to start and stop in walking
18 months	Seldom falls Runs stiffly with eyes on ground
Release	
0–1 months	No release; grasp reflex is strong
1–4 months	Involuntary release
4 months	Mutual fingering in midline
4–8 months	Transfers object from hand to hand
5–6 months	Two-stage transfer; taking hand grasps before releasing hand lets go

Table 5-4

Sensorimotor Development Mobility and Stability (Continued)

AGE	GROSS MOTOR SKILL
Release (cont.)	
6–7 months	One-stage transfer; taking hand and releasing hand perform actions simultaneously
7–9 months	Volitional release
7–10 months	Presses down on surface to release
8 months	Releases above a surface with wrist flexion
9–10 months	Releases into a container with wrist straight
10–14 months	Clumsy release into small container; hand rests on edge of container
12–15 months	Precise, controlled release into small container with wrist extended

Modified from Bly, L. (1993). *Normal development in the first year of life.* Tucson, AZ: Therapy Skill Builders; Illingworth, R. S. (1991). *The normal child: Some problems of the early years and their treatment* (10th ed.). Edinburgh: Churchill-Livingstone; Knobloch, H., & Pasamanick, B. (1974). *Gesell and Amatruda's developmental diagnosis: The evaluation and management of normal and abnormal neuropsychological development in infancy and early childhood.* Hagerstown, MD: Harper and Row; Gilfoyle, E., Grady, A., & Moore, J. (1990). *Children adapt.* Thorofare, NJ: Slack.

Reference: Case-Smith, J., Allen, A. S., & Pratt, P. N. (1996). *Occupational therapy for children* (3rd ed., pp. 49–50). St. Louis, MO: Mosby-Year Book. Reprinted with permission.

(g) Pincer grasp: between distal pads of thumb and index finger, distal thumb joint slightly flexed, thumb opposed (10 months).
(h) Fine pincer grasp: between fingertips or fingernails, distal thumb joint flexed (12 months).
(i) Refer to Figure 5-10.
(2) Grasp of the cube.
  (a) Neonate visually attends to object, grasp is reflexive.
  (b) Infant visually attends to object and may swipe. Sustained voluntary grasp possible only upon contact, ulnar side used, no thumb involvement, wrist flexed (3 months).
  (c) Primitive squeeze grasp: the infant visually attends to object, approaches it if within 1 inch, contact results in hand pulling object back to squeeze precariously against the other hand or body, no thumb involvement (4 months).
  (d) Between 4 and 5 months the infant begins to progress toward a palmar grasp, the

Table 5-5

Development of Stair Climbing and Jumping/Hopping Skills

AGE	SKILL
Stair Climbing	
15 months	Creeps up stairs
18–24 months	Walks up stairs while holding on Walks down stairs while holding on
18–23 months	Creeps backwards down stairs
2–2½+ years	Walks up stairs without support, marking time Walks down stairs without support, marking time
2–2½–3 years	Walks up stairs, alternating feet
3–3½ years	Walks down stairs, alternating feet
Jumping and Hopping	
2 years	Jumps down from step
2½+ years	Hops on one foot, few steps
3 years	Jumps off floor with both feet
3–5 years	Jumps over objects
3½–5 years	Hops on one foot
3–4 years	Gallops, leading with one foot and transferring weight smoothly and evenly
5 years	Hops in straight line
5–6 years	Skips on alternating feet, maintaining balance

Modified from Gesell, A., & Amatruda, C. S. (1947). *Developmental diagnosis*. New York, NY: Harper and Row; Bayley, N. (1993). *Bayley scales of infant development* (rev. ed.). New York, NY: Psychological Corporation; Knobloch, H. & Pasamanick, B. (1974). *Gesell and Amatruda's developmental diagnosis: The evaluation and management of normal and abnormal neuropsychological development in infancy and early childhood*. Hagerstown, MD: Harper and Row.
Reference: Case-Smith, J., Allen, A. S., & Pratt, P. N. (1996). *Occupational therapy for children* (3rd ed., p. 59). St. Louis, MO: Mosby-Year Book. Reprinted with permission.

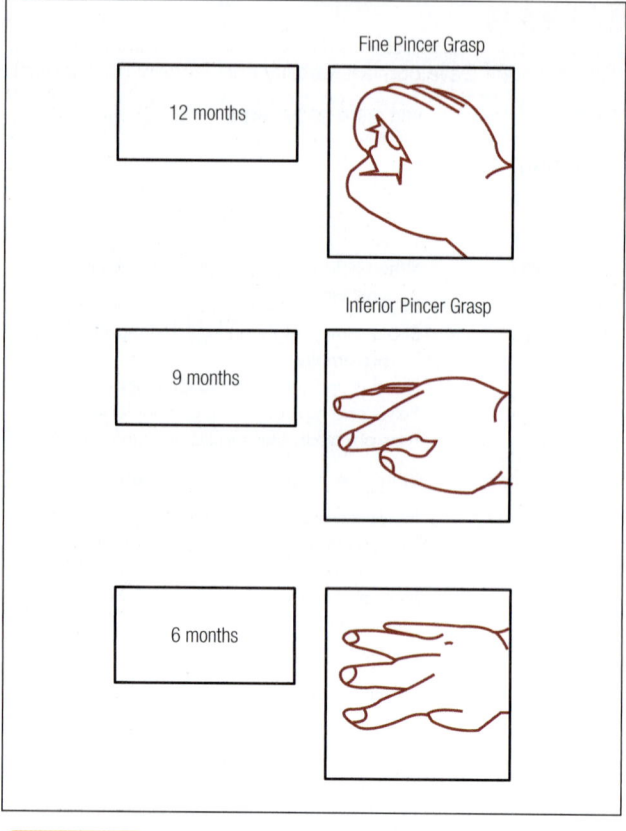

Figure 5-10 Developmental Levels: Grasp of the Pellet.

Illustrations from *The Erhardt Developmental Prehension Assessment*, copyright 1994 by Rhoda P. Erhardt. Published by Erhardt Developmental Products, 2379 Snowshoe Court, Maplewood, MN 55119, (651) 730-9004. Reprinted with permission.

infant's thumb begins to adduct with fingers pressed against the ulnar side of the palm, progressing in the direction of the center of the palm toward a palmar grasp. This is sometimes referred to as an ulnar-palmar grasp.
  (e) Palmar grasp: fingers on top surface of object press it into center of palm with thumb adducted (5 months).
  (f) Radial-palmar grasp: fingers on far side of object press it against opposed thumb and radial side of palm (6 months), with wrist straight (7 months).
  (g) Radial-digital grasp: object held with the opposed thumb and fingertips, space visible between (8 months) with wrist extended (9 months).
  (h) Refer to Figure 5-11.
 c. Mature grasping skills are needed to complete functional activities.
  (1) Grasp patterns are described according to the need to use precision and power to perform a task.
  (2) See Table 5-6.
 d. Releasing skills: initially, involuntary dropping, then object is pulled out of one hand by the other hand. See Table 5-4.
  (1) Development progresses from no release (0–1 month) to involuntary release (1–4 months) to two-stage transfer (5–6 months) to one-stage transfer (6–7 months) to voluntary release (7–9 months).
  (2) By 9 months, release by full arm extension.
  (3) Refinement continues up to age 4 years with the attainment of graded release.

Table 5-6

Mature Grasping Patterns Used in Functional Activities

GRASP PATTERN	FUNCTIONALITY	DESCRIPTION
Power grasp	Used to control tools or other objects. Used with hand strength is required in activity	The object is help obliquely in the hand; ulnar fingers are flexed; radial fingers are less flexed. Thumb is in extension and adduction. The child stabilizes the object with the ulnar side of the hand and controls the object using the radial side of the hand.
Hook grasp	Used to carry objects such as a purse or briefcase	The transverse metacarpal arch is flat; the fingers are adducted with flexion at the interphalangeal (IP) joints. The metacarpophalangeal (MCP) joints may be flexed or extended.
Spherical grasp	Used to hold a small ball	The wrist is extended, fingers abducted, with some flexion at the MCP and IP joints. Stability of the longitudinal arch is needed to use this pattern to grasp a larger ball. The hypothenar eminence assists in cupping the hand for control of the object.
Cylindrical grasp	Used to hold a glass, cup, or can with hand around the object	The transverse arch is flattened to allow the fingers to hold against the object. The fingers are only slightly abducted, and IP and MCP joint flexion is graded according to the size of the object. When additional force is required, more of the palmar surface of the hand contacts the object.
Disk grasp	Used to hold a disk such as a jar lid	Thee fingers hold the disk with extension of the MCP joints and flexion of the IP joints. The wrist flexes and thumb extends when objects are larger, and only the pads of the fingers contact the object. This pattern involves dissociation of flexion and extension movements and use of a combination of wrist flexion with MCP extension and IP flexion.
Lateral pinch	Used to exert power on or with a small object	The index finger is slightly flexed and the thumb is flexed and adducted. The pad of the thumb is placed against the radial side of the index finger at or near the distal interphalangeal (DIP) joint.
Pincer grasp	Used to hold and handle small objects and precision tools (e.g., a pencil)	The thumb is opposed to the index finger pad and the object is held within the finger pads. The ulnar fingers are often flexed.
Three-jaw chuck or tripod grasp	Used to hold and manipulate a writing utensil or eating utensil	The thumb is simultaneously opposed to the index and middle finger pads. These fingers provide stability for prehension of a tool. The thumb forms an oval or modified oval shape with the fingers. When using a tripod grasp on a tool, the forearm is slightly supinated.
Tip pinch	Used to prehend and hold tiny objects	The thumb is opposed with thumb tip meeting index finger tip, forming a circle. All joints of the index finger and thumb are partly flexed.

Reference: Case-Smith, J., & Exner, C. E. (2015). Hand function evaluation and intervention. In J. Case-Smith, & J. C. O'Brien (Eds.), *Occupational therapy for children and adolescents* (7th ed., p. 224). St. Louis, MO: Elsevier.

---

e. Carrying skills: involves a combination of movements of the shoulder, body, and distal joints of the wrist and hand to hold the item, making appropriate adjustments as necessary to maintain this hold.

f. Bilateral hand use: asymmetric movements prevail until 3 months, and then symmetric movements emerge until 10 months.
  (1) By 12–18 months, the baby uses both hands for different functions.
  (2) At 18–24 months, manipulation skills emerge.
  (3) At 2½ years, the ability to use two different hands for two very different functions emerges.

g. Manipulating skills according to Exner's Classification System.
  (1) Finger-to-palm translation: a linear movement of an object from the fingers to the palm of the hand, e.g., picking up coins (12–15 months).
  (2) Palm-to-finger translation: with stabilization, a linear movement of an object from the palm of the hand to the fingers, e.g., placing coins in a slot (2–2½ years).
  (3) Shift: a linear movement of an object by the fingers allow for repositioning of the object relative to the finger pads, e.g., separating two pieces of paper (3–5 years), rolling a piece of clay into a ball (3–6+ years), shifting on marker or pencil (5–6+ years).
  (4) Simple rotation: the turning or rolling of an object held at the finger pads approximately 90° or less, e.g., unscrewing a small bottle cap (2–2½ years).
  (5) Complex rotation: the rotation of an object 360°, e.g., turning a pencil over to erase (6–7 years).
  (6) In-hand manipulation with stabilization: several objects are held in the hand and manipulation of one object occurs, while simultaneously stabilizing the others, e.g., picking up pennies

with thumb and forefinger while storing them in the ulnar side of the same hand (6–7 years).
h. Pre-writing skills.
(1) Palmar-supinate grasp: writing tool held with fisted hand, wrist slightly flexed and slightly supinated away from mid-position; arm moves as a unit (1–1½ years).
(2) Digital-pronate grasp: writing tool held with fingers, wrist neutral with slight ulnar deviation, and forearm pronated; arm moves as a unit (2–3 years).
(3) Static tripod posture: writing tool held with crude approximation of thumb, index, and middle fingers, ring and little fingers only slightly flexed, grasped proximally with continual adjustments by other hand, no fine localized movements of digit components; hand moves as a unit (3½–4 years).
(4) Dynamic tripod posture: writing tool held with precise opposition of distal phalanges of thumb, index, and middle fingers, ring and little fingers flexed to form a stable arch, wrist slightly extended, grasped distally, MCP joints stabilized during fine, localized movements of PIP joints (4½–6 years).
(5) Refer to Figure 5-12.

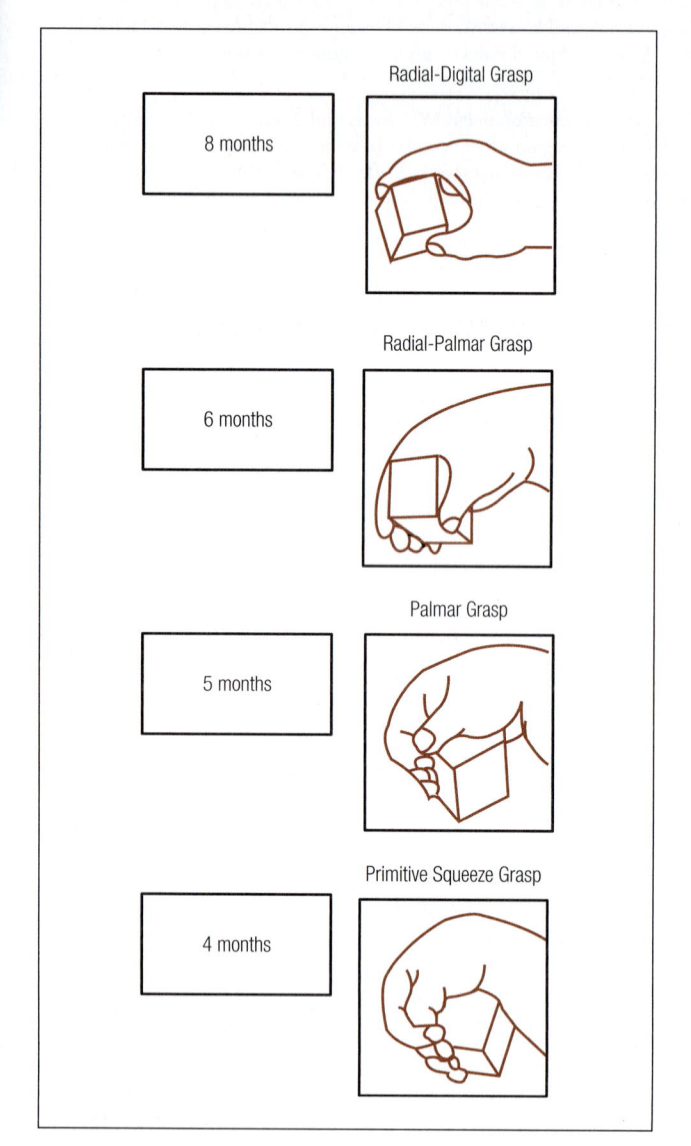

Figure 5-11 Developmental Levels: Grasp of the Cube.

Illustrations from *The Erhardt Developmental Prehension Assessment*, copyright 1994 by Rhoda P. Erhardt. Published by Erhardt Developmental Products, 2379 Snowshoe Court, Maplewood, MN 55119, (651) 730-9004. Reprinted by permission.

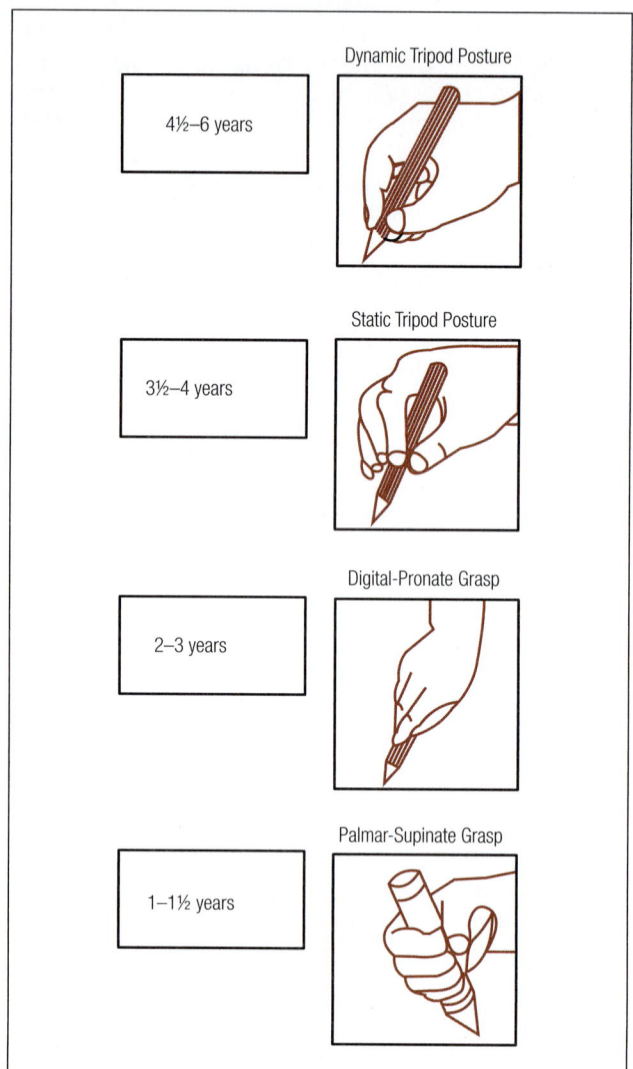

Figure 5-12 Developmental Levels: Prewriting Skills.

Illustrations from *The Erhardt Developmental Prehension Assessment*, copyright 1994 by Rhoda P. Erhardt. Published by Erhardt Developmental Products, 2379 Snowshoe Court, Maplewood, MN 55119, (651) 730-9004. Reprinted by permission.

i. Scissor use skills.
   (1) Prerequisite skills for using scissors include the ability to:
      (a) Open and close a hand.
      (b) Isolate or combine the movements of the thumb, index, and middle fingers.
      (c) Use hands bilaterally; one hand cuts using the scissors, while the other hand stabilizes the item being cut.
      (d) Coordinate arm, hand, and eye movements.
      (e) Stabilize the wrist, elbow, and shoulder joints so that movement can occur at the distal joints.
      (f) Interact with the environment in the constructive developmental play stage.
   (2) Stages of development in scissor use, the child sequentially:
      (a) Shows an interest in scissors (2–3 years).
      (b) Holds and snips with scissors (2–3 years).
      (c) Opens and closes scissors in a controlled fashion (2–3 years).
      (d) Manipulates scissors in a forward motion (3–4 years).
      (e) Coordinates the lateral direction of the scissors (3–4 years).
      (f) Cuts a straight, forward line (3–4 years).
      (g) Cuts simple geometric shapes (3–4 years).
      (h) Cuts circles (3½–4½ years).
      (i) Cuts simple figure shapes (4–6 years).
      (j) Cuts complex figure shapes (6–7 years).

Psychosocial Development and Major Theorists

Overview

EXAM HINT: The COTA® exam will likely not ask specific questions about psychosocial developmental theories. However, the application of knowledge about lifespan psychological theories can help determine a developmentally correct answer to COTA® exam items about working with persons across the lifespan. For example, knowing that the typical crisis experienced during the teen years, as described by Erikson, is self-identity versus role confusion can be relevant to answering a question about an OTA collaborating with an occupational therapist to develop a transition program in a high school. An answer choice that includes an exploration of students' unique interests and personal aspirations would be correct. Similarly, the application of Maslow's hierarchy of needs can help you determine the correct answer to an exam item about an OTA working with an occupational therapist to design a program in a homeless shelter. According to Maslow, the program should first focus on meeting the participants' physiological and safety needs. Subsequent interventions would address participants' love, belonging, and self-esteem needs followed by referrals to resources and programs that would support the attainment of self-actualization.

1. Occupational therapy practitioners need to know and understand maturation, which is dependent on biological processes.
   a. These stages of development influence an individual's occupational performance.
2. Developmental psychological theories contribute to, but are not sufficient to understand, the complexity involved in human occupational performance.

Erik Erikson

1. Ego adaptation is the adaptive response of the ego in the development of the personality.
2. Eight stages of individuals' development are identified including a critical personal-social crisis that, when resolved, gives individuals a sense of mastery and results in the acquisition of personality qualities.
   a. Stage 1. Basic trust versus mistrust: infants/toddlers realize that survival and comfort needs will be met; hope is integrated into their personalities (birth–18 months).
   b. Stage 2. Autonomy versus doubt and shame: children realize that they can control bodily functions; self-controlled will is integrated into their personalities (2–4 years).
   c. Stage 3. Initiative versus guilt: children gain social skills and gender role identities; a sense of purpose is integrated into their personalities (preschool age).
   d. Stage 4. Industry versus inferiority: children gain a sense of security through peers and gain mastery over activities of their age group; a feeling of competency is integrated into their personalities (elementary school age).
   e. Stage 5. Self-identity versus role confusion: teenagers begin to make choices about adult roles, and with resolution of this identity crisis comes a sense

of fidelity or membership with society, which is integrated into their personalities (teenage years).
  f. Stage 6. Intimacy and solidarity versus isolation: young adults establish intimate relationships with a partner and family; the capacity to love is achieved (young adulthood).
  g. Stage 7. Generativity versus self-absorption: adults find security in the contribution of their chosen personal/professional roles; the capacity to care is achieved (middle adulthood).
  h. Stage 8. Integrity versus despair: mature adults reflect on their own values and share with the younger generation the knowledge gained; wisdom is acquired (maturity, older adulthood).

Lawrence Kohlberg

1. Stages of moral development.
   a. Level 1. Preconventional morality: occurs up until the age of 8 years.
      (1) Stage 1. Punishment and obedience: the child is obedient in order to avoid punishment.
      (2) Stage 2. Instrumental relativism: the child makes moral choices based on the benefit to self and sometimes to others.
   b. Level 2. Conventional morality: occurs at about 9 or 10 years of age.
      (1) Stage 1. Social conformity: the child desires to gain the approval of others.
      (2) Stage 2. Law and order: rules and social norms are internalized.
   c. Level 3. Postconventional morality: age range can vary, and not all will achieve this level.
      (1) Social contracts: The young adult has social awareness and an awareness of the legal implications of decisions/actions.

Abraham Maslow

1. Maslow developed a hierarchy of basic human needs, proposing that if the lower-level needs are not met, the individual is unable to work on higher-level pursuits.
   a. Physiological: basic survival needs (i.e., food, water, rest, warmth).
   b. Safety: the need for physical and physiologic security.
   c. Love and belonging: the need for affection, emotional support, and group affiliation.
   d. Self-esteem: the need to believe in oneself as a competent and valuable member of society.
   e. Self-actualization: after attaining all of the physiological and psychosocial developmental milestones, an individual's development of creativity, morality, spontaneity, lack of prejudice, acceptance of facts, and problem-solving becomes integrated at this highest level of capability.

Ryan and Deci

1. Ryan and Deci's self-determination theory examines how self-determination can enhance or weaken intrinsic motivation, self-regulation, and well-being.
2. The key elements of self-determination are competence, autonomy, and relatedness.
   a. Competence promotes children's desire to continue engaging in an activity with the belief that they will succeed.
      (1) Success leads to continued engagement, and additional success.
      (2) Children who consistently fail during engagement in activities tend to discontinue engaging, due to a perceived sense of failure.
   b. Autonomy promotes intrinsic motivation, which leads children to enthusiastic, self-directed behaviors and a desire to explore.
      (1) These characteristics are associated with a high level of self-esteem and well-being.
      (2) External pressures to engage can result in decreased initiative and learning.
   c. Relatedness, which is dependent on secure relationships, promotes motivation for increased engagement, exploration autonomy, and success.

Cognitive Development

Jean Piaget

1. Described the process of cognitive development from birth to adolescence.
2. Major constructs.
   a. Adaptation: responding to environmental challenges as they occur.
   b. Mental schemes: organizing experiences into concepts.
   c. Operations: the cognitive methods used by the child to organize schemes and experiences to direct subsequent actions.
   d. Adapted intelligence or cognitive competence.

e. Equilibrium: the balance between what the child knows and can act on, and what the environment provides.
f. Assimilation: the ability to take a new situation and change it to match an existing scheme or generalization.
g. Accommodation: the development of a new scheme in response to the reality of a situation, or discrimination.

> **EXAM HINT:** The following information about the developmental sequence of cognitive development and cognitive milestones provides foundational knowledge for answering COTA® exam items about working with children with typical and atypical cognitive development. For example, the correct answer to an exam item that asks how best to present an activity to a child at the developmental level of a 5-year-old would include demonstration. At this age, the child is at the phase of the pre-operational cognitive level, during which children will imitate what they see and hear.

3. Hierarchical development of cognition.
   a. Sensorimotor period (birth–2 years).
      (1) Reflexive stage: schemes begin in response to reflexes (1 month).
      (2) Primary circular reactions: child learns about cause and effect as a result of reflexive sensorimotor patterns that are repeated for enjoyment (2–4 months).
      (3) Secondary circular reactions: voluntary movement patterns emerge due to coordination of vision and hand function, and an early awareness of cause and effect develops (5–8 months).
      (4) Coordination of secondary schemata: voluntary movement in response to stimuli that cannot be seen such as in object permanence, and early development of de-centered thought (9–12 months).
      (5) Tertiary circular reactions: the child seeks out new schemes, with improved gross and fine motor abilities; tool use begins (12–18 months).
      (6) Inventions of new means through mental combinations: the child demonstrates insight and purposeful tool use and explores problem-solving options. The ability to represent concepts without direct manipulation emerges (18 months–2 years).
      (7) Child progresses from reflexive activity to mental representation to cognitive functions of combining and manipulating objects in play.
   b. Pre-operational period, ages 2–7 years.
      (1) Classification: categorizing objects according to similarities and differences.
      (2) Seriation: the relationship of one object or classification of objects to another.
      (3) Conservation: the end product of the preoperational period. The child is able to recognize the continuities of an object or class of objects in spite of apparent changes.
      (4) The pre-operational period is divided into two phases.
         (a) Preconceptual: the child expands vocabulary and symbolic representations (2–4 years).
         (b) Intuitive thought phase: the child imitates, copies, or repeats what is seen or heard and bases conclusions on what the child believes to be true rather than on logic. Inductive reasoning denotes a transition to the next stage (4–7 years).
      (5) Child progresses from dependence on perception, and egocentric orientation to logical thought, for solving problems. Child enjoys verbal and symbolic play.
   c. Concrete operations, ages 7–11 years.
      (1) Reversibility an expansion of conservation, leads to increased spatial awareness.
      (2) Rules: as rules are better understood, they are also applied.
      (3) Empiric-inductive thinking: the child solves problems with the information that is obvious and present.
      (4) Child uses logical thinking on observed or mentally represented objects, enjoying games with rules, which helps the child adjust to social demands.
   d. Formal operations, ages 11 through the teen years.
      (1) Hypothetic-deductive thinking, the ability to analyze and plan.
      (2) Child uses logic to hypothesize many ways to solve problems and can draw from past and present experiences to imagine what can have an effect on future situations.
4. Piaget stated that maturation of cognition is dependent upon:
   a. Organic growth, especially the maturation of the nervous system and endocrine glands.
   b. Experience in the actions performed on objects.
   c. Social interaction and transmission.
   d. A balance of opportunities for both assimilation and accommodation.

Major Milestones in Cognitive Development

1. Early object use.
   a. Child focuses on action performed with objects, e.g., banging, shaking (3–6 months).

b. Child explores characteristics of objects and expands the range of schemes, e.g., pulling, turning, poking, tearing (6–9 months).
c. Child combines objects in relational play, such as objects in containers (8–9 months).
d. Child notices the relation between complex actions and consequences such as opening doors, placing lids on containers, and differential use of schemes based on the toy being played with, e.g., pushing a train or rolling a ball (9–12 months).
e. Child acts on objects with a variety of schemes (12+ months).
f. Child links schemes in simple combinations, e.g., placing a baby doll in a carriage and then pushing the carriage (12–15 months).
g. Child links multi-scheme combinations into a meaningful sequence, e.g., putting food in a bowl, scooping the food using a spoon, and feeding a doll (24–36 months).
h. Child links schemes into a complex script (36–42 months).

2. Problem-solving skills.
   a. 6–9 months.
      (1) Child finds object after watching it disappear (e.g., toy covered by cloth).
      (2) Child uses movement as a means to an end (e.g., rolling to secure a toy).
      (3) Child anticipates movement of objects in space (e.g., looking toward trajectory of object circling the child's head).
      (4) Child attends to consequences of actions (e.g., banging toy and realizing it makes noise).
      (5) Child repeats actions to repeat consequences (e.g., banging toy to hear noise).
   b. 9–12 months.
      (1) Child is able to use a tool after demonstration (e.g., using a stick to secure a toy that is out of reach).
      (2) Child's behavior becomes more goal directed.
      (3) Child performs an action to produce a response.
   c. 12–15 months.
      (1) Child recruits the help of an adult to achieve a goal.
      (2) Child attempts to activate a simple mechanism.
      (3) Child turns and inspects objects.
      (4) Child uses a trial and error approach to new challenges.
   d. 18–21 months.
      (1) Child attends to shapes of things and uses them appropriately.
      (2) Child begins to think before acting.
      (3) Child uses tool to obtain a favored object.
      (4) Child begins to replace trial and error with a thought process in order to attain a goal.
      (5) Child can operate a mechanical toy (e.g., an on-off switch).
      (6) Child can predict effects or presume causes.
   e. 21–24 months.
      (1) Child recognizes operations of several mechanisms.
      (2) Child matches circles, squares, triangles, and manipulates objects into small openings (e.g., shape sorters).
   f. 24–27 months.
      (1) Child discriminates sizes.
   g. 24–30 months.
      (1) Child can build with blocks horizontally and vertically.
   h. 27–30 months.
      (1) Child begins to relate experiences to one another, based on logic and knowledge of previous experiences.
      (2) Child can make a mental plan of actions without acting it out.
      (3) Child can see relationships between experiences (e.g., if the balloon is popped, it will make a loud noise).
   i. 36–48 months.
      (1) Child can build a tower of nine cubes, demonstrating balance and coordination.
      (2) Child can organize objects by size and builds a structure from a mental image.
   j. 48–60 months.
      (1) Child can build involved structures combining various planes, along with symmetrical designs.
      (2) Child is able to utilize spatial awareness, cause and effect, and mental images in problem solving.

3. Symbolic play.
   a. 12–16 months.
      (1) Basic 'make believe' play, primarily involving self (e.g., eating, sleeping).
   b. 12–18 months.
      (1) Child can project 'make believe' play on objects and others.
      (2) Child uses a variety of schemes in imitating familiar activities.
   c. 18–24 months.
      (1) Child increases the use of non-realistic objects in pretending (e.g., substituting a block for a train).
      (2) Child can have inanimate objects perform familiar activities (e.g., a doll washing itself).
   d. 24–48 months.
      (1) See the following section.

Development of Play

> **EXAM HINT:** Pediatric OT practitioners often use play activities to achieve intervention goals; thus, the following developmental information about play provides foundational knowledge for answering COTA® exam items about working with children. For example, the correct answer to an exam item about working with a child at the developmental level of a 3-year-old would include symbolic parallel play, while an option that included creative cooperative play would be the correct answer to a COTA® exam item about working with a child at the developmental level of a 6-year-old.

Categories of Play

1. Exploratory play, 0–2 years.
   a. Child engages in play experiences, in which the child develops a body scheme.
   b. Sensory integrative and motor skills are also developed as the child explores the properties and effects of actions on objects and people.
   c. Child plays mostly with parents/caregiver(s).
2. Symbolic play, 2–4 years.
   a. Child engages in play experiences through which the child formulates, tests, classifies, and refines ideas, feelings, and combined actions.
   b. This form of play is associated with language development.
   c. Objects that are manageable for the child in terms of symbolization, control, and mastery are preferred by the child.
   d. Child is mostly involved in parallel play with peers and begins to become more cooperative over time.
3. Creative play, 4–7 years.
   a. Child engages in sensory, motor, cognitive, and social play experiences in which the child refines relevant skills.
   b. Child explores combinations of actions on multiple objects.
   c. Child begins to master skills that promote performance of school- and work-related activities.
   d. Child participates in cooperative peer groups.
4. Games, 7–12 years.
   a. Child participates in play with rules, competition, social interaction, and opportunities for development of skills.
   b. Child begins to participate in cooperative peer groups with a growing interest in competition.
   c. Friends become important for validation of play items and performance, while parents assist and validate in the absence of peers.

Self-Care Development

Feeding

1. Oral-motor development.
   a. Prior to 33 weeks of gestation: an infant is fed by non-oral means.
   b. At 35 weeks of gestation or after: jaw and tongue movements are strong enough to allow for feeding.
   c. At 40 weeks of gestation: rooting, gag, and cough reflexes are present for up to 4 months, protecting the airway and decreasing the chances of aspiration.
   d. At 4–5 months: munching occurs, consisting of a phasic bite and release of a soft cookie.
   e. At 6 months: strong up and down movement of the tongue.
   f. At 7–8 months: beginning of mastication of soft and mashed foods with diagonal jaw movement.
   g. At 9 months: lateral tongue movements make mastication of soft and mashed foods effective, able to drink from a cup; however, jaw is not firm.
   h. At 12 months: jaw is firm, there is rotary chewing allowing for a good bite on a hard cookie.
   i. At 24 months: able to chew most meats and raw vegetables.

> **EXAM HINT:** The NBCOT® exam outline for the COTA® identifies the task of recognizing "the influence of development; body functions and body structures . . . on a client's occupational performance" (NBCOT®, 2018, p. 21) and knowledge of the "technical level intervention strategies and techniques used to facilitate oral motor skills for drinking, eating, and swallowing consistent with developmental level, client condition, caregiver interaction, and mealtime environment and context" (NBCOT®, 2018, p. 25) as essential for competent and safe practice. Thus, the application of knowledge about oral-motor development previously described and the feeding evaluation standards and interventions to develop oral motor control described below can help you determine the correct answer for exam items about working with children who have oral-motor dysfunction.

2. Evaluation of feeding.
   a. Parent interview including parent's concerns, feeding history, behavior during feeding, weight gain or loss.
   b. Medical and developmental history.
   c. Observation of feeding including postural control; oral sensitivity; motor control of the jaw, lip, tongue, and cheek; and coordination and endurance of all.
   d. Recommendation for video fluoroscopy swallow study, especially if the child has a high risk of aspiration.
3. Intervention for oral motor control.
   a. Appropriate positioning to allow for neutral pelvic alignment and trunk stability, either in caregiver's lap or chair (infant seat or wheelchair); avoid head extension to prevent asphyxiation as a result of closing of the airway.
   b. Hand positioning of the caregiver: place the index finger longitudinally under the child's lip, middle finger under the jaw, and place the thumb on the lateral end of the mandible.
   c. Facilitate lip closure by applying slight upward pressure of the index finger under the child's lip.
   d. Facilitate jaw closure by firm upper pressure of the middle finger under the jaw.
   e. Hand positioning of the index and middle fingers to assist in inhibiting tongue thrust.
      (1) Press bowl of spoon downward and hold onto tongue.
   f. Facilitate swallow by lip closure and by placement and slight downward pressure of the spoon on the middle aspect of the tongue.
   g. Facilitate chewing by placement of foods, such as long soft-cooked vegetables, between the gum and teeth.
   h. Integrate preventive measures to work out of abnormal movement patterns.
      (1) Provide firm downward pressure, using a spoon, on the middle aspect of the tongue in presence of a tonic bite reflex.
      (2) Prevent tongue retraction to avoid choking.
      (3) Facilitate lip closure for a tongue thrust that can result in loss of liquid and food, drooling, and failure to thrive.
      (4) Decrease tactile sensitivity prior to feeding as well as at other times, by providing firm pressure; encourage sucking/chewing on a cloth; rub gums, palate, and tongue; promote oral exploration of toys; use a NUK toothbrush; and vary textures of foods, gradually introducing mashed potatoes mixed with other vegetables and soft meats.
   i. Consider and utilize the appropriate texture of foods as related to the child's feeding problems.
      (1) Thick foods are easier to swallow and manage, especially if a tongue thrust is present.
   j. A major role of the therapist and the OTA is to assist the caregiver in considering and promoting a pleasant social atmosphere for feeding by utilizing positioning and handling techniques to promote eye contact and bonding in a relaxed environment.
   k. Consider the developmental sequence of feeding skills.
      (1) Refer to Table 5-7.

> **EXAM HINT:** The NBCOT® exam outline for the COTA® identifies knowledge of the "clinical decision-making for implementing modifications to the intervention plan and prioritizing goals under the supervision of the OTR in response to . . . (the) developmental needs of the client" (NBCOT®, 2018, p. 23) as essential for competent practice. The application of knowledge about the developmental sequence for all areas of occupation outlined in this chapter's tables and text can help you determine the correct answer for exam items about working with typically and atypically developing children.

Table 5-7

Developmental Continuum in Self-Feeding and Associated Component Areas

AGE (MONTHS)	EATING AND FEEDING PERFORMANCE	SENSORIMOTOR	COGNITION	PSYCHOSOCIAL
5–7	Takes cereal or poured baby food from spoon.	Has good head stability and emerging sitting abilities; reaches and grasps toys; explores and tolerates various textures (e.g., fingers, rattles); puts objects in mouth.	Attends to effect produced by actions, such as hitting or shaking.	Plays with caregiver during meals and engages in interactive routines.
6–8	Attempts to hold bottle but may not retrieve it if it falls; needs to be monitored for safety reasons.		Object permanence is emerging and infant anticipates spoon or bottle.	Is easily distracted by stimuli (especially siblings) in the environment.
6–9	Holds and tries to eat cracker but sucks on it more than bites it; consumes soft foods that dissolve in the mouth; grabs at spoon but bangs it or sucks on either end of it.	Good sitting stability emerges; able to use hands to manipulate smaller parts of rattle; guided reach and palmer grasp applied to hand-to-mouth actions with objects.	Uses familiar actions initially with haphazard variations; seeks novelty and is anxious to explore objects (may grab at food on adult's plate).	Recognizes strangers; emerging sense of self.
9–13	Finger-feeds self a portion of meals consisting of soft table foods (e.g., macaroni, peas, dry cereal) and food if fed by an adult.	Uses various grasps on objects of different sizes; able to isolate radial fingers on smaller objects.	Has increased organization and sequencing of schemes to do desired activity; may have difficulty attending to events outside visual space (e.g., position of spoon close to mouth).	Prefers to act on objects than be passive observer.
12–14	Dips spoon in food, brings spoonful of food to mouth, but spills food by inverting spoon before it goes into mouth.	Begins to place and release objects; likely to use pronated grasp on objects like crayon or spoon.	Recognizes that objects have function and uses tools appropriately; relates objects together, shifting attention among them.	Has interest in watching family routines.
15–18	Scoops food with spoon and brings it to mouth.	Shoulder and wrist stability demonstrate precise movements.	Experiments to learn rules of how objects work; actively solves problems by creating new action solutions.	Internalizes standards imposed by others for how to play with objects.
24–30	Demonstrates interest in using fork; may stab at food such as pieces of canned fruit; proficient at spoon use and eats cereal with milk or rice with gravy with utensil.	Tolerates various food textures in mouth; adjusts movements to be efficient (e.g., forearm supinated to scoop and lift spoon).	Expresses wants verbally; demonstrates imitation of short sequence of occupation (e.g., putting food on plate and eating it).	Has increasing desire to copy peers; looks to adults to see if they appreciate success in an occupation; interested in household routines.

Shepherd, J. (2005). Activities of daily living and adaptations for independent living. In J. Case-Smith, (Ed.), *Occupational therapy for children* (5th ed., p. 489). St. Louis, MO: Elsevier Mosby. Reprinted with permission.

Development of Dressing Skills

1. Refer to Table 5-8.

Development of Toileting Skills

1. Refer to Table 5-9.

Development of Home Management Skills

1. Refer to Table 5-10.

Table 5-8

Development of Self-Dressing Skills

AGE (YEARS)	SELF-DRESSING SKILL
1	Cooperates with dressing (holds out arms and feet) Pulls off shoes, removes socks Pushes arms through sleeves and legs through pants
2	Removes unfastened coat Removes shoes if laces are untied Helps pull down pants Finds armholes in pullover shirt
2½	Removes pull-down pants with elastic waist Assists in pulling on socks Puts on front-button coat or shirt Unbuttons large buttons
3	Puts on pullover shirt with minimal assistance Puts on shoes without fasteners (may be on wrong foot) Puts on socks (may be with heel on top) Independently pulls down pants Zips and unzips jacket once on track Needs assistance to remove pullover shirt Buttons large front buttons
3½	Finds front of clothing Snaps or hooks front fastener Unzips front zipper on jacket, separating zipper Puts on mittens Buttons series of three or four buttons Unbuckles shoe or belt Dresses with supervision (needs help with front and back)
4	Removes pullover garment independently Buckles shoes or belt Zips jacket zipper Puts on socks correctly Puts on shoes with assistance in tying laces Laces shoes Consistently identifies the front and back of garment
4½	Puts belt in loops
5	Ties and unties knots Dresses unsupervised
6	Closes back zipper Ties bows Buttons back buttons Snaps back snaps

Shepherd, J. (2005). Activities of daily living and adaptations for independent living. In J. Case-Smith (Ed.), *Occupational therapy for children* (5th ed., p. 547). St. Louis, MO: Elsevier Mosby. Reprinted with permission.

Table 5-9

Typical Developmental Sequence of Toileting

APPROXIMATE AGE (YEAR)	TOILETING SKILL
1	Indicates discomfort when wet or soiled Has regular bowel movements
1½	Sits on toilet when placed there and supervised (short time)
2	Urinates regularly
2½	Achieves regulated toileting with occasional daytime accidents Rarely has bowel accidents Tells someone that he or she needs to go to the bathroom May need reminders to go to the bathroom May need help with getting on the toilet
3	Goes to bathroom independently; seats himself or herself on the toilet May need help with wiping May need help with fasteners or difficult clothing
4–5	Is independent in toileting (e.g., tearing toilet paper, flushing, washing hands, managing clothing)

Shepherd, J. (2005). Activities of daily living and adaptations for independent living. In J. Case-Smith (Ed.), *Occupational therapy for children* (5th ed., p. 543). St. Louis, MO: Elsevier Mosby. Reprinted with permission.

Table 5-10

Developmental Sequence for Household Management Tasks

AGE	TASK
13 months	Imitates housework
2 years	Picks up and puts toys away with parental reminders Copies parents' domestic activities
3 years	Carries things without dropping them Dusts with help Dries dishes with help Gardens with help Puts toys away with reminders Wipes up spills
4 years	Fixes dry cereal and snacks Helps with sorting laundry
5 years	Puts toys away neatly Makes a sandwich Takes out trash Makes bed Puts dirty clothes in hamper Answers telephone correctly

Table 5-10

Developmental Sequence for Household Management Tasks (*Continued*)

AGE	TASK
6 years	Does simple errands Does household chores without redoing Cleans sink Washes dishes with help Crosses street safely
7–9 years	Begins to cook simple meals Puts clean clothes away Hangs up clothes Manages small amounts of money Uses telephone correctly

Table 5-10

Developmental Sequence for Household Management Tasks (*Continued*)

AGE	TASK
10–12 years	Cooks simple meals with supervision Does simple repairs with appropriate tools Begins doing laundry Sets table Washes dishes Cares for pet with reminders
13–14 years	Does laundry Cooks meals

Shepherd, J. (2005). Activities of daily living and adaptations for independent living. In J. Case-Smith (Ed.), *Occupational therapy for children* (5th ed., p. 558) St. Louis, MO: Elsevier Mosby. Reprinted with permission.

Lifespan and Occupational Therapy Developmental Theorists

Overview

EXAM HINT: The NBCOT® exam outline for the COTA® identifies knowledge of the "influence of theoretical approaches, models of practice, and frames of reference on information-gathering and the intervention process" (NBCOT®, 2018, p. 22) as essential for competent practice. The application of knowledge about the lifespan and OT developmental theories, OT frames of reference, and models of practice described in this chapter can help you determine the correct answer to COTA® exam items that include scenarios about a person's and/or population's age and/or developmental stage. Understanding that development occurs in many dimensions throughout the lifespan, with specific tasks being considered typical for each life stage, can be helpful in determining an answer that is developmentally appropriate for an exam item.

Havighurst

1. Proposed that people need to develop certain skills at different ages to meet social standards.
2. Believed that these developmental tasks rely on biological, psychological, and sociological conditions that are optimal for the accomplishment of a developmental task.
    a. Proposed that there are certain sensitive periods when biological, psychological, and sociological conditions are optimal for the accomplishment of a developmental task.
    b. Described 'teachable moments,' referring to the sensitive periods when conditions are optimal for integration of previous knowledge and the accomplishment of new developmental tasks with assistance.
3. Six stages of development are described along with specific developmental tasks for each stage.
4. In contemporary society, the tasks of adolescent and adult stages may occur later than described by Havighurst.
5. Tasks of infancy and childhood.
    a. Walk.
    b. Take in solid food.
    c. Talk.
    d. Control elimination of body wastes.
    e. Develop sex differences and sexual modesty.
    f. Develop physiological stability.
    g. Understand concepts of social and physical reality.
    h. Develop emotional ties with parents, siblings, and others.
    i. Understand right from wrong, conscience evolves.
6. Tasks of middle childhood.
    a. Develop physical skills needed for games.
    b. Establish healthy self-concept.
    c. Make friends with children of the same age.
    d. Read, write, and calculate.
    e. Acquire a fund of information necessary for everyday life.

f. Develop morality and values.
  g. Formulate opinions about social groups and institutions.
7. Tasks of adolescence.
  a. Establish relationships with male and female friends of same age, increasing in quantity and quality.
  b. Develop gender social roles.
  c. Become comfortable with and respect one's changing body.
  d. Decrease emotional reliance on parents/other adults.
  e. Prepare for marriage and family life.
  f. Prepare for economic career.
  g. Develop a value system to shape behavior or develop one's own philosophy.
  h. Behave in a socially responsible manner.
8. Tasks of early adulthood.
  a. Choose a partner.
  b. Adjust to a partner.
  c. Start a family.
  d. Raise children.
  e. Manage a home.
  f. Pursue an occupation.
  g. Develop civic responsibility.
  h. Join/form a compatible social group.
9. Tasks of middle adulthood.
  a. Guide adolescents toward becoming responsible and well-adjusted adults.
  b. Engage in adult civic and social responsibility.
  c. Progress in an occupational career.
  d. Pursue leisure-time activities.
  e. Relate to partner as a person.
  f. Deal with and accept physiological changes of middle age.
  g. Accept aging parents.
10. Tasks of later adulthood.
  a. Cope with decreasing physical strength and health.
  b. Adjust to retirement and reduced income.
  c. Adjust to death of a spouse/partner.
  d. Affiliate with one's age group.
  e. Change social roles.
  f. Arrange for the most appropriate and appealing living environment.

Lela Llorens

1. Individual is viewed from two perspectives.
  a. Specific period of time, referred to as horizontal development.
  b. Over the course of time, referred to as longitudinal/chronological development.
2. Both of these perspectives occur simultaneously.
3. The integration of these two aspects is critical to normal development.
4. The role of OT is to facilitate development and to assist in the mastery of life tasks and the ability to cope with life expectations.
5. Lloren's frame of reference integrated many of the concepts of Gesell, Amatruda, Erikson, Havighurst, and Freud.

Anne Mosey

1. Recapitulation of ontogenesis frame of reference.
  a. The development of adaptive skills, essential learned behaviors that are considered critical for successful participation and occupational performance.
2. Six major adaptive skills along with subskills are delineated.
  a. Sensory integration of vestibular, proprioceptive, and tactile information for functional use.
     (1) Integration of the tactile subsystems (0–3 months).
     (2) Integration of primitive postural reflexes (3–9 months).
     (3) Maturation of righting and equilibrium reactions (9–12 months).
     (4) Integration of two sides of the body, awareness of body parts and their relationship for motor planning gross movements (1–2 years).
     (5) Motor plan fine movements (2–3 years).
  b. Cognitive skill: ability to perceive, represent, and organize sensory information to think and problem-solve.
     (1) Using inborn behavioral patterns for environmental interaction (0–1 month).
     (2) Interrelating visual, manual, auditory, and oral responses (1–4 months).
     (3) Early exploring of the environments and interest in outcomes of actions: remembers action responses, believes that own actions cause responses, and awareness of the relation of these actions and events (4–9 months).
     (4) Deliberate actions to achieve a goal: object permanence begins, anticipation of familiar events, imitation, interest in sizes/shapes, and perception of other objects as partially causal (9–12 months).
     (5) Using a trial-and-error approach to problem-solving: tool use, begins to realize that alternate approaches can be used, remembers the order of a simple sequences, and realizes that others can cause events to happen (12–18 months).
     (6) Formulating mental pictures: pretending, early understanding of cause and effect, manipulating objects in space, and having a clearer

understanding that others can manipulate the environment (18 months–2 years).
- (7) Represents objects in terms of felt experiences: understands that there are consequences to actions, that others cannot read your mind, and recognizes that events have causes (2–5 years).
- (8) Represents objects by name: begins to understand that other people may have differing opinions (6–7 years).
- (9) Comprehends that different labels can be used for the same object, uses formal logic and speculation (11–13 years).

c. Dyadic interaction skill: the ability to participate in a variety of dyadic relationships.
  (1) Family relationships (8–10 months).
  (2) Playmate relationships (3–5 years).
  (3) Superior/authority relationship interactions (5–7 years).
  (4) Friend relationships (10–14 years).
  (5) Peer-superior relationships (15–17 years).
  (6) Intimate/sharing/committed relationships (18–25 years).
  (7) Caring/unselfish relationships (20–30 years).

d. Group interaction skills: the ability to engage in a variety of primary groups.
  (1) Parallel group: minimal awareness of others and interaction with others (18 months–2 years).
  (2) Project group: limited in duration, cooperation, and sharing (2–4 years).
  (3) Egocentric group: cooperation, competition, longer in duration, builds self-esteem (5–7 years).
  (4) Cooperative group: compatible group, members concerned with meeting the needs of fellow members (9–12 years).
  (5) Mature group: differing roles, concerned with completion of task as well as meeting the needs of fellow members (15–18 years).

e. Self-identity skills: the ability to perceive the self as a relatively autonomous, holistic, and acceptable person who has permanence and continuity over time.
  (1) Self as a valued person (9–12 months).
  (2) Assets and limitations of the self (11–15 years).
  (3) Self as self-directed (20–25 years).
  (4) Self as a productive, contributing member of a society (30–35 years).
  (5) Self-identity as an independent individual (35–50 years).
  (6) Understanding the aging process of one's self and eventual death as part of the life cycle (45–60 years).

f. Sexual identity skill: the ability to feel comfortable about one's sexual nature and to engage in continued sexual relationship that takes into account mutual satisfaction of sexual needs.
  (1) Act on the basis of one's pregenital sexual nature (4–5 years).
  (2) Sexually mature as a positive growth experience (12–16 years).
  (3) Give and receive sexual gratification (18–25 years).
  (4) Sustain sexual relationship with mutual satisfaction of sexual needs (20–30 years).
  (5) Accept sex-related physiological changes that occur as a natural part of the aging process (40–60 years).

CAUTION: Since the publication of the lifespan theories and frames of reference described in this chapter, there have been significant social, cultural, and demographic changes in the United States. Thus, before applying these conceptual frameworks to a COTA® exam item, you should carefully consider the social, cultural, and demographic information that is provided in an exam scenario to determine a correct answer. For example, a multi-select multiple choice exam item can include a scenario about an OTA collaborating with an occupational therapist to plan OT evaluation with an older adult who incurred a concussion and multiple fractures due to a skiing accident. The item states that the individual is an independent business owner, a community activist, and partner in a sexually intimate relationship and asks you to identify the best foci for evaluation according to an occupation-based frame of reference. Correct answers to select from the six available options provided in this multi-select exam item may include assessing the effect of these injuries on the person's desired work, leisure, volunteer, and/or sexual activities.

Role of the Occupational Therapy Assistant (OTA) in Pediatric Evaluation

1. The OTA contributes to the evaluation process with supervision from the occupational therapist.
   a. The OTA can assist with the collection of data for the evaluation once service competency has been established.
   b. The level of supervision required will be determined by the OTA's experience and their established service competency.
   c. The OTA cannot independently evaluate or interpret evaluation results.
2. Evaluation methods can include parent/family member/teacher interview, medical and developmental history, formal and informal observations, and some standardized developmental assessments.

3. Primary purposes of parent/family member/teacher interviews and home/classroom observations.
   a. To explore environmental and contextual aspects related to the child's development and occupational performance.
   b. To identify family supports and community resources.
   c. To understand cultural and spiritual values.
4. Developmental considerations in the evaluation of children.
   a. Understand the appropriate developmental levels in selecting toys and activities, and in considering other evaluation media.
   b. Observe symmetries/asymmetries, stability of trunk, pelvis, hips, and shoulders, at rest and during movement.
   c. Observe transitional movement in and out of prone, supine, side-lying, quadruped, sitting, standing, kneeling, half-kneel, and in various sitting positions such as tailor, long, heel, or side-sitting.
   d. Assess the quality of movement in and out of the above positions.
   e. Assess fine motor coordination.
   f. Consider proper positioning and adaptive equipment, seating, and technology needs.
   g. Assess cognition in the context of play and other occupations.
5. Assist in the assessment of psychosocial skills such as the child's coping style, frustration tolerance, and social interaction.
6. Assist in the evaluation of sensorimotor development.

Role of the OTA in Pediatric Intervention

1. The OTA implements intervention with supervision from the occupational therapist.
   a. The level of supervision required depends upon the OTA's experience and established service competency.
   b. During the implementation of intervention, the OTA informs the supervising OT of any change in the child's status and any other relevant information that may affect interventions.
2. Developmental considerations in interventions with children.
   a. All activities, toys, and other intervention media must be appropriate to the child's developmental level.
   b. Play activities should be the primary occupation for intervention.
   c. Family education is essential.
      (1) Identify environmental and contextual aspects that facilitate the child's development.
      (2) Provide advocacy training to link families to community.
      (3) Identify psychosocial factors that promote the child's development.
      (4) Teach avoidance of behaviors that may interfere with learning.
      (5) Consider and respect the family's cultural and spiritual background.
   d. Provide consultation or direct intervention to facilitate school performance and achieve educational goals.
   e. Provide intervention to facilitate sensorimotor, cognitive, and psychosocial development.
   f. Fabricate or requisition positioning equipment and assistive technology for home and/or school.
   g. Ensure the proper visual and auditory aides are used during intervention sessions.
   h. See this chapter's section on psychosocial development and Chapter 10 for information on pediatric and developmental clinical conditions and diagnostic-specific interventions.

Child Abuse

Facts and Figures

1. In the United States, child abuse is a major social justice crisis.
   a. A report of child abuse is made every 10 seconds. In 2017, the national estimate was 674,000 victims of child abuse and neglect.
   b. In 2017, an estimated 4.1 million child abuse reports and allegations were made involving approximately 7.5 million children.
   c. National estimates were 1,720 childhood fatalities per year from abuse or neglect, which is almost five child deaths each day.
      (1) Approximately 72% of these deaths are children under the age of three.
      (2) The death of children as a result of maltreatment is thought to be significantly underreported with the majority of child fatalities caused by maltreatment not recorded on death certificates.

2. Child abuse can occur in any family. It is evident at all socioeconomic levels, in all ethnicities, cultural groups, and religions and at all levels of education.
3. The effects of child abuse and neglect continue into adulthood.
   a. It is estimated that the cycle of abuse is continued by 30% of abused and neglected children who, as parents, abuse their own children.
   b. Approximately 80% of 21-year-olds who survived child abuse have at least one diagnosed psychological disorder.
   c. Approximately 37% of women in prison and 14% of men in prison in the United States are survivors of child abuse.
   d. Over 60% of adults in drug rehabilitation centers report being survivors of child abuse or neglect.

EXAM HINT: The above facts are provided to support the critical need for everyone to address this societal crisis and highlight the need for OT practitioners to be vigilant about the potential of child abuse and neglect in all interactions with children and adult survivors. These statistics will not be on the COTA® exam. However, because the occupational therapy code of ethics requires OT personnel to "demonstrate a concern for the safety and well-being of the recipients of their services" (AOTA, 2015, p. 2), it is likely that the COTA® exam will include items about the OTA's role in identifying and responding to child abuse. The application of knowledge about the prevalence, signs, and symptoms of child abuse and occupational intervention for cases of abuse can help you determine the correct answer to these items.

Definition of Child Abuse

1. Any behavior directed toward a child by a parent, guardian, caregiver, other family member, or other adult that endangers or impairs a child's physical or emotional health and development.

Types of Child Abuse

1. Physical.
2. Emotional or mental.
3. Sexual.
4. Neglect.

Signs of Abuse

1. General signs of abuse.
   a. Withdrawal.
   b. Nightmares.
   c. Running away.
   d. Anxiety or depression.
   e. Guilt.
   f. Mistrust of adults.
   g. Fear.
   h. Aggressiveness.
2. Signs and symptoms of physical abuse.
   a. The child reports being physically mistreated.
   b. Unexplained injuries.
   c. Repeated injuries.
   d. Abrasions and lacerations.
   e. Small circular burns such as cigarette or cigar burns.
   f. Burns with a 'doughnut' shape on the buttocks that may indicate scalding, or any burn that shows the pattern of an object used to inflict injury, such as an iron.
   g. Friction burns such as those from a rope.
   h. Unexplained fractures.
   i. Denial, unlikely explanations, or delays in treatment on the part of the caregiver.
   j. Unconsciousness and/or symptoms of a traumatic brain injury due to shaken baby syndrome.
3. Signs and symptoms of emotional or mental abuse.
   a. The child reports being verbally and/or emotionally mistreated.
   b. Aggressive or acting out behavior such as lying or stealing.
   c. Shy, dependent, or defensive appearance.
   d. Verbally abuses others with language that appears to have been directed toward him/her.
4. Signs and symptoms of sexual abuse.
   a. The child reports being inappropriately approached, touched, and/or assaulted.
   b. Abuse may be physical (e.g., touching), non-physical (e.g., indecent exposure), or violent (e.g., rape), so signs may include emotional and physical indicators.
   c. Precocious sexual behavior or knowledge.
   d. Copying adult sexual behavior.
   e. Inappropriate sexual behavior (e.g., putting tongue in other's mouth when kissing).
   f. Soreness or injury around the genitals.
   g. Reluctance or refusal to let caregivers wash parts of the body.
   h. Sexual play.
5. Signs and symptoms of neglect.
   a. Poorly nourished appearance or inadequately clothed.
   b. Consistently tired or listless behavior.
   c. Inconsistent attendance at school.
   d. Poor hygiene or obsession with cleanliness.
   e. Left alone in dangerous situations, for long periods of time, and/or at an inappropriate young age.
   f. Unable to relate well to adults or form friendships.

Role of Occupational Therapy

> **EXAM HINT:** The NBCOT® exam outline for the COTA® identifies the task of providing "occupational therapy service in accordance with laws (and) regulations . . . in order to protect consumers" (NBCOT®, 2018, p. 29) as essential for competent practice. The application of knowledge about the following federal and state mandates for the reporting of child abuse and the previous descriptions of types of child abuse can help you determine the correct answer to NBCOT® Domain 03 exam items related to child abuse.

1. Mandatory reporting.
   a. The federal Child Abuse Prevention and Treatment Act (CAPTA) defined child abuse and neglect and established mandates for professionals to report abuse and neglect to law enforcement officials. See Chapter 4.
   b. All states must have child abuse and neglect reporting laws to qualify for federal funding under CAPTA.
   c. All states require reporting of known or suspected cases of child abuse or neglect by health care providers.
      (1) Standards for reporting may vary.
      (2) Reporting to the OTA's direct supervisor may/may not be sufficient.
         (a) OTAs should immediately report any and all concerns to their supervisor but must be prepared to follow-up as necessary.
   d. Failure to report suspected child abuse may be considered a crime.
   e. In most states, good faith reporting is immune from liability.
   f. All states require reporting to be made to a law enforcement agency or child protective services.
2. OT intervention.
   a. Treat physical injuries, emotional injuries, and developmental delays.
   b. Develop a trusting relationship with child and non-abusive caregivers.
   c. Provide support to non-abusive family members/caregivers.
   d. Refer to appropriate disciplines and agencies.

Aging

General Concepts and Definitions

> **EXAM HINT:** The NBCOT® exam outline identifies knowledge of the "impact of . . . aging on occupational performance, health, and wellness across the lifespan" (NBCOT®, 2018, p. 21) as essential for competent and safe practice. The application of knowledge about information provided in this section can help you correctly answer exam items about working with older adults throughout the OT process.

1. Aging: the process of growing old.
   a. Describes a wide array of physiological changes in the body systems.
   b. A complex and variable process.
   c. Common to all members of a given species.
   d. Aging is developmental, occurs across the lifespan.
   e. Progressive with time.
   f. Evidence of aging.
      (1) Decline in homeostatic efficiency.
      (2) Decline in reaction time.
         (a) Increased probability that the reaction to injury will not be successful.
   g. Varies among and within individuals.
2. Aging changes.
   a. Cellular changes.
      (1) Increase in size; fragmentation of Golgi apparatus and mitochondria.
      (2) Decrease in cell capacity to divide and reproduce.
      (3) Arrest of DNA synthesis and cell division.
   b. Tissue changes.
      (1) Accumulation of pigmented materials, lipofuscins.
      (2) Accumulation of lipids and fats.
      (3) Connective tissue changes: decreased elastic content, degradation of collagen; presence of pseudoelastins.
   c. Organ changes.
      (1) Decrease in functional capacity.
      (2) Decrease in homeostatic efficiency.
3. Gerontology: the scientific study of the factors impacting the normal aging process and the effects of aging.
4. Geriatrics: the branch of medicine concerned with the illnesses of old age and their care.
5. Ageism: discrimination and prejudice leveled against individuals on the basis of their age.
   a. Isolates older adults socially.

b. Permits attitudes and policies that discourage older adults from full participation in work, leisure, and other meaningful occupations.
c. Perpetuates fears of aging.
d. Diminishes quality of life.

Demographics, Mortality, and Morbidity

1. Lifespan: maximum survival potential, the inherent natural life of the species; in humans 110–120 years.
2. Senescence: the weakening of the body at a gradual but steady pace during the last stages of adulthood through death.
3. Life expectancy: the number of years of life expectation from year of birth.
   a. Overall life expectancy is 78.8 years in United States; women live five years longer than men (81 versus 76 years).
   b. For decades, the following trends have contributed to increased life expectancy.
      (1) Advances in health care, improved infectious disease control.
      (2) Advances in infant/child care, decreased mortality rates.
      (3) Improvements in nutrition and sanitation.
   c. In recent years, life expectancy in the United States has declined slightly. This decline has been attributed to an increase in deaths due to drug overdoses and suicide.
4. Categories of older adults.
   a. Young-old: ages 65–74.
   b. Middle-old: ages 75–84.
   c. Very old: ages >85.
5. Persons over 65 years: represents a rapidly growing segment with lengthening of life expectancy; currently 15.2% of the U.S. population.
   a. By 2040, it is expected that there will be 82 million people over age 65 years, which is 21.7% of the U.S. population.

> **EXAM HINT:** The above demographics and the following characteristics of older adults are provided to emphasize that there is a significant need for OT practitioners to work with older adults in a manner that recognizes their lived experiences. Correct answers to COTA® exam items about OT intervention for older adults will reflect these realities.

6. Social and economic characteristics of older adults.
   a. Approximately 33% of all older women are widows, which is triple the widow rate for older men. Older men are 25% more likely to be married compared to older women.
   b. The educational level of older adults is increasing. Approximately 86% of older persons have completed high school, and 30% have a bachelor's degree or higher.
   c. About 3% of persons over 65 reside in nursing homes; the percentage of institutionalized older adults increase dramatically with age (i.e., 92% of persons over 85).
      (1) The number of older adults residing in institutional settings has been decreasing as more people choose to age in place and more community-based living options have become available.
   d. The need for caregiving increases with age. About one-third of older adults need assistance with personal care.
   e. Most noninstitutionalized older adults live in a family setting, usually with their spouse. About 28% of older adults live alone.
   f. Most older adults live on fixed incomes.
      (1) Social security is the major source of income.
      (2) Poverty rate for persons over 65 years is 9.3%; another 5.2% live near the poverty rate.
   g. In 2017, about 20% of older adults were working, comprising ~6% of the U.S. labor force. The number of employed older adults has been increasing since 2002.
7. Leading causes of death (mortality) in persons over 65, in order of frequency are coronary heart disease (CHD), cancer, chronic respiratory diseases (e.g., chronic obstructive pulmonary disease [COPD]), cerebrovascular disease (i.e., stroke), and neurocognitive disorders
8. Leading causes of disability/chronic conditions (morbidity) in persons over 65 years, include hypertension, hyperlipidemia, arthritis, heart disease, and diabetes.
   a. Most older persons (75%) report having one or more chronic conditions.
9. Health-care costs.
   a. Older persons account for 14% of population and 34.5% of total health-care expenditures.
   b. Older persons account for 27% of all hospital stays.

Muscular System Changes and Adaptation in the Older Adult

1. Age-related changes.
   a. Changes may be due more to decreased activity levels (hypokinesis) and disuse than from the aging process.
   b. Loss of muscle strength: peaks at age 30, remains fairly constant until age 50; after which there is an accelerating loss, 20%–40% loss by age 65 in the nonexercising adult.

c. Loss of power (force/unit time): significant declines, due to losses in speed of contraction and changes in nerve conduction and synaptic transmission.
d. Loss of skeletal muscle mass (atrophy): both size and number of muscle fibers decrease; by age 70, most lose 33% of skeletal muscle mass.
e. Changes in muscle fiber composition: selective loss of Type II, fast-twitch fibers, with increase in proportion of Type I fibers.
f. Changes in muscular endurance: muscles fatigue more readily.
   (1) Decreased muscle tissue oxidative capacity.
   (2) Decreased peripheral blood flow, oxygen delivery to muscles.
   (3) Altered chemical composition of muscle: decreased myosin ATPase activity, glycoproteins, and contractile protein.
   (4) Collagen changes: denser, irregular due to cross-linkages, loss of water content and elasticity; affects tendons, bone, cartilage.
2. Clinical implications.
   a. Movements become slower.
   b. Increased complaints of fatigue.
   c. Connective tissue becomes denser and stiffer.
      (1) Loss of range of motion: highly variable by joint and individual's activity level.

> **CAUTION:** Increased risk of muscle sprains, strains, and tendon tears and increased tendency for fibrinous adhesions and contractures.

   d. Decreased functional mobility, limitations to movement.
   e. Gait may become unsteady due to changes in balance and strength; increased need for assistive devices.

> **RED FLAG:** Increased risk of falls.

3. Strategies to slow, reverse, and/or compensate for age-related muscular system changes.
   a. Improve health.
      (1) Correct medical problems that may cause weakness.
      (2) Improve nutrition.
      (3) Address alcoholism/substance abuse.
   b. Increase levels of physical activity, stress functional activities, and activity programs.
      (1) Gradually increase intensity of activity to avoid injury.
      (2) Plan and include adequate warm-ups and cool downs; appropriate pacing and rest periods.
   c. Provide strength training to increase/maintain muscle strength required for functional activity.
      (1) Significant increases in strength are noted in older adults with isometric and progressive resistive exercise regimes.
      (2) High-intensity training programs (70%–80% of one-repetition maximum) produce quicker and more predictable results than moderate intensity programs; both have been successfully used with the older adults.
      (3) Age is not a limiting factor; significant improvements noted in 80- and 90-year-old older adults who were frail and institutionalized.
      (4) Improvements in strength can improve functional abilities and occupational performance.
      (5) Maintain newly gained and existing strength and incorporate into functional activities.
   d. Provide flexibility and range of motion exercises to increase range of motion needed for functional activity.
      (1) Utilize slow, prolonged stretching, maintained for 20–30 seconds.
      (2) Tissues heated prior to stretching are more distensible, e.g., warm pool.
      (3) Maintain newly gained range: incorporate into functional activities.
      (4) Mobility gains are slower with older adults.
4. See Chapter 6 for additional information on musculoskeletal system disorders and Chapter 11 for information on biomechanical evaluation and intervention approaches.

Skeletal System Changes and Adaptations in the Older Adult

1. Age-related changes.
   a. Cartilage changes: decreased water content, becomes stiffer, fragments, and erodes; by age 60, more than 60% of adults have degenerative joint changes, cartilage abnormalities.
   b. Loss of bone mass and density: peak bone mass at age 40; between 45 and 70, bone mass decreases (women by about 25%; men 15%); decreases another 5% by age 90.
      (1) Loss of calcium, bone strength: especially trabecular bone.
      (2) Decreased bone marrow red blood cell production.
   c. Intervertebral discs: flatten, less resilient due to loss of water content (30% loss by age 65 years) and loss of collagen elasticity; trunk length and overall height decreases.
   d. Senile postural changes.
      (1) Forward head.
      (2) Kyphosis of thoracic spine.
      (3) Flattening of lumbar spine.

> **CAUTION:** With prolonged sitting, the tendency to develop hip and knee flexion contractures increases.

2. Clinical implications.
   a. Maintenance of weight bearing is important for cartilaginous/joint health and mobility.

   > **RED FLAG:** Increased risk of falls and fractures.

3. Strategies to slow, reverse, and/or compensate for age-related skeletal system changes.
   a. Postural exercises: stress components of good posture.
   b. Weight-bearing (gravity-loading) exercise can decrease bone loss in older adults (e.g., walking, stair climbing, all activities that are performed in standing).
   c. Nutritional, hormonal, and medical therapies.
   d. See Chapter 15 for information on fall prevention.
4. See Chapter 6 for additional information on musculoskeletal system disorders and Chapter 11 for information on biomechanical evaluation and intervention approaches.

Neurological System Changes and Adaptations in the Older Adult

1. Age-related changes.
   a. Atrophy of nerve cells in cerebral cortex.
   b. Changes in brain morphology.
      (1) Gyral atrophy: narrowing and flattening of gyri with widening of sulci.
      (2) Ventricular dilation.
      (3) Generalized cell loss in cerebral cortex: especially frontal and temporal lobes, association areas (prefrontal cortex, visual).
      (4) Presence of lipofuscins, senile or neuritic plaques, and neurofibrillary tangles (NFT): significant accumulations associated with pathology, for example, neurocognitive disorders.
      (5) More selective cell loss in basal ganglia (substantia nigra and putamen), cerebellum, hippocampus, locus coeruleus; brain stem minimally affected.
   c. Decreased cerebral blood flow and energy metabolism.
   d. Changes in synaptic transmission.
      (1) Decreased synthesis and metabolism of major neurotransmitters, for example, acetylcholine, dopamine.
      (2) Slowing of many neural processes, especially in polysynaptic pathways.
   e. Changes in spinal cord/peripheral nerves.
      (1) Neuronal loss and atrophy.
      (2) Loss of motoneurons results in increase in size of remaining motor units (development of macro motor units).
      (3) Slowed nerve conduction velocity: sensory greater than motor.
      (4) Loss of sympathetic fibers: may account for diminished autonomic stability, increasing the incidence of postural hypotension in older adults.
   f. Age-related tremors (essential tremor [ET]).
      (1) Occur as an isolated symptom, particularly in hands, head, and voice.
      (2) Characterized as postural or kinetic, rarely resting.
      (3) Benign, slowly progressive; in late stages may limit function.
      (4) Exaggerated by movement and emotion.
2. Clinical implications.
   a. Effects on movement.
      (1) Overall speed and coordination are decreased; increased difficulties with fine motor control.
      (2) Slowed recruitment of motoneurons contributes to loss of strength.
      (3) Both reaction time and movement time are increased.
      (4) Older adults are affected by the speed/accuracy trade-off.
         (a) The simpler the movement, the less is the change.
         (b) More complicated movements require more preparation, leading to longer reaction and movement times.
         (c) Faster movements decrease accuracy, increase errors.
      (5) Older adults typically shift in motor control processing from open to closed loop (e.g., demonstrate increased reliance on visual feedback for movement).
      (6) Demonstrate increased cautionary behaviors, an indirect effect of decreased capacity.
   b. General slowing of neural processing: learning and memory may be affected.
   c. Problems in homeostatic regulation: stressors (heat, cold, excess exercise) can be harmful, even life-threatening.
3. Strategies to slow, reverse, and/or compensate for age-related neurological system changes.
   a. Correct medical problems: improve cerebral blood flow.
   b. Improve health: diet, smoking cessation.
   c. Increase levels of physical activity: may encourage neuronal branching, slow rate of neural decline, and improve cerebral circulation.
   d. Provide effective strategies to improve motor learning and control.
      (1) Allow for increased reaction and movement times: will improve motivation, accuracy of movements.

(2) Allow for limitations of memory: avoid long sequences of movements.
(3) Allow for increased cautionary behaviors: provide adequate explanation, demonstration when teaching new movement skills.
(4) Stress familiar, well-learned skills and repetitive movements.
4. See Chapter 7 for additional information on neurological system disorders and Chapter 12 for information on neurological evaluation and intervention approaches.

Sensory Systems Changes and Adaptations in the Older Adult

1. Age-related changes: older adults experience a loss of function of the senses.
   a. May lead to sensory deprivation, isolation, disorientation, confusion, appearance of senility, and depression.
   b. May strain social interactions and decrease ability to interact socially and with the environment.
   c. Alters quality of life.

   > **CAUTION:** May lead to decreased functional mobility and increased risk of injury.

2. Visual system changes, conditions, and clinical implications.
   a. Age-related changes: there is a general decline in visual acuity; gradual prior to sixth decade, rapid decline between ages 60 and 90; visual loss may be as much as 80% by age 90. These changes include:
      (1) Presbyopia: visual loss in middle and older ages characterized by inability to focus properly and blurred images; due to loss of accommodation, diminished elasticity of lens.
      (2) Decreased ability to adapt to dark and light.
      (3) Increased sensitivity to light and glare.
      (4) Loss of color discrimination, especially for blues and greens.
      (5) Decreased pupillary responses, size of resting pupil increases.
      (6) Decreased sensitivity of corneal reflex: less sensitive to eye injury or infection.
      (7) Oculomotor responses diminished: restricted upward gaze, reduced pursuit eye movements; ptosis may develop.
   b. Additional vision loss associated with pathology.
      (1) Low vision: a visual impairment that standard eyeglasses, contact lenses, medication, or surgery cannot correct.
         (a) Persons with low vision have some usable vision, but impairments are severe enough to make it difficult to perform everyday activities.
         (b) One in 28 Americans over the age of 40 years qualify as having low vision.
         (c) Four chronic, progressing eye diseases are the main conditions contributing to the development of low vision: i.e., age-related macular degeneration (AMD), diabetic retinopathy, glaucoma, and cataracts.
      (2) Age-related macular degeneration (AMD).
         (a) Affects the macula, the part of the eye that allows you to see fine detail.
         (b) Appears as a "blank spot" in the central visual field, blurring details and the sharp/central vision needed for many daily activities.
         (c) AMD can be dry (80%–90% of cases) or wet (10%–20% of cases). In dry AMD, drusen block vision; in wet AMD, hemorrhagic bleeding on the macula blocks vision. Dry AMD can progress to wet AMD.
         (d) There is no treatment available for dry AMD; however, wet AMD can progress quickly, and medical treatment (i.e., eye injections) is available.
         (e) The affected area on the macula is called a scotoma. Scotomas can be relative (e.g., some vision can be processed with increased light) or dense (no vision despite light changes).
         (f) All scotomas are not the same; they can be in different sizes, different shapes, and different locations. Variations may also exist between the two eyes.

         > **CAUTION:** Use of magnifiers is *not* indicated for certain scotomas because it may enlarge images into the non-seeing portion of the macula.

         (g) Less common symptoms of AMD include metamorphopsia, which is the appearance of spinning and swirling of images, and Charles Bonnet syndrome (also known as "phantom vision") which leads to visual hallucinations that the individual knows are not real.
         (h) Affects occupational performance such as reading, driving, managing medication, and watching television.
      (3) Diabetic retinopathy.
         (a) A complication of diabetes that affects the eyes. This is caused by damage to the blood vessels of the light-sensitive tissue at the back of the eye—the *retina*.
         (b) This condition affects central and peripheral vision, causing blurred or hazy vision in affected areas.

(c) Can develop in anyone who has type 1 or type 2 diabetes.
(d) There are two types of diabetic retinopathy: nonproliferative and proliferative.
(e) Nonproliferative diabetic retinopathy is the early stage of the disease, in which symptoms will be mild or not apparent, leaving more vision intact. This form can progress to proliferative.
(f) Proliferative diabetic retinopathy is a more advanced form of the disease, characterized by new blood vessel growth in the retina and leakage of blood vessels, which causes scar formation and possibly retinal detachment.

> **RED FLAG:** This can lead to total blindness.

(g) Maintaining control of blood glucose levels helps prevent vison loss.
(4) Glaucoma.
   (a) Chronic elevated pressure in the eye that may cause optic nerve atrophy and loss of peripheral vision. This is more prevalent in persons over 40 years old.
   (b) Vision loss starts peripherally and moves toward central vision (also referred to as 'tunnel vision').
   (c) Symptoms include difficulty scanning the environment and decreased visual acuity, contrast sensitivity, light sensitivity, and sensitivity to glare. Orientation and mobility within the environment are often affected, especially with dim illumination and at night.
   (d) Medical intervention is available to decrease the intraocular pressure. Glaucoma can also be prevented with eye drops.
   (e) This condition is painless and is often detected too late when the person experiences vision deficits. At that point, the goal is to decrease further vision loss.
(5) Cataracts.
   (a) Opacity of the lens, including protein changes and lens hardening/thickening, which results in diminished visual acuity and gradual loss in vision.
   (b) Field of vison is not affected.
   (c) Vision is overall hazy and blurry, especially in glaring light or when reading printed materials.
   (d) Central vision is predominantly affected because of the glare, haziness, and decrease in contrast sensitivity.
   (e) If surgery is indicated, the lens is removed and an intraocular lens (plastic implant) is inserted to correct visual deficits.

(6) Neurological injuries (e.g., cerebrovascular accident [CVA], traumatic brain injury [TBI], and brain tumors) can also lead to irreversible vision damage.
   (a) With neurological diagnoses, the structures of the eye remain functionally intact; impairment depends on where damage in the visual pathway occurs.
   (b) Aspects of vision that may be affected include visual acuity, visual fields, oculomotor control, binocularity, contrast sensitivity, visual attention, visual scanning, vision perception, and visual memory.
   (c) Homonymous hemianopsia: a visual field deficit in which half of the visual field is lost in each eye (i.e., nasal half of one eye and temporal half of other eye); occurs after neurological injury, especially CVA. This results in an inability to receive information from right or left sides, corresponding to the side of sensorimotor deficit.

c. Strategies to slow, reverse, and/or compensate for age-related visual system changes.
   (1) Assess for visual deficits: visual acuity, visual fields, contrast sensitivity, light and dark adaptation, depth perception, diplopia, eye fatigue, and eye pain.
   (2) Maximize visual function: assess for use of magnification as indicated, or the need for environmental adaptations.
   (3) Sensory thresholds are increased: allow extra time for visual discrimination and response.
   (4) When considering compensatory strategies, consider other client factors that may impact function, such as tremors or decreased range of motion, strength, sensation, cognition, hearing, and/or ambulation.
   (5) Work in adequate light, increase intensity, reduce glare; avoid abrupt changes in light, for example, light to dark.
   (6) Use large, high-contrast print for written materials.
   (7) Provide magnifying glasses (either portable or attached to a stand/work table) to view objects and complete tasks. Remember that magnificent level must be prescribed by a doctor.
   (8) Provide an eye patch for diplopia.
      (a) Some state OT licensure practice acts do not allow OT practitioners to give clients eye patches. In these states, the occupational therapist should refer the person to an ophthalmologist.
   (9) Decreased peripheral vision may limit social interactions; therefore, stand directly in front of the person at eye level when communicating with them.

(10) Assist in color discrimination: use warm colors (i.e., yellow, orange, red) for identification and color coding.
(11) Provide other sensory cues when vision is limited (e.g., verbal descriptions to new environments, sighted guide techniques, touching to communicate you are listening, and 'talking' clocks and watches).
(12) Provide safety education; reduce fall risk.
(13) Chapter 15 provides additional information about evaluation methods and intervention approaches for low vision.

3. Auditory system changes, conditions, and clinical implications.
   a. Hearing age-related changes: occur as early as fourth decade; affects a significant number of older adults (33% of individuals aged 65–74 have hearing impairments and 50% over age 75 have hearing loss; rate of loss in men is twice the rate of women, also starts earlier).
      (1) Outer ear: buildup of cerumen (ear wax) may result in conductive hearing loss; common in older men.
      (2) Middle ear: minimal degenerative changes of bony joints.
      (3) Inner ear: significant changes in sound sensitivity, understanding of speech, and maintenance of equilibrium may result with degeneration and atrophy of cochlea and vestibular structures, loss of neurons.
   b. Types of hearing loss.
      (1) Conductive: mechanical hearing loss from damage to external auditory canal, tympanic membrane, or middle ear ossicles; results in hearing loss (all frequencies); tinnitus (ringing in the ears) may be present.
      (2) Sensorineural: central or neural hearing loss from multiple factors (e.g., noise damage, trauma, disease, drugs, arteriosclerosis, etc.).
      (3) Presbycusis: sensorineural hearing loss associated with middle and older ages; characterized by bilateral hearing loss, especially at high frequencies at first, then all frequencies; poor auditory discrimination and comprehension, especially with background noise; tinnitus.
   c. Additional hearing loss with pathology.
      (1) Otosclerosis: immobility of stapes results in profound conductive hearing loss.
      (2) Paget's disease.
      (3) Hypothyroidism.
   d. Strategies to slow, reverse, and/or compensate for age-related auditory system changes.
      (1) Assess for hearing: acuity, speech discrimination/comprehension; tinnitus, dizziness, vertigo, pain.
      (2) Assess for use of hearing aids; check for proper functioning.
      (3) Minimize auditory distractions, work in quiet environment.
      (4) Speak slowly and clearly, directly in front of person at eye level.
      (5) Use nonverbal communication to reinforce your message, for example, gesture, demonstration.
      (6) Provide written and demonstrated directions/guidelines for activities.
      (7) Orient person to topics of conversation he/she cannot hear to reduce paranoia, isolation.
      (8) Provide assistive devices to compensate for functional effects of hearing loss and to ensure person's safety (e.g., vibrating and flashing smoke alarms, telephones, doorbells, and clocks).

4. Vestibular system changes, conditions, and clinical implications.
   a. Age-related changes: degenerative changes in otoconia of utricle and saccule; loss of vestibular hair-cell receptors; decreased number of vestibular neurons; vestibular ocular reflex gain decreases; beginning at age 30, at ages 55-60 there is accelerating decline which results in diminished vestibular sensation.
      (1) Diminished acuity, delayed reaction times, longer response times.
      (2) Reduced function of vestibular ocular reflex; affects retinal image stability with head movements, produces blurred vision.
      (3) Altered sensory organization: older adults more dependent upon somatosensory inputs for balance.
      (4) Less able to resolve sensory conflicts when presented with inappropriate visual or proprioceptive inputs due to vestibular losses.
      (5) Postural response patterns for balance are disorganized: characterized by diminished ankle torque, increased hip torque, increased postural sway.

> **RED FLAG:** Increased incidence of falls in older adults.

   b. Additional loss of vestibular sensitivity with pathology.
      (1) Ménière's disease: episodic attacks characterized by tinnitus, dizziness, and a sensation of fullness or pressure in the ears; may also experience sensorineural hearing loss.
      (2) Benign paroxysmal positional vertigo (BPPV): brief episodes of vertigo (less than 1 minute) associated with position change; the result of degeneration of the utricular otoconia that settle on the cupula of the posterior semicircular canal; common in older adults.

(3) Medications: antihypertensives (postural hypotension); anticonvulsants; tranquilizers, sleeping pills, aspirin, nonsteroidal anti-inflammatory drugs.
(4) Cerebrovascular disease: vertebrobasilar artery insufficiency (transient ischemic attack, stroke); cerebellar artery stroke, lateral medullary stroke.
(5) Cerebellar dysfunction: hemorrhage, tumors (acoustic neuroma, meningioma); degenerative disease of brain stem and cerebellum; progressive supranuclear palsy.
(6) Migraine.
(7) Cardiac disease.
c. Strategies to slow, reverse, and/or compensate for changes.
(1) Refer to Chapter 15 for information on fall prevention.
5. Somatosensory system changes, conditions, and clinical implications.
a. Age-related changes.
(1) Decreased sensitivity of touch associated with decline of peripheral receptors, atrophy of afferent fibers, lower extremities more affected than upper.
(2) Proprioceptive losses, increased thresholds in vibratory sensibility, beginning around age 50; greater in lower extremities than upper extremities, greater in distal extremities than proximal.
(3) Loss of joint receptor sensitivity; losses in lower extremities and/or cervical joints may contribute to loss of balance.
(4) Cutaneous pain thresholds increase, greater changes in upper body areas (e.g., upper extremities, face) than in lower extremities.
b. Additional loss of sensation with pathology.
(1) Diabetes, peripheral neuropathy.
(2) CVA, central sensory losses.
(3) Peripheral vascular disease, peripheral ischemia.
c. Strategies to slow, reverse, and/or compensate for age-related somatosensory system changes.
(1) Assess carefully: check for increased thresholds to stimulation, sensory losses by modality, area of body.
(2) Allow extra time for responses with increased thresholds.
(3) Use touch to communicate: maximize physical contact (e.g., rubbing, stroking, tapping).
(4) Provide augmented feedback through appropriate sensory channels (e.g., using kitchen utensils with wide textured grips may be easier than narrow, smooth handles).
(5) Teach compensatory strategies to prevent injury to anesthetic limbs.

(6) Provide assistive devices and environmental modifications as needed for fall prevention. See Chapter 15 for further information.
(7) Provide biofeedback devices as appropriate (e.g., limb load monitor).
6. Gustatory and olfactory system changes, conditions, and clinical implications.
a. Taste and smell age-related changes.
(1) Gradual decrease in taste sensitivity.
(a) As a result, older adults frequently increase their use of taste enhancers (e.g., salt and/or sugar).
(b) Decreased taste can diminish the enjoyment of food and contribute to a poor diet and inadequate nutrition.
(2) Decreased smell sensitivity.
(a) Decreased home safety can result (e.g., the inability to detect gas leaks or smoke).
b. Conditions resulting in additional loss of sensation.
(1) Smoking.
(2) Chronic allergies, respiratory infections.
(3) Dentures.
(4) CVA, involvement of hypoglossal nerve.
c. Strategies to slow, reverse, and/or compensate for age-related gustatory and olfactory system changes.
(1) Assess for identification of odors, tastes (i.e., sweet, sour, bitter, salty); somatic sensations (i.e., temperature, touch).

Cognitive Changes and Adaptations in the Older Adult

1. Age-related cognitive changes, conditions, and clinical implications.
a. No uniform decline in intellectual abilities throughout adulthood.
(1) Cognitive changes do not typically show up until mid-60s; significant declines affecting everyday life do not show up until early 80s.
(2) Most significant decline in measures of intelligence occurs in the years immediately preceding death (termed 'terminal drop').
b. Tasks involving perceptual speed show early declines (by age 39); require increased time to complete tasks.
c. Numeric ability (tests of adding, subtracting, multiplying): abilities peak in mid-40s, well maintained until 60s.
d. Verbal ability: abilities peak at age 30, well maintained until 60s.
e. Memory.
(1) Impairments are typically noted in short-term memory; long-term memory retained.

(2) Impairments are task dependent (e.g., deficits primarily with novel conditions, new learning).
f. Learning: all age groups can learn. Factors affecting learning in older adults include:
   (1) Increased cautiousness.
   (2) Anxiety.
   (3) Sensory deficits.
   (4) Pace of learning: fast pace is problematic.
   (5) Interference from prior learning.
2. Clinical implications.
   a. Older adults utilize different strategies for memory: context-based strategies versus memorization (young adults).
3. Strategies to slow, reverse, and/or compensate for age-related cognitive changes.
   a. Improve health.
      (1) Correct medical problems: imbalances between oxygen supply and demand to CNS (e.g., cardiovascular disease, hypertension, diabetes, and hypothyroidism).
      (2) Assess needed pharmacological changes: drug re-evaluation; decrease use of multiple drugs; monitor closely for drug toxicity.
      (3) Reduce chronic use of tobacco and alcohol.
      (4) Correct nutritional deficiencies.
   b. Increase physical activity.
   c. Increase mental activity.
      (1) Keep mentally engaged, 'use it or lose it' (e.g., chess, crossword puzzles, book discussion groups, reading to children).
      (2) Maintain an engaged lifestyle: socially active (e.g., clubs, travel, work, volunteerism; allow for personal choice in activity).
      (3) Use cognitive training activities.
   d. Provide multiple sensory cues to compensate for decreased sensory processing and sensory losses and to maximize learning (e.g., provide visual demonstrations, written instructions, verbal cues).
   e. Provide stimulating, 'enriching' environment; avoid environmental dislocation (e.g., hospitalization or institutionalization may produce disorientation and agitation in some older adults).
   f. Reduce stress; provide counseling and family support.

Cardiopulmonary System Changes and Adaptations in the Older Adult

1. Cardiovascular age-related changes.
   a. Changes due more to inactivity and disease than aging.
   b. Degeneration of heart muscle.
   c. Decreased coronary blood flow.
   d. Cardiac valves thicken and stiffen.
   e. Changes in conduction system: loss of pacemaker cells in SA node.
   f. Changes in blood vessels: arteries thicken, less distensible; slowed exchange capillary walls; increased peripheral resistance.
   g. Resting blood pressures rise: systolic greater than diastolic.
   h. Decreased blood volume, hemopoietic activity of bone.
   i. Increased blood coagulability.
2. Clinical implications for cardiovascular changes.
   a. Changes at rest are minor: resting heart rate and cardiac output relatively unchanged; resting blood pressures increase.
   b. Cardiovascular responses to exercise: blunted, decreased heart rate acceleration, decreased maximal oxygen uptake and heart rate; reduced exercise capacity, increased recovery time.
   c. Decreased stroke volume due to decreased myocardial contractility.
   d. Maximum heart rate declines with age.
   e. Cardiac output decreases, 1% per year after age 20 due to decreased heart rate and stroke volume.
   f. Orthostatic hypotension: common problem in older adults due to reduced baroreceptor sensitivity and vascular elasticity.
   g. Increased fatigue; anemia common in older adults.
   h. Systolic ejection murmur common in older adults.
   i. Possible electrocardiogram changes: loss of normal sinus rhythm; increased arrhythmias.
3. Pulmonary system age-related changes.
   a. Chest wall stiffness, declining strength of respiratory muscles results in increased work of breathing.
   b. Loss of lung elastic recoil, decreased lung compliance.
   c. Changes in lung parenchyma: alveoli enlarge, become thinner; fewer capillaries for delivery of blood.
   d. Changes in pulmonary blood vessels: thicken, less distensible.
   e. Decline in total lung capacity: residual volume increases, vital capacity decreases.
   f. Forced expiratory volume (air flow) decreases.
   g. Altered pulmonary gas exchange: oxygen tension falls with age (at a rate of 4 mm Hg/decade; PaO_2 at age 70 is 75, versus 90 at age 20).
   h. Blunted ventilatory responses of chemoreceptors in response to respiratory acidosis: decreased homeostatic responses.
   i. Blunted defense/immune responses: decreased ciliary action to clear secretions, decreased secretory immunoglobulins.
4. Clinical implications for pulmonary changes.
   a. Respiratory responses to exercise: similar to younger adult at low and moderate intensities; at higher

intensities, responses include increased ventilatory cost of work, greater blood acidosis, increased likelihood of breathlessness, and increased perceived exertion.
   b. Clinical signs of hypoxia are blunted; changes in mentation and affect may provide important cues.
   c. Cough mechanism is impaired.
   d. Gag reflex is decreased, increased risk of aspiration.
   e. Recovery from respiratory illness: prolonged in older adults.
   f. Significant changes in function with chronic smoking, exposure to environmental toxic inhalants.
5. Strategies to slow, reverse, and/or compensate for age-related changes in cardiopulmonary systems.
   a. Complete a cardiopulmonary assessment prior to commencing an exercise program.

> **CAUTION:** This is essential in older adults due to their high incidence of cardiopulmonary pathologies.

   (1) Select an appropriate graded exercise testing protocol.
   (2) Standardized test batteries and norms for older adults are not available.

> **CAUTION:** Many older adults cannot tolerate maximal testing; submaximal testing commonly used.

   (3) Testing and training modes should be similar.
   b. Individualized exercise prescription is essential.
      (1) Choice of training program is based on: fitness level, presence or absence of cardiovascular disease, musculoskeletal limitations, and the individual's goals, roles, and activity interests.
      (2) Prescriptive elements (i.e., frequency, intensity, duration, mode) are the same as for younger adults.
      (3) Walking, chair and floor exercises, yoga, tai-chi, and modified strength/flexibility calisthenics are well-tolerated by most older adults.
      (4) Consider pool programs (e.g., exercises, ai-chi, walking, swimming) for persons with musculoskeletal and neurological impairments.
      (5) Consider multiple modes of exercise on alternate days to maintain interest and reduce likelihood of muscle injury, joint overuse, pain, fatigue, and boredom.
   c. Aerobic training programs can significantly improve cardiopulmonary function in older adults.
      (1) Decreases heart rate at a given submaximal power output.
      (2) Improves maximal oxygen uptake (VO_2 max).
      (3) Improves peripheral adaptation and muscle oxidative capacity.
      (4) Improves recovery heart rates.
      (5) Decreases systolic blood pressure, may produce a small decrease in diastolic blood pressure.
      (6) Increases maximum ventilatory capacity: vital capacity.
      (7) Reduces breathlessness, lowers perceived exertion.
      (8) Improves sense of well-being and self-image.
      (9) Improves functional capacity.
   d. Improve overall daily activity levels for independent living.
      (1) Lack of exercise/activity is an important risk factor in the development of cardiopulmonary diseases.
      (2) Lack of exercise/activity contributes to problems of immobility and disability in older adults.
6. See Chapter 8 for additional information on cardiovascular and pulmonary system disorders and cardiopulmonary evaluation and intervention approaches.

Other Systems Changes and Adaptations in the Older Adult

1. Integumentary changes.
   a. Changes in skin composition.
      (1) Dermis thins with loss of elastin.
      (2) Decreased vascularity; vascular fragility results in easy bruising (senile purpura).
      (3) Decreased sebaceous activity and decline in hydration.
      (4) Appearance: skin appears dry, wrinkled, yellowed, and inelastic; aging spots appear (clusters of melanocyte pigmentation); increased with exposure to sun.
      (5) General thinning and graying of hair due to vascular insufficiency and decreased melanin production.
      (6) Nails grow more slowly, become brittle and thick.
   b. Loss of effectiveness as protective barrier.
      (1) Skin grows and heals more slowly; less able to resist injury and infection.
      (2) Inflammatory response is attenuated.

> **CAUTION:** Decreased sensitivity to touch and diminished perception of pain and temperature can contribute to increased risk for injury from concentrated pressures or excess temperatures.

> **CAUTION:** Decreased sweat production with loss of sweat glands results in decreased temperature regulation and homeostasis.

2. Gastrointestinal changes.
   a. Decreased salivation, taste, and smell along with inadequate chewing (tooth loss, poorly fitting dentures); poor swallowing reflex may lead to poor dietary intake, nutritional deficiencies.

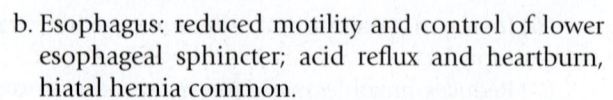

b. Esophagus: reduced motility and control of lower esophageal sphincter; acid reflux and heartburn, hiatal hernia common.
c. Stomach: reduced motility, delayed gastric emptying; decreased digestive enzymes and hydrochloric acid; decreased digestion and absorption; indigestion common.
d. Decreased intestinal motility; constipation common.
3. Renal, urogenital changes.
   a. Kidneys: loss of mass and total weight with nephron atrophy, decreased renal blood flow, decreased filtration.
      (1) Blood urea rises.
      (2) Decreased excretory and reabsorptive capacities.
   b. Bladder: muscle weakness; decreased capacity causing urinary frequency; difficulty with emptying causing increased retention.
      (1) Urinary incontinence common (affects over 10 million adults; over half of nursing home residents and one-third of community dwelling older adults); affects older women with pelvic floor weakness and older men with bladder or prostate disease.
      (2) Increased likelihood of urinary tract infections.

Nutrition and Older Adults

Overview and Contributing Factors to Poor Nutrition

1. Many older adults have primary nutrition problems.
   a. Nutritional problems in older adults are often linked to health status and poverty rather than to age itself.
      (1) Chronic diseases alter the overall need for nutrients, the abilities to take in and utilize nutrients, energy demands, and overall activity levels (e.g., neurocognitive disorders, CVA, diabetes).
      (2) Limited, fixed incomes severely limit food choices and availability.
   b. There is an age-related slowing in basal metabolic rate and a decline in total caloric intake; most of the decline is associated with a concurrent reduction in physical activity.
      (1) Both undernourishment and obesity exist in older adults and contribute to decreased levels of vitality and fitness.
   c. Contributing factors to poor dietary intake.
      (1) Decreased sense of taste and smell.
      (2) Poor teeth or poorly fitting dentures.
      (3) Reduced gastrointestinal function.
         (a) Decreased saliva.
         (b) Gastromucosal atrophy.
         (c) Reduced intestinal mobility; reflux.
      (4) Loss of interest in foods.
      (5) Isolation, lack of social support, no socialization during meals, loss of spouse, loss of friends.
      (6) Lack of functional mobility.
         (a) Inability to get to a grocery store to shop.
         (b) Inability to prepare foods.

Outcomes of Poor Nutrition

1. Dehydration is common in older adults, resulting in fluid and electrolyte disturbances.
   a. Thirst sensation is diminished.
   b. May be physically unable to acquire/maintain fluids.

> **RED FLAG:** Environmental heat stresses can contribute to dehydration (e.g., having no air conditioning during a summer heat wave) which can be life threatening and should be treated as medical emergencies.

   c. Diets are often deficient in nutrients, especially vitamins A and C, B12, thiamine, protein, iron, calcium, vitamin D, folic acid, and zinc.
   d. Increased use of alcohol or taste enhancers (e.g., salt and sugar) influences nutritional intake.
   e. Drug/dietary interactions influence nutritional intake (e.g., reserpine, digoxin, antitumor agents, excessive use of antacids).

Assessment of Nutrition

1. The role of the occupational therapy assistant (OTA).
   a. The OTA contributes to the evaluation process in collaboration with the OT supervisor.
      (1) Supervision is required.

(2) The level of supervision required will be determined by the OTA's experience and established service competence.
   b. Service competency must be established.
   c. The OTA cannot independently evaluate or interpret assessment results.
2. Evaluation foci.
   a. Dietary history: patterns of eating, types of foods.
   b. Psychosocial: mental status, desire to eat, depression, grief, social isolation, social supports.
   c. Body composition.
      (1) Weight/height measures.
      (2) Skin-fold measurements: triceps/subscapular skin-fold thickness.
      (3) Upper arm circumference.
   d. Olfactory and gustatory sensory function.
   e. Dental and periodontal disease, fit of dentures.
   f. Ability to feed self: mastication, swallowing, hand/mouth control, posture, physical weakness, and fatigue.
   g. Integumentary: skin condition, edema.
   h. Compliance to special diets.
   i. Functional assessment: basic activities of daily living, feeding; overall exercise/activity levels.

Goals and Interventions

1. Assist in monitoring adequate nutritional intake.
2. Assist in maintaining nutritional support.
   a. Refer to dietitian, nutritional consultants, and/or nutritional education programs as needed.
   b. Make recommendations for home health aide to assist with grocery shopping and meal preparation.
   c. Refer to older adults' food programs: home delivered (i.e., Meals on Wheels); congregate meals/senior center daily meal programs; federal supplemental nutrition assistance program (SNAP).
3. Maintain physical function and promote adequate activity levels.
4. Maintain independence in food preparation and self-feeding.
   a. Teach work simplification and energy conservation techniques to maximize function.
   b. Modify the environment and adapt activities to enhance mastery and ensure safety.
   c. See Chapters 14 and 15 for more details.

Elder and Vulnerable Adult Abuse

Overview: Facts and Statistics

1. In the United States, the abuse of vulnerable and older adults is a social justice and health care crisis.

EXAM HINT: The following facts are provided to support the critical need for everyone to address this societal crisis and highlight the need for OT practitioners to be vigilant about the potential of abuse, neglect, and exploitation in all interactions with vulnerable and older adults. These statistics will not be on the COTA® exam. However, because the AOTA code of ethics requires OT personnel to "demonstrate a concern for the safety and well-being of the recipients of their services" (AOTA, 2015, p. 2), it is likely that the exam will include items about the OTA's role in identifying and responding to elder and vulnerable adult abuse. The application of knowledge about the prevalence, signs, and symptoms of elder abuse and OT intervention for cases of abuse can help you determine the correct answer to these items.

   a. According to the best available estimates, in the United States, five million older adults (age 65 or older) are victims of abuse, neglect, and/or exploitation.
   b. Elder and vulnerable adult abuse is underreported; approximately one in 14–24 cases is reported to authorities.
   c. Two-thirds (67%) of reported elder abuse victims were female.
   d. The vast majority (86%) of reported elder abuse is committed by someone familiar to the victim.
2. Definitions vary; however, there are three basic categories.
   a. Domestic elder abuse.
   b. Institutional elder abuse.
   c. Self-neglect or self-abuse.

Signs and Symptoms of Elder Abuse

1. Physical abuse signs and symptoms.
   a. An older adult's report of being physically mistreated.
   b. Bruises, black eyes, welts, and/or lacerations.
   c. Rope marks and/or other signs of restraint.

d. Bone and skull fractures, sprains, and/or dislocations.
   e. Open wounds, cuts, and untreated injuries in various stages of healing.
   f. Internal injuries/bleeding.
   g. Broken eyeglasses.
   h. Under- or overdosing of prescribed drugs.
   i. A sudden change in behavior.
   j. The caregiver's refusal to allow visitors to see an older adult alone.
2. Sexual abuse signs and symptoms.
   a. An older adult's report of sexual assault or rape.
   b. Bruises around the breasts or genital area.
   c. Unexplained venereal disease or genital infection.
   d. Unexplained vaginal or anal bleeding.
   e. Torn, stained, or bloody underclothing.
3. Emotional/psychological abuse signs and symptoms.
   a. An older adult's report of being verbally or emotionally mistreated.
   b. Emotionally upset or agitated behavior.
   c. Extremely withdrawn and non-communicative or non-responsive behavior.
   d. Unusual behavior such as sucking, biting, or rocking.
4. Neglect signs and symptoms.
   a. An older adult's report of being mistreated.
   b. Dehydration, malnutrition, untreated bedsores, and poor personal hygiene.
   c. Unattended or untreated health problems.
   d. Hazardous or unsafe living conditions.
5. Financial or material exploitation signs and symptoms.
   a. An older adult's report of financial exploitation.
   b. Sudden changes in bank account or banking practice.
   c. The inclusion of additional names on an older adult's bank signature card.
   d. Unauthorized withdrawal using an ATM card.
   e. Abrupt changes in a will or other financial documents.
   f. Substandard care or unpaid bills despite the availability of funds.
   g. Discovery of a forged signature.
   h. Sudden appearance of relatives claiming rights to decisions, money, or possessions.
   i. Unexplained transfer of funds.
   j. The provision of unnecessary services.

Role of Occupational Therapy

1. Mandatory reporting.
   a. Elder abuse per se may or may not be designated as a specific crime in a state; however, most physical, sexual, and financial/material abuse are crimes in all states.
   b. Health care workers are required to report suspected or observed cases of elder abuse.
   c. Failure to report may be considered a crime.
   d. In most states, Adult Protective Services, the area Agency on Aging, or the county Department of Social Services are designated to provide investigation and services.
2. OT intervention.
   a. Treat for physical and emotional injuries.
   b. Develop a trusting relationship.
   c. Assist in developing a support system.
   d. Refer to appropriate disciplines and/or agencies.

References

American Occupational Therapy Association. (2015). Occupational therapy code of ethics and ethics standards, *American Journal of Occupational Therapy, 69* (Suppl. 3), S1–S8.

Amini, D. A. (2014). Motor and praxis assessments. In I. E. Asher (Ed.), *Occupational therapy assessment tools: An annotated index* (4th ed., pp. 441–499). Bethesda, MD: AOTA Press.

Anzalone, M. E., & Lane, S. J. (2012). Sensory processing disorder. In S. J. Lane & A. C. Bundy (Eds.), *Kids can be kids: A childhood occupations approach* (pp. 437–459). Philadelphia, PA: F.A. Davis.

Asher, I. E. (2014). *An annotated index of occupational therapy evaluation tools* (4th ed.). Bethesda, MD: AOTA Press.

Ayres, A. J. (1998). *Sensory integration and the child* (13th ed.). Los Angeles, CA: Western Psychological Services.

Beery, K. E., Buktenica, N. A., & Beery, N. A. (2010). *Beery-Buktenica Developmental Test of Visual-Motor Integration (BEERY™ VMI)* (6th ed.). San Antonio, TX: Pearson Education.

Berkow, R., & Beers, R. (Eds.). (2000). *The Merck manual of geriatrics* (3rd ed.). Whitehouse Station, NJ: Merck and Co.

Bigsby, E., & Vergara, R. (2003). *Developmental and therapeutic interventions in the NICU*. Baltimore, MD: Paul H. Brookes.

Bundy, A. C., & Murray, E. A. (2002). Sensory integration: A. Jean Ayres' theory revisited. In A. C. Bundy, S. J. Lane, & E. A. Murray (Eds.), *Sensory integration: Theory and practice* (2nd ed., pp. 3–33). Philadelphia, PA: F. A. Davis.

Case-Smith, J. (2015). Development of childhood occupations. In J. Case-Smith & J. C. O'Brien (Eds.), *Occupational therapy for children and adolescents* (7th ed., pp. 65–101). St. Louis, MO: Elsevier.

Case-Smith, J., & Humphry, R. (2005). Feeding intervention. In J. Case-Smith (Ed.), *Occupational therapy for children* (5th ed., pp. 485–520). St. Louis, MO: Elsevier Mosby.

Case-Smith, J., & O'Brien, J. C. (2015). *Occupational therapy for children* (7th ed.). Maryland Heights, MO: Mosby Elsevier.

Centers for Disease Control and Prevention. (2018). *Deaths: Leading causes for 2016* (DHHS Publication No. 2018-1120). Retrieved from https://www.cdc.gov/nchs/data/nvsr/nvsr67/nvsr67_06.pdf

Centers for Medicare and Medicaid Services. (2018, December 6). *NHE fact sheet*. Retrieved from https://www.cms.gov/research-statistics-data-and-systems/statistics-trends-and-reports/nationalhealthexpenddata/nhe-fact-sheet.html

Child help. (2018). *National child abuse statistics*. Retrieved from https://www.childhelp.org/child-abuse-statistics/

Coker-Bolt, P. C., Garcia, T., & Naber, E. (2015). Neuromotor cerebral palsy. In J. Case-Smith & J. C. O'Brien (Eds.), *Occupational therapy for children and adolescence* (7th ed., pp. 793–811). St. Louis, MO: Elsevier.

Cyberparent. (2010). *Abuse of children: The signs and symptoms*. Retrieved from http://www.cyberparent.com/abuse/childabuse

Dunbar, S. B. (2007). Theory, frame of reference and model: A differentiation for practice considerations. In S. B. Dunbar (Ed.), *Occupational therapy models for intervention with children and families* (pp. 1–9). Thorofare, NJ: Slack.

Erhardt, R. P. (1994). *The Erhardt Developmental Prehension Assessment*. Maplewood, MN: Erhardt Developmental Products.

Gench, B., Hinson, M., & McNurlen, G. (1996). *Human reflexes and reacting resource cards*. Dubuque, IA: Eddie Bowers.

Gesell, A., & Amatrunda, G. (1947). *Developmental diagnosis* (2nd ed.). New York, NY; Harper & Row.

Humphry, R., & Womack, J. (2012). Transformations of occupations: A life course perspective. In B. A. B. Schell, G. Gillen, & M. E. Scaffa (Eds.), *Willard and Spackman's occupational therapy* (12th ed., pp. 60–71). Philadelphia, PA: Lippincott Williams & Wilkins.

Jaffe, L., & Cosper, S. (2015). Working with families. In J. Case-Smith & J. C. O'Brien (Eds.), *Occupational therapy for children and adolescence* (7th ed., pp. 129–161). St. Louis, MI: Elsevier.

Kahn-D'Angelo, L. (2013). Theories of development, motor control, and motor learning. In S. B. O'Sullivan & R. P. Siegelman (Eds.), *National physical therapy examination review & study guide* (16th ed., pp. 283–299). Evanston, IL: Therapy Ed.

Kang, P. (2013). Muscles, bones and nerves. In M. L. Batshaw, N. J. Roizen, & G. Lotrecchiano (Eds.), *Children with disabilities* (7th ed., pp. 213–231). Baltimore, MD: Paul H. Brookes.

Klein, M. (1987). *Pre-scissor skills* (rev. ed.). Tuscon, AZ: Therapy Skill Builders.

Korth, I., & Rendell, L. (2015). Feeding interventions. In J. Case-Smith & J. C. O'Brien (Eds.), *Occupational therapy for children and adolescents* (7th ed., pp. 385–415). St. Louis, MO: Elsevier.

Lane, S. J. (2002). Sensory modulation. In A. C. Bundy, S. J. Lane, & E. A. Murray (Eds.), *Sensory integration: Theory and practice* (2nd ed., pp. 101–122). Philadelphia, PA: F.A. Davis.

Law, M., Missiuna, C., Pollock, N., & Stewart, D. (2005). Foundations for occupational therapy practice with children. In J. Case-Smith (Ed.), *Occupational therapy for children* (5th ed., pp. 53–87). St. Louis, MO: Elsevier Mosby.

Lewis, C. & Bottomley, J. (2007). *Geriatric rehabilitation: A clinical approach* (3rd ed.). Upper Saddle River, NJ: Prentice Hall.

Mandich, A., Wilson, J., & Gain, K. (2015). Cognitive interventions for children. In J. Case-Smith & J. C. O'Brien (Eds.), *Occupational therapy for children and adolescents* (7th ed., pp. 304–320). St. Louis, MO: Elsevier.

Miller, L. J. (2014). *Sensational kids: Hope and help for children with sensory processing disorders (SPD)* (rev ed.). New York, NY: G. P. Putnam's Sons.

Mosey, A. C. (1996). *Psychosocial components of occupational therapy*. Philadelphia, PA: Lippincott-Raven.

Myers, C. T., Case-Smith, J., & Cason, J. (2015). Early intervention. In J. Case-Smith & J. C. O'Brien (Eds.), *Occupational therapy for children and adolescents* (7th ed., pp. 636–663). St. Louis, MO: Elsevier.

National Board for Certification in Occupational Therapy (NBCOT®). (2018). *Practice analysis of the certified occupational therapy assistant: Executive summary*. Gaithersburg, MD: Author. Retrieved from https://www.nbcot.org/-/media/NBCOT/PDFs/2017-Practice-Analysis-Executive-COTA.ashx?la=en

National Center on Elder Abuse. (2013). *Elder abuse and its impact: What you must know*. Retrieved from https://ncea.acl.gov/resources/docs/EA-Impact-What-You-Must-Know-2013.pdf

National Council on Aging. (2016). *Fact sheet*. Retrieved from https://www.ncoa.org/wp-content/uploads/NCOA-Economic-Security.pdf

National Institute on Deafness and Other Communication Disorders. (2018, July 17). *Age-related hearing loss*. Retrieved from https://www.nidcd.nih.gov/health/age-related-hearing-loss

Odhayani, A. A., Watson, W. J., & Watson, L. (2013). Behavioural consequences of child abuse. *Canadian Family Physician, 59*, 831–836.

Office for Victims of Crime. (2016). *Elder abuse*. Retrieved from https://ovc.ncjrs.gov/ncvrw2016/content/section-6/PDF/2016NCVRW_6_ElderAbuse-508.pdf

Office for Victims of Crime. (2018). *Crimes against older adults*. Retrieved from https://ovc.ncjrs.gov/ncvrw2018/info_flyers/fact_sheets/2018NCVRW_OlderAdults_508_QC.pdf

Parham, D., & Mailoux, Z. (2015). Sensory integration. In J. Case-Smith & J. C. O'Brien (Eds.), *Occupational therapy for children and adolescents* (7th ed., pp. 258–303). St. Louis, MO: Elsevier.

Reeves, G. D., & Cermak, S. A. (2002). Disorders of praxis. In A. C., Bundy, S. J. Lane, & E. A. Murray (Eds.), *Sensory integration: Theory and practice* (2nd ed., pp. 71–100). Philadelphia, PA: F. A. Davis.

Rodger, S., & Liu, S. (2008). Cognitive orientation to (daily) occupational performance: Changes in strategy and session time use over the course of intervention. *OTJR: Occupation, Participation and Health, 38*, 168–179.

Rogers, S. (2005). Common conditions that influence children's participation. In J. Case-Smith (Ed.), *Occupational therapy for children* (5th ed., pp. 160–215). St. Louis, MO: Elsevier Mosby.

Sadock, B. J., & Sadock V. A. (2007). *Kaplan and Sadock's synopsis of psychiatry: Behavioral sciences/clinical psychiatry* (10th ed.). Philadelphia, PA: Lippincott Williams & Wilkins.

Schneck, C. M., & Case-Smith, J. (2015). Pre-writing and hand skills. In J. Case-Smith & J. C. O'Brien (Eds.), *Occupational therapy for children and adolescents* (7th ed., pp. 498–524). St. Louis, MO: Elsevier.

Shapiro, B. K., & Batshaw, M. L. (2013). Developmental delay and intellectual disability. In M. L. Batshaw, N. J. Roizen, & G. R. Lotrecchiano (Eds.), *Children with disabilities* (7th ed., pp. 291–306). Baltimore, MD: Paul H. Brookes.

Shepherd, J. (2015). Activities of daily living and sleep and rest. In J. Case-Smith & J. C. O'Brien (Eds.), *Occupational therapy for children* (7th ed., pp. 416–460). St. Louis, MO: Elsevier Mosby.

Smith, S. K. (2001). *Mandatory reporting of child abuse and neglect*. Retrieved from http://www.smithlawfirm.com/mandatoryreporting

Statista. (2019). *Average life expectancy in North America for those born in 2018, by gender and region (in years)*. Retrieved from https://www.statista.com/statistics/274513/life-expectancy-in-north-america/

Turnbull, A. P., & Turnbull, H. R. (1990). *Families professions and exceptionality: A special partnership* (pp. 156–157). Columbus, OH: Merrill.

U.S. Census Bureau. (2018). *The population 65 years and older in the United States: 2016*. Retrieved from https://www.census.gov/content/dam/Census/library/publications/2018/acs/ACS-38.pdf

U.S. Department of Health and Human Services, The Administration for Community Living. (2018). *2017 profile of older Americans*. Retrieved from https://acl.gov/sites/default/files/Aging%20and%20Disability%20in%20America/2017OlderAmericansProfile.pdf

U.S. Department of Health and Human Services, Administration for Children and Families, and Administration on Children, Youth and Families. (2019). *Child maltreatment 2017*. Retrieved from https://www.acf.hhs.gov/cb/research-data-technology/statistics-research/child-maltreatment

Vergara, E. (1993). *Foundations for practice in the neonatal intensive care unit and early intervention* (Vol. 2, pp. 34–35). Baltimore, MD: AOTA Press.

Review Questions

Human Development Across the Lifespan: Considerations for Occupational Therapy Practice

Following are five questions about key content covered in this chapter. These questions are not inclusive of the entirety of content about human development across the lifespan and pediatric through geriatric considerations for occupational therapy practice that you must know for success on the COTA® exam. These questions are provided to help you jump-start the thought processes you will need to apply your studying of content to the answering of exam questions; hence they are not in the COTA® exam format. Exam items in the COTA® format that cover the depth and breadth of content you will need to know to pass the exam are provided on this text's online exams. The answers to the following questions are provided in Appendix 3.

1. A typically developing child with no developmental delays independently creates a building made of blocks from a mental image. Identify the child's age range and describe the skills the child would use during this play activity.

2. You are part of an intraprofessional screening team to determine children's readiness for kindergarten. A 5-year-old child whom you and the occupational therapist are evaluating has performed at or above level on every aspect of the screening. The child has not demonstrated any fine motor, visual motor, or gross motor delays. The child has no cognitive deficits. Given the child's performance, which of Erhardt's developmental levels of prewriting skills would you expect the child to use for writing tasks? Explain your answer.

3. A 15-year-old has a group of friends who have recently become involved in experimenting with drugs, alcohol, and other risky behaviors. The teen is torn between wanting to remain friends with this group and not wanting to join them in these behaviors. The teen decides to join another group of teens who are engaged in a competitive soccer league in order to meet and become connected to a new group of friends. According to Erikson's eight stages of man, what stage of development is the teenager undergoing? Describe the characteristics of this stage.

4. A 16-month-old toddler is brought to occupational therapy for an evaluation. The parents are concerned with the frequency of the toddler's falls, which result in bangs to the head. The child demonstrates delayed motor skills. The occupational therapist and you notice that the toddler has not yet integrated primitive reflexes. Which primary primitive reflex is most likely absent in this toddler? Explain its relevance to the toddler's health status and safety and its impact on occupational performance.

5. You provide wellness and prevention services to older adults who attend a community-based senior center. What strategies to slow, reverse, and/or compensate for age-related changes to their muscular, skeletal, and neurological systems can you share with these older adults?

6

Musculoskeletal System Disorders

COLLEEN MAHER

Chapter Outline

- Anatomy of the Musculoskeletal System, 158
- Hand and Upper Extremity Disorders and Injuries, 162
- Arthritis, 169
- Osteogenesis Imperfecta (OI), 171
- Hip Fractures, 173
- Total Hip Replacement (THR)/Total Hip Arthroplasty, 174
- Amputations, 175
- Burns, 179
- Pain, 181
- References, 182
- Review Questions, 184

Anatomy of the Musculoskeletal System

Relationship to the Examination

1. It is not likely that the NBCOT® exam will ask direct questions about anatomy or physiology.
2. As a result, this chapter does not provide a complete anatomy and physiology review.

> **EXAM HINT:** The NBCOT® exam outline for the certified occupational therapy assistant (COTA®) identifies knowledge of the "impact of body functions (and) body structures, . . . on occupational performance" (NBCOT®, 2018, p. 21) as essential for competent and safe practice. Thus, knowing the major structures and functions of the musculoskeletal system can help you correctly answer exam items about the functional implications of damage to the musculoskeletal system. For example, damage to the opponens pollicis would result in the need to engage in activities that do not require opposition.

Anatomy of the Hand

1. Intrinsic muscles innervated by the median nerve (see Figure 6-1).
   a. Abductor pollicis brevis.
      (1) Origin: scaphoid, trapezium, flexor retinaculum, and tendon of the abductor pollicis longus.
      (2) Insertion: base of proximal phalanx, radial side of thumb.
      (3) Function: palmar abduction.
   b. Opponens pollicis.
      (1) Origin: trapezium and flexor retinaculum.
      (2) Insertion: first metacarpal.
      (3) Function: opposition.
   c. Flexor pollicis brevis: superficial head.
      (1) Origin: trapezium, trapezoid, capitate, and flexor retinaculum.
      (2) Insertion: base of proximal phalanx, radial side of thumb.
      (3) Function: thumb MCP flexion, deep head innervated by ulnar nerve.
   d. Lumbricals (radial side).
      (1) Origin: tendons of flexor digitorum profundus, index and middle fingers (radial and palmar sides).
      (2) Insertion: radial side of digits II and III into extensor expansion.
      (3) Function: metacarpophalangeal (MCP) flexion and extension of interphalangeal (IP) joints.
2. Intrinsic muscles innervated by the ulnar nerve (see Figure 6-2).
   a. Abductor digiti minimi.
      (1) Origin: pisiform and tendon of flexor carpi ulnaris.
      (2) Insertion: proximal phalanx of the fifth digit.
      (3) Function: abduction of the fifth digit.

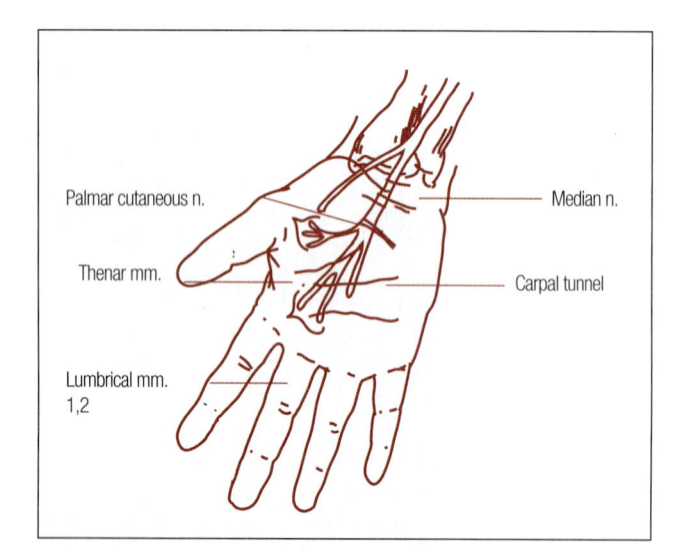

Figure 6-1 Median Nerve.
Malick, M., & Kasch, M. (1984). *Manual on management of specific hand problems.* Pittsburgh, PA: AREN. Reprinted with permission.

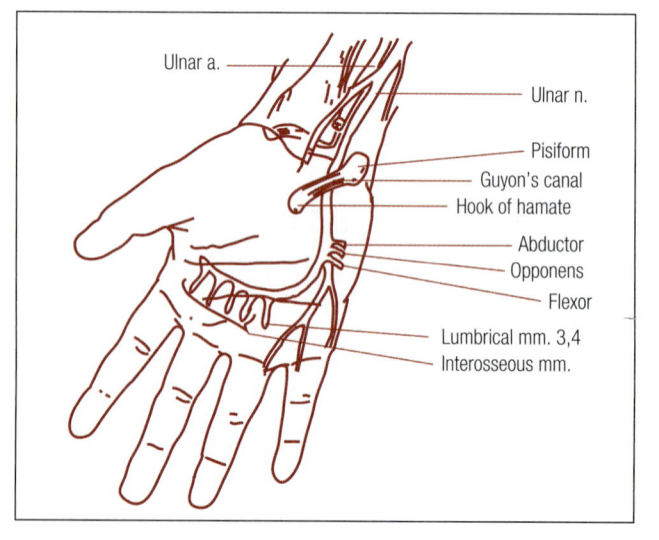

Figure 6-2 Ulnar Nerve.
Malick, M., & Kasch, M. (1984). *Manual on management of specific hand problems.* Pittsburgh, PA: AREN. Reprinted with permission.

b. Opponens digiti minimi.
   (1) Origin: hook of hamate and flexor retinaculum.
   (2) Insertion: fifth metacarpal.
   (3) Function: opposition of the fifth digit.
c. Flexor digiti minimi.
   (1) Origin: hook of hamate and flexor retinaculum.
   (2) Insertion: proximal phalanx of fifth digit.
   (3) Function: flexion of MCP joint and opposition of the fifth digit.
d. Adductor
   (1) Origin: oblique head: base of the second and third metacarpal, trapezoid, and capitate. Transverse head: palmar border and shaft of third metacarpal.
   (2) Insertion: sesamoid, base of proximal phalanx, tendon of extensor pollicis longus.
   (3) Function: adducts carpometacarpal (CMC) joint of thumb.
e. Lumbricals (ulnar side).
   (1) Origin: tendons of flexor digitorum profundus for digits IV and V.
   (2) Insertion: radial side of digits IV and V into extensor expansion.
   (3) Function: MCP flexion and extension of IP joints of digits IV and V.
f. Palmar interossei.
   (1) Origin: first palmar: ulnar surface of second metacarpal; second palmar; radial surface of fourth metacarpal; third palmar; radial surface of fifth metacarpal.
   (2) Insertion: first palmar; ulnar surface of second proximal phalanx; second palmar; radial surface of fourth proximal phalanx; third palmar; radial surface of fifth proximal phalanx.
   (3) Function: adduction and assistance with MCP flexion and extension of IP joints of digits II through V.
g. Dorsal interossei.
   (1) Origin: all four muscles arise from the adjacent sides of the metacarpals.
   (2) Insertion: proximal phalanx on the radial aspect of the index, radial and ulnar sides of middle finger, and ulnar side of ring finger (all into extensor digitorum).
   (3) Function: abduction and assists with MCP flexion and extension of IP joints of digits II through V.
3. Extrinsic flexor muscles of the hand innervated by the median nerve (see Figure 6-3).
   a. Flexor digitorum superficialis (sublimis) (FDS).
      (1) Origin: medial epicondyle.
      (2) Insertion: middle phalanx (two slips).
      (3) Function: flexion of PIP joints.
   b. Flexor digitorum profundus (FDP).
      (1) Origin: proximal two-thirds of the ulna and interosseous membrane.
      (2) Insertion: distal phalanx.

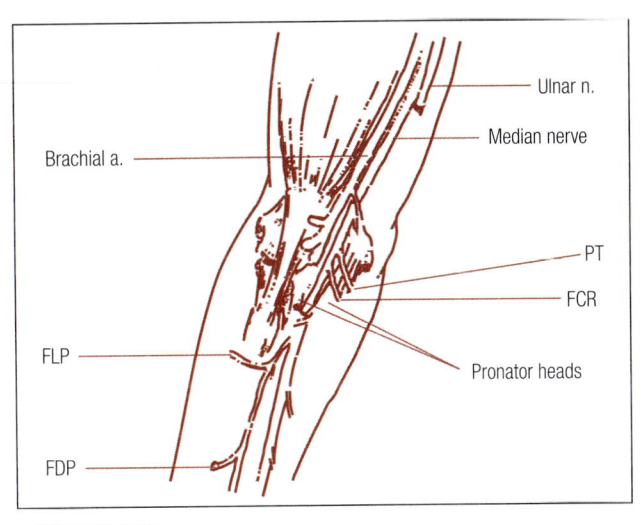

Figure 6-3 Median Nerve.

Malick, M., & Kasch, M. (1984). *Manual on management of specific hand problems.* Pittsburgh, PA: AREN. Reprinted with permission.

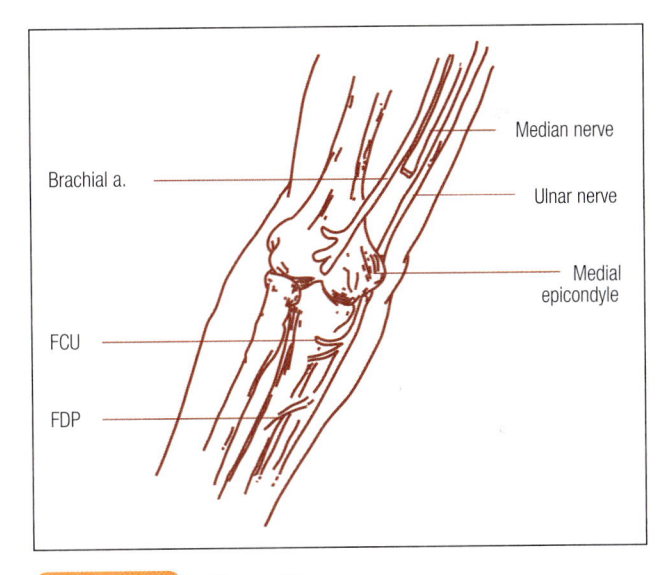

Figure 6-4 Ulnar Nerve.

Malick, M., & Kasch, M. (1984). *Manual on management of specific hand problems.* Pittsburgh, PA: AREN. Reprinted with permission.

   (3) Function: flexion of distal interphalangeal (DIP) joints to digits II and III. (See ulnar nerve for digits IV and V.)
   c. Flexor pollicis longus (FPL).
      (1) Origin: radius, middle one-third.
      (2) Insertion: distal phalanx of thumb.
      (3) Function: flexion of IP joint of thumb.
4. Extrinsic flexors of the hand innervated by the ulnar nerve (see Figure 6-4).
   a. Flexor digitorum profundus (FDP).
      (1) Origin: proximal two-thirds of the ulna and interosseous membrane.

f. Abductor pollicis longus (APL).
   (1) Origin: middle one-third of ulna and radius.
   (2) Insertion: first metacarpal, radial side.
   (3) Function: abduction and extension of CMC joint.

Anatomy of the Wrist

1. Wrist flexors innervated by the median nerve (see Figure 6-3).
   a. Flexor carpi radialis (FCR).
      (1) Origin: medial epicondyle.
      (2) Insertion: second and third metacarpal, base.
      (3) Function: flexion of wrist and radial deviation.
   b. Palmaris longus (PL).
      (1) Origin: medial epicondyle.
      (2) Insertion: palmar aponeurosis.
      (3) Function: flexion of wrist.
2. Wrist flexors innervated by the ulnar nerve (see Figure 6-4).
   a. Flexor carpi ulnaris (FCU).
      (1) Origin: medial epicondyle and proximal two-thirds of the ulna.
      (2) Insertion: pisiform and fifth metacarpal.
      (3) Function: flexion of wrist and ulnar deviation.
3. Wrist extensors innervated by the radial nerve (see Figure 6-5).
   a. Extensor carpi radialis brevis (ECRB).
      (1) Origin: lateral epicondyle.
      (2) Insertion: third metacarpal, base.
      (3) Function: extension of wrist and radial deviation.
   b. Extensor carpi radialis longus (ECRL).
      (1) Origin: supracondylar ridge of the humerus.
      (2) Insertion: second metacarpal, base.
      (3) Function: extension of wrist and radial deviation.
   c. Extensor carpi ulnaris (ECU).
      (1) Origin: lateral epicondyle.
      (2) Insertion: fifth metacarpal.
      (3) Function: extension of wrist and ulnar deviation.

Anatomy of the Forearm

1. Volar forearm muscles innervated by the median nerve.
   a. Pronator teres.
      (1) Origin: medial epicondyle and coronoid process of ulna.
      (2) Insertion: lateral surface of radius.
      (3) Function: forearm pronation.
   b. Pronator quadratus.
      (1) Origin: distal ulna.
      (2) Insertion: distal radius.
      (3) Function: forearm pronation.

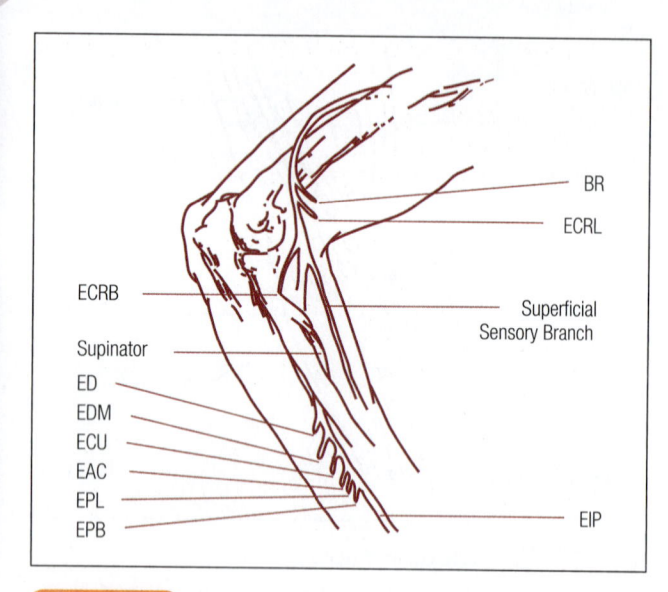

Figure 6-5 Radial Nerve.

Malick, M., & Kasch, M. (1984). *Manual on management of specific hand problems.* Pittsburgh, PA: AREN. Reprinted with permission.

   (2) Insertion: distal phalanx.
   (3) Function: flexion of DIP joints to digits IV and V.
5. Extrinsic extensor muscles of the hand innervated by the radial nerve (see Figure 6-5).
   a. Extensor digitorum communis (EDC).
      (1) Origin: lateral epicondyle.
      (2) Insertion: medial band to middle phalanx and lateral band to distal phalanx.
      (3) Function: extension of MCP joints and contributes to extension of the IP joints.
   b. Extensor digiti minimi (EDM).
      (1) Origin: lateral epicondyle.
      (2) Insertion: inserts into EDC at MCP level of the fifth digit.
      (3) Function: extension of MCP joint of the fifth digit and contributes to extension of the IP joints.
   c. Extensor indicis proprius (EIP).
      (1) Origin: ulna, middle one-third.
      (2) Insertion: inserts into EDC at MCP level.
      (3) Function: extension of MCP joint of the second digit and contributes to extension of the IP joints.
   d. Extensor pollicis longus (EPL).
      (1) Origin: ulna, middle one-third.
      (2) Insertion: distal phalanx of thumb.
      (3) Function: extension of IP joint of thumb.
   e. Extensor pollicis brevis (EPB).
      (1) Origin: radius, middle one-third.
      (2) Insertion: proximal phalanx of thumb.
      (3) Function: extension of MCP and CMC joints of thumb.

2. Dorsal forearm muscles innervated by the radial nerve.
   a. Supinator.
      (1) Origin: lateral epicondyle and ulna.
      (2) Insertion: radius.
      (3) Function: forearm supination.

Anatomy of the Elbow

1. Elbow flexion: biceps and brachialis innervated by musculocutaneus nerve; brachioradialis innervated by radial nerve.
   a. Biceps.
      (1) Origin: coracoid process and supraglenoid tubercle.
      (2) Insertion: radial tuberosity.
      (3) Function: elbow flexion with forearm supinated.
   b. Brachialis.
      (1) Origin: distal two-thirds of humerus.
      (2) Insertion: ulnar tuberosity.
      (3) Function: elbow flexion with forearm pronated.
   c. Brachioradialis.
      (1) Origin: supracondylar ridge.
      (2) Insertion: distal radius.
      (3) Function: elbow flexion with forearm neutral.
2. Elbow extension: triceps and anconeus innervated by radial nerve.
   a. Triceps.
      (1) Origin: long head; infraglenoid tuberosity. Lateral head; posterior humerus. Medial head; distal to lateral head.
      (2) Insertion: olecranon.
      (3) Function: elbow extension.
   b. Anconeus.
      (1) Origin: lateral epicondyle and capsule of elbow joint.
      (2) Insertion: olecranon and upper one-quarter of dorsal ulna.
      (3) Function: elbow extension.

Anatomy of the Shoulder

1. Rotator cuff muscles.
   a. Subscapularis innervated by the subscapular nerve.
      (1) Origin: anterior surface of scapula.
      (2) Insertion: lesser tuberosity.
      (3) Function: internal rotation.
   b. Supraspinatus innervated by the suprascapular nerve.
      (1) Origin: supraspinatus fossa.
      (2) Insertion: greater tuberosity.
      (3) Function: abduction and flexion.
   c. Infraspinatus innervated by the suprascapular nerve.
      (1) Origin: infraspinatus fossa.
      (2) Insertion: greater tuberosity.
      (3) Function: external rotation.
   d. Teres minor innervated by the axillary nerve.
      (1) Origin: axillary border of scapula.
      (2) Insertion: greater tuberosity.
      (3) Function: external rotation.
2. Shoulder flexion muscles.
   a. Anterior deltoid innervated by axillary nerve.
      (1) Origin: clavicle.
      (2) Insertion: deltoid tuberosity.
   b. Coracobrachialis innervated by the musculocutaneus nerve.
      (1) Origin: coracoid process.
      (2) Insertion: medial aspect of deltoid.
   c. Supraspinatus (as previously discussed).
3. Shoulder abduction muscles.
   a. Middle deltoid innervated by the axillary nerve.
      (1) Origin: acromion.
      (2) Insertion: deltoid tuberosity.
   b. Supraspinatus (as previously discussed).
4. Horizontal abduction muscles.
   a. Posterior deltoid innervated by the axillary nerve.
      (1) Origin: spine of scapula.
      (2) Insertion: deltoid tuberosity.
5. Horizontal adduction muscles.
   a. Pectoralis major innervated by the lateral pectoral nerve.
      (1) Origin: medial clavicle, sternum, and ribs 1–7.
      (2) Insertion: greater tuberosity.
6. Shoulder extension muscles.
   a. Latissimus dorsi innervated by the thoracodorsal nerve.
      (1) Origin: T6–T12, L1–L5, sacral vertebrae, ribs 9–12, iliac crest, and inferior angle of scapula.
      (2) Insertion: intertubercular groove of the humerus.
   b. Teres major innervated by the subscapular nerve.
      (1) Origin: inferior angle of scapula.
      (2) Insertion: intertubercular groove of the humerus.
   c. Posterior deltoid (as previously discussed).

Anatomy of the Scapula

1. Upward rotation muscles.
   a. Trapezius (upper, middle, and lower) innervated by the spinal accessory nerve (CNXI).
      (1) Origin.
         (a) Upper fibers: occiput and ligamentum nuchae.

162　TherapyEd • Musculoskeletal System Disorders

  (b) Middle fibers: spinous processes of T1–T5.
  (c) Lower fibers: spinous processes of T6–T12.
 (2) Insertion.
  (a) Upper fibers: lateral one-third of the clavicle.
  (b) Middle fibers: acromion and spine of scapula.
  (c) Lower fibers: medial end of spine of scapula.
 b. Serratus anterior innervated by the long thoracic nerve.
  (1) Origin: ribs 1–8 and aponeurosis of intercostals.
  (2) Insertion: superior and inferior angles of scapula and vertebral border of scapula.
2. Downward rotation muscles.
 a. Levator scapulae innervated by C3–C4 nerves.
  (1) Origin: C1–C4 transverse processes.
  (2) Insertion: vertebral border of scapula.
 b. Rhomboids (major and minor) innervated by the dorsal scapular nerve.
  (1) Origin: C7–T5 spinous processes.
  (2) Insertion: vertebral border, distal to the spine of the scapula.
 c. Serratus anterior (as previously discussed).
 d. Latissimus dorsi (as previously discussed).
3. Scapula adduction muscles.
 a. Middle trapezius (as previously discussed).
 b. Rhomboid major (as previously discussed).
4. Scapula abduction muscles.
 a. Serratus anterior (as previously discussed).
5. Scapula elevation muscles.
 a. Trapezius (upper) (as previously discussed).
 b. Levator scapulae (as previously discussed).
6. Scapula depression muscles.
 a. Trapezius (lower) (as previously discussed).

Dermatome Distribution

1. Refer to Table 11-3.
2. Refer to Figure 6-6.

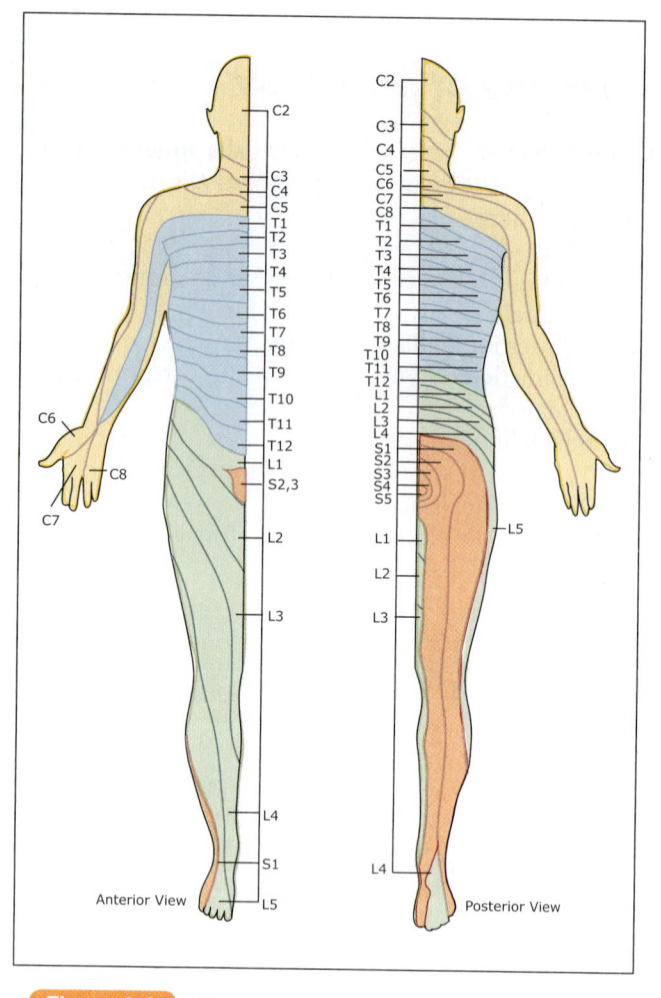

Figure 6-6 Dermatomes.

Hand and Upper Extremity Disorders and Injuries

Dupuytren's Disease

1. Disease of the fascia of the palm and digits.
 a. The fascia becomes thick and contracted; develops cords and bands that extend into the digits.
 b. Results in flexion deformities of the involved digits (see Figure 6-7).
2. Etiology: unknown.
3. Conservative treatment such as splinting has not been successful.
4. Medical treatments.
 a. Fasciotomy with Z-plasty.
 b. Aponeurotomy.
 c. McCash procedure (open palm).
 d. Collagenase enzymatic injection (nonsurgical: no wound care or scar management required).
5. Occupational therapy (OT) intervention.
 a. Wound care: dressing changes.
  (1) The OTA may be asked to assist with maintaining a sterile field.

Figure 6-7 Dupuytren's Contractures.

Adapted from Magee DJ: Orthopedic Physical Assessment, 2nd ed. Saunders, 1992.

b. Edema control: elevation above the heart.
c. Extension splint: initially at all times except to remove for range of motion (ROM) and bathing.
   (1) This splint is commonly hand based and can be dorsal or volar.
   (2) The OTA may be asked to assist with modifying the splint (especially extension as ROM improves).

CAUTION: The ideal splint is full extension; however, this is not always possible due to the severity of contracture and the quality of the tendon and nerves. The occupational therapist should consult with the surgeon to obtain clarification.

d. Active range of motion (AROM)/passive range of motion (PROM); progress to strengthening when wounds are healed.
e. Scar management (massage, scar pad, and compression garment).
f. Purposeful and occupation-based interventions that emphasize flexion (gripping) and extension (release).

Skier's Thumb (Gamekeeper's Thumb)

1. Rupture of the ulnar collateral ligament of the MCP joint of the thumb.
2. Etiology: most common cause is a fall while skiing with the thumb held in a ski pole.
3. OT intervention.
   a. Conservative treatment including a thumb splint (for four to six weeks).
   b. AROM and pinch strengthening (at six weeks).
   c. Focus on activities of daily living (ADL) that require opposition and pinch strength.

d. Postoperative treatment includes thumb splint for six weeks, followed by AROM. PROM can begin at eight weeks and strengthening at 10 weeks.

Complex Regional Pain Syndrome (CRPS)

1. Type 1 formerly known as reflex sympathetic dystrophy (RSD).
2. Type 2 formerly known as causalgia.
3. Vasomotor dysfunction as a result of an abnormal reflex.
4. It can be localized to one specific area or spread to other parts of the extremity.
5. Etiology: may follow trauma (e.g., Colles' fracture) or surgery, but actual cause is unknown.
6. Symptoms include severe pain, edema, discoloration, osteoporosis, sudomotor changes (sweating), temperature changes, trophic changes (skin, nail, and fingertip appearance), and vasomotor instability.
7. OT intervention (the focus should be on decreasing pain and increasing participation in occupations as tolerated):
   a. Modalities to decrease pain.
   b. Edema management: elevation, manual edema mobilization, and compression glove.
   c. AROM to involved joints.
   d. ADL to encourage pain-free active use.
   e. Stress loading (weightbearing and joint distraction activities, including scrubbing and carrying activities).
   f. Splinting to prevent contractures and enable ability to engage in occupation-based activities.
   g. Encourage self-management.
   h. Interventions to avoid include or to proceed with caution include PROM, passive stretching, joint mobilization, dynamic splinting, and casting.

Fractures

EXAM HINT: In the NBCOT® practice analysis, 55.4% of COTA®s who provided services to persons with musculoskeletal/orthopedic disorders indicated they provided services to individuals with fractures (NBCOT®, 2018, p. 14). Due to this high prevalence, it is likely that the COTA® exam will have items about working with persons recovering from fractures.

1. Types of fractures.
   a. Intraarticular versus extraarticular.
   b. Closed versus open.
   c. Dorsal displacement versus volar displacement.

d. Midshaft versus neck versus base.
e. Complete versus incomplete.
f. Transverse versus spiral versus oblique.
g. Comminuted.
2. Medical treatment.
    a. Closed reduction: types of stabilization include short arm cast (SAC), long arm cast (LAC), splint, sling, or fracture brace.
    b. Open reduction internal fixation (ORIF): types include nails, screws, plates, or wire.
    c. External fixation.
    d. Arthrodesis: fusion.
    e. Arthroplasty: joint replacement.
3. Most common upper extremity fractures.
    a. Colles' fracture: fracture of the distal radius with dorsal displacement.
    b. Smith's fracture: fracture of the distal radius with volar displacement.
    c. Carpal fractures: most common is scaphoid fracture (60% of carpal fractures). The proximal scaphoid has a poor blood supply and may become necrotic.
    d. Metacarpal fractures: classified according to location (head, neck, shaft, or base). A common complication is rotational deformities. A boxer's fracture is a fracture of the fifth metacarpal (requires an ulnar gutter splint).
    e. Proximal phalanx fractures: most common with thumb and index. A common complication is loss of PIP AROM/PROM.
    f. Middle phalanx fractures: not commonly fractured.
    g. Distal phalanx fracture: most common finger fracture. May result in mallet finger (which involves terminal extensor tendon).
    h. Elbow fracture: involvement of the radial head may result in limited rotation of the forearm.
    i. Humerus fractures: nondisplaced vs. displaced fractures.
        (1) Etiology: fall onto an outstretched upper extremity.
        (2) Fractures of the greater tuberosity may result in rotator cuff injuries.
        (3) Humeral shaft fractures may cause injury to the radial nerve resulting in wrist drop.
4. OT evaluation.
    a. Occupational profile.
    b. History should include mechanism of injury and fracture management.
    c. Review results of special tests (x-rays, magnetic resonance imaging, and computed tomography scan).
    d. Edema: volumeter if the swelling is throughout the hand. If it's an individual finger, then a tape measure should be used.
    e. Pain.
    f. AROM.
        (1) Do not assess PROM or strength until ordered by physician.
        (2) Exceptions are humerus fractures, that often begin with PROM or active assistive range of motion (AAROM).
    g. Sensation.
    h. Occupations, ADL, and activities related to roles.
5. OT intervention.
    a. Immobilization phase: stabilization and healing are the goals.
        (1) AROM of joints above and below the stabilized part.
        (2) Edema control: elevation, manual edema mobilization, gentle retrograde massage, and compression garments.
        (3) Light ADL and role activities with no resistance, progress as tolerated.
            (a) If the patient is in a sling, shoulder immobilizer, LAC, fracture brace, or ORIF, instruction in one-handed techniques should be provided.
    b. Mobilization phase: consolidation is the goal.
        (1) Edema control: elevation, manual edema mobilization, gentle retrograde massage, contrast baths and compression garments. (e.g., Tubigrip, Isotoner glove).
        (2) Some patients will require a splint for protection.
        (3) AROM.
            (a) Progress to PROM when approved by physician (4–8 weeks).
            (b) Exceptions are humerus fractures that often begin with PROM or AAROM.
        (4) Light purposeful or occupation-based activities.
            (a) Progress to occupation-based activities.
        (5) Pain management: positioning and physical agent modalities.
        (6) Strengthening: begin with isometrics when approved by physician.
            (a) Shoulder fractures most commonly begin with isometric exercises.

Cumulative Trauma Disorders (CTD)

1. Also known as repetitive strain injuries (RSIs) and/or overuse syndromes, and/or musculoskeletal disorders.
2. Risk factors: repetition, static position, awkward postures, forceful exertions, and vibration.
3. Nonwork risk factors: acute trauma, pregnancy, diabetes, arthritis, and wrist size and shape.

4. Most common types.
   a. de Quervain's.
      (1) Stenosing tenosynovitis of the abductor pollicis longus (APL) and the extensor pollicis brevis (EPB). (See Figure 6-8.)
      (2) Pain and swelling over the radial styloid.
      (3) Positive Finkelstein's test.
      (4) Conservative treatment.
         (a) Thumb spica splint (IP joint free).
         (b) Activity/work modification.
         (c) Ice massage over radial wrist.
         (d) Gentle AROM of wrist and thumb to prevent stiffness.
      (5) Postoperative treatment.
         (a) Thumb spica splint and gentle AROM (0–2 weeks).
         (b) Strengthening, ADL and role activities (2–6 weeks).
         (c) Unrestricted activity (6 weeks).
   b. Lateral and medial epicondylitis.
      (1) Degeneration of the tendon origin as a result of repetitive microtrauma.
      (2) Lateral epicondylitis: overuse of wrist extensors, especially the extensor carpi radialis brevis. Also called tennis elbow.
      (3) Medial epicondylitis: overuse of wrist flexors. Also called golfer's elbow.
      (4) Conservative treatment.
         (a) Elbow strap, wrist splint.
         (b) Ice and deep friction massage.
         (c) Stretching.
         (d) Activity/work modification.
         (e) As pain decreases, begin strengthening. Begin with isometric exercises and then progress to isotonic and eccentric exercises.
   c. Trigger finger.
      (1) Tenosynovitis of the finger flexors: most commonly is the A1 pulley.
      (2) Caused by repetitive gripping and the use of tools that are placed too far apart.
      (3) Conservative treatment.
         (a) Hand- or finger- based trigger finger splint (MCP extended, IP joints free).
         (b) Scar massage.
         (c) Edema control.
         (d) Tendon gliding.
         (e) Activity/work modification: avoid repetitive gripping activities and using tools with handles too far apart.
   d. Nerve compressions: refer to next section on peripheral nerve compressions.

Peripheral Nerve Injuries

1. Three major nerves: median, ulnar, and radial.
2. Two types of nerve injuries.
   a. Incomplete: such as a compression or nerve entrapment.
   b. Complete: such as a laceration or avulsion injury.
3. Carpal tunnel syndrome (CTS): a median nerve compression.
   a. Etiology: repetition, awkward postures, vibration, anatomical anomalies, and pregnancy.
   b. Symptoms: numbness and tingling of the thumb, index, middle, and radial half of the ring fingers.
      (1) Paresthesias usually occur at night (most characteristic).
      (2) Person will complain of dropping things.
      (3) Positive Tinel's sign at wrist. Positive Phalen's sign.
      (4) Advanced stage of CTS can result in muscle atrophy of the thenar eminence.
   c. Conservative treatment.
      (1) Wrist splint in neutral: should be worn at night and during the day if performing repetitive activity.
      (2) Median nerve gliding exercises (gentle sliding, should not place tension on the nerve) and differential tendon gliding exercises.

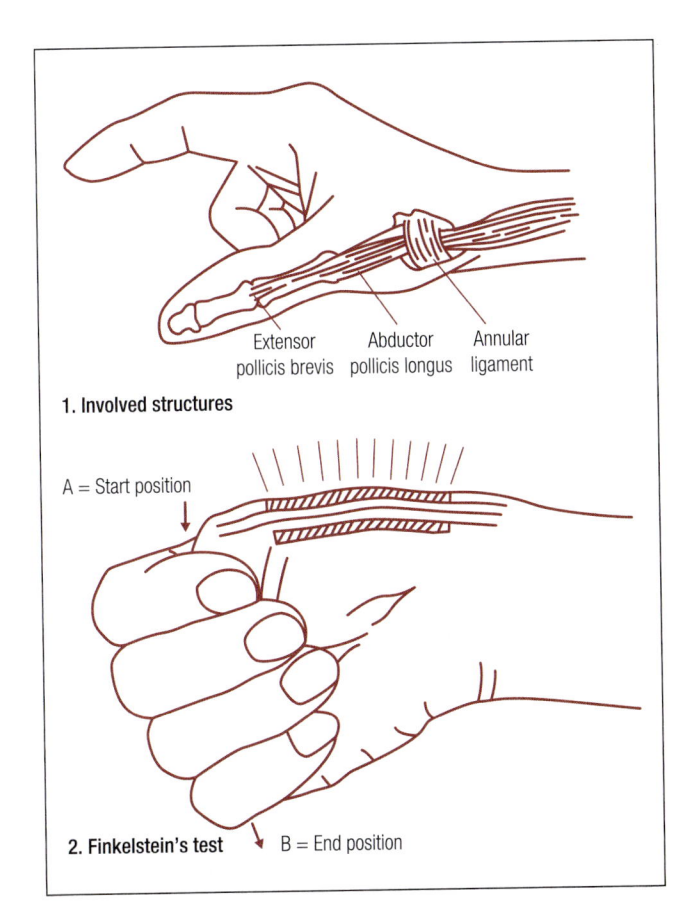

Figure 6-8 de Quervain's.

(3) Activity modification: avoid activities with extreme positions of wrist flexion, wrist flexion with repetitive finger flexion, and wrist flexion with a static grip.
(4) Ergonomics: appropriate workstation design. See Chapter 14.
 (a) CTS is the most common work-related injury of the upper extremity.
d. Surgical intervention: carpal tunnel release (CTR).
e. Postoperative treatment of CTR.
(1) Edema control: elevation, retrograde massage, compression glove, and/or contrast bath.
(2) AROM.
(3) Nerve and tendon gliding exercises.
(4) Sensory reeducation.
(5) Strengthening of thenar muscles (usually six weeks postoperative).
(6) Work/activity modification.
4. Cubital tunnel syndrome: an ulnar nerve compression at the elbow.
a. Etiology: second most common compression; pressure at elbow (leaning on elbow) and extreme elbow flexion.
b. Symptoms.
(1) Numbness and tingling along ulnar aspect of forearm and hand.
(2) Pain at elbow with extreme position of elbow flexion.
(3) Weakness of power grip.
(4) Positive Tinel's sign at elbow.
(5) Advanced stages can lead to atrophy of FCU, FDP to digits IV and V, and ulnar nerve-innervated intrinsic muscles of the hand.
c. Conservative treatment.
(1) Elbow splint at 30° of flexion to prevent positions of extreme flexion (especially at night).
(2) Elbow pad to decrease compression of nerve when leaning on elbows.
(3) Activity/work modification.
d. Surgical intervention: decompression or transposition.
e. Postoperative treatment.
(1) Edema control.
(2) Scar management.
(3) AROM and nerve gliding (2 weeks postoperative).
(4) Strengthening (4 weeks postoperative).
(5) MCP flexion anticlaw splint if clawing noted.
5. Radial nerve palsy: a radial nerve compression.
a. Etiology: Saturday night palsy, a term used to describe sleeping in a position that places stress on the radial nerve. Also, compression as a result of a humeral shaft fracture.
b. Symptoms: weakness or paralysis of extensors to the wrist, MCPs, and thumb; wrist drop.

c. Conservative treatment.
(1) Dynamic wrist and MCP extension splint. The OTA would most likely not fabricate this splint, but should be aware of its purpose (to extend wrist and fingers).
(2) Work/activity modification while using dynamic splint.
(3) Strengthening wrist and finger extensors when motor function returns.
d. Surgical intervention: decompression.
e. Postoperative treatment.
(1) AROM.
(2) Strengthening (6–8 weeks postoperative).
(3) ADL and meaningful role activities.

> **CAUTION:** Avoid combined forearm pronation, elbow extension, and wrist flexion, as this can place tension on the nerves.

6. Median nerve laceration.
a. Sensory loss.
(1) Central palm (thumb to radial half of ring finger).
(2) Palmar surface of thumb, index, middle, and radial half of ring fingers.
(3) Dorsal surface of index, middle, and radial half of ring fingers (middle and distal phalanges).
b. Motor loss for a low lesion at the wrist.
(1) Lumbricals I and II (MCP flexion of digits II and III).
(2) Opponens pollicis (opposition).
(3) Abductor pollicis brevis (abduction).
(4) Flexor pollicis brevis (flexion of thumb MCP).
c. Motor loss for a high lesion at or proximal to the elbow.
(1) All of the above in b.
(2) FDP to index and middle fingers, and FPL (flexion of tip of index, middle fingers, and thumb).
(3) FCR (inability to flex to radial aspect of wrist).
d. Deformity.
(1) Flattening of thenar eminence, 'ape hand' (Figure 6-9).
(2) Clawing of index and middle fingers for a low lesion.
(3) Benediction sign for a high lesion (Figure 6-10).
e. Functional loss.
(1) Loss of thumb opposition.
(2) Weakness of pinch.
f. OT intervention.
(1) Dorsal protection splint with wrist positioned in 30° flexion if a low lesion. Include elbow (90° flexion) if a high lesion.
(2) Begin A/PROM of digits with wrist in flexed position at two weeks postoperative.
(3) Scar management.

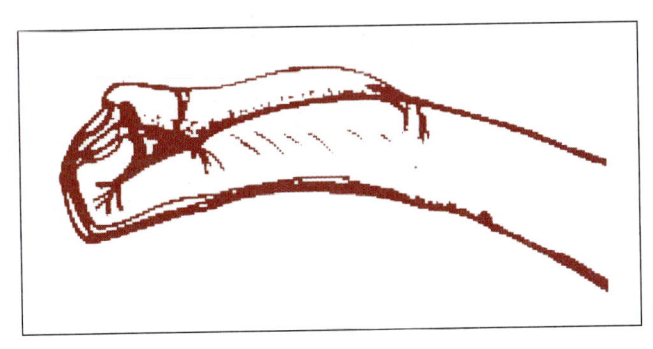

Figure 6-9 Ape Hand: Due to injury of the distal median nerve.

Darlington, Vicki, OTR/L, CHT with permission.

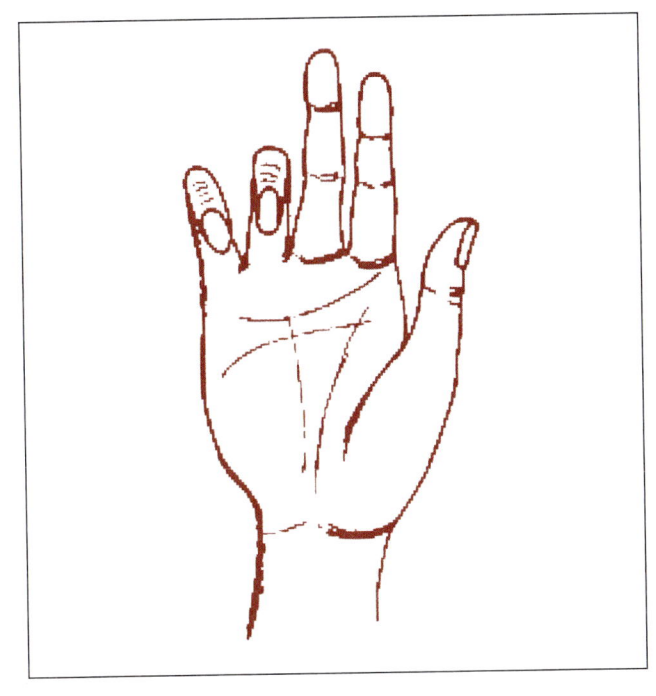

Figure 6-10 Benediction Sign: Due to a high injury of the median nerve.

Darlington, Vicki, OTR/L, CHT with permission.

      (4) AROM of wrist at four weeks; include elbow if a high lesion.
      (5) Begin strengthening at nine weeks.
  g. Splinting considerations: C-bar to prevent thumb adduction contracture.
  h. Sensory reeducation: begin when individual demonstrates a level of diminished protective sensation (4.31) on Semmes-Weinstein.
7. Ulnar nerve laceration.
  a. Sensory loss.
    (1) Ulnar aspects of palmar and dorsal surfaces.
    (2) Ulnar half of ring and little fingers on palmar and dorsal surfaces.

  b. Motor loss: low lesion at the wrist.
    (1) Palmar and dorsal interossei (adduction and abduction of MCP joints).
    (2) Lumbricals III and IV (MCP flexion of digits 4 and 5).
    (3) FPB and adductor pollicis (flexion and adduction of thumb).
    (4) ADM, ODM, FDM (abduction, opposition, and flexion of fifth digit).
  c. Motor loss: high lesion wrist or above.
    (1) Same as above, including FCU (flexion toward ulnar wrist).
    (2) FDP IV and V (flexion of DIPs of ring and little fingers).
  d. Deformity.
    (1) Claw hand.
    (2) Flattened metacarpal arch.
    (3) Positive Froment's sign (assessment of thumb adductor while laterally pinching paper).
  e. Functional loss.
    (1) Loss of power grip.
    (2) Decreased pinch strength.
  f. OT intervention.
    (1) See median nerve repair.
    (2) Splinting consideration: MCP flexion block splint.
    (3) Sensory reeducation: same as median nerve.
8. Radial nerve injury.
  a. Sensory loss: high lesions at the level of the humerus.
    (1) Medial aspect of dorsal forearm. Radial aspect of dorsal palm, thumb, and index, middle and radial half of ring phalanges.
  b. Motor loss: low lesion at the level of the forearm.
    (1) Loss of wrist extension due to absent or impaired innervation to ECU.
    (2) EDC, EI, EDM (MCP extension).
    (3) EPB, EPL, APL (thumb extension).
  c. Motor loss: high lesion at the level of the humerus.
    (1) All of the above, including ECRB, ECRL, and brachioradialis.
    (2) If level of axilla, loss of triceps (elbow extension).
  d. Functional loss.
    (1) Inability to extend digits to release objects.
    (2) Difficulty manipulating objects.
  e. Deformity.
    (1) Wrist drop (Figure 6-11).
  f. OT intervention.
    (1) Dynamic extension splint.
    (2) ROM.
    (3) Sensory reeducation if needed.
    (4) Instruct in home program.
    (5) Activity modification.
    (6) Neuromuscular electrical stimulation (NMES) to aide in muscle reeducation.

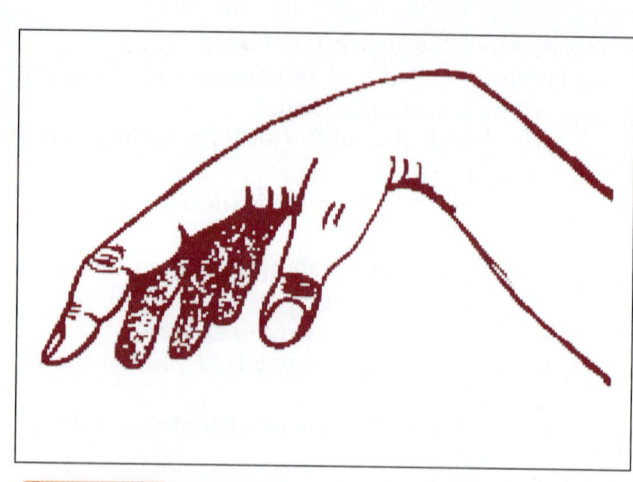

Figure 6-11 Wrist Drop: Due to injury of the radial nerve.

Darlington, Vicki, OTR/L, CHT with permission.

Nerve and Tendon Repairs

1. These are diagnoses that are more commonly treated by the occupational therapist in the acute phase following surgery.
    a. With established service competency, the OTA may work collaboratively with the occupational therapist to treat these more complex hand injuries in the late phase of healing.

Rotator Cuff Tendonitis

1. Anatomy of rotator cuff.
    a. Supraspinatus.
        (1) Function: abduction and flexion.
    b. Infraspinatus and teres minor.
        (1) Function: external rotation.
    c. Subscapularis.
        (1) Function: internal rotation.
    d. The rotator cuff functions together to control the head of the humerus in the glenoid fossa.
    e. Site of impingement: coracoacromial arch (acromion, coracoacromial ligament, and coracoid process).
2. Etiology.
    a. Repetitive overuse.
    b. Curved or hook acromion.
    c. Weakness of rotator cuff.
    d. Weakness of scapula musculature.
    e. Ligament and capsule tightness.
    f. Trauma.
3. OT conservative intervention.
    a. Activity modification: avoid above-shoulder level activities until pain subsides.
    b. Educate in sleeping posture: avoid sleeping with arm overhead or combined adduction and internal rotation.
    c. Decrease pain: positioning, modalities, and rest.
    d. Restore pain-free ROM.
    e. Strengthening: below shoulder level.
    f. Purposeful and occupation-based activities.
4. Surgical interventions.
    a. Arthroscopic surgery.
    b. Open repair: small, medium, large, and massive tears.
5. OT postoperative intervention (note: time frames will vary depending on surgeon).
    a. Begin with PROM (may be initiated anytime from 0–6 weeks); progress AAROM/AROM (commonly initiated from 6 to 8 weeks).

> **CAUTION:** The surgeon will determine when exercise should begin based on the size of the tear and tension of the repair site. The occupational therapist must communicate with the surgeon about when exercise can be initiated and what types of exercise should be used.

   (1) Patients will be placed in a sling or abduction orthosis to be worn in between exercises.
    b. Decrease pain: begin with ice, progress to heat.
    c. Strengthening: begin with isometrics, progress to isotonic (below shoulder level- usually begins 8-10 weeks).
    d. Activity modification: light ADL and meaningful role activities; progress as tolerated.
    e. Leisure and work activities (8–12 weeks postoperative).

Adhesive Capsulitis

1. Also known as frozen shoulder.
2. Restricted passive shoulder range of motion.
    a. Greatest limitation is external rotation, then abduction, internal rotation, and flexion.
3. Anatomy: glenohumeral ligaments and joint capsule.
4. Etiology.
    a. Inflammation and immobility.
    b. Linked to diabetes mellitus and Parkinson's disease.
5. OT conservative intervention.
    a. Encourage active use through ADL and role activities.
    b. PROM.
    c. Modalities.
6. Surgical interventions: manipulation and arthroscopic surgery.
7. OT postoperative intervention.
    a. PROM immediately following surgery.
    b. Pain relief: modalities.
    c. Encourage use of extremity for all ADL and role activities.

Shoulder Dislocations

1. Anterior dislocation most common.
2. Etiology.
    a. Trauma.
    b. Repetitive overuse.
3. OT intervention.
    a. Regain ROM: avoid combined abduction and external rotation with anterior dislocation.
    b. Pain-free ADL and role activities.
    c. Strengthen rotator cuff.

> **EXAM HINT:** The NBCOT® exam outline for the COTA® identifies knowledge of the "expected patterns, progressions, and prognoses associated with conditions that limit occupational performance" (NBCOT®, 2018, p. 21) as essential for competent and safe practice. The application of knowledge about the hand and upper extremity disorders and injuries previously described and the musculoskeletal system disorders described in subsequent sections of this chapter will be required to correctly answer COTA® exam items about working with people with musculoskeletal system disorders.

The Role of the Occupational Therapy Assistant (OTA) in Evaluation

1. The OTA contributes to the evaluation process with supervision from the occupational therapist.
2. The OTA can assist with the collection of data for the evaluation once service competency has been established.
3. The level of supervision required will be determined by the OTA's experience and established service competence.
4. The OTA cannot independently evaluate or interpret evaluation results.

The Role of the OTA in Intervention

1. The OTA implements intervention with supervision from the occupational therapist.
2. The level of supervision required depends upon the OTA's experience and established service competence.
3. During the implementation of intervention, the OTA informs the supervising occupational therapist of any change in the individual's status and any other relevant information that may affect treatment.

> **EXAM HINT:** In the NBCOT® exam outline for the COTA®, Domain 02 Selecting and Implementing Interventions comprises 55% of the NBCOT® exam. This domain focuses on the OTA's ability to "implement interventions under the supervision of the OTR in accordance with the intervention plan and level of service competence to support client participation in areas of occupation throughout the occupational therapy process" (NBCOT®, 2018, p. 24). The application of knowledge about the diagnostic-specific interventions previously described for each condition in this section can help you correctly answer NBCOT® Domain 02 exam items about intervention management for persons with hand and upper extremity disorders and injuries.

Arthritis

Definition

1. An inflammation of a joint or joints.

Types

1. Rheumatoid arthritis (RA).
    a. Systemic, symmetrical, and affects many joints.
        (1) Most commonly attacks the small joints of the hands.
        (2) Characterized by remissions and exacerbations.
        (3) Begins in the acute phase as an inflammatory process of the synovial lining.

> **EXAM HINT:** In the NBCOT® practice analysis, 24.7% of COTA®s provided services to persons with musculoskeletal/orthopedic disorders indicated they provided services to individuals with RA (NBCOT®, 2018, p. 15). Due to this prevalence, the exam may have items about working with persons recovering from and living with RA.

    b. Etiology is unknown but there are two main theories.
        (1) Infection theory.
        (2) Autoimmune theory.
    c. Symptoms.
        (1) Pain.
        (2) Stiffness.

(3) Limited range of motion.
(4) Fatigue.
(5) Weight loss.
(6) Limited ADL status, diminished ability to perform role activities.
(7) Swelling.
(8) Deformities.
d. Types of deformities common with RA.
(1) Ulnar deviation and subluxation of the wrists and MCP joints.
(2) Boutonniere deformity: flexion of PIP joint and hyperextension of DIP joint (see Figure 6-12).
(3) Swan neck deformity: hyperextension of PIP joint and flexion of DIP joint (see Figure 6-13).
2. Osteoarthritis (OA).
a. Degenerative joint disease.
(1) Not systemic but wear and tear.
(2) Commonly affects large weight-bearing joints.
(3) Attacks hyaline cartilage.
b. Etiology.
(1) Genetic.
(2) Trauma.
(3) Inflammation.
(4) Cumulative trauma.
(5) Endocrine and metabolic diseases.
c. Symptoms.
(1) Pain.
(2) Stiffness.
(3) Limited ROM.
(4) Bone spurs.
d. Types of bone spurs.
(1) Heberden's nodes at the DIP joints.
(2) Bouchard's nodes at the PIP joints.

EXAM HINT: In the NBCOT® practice analysis, 45.6% of COTA®s who provided services to persons with musculoskeletal/orthopedic disorders indicated they provided services to individuals with OA (NBCOT®, 2018, p. 15). Due to this prevalence, it is likely that the COTA® exam will have items about working with persons recovering living with OA.

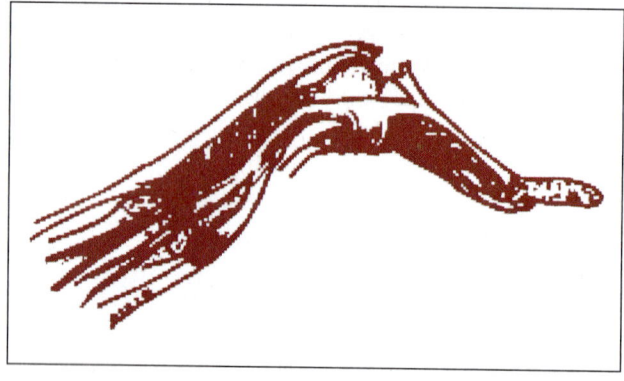

Figure 6-12 Boutonniere Deformity.
Darlington, Vicki, OTR/L, CHT with permission.

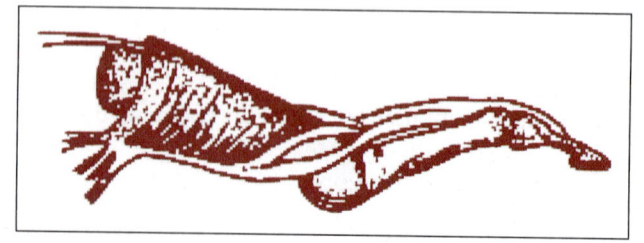

Figure 6-13 Swan Neck Deformity.
Darlington, Vicki, OTR/L, CHT with permission.

Occupational Therapy Evaluation

EXAM HINT: The NBCOT® exam outline for the COTA® identifies knowledge of the "expected patterns, progressions, and prognoses associated with conditions that limit occupational performance (and the) impact of . . . body functions and body structures . . . on occupational performance" (NBCOT®, 2018, p. 21) as essential for competent and safe practice. The application of knowledge about the presenting symptoms of RA and OA described previously and the following assessment approaches will be required to correctly answer exam items about the evaluation of persons with arthritis.

1. Role of the OTA in the evaluation process.
    a. The OTA contributes to the evaluation process with supervision from the occupational therapist.
    b. The OTA can assist with the collection of data for the evaluation once service competency has been established.
    c. The level of supervision required will be determined by the OTA's experience and established service competence.
    d. The OTA cannot independently evaluate or interpret evaluation results.
2. Occupational profile.
3. ROM: focus on AROM.

CAUTION: PROM should be avoided, especially in the inflammatory stage. Note deformities and nodules.

4. Muscle strength.
    a. Avoid muscle testing unless requested by physician.
    b. Document strength in relation to function.
5. Grip strength: use sphygmomanometer or bulb dynamometer.
6. ADL and role activities: note if ADL and role activity deficits are related to pain, limitation in motion, deformity, weakness, or fatigue.

7. Pain: use pain scales.
8. Edema: volumeter or tape measure.
9. Chapter 11 provides detailed information about the above biomechanical evaluation methods.

> **EXAM HINT:** In the NBCOT® exam outline for the COTA®, Domain 02 Selecting and Implementing Interventions comprises 55% of the exam. This domain focuses on the OTA's ability to "implement interventions under the supervision of the OTR in accordance with the intervention plan and level of service competence to support client participation in areas of occupation throughout the occupational therapy process" (NBCOT®, 2018, p. 24). The application of knowledge about the following interventions can help you correctly answer NBCOT® Domain 02 exam items about intervention management for persons with arthritis.

Occupational Therapy Intervention

1. Role of the OTA.
   a. The OTA implements intervention with supervision from the occupational therapist.
      (1) The level of supervision required depends upon the OTA's experience and established service competence.
      (2) During the implementation of intervention, the OTA informs the supervising occupational therapist of any change in the individual's status and any other relevant information that may affect treatment.
2. Splinting.
   a. Resting hand splints in the acute stage until inflammation decreases.
   b. Wrist splint only if arthritis specific to wrist.
   c. Ulnar drift splint to prevent ulnar deviation deformity.
   d. Swan neck deformity: silver rings, buttonhole/hyperextension block splint or digital dorsal splint in slight PIP flexion. These splints all prevent hyperextension of the PIP joint while allowing digital flexion.
   e. Boutonniere deformity: silver rings or PIP extension splint.
   f. Dynamic MCP extension splint with radial pull for postoperative MCP arthroplasties.
      (1) Some surgeons may order a night resting splint.
   g. Hand base thumb splint for CMC arthritis.
3. Joint protection techniques.
4. Energy conservation techniques.
5. ROM: focus on AROM.
   a. Gentle PROM if person unable to perform AROM.
   b. All exercises should be pain free.
6. Heat modalities.
   a. Hot packs can be used before exercise.
      (1) An exception is during the acute inflammatory stage when heat should be avoided.
   b. Paraffin is recommended for the hands.
7. Strengthening.
   a. Avoid during inflammatory stage.
   b. Gentle strengthening while avoiding positions of deformity.
   c. Strengthen through functional activities.
8. Chapter 11 provides detailed information about the above biomechanical intervention approaches.
9. Purposeful and occupation-based activities
   a. Joint protection and energy conservation techniques should be incorporated. Refer to Chapter 11.
   b. Adaptive equipment should be provided to prevent deformity, decrease stress on small joints, and extend reach. Refer to Chapter 14.
   c. Chapter 14 provides detailed information about intervention approaches to enable occupational performance.

Osteogenesis Imperfecta (OI)[1]

Etiology

1. Disorder caused by the dysfunction of one of several genes responsible for producing collagen to strengthen bones.
2. The genes responsible for osteogenesis imperfecta OI can be inherited from one or both parents.

Signs and Symptoms

1. Malformed bones.
   a. Short, small body.
   b. Triangular face.
   c. Barrel-shaped rib cage.
   d. Brittle bones that fracture easily.
   e. Multiple fractures as the child grows.
   f. Developmental growth problems.
2. Loose joints.

---
[1] Marge E. Moffett Boyd contributed this section on osteogenesis imperfecta.

3. Sclera of the whites of the eyes look blue or purple.
4. Brittle teeth.
5. Hearing loss (often starting in the 20s or 30s).
6. Respiratory problems.
7. Insufficient collagen.

Classification

1. Eight main types of OI: classified by the genes that are involved.
   a. Types 2, 3, 7, and 8: severe symptoms.
   b. Types 4, 5, and 6: moderate symptoms.
   c. Type 1: mild symptoms.

Diagnosis

1. Family and medical history.
2. Results from a physical examination and medical including x-rays, collagen, and blood test.

Medical Management

1. Care for broken bones.
   a. See this chapter's section on the medical treatment of fractures.
2. Dental care for brittle teeth.
3. Medication for pain.
4. Surgery.
   a. Fix bone malformations.
   b. Prevent bone malformations.
   c. "Rodding," in which metal rods are put inside the long bones.

Occupational Therapy Evaluation

1. Role of the OTA in the evaluation process.
   a. The OTA contributes to the evaluation process with supervision from the occupational therapist.
   b. The OTA can assist with the collection of data for the evaluation once service competency has been established.
   c. The level of supervision required will be determined by the OTA's experience and established service competence.
   d. The OTA cannot independently evaluate or interpret evaluation results.
2. Evaluation focus.
   a. Activity interests that can be safely pursued.
   b. Environmental risk factors.
3. See this chapter's section on OT evaluation for fractures.

Occupational Therapy Intervention

1. Role of the OTA.
   a. The OTA implements intervention with supervision from the occupational therapist.
      (1) The level of supervision required depends upon the OTA's experience and established service competence.
      (2) During the implementation of intervention, the OTA informs the supervising occupational therapist of any change in the individual's status and any other relevant information that may affect treatment.

> **EXAM HINT:** In the NBCOT® exam outline for the COTA®, "Domain 02 Select interventions under the supervision of the OTR in accordance with the intervention plan and level of service competence to support client participation in areas of occupation throughout the occupational therapy process." (NBCOT®, 2018, p. 24) comprises 55% of the exam. The application of knowledge about the following interventions can help you effectively determine the correct answers to Domain 02 exam items that address intervention management for persons with OI.

2. Weightbearing activities to facilitate bone growth.
3. Activity adaptation and assistive device prescription and fabrication to facilitate safe participation in daily occupations. Refer to Chapter 14.
4. Environmental modifications to maintain safety. Refer to Chapter 15.
5. Preventive positioning and protective splinting/padding. Refer to Chapter 11.
6. Activities to increase muscle strength. Refer to Chapter 11.
7. Health education to promote a healthy lifestyle.
   a. Healthy diet and weight control.
   b. Avoid smoking, caffeine, alcohol, steroids.
   c. Exercise: swimming, water therapy, walking.
8. Family, caregiver and teacher education about proper handling, positioning, activity adaptations, environmental modifications, and the need to observe all safety precautions.
9. See this chapter's section on OT intervention for fractures and musculoskeletal pain.

Hip Fractures

EXAM HINT: In the NBCOT® practice analysis, 59.1% of COTA®s who provided services to persons with musculoskeletal/orthopedic disorders indicated they provided services to individuals with fractures (NBCOT®, 2018, p. 14). Due to this prevalence, it is very likely that the COTA® exam will have items about working with persons recovering from hip fractures.

EXAM HINT: In the NBCOT® exam outline for the COTA®, Domain 01 Collaborating and Gathering Information comprises 28% of the exam and Domain 02 Selecting and Implementing Interventions (NBCOT®, 2018, p. 24) comprises 55% of the exam. The application of knowledge about the previous evaluation foci and the following intervention foci can help you effectively determine the correct answers to exam items about working with persons with hip fractures.

Etiology

1. Trauma.
2. Osteoporosis.
3. Pathological fractures (i.e., cancer).

Types

1. Femoral neck fracture.
2. Intertrochanteric fracture.
3. Subtrochanteric fracture.

Medical Management

1. Closed reduction for minimally displaced fractures.
2. ORIF.
3. Joint replacement.

Occupational Therapy Evaluation

1. Role of the OTA in the evaluation process.
    a. The OTA contributes to the evaluation process with supervision from the occupational therapist.
    b. The OTA can assist with the collection of data for the evaluation once service competency has been established.
    c. The level of supervision required will be determined by the OTA's experience and established service competence.
    d. The OTA cannot independently evaluate or interpret evaluation results.
2. Review precautions and weightbearing status before initiating evaluation.
3. Occupational role requirements and expectations.
4. ADL: focus on dressing, bathing, functional mobility with a focus on transfers.
5. ROM and strength of upper extremities.
6. Conduct other assessments as needed (e.g., cognitive).
7. Chapters 11–15 provide detailed information about evaluation methods and approaches.

Occupational Therapy Intervention

1. Role of the OTA.
    a. The OTA implements intervention with supervision from the occupational therapist.
        (1) The level of supervision required depends upon the OTA's experience.
        (2) During the implementation of intervention, the OTA informs the supervising OT of any change in the individual's status and any other relevant information that may affect treatment.
2. Bed mobility and bedside ADL. Refer to Chapter 14.
3. Upper extremity strengthening. Refer to Chapter 11.
4. Functional mobility/ambulation and transfers with appropriate weightbearing status and appropriate ambulation device (i.e., walker, crutches). Refer to Chapter 15.
    a. The type of ambulation device is determined by the person's weightbearing status.
5. Instruct in and practice use of assistive devices for use in the home (e.g., shower chair, elevated commode seat). Refer to Chapter 15.
6. Practice occupation-based activities (e.g., small meal preparation) using proper weight-bearing status and ambulatory device.

CAUTION: Weight-bearing status, the amount of ROM allowed at the hip, and time frames for beginning OT intervention will be determined by the surgeon.

Complications

1. Avascular necrosis.
2. Nonunion.
3. Degenerative joint disease.

Total Hip Replacement (THR)/Total Hip Arthroplasty

EXAM HINT: In the NBCOT® practice analysis, 60.4% of COTA®s who provided services to persons with musculoskeletal/orthopedic disorders indicated they provided services to individuals with joint replacements (NBCOT®, 2018, p. 14). Due to this high prevalence, it is very likely that the COTA® exam will have items about working with persons recovering from joint replacements.

Etiology

1. Trauma from hip fracture.
2. Disease, most often arthritis; surgery is then elective.

Types

1. Total hip joint implant: replaces acetabulum and femoral head
2. Austin Moore: partial hip replacement. Replaces femoral head.
3. See Figure 6-14.

Surgical Procedures

1. Cemented or uncemented.
2. Anterolateral or posterolateral.

Occupational Therapy Evaluation

1. Role of the OTA in the evaluation process.
   a. The OTA contributes to the evaluation process with supervision from the occupational therapist.
   b. The OTA can assist with the collection of data for the evaluation once service competency has been established.
   c. The level of supervision required will be determined by the OTA's experience and established service competence.
   d. The OTA cannot independently evaluate or interpret evaluation results.

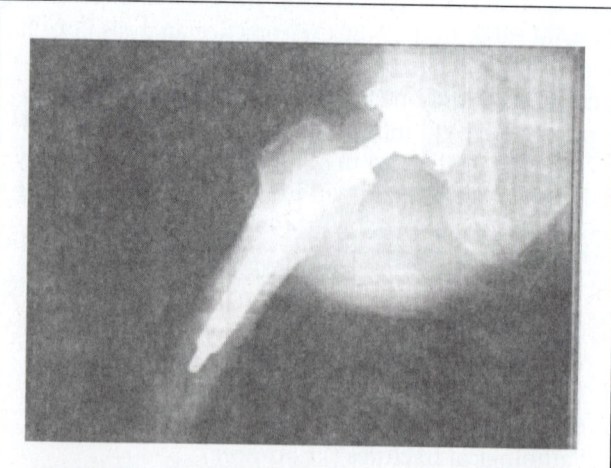

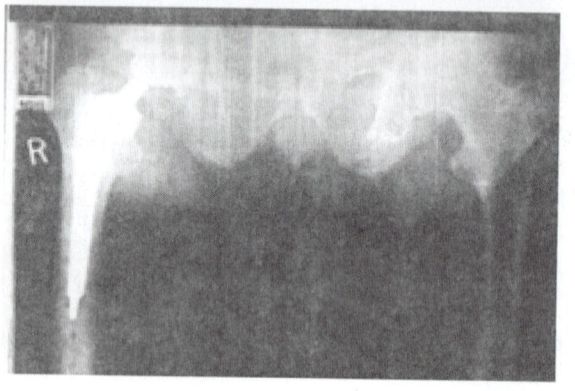

Figure 6-14 Hybrid Cemented Total Hip Arthroplasty.
(Biomet Integral Design, Warsaw, IN).
From Maxey, L., & Magnusson, J. (2006). *Rehabilitation for the postsurgical orthopedic patient* (p. 173). Mosby Publications. Reprinted with permission.

CAUTION: Review precautions and weightbearing status before initiating evaluation.

2. Complete an occupational profile.
3. Assess ADL; focus on dressing, bathing, and transfers. Refer to Chapter 15.
4. Assess ROM and strength of upper extremities. Refer to Chapter 11.
5. Conduct other assessments as needed (e.g., cognitive).
6. Chapters 11–15 provide detailed information about evaluation methods and approaches.

EXAM HINT: The NBCOT® exam outline for the COTA®, identifies knowledge of "the influence of . . . body functions and body structures . . . on a client's occupational performance" (NBCOT®, 2018, p. 21) and "methods for selecting, preparing, and adapting the intervention technique and environment to support optimal engagement in the intervention and promote goal achievement" (NBCOT®, 2018, p. 24) as essential for competent and safe practice. The application of knowledge about the previous evaluation foci and the following interventions can help you effectively determine the correct answers to COTA® exam items about working with persons with total hip replacements.

Occupational Therapy Intervention

1. Role of the OTA.
   a. The OTA implements intervention with supervision from the occupational therapist.
      (1) The level of supervision required depends upon the OTA's experience and established service competence.
      (2) During the implementation of intervention, the OTA informs the supervising OT of any change in the individual's status and any other relevant information that may affect treatment.
2. Educate the individual in hip precautions.
   a. Posterolateral.
      (1) Do not flex beyond 90°.
      (2) Do not adduct or cross legs.
         (a) Do not internally rotate.
      (3) Do not pivot at hip.
      (4) Sit only on raised chair and raised toilet seat.
      (5) Transfer sit to stand by keeping operated hip in slight abduction and extended out in front.

   RED FLAG: If these posterolateral precautions are not followed, a dislocation could result.

   b. Anterolateral.
      (1) Do not externally rotate.
      (2) Do not extend hip.
      (3) Precautions vary for anterior total hip arthroplasty (THA). Some surgeons follow a no restriction protocol.
3. Instruct in and practice use of long-handled equipment.
4. Provide transfer training. Refer to Chapter 15.
   a. Practice with tub bench, raised toilet seat.
   b. Practice car transfers.
   c. Practice bed-to-chair-transfers.
5. Practice occupation-based activities (e.g., small meal preparation) using proper weightbearing status and ambulatory device. Refer to Chapter 15.

Amputations

EXAM HINT: In the NBCOT® practice analysis, 31.2% of COTA®s who provided services to persons with musculoskeletal/orthopedic disorders indicated they provided services to individuals with upper and/or lower extremity amputations (NBCOT®, 2018, p. 14). Due to this prevalence, it is likely that the COTA® exam will have items about working with persons recovering from and living with upper and/or lower extremity amputations.

Etiology

1. Congenital, peripheral vascular disease, trauma, cancer, and infection.

Classification of Amputations

1. Upper extremity level of amputation.
   a. Forequarter: loss of clavicle, scapula, and entire upper extremity.
   b. Shoulder disarticulation: loss of entire upper extremity.
   c. Transhumeral short.
   d. Transhumeral long.
   e. Elbow disarticulation: amputation of the upper extremity distal to the elbow joint.
   f. Transradial short.
   g. Transradial long.
   h. Wrist disarticulation: amputation distal to the wrist joint. Loss of entire hand.
   i. Transmetatarsal.

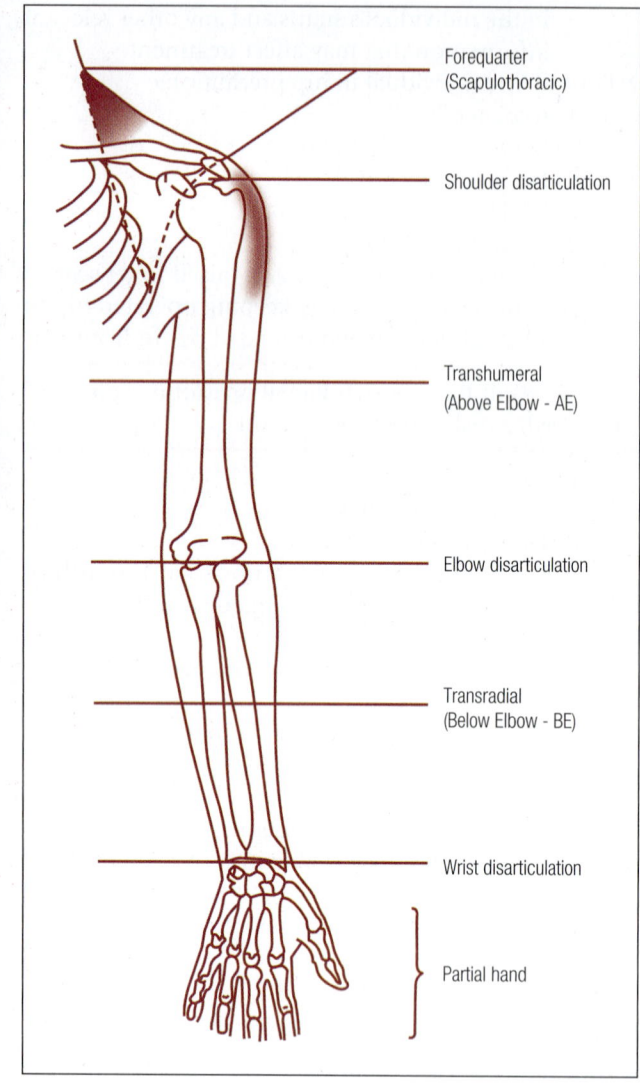

Figure 6-15 Levels of Amputation.

Labels (top to bottom): Forequarter (Scapulothoracic); Shoulder disarticulation; Transhumeral (Above Elbow – AE); Elbow disarticulation; Transradial (Below Elbow – BE); Wrist disarticulation; Partial hand.

Mitsch, S., Smurr Walters, L., & Yancosek, K. (2014). Amputations and prosthetics. In M.V. Radomski & S.A. Trembly Latham (Eds.), *Occupational therapy for physical dysfunction* (7th ed., p. 1267). Philadelphia: Lippincott Williams & Wilkins. Reprinted with permission.

---

f. Syme's amputation or ankle disarticulation.
g. Ray amputation (amputation of the entire digit from the metacarpal and distal).
h. Complete phalanges: amputation of toe(s).

Prosthetic Terminal Devices (TDs)

1. Function to grasp and maintain hold on an object.
2. Body-operated prostheses: use specific scapula and shoulder movements to place tension on the cable that opens or closes the TD.
   a. The two main types of body-operated TDs are the hook and the prosthetic hand.
      (1) Both hooks and hands are operated in one of two ways.
         (a) Voluntary opening (VO): hook remains closed until tension is placed on cable and then it opens. This is prescribed more than the VC.
         (b) Voluntary closing (VC): hook remains opened until tension is placed on cable and then it closes.
         (c) Cosmetic device: minimal function.
3. Myoelectric prostheses: use muscle contractions detected by electrodes to open and close the TD. Common muscle contractions include:
   a. Wrist: use flexors and extensors to open and close the TD.
   b. Transhumeral amputations: use biceps and triceps.
   c. Shoulder disarticulation: use pectoralis major or infraspinatus.
4. Refer to Table 6-1.
5. Determination of the most appropriate TD is based on the person's interests, roles, and preferences.
   a. TDs can be interchangeably used with a prosthesis if the shaft size is the same.

Complications

> **CAUTION:** The occurrence of the following complications can negatively impact a person's health, impede function, and compromise the safe and effective use of prosthetic devices.

1. Neuromas: nerve endings adhered to scar tissue.
   a. These can be very painful and hypersensitive.
2. Skin breakdown.
3. Phantom limb syndrome: sensation of the presence of the amputated limb.
4. Phantom limb pain: sensation of the presence of the amputated limb but is also painful.
5. Infection.
6. Knee flexion contractures in transtibial amputation.
7. Psychological impairments due to shock/grief.

---

   j. Finger amputation: amputation of digit(s) at any level.
   k. See Figure 6-15.
2. Lower extremity (LE) level of amputation.
   a. Hemipelvectomy: amputation of half of pelvis and entire LE.
   b. Hip disarticulation: amputation at the hip joint. Loss of the entire LE.
   c. Above-knee amputation (transfemoral): amputation above knee at any level on the thigh.
   d. Knee disarticulation: amputation at the knee joint.
   e. Below-knee amputation (transtibial): amputation below knee at any level on the calf. Most common.

Table 6-1

Hooks and Hands Compared

FEATURES	HOOKS VO (BODY POWER)	VC TRS GRIP (BODY POWER)	HANDS (EXTERNAL POWER)	HANDS VO (BODY POWER)	GREIFER (EXTERNAL POWER)
Cosmesis	**Unfavorable**	**Unfavorable**	**Favorable**	**Favorable**	**Unfavorable**
Pinch Force	1 lb/rubber band; more rubber bands yield stronger grip but require more effort to open	Controlled strong grip >40 lb dependent on force exerted on cable	Strong grip, 22 lb; may have proportional control	Pinch stronger than VO hook but weaker than externally powered TD; relies on internal springs, adjustable	Strong pinch, 32 lb
Prehension pattern	Precise, exact pinch	Pinch more precise than hand, less than hook	Cylindrical grasp 3-point pinch; configuration same as BP hand	Cylindrical grasp, 3-point pinch; configuration same as external powered hand	Precise pinch and cylindrical grasp
Weight	Lighter than hands; aluminum to stainless steel; 3–8.7 oz	Aluminum, polymer, stainless steel; 4–16 oz	Heavy; 16.2 oz	Heavy; 10.5–14 oz	Heavy; 19oz
Durability	Durable; stainless steel is strongest	Durable and rugged; especially stainless	Not durable; delicate inner electronics and glove	Not durable; delicate inner spring mechanism and glove	Durable and rugged
Reliability	Very good; requires minimal service	Very good; requires minimal service	Good if not used for rugged activities	Good if not used for rugged activities	Very good
Feedback	Some proprioceptive feedback from tension on harness and limb in socket when operating TD/elbow	Better proprioceptive feedback, as tension on cable must be maintained for sustained grasp	Some feedback through intensity of muscle contraction, particularly for proportional control	Feedback similar to VO hook	Same as externally powered hand
Ease of use	Effort increases with more rubber bands	More effort to sustain grasp; lock available	Low effort to activate	More effort to open; can relax for grasp	Same as externally powered hand
Use in various planes	Difficult for high planes	Similar to VO hook	Very good for transradial amputation	Similar to VO hook/hand because of harness	Same as externally powered hand
Visibility of items grasped	Very good	Good; less than VO	Poor for small items	Poor for small items	Poor for small items
Cost	Lowest	Higher than hook, less than hand	Highest cost	Higher than hooks; lower than externally powered hand	About the same as externally powered hand

Stubblefield, K., & Armstrong, A. (2008). Amputations and prosthetics. In M. V. Radomski & C. A. Trombly-Latham (Eds.), *Occupational therapy for physical dysfunction* (6th ed., p. 1272). Baltimore, MD: Lippincott Williams and Wilkins. Reprinted with permission.

Preprosthetic Treatment

1. Change of dominance activities, if needed.
2. ROM of uninvolved joints.
3. Prepare limb for a prosthesis.
4. Desensitization.
5. Wrapping to shape and shrink the residual limb.
   a. Wrap distal to proximal.
   b. Tension should decrease with proximal wrapping.
6. ADL training, including education in skin care.
7. Supportive counseling to facilitate adjustment.
8. Individualize treatment to enhance physical and psychological adjustment.

Prosthetic Treatment

EXAM HINT: The NBCOT® exam outline for the COTA® identifies knowledge of the "training methods regarding the safe and effective use of . . . prosthetic devices consistent with the client's prioritized needs, goals, and task demands in order to optimize or enhance function" (NBCOT®, 2018, p. 26) as essential for competent and safe practice. Based on this requirement, it is likely that the COTA® exam will include items about the OTA's role in prosthetic training.

1. Functional training with prosthesis.
   a. Practice engagement in activities of interest and occupational role activities.
   b. Refer to Table 6-2.
2. Donning and doffing the prosthesis.
3. Increase prosthetic wearing tolerance.
4. Individualize treatment to enhance physical and psychological adjustment.

Treatment for Lower Extremity (LE) Amputations

1. Wrapping to shape residual limb and decrease swelling.
2. Desensitization.
3. Strengthening (UE) with the focus on triceps.
4. Transfer training, stand pivot.
5. ADL training; LE dressing is the most difficult.
6. Standing tolerance.
7. Wheelchair mobility.
8. Chapters 11–15 provide detailed information about the previous intervention methods and approaches.

Table 6-2

Procedures for Practice Controls Training for Body Powered Prostheses

COMPONENT	MOVEMENT	INTERVENTION
Terminal device	Humeral flexion with scapular abduction (protraction) on side of amputation; bilateral scapular abduction for midline use of TD or when strength is limited.	Manually guide patient through motions. For transhumeral prostheses, keep elbow unit locked in 90 degree flexion; teach TD control first.
Wrist unit	Rotate TD to supination (fingers of hook up), midposition (fingers toward midline), or pronation (fingers down). For unilateral amputation, patient uses sound hand to rotate TD. For bilateral amputation, rotate TD against stationary object, between knees, or with contralateral TD.	Have patient analyze the task and determine the most efficient approach for grasp, avoiding excessive or awkward movements. Examples: TD in midposition for carrying a tray, in pronation for grasping small box from table.
Elbow unit	Depress arm while extending and abducting humerus to lock or unlock elbow mechanism. Practice flexing and locking elbow in several planes.	Manually guide patient through motions. Begin with elbow unlocked. Patient listens for click as lock activates. Have patient exaggerate movements initially. Use a mirror. Use humeral flexion to flex the elbow; go beyond desired height, since the arm will drop with gravity pull as patient is in process of locking the elbow unit.
Turntable	Rotate elbow turntable toward or away from body using sound hand. With bilateral amputations, push or pull against stationary object to rotate.	Teach patient to analyze task to determine need to use this component for more efficiency.

Stubblefield, K., & Armstrong, A. (2008). Amputations and prosthetics. In M. V. Radomski & C. A. Trombly-Latham (Eds.), *Occupational therapy for physical dysfunction* (6th ed., p. 1280). Baltimore, MD: Lippincott Williams and Wilkins. Reprinted with permission.

Burns

Classification

1. Superficial (first-degree burn) involves the epidermis only.
   a. Minimal pain and edema, but no blisters.
   b. Healing time is three–seven days.
2. Superficial partial-thickness burn.
   a. Second-degree burns involve the epidermis and upper portion of dermis (e.g., sunburn).
   b. Appearance: red, blistering, and wet.
   c. Painful, no grafting necessary, heals on its own.
   d. Healing time is 7–21 days.
3. Deep partial-thickness burn.
   a. Deep second-degree burn involving the epidermis and deep portion of dermis, hair follicles, and sweat glands.
   b. Appearance: red, white, and elastic.
   c. Sensation may be impaired.
   d. Healing time is 21–35 days.

> **CAUTION:** Potential to convert to full-thickness burn due to infection.

4. Full-thickness burn.
   a. Third-degree burn involving the epidermis and dermis; hair follicles, sweat glands, and nerve endings.
   b. Appearance: white, waxy, leathery, and nonelastic.
   c. Sensation is absent, requires skin graft.
   d. Hypertrophic scar.
   e. Healing time can take months.
5. Fourth-degree burn.
   a. Involves fat, muscle, and bone.
   b. Electrical burn: destruction of nerve along pathway.
6. Rule of nines is a method of assessing burn wound size.
   a. See Figure 6-16.

Occupational Therapy Evaluation and Intervention

1. Role of the OTA in the evaluation process.
   a. The OTA contributes to the evaluation process with supervision from the occupational therapist.
   b. The OTA can assist with the collection of data for the evaluation once service competency has been established.
   c. The level of supervision required will be determined by the OTA's experience and established service competence.
   d. The OTA cannot independently evaluate or interpret evaluation results.
2. Role of the OTA in intervention.
   a. The OTA implements intervention with supervision from the occupational therapist.
      (1) The level of supervision required depends upon the OTA's experience and established service competence.
      (2) During the implementation of intervention, the OTA informs the supervising OT of any change in the individual's status and any other relevant information that may affect treatment.
      (3) During intervention, the psychosocial impact of burns on the person's body image, personal identity, emotional regulation skills, and social participation must be considered and integrated into the intervention process.

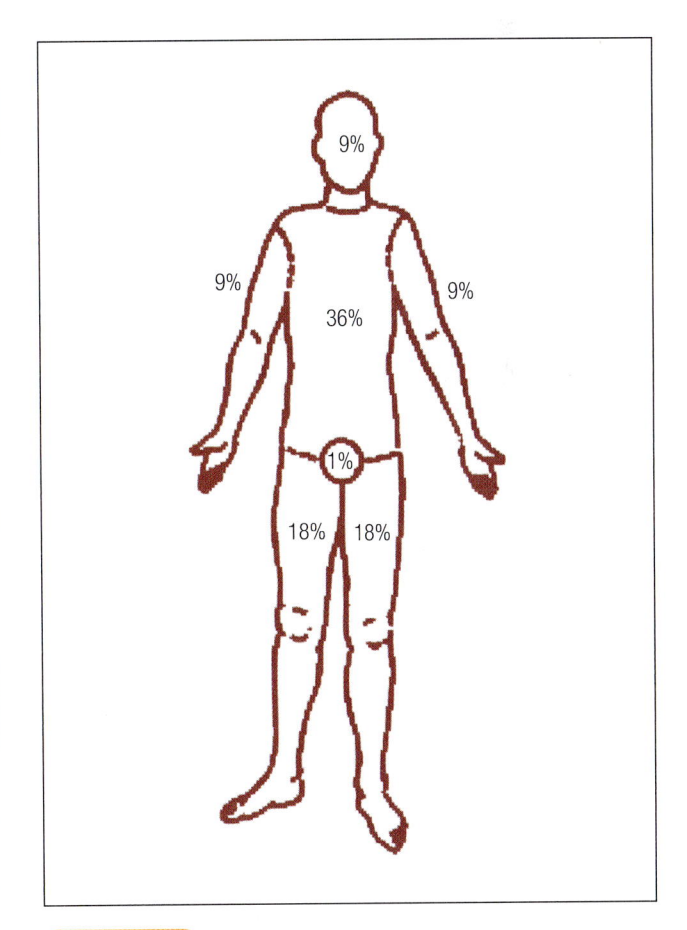

Figure 6-16 Rule of Nines.

Adult Pedretti, L.W. (1996). *Occupational therapy: Practice skills for physical dysfunction*, 4th ed. (p. 615). St. Louis, MO: Mosby. Reprinted with permission.

EXAM HINT: In the NBCOT® exam outline for the COTA® identifies knowledge of the "expected patterns, progressions, and prognoses associated with conditions that limit occupational performance (and the) impact of . . . body functions, (and) body structures . . . on a client's occupational performance" (NBCOT®, 2018, p. 21) and "methods for selecting, preparing, and adapting the intervention technique and environment to support optimal engagement in the intervention and promote goal achievement" (NBCOT®, 2018, p. 24) as essential for competent and safe practice. The application of knowledge about the following evaluation and intervention foci can help you effectively determine the correct answers to exam items about working with persons with burns.

3. Superficial partial-thickness burns.
   a. Evaluation.
      (1) Occupational profile.
      (2) ROM, 72 hours postoperative.
      (3) Sensation, when wounds are healed.
      (4) Strength, when wounds are healed.
      (5) Observe ADL and meaningful role activities, as soon as possible.
   b. Intervention.
      (1) Wound care and débridement, sterile whirlpool, and dressing changes. See Chapter 9.
      (2) Gentle AROM and PROM to individual's tolerance.
      (3) Edema control.
      (4) Splinting, if necessary.
      (5) ADL and role activities.
4. Deep partial-thickness burns.
   a. Evaluation.
      (1) Same as superficial partial-thickness burns.
   b. Intervention.
      (1) Wound care and débridement, sterile whirlpool, and dressing changes. See Chapter 9.
      (2) Gentle AROM and PROM to individual's tolerance.
      (3) Edema control.
      (4) Splinting.
      (5) Occupational role activities and ADL.
      (6) Strengthening (when wounds are healed).
5. Full-thickness burn—requires grafting.
   a. Evaluation.
      (1) ROM (five–seven days postoperative).
      (2) All other evaluations same as previously described.
   b. Postoperative intervention.
      (1) At 72 hours: dressing changes, splint at all times.
      (2) Five to 7 days: begin AROM, light ADL and meaningful activities, sterile whirlpool.
      (3) Over 7 days: PROM as tolerated, ADL and meaningful activities.
      (4) When wounds are healed, use massage.
      (5) Order compression garments.
      (6) Provide Otoform/elastomer inserts.
      (7) Strengthening.

Antideformity Positions Following Burn Injury

1. See Table 6-3.

Hand Splints

EXAM HINT: The NBCOT® exam outline for the COTA® identifies the task of applying "anatomical, physiological, biomechanical, and healing principles to select or fabricate orthotic devices" (NBCOT®, 2018, p.26) as essential for competent and safe practice. The application of knowledge about the following splints will be required to determine the correct answer to the exam items about the OTA's role in the selection and fabrication of splints for persons with burns.

1. Burns to the hand.
   a. Wrist in 20° – 30° extension.
   b. MCP joints in 70° flexion.
   c. IP joints in full extension.
   d. Thumb abducted and extended.
2. If burns to volar surface of hand, flexion contractures develop. Palmar extension splint:
   a. Wrist in 0° – 30° extension.
   b. MCP joints in neutral to slight extension and abducted (monitor collateral ligaments).
   c. IP joints in full extension.
   d. Thumb abducted and extended.
3. Web space burn.
   a. C-splint.

Hypertrophic Scar

1. Most common with deep second- and third-degree burns.
2. Appears 6 - 8 weeks after wound closure.
3. One to 2 years to mature.
4. Compression garments should be worn 24 hours daily.
   a. Applied when wounds are healed.
   b. Recommendation is to wear 24 hours a day for 1–2 years until scar is matured.
5. Additional interventions include ROM, skin care, ADL, role activities, and patient/family support.

Table 6-3

Anticontracture Positioning by Location of Burn

LOCATION OF BURN	CONTRACTURE TENDENCY	ANTI-CONTRACTURE POSITIONING AND/OR TYPICAL SPLINT
Anterior neck	Neck flexion	Remove pillows; use half-mattress to extend the neck; neck extension splint or collar
Axilla	Adduction	120° abduction with slight external rotation; axilla splint or positioning wedges; watch for signs of brachial plexus strain
Anterior elbow	Flexion	Elbow extension splint in 5°–10° flexion
Dorsal wrist	Wrist extension	Wrist support in neutral
Volar wrist	Wrist flexion	Wrist cockup splint in 5°–10° extension
Hand dorsal	Claw hand deformity	Functional hand splint with MP joints 70°–90°, IP joints fully extended, first web open, thumb in opposition
Hand volar	Palmar contracture	Palm extension splint
	Cupping of hand	Myofascial pain syndrome (MPS) in slight hyperextension
Hip-anterior	Hip flexion	Prone positioning; weights on thigh in supine; knee immobilizers
Knee	Knee flexion	Knee extension positioning and/or splints; prevent external rotation, which may cause peroneal nerve compression
Foot	Foot drop	Ankle at 90° with foot board or splint; watch for signs of heel ulcer

Radomski, M. V., & Trombly-Latham, C. A. (Eds.). (2014). *Occupational therapy for physical dysfunction* (6th ed., p. 1249). Baltimore, MD: Lippincott Williams and Wilkins. Reprinted with permission.

Pain

Definition

1. Personal sensation of hurt that can significantly affect an individual's quality of life.

Types of Pain

1. Acute pain has a recent onset and usually lasts for a short duration.
2. Chronic pain is of a long duration and can lead to depression and prescription drug misuse. See Chapter 7.
3. Myofascial pain is specific to muscles, tendons, or fascia.
   a. Myofascial pain syndrome (MPS).
      (1) Persistent, deep aching pains in muscle, nonarticular in origin.
      (2) Characterized by well-defined, highly sensitive tender spots (trigger points).
4. Fibromyalgia syndrome (FMS) is a musculoskeletal pain and fatigue disorder that can vary in intensity.
   a. Widespread pain accompanied by tenderness of muscles and adjacent soft tissues.
   b. A nonarticular rheumatic disease of unknown origin.
5. Low back pain.
   a. Most common work-related injury.
   b. Location: lumbar lordosis.
   c. Etiology.
      (1) Poor posture: seated and standing.
      (2) Repetitive bending using poor body mechanics.
      (3) Heavy lifting.
      (4) Sleeping with poor posture.
   d. Symptoms.
      (1) Pain.
      (2) Difficulty with self-care activities and other role activities (especially LE activities).
      (3) Difficulty sleeping.

EXAM HINT: The NBCOT® exam outline for the COTA® identifies knowledge of the "expected patterns, progressions, and prognoses associated with conditions that limit occupational performance (and the) the impact of . . . body functions and body structures . . . on occupational performance" (NBCOT®, 2018, p. 21) as essential for competent and safe practice. The application of knowledge about the previously described types, causes, and symptoms of pain and the following assessment foci can help you effectively determine the correct answers to NBCOT® Domain 01 exam items about the assessment of pain.

Assessment of Pain

1. Role of the OTA in the evaluation process.
   a. The OTA contributes to the evaluation process with supervision from the occupational therapist.
   b. The OTA can assist with the collection of data for the evaluation once service competency has been established.
   c. The level of supervision required will be determined by the OTA's experience and established service competence.
   d. The OTA cannot independently evaluate or interpret evaluation results.
2. Determine location of pain.
   a. Localized or diffuse.
3. Evaluate intensity of pain.
   a. Pain intensity scale of 0–10 is most commonly used.
   b. Identify the time of day, positions, and activities during which the pain is most intense.
4. Determine the onset and duration of pain.
   a. Gradual or sudden onset.
   b. The length of time pain has been experienced.
5. Description of pain.
   a. Common descriptors include sharp, throbbing, tender, burning, and shooting.
6. Functional assessment of pain.
   a. Pain scales that commonly address function.
      (1) McGill Pain Questionnaire.
      (2) Pain Disability Index.
      (3) Functional Interference Estimate.
   b. Refer to pain management section in Chapter 7.

Occupational Therapy Intervention

1. Role of the OTA.
   a. The OTA implements intervention with supervision from the occupational therapist.
      (1) The level of supervision required depends upon the OTA's experience and established service competence.
      (2) During the implementation of intervention, the OTA informs the supervising OT of any change in the individual's status and any other relevant information that may affect treatment.

> **EXAM HINT:** The NBCOT® exam outline for the COTA® identifies knowledge of "technical level techniques for implementing . . . pain management . . . programs" (NBCOT®, 2018, p. 26) as essential for competent and safe practice. Based on this requirement and the recognition of OT as a nonpharmacological intervention for pain, it is likely that the COTA® exam will include items about the following interventions for pain.

2. Utilize physical agent modalities and massage in preparation for functional activities.
3. Teach proper positioning techniques.
4. Splint in the resting position.
5. Gentle ROM.
6. Teach relaxation exercises.
7. Utilize proper body mechanics during self-care, leisure, and work activities.
8. Correct environmental factors.
9. Correct standing and seated posture.
10. Modify activities and provide ADL training and adaptive equipment, as needed.
11. Provide alternative exercise programs (e.g., aquatic therapy, ai chi, tai chi).
12. Refer to pain management section in Chapter 7.

References

American Occupational Therapy Association. (2005). Standards of practice for occupational therapy. *American Journal of Occupational Therapy, 59,* 663–665.

American Society of Hand Therapists. (1992). *Clinical assessment recommendations.* (2nd ed.). Chicago, IL: Author.

Batshaw, M. L., & Perret, Y. M. (1995). *Children with disabilities: A medical primer.* (4th ed.). Baltimore, MD: Paul Brooke.

Butler, M. W. (2014). Common shoulder diagnoses. In C. Cooper (Ed.), *Fundamentals of hand therapy: Clinical reasoning and treatment guidelines for common diagnoses of the upper extremity.* St. Louis, MO: Elsevier.

Cooper, C. (2014). Hand impairments. In M. V. Radomski & C. A. Trombly Latham (Eds.), *Occupational therapy for physical dysfunction* (7th ed., pp. 1129–1167). Philadelphia, PA: Lippincott Williams & Wilkins.

Cooper, C. (2007). *Fundamentals of hand therapy: Clinical reasoning and treatment guidelines for common diagnoses of the upper extremity.* St. Louis, MO: Elsevier.

Cowdry, J. (2014). Perspectives on pain. In C. Cooper (Ed.), *Fundamentals of hand therapy: Clinical reasoning and treatment guidelines for common diagnoses of the upper extremity.* (2nd ed., pp. 145–150). St. Louis, MO: Elsevier.

De Herder, E. (2015). *Evidence based hands and upper extremity protocol: A practical guide for therapists and physicians.* USA: Elizabeth de Herder.

Deshaies, L. (2014). Burns. In C. Cooper (Ed.), *Fundamentals of hand therapy: Clinical reasoning and treatment guidelines for common diagnoses of the upper extremity* (2nd ed., pp. 479-490). St. Louis, MO: Elsevier.

Escolar, D., Tosi, L. Rocha, A., & Kennedy, A. (2007). Muscles, bones, and nerves. In M. Batshaw, L. Pellegrino, & N. Roizen (Eds.), *Children with disabilities* (6th ed., pp. 203-215). Baltimore: Paul Brookes.

Falkenstein, N., & Weiss-Lessard, S. (1999). *Hand rehabilitation: A quick reference guide and review.* St. Louis, MO: Mosby.

Greene, D. P., & Roberts, S. L. (2005). *Kinesiology: Movement in the context of activity.* (3rd ed.). St. Louis, MO: Mosby.

Klein, L. J. (2014). Flexor tendon repairs. In C. Cooper (Ed.). *Fundamentals of hand therapy: Clinical reasoning and treatment guidelines for common diagnoses of the upper extremity.* (2nd ed., pp. 412-425). St. Louis, MO: Elsevier.

Magee, D.J. (1992). *Orthopedic physical assessment, 2nd ed.* Philadelphia: Saunders.

Maher, C. (2014). Orthopaedic conditions. In M. V. Radomski & C. A. Trombly Latham (Eds.), *Occupational therapy for physical dysfunction.* (7th ed., pp. 1103-1128). Baltimore, MD: Lippincott Williams and Wilkins.

Malick, M., & Kasch, M. (1984). *Manual on management of specific hand problems.* Pittsburgh, PA: AREN.

Maxey, L., & Magnusson, J. (2006). *Rehabilitation for the postsurgical orthopedic patient.* St. Louis, MO: Mosby.

Mitsch, S., Smurr Walters, L., & Yancosek, K. (2014). Amputations and prosthetics. In M. V. Radomski & C. A. Trombly Latham (Eds.), *Occupational therapy for physical dysfunction.* (7th ed., pp. 1266-1299). Baltimore, MD: Lippincott Williams and Wilkins.

Moscony, A. (2014). Peripheral nerve problems. In C. Cooper (Ed.), *Fundamentals of hand therapy: Clinical reasoning and treatment guidelines for common diagnoses of the upper extremity* (2nd ed., pp. 273-311). St. Louis, MO: Elsevier.

National Board for Certification in Occupational Therapy (NBCOT®). (2018). *Practice analysis of the certified occupational therapy assistant registered: Executive summary* [PDF file]. Gaithersburg, MD: Author. Retrieved from https://www.nbcot.org/-/media/NBCOT/PDFs/2017-Practice-Analysis-Executive-OTR.ashx?la=en

Neer, C. (1990). *Shoulder reconstruction.* Philadelphia: PA. Saunders.

Pendeleton, H. M., & Schultz-Krohn, W. (2013). *Pedretti's occupational therapy: Practice skills for physical dysfunction.* (7th ed.). St. Louis, MO: Mosby

Pessina, M. A., & Orroth, A. C. (2014) Burn injuries. In M. V. Radomski & C. A. Trombly Latham (Eds.), *Occupational therapy for physical dysfunction* (7th ed., pp. 1244-1265). Baltimore, MD: Lippincott Williams and Wilkins.

Radomski. M. V., & Trombly Latham, C. A. (2014). *Occupational therapy for physical dysfunction.* (7th ed.). Baltimore: Lippincott Williams and Wilkins.

Restrepo, C., Javad Mortazavi, S. M., Brothers, J., Parvizi, J., & Rothman, R. H. (2011). Hip dislocations: Are hip precautions necessary in anterior approaches? *Clinical Orthopedics Related Research, 469*(2), 417-422.

Sladyk, K., Jacobs, K., & MacRae, N. (2010). *Occupational therapy essentials for clinical competence.* Thorofare, NJ: Slack.

Stoykov, M. E. (2001, August 20). OT treatment for complex regional pain syndrome. *OT Practice,* 10-14.

Weiss, S., & Falkenstein, N. (2005). *Hand rehabilitation: A quick reference guide and review.* (2nd ed.). St. Louis, MO: Elsevier/Mosby.

Review Questions

Musculoskeletal System Disorders

Following are six questions about key content covered in this chapter. These questions are not inclusive of the entirety of content related to musculoskeletal system disorders that you must know for success on the COTA® exam. These questions are provided to help you jump-start the thought processes you will need to apply your studying of content to the answering of exam questions; hence, they are not in the COTA® exam format. Exam items in the COTA® format that cover the depth and breadth of content you will need to know to pass the exam are provided on this text's computer-based exams. The answers to the following questions are provided in Appendix 3.

1. Your client is status post a below-knee amputation. You assess the strength of the client's triceps in preparation for transfer training. The results of the manual muscle testing (MMT) reveal that the client can extend the elbows full range against gravity. When placed in the test position, the client can take moderate resistance and then break. What muscle grade would you document the client possesses?

2. A client incurred a right Colles' fracture. One week ago, the client's cast was removed. You have worked with this client for several intervention sessions. When arriving for the current therapy session, the client is tearful and holding the right arm in a protected position. The client reports that severe pain developed over the weekend in the wrist, hand, and shoulder and that it has not gone away. The right hand is swollen and skin is shiny. On a pain scale of 0–10, the client reports a 10+. The client describes an inability (over the past 2 days) to complete exercises and basic self-care activities due to the pain. You discuss the change in client's status with the occupational therapist. What may be causing the client's increase in symptoms? How should you and the occupational therapist address the client's new presenting symptoms?

3. You begin intervention with a client with a diagnosis of de Quervain's. Upon evaluation, the client's major complaint was pain when lifting (e.g., the client's newborn child, grocery bags). Pain is reported as 8/10. What interventions should you implement?

4. You work with a client with a third-degree burn to the hand. The physician has prescribed a splint for the client. What is the optimal antideformity position you should use to guide your splint construction? Explain your reasoning.

(Continued)

Review Questions

Musculoskeletal System Disorders (Continued)

5. You begin intervention with a person with a diagnosis of carpal tunnel syndrome (CTS). What conservative treatment methods are indicated for this diagnosis?

6. A child with a diagnosis of osteogenesis imperfecta receives occupational therapy services. What should be the primary foci of occupational therapy intervention? Describe the safety precautions you and the occupational therapist should integrate into the treatment of a child with osteogenesis imperfecta.

7

Neurological System Disorders

GLEN GILLEN, SUSAN B. O'SULLIVAN, JAN G. GARBARINI, AND MARGE E. MOFFETT BOYD

Chapter Outline

- Anatomy and Physiology of the Nervous System, 188
- Stroke/Cerebral Vascular Accident (CVA), 192
- Trauma, 194
- Disorders of Movement/Neuromuscular Diseases, 201
- Disorders of the Peripheral Nervous System/Neuromuscular Diseases, 206
- Demyelinating Disease, 209
- Occupational Therapy Evaluation and Intervention for Neurological System Disorders, 209
- Pain, 211
- Sensory Processing Disorders, 213
- Seizure Disorders, 216
- References, 218
- Review Questions, 221

Anatomy and Physiology of the Nervous System

Relationship to the Examination

1. It is not likely that the COTA® exam will ask direct questions about anatomy or physiology. As a result, this chapter does not provide a complete anatomy and physiology review.

> **EXAM HINT:** In the NBCOT® exam outline for the certified occupational therapy assistant (COTA®), the task of recognizing the influence of "body functions and body structures . . . on a client's occupational performance" (NBCOT®, 2018, p. 21) is identified as essential for competent and safe practice. The application of knowledge about the major structures and functions of the nervous system can help you correctly answer COTA® exam items about the functional implications of damage to the nervous system. For example, damage to the left temporal lobe would result in the need to communicate nonverbally.

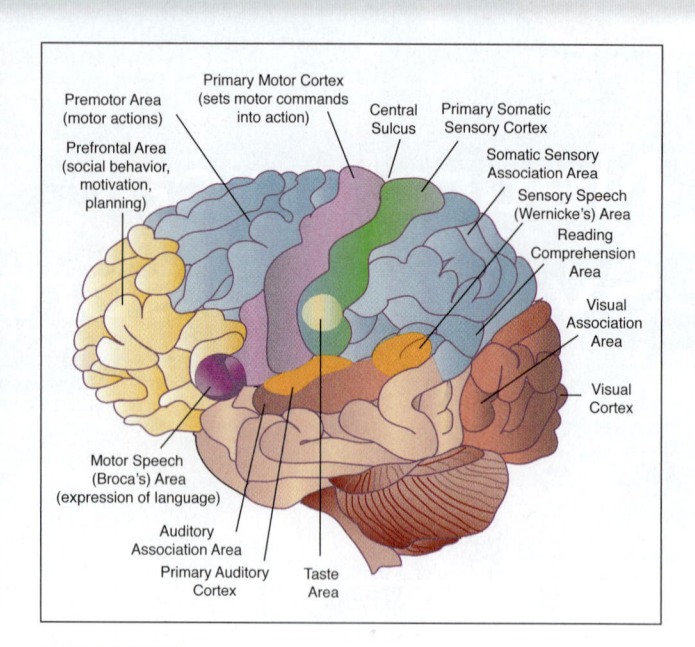

Figure 7-1 Functional Areas of the Brain.

Brain

1. See Figure 7-1.
2. Cerebral hemispheres (telencephalon).
   a. Convolutions of gray matter composed of gyri (crests) and sulci (fissures).
      (1) Lateral central fissure (Sylvian fissure) separates temporal lobe from frontal and parietal lobes.
      (2) Longitudinal cerebral fissure separates the two hemispheres.
      (3) Central sulcus separates frontal lobe from the parietal lobe.
   b. Paired hemispheres, consisting of six lobes on each side: frontal, parietal, temporal, occipital, insular, limbic.
      (1) Frontal lobe.
         (a) Precentral gyrus: primary motor cortex for voluntary muscle activation. Damage to this is area would result in contralateral weakness of the limbs and trunk.
         (b) Prefrontal cortex: controls emotions, judgments, higher-order cognitive functions such as ideation and abstraction. Damage to this is area would result in executive dysfunction, ideational apraxia, decreased organization and sequencing, etc.
         (c) Premotor cortex related to planning of movements including Broca's area, which controls motor aspects of speech. Damage to this area would result motor apraxia and expressive aphasia.
      (2) Parietal lobe.
         (a) Postcentral gyrus: primary sensory cortex for integration of sensation. Damage to this area would result in contralateral sensory loss.
         (b) Receives fibers conveying touch, proprioceptive, pain, and temperature sensations from opposite side of body.
      (3) Temporal lobe.
         (a) Primary auditory cortex: receives/processes auditory stimuli.
         (b) Associative auditory cortex: processes auditory stimuli.
         (c) Wernicke's area: language comprehension. Damage to this area would result in receptive aphasia.
      (4) Occipital lobe.
         (a) Primary visual cortex: receives/processes visual stimuli.
         (b) Visual association cortex: processes visual stimuli. Damage to this area would result in visual impairments such as visual spatial relations impairment.
      (5) Insula: deep within lateral sulcus, associated with visceral functions.

(6) Limbic system.
   (a) Consists of the limbic lobe, hippocampal formation, amygdaloid nucleus, hypothalamus, anterior nucleus of thalamus.
   (b) Phylogenetically oldest part of the brain, concerned with instincts and emotions contributing to preservation of the individual.
   (c) Basic functions include feeding, aggression, emotions, endocrine aspects of sexual response, and long-term memory. Damage to this area would result in poor emotional regulation in addition to long term memory loss.

c. White matter: myelinated nerve fibers located centrally.
   (1) Transverse (commissural) fibers: interconnect the two hemispheres, including the corpus callosum (the largest), anterior commissure, and hippocampal commissure.
   (2) Projection fibers: connect cerebral hemispheres with other portions of the brain and spinal cord.
   (3) Association fibers: connect different portions of the cerebral hemispheres (within the same hemisphere), allowing cortex to function as an integrated whole.

d. Basal ganglia.
   (1) Masses of gray matter deep within the cerebral hemispheres, including the corpus striatum, amygdaloid nucleus, and claustrum. The lenticular nuclei are further subdivided into the putamen and globus pallidus.
   (2) Forms an associated motor system (extrapyramidal system) with other nuclei in the subthalamus and midbrain.
   (3) Has numerous fiber interconnections.
      (a) Caudate loop (complex loop) functions in conjunction with association cortex in the formation of motor plans.
      (b) Putamen loop (motor loop) functions in association with sensorimotor cortex to scale and adjust movements.
   (4) Damage to the basal ganglia will result in problems controlling speech, movement, and posture. These impairments are common in those living with Parkinson's disease.

3. Cerebellum.
   a. Located behind dorsal pons and medulla in posterior fossa.
   b. Structure.
      (1) Joined to brain stem by three pairs of peduncles: superior, middle, and inferior.
      (2) Comprised of two hemispheres and midline vermis; have cerebellar cortex, underlying white matter, and four paired deep nuclei.
   c. Damage to the cerebellum will result in decreased motor coordination such as ataxia.

Spinal Cord

1. General structure.
   a. Cylindrical mass of nerve tissue extending from the foramen magnum in skull continuous with medulla to the lower border of first lumbar vertebra in the conus medullaris.
   b. Divided into 30 segments: 7 cervical, 12 thoracic, 5 lumbar, 5 sacral, a few coccygeal segments.
2. Central gray matter contains: two anterior (ventral) and two posterior (dorsal) horns united by gray commissure with central canal. See Figure 7-2.
   a. Anterior horns contain cell bodies that give rise to efferent (motor) neurons: alpha motor neurons to effect muscles and gamma motor neurons to muscle spindles.
   b. Posterior horns contain afferent (sensory) neurons with cell bodies located in the dorsal root ganglia.

> **EXAM HINT:** Applying knowledge of the anterior (ventral) and posterior (dorsal) spinal cord tracts can help you correctly answer COTA® exam items about the functional implications of incomplete spinal cord lesions and specific cord syndromes (e.g., anterior cord, central cord, and Brown-Sequard syndromes). See Table 7-1.

   c. Two enlargements, cervical and lumbosacral, for origins of nerves of upper and lower extremities.

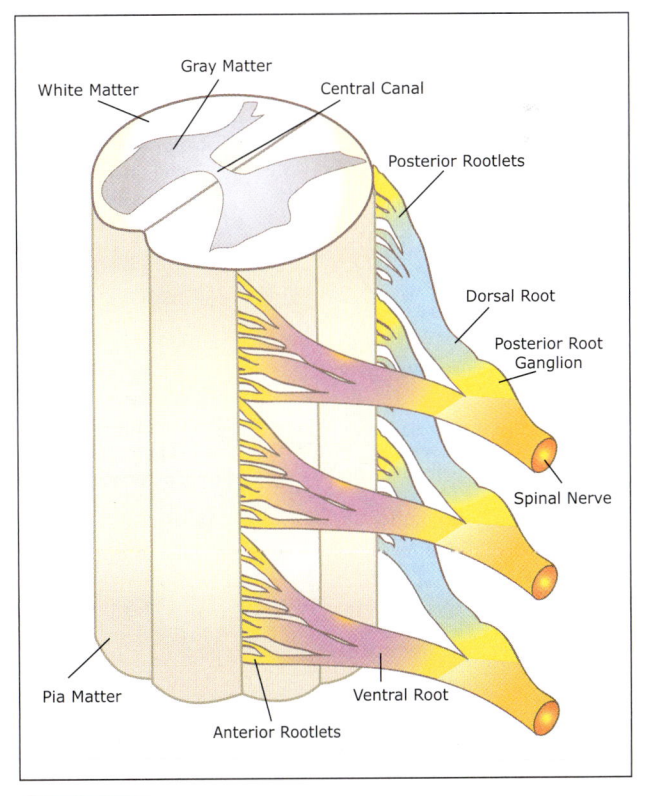

Figure 7-2 Spinal Cord: Anterior Cross Section.

Table 7-1

Spinal Cord Syndromes

LESION	CHARACTERISTICS
Complete Cord Lesion: UMN lesion	Complete bilateral loss of all sensory modalities Bilateral loss of motor function with spastic paralysis below level of lesion Loss of bladder and bowel functions with spastic bladder and bowel
Central Cord Lesion: UMN lesion	Cavitation of central cord in cervical section Loss of spinothalamic tracts with bilateral loss of pain and temperature Loss of ventral horn with bilateral loss of motor function: primarily upper extremities Preservation of proprioception and discriminatory sensation
Brown-Sequard Syndrome: UMN lesion	Hemisection of spinal cord Ipsilateral loss of dorsal columns with loss of tactile discrimination, pressure, vibration, and proprioception Ipsilateral loss of corticospinal tracts with loss of motor function and spastic paralysis below level of lesion Contralateral loss of spinothalamic tract with loss of pain and temperature below level of lesion; at lesion level, bilateral loss of pain and temperature
Anterior Cord Syndrome: UMN lesion	Loss of anterior cord Loss of lateral corticospinal tracts with bilateral loss of motor function, spastic paralysis below level of lesion Loss of spinothalamic tracts with bilateral loss of pain and temperature Preservation of dorsal columns: proprioception, kinesthesia, and vibratory sense
Posterior Cord Syndrome: UMN lesion	Loss of dorsal columns bilaterally Bilateral loss of proprioception, vibration, pressure, and epicritic sensations (stereognosis, two-point discrimination) Preservation of motor function, pain, and light touch
Cauda Equina Injury: LMN lesion	Loss of long nerve roots at or below L1 Variable nerve root damage (motor and sensory signs); incomplete lesions common Flaccid paralysis with no spinal reflex activity Flaccid paralysis of bladder and bowel Potential for nerve regeneration; regeneration often incomplete, slows and stops after about 1 year

LMN = lower motor neuron; UMN = upper motor neuron

d. Lateral horn is found in thoracic and upper lumbar segments for preganglionic fibers of the autonomic nervous system.
3. White matter: anterior (ventral), lateral, and posterior (dorsal) white columns or funiculi.
   a. Ascending fiber systems (sensory pathways). Damage to these pathways will result in various patterns of loss of sensation such as proprioception, temperature sense, and light touch.
   b. Descending fiber systems (motor pathways). Damage to these pathways will result in motor dysfunction such as weakness, spasticity, or flaccidity.
4. Autonomic nervous system (ANS).
   a. Concerned with innervation of involuntary structures: smooth muscle, heart, glands; helps maintain homeostasis (constant internal body environment).
   b. Divided into two divisions: sympathetic and parasympathetic; both have afferent and efferent nerve fibers; preganglionic and postganglionic fibers.
      (1) Sympathetic (thoracolumbar) division: prepares body for fight-or-flight, emergency responses, raises heart rate and blood pressure, constricts peripheral blood vessels and redistributes blood; inhibits peristalsis.
      (2) Parasympathetic (craniosacral) division: conserves and restores homeostasis; slows heart rate and reduces blood pressure, increases peristalsis and glandular activity.

Neurons

1. Structure.
   a. Neurons vary in size and complexity.
      (1) Cell bodies (genetic center) with dendrites (receptive surface area to receive information via synapses).
      (2) Axons conduct impulses away from the cell body (one-way conduction).
      (3) Synapses allow communication between neurons; chemical neurotransmitters are released (chemical synapses) or electrical signals pass directly from cell to cell (electrical synapses).
   b. Neuron groupings and types.
      (1) Nuclei are compact groups of nerve cell bodies; in the peripheral nervous system these groups are called ganglia.
      (2) Projection neurons carry impulses to other parts of the CNS.
      (3) Interneurons are short relay neurons.
      (4) Axon bundles are called tracts or fasciculi; in spinal cord, collections of tracts are called columns, or funiculi.
2. Lower motor neuron system and upper motor neuron system.
   a. See Table 7-2.

Table 7-2

Differential Diagnosis: Comparison of Upper Motor Neuron (UMN) and Lower Motor Neuron (LMN) Syndromes

	UMN LESION	LMN LESION
Location of Lesion	Central nervous system	Peripheral nervous system
Structures Involved	Cortex, brainstem, corticospinal tracts, spinal cord	SC: anterior horn cell, spinal roots, peripheral nerves CN: cranial nerves
Disorders	Stroke, traumatic brain injury, spinal cord injury	Polio, Guillain-Barré, PNI, peripheral neuropathy, radiculopathy
Tone	Increased: hypertonia Velocity-dependent	Decreased or absent: hypotonia, flaccidity Not velocity dependent
Reflexes	Increased: hyperreflexia, clonus Exaggerated cutaneous and autonomic reflexes: + Babinski response	Decreased or absent: hyporeflexia Cutaneous reflexes decreased or absent
Involuntary Movements	Muscle spasms: flexor or extensor	With denervation: fasciculations
Strength	Stroke: weakness or paralysis on one side of the body Corticospinal lesions: contralateral if above decussation in medulla, ipsilateral if below Spinal cord lesions: bilateral loss below level of lesion	Limited distribution: segmental or focal pattern Root-innervated pattern
Muscle Bulk	Variable, disuse atrophy	Neurogenic atrophy: rapid, focal, severe wasting
Voluntary Movements	Impaired or absent: dyssynergic patterns, obligatory synergies	Weak or absent if nerve interrupted

Key: CN = cranial nerve; PNI = peripheral nerve injury; SC = spinal cord

Peripheral Nervous System

1. Peripheral nerves are referred to as lower motor neurons (LMNs). See Figure 7-3. Functional components include:
   a. Motor (efferent) fibers originate from motor nuclei (cranial nerves) or anterior horn cells (spinal nerves).
      (1) Damage to the motor fibers will result in weakness.
   b. Sensory (afferent) fibers originate in cells outside of brain stem or spinal cord with sensory ganglia (cranial nerves) or dorsal root ganglia (spinal nerves).
      (1) Damage to the sensory fibers will result in sensory impairments such as loss of light touch, moving touch, and two-point discrimination.
   c. ANS fibers: sympathetic fibers at thoracolumbar spinal segments and parasympathetic fibers at craniosacral segments.
2. Cranial nerves: 12 pairs of cranial nerves, all nerves are distributed to head and neck except C.N. X, which is distributed to thorax and abdomen.
3. Spinal nerves: 31 pairs of spinal nerves; spinal nerves are divided into groups (8 cervical, 12 thoracic, 5 lumbar, 5 sacral, coccygeal) and correspond to vertebral segments; each has a ventral root and a dorsal root.
   a. Ventral (anterior) root: efferent (motor) fibers to voluntary muscles (alpha motoneurons, gamma motoneurons), and to viscera, glands, and smooth muscles (preganglionic ANS fibers).
   b. Dorsal (posterior) root: afferent (sensory) fibers from sensory receptors from skin, joints, and muscles; each dorsal root possesses a dorsal root ganglion (cell bodies of sensory neurons); there is no dorsal root for C1.
   c. The term dermatome refers to a specific segmental skin area innervated by sensory spinal axons. See Figure 6-6 in Chapter 6 and Table 11-3 in Chapter 11.

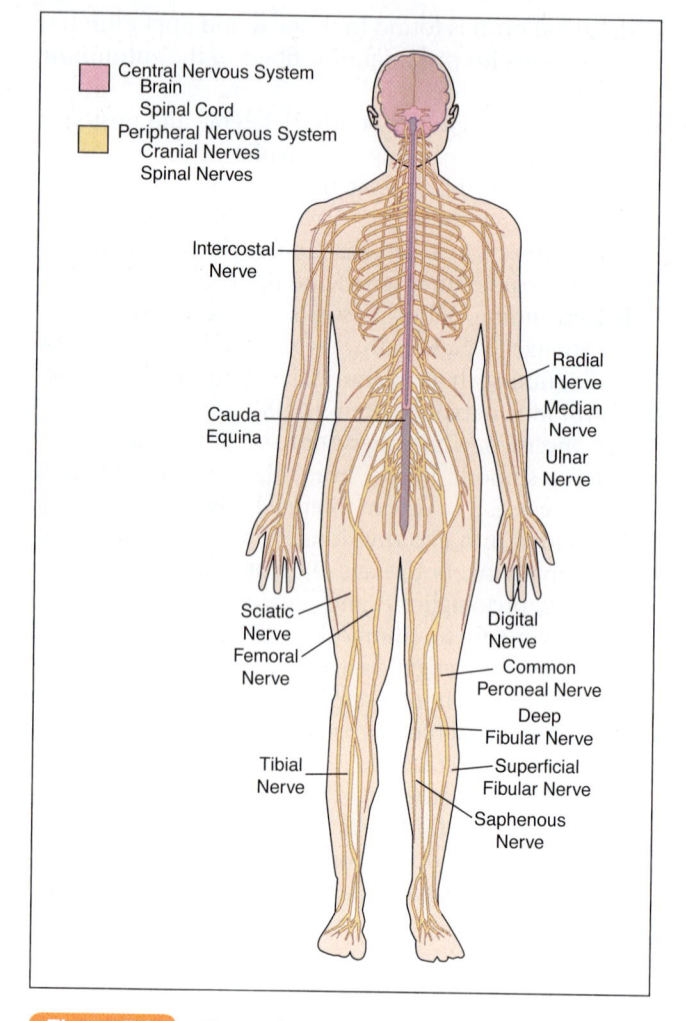

Figure 7-3 Overview of Nervous System.

Stroke/Cerebral Vascular Accident (CVA)

Specific Types and Etiology

1. The term CVA or stroke apply to clinical syndromes that accompany ischemic or hemorrhagic lesions.
   a. Cerebral insufficiency: due to transient disturbances of blood flow, for example, transient ischemic attack (TIA).
      (1) A transient ischemic attack (TIA) is a transitory stroke that for the most part lasts only a few minutes.
         (a) TIAs occur when the blood supply to part of the brain is briefly interrupted.
         (b) TIA symptoms, which usually occur suddenly, are similar to those of stroke but do not last as long. Most symptoms of a TIA disappear within an hour, although they may persist for up to 24 hours.
         (c) Symptoms can include: numbness or weakness in the face, arm, or leg, especially on one side of the body; confusion or difficulty in talking or understanding speech; trouble seeing in one or both eyes; difficulty with walking, dizziness, and/or loss of balance and coordination.

> **RED FLAG:** TIAs are often warning signs that a person is at risk for a more serious and debilitating stroke. About one-third of those who have a TIA will have an acute stroke in the future.

   b. Cerebral infarction: due to either embolism or thrombosis of the intra- or extracranial arteries.
   c. Cerebral hemorrhage: bleed secondary to hypertension or aneurysm.
   d. Cerebral arteriovenous malformation (AVM): abnormal, tangled collections of dilated blood vessels that result from congenitally malformed vascular structures.

Prevalence, Onset, and Prognosis

1. On average, a US citizen incurs a stroke every 40 seconds; every four minutes someone dies of a stroke.
2. It is the third largest cause of death ranking behind heart diseases and all forms of cancer.
3. Stroke is the leading cause of serious, long-term disability in the United States.
4. The prevalence of stroke is 7,200,000 based on current data.
5. Data show that about 795,000 people incur a new or recurrent stroke each year. About 610,000 of these are first attacks and 185,000 are recurrent attacks.

> **EXAM HINT:** In the NBCOT® practice analysis for the COTA®, 62.9% of COTA®s who provided services to persons with neurological disorders indicated they provided services to individuals with strokes (NBCOT®, 2018, p. 12). Due to this high prevalence, it is very likely that the COTA® exam will have items about working with persons recovering from CVAs.

Symptoms of CVA

1. Abrupt onset of usually unilateral neurological signs (i.e., weakness, vision loss, sensory changes, etc.).
2. Symptoms progress over several hours to two days.
3. Specific symptoms are determined by the site of the infarct and the involved artery.
   a. Refer to Table 7-3 for hemispheric specialization information, which is based on lateralization in most individuals.
      (1) Hemispheric asymmetry and functional localization can vary in individuals.

Table 7-3

Hemispheric Specialization*

LEFT HEMISPHERE	RIGHT HEMISPHERE
Movement of right side of body	Movement of left side of body
Processing of sensory information from right side of body	Processing of sensory information from left side of body
Visual reception from right field	Visual reception from left field
Visual verbal processing	Visual spatial processing
Bilateral motor praxis	Left motor praxis
Verbal memory	Nonverbal memory
Bilateral auditory reception	Attention to incoming stimuli
Speech	Emotional lability
Processing of verbal auditory information	Processing of nonverbal auditory information
	Interpretation of abstract information
	Interpretation of tonal inflections

*Based on hemispheric lateralization in most clients. It must be recognized that hemispheric asymmetry and functional localization varies in individuals.

> **EXAM HINT:** When determining the correct answers to COTA® exam items about persons with strokes/CVAs, be sure to consider the reported site of the infarct. For example, the correct answer to an exam item about an OTA working with a person recovering from a left CVA will need to consider its impact on the person's communication abilities; whereas, the correct answer to an exam item about recovering from a right CVA will need to consider its impact on the person's ability to attend to the left side of the environment and body.

Risk Factors

1. Modifiable risk factors.
   a. Hypertension.
   b. Cardiac disease.
   c. Atrial fibrillation.
   d. Diabetes mellitus.
   e. Smoking.
   f. Alcohol abuse.
   g. Hyperlipidemia.
2. Nonmodifiable risk factors.
   a. Age: relative risk increases with age.
   b. Gender: males are at higher risk.
   c. Race: African-American and Latino are at greater risk.
   d. Heredity.

Diagnosis

1. Usually diagnosed clinically using symptoms as a guide to lesion location.
2. Infarction visualized via computerized axial tomography (CT) scan (may initially read as negative).
3. Arteriography.
4. Positron emission tomography (PET) and single photon emission computerized tomography (SPECT) scanning to distinguish between infarcted and non-infarcted tissue.
5. Magnetic resonance imaging (MRI) to rule out other conditions and screen for acute bleeding.
6. Diagnostic testing
   a. Transcranial and carotid Doppler for noninvasive visualization of plaque or occlusion of the cerebral vessels.
   b. Electrocardiogram (ECG) to detect arrhythmias.
   c. Echocardiography to evaluate presence of cardiac emboli and cardiac disease.
   d. Blood work to rule out metabolic abnormalities.

Medical Management

1. Immediate care.
   a. Airway maintenance.
   b. Adequate oxygenation.
   c. Nutritional intervention (IV fluids, alternative feeding routes).
   d. Decubiti prevention.
   e. Treatment of underlying cardiac dysfunction (dysrhythmias).
2. Pharmacologic therapies.
   a. Antithrombotic therapy (antiplatelet and anticoagulation) is used for rapid recanalization and reperfusion of occluded vessels to reduce infarction area, e.g., aspirin, heparin.
   b. Thrombolytic therapy is used in acute strokes to open occluded cerebral vessels and restore blood flow to ischemic areas, e.g., tissue plasminogen activator (t-PA).

Trauma

Traumatic Brain Injury (TBI)

1. Etiology.
2. Damage results from penetration of the skull (open TBI), or from rapid acceleration or deceleration of the brain (closed TBI), or blunt external force (closed TBI).
   a. Injury occurs in the tissue at the point of impact (coup), at the opposite pole (contrecoup), and diffusely along the frontal and temporal lobes.
   b. Injury can result from a variety of occurrences.
      (1) Skull fractures.
      (2) Closed head injuries.
      (3) Penetrating wounds of the skull and brain.
      (4) Traumatic injury to extracranial blood vessels.
      (5) Nerve tissues, blood vessels, and meninges are sheared, torn, or ruptured, resulting in hemorrhage, edema, and ischemia.
3. Prevalence, onset, and prognosis.
   a. Responsible for more deaths and disabilities than any other neurologic cause in the population under age 50.
   b. Males are twice as likely to incur a TBI, with the highest risk group being 15- to 29-year-olds.
   c. Between 2.5 and 6.5 million Americans alive today have had a TBI.
   d. 1.7 million new head injuries are reported each year.

> **EXAM HINT:** In the NBCOT® practice analysis for the COTA®, 15.6% of COTA®s who provided services to persons with neurological disorders indicated they provided services to individuals with TBIs (NBCOT®, 2018, p. 12). Due to this prevalence, the COTA® exam may have items about working with persons recovering from TBIs.

4. Symptoms.
   a. Concussion characterized by post-traumatic loss of consciousness and memory disturbances.
   b. Cerebral contusion/laceration/edema accompanied by surface wounds and skull fractures.
   c. A variety of symptoms can result.
      (1) Hemiplegia or monoplegia and abnormal reflexes.
      (2) Decorticate or decerebrate rigidity.
      (3) Fixed pupils.
      (4) Coma.
      (5) Changes in vital signs.
5. Diagnostic testing.
   a. Administration of the Glasgow Coma Scale.
      (1) This scale rates a person's eye opening, motor responses, and verbal responses.
         (a) The scale ranges from 3 (deep coma or death) to 15 (fully awake person).
         (b) See Table 7-4.

Table 7-4

Glasgow Coma Scale

Best eye response (E)	Eyes opening spontaneously	4
	Eyes opening to speech	3
	Eyes opening in response to pain	2
	No eye opening	1
Best verbal response (V)	Oriented (patient responds coherently and appropriately to questions such as the patient's name and age, where they are and why, the year, month, etc.)	5
	Confused (patient responds to questions coherently but there is some disorientation and confusion)	4
	Inappropriate words (random or exclamatory speech, but not conversational exchange)	3
	Incomprehensible sounds (moaning but no words)	2
	None	1
Best motor response (M)	Obeys commands (the person does simple things as asked)	6
	Localizes to pain (purposeful movements towards changing painful stimuli)	5
	Withdraws from pain (pulls part of body away when pinched)	4
	Flexion in response to pain (decorticate response)	3
	Extension to pain (decerebrate response)	2
	No motor response	1

Reprinted from *The Lancet*, 304., Teasdale G, Jennett B. Assessment of coma and impaired consciousness. A practical scale, 81–84. Copyright 1974, with permission from Elsevier.

b. Administration of the Rancho Los Amigos Levels of Cognitive Functioning Scale.
　(1) Refer to Table 7-5.
c. CT scan and MRI to visualize intracranial structure damage.

EXAM HINT: COTA® exam items about working with a person recovering from a TBI may include behavioral descriptions that indicate a specific level on the Glasgow Coma or Rancho Los Amigos Levels of Cognitive Functioning Scale. Correct answers about the implementation of an OT intervention plan should consider the person's current capabilities and include treatment approaches that are designed to develop the person's abilities to progress to the next level on these scales.

6. Medical management.
　a. Resuscitation.
　b. Management of respiratory dysfunction.
　c. Cardiovascular monitoring.
　d. Surgical, pharmacologic, or mechanical means to decrease intracranial pressure.
　e. Neurosurgery to manage lacerated vessels and depressed skull fractures.
　f. Pharmacologic interventions.
　　(1) Antibiotics.
　　(2) Anticonvulsants.
　　(3) Sedatives.
　　(4) Antidepressants.

Postconcussion Syndrome

1. A set of symptoms that may continue for weeks, months, or a year or more after a concussion.
2. Prevalence, onset, and prognosis.
　a. The prevalence of postconcussion syndrome in the first weeks after TBI varies from 40% to 80%.
　b. As many as 50% of patients report symptoms for up to three months and 10% to 15% for more than a year.
　c. Symptoms may develop in the days or weeks after concussion. However, this will affect a minority of individuals.
　d. Symptoms usually subside in a few weeks, but some individuals will have longer-lasting symptoms.
3. Symptoms.
　a. Concussion with or without loss of consciousness.
　b. A variety of symptoms can result. These include:
　　(1) Headache.
　　(2) Fatigue.
　　(3) Cognitive impairment.
　　(4) Dizziness.
　　(5) Depression.
　　(6) Impaired balance.
　　(7) Irritability.
　　(8) Apathy.
4. Diagnostic testing.
　a. Exercise testing such as treadmill exercise.

CAUTION: Concussion symptoms are typically exacerbated by exercise.

　b. Neuropsychiatric evaluation.
　c. Neuro-ophthalmologic examination.
　d. Vestibular testing.
5. Medical management
　a. Prescribing a period of cognitive and physical rest.
　b. Cognitive behavioral therapy (CBT).
　c. Anti-depression medications.

Table 7-5

Rancho Los Amigos Levels of Cognitive Functioning Scale

Level I - No Response: Total Assistance
- Complete absence of observable change in behavior when presented visual, auditory, tactile, proprioceptive, vestibular, or painful stimuli.

Level II - Generalized Response: Total Assistance
- Demonstrates generalized reflex response to painful stimuli.
- Responds to repeated auditory stimuli with increased or decreased activity.
- Responds to external stimuli with physiological changes generalized, gross body movement, and/or not purposeful vocalization.
- Responses noted above may be same regardless of type and location of stimulation.
- Responses may be significantly delayed.

Level III - Localized Response: Total Assistance
- Demonstrates withdrawal or vocalization to painful stimuli.
- Turns toward or away from auditory stimuli.
- Blinks when strong light crosses visual field.
- Follows moving object passed within visual field.
- Responds to discomfort by pulling tubes or restraints.
- Responds inconsistently to simple commands.
- Responses directly related to type of stimulus.
- May respond to some persons (especially family and friends) but not to others.

Level IV - Confused/Agitated: Maximal Assistance
- Alert and in heightened state of activity.
- Purposeful attempts to remove restraints or tubes or crawl out of bed.
- May perform motor activities such as sitting, reaching, and walking but without any apparent purpose or upon another's request.
- Very brief and usually nonpurposeful moments of sustained alternatives and divided attention.
- Absent short-term memory.
- May cry out or scream out of proportion to stimulus even after its removal.
- May exhibit aggressive or flight behavior.
- Mood may swing from euphoric to hostile with no apparent relationship to environmental events.
- Unable to cooperate with treatment efforts.
- Verbalizations are frequently incoherent and/or inappropriate to activity or environment.

Level V - Confused, Inappropriate, Nonagitated: Maximal Assistance
- Alert, not agitated but may wander randomly or with a vague intention of going home.
- May become agitated in response to external stimulation and/or lack of environmental structure.
- Not oriented to person, place, or time.
- Frequent brief periods, nonpurposeful sustained attention.
- Severely impaired recent memory, with confusion of past and present in reaction to ongoing activity.
- Absent goal-directed, problem solving, self-monitoring behavior.
- Often demonstrates inappropriate use of objects without external direction.
- May be able to perform previously learned tasks when structured and cues provided.
- Unable to learn new information.
- Able to respond appropriately to simple commands fairly consistently with external structures and cues.
- Responses to simple commands without external structure are random and nonpurposeful in relation to command.
- Able to converse on a social, automatic level for brief periods of time when provided external structure and cues.
- Verbalizations about present events become inappropriate and confabulatory when external structure and cues are not provided.

Level VI - Confused, Appropriate: Moderate Assistance
- Inconsistently oriented to person, time, and place.
- Able to attend to highly familiar tasks in nondistracting environment for 30 minutes with moderate redirection.
- Remote memory has more depth and detail than recent memory.
- Vague recognition of some staff.
- Able to use assistive memory aide with maximum assistance.
- Emerging awareness of appropriate response to self, family, and basic needs.
- Moderate assist to problem solve barriers to task completion.
- Supervised for old learning (e.g., self-care).
- Shows carryover for relearned familiar tasks (e.g., self-care).
- Maximum assistance for new learning with little or no carryover.
- Unaware of impairments, disabilities, and safety risks.
- Consistently follows simple directions.
- Verbal expressions are appropriate in highly familiar and structured situations.

Level VII - Automatic, Appropriate: Minimal Assistance for Daily Living Skills
- Consistently oriented to person and place, within highly familiar environments. Moderate assistance for orientation to time.
- Able to attend to highly familiar tasks in a nondistracting environment for at least 30 minutes with minimal assist to complete tasks.
- Minimal supervision for new learning.

(Continued)

Table 7-5

Rancho Los Amigos Levels of Cognitive Functioning Scale *(Continued)*

Level VII - Automatic, Appropriate: Minimal Assistance for Daily Living Skills *(Continued)*

- Demonstrates carryover of new learning.
- Initiates and carries out steps to complete familiar personal and household routine but has shallow recall of what he/she has been doing.
- Able to monitor accuracy and completeness of each step in routine personal and household ADL and modify plan with minimal assistance.
- Superficial awareness of his/her condition but unaware of specific impairments and disabilities and the limits they place on his/her ability to safely, accurately, and completely carry out his/her household, community, work, and leisure ADL.
- Minimal supervision for safety in routine home and community activities.
- Unrealistic planning for the future.
- Unable to think about consequences of a decision or action.
- Overestimates abilities.
- Unaware of others' needs and feelings.
- Oppositional/uncooperative.
- Unable to recognize inappropriate social interaction behavior.

Level VIII - Purposeful, Appropriate: Stand-By Assistance

- Consistently oriented to person, place, and time.
- Independently attends to and completes familiar tasks for one hour in distracting environments.
- Able to recall and integrate past and recent events.
- Uses assistive memory devices to recall daily schedule, recall "to do" lists, and record critical information for later use with stand-by assistance.
- Initiates and carries out steps to complete familiar personal, household, community, work, and leisure routines with stand-by assistance and can modify the plan when needed with minimal assistance.
- Requires no assistance once new tasks/activities are learned.
- Aware of and acknowledges impairments and disabilities when they interfere with task completion but requires stand-by assistance to take appropriate corrective action.
- Thinks about consequences of a decision or action with minimal assistance.
- Overestimates or underestimates abilities.
- Acknowledges others' needs and feelings and responds appropriately with minimal assistance.
- Depressed.
- Irritable.
- Low frustration tolerance/easily angered.
- Argumentative.
- Self-centered.
- Uncharacteristically dependent/independent.
- Able to recognize and acknowledge inappropriate social interaction behavior while it is occurring and takes corrective action with minimal assistance.

Level IX - Purposeful, Appropriate: Stand-By Assistance on Request

- Independently shifts back and forth between tasks and completes them accurately for at least two consecutive hours.
- Uses assistive memory devices to recall daily schedule, "to do" lists, and record critical information for later use with assistance when requested.
- Initiates and carries out steps to complete familiar personal, household, work, and leisure tasks independently and unfamiliar personal, household, work, and leisure tasks with assistance when requested.
- Aware of and acknowledges impairments and disabilities when they interfere with task completion and takes appropriate corrective action but requires stand-by assist to anticipate a problem before it occurs and take action to avoid it.
- Able to think about consequences of decisions or actions with assistance when requested.
- Accurately estimates abilities but requires stand-by assistance to adjust to task demands.
- Acknowledges others' needs and feelings and responds appropriately with stand-by assistance.
- Depression may continue.
- May be easily irritable.
- May have low frustration tolerance.
- Able to self-monitor appropriateness of social interaction with stand-by assistance.

Level X - Purposeful, Appropriate: Modified Independent

- Able to handle multiple tasks simultaneously in all environments but may require periodic breaks.
- Able to independently procure, create, and maintain own assistive memory devices.
- Independently initiates and carries out steps to complete familiar and unfamiliar personal, household, community, work, and leisure tasks but may require more than usual amount of time and/or compensatory strategies to complete them.
- Anticipates impact of impairments and disabilities on ability to complete daily living tasks and takes action to avoid problems before they occur but may require more than usual amount of time and/or compensatory strategies.
- Able to independently think about consequences of decisions or actions but may require more than usual amount of time and/or compensatory strategies to select the appropriate decision or action.
- Accurately estimates abilities and independently adjusts to task demands.
- Able to recognize the needs and feelings of others and automatically respond in appropriate manner.
- Periodic periods of depression may occur.
- Irritability and low frustration tolerance when sick, fatigued, and/or under emotional stress.
- Social interaction behavior is consistently appropriate.

Reprinted with permission from the author Chris Hagen.

Spinal Cord Injury (SCI)

1. Etiology.
   a. Trauma to the spinal cord as a result of compression, shearing force, contusion secondary to motor vehicle accident, diving accident, penetration wound (gunshot or knife), sports injury, or fall.
   b. Nontraumatic cord injuries may be a result of tumor, progressive degenerative disease.
2. Classification of injury/signs and symptoms.
   a. Degree of impairment and severity of injury is graded using the ASIA Impairment Scale:
      (1) A = complete, no sensory or motor function is preserved in the sacral segments S4–S5.
      (2) B = incomplete, sensory but no motor function is preserved below the neurological level and extends through the sacral segments.
      (3) C = incomplete, motor function is preserved below the neurological level, and the majority of key muscle groups below the neurological level have a muscle grade less than 3/5.
      (4) D = incomplete, motor function is preserved below the neurological level, and the majority of key muscle groups below the level have a muscle grade greater than or equal to 3/5.
      (5) E = normal, sensory, and motor function are normal.
3. Specific symptoms.
   a. Spinal shock (4–8 weeks), all reflex activity is obliterated below the level of the injury presenting as flaccid paralysis.
   b. Sensory deficits may be partial loss or complete.
   c. Loss of bowel/bladder control.
   d. Loss of temperature control below the lesion.
   e. Decreased respiratory function.
   f. Sexual dysfunction.
   g. Changes in muscle tone.
      (1) Spasticity in upper motor neuron lesions.
      (2) Flaccidity in lesions below L1.
   h. Loss of motor function resulting in tetraplegia (quadriplegia) or paraplegia; may be complete or incomplete.
4. Clinical syndromes. See Table 7-1
5. Complications.
   a. Respiratory complications, decreased vital capacity, pneumonia.
   b. Decubitus ulcer formation.
   c. Orthostatic hypotension: an excessive fall in blood pressure upon assuming the upright position.
   d. Deep vein thrombosis (DVT): inflammation of a vein in association with the formation of a thrombus; usually occurs in lower extremities.
      (1) See Chapter 8's section on peripheral vascular disease (PVD) for more information about the presenting symptoms of DVT.

RED FLAG: Deep vein thrombosis can be life threatening as it can turn into a pulmonary embolism; thus, its presenting symptoms require immediate medical attention.

   e. Autonomic dysreflexia[1]: an abnormal response to a noxious stimulus that results in extreme rise in blood pressure, pounding headache, and profuse sweating.
      (1) Irritants that would normally cause pain to areas below the spinal injury specific to the bowel include bowel irritation or overdistention (e.g., constipation/impaction, distention during bowel program [digital stimulation], hemorrhoid infection or irritation).
      (2) Irritants specific to the bladder include bladder infection or over distention (e.g., urinary tract infection [UTI], urinary retention, blocked catheter, overfilled urine collection bag, non-compliance with intermittent catheterization program).
      (3) Skin-related irritants can include any skin irritation below area of injury (e.g., decubitus ulcers, ingrown toenails, burns, tight or restrictive clothing or pressure to skin from clothing restrictions or wrinkles in clothing).
      (4) Sexual activity irritants can include overstimulation during sex, stimuli to the pelvic region that would be felt as pain if sensation were intact, menstrual cramps, labor and delivery.
      (5) Other irritants can include heterotopic ossification/myositis ossificans, skeletal fractures, and appendicitis.

RED FLAG: Autonomic dysreflexia is a medical emergency if not reversed by removing the irritating stimulus quickly.

      (6) Management of autonomic dysreflexia.
         (a) Identify the offending stimulus and relieve the underlying issue immediately.
         (b) Medications if no impact can be made by removing the irritant.
      (7) Prevention of autonomic dysreflexia.
         (a) Teach person/caregiver frequent pressure relief principles.
         (b) Ensure compliance with intermittent catheterization.
         (c) Practice well-balanced diet habits.
         (d) Ensure medication compliance.
         (e) Educate the person with the condition (and/or at risk) and caregivers on how to use prevention methods; recognize the cause, signs, and symptoms (i.e., sweating, headache); and initiate first aid procedures to deal effectively with the occurrence of this condition.

---

[1] Ann Burkhardt contributed to this section on autonomic dysreflexia.

f. Urinary tract infection.
g. Heterotopic ossification, the formation of bone in abnormal anatomical locations.

> **EXAM HINT:** The maintenance of people's health and safety is an OT practice priority and an ethical responsibility; thus, it is likely that the COTA® exam will have items about the potential complications of a SCI.

6. Medical management.
   a. Prevention of further cord damage via stabilization.
   b. Traction and rest for unstable injuries.
   c. Surgery with internal or external fixation.
   d. Diuretic prescription to decrease inflammation.
   e. Bladder care.
   f. Decubiti prevention.
   g. Control of autonomic dysreflexia and orthostatic hypotension.
   h. Prevention of thrombus formation.
   i. Treatment for heterotopic ossification.

Cerebral Palsy (CP)

1. Etiology.
   a. Caused by an injury and/or disease prior to, during, or shortly after birth resulting in brain damage and neurological and muscular deficits.
   b. Common causes during the perinatal period include lack of oxygen, intracranial hemorrhage, meningitis, chronic alcohol abuse, toxicosis, infections, genetic factors, and endocrine and metabolic disorders.
2. Onset, prevalence, and prognosis.
   a. Occurs in 1.5 to 4 per 1,000 live births.
      (1) In the United States, 1 in 323 children are diagnosed with CP.
   b. An increase in the number of infants surviving pre-maturely and an increase in low birth weight have resulted in a higher incidence of the spastic diplegia type of CP.

> **EXAM HINT:** In the NBCOT® practice analysis for the COTA®, 15.7% of COTA®s who provided services to persons with neurological disorders indicated they provided services to individuals with cerebral palsy (NBCOT®, 2018, p. 12). Due to this prevalence, the COTA® exam may have items about working with children, youth, and adults with cerebral palsy.

   c. Prognosis is dependent on the severity of the brain injury and the location.
   d. It is nonprogressive; however, deformities and contractures may develop depending on the level of involvement.
   e. It may be accompanied with seizure, intellectual, and/or behavioral disorders.
   f. The individual can have normal intelligence, which is masked by significant motor deficits.
3. Diagnosis.
   a. Detected usually by 12 months of age.
   b. Sometimes diagnosis may not be identified in early infancy.
      (1) An infant may initially present with hypotonia.
      (2) As the child's neuromotor status evolves spasticity may develop.
      (3) The child may present with primitive reflexes and automatic reactions, hyperresponsive reflexes, clonus, variable tone, asymmetry, involuntary movements, feeding difficulties due to oral motor impairments, cognitive and other developmental delays.
   c. Persistence of primitive reflexes contributes to diagnosis.
      (1) These may extend into adulthood.
   d. The location and severity of the lesion determines the type of cerebral palsy. Types include:
      (1) Spastic cerebral palsy: a lesion of the motor cortex will result in spasticity with flexor and extensor imbalance. Spasticity can express itself as:
         (a) Hypertonia: increased muscle tone.
         (b) Hyperreflexia: increased intensity of reflex responses.
      (2) Dyskinetic cerebral palsy: a lesion in the basal ganglia results in fluctuations in muscle tone. This lesion expresses itself as:
         (a) Dystonia: excessive or inadequate muscle tone.
         (b) Athetosis: writhing involuntary movements that are more distal than proximal.
         (c) Chorea: spasmodic involuntary movements that are more proximal than distal and a lack of cocontractions.
      (3) Ataxic cerebral palsy: a lesion in the cerebellum results in hypotonia and ataxic movements; characterized by a lack of stability so coactivation is difficult, resulting in more primitive total patterns of movement. Classification is according to level of severity.
         (a) Previously classified as mild, moderate, and severe.
         (b) Current gross motor classification: The Gross Motor Functional Classification System (GMFCS) that delineates five levels of functional motor performance for children aged 6 to 12 years. See Table 7-6.
         (c) Current manual ability classification: The Manual Ability Classification System (MACS) for Children with Cerebral Palsy, which describes five levels of handling objects placed within easy reach and everyday functional tasks. See Table 7-6.

Table 7-6

Summary of Functional Motor Performance of Children with Cerebral Palsy

LEVEL	DESCRIPTION OF FUNCTIONAL MOTOR PERFORMANCE
For Each Level of the Gross Motor Functional Classification System	
I	Walks without restrictions; limitations in more advanced gross motor skills.
II	Walks without assistive devices; limitations walking outdoors and in the community.
III	Walks with assistive mobility devices; limitations walking outdoors and in the community.
IV	Self-mobility with limitations; children are transported or use power mobility outdoors and in the community.
V	Self-mobility is severely limited, even with the use of assistive technology.
For Each Level of the Manual Ability Classification System for Children With Cerebral Palsy	
I	Handles objects easily and successfully.
II	Handles most objects but with somewhat reduced quality and/or speed of achievement.
III	Handles objects with difficulty; needs help to prepare and/or modify activities.
IV	Handles a limited selection of easily managed objects in adapted situations.
V	Does not handle objects and has severely limited ability to perform even simple actions.

Missiuna, C., Polatajko, H., Pollock, N., & Cameron, D. (2012). Neuromotor disorders. In S. J. Lane and A. C. Bundy (Eds.). *Kids can be kids: A childhood occupation.* Philadelphia: FA Davis.

---

e. The distribution of the disorder in limbs determines the classification.
   (1) Monoplegia involves one extremity.
   (2) Hemiplegia involves the upper and lower extremity on the same side.
   (3) Paraplegia involves the lower extremities.
   (4) Quadriplegia involves all extremities.
   (5) Diplegia involves less upper extremity involvement and greater lower extremity functional impairment.
4. Complications.
   a. Seizures occur in 50% of children with cerebral palsy.
   b. Language and intellectual deficits occur in 50%–75% of children with cerebral palsy. These include:
      (1) Speech and language deficits.
      (2) Difficulty coordinating breathing with swallowing which is a necessary function for speech.
      (3) Dysarthria
      (4) Aphasia
      (5) Cognitive deficits are more typical associated with the presence of seizures.
   c. Visual impairments occur in 40%-50% of children with cerebral palsy.
      (1) Strabismus: deviation of how one eye aligns with the other.
      (2) Nystagmus: a reflexive response of the eyes triggered by head movement.
      (3) Refractive errors:
         (a) Myopia (nearsightedness).
         (b) Hyperopia (farsightedness).
         (c) Presbyopia: difficulty in accommodation when focusing on objects nearby and when shifting focus from near to far.
   d. Feeding disturbances (e.g., difficulty swallowing, chewing).
   e. Diminished sensation is common in spastic hemiplegia.
5. Medical management.
   a. Antispasticity drugs (e.g., benzodiazepines).
   b. Medication to reduce tremors and relax muscles (e.g., baclofen pumps).
   c. Medication to relax muscles to decrease muscle stiffness and increase controlled movement (e.g., botulinum toxin [Botox]).
   d. Orthopedic management to address development of scoliosis and joint contractures.
   e. Surgery may be indicated to decrease contractures and improving functional movement (e.g., dorsal rhizotomy surgery).
   f. Medications for seizures if present.
   g. Dietary interventions and special feeding techniques for regularity in elimination and/or other medical complications.
6. Occupational therapy evaluation and intervention.
   a. See Chapter 5: Human Development Across the Life Span.
   b. See Chapter 12: Neurological Approaches: Evaluation and Intervention.
   c. See Chapter 14: Evaluation and Intervention for Performance in Areas of Occupation.

> **EXAM HINT:** The NBCOT® exam outline for the COTA® identifies knowledge of the "expected patterns, progressions, and prognoses associated with conditions that limit occupational performance" (NBCOT®, 2018, p. 21) as essential for competent and safe practice. The application of knowledge about the neurological system disorders described in previous chapter sections and the disorders of movement and neuromuscular diseases described in the following chapter section will be required to correctly answer exam items about working with people with these disorders and diseases.

Disorders of Movement/Neuromuscular Diseases

Classification of Symptoms

1. Ataxia: describes a lack of coordination while performing voluntary movements. It may appear as clumsiness, inaccuracy, or instability. Movements are not smooth and may appear disjointed or jerky.
2. Chorea: brief, purposeless, involuntary movements of the distal extremities and face. Usually considered to be a manifestation of dopaminergic overactivity in the basal ganglia.
3. Dyskinesias: involuntary, nonrepetitive, but occasionally stereotyped movements affecting distal, proximal, and axial musculature in varying combinations. Most dyskinesias are representative of basal ganglia disorders.
4. Dystonia: results in sustained abnormal postures and disruptions of ongoing movement resulting from alterations of muscle tone. Dystonias may be generalized or focal.
5. Hemiballismus: usually characterized by involuntary flinging motions of the extremities. The movements are often violent and have wide amplitudes of motion. They are continuous and random and can involve proximal and/or distal muscles on one side of the body.
6. Myoclonus: a brief and rapid contraction of a muscle or group of muscles.
7. Tics: brief, rapid, involuntary movements, often resembling fragments of normal motor behavior. They tend to be stereotyped and repetitive, but not rhythmic.
8. Tremor: rhythmic, alternating, oscillatory movements produced by repetitive patterns of muscle contraction and relaxation. They are classified by rate, rhythm, distribution. Tremors are identified as to whether they occur at rest (resting tremor) or during activity (action or intention tremor).

> **EXAM HINT:** Understanding how neuromuscular symptoms affect functional abilities can help you correctly answer COTA® exam items about the best approach to use to enable occupational performance. For example, the functional effects of intention tremors can be minimized by teaching the person to use the environment for proximal stability.

Parkinson's Disease

1. Etiology: a hypokinetic CNS movement disorder that is idiopathic, slowly progressive, and degenerative.
2. Prevalence, onset, and prognosis.
   a. Onset of the disease is usually after age 40, with increasing incidence in older age groups.
   b. Occurs in 1% of the population over 50.
   c. Rate of deterioration ranges from 2 to 20 years.

> **EXAM HINT:** In the NBCOT® practice analysis for the COTA®, 28.6% of COTA®s who provided services to persons with neurological disorders indicated they provided services to individuals with Parkinson's disease (NBCOT®, 2018, p. 12). Due to this prevalence, it is likely that the exam will have items about working with persons with Parkinson's disease.

3. Symptoms.
   a. Begins insidiously with a resting 'pill-rolling' tremor of one hand.
   b. Cardinal signs include tremor, rigidity, resistance to passive motion that is not velocity dependent (cogwheel or lead pipe), akinesia, postural instability, festinating gait, falling backward (retropulsion) or forward (propulsion), mask face, micrographia.
4. Diagnostic testing.
   a. Presence of cardinal signs.
   b. Degeneration in dopaminergic pathways in the basal ganglia, primarily in the substantia nigra.
   c. Positive response to Sinemet (levodopa-carbidopa).
   d. Stage of disease progression is diagnosed using Hoehn and Yahr's five-stage scale.
      (1) Stage I = unilateral tremor, rigidity, akinesia, minimal or no functional impairment.
      (2) Stage II = bilateral tremor, rigidity or akinesia, with or without axial signs, independent with activities of daily living (ADL), no balance impairment.
      (3) Stage III = worsening of symptoms, first signs of impaired righting reflexes, onset of disability in ADL performance, can lead independent life.
      (4) Stage IV = requires help with some or all ADL, unable to live alone without some assistance, able to walk and stand unaided.
      (5) Stage V = confined to a wheelchair or bed, maximally assisted.
5. Medical management.
   a. Surgical interventions: thalamotomy, pallidotomy, fetal tissue transplant, deep brain stimulators.
   b. Pharmacology: Levodopa (the metabolic precursor of dopamine), Sinemet (levodopa-carbidopa), dopamine agonists, anticholinergics (Benadryl, Artane, Cogentin) for rigidity and tremors, dopamine releasers (amantadine).

c. Side effects are common when the disease is being managed pharmacologically.
   (1) During early treatment, side effects from carbidopa/levodopa therapy are usually not a major problem.
   (2) As the disease progresses, the drug works less evenly and predictably.
      (a) As a result, some people may experience involuntary movements (dyskinesia), primarily when the medication is having its peak effects.
      (b) The length of time for which each dose is effective may begin to shorten (wearing-off effect), leading to more frequent doses.

CAUTION: The on-off effect of long-term carbidopa/levodopa usage may cause Parkinson's-related movement problems to appear and disappear suddenly and unpredictably.

   (3) Other side effects may include:
      (a) Hallucinations.
      (b) A drop in blood pressure when standing (orthostatic hypotension).
      (c) Nausea.
d. Despite the above potential side effects, carbidopa/levodopa typically allows people with Parkinson's disease to extend the time that they are able to lead relatively normal lives and in many cases is effective for a number of years.

Spina Bifida

1. Etiology is unknown.
   a. Genetic, intrauterine, and/or environmental factors contribute to the failure of the spinal column's vertebral arches to fully form to enclose and to protect the neural tube. This defect may result in a protrusion of the neural tube.
   b. Some studies suggest certain medications and a lack of folic acid may induce neural tube defects.
2. Onset, prevalence, and prognosis.
   a. Occurs in about 1 in every 1,000 births.
      (1) The most common neural tube disorder, affecting approximately 166,000 individuals in the United States.
      (2) Incidence has decreased with folic acid being prescribed to women before and during pregnancy.
         (a) Selective abortion has also decreased incidence.
      (3) The first-year survival rate for infants has increased to over 92%.
      (4) The survival rate of infants with encephalocele is over 75%.
   b. The prognosis and degree of impairment is dependent on the level of the lesion and the extent of the neural tube defect of the vertebral arches and the spinal column.
      (1) Lesions usually occur in the thoracic or lumbar spine.
3. Diagnosis.
   a. Detected prenatally through amniocentesis for levels of alpha-fetoprotein (AFP) and acetylcholinesterase, and ultrasound if indicated.
   b. A less reliable means of prenatal detection involves determining the amount of AFP the unborn baby produces in the mother's blood.
4. Classification of spina bifida is dependent on the level of the lesion and the extent of tissue involved.
   a. Spina bifida occulta: a bony malformation with separation of vertebral arches of one or more vertebrae with no external manifestations; may not be discovered until late childhood.
      (1) Occult spinal dysraphism (OSD): when external manifestations such as a red birthmark (hemangioma or flame nervus), patch of hair, a dermal sinus (opening in skin), a fatty benign tumor (lipoma), or dimple covering the site are present.
   b. Spina bifida cystica: an exposed pouch.
      (1) Spina bifida with meningocele: protrusion of a sac through the spine, containing cerebral spinal fluid and meninges; however, does not include the spinal cord.
      (2) Spina bifida with myelomeningocele: protrusion of a sac through the spine, containing cerebral spinal fluid and meninges as well as the spinal cord or nerve roots.
         (a) Most commonly located in the lumbar region; however, it can occur at any point along the spinal column.
5. Specific symptoms.
   a. Spina bifida occulta usually does not result in any symptoms.
      (1) Occasionally slight instability and neuromuscular impairments, such as mild gait involvement and bowel or bladder problems may occur.
   b. Occult spinal dysraphism may result in the spinal cord being split (diplomyelia) or being tied down and tethered (diastematomyelia), which may lead to neurological damage and developmental abnormality as the child grows.
   c. Spina bifida meningocele usually does not present with symptoms impacting on function as the spinal cord itself is not entrapped.
      (1) Occasionally slight instability and neuromuscular impairments, such as mild gait involvement and bowel or bladder problems may occur.
   d. Spina bifida with a myelomeningocele results in sensory and motor deficits occurring below the

level of the lesion and may result in lower extremity paralysis and/or deformities, bowel and bladder incontinence, decubitus ulcer, and DVT.
   (1) The level of lesions impact leg movements.
   (2) Lesions of S2–S4 results in bladder and bowel problems.
      (a) A neurogenic bladder impacts on the sensation to urinate and the control of the urinary sphincter.
      (b) Incomplete emptying of the bladder results; this often leads to infections.
      (c) A neurogenic bowel causes constipation and incontinence.
6. Tethered cord syndrome occurs in the tail end of the spinal cord when the cord is stretched as a result of compression, being trapped with a fatty mass or scar tissue, developmental abnormality, or injury.
   a. Visible signs include a hairy patch of skin, a hemangioma, and/or a dimple of the lower spine.
   b. Difficulties with bowel and bladder control, gait disturbances, and/or deformities of the feet, low back pain, and scoliosis may result.
   c. May go undiagnosed until the above symptoms emerge.
   d. Symptoms may be exacerbated with pregnancy or with age due to spinal stenosis.
   e. In children and adolescents, symptoms may be exacerbated by growth spurts. During growth spurts, it is also possible for the spine to re-tether even after surgery has occurred, which may warrant additional surgery to correct.
7. Medical management.
   a. During the neonatal period, precautions are taken to protect the sac from rupturing and from infection, which may result in meningitis.
      (1) All or part of the sac may be removed 24 to 48 hours after birth.
   b. A ventriculoperitoneal or other type of shunt is indicated should the complication of hydrocephalus occur, in which the cerebral spinal fluid is not absorbed, resulting in an increase in size of the ventricles and the infant's head.
      (1) Brain damage as a result of increased intracranial pressure can cause an intellectual disability.
      (2) Increased pressure may also result in Arnold-Chiari syndrome in which a portion of the cerebellum and medulla oblongata slip down through the foramen magnum to the cervical spinal cord.
      (3) Shunts can become blocked, resulting in increased intracranial pressure.
         (a) Signs and symptoms during the first year of life include extreme head growth and often a soft spot on the forehead.
         (b) Signs and symptoms by the second year of life include severe headache, vomiting, and/or irritability.
         (c) Signs and symptoms in adolescents include increasing head size, change in the function of upper extremities, regression in milestones or decline in academic performance, neck pain, severe headache, and/or loss of balance.
         (d) Signs and symptoms in adults can include vomiting, severe headache, vision or memory problems, irritability, personality change, loss of coordination, numbness in the upper extremities, head and neck pain, and/or difficulty swallowing.
         (e) Intracranial pressure may contribute to seizure disorders and deterioration of physical and/or cognitive functioning.
         (f) Intracranial pressure may contribute to seizure disorders and deterioration of physical and/or cognitive functioning.
         (g) Blocked shunts are revised by removing the blocked section and replacing it with a catheter.
      (4) Shunts can become infected.
         (a) Signs and symptoms include vomiting, lethargy, and/or fever.
         (b) Seizures and deterioration of physical and/or cognitive functioning may result.
         (c) Infections are treated by withdrawing fluid through or replacing the tubing. Intravenous antibiotics are also administered.
         (d) Medications to reduce cerebrospinal fluid production and intracranial pressure are sometimes used as an interim measure.

RED FLAG: Early identification of blocked and infected shunts is vital, as these conditions are life threatening. Immediate notification of signs and symptoms to the child's/facility's neurosurgeon is required.

   c. Urological management, and if indicated intermittent catheterization.
   d. Orthopedic management for motor deficits.
   e. Surgical intervention may be indicated for tethered cord syndrome.

Muscular Dystrophies/Atrophies

1. Etiology: a group of degenerative disorders resulting in muscle weakness and decreased muscle mass due to a hereditary disease process.
   a. Muscular dystrophies are due to an absent muscle protein product, dystrophin.
      (1) The responsible genes and biochemical abnormalities can be tested through a muscle biopsy to determine the level or absence of dystrophin.
2. Onset, prevalence, and prognosis.
   a. Muscular dystrophies/atrophies can begin in infancy, childhood, or adulthood.

b. First symptoms may not be apparent until 2.5 years of age.
c. Average age of diagnosis is five years, unless there is a known family history; whereby, earlier detection is more likely to occur.
d. The estimated prevalence for Duchenne's and Becker's muscular dystrophies is 1 per 7,250 males aged 5–24 years. Across all types of muscular dystrophies, it is estimated that 250,000 individuals are affected in the United States.
   (1) Prenatal testing and selective abortion accounts for a decrease in the number of children born with muscular dystrophies.
e. Progress may be rapid and fatal or may remain stable throughout life.
   (1) Those starting early in life tend to be more severe and to progress more rapidly.
3. Diagnosis.
   a. Detection is confirmed by blood tests for muscle enzymes or muscle proteins, nerve conduction velocity, electromyography, and, if indicated, muscle or nerve biopsy.
   b. In muscular dystrophies blood tests demonstrate a high elevated level of creatine kinase (CK).
   c. Common symptoms include hypotonia, muscle weakness, and atrophy.
4. Major types.
   a. Duchenne's muscular dystrophy is the most common form of muscular dystrophy.
      (1) It is detected between three and five years of age.
      (2) It is inherited, sex-linked, and recessive; occurring in 1 per 3,500 male births.
      (3) Symptoms include pseudohypertrophy which is enlargement of calf muscles, and at times enlargement of the forearm and thigh muscles, giving an appearance the child is muscular and healthy.
      (4) Weakness of the proximal joints progresses to the point that the child has significant functional mobility impairments. These include:
         (a) Ambulating with a Trendelenburg (i.e., waddling) gait with frequent falls.
         (b) Difficulty getting up from the floor to a standing position; uses hands to crawl up the thighs to get to the standing position, known as Gower's sign.
      (5) Weakness occurs in all voluntary muscles, including the heart and diaphragm.
      (6) Behavioral and learning difficulties and delayed speech may occur.
      (7) Individuals rarely survive beyond their early 20s due to respiratory problems, infections, and/or cardiovascular complications; however, advancements in supportive care enable some individuals to live longer.
   b. Becker's muscular dystrophy.
      (1) A variant of Duchenne's muscular dystrophy that is slower to progress, less severe, and less predictable.
      (2) Presenting symptoms include:
         (a) Loss of motor function of the hips, thighs, pelvic area, and shoulders.
         (b) Enlarged calves.
         (c) Cardiac system can be involved.
      (3) Survival can be until late adulthood.
         (a) A normal life span can be attained if there is minimal cardiac involvement.
   c. Arthrogryposis multiplex congenita.
      (1) It is detected at birth and associated with loss of anterior horn cells.
      (2) Presence of weakness, deformities, and associated joint contractures.
      (3) Position of rest for the upper extremities tends to be internal rotation of the shoulders, extension of the elbows, and flexion of the wrists; for the lower extremities, there is flexion and internal rotation of the hips and clubfeet.
      (4) It may be stable, mildly progressive, or may improve.
      (5) Related problems include congenital heart defects, spinal defects, torticollis, and involvement of the diaphragm.
   d. Limb-girdle muscular dystrophy.
      (1) Onset begins between the first and third decades of life.
      (2) Proximal muscles of the pelvis and shoulder are initially affected.
      (3) Typically progresses slowly.
   e. Facioscapulohumeral muscular dystrophy.
      (1) Occurs in early adolescence.
      (2) Involves the face, upper arms, and scapular region, causing masking and decreased mobility of the face and the inability to lift the arms above shoulder level.
      (3) As it progresses, the weakness can extend to the abdominal muscles and sometimes the hip muscles.
      (4) Progresses slowly and rarely affects the cardiac or respiratory systems; thus, life expectancy can be relatively normal.
   f. Spinal muscular atrophy.
      (1) Caused by a decrease of a motor neuron protein called Survival of Motor Neuron (SMN), Chromosome 5.
      (2) Weakness of the voluntary muscles of the shoulders, hips, thighs, and upper back which can result in spinal curvatures.
      (3) Muscles for breathing and swallowing can be affected.

(4) The earlier the age of diagnosis, the greater the severity of functional deficits and the shorter the life expectancy.
  (a) Type I, birth or infancy: the infantile form known as Werdnig-Hoffman disease has a life expectancy up to approximately two years of age.
  (b) Type II, children: the intermediate form is detected six months to three years of age and progresses rapidly with a life expectancy of early childhood.
  (c) Type III, older children: later onset, less severe form.
  (d) Types IV, adolescent or adult: later onset, less severe form.
g. Congenital myasthenia gravis.
  (1) A disorder involving transmission of impulses in the neuromuscular junction.
  (2) Onset starting near birth and occurring more frequently in males.
h. Charcot-Marie-Tooth disease.
  (1) A disease involving the peripheral nerves marked by progressive weakness, primarily in peroneal (fibular) and distal leg muscles.
  (2) Typically occurs in the teenage years or earlier.
i. Myopathies.
  (1) Symptoms are similar to dystrophies; however, myopathies progress slowly, resulting in a better prognosis.
  (2) Weakness of the face, neck, and limbs is characteristic.
5. Specific symptoms.
  a. Low muscle tone and weakness contributes to abnormal movement patterns and delayed developmental milestones.
  b. There may be difficulty with oral motor feeding, necessitating a nasogastric or gastrostomy tube.
  c. Weakness contributes to deformities of the extremities and spine.
  d. Difficulty with breathing may require tracheostomies or mechanical ventilators, and frequently results in death.
6. Medical management.
  a. Prescribed medications to decrease pulmonary complications, prolong life.
  b. Nutritional management for difficulties with feeding and the tendency to gain weight secondary to inactivity.
  c. Prevention of skin breakdown and decubitus ulcers.
  d. Steroids to help delay or reverse muscle weakness; however, the undesirable side effects associated with steroids bring their use into question.

Progressive Supranuclear Palsy

1. Etiology: manifested by loss of voluntary, but preservation of reflexive, eye movements, bradykinesia, rigidity, axial dystonia, pseudobulbar palsy, and dementia.
2. Onset, prevalence, and prognosis.
  a. Occurs in later middle life, with onset typically occurring between 45 and 75 years of age.
  b. Affects approximately 20,000 people in the United States; however, it is underdiagnosed. This disorder is estimated to affect as many as 5 per 100,000 people.
  c. Death occurs approximately 15 years after onset.

Huntington's Chorea

1. Etiology: an autosomal dominant disorder.
2. Onset, prevalence, and prognosis.
  a. Begins in middle age.
  b. Onset of this disease process is insidious.
  c. Occurs in 1 in 10,000.
  d. Characterized by choreiform movements and progressive intellectual deterioration.
  e. Psychiatric disturbance (personality change, manic-depressive symptoms, and schizophreniform illness) may precede the onset of the movement disorder.
  f. Signs and symptoms are progressive until the end of life.

Cerebellar/Spinocerebellar Disorders

1. Etiology: characterized by ataxia, dysmetria, dysdiadochokinesia, hypotonia, movement decomposition, tremor, dysarthria, and nystagmus.

Structural Cerebellar Lesions

1. Etiology: includes vascular lesions (stroke) and tumor deposits, producing symptoms and signs appropriate to their locus within the cerebellum.
  a. Demyelinating plaques of multiple sclerosis may also arise in the cerebellum white matter and give rise to cerebellar symptoms.
  b. Alcoholism and nutritional deprivation can cause degeneration of the vermis and anterior cerebellum.

Spinocerebellar Degenerations

1. Etiology: a group of degenerative disorders, characterized by progressive ataxia due to the degeneration of the cerebellum, brain stem, spinal cord, peripheral nerves, and the basal ganglia.
2. These disorders are grouped as spinal ataxias, cerebellar ataxias, and multiple system degeneration.
   a. Friedreich's ataxia.
      (1) Etiology: autosomal recessive inheritance.
      (2) Onset occurs in childhood or early adolescence.
      (3) Symptoms: the prototype of spinal ataxia.
         (a) This process is characterized by gait unsteadiness, upper extremity ataxia, and dysarthria.
         (b) Tremor may be a minor feature.
         (c) Presentation also includes areflexia and loss of large fiber sensory modalities.
         (d) As the disease progresses, scoliosis and cardiomyopathy are common.
   b. Cerebellar cortical degeneration.
      (1) Etiology: pathologic changes are seen in the cerebellum and the inferior olives.
      (2) Onset begins between ages 30 and 50.
      (3) Symptoms: cerebellar symptoms are the only signs detectable.
   c. Multiple systems degeneration (olivopontocerebellar atrophies).
      (1) Etiology: characterized by spasticity, extrapyramidal, sensory, lower motor neuron, and autonomic dysfunction.
      (2) Onset occurs in young to middle life.
3. Medical management for movement disorders is limited in many cases.
   a. Pharmacologic intervention may be able to dampen effects of the movement disorders.
   b. Agents utilized for this population include propranolol, clonazepam, clonidine, and anticholinergic agents, depending upon symptomatology.

Disorders of the Peripheral Nervous System/Neuromuscular Diseases

Amyotrophic Lateral Sclerosis (ALS)

1. Etiology: motor neuron disease of unknown etiology characterized by progressive degeneration of corticospinal tracts and anterior horn cells or bulbar efferent neurons.
2. Onset, prevalence, and prognosis.
   a. The disease is more prevalent in men than women at a ratio of 1.2:1. The prevalence of ALS in the United States is estimated to be 3.9 cases per 100,000 persons in the general population.
   b. Onset occurs at an average age of 57.
   c. Death usually occurs in two to five years.
3. Symptoms.
   a. Muscle weakness and atrophy, evidence of anterior horn cell destruction, often begins distally and asymmetrically.
   b. Cramps and fasciculations precede weakness.
   c. Signs usually begin in the hands.
   d. LMN signs are soon accompanied by spasticity, hyperactive deep tendon reflexes, and evidence of corticospinal tract involvement.
   e. Dysarthria and dysphagia are evident.
   f. Sensory systems, eye movements, and urinary sphincters are often spared.
   g. Symptom severity is documented by scores on the ALS Functional Rating Scale.
      (1) Symptoms that are quantified include speech, salivation, swallowing, handwriting, cutting food, dressing/hygiene, turning in bed, walking, climbing stairs, dyspnea, orthopnea, respiratory insufficiency, and number of years with symptoms.
4. Diagnosis.
   a. Usually clinical, with generalized motor involvement unaccompanied by sensory abnormalities.
   b. Electromyography can support the diagnosis.
   c. Other processes such as spinal cord tumors and myopathies must be ruled out.
5. Medical management.
   a. There is no specific treatment to slow the disease process.
   b. Treatment is aimed at treating secondary complications such as spasticity (treated with antispasmodics), prevention of aspirations (gastrostomy and modified diets), prevention of decubiti, prevention of contracture, and pain management.

Brachial Plexus Disorder

1. Etiology: secondary to traction during birth, invasion of metastatic cancer, after radiation treatment secondary to fibrosis, or traction injury.
2. Symptoms.
   a. Mixed motor and sensory disorders of the corresponding limb.

b. Rostral injuries produce shoulder dysfunction while caudal injuries produce dysfunction in the hand.
3. Diagnosis.
   a. Made via CT scanning of the plexus in cases where a mass is present.
   b. EMG/nerve conduction velocities are used to localize the plexus lesion.
4. Common injuries of the brachial plexus seen in children include:
   a. Erb's palsy: a paralysis of the upper brachial plexus including the fifth and sixth cervical nerves; C7 may also be involved in some cases.
      (1) Muscles most often paralyzed include the supraspinatus and infraspinatus as well as the deltoid, biceps, brachialis, and subscapularis.
      (2) The arm cannot be raised; elbow flexion is weakened and weakness in retraction and protraction of scapula may be noted.
      (3) The arm grossly presents with the arm straight and wrist fully bent (the "waiter's tip" position).
      (4) After the age of six months, contractures may begin to develop (adduction and internal rotation contractures).
         (a) Supination deformity of the forearm may also develop from the imbalance between the supinator and the paralyzed pronator muscles.
      (5) Positioning and ROM exercises are necessary to retain external rotation, abduction, and flexion at the shoulder as well as distal flexibility.
   b. Klumpke's palsy: a paralysis of the lower brachial plexus including the seventh and eighth cervical and first thoracic nerves.
      (1) Relatively rare when compared to the prevalence of Erb's palsy.
      (2) It results in paralysis of the hand and wrist, often with ipsilateral Horner's syndrome (miosis, ptosis, and facial anhidrosis).
      (3) Characteristic signs are that the hand is limp and the fingers do not move.

Peripheral Neuropathies

1. Etiology: peripheral neuropathy of a single nerve may be the result of trauma, pressure paralysis, forcible overextension of a joint, hemorrhage into a nerve, exposure to cold or radiation, or ischemic paralysis.
   a. Multiple nerves may be affected in cases of collagen vascular disease, metabolic diseases (diabetes mellitus), or infectious agents (Lyme disease).
   b. Other causes include nutritional deficiency, malignancy, microorganisms, exposure to toxic agents, and chronic alcohol abuse.

2. Diagnosis.
   a. Focused on the cause of the symptoms.
   b. Specific tests utilized include electromyography, nerve conduction velocity, muscle biopsy, and examinations to identify systemic disorders.
3. Symptoms.
   a. A syndrome of sensory, motor, reflex, and vasomotor symptoms.
   b. Symptoms include pain, weakness, and paresthesias in the distribution of the affected nerve.
4. Medical management.
   a. Guided by the underlying disease process, not the symptoms of the neuropathy.
   b. Treatment of the underlying systemic disorder (diabetes, tumor, multiple myeloma), may slow progression, although recovery is slow.

Guillain-Barré Syndrome

1. Etiology is unknown. May occur after an infectious disorder, surgery, or an immunization.
2. Onset prevalence and prognosis.
   a. The prevalence of Guillain-Barré syndrome is estimated to be 6–40 cases per one million people. It affects both sexes at any age.
   b. Onset of recovery is two to four weeks after first symptoms.
   c. Long-term prognosis.
      (1) 50% exhibit mild neurological deficits.
      (2) 15% exhibit residual functional deficits.
      (3) 80% are ambulatory in six months.
      (4) 5% die of complications.
3. Diagnosis.
   a. Diagnosis is based on clinical symptoms.
   b. Lumbar puncture reveals increased protein without cells in the cerebrospinal fluid.
   c. Electromyography and nerve conduction studies may support the diagnosis.
   d. Segmental demyelination is apparent, and in severe cases, axonal degeneration accompanies the demyelination.
4. Symptoms.
   a. Acute, rapidly progressive form of polyneuropathy characterized by symmetric muscular weakness and mild distal sensory loss/paresthesias.
   b. Weakness is always more apparent than sensory findings and is at first more prominent distally.
   c. Relatively minor sensory signs and symptoms occur.
      (1) The patient may complain of painful extremities.
      (2) Subjective and objective sensory disturbances are common initially.
         (a) Most commonly occurring in a distal (stocking-glove) distribution.
   d. Deep tendon reflexes are lost and sphincters are spared.

e. Respiratory failure and dysphagia may be seen in some cases.
5. Medical management.
   a. Severe cases constitute a medical emergency requiring constant monitoring of vital signs.
   b. Respiratory support may be necessary in some cases.
   c. Plasmapheresis may be utilized to slow symptoms or halt progression.
   d. Intravenous immunoglobulin has been utilized effectively.

Myasthenia Gravis

1. Etiology: the disease is caused by an autoimmune attack on the acetylcholine receptor of the postsynaptic neuromuscular junction.
   a. This process is considered a disorder of neuromuscular transmission.
   b. The initiating event leading to antibody production is unknown.
2. Onset, prevalence, and prognosis.
   a. Occurs at any age but most often affects younger women and older men.
   b. Occurs in 14 per 100,000.
   c. Prognosis varies, but usually is a progressive disabling process.
   d. Death may occur from respiratory complications.
3. Diagnosis.
   a. Diagnosis is often missed because of the rarity of the disease and the vagueness of symptoms.
   b. Characterized by episodic muscle weakness, chiefly in muscles innervated by cranial nerves.
   c. The possibility of myasthenia gravis is suggested by any of the below symptoms and is confirmed by response to anticholinesterase drugs.
4. Symptoms.
   a. Common symptoms include ptosis, diplopia, muscle fatigue after exercise, dysarthria, dysphagia, and proximal limb weakness.
   b. Sensation and deep tendon reflexes are intact.
   c. Symptoms fluctuate over the course of the day.
   d. In relapsing periods, quadriparesis may develop.
   e. Life-threatening respiratory muscle involvement may occur.
5. Medical management.
   a. Treatment includes cholinesterase inhibitors, corticosteroids, immunosuppressive agents, and plasmapheresis.
   b. The anticholinergics and plasmapheresis treat current symptoms.
   c. Corticosteroids and immunosuppressives may alter the disease course by interfering with autoimmune pathogenesis.

Post-Polio Syndrome (PPS)

1. Etiology: some motor neurons infected with the polio virus die (leaving paralyzed muscle cells), others survive. Recovered motor neurons develop new terminal axon sprouts that reinnervate muscle cells. After years of stability, these motor units break down, causing new muscle weakness.
   a. Degeneration of the axon sprouts explains the new weakness and fatigue, but the mechanism remains controversial.
   b. A current explanation is related to the overuse of individual motor neurons over time.
2. Onset, prevalence, and prognosis.
   a. 250,000 people live with post-polio syndrome.
   b. Onset is typically 15 years after recovery from polio.
   c. Progress is slow, with a good prognosis unless breathing or swallowing difficulties occur.
3. Diagnosis.
   a. Based on clinical symptoms.
   b. Characterized by the onset of new muscle weakness after years of stable functioning.
   c. Disuse weakness should be ruled out.
4. Symptoms.
   a. New onset of weakness.
   b. Easily fatigued.
   c. Muscle pain.
   d. Joint pain.
   e. Cold intolerance.
   f. Atrophy.
   g. Loss of functional skills.
5. Medical management.
   a. Bracing with orthoses and pacing daily activity.
   b. Stretching programs.
   c. Exercise program.
   d. Low doses of tricyclic antidepressants to relieve muscle pain.
   e. Pyridostigmine to reduce fatigue and improve strength.

EXAM HINT: The NBCOT® exam outline for the COTA® identifies knowledge of the "expected patterns, progressions, and prognoses associated with conditions that limit occupational performance" (NBCOT®, 2018, p. 21) as essential for competent and safe practice. The application of knowledge about multiple sclerosis as described in the following chapter section and the disorders of the peripheral nervous system and neuromuscular diseases described in the preceding chapter section will be required to correctly answer COTA® exam items about working with people with these disorders and diseases.

Demyelinating Disease

Multiple Sclerosis (MS)

1. Etiology: the exact cause is unknown.
   a. The myelin damage is probably mediated by the immune system.
   b. Postulated etiologies include infection by a slow or latent virus and the possibility of environmental factors contributing to the disease.
2. Onset, prevalence, and prognosis.
   a. More prevalent in areas further north of the equator.
   b. Approximately 400,000 people are living with MS in the United States.
   c. Occurs most often between the ages of 20 and 50; it is most often diagnosed when persons are in their 30s.
   d. Overall prognosis is variable with an unpredictable disease course.
3. Diagnosis.
   a. Diagnosis is largely based on symptoms.
   b. Slowly progressive CNS disease characterized by patches of demyelination in the brain and spinal cord.
   c. Basic diagnostic criteria are evidence of multiple CNS lesions and evidence of at least two episodes of neurological disturbance in an individual between 10 and 59 years.
   d. Diagnostics may include MRI to detect lesions, evoked potentials to measure conduction along sensory pathways, and cerebrospinal fluid examination.
4. Symptoms.
   a. Multiple and varied neurologic symptoms and signs, usually with remissions and exacerbations.
   b. Onset of symptoms is usually insidious.
   c. Paresthesias in one or more extremities, on the trunk, or in the face.
   d. Weakness or clumsiness in the leg or hand is common.
   e. Visual disturbance (diplopia, partial blindness, nystagmus, eye pain, etc.).
   f. Emotional disturbances (lability, euphoria, and reactive depression).
   g. Balance loss and/or vertigo.
   h. Bladder dysfunction.
   i. Cognitive features may include apathy, memory loss, lack of judgment, and inattention.
   j. Sensorimotor findings may include: spasticity, increased reflexes, ataxia, weakness, gait instability, easy fatigue, hemiplegia or quadriplegia.
   k. The course of the symptoms is highly variable and may follow one of four patterns.
      (1) Relapsing remitting.
      (2) Secondary progressive.
      (3) Primary progressive.
      (4) Progressive relapsing.
5. Medical management is symptom specific.
   a. During acute exacerbation, anti-inflammatory drugs are used to control symptoms.
   b. Antispasmodics (baclofen) may be effective to counteract spasticity.
   c. Management of bowel and bladder dysfunction may require pharmacologic intervention.
      (1) Catheterization (indwelling or intermittent) is necessary in many cases of bladder dysfunction.
   d. Disease-modifying drugs are used to slow progression.

Occupational Therapy Evaluation and Intervention for Neurological System Disorders

Role of the Occupational Therapy Assistant (OTA) in Evaluation

1. The OTA contributes to the evaluation process.
   a. The OTA can assist with the collection of data for the evaluation once service competency has been established.
   b. The level of supervision required will be determined by the OTA's established service competency.
   c. The OTA cannot independently evaluate or interpret evaluation results.

EXAM HINT: In the NBCOT® exam outline for the COTA®, "Domain 01 Collaborating and Gathering Information comprises 28% of the exam. This domain focuses on the OTA's ability to "assist the OTR to acquire information regarding factors that influence occupational performance on an ongoing basis throughout the occupational therapy process" (NBCOT®, 2018, p. 18). The application of knowledge about the role of the OTA in evaluation described here and the following evaluation foci can help you effectively determine the correct answers to NBCOT® Domain 01 exam items about working with persons with neurological system disorders.

d. The occupational profile is the initial step in the evaluation process that provides an understanding of the client's occupational history and experiences, patterns of daily living, interests, values, and needs.
e. The client's problems and concerns about performing occupations and daily life activities are identified, and the client's priorities are determined.

Analysis of Performance in Areas of Occupation

1. Basic activities of daily living (BADL).
2. Instrumental activities of daily living (IADL).
3. Education.
4. Work.
5. Play and leisure.
6. Rest and sleep.
7. Social participation.
8. See Chapter 15 for more information on the evaluation of occupational performance.

Client Factors and Performance Skills Evaluation

1. Determine sensory and motor dysfunction and strengths.
   a. Extent of paralysis/weakness.
   b. Severity and distribution of spasticity.
   c. Gross and fine motor coordination loss.
   d. Evaluation of sensory modalities: light touch, pain, pressure, proprioception, kinesthesia, temperature, gustatory, olfactory, auditory.
   e. Postural control evaluation.
   f. Range of motion testing.
   g. Manual muscle testing.
   h. Skin integrity.
2. Cognitive/perceptual dysfunction.
   a. Evaluation of foundational visual skills: acuity, visual fields, ocular range of motion, accommodation, pursuits, saccades.
   b. Evaluation of pervasive impairments: decreased arousal, decreased alertness, loss of selective/sustained attention, concrete thinking, decreased insight, impaired judgment, confusion, disorientation, language dysfunction, impaired motivation, and impaired initiative.
   c. Evaluation of the impact of specific deficits on basic and instrumental activities of daily living and mobility including apraxia, spatial neglect, body neglect, perseveration, spatial relations dysfunction, various agnosias, organization and sequencing dysfunction, and memory loss.
3. Determine psychosocial dysfunction and strengths.
   a. Evaluation of emotional/affective disturbances: lability, euphoria, apathy, depression, aggression, irritability, frustration tolerance.
   b. Coping mechanisms.
   c. Adaptation to change in occupational role functioning or to difficulty in assuming occupational roles.
4. See subsequent evaluation chapters for more information on each of the above areas.

Performance Context Evaluation

1. Cultural barriers.
2. Architectural barriers.
3. Societal limitations.
   a. Financial barriers.
   b. Stigma.
4. Home evaluation.
5. School/work site evaluations.
6. See Chapter 15 for more information on mastery of the environment.

General Intervention/Treatment Guidelines

1. Role of the OTA.
   a. The OTA implements intervention with the supervision of the occupational therapist.
      (1) The level of supervision required depends upon the OTA's experience and established service competency.
      (2) During the implementation of intervention, the OTA informs the supervising therapist of any change in the individual's status and any other relevant information that may affect treatment.

> **EXAM HINT:** In the NBCOT® exam outline for the COTA®, Domain 02 Selecting and Implementing Interventions comprises 55% of the NBCOT® exam. This domain focuses on the OTA's ability to "implement interventions under the supervision of the OTR in accordance with the intervention plan and level of service competence to support client participation in areas of occupation throughout the occupational therapy process" (NBCOT®, 2018, p. 18). The application of knowledge about the role of the OTA in intervention described above and the following intervention foci can help you correctly answer NBCOT® Domain 02 exam items about intervention management for persons with neurological system disorders.

2. Positioning.
   a. Seating and wheeled mobility prescription.
   b. Bed positioning.
   c. Pressure reduction and pressure relief techniques.
3. Postural control training for seated and standing activities.
4. Motor learning approaches.
5. Motor control retraining/relearning for functional integration of affected limbs.
6. Specific ADL training/retraining/adaptation.
7. Prescription of assistive devices and technology.
8. Splinting for contracture prevention and/or enhancement of function (e.g., tenodesis splint).
9. Family/caregiver education.
10. Cognitive-perceptual retraining/compensation in the context of functional activities.
11. Visual skills retraining and/or adaptation (e.g., visual occlusion for diplopia).
12. Intervention for sexual dysfunction.
13. Bowel and bladder training with adaptive techniques and equipment.
14. Skin care education.
15. Durable medical equipment prescription.
16. Sensory re-education, compensation, and safety training for those without return of sensation.
17. Assistance with the development of coping strategies.
18. Community reintegration.
19. Return to work or work hardening programs for adults.
20. Collaboration with educational team for children.
21. See subsequent intervention chapters in this text for more information on each of the above areas.

> **EXAM HINT:** Understand that the prognosis of neurological system disorders must be considered during intervention planning and implementation. To determine correct answers for COTA® exam items about working with clients with these conditions, remember that compensatory approaches are best to use with people with progressive disorders (e.g., ALS, muscular dystrophy) while a combination of remediation and rehabilitative approaches are best for people with nonprogressive disorders (e.g., TBI, SCI).

Pain

Definition

1. The sensory and emotional experience associated with actual or potential tissue damage.

Acute Pain

1. Pain provoked by noxious stimulation.
2. Associated with an underlying pathology (injury or acute inflammation/disease).
3. Signs include sharp pain and sympathetic changes (increased heart rate, increased blood pressure, pupillary dilation, sweating, hyperventilation, anxiety, protective/escape behaviors).

Chronic Pain

1. Pain that persists beyond the usual course of healing.
2. Symptoms present for greater than six months for which an underlying pathology is no longer identifiable or may never have been present.

Pain Syndromes

1. Neuropathic pain: pain as a result of lesions in some part of the nervous system (central or peripheral); usually accompanied by some degree of sensory deficit.
   a. Thalamic pain: continuous, intense pain occurring on the contralateral hemiplegic side; the result of a stroke involving the ventral posterolateral thalamus; poor rehabilitation potential.
   b. Complex Regional Pain Syndrome Type 1 (formerly known as reflex sympathetic dystrophy, [RSD]): pain maintained by efferent activity of sympathetic nervous system.
      (1) Characterized by abnormal burning pain (causalgia), hypersensitivity to light touch, and sympathetic hyperfunction (coldness, sweating, etc.).
      (2) Usually associated with traumatic injury.
   c. Disorders of peripheral roots and nerves.
      (1) Complex Regional Pain Syndrome Type II (formerly known as neuralgia): pain occurring along the branches of a nerve; frequently paroxysmal.
      (2) Radicalgia: neuralgia of nerve roots.
      (3) Paresthesias, allodynia: with nerve injury or transection.

d. Herpes Zoster (shingles): an acute, painful mononeuropathy caused by the varicella zoster virus.
   (1) Characterized by vesicular eruption and marked inflammation of the posterior root ganglion of the affected spinal nerve or sensory ganglion of the cranial nerve; ventral root involvement (motor weakness) in 5%–10% of cases.
   (2) Infection can last from 10 days to 5 weeks.
   (3) Pain may persist for months (postherpetic neuralgia).
e. Phantom limb pain: pain in a limb following amputation of that limb; differentiated from far more common phantom limb sensation.
f. Musculoskeletal pain: see Chapter 6.
g. Psychosomatic pain: the origin of the pain experience is due to mental or emotional disorders.
h. Headache and craniofacial pain, for example, temporomandibular joint syndrome (TMJ).
i. Referred pain: pain arising from deep visceral tissues that is felt in a body region remote from the site of pathology, resulting in tenderness and cutaneous hyperalgesia (e.g., medial left arm pain with heart attack; right subscapular pain from gallbladder attack).

Assessment of Chronic Pain

1. Role of the OTA in evaluation.
   a. The OTA can assist with the collection of data for the evaluation of pain once service competency has been established.
   b. The level of supervision required will be determined by the OTA's experience and established service competency.
   c. The OTA cannot independently evaluate or interpret evaluation results.

> **EXAM HINT:** The NBCOT® exam outline for the COTA® identifies knowledge of the "expected patterns, progressions, and prognoses associated with conditions that limit occupational performance (and the) the impact of . . . body functions and body structures . . . on occupational performance" (NBCOT®, 2018, p. 21) as essential for competent and safe practice. The application of knowledge about the previously described types, causes, and symptoms of pain and the following evaluation foci and approaches can help you effectively determine the correct answers to NBCOT® Domain 01 exam items about the assessment of pain.

2. Evaluation focus.
   a. History: determine chief complaints, description of onset, and mechanism of injury.
   b. Determine localization: chronic pain is poorly localized, not well defined.
   c. Identify nature of pain: constant, intermittent.
   d. Determine irritating stimuli/activities.
   e. Determine subjective assessment using pain intensity rating scales.
      (1) Simple descriptive scales: verbal report (e.g., select the words that best describe your pain).
      (2) Semantic differentiation scales (e.g., McGill Pain Questionnaire).
      (3) Numerical rating scales (rate pain on a scale of 1 to 10, e.g., 8/10).
      (4) Visual analog scale (e.g., bisect line where your pain falls, from mild to severe pain).
      (5) Spatial distribution of pain: using drawings to plot location, type of pain.
      (6) Visual scales (e.g., Wong-Baker FACES® Pain Rating Scale).
   f. Physical examination: identification of underlying pathology (cause of pain); objective physical findings are usually not readily identified.
      (1) Assess all systems: musculoskeletal, neurologic, and cardiopulmonary. Check for muscle guarding.
      (2) Check for postural stress syndrome (PSS): chronic muscle lengthening and/or shortening that causes postural malalignment and stress to soft tissues.
      (3) Check for movement adaptation syndrome (MAS): habituated movement dysfunction.
      (4) Check for autonomic changes (sympathetic activity): typically present with acute pain but not with chronic pain.
      (5) Assess for abnormal movements.
   g. Assess degree of suffering.
      (1) Verbal complaints are out of proportion to degree of underlying pathology; include emotional content.
      (2) The person exhibits a stooped posture, antalgic gait.
      (3) The person exhibits facial grimacing.
   h. Assess for functional changes.
      (1) Check for self-imposed limited activity; disrupted lifestyle; disuse syndrome.
      (2) Check for avoidance of work, home management, leisure, social, and/or sexual activity.
   i. Assess for consequences of pain, behavioral impact, secondary gains.
      (1) Monetary benefits (malingering, insurance claims).
      (2) Sympathy and attention.
      (3) Avoidance of undesirable tasks.
   j. Assess for depression and anxiety.
   k. Assess for prescription drug misuse.
   l. Assess for dependence on health care system: multiple health care providers, clinical services; 'shopping around' behaviors.
   m. Determine responsiveness of pain to physiological interventions/treatments: chronic pain is often unresponsive.

n. Determine motivational/affective components.
   (1) Previous experience with pain.
   (2) Learned responses to pain.
   (3) Perception of control over pain.
   (4) Ethnic/cultural aspects of pain.
   (5) Familial response to pain behavior.

Occupational Therapy Intervention

1. Role of the OTA in intervention.
   a. The OTA implements intervention with OT supervision.
      (1) The level of supervision required depends upon the OTA's experience and established service competency.
      (2) During the implementation of intervention, the OTA informs the supervising therapist of any change in the individual's status and any other relevant information that may affect treatment.

EXAM HINT: The NBCOT® exam outline for the COTA® identifies knowledge of "technical level techniques for implementing . . . pain management . . . programs" (NBCOT®, 2018, p. 26) as essential for competent and safe practice. Based on this requirement and the recognition of occupational therapy as a non-pharmacological intervention for pain, it is likely that the COTA® exam will include items about interventions for pain. The application of knowledge about the role of the OTA in intervention described above and the following intervention foci can help you correctly answer NBCOT® Domain 02 exam items about intervention management for persons with pain.

2. Intervention focus.
   a. Educate the individual about contributing factors.
   b. Assist the individual in identifying and responding adaptively to pain behaviors.
      (1) Remove behavioral reinforcers.
      (2) Establish a behavior contract.
      (3) Provide positive reinforcers and educational support.
      (4) Demonstrate change, allow person to experience success.
      (5) Practice well behaviors.
   c. Assist the individual in developing strategies and using techniques to manage pain.
      (1) Teach coping skills/stress management/assertive communication.
      (2) Provide relaxation training.
         (a) Progressive relaxation techniques (e.g., Jacobson's), deep breathing exercises.
         (b) Guided imagery.
         (c) Yoga, tai chi, ai chi.
         (d) Biofeedback.
   d. Establish a realistic, person-directed daily activity program.
      (1) Improve overall level of conditioning: daily walking program.
      (2) Improve overall functional capacity and functional mobility skills.
      (3) Increase engagement in activities of daily living and meaningful occupations.
      (4) Teach energy conservation techniques.
      (5) Provide meaningful diversional activities.
   e. Prescribe assistive devices as appropriate.
   f. Provide family education.
   g. Refer to other professionals for direct pain/symptoms control interventions.

Sensory Processing Disorders

EXAM HINT: In the NBCOT® practice analysis for the COTA®, 33.6% of COTA®s who provided services across diagnostic categories indicated they provided services to individuals with sensory processing/sensory integrative disorder (NBCOT®, 2018, p. 13). Due to this prevalence, it is likely that the COTA® exam will have items about working with children, youth, and adults with sensory processing/sensory integrative disorders.

Etiology

1. Unknown.
2. Subtle, primarily subcortical, neural dysfunction with impaired processing of sensory information and modulation of multisensory systems.

Symptom Classification

1. Ayers Sensory Integration® model; see Chapter 12.
2. Dunn's model: symptoms are classified according to the interaction of sensory stimuli that are needed to stimulate a behavioral response.

a. There are two types of neurological thresholds: high neurological threshold and low neurological threshold.
   (1) High neurological threshold: failure to register or respond to routine environmental sensation or sensation must be experienced over a prolonged time period to elicit a behavioral response.
   (2) Low neurological threshold: the minimal sensation facilitates a behavioral response.
b. There are two types of behavioral responses.
   (1) Passive behavioral response: the individual makes no attempt to change the intensity or duration of sensory input.
   (2) Active behavioral response: the individual avoids or seeks to avoid sensory stimuli.
c. Neurological thresholds and behavioral responses combine to form four categories. These include:
   (1) Poor registration: high neurological thresholds and passive behavioral responses.
   (2) Sensory seeking: high neurological thresholds and active behavioral responses.
   (3) Sensory sensitivity: low neurological thresholds and passive behavioral responses.
   (4) Sensory avoiding: low neurological thresholds and active behavioral responses.
3. Ecological model of sensory modulation disorder describes individuals' unique response to interactions between external and internal dimensions of sensory processing in the context of their lives.
   a. External dimensions include culture, relationships, and chosen tasks.
   b. Internal dimensions include sensation, emotion, and attention.
   c. Difficulty with modulation either can result in:
      (1) Difficulties with social and environmental interactions.
      (2) Difficulties with self-regulation due to a mismatch between internal capabilities and external environment and activities.
4. Sensory-processing nosology has been put forth for inclusion in diagnostic manuals that classify symptoms under the categories of:
   a. Sensory modulation disorder (SMD) in any sensory system.
      (1) Sensory overresponsivity (SOR).
      (2) Sensory underresponsivity (SUR).
      (3) Sensory seeking/craving (SS).
   b. Sensory-based motor disorder (SBMD) includes underlying sensory discrimination disorder as well as possible sensory modulation disorder.
      (1) Dyspraxia.
      (2) Sensory-based postural disorders.
   c. Sensory discrimination disorder (SDD).
      (1) Visual.
      (2) Auditory.
      (3) Tactile.
      (4) Vestibular.
      (5) Proprioceptive.
      (6) Taste/smell.

Presenting Signs and Symptoms

1. Fluctuating or extreme responsiveness while engaging in everyday activities (e.g., stress and frustration demonstrated in performance of everyday activities).
2. Difficulties with the environment in play, learning, social situations, and while engaging in other developmental and health-promoting activities.
3. Difficulty with conceiving, planning, and sequencing, or executing novel actions (dyspraxia).
   a. Tendency to avoid or reject simple motor challenges.
4. Poor initiation of activities as demonstrated in some children due to difficulty generating ideas (ideation).
5. Difficulty with goal directed action on the environment, known as an adaptive response.
6. Responses may present along a continuum of underresponsivity to overresponsivity of multisensory processing and sensory seeking.
7. Tactile processing dysfunction manifestations.
   a. Deficits in modulation (regulation and organization).
      (1) Tactile defensiveness: overresponsivity to ordinary touch sensations.
         (a) The individual may demonstrate irritation and discomfort from a variety of textures such as clothing, sand, grass, glue, water, paint, and/or food.
         (b) The individual may dislike brushing their teeth or hair.
         (c) The individual may demonstrate various behavioral responses including distractibility, anger, hostility, temper tantrums, fear, and/or distress.
      (2) Underresponsivity to tactile stimuli as demonstrated by diminished sensory registration and responsiveness.
         (a) The individual may not respond to normal levels of tactile input and may seek disproportionate amounts of stimuli to gain environmental information (e.g., excessive touching of people or objects).
   b. Deficits in tactile discrimination.
      (1) Difficulty interpreting tactile information in a precise and efficient manner.
         (a) Contributes to impaired body scheme and somatodyspraxia (a disorder in motor planning due to poor tactile perception and proprioception).

(b) Contributes to awkwardness in fine and gross motor tasks, impaired manipulation skills, visual perception, and eye-hand coordination.
(c) Hinders ability to learn about properties and substances.
(2) Difficulty with localizing tactile stimuli.
c. Impaired stereognosis and decreased fine motor and eye-hand coordination skills may be demonstrated in difficulties with writing and cutting with a scissors and knife.
8. Proprioceptive processing dysfunction manifestations.
a. Deficits in modulation.
b. Discrimination deficits demonstrated by poor awareness of position of body, body parts, and body schema.
c. Clumsiness, awkwardness.
d. Distractibility.
e. Motor planning and movement difficulties.
f. Reliance on visual cues or other cognitive strategies to motor plan, guide movements, and perform tasks.
g. Use of too much or too little force; e.g., stomping when walking, breaking objects unintentionally.
h. Poor awareness of personal space.
i. Seek heavy resistance and pressure.
9. Vestibular processing dysfunction manifestations.
a. Deficits in modulation.
(1) Hypersensitivity to movement, characterized by aversion to movement impacting on the sympathetic system.
(2) Hyposensitivity to movement characterized by the individual seeking intense vestibular stimulation without complaints of feeling dizzy and by a tendency to be a thrill seeker unaware of potential danger.
(3) Gravitational insecurity characterized by excessive fear during typical activities when the head is not upright, especially when the individual's feet are off the ground, when moving backward or upward in space, walking on uneven terrain, jumping, getting on/off elevators, using any playground equipment involving movement, and when handling even minimal heights.
b. Vestibular discrimination deficits, characterized by the above symptoms; however, symptoms are demonstrated on a subtle level.
c. Low muscle tone.
d. Postural-ocular deficits.
e. Decreased balance and equilibrium reactions.
f. Deficits in bilateral coordination.
g. Poor endurance.
h. Deficient motor planning and sequencing.
i. Behavior responses include difficulty with attention, organization of behavior, communication.

10. Sensory-based motor disorder.
a. Deficits in proprioceptive and vestibular systems.
b. Dyspraxia: difficulty with planning movements, particularly those that are complex or new.
c. Postural disorders: decreased muscle tone impacting on stability.

Medical Management

1. Possible pharmacology intervention to decrease activity level.

Occupational Therapy Evaluation

EXAM HINT: In the NBCOT® exam outline for the COTA®, Domain 01 Collaborating and Gathering Information comprises 28% of the exam (NBCOT®, 2018, p. 18). This domain focuses on the OTA's ability to "assist the OTR to acquire information regarding factors that influence occupational performance on an ongoing basis throughout the occupational therapy process" (NBCOT®, 2018, p. 18). The application of knowledge about the symptom classification for sensory processing disorders and their presenting signs and symptoms described in prior sections and the evaluation foci described below can help you effectively determine the correct answers to NBCOT® Domain 01 exam items about working with persons with sensory processing disorders.

1. Parent/caregiver interview regarding medical and developmental history.
2. Teacher interview regarding school performance, play, and behaviors.
3. Formal assessment of sensory processing.
4. Informal observations of performance and behavior in a variety of settings (e.g., classroom, playground, home and work).
5. Formal assessment of clinical observations using the Ayres unpublished and nonstandardized tools.
a. Items to be observed include specific reflexes, crossing body midline, bilateral coordination, muscle tone.
6. Standardized tests for tactile processing, vestibular-proprioceptive processing, visual perception, practical ability, and their impact on occupational functioning (e.g., SPM; see Chapter 12).
7. Role of the OTA in evaluation.
a. The OTA contributes to the evaluation process.
(1) The OTA can assist with the collection of data for the evaluation once service competency has been established.
(2) The level of supervision required will be determined by the OTA's established service competency.

(3) The OTA cannot independently evaluate or interpret evaluation results.

Occupational Therapy Intervention

1. Role of the OTA.
   a. The OTA implements intervention with supervision of the occupational therapist.
      (1) The level of supervision required depends upon the OTA's experience and established service competency.
      (2) During the implementation of intervention, the OTA informs the supervising therapist of any change in the individual's status and any other relevant information that may affect treatment.
2. See Chapter 12 for information on the sensory integration (SI) frame of reference and intervention approaches.

Seizure Disorders

Etiology

1. Seizure disorders must be differentiated from epilepsy.
   a. Epilepsy is a chronic state of recurrent seizures.
   b. Seizure disorder refers to a temporary disturbance in brain activity causing a group of nerve cells to fire excessively, interfering with normal brain function.
2. Seizures are typically idiopathic; they also can be hereditary.
   a. In almost two-thirds of all epilepsy cases, the cause remains unknown.
3. Seizures are often associated with conditions. These include:
   a. Oxygen deprivation (e.g., during childbirth).
   b. Severe head injuries or brain hemorrhage.
   c. Cerebral palsy.
   d. Stroke.
   e. Brain tumors.
   f. Other neurological disorders (e.g., Alzheimer's disease).
   g. Hydrocephalus.
   h. Metabolic disorders.
   i. Infections, meningitis, encephalitis, congenital infections.
   j. Rubella.

Prevalence

1. Three million adults and 470,000 children (ages 0–17) in the United States have epilepsy.
2. Approximately 35–71 people of 100,000 Americans develop the condition each year.

Specific Classifications of Seizures and Presenting Signs and Symptoms

1. Two broad groups.
   a. Primary generalized seizures: seizures begin with widespread involvement of both sides of the brain.
   b. Partial seizures begin with involvement of a smaller, localized area.
      (1) The disturbance can still spread within seconds or minutes to widespread areas of the brain (known as secondary generalized seizure).
2. Generalized seizures.
   a. Tonic-clonic seizures/grand mal seizures.
      (1) Most common type of seizure disorder in children.
      (2) A brief warning/aura such as numbness, taste, smell, or other sensation occurs.
      (3) Tonic phase includes a loss of consciousness, stiffening of the body, heavy and irregular breathing, drooling, skin pallor, and occasional bladder and bowel incontinence for a few seconds before the clonic phase begins.
      (4) Clonic phase includes alternating rigidity and relaxation of muscles.
      (5) Postictal state follows the clonic phase and includes a period of drowsiness, disorientation, or fatigue.
   b. Myoclonic-akinetic seizure.
      (1) Myoclonic seizures are not the same as infantile myoclonic seizures.
      (2) Myoclonic seizures are brief, involuntary jerking of the extremities, with or without loss of consciousness.

(3) Akinetic seizures include a loss of tone.
(4) Myoclonic-akinetic seizures are difficult to control.
c. Petit mal seizures, also called absence seizures.
  (1) Typically occur between ages of 4 and 12 years.
  (2) A loss of consciousness without loss of muscle tone occurs.
  (3) Rapid blinking or staring into space.
  (4) The child does not fall down.
  (5) The child does not recall the episode or any lapse in time.
3. Partial focal seizures.
  a. Simple partial seizures.
    (1) Abnormal electrical impulses occur in a localized area of the brain, often in the motor strip of the frontal lobe.
    (2) Involuntary, repetitive jerking of the hand and arm occurs, but the individual can maintain interaction with their environment.
    (3) Focal seizures may become generalized and result in a loss of consciousness.
  b. Complex partial or psychomotor seizures.
    (1) Symptoms vary.
    (2) There are alterations in consciousness and unresponsiveness.
    (3) May appear confused or dazed, unable to respond to questions or directions.
    (4) Automatic motions, such as lip smacking, chewing and swallowing, and nervous movement of the hands/fingers, and repetitive movements occur.
    (5) Visual or auditory sensations occur just before the seizure.
4. Selected seizure syndromes.
  a. Infantile spasms or West syndrome, infantile myoclonic seizures or jackknife epilepsy.
    (1) Begins at three to nine months of age.
    (2) Dropping of the head and flexion of the arms occurs.
    (3) Seizures may occur hundreds of times per day.
    (4) Prognosis is generally poor.
    (5) Spasms sometimes decrease after several years, but are often replaced by other seizure disorders.
    (6) These seizures often indicate an underlying disorder such as tuberous sclerosis.
  b. Lennox-Gastaut syndrome.
    (1) Children with severe seizures, intellectual disability, and a specific EEG pattern.
    (2) Seizures of different types begin during the first three years of life and are difficult to control.
    (3) Associated with various brain disorders from structural abnormalities to birth asphyxia.
    (4) A regression of developmental status can occur in some cases.
  c. Landau-Kleffner syndrome or acquired epileptic aphasia.
    (1) Progressive encephalopathy.
    (2) Loss of language skills.
    (3) Auditory agnosia (inability to distinguish different sounds).
    (4) Behavioral disturbances such as inattention.
5. Simple febrile seizures.
  a. Most common type of seizure, occurring in 5%–10% of children under the age of five, precipitated by a fever.
  b. The seizure lasts less than 10 minutes and it includes a loss of consciousness and involuntary, generalized jerking of a grand mal seizure.
  c. These seizures usually do not cause damage and they do not lead to epilepsy.
6. Status epilepticus: prolonged seizures or seizures in rapid succession.

> **CAUTION:** Status epilepticus can sometimes be triggered when medication is stopped abruptly.

  a. Can be life threatening; sometimes triggered when medication is stopped abruptly.
  b. Rarely does sudden death occur; however, it is possible due to resulting erratic heart rhythm.
    (1) Typically occurs with tonic-clonic seizures that are not well controlled.

Diagnostic Criteria

1. Clinical observations of the obvious manifestations associated with the specific seizure disorder.
2. The EEG alone is not sufficient to diagnose a seizure disorder since the disorder does not always show up on the EEG and conversely abnormal EEGs may appear when there is no clinical evidence of seizures.

Impact on Occupational Performance

1. The seizure disorder and/or the anticonvulsive medication(s) prescribed to control the seizures may affect the individual's alertness and learning potential.
2. The amount of brain damage incurred by the seizures and associated conditions and the effects of medication can influence performance in all areas of occupation.

Medical Management

1. A neurologist is most often required to medically manage seizures.

2. Seizure disorders are treated with anticonvulsive medications.
   a. Phenobarbital (Luminal), carbamazepine (Tegretol), phenytoin (Dilantin), and valproic acid (Depakene) are used with grand mal seizures.
   b. Ethosuximide (Zarontin) is used with petit mal seizures.
   c. Carbamazepine and primidone are used with psychomotor seizures.
   d. Clonazepam (Clonopin), steroids, and CTH (hormone secreted by the pituitary gland) are used with myoclonic seizures.

Intervention for Seizure Disorders

1. First-aid procedures for seizures.
   a. Remain calm.

   RED FLAG: Status epilepticus can be life threatening; thus, it is a medical emergency, and immediate medical attention must be obtained.

   b. Remove dangerous objects from the area.
   c. Protect the individual from harm, without interfering with the individual's movements.
   d. If the person is in a hospital bed, raise the bed rails.
   e. Do not place anything in the mouth.
   f. Turn the individual on their side if there is a risk of aspiration (e.g., person is salivating or vomiting and could aspirate fluid).
   g. Allow the seizure to happen, protecting the head and/or extremities if injury could occur from violent shaking.
   h. Once the clonus activity is over (for tonic-clonic type), place the person in the recovery position (side-lying).
   i. Monitor for improving mental state postictal.
   j. Do not be alarmed if the individual seems to stop breathing momentarily.
      (1) If the individual's breathing actually stops, use standard rescue breathing techniques.
   k. Call for medical attention during seizures:
      (1) If this is the individual's first seizure.
      (2) The person has a seizure in water.
      (3) If the person has a second seizure.
      (4) If the individual does not regain consciousness within 5 or 10 minutes following the seizure.
      (5) If the seizure lasts five minutes or more.
      (6) If the individual is diabetic or pregnant.
2. Postseizure care.
   a. Allow the individual to rest or sleep after the seizure.
   b. Call a physician if this is the individual's first seizure, if the seizure is followed by another seizure (status epilepticus), or if the seizure lasts more than five minutes.
   c. Notify the physician and parents/guardians/caregivers or designated emergency contact person that a seizure has occurred.
   d. Observe safety precautions if the individual seems groggy, confused, or weak following the seizure.

   EXAM HINT: The maintenance of people's health and safety is an OT practice priority and an ethical responsibility; thus, it is likely that the COTA® exam will have items about the management of seizures.

3. Occupational therapy evaluation and intervention.
   a. Assess and intervene for developmental delays as necessary.
   b. Observe all medical and safety precautions.
   c. Document and report any seizure activity, medication side effects, or behavioral changes.
   d. Refer to Chapter 14 for information on evaluation and intervention for deficits in performance in areas of occupation.

References

American Epilepsy Society. (2019). *Facts and figures*. Retrieved from https://www.aesnet.org/for_patients/facts_figures.

American Heart Disease Association. (2017). Heart disease and stroke statistics update. *Circulation*, 135:00.

Anzalone, M. E., & Lane, S. J. (2012). Sensory processing disorder. In S. J. Lane & A. C. Bundy (Eds.), *Kids can be kids: A childhood occupations approach* (pp. 437–459). Philadelphia: F.A. Davis.

Blackman, J. A. (1997a). Spina bifida. In J. A. Blackman (ed.), *Medical aspects of developmental disabilities in children birth to three* (3rd ed., pp. 36–39). Gaithersburg, MD: Aspen.

Blackman, J. A. (1997b). Seizure disorders. In J. A. Blackman (ed.), *Medical aspects of developmental disabilities in children birth to three* (3rd ed., pp. 238–246). Gaithersburg, MD: Aspen.

Boston Children's Hospital. (n.d.). *Tethered spinal cord: Frequently asked questions*. Retrieved from http://www.childrenshospital.org/conditions-and-treatments/conditions/t/tethered-spinal-cord/research-and-clinical-trials.

Bundy, A. C., & Murray, E. A. (2002). Sensory integration: A. Jean Ayers' theory revisited. In A. C. Bundy, S .J. Lane, & E. A. Murray (Eds.), *Sensory integration: Theory and practice* (2nd ed., pp. 3–33). Philadelphia: F.A. Davis.

References

Carpenter Rowe, N., & Lowe Breeden K. (2018, August). Opioid guidelines and their implications for occupational therapy. *OT Practice*, CE-1–CE-10.

Case-Smith, J., & O'Brien, J. C. (Eds.). (2015). *Occupational therapy for children and adolescents* (7th ed.). St. Louis, MO: Elsevier Mosby.

Centers for Disease Control and Prevention. (2013). *Data and statistics, muscular dystrophy–NCBDDD*. Retrieved from http://www.cdc.gov/ncbddd/musculardystrophy.data.html.

Centers for Disease Control and Prevention. (2013). *Epilepsy. Frequently asked questions*. Retrieved from http://www.cdc.gov/epilepsy/basics/faqs.htm.

Centers for Disease Control and Prevention. (2013). *Facts about muscular dystrophy*. Retrieved from http://www.cdc.gov/ncbdd/musculardystrophy/facts.html.

Centers for Disease Control and Prevention. (2013). *Spina bifida. Facts*. Retrieved from http://www.cdc.gov/ncbdd/spinalbifida/facts.html.

Centers for Disease Control and Prevention. (2013). *Treatments. Muscular dystrophy*. Retrieved from http://www.cdc.gov/ncbdd/musculardystrophy/treatment.html

Centers for Disease Control and Prevention. (2013). *Spina bifida—Facts*. Retrieved from http://www.cdc.gov/ncbdd/spinalbifida/facts.html.

Centers for Disease Control and Prevention. (2018). *Data and statistics for cerebral palsy*. Retrieved from https://www.cdc.gov/ncbddd/cp/data.html.

Centers for Disease Control and Prevention. (2018). *Epilepsy fast facts*. Retrieved from https://www.cdc.gov/epilepsy/about/fast-facts.htm.

Centers for Disease Control and Prevention. (2018). *Muscular dystrophy*. Retrieved from https://www.cdc.gov/ncbddd/musculardystrophy/data.html.

Escolar, D. M., & Toisi, L. L. (2007). Muscles, bones and nerves. In M. L. Batshaw, L. Pellegrino, & N. J. Roizen (Eds.), *Children with disabilities* (6th ed., pp. 203–215). Baltimore: Paul H. Brookes.

Gillen, G. (Ed.). (2016). *Stroke rehabilitation: A function-based approach* (4th ed.). St. Louis, MO: Elsevier/Mosby.

Gutman, S. A. (2017). *Quick reference neuroscience for rehabilitation professionals: The essential neurologic principles underlying rehabilitation practice* (3rd ed.). Thorofare, NJ: Slack.

Gutman, S. A., & Schonfeld, A. B. (2009). *Screening adult neurologic populations: A step-by-step instruction manual* (2nd ed.). Bethesda, MD: AOTA Press.

Humphry, R., & Wakeford, L. (2006). An occupation-centered discussion of development and implications for practice. *American Journal of Occupational Therapy*, 60, 258–267.

Kandell, E. R., Schwartz, T. H., & Tessel, T. M. (Eds.). (2012). *Principles of neural science* (5th ed.). New York: McGraw Hill.

Lane, S. J. (2002). Structure and function of the sensory systems. In A. C. Bundy, S. J. Lane, & E. A. Murray (Eds.), *Sensory integration: Theory and practice* (2nd ed., pp. 35–68). Philadelphia: F.A. Davis.

Lane, S. J. (2002). Sensory modulation. In A. C. Bundy, S. J. Lane, & E. A. Murray (Eds.), *Sensory integration: Theory and practice* (2nd ed., pp. 101–122). Philadelphia: F.A. Davis.

Liptak, G. S. (2005). Neural tube defects. In M. L. Batshaw, L. Pellegrino, & N. J. Roizen (Eds.), *Children with disabilities* (6th ed., pp. 419–438). Baltimore, MD: Paul H. Brooks.

Madsen, J. H. *Tethered cord syndrome: Questions and answers*. Retrieved from www.boston-neurosurg.org/amphitheater/tetheredcord.html.

Medline Plus. (2017). *Duchenne muscular dystrophy*. Retrieved from https://medlineplus.gov/ency/article/000705.htm.

Miller, L. J. (2006). *Sensational kids hope and help for children with sensory processing disorders (SPD)*. New York: G.P. Putnam's Sons.

Miller, L. S., Anzalone, M. E., Lane, S. J., Cermak, S. A., & Osten, E. T. (2007). Concept evolution in sensory integration: A proposed nosology for diagnosis. *American Journal of Occupational Therapy*, 61, 135–140.

Missiuna, C., Polatajko, H., Pollock, N., & Cameron, D. (2012). Neuromotor disorders. In S. J. Lane and A. C. Bundy (Eds.), *Kids can be kids: A childhood occupations approach*. Philadelphia: F.A. Davis.

Muscular Dystrophy Association. (2019). About neuromuscular *diseases*. Retrieved from http://www.mda.org/disease.

National Eye Institute (2019). *Refractive errors*. Retrieved from https://nei.nih.gov/health/errors

National Institutes of Neurological Disorders and Stroke. (2012). *Tethered spinal cord syndrome information page*. Retrieved from http://www.ninds.nih.gov/disorders/tethered_cord/tethered_cord.h.

National Organization for Rare Disorders. (2019). *Duchenne muscular dystrophy*. Retrieved from https://rarediseases.org/rare-diseases/duchenne-muscular-dystrophy/

National Organization for Rare Disorders. (2017). *Progressive supranuclear palsy*. Retrieved from https://rarediseases.org/rare-diseases/progressive-supranuclear-palsy/.

Parham, L. D., & Mailoux, Z. (2015). Sensory integration. In J. Case-Smith & J. C. O'Brien (Ed.), *Occupational therapy for children and adolescents* (7th ed., pp. 258–303). St. Louis, MO: Elsevier Mosby.

Pellegrino, L. (2007). Cerebral palsy. In M. L. Batshaw, L. Pellegrino, & N. J. Roizen (Eds.), *Children with disabilities* (6th ed., pp. 387–408). Baltimore, MD: Paul H. Brooks.

Pendleton, H., & Schultz-Krohn, W. (Eds.). (2013). *Pedretti's occupational therapy: Practice skills for physical dysfunction* (7th ed.). St. Louis, MO: Elsevier Mosby.

Reeves, G. D., & Cermak, S. A. (2002). Disorders of praxis. In A. C. Bundy, S. J. Lane, & E. A. Murray, (Eds.), *Sensory integration: Theory and practice* (2nd ed., pp. 71–100). Philadelphia: F.A. Davis.

Rogers, S. (2005). Common conditions that influence children's participation. In J. Case-Smith (Ed.), *Occupational therapy for children* (5th ed., pp. 160–215). St. Louis, MO: Elsevier Mosby.

Shaf, R., & Lane, S. (2009). Neuroscience foundations of vestibular, proprioceptive, and tactile sensory strategies. *Occupational Therapy Practice*, 14(22), CE1–CE8.

Spina Bifida Association. (2015). *Neurologic needs & care*. Retrieved from http://spinabifidaassociation.org/resource-directory/neurologic-needs-and-care/.

Spina Bifida Association. (n.d.). *Spinal cord tethering*. Retrieved from https://spinabifidaassociation.org/wp-content/uploads/2015/07/Spinal-Cord-Tethering1.pdf.

United Cerebral Palsy (UCP). (2010). *Cerebral palsy information*. Retrieved from http://ucp.org.

Vining-Radomski, M., & Trombly-Latham, C. A. (2014). *Occupational therapy for physical dysfunction* (7th ed.). Baltimore, MD: Williams & Wilkins.

Weinstein, S. L., & Gaillard, W. D. (2005). Epilepsy. In M. L. Batshaw, L. Pellegrino, & N. J. Roizen (Eds.), *Children with disabilities* (6th ed., pp. 439–460). Baltimore, MD: Paul H. Brookes.

Review Questions

Neurological System Disorders

Below are five questions about key content covered in this chapter. These questions are not inclusive of the entirety of content related to neurological disorders that you must know for success on the COTA® exam. These questions are provided to help you "jump-start" the thought processes you will need to apply your studying of content to the answering of exam questions; hence they are not in the COTA® exam format. Exam items in the COTA® format which cover the depth and breadth of content you will need to know to pass the exam are provided on this text's computerized exams. The answers to the questions below are provided in Appendix 3.

1. You will be working with two persons who have survived strokes. One incurred a left MCA stroke and one incurred a right MCA stroke. What symptoms might each patient present during their respective intervention session?

2. You are working on a spinal cord unit. You are about to evaluate a client who has injury classified as ASIA A. The injury is at the C5 level. What is the expected sensory and motor status of your client?

3. You have collaborated with the occupational therapist to evaluate a client who sustained a TBI two weeks ago. Your findings include that the patient was alert and in a heightened state of activity (easily overstimulated) and attempting to pull out the IV and feeding tube. The patient could not remember directions, exhibiting poor short-term memory. The patient screamed out for no reason several times during the session and was observed to be aggressive (e.g., attempting to hit you and the occupational therapist). The patient required maximum assist for BADL. Your facility requires the documentation of each TBI patient's Rancho Level of Cognitive Function. What level should be recorded for this client?

4. During an occupational therapy session with a toddler, you observe that the child tends to sit or lay as placed, without moving. The parent reports that the child shows interest in toys, but never seems to reach out to them or handle them. The child is reported to be a "picky eater," who shows no interest in self-feeding. When you attempt to approach or make eye contact, the child cries. Based on this information, how would you explain the child's behaviors as related to possible underlying conditions to the parent?

5. You are working with a child who suddenly has a series of seizures that occur in rapid succession and are prolonged. The parents are present, and they report that they ran out of the child's medication the day before. What type of seizure do these symptoms represent? How should you respond to this situation?

8

Cardiovascular and Pulmonary System Disorders

REGINA M. LEHMAN, KELLY MACAULEY, SUSAN O'SULLIVAN, THOMAS SUTLIVE, AND TODD SANDERS

Chapter Outline

- Cardiovascular System, 224
- Coronary Artery Disease (CAD), 228
- Pulmonary System, 235
- Pulmonary Dysfunction, 235
- Occupational Therapy Cardiopulmonary Assessment, 239
- Occupational Therapy Cardiopulmonary Rehabilitation, 244
- Pediatric Pulmonary Disorders, 251
- References, 254
- Review Questions, 255

Cardiovascular System

Function

1. Delivers oxygen to organs and tissues.
2. Removes carbon dioxide and other by-products from body.
3. Assists in the regulation of core body temperature.

Cardiovascular Anatomy and Physiology

1. Relationship to the NBCOT® exam.
   a. It is not likely that the NBCOT® exam will ask direct questions about anatomy and physiology.
   b. As a result, this chapter does not provide a complete anatomy and physiology review.
   c. Major structures and functions are outlined because knowledge of these can increase understanding of cardiovascular function.

> **EXAM HINT:** In the NBCOT® exam outline for the certified occupational therapy assistant (COTA®) the task of recognizing" the influence of . . . body functions and body structures . . . on a client's occupational performance" (NBCOT®, 2018, p. 21) is identified as essential for competent and safe practice. Thus, knowing the major structures and functions of the cardiovascular system can help you correctly answer COTA® exam items about the functional implications of cardiovascular conditions. This knowledge will improve your ability to understand pathology, presenting symptoms, medical interventions, and occupational therapy (OT) treatment rationales. For example, the left ventricle is the main pump of the heart, pumping blood from the heart to the rest of the body. This is usually the first area to be affected by a deficiency in coronary artery perfusion because it has a higher workload than the rest of the heart. Decreased function of the left ventricle can result in left-sided congestive heart failure with tachycardia, shortness of breath, decreased endurance, weakness, and fatigue.

The Heart and Circulation

1. Heart tissue.
   a. Pericardium: fibrous protective sac enclosing heart.
   b. Epicardium: inner layer of pericardium.
   c. Myocardium: heart muscle, the major portion of the heart.
   d. Endocardium: smooth lining of the inner surface and cavities of the heart.
2. Heart chambers.
   a. Four chambers arranged in pairs, functioning as two pumps working in sequence.
      (1) Right atrium (RA): receives blood from systemic circulation (from the superior and inferior vena cava); during systole (contraction) blood is sent into right ventricle.
      (2) Right ventricle (RV): pumps blood via the pulmonary artery to the lungs for oxygenation; the low-pressure pulmonary pump.
      (3) Left atrium (LA): receives oxygenated blood from the lungs (from the four pulmonary veins); during systole, blood is sent into the left ventricle.
      (4) Left ventricle (LV): pumps blood via the aorta throughout the entire systemic circulation; walls of left are thicker and stronger than right ventricle and form most of the left side and apex of the heart; the high-pressure systemic pump.

> **EXAM HINT:** Understanding the mechanism of blood flow through the heart can help you understand what systems and structures could be affected by damage in a specific area. For example, a compromise in right ventricle function could result in right-sided heart failure with poor peripheral circulation, lower extremity edema, and decreased endurance and mobility.

   b. See Figure 8-1
   c. Blood flow.
      (1) Systemic circulation to RA to RV then to lungs for oxygenation.
      (2) LA receives oxygenated blood from the lungs, sends blood to LV.
      (3) LV pumps blood to the body via the aorta.
3. Valves: ensure unidirectional blood flow through the heart; provide one-way flow of blood into, out of, and within heart.
   a. Atrioventricular valves: prevent backflow of blood into the atria during ventricular systole; valves close when ventricular walls contract.
      (1) Tricuspid valve (three cusps of leaflets): right heart valve.
      (2) Bicuspid or mitral valve (two cusps or leaflets): left heart valve.
   b. Semilunar valves: prevent backflow of blood from aorta and pulmonary arteries into the ventricles during diastole.
      (1) Pulmonary valve: prevents right backflow.
      (2) Aortic valve: prevents left backflow.

Cardiovascular System

4. Cardiac cycle.
   a. The rhythmic pumping action of the heart.
   b. Systole: the period of ventricular contraction.
   c. Diastole: the period of ventricular relaxation and filling of blood.
   d. Atrial contraction occurs during the last third of diastole and completes ventricular filling.
5. Coronary circulation.
   a. Right coronary artery (RCA): supplies right atrium, most of right ventricle, and in most individuals the inferior wall of left ventricle, atrioventricular (AV) node, and bundle of His; 60% of time supplies the sinoatrial (SA) node.
   b. Left coronary artery (LCA): supplies most of the left ventricle; has two main divisions.
      (1) Left anterior descending (LAD) supplies the anterior wall of the left ventricle.
      (2) Circumflex supplies the lateral and inferior walls of the left ventricle and portions of the left atrium; supplies SA node 40% of the time.
   c. Veins: parallel arterial system.
   d. See Figure 8-2.
6. Conduction: specialized tissue allows rapid transmission of electrical impulses in the myocardium; includes nodal tissue and Purkinje fibers.
   a. Sinoatrial (SA) node: main pacemaker of the heart; initiates sinus rhythm; has sympathetic and parasympathetic innervation affecting both heart rate and strength of contraction.

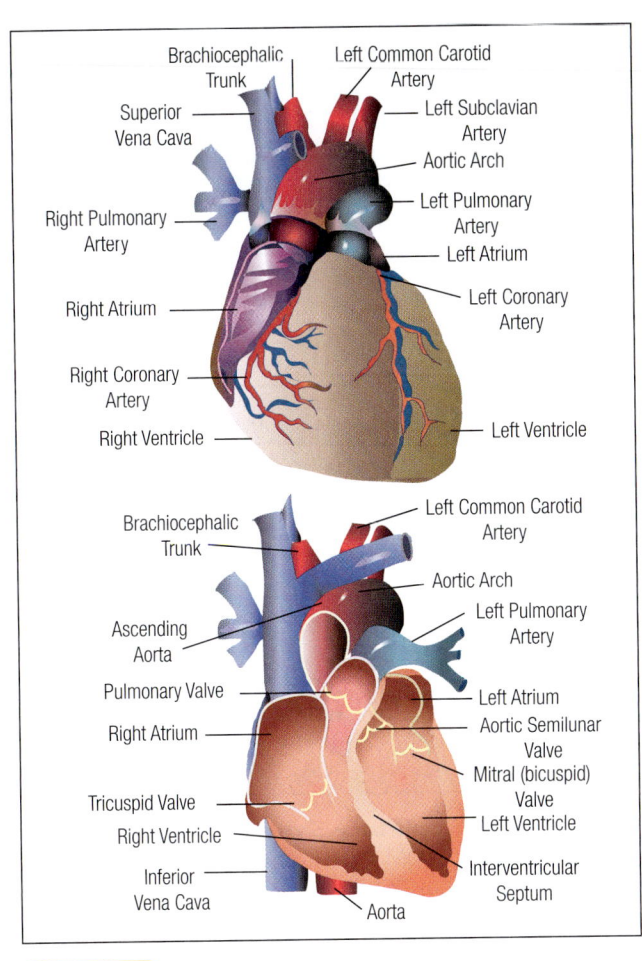

Figure 8-1 The Heart.

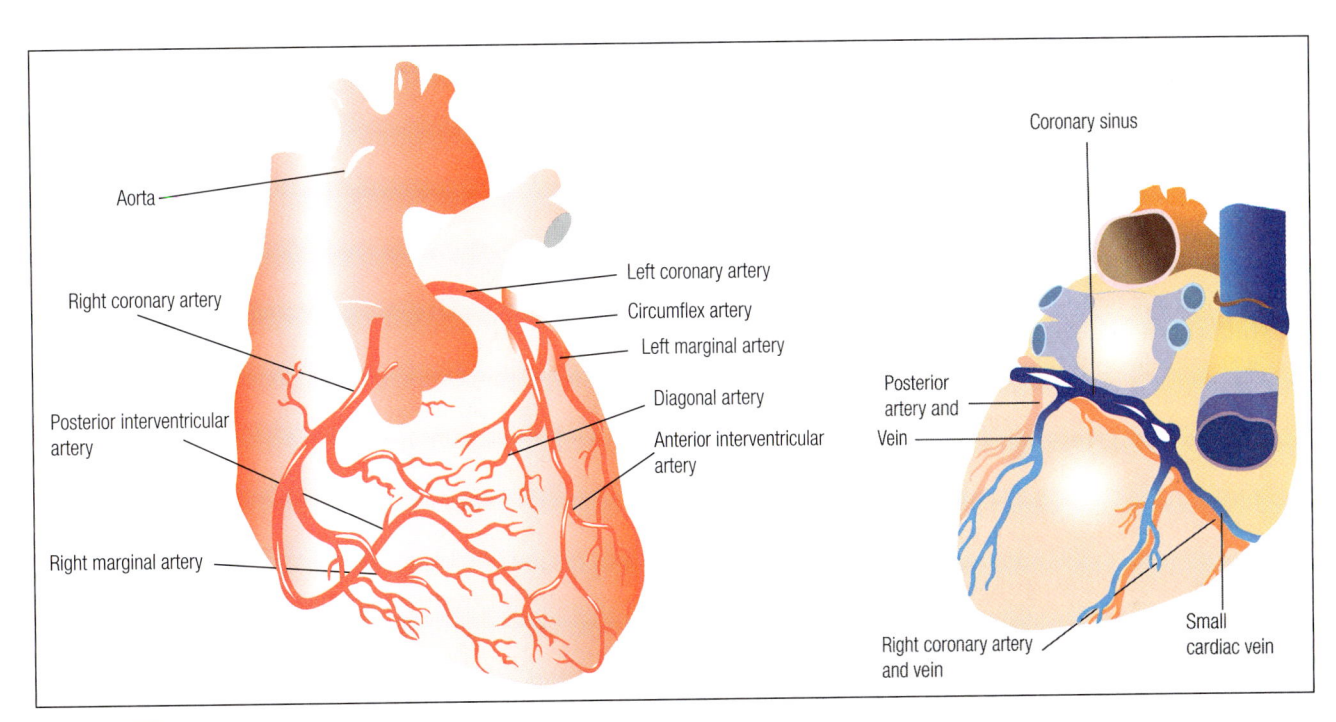

Figure 8-2 Coronary Arteries.

(1) This controls the flow of blood through the heart and thereby the normal perfusion of the body's systems and structures.
(2) SA node dysfunction results in irregular heart rhythm and atrial fibrillation, and it also increases the risk of stroke.
  b. Atrioventricular (AV) node: has sympathetic and parasympathetic innervation; merges with bundle of His.
  c. Purkinje tissue: specialized conducting tissue of the ventricles.
  d. Conduction of heartbeat.
    (1) Impulse originates in SA node and spreads throughout both atria, which contract together.
    (2) Impulse stimulates AV node, is transmitted down bundle of His to the Purkinje fibers; impulse spreads throughout the ventricles, which contract together.
7. Myocardial fibers: striated muscle tissue/fibers that exhibit rhythmicity of contraction as fibers contract as a functional unit; myocardial metabolism is primarily aerobic, sustained by continuous O_2 delivery from the coronary arteries.
8. Hemodynamics.
  a. Cardiac output: amount of blood ejected from the heart per minute; dependent upon heart rate and stroke volume.
  b. Stroke volume: average amount of blood ejected per heartbeat.
  c. Ejection fraction: percentage of blood emptied from the ventricle during systole; a clinically useful measure of LV function.
    (1) This measure is used in the diagnosis and monitoring of left-sided heart failure.

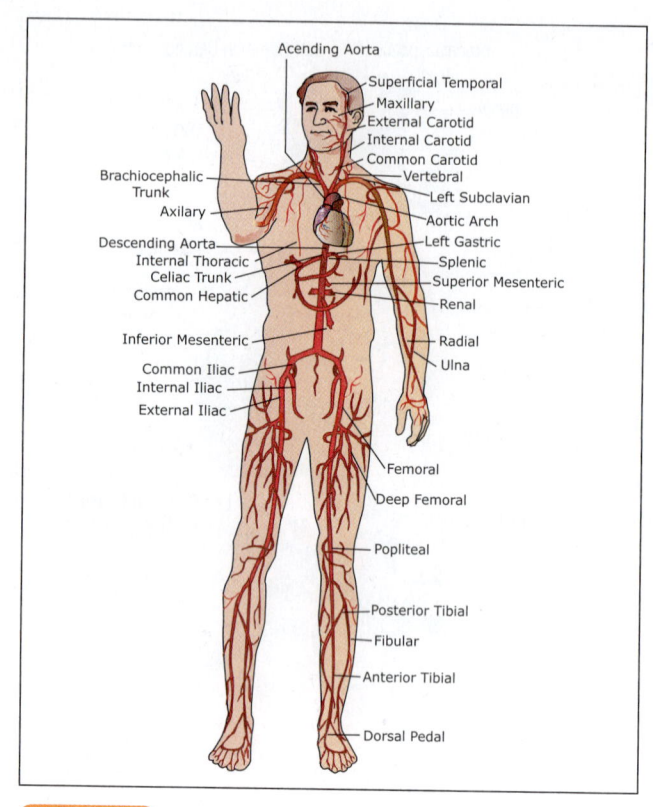

Figure 8-3 Circulatory System: Arteries.

Peripheral Circulation

1. Arteries.
   a. Transport oxygenated blood from areas of high pressure to lower pressures in the body tissues.
   b. Arterial circulation maintained by heart pump.
   c. Influenced by elasticity and extensibility of vessel walls, peripheral resistance, and amount of blood in body.
   d. See Figure 8-3.
2. Capillaries.
   a. Minute blood vessels that connect the ends of arteries (arterioles) with the beginning of veins (venules); forms an anastomosing network.
   b. Function for the exchange of nutrients and fluids between blood and tissues.
   c. Capillary walls are thin, permeable.
3. Veins.
   a. Transport dark, unoxygenated blood from tissues back to the heart.
   b. Larger capacity, thinner walls than arteries, greater number.
   c. One-way valves to prevent backflow.
   d. Venous system includes both superficial and deep veins (deep veins accompany arteries, while superficial ones do not).
   e. See Figure 8-4.
4. Lymphatic system.
   a. Includes lymphatics (superficial, intermediate, and deep), lymph fluid, lymph tissues, and organs (lymph nodes, tonsils, spleen, thymus, and the thoracic duct).
   b. Drains lymph from bodily tissues and returns it to venous circulation.
   c. Lymph travels from lymphatic capillaries to lymphatic vessels to ducts to left subclavian vein. Lymphatic contraction occurs by.
      (1) Parasympathetic, sympathetic, and sensory nerve stimulation.
      (2) Contraction of adjacent muscles.
      (3) Abdominal and thoracic cavity pressure changes during normal breathing.
      (4) Mechanical stimulation of dermal tissues.
      (5) Volume changes within each lymphatic vessel.
   d. Major lymph nodes are submaxillary, cervical, axillary, mesenteric, iliac, inguinal, popliteal, and cubital.

Figure 8-4 Circulatory System: Veins.

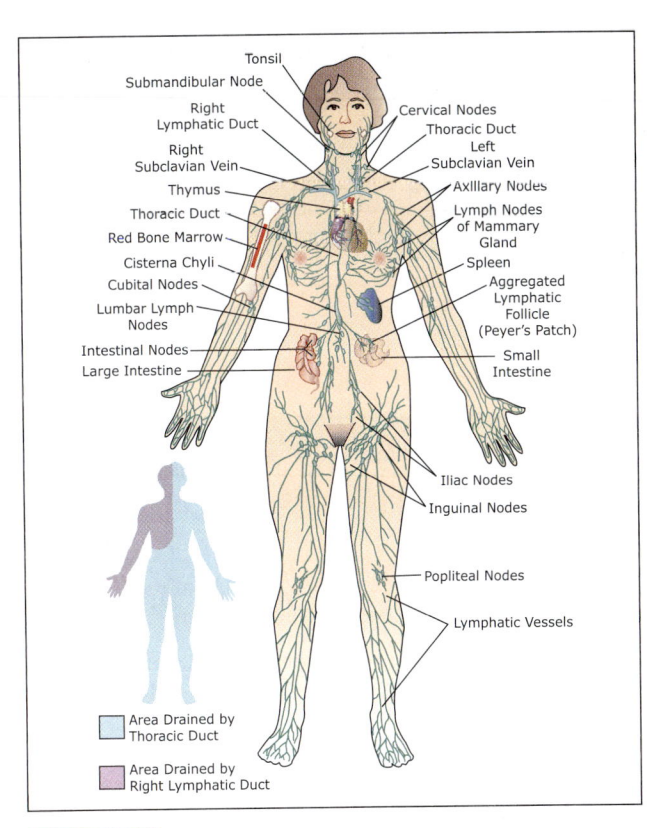

Figure 8-5 Lymphatic System.

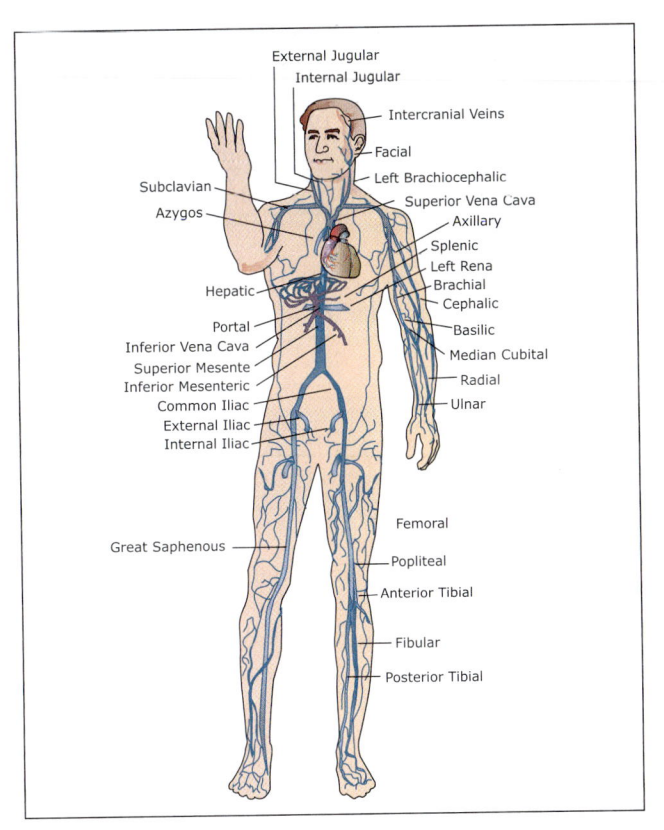

e. Contributes to immune system function; lymph nodes collect cellular debris and bacteria; remove excess fluid, blood waste, and protein molecules; and produce antibodies.
f. See Figure 8-5.

Neurohumoral Influences

1. Neural control of heart rate and blood vessels.
2. Parasympathetic control (cholinergic): cardioinhibitory center; slows rate and force of myocardial contraction; decreases myocardial metabolism; causes coronary artery vasodilation.
   a. A gradual decrease in heart rate is expected during the recovery phase following engagement in exercise or activity.
      (1) Abnormal, consistent decrease in heart rate (i.e., bradycardia) decreases the supply of oxygen-rich blood to the body.
      (2) Syncope, shortness of breath, angina, confusion, and decreased endurance can result.

   CAUTION: Monitoring vital signs to track changes in heart rate during interventions is required to ensure safety.

3. Sympathetic control (adrenergic): cardioaccelleratory center; causes an increase in the rate and force of myocardial contraction and myocardial metabolism; causes coronary artery vasoconstriction.
   a. A gradual increase in heart rate is expected during active engagement in exercise or other activities.
4. Additional control mechanisms.
   a. Baroreceptors: main mechanism controlling heart rate; respond to changes in blood pressure.
      (1) A rapid decrease in blood pressure could result in syncope.
   b. Chemoreceptors: sensitive to changes in blood chemicals (i.e., O_2, CO_2, lactic acid).
   c. Body temperature: heart rate changes analogously to temperature.
   d. Ion concentrations.
      (1) Hyperkalemia: increased potassium ions, decreases the rate and force of contraction, and produces ECG changes.
      (2) Hypokalemia: decreased potassium ions, produces ECG changes; arrhythmias, may progress to ventricular fibrillation.
      (3) Hypercalcemia: increased calcium concentration; increases heart rate.
      (4) Hypocalcemia: decreased calcium concentration; depresses heart action.

e. Peripheral resistance.
    (1) Increased peripheral resistance increases arterial blood volume and pressure.
    (2) Decreased peripheral resistance decreases arterial blood volume and pressure.
    (3) Influenced by arterial blood volume: viscosity of blood and diameter of arterioles and capillaries.

> **EXAM HINT:** The NBCOT® exam outline for the COTA® identifies knowledge of the "expected patterns, progressions, and prognoses associated with conditions that limit occupational performance" (NBCOT®, 2018, p. 21) as essential for competent and safe practice. The application of knowledge about the following conditions will be required to correctly answer COTA® exam items about working with persons with cardiovascular disorders.

▶ Coronary Artery Disease (CAD)

Definition

1. Atherosclerotic disease process that narrows the lumen of coronary arteries resulting in ischemia to the myocardium.

Atherosclerosis

1. Etiology.
    a. Disease of lipid-laden plaques (lesions) affecting moderate and large-size arteries.
    b. Characterized by thickening of the intimal layer of the blood vessel wall from the focal accumulation of lipids, platelets, monocytes, plaque, and other debris.
2. Onset: variable depending on presence or absence of risk factors.
3. Prevalence: increases with age and presence of risk factors.
4. Prognosis: good with early detection and treatment.
5. Multiple risk factors.
    a. Nonmodifiable risk factors: age, sex, race, significant family history of CAD.
    b. Modifiable risk factors: cigarette smoking, high blood pressure, elevated cholesterol levels, and low-density lipoprotein (LDL) levels, elevated blood homocystine, emotional stress.
    c. Contributory risk factors: diabetes, obesity, sedentary lifestyle, and elevated blood homocystine and fibrinogen levels.

> **CAUTION:** Two or more of the above risk factors increase the risk of CAD.

Main Clinical Syndromes of CAD

1. Characteristics.
    a. Involves a spectrum of clinical entities ranging from angina to infarction to sudden cardiac death.
    b. An imbalance of myocardial oxygen supply and demand resulting in ischemic chest pain.
    c. Subacte occlusion may produce no symptoms.
    d. Symptoms present when lumen is at least 70% occluded.
2. Angina pectoris: clinical manifestation of ischemia characterized by mild to moderate substernal chest pain/discomfort, most commonly felt as pressure or dull ache in the chest and left arm but may be felt anywhere in the upper body including neck, jaw, back, arm, epigastric area.
    a. Usually lasts less than 20 minutes due to transient ischemia.
    b. Represents an imbalance in myocardial oxygen supply and demand; brought on by:
        (1) Increased demands on heart: exertion/exercise, emotional upsets, smoking, extremes of temperature (especially cold), overeating, tachyarrhythmias.
        (2) Vasospasm: symptoms may be present at rest.
    c. Types of angina.
        (1) Stable angina: classic exertional angina occurring during exercise or activity; relieved with rest and/or sublingual nitroglycerin.
        (2) Unstable angina (preinfarction, crescendo angina): coronary insufficiency at rest without any precipitating factors or exertion; pain is difficult to control.

> **RED FLAG:** If chest pain increases in severity, frequency, and duration, there is an increased risk for myocardial infarction or sudden death (i.e., lethal arrhythmia).

        (3) Variant angina (Prinzmetal's angina): caused by vasospasm of coronary arteries in the absence of occlusive disease. Responds well to nitroglycerin or calcium channel blocker long term.

3. Myocardial infarction (MI): prolonged ischemia, injury, and death of an area of the myocardium caused by occlusion of one or more of the coronary arteries; results in necrosis of heart tissue.

> **EXAM HINT:** In the NBCOT® practice analysis for the COTA®, 29.8% of COTA®s who provided services to persons with cardiopulmonary disorders indicated they provided services to individuals with MIs (NBCOT®, 2018, p. 13). Due to this prevalence, it is likely that the exam will have items about working with persons recovering from MIs.

  a. Precipitating factors: atherosclerotic heart disease with thrombus formation, coronary vasospasm or embolism; cocaine toxicity.
  b. Presenting signs and symptoms.
     (1) Severe substernal pain of more than 20 minutes' duration which may radiate to neck, jaw, arm, and/or epigastric area.

> **CAUTION:** Pain may be misinterpreted as indigestion.

     (2) Dyspnea, rapid respiration, shortness of breath.
     (3) Indigestion, nausea, and vomiting.
     (4) Pain unrelieved by rest and/or sublingual nitroglycerin.
     (5) Women are more likely than men to experience the common symptoms of shortness of breath, nausea/vomiting, and back or jaw pain.

> **CAUTION:** Presenting signs in women may vary and are often mistaken as something else (e.g., the flu or acid reflux) and not a MI. These include:
> - Chest pain that is not severe or long-lasting but characterized by uncomfortable pressure, squeezing, fullness, or pain in the center of the chest that may persist for more than a few minutes or go away and come back.
> - Pain or discomfort in one or both arms, the back, neck, jaw, or stomach with or without chest pain.
> - Breaking out in a cold sweat and/or being lightheaded.

  c. Infarction sites.
     (1) Transmural (Q-wave infarction); full thickness of myocardium.
     (2) Nontransmural (non-Q wave infarction); subendocardial, subepicardial, intramural infarctions.
     (3) Coronary artery occlusion.
        (a) Inferior MI, right ventricle infarction, disturbances of upper conduction system: right coronary artery.
        (b) Lateral MI, ventricular ectopy: circumflex artery.
        (c) Anterior MI, disturbances of lower conduction system: left anterior descending artery.
  d. Results of impaired ventricular function.
     (1) Decreased stroke volume, cardiac output, and ejection fraction.
     (2) Increased end diastolic ventricular pressure.
  e. Electrical instability and arrhythmias, present in injured and ischemic areas.
4. Heart failure (HF).
  a. A clinical syndrome in which the heart is unable to maintain adequate circulation of the blood to meet the metabolic needs of the body.
  b. Etiology: may be caused by coronary artery disease, valvular disease, congenital heart disease, hypertension, infections.
  c. Physiological abnormalities: decreased cardiac output, elevated end diastolic pressures (preload); increased heart rate; impaired ventricular contractility.
  d. Types of heart failure.
     (1) Left-sided heart failure (congestive heart failure [CHF]): blood is not adequately pumped into systemic circulation.
        (a) Characterized by pulmonary congestion, edema, and low cardiac output due to backup of blood from left ventricle (LV) to the left atrium (LA) and lungs.
        (b) Occurs with insult to the left ventricle from myocardial disease; excessive workload of the heart (hypertension, valvular disease, or congenital defects); cardiac arrhythmias; or heart damage.

> **EXAM HINT:** In the NBCOT® practice analysis for the COTA® 59.8% of COTA®s who provided services to persons with cardiopulmonary disorders indicated they provided services to individuals with CHF (NBCOT®, 2018, p. 13). Due to this prevalence, it is likely that the exam will have items about working with persons recovering from and living with CHF.

     (2) Right heart failure: blood is not adequately returned from the systemic circulation to the heart.
        (a) Characterized by increased pressure load on the right ventricle (RV) with higher pulmonary vascular pressures.
        (b) Occurs with insult to the right ventricle (RV) from LV failure, mitral valve disease of chronic lung disease (or pulmonale); produces hallmark signs of jugular vein distension and peripheral edema.
     (3) Biventricular failure: severe LV pathology producing back up into the lungs, increased PA pressure, and RV signs of HF.

e. Associated symptoms: muscle wasting, myopathies, osteoporosis.
f. Possible clinical manifestations of heart failure. See Table 8-1.

Classification of Heart Failure

1. The New York Heart Association (NYHA) Functional Classification is the most commonly used classification system to assess the stage of heart failure.
    a. The NYHA places patients in one of four categories based on their functional capacity.
        (1) Functional capacity is how a patient with cardiac disease feels while engaged in physical activity.

> **EXAM HINT:** The NYHA classification relates symptoms to everyday activities and quality of life, and its categories describe functional limitations experienced during physical activity. The application of knowledge about the NYHA categories can be used to correctly answer COTA® exam items about implementing interventions based on "cardiopulmonary response, and current stage of recovery or condition in order to support occupational performance" (NBCOT®, 2018, p. 26), which has been identified as a key task for competent and safe practice in the NBCOT® exam outline for the COTA®.

2. NYHA categories.
    a. Class I: persons with cardiac disease but resulting in no limitation of physical activity.
        (1) Ordinary physical activity does not cause undue fatigue, palpitation, dyspnea, or angina pain.
    b. Class II: persons with cardiac disease resulting in slight limitation of physical activity. They are comfortable at rest.
        (1) Ordinary physical activity results in fatigue, palpitation, dyspnea, or angina pain.
    c. Class III: persons with cardiac disease resulting in marked limitation of physical activity. They are comfortable at rest.
        (1) Less than ordinary activity causes fatigue, palpitation, dyspnea, or angina pain.
    d. Class IV: persons with cardiac disease resulting in inability to carry on any physical activity without discomfort.
        (1) Symptoms of heart failure or the angina syndrome may be present even at rest. If any physical activity is undertaken, discomfort increases.
3. Objective assessment: based on measurements such as electrocardiograms, stress tests, x-rays, echocardiograms, and radiological images.
    a. Class A: No objective evidence of cardiovascular disease. No symptoms and no limitation in ordinary physical activity.

Table 8-1

Possible Clinical Manifestations of Cardiac Failure

LEFT VENTRICULAR FAILURE	RIGHT VENTRICULAR FAILURE
Signs and symptoms of pulmonary congestion:	
Dyspnea, dry cough	Dependent edema
Orthopnea	Weight gain
Paroxysmal nocturnal dyspnea (PND)	Ascites
Pulmonary rales, wheezing	Liver engorgement (hepatomegaly)
Signs and symptoms of low cardiac output:	
Hypotension	Anorexia, nausea, bloating
Tachycardia	Cyanosis (nail beds)
Lightheadedness, dizziness	Right upper quadrant pain
Cerebral hypoxia: irritability, restlessness, confusion, impaired memory, sleep disturbances	Jugular vein distension
Fatigue, weakness	Right-sided S_3 heart sounds
Poor exercise tolerance	Murmurs of pulmonary or tricuspid insufficiency
Enlarged heart on chest x-ray	
S_3 heart sound, possibly S_4	
Murmurs of mitral or bicuspid regurgitation	

b. Class B: Objective evidence of minimal cardiovascular disease. Mild symptoms and slight limitation during ordinary activity. Comfortable at rest.
c. Class C: Objective evidence of moderately severe cardiovascular disease. Marked limitation in activity due to symptoms, even during less-than-ordinary activity. Comfortable only at rest.
d. Class D: Objective evidence of severe cardiovascular disease. Severe limitations. Experiences symptoms even while at rest.

Medical and Surgical Management/Relevant Pharmacology

1. Diagnostic procedures.
   a. Chest x-ray: done to evaluate evidence of congestion in lungs, heart chamber hypertrophy, and structural abnormalities.
   b. Electrocardiogram (ECG): done to identify cardiac arrhythmias, assess amount and location of damage to myocardium, determine adequacy of oxygenation of myocardium.
   c. Holter monitor: records ECG signals over a 24-hour period while person engages in normal daily routine to determine heart function during various activities.
   d. Echocardiogram: ultrasound used to record size, structure, and motion of the heart and vessels; reveals valvular defects and structural abnormalities.
   e. Cardiac stress test: records cardiac activity during graded exercise; used to determine the extent to which cardiac disease affects functional capacity; provides guidelines related to the type and amount of physical activity that a person can engage in safely.
   f. Cardiac catheterization: invasive procedure used to visualize coronary circulation to determine the degree of CAD, congenital heart defect, valvular disease, myocardial damage.
   g. Pulmonary function test: used to determine cause of dyspnea, degree of lung disease; provides information related to endurance potential for functional activities.
2. Dietary and lifestyle interventions: healthy food choices, low-salt and low-cholesterol diets, physical activity, weight reduction, and smoking cessation.
3. Pharmaceutical interventions: medications designed to manage specific aspects of existing cardiovascular function or prevent or decrease the risk of cardiac events and the progression of related diseases; drugs aimed at reducing oxygen demand on the heart and increasing coronary blood flow; drugs may be prescribed alone or in combinations.
   a. Types of medications.
      (1) Nitrates/vasodilators (Isordil, minoxidil, nitroglycerin): relax blood vessels, increase blood flow and oxygen to heart, reduce cardiac workload; ease angina.
      (2) Angiotensin-converting enzyme (ACE) inhibitors (Capoten, Monopril, and Vasotec): decrease preload through peripheral vasodilation, reduce myocardial oxygen demand, improve blood flow; antihypertensive.
      (3) Angiotensin II receptor (ARB) inhibitors (Cozaar, Micardis): block effects of angiotensin to prevent blood pressure from rising; antihypertensive.
      (4) Beta-blockers (e.g., atenolol, Corgard, Inderal, metoprolol/Lopressor): reduce myocardial demand by reducing heart rate and contractility; control arrhythmias, chest pain; antihypertensive.
      (5) Calcium channel blockers (e.g., Cardizem, Norvasc, Procardia): inhibit flow of calcium ions; decrease heart rate, decrease contractility, dilate coronary arteries, act as antihypertensive, control arrhythmias, control angina.
      (6) Digitalis (cardiac glycosides): increase contractility and decrease heart rate; mainstay in the treatment of CHF (e.g., digoxin).
      (7) Diuretics (e.g., Esidrix, Lasix, Microzide): decrease myocardial work (reduce preload and afterload); antihypertensive.
      (8) Tranquilizers: decrease anxiety, sympathetic effects (e.g., drowsiness, decreased heart and respiration rate, decreased blood pressure).
      (9) Hypolipidemic agents (e.g., Colestid, Mevacor, and Zocor): reduce serum lipid levels when diet and weight reduction are not effective.
      (10) Anticoagulants: also known as blood thinners; work to prevent blood clot formation that may interfere with blood circulation or cause venous thrombosis; used to treat certain blood vessel, heart, and lung conditions; often prescribed to prevent first or recurrent strokes.
      (11) Antiplatelet agents: prevent platelets from forming clots; usually prescribed for unstable angina, after MI or transient ischemic attack, or as a preventative measure in early stages of coronary artery disease (e.g., aspirin, Plavix); dual antiplatelet therapy (DAPT) prescribes aspirin and another antiplatelet agent together.
   b. Medication implications for occupational therapy assessment and intervention.

> **CAUTION:** All medications have potential side effects. OTAs must be aware of the following potential negative impact(s) of medications on the person and respond accordingly.
> - Unusual symptoms during assessment or intervention may indicate an adverse drug reaction; the OTA must alert the cardiologist or attending physician if these occur.
> - For clients taking anticoagulants, the OTA should be aware of bruising or cuts; if a cut occurs, it may take longer to stop bleeding or require immediate medical attention.
> - Clients taking beta-blockers may not demonstrate the expected increase in heart rate or blood pressure during activity or exercise; therefore, the OTA should adjust expected parameters accordingly and utilize rate of perceived exertion scales as an indication of the effects of activity or exercise.

> **RED FLAG:** Combinations of medications could have an adverse effect on blood pressure during position changes (moving from supine to sit; sit to stand) and during activity; careful monitoring of vital signs during position changes is required.

4. Surgical interventions: surgical procedures often result in deconditioning and impact on the client's occupational performance.
   a. Angioplasty (percutaneous transluminal coronary angioplasty [PCTA]): under fluoroscopy, surgical dilation of a blood vessel using a small balloon-tipped catheter inflated inside the lumen.
      (1) Catheter is inserted into the femoral artery and guided through the arterial system into the coronary arteries.
      (2) Relieves obstructed blood flow in acute angina or acute MI.
      (3) Results in improved coronary blood flow, improved left ventricular function, anginal relief.
   b. Intravascular stents: an endoprosthesis (pliable wire mesh) implanted postangioplasty to prevent restenosis and occlusion in coronary or peripheral arteries.
   c. Revascularization surgery (coronary artery bypass grafting [CABG]): surgical circumvention of an obstruction in a coronary artery using an anastomosing graft (saphenous vein, internal mammary artery).
      (1) Multiple grafts may be necessary.
      (2) Results in improved coronary blood flow and left ventricular function, anginal relief.

> **CAUTION:** Surgery results in deconditioning that must be addressed.

   d. Transplantation: used in end-stage myocardial disease, e.g., cardiomyopathy, ischemic heart disease, valvular heart disease.
      (1) Heterotopic: involves leaving the natural heart and piggy-backing the donor heart.
      (2) Orthotopic: involves removing the diseased heart and replacing it with a donor heart.
      (3) Heart and lung transplantation: involves removing both organs and replacing them with donor organs.
      (4) Major problems post-transplantation: rejection, infection, complications on immunosuppressive therapy.
   e. Ventricular assistive devices (VADs).
      (1) Implanted device (accessory pump) that improves tissue perfusion and maintains cardiogenic circulation.
      (2) Used with severely involved patients (e.g., cardiogenic shock, unresponsive to medications, severe ventricular dysfunction; those awaiting heart transplant).
      (3) Often called the "bridge to transplantation."
5. Thrombolytic therapy for acute MI.
   a. Medications administered to activate body's fibrinolytic system, dissolve clot, and restore coronary blood flow (e.g., streptokinase, tissue plasminogen [TPA], urokinase).

Peripheral Vascular Disease (PVD)

1. Arterial disease.
   a. Occlusive peripheral arterial disease (PAD). See Table 8-2.
      (1) Chronic, occlusive arterial disease of medium- and large-sized vessels.
      (2) Associated with hypertension and hyperlipidemia; patients may also have CAD, diabetes, cerebrovascular disease, metabolic syndrome, history of smoking.
      (3) Diminished blood supply to affected extremities with pulses decreased or absent.
      (4) Early stages: patients exhibit intermittent claudication. Pain is described as burning, searing, aching, tightness, or cramping. Occurs regularly and predictably with walking and is relieved by rest.
      (5) Late stages: patients exhibit rest pain, muscle atrophy, trophic changes (hair loss, skin and nail changes).
      (6) Affects primarily lower extremities.
   b. Thromboangiitis obliterans (Buerger's disease): chronic inflammatory vascular occlusive disease of small arteries and also veins.

Table 8-2
Differential Diagnosis: Peripheral Vascular Diseases

	CHRONIC ARTERIAL INSUFFICIENCY	CHRONIC VENOUS INSUFFICIENCY	CHRONIC LYMPHATIC INSUFFICIENCY
Etiology	Atherosclerosis Thrombosis Emboli Inflammatory process	Thrombophlebitis Trauma Vein obstruction (clot) Vein incompetence	Primary lymphedema Secondary lymphedema
Risk factors	Age: >60 years Smoking Diabetes mellitus Gender: slightly higher in men Dyslipidemia Hypertension Hyperhomocysteinemia Race (African American)	Venous hypertension Varicose veins Inherited trait Gender: female Age Increased BMI Sedentary lifestyle/prolonged sitting Ligamentous laxity	Lymphadenectomy Radiation treatment Inflammatory arthritis Obesity
Signs and symptoms: determined by location and degree of vascular involvement			
Pain	Severe muscle ischemia/intermittent claudication Worse with exercise, relieved by rest Rest pain indicates severe involvement Muscle fatigue, cramping, numbness Paresthesias over time	Minimal to moderate steady pain Aching pain in lower leg with prolonged standing or sitting (dependency) Superficial pain along course of vein	Heaviness, tightness, aching, or discomfort
Location of pain	Usually calf, lower leg, or dorsum of foot May occur in thigh, hip, or buttock	Muscle compartment tenderness	Edematous limb
Vascular	Decreased or absent pulses Pallor of forefoot on elevation Dependent rubor	Venous dilatation or varicosity Edema: moderate to severe, especially after prolonged dependency	Rare complications unless severe and untreated edema
Skin changes	Pale, shiny, dry skin Loss of hair Nail changes Coolness of extremity	Hemosiderin deposition: dark, cyanotic, thickened, brown skin Lipodermatosclerosis: fibrosing of the subcutaneous tissue May lead to stasis dermatitis, cellulitis	Cutaneous fibrosis May lead to cellulitis, lymphangitis
Acute	Acute arterial obstruction: distal pain, paresthetic, pale, pulseless, sudden onset	Acute thrombophlebitis (deep venous thrombosis, DVT): Calf pain, aching, edema, muscle tenderness, 50% asymptomatic	Rarely acute, usually progressive over time except with changes in pressure to limb altering flow (repeated blood pressure measurements, airplane flights)
Ulceration	May develop in toes, feet, or areas of trauma; pale or yellow to black eschar, gangrene may develop; regular in shape and may appear punched out	May develop at sides of ankles, especially medial malleolus along the course of veins; gangrene absent; painful, shallow, exudative and have granulation tissue in the base; irregular borders	Unusual

Adapted from Bickley, L., & Szilagyi, P. G. (2003). *Bates' Guide to physical examination and history taking* (8th ed.). Philadelphia, PA: Lippincott Williams & Wilkins.

---

(1) Most common in young males who smoke.
(2) Begins distally and progresses proximally in both lower and upper extremities.
(3) Symptoms include pain, paresthesias, cold extremities, diminished temperature sensation, fatigue; risk of ulceration and gangrene.

c. Diabetic angiopathy: consistent and noncontrolled elevation of blood glucose levels and accelerated atherosclerosis; neuropathies are a major problem; ulcers and diabetic retinopathy are common outcomes.

CAUTION: Untreated ulcers can lead to gangrene and amputation. See Chapter 9 for information on the prevention and management of ulcers. Unmanaged diabetic retinopathy can result in blindness. See Chapter 5.

d. Raynaud's phenomenon: episodic spasm of small arteries and arterioles; abnormal vasoconstriction reflex exacerbated by exposure to cold or emotional stress; tips of fingers develop pallor, cyanosis, numbness, and tingling; affects largely females. See Chapter 9.

2. Venous disease.
   a. Varicose veins: distended, swollen superficial veins; tortuous in appearance; may lead to varicose ulcers.
   b. Superficial vein thrombophlebitis: clot formation and acute inflammation in a superficial vein; localized pain usually in saphenous vein.
   c. Deep vein thrombosis (DVT): inflammation of a vein in association with the formation of a thrombus; usually occurs in lower extremities.
      (1) Associated with venous stasis (e.g., bed rest, lack of leg exercise), hyperactivity of blood coagulation, and vascular trauma.
      (2) Early mobility (i.e., out of bed activities) after surgery helps to eliminate venous stasis.
      (3) DVY may be a contributing factor to or a complication of cerebral vascular accident (CVA) or the result of prolonged bed rest during serious illness.
      (4) Initially, rhe person may be asymptomatic.
      (5) Signs and symptoms include progressive inflammation with tenderness to palpation; change in lower extremity temperature, color circumference, appearance, or tenderness/pain.

   RED FLAG: DVT may be life threatening; thus, its symptoms require *immediate* medical attention.

   d. Chronic venous insufficiency (Table 8-2).
      (1) Characterized by chronic leg edema; skin pigmentation changes, scaly appearance, itchy.
3. Lymphedema.
   a. Chronic disorder with excessive accumulation of fluid due to obstruction of lymphatics.
   b. Causes swelling of the soft tissues in arms and legs.
   c. Results from mechanical insufficiency of the lymphatic system.
   d. Primary lymphedema: congenital condition with abnormal lymph node or lymph vessel formation (hypoplasia or hyperplasia).
   e. Secondary lymphedema: acquired, due to injury of one or more parts of the lymphatic system. Possible causes include:
      (1) Surgery: e.g., radical mastectomy, femoropopliteal bypass (femoral popliteal bypass), lymph node removal.
      (2) Tumors, trauma, or infection affecting the lymph nodes.
      (3) Radiation therapy with fibrosis of tissues.
      (4) Chronic venous insufficiency.
      (5) In tropical and subtropical areas, filariasis (i.e., nematode worm larvae in the lymphatic system).
   f. Initiating factors that can trigger lymphedema.
      (1) Inactivity and changes in cabin pressure during air flight.
      (2) Fluctuation in weight gain and fluid volumes.
      (3) Hyperemia.
      (4) Hypoproteinemia.
   g. Stages of lymphedema (progressive disease).
      (1) Stage 0, no visible changes in limb or upper body, may notice difference in feeling—mild tingling, unusual tiredness, or slight heaviness, may remain in this stage for months or years before obvious symptoms develop.
      (2) Stage 1, reversible lymphedema: limb is soft and pitting; swelling may increase overnight.
      (3) Stage 2, spontaneously irreversible lymphedema: swelling with increase in fibrotic tissue; risk for infection.
      (4) Stage 3, lymphostatic elephantiasis: extreme increase in swelling, skin changes (e.g., fibrosis, sclerosis, papillomas).
   h. See Table 8-3.

Table 8-3

Lymphedema Summary	
ETIOLOGY	Primary lymphedema: congenital Secondary lymphedema: occurs as a result of injury to lymphatic vessels (e.g., cancer surgery and/or radiation, chronic venous insufficiency) or parasitic infection (filariasis)
PROGRESSIVE OVER TIME	Without treatment, may develop into fibrosis, chronic infection (cellulitis, lymphangitis) or loss of limb function
SYMPTOMS	Heaviness, tightness or pain; swelling and persistent edema; loss of ROM and function in an arm or leg
SKIN CHANGES	Hardening and/or discoloration of skin
DIAGNOSIS	History, visual inspection and palpation, girth measurements Tests may include: MRI and CT scans; Doppler ultrasound, radionuclide imaging of the lymphatic system (lymphoscintigraphy)
STAGING	4 stage system: 0 – latent; 1 – spontaneously reversible; 2 – spontaneously irreversible; 3 – lymphostatic elephantiasis
TREATMENT	Complete decongestive therapy (CDT): Manual lymph drainage, short-stretch compression bandages, exercises, functional training, skin care, and lymphedema education.

Pulmonary System

Function

1. Respiration, delivers oxygen to cardiovascular system.
2. Removes carbon dioxide and other by-products from body.

Anatomy and Physiology

> **EXAM HINT:** In the NBCOT® exam outline for the COTA®, the task of recognizing the "influence of body functions and body structures . . . on a client's occupational performance" (NBCOT®, 2018, p. 21) is identified as essential for competent and safe practice. Thus, knowing the major structures and functions of the pulmonary system can help you correctly answer COTA® exam items about the functional implications of pulmonary dysfunction. For example, damage to the bronchioles and alveoli results in decreased gas exchange, compromised lung function, and signs and symptoms of chronic obstructive pulmonary disease (COPD).

1. Bony thorax: anterior border is the sternum, lateral border is the ribcage, posterior border is the vertebral column; shoulder girdle can affect the motion of the thorax. Musculoskeletal structures support the ability of the lungs to fully inflate during inspiration and deflate during expiration.
2. Airways.
   a. Upper airways: nose, pharynx, larynx.
   b. Lower airways: conducting airways (trachea to terminal bronchioles) and the respiratory unit (respiratory bronchioles, alveolar ducts, alveolar sacs, and alveoli).
3. Lungs.
4. Pleura.
5. Muscles of ventilation.
   a. Primary muscles of inspiration: diaphragm, intercostals.
   b. Accessory muscles of inspiration: used when a more rapid or deeper inhalation is required or in disease; include sternocleidomastoid, scalenes, levator costarum, serratus, trapezius, and pectorals.
   c. Expiratory muscles.
      (1) Resting expiration: done by passive relaxation of inspiratory muscles and elastic recoil tendency of lungs.
      (2) Expiratory muscles used when quicker, fuller expiration is desired or in disease; include quadratus lumborum, intercostals, rectus abdominis, triangularis sterni.
6. Mechanics of breathing: forces acting upon the rib cage include elastic recoil of lungs, bony thorax, muscles.
7. Ventilation and perfusion: the movement of gas in and out of the pulmonary system.
   a. Measurements include volumes, capacities, flow rates.
   b. Optimal respiration occurs when ventilation and perfusion (blood flow to lungs) are matched.
   c. Body position/gravity affects distribution of ventilation and perfusion. Breathing patterns and rate of respiration may change depending on the person's position.
8. Respiration: diffusion of gas across the alveolocapillary membrane.
9. Control of ventilation.
   a. Receptors: baroreceptors, chemoreceptors, irritant receptors, stretch receptors.
   b. Central control centers: brain and autonomic nervous system.
   c. Ventilatory muscles.

Pulmonary Dysfunction

> **EXAM HINT:** The NBCOT® exam outline for the COTA® identifies knowledge of the "expected patterns, progressions, and prognoses associated with conditions that limit occupational performance" (NBCOT®, 2018, p. 21) as essential for competent practice. The application of knowledge about the following clinical conditions will be required to correctly answer COTA® exam items about working with persons with pulmonary dysfunction.

Acute Diseases

1. Bacterial pneumonia: an intra-alveolar bacterial infection.
   a. Gram-positive bacteria usually acquired in the community; pneumococcal pneumonia (streptococcal) is the most common type.
   b. Gram-negative bacteria usually develop in a host who has an underlying chronic condition, acute

illness, recent antibiotic therapy; usually results in early tissue necrosis and abscess formation.
2. Viral pneumonia: an interstitial or interalveolar inflammatory process caused by viral agents (influenza, adenovirus, cytomegalovirus, herpes, parainfluenza, respiratory syncytial virus, measles).
3. Aspiration pneumonia: aspirated material causes an acute inflammatory reaction within the lungs; usually found in persons with impaired swallowing ability (dysphagia).

> **EXAM HINT:** In the NBCOT® practice analysis for the COTA®, 42.2% of COTA®s who provided services to persons with cardiopulmonary disorders indicated they provided services to individuals with pneumonia (NBCOT®, 2018, p. 13). Due to this prevalence, it is likely that the COTA® exam will have items about working with persons with and recovering from pneumonia.

4. Tuberculosis: see subsequent section.
5. Pneumocystis pneumonia (PCP): pulmonary infection caused by a fungus (*Pneumocystis carinii*) in immunocompromised hosts; most often found in patients following transplantation, neonates, those infected with HIV.
6. SARS (severe acute respiratory syndrome).
   a. An atypical respiratory illness caused by a coronavirus.

Tuberculosis (TB)[1]

1. Etiology: an airborne infection caused by a bacterium (*Mycobacterium tuberculosis*).
   a. People who have weakened immune systems are at greater risk for rapid onset of TB disease, such as people with:
2. Transmission and risk factors.
   a. A person with TB of the throat or chest can pass the infection by sneezing or coughing.

> **CAUTION:** People most at risk for infection are those who are in close contact with an infected individual on a daily/regular basis, including family members, neighbors, friends, co-workers, and health-care personnel.

   b. The risk for rapid onset of TB disease increases for persons with:
      (1) HIV/AIDS.
      (2) Substance abuse.
      (3) Diabetes.
      (4) Scoliosis.
      (5) Cancer of the head or neck.
      (6) Leukemia or Hodgkin's disease.
      (7) Severe kidney disease.
      (8) Low body weight.
      (9) Certain medical conditions receiving special treatments (e.g., steroid users or organ recipients).
   c. Infants, young children, older adults, and people who use intravenous drugs have a higher risk for TB.
   d. People who have had a TB infection within two years of treatment are at high risk for reinfection.
3. TB infection: People who breathe in TB bacteria and become infected may be able to fight the infection. The TB cells become inactive but remain alive in the body. TB-infected people:
   a. Are asymptomatic.
   b. Do not feel ill.
   c. Are not contagious.
   d. Do usually have a positive TB skin test.
   e. Can develop full-blown TB later, if they do not get drug treatment for the TB infection.
4. Signs and symptoms of TB.
   a. A bad cough for more than two weeks.
   b. Chest pain.
   c. Blood-tinged sputum or phlegm.
   d. Weakness or fatigue.
   e. Weight loss.
   f. Loss of appetite.
   g. Chills/fever.
   h. Night sweats.
5. Prevention, detection, and early intervention.
   a. Avoid high-risk situations that contribute to possible exposure.
      (1) Spending time with a person who is infected with TB.
      (2) Traveling to countries where TB is prevalent.
      (3) Residence in a setting where TB is common.
         (a) Homeless shelters.
         (b) Migrant farm residences.
         (c) Prisons and jails.
         (d) Some nursing homes.
   b. Get checked frequently (every one to two years) for TB by having a skin test if person has no history of a positive skin test.
   c. Get a chest x-ray if person is TB positive or if person was injected with BCG (a vaccine for TB that is given outside of the United States).
   d. Frequent checkups are essential if:
      (1) The immune system is impaired or weakened (e.g., due to HIV/AIDS, lupus, cancer, multiple sclerosis [MS]).
      (2) The person lives in an area of the United States where TB is common.

---

[1] This section was completed by Ann Burkhardt.

e. It takes 10–12 weeks after exposure to TB for a skin test to detect infection.
   (1) BCG vaccination can make a skin test appear positive. Individuals who were given BCG can still get TB infected.
      (a) If they become TB infected, they may have a large skin reaction.
   (2) Additional reasons individuals who have been vaccinated may become infected with TB.
      (a) Vaccination was many years before being skin tested.
      (b) Someone in their family has TB.
      (c) Their origin is from a country where TB is common.

6. Medical treatment.
   a. Drug therapy is frequently used to treat TB infection or prevention after an exposure.
   b. Persons who have TB disease may need to take several different drugs to effectively kill the bacteria.
   c. If a person stops taking the drugs before the prescribed interval, the drugs may become ineffective in fighting the infection.
   d. Development of multidrug-resistant TB (MDR TB) can occur.
   e. Types of drugs.
      (1) Isoniazid (INH) which must be taken for six months.
         (a) People with weakened or undeveloped immune systems may have to take INH longer.
         (b) All of the INH pills prescribed must be taken.
         (c) People on INH must see the doctor/nurse regularly, or they may develop a resistance to the drug therapy.
         (d) Side effects of INH therapy include loss of appetite, nausea, vomiting, jaundice, and fever lasting more than three days, abdominal pain, tingling in the fingers or toes.
         (e) A person receiving INH should avoid alcoholic beverages while receiving drug therapy.
      (2) Rifampin.
         (a) Side effects include orange tint to urine, saliva, or tears; inability to wear contact lenses; sun sensitivity.
         (b) Affects birth control pills and implants, rendering them ineffective.
         (c) Lessens effectiveness of methadone therapy for drug addiction.
      (3) Pyrazinamide.
      (4) Ethambutol.
      (5) Streptomycin.
   f. Serious side effects of all of the above drug therapies.
      (1) No appetite.
      (2) Nausea, vomiting.
      (3) Jaundice.
      (4) Fever lasting more than three days.
      (5) Abdominal pain.
      (6) Tingling in the fingers or toes.
      (7) Easy bruising.
      (8) Blurred vision.
      (9) Tinnitus, hearing loss.

7. Sequelae of TB.
   a. Once the infection settles into a person's lungs, it can spread to other parts of the body.
      (1) Kidney dysfunction can occur.
      (2) Spine: Rood's disease can occur, which is vertebral collapse caused by TB, resulting in compression of the spinal cord.

> **CAUTION:** Outcomes can include the following:
> - Compromised spinal structural integrity.
> - Cervical spinal lesions resulting in hand functional impairment, sensory impairment, postural changes.
> - Thoracic spinal lesions resulting in paraparesis, neurogenic bowel/bladder, altered mobility, and altered activities of daily living (ADL).
> - Space-occupying lesions in the brain resulting in stroke-like symptoms.

Chronic Obstructive Diseases

1. COPD: a disorder characterized by poor expiratory flow rates.
   a. Peripheral airways disease: inflammation of the distal conducting airways; association with smoking.

> **EXAM HINT:** In the NBCOT® practice analysis for the COTA®, 60.3% of COTA®s who provided services to persons with cardiopulmonary disorders indicated they provided services to individuals with COPD (NBCOT®, 2018, p. 13). Due to this high prevalence, it is likely that the COTA® exam will have items about working with persons living with COPD.

   b. Chronic bronchitis: chronic inflammation of the tracheobronchial tree with cough and sputum production lasting at least three months for two consecutive years.
   c. Emphysema: permanent abnormal enlargement and destruction of air spaces distal to terminal bronchioles; may result in destruction of acini, the functional units for gas exchange in the lungs.
      (1) Etiology: based on the assumption that there is an imbalance between protease and antiprotease enzymes.
         (a) Causes tissue breakdown, and antiprotease enzymes.

(b) Leads to loss of lung parenchyma, elastic recoil during exhalation, and normal airway resistance during inspiration.
(c) Results in airway dilation, premature airway closure, air trapping, and increased residual air volume or hyperinflation.
(2) Signs and symptoms: patients present with a mixture of clinical features. These include the following.
(a) Primary complaint of dyspnea on exertion.
(b) Diminished breath sounds, wheezing (typically associated with exertion).
(c) Prolonged expiratory phase.
(d) Pursed lip breathing.
(e) Physical presentation may include: enlarged anterior/posterior dimensions of the chest wall (barrel chest), hypertrophied accessory muscle from overuse, use of accessory muscles for breathing, forward leaning posture.
(f) Presence of a chronic cough and sputum production will vary and depend on the infectious history of the person.
(g) Disease advancement may result in patient becoming cachectic (emaciated), signs of right heart failure due to secondary pulmonary hypertension.
(3) Interventions.
(a) Smoking cessation.
(b) Short-acting and long-acting β2 agonists/bronchodilators.
(c) Anticholinergic drugs to block bronchoconstriction (e.g., Atrovent, Ventolin, Proventil, Maxair); not the first line of medications.
(d) Xanthine derivatives (e.g., theophylline) for bronchodilation, limitation of inflammatory response.
(e) Corticosteroids for anti-inflammatory effects.
(f) Preventive vaccination against influenza and pneumococcus.
(g) Oxygen therapy to:
- reduce level of dyspnea.
- improve/decrease maximal voluntary ventilation, polycythemia, by correcting hypoxemia.
- decrease pulmonary hypertension.
- improve quality and quantity of sleep.
- improve cognitive function and exercise tolerance.
(h) Surgeries may include bullectomy, volume reduction, lung transplantation.
(4) Prognosis: varies depending upon degree on obstruction, presence of hypercapnia (increased levels of CO_2), recurrence of infections, and development of right heart failure.

2. Asthma: an increased reactivity of the trachea and bronchi to various stimuli (allergens, exercise, cold).
   a. Etiology: unknown.
      (1) Factors associated with the development of asthma include maternal smoking, early infections (respiratory syncytial virus), and genetics.
   b. Risk factors: childhood asthma, family history, maternal smoking, occupational exposures, environmental exposure, exposure to secondhand smoke.
   c. Manifests by widespread narrowing of the airways due to inflammation, smooth muscle constriction, and increased secretions.
   d. Sign and symptoms: wheezing, dyspnea, chest pain, facial distress, nonproductive cough with acute exacerbation, where airways may become obstructed with vicious, tenacious mucus (more severe in children than adults).
      (1) Symptoms in adults may include paroxysmal nocturnal dyspnea, morning chest pain, and increased symptoms with exposure to cold.
   e. Intervention.
      (1) Prevention.
      (2) Smoking cessation and minimizing exposure to secondhand smoke for pregnant women.
      (3) Annual flu shot.
      (4) Avoidance of stimulants that precipitate asthmatic episode.
      (5) Use of short- and long-acting dilators.
      (6) Common medications: albuterol (e.g., Ventolin, Proventil), Atrovent w/albuterol, Combivent).
      (7) Establishment of a routine exercise program.
   f. Reversible in nature.
3. Cystic fibrosis (see "Pediatric Pulmonary Disorders" section.)
4. Hyaline membrane disease/respiratory distress syndrome. (See "Pediatric Pulmonary Disorders" section.)

Chronic Restrictive Diseases

1. Etiology varies.
2. Diseases are all characterized by difficulty expanding the lungs causing a reduction in lung volumes.
3. Restrictive disease due to alterations in lung parenchyma and pleura: fibrotic changes within the pulmonary parenchyma or pleura due to idiopathic pulmonary fibrosis, asbestosis, radiation pneumonitis, oxygen toxicity.
4. Restrictive disease due to alteration in the chest wall: restricted motion of the bony thorax, with diseases such as ankylosing spondylitis, arthritis, scoliosis, pectus excavatum, arthrogryposis, or the integumentary changes of the chest wall such as thoracic burns or scleroderma.
5. Restrictive disease due to alteration in the neuromuscular apparatus: decreased muscular strength results

in an inability to expand rib cage, seen in disease states such as MS, muscular dystrophy, Parkinson's disease, spinal cord injury, or CVA.

Carcinomas

1. Refer to Chapter 9.

Other Pulmonary Conditions

1. Pulmonary edema: excessive seepage of fluid from the pulmonary vascular system into the interstitial space; may eventually cause alveolar edema.
2. Pulmonary emboli: a thrombus from the peripheral venous circulation becomes embolic and lodges in the pulmonary circulation.
   a. Small emboli do not necessarily cause infarction.
3. Pleural effusion: excessive fluid between the visceral and parietal pleura, caused mainly by increased pleural permeability to proteins from inflammatory diseases (e.g., pneumonia, rheumatoid arthritis, systemic lupus), neoplastic disease, increased hydrostatic pressure within pleural space (e.g., congestive heart failure), decrease in osmotic pressure (i.e., hypoproteinemia), peritoneal fluid within the pleural space (i.e., ascites in cirrhosis), or interference of pleural reabsorption from a tumor invading pleural lymphatics.
4. Atelectasis: collapsed or airless alveolar unit, caused by hypoventilation secondary to pain during the ventilator cycle (due to pleuritis, postoperative pain, rib fracture), internal bronchial obstruction (e.g., aspiration, mucus plugging), external bronchial compression (e.g., tumor or enlarged lymph nodes), low tidal volumes (due to narcotic overdose, inappropriately low ventilator settings), or neurologic insult.

Occupational Therapy Cardiopulmonary Assessment

EXAM HINT: In the NBCOT® exam outline for the COTA®, Domain 01 Collaborating and Gathering Information comprises 28% of the exam. This domain focuses on the OTA's ability to "assist the OTR to acquire information regarding factors that influence occupational performance on an ongoing basis throughout the occupational therapy process" (NBCOT®, 2018, p. 18). The application of knowledge about the following assessment methods can help you correctly answer Domain 01 exam items about the evaluation of persons with cardiopulmonary disorders.

Role of the OTA

1. Contribute to the evaluation process in collaboration with the occupational therapist.
   a. The level of supervision required will be determined by the OTA's experience and established service competency.
   b. The OTA cannot independently evaluate or interpret evaluation results.
   c. The OTA can conduct specific assessments with OT supervision upon establishment of service competency.
2. The occupational profile obtains information from the person's medical record and interview to determine their medical and occupational history, activity patterns, roles, interests, values, priorities, needs, and desired outcomes.
   a. Medical record review.
      (1) Review current medical record and past medical history to learn about the onset of a cardiac incident and/or cardiopulmonary condition, past and current diagnoses, chronic and/or co-occurring conditions, medications, and prognosis.
         (a) The review of a person's medical record can provide insights into their premorbid status and current functional level.
         (b) This information can inform the occupational therapy evaluation process, assist with person-centered goal setting and intervention planning, and guide the selection of treatment modalities and activities.
      (2) Review diagnostic tests (see "Medical and Surgical Management" section).
         (a) Review results to determine implications for OT intervention including activity restrictions, vital sign parameters, and prognosis.
   b. Client interview.
      (1) Interview person and/or family member(s)/caregiver(s) to:
         (a) Establish client-centered priorities and outcomes through formal interview and casual conversation.
         (b) Establish rapport and foundation for therapeutic relationship with person and their family member(s)/caregiver(s).
      (2) Obtain social history.
         (a) Information used to determine implications for OT intervention including activity

selection, educational/learning needs, social supports, discharge needs.
- (b) Areas include educational history, vocational/avocational history, leisure pursuits and activities history, presence/absence of substance abuse, diet, family configuration, and social supports.
- (3) Discuss discharge environment and anticipated level of activity.
  - (a) Identify the physical and social aspects of the discharge environment to determine support and barriers to person's ability to engage in targeted occupations following the completion of OT services

3. Analysis of occupational performance.
   a. Identify the impact of presenting symptoms on occupational performance through the client interview and observation of performance.

> **EXAM HINT:** The NBCOT® exam outline for the COTA® identifies knowledge of the "expected patterns, progressions, and prognoses associated with conditions that limit occupational performance (and the) the impact of . . . body functions and body structures . . . on occupational performance" (NBCOT®, 2018, p. 21) as essential for competent and safe practice. The application of knowledge about the previously described types, causes, and symptoms of cardiopulmonary disorders and the following evaluation foci and approaches can help you effectively determine the correct answers to NBCOT® Domain 01 exam items about the evaluation of persons with cardiopulmonary disorders.

   b. Pain/angina: note location, severity, type. See Table 8-4.
   c. Dyspnea (i.e., shortness of breath): note severity, position, or times at which discomfort is experienced. See Table 8-5.
   d. Fatigue/perceived exertion: note severity, time of occurrence, association with activities.
   e. Palpitations: note person's awareness of heart rhythm abnormalities including pounding, fluttering, racing heartbeat, skipped beats.
   f. Dizziness: note time of occurrence and association with postural changes during activity.
   g. Edema.
      (1) Fluid retention may be identified by swelling, especially in the lower extremities, or sudden weight gain.
      (2) Note location, measurements, time of day when edema is most prominent, resolution with activity.

Vital Signs

1. Important and reliable indicator of activity tolerance/response to evaluation and treatment.
   a. See Table 8-6 for normal vital sign values for infants and adults.

Table 8-4

Intermittent Claudication Rating Scale

0	No claudication pain
1	Initial, minimal pain
2	Moderate, bothersome pain
3	Intense pain
4	Maximal Pain, cannot continue

Republished with permission of Human Kinetics from *Guidelines for cardiac rehabilitation and secondary prevention programs*. Williams, M. (Ed.). AACVPR. 4th ed., p. 81, 2004. Permission conveyed through Copyright Clearance Center, Inc.

Table 8-5

Common Angina and Dyspnea Rating Scales

5-GRADE ANGINA SCALE

0	No angina
1	Light, barely noticeable
2	Moderate, bothersome
3	Severe, very uncomfortable
4	Most pain ever experienced

5-GRADE DYSPNEA SCALE

0	No dyspnea
1	Mild, noticeable
2	Mild, some difficulty
3	Moderate difficulty, but can continue
4	Severe difficulty, cannot continue

10-GRADE ANGINA/DYSPNEA SCALE

0	Nothing
0.5	Very, very slight
1	Very slight
2	Slight
3	Moderate
4	Somewhat severe
5	Severe
6	
7	Very severe
8	
9	
10	Very, very severe Maximal

Republished with permission of Human Kinetics from *Guidelines for cardiac rehabilitation and secondary prevention programs*. Williams, M. (Ed.). AACVPR. 4th ed., p. 81, 2004. Permission conveyed through Copyright Clearance Center, Inc.

Table 8-6

Normal Values for Infants and Adults

PARAMETER	INFANT	ADULT
Heart Rate	120 bpm	60–100 bpm
Blood Pressure	75/50 mm Hg	<120/80 mm Hg
Respiratory Rate	40 br/min	12–20 br/min
PaO_2	75–80 mm Hg	80–100 mm Hg
$PaCO_2$	34–54 mm Hg	35–45 mm Hg
pH	7.26–7.41	7.35–7.45
Tidal Volume	20 mL	500 mL

   b. Must be monitored before activity, during activity, and after activity to ensure compliance with parameters.

> **CAUTION:** Possible side effects of medications must be reviewed and taken into account when monitoring vital signs.

2. Pulse/heart rate: rhythmical throbbing of arterial wall as a result of each heartbeat; influenced by force of contraction, volume and viscosity of blood, diameter and elasticity of vessels, emotions, exercise, blood temperature, and hormones.
   a. Assessment: done by palpation of peripheral pulses; with normal rhythm palpate 30 seconds; with irregular rhythm palpate one to two minutes; taken prior to activity, during activity, and after activity.
   b. Palpation sites.
      (1) Radial: most common monitoring site; radial artery, radial wrist at base of thumb.
      (2) Temporal: superior and lateral to eye.
      (3) Carotid: on either side of anterior neck between sternocleidomastoid muscle and trachea; best reflects cardiac function.
      (4) Brachial: medial aspect of the antecubital fossa; used to monitor blood pressure.
      (5) Femoral.
      (6) Popliteal.
      (7) Pedal.
3. Pulse/heart rate (HR) parameters:
   a. Normal adult HR is 70 beats per minute (bpm); range 60–100 bpm.
      (1) As an individual ages, the normal resting heart rate range may increase up to 100 bpm.
   b. Pediatric: newborn is 120 bpm; range 70–170 bpm.
   c. Tachycardia: greater than 100 bpm.
   d. Bradycardia: less than 60 bpm.
   e. Irregular: force and frequency vary; may be due to arrhythmia, myocarditis.
   f. Weak, thready pulse.
   g. Bounding, full pulse.
   h. Bruit: abnormal sound or murmur; associated with atherosclerosis.

4. Auscultation of heart: done with stethoscope to assess heart sounds. Note the addition of extra, abnormal heart sounds.
5. Blood pressure (BP).
   a. Monitor at rest, during evaluation/activity, after activity.
   b. Normal adult BP is <120/<80 mm Hg (systolic/diastolic); range between 110 and 140 systolic, 60 and 80 diastolic.
   c. Pediatric: 1 month—80 systolic, 45 diastolic; 6 years—105–125 systolic, 60–80 diastolic.
   d. Hypertension: BP above 120/80.
   e. Increased BP may be related to stress, pain, hypoxia, drugs, and disease.
   f. Decreased BP may be related to bed rest, drugs, arrhythmias, blood loss/shock, and MI.
   g. Orthostatic hypotension: a sudden drop in blood pressure that can occur with positional changes, especially from supine or sitting to standing.
      (1) Also called postural hypotension, it can cause dizziness, weakness, blurred vision, and syncope (i.e., fainting).
      (2) Orthostatic hypotension can occur after surgery, several days of bed rest, secondary to other conditions (e.g., Parkinson's disease, SCI), and as a side effect of medications.

> **CAUTION:** People at risk for orthostatic hypotension should be advised to move slowly when changing positions (e.g., standing up slowly after crouching to garden).

6. Respiration.
   a. Monitor at rest, during evaluation/activity, after activity.
   b. Rate and depth of breathing: normal is 12–18 breaths per minute.
   c. Auscultation of lungs/respiratory sounds.
      (1) Normal: soft, rustling sound heard throughout all inspiration and start of expiration.
      (2) Abnormal: crackles/rales.
         (a) Rattling, bubbling sounds; may be due to secretions in lungs.
         (b) Wheezes, whistling sounds.

Condition of Extremities

1. Diaphoresis: excessive sweating associated with decreased cardiac output.
2. Pulses: decreased or absent pulses associated with peripheral vascular disease (PVD). See Table 8-7.
3. Skin color and vascular status.
   a. Cyanosis: bluish color related to decreased cardiac output or cold; especially lips, fingertips, nail beds.

Table 8-7

Grading Scale for Peripheral Pulses

0	Absent pulse, not palpable
1+	Pulse diminished, barely perceptible
2+	Easily palpable, normal
3+	Full pulse, increased strength
4+	Bounding pulse

Table 8-8

Grading Scale for Edema

1+	Mild, barely perceptible indentation; <¼ inch pitting
2+	Moderate, easily identified depression; returns to normal within 15 seconds; ¼–½ inch pitting
3+	Severe, depression takes 15–30 seconds to rebound; ½–1 inch pitting
4+	Very severe, depression lasts for >30 seconds or more; >1 inch pitting

b. Pallor: absence of rosy color in light-skinned individuals, associated with decreased peripheral blood flow, PVD.
c. Rubor: dependent redness with PVD.
d. Temperature.
e. Skin changes: clubbing of fingernails; pale, shiny, dry, abnormal pigmentation; ulceration, dermatitis; gangrene.
f. Intermittent claudication: pain, cramping, fatigue occurring during exercise and relieved by rest, associated with PVD; pain is typically in calf.
g. Edema. See Table 8-8.

Mobility Assessment

1. Evaluation is ongoing during activity performance. The OTA contributes to the evaluation process to assess:
   a. Bed mobility.
   b. Transfers.
   c. Wheelchair mobility.
   d. Ambulation status.
2. The OTA observes and reports any overt signs/symptoms of distress, the optimal position(s) for activities, and the person's endurance.
3. Refer to Chapter 15.

Cognition

1. Evaluation determines the baseline of the person's ability to understand, process, retain, and apply information taught during rehabilitation.
2. The OTA contributes to the evaluation process to assess:
   a. Orientation.
   b. Memory.
   c. Concentration.
   d. Judgment.
3. Refer to Chapter 13.

Activities of Daily Living/Instrumental Activities of Daily Living

1. The OTA contributes to the evaluation process to assess:
   a. Self-care.
   b. Household management tasks.
   c. Leisure activities.
   d. Community activities.
   e. Note level of function and type of assistance required.
   f. Note level of dyspnea and angina reported during activities. See Table 8-5.
2. See Chapter 14 for more information on evaluation of ADL and instrumental activities of daily living (IADL).

Activity Tolerance

1. The OTA contributes to the evaluation process by:
   a. Observing activities and monitoring of vital signs (heart rate, blood pressure, respiration rate, rate of perceived exertion).
   b. Periodically monitoring dyspnea, angina, and claudication pain. See Tables 8-4 and 8-5.
   c. Periodically monitoring exertion.
      (1) Borg rate of perceived exertion: a self-report rating scale that ranges from no exertion at all (e.g., sitting or lying) to maximal exertion (e.g., hard work that is not advisable to engage in).
   d. Using metabolic equivalent levels (METs) to determine the energy expenditure required for activity performance. See Table 8-9.

EXAM HINT: When answering COTA® exam items about the use of METs during the assessment of a person's activity tolerance, remember that the person's current physical status and pattern of activities prior to the cardiac event must be considered to determine the correct answer.

Psychosocial Assessment

1. The OTA contributes to the evaluation process. The foci of assessment include:
   a. Overt signs and symptoms of depression, anxiety, and/or stress and the potential effects on the individual's ability to complete/engage in activities.

Table 8-9

Metabolic Equivalent Levels for Common Activities

MET LEVELS	ACTIVITIES OF DAILY LIVING (MET LEVEL)	INSTRUMENTAL ACTIVITIES OF DAILY LIVING (MET LEVEL)	LEISURE AND WORK ACTIVITIES (MET LEVEL)
<1.5 METs Very light activities	Grooming done by another person (1.3) Passive sexual activity, kissing, hugging (1.3)	Repairing clothing, sewing a button or a hem while seated (1.3) Wrapping a present while seated (1.3)	Keyboarding, writing, playing a low–key video game while seated (1.0) Reading (1.3) Knitting, crocheting (1.3)
1.5 to <3 METs Light activities	Eating, bathing while seated (1.5) Toileting, eliminating, seated or standing (1.8) Grooming, seated or standing (2.0) Showering, dressing/ undressing, hair styling in standing (2.5) Active sexual activity (2.8)	Light homemaking: washing dishes while standing, straightening a bed, preparing food (1.8–2.5) Loading/unloading washer and dryer, folding and hanging clothes (1.8–2.0) Ironing (1.8) Gardening, light (2.0) Putting away groceries (2.5) Mowing lawn with a rider mower (2.5)	Doing arts and crafts, seated (1.5–3.0), standing arts and crafts (2.5–3.0) Driving a car, motorcycle, golf power cart (1.5–3.0) Walking slowly around home, store, or office; up to 2.5 mph pace (2.0–2.8) Playing a musical instrument (2.0–2.5) Stretching (2.3) Physically active video gaming (2.3) Doing calisthenics (2.8) Playing pool, bowling (2.0–3.0)
3 to <6 METs Moderate activities		Sweeping, vacuuming, mopping interior floors (3.0–3.5) Making a bed and changing its linens (3.3) Preparing meals and cooking (3.5) Heavy cleaning: washing windows or a car, cleaning a garage (3.0–4.0) Pushing a wheelbarrow (220 lb. load) (3.0–4.0) Doing moderate yard work; raking, pruning, sweeping (4.0) Digging a garden (3.5–5.0) Mowing lawn with a walking power mower (5.5)	Walking, 3.0 mph to 4.0 mph (3.0–6.0) Cycling, 6 mph to 10 mph (3.0–6.0) Playing recreational sports; basketball, tennis, volleyball, archery, golfing while pulling a bag cart, fly fishing (3.0–4.5) Brick laying (3.0–4.0) General carpentry (3.6) Calisthenics, moderate; resistance training, 8–15 repetitions (3.5) Endurance promoting video gaming (3.8) Upper body exercise (4.3) Water aerobics and water exercise (5.3) Ice or roller skating, 9 mph (5.0–6.0) Canoeing, kayaking, 4 mph (5.0–6.0)
≥6 to 10 METs Vigorous activities		Doing vigorous yard work (6.0) Scrubbing a bathroom (6.5) Carrying heavy loads (7.5) Carrying groceries up stairs (7.5) Shoveling, 10 min./22lbs (6.0–7.0), 10 min./31lbs (8.0–9.0) Carrying boxes or furniture up stairs (9.0)	Walking very briskly, 4.5 mph (6.3) Jogging, 5.0 mph, and running at <6.0 mph (8.0–10.0) Cycling, 11 mph to 13 mph (6.0–10.0) Calisthenics, vigorous (8.0) Stair climbing, fast pace (8.8) Walking/hiking, up to steep grades with a backpack (7.0–9.0) Bicycling on flat land, light effort (6.0), moderate (8.0), fast pace (10.0) Swimming, leisurely (6.0), moderately (8.0) Competitive sports, i.e., skiing, soccer, tennis singles, badminton (6.0–8.0) Manual lawn mowing (6.0–7.0) Ice hockey (7.0–8.0) Canoeing, kayaking 5 mph (7.0–8.0)
10+ METs Very vigorous activities		Shoveling, 10 min./35lbs (6.0–7.0),	Cross country skiing, 5+ mph Running, 6 mph (10,0), 7 mph (11.5), 8 mph (13.5), 9 mph (15.0), 10 mph (17.0) Swimming, very vigorously (11.0)

References
American College of Sports Medicine. (2014). *ACSM's guidelines for exercise testing and prescription* (9th ed.). Baltimore, MD: Lippincott Williams & Williams.
Causey–Upton, R., Hatch, B.C., & Benthall, D.H. (2019). Cardiopulmonary conditions and treatment. In A.J. Mahle & A.L. Ward (Eds.), *Adult physical conditions: Intervention strategies for occupational therapy assistants* (pp. 680–681). Philadelphia: F.A. Davis.

b. Stress management, coping styles, and psychosocial, family/caregiver, and spiritual supports.
2. Refer to Chapters 10 and 13.

Environmental Assessment

1. Accomplished via a visit to the discharge environment and completion of an on-site assessment.
   a. May also be done via patient and/or family/caregiver self-report, which includes measurements and photos or videos of the environment.
2. The OTA contributes to the evaluation process. The foci of assessment include:
   a. Accessibility issues related to safety, risk for falls, environmental barriers in the discharge environment.
      (1) Barriers may include stairs, clutter, spatial limitations.
   b. Physical demands of the discharge environment, that is, presence of stairs, airborne irritants.
3. Refer to Chapter 15.

▶ Occupational Therapy Cardiopulmonary Rehabilitation

EXAM HINT: In the NBCOT® exam outline for the COTA®, "Domain 02 Selecting and Implementing Interventions comprises 55% of the exam. This domain focuses on the COTA®'s ability to "implement interventions under the supervision of the OTR in accordance with the intervention plan and level of service competence to support client participation in areas of occupation throughout the occupational therapy process." (NBCOT®, 2018, p. 18). The application of knowledge about the cardiopulmonary interventions described in the following section can help you effectively determine the correct answers to Domain 02 exam items that address intervention management for persons with cardiopulmonary conditions.

Phase 1: Inpatient Rehabilitation/Hospitalization Stage (Acute)

1. Begins when the patient is determined to be medically stable following the cardiac or pulmonary event (MI, CABG, angioplasty, valve repair/replacement, CHF, etc.).
   a. Typically, after 24 hours or until the patient is stable for 24 hours.
2. Program focus.
   a. Patient and family education regarding disease process and recovery.
      (1) Increase knowledge of energy conservation and work simplification principles and techniques. (see Chapter 11.)
      (2) Increase knowledge of the approximate metabolic cost of activities (Table 8-9).
   b. Improve ability to carry out self-care and low-level functional activities.
   c. Decrease anxiety.
   d. Promote risk factor modification: support smoking cessation and dietary modification efforts if warranted.
   e. Discharge to home.
3. Intervention.
   a. The OTA implements intervention with OT supervision.
      (1) During the implementation of intervention, the OTA informs the supervising therapist of any change in the individual's status and any other relevant information that may affect treatment.
   b. Initiated at bedside with a monitored, functional assessment of self-care and mobility.
   c. If person is pain free, exhibits no arrhythmia, and has regular pulse of 100 or less, an activity program is initiated.

CAUTION: Intense monitoring is required during activity, especially in the coronary care unit (CCU).

   d. Beginning activities at MET level = 1–2.
      (1) Bed mobility, static standing.
      (2) Transfer from bed to chair/bedside commode.
      (3) Bed bath, feeding, grooming at sink in sitting.
      (4) Active range of motion/warm-up exercises.
      (5) Wheelchair mobility/ambulation in room.
   e. All activities use energy conservation techniques. General principles of energy conservation and work simplification include:
      (1) Pace oneself.
      (2) Monitor body position during activities.

(3) Organize daily activities and work areas.
(4) Delegate responsibilities.
(5) See Chapter 11

EXAM HINT: The NBCOT® exam outline for the COTA® identifies knowledge of "technical level techniques and activities for promoting or improving . . . efficient breathing patterns during functional tasks to support engagement in occupation" (NBCOT®, 2018, p. 26) as essential for competent practice. Thus, the application of knowledge about the following techniques will be required to correctly answer exam items about working with persons with cardiopulmonary disorders.

f. Breathing exercises.
  (1) Specific training needed to establish OTA service competence.
  (2) Abdominal diaphragmatic breathing: strengthens diaphragm, decreases need to use neck and shoulder muscles, decreases energy required for activity.
  (3) Pursed lip breathing: controls respiratory rate; decreases rate of breathing, helps remove trapped air from lungs.
  (4) Techniques are done during all exercises and activities.
g. Vital signs (BP, HR, rate of respiration, oxygen saturation) and exertion scales are monitored prior to each activity, at peak of each activity, immediately upon cessation of activity, and four to five minutes postactivity.
h. Exertion scales are monitored prior to each activity, at the peak of each activity, 30 seconds before the cessation of activity, immediately upon cessation of activity, and three to five minutes post-activity.
  (1) To ensure the validity of the person's responses on exertion scales, clear and accurate instructions must be provided.
    (a) Occupational therapy practitioners must make sure that the person has a clear understanding of what the ratings mean (i.e., all ratings should reflect the person's perceptions of how the exercise is making them feel; how hard they are working to perform the exercise).
i. Adhere to activity guidelines and MET levels. See Table 8-9.
  (1) As the patient's activity tolerance improves, more strenuous, higher MET level activities are added in progression from basic ADL to IADL.

EXAM HINT: The most NBCOT® exam outline for the COTA® identifies knowledge of "clinical decision-making for implementing modifications to the intervention plan and prioritization of goals under the supervision of the OTR in response to physiological changes . . . of the client" (NBCOT®, 2018, p. 23) as essential for the competent management of the intervention plan. Thus, the application of knowledge about the following contraindications/precautions can help determine the correct answer to COTA® exam items about working with persons with cardiopulmonary disorders.

j. Adhere to any contraindications/precautions as per physician orders.
  (1) Observe/monitor for shortness of breath (SOB), chest pain, nausea, vomiting, dizziness, and/or fatigue.
  (2) Adhere to activity guidelines and MET levels. See Table 8-9.
  (3) Observe for decrease in systolic BP greater than 20 mm Hg.
  (4) Observe facial expression; be alert to facial changes.
  (5) Monitor heart rate (some facilities have specific guidelines).
    (a) Max HR 100 very light activity—very high risk.
    (b) Max HR 120 light activity—less than six weeks after MI, surgery.
    (c) Max HR 130 recent bypass surgery, cardiomyopathy, CHF.
    (d) Target HR 60%–80% patient's maximum HR—treadmill test.
  (6) Monitor BP also for resting systolic BP <120 mmHg; dystolic 80 mmHg.
  (7) Monitor oxygen saturation (O_2 sat); below 86% for pulmonary patients, below 90% for cardiac patients.
  (8) Monitor exertion scales for signs and symptoms of distress during activity, speed of recovery. See Tables 8-4 and 8-5.

CAUTION: The following precautions should be followed
- Avoid isometric muscle work, straining, breath holding (Valsalva).
- Avoid overhead exercises or holding UEs over head for extensive time periods.
- Avoid lateral arm movements and exercises that stretch chest and pull incision.

> **RED FLAG:** There are clinical signs/symptoms and diagnoses for which therapy is contraindicated and should not be implemented. These include uncontrolled atrial/ventricular arrhythmias, recent embolism/thrombophlebitis, dissecting aneurysm, severe aortic stenosis, acute systemic illness, acute MI, digoxin toxicity, acute hypoglycemia or metabolic disorder, third-degree heart block, and unstable angina.

   k. Patients are generally discharged to Phase 2 when they are able to carry out activities at MET level 3.5. See Table 8-9.
      (1) MET tables should be used as a general reference to determine the approximate level of energy required to perform an activity.
      (2) MET levels are used to quantify the amount of energy required to perform an activity and to provide practitioners with a guideline for grading activities used in treatment.
         (a) Selection of activities based on MET level must take into consideration the patient's physical status and activity patterns prior to the cardiac or pulmonary event, as well as the patient's subjective report of level of exertion during activity performance.
   l. Educate individual about heart disease and the recovery process, provide emotional support.
4. Length of stay 5–14 days in the hospital.
   a. Commonly 3–5 days for uncomplicated MI (no post-MI angina, malignant arrhythmias, or heart failure).
   b. Continued inpatient services may be required in a transitional setting for up to six weeks post cardiac event, surgery, or pulmonary disease exacerbation.

> **RED FLAG:** The contraindications for inpatient cardiac rehabilitation and adverse responses to inpatient exercise leading to exercise termination must be considered. See Box 8-1.

   c. Box 8-2 identifies the possible outcomes of cardiac rehabilitation.

Phase 2: Outpatient Rehabilitation/Convalescence Stage (Subacute)

1. Begins as early as 24 hours after discharge from the hospital.
   a. Frequency of visits depends on the clinical needs of the patient.
2. Program focus.
   a. Educate person on the importance of continued exercise.
   b. Build up activity tolerance.

BOX 8-1 ▷ Contraindications for Inpatient and Outpatient Cardiac Rehabilitation

Absolute Contraindications

- Acute MI (within 2 days)
- Unstable angina not previously stabilized by medical therapy
- Uncontrolled cardiac arrhythmias causing symptoms or hemodynamic compromise
- Acute PE or pulmonary infarction
- Acute myocarditis or pericarditis
- Acute aortic dissection

Relative Contraindications

- Left main coronary stenosis
- Moderate stenotic valvular heart disease
- Electrolyte abnormalities
- Severe arterial hypertension
- Tachyarrhythmias or bradyarrhythmias
- Hypertrophic cardiomyopathy and other forms of outflow tract obstruction
- Mental or physical impairment leading to inability to exercise adequately
- High-degree atrioventricular block

> **BOX 8-2 ○ Possible Effects of Physical Training/Cardiac Rehabilitation**
>
> - Decreased HR at rest and during exercise; improved HR recovery after exercise
> - Increased stroke volume
> - Increased myocardial oxygen supply and myocardial contractility; myocardial hypertrophy
> - Improved respiratory capacity during exercise
> - Improved functional capacity of exercising muscles
> - Reduced body fat, increased lean body mass; successful weight reduction requires multifactorial interventions
> - Decreased serum lipoproteins (cholesterol, triglycerides)
> - Improved glucose tolerance
> - Improved blood fibrinolytic activity and coagulability
> - Improvement in measures of psychological status and functioning: self-confidence and sense of well-being
> - Increased participation in exercise; improved outcomes with adherence to rehabilitation programming
>   - Decreased angina in patients with CAD: anginal threshold is raised secondary to decreased myocardial oxygen consumption
>   - Reduced total and cardiovascular mortality in patients following myocardial infarction
>   - Decreased symptoms of heart failure, improved functional capacity in patients with left ventricular systolic dysfunction
>   - Improved exercise tolerance and function in patients with cardiac transplantation

    c. Improve ability to carry out IADL and community tasks.
    d. Improve ability to perform work activities.
    e. Support person's efforts in smoking cessation and lifestyle changes as needed.
3. Evaluation and Intervention.
    a. The OTA implements intervention with OT supervision.
    b. Intervention foci include:
       (1) Home evaluation.
       (2) Consumer and family education.
       (3) Graded exercise program with slow and gradual increase of weight.
       (4) Begin with activities at MET level 4 - 5, gradually increasing as person's tolerance improves.
       (5) Resumption of sexual activity, usually at 5 - 6 MET level as per physician.
       (6) Practice of functional activities in the discharge environment.
       (7) Use of energy conservation techniques and compensatory techniques in daily tasks.
       (8) Community activities.
       (9) Work site evaluation if applicable.
    c. The OTA needs to establish service competence to monitor status.
    d. The OTA observes and reports any overt signs/symptoms of distress, the optimal position(s) for activities and the person's endurance.
4. Length of outpatient program is dependent upon several factors, including person's physical and mental status postevent and/or surgery, progress through MET levels, activity tolerance, and prognosis.
5. The contraindications provided in Box 8-1 and the effects provided in Box 8-2 are applicable to outpatient cardiac rehabilitation.

Phase 3: Maintenance/Training Stage (Community Exercise Programs)

1. Patients generally attend maintenance/training sessions once a week following the completion of Phase 2.
2. Groups may be integrated into individual exercise programs.
3. OT intervention is provided as necessary for IADL, leisure pursuits, and work.
4. Maintenance gym program.
    a. Weight training to maintain upper and lower body strength.
    b. Cardiovascular training to maintain cardiopulmonary health.
5. See Table 8-10 for the recommended continuum of care for cardiac rehabilitation services and lifelong maintenance.

Rehabilitation Guidelines for Lymphatic Disease

1. Occupational therapy evaluation tools and foci.
    a. Occupation-based assessments to determine impact on occupational performance.

Table 8-10

Recommended Continuum of Care for Cardiac Rehabilitation

WEEKS													
0	1	2	3	4	5	6	7	8	9	10	11	12	Beyond

- Inpatient—hospital clinical pathway (weeks 0–1)
- Transitional care—subacute facility, home care, pretraining at home (weeks 1–4)
- Outpatient programming—cardiac rehabilitation center (weeks 3–8)
- Maintenance, lifelong—community facility or at home (weeks 6–Beyond)

Republished with permission of Human Kinetics from *Guidelines for cardiac rehabilitation and secondary prevention programs*. Williams, M. (Ed.). AACVPR. 4th ed., p. 32, 2004. Permission conveyed through Copyright Clearance Center, Inc.

---

b. Biomechanical assessments: upper extremity ROM and manual muscle testing (MMT), pain, activity tolerance, endurance, and edema.
  (1) Measurement of lymphedema swelling: circumferential girth measurement.
    (a) The volumeter is the best objective measurement tool.
    (b) The time of day when measurements are taken should be recorded.
  (2) See Chapter 11 for more information about biomechanical assessments.

> **EXAM HINT:** In the NBCOT® exam outline for the COTA®, "Domain 01 Collaborating and Acquiring Information (to) assist the OTR to acquire information regarding factors that influence occupational performance on an ongoing basis throughout the occupational therapy process." (NBCOT®, 2018, p. 18) and "Domain 02 Selecting and Implementing Interventions (to) implement interventions under the supervision of the OTR in accordance with the intervention plan and level of service competence to support client participation in areas of occupation throughout the occupational therapy process" (NBCOT®, 2018, p. 18) comprise 28% and 55% of the exam, respectively. The application of knowledge about the preceding evaluation foci and tools and the following interventions can help you effectively determine the correct answers to exam items that address OT evaluation and interventions for persons with lymphatic disease.

2. Occupational therapy intervention.
  a. Phase I management: edema secondary to lymphatic dysfunction.
    (1) Short-stretch compression bandages, worn 24 hours/day.
      (a) These provide slow resting pressure and high working pressure to enhance lymphatic return at rest, improve activity of lymphatic system, and facilitate return during muscle pumping activities.
    (2) Manual lymph drainage (MLD) with complete decongestive therapy.
      (a) Massage and passive range of motion (PROM) to assist lymphatic flow.
      (b) Emphasis on decongesting proximal segments first (trunk quadrant), then extremities, directing flow distal to proximal.
      (c) Compression using multilayered padding and short-stretch bandages.
    (3) Exercise; stretching and low-to-moderate intensity aerobic exercise combined with rest; tai chi, yoga, movement to support lymphatic drainage.

> **RED FLAG:** Strenuous activities, jogging, ballistic movements, and rotational motions are contraindicated, as they are likely to exacerbate lymphedema.

   (4) Relaxation, deep-breathing, and energy conservation/work simplification techniques to address stress, pain, fatigue, and breathing.
   (5) Custom compression garments; provided once limb reduction plateaus (four to six months).
   (6) Referral to a certified lymphedema therapist.
  b. Occupation-based interventions.
    (1) Engagement in ADL, IADL, work, and leisure activities with adaptations, if needed.
    (2) Energy conservation techniques to minimize exacerbation of swelling.
  c. Patient and family education.
    (1) Skin care, donning and doffing compression garments, environmental modifications to improve mobility and function.
    (2) Psychosocial issues including stress, distress, depression, anxiety.
3. Phase II intervention; self-management and daily home program.
  a. Skin care.
  b. Compression bandages.
  c. Exercise.
  d. Lymphedema bandaging at night.

e. MLD as needed.
f. Compression pumps: use with caution; limited benefits.

> **RED FLAG:** Pressures >45 mm Hg are contraindicated.

4. Education.
   a. Skin and nail care.
   b. Self-bandaging, garment care.
   c. Infection management.
   d. Maintain exercise while preventing lymph overload.
   e. Incorporation of home management program into daily routine.

Basic Life Support (BLS) and Cardiopulmonary Resuscitation (CPR)

> **RED FLAG:** If a person appears to be experiencing cardiac arrest (as evident by a sudden loss of responsiveness and/or no normal breathing), this is a medical emergency and the practitioner must call 911 *immediately* and implement and maintain CPR until emergency personnel arrive.

1. Current CPR guidelines.
   a. Compressions come first; then focus on airway and breathing (CAB). Only exception is a newborn babies.
   b. No more looking, listening, and feeling. Call 911 immediately.
   c. Push a little harder for adult CPR: at least two inches deep on chest.
   d. Push a little faster: about 100 compressions/minute.
   e. Hands-only CPR for untrained lay rescuers.
   f. Do not stop pushing, no interruptions.
   g. See Figure 8-6 and Table 8-11.

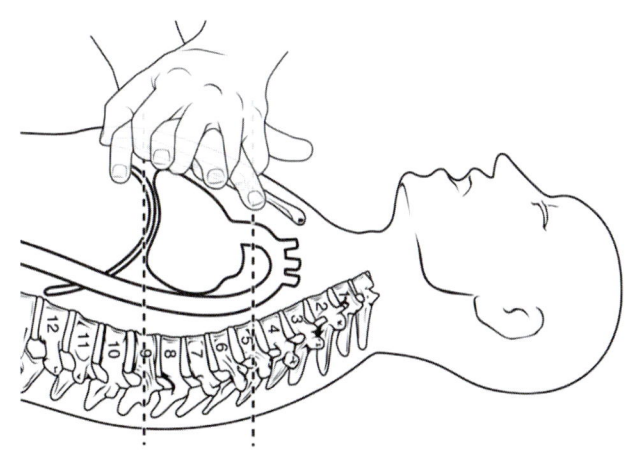

Figure 8-6 CPR Technique.

First Aid

> **EXAM HINT:** The NBCOT® exam outline for the COTA® identifies knowledge of "basic first aid in response to minor injuries and adverse reactions" (NBCOT®, 2018, p. 29) as essential for competent practice. Thus, the application of knowledge about the following techniques will be required to correctly answer COTA® exam items about responding to situations that require the OT practitioner to administer first aid (e.g., a person accidentally incurs a cut during a cooking activity).

1. External bleeding.
   a. Minor bleeding.
      (1) Usually clots within 10 minutes.

> **CAUTION:** If a person is taking aspirin or nonsteroidal anti-inflammatory drugs (NSAIDS), clotting may take longer.

   b. Severe bleeding characteristics.
      (1) Blood spurting from a wound.
      (2) Blood fails to clot even after measures to control bleeding have been taken.
      (3) Arterial bleed: high pressure, spurting, red.
      (4) Venous bleed: low pressure, steady flow, dark red or maroon blood.
      (5) Capillary bleed: low pressure, oozing, dark red blood.
   c. Controlling external bleeding.
      (1) Use standard precautions such as wearing gloves. See Appendix 3-A in Chapter 3.
      (2) Apply gauze pads using firm pressure. If no gauze available, use a clean cloth, towel, a gloved hand, or person's own hand. If blood soaks through, do not remove any gauze, add additional layers.
      (3) Elevate the part if possible unless it is anatomically misaligned or it causes significant pain when elevated.
      (4) Apply a pressure bandage, such as roller gauze, over the gauze pads.
      (5) If necessary, apply pressure with the heel of your hand over pressure points. The femoral artery in the groin and the brachial artery in the medial aspect of the upper arm are two such points.
      (6) Monitor A, B, Cs, and overall status of the patient. Administer supplemental oxygen if nearby. Seek more advanced care as necessary.
2. Internal bleeding.
   a. The possible result of a fall, blunt force trauma, or a fracture rupturing a blood vessel or organ.

Table 8-11

Summary of Key Basic Life Support (BLS) Components for Adults, Children, and Infants

COMPONENT	ADULTS	CHILDREN	INFANTS
Recognition	Unresponsive (all ages) No breathing, not breathing normally (e.g., only gasping)	Same as for adults	Same as for adults
CPR Sequence	CAB	CAB	CAB (ABC for neonates)
Compression Rate	At least 100/minute	Same as for adults	Same as for adults
Compression Depth	At least 2 inches (5 cm)	At least 1/3 AP depth, about 2 inches (5 cm)	At least 1/3 AP depth, about 1½ inches (4 cm)
Chest Wall Recall	Allow complete recoil between compressions, HCPs rotate compressors every 2 minutes	Same as for adults	Same as for adults
Compression Interruption	30:2 (1 or 2 rescuers)	30:2 single rescuer, 15:2 2 HCP rescuers	30:2 single rescuer, 15:2 2 HCP rescuers
Airway	Head tilt-chin lift (HCP suspected trauma: jaw thrust)	Same as for adults	Same as for adults
Compression-to-Ventilation Ratio (until advanced airway placed)	30:2 (1 or 2 rescuers)	30:2 single rescuer or 15:2 2 HCP rescuers	30:2 single rescuer or 15:2 2 HCP rescuers
Ventilations: when rescuer untrained or trained and not proficient	Compressions only	Compressions only	Compressions only
Ventilations with Advanced Airway (HCP)	One breath every 6–8 seconds (8–10 breaths/min) Asynchronous with chest compressions About 1 second per breath Visible chest rise	Same as for adults	Same as for adults
Defibrillation	Attach and use AED as soon as available. Minimize interruptions in chest compressions before and after shock, resume CPR, beginning with compressions immediately after each shock	Same as for adults	Same as for adults

Key: ABC, airway, breathing, compression; AED, automatic electronic defibrillator; CAB, compressions, airway, breathing; CPR, cardiopulmonary resuscitation; HCP, health-care provider.
From 2010 American Heart Association Guidelines for CPR and ECG. Downloaded from circ.ahajournals.org on July 5, 2011.

> **RED FLAG:** Severe internal bleeding may be life threatening. Knowledge of the following signs/characteristics of severe internal bleeding is essential to effectively manage internal bleeding and ensure emergency medical care is obtained, if needed.

   b. Severe internal bleeding signs/characteristics.
      (1) Ecchymosis (black and blue) in the injured area.
      (2) Body part, especially the abdomen, may be swollen, tender, and firm.
      (3) Skin may appear blue, gray, or pale and may be cool or moist.
      (4) Respiratory rate is increased.
      (5) Pulse rate is increased and weak.
      (6) Blood pressure is decreased.
      (7) Patient may be nauseated or vomit.
      (8) Patient may exhibit restlessness or anxiety.
      (9) Level of consciousness may decline.
   c. Management of internal bleeding.
      (1) If minor, follow RICE procedure: rest, ice, compression, elevation.
      (2) Major internal bleeding.
         (a) Summon advanced medical personnel.
         (b) Monitor A, B, Cs, and vital signs.
         (c) Keep the person comfortable and quiet. Keep the person from getting chilled or overheated.

(d) Reassure the person.
   (e) Administer supplemental oxygen if available and nearby.
3. Shock (hypoperfusion).
   a. Failure of the circulatory system to perfuse (i.e., supply) vital organs.
   b. At first, blood is shunted from the periphery to compensate.
      (1) The victim may lose consciousness as the brain is affected.
      (2) The heart rate increases, resulting in increased oxygen demand.

RED FLAG: Organs ultimately fail when deprived of oxygen. Heart rhythm is affected, ultimately leading to cardiac arrest and death. Knowledge about the types, causes, signs, and symptoms of shock is essential to effectively recognize shock, provide needed care, and obtain emergency medical care.

   c. Types and causes of shock.
      (1) Hemorrhagic: severe internal or external bleeding.
      (2) Psychogenic: emotional stress causes blood to pool away from the brain.
      (3) Metabolic: loss of body fluids from heat or severe vomiting or diarrhea.
      (4) Anaphylactic: allergic reaction to drugs, food, or insect stings.
      (5) Cardiogenic: MI or cardiac arrest results in pump failure.
      (6) Respiratory: respiratory illness or arrest results in insufficient oxygenation of the blood.
      (7) Septic: severe infections cause blood vessels to dilate.
      (8) Neurogenic: traumatic brain injury (TBI), spinal cord injury (SCI), or other neural trauma causes disruption of autonomic nervous system resulting in disruption of blood vessel dilation/constriction.
   d. Signs and symptoms.
      (1) Pale, gray, or blue, cool skin.
      (2) Increased, weak pulse.
      (3) Increased respiratory rate
      (4) Decreased blood pressure.
      (5) Irritability or restlessness.
      (6) Diminishing level of consciousness.
      (7) Nausea or vomiting.
   e. Care for shock.
      (1) Obtain history if possible.
      (2) Examine the person for airway, breathing, circulation, and bleeding.
      (3) Assess level of consciousness.
      (4) Determine skin characteristics and perform capillary refill test of fingertips.
         (a) Capillary refill test: squeeze fingernail for two seconds.
         (b) In healthy individuals, the nail will blanch and turn pink when pressure is released.
         (c) If nail bed does not refill and turn pink within two seconds, the cause could be that blood is being shunted away from the periphery to vital organs to maintain core temperature.
      (5) Treat any specific conditions if possible, e.g. control bleeding, splint a fracture, use an EpiPen for anaphylaxis.
      (6) Keep the person from getting chilled or overheated.
      (7) Elevate the legs 12 inches unless there is suspected spinal injury or painful deformities of the lower extremities.
      (8) Reassure the person and continue to monitor A, B, Cs.
      (9) Administer supplemental oxygen if nearby.
      (10) Do not give any food or drink.

Pediatric Pulmonary Disorders[2]

Cystic Fibrosis (CF)

1. Etiology.
   a. Genetically inherited autosomal recessive trait, gene mutation.
   b. Both parents must be carriers. Neither parent will have the disease.

2. Prevalence and prognosis.
   a. 30,000 children and adults in the United States (70,000 worldwide).
   b. Currently, individuals with CF can expect to live into their 30s and 40s, and beyond.
3. Diagnosis.
   a. Chronic, progressive lung disease (production of abnormal mucus).
   b. Salt concentration in the sweat.
   c. Decreased release of certain enzymes by the pancreas.

---

[2] This section was completed by Marge E. Moffett Boyd and Jan G. Garbarini.

d. Certain abnormalities revealed on x-rays.
   e. Failure to grow properly.
4. Complications.
   a. Reduced life expectancy.
      (1) The abnormal mucous clogs the lungs and leads to life-threatening lung infections.
      (2) The mucous obstructs the pancreas and stops natural enzymes from helping the body break down and absorb food.
   b. Cardiac symptoms are a possible complication of CF.
   c. Diabetes, cirrhosis, and rectal prolapse are rare complications of CF.
   d. 10%–20% of children with CF present with intestinal blockage.
5. Medical management/relevant pharmacology.
   a. Aerosol (mist).
   b. Chest physical therapy to loosen secretions that block lung airways.
   c. Vitamin and mineral supplements, enzymes.
   d. Antibiotics.
6. Effect on function.
   a. Exercise intolerance.
   b. Poor nutrition due to malabsorption may contribute to developmental delays.

Respiratory Distress Syndrome (RDS)

1. Etiology.
   a. Premature birth.
   b. Insufficient production of surfactant to keep alveoli (air pockets of the lungs) open.
2. Diagnosis.
   a. Lungs collapse after each breath.
   b. X-ray of lungs reveals 'ground glass' appearance.
   c. Collapsed alveoli are dense and appear white on the x-ray as opposed to the black appearance on an x-ray of air-filled alveoli.
   d. RDS is also called hyaline membrane disease (HMD).
3. Prenatal management.
   a. To stimulate surfactant production and to reduce the risk of RDS, the mother is treated prophylactically with steroid medication 24–36 hours before delivery of a premature infant.
4. Medical management/relevant pharmacology.
   a. Mild case.
      (1) Supplemental oxygen alone or in combination with positive airways pressure (CPAP), a mixture of oxygen and air provided under pressure through short, two-pronged tubes placed in the nose.
   b. Severe case.
      (1) Intubation and a mixture of oxygen and air provided by a ventilator under positive end-expiratory pressure (PEEP).
   c. To reduce the severity of RDS and the risk of chronic lung disease, a single dose of surfactant replacement is given within six hours of development of RDS.
5. Complications/secondary diagnosis.
   a. Risk of severe intracranial hemorrhage (approximately 35%).
   b. Risk of bronchopulmonary dysplasia (BPD) (approximately 35%).
   c. Risk for developmental delay, severe developmental delay (less than 15%).

> **CAUTION:** The risk for these complications is far greater for infants who do not receive the above-mentioned treatments.

6. Effect on function.
   a. The future intellectual development of the premature infant who had RDS and who received the latest treatments appears to be good.
   b. The functional effects for infants who develop BPD or who incur a severe intracranial hemorrhage may include motor, sensory, cognitive, and/or language impairments.
   c. For premature infants with RDS, functional effects may include visual defects, hypotonia, and other health issues that can impact development.

Bronchopulmonary Dysplasia (BPD)

1. Etiology.
   a. Respiratory disorder often as a result of barotrauma.
      (1) High inflating pressures.
      (2) Infection.
      (3) Meconium aspiration.
      (4) Asphyxia.
   b. A complication of prematurity.
   c. The walls of the immature lungs thicken, making the exchange of oxygen and carbon dioxide more difficult.
   d. The mucous lining of the lung is reduced along with the airway diameter.
2. Diagnosis.
   a. Infant must work harder than normal to obtain sufficient oxygen for survival.
3. Medical management/relevant pharmacology.
   a. Months or years of oxygen therapy and artificial ventilation.
   b. Bronchodilators and diuretics to keep the airways and lungs dry.

4. Complications.
   a. Greater risk for hypotonia and gross motor delays.
   b. Feeding problems can lead to poor nutrition.
      (1) Malabsorption problems.
      (2) Fragile bones with an increased risk of fractures.
   c. Central nervous system problems, such as damage to parts of the brain, can lead to delays or impairments in motor, sensory, speech, and cognitive function.
   d. Recurrent otitis media can lead to conductive hearing loss that can affect the development of speech and language as well as cognition.
5. Effect on function.
   a. Poor autonomic and sensory state regulation can impact on the alert state which is necessary for proper feeding.
   b. Poor exercise/activity tolerance due to illness and compromised respiration.
   c. Reduced ability to socialize due to long periods of poor health and the increased susceptibility to infection.
   d. Isolation and stress on the child and family members can lead to psychosocial problems.
   e. Greater risk for attachment disorder, affecting the child's ability to relate to others due to isolation and dependence on technological equipment.

Occupational Therapy Evaluation Foci for Pediatric Pulmonary Disorders

1. Assess for developmental strengths/capabilities (e.g., developmentally appropriate cognitive and communication skills).
2. Assess for developmental delays/deficits (e.g., difficulty engaging in developmentally appropriate play due to decreased vital capacity, poor strength, low endurance, and pain).
3. Assess the psychosocial status of the child and family/caregivers. Typical areas of concern include:
   a. Social isolation related to frequent hospitalizations, ongoing home treatment, and school absences.
   b. Physical and emotional fatigue related to the intense level of care that is required.
   c. Emotional stress related to complications (e.g., infections), related symptoms (e.g., pain), and prognosis (e.g., decreased life expectancy).
4. Assess the environment to determine needed modifications to conserve energy and enable occupational performance.
5. Assess positioning equipment needs and activity adaptations to enable occupational performance.
6. Determine the family's need for additional supports (e.g., support groups, respite care).

EXAM HINT: The most recent NBCOT® exam outline for the COTA® identifies knowledge of the "impact of typical development and aging on occupational performance, health, and wellness across the life span" (NBCOT®, 2018, p. 21) as essential for competent and safe practice. The application of knowledge about child development to the preceding evaluation foci and the following intervention foci will help you determine the correct answers to COTA® exam items about working with children with pediatric pulmonary disorders.

Occupational Therapy Intervention Foci for Pediatric Pulmonary Disorders

1. Monitor development.
2. Provide treatment to facilitate cognitive, sensorimotor, and psychosocial development.
3. Provide treatment to improve endurance, postural stability, and feeding.
4. Use positioning to promote postural drainage.
5. Provide environmental modifications and activity adaptations to enhance occupational performance.
6. Train in energy conservation methods to enable occupational performance.
7. Promote engagement in physical activity (especially play) within child's capabilities.
8. Address psychosocial issues that arise.
9. Provide parent/caregiver/teacher education.
   a. Treatment protocols for the preceding interventions.
   b. Precautions for participation in activities of daily living, play, and other healthful physical activities.
10. Foster the parents'/caregiver's advocacy skills to obtain respite and support services as needed and necessary modifications, equipment, and services for the child in the home and school.
11. Refer as necessary to ophthalmologist and other relevant services (e.g., support groups, respite programs).
12. Observe medical precautions during all occupational therapy sessions (i.e., respiratory/cardiac contraindications).

EXAM HINT: The NBCOT® exam outline for the COTA® identifies knowledge of the "precautions or contraindications associated with a client condition or stage of recovery . . . essential safety procedures to implement during interventions . . . (and) preventive measures for minimizing risk in the intervention environment" (NBCOT®, 2018, p. 29) as essential for competent practice. Thus, the application of knowledge about *all* of the precautions, contraindications, preventative measures, safety techniques, and emergency response approaches described in this chapter will be required to correctly answer COTA® exam items about working with persons with cardiopulmonary disorders.

References

American Heart Association. (2015). Cardiac medications. Retrieved from https://www.heart.org/en/health-topics/heart-attack/treatment-of-a-heart-attack/cardiac-medications.

American Heart Association. (2015). Heart attack symptoms in women. Retrieved from https://www.heart.org/en/health-topics/heart-attack/warning-signs-of-a-heart-attack/heart-attack-symptoms-in-women#.W14JsdJKg2w.

American Heart Association. (2015). The American Heart Association's diet and lifestyle recommendations. Retrieved from https://www.heart.org/en/healthy-living/healthy-eating/eat-smart/nutrition-basics/aha-diet-and-lifestyle-recommendations#.W2ScvYWfL-A.

American Occupational Therapy Association. (2014). Occupational therapy practice framework: Domain and process, 3rd ed. *American Journal of Occupational Therapy, 62,* 625–683.

Atchison, B. (1995). Cardiopulmonary diseases. In Trombly, C. A. (Ed.), *Occupational therapy for physical dysfunction* (4th ed., pp. 884–885). Baltimore, MD: Williams & Wilkins.

Batshaw, M. L., Pellegrino, L., & Roizen, N.J. (2007). *Children with disabilities: A medical primer* (6th ed., pp. 107–122, 638). Baltimore, MD: Paul H. Brookes.

Batshaw, M. L., & Perret, Y. M. (2002). *Children with disabilities: A medical primer* (5th ed.). Baltimore, MD: Paul H. Brookes.

Batshaw, M. L., Roizen, N. J., & Lotrecchiano, G. R. (2013). *Children with disabilities* (7th ed.). Baltimore, MD: Paul H. Brookes.

Ciccone, C. (2010). Medication. In W. Turk & L. Cahalin (Eds.), *Cardiovascular and pulmonary physical therapy: An evidence-based approach* (pp. 209–242). New York, NY: McGraw-Hill.

Collins, S., & Cocanour, B. (2010). Anatomy of the cardiopulmonary system. In W. Turk & L. Cahalin (Eds.), *Cardiovascular and pulmonary physical therapy: An evidence-based approach* (pp. 85–106). New York, NY: McGraw-Hill.

Criteria Committee of the New York Heart Association. (1994). *Nomenclature and criteria for diagnosis of diseases of the heart and great vessels* (9th ed.). Boston, MA: Little, Brown & Co.

Executive Committee. (2016). The diagnosis and treatment of peripheral lymphedema: 2016 Consensus Document of the International Society of Lymphology. *Lymphology, 42,* 170–184.

Hillegass, E., & Sadowsky, S. (2017). *Essentials of cardiopulmonary physical therapy* (4th ed.). Philadelphia, PA: Saunders.

Hunter, E. G., Gibson, R. W., Arbesman, M., & D'Amico, M. (2017). Systematic review of occupational therapy and adult cancer rehabilitation: Part 1. Impact of physical activity and symptom management interventions. *American Journal of Occupational Therapy, 71,* 7102100030p1–7102100030p11. https://doi.org/10.5014/ajot.2017.023564

Huntley, N. (2014). Cardiac and pulmonary diseases. In M.V. Radomski & C. A. Trombly Latham (Eds.), *Occupational therapy for physical dysfunction* (7th ed., pp. 1300–1326). Baltimore, MD: Lippincott Williams & Wilkins.

Johns Hopkins Cystic Fibrosis Center. (2018). *Effects of CF.* Retrieved from /https://www.hopkinscf.org/what-is-cf/effects-of-cf/.

Lymph Notes. (2015). Lymphedema stages. Retrieved from http://www.lymphnotes.com/article.php/id/474/.

Matthews, M. (2018). Cardiac and pulmonary diseases. In H. Pendleton & W. Schultz-Krohn (Eds.), *Pedretti's occupational therapy: Practice skills for physical dysfunction* (8th ed., pp. 1117–1133). St. Louis, MO: Elsevier Science/Mosby.

McClure, M. K., McClure, R. J., Day, R., & Brufsky, A. M. (2010). Randomized controlled trial of the Breast Cancer Recovery Program for women with breast cancer–related lymphedema. *American Journal of Occupational Therapy, 64,* 59–72.

McIntyre, M. (2007, March 5). Keeping VAD patients functional. *ADVANCE for Occupational Therapy Practitioners, 23,* 43–45.

National Board for Certification in Occupational Therapy (NBCOT®). (2018). *Practice analysis of the certified occupational therapy assistant registered: Executive summary* [PDF file]. Gaithersburg, MD: Author. Retrieved from https://www.nbcot.org/-/media/NBCOT/PDFs/2017-Practice-Analysis-Executive-OTR.ashx?la=en.

National Institutes of Health. (2013). *Bronchopulmonary dysplasia.* Retrieved from http://www.nhlbi.nih.gov/health/health-topics/topics/bpd/.

OpenStax College. (2013). *Anatomy and physiology.* OpenStax College. Retrieved from https://opentextbc.ca/anatomyandphysiology/chapter/19-1-heart-anatomy/.

Rais-Bahrami, K., & Short, B. L. (2013). Premature and small-for-dates infants. In M. L.

Batshaw, N. J. Roizen, & G. R. Lotrecchiano (Eds.), *Children with disabilities* (7th ed., pp. 87–104). Baltimore, MD: Paul H. Brookes.

Rogers, S. L. (2005). Common conditions that influence children's participation. In J. Case-Smith (Ed.), *Occupational therapy for children* (6th ed., pp. 160–215). St. Louis, MO: Elsevier/Mosby.

Rubio, K. (2018). Lymphedema self-management: Helping clients value home care programs. *OT Practice, 23*(1), 8–12.

Sandhu, S. (2009). *AOTA comments on lymphedema for meeting of Medicare Evidence Development and Coverage Advisory Committee on November 18, 2009.* Retrieved from https://www.aota.org/-/media/Corporate/Files/Advocacy/Reimb/News/Archives/Archived-Letters/Lymphedema%20letter%20to%20MedCAC.pdf.

Vining-Radomski, M., & Trombly-Latham, C. A. (2017). *Occupational therapy for physical dysfunction* (7th ed.). Baltimore, MD: Williams & Wilkins.

Wells, C. (2004). Pulmonary pathology. In W. DeTurk & L. Cahalin (Eds.), *Cardiovascular and pulmonary physical therapy: An evidence-based approach* (pp. 151–188). New York, NY: McGraw-Hill.

Williams, M. (Ed.). (2013). *Guidelines for cardiac rehabilitation and secondary prevention programs* (5th ed.) Champaign, IL: Human Kinetics.

Review Questions

Cardiovascular and Pulmonary System Disorders

Following are five questions about key content covered in this chapter. These questions are not inclusive of the entirety of content related to cardiovascular and pulmonary system disorders that you must know for success on the COTA® exam. These questions are provided to help you "jump-start" the thought processes you will need to apply your studying of content to the answering of exam questions; hence they are not in the COTA® exam format. Exam items in the COTA® format that cover the depth and breadth of content you will need to know to pass the exam are provided on this text's computerized exams. The answers to the following questions below are provided in Appendix 3.

1. An adult with a diagnosis of left ventricular failure congestive heart failure (CHF) has been referred to occupational therapy for Phase I cardiac rehabilitation during an acute hospitalization. What are the primary goals of inpatient cardiac rehabilitation? What symptoms of CHF do you need to be aware of that might manifest during therapeutic activities?

2. What are the clinical indications that may lead you to stop an activity during a cardiac rehabilitation intervention session? How would you monitor the patient during activity for signs/symptoms of distress?

3. An older adult status-postmyocardial infarction (S/P MI) has been referred to occupational therapy for Phase II outpatient cardiac rehabilitation. The client is able to carry out all basic ADL independently and has fair tolerance for activities that require standing and overhead movements. The client lives with a spouse and identifies being a partner, home maintainer, and gardener as primary roles. The client would like to be able to resume role-related activities. The occupational therapy prescription calls for activities beginning at MET level 3 and increasing to MET level 5 according to the client's activity tolerance. Taking into consideration the therapy prescription, the client's current status, desired occupational roles, and activity preferences, which treatment approaches and activities should you include in intervention?

4. You have been asked to consult with a teacher to discuss precautions for a student who has a diagnosis of cystic fibrosis. What precautions should you would discuss with the teacher? Provide a rationale for your recommendations.

5. You are working with a 20-month-old toddler who was diagnosed with bronchopulmonary dysplasia (BPD) shortly after birth. What are the typical deficits resulting from BPD that the child may exhibit during occupational therapy intervention sessions? Provide an explanation for your answers.

9

Gastrointestinal, Renal-Genitourinary, Endocrine, Immunological, and Integumentary Systems Disorders

ANN BURKHARDT, RITA P. FLEMING-CASTALDY, AND CHRISTINA GAVALAS

Chapter Outline

- Gastrointestinal System Disorders, 258
- Gastric Esophageal Reflux Disease (GERD), 261
- Renal-Genitourinary System Disorders, 261
- Immunological System Disorders, 264
- Endocrine System and Metabolic System Disorders, 270
- Integumentary System Disorders, 274
- Whole Body System Disorders, 277
- References, 278
- Review Questions, 281

Gastrointestinal System Disorders

Dysphagia and Swallowing Disorders

1. Structures involved and functions. See Figure 9-1.
   a. Oral facial musculature.
      (1) Controls maintenance of the bolus in the oral cavity during mastication and swallowing.
   b. Pharyngeal and laryngeal structures.
      (1) The pharynx extends from the nares (nostrils) to the mouth and larynx; all a part of the alimentary canal.
         (a) Both air and food pass through the pharynx.
      (2) The larynx is also called the voice box.
         (a) It functions to protect the airway from the aspiration of food.
         (b) The larynx houses the vocal folds and manipulates the pitch and volume of someone's voice.
   c. Piriform sinuses.
      (1) A pear-shaped fossa located laterally to the laryngeal entrance that channels swallowed material just before it enters the esophagus.
   d. Vocal folds.
      (1) Tissue that opens when breathing or vibrating (e.g., when speaking or singing); also called the vocal cords.
         (a) Controlled by the vagus nerve.
         (b) The vocal cords protect the airway from choking and regulate the flow of air into the lungs.
         (c) They are also important in producing sounds used for speech.
   e. Bronchioles/bronchi.
      (1) The major air passages of the lungs that diverge from the windpipe.
   f. Lungs.
      (1) In normal swallowing, the bolus does not enter the airway and the lungs.
      (2) A person who aspirates food or drink into their airway are at risk for pneumonia.
      (3) All people aspirate saliva in their sleep; however, for people with impaired immune systems, the risk for repeat pneumonia escalates.
   g. Esophagus.
      (1) Food or liquid normally enters the esophagus during a swallow.
      (2) The upper esophageal sphincter (UES) is a bundle of muscles at the top of the esophagus.
         (a) The muscles of the UES are consciously controlled and used when breathing, eating, belching, and vomiting.

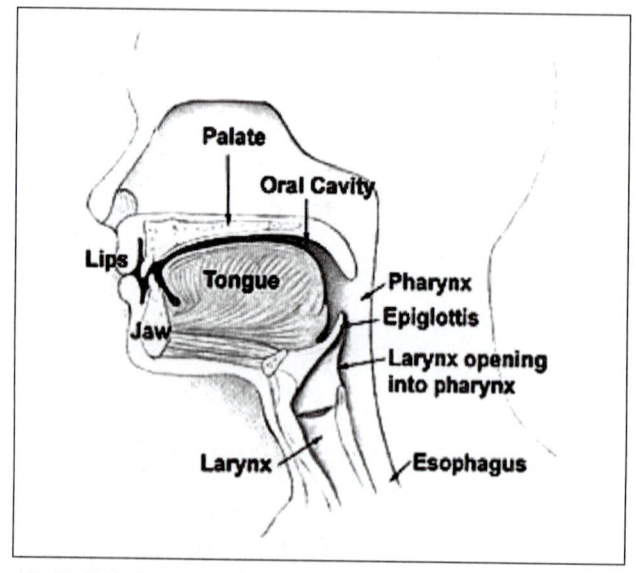

> **EXAM HINT:** The NBCOT® exam outline for the COTA®, identifies knowledge of the "influence . . . of body functions (and) body structures, . . . on occupational performance" (NBCOT®, 2018, p. 21) as essential for competent and safe practice. The application of knowledge about the major structures and functions of the gastrointestinal system described above and the conditions and impairments discussed in this chapter can help you correctly answer NBCOT® Domain 01 exam items about the functional implications of damage to the gastrointestinal system.

2. Conditions and functional impairments.
   a. Facial paralysis.
      (1) Incomplete closure of the mouth.
      (2) Loss of the bolus out of the front of the oral cavity.
   b. Praxis/motor planning deficits.
      (1) Inability to effectively chew and coordinate tongue movements to propel the bolus toward the base of the tongue.
      (2) Residual food centrally located in the oral cavity.
      (3) Difficulty forming a bolus with smoother consistencies.
   c. Sensory impairment of the oral cavity.
      (1) Lack of awareness of residual food on the side of the mouth that has decreased sensation.

Figure 9-1 Anatomy of Swallowing Structure

National Cancer Institute (n.d.). Head and neck cancer module. Retrieved from https://training.seer.cancer.gov/head-neck/anatomy/overview.html

(2) Pocketing of food.
(3) Spillage of residual food into the airway at a time when the vocal cords are open; timing of the swallow sequence is off.
d. Weakness of the tongue/base of tongue structures.
  (1) Inefficient propulsion of bolus into the pharyngeal cavity.
  (2) Lack of closure at the cricopharyngeal junction can result in:
    (a) Suboptimal propulsion of the bolus.
    (b) Interference with the normal timing of the swallow sequence.
    (c) Failure to trigger closure of the vocal folds during swallow; aspiration.
e. Weakness of the elevation of the pharynx during swallow.
  (1) Incomplete triggering (diminished neural stimulation) of the pharyngeal phase of swallowing.
f. Vocal cord paralysis.
  (1) Inefficient closure of the vocal folds during the pharyngeal phase of swallow.
    (a) Vocal cords are in paramedian position; swallow may be safe.
    (b) Vocal cords fail to meet/close to protect airway; aspiration may occur.
g. Penetration of the bronchioles/bronchi by the bolus when aspiration occurs.
  (1) Food enters the lung; true aspiration occurs.
    (a) Bacteria can cause pneumonia (aspiration pneumonia). If the person's immune system is functioning well, they may not experience pneumonia.
h. Clinical aspiration.
  (1) Food enters the airway.
    (a) Person can clear airway by coughing (reflex intact).

RED FLAG: Silent aspiration occurs when the:
- Bolus enters the lung and person does not react.
- Bolus enters the lung and person experiences respiratory distress without a cough.
- Person coughs too weakly to raise the bolus in order to expel it.

i. Diminished esophageal motility.
  (1) Bolus sits in the esophagus and can slowly either move toward the stomach or upward toward the pharynx.

CAUTION: Person may report feeling that food is stuck in the esophagus. Person aspirates when food propels upward and they cannot swallow it.

3. Functional observations.
  a. Staff report questioning swallowing dysfunction.
    (1) Person coughs during or after drinking water or other thin liquid.
    (2) The person's face changes color during or after eating.
      (a) Flushed/reddened color, ashened appearance for persons with darker skin.
      (b) Blanches.

CAUTION: The person gasps for breath, possibly indicating a partial or complete airway obstruction.

    (3) If an obstruction is visualized, it may be possible to remove the object and restore respiratory function.

RED FLAG: Aspiration requires *immediate* action.
- The Heimlich maneuver is used to clear the obstruction and raise the bolus that has been aspirated, as long as the person is awake and responsive. See Figure 9-2.
- If the person loses consciousness, basic life support procedures are used to continue to try to reestablish the airway. This includes abdominal thrusts, back blows, and periodically looking in the oral cavity to try to visualize the object.

4. Swallowing assessment.
  a. The occupational therapy assistant (OTA) can contribute to the evaluation process in collaboration with the occupational therapist.
    (1) Supervision is required.
    (2) The level of supervision required will be determined by the OTA's experience.
  b. Service competency must be established.
  c. The OTA cannot independently evaluate or interpret evaluation results.
5. Relationship of swallowing dysfunction to occupation.
  a. Disruption of family role; e.g., ability to comfortably eat at the dinner table.
    (1) Modified diet can be infantilizing.
    (2) Tube feeding may preempt the person's ability to partake in the family meal in cultural/social context.
  b. Disruption of ability/comfort level for eating out in public.
    (1) Tube feeding may preempt the person's ability to partake in a meal in a cultural/social context.
  c. Disruption of swallowing ability may contribute to decreased comfort level for eating out in public.
    (1) Person may choose not to dine in a public social context.
    (2) If business lunches or dinners are part of a vocational role, the person may not be able to resume their vocation without modification of expectations regarding how participation in social meals relates to vocational performance.

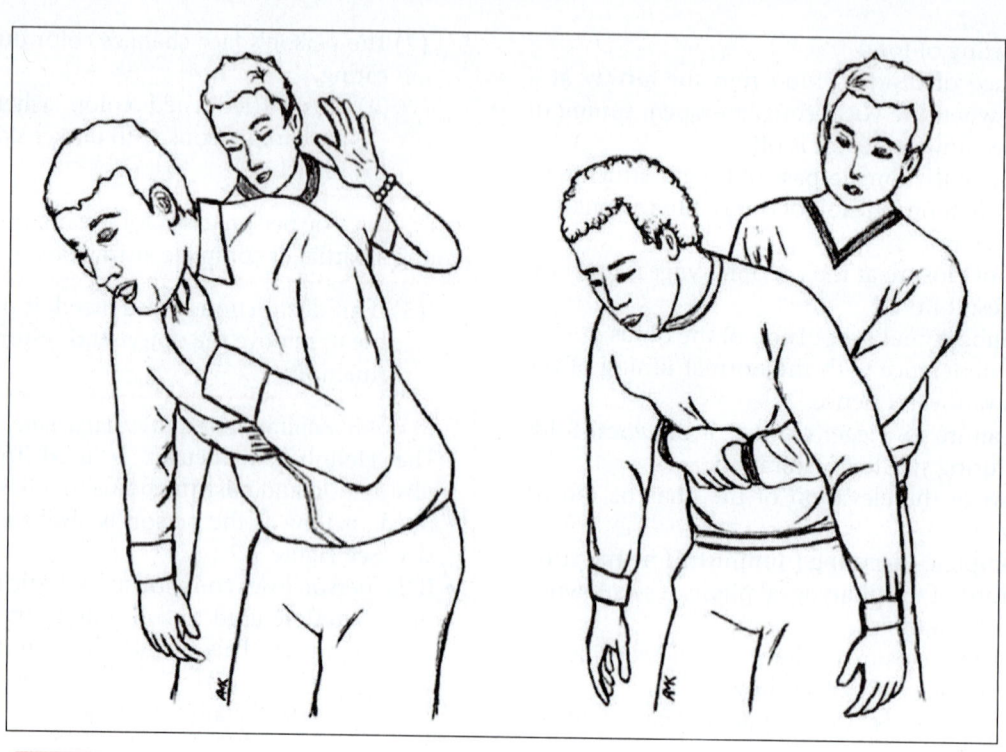

Figure 9-2 The Heimlich Maneuver

Abdominal Thrust/Heimlich Maneuver (2014). Retrieved January 10, 2018 from https://commons.wikimedia.org/wiki/Category:Abdominal_thrusts

d. Alteration of self-concept concerning life roles and appearance.
  (1) If person is tube fed, how does that alter how they perceive self?
    (a) Sex appeal can be questioned.
    (b) Self-image as it impacts on life roles (e.g., a 'foodie' or 'fashionista') can be altered.
  (2) If tube fed, how does that alter how others perceive them?
    (a) Accepted, feared, or pitied by children, grandchildren, family, friends, and colleagues.

> **EXAM HINT:** The NBCOT® exam outline for the COTA® identifies knowledge of "technical level intervention strategies and techniques used to facilitate oral motor skills for drinking, eating, and swallowing consistent with developmental level, client condition, caregiver interaction, and mealtime environment and context" (NBCOT®, 2018, p. 25) as essential for competent practice. The application of knowledge about the relationship of swallowing dysfunction to occupation described above and the intervention approaches described below can help you determine the correct answer for NBCOT® Domain 02 Selecting and Implementing Intervention exam items about swallowing disorders.

6. Intervention.
  a. Provide family-centered intervention to determine an acceptable dinner table alternative for family interaction.
  b. Work with the person toward developing new roles and occupations to transition from old role (i.e., head of table).
  c. Provide ongoing education and information to the family regarding the person's feeding/nutrition.
  d. The role of the OTA in intervention.
    (1) The OTA implements intervention with the supervision of the occupational therapist.
    (2) The level of supervision required depends upon the OTA's experience and established service competence.
    (3) During the implementation of intervention, the OTA informs the supervising therapist of any change in the individual's status and any other relevant information that may affect treatment.
  e. See Chapter 12 for further information on interventions for swallowing disorders, Chapter 13 for further information on psychosocial interventions, and Chapter 14 for further information on interventions for performance in areas of occupation.

> **EXAM HINT:** Correct answers to COTA® exam items about occupational therapy intervention for persons with swallowing disorders should include collaboration with the person. Depending on the exam item, the scenario may include collaboration with speech-language pathologists, dieticians, nurses, and/or family members.

Gastric Esophageal Reflux Disease (GERD)

1. Structures involved include the lower esophagus and gastric sphincter.
   a. Food enters stomach and mixes with stomach acid/digestive juices.
   b. Lower esophageal sphincter inefficiently closes; stomach contraction propels acid/acidic bolus back into the esophagus.
      (1) Person reports heartburn sensation, indigestion, or dull chest pain.
   c. Positional elevation of the head above the stomach, when the person is reclined, may discourage upward retropulsion of the bolus from the stomach.
2. Frequent complaints of people who have GERD.
   a. Heartburn/indigestion.
   b. Swallowing problems.
      (1) A sensation of feeling that something is getting 'stuck' in their throat.
      (2) Chest pressure or pain.
      (3) Regurgitation after swallowing.
      (4) Increased production of mucus, mimics postnasal drip symptoms.
3. Intervention.
   a. Sleeping with more than one pillow (elevating the head to discourage regurgitation associated with body posture).
   b. Drug therapy.
   c. Diet modification.
      (1) Less spice.
      (2) Small meals on a more frequent basis.
   d. Mechanical stretching of the esophagus, when stricture plays a role in the condition.
   e. Stress management.

Small Bowel Obstruction

1. Etiology.
   a. Secondary to scar tissue.
   b. Secondary to radiation of the abdomen; a long-term effect.
   c. Result of tumor obstruction.
2. Surgical treatment.
   a. Resection with open stoma (i.e., colostomy).
   b. Closed abdominal surgery.
3. Rehabilitation issues.
   a. Self-care aspects of stoma care must be addressed for persons with decreased fine motor skills (e.g., individuals with peripheral neuropathy secondary to chemotherapy treatment).
   b. Decreased mobility in gross movements (i.e., bending or stooping during daily tasks, including lower body dressing) can cause traction on the healing scar.
   c. Appetite may be altered in postoperative phase.

CAUTION: Cognitive impairments may impede a person's ability to safely maintain stoma care (e.g., forgetting to properly clean and restore the collection bag can lead to the development of abscesses).

Neurogenic Bowel

1. Etiology: sympathetic nerve impairment, generally occurring in persons who have spinal cord injury above the (thoracic) T6 level.
   a. Loss of control of anal sphincter.
   b. Sensory loss resulting in a lack of awareness of feces in the bowel.
   c. Motor loss, decreased or lost ability to self-initiate or control a bowel movement.
2. Flaccidity of muscles results in incontinence.
3. Autonomic dysreflexia, an extreme rise in blood pressure can result.

RED FLAG: Autonomic dysreflexia is a medical emergency if not reversed.

   a. See Chapter 7's section on the complications of spinal cord injury for more information about the prevention and management of autonomic dysreflexia.

Renal-Genitourinary System Disorders

Kidney Disease

1. Risk factors.
   a. Diabetes.
      (1) Three of every 10 individuals with diabetes develop kidney failure.
      (2) 60%–65% of all persons with diabetes also have high blood pressure.

(3) 10%–40% of people with type 2 diabetes develop severe kidney disease and end-stage renal disease (ESRD).
(4) Diabetes can contribute to the development of nephrotic syndrome.
b. Hypertension (HTN).
(1) Uncontrolled or poorly controlled hypertension is the primary diagnosis for 26% of all new cases of chronic kidney failure each year.
(2) 65% of HTN in women and 78% of HTN in men can be directly attributed to obesity.
c. Systemic lupus erythematosus.
(1) Lupus can contribute to development of nephrotic syndrome.

> **CAUTION:** Personal lifestyle and habits can damage the kidneys. See Box 9-1.

2. Stages of kidney disease.
    a. There are five stages of kidney disease, with progressive worsening of the glomerular filtration rate (GFR) which characterizes each stage of the disease.
    b. Focus of medical care and interventions.
        (1) Stage 1: prevention of progression of the kidney disease.
        (2) Stage 2: management of health conditions.
        (3) Stage 3: management of anemia and bone loss.
        (4) Stage 4: education for further management of kidney failure should be provided (i.e., hemodialysis versus peritoneal dialysis versus transplantation).
        (5) Stage 5: for life to be sustained, the person must receive either dialysis or a kidney transplant.

> **RED FLAG:** Signs and symptoms of chronic kidney disease are critical to recognize. These are provided in Box 9-2.

3. Medical treatment of kidney disease and related conditions.
    a. Nephrotic syndrome treatment.
        (1) Treat with diuretics and drugs that prevent spillage of protein in the urine.
        (2) Drug control of fluid overload and/or spillage of protein into the urine (proteinuria).
        (3) Encourage compliance with drug therapy and dietary and exercise recommendations.
    b. Acute renal failure treatment.
        (1) Drug control of underlying medical contributory conditions.
        (2) Emergent, acute dialysis.
    c. End stage renal disease (ESRD) treatment.
        (1) Dialysis required to stay alive.
        (2) Hemodialysis, which requires presence of vascular access via a shunt or fistula.
        (3) Peritoneal dialysis (PD): inpatient treatment, continuous ambulatory peritoneal dialysis (CAPD).
        (4) Continuous cycling peritoneal dialysis (CCPD).
        (5) Nocturnal intermittent PD (NIPD).

BOX 9-1 ▶ Habits that can Cause Kidney Damage

- Insufficient water consumption: dehydration stresses renal function.
- Smoking: causes microvascular disease.
- Alcohol: over 8 oz. of alcohol daily can suppress function. Alcohol also causes release of water from the body and can lead to dehydration.
- Medications: if chemically based, may tax the organ's ability to filtrate out by-products.
- High-protein diet: too much protein in the diet taxes the metabolic capacity of the kidney.
- Physical inactivity: generates kidney stones.
- Sleeplessness: increases toxins that the kidney must filtrate.
- Overconsumption of salt and sugar.
- Delaying urine release: leads to urinary tract infection and absorption of bacteria into the bloodstream.
- Dietary deficiencies: the kidney needs vitamins and minerals. Most people lack adequate amounts of magnesium.
- Failing to medically treat viral and bacterial infections: many infections can be a signal of reduced kidney function brought on by a toxin buildup.
- Ignoring symptoms: changes in urine color, loss of breath, fatigue, bad breath, leg and waist pain, swelling, frequent feelings of coldness, dizziness, vomiting, and itchy skin.

BOX 9-2 ▶ Signs and Symptoms of Chronic Kidney Disease

- Vomiting.
- Loss of appetite.
- Fatigue and weakness.
- Sleep problems.
- Changes in urination output.
- Decreased mental sharpness.
- Muscle twitches and cramps.
- Swelling of feet and ankles.
- Persistent itching.
- Chest pain, if fluid builds up around the lining of the heart.
- Shortness of breath, if fluid builds up in the lungs.
- High blood pressure (hypertension) that is difficult to control.

Mayo Clinic. (2017). *Patient care and health information. Diseases and conditions: Chronic kidney disease*. Retrieved from https://www.mayoclinic.org/diseases-conditions/chronic-kidney-disease/symptoms-causes/dxc-20207466

(6) Transplantation.
(7) Hypertension treatment: diet, medication, exercise, stress reduction, and smoking cessation. See Chapter 8 for more information on hypertension treatment.
d. Diabetes treatment. See this chapter's section on diabetes.
e. Systematic lupus erythematosus treatment.
(1) Control symptoms to prevent complications.
(2) Treat with diuretics and drugs that prevent spillage of protein in the urine (angiotensin converting enzyme-ACE).
(3) See this chapter's section on systematic lupus erythematosus treatment.
4. Impact on performance skills and client factors.
a. Motor skills can be affected by fatigue, muscle pain, edema, and weakness.
b. Sensory skills can be affected by neuropathy (diabetes related, toxicity related, cyclosporin, antirejection (drug related), and vision loss (diabetes related).
c. Delusions due to sepsis or toxicity and neurocognitive disorders (i.e., multi-infarct or metabolic) can affect process skills.
d. Neurocognitive disorders (i.e., multi-infarct or metabolic) can affect motor and process skills.
e. Perceptual (neurobehavioral) impairment can affect motor and process skills.
f. Psychological/emotional dysfunction can affect social interaction skills.
g. Impact on performance in basic activities of daily living (BADL).
(1) Bowel and bladder training and self-management.
(2) Practice meticulous sanitary technique with self-dialysis.
(3) Adhere to a disease-specific/highly restrictive diet.
(4) Cope with the impact of impotence on sexual participation and alterations in self-esteem and body image.
(5) Use adapted equipment to enable performance of self-care tasks.
(6) Pace oneself when fatigue limits performance.
h. Impact on instrumental activities of daily living (IADL).
(1) Home establishment and management.
(a) Accept impact of physical limitations (e.g., the need for lighter workload and housekeeping assistance).
(b) Cope with having an altered home maintainer role.
(2) Meal preparation.
(a) Adhere to changes in usual meal preparation habits to accommodate dietary limitations.
(3) Management of personal finances.
(a) Identify solutions and resources to cover the cost of care, which can be prohibitive if insurance does not provide adequate coverage.
(b) Plan and seek alternative participation means for coping with dialysis-related fatigue and its impact on community banking.
(4) Community mobility.
(a) Cope with the presence of fatigue and impaired functional mobility that limits community participation.
(b) Cope with altered functional mobility and accept assistive technology solutions.
(c) Engage in additional planning that is needed for long distance travel.
i. Leisure/sports activities.
(1) Cope with the presence of fatigue and impaired functional mobility to participate in chosen activities.
(2) Attend to participation precautions (e.g., the need to pace self and self-regulate to decrease fatigue) and engage in activities that minimize risk.
(3) Access leisure resources and sports facilities that provide adaptations that enable social participation and active engagement for persons whose condition and treatment (i.e., dialysis) tend to isolate them.
5. Impact on performance contexts.
a. Social context.
(1) How disease affects role in the family.
(2) How disease affects role in the workplace.
(3) How disease affects role in the community, including spiritual communities, social groups, and special interests.
b. Sociocultural context.
(1) How a cultural and/or religious group accepts or does not accept a condition and/or its treatment (e.g., resisting invasive interventions, such as dialysis).
(a) Explicit taboos on invasive treatments; some people will choose to end their lives by not starting dialysis based on cultural/religious beliefs.
(2) The individual's acceptance or nonacceptance of the impairment/disease (i.e., the personal meaning of having a machine perform a bodily function).
6. Occupational therapy evaluation and intervention.
a. Assess performance skills, client factors, areas of occupation, and performance contexts to develop an individualized intervention plan. Chapters 11–15 provide information about evaluation approaches.

b. Provide interventions to remediate deficits and compensate for limitations to enable occupational performance. Interventions can include:
   (1) Education about activity and participation precautions to minimize risks (e.g., behaviors and habits that can cause strain to kidney function).
   (2) Training in the safe and effective use of adaptive equipment (e.g., tub bench, built-up handled utensils, reachers, button hooks).
   (3) Training in the safe and effective use of assistive mobility devices (e.g., ankle-foot orthoses, canes, walkers) and/or wheeled mobility.
   (4) Energy conservation and work simplification techniques to compensate for fatigue during BADL, IADL, leisure, and/or work.
   (5) Lifestyle redesign to change unhealthy habits and routines, develop new habits that support health and well-being, and implement new routines that include activities that promote health and well-being.
   (6) Health promotion and prevention to facilitate health management and maintenance.
   (7) Education in community resources that enable participation (e.g., accessible public transportation).
   (8) Referrals to obtain supportive counseling and social support, drug therapy, and complementary medicine, if indicated.
   (9) Referrals to driving rehabilitation programs, if needed.
   (10) Physical or cognitive assistance may be indicated for complex BADL and IADL.
c. Dialysis treatment-specific interventions.
   (1) Manufacture devices to protect shunts postoperatively that are used for hemodialysis.
   (2) Encourage movement and engage the person in activity participation during dialysis.
      (a) When active, the body has a better ability to eliminate the lactic acid generated during dialysis.

CAUTION: If the person remains inactive, fatigue and muscle soreness/stiffness will result from treatment.

   (3) Teach the person to implement energy conservation and work simplification techniques when and if they experience chronic fatigue with dialysis treatment.

Neurogenic Bladder/UTI

1. See this chapter's gastrointestinal system section.

Stress Incontinence

1. Etiology: local damage to bladder sphincter associated with the aftereffects of bearing children, morbid obesity, and weakening of accessory musculature associated with normal aging.
   a. Intervention.
      (1) Kegel exercises to strengthen pelvic floor.
      (2) Timed routines for emptying bladder before it is full enough to cause spillage.
      (3) Lifestyle adjustments to use incontinence supporting garments for a socially acceptable solution and to decrease public attention to the incontinence.
      (4) Medications may be used when the physician feels the client can tolerate the side effects of drug therapy support.
      (5) Electric stimulation may be used, if client fits the parameters of recovery for the condition.

Immunological System Disorders

Cancer

1. Etiology: Unknown for some cancers, strong link to risk factors for others.
2. Prevalence and general statistics.
   a. Cancer is among the leading causes of death worldwide.
   b. Approximately 38.4% of all people will be diagnosed with cancer at some point in their lives. In 2018, it is estimated that over 1.7 million new cases of cancer will be diagnosed.
   c. Cancer incidence is 439.2 cases per 100,000 people; cancer mortality is 163.5 cases per 100,000.
   d. The three most common cancers, from most to least prevalent, are breast cancer, lung/bronchus cancer, and prostate cancer.
   e. If cancer is controlled at the five-year mark after initial diagnosis, the person is considered to be in remission. In the United States, the number of cancer survivors is expected to increase from 15.5 million (currently) to 20.3 million by 2026.

EXAM HINT: In the NBCOT® practice analysis, 25.8% of certified occupational therapy assistants (COTA®s) who provided services to persons with general medical/systemic disorders indicated they provided services to individuals with cancer (NBCOT®, 2018, p. 15). Due to this prevalence, it is likely that the COTA® exam will have items about working with persons with cancer.

3. Risk factors for cancer.
   a. Heredity.
      (1) Some tumors (i.e., breast, prostate, skin, and colon) seem to have a high hereditary risk.
   b. Environmental.
      (1) Cluster patterns related to chemical pollution.
   c. Habit or lifestyle related.
      (1) Smoking, alcohol consumption, high-fat diets, and obesity may be linked to increased risk.
4. Prevention, early intervention, and control.
   a. Specific to type of cancer.
      (1) Recommended screening tests include mammograms and ultrasound, prostate and testicular exams, skin checks, colonoscopies, pap smears, blood tests, and abdominal ultrasound.
         (a) Cancer type and family history determine the screening method and its frequency.
   b. Recommended preventative measures.
      (1) Avoid environmental contributing factors (e.g., chemically contaminated land, lead paint).
      (2) Avoid and/or change contributory habits.
         (a) OT practitioners can provide wellness interventions for people who want to quit or change habits (e.g., cease smoking).
         (b) Wellness interventions can:
            - Foster the use of self-regulatory behaviors.
            - Support person-directed actions to change habits.
            - Provide health-promoting, occupation-based alternatives to unhealthy habits.
            - Promote participation in programs that increase engagement in health-promoting behaviors (e.g., 12-step programs, support groups, individual treatment).

EXAM HINT: The NBCOT® exam outline for the COTA® identifies knowledge of "fundamental strategies used for addressing health literacy ... to promote positive health behaviors, enable informed decisions, (and) ... support positive outcomes" (NBCOT®, 2018, p. 22) as essential for competent practice. Based on this requirement, it is likely that the exam will include items about the COTA®'s role in health promotion for persons with cancer and other conditions (e.g., diabetes, obesity) that can benefit from interventions focused on enabling personal wellness.

5. Diagnostic staging of cancer.
   a. Stage 1: tumor present, no perceived spread of disease.
      (1) Lesion operable.
      (2) Prognosis good (70%–90% mean survival at five years).
         (a) No spread of disease to the lymph nodes.
         (b) No metastatic lesions.
   b. Stage 2: localized spread of the tumor.
      (1) Lesion is operable and can be removed with margins.
      (2) Spread is limited and usually responds well to treatment (chemo/radiation/immunotherapy).
      (3) Mean five-year survival rate is 45%–55%.
   c. Stage 3: extensive evidence of a primary tumor that has spread to other organs in the body.
      (1) Tumor can be surgically debulked, but some cells may remain behind.
      (2) There is deeper spread of the tumor cells in the lymphatics.
      (3) Widespread evidence of cancer throughout multiple organs of the body.
      (4) Mean five-year survival rate is 15%–25%
   d. Stage 4: inoperable primary lesion.
      (1) Survival is dependent on the depth and extent of the tumor spread as well as the ability to have the tumor respond to therapy (mean five-year survival rate is less than 5%).
      (2) Multiple metastases.
6. Medical treatment.
   a. Surgery.
      (1) Lumpectomy. Surgery (i.e., lumpectomy, en bloc resection, reconstruction, and amputation).
      (2) Positioning postoperatively in the operating room.
      (3) Early movement postoperatively.
      (4) Client education for prevention of complications, such as lymphedema and loss of active range of motion (AROM), if the shoulder joint capsule tightens after surgery.
   b. Chemotherapy (i.e., intravenous, shunt, oral).
      (1) When people are receiving chemotherapy, they may experience:
         (a) Fatigue.
         (b) Increased risk of excessive bleeding if cut or abraded (e.g., brushing teeth).
         (c) Acute onset of neuropathy resulting in difficulty using feeding utensils and ADL tools.
         (d) Loss of protective sensation.
   c. Radiation.
      (1) Radiation burns to skin and soft tissues in the line of radiation.
         (a) The person may need to learn new skin care regimens that do not alter the pH of the skin to either intensify or lessen the impact of the radiation dose.

d. Immunotherapy.
  (1) Adherence to medication management, if part of the immunotherapy regime is important.
e. Hormonal therapy.
  (1) People receiving treatment may experience intensified signs and symptoms of estrogen withdrawal, such as hot flashes. Mood swings and behavioral changes can also occur.
f. Transplantation.
  (1) People who are undergoing bone marrow transplantation will be kept in physical isolation.

> **RED FLAG:** The risk for developing infections that can be life threatening is great.

    (a) Providing strategies to lessen the impact of anxiety, depression, and social isolation can be useful.
7. Rehabilitation.
  a. Preoperative.
    (1) Preoperative functional assessments and preparation of the client for post-operative phase and care.
    (2) Client and caregiver education concerning recovery and follow-up care, functional expectations, and client engagement.
  b. Postoperative.
    (1) Intervention planning based on a client's medical status and blood value guidelines that can affect safety during activity (platelets, hemoglobin level).

> **CAUTION:** Postoperative precautions related to structural changes resulting from surgery must be followed. These will be dependent on the location of the tumor and the procedure done; for example, abdominal precautions when the tumor is in the abdominal cavity and regional precautions when there is an incision near a joint.

  c. Convalescence.
    (1) Rehabilitation of motor, sensory, cognitive, and/or neurobehavioral impairments.
    (2) Psychological support to enhance coping ability during recovery from cancer treatment phase.
      (a) Liminality: self-recognition of vulnerability and self-sense of mortality.
      (b) Occupational role and body image adjustment.
      (c) Obtainment of social support.
    (3) Development of health-supporting behaviors with follow-up support (e.g., diet, exercise, stress management, vocational skill support, or assistance for occupational role performance).
  d. Palliative care.
    (1) Prevent and relieve suffering for persons with life-threatening illness through early identification, assessment, and treatment of pain.
    (2) Address physical, psychosocial, and spiritual needs.
    (3) Enhance quality of life by supporting clients' engagement in daily life occupations that they find meaningful and purposeful.
    (4) Consider environmental and contextual factors (e.g., accessibility of objects or places in the environment, social contacts available to prevent isolation) and client factors (e.g., decreased endurance, increased anxiety) that may limit a client's abilities and satisfaction when performing desired occupations.
    (5) Collaborate with the client and family members throughout the OT process to identify occupations that are meaningful, incorporate strategies that support occupational engagement, and provide caregiver training as needed.
  e. End-of-life care (hospice).
    (1) Support quality of life as disease advances and functional status declines.
    (2) Provide client with as much control as they can have and desire to have on their day-to-day life and lifestyle support.
    (3) Be present, be accountable, listen, and counsel as needed concerning the progression of the disease and sense of liminality.
    (4) Encourage planning for death (e.g., advanced directives and control over goodbyes and funeral arrangements).
    (5) Empower life celebration and life reflection (e.g., journaling, scrapbooks, phone call contact, and recontact, letter writing).
    (6) Refer for legal support, if needed and requested.
    (7) See Chapter 13 for additional information on psychosocial issues related to the end of life and dying.

> **EXAM HINT:** When determining the correct answer to an exam item about a COTA® working with a person with cancer, be sure to consider the reported cancer stage. The correct answer to an exam item about a person recovering from the surgical removal of a Stage 2 breast tumor will likely include a rehabilitative approach; whereas, the correct answer to an exam item about a person with Stage 4 brain cancer that has reoccurred multiple times will likely include a palliative approach.

Scleroderma

1. Rheumatic, connective tissue disease associated with impaired immune response.

2. Etiology: unknown.
   a. Three main components.
      (1) Vascular (Raynaud's phenomenon, pulmonary hypertension, decreased esophageal motility).
      (2) Fibrotic.
         (a) Scar tissue resulting from excess collagen (protein) causing thickness of skin and a burning sensation in the skin.
         (b) Fibrosis of the lungs causing restrictive lung disease.
      (3) Autoimmunity.
         (a) B cell-produced antibodies (anti-centromere, anti-topisomerase I antibodies).
   b. Two basic types of the disease.
      (1) Limited.
         (a) Skin involvement (with a good prognosis).
         (b) Linear scleroderma (bands of thicker skin, with a good prognosis).
      (2) Systemic.
         (a) Systemic sclerosis of internal organs, which is life threatening.
         (b) CREST syndrome (with a good prognosis).
            • Calcinosis or calcium in the skin.
            • Raynaud's phenomenon.
            • Esophageal dysfunction.
            • Sclerodactyly of fingers and toes.
            • Telangiectasis or red spots covering the hands, feet, forearms, face, and hips.
         (c) General morphea.
3. Risk factors: unknown, two main theories.
   a. Genetic.
   b. Environment.
4. Prevalence: 300,000 cases in the United States, but only about 49,000 have the systemic form.
   a. 80% of persons with scleroderma are women 30–50 years old at diagnosis.
5. Prevention.
   a. Control symptoms of Raynaud's phenomenon.
   b. Have screening echocardiograms to rule out pulmonary hypertension.
   c. Smoking cessation.
6. Intervention.
   a. Raynaud's phenomenon.
      (1) Keep fingers and toes warm.
      (2) Dress in layers.
      (3) Drug therapy: vasodilators.
      (4) Biofeedback.
   b. Pulmonary artery problems.
      (1) Drug therapy: Procardia SL, anticoagulation therapy.
      (2) Nasal canula oxygen.
   c. Gastrointestinal problems.
      (1) Drug therapy: antacids.
      (2) Dietary modifications: soft diet, avoidance of alcoholic beverages and spicy foods.
      (3) Treatment of infection.
   d. Fibrosis of the skin.
      (1) Protective gloves: cotton, insulated, mildly compressive.
      (2) Drug therapy.
   e. Myositis: inflammatory muscle disease.
      (1) Cessation of exercise.
      (2) Drug therapy: low dose of oral steroids.
   f. Fibrosis of the lungs.
      (1) Drug therapy.
7. Sequelae of scleroderma and recommendations.
   a. Poor circulation, as in Raynaud's phenomenon.
      (1) Use of dressing in layers of clothing and clothing style modifications for neutral warmth.
      (2) Biofeedback, guided imagery to concentrate on improving distal circulation.
      (3) Education to encourage skin inspection.
      (4) Activity modifications to prevent trauma to fingers and toes.
   b. Contractures.
      (1) Splinting at optimal resting length for hands/wrists to attempt to slow progressive development of contractures.
      (2) Use of silicone gel in the palms of the hands.
      (3) Use of electrical/mechanical vibration (muffled) to stimulate rapidly adapting-type A-nerve fibers and decrease burning sensation in hands.
   c. Facial disfigurement and alteration in body image and self-identity.
      (1) "Look good/feel better" programs.
      (2) Work with people to help them choose adaptations and new accessories to ease their adjustment to their changing appearance.
      (3) Support groups: in person and online.
   d. Thoracic spinal lesions can result in paraparesis, neurogenic bowel/bladder, altered mobility, and altered occupational performance.
      (1) Neurorehabilitation and biomechanical approaches as indicated.
   e. Space-occupying lesions in the brain produce stroke-like symptoms.
      (1) Rehabilitation for functional deficits.

Acquired Immunodeficiency Syndrome (AIDS)

1. Etiology: infection by the human immunodeficiency virus (HIV).
2. Risk factors for infection.
   a. Unprotected sex.
   b. Contact with blood or body fluids.
3. Prevention.
   a. Avoid unprotected sex via abstinence or use of condoms.

b. Avoid contact with body fluids.
c. Practice standard precautions with all persons. Refer to Appendix 3A in Chapter 3.
4. Human immunodeficiency virus (HIV) infection.
   a. Retrovirus.
      (1) The virus can eclipse into the cell, remaining dormant until stimulated by the body.
   b. HIV attacks the lymphatic system, the system that protects the body's immunity to opportunistic infections.
      (1) The T cells (also known as CD4+ cells) attack the cells of the body, including central nervous system cells (CNS), gastrointestinal tract cells, and uterine/cervical cells.
   c. Four stages of infection.
      (1) Acute infection: flu-like response to initial contact with the virus.
      (2) Asymptomatic disease: HIV replicates and affects the immune system, but no visible signs other than blood abnormalities are detectable.
      (3) Symptomatic HIV: signs and symptoms appear.
      (4) Advanced disease, or AIDS: severely compromised immunity.
   d. Sequelae of HIV infection.
      (1) Generalized lymphadenopathy/enlarged lymph nodes.
         (a) Fatigue.
         (b) Weight loss, malabsorption of nutrients (wasting syndrome).
         (c) General malaise.
      (2) Fever.
      (3) Diarrhea.
      (4) All of these result in decreased tolerance for activity participation and lack of energy.
      (5) Neurological impairment.
         (a) Cognitive impairment (i.e., safety issues, communication and expression impairments, alteration of personality, decreased ability to engage as before in interpersonal relationships).
         (b) Affective changes.
         (c) Sensory changes (associated with neurocognitive disorders).
         (d) BADL impairments such as inability to hold and manipulate objects for use (e.g., money, combs, toothbrushes, writing implements, feeding utensils, telephone, remote control, etc.).
         (e) Myelopathy (spinal cord pathology).
         (f) Peripheral neuropathy.
         (g) Visual impairment.
   e. Drug therapy.
      (1) Protease inhibitors work to suppress the viral load in the bloodstream.
         (a) Has resulted in a dramatic change in the management, treatment, and survivability of persons with a diagnosis of HIV/AIDS.

CAUTION: Protease inhibitors must be taken consistently on time or effectiveness is lost.

      (2) Chemotherapy.
         (a) Less effective than protease inhibitors.
         (b) Several side effects (specific to drugs used).
         (c) Drugs used related to observed neoplastic processes (e.g., Kaposi's sarcoma, lymphoma).
         (d) Drugs used to treat opportunistic infections (e.g., Foscarnet).
   f. Complications of advanced disease occur with less frequency in the current medical environment.
   g. Treatment advances using drugs in combination and personal adherence to drug treatment regimens that suppress the infection has resulted in transforming the outcome of AIDS from an immediate life-threatening diagnosis to a chronic condition.

Hepatitis

1. Etiology: a viral infection.
2. Risk factors.
   a. Type A.
      (1) Contaminated seafood.
      (2) Protective immunization possible.
   b. Types B, C, and other identified forms.
      (1) Body-borne and bloodborne exposure.
      (2) Protective immunization possible for type B.
         (a) Health-care workers are most susceptible to hepatitis B.
         (b) It is estimated that many people in the US population may have undetected hepatitis C infections that they can potentially (and unknowingly) communicate to others.

CAUTION: Standard precautions must be used with all persons in all situations to prevent contact with blood or body fluids. Refer to Appendix 3A in Chapter 3.

3. Sequelae.
   a. Fever.
   b. Fatigue.
   c. These contribute to decreased tolerance for activity participation and lack of energy.
   d. Hepatitis C infections can cause life-threatening cirrhosis over time and may contribute to chronic fatigue and disability.

Tuberculosis (TB)

1. See Chapter 8.

Methicillin-Resistant Staphylococcus aureus (MRSA)

1. Etiology: usually mild infections (pimples or boils) on the skin; or more serious infections on skin; or infection in surgical wounds.
    a. The infection can be locally confined or systemic (entering the bloodstream and affecting primarily the lungs or the urinary tract).
2. Risk factors.
    a. Having a weakened immune system.
    b. Confinement in a hospital or other health-care institutions.
    c. Living in close quarters (military barracks, college dormitory, etc.).
    d. Direct skin contact with an infected body part of another person (e.g., contact sports).
    e. Secondary skin contact from something used by someone with an infection (e.g., shared towels during sports activities).
3. The infection resists treatment from known antibiotics, even broad-spectrum antibiotics. Some antibiotics still work to fight it.
4. Signs and symptoms.
    a. Redness accompanied by swelling and pain in the area of the wound.
    b. Drainage such as pus in the local area of the wound.
    c. Fever.
    d. Skin abscess.
    e. Chest pain.
    f. Cough.
    g. Fatigue.
    h. Headache.
    i. Muscle ache.
    j. Rash.
    k. Shortness of breath.
5. Testing.
    a. Cultures of blood, sputum, skin, or urine.
6. Prevention, detection, and early intervention.
    a. Avoid high-risk situations that contribute to possible exposure.
    b. Take preventative measures.
        (1) Wash your hands.
        (2) Avoid sharing personal items (e.g., razors or towels).
        (3) Keep any wounds or cuts covered.
        (4) Avoid communal bathing/swimming where infected persons may have been.
        (5) Assure facilities you use are clean.
7. Medical treatment for MRSA.
    a. Draining of a skin sore by a physician.
    b. Antibiotic treatment.
    c. Additional measures depending on severity and location of infection.
        (1) Intravenous fluids.
        (2) Oxygen.
        (3) Dialysis (if kidney failure occurs).
8. Sequelae of MRSA.
    a. Chance of recurrence of infection in the future.
    b. Any organ system damage that occurs as a result from untreated or unmanaged infections.

Rehabilitation for Immunological System Disorders

1. Overall goals and approaches can be preventive, restorative, supportive, and/or palliative depending on treatment setting, diagnosis, stage of illness, and expected outcomes.
2. The role of the OTA in intervention.
    a. The OTA implements intervention with OT supervision.
    b. The level of supervision required depends upon the OTA's experience and established service competence.
    c. During the implementation of intervention, the OTA informs the supervising OT of any change in the individual's status and any other relevant information that may affect treatment.
3. Interventions for impairment-level problems.
    a. Counsel people to follow screening and treatment regimens.
    b. Set personal goals to invest behaviorally in one's health.
    c. Provide support to those dealing with immunological system disorders that are chronic illnesses (i.e., AIDS).
    d. Provide supportive counseling and social support for psychological disorders that can develop (e.g., anxiety disorder, depression, and/or adjustment disorders).
    e. Refer to physician for drug therapy and complementary medicine as indicated for accompanying physical and/or psychiatric disorders (e.g., kidney disease, depression).
4. Interventions for activity-level problems.
    a. Self-care.
        (1) Adaptations and training to do self-care tasks with greatest ease while conserving energy. For example, for an individual with scleroderma:
            (a) Alter grasp/pinch patterns and level of demand and upper extremity demand.
            (b) Alter size of feeding utensils and toothbrushes to accommodate decreased ability to open mouth.
            (c) Prevent shearing forces on skin during specific personal ADL tasks.

b. Work.
      (1) Modifications to work site to allow participation in component tasks and activities.
      (2) Counseling and intervention for transition to disability status when work is no longer possible.
  c. Leisure/sports.
      (1) Modify specific tasks and activities (e.g., to protect body parts involved by sclerodermic changes).
      (2) Determine interests and skills to introduce new leisure or sports activities of interest to the person to transition to less physically demanding tasks as a disease progresses.
  d. Rest and sleep.
      (1) Monitor and intervene to maximize the ability to be well positioned during rest and sleep.
      (2) Monitor rest and sleep habits and patterns and intervene when strategies are needed to relax and unwind or to schedule time and opportunity for relaxation.
      (3) Refer to Chapter 14 for more information on rest and sleep evaluation and intervention.
5. Interventions for participation problems.
  a. Needs assessment to determine individual issues the person has with mobility, social, or political access to their personal, home, or community environments.
  b. Identification and facilitation of procurement of system changes to allow the person to access and participate in their community as a contributing member.
6. Acute hospitalization phase.
  a. Early mobilization.
  b. Preservation of function.
  c. Positioning.
  d. Psychological/emotional support.
  e. Prevention of long-term disability.
7. Inpatient rehabilitation.
  a. Restoration of functional abilities.
      (1) BADL.
      (2) IADL.
      (3) Energy conservation and work simplification.
  b. Restoration of activity/exercise tolerance.
  c. Achievement and maintenance of quality of life.
  d. Role readjustment intervention.
  e. Planning to return to community.
      (1) Access to environment.
      (2) Participation issues.
8. Home care.
  a. Restoration of functional ability.
  b. Restoration of activity/exercise tolerance.
  c. Community mobility.
      (1) To inner and outer boundaries of home environment.
      (2) Into the street/block.
      (3) Further ability to venture out into the community (i.e., marketing, use of transportation, medical/business appointments, leisure access).
9. Community-based care.
  a. School related.
      (1) Transition from home schooling back to school for the returning child.
      (2) Transition of having student return to the class for the classmates.
  b. Work related.
      (1) Participation as per Americans with Disabilities Act (ADA). See Chapters 4 and 14.
  c. Population-related intervention.
      (1) Coalition-related and grant-funded initiatives for prevention and outreach programs.

Endocrine System and Metabolic System Disorders

Diabetes

1. Prevalence: 9.4% of the population of the United States has diabetes.
  a. Of the 30.3 million adults with diabetes, 23.1 million were diagnosed and 7.2 million were undiagnosed.
      (1) The percentage of Americans age 65 and older with diagnosed and undiagnosed diabetes remains high, at 25.2%, or 12 million.
  b. 1.5 million Americans are diagnosed with diabetes every year.
  c. 84.1 million Americans age 20 and older have pre-diabetes.
2. Prognosis: diabetes remains the seventh leading cause of death in the United States in 2015.
  a. Diabetes is listed as the cause of death in 80,000 cases.
  b. Diabetes is an underlying or contributing cause of death for an additional 170,000 persons per year (Centers for Disease Control and Prevention [CDC], 2018).

EXAM HINT: In the NBCOT® practice analysis, 42.5% of COTA®s who provided services to persons with general medical/systemic disorders indicated they provided services to individuals with diabetes (NBCOT®, 2018, p. 15). Due to this prevalence, it is likely that the COTA® exam will have items about working with persons with diabetes.

3. Types, etiology, and risk factors.
   a. Type 1 diabetes (insulin-dependent; ~5% of all diagnosed cases of diabetes).
      (1) Autoimmune.
      (2) Genetic.
      (3) Environmental factors.
   b. Type 2 diabetes (non-insulin-dependent; ~90%–95% of all cases of diabetes).
      (1) Older age.
      (2) Obesity.
      (3) Family history.
      (4) Prior history of gestational diabetes.
      (5) Impaired glucose tolerance.
      (6) Physical inactivity.
      (7) Race/ethnicity.
   c. Gestational diabetes (2%–10% of all pregnancies; 50% may go on later to develop type 2 diabetes in later life).
      (1) Usually resolves after pregnancy.
      (2) Occurs at a greater frequency in race/ethnicity risk groups.
      (3) Obesity is another risk factor.
   d. Other types of diabetes (1%–2% of all cases of diabetes).
      (1) Genetic syndromes.
      (2) Surgery.
      (3) Drugs (e.g., steroids).
      (4) Malnutrition.
      (5) Infections.
4. Signs and symptoms.
   a. Frequent urination.
   b. Excessive thirst.
   c. Unexplained weight loss.
   d. Extreme hunger.
   e. Visual changes.
   f. Sensory changes (tingling/numbness) in the hands or feet.
   g. Fatigue.
   h. Very dry skin.
   i. Slow-healing wounds.
   j. Increased rate of infections.
5. Prevention.
   a. Regular physical activity may reduce the risk of type 2 diabetes.
   b. Maintaining normal body weight may prevent type 2 diabetes.
6. Sequelae/complications.
   a. Fatigue/decreased activity tolerance.
   b. Urinary disturbance.
   c. Visual loss, low vision, blindness.
   d. Peripheral neuropathy.
      (1) Amputations.
   e. Propensity to develop wounds.
   f. Connective tissue disease associated with diabetes.
      (1) There is a significantly higher incidence of Dupuytren's disease, limited joint motion, carpal tunnel syndrome, and flexor tenosynovitis in the diabetic population.
      (2) Characterized by development of soft tissue thickening in the palms of the hands and soles of the feet.
   g. Poor general health/increased rate of infections disrupt life roles and activity participation.
   h. Hypoglycemia: very low blood sugar.

> **RED FLAG:** Hypoglycemic symptoms include vagueness, dizziness, tachycardia, pallor, weakness, diaphoresis, seizures, and/or coma.
> - If the person is conscious, immediately provide carbohydrates in the form of hard candy, fruit juice, or honey.
> - If the person is unconscious, immediately call for emergency medical care.

   i. Hyperglycemic crisis: A metabolic emergency.

> **RED FLAG:** Ketoacidosis signs include dehydration, rapid and weak pulse, and acetone breath. Hyperosmolar coma: signs include stupor, thirst, polyuria, and neurologic abnormalities.
> - Call for emergency medical services *immediately* as IV fluids and insulin are required.

7. Rehabilitation.
   a. Preventive exercise.
   b. Education concerning compliance and need for medical management of condition.
   c. Psychological and emotional support to improve self-care habits.
   d. Lifestyle readjustment to complications when and if they occur.
      (1) Low vision.
      (2) Safety assessment and intervention.
      (3) Physical adaptations.
   e. Protective issues regarding peripheral neuropathy.
      (1) Safety assessment.
      (2) Education concerning risk associated with sensory loss.
      (3) Skin care.
      (4) Pain management.
      (5) Adapted equipment/techniques to facilitate participation in lifestyle.
      (6) Instrumental activities supporting compliance of self-management.
   f. Early attention to wound management.
      (1) Teach skin care and inspection techniques.
      (2) Teach person to self-advocate quickly when changes are observed.
   g. Assistance in problem-solving and modifying self-care as changes occur in the medical status of the condition.
      (1) Problem-solve resources for specialized treatment.

(2) Teach person to recognize changes in their functional status that warrant further attention and intervention.

Obesity and Bariatric Issues[1]

1. Obesity is defined as a condition characterized by excess body fat.
2. Body mass index (BMI): a formula for determining obesity. BMI is calculated by dividing an individual's weight in kilograms by the square of the person's height in meters.
    a. World Health Organization Classification adopted by the National Institutes of Health.
       (1) Overweight defined as BMI ranging from 25 to 29.9.
       (2) Obesity defined as BMI > 30.
       (3) Morbidly obese defined as BMI > 0.
3. A national health problem: overweight (65% of Americans) and obesity (31% of Americans).
    a. Health risks and resultant conditions associated with obesity: metabolic syndrome, hypertension, hyperlipidemia, type 2 diabetes, cardiovascular disease, stroke, glucose intolerance, sleep apnea, gallbladder disease, menstrual irregularities, infertility, cancer (endometrial, breast, prostate, and colon), and chronic low back pain.
    b. The result is premature death and an increased mortality rate.
    c. Waist circumference is used to determine distribution of body fat. Abdominal obesity (central accumulation of fat) is an independent predictor of morbidity and mortality.
    d. Childhood obesity: most prevalent nutritional disorder affecting children in the United States.
4. Prevalence.
    a. Obesity affected about 93.3 million of US adults (39.8%) in 2015–2016.
       (1) The prevalence of obesity was 35.7% among young adults aged 20–39 years, 42.8% among middle-aged adults aged 40–59 years, and 41.0% among older adults aged 60 and older.

> **EXAM HINT:** In the NBCOT® practice analysis, 19.4% of COTA®s who provided services to persons with general medical/systemic disorders indicated they provided services to bariatric individuals (NBCOT®, 2018, p. 15). Due to this prevalence, the COTA® exam may have items about bariatric practice.

5. Etiology: health disparity; result of complex social, behavioral, cultural, environmental, physiological, and genetic factors.
    a. Social.
       (1) Education and income level.
       (2) Occupation.
       (3) Family background.
    b. Behavioral.
       (1) Eating on the run/fast food.
       (2) Eating alone.
       (3) Eating for solace/'comfort' foods.
       (4) Binge eating.
    c. Cultural.
       (1) 'Food and love' cultures (food given as a sign of affection).
       (2) Larger body size is more highly valued in several cultures.
       (3) Post-Depression-era eating (i.e., consuming more because there is money to buy).
       (4) Restaurant cultures' (larger proportions, greater food diversity, higher fat content).
    d. Environmental.
       (1) Lack of time to devote to meal planning and preparation.
       (2) Lack of time to develop and maintain a proper exercise routine (e.g., the 'sandwich' generation who provides simultaneous caregiving for their parents and children resulting in a real or perceived lack of time for self).
       (3) Lack of access to resources.
           (a) No facilities in which to exercise.
           (b) No exercise coach/partner.
    e. Physiological.
       (1) A nutritionally related imbalance that occurs resulting in excess body fat.
           (a) Poor diet and nutrition.
           (b) Eating processed foods.
           (c) Excessive food consumption: excess calories are consumed that are not expended by work or exercise.
           (d) Activity level: lack of exercise; poor choice of exercise in proportion to what is consumed.
           (e) Compulsive overeating: psychiatric disorder.
       (2) Excess body fat that occurs from a metabolic imbalance.
           (a) Gestational diabetes (passively introduced to fetus: results in oversized infants at birth).
           (b) Adrenal disorders: cortisol and stress.
       (3) Side effects of the atypical second-generation antipsychotic (SGAs) medications.
           (a) SGAs affect the metabolism process, alter resting metabolic rate, and increase cravings for carbohydrates.
           (b) The rate of metabolic syndrome is substantially higher for persons with mental illness as compared to the general population.

---
[1] Susan O'Sullivan contributed to this section.

6. Prevention.
   a. Education.
      (1) Raising awareness of behavioral factors that contribute to obesity (e.g., sedentary lifestyle).
      (2) Promoting community-driven group intervention options focused on health promotion and wellness.
   b. Habit intervention with occupations and activities that contribute to obesity (e.g., choose this/not that approaches, not eating while stressed, mindful eating).
   c. Tertiary intervention when overcoming obesity is not the issue-focus on occupational needs of the client.
7. Sequelae.
   a. Decreased ability in performance areas of occupations (BADL, IADL, community mobility, social participation).
   b. Symptomatology related to larger body size: musculoskeletal pain, limited mobility, lower activity tolerance.
8. Rehabilitation.
   a. Lifestyle redesign: combination of changes in daily habits, patterns, and routines to reduce body weight through nutritional changes (e.g., emphasis on fruits, vegetables, whole grains, and lean protein) and changes in activity time engagement combined with increased physical activity.
      (1) Personalized plan to change lifestyle habits that contribute to obesity risk.
      (2) Personalized activity-focused exercise program combining personal interests, desired participation, goals, and positive meaning (e.g., participating in the OT walks with National Alliance on Mental Illness [NAMI] program for persons with metabolic syndrome caused by SGAs).
      (3) Instruction in self-monitoring of exercise responses (i.e., heart rate, perceived exertion).
      (4) Supportive coaching/counseling to improve compliance and make long-term, life-altering change.
   b. Inpatient rehabilitation tertiary care.
      (1) Access devices and equipment to maximize client participation in daily activities of meaning (BADL, IADL, mobility, and community participation).
         (a) Bariatric equipment: wheeled mobility, assistive devices, lifters, seating adaptations, clothing adaptations. See Chapter 15.
      (2) Activity participation to relearn lifestyle modifications and to offer practice in altering habits and patterns that require adjustment in order to maximize the individual's participation and meaningful engagement.
   c. Comorbidities, risks, and complications.
      (1) Cardiopulmonary compromise is typically exhibited (i.e., shortness of breath, elevated blood pressure, and angina).
      (2) Altered biomechanics affects hips, knees, ankle/foot; back and joint pain are common.
         (a) Increased risk of orthopedic injury.
      (3) Increased risk of skin breakdown due to shear forces.
      (4) Increased heat intolerance, risk of hyperthermia, and heat exhaustion.
      (5) Increased risk of practitioner injury when using poor body mechanics or inadequate assistance during transfers and lifts.

Lyme Disease

1. The incidence of Lyme disease in the United States has approximately doubled since 1991, from 3.74 reported cases per 100,000 people to 7.95 reported cases per 100,000 people in 2014. There are approximately 30,000 new cases of Lyme disease each year.
2. Etiology.
   a. Tick bites.
      (1) Ticks are usually found on animals, on the tips of grasses and shrubs.
      (2) Ticks attach to people as they brush by the object to which the tick is attached.
3. Prevention.
   a. Walk on trails to avoid contact with grass and brush.
   b. Avoid tick-infested areas especially in May, June, and July.
   c. Wear light-colored clothing, so ticks can be easily seen.
   d. Tuck in clothing and tape clothing seams (i.e., where pants meet socks) to prevent entry.
   e. Spray insect repellent containing DEET on clothes and exposed skin, excluding the face.
   f. After being outdoors, change clothes and inspect skin for the presence of ticks.
   g. Remove any ticks with tweezers, grasping the tick as close to the skin surface as possible and pulling straight back.
4. Sequelae and symptoms.
   a. Impairs the immune response and affects the neurological and orthopedic systems.
   b. Early symptoms.
      (1) Fatigue.
      (2) Headache.
      (3) Chills and fever.
      (4) Muscle and joint pain.
      (5) Swollen lymph nodes.
      (6) Rash, erythema migrans: a circular red patch occurring three days to one month after the bite from an infected tick.
         (a) The center of the rash may clear as it enlarges, resembling a bulls-eye.

c. Late symptoms.
  (1) Arthritis: brief bouts of pain and swelling in one or more of the large joints.
    (a) Knees are most commonly affected joints.
  (2) Nervous system abnormalities.
    (a) Numbness.
    (b) Pain.
    (c) Bell's palsy.
    (d) Meningitis.
    (e) CNS involvement may contribute to neurocognitive disorders and balance impairments.
  (3) Heart rate irregularities.
  (4) Bowel and bladder control problems associated with the antibiotics used to treat Lyme disease.
5. Medical treatment.
  a. Antibiotics, oral or intravenous.
  b. Management of joint-related symptoms from the accompanying arthritis.
6. Rehabilitation.
  a. Treat joint pain and swelling.
    (1) Provide education regarding acute arthritic flares.
      (a) Rest.
      (b) Anti-inflammatory medicine compliance.
      (c) Splinting or wrapping to protect inflamed joints and prevent overstretching of enlarged joint.
      (d) Teach energy conservation and work simplification.
    (2) Following flare, in subacute phase, provide gradual reintroduction of normal performance of daily tasks and activities.
  b. Treat nervous system abnormalities.
    (1) Numbness.
      (a) Safety assessment and intervention to preserve safety and prevent injury.
      (b) Management of esthesias that are perceived as painful.
      (c) Occupation-based interventions to encourage and preserve function and to cope with chronic pain conditions.
    (2) Pain.
      (a) Use of physical agent modalities to reduce pain.
      (b) Use of stress management (complementary care) techniques to control the intensity of the pain and to increase coping ability.
      (c) Use of neutral warmth to decrease intensity of pain.
      (d) Use of adapted techniques to avoid triggering of movements that exacerbate pain during activity (e.g., sit on higher seat to decrease stress load in sit or stand).
    (3) Bell's palsy.
      (a) Make a facial splint to prevent long-term asymmetry of facial muscles. Clip or pincer mold of the inside and outer lip of the mouth on the involved side. Elastic attaching mouth mold to earpiece (similar to eyeglass ear rim).
      (b) Use electric stimulation to stimulate denervated muscles.
      (c) Teach person to use their fingers to assist buccal closure and prevent spillage of the bolus through the lips.
      (d) Provide counseling concerning alteration in body image, since the individual is coping with a facial deformity.
    (4) Meningitis.
      (a) Acute care: positioning, splinting, supportive care while hospitalized.
      (b) Rehabilitation if there is recovery-related sequelae (i.e., neurologic impairment, motor impairment, sensory impairment, cognitive impairment, and/or ADL impairment).
    (5) Heart rate irregularities.
      (a) Telemetry during daily performance of tasks and activities that support role performance.
      (b) Pulse oximetry measurements, if oxygenation is poor during performance of daily tasks and activities.
      (c) Work simplification, adaptation, and modification to prevent further complications associated with arrhythmia.

Integumentary System Disorders

Wounds and Pressure/Decubitus Ulcers

1. Prevalence.
  a. Chronic wounds affect nearly 14.5% of Medicare beneficiaries (8.2 million people).
    (1) The most expensive mean Medicare spending per beneficiary was for surgical wounds, followed by diabetic wounds.
  b. Among persons with diabetes, 15%–25% develop a foot ulcer; 20% of individuals with a foot ulcer require amputation.

(1) Hospitalizations for persons with diabetes due to lower-extremity amputations caused by non-healing wounds were 5 per 1,000 persons with diabetes.

> **CAUTION:** Be aware that wounds can be a complication of any diagnosis that compromises the person's sensorimotor, cardiopulmonary, renal-genitourinary, immunological, and/or endocrine systems.

> **EXAM HINT:** In the NBCOT® practice analysis, 18.0% of COTA®s who provided services to persons with general medical/systemic disorders indicated they provided services to persons with open wounds and pressure ulcers (NBCOT®, 2018, p. 15). Due to this prevalence and practitioners' ethical responsibility to ensure people's health and safety, it is likely that the COTA® exam will have items about the prevention, evaluation, and management of wounds and decubiti.

2. Types of wounds or impaired skin integrities.
   a. Abrasions: trauma to the skin resulting in a breakage in skin integrity, often caused by a fall, or sliding impact to the body part.
   b. Punctures: small holes in the skin, allowing air passage into the wound.
   c. Bites: insect, animals, human.
   d. Surgical wounds: incisions, resections, grafts, amputations.
   e. Diabetic ulcers.
   f. Pressure injuries: prolonged exposure to pressures exceeding capillary pressure.
   g. Traumatic wounds: burns/thermal injuries, gunshot wounds, degloving injuries, compression and crash injuries.
   h. Venous stasis ulcers: poor lower extremity circulation, varicose veins.
   i. Arterial ulcers: result from damage to the arteries due to lack of blood flow to tissue.
   j. Surgical infections were the largest prevalence category, followed by diabetic wound infections.
3. Etiology and risk factors.
   a. Pressure that interrupts normal circulation causing localized areas of cellular necrosis.
      (1) Greatest risk is over bony prominences (e.g., ischial tuberosity).
      (2) Intensity and duration of the pressure determines the severity of the decubiti.
   b. Refer to Box 9-3 for factors that predispose the development of decubitus ulcers.
4. Stages and signs of pressure ulcers.
   a. The National Pressure Ulcer Advisory Panel has updated the definitions and stage classifications of pressure ulcers.
      (1) This revision includes the original four stages and two additional stages of deep tissue injury and unstageable pressure ulcers.
   b. Suspected deep tissue injury.
      (1) Localized discoloration of intact skin (purple or maroon) or a blister filled with blood resulting from damage of underlying soft tissue.
      (2) Deep tissue injury may be difficult to detect in individuals with darkly pigmented skin.
      (3) This stage may further evolve and can rapidly expose additional layers of tissue.
   c. Stage I pressure ulcer.
      (1) Skin is intact with visible nonblanchable redness over a localized area, typically over a bony prominence. See Figure 9-3.
      (2) Visible blanching may not be evident in darkly pigmented skin; the color may appear different from the surrounding area.
      (3) The area may be soft or firm and/or cooler or warmer when compared to adjacent skin.
      (4) The area may be painful or itchy.

BOX 9-3 Factors that Predispose Formation of Decubitus Ulcers

- Immobility or altered mobility.
- Significant weight loss.
- Edema.
- Incontinence.
- Sensory deficiencies.
- Circulatory abnormalities.
- Dehydration.
- Inadequate nutrition.
- Obesity.
- Age-related skin changes.
- Multiple comorbidities.
- Certain pathological conditions, including spinal cord injury (SCI), cerebral palsy, diabetes, cancer, burns, and hand injuries.

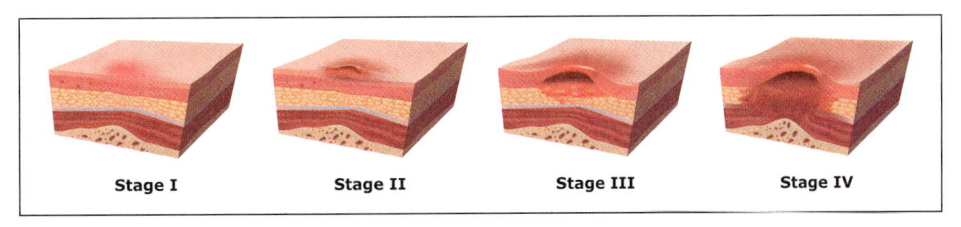

Stage I   Stage II   Stage III   Stage IV

Figure 9-3 Stages of Pressure Ulcers

> **CAUTION:** A Stage I pressure ulcer may indicate "at risk" persons, but its signs can be difficult to detect.

    d. Stage II pressure ulcer.
      (1) Involves the dermis with partial-thickness loss, which presents as a shallow open ulcer that can be shiny or dry. See Figure 9-3.
      (2) A Stage II ulcer can also present as a blister that is intact or open/ruptured.
      (3) The wound bed is a red/pink color without slough or bruising.
    e. Stage III pressure ulcer.
      (1) Involves full-thickness tissue loss with subcutaneous fat possibly visible. See Figure 9-3.
      (2) The depth of tissue loss is not obscured if slough (i.e., dead matter/necrotic tissue) is present.
      (3) Bone, tendon, or muscle are not exposed or directly palpable.
      (4) The depth of a Stage III pressure ulcer can vary according to anatomical location and can range from shallow in areas that do not have subcutaneous tissue (e.g., the nose, ear) to very deep in areas with significant fat (e.g., the buttocks).
    f. Stage IV pressure ulcer.
      (1) Involves full-thickness tissue loss with bone, tendon, or muscle visible or directly palpable. See Figure 9-3.
      (2) Similarly, the depth of a Stage IV pressure ulcer can vary according to anatomical location and can range from shallow in areas that do not have subcutaneous tissue (e.g., the nose, ear) to very deep in areas with significant fat (e.g., the buttocks).
      (3) Osteomyelitis is possible if Stage IV ulcers extend into muscle, fascia, tendon, and/or the joint capsule.
    g. Unstageable pressure ulcers.
      (1) Involves full-thickness tissue loss in which the wound bed has slough and/or eschar (i.e., a scab or dark crusted ulcer) which covers the base of the ulcer.
5. Medical management including occlusive dressings, débridement, surgery, and/or grafting may be needed depending on the severity of the decubitus ulcer.
6. Impact of wounds.
    a. Wounds and related conditions can negatively affect a person's ability to participate in their life roles, routines, and useful habits and can affect performance with self-care, work, educational activities, leisure activities, social participation, and rest and sleep.
    b. Wounds affect both the physical and psychological well-being of individuals.
    c. Wounds can adversely affect quality of life.
    d. Reduced social participation, self-efficacy, and reported quality of life due to discoloration of the skin, visible scars, contracting or hypertrophic scars, and conspicuous use of compression garments.
    e. Pain, depression, social isolation, and anxiety can result from the existence of wounds in the acute and chronic phases.
    f. Financial stability that can be affected by the inability to work due to a significant wound. (AOTA, 2018.)

> **EXAM HINT:** The NBCOT® exam outline for the COTA® identifies knowledge of the "technical level indications, contraindications, and precautions associated with wound management, considering the characteristics of a wound, the stage of wound healing, and the influence of the wound on engagement in occupation as guided by evidence, best practice standards, scope of practice, and state licensure practice acts in order to support functional outcomes" as essential for competent practice. The application of knowledge about the types, causes, risks, and impact of wounds and the stages of pressure ulcers previously described and the information about the evaluation, intervention, and prevention of wounds described in the following can help you determine the correct answer for exam items about persons with wounds and decubiti.

7. Evaluation.
    a. Early assessment is critical to prevent wounds from developing and/or progressing.
      (1) The skin integrity of all persons should be assessed.
      (2) The presence of risk factors for wounds should be assessed to determine the person's potential for developing a wound.
        (a) Refer to Box 9-3 for a list of risk factors for the development of decubiti ulcers.
    b. While nursing staff in medical model settings typically assume the responsibility for skin and risk assessments, OT practitioners can (and should) contribute to this process.
      (1) In nonmedical model settings (e.g., home care), the OT practitioner may need to take a more active role in the evaluation/reevaluation process.
    c. During the provision of OT services, the OTA should monitor the person's skin integrity and risk factors and inform the supervising therapist of any change in the individual's status and any other relevant information that may affect their skin integrity.
8. Intervention.
    a. The need for assistance and/or accommodations for participation in activities and contexts specifically

related to the wound should be addressed. Interventions include:
- (1) Management of the wound site, including applying wound care treatments and products to promote healing as well as manage drainage or odor.
- (2) Management of clothing and footwear that may no longer fit correctly or that may worsen the wound condition.
- (3) Education regarding donning/doffing, care of, and recommended wear schedule for pressure garments for scar management.
- (4) The promotion of restful sleep, despite the presence of pain.
- (5) Physical activity and functional mobility to prevent impairments in endurance, overall strength, cardiovascular status, pulmonary status, and cognition, as well as reduce pain at the wound site.
- (6) Bed mobility and positioning to relieve pressure on wounds, minimize pain, and prevent further skin breakdown from occurring.
- (7) Social participation opportunities to address potential self-efficacy and body image issues due to skin discoloration or scarring, and/or compression garment use.

b. Prevention is the most effective intervention for all wound types.
- (1) Use of wheelchair cushions, flotation pads, and pressure-relief bed aids to distribute pressure over a larger skin surface. The Centers for Medicare and Medicaid Services has divided pressure-reducing devices into three categories for reimbursement purposes. These are:
  - (a) Group 1: cushions or mattresses that use nonelectrical means (e.g., air, foam, gel, or water) to distribute pressure.
  - (b) Group 2: dynamic, electric-powered devices (e.g., alternating and low air loss mattresses) for persons with full-thickness ulcers or those at moderate to high risk.
  - (c) Group 3: dynamic, electric-powered devices (e.g., air-fluidized beds) for persons with nonhealing full-thickness ulcers.
- (2) Train the individual and/or caregivers in positioning and weight-shifting techniques and schedules.
  - (a) Full push-ups, lateral leans, forward leans, or wheelchair tilt/recline options are common techniques, used depending upon the abilities of the individual.
  - (b) Weight shifts should occur every 30 minutes for 30 seconds or every 60 minutes for 60 seconds.
  - (c) Integrate weight shifting into daily activities (e.g., lean forward to pick up the phone, lean sideways when reading the mail).

CAUTION: The presence of substance abuse, cognitive deficits, and/or psychological impairments can jeopardize the individual's ability to understand and complete the required daily wound prevention regimen, thus increasing their risk for the development of wounds.

- (3) Train the individual and/or caregivers in proper skin care.
  - (a) Keep skin free of excessive moisture, dryness, and heat.
  - (b) Check skin at least two times per day for any evidence of breakdown. Most individuals perform this in bed in the morning before arising and in the evening before sleep.
  - (c) Target the scapula, elbows, ischia, sacrum/coccyx, trochanters, heels, ankles, and knees for inspection when checking for pressure sores.
- (4) Encourage adequate intake of fluids and food to maintain nutrition, promote healing, and achieve a recommended body weight.

c. Occupation-based interventions.
- (1) Encourage participation in meaningful and productive activities.
- (2) Individuals who pursue active lifestyles have fewer decubiti.

Whole Body System Disorders

Heat Syndromes/ Hyperthermia

1. Etiology and risk factors.
   a. Heat production increases with infection, exercise, and/or drugs.
   b. Heat loss decreases with high humidity and/or temperature, excess clothing, obesity, cardiovascular disease, dehydration, sweat gland dysfunction, lack of acclimatization, and/or drugs.
   c. When an individual's heat loss is not sufficient to offset their heat production, their body will retain heat and a heat syndrome can develop.
   d. Older adults and individuals who are obese or taking drugs are at increased risk.

2. Prevention.
   a. In hot weather, wear lightweight, loose-fitting clothing.
   b. Avoid hot places; seek shade, use fans and/or air conditioners.
   c. Rest frequently.
   d. Increase fluid intake.
3. Types, signs, and symptoms.
   a. Heat cramps are characterized by a normal body temperature, nausea, diaphoresis, muscle twitching or spasms, weakness, and/or severe muscle cramps.
   b. Heat exhaustion is characterized by a rapid pulse, decreased blood pressure, nausea, vomiting, cool, pallid skin, mental confusion, headache and/or giddiness, but no fever.

RED FLAG: Heat stroke is characterized by hot, dry red skin; a body temperature higher than 104°; slow, deep respiration; tachycardia; dilated pupils; confusion; progressing to seizures and possibly loss of consciousness. Heat stroke is a medical emergency and emergency medical services must be called immediately.

4. Intervention.
   a. Heat stroke: while waiting for emergency medical services to arrive, lower the person's body temperature by any and all means possible. For example, getting them to a cooler area, placing ice packs on arterial pressure points, spraying the person's body with a cool mist and/or covering the person with cold wet sheets.
      (1) Hypothermia blankets, IV infusions, and medications are necessary.
   b. Heat cramps and heat exhaustion usually do not require hospitalization.
      (1) Loosen clothing and have the person lie in a cool place.
      (2) Replace fluid and electrolytes with salt tablets and a balanced electrolyte drink. If these are not available, give fluids and seek additional medical care.
      (3) Massage muscles if cramps are severe.
      (4) IV infusions and oxygen may be indicated if symptoms are severe.

References

American Cancer Society. (2019). *Cancer facts and figures.* Retrieved from https://www.cancer.org/content/dam/cancer-org/research/cancer-facts-and-statistics/annual-cancer-facts-and-figures/2019/cancer-facts-and-figures-2019.pdf

American Diabetes Association. (2019). *Fast facts: Data and statistics about diabetes.* Retrieved from https://professional.diabetes.org/sites/professional.diabetes.org/files/media/sci_2019_diabetes_fast_facts_sheet.pdf

American Occupational Therapy Association. (2007). Position paper: Obesity and occupational therapy. *American Journal of Occupational Therapy, 61,* 701–703.

American Occupational Therapy Association. (2011). The role of occupational therapy in end-of-life care. *American Journal of Occupational Therapy, 65,* S66-S75.

American Occupational Therapy Association. (2014). Occupational therapy practice framework: Domain and process (3rd ed.). *American Journal of Occupational Therapy, 68*(Suppl. 1), S1–S48.

American Occupational Therapy Association. (2018). Position paper: The role of occupational therapy in wound management. *American Journal of Occupational Therapy, 72*(Suppl. 2), 212410057p1–7212410057p9.

Armstrong, D. G., Boulton, A. J. M., & Bus, S. A. (2017). Diabetic foot ulcers and their recurrence. *New England Journal of Medicine, 376,* 2367–2375.

Balasundaram, I., et al. (2013). Rehabilitation interventions and their effect on quality of life in patients following major head and neck cancer surgery: Part 1. *Face Mouth and Jaw Surgery, 2*(2).

Balducci, L., & Fossa, S. D. (2013). Rehabilitation of older cancer patients. *Acta Oncologica, 52,* 233–238.

Balsara, Z., Ross, S. S., Dolber, P. C., Wiener, J. S., Tang, Y., & Seed, P. (2013). Enhanced susceptibility to urinary tract infection in the spinal cord-injured host with neurogenic bladder. *Infection and Immunity, 81,* 3018–3026.

Bergholdt, S. H., Søndergaard, J., Larsen, P. V., Holm, L. V., Kragstrup, J., & Hansen, D. G. (2013). A randomised controlled trial to improve general practitioners' services in cancer rehabilitation: Effects on general practitioners' proactivity and on patients' participation in rehabilitation activities. *Acta Oncologica, 52*(2), 400–409.

Blanchard, S. A. (2009). Variables associated with obesity among African-American women in Omaha. *American Journal of Occupational Therapy, 63,* 58–68.

Burkhardt, A., & Joachim, J. (1996). *A therapist's guide to oncology: Medical issues affecting management.* San Antonio, TX: Therapy Skill Builders.

Braveman, B., & Hunter, E. G. (2017). *Occupational therapy practice guidelines for cancer rehabilitation with adults.* Bethesda, MD: AOTA Press.

Buenaver, L., McGuire, L., & Haythornthwaite, J. (2006). Cognitive-behavioral self-help for chronic pain. *Journal of Clinical Psychology, 62,* 1389–1396.

Burkhardt, A. (2006). Oncology. In W. Schultz-Krohn & H. Pendleton (Eds.), *Occupational therapy: Practice skills for physical dysfunction* (6th ed., pp. 1157–1168). St. Louis, MO: Elsevier Science/Mosby.

Casale, R., Buounocore, M., & Matucci-Cerinic, M. (1997). Review article: Systemic sclerosis (scleroderma): An integrated challenge in rehabilitation. *Archives of Physical Medicine and Rehabilitation. 78*, 767–773.

Centers for Disease Control and Prevention. (2010). *Diabetes Public Health Resource*. Retrieved from http://www.cdc.gov/diabetes/

Centers for Disease Control and Prevention. (2014). *HIV/AIDS prevention*. Retrieved, from http://www.cdc.gov/nchstp/hiv_aids/pubs/faq/faq11.htm.

Centers for Disease Control and Prevention. (2015, October 15). *Testing recommendations for hepatitis C virus infection*. Retrieved from https://www.cdc.gov/hepatitis/hcv/guidelinesc.htm

Centers for Disease Control and Prevention. (2016, August 17). *Healthcare-associated infections: MRSA in healthcare settings*. Retrieved from https://www.cdc.gov/hai/organisms/mrsa-infection.html

Centers for Disease Control and Prevention. (2017, January 31). *HIV/ADIS: Surveillance overview*. Retrieved from https://www.cdc.gov/hiv/statistics/surveillance/index.html

Centers for Disease Control and Prevention. (2017, July 25). *Gestational diabetes*. Retrieved from https://www.cdc.gov/diabetes/basics/gestational.html

Centers for Disease Control and Prevention. (2018). *About HIV/AIDS*. Retrieved from https://www.cdc.gov/hiv/basics/whatishiv.html

Centers for Disease Control and Prevention. (2018, August 13). *Adult obesity facts*. Retrieved from https://www.cdc.gov/obesity/data/adult.html

Centers for Disease Control and Prevention. (2019, February 5). *Lyme disease statistics*. Retrieved from https://www.cdc.gov/lyme/datasurveillance/index.html

Clark, F. A., Blanchard, J., Sleight, A., Cogan, A., Floríndez, L., Gleason, S., . . ., & Vigen, C. (2015). *Lifestyle redesign: The intervention tested in the USC Well Elderly Studies* (2nd ed.). Bethesda, MD: AOTA Press.

Cox, M., Holm, S., Kurfuerst, S., Lynch, A., & Schuberth, L. (2007). Specialized knowledge and skills in feeding, eating, and swallowing for occupational therapy practice. *American Journal of Occupational Therapy, 61*, 686–700.

Curtin, R., Mapes, D., Schatell, D., & Burrows-Hudson, S. (2005). Self-management in patients with end stage renal disease: Exploring domains and dimensions. *Nephrology Nursing Journal, 32*, 389–395.

Dickman, R., Green, C., Fass, S., Quan, S., Dekel, R., Risner-Adler, S., & Fass, R. (2007). Relationships between sleep quality and pH monitoring findings in persons with gastroesophageal reflux disease. *Journal of Clinical Sleep Medicine, 15*, 505–513.

Dorsher, P. T., & McIntosh, P. M. (2012). Neurogenic bladder. *Advances in Urology*, 816274p1–816274p16.

Eades, M., Murphy, J., Carney, S., Amdouni, S., Lemoignan, J., Jelowicki, M., & Gagnon, B. (2012). Effect of an interdisciplinary rehabilitation program on quality of life in patients with head and neck cancer: Review of clinical experience. *Head and Neck, 35*(3), 343–349.

Ekberg, O., Hamdy, S., Woisard, V., Wuttge-Hannig, A., & Ortega, P. (2002). Social and psychological burden of dysphagia: Its impact on diagnosis and treatment. *Dysphagia, 17*(2), 139–146.

Farri, A., Accornero, A., & Burdese, C. (2007). Social importance of dysphagia: Its impact on diagnosis and therapy. *ACTA Otorhinolaryngol Italia, 27*, 83–86.

Foley, R. N., & Collins, A. J. (2007). End-stage renal disease in the United States: An update from the United States Renal Data System. *Journal of the American Society for Nephrology, 18*, 2644–2648.

Forhan, M., Bhambhani, Y., Dyer, D., Ramos-Salas, X., Ferguson-Pell, M., Sharma, A. (2010). Rehabilitation in bariatrics: Opportunities for practice and research. *Disability & Rehabilitation, 32*, 952–959.

Forhan, M., Bhambhani, Y., Dyer, D., Ramos-Salas, X., Ferguson-Pell, M., & Sharma, A. (2010). Rehabilitation in bariatrics: Opportunities for practice and research. *Disability and Rehabilitation, 32*(11), 952–959.

Frolek Clark, G., Roberts, P., Cox, M. S., Holm, S., Kurfuerst, S. T., Lynch, A. K., & Schuberth, L. M. (2007). Specialized knowledge and skills in feeding, eating, and swallowing for occupational therapy practice. *American Journal of Occupational Therapy, 61*, 686–700.

Furusawa, K., Sugiyama, H., Ikeda, A., Tokohiro, A., Koyoshi, H., Takahashi, M., & Tajima, F. (2007). Autonomic dysreflexia during a bowel regimen program in patients with cervical spinal cord injury. *Acta Medica Okayama, 61*, 221–227.

George, B., & Malkenson, G. (2008). Pressure ulcers: A clinical review. *Rehabilitation Management, 21*(10), 16–19.

Haig, A. J. (2007). Developing world rehabilitation strategy II: Flex the muscles, train the brain, and adapt to the impairment. *Disability and Rehabilitation, 29*, 977–979.

Hales, C. M., Carroll, M. D., Fryar, C. D., & Ogden, C. L. (2017). *Prevalence of obesity among adults and youth: United States, 2015–2016* (NCHS Data Brief No. 288). Hyattsville, MD: National Center for Health Statistics.

Healthline Editorial Team. (2018, January 2). *HIV treatments: List of prescription medications*. Retrieved from https://www.healthline.com/health/hiv-aids/medications-list#combination-drugs

Jung, T.-D., & Park, S.-H. (2011). Intradialytic exercise programs for hemodialysis patients. *Chonnam Medical Journal, 47*(2), 61–65.

Kaiser, F., Spiridigliozzi, A. M., & Hunt, M. P. (2001). Promoting shared decision-making in rehabilitation: Development of a framework for situations when patients with dysphagia refuse diet modification recommended by the treating team. *Dysphagia, 27*(1), 81–87.

Karlsson, A. K. (1999). Scientific review: Autonomic dysreflexia. *Spinal Cord, 37*, 383–391.

Kielhofner, G., Braveman, B., Fogg, L., & Levin, M. (2008). A controlled study of services to enhance productive participation among people with HIV/AIDS. *American Journal of Occupational Therapy, 62*, 36–45.

Kimmel, P., & Rosenberg, M. (Eds.). (2015). *Chronic renal disease*. Burlington, MA: Elsevier Science.

King, J. M., & Ligman, K. (2011). Patient noncompliance with swallowing recommendations: Reports from speech-language pathologists. *Contemporary Issues in Communication Science and Disorders, 38*, 53–60.

Lin, Y. H., & Pan, P. J. (2012). The use of rehabilitation among patients with breast cancer: A retrospective longitudinal cohort study. *BMC Health Services Research, 12*(1), 282.

Mayo Clinic. (2018). *Chronic kidney disease.* Retrieved from https://www.mayoclinic.org/diseases-conditions/chronic-kidney-disease/symptoms-causes/syc-20354521

McDevitt, J., Wilbur, J., Kogan, J., & Briller, J. (2005). A walking program for outpatients in psychiatric rehabilitation: Pilot study. *Biological Research for Nursing, 7*(2), 87–97.

Mewes, J. C., Steuten, L. M., Ijzerman, M. J., & van Harten, W. H. (2012). Effectiveness of multidimensional cancer survivor rehabilitation and cost-effectiveness of cancer rehabilitation in general: A systematic review. *Oncologist, 17*(12), 1581–1593.

Mittalhenkle, A., Stehman-Breen, C., Shlipak, M., Fried, L. F., Katz, R., Young, B., . . ., & Siscovick, D. (2008). Cardiovascular risk factors and incident acute renal failure in older adults: The cardiovascular health study. *Clinical Journal of the American Society of Nephrology, 3,* 450–456.

Moinuddin, I., & Leehey, D. J. (2008). A comparison of aerobic exercise and resistance training in patients with and without chronic kidney disease. *Advances in Chronic Kidney Disease, 15,* 83–96.

National Board for Certification in Occupational Therapy (NBCOT®). (2018). *Practice analysis of the certified occupational therapy assistant: Executive summary* [PDF file]. Retrieved from https://www.nbcot.org/-/media/NBCOT/PDFs/2017-Practice-Analysis-Executive-

National Cancer Institute. (2018, April 27). *Cancer statistics.* Retrieved from https://www.cancer.gov/about-cancer/understanding/statistics

National Institutes of Health. (2019, January 28). *HIV treatment: Drug resistance.* Retrieved from https://aidsinfo.nih.gov/understanding-hiv-aids/fact-sheets/21/56/drug-resistance

National Kidney Foundation. (2015). *Nephrotic syndrome.* Retrieved from http://www.kidney.org/atoz/content/nephrotic.cfm

National Kidney Foundation. (2017). *The facts for peritoneal dialysis.* Retrieved from https://aakp.org/dialysis/the-facts-of-peritoneal-dialysis/

National Pressure Ulcer Advisory Panel. (2017). *NPUAP pressure ulcer stages/categories.* Retrieved from https://www.npuap.org/wp-content/uploads/2012/01/NPUAP-Pressure-Ulcer-Stages-Categories.pdf.

Nussbaum, S. R., Carter, M. J., Fife, C. E., DaVanzo, J., Haught, R., Nusgart, M., & Cartwright, D. (2018). An economic evaluation of the impact, cost, and Medicare policy implications of chronic nonhealing wounds. *Value Health, 21,* 27–32.

Padilla, R. (2003). Clara: A phenomenology of disability. *American Journal of Occupational Therapy, 57,* 413–423.

Patil, N. J., Nagaratna, R., Garner, C., Raghuram, N. V., & Crisan, R. (2012). Effect of integrated Yoga on neurogenic bladder dysfunction in patients with multiple sclerosis: A prospective observational case series. *Complementary Therapies in Medicine, 20*(6), 424–430.

Pearl, R. K., Felix, E. L., Hasselberg, K., & LeVine L. (1980). The use of a moldable plastic splint to minimize early postoperative thrombosis of an internal arteriovenous fistula in the high-risk renal dialysis patient. *American Surgery, 46,* 333–334.

Pizzi, M., & Burkhardt, A. (2003). Adult immunological diseases. In E. Crepeau, B. Schell, & E. Cohn (Eds.), *Willard and Spackman's occupational therapy* (10th ed., pp. 821–834). Philadelphia, PA: Lippincott.

Poole, J. L. (2010) Musculoskeletal rehabilitation in the person with scleroderma. *Current Opinions in Rheumatology, 22,* 205–212.

Prieto, L., Thorsen, H., & Juul, K. (2005). Development and validation of a quality of life questionnaire for patients with colostomy or ileostomy. *Health and Quality of Life Outcomes, 12,* 62.

Reingold, F. S., & Jordan, K. (2013). Obesity and occupational therapy. *American Journal of Occupational Therapy, 67*(Suppl.), S39–S46.

Rosenbloom, A. L. (2004). Connective tissue disorders in diabetes. In R.A. DeFronzo, E. Feraninni, H. Keen, & P. Zimmet (Eds.), *International Textbook of Diabetes Mellitus* (3rd ed., pp. 1283–1309). Chichester, England: John Wiley and Sons.

Salyers, W. J., Mansour, A., El-Haddad, B., Golbeck, A. L., & Kallail, K. J. (2007). Lifestyle modification counseling in patients with gastroesophageal reflux disease. *Gastroenterological Nursing, 30,* 302–304.

Silver, J. K., Baima, J., & Mayer, R. S. (2013). Impairment-driven cancer rehabilitation: An essential component of quality care and survivorship. *CA: A Cancer Journal for Clinicians, 63,* 295–317.

Siracusa, G., Sparacino, A., & Lentini, V. L. (2013). Neurogenic bladder and disc disease: A brief review. *Current Medical Research and Opinion, 29*(8), 1–19.

Takaya, Y., Kumasaka, R., Arakawa, T., Ohara, T., Nakanishi, M., Noguchi, T., . . ., & Goto, Y. (2014). Impact of cardiac rehabilitation on renal function in patients with and without chronic kidney disease after acute myocardial infarction. *Circulation Journal, 78,* 377–384.

Toalson, P., Ahmed, S., Hardy, T., & Kabinoff, G. (2004). The metabolic syndrome in patients with severe mental illnesses. *Primary Care Companion to the Journal of Clinical Psychiatry 6,* 152–158.

Tubaro, A., Puccini, F., De Nunzio, C., Digesu, G. A., Elneil, S., Gobbi, C., & Khullar, V. (2012). The treatment of lower urinary tract symptoms in patients with multiple sclerosis: A systematic review. *Current Urology Reports, 13,* 335–342.

Wild, C. P., Bucher, J. R., de Jong, B. W., Dillner, J., von Gertten, C., Groopman, J. D., . . ., & McLaughlin, J. (2014). Translational cancer research: Balancing prevention and treatment to combat cancer globally. *Journal of the National Cancer Institute, 107,* 353.

Wilson, H., & Vincent, R. (2006). Autoimmune connective tissue disease: Scleroderma. *British Journal of Nursing. 15,* 805–809.

World Health Organization. (n.d.). *Definition of palliative care.* Retrieved from https://www.who.int/cancer/palliative/definition/en/

Review Questions

Gastrointestinal, Renal-Genitourinary, Endocrine, Immunological, and Integumentary Systems Disorders

Below are five questions about key content covered in this chapter. These questions are not inclusive of the entirety of content related to disorders of the gastrointestinal, renal-genitourinary, endocrine, immunological, and integumentary systems that you must know for success on the COTA® exam. These questions are provided to help you jump-start the thought processes you will need to apply your studying of content to the answering of exam questions; hence, they are not in the COTA® exam format. Exam items in the COTA® format that cover the depth and breadth of content you will need to know to pass the exam are provided on this text's computerized exams. The answers to the questions below are provided in Appendix 3.

1. You work with clients who have dysphagia and swallowing disorders to develop their feeding skills. What would you do if a client chokes and cannot clear their airway during the activity?

2. You are working with clients who have a colostomy or a stoma due to surgery to their bowel. Some clients do not have the intact fine motor functioning to learn to manage their stoma independently. What can you do to work with these clients to develop their ability to manage their stoma care independently?

3. Describe options that could be useful in providing intervention for someone who has bladder urgency with stress urinary incontinence and a diagnosis of non-insulin-dependent diabetes mellitus.

4. You are treating an adult client with a diagnosis of scleroderma and colon cancer who was referred to occupational therapy because soft tissue/connective tissue changes are affecting hand function. Would it be appropriate to have a restorative goal for evolving contractures? Describe your rationale.

5. You work in a community-based setting that serves people with spinal cord injuries. Several of your clients report reddening of skin in their sacral regions. What should you do to work with these clients to improve their skin integrity and prevent decubiti?

10

Psychiatric and Cognitive Disorders

WILLIAM L. LAMBERT, RITA P. FLEMING-CASTALDY, AND JANICE L. ROMEO

Chapter Outline

- Signs and Symptoms of Psychiatric Illness and/or Cognitive Disorders, 284
- Diagnosis of Psychiatric Disorders, 286
- Schizophrenia Spectrum and Other Psychotic Disorders, 288
- Bipolar and Related Disorders, 290
- Depressive Disorders, 293
- Substance-Related and Addictive Disorders, 294
- Anxiety Disorders, 296
- Personality Disorders, 297
- Obsessive-Compulsive and Related Disorders, 298
- Trauma- and Stressor Related Disorders, 300
- Neurocognitive Disorders, 301
- Feeding and Eating Disorders, 305
- Disruptive, Impulse-Control, and Conduct Disorders, 307
- Neurodevelopmental Disorders, 308
- Occupational Therapy Mental Health Evaluation, 313
- Occupational Therapy Mental Health Intervention, 314
- References, 315
- Review Questions, 317

Signs and Symptoms of Psychiatric Illness and/or Cognitive Disorders

> **EXAM HINT:** Understanding how the following signs and symptoms of psychiatric illnesses and cognitive disorders impact functional performance can help you correctly answer NBCOT® Domain 01 exam items about collaborating and gathering information to "assist the OTR to acquire information regarding factors that influence occupational performance on an ongoing basis throughout the occupational therapy process" (NBCOT®, 2018, p. 21).

Attention

1. The ability to remain focused on an activity or experience or the ability to concentrate.
2. Disturbances of attention.
   a. Distractibility is the inability to concentrate one's attention without attention being drawn to unimportant or irrelevant stimuli.
   b. Selective inattention is blocking out those activities, objects, or concepts that produce anxiety.
   c. Hypervigilance is excessive attention and alertness that guards against potential danger.

Consciousness

1. A state of awareness that responds to external stimuli.
2. Disturbances of consciousness.
   a. These disturbances are usually a result of brain pathology.
   b. Disorientation is a disturbance of orientation to person, place, or time. Situation is sometimes used as a fourth consideration.
   c. Delirium is an acute, reversible disorder that presents as a disoriented reaction with confusion, lability, and disturbances in behavior, e.g., aggression.
      (1) It may be associated with fear and hallucinations.
   d. Confusion involves inappropriate reactions to environmental stimuli, manifested by a disordered orientation in relation to person, place, and time.
   e. Sundowner syndrome occurs in the late afternoon and at night in older people, often seen in individuals with dementia.
      (1) Characterized by drowsiness, confusion, ataxia, falling, agitation, and sometimes aggression.
      (2) It is associated with sedation, dementia, and changes in orienting cues such as light and familiar people and objects.

Emotion

1. A feeling state associated with affect and mood that consists of psychological and physical components (e.g., fear, anger, joy).
   a. Physiological disturbances associated with mood are frequently autonomic in nature.
2. Affect is the observable component of emotions.
   a. Appropriate affect is consistent with the accompanying idea, thought, or speech.
   b. Disturbances of affect.
      (1) Inappropriate affect is inconsistent with the accompanying idea, thought, or speech.
      (2) Blunted affect is a severe lack of affect. As seen clinically, an affect that does not demonstrate the ability to change is observed.
      (3) Restricted or constricted affect is observed as reduced affect, but less so than blunted affect.
      (4) Flat affect is the absence of any affective signs of emotion.
      (5) Labile affect is rapid and abrupt changes in affect.
3. Mood is a pervasive and sustained emotion manifested by thoughts and actions (e.g., elation, anger, depression).
   a. Rapid changes in affect (lability) are usually accompanied by rapid changes in mood.
   b. These rapid changes are frequently referred to as "mood swings."
4. Other emotions.
   a. Anxiety is a feeling of apprehension or worry associated with anticipation of future danger.
      (1) Free-floating anxiety is a pervasive anxiety that does not have a specific focus.
   b. Fear is an anxiety that is focused on a real danger.

Memory

1. A process whereby what has been experienced or learned is registered and stored, can be retained to varying degrees, and can be recalled at will.
2. Levels of memory.
   a. Immediate memory is the ability to recall material within seconds or minutes, also known as short-term memory
   b. Recent memory is the ability to recall events of the past few days.
   c. Recent past memory is the ability to recall events of the past few months.

d. Remote memory is the ability to recall events of the distant past, also known as long-term memory.
e. Procedural memory is an automatic sequence of behavior such as conditioned responses.
f. Declarative memory is recall specific to consciously learned facts, such as school subjects.
g. Semantic memory is knowing the meaning of words and the ability to classify information.
h. Episodic memory is the knowledge of one's personal experiences.
i. Prospective memory is the capacity to remember to carry out actions in the future, such as knowing you have appointments scheduled, to turn off the stove, and to pay bills on time.
   (1) Prospective memory is clinically important, especially with regard to an individual's ability to live safely and independently.
3. Disturbances of memory.
   a. Amnesia is an inability to recall past experiences or personal identity.
      (1) It may be caused by organic or emotional dysfunction.
      (2) Retrograde amnesia is the inability to remember events that occurred prior to the precipitating event.

Motor Behavior

1. Behavioral and motoric expressions of impulses, drives, wishes, motivations, and cravings.
2. Disturbances of motor behavior.
   a. Echopraxia is the meaningless imitation of another person's movements.
   b. Catatonia is characterized by immobility or rigidity.
   c. Stereotypy is the repetition of fixed patterns of movement and speech (e.g., echolalia).
   d. Psychomotor agitation is excessive motor and cognitive activity, usually nonproductive and in response to inner tension.
   e. Hyperactivity is restless, sometimes aggressive or destructive activity, often associated with brain pathology.
   f. Psychomotor retardation is decreased or slowed motor and cognitive activity.
   g. Aggression is forceful, angry, or destructive speech or behavior.
   h. Acting out is the physical expression of thoughts and impulses.
   i. Akathisia is the state of restlessness characterized by an urgent need for movement, usually as a side effect of medication.
   j. Ataxia is the irregularity or failure of muscle coordination upon movement.

Perception

1. The process of interpreting sensory information received from the environment.
2. Disturbances of perception.
   a. Hallucinations are false sensory perceptions that are not in response to an external stimulus.
      (1) Often referred to clinically as "responding to internal stimuli."
   b. Illusions are misperceptions or misinterpretations of real sensory events.
   c. Disturbances associated with cognitive disorders.
      (1) Agnosia is the inability to understand and interpret the significance of sensory input.
         (a) Visual agnosia is the inability to recognize people and objects.
      (2) Astereognosis is the inability to identify objects through touch.
      (3) Apraxia is the inability to carry out specific motor tasks in the absence of sensory or motor impairment.
      (4) Adiadochokinesia is the inability to perform rapidly alternating movements.
      (5) See Chapter 12 for additional information about cognitive-perceptual deficits.
3. Disturbances associated with conversion and dissociative phenomena.
   a. These disturbances are in response to repressed material and involve physical symptoms and distortions that are not under voluntary control or associated with a physical disorder.
   b. Depersonalization is a subjective sensation of unreality about oneself or the environment.
   c. Derealization is a subjective sense that the environment is unreal.
   d. Fugue is a state of serious depersonalization, often involving travel or relocation, in which the individual takes on a new identity with amnesia for their old identity.
   e. Dissociative identity disorder involves the appearance that an individual has developed two or more distinct personalities.
   f. Dissociation involves the separation of a group of mental or behavioral processes from the rest of the person's psychic activity.
      (1) It may involve separating an idea from its emotional tone.

Speech

1. The expression of ideas, thoughts, and feelings through language.
2. Disturbances in speech.
   a. Pressured speech is rapid and increased in amount. It may be difficult to understand and/or interrupt.

b. Poverty of speech is limited in amount, i.e., one-word answers to questions.
c. Poverty of content in speech is speech that is adequate in amount but conveys little information due to vagueness, lack of specificity, and limited detail.
d. Nonspontaneous speech consists of responses that are given only when spoken to directly.
e. Stuttering consists of the repetition or prolongation of sounds or syllables.
f. Perseveration in speech is continued, persistent repetition of a word or phrase, often in response to different stimuli or different questions.
3. Disturbances in language output.
   a. Expressive aphasia (i.e., Broca's) is a disturbance in which the individual knows what they wants to say, but cannot say it.
   b. Receptive aphasia (i.e., Wernicke's) is an organic loss of the individual's ability to comprehend what has been said to him/her.
   c. Nominal aphasia (also known as anomial or amnestic) is the inability to name objects.
   d. Global aphasia involves all forms of aphasia.

Thought

1. Thinking is a goal-directed reasoned flow of ideas and associations.
   a. When thinking follows a logical sequence, it is considered normal.
2. Disturbances in form of thought.
   a. Circumstantiality is speech that is delayed in reaching the point and contains excessive or irrelevant details.
   b. Tangentiality is the abrupt changing of focus to a loosely associated topic.
   c. Perseveration is a persistent focus on a previous topic or behavior after a new topic or behavior has been introduced.
   d. Flight of ideas refers to rapid shifts in thoughts from one idea to another.
   e. Thought blocking is the interruption of a thought process before it is carried through to completion.
3. Disturbances in content of thought.
   a. Delusions are false beliefs about external reality without an appropriate stimulus that cannot be explained by the individual's intelligence or cultural background.
   b. Compulsions are a need to act on specific impulses to relieve associated anxiety.
   c. Obsessions constitute a persistent thought or feeling that cannot be eliminated by logical thought.
   d. Concrete thinking is characterized by actual things, events, and immediate experience; the inability to think abstractly.

EXAM HINT: The application of knowledge about how the above signs and symptoms of psychiatric illnesses and cognitive disorders impact functional performance can help you determine the correct answer to a COTA® exam item. For example, an exam item can include a scenario about an OTA contributing to the evaluation of a person with poor episodic memory. Answer choice options which include assessments that use an interview as their method of data collection will be incorrect. It is also important to recognize that compensations for functional deficits should be provided during evaluation and intervention. An item can also include a scenario about an OTA working with a distractible person. A correct answer choice would include the use of a structured approach and a quiet environment.

Diagnosis of Psychiatric Disorders

Determination of Diagnosis by the Psychiatrist

1. The individual's psychiatric history and physical status is reviewed.
2. A clinical interview, which includes a mental status examination, is conducted.
3. Clinical observation of the individual. This includes:
   a. Appearance.
   b. Speech.
   c. Actions.
   d. Thoughts.

The Mental Status Examination

1. General description of the individual.
   a. Appearance.
   b. Behavior and psychomotor activity.
   c. Attitude toward examiner.
2. Mood and affect.
   a. Mood (pervasive, sustained emotion).
   b. Affect (observable expression of mood).
   c. Appropriateness of mood and affect.
3. Speech.
4. Perceptual disturbances.
5. Thought.
   a. Process or form of thought.
   b. Content of thought.
6. Sensorium and cognition.
   a. Alertness and level of consciousness.
   b. Orientation to person, place, time, and situation.
   c. Memory.
   d. Concentration and attention.
   e. Capacity to read and write.
   f. Abstract thinking.
   g. Fund of information and intelligence.
7. Impulse control.
8. Judgment and insight.
9. Reliability.

Shortened Forms of the Mental Status Examination

1. Occupational therapy practitioners often use the below shortened forms as screening tools to assess mental status and cognitive functioning.
   a. The Mini-Mental State Examination (also known as Folstein Mini-Mental).
   b. The Short Portable Mental.

Diagnostic Information According to Diagnostic and Statistical Manual of Mental Disorders, 5th edition (DSM-5™)

Overview of DSM-5™ Changes

1. The DSM-5™, published by the American Psychiatric Association (APA), provides a categorical guide to mental health diagnoses.
   a. DSM-5™ delineates the specific symptoms of each diagnosis and enables a universal understanding of what constitutes psychiatric disorders.
      (1) DSM-5™ helps mental health professionals (i.e., psychologists, social workers, nurses, OT practitioners, and others) assist the attending psychiatrist in formulating as accurate a diagnosis as possible.
      (2) DSM-5™ is an essential guide that provides uniformity in how each mental health disorder may be viewed, discussed, and addressed by OT practitioners and other clinicians.
      (3) Using the standardized diagnostic language of the DSM-5™ can help the treatment team formulate an effective interdisciplinary evaluation and intervention plan.
2. The following sections provide information about major mental disorders including DSM-5™ diagnostic criteria, onset, prevalence, prognosis, and diagnostic-specific considerations for OT.

> **EXAM HINT:** Information about prevalence of different diagnoses can help determine disorders that will most likely be on the COTA® exam. While less common disorders may be on the exam, the number of potential exam items about rare disorders (e.g., Rett Syndrome) in the exam item pool will likely be less than more common disorders (e.g., anxiety and substance use disorders).

> **EXAM HINT:** The NBCOT® exam outline for the COTA® identifies knowledge of the "impact of typical development and aging on occupational performance, health, and wellness across the life span" (NBCOT®, 2018, p. 21) as essential for competent practice. Correct answers to COTA® exam items will be developmentally appropriate. Therefore, the application of knowledge about the typical onset age of psychiatric and cognitive disorders can help you determine a correct answer about working with a person with one of these diagnoses. For example, eating disorders often develop during adolescence; thus, issues of role identity and peer relationships would be important to consider when selecting the correct answer to an exam item. Prognosis information can help determine the most appropriate frame of reference/model of practice to use to guide the OT process. See Chapter 13.

Schizophrenia Spectrum and Other Psychotic Disorders[1]

Schizophrenia

1. Diagnostic criteria.
   a. Criterion A: the presence of two or more of the following symptoms, referred to clinically as positive symptoms. These include:
      (1) Delusions.
      (2) Hallucinations.
      (3) Disorganized speech.
      (4) Grossly disorganized or catatonic behavior (positive symptoms).
      (5) Negative symptoms (see the following text).
   b. Criterion B: disturbance in one or more areas of function such as work, interpersonal relations, or self-care.
   c. Criterion C: continuous signs of the illness for 6 months including at least 1 month of symptoms that meet criterion A.
   d. Criterion D: other related disorders, including schizoaffective disorder or depressive/bipolar disorder with psychotic features, have been ruled out as diagnoses.
   e. Criterion E: the disturbance is not being caused by another medical condition.
   f. Criterion F: if an already-existing neurodevelopmental or childhood communication disorder is diagnosed, schizophrenia is only diagnosed if all required symptoms plus prominent delusions/hallucinations are present for at least 1 month without treatment.
   g. Positive symptoms are the excesses or distortions of normal function as found in criterion A.
   h. Negative symptoms represent a loss or absence of function.
      (1) Restricted emotion (i.e., affective flattening).
      (2) Difficulty in experiencing pleasure (i.e., anhedonia).
      (3) Decreased thought and speech (i.e., alogia).
      (4) Lack of energy (i.e., anergia) and initiative.

   > **CAUTION:** Anergia is often *incorrectly* interpreted as lack of motivation.

      (5) Inability to relate to others.
2. Specifiers are provided for each diagnosis to further describe and clarify what the presenting individual is experiencing in terms of the disorder. These include:
   a. The identification of the frequency of the presenting condition (e.g., first episode or multiple episodes) and the current status of the presenting condition (e.g., acute episode, in partial remission, or in full remission).
   b. Additional specifiers can include noting if the condition is continuous, unspecified, or with catatonia.
   c. The current severity of the condition is also specified.
3. Onset, prevalence, and prognosis.
   a. The onset of schizophrenia is usually between early adolescence and the mid-thirties.
   b. Prevalence estimates for schizophrenia and related psychotic disorders range from 0.25% to 0.64% in the United States.
   c. Recovery is possible with effective intervention. Chapter 13 provides information about the recovery model and effective interventions for persons with psychiatric disorders.
      (1) 50% of diagnosed cases have been found to sustain a good outcome of either a complete recovery or sufficient recovery to live an independent, satisfying life.
      (2) 25% are able to lead satisfying lives with ongoing supports.
      (3) The prognosis is poorer for the remaining 25% of individuals with schizophrenia who have repeated hospitalizations, periods of exacerbation, and episodes of major mood disorders.

Other Psychotic Disorders

1. Schizoaffective disorder.
   a. Diagnostic criteria.
      (1) The person has an uninterrupted period of illness during which, at some point, there is a major depressive, manic, or mixed episode concurrent with positive or negative symptoms associated with schizophrenia (APA, 2013).
2. Schizophreniform disorder.
   a. Diagnostic criteria.
      (1) The individual meets the criteria for schizophrenia; however, the episode lasts more than one month but less than the six months required for a diagnosis of schizophrenia.
3. Delusional disorder.
   a. Diagnostic criteria.
      (1) The presence of one or more delusions for the duration of one month or longer and the criteria for schizophrenia has not been met.

---

[1] Psychotic is often used interchangeably with *thought disorder*. A *thought disorder* is any disturbance of thinking that affects language, communication, or thought content and is a predominate feature of schizophrenia.

4. Brief psychotic disorder.
   a. Diagnostic criteria.
      (1) Criterion A: presence of one or more sensory, behavioral, cognitive, or psychomotor symptoms, including delusions, hallucinations, disorganization of speech or behavior, and/or catatonia.
      (2) Criterion B: symptoms range from one day to one month in duration, followed by complete resolution of symptoms and return to prior level of functioning (APA, 2013).

Impact on Function

1. Many individuals with psychotic disorders demonstrate deficits in cognitive-perceptual and social interaction skills that affect all areas of function.
   a. The deficits in the processing of sensory information that are experienced by some individuals make interaction with the environment difficult and frightening.
   b. Individuals who have difficulty with their own ego boundaries often exhibit socially inappropriate, sometimes intrusive, behaviors.
   c. Some individuals have lost or failed to develop the social and communication skills necessary for effective and satisfying interpersonal interactions and relationships.
   d. Cognitive deficits due to thought disorders and difficulty performing basic skills interfere with all areas of occupation from basic activities of daily living and leisure pursuits to social participation, education, and work activities.
   e. It is important to assess and continue to monitor the degree of assistance and structure needed to maintain optimum independence in all areas of occupation.

Symptom Management

1. Treatment consists primarily of the use of antipsychotic medications, the provision of a structured supportive environment, and the implementation of an individualized intervention program to develop illness management skills and competencies to enable occupational performance.
2. Psychopharmacology.
   a. Traditional antipsychotic medications.
      (1) Thorazine, Prolixin, Haldol, Navane, Mellaril, Stelazine, and Trilafon. These are infrequently used, but occasionally still prescribed.
      (2) Long-acting injections are available for Haldol (once a month) and Prolixin (once every two weeks).
         (a) Long-acting injections improve/assist in medication compliance.
      (3) Side effects of traditional antipsychotic medications may include: dry mouth, blurry vision, photosensitivity, constipation, orthostatic hypotension, Parkinsonism, dystonias (i.e., impaired tonicity), akathisia (i.e., restless, anxiety provoking need for movement), and cardiovascular disorders.
      (4) Complications of traditional antipsychotic medications may include:
         (a) Neuroleptic malignant syndrome: an autonomic emergency leading to increased blood pressure, tachycardia, sweating, convulsions, and coma.
         (b) Tardive dyskinesia: a neurological disorder resulting from long-term or high-dose use of antipsychotic medications characterized by abnormal, involuntary, irregular movements of the head, limbs, and trunk, often presenting as slow, rhythmic, automatic, stereotyped movements.
         (c) Neuroleptic-induced Parkinsonism (pseudo-Parkinson's): a disorder that presents with muscle stiffness, cogwheel rigidity, shuffling gait, stooped posture, and drooling. The pill-rolling tremor of idiopathic Parkinsonism is rare, but regular, coarse tremors may be present, and tremors of the lips and mouth can also be seen with this disorder, which also results from use of antipsychotic medications.
      (5) Atypical antipsychotics are not as problematic as the use of older medications such as Stelazine, Thorazine, and Mellaril.
   b. Atypical antipsychotics.
      (1) Clozaril, Risperdal, Zyprexa, Seroquel, Geodon, Saphris, Fanapt, Latuda, Symbyax, Invega, and Abilify.
         (a) Long-acting atypical injections are available for Risperdal Consta (once every 2 weeks) and Invega Sustenna (once every 4 weeks).
            • Long-acting injections can support an individual's ability to effectively self-manage their medication regimen.
      (2) Side effects vary with individual medications.
   c. Neuromuscular side effects of antipsychotics may be treated by Cogentin, Artane, Benadryl, and Symmetrel.
      (1) Side effects include dry mouth, blurry vision, sedation, dizziness, hypotension, insomnia, and confusion.

> **CAUTION:** Complications of Clozaril may include agranulocytosis, which is a decrease in certain white blood cells that is potentially fatal. A result of this potentiality necessitates weekly blood count monitoring initially, biweekly after six months, and monthly after a year of treatment. The resulting disruptions in lifestyle can be problematic for those on this medication, which can negatively impact adherence to medication regimen.

Diagnostic-Specific Considerations for Occupational Therapy

1. When working with persons with psychotic disorders, the presence of disordered thinking requires the OTA to communicate simply, clearly, and concretely.
2. External structure to organize the individual's thinking, environment, and daily activities are often required.
3. The provision of supports and tools to enable recovery is essential (e.g., Wellness and Recovery Action Plan [WRAP]; see Chapter 13).
4. See this chapter's sections on OT mental health evaluation and OT mental health intervention for additional guidelines.
5. Chapter 13 provides further information on general OT psychosocial evaluation and intervention approaches and specific interventions to manage psychotic behaviors (i.e., delusions and hallucinations).

Bipolar and Related Disorders

Overview

1. Bipolar and related disorders are diagnosed based on the incidence of manic, hypomanic, and/or major depressive episodes. (See below for descriptions of specific episodes.)
2. Mood episodes are not coded diagnoses in and of themselves.
3. Treatment addresses the symptoms of the episode experienced by the person.
    a. Intervention will vary with shifts in mood.

Diagnostic Criteria for Specific Mood Disorders

1. Bipolar I disorder.
    a. One or more manic episodes.
    b. May be combined with hypomanic or major depressive episodes.
2. Bipolar II disorder.
    a. One or more major depressive episodes.
    b. There must be at least one hypomanic episode.
    c. There is no history of a manic episode.
3. Other related disorders.
    a. Cyclothymic disorder is characterized by several periods of hypomanic and depressive symptoms, which do not meet the criteria for a manic, hypomanic, or major depressive episode, lasting for at least two years.

Onset, Prevalence, and Prognosis

1. The median age of onset for bipolar disorder is 25 years, although the illness can start in early childhood or as late as the 40s and 50s.
2. Bipolar disorders have a lifetime prevalence of 1.0%–2.4%.
3. While the prognosis for repeated recurrences of mood disorders is poor, recovery is possible.
    a. Early intervention is more effective than later intervention.
    b. The use of effective medications and interventions based on a recovery model have increased the number of individuals with bipolar and related disorders who are able to maintain satisfying lifestyles, resulting in a more favorable overall prognosis.
    c. Minimizing the frequency of episodes helps with recovery.

Manic Episode

1. Diagnostic criteria.
    a. At least three of the following symptoms must persist for the period of at least one week:
        (1) Mood is uncharacteristically and consistently elevated or irritable.
        (2) Increase in targeted, goal-directed behavior or restless, purposeless behaviors (psychomotor agitation).
        (3) Inflated self-esteem or thoughts of grandeur, potentially resulting in grandiose and/or impulsive behaviors.
        (4) Decreased need for sleep.
        (5) Pressured or quick speech, potentially related to feelings of rushed/racing thoughts.
        (6) Increased engagement in subjectively pleasurable activities that may be high-risk, painful, harmful, or have adverse consequences.
    b. Symptoms of mood disturbance or psychotic features may cause a marked impairment in daily function or require hospitalization to prevent harm, whether to self or to others (APA, 2013).
    c. Behaviors often associated with a manic episode.
        (1) Treatment resistance resulting from failure to recognize illness.
        (2) Suggestive or flamboyant dress.

(3) Gambling, promiscuity, excessive spending, or giving things away.
(4) Irritable, assaultive, or suicidal behavior.
2. Impact on function.
   a. The lack of inhibition experienced during a manic phase may lead to excessive spending, impulsive travel, flamboyant and promiscuous dress and/or behavior, etc.
   b. Individuals may be euphoric in early phases, but may become labile, threatening, and assaultive.
   c. Individuals may have high, often undirected, energy levels and require little sleep.
   d. Poor judgment can lead to dangerous situations, poor self-care, problems in relationships, and decreased or irresponsible work performance.
   e. The incidence of substance abuse is increased.
3. Symptom management.
   a. Antipsychotics (refer to prior section on psychotic disorders).
   b. Mood-stabilizing medications (first line of psychopharmacological treatment).
      (1) Lithium: Eskalith, Lithobid, and time-released forms.
         (a) Side effects include excessive thirst, tremors, excessive urination, weight gain, nausea, diarrhea, and cognitive impairment.

> **CAUTION:** Blood levels must be monitored to maintain the narrow therapeutic window. High levels of lithium may cause nerve damage and death.

> **RED FLAG:** Early symptoms of toxicity include motoric disturbances.

      (2) Anticonvulsants.
         (a) Depakote, Tegretol, Lamictal, Topamax, Neurontin, and Trileptal.
         (b) Side effects include dizziness, drowsiness, ataxia, weight gain, and sedation.
      (3) Mood stabilizers are also used to prevent bipolar disorder.
      (4) Antipsychotic medications such as Zyprexa, Seroquel, Risperdal, Geodon, and Abilify are also used to treat symptoms of bipolar disorder.
4. Diagnostic-specific considerations for OT.
   a. Limit-setting to reduce the individual's fears of losing control, increase participation in the treatment process, and promote safety.
   b. Engagement in activities that provide structure and the opportunity for release of excess energy in a positive and therapeutic manner.
   c. Periods between manic episodes should be used to educate the individual and the family on symptom management.
   d. See this chapter's sections on OT mental health evaluation and occupational therapy mental health intervention for additional guidelines.
   e. Chapter 13 provides additional information on general OT psychosocial evaluation and intervention approaches and specific intervention approaches for managing manic or monopolizing behaviors.

Major Depressive Episode

1. Diagnostic criteria.
   a. Five or more diagnostic symptoms must be present for at least two weeks:
      (1) One of the five symptoms must include a depressed mood or a notable loss of interest/pleasure.
      (2) Significant fluctuations in weight, potentially along with appetite changes.
      (3) Difficulty falling or staying asleep (insomnia), or excessive sleeping throughout the day (hypersomnia).
      (4) Changes in thinking or behavior, such as a slowing down of thinking and motor speed (psychomotor retardation) or restless, purposeless movement patterns (psychomotor agitation).
      (5) Fatigue or a loss of energy that impacts completion of daily activities.
      (6) Changes in mood or self-perception, including feelings of worthlessness, inadequacy, or extreme guilt about thoughts/feelings.
      (7) Decreased ability to concentrate on tasks, which may be an isolated symptom or related to difficulty sleeping, fatigue, and/or psychomotor changes.
      (8) Recurrent suicidal thoughts, with or without a plan or attempt at suicide (APA, 2013).
   b. Behaviors often associated with depressive episodes.
      (1) Irritability, anxiety, phobias, and obsessive thinking.
      (2) Difficulties in social interactions, relationships, and sexual functioning.
      (3) Self-destructive behavior including suicide and substance abuse.
      (4) May be manifested as somatic complaints.
      (5) There may be an increased use of medical services.
   c. Symptoms are significant enough to cause marked disruption in important areas of daily function, including social or occupational contexts (APA, 2013).
2. Impact on function.
   a. Individuals are often tearful, brooding, and isolative.
   b. Anxiety leads to excessive concerns about physical health, complaints of pain, and alcohol abuse.
   c. Hopelessness, lack of energy, and slow thought processing lead to limited interest in activity and difficulty performing tasks in all areas of occupation, including basic and instrumental activities of daily living, leisure, social participation, education, and work activities.

3. Symptom management.
   a. Antidepressant medications.
      (1) Selective serotonin reuptake inhibitors (SSRIs) include Prozac, Zoloft, Paxil, Celexa, and Lexapro.
         (a) Side effects include nausea, headache, sexual dysfunction, and insomnia.
      (2) Tricyclics include Elavil, Tofranil, and Norpramin. However, these are rarely used secondary to the efficacy of the SSRIs and selective norepinephrine or serotonin and norepinephrine inhibitors (SNRIs).
         (a) Side effects include dry mouth, blurred vision, sedation, postural hypotension, and other anticholinergic effects.
      (3) SNRIs include Effexor, Cymbalta.
         (a) Side effects vary but may include hypertension, anxiety, dizziness, sedation, nervousness, weight gain, nausea, and sweating.
      (4) Atypical antidepressants include Wellbutrin and Remeron.
         (a) Similar in effect to SSRIs and SNRIs.
         (b) Wellbutrin has fewer sexual side effects.
      (5) Monoamine oxidase inhibitors (MAOIs) include Nardil and Parnate.
         (a) Side effects include weight gain, hypotension, insomnia, and liver damage.

CAUTION: Dietary restrictions for individuals taking MAOIs must be followed:
- Ingesting foods or beverages that contain the amino acid tyramine can suddenly increase blood pressure and may lead to stroke or other serious cardiac reactions.
- Foods and beverages with tyramine must be completely avoided. These include aged cheeses (e.g., cheddar), pickled foods (e.g., sauerkraut, herring), cured or smoked meats (e.g., salami, sausage, pepperoni, hot dogs), liver, yogurt, sour cream, fruits that must ripen to eat (e.g., avocados, bananas), fava beans, peapods, chocolate, beer and red wine (including non-alcoholic and alcohol-reduced), meat tenderizers, soy products (soy sauce, tofu), yeast extracts, and any product that has been improperly stored, over-ripened, not fresh, and/or past an expiration date.
- Many over the counter drugs also contain ingredients that can cause a serious interaction with MAOIs. These include cold, sinus, and hay fever medications, nasal decongestants, asthma inhalants, 'pep' pills, and appetite suppressants.

RED FLAG: Severe headaches or palpations can be the first sign of a hypertensive crisis.
- The medication should be stopped immediately, and a physician consulted.

      (b) MAOIs that are administered via a skin (transdermal) patch (e.g., Selegiline [Emsam]) may have fewer side effects than MAOIs taken orally.
         • Persons who take the lowest dose patch may be advised by their physician that they do not need to follow the MAOI dietary restrictions.

CAUTION: A doctor's opinion should be sought before anyone taking a MAOI decides to not follow the MAOI food and over-the-counter medication restrictions.

EXAM HINT: The NBCOT® exam outline for the COTA® identifies knowledge of the "precautions or contraindications associated with a client condition" (NBCOT®, 2018, p. 29) as essential for competent and safe practice. Knowing that a lack of adherence to MAOI dietary restrictions may seriously impact a person's health can assist with selecting the correct answer to a COTA® exam item. For example, the correct answer for an exam item that includes a participant in a meal preparation group who is taking a MAOI would be preparing a meal which adhered to MAOI dietary restrictions.

   b. The most effective treatment involves antidepressant medication combined with psychotherapy.
   c. Cognitive approaches (i.e., CBT) are helpful for those who demonstrate self-awareness, intact cognitive skills, and the ability to actively participate in the intervention process. See Chapter 13.
   d. Electroconvulsive therapy (ECT) is very effective and the treatment of choice for those who have been unresponsive to trials on medications and other interventions.
      (1) How ECT works is not fully understood.
         (a) A limiting factor is that ECT often produces memory loss and confusion for the period surrounding treatment. Both are reversible, and evolution of ECT over the past decades has produced innovations that diminish cognitive effects while maintaining benefits.
4. Diagnostic-specific considerations for OT.
   a. The provision of a safe environment and the management of behaviors that threaten the safety and well-being of the individual are paramount.
      (1) Individuals must be closely monitored for self-destructive and/or suicidal behavior.

CAUTION: The most dangerous time for self-destructive and/or suicidal behaviors may be when the depression begins to lift and the person becomes mobilized. This includes the days after inpatient admission and just prior to discharge.

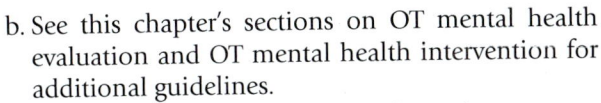

b. See this chapter's sections on OT mental health evaluation and OT mental health intervention for additional guidelines.
c. Chapter 13 provides further information on general OT psychosocial evaluation and intervention approaches and specific interventions to manage suicidal behaviors and other depressive symptoms.

Hypomanic Episode

1. Symptoms are the same as for a manic episode; however, they are not severe enough (i.e., they last for four days rather than 1 week) to cause marked impairment in social or occupational function or to require hospitalization.

> **EXAM HINT:** In the NBCOT®'s practice analysis, 17.4% of COTAs® who provided services to persons with psychosocial disorders indicated they provided services to individuals with mood disorders. The application of knowledge about the bipolar and related disorders information provided above and the depressive disorders information provided below can help you determine the correct answer to COTA® exam items about working with persons with mood disorders.

Depressive Disorders

Overview

1. Depressive disorders share the common presentations of sad, sometimes irritable mood that along with changes in cognitive and physical health affect one's ability to function.
2. They are differentiated by length of time, number of episodes, and specific type and number of symptoms.

Diagnostic Criteria for Depressive Disorders

1. Major depressive disorder.
   a. The presence of one or more major depressive episodes.
2. Persistent depressive disorder (dysthymia).
   a. Characterized by at least two years of a depressed mood, most days, with depressive symptoms.
   b. Criteria for a major depressive disorder may be continuously present for two years.
3. Disruptive mood dysregulation disorder.
   a. Temper outbursts that are characterized as:
      (1) Severe and recurrent verbal or behavioral episodes.
      (2) Uncharacteristic for expectations consistent with developmental level.
      (3) The outbursts are considered an over-reaction (either in intensity or duration of response) based on the stimuli (APA, 2013).
   b. Diagnosis is made between the ages of 6 and 18 based on observations from others such as parents, teachers, and/or peers.
4. Premenstrual dysphoric disorder
   a. Symptoms include marked affective lability, irritability or anger, increased interpersonal conflicts, depressive symptoms, depressed mood, and/or marked anxiety.

Onset, Prevalence, and Prognosis

1. While major depressive disorder can develop at any age, the median age at onset is 32.
2. It is estimated that 6.7% of Americans over the age of 18 and 9% of Americans age 12–17 have had at least one major depressive episode according to the National Institute of Mental Health (NIMH).

Impact on Function

1. Major depressive disorder and persistent depressive disorder (dysthymia).
   a. See prior section on major depressive episode.

Symptom Management

1. See prior section on major depressive episode.

Diagnostic-Specific Considerations for Occupational Therapy

1. See prior section on major depressive episode.

Substance-Related and Addictive Disorders

Overview

1. Substance-related disorders are diagnosed based on the taking of a drug of abuse (including alcohol and prescription medications), the side effects of medication(s), and/or exposure to toxins (inhalants, lead).
2. Substance-related disorders are categorized by the specific substance (i.e., alcohol or opioid).
   a. Substance use disorders include dependence and abuse.
      (1) Use: consumption that causes impairment that adversely affects daily functioning in occupational roles, fulfilling personal responsibilities, and interacting socially; it may cause personal harm (e.g., alcohol use disorder).
      (2) Intoxication: use that causes problems both behaviorally and mentally and changes in the pupils, followed by feeling drowsy, slurring words, and/or experiencing attention and memory problems (e.g., opioid intoxication disorder).
      (3) Withdrawal: stopping significant consumption which causes physical symptoms (e.g., tremors, difficulty sleeping) as well as mental symptoms (e.g., hallucinations, anxiety).
   b. Non-substance-related disorders
      (1) Gambling disorder.
3. Addictive disorders include gambling disorders that produce addictive behaviors that appear comparable to the substance use disorders.

Substance Use Disorders

1. Diagnostic criteria.
   a. Two of the following symptoms must be present within a 12-month period, due to problematic substance use resulting in significant impairment in occupational performance.
      (1) Substances are used in larger quantities than intended and/or effects last for longer than anticipated.
         (a) Over time, this may result in the development of tolerance to substances, in which larger quantities are intentionally used to obtain similar or desired effects.
      (2) A significant amount of time is dedicated to substance acquisition or use.
      (3) The desire to use substances is strong throughout the day and attempts to reduce substance use are unsuccessful despite efforts.
         (a) Behaviors continue despite the potential for physical harm due to recurrent substance use.
         (b) Attempts to cease/reduce substance use may result in withdrawal after prolonged, frequent substance use. Withdrawal signs and symptoms include sensory, motor, and psychological changes (including autonomic hyperactivity, insomnia, nausea, vomiting, hallucinations, psychomotor agitation, anxiety, or generalized tonic-clonic seizures) which may result in recurring substance use.
      (4) Ongoing substance use causes marked disruption in social, occupational, vocational, educational, and/or recreational aspects of daily life. This may cause a reduction in engagement in valued activities or an inability to meet expectations associated with roles.
         (a) Substance use continues despite the individual's awareness of the impact on function (APA, 2013).

Onset, Prevalence, and Prognosis

1. The onset of substance abuse beginning in early adolescence is increasing.
   a. A majority of adolescents consumed alcohol in the past year and thousands of deaths are attributed to the use of alcohol.
   b. Illicit drug use in the United States has increased among those 12 and older.
2. The misuse of prescribed medications and opioids is increasing.
   a. The inappropriate use of prescribed medications is a major drug problem in the United States.
   b. In the past 10 years there has been a dramatic increase in opioid overdoses in America.
   c. A major number of overdose deaths are related to opioid use.
3. Prevalence, statistics, and demographics.
   a. Men are more likely to use illicit drugs and are almost three times as likely to report heavy alcohol use than women.
   b. More than 50% of Americans aged 12 and older report drinking alcohol.

c. After alcohol, marijuana has the highest rate of substance abuse among all drugs.
4. Prognosis varies depending on several factors including motivation, substance used, and degree and type of support.
   a. Various adverse effects of substance use may include brain and liver damage, heart disease, and fetal damage during pregnancy.

> **EXAM HINT:** In the NBCOT®'s practice analysis, 19.8% of COTAs® who provided services to persons with psychosocial disorders indicated they provided services to individuals with substance abuse disorders. Due to this prevalence, it is likely that the COTA® exam will have items about working with this population.

Impact on Function

1. The impact that substance use has on the individual depends on the type of substance used and on whether the individual is abusing the substance or is dependent upon it.
2. Results of disorders of use.
   a. Disinterest and inability to care for self and others.
   b. Difficulty with and loss of personal relationships.
   c. Inability to be productive and/or maintain employment.
   d. Absence of leisure and/or social pursuits that do not involve substance use.
   e. Involvement with the legal system.
3. Prolonged use may lead to severe physical, cognitive, and psychiatric problems and can result in death.

Symptom Management

1. Medications to help the individual refrain from substance use can be provided.
2. This medical management is typically supplemented with psychotherapy and support groups (e.g., Alcoholics Anonymous, Narcotics Anonymous).
3. Methadone clinics and the use of methadone for detoxification and maintenance for opioid dependence is the most accepted approach for heroin addiction.
4. Assist with concrete practical services, such as obtaining social security, housing, and food stamps, as needed.

Diagnostic-Specific Considerations for Occupational Therapy

1. Due to the presence of learned 'survival skills,' the individual's abilities and potential may be overestimated.
   a. The OTA can apprise the team of the person's actual skills and deficits.
   b. The OTA assists the team in identifying realistic expectations and discharge plans.
2. The individual's identification of the reasons for substance use is important.
3. The development of the skills necessary to cope with life stressors without substance use is critical for a substance-free lifestyle. Skills needed include:
   a. Communication and social skills to support substance-free social participation.
   b. Skills to engage productively in work, education, and/or other productive activities (e.g., volunteering).
   c. Skills to use leisure time without using substances.
4. Life-long patterns of denial, resistance, and other defensive behaviors can make treatment challenging and difficult.
5. Referrals to support groups, including Alcoholics Anonymous, Narcotics Anonymous, and specialized addiction providers can sustain recovery.
6. See this chapter's sections on occupational therapy mental health evaluation and occupational therapy mental health intervention for additional guidelines.
7. Chapter 13 provides further information on general OT psychosocial evaluation and intervention approaches.

Gambling Disorder

1. Diagnostic criteria.
   a. Four or more of the following gambling behaviors must be true for at least 12-months:
      (1) Thoughts of gambling occupy the mind most of the day.
      (2) The individual has made multiple attempts to decrease gambling behaviors unsuccessfully, and is usually restless, irritable, unhappy, or preoccupied with gambling due to efforts to control behaviors.
      (3) Gambling behaviors increase in the presence of stress.
      (4) The individual is in serious financial trouble due to betting larger amounts of money to experience desired effects.
         (a) The individual may ask for or rely on money from close friends or family members to relieve financial stress caused by gambling behavior.
      (5) Excessive gambling behavior continues on subsequent days after losing money to attempt to break-even or 'chase' losses.
      (6) The individual lies to downplay the frequency or effects of gambling, which causes marked stress in vocational, educational, and personal/social areas of functioning.
      (7) Gambling behavior must be problematic and recurrent, causing clinically-significant impairment that is not better explained by mania (APA, 2013).

Anxiety Disorders

Overview

1. Anxiety disorders include a range of disorders that include episodic periods of intense anxiety to chronic periods of lower levels of anxiety.
2. Anxiety is an internal sense of apprehension and psychological distress. It may or may not have a specific focus.

Panic Attacks and Agoraphobia

1. Panic attacks are symptoms of anxiety.
   a. They are not coded diagnoses.
2. Panic attacks are discrete periods of intense fear or discomfort, in which four or more symptoms develop abruptly and reach a peak within 10 minutes.
   a. Physical symptoms: heart palpitations, sweating, trembling/shaking, sensations of choking or feeling short of breath, chest pain, nausea/vomiting, feeling dizzy or faint, and chills or hot flashes.
   b. Psychological symptoms: de-realization, feelings of loss of control, and fear of dying.
   c. Neurological symptoms: paraesthesia (APA, 2013).
3. Agoraphobia associated with panic attack.
   a. Anxiety about being in places or situations from which escape may be difficult or embarrassing or in which help may not be available if needed.
   b. Situations are avoided or endured with anxiety about having a panic attack.

Specific Anxiety Disorders

1. Generalized anxiety disorder.
   a. Consists of six months of persistent and excessive unfocused anxiety and worry.
2. Panic disorder.
   a. Recurrent panic attacks followed at least once by concern for recurrence.
3. Selective mutism.
   a. Consistent inability to speak in social situations when it is expected (i.e., in school), despite being able to speak in other circumstances.
   b. This behavior must persist for at least one month and not be better explained by a developmental or communication disorder (APA, 2013).
4. Separation anxiety disorder.
   a. Individuals, typically young children, became excessively attached to another individual and experience severe anxiety when separated.
   b. The level of anxiety caused by separation is considered developmentally inappropriate and unwarranted given the circumstances (APA, 2013).
5. Social phobia.
   a. A clinically significant anxiety from certain types of social or performance situations leading to avoidance.
6. Specific phobia.
   a. A clinically significant anxiety from a specific object or situation leading to avoidant behavior.

Onset, Prevalence, and Prognosis

1. Anxiety disorders often begin in childhood but may develop at any time.
2. Prevalence and prognosis vary with the specific disorder.

Impact on Function

1. The degree of impact varies with the severity and type of anxiety disorder.
2. Reactions may vary from temporary discomfort to severely avoidant and paralyzing behavior.

Symptom Management

1. Psychotherapy to explore psychodynamic issues.
2. Cognitive-behavioral therapy to develop skills to manage symptoms.
3. Several types of medications may be helpful, depending on the specific disorder.
   a. Anxiolytic medications include Xanax, Valium, Ativan, Klonopin, Serax, and BuSpar.
      (1) Side effects include drowsiness, ataxia, headache, nausea, depression, and dependence.
   b. Antidepressant medications are helpful in some cases.
      (1) Refer to mood disorder section for side-effect profiles.
   c. In some cases, hypnotic medications to induce sleep may be used briefly.
      (1) Hypnotic medications include Restoril, Dalmane, Ambien, and Benadryl.
      (2) Side effects are similar to those of the anxiolytics.

Diagnostic-Specific Considerations for Occupational Therapy

1. Skills training and using cognitive behavioral approaches may reduce anxiety and avoidant behavior.
2. Development of relaxation and stress management skills may decrease the incidence and severity of symptoms.

3. Providing graded activities designed to promote self-efficacy may increase self-confidence, motivation, and participation in intervention.
4. See this chapter's sections on OT mental health evaluation and OT mental health intervention for additional guidelines.
5. Chapter 13 provides further information on general OT psychosocial evaluation and intervention approaches.

> **EXAM HINT:** In the NBCOT® practice analysis, 46.4% of COTA®s who provided services to persons with psychosocial disorders indicated they provided services to individuals with anxiety disorders (NBCOT®, 2018). Due to this prevalence, it is likely that the COTA® exam will have items about working with persons with anxiety disorders.

Personality Disorders

Diagnostic Criteria

1. Persistent patterns in cognition, affect, behavior, or interpersonal functioning are experienced or expressed despite being notably different from the expectations and norms of one's culture (APA, 2013).
   a. The pattern is stable, inflexible, and evident in wide-ranging social and personal situations.
   b. This long-lasting pattern typically begins in adolescence or early adulthood.

Specific Personality Disorders

1. Antisocial personality disorder.
   a. This disorder is characterized by continual antisocial or criminal acts, but it is not synonymous with criminality.
   b. It is an inability to conform to social norms that involves many aspects of the individual's adolescent and adult development.
   c. Persons with antisocial personality disorder have no regard for the safety or feelings of others, and they lack remorse.
   d. Individuals diagnosed with a conduct disorder that does not respond to treatment or is untreated can be a precursor to developing this disorder.
2. Avoidant personality disorder.
   a. Persons with this disorder show an extreme sensitivity to rejection, which may lead to a socially withdrawn life.
   b. These individuals are not, however, asocial. They show a great desire for companionship but consider themselves inept or unworthy.
   c. Individuals with avoidant personality disorder need unusually strong and repeated guarantees of uncritical acceptance.
   d. These persons are commonly referred to as having an inferiority complex.
3. Borderline personality disorder.
   a. Individuals with borderline personality disorder experience extraordinarily unstable affect, mood, behavior, relationships, and self-image.
   b. Fear of real or imagined abandonment leads to frantic efforts to avoid it.
   c. A pattern of unstable and intense interpersonal relationships with alternating extremes of idealization and devaluation (splitting).
   d. Recurrent self-destructive or self-mutilating behavior may be threatened or carried out.
   e. Chronic feelings of emptiness.
   f. Majority of persons with borderline personality disorder have a history of trauma (i.e., physical, sexual, emotional abuse).
4. Dependent personality disorder.
   a. Persons with this disorder subordinate their own needs to those of others and need others to assume responsibility for major areas in their lives.
   b. Individuals with dependent personality disorder lack self-confidence.
   c. They may experience discomfort when alone for more than a brief period.
5. Histrionic personality disorder.
   a. This disorder is characterized by colorful, dramatic, extroverted behavior in excitable, emotional persons.
   b. An inability to maintain deep, long-lasting attachments with accompanying flamboyant presentation is often characteristic.
6. Narcissistic personality disorder.
   a. Persons with this disorder are characterized by a heightened sense of self-importance and a grandiose feeling that they are special in some way.
7. Obsessive-compulsive personality disorder.
   a. Characterized by emotional constriction, orderliness, perseverance, stubbornness, and indecisiveness.
   b. The essential feature is a pervasive pattern of perfectionism and inflexibility.
   c. It should not be confused with obsessive-compulsive disorder.
8. Paranoid personality disorder.
   a. Persons with this disorder are characterized by long-standing suspiciousness and mistrust of people in general.
   b. They can often appear hostile, irritable, and angry.

9. Personality disorders not otherwise specified (NOS).
   a. Passive-aggressive.
   b. Depressive.
   c. Sadomasochistic.
   d. Sadistic.
10. Schizoid personality disorder.
    a. This is frequently diagnosed in individuals who display a lifelong pattern of social withdrawal.
    b. Their discomfort with human interaction, their introversion, and their bland, constricted affect are noteworthy.
    c. Persons with schizoid personality disorder are often seen by others as eccentric, isolated, or lonely.
11. Schizotypal personality disorder.
    a. Persons with this disorder appear odd or strange in their thinking and behavior to those who come in contact with them.
    b. Magical thinking, peculiar ideas, ideas of reference, illusions, and derealization are part of this individual's everyday world.

Onset, Prevalence, and Prognosis

1. Symptoms of personality disorders usually begin in childhood or early adolescence.
2. The prevalence of personality disorders varies with the specific disorder from rare to approximately 12.16% of adults.
3. The prognosis for individuals with personality disorders varies, with the condition often remaining unchanged.
   a. There is an increased risk of the development of depressive disorders among persons with personality disorders.
   b. There is some evidence that the symptoms of avoidant, borderline, and antisocial personality disorders may decrease with age.

Impact on Function

1. The type and degree of impact on areas of occupation, personal relationships, and daily life depend on the severity and type of personality disorder.

Symptom Management

1. Psychotherapy and certain medications may reduce symptomatology for some patients.
2. Dialectical behavior therapy (DBT) has demonstrated success in the treatment of borderline personality disorder.
3. Monitoring, supervision, and hospitalization may be required during periods of increased symptoms and/or aggressive or self-destructive behavior.

Diagnostic-Specific Considerations for Occupational Therapy

1. Individualized assistance to help the person identify the previous diagnostic-specific issues may increase commitment to treatment and the pursuit of behavioral change.
2. Cognitive behavioral approaches (including dialectical behavioral therapy) can increase functional and coping skills and may decrease symptomatic behavior.
3. See this chapter's sections on OT mental health evaluation and OT mental health intervention for additional guidelines.
4. Chapter 13 provides further information on general OT psychosocial evaluation and intervention approaches.

Obsessive-Compulsive and Related Disorders

1. Obsessive-compulsive disorder.
   a. Obsessions are persistent thoughts or feelings that are unwanted, intrusive, and inappropriate based on the stimulus or situations.
   b. Compulsions are irresistible urges that take the form of repetitive behaviors carried out in an attempt to reduce anxiety or anticipated negative consequences related to obsessions.
      (1) Behaviors are typically executed according to strict or specific rules that manifest as ritualistic (i.e., washing hands three times prior to eating, locking and unlocking a door four times before exiting the house).
   c. Obsessive thoughts and compulsive behaviors are time-consuming and intrusive, although the individuals realize they're not rational.
2. Body dysmorphic disorder.
   a. The person is preoccupied with perceived physical flaws (whether imagined or slight) that are imperceptible, acceptable, or insignificant to others.
   b. Concerns regarding appearance cause repetitive thoughts or behaviors as an attempt to conceal or improve perceived flaws.
   c. Recurring thoughts of imperfections cause clinically-significant interruptions in social and occupational areas of functioning in daily life.

3. Hoarding disorder.
   a. There is a perceived need to save items associated with significant difficulty discarding possessions, regardless of value, need, or practicality.
   b. The thought of parting with items may result in marked distress and attempts to justify why the items are needed or will be needed in the future.
   c. Accumulation of items results in cramped, cluttered living conditions that may compromise cleanliness and safety within the home.
4. Trichotillomania.
   a. Compulsive, irresistible desire to pull out one's hair, typically of the scalp, eyelashes, or eyebrows although sites may vary over the body, resulting in hair loss.
   b. Hair-pulling often results in bald or patchy spots, potentially impacting social and occupational functioning.
5. Excoriation disorder.
   a. Repeated picking at one's own skin, resulting in skin lesions and causing significant disruption in daily occupations (APA, 2013).

Onset, Prevalence, and Prognosis

1. Obsessive-compulsive and related disorders can develop in childhood but may develop at any time.
2. Prevalence and prognosis vary with the specific disorder.

Impact on Function

1. The degree of impact varies with the severity and type of disorder.
2. Reactions may vary from temporary discomfort to severely avoidant and paralyzing behavior.

Symptom Management

1. Psychotherapy to explore psychodynamic issues.
2. Cognitive-behavioral therapy to develop skills to manage symptoms.
3. Several types of medications may be helpful depending on the specific disorder.
   a. Anxiolytic medications include Xanax, Valium, Librium, Ativan, Klonopin, and BuSpar.
      (1) Side effects include drowsiness, ataxia, headache, nausea, depression, and dependence.
   b. Antidepressant medications are helpful in some cases such as Anafranil, Paxil, Prozac, and Zoloft.
   c. Anti-obsessional medications Luvox may be used.
      (1) Side effects are similar to that of the Selective Serotonin Reuptake Inhibitors.
   d. In some cases, hypnotic medications to induce sleep may be used briefly.
      (1) Hypnotic medications include Restoril, Dalmane, Ambien, and Benadryl.
      (2) Side effects are similar to those of the anxiolytics.

Diagnostic-Specific Considerations for Occupational Therapy

1. Skills training and using cognitive behavioral approaches may reduce obsessive thoughts and compulsive behaviors.
2. Developing relaxation and stress management skills may decrease the incidence and severity of symptoms.
3. Providing graded activities designed to promote self-efficacy may increase self-confidence, motivation, and participation in intervention.
4. See this chapter's sections on OT mental health evaluation and OT mental health intervention for additional guidelines.
5. Chapter 13 provides further information on general OT psychosocial evaluation and intervention approaches.

EXAM HINT: The NBCOT® exam outline for the COTA® identifies knowledge of the "precautions or contraindications associated with a client condition or stage of recovery" (NBCOT®, 2018, p. 29) as essential for competent and safe practice. Because the medical management of psychiatric disorders includes the prescription of medications, OT practitioners should know how medication side effects can diminish performance (e.g., blurring vision) and impact health (e.g., increasing blood pressure) to effectively address these effects. OT practitioners should also know the positive effects of medications that can enhance performance (e.g., decreasing hallucinations/delusions; alleviating anxiety/depression) and use this knowledge to support the effective use of medications. The application of knowledge about the medications prescribed for each of the diagnoses included in this chapter can help determine the correct answer to exam items about medication precautions and activity contraindications during evaluation and intervention. Correct answers will adhere to medication precautions and consider activity contraindications during evaluation and intervention (e.g., providing assessment materials in large, high contrast print, addressing the side effect of photosensitivity before initiating a horticulture group).

Trauma- and Stressor Related Disorders

Reactive Attachment Disorder (RAD) of Infancy or Early Childhood

1. Diagnostic criteria.
   a. Childhood is characterized by social neglect or instability/inconsistency of primary caregivers, leading to insufficient or frequently changing care that alters the nature of interactions with caregivers.
   b. Reactive attachment disorder, inhibited type, is characterized by:
      (1) Persistent failure to initiate or respond in a developmentally appropriate fashion to most social interactions.
      (2) Interactions are excessively inhibited, hypervigilant, or highly ambivalent and contradictory in nature.
   c. Reactive attachment disorder, disinhibited type, is characterized by:
      (1) Indiscriminate sociability with inability to exhibit appropriate selective attachments.
      (2) Demonstrated by excessive familiarity with relative strangers or lack of selectivity.
2. Etiology.
   a. Exact cause is unknown.
   b. Early poor experiences with initial caregivers and/or pathogenic care may contribute to the disorder.
      (1) Indicators of pathogenic care:
         (a) Persistent disregard of the child's basic emotional needs.
         (b) Persistent disregard of the child's basic physical needs.
         (c) Repeated changes of primary caregiver or a succession of caregivers prevents the establishment of stable, appropriate attachments.
3. Onset, prevalence, and prognosis.
   a. Onset begins before 5 years of age.
   b. Exact prevalence or incidence of RAD is unknown.
   c. There is a high risk of prevalence for toddlers and children in foster care and orphanages and for children with frequently changing caregivers.
   d. Prognosis: unknown.
4. Impact on function.
   a. Children with RAD exhibit challenging behaviors. These include:
      (1) A high need to be in control.
      (2) Frequent lying.
      (3) Affectionate and overly related with strangers.
      (4) Frequent episodes of hoarding or gorging on food without physical need.
      (5) Denial of responsibility.
      (6) Projecting blame for their actions on others.
   b. Due to the above behaviors, children with RAD can be frustrating to work with and difficult to parent.
5. Symptom management.
   a. No one standard effective treatment for RAD is apparent in the literature.
6. Diagnostic-specific considerations for occupational therapy
   a. Close and ongoing collaboration with the child's family facilitates successful outcomes.
   b. Actively involve parents in treatment.
   c. Assist children to form a more secure sense of self.
   d. Limit the child's exposure to multiple caregivers.
   e. Provide high levels of structure and consistency.
   f. Goals need to be specific, realistic and attainable.
   g. See this chapter's sections on occupational therapy mental health evaluation and occupational therapy mental health intervention for additional guidelines.
7. Chapter 13 provides further information on general OT psychosocial evaluation and intervention approaches and specific interventions to manage behaviors.

Disinhibited Social Engagement Disorder

1. Diagnostic criteria.
   a. A child initiates active interaction with unfamiliar adults, while displaying at least two of the following behaviors:
      (1) Little reservation when approaching unfamiliar adults.
      (2) Overly familiar use of words or actions despite novelty and unfamiliarity of relationship.
      (3) The child is willing to leave with an unfamiliar adult without much or any hesitation, consideration, or checking back with the primary caregiver.
   b. The child's upbringing is characterized by patterns of social neglect, deprivation, or constant changing of primary caregivers, resulting in insufficient care for forming stable relationships with adults and caregivers.
   c. The child has a minimum of a 9-month-old developmental age (APA, 2013).

Post-traumatic Stress Disorder

1. Diagnostic criteria.
   a. Exposure to threats or actual events which can result in sexual violence, bodily injury, or death, by:
      (1) Personally and directly experiencing the trauma.
      (2) Firsthand witnessing of the traumatic event happening to another individual.
      (3) Learning about traumatic events experienced by close friends or family, after the fact.
      (4) Repeated or extreme exposure to visuals or explanations of aversive details associated with the traumatic events and negative consequences.
   b. Presence of intrusion symptoms (for more than one month):
      (1) Recurrent, unwanted, intrusive memories and/or dreams related to or depicting the traumatic event.
      (2) Physical or mental exposure to the traumatic event or related situations causes the individual to believe and/or act as if the traumatic event is reoccurring.
      (3) Experience of marked, prolonged physiological reactions and/or psychological distress associated with exposure to internal or external cues related to the traumatic event.
   c. Notable changes in patterns or behaviors as an attempt to avoid external stimuli or reminders associated with the traumatic event.
   d. Reminders of the traumatic event may have adverse reactions on cognition, focus, mood, sleep patterns, arousal, and reactivity or exaggerate vigilance, startle responses, and irritability (APA, 2013).

Acute Distress Disorder

1. Similar to post-traumatic stress disorder; however, it immediately follows the event. The symptoms do not persist beyond one month.

Adjustment Disorders

1. Diagnostic criteria.
   a. A clearly identifiable stressor causes onset of emotional and/or behavioral symptoms within three months of experiencing the stressor.
      (1) Symptoms resolve and disappear within 6 months of the stressor or its consequences being removed.
   b. Symptoms cause marked distress in important areas of function, including social and occupational, due to reactions that are unproportionate to the frequency or severity of the stressor.
   c. The symptoms are not better explained by another disorder, attributable to an exacerbation of symptoms from a pre-existing diagnosis or warranted as part of a normal bereavement response.

Neurocognitive Disorders

Diagnostic Criteria

1. Conditions for which the primary symptoms are cognitive deficits. This may be from substance abuse, medical conditions, or other known or unknown causes.
2. Delirium.
   a. A disturbance of consciousness (awareness of environment) with a decreased ability to attend.
   b. There is a change from previous cognition and/or perception.
   c. It covers a short period of time (hours to days) and tends to fluctuate.
   d. There are many causes.
      (1) Brain dysfunction.
      (2) Medication.
      (3) Endocrine disorders.
      (4) Cardiac disorders.
      (5) Infections and inflammations (e.g., fever, UTI).
      (6) Liver function disorders.
3. Major neurocognitive disorder.
   a. Clinical assessment reveals significant impairment in cognitive functioning that is a marked decline from a prior level of performance, as reported by the individual, clinician, or other knowledgeable source (APA, 2013).

> **EXAM HINT:** This condition was previously termed dementia in prior editions of the DSM™ and the term dementia is still typically used in clinical practice. In the NBCOT® practice analysis, 42.3% of COTA®s who provided services to persons with neurologic disorders indicated they worked with people with neurocognitive disorders/dementia (NBCOT®, 2018). Due to this prevalence, it is likely that the COTA® exam will have items about working with persons with neurocognitive disorders/dementia.

4. Mild neurocognitive disorder.
   a. Similar to major neurocognitive disorder, with the difference that the cognitive deficits do not interfere with independence in everyday activities.

Onset, Prevalence, and Prognosis

1. Delirium occurs in approximately one in five hospitalized individuals, with greater prevalence reported for older patients.
   a. It may resolve quickly or take several days.
   b. It is more severe with advanced age.
   c. It may indicate a poor prognosis over time.
2. The prevalence of neurocognitive disorder increases with age.
   a. There may be periods of plateauing with a gradual decline over time.

Impact on Function

1. The degree of impact varies according to the nature and severity of the symptoms.
2. The individual may require intervention varying from education in compensatory strategies to the need for total care.
3. Table 10-1. describe the progressive impact of neurocognitive disorders/dementia on functional abilities and occupational performance according to DSM-V and the Global Deterioration Scale for Assessment of Primary Degenerative Dementia (typically called the Reisberg levels).

Table 10-1

Neurocognitive Disorders: Presenting Signs and Functional Impact

STAGE/LEVEL	PRESENTING SIGNS	FUNCTIONAL ABILITIES	FUNCTIONAL LIMITATIONS
Very Mild Cognitive Decline Reisberg Level 2	The person experiences typical age-related memory loss (e.g., the person forgets the location of their keys); changes are not noticed by others.	Independent in activities daily living (ADL), instrumental activities of daily (IADL), work, leisure, and social participation.	Participation in activities may require more concentration and time and/or the use of compensatory strategies (e.g., 'talking' pill bottles)
Mild Cognitive Impairment Reisburg Level 3	One or more cognitive domains is affected at a level that is noticeable to themselves and others and evident on mental status exams.	Activity adaptations and compensation strategies can be used to maintain independence in familiar, noncomplex ADL, IADL, work, leisure, and social participation activities. Challenging situations (e.g., a noisy environment) are recognized by the person and avoided to minimize their deficits (e.g., distractibility)	Participation in activities requires more concentration and time and the use of compensatory strategies (e.g., written directions for a work task that was once intuitive). The difficulties experienced when completing complex occupational tasks can result in the person withdrawing from situations that will call attention to their deficits. Learning, remembering, and using new information (e.g., the names of new neighbors, following directions to a new restaurant) is difficult.
Moderate Neurocognitive Decline Reisburg Level 4	Moderate cognitive decline in one or more cognitive domains (e.g., the person is more forgetful, has difficulty finding words). The person and others express concern about the cognitive decline and modest impairments are evident on objective cognitive assessments.	Independent in simple, repetitive ADL (e.g., grooming) and following simple verbal cues and demonstration to complete other IADL, leisure, and social participation tasks (e.g., tearing lettuce to make a salad, setting the table for dinner) The person can live in their home with assistance.	The person cannot independently perform familiar, challenging activities or follow and sequence written cues (e.g., following the directions on a can of soup to cook the soup for lunch).
Major/Moderately Severe Neurocognitive Decline Reisburg Level 5	Significant cognitive decline in two or more cognitive domains. The person and others express concern about significant cognitive decline and substantial impairments are evident on objective cognitive assessments.	Able to perform ADL and very structured, repetitive, and highly familiar IADL, leisure, and social participation activities with encouragement, cues, and assistance (e.g., sweeping a floor, weeding a garden). The person can live in their home with substantial assistance.	The person is unable to use judgement to make decisions (e.g., what to wear based on the weather). The person cannot perform most IADL and cannot drive.

Table 10-1

Neurocognitive Disorders: Presenting Signs and Functional Impact

STAGE/LEVEL	PRESENTING SIGNS	FUNCTIONAL ABILITIES	FUNCTIONAL LIMITATIONS
Severe Neurocognitive Decline Reisburg Level 6	Severe impairment in multiple cognitive domains documented by objective cognitive assessments.	Able to perform components of familiar ADL tasks (e.g., self-feeding) and follow demonstration and hand-over-hand cues (e.g., brushing teeth). Able to make emotional connections with people and respond to pleasant sensory input (e.g., swaying to music).	The person needs assistance to complete ADL, cannot speak in full sentences, and is incontinent. The person needs 24/7 care.
Very Severe Neurocognitive Decline Reisburg Level 7	Very severe impairment in multiple cognitive domains.		The person is dependent in all ADL, loses speech and motor abilities, and is nonresponsive to others. The person requires 24/7 care.

References:
Hugo, J. & Ganguli, M. (2014). Dementia and cognitive impairment: Epidemiology, diagnosis, and treatment. *Clinics in Geriatric Medicine, 30*(3), 421–442. doi: 10.1016/j.cger.2014.04.001.
Reisberg, B., Ferris, S. H., de Leon, M. J., & Crook, T. (1982). The global deterioration scale for assessment of primary degenerative dementia. *American Journal of Psychiatry, 139*, 1136–1139.

---

a. The cognitive domains referred to in Table 10-1 are complex attention, executive function, learning and memory, language, perceptual motor, and social cognition.

Symptom Management

1. Medical treatment involves resolution of the causes of the disorder, if possible.
2. There are a limited number of newer medications that appear to maintain or slow the decline of cognitive function (e.g., Aricept, Cognex).
3. If causes of the disorder are not treatable, attempts are made to mitigate symptoms where possible.

Diagnostic-Specific Considerations for Occupational Therapy

1. Maintenance of quality of life through activity adaptation and environmental modification. See Chapters 14 and 15.
2. Family education to understand the nature of the person's disorder and improve the management of its symptoms and functional effects. See Table 10-2.
3. See this chapter's sections on OT mental health evaluation and OT mental health intervention for additional guidelines.

CAUTION: All OT practitioners should be aware that some of the causes of cognitive decline and neurocognitive disorders can be reversed with treatment. Table 10-3 identifies reversible causes of mental confusion that should be considered before a diagnosis of a neurocognitive disorder is made. The OTA should collaborate with the supervising occupational therapist to screen for these causes and act accordingly.

EXAM HINT: If a COTA® exam item includes a scenario in which a person is confused due to a potentially reversible cause, a correct answer may be instructing caregivers on how to provide an environment that meets a person's sensory needs and/or cues that enable performance. Additional correct answers could include the OTA collaborating with the supervising occupational therapist to refer a client to an audiologist for a hearing evaluation or to a primary care physician for an evaluation of polymedication.

4. Chapter 13 provides further information on general OT psychosocial evaluation and intervention approaches and specific interventions to manage the effects of neurocognitive disorders.

Table 10-2

Task Management Strategy Index Items Used by Caregivers of Persons Living with Dementia
Keep things that the person likes to use, look at, or touch in easy reach.
Put items that are needed by the person in a place where he/she will notice them.
Show the person what to do by demonstrating the activity.
Put away items that are not needed for what the person is doing.
Use pictures to help the person remember what to do.
Use bright colors or signs to help the person notice an item.
Use clothing that is easy to put on or take off.
Have the person do simple, repetitive chores such as folding laundry, making beds, or drying dishes.
Try to ignore the person's mistakes.
Plan a routine for the person and try to stick to it.
Use intercom or other monitoring device to supervise the person when he/she is in another room.

Gitlin, L., Winter, L., Dennis, M. P., Corcoran, M., Schinfeld, S., & Hauck, W. W. (2002). Strategies used by families to simplify tasks for individuals with Alzheimer's disease and related disorders: Psychometric analysis of the Task Management Strategy Index (TMSI). *Gerontologist, 42(1),* 61–69.

Table 10-3

Reversible Causes of Mental Confusion

Sensory changes and problems

Age-related losses in hearing, vision, touch, etc.

Unavailable or inadequate prostheses such as hearing aids, glasses, dentures, etc.

Sensory overload; too much, too long, too fast.

Sensory deprivation; too little stimulation, isolation, restraints.

Loss of cues to aid orientation and memory such as clocks, magazines, calendars, and strict adherence to routines and rituals.

Depression

Drug use and misuse

Drug interactions, side effects, and buildup from longer absorption and elimination times.

Over-the-counter cold, sleeping, and pain remedies; often taken without the physician's knowledge and which react with prescribed drugs.

Infections/Inflammation

Viral or bacterial infections; may be accompanied by fever.

Urinary tract infections, pneumonia, etc.

Gallbladder disease.

Metabolic problems caused by

Liver or kidney disease.

Thyroid disorders (hyperthyroidism and hypothyroidism).

Dehydration from diuretics, low fluid intake, hot weather.

Poorly controlled diabetes.

Feeding and Eating Disorders

Anorexia Nervosa

1. Diagnostic criteria.
   a. Low body weight due to difficulty maintaining body weight within or above normal parameters for sex, age, and height or due to an inability to gain weight as expected during growth periods (in this case, body weight is 85% or less than expected).
   b. Despite being underweight, there is a fear of gaining weight or becoming fat; the individual tends to perceive self as being heavier than in actuality.
   c. Alteration in self-perception of body weight or shape.
      (1) Physical body weight or shape is considered important in determination of self-evaluation or self-worth.
      (2) The individual may not realize, or may deny, the presence of low body weight and/or the seriousness of the effects despite being ill or hospitalized.
   d. Two types may be identified, either food restrictive type or binge eating/purging type (APA, 2013).
2. Onset, prevalence, and prognosis.
   a. It has a lifetime prevalence of 0.5%–1%.
   b. It is more common in girls than in boys.
   c. The long-term prognosis may not be good, with mortality rates of approximately 5.35%.
3. Behavioral characteristics.
   a. Individuals often exhibit obsessive/compulsive behavior, depression, anxiety, rigidity, perfectionism, and poor sexual adjustment.

Bulimia Nervosa

1. Diagnostic criteria.
   a. Ongoing binge eating of much larger portions than would be expected and feeling the inability to control consumption to avoid gaining weight.
   b. Attempts are made to avoid gaining weight through vomiting, using laxatives, fasting and engaging in extreme amounts of exercise.
   c. Personal self-concept defined by body proportions and size.
   d. Symptoms are not occurring as part of anorexia nervosa.
2. Onset, prevalence, and prognosis.
   a. The usual age of onset of bulimia is later than that of anorexia.
      (1) It begins in adolescence or in early adulthood.
      (2) It has an estimated lifetime prevalence of 0.5%–3%.
      (3) It is significantly more common in women than in men.

CAUTION: Adolescents with bulimia have reported higher rates of suicide ideation and suicide attempt than adolescents with anorexia.

3. Behavioral characteristics.
   a. Obsession with personal appearance and attractiveness to others.
   b. Individuals maintain a normative weight.

Binge-Eating Disorder

1. Diagnostic criteria.
   a. Inability to control recurrent periods of consuming an exorbitant amount of foods in a discrete situation.
   b. Binge-eating episodes may include:
      (1) Eating until uncomfortably full or when not feeling physically hungry.
      (2) Eating more and at a faster pace than usual.
      (3) Experiencing feelings of guilt or depression after excessive eating.
      (4) Frequent solitary eating due to embarrassment over behaviors.
   c. Binge eating behaviors result in clinically significant distress.
   d. The average frequency for a clinical diagnosis is a minimum of one time per week for at least three months (APA, 2013).

Other Feeding and Eating Disorders

1. Pica.
   a. Persistent eating of nonfood substances, which is inconsistent with cultural or developmental expectations.
   b. Recurrent patterns of behavior must be present for at least one month.

2. Rumination disorder.
   a. Repeated, unintentional regurgitation of undigested or partially digested food, followed by rechewing and either swallowing or spitting food out, for at least one month.
3. Avoidant/restrictive food intake disorder.
   a. Persistent failure to meet nutritional needs and expectations, resulting in any of the following symptoms:
      (1) Nutritional deficiency.
      (2) Significant weight loss.
      (3) Reliance on oral nutritional supplements or alternative feeding methods (i.e., enteral feeding via pump).
      (4) Clinical disturbance in psychological functioning (APA, 2013).

Impact on Function

1. Activities of daily living (ADL) such as self-care, eating, and feeding can be severely disrupted.
2. Instrumental activities of daily living (IADL) such as shopping for clothing and food, meal preparation and clean-up, and health management and maintenance can be significantly affected.
3. Work skills can be intact unless food-restricting behaviors and/or medical problems interfere with work performance or prevocational/vocational skill development.
   a. Focus on weight control may interfere with pursuit of vocational goals and/or the development of prerequisite skills.
4. Leisure skills can be intact unless affected by food-restricting behaviors and/or medical complications.
   a. Activities may focus mainly on appearance, rather than on those that have meaning or purpose.
   b. Exercise activities previously done for fun (e.g., running, swimming, cycling) may now be done excessively without enjoyment to decrease weight.
5. Social participation (including family, community, and peer/friend) can be greatly impacted by the excessive use of food-restricting behaviors, the need to maintain secrecy about the behaviors, and feeling ashamed, guilty, embarrassed, and/or depressed about atypical and disturbed eating habits and patterns.

Symptom Management

1. The use of antidepressant medications may be used in anorexia nervosa, but they are more effective for individuals with bulimia.
   a. Antipsychotics can be used to improve distorted thinking and perceptions.
2. Treatment of any of the resulting medical complications such as cardiac disturbances (hypotension, slow heart rate), reduced thyroid metabolism, osteoporosis, seizures, severe dehydration, electrolyte imbalances, irregular bowel movements, pancreatitis, peptic ulcers, gastric and/or esophageal inflammation, and possible rupture, and tooth decay may also be necessary.
3. Treatment most often takes place in outpatient or day care programs.
4. Hospitalization may be necessary if the individual has medical difficulties, is suicidal, cannot care for themself, or needs to be removed from their environment.
5. Behavioral programs designed around a privileging system are often used.
   a. Consistency among staff is crucial for program effectiveness.
6. Symptom management also typically includes individual psychotherapy, family counseling, and behavioral and/or cognitive therapies.

Diagnostic-Specific Considerations for Occupational Therapy

1. The building of trust is essential to effective intervention due to the secrecy, guilt, anger, resistance, and ego fragility often associated with the disorder and its stages of recovery.
2. The OT practitioner must be honest, supportive, and gently confrontational when indicated.
3. Evaluation and intervention must include the identification of the socioemotional needs the eating disorder had fulfilled for the person so that health-promoting occupation-based alternatives can be explored and developed.
   a. Non-food-related areas of interest and meaningful purposeful activities should be pursued to promote a reality-based body image and foster improved coping.
4. Education about nutritional food management and the development of healthy leisure time (i.e., does not involve excessive exercise) are key.
5. See this chapter's sections on OT mental health evaluation and OT mental health intervention for additional guidelines.
6. Chapter 13 provides further information on general OT psychosocial evaluation and intervention approaches.

Disruptive, Impulse-Control, and Conduct Disorders

Diagnostic Criteria

1. Oppositional defiant disorder (ODD).
   a. Negativistic, hostile, and defiant behaviors that result in functional impairment.
2. Conduct disorder.
   a. Disregard for the rights of others leading to aggression toward people and animals, destruction of property, deceitfulness, theft, or serious violation of rules.
3. Unspecified disruptive, impulse control, and conduct disorder.
   a. Children who do not meet the criteria for conduct disorder or ODD; however, they display significant functional impairment and conduct and oppositional behaviors are present.

Onset, Prevalence, and Prognosis

1. ODD.
   a. Oppositional, negative behavior begins in early childhood and occurs in 2%–16% of children, with a higher prevalence reported in boys.
   b. The course and prognosis depend on the severity of behaviors, the presence of other disorders, and the intactness of the family.
   c. It is most likely to progress into a conduct disorder if aggression is prominent.
   d. Lifetime prevalence of ODD is estimated to be 12.6%.
2. Conduct disorder.
   a. It is estimated that 3.3%–4% of boys and 1.4%–1.7% of girls ages 5–19 have a conduct disorder.
   b. Prognosis is related to the age of onset and the severity of symptoms and behavior.
      (1) Severe conduct disorder is often associated with the development of other disorders and substance abuse later in life.
   c. Assaultive behavior and parental criminality correlate highly with future incarceration.

EXAM HINT: In the NBCOT®'s practice analysis, 37.1% of COTAs® who provided services to persons with psychosocial disorders indicated they provided services to individuals with behavior disorders. Due to this prevalence, it is likely that the COTA® exam will have items about working with this population.

Impact on Function

1. Children with these behavior disorders have difficulty at school and with the formation of healthy social and familial relationships.
2. Difficulties within the family affect not only the child but all family members, impacting on their role performance.

Symptom Management

1. Behavioral techniques are often the most effective forms of intervention with adolescents.
2. The identification and treatment of other disorders, (e.g., attention deficit hyperactivity disorder [ADHD], learning disorders, substance use, depression, etc.) is important.
3. The use of medications such as antipsychotics, antidepressants, anxiolytics, and mood stabilizers may be helpful.
4. A consistent approach from all team members is essential.

Diagnostic-Specific Considerations for Occupational Therapy

1. Contributing disorders (ADHD, mood disorders, learning disorders, etc.) and their effect on performance skills and areas of occupation must be evaluated and addressed in intervention.
2. The child's goals, stressors, and family and social relationships should be considered.
3. Skill development may improve emotional adjustment.
4. Behavioral approaches must be consistent throughout all programming.
5. The OT practitioner should assist the parents, other family members, teachers, and other school personnel to understand the nature of the child's condition and to develop consistent strategies for behavior management.
6. See this chapter's sections on OT mental health evaluation and OT mental health intervention for additional guidelines.
7. Chapter 13 provides further information on general OT psychosocial evaluation and intervention approaches and specific interventions to manage offensive, intrusive, and escalating behaviors.

Neurodevelopmental Disorders

Autism Spectrum Disorders (ASDs)[2]

1. Etiology.
   a. Organic brain pathology.
   b. May or may not be seen with other disorders.
      (1) Rett's syndrome, if associated with ASD, is now specified as "Known Genetic Condition" (see section that follows).
2. Onset, prevalence, and prognosis.
   a. May occur from birth up to three years of age.
   b. About 1 in 59 children has been identified with ASD according to estimates from the Centers for Disease Control and Prevention's Autism and Developmental Disabilities Monitoring (ADDM) network.
   c. ASD is about four times more common among boys than girls.
   d. ASD is reported to occur in all racial, ethnic, and socioeconomic groups.

> **EXAM HINT:** In the NBCOT®'s practice analysis, 27.4% of COTAs® who provided services to persons with psychosocial disorders indicated they provided services to individuals with ASD. Due to this prevalence, it is likely that the COTA® exam will have items about working with persons with ASD.

   e. The prognosis for children with ASD is dependent upon the combined impact of the following three parameters:
      (1) Severity of ASD.
      (2) Level of general intelligence.
      (3) Change in symptom expression over time.
   f. Life expectancy is not affected, although a supervised living setting may be necessary for those with severe ASD.
3. Diagnostic characteristics.
   a. Presence of at least two core symptom domains:
      (1) Impaired social communication and social interaction.
      (2) Restricted, repetitive patterns of behavior, interests, or activities.
   b. Behavioral characteristics.
      (1) Impaired nonverbal behaviors (e.g., infrequent/poor eye contact, impaired attachment behavior, anxiety with changes in typical routines).
      (2) Difficulty relating to others and forming relationships at an age-appropriate level.
      (3) Lack of spontaneous social-seeking behavioral interactions with others and lack of awareness of others who are seeking interactions (e.g., sharing a snack, pointing at an object of interest).
      (4) Lack of social reciprocation due to decreased ability to infer feelings and intentions of others (e.g., the child does not understand that sharing is expected; the child does not point at an object to have the parents name the object or point to pictures in a book and look to the reader for a response).
      (5) Difficulty with communication.
         (a) Lack of initiation, reflection, and/or development of spoken language or alternative means for communication.
         (b) If speech is developed, difficulty in initiating or engaging in conversation and lack of appropriate context.
         (c) Stereotyped echolalia and/or use of indiscernible language.
      (6) Lack of spontaneous pretend, imitative, or exploratory play.
      (7) Repetitive and stereotyped behaviors and movements in one or more of the following:
         (a) Ritualistic nonfunctional routines, preoccupation.
         (b) Rigid observance of nonfunctional routines or behavioral patterns.
         (c) Repetitive motor action (e.g., flapping and wiggling of fingers, head banging, rocking of the head or body).
         (d) Restrictive fixation on parts of a whole object (e.g., wheel of a toy car).
   c. Delay or impairment in social interaction, language, and/or play (symbolic or imaginative) is present before three years of age.
   d. Not better described as Rett's syndrome or childhood disintegrative disorder.
   e. Difficulty with sensory processing and perception of various sensory stimuli; difficulty in modulation of stimuli at various levels of the continuum, e.g., hyper- or hyporesponsiveness.
   f. Common associated behaviors may include unanticipated mood swings, temper tantrums, lack of ability to focus, insomnia, and enuresis.
   g. Deficits tend to be more severe in verbal sequencing and abstraction versus abilities in visuospatial and rote memory skills (e.g., calculation, musical abilities) (APA, 2013).
4. Symptom management.
   a. Medications prescribed will depend on the presenting symptoms.

---
[2] Jan G. Garbarini and Marge E. Moffet Boyd contributed this section on autism spectrum disorders.

(1) Seizure medications.
(2) Medication for muscle deterioration and/or complications due to abnormal tone.
(3) Medications to increase alertness.
(4) Medications to modulate behaviors.

5. Diagnostic specific considerations for OT.
   a. Evaluate developmental and functional levels. See Chapter 5.
   b. Develop sensorimotor, social interaction, vocational readiness, and community participation skills relevant to the child's level. See Chapter 5 and Chapter 14.
   c. Provide sensory integrative intervention, if indicated. See relevant sections in Chapter 5 and Chapter 12.
   d. If indicated, prescribe and train in technologically-based augmentive communication. See Chapter 15.
   e. Provide adaptive and positioning equipment to facilitate function (e.g., the stereotypical movements of licking, biting, and slapping of the hands in a child with Rett's Syndrome may require adaptations to maintain the integrity of the skin, such as dynamic elbow splints that inhibit a hand-to-mouth pattern by limiting full elbow flexion).
   f. Table 10-4 outlines specific strategies that OT practitioners can use when working with children with ASD.
   g. Collaborate with the family and interdisciplinary team to promote occupational performance and social participation.
   h. See this chapter's sections on OT mental health evaluation and OT mental health intervention for additional guidelines.
   i. Chapter 13 provides further information on general OT psychosocial evaluation and intervention approaches and specific interventions to manage behaviors.

Table 10-4

Specific Strategies for Occupational Therapy Sessions when Working with Children with Autism Spectrum Disorder

Improve Engagement and Interaction, Reduce Fear or Anxiety
- Imitate the child and wait for the child to initiate interaction via eye contact, touch, or moving into closer physical proximity.
- Alter your proximity to the child.
- Reduce the use of direct eye contact.
- Alter the therapist's motor and verbal pace.
- Alter the therapist's voice volume or intonation.
- Use musical or sing-song vocalizations that the child finds humorous.
- Use preferred objects, colors, or movements within therapy tasks to elicit desired gross or fine motor skills. This should be a fun game.
- Interact playfully, make work into play.
- Create fun problems to solve (e.g., "Oh no, the pig (stuffed toy) is trapped in the mud, you have to help get him out. How can we save him?").
- Sing familiar songs and leave out the last word, to encourage the child to vocalize to fill in where you have omitted the word.

Improve Motor Skills/Praxis
- Create fun obstacles/challenges that encourage therapeutically desired movements while engaging the child in a preferred activity of his/her choice.
- Climb, walk, or crawl on raised surfaces to increase attention to motion. For example, climb across a wide balance beam or a horizontal ladder at two to three feet off the ground (while maintaining safety).
- Gradually increase motoric sequences that are completed before a desired event or object is provided (e.g., placing a favorite toy in an increasing number of layers to open prior to placing it up a ramp or ladder).
- Alternate preferred sensory activities with more challenging motor tasks.
- Sing about the motor activity you are doing using a familiar tune (e.g., use the tune of "Row, Row, Row Your Boat," to sing "push, push, push that cart gently down the hall").

Improve Comfort, Reduce Fear and Anxiety
- Carefully grade the introduction of novelty into a session.
- Attend to the sensory environment and the child's response (i.e., nonverbal responses, facial expression) to the sensory environment.
- Alter lighting, noise, smells.
- Provide opportunities for deep pressure and proprioception through active play.

Improve Behavior and Task Completion, Reduce Fear or Anxiety
- Use objects, visual cues, or schedules to help the child predict what will come next, what will happen, or how many times a particular action/behavior is expected.
- Use prompts that are familiar to the child.
- Know and use the child's preferred reinforcers throughout the OT "work."
- Provide clear boundaries regarding areas of the intervention space so that it is clear which type of activity occurs in each area.
- Provide choices or choice boards, visual schedules, or other visual materials to aid in understanding what is to be done.
- Provide written instructions if a child can read.

Improve Play and Ideational Praxis
- Use realistic prompts to introduce role play (e.g., fireman's hat, realistic dress-up clothing).
- Use movie characters and stories to begin to introduce pretend play.
- Promote imagination in your sessions.
- Have the child help you create a game out of unusual materials.
- Have the child help you build an obstacle course or sensorimotor activity.
- Discuss the different ways you can use certain objects based on their properties (affordances).
- Try to add to current ideas with prompting (e.g., "can you think of another way to do that?").
- Take turns between imitating the child and having the child attempt to imitate you.
- Use silly motions, vocalizations, and sequences to be playful.

Adapted from Miller-Kuhaneck, H. (2016). Autism spectrum disorder. In J. Case-Smith & J. C. O'Brien (Eds.), *Occupational therapy for children and adolescence* (7th ed., p. 777). St. Louis, MO: Elsevier. Reprinted with permission.

Known Genetic Condition (Previously Rett's Syndrome)

1. Etiology is unknown; however, since deterioration occurs after a period of normal development, it is thought to be attributed to a genetic metabolic disorder.
2. Onset, prevalence, and prognosis.
   a. Motor and social skills are age appropriate from six months to two years of development when the onset of progressive encephalopathy develops.
   b. The exact prevalence is unknown; however, current estimates suggest it occurs in 1 in 10,000 girls to 1 in 22,000 girls in the United States.
   c. Development of physical growth and head circumference plateau resulting in progressive encephalopathy.
   d. A child may live for over 10 years following the onset.
3. Diagnostic characteristics and sequelae.
   a. Deterioration of language; receptive and expressive communication and social skills may plateau at a six-month to one-year developmental level.
   b. Motor deterioration is characterized by a loss of purposeful hand movements with the development of stereotypical movements, such as hand wringing and licking, biting, and slapping of fingers.
      (1) Deterioration of the integrity of the skin results from these repetitive stereotypical movements.
   c. Muscle tone becomes hypotonic and then progresses to spasticity and then rigidity.
      (1) The result is an ataxic, uncoordinated, and stiff gait.
   d. Muscle wasting can make these children prone to scoliosis and eventually may necessitate the use of a wheelchair.
   e. Breathing patterns become irregular, marked by hyperventilation, apnea, and holding of breath.
   f. Regression occurs in cognition and praxis.
   g. Electroencephalograms are abnormal and seizures are common.

Social (Pragmatic) Communication Disorder (SCD)

1. Formerly known as Asperger's disorder.
2. Etiology is unknown; however, studies indicate a strong relation to autism. It is hypothesized to be due to genetic, metabolic, infectious, or perinatal causes.
3. Onset, prevalence, and prognosis.
   a. Little is known, and course and prognosis are variable.
   b. Individuals with a normal IQ and high-level social skills appear to have a good prognosis, although they tend to be socially uncomfortable and demonstrate illogical thinking.
4. Diagnostic characteristics.
   a. Difficulty with social interaction.
   b. Restricted interests and behaviors.
   c. Characterized by clumsiness.
   d. Delayed developmental motor milestones.
   e. Differentiated from ASD by adequate language and the level of social interaction and engagement in activities with others.

Attention-Deficit/Hyperactivity Disorders

1. Etiology.
   a. Brain development correlates with ASD.
   b. Unknown, however, there are suggested contributing factors. These include:
      (1) Genetic factors include higher occurrence in monozygotic twins than in dizygotic twins, and twice the occurrence in siblings of hyperactive children.
      (2) Neurological factors include the possibility of minimal or subtle brain damage due to circulatory, toxic, metabolic, or mechanical effects during fetal or perinatal periods; and infection, inflammation, and/or trauma during early childhood.
      (3) Neurochemical dysfunction related to neurotransmitters in the adrenergic and the dopaminergic systems.
      (4) Psychosocial factors include stress, anxiety, or predisposing factors such as temperament.
2. Subtypes of attention deficit hyperactivity disorders specify whether:
   a. Combined presentation.
   b. Predominantly inattentive presentation.
   c. Predominantly hyperactive/impulsive presentation.
3. Onset, prevalence, and prognosis.
   a. Symptoms are often noted during the toddler years, usually by the age of three.
      (1) Caution is advised to not make a diagnosis in early childhood years.
      (2) Diagnosis is most often made during elementary school years when behavior interferes with adjustment to school.
   b. Occurs in 5%–9% children between the ages of 2 and 17.
      (1) Incidence in boys to girls is a 3 to 1 ratio, most common in firstborn boys.
   c. Partial remission may occur between the ages of 12 and 20, allowing for a productive adolescence and adulthood.
      (1) Although hyperactivity may disappear, distractibility and impulsivity can persist.
   d. Symptoms persist into adulthood in 60% of cases.

> **EXAM HINT:** In the NBCOT®'s practice analysis, 23.6% of COTAs® who provided services to persons with psychosocial disorders indicated they provided services to individuals with ADHD. Due to this prevalence, it is likely that the COTA® exam will have items about working with persons with ADHD.

4. Diagnostic criteria.
   a. Children.
      (1) The presence of six or more symptoms in the inattention domain, the hyperactivity-impulsivity domain, or both.
      (2) Symptoms in the inattention domain or hyperactivity-impulsivity domain that interfere with occupational activities are present for at least six months or more.
         (a) Symptoms of the inattention domain may include lack of attention to detail, poor listening, limited follow-through of tasks, difficulty with organization, and avoidance of tasks that require sustained attention, tendency to lose things, distractibility, and forgetfulness.
         (b) Symptoms of the hyperactivity domain may include fidgeting, inability to remain seated, inappropriate activity level for a given situation, difficulty with quiet sedentary activities, frequent movement, and excessive talking.
         (c) Symptoms of impulsivity include answering questions before they are fully stated, difficulty with turn taking, and interrupting the conversations or activities of others.
      (3) Visual-perceptual, auditory-perceptual, language, and/or cognitive problems may be present.
      (4) Some of the symptoms that result in impairment were evident before seven years of age.
      (5) Symptoms that result in impairment are present in two settings, such as school, home, and/or work.
   b. Adolescents/adults.
      (1) Adolescents and adults (aged ≥17) are required to present with a minimum of five (rather than six) symptoms.
      (2) Symptoms should have been present before age 12 (not before age seven).
      (3) Motor symptoms of hyperactivity may appear less in adolescence and adulthood; however, restlessness, inattention, poor planning, and impulsivity may persist.
      (4) Impairments tend to be present into adulthood.
      (5) A diagnosis of ASD may accompany a diagnosis of ADHD.
5. Impact on function.
   a. Infants are over-active, difficult to soothe when crying, and demonstrate poor sleeping habits.
   b. Defensiveness to environmental stimuli, frequent irritability, aggressive behavior, emotional lability, and fluctuating and unpredictable performance.
   c. Difficulty with delayed gratification in the school and home.
   d. Deficits in perceptual motor tasks with disorders in reading, mathematics, written expression, and general coordination resulting.
   e. Disorders of memory, thinking, speech, and hearing.
   f. Depression secondary to frustration and difficulty with learning.
   g. This often leads to low self-esteem and conduct disorders.
   h. Individuals with symptoms remaining in adolescence and adulthood are prone to antisocial personality disorders and are at risk for substance-related disorders.
6. Symptom management.
   a. Prescribed medications depend on presenting symptoms.
      (1) Stimulants.
         (a) Most commonly used include dextroamphetamine (e.g., Dexedrine, Focalin) for children three years and older, and methylphenidate (e.g., Concerta, Ritalin, Adderall, Metadate) for children six years and older.
         (b) Side effects include loss of appetite, weight loss, loss of appetite, disturbed sleep patterns, and slow growth.
      (2) Antidepressants.
         (a) Imipramine.
         (b) Used when stimulants are unable to be used.
         (c) Careful monitoring of cardiac functioning is required.
      (3) Anxiolytics.
         (a) Clonidine (Catapres).
         (b) Guanfacine (Tenex).
         (c) Require careful dosing and competent adults for administration.
         (d) Medications cannot be stopped suddenly because this could medically compromise the child.
   b. Monitoring of medication and its impact on cognitive and psychosocial function (e.g., learning and self-esteem).
   c. Psychotherapy, behavior modification, parent and individual counselling may be indicated.
7. Diagnostic-specific considerations for occupational therapy.
   a. Behavior's impact on school, home, play/leisure, and social participation must be considered.
   b. Environmental modifications and activity adaptations to structure the client's home environment can enhance function.

c. Environmental modifications and activity adaptations to structure the child's environment at school and the adult's environment at work can support more successful outcomes (e.g., the elimination of sensory distracters, the use of lists, datebooks, and/or texted reminders).
d. Training in social skills and self-management (i.e., the use of humor, personally initiated time-outs) can improve adaptive behaviors.
e. Interventions to promote sensory modulation are emphasized. See Chapter 12.
f. Consultation is provided to parents, family members, teachers, and employees regarding strategies for the provision of structure and expectations in a manner that fosters the person's psychosocial adaptation.
g. In school-based practice, ongoing collaboration with individualized education planning team members and parents is vital.
h. See this chapter's sections on OT mental health evaluation OT mental health intervention for additional guidelines.
i. Chapter 13 provides further information on general OT psychosocial evaluation and intervention approaches and specific interventions to manage problem behaviors.

Intellectual Disorders

1. Etiology.
   a. Genetic conditions such as chromosomal abnormalities (e.g., Down syndrome, fragile X syndrome, Prader-Willi syndrome, and Klinefelter's syndrome).
   b. Metabolic conditions such as phenylketonuria, hypothyroidism, and Tay-Sachs disease.
   c. Prenatal infections such as rubella, toxoplasmosis, and AIDS.
   d. Maternal substance abuse.
   e. Perinatal factors such as trauma and prematurity.
   f. Acquired conditions, including infections such as encephalitis and meningitis.
   g. Head trauma sustained in motor vehicle accidents, falls, child abuse, etc.
2. Onset, prevalence, and prognosis.
   a. Onset of deficits begins in the developmental period.
   b. Occurs in 0.05%–1.55% of the population.
   c. Likely lifelong disorders with treatment focused on rehabilitation, management of symptoms, and adaptive strategies.
3. Diagnostic classification and functional implications.
   a. The essential features include:
      (1) Criterion A: deficits in general mental abilities.
      (2) Criterion B: impairment in everyday adaptive functioning, in comparison to an individual's age-, gender-, and socioculturally matched peers.
      (3) Criterion C: Onset is during the developmental period.
   b. The diagnosis of intellectual disability is determined by clinical assessment and standardized testing of intellectual and adaptive functioning.
   c. Deficits in adaptive functioning impact the everyday life activities (occupations) and are a central focus of OT intervention.
   d. The American Association on Intellectual and Developmental Disabilities has categorized adaptive functioning into three domains:
      (1) Conceptual skills—language and literacy; money, time, and number concepts; and self-direction.
      (2) Social skills—interpersonal skills, social responsibility, self-esteem, gullibility, naïveté (i.e., wariness), social problem-solving, and the ability to follow rules/obey laws and to avoid being victimized.
      (3) Practical skills—activities of daily living (personal care), occupational skills, healthcare, travel/transportation, schedules/routines, safety, use of money, use of the telephone.
   e. Diagnosis is based on the measurement of intelligence or IQ tests; however, it should be noted that IQ scores do not provide a full profile of individuals' capabilities.
      (1) Individuals who score more than two standard deviations below the norm, or below an IQ of 70, are considered to have an intellectual disability.
   f. An IQ range of 50 to approximately 70 indicates a mild intellectual disability.
      (1) Focus is placed on the individual acquiring social and vocational skills to function independently in desired occupational roles.
      (2) Minimal support is required.
      (3) Additional intermittent support may be required in special circumstances.
   g. An IQ range of 35 to approximately 50 indicates a moderate intellectual disability.
      (1) Focus is usually placed on the individual acquiring independence in routine daily skills and skills necessary to perform in desired occupational roles with supports and structure (e.g., work in a vocational rehabilitation [sheltered] workshop).
      (2) Limited support and assistance may be required in specific occupational performance areas on a daily basis.
      (3) Supervised living is required.
   h. An IQ range of 20 to approximately 35 indicates a severe intellectual disability.
      (1) Focus is usually placed on the individual acquiring communication skills and some basic health habits.
      (2) Assistance is required for performance of most tasks in all areas of occupation on a daily basis.

(3) Supervised living is required.
(4) Significant impairments in motor functioning and physical development are typical.
i. IQ of below 20–25 indicates a profound intellectual disability.
(1) Assistance and ongoing supervision are required for basic survival skills.
(2) Significant impairments in motor functioning and physical development are typical.
(3) Supervised living is required.
j. Multiple disabilities such as hearing and other sensory impairments, seizures, and other neurologic abnormalities may be associated with various syndromes (e.g., fetal alcohol syndrome).
4. Impact on development.
a. The developmental impact of intellectual disability can vary greatly.
(1) The impact is greatest in children with severe and profound intellectual disability.
b. Cognitive development.
(1) Slower learning ability.
(2) Shorter attention span.
(3) Difficulty with problem-solving and critical thinking.
(4) Difficulty generalizing information and mastering abstract thinking.
(5) Increased distractibility.
c. Motor development.
(1) Slower development with the attainment of physical milestones occurring at a later age than typical.
(2) Uncoordinated appearance and movements.
(3) Low muscle tone.
d. Sensory development.
(1) Diminished sensory modulation abilities.
(2) Hyper- or hyposensitivity to all sensory stimuli.
e. Language development.
(1) Decreased ability in recalling and retrieving words secondary to cognitive deficits (e.g., inattention and impaired memory).
(2) Difficulty grasping and expressing concepts secondary to cognitive deficits (e.g., impaired abstract thinking).
(3) Difficulty with the motor aspects of creating language secondary to motor deficits (e.g., low tone).
f. Psychosocial development.
(1) Impaired ability to respond to social cues can result in a number of behavioral outcomes. These can include:
(a) Excessive shyness.
(b) Aggressiveness.
(2) Hyperactivity and distractibility can also impede psychosocial development.
5. Symptom management.
a. Dependent upon presenting symptoms and complications.
b. Psychological, audiological, and speech evaluations and interventions may be indicated.
c. Intermittent support may be required in special circumstances.
6. Diagnostic-specific considerations for OT.
a. Self-determination and person-centered planning within the person's capabilities should be a priority.
b. Support and assistance may be required to address performance skills and patterns in areas of occupation.
c. Development of community and social participation skills are a major focus.
d. Interdisciplinary team and family collaboration is helpful to support the development of the person's functional and social skills and to promote participation in areas of occupation.
e. If individual is of school age, collaboration with the educational team is needed to develop a comprehensive educational program. See Chapter 4.

EXAM HINT: The NBCOT® exam outline for the COTA® identifies knowledge of the "expected patterns, progressions, and prognoses associated with conditions that limit occupational performance" (NBCOT®, 2018, p. 21) as essential for competent and safe practice. The application of knowledge about the DSM-5™ diagnostic information provided in this chapter can help you determine the correct answers to exam items about working with persons with psychiatric and cognitive disorders.

Occupational Therapy Mental Health Evaluation

Role of the Occupational Therapy Assistant (OTA)

1. The OTA can contribute to the evaluation process in collaboration with the occupational therapist.
a. Supervision by an occupational therapist is required.
b. The level of supervision required will be determined by the OTA's experience and established service competency.
2. The OTA can assist with the collection of data for the evaluation once service competency has been established.
3. The OTA cannot independently evaluate or interpret evaluation results.

Evaluation Focus

1. Determination of values, interests, desired occupational roles, and self-determined goals.
2. Identification of cognitive, perceptual, and psychosocial strengths and skills, and their ability to facilitate recovery.
3. Identification of cognitive, perceptual, and psychosocial deficits and limitations, and their impact on function and life style.
4. Determination of functional problems associated with psychiatric symptoms (e.g., safety awareness and judgment).
5. Treatment history and ability and interest to engage in recovery (i.e., readiness for change).
6. Identification of coping skills, stressors, and environmental and social supports.
7. See Chapter 13 for additional information about psychosocial evaluation methods and specific assessment tools.

Occupational Therapy Mental Health Intervention

The Role of the OTA

1. The OTA implements intervention with supervision of the occupational therapist.
2. The level of supervision required depends on the OTA's experience and established service competency.
3. During the implementation of intervention, the OTA informs the supervising therapist of any change in the individual's status and any other relevant information that may affect treatment.

EXAM HINT: The NBCOT® exam outline for the COTA® identifies the tasks of providing "information regarding the influence of current conditions, contexts, and task demands on occupational performance in order to assist the OTR in planning interventions and monitoring progress as guided by the practice setting and theoretical construct" (NBCOT®, 2018, p. 22) and "using a culturally sensitive, client-centered approach and therapeutic use of self to provide quality services guided by evidence, scope of practice, service competence, and principles of best practice" (NBCOT®, 2018, p. 22) as essential to competent practice. The application of knowledge about the general intervention foci described below, the diagnostic-specific interventions described throughout this chapter, and the intervention methods and approaches described in Chapter 13 can help you effectively determine the correct answers to exam items about OT interventions for persons with psychiatric and cognitive disorders

Intervention Foci

1. The foci of intervention during periods of acute hospitalization includes:
   a. Management of all behaviors that threaten the safety and well-being of the individual as well as that of others on the unit.
   b. Stabilization of behavior to enable engagement in intervention.
   c. Engagement in activities that are 'do-able' (e.g., brief and structured) to enable success and promote reality-based thinking.
      (1) Graded activities are designed to promote self-efficacy, which can increase self-confidence, motivation, and participation in treatment.
   d. Engagement of the person in the treatment process.
   e. Development of relaxation and stress management skills to help decrease the incidence and severity of symptoms and facilitate recovery.
   f. Development of the skills needed to pursue desired occupational roles and attain self-determined goals.
   g. Engagement in activities to improve communication skills and self-expression.
   h. The gathering and sharing of ongoing assessment information with the treatment team.
      (1) The person's status typically changes drastically during the course of an acute hospitalization due to the stabilizing effects of psychotropic medications.
         (a) The input of OT practitioners about a patient's observed symptoms and functional behaviors is critical in assisting with the effective titration of psychotropic medications.
   i. Assistance with discharge planning to support recovery and a healthy lifestyle.
2. The foci of intervention during periods of long-term hospitalization include:
   a. Development and implementation of a plan for self-determined goal achievement.
   b. Provision of a normalizing environment that enables participation in meaningful and desired occupational roles.
   c. Engagement of the person in the treatment process.
   d. Provision of graded activities to develop the skills needed for competence in ADL, IADL, social participation, leisure, school, and/or work.

e. Development of relaxation and stress management skills to help decrease the incidence and severity of symptoms and facilitate recovery.
f. Continuation of assessment to determine realistic and meaningful discharge goals.
g. Development of the skills and external supports needed to pursue desired post-discharge occupational roles, participate in the anticipated discharge environment, and attain self-determined discharge goals.
3. The foci of intervention in community settings.
a. Provision of services that facilitate recovery and assist in the maintenance of existing skills.
b. Assistance with the continued development of skills needed for community living, social participation, and the pursuit of valued occupational roles.
c. Development of skills and supports to enable ongoing recovery (e.g., WRAP, NAMI [National Alliance for the Mentally Ill]).
d. Development of skills and the provision of assistance, if needed, to obtain concrete practical resources to support community living (e.g., supplemental social security [SSI], affordable housing, and food stamps).
e. Monitoring of the individual for changing clinical, personal, and social needs.

References

American Academy of Child and Adolescent Psychiatry. (2009). *Facts for families: Children with oppositional defiant disorder.* Retrieved from http://www.aacap.org/galleries/FactsForFamilies/72_children_with_oppositional_defiant_disorder.pdf

American Association on Intellectual and Developmental Disabilities. (2013). *Definition of intellectual disability.* Retrieved from http://aaidd.org/intellectual-disability/definition

American Occupational Therapy Association. (2007). Societal statement on family caregivers. *American Journal of Occupational Therapy, 61,* 710.

American Occupational Therapy Association. (2010). The scope of practice of occupational therapy service for individuals with autism spectrum disorders across the life span. *American Journal of Occupational Therapy, 64,* 467–468.

American Occupational Therapy Association. (2014). Occupational therapy practice framework: Domain and process (3rd ed.). *American Journal of Occupational Therapy, 6*(Suppl. 1), S1-S48. http://dx.doi.org/10.5014/ajot.2014.682006

American Occupational Therapy Association. (2018). *Occupational therapy included in new law to address opioid epidemic.* Retrieved from https://www.aota.org/publications-news/otp/archive/2018/support-act.aspx

American Psychiatric Association (2013). *Diagnostic and statistical manual of mental disorders: DSM-5™* (5th ed.). Arlington, VA: Author.

Anxiety and Depression Association of America. (2010). *Facts and statistics.* Retrieved from https://adaa.org/about-adaa/press-room/facts-statistics

Autism Speaks. (2017). *What is autism?* Retrieved from https://www.autismspeaks.org/what-autism

Ayd, F. J. (1995). *Lexicon of psychiatry, neurology, and the neurosciences.* Baltimore, MD: Williams & Wilkins.

Batshaw, M. L., Roizen, N. J., & Lotrecchiano, G. R. (2013). *Children with disabilities* (7th ed.). Baltimore: Paul H. Brookes.

Bonder, B. (1991). *Psychopathology and function.* Thorofare, NJ: Slack.

Cara, E., & MacRae, A. (Eds.). (2013). *Psychosocial occupational therapy: An evolving practice* (3rd ed.). Clifton Park, NY: Delmar Cengage Learning.

Case-Smith, J., & O'Brien, J. C. (Eds.). (2015). *Occupational therapy for children and adolescents* (7th ed.). Maryland Heights, MO: Mosby Elsevier.

Centers for Disease Control and Development. (2018a). *Autism and Developmental Disabilities Monitoring (ADDM) Network.* Retrieved from https://www.cdc.gov/ncbddd/autism/addm.html

Centers for Disease Control and Prevention. (2018b). *Attention-deficit hyperactivity disorder (ADHD).* Retrieved from https://www.cdc.gov/ncbddd/adhd/data.html

Cleveland Clinic. (2018). *Oppositional defiant disorder.* Retrieved from https://my.clevelandclinic.org/health/diseases/9905-oppositional-defiant-disorder

Cornell, C., & Hamrin, V. (2008). Clinical interventions for children with attachment problems. *Journal of Child and Adolescent Psychiatric Nursing, 21,* 35–47.

Costa, D. (2009, June 29). Eating disorders: Occupational therapy's role. *Occupational Therapy Practice,* 13–16.

Crnic, K., Neece, C., McIntyre L., Blacher, J., & Baker, B. (2017). Intellectual disability and developmental risk: Promoting intervention to improve child and family well-being. *Child Development, 88,* 436–445.

Erskine, H., Ferrari, A., Nelson, P., Polanczyk, G., Flaxman, A., Vos, T., . . . Scott, J. (2013). Epidemiological modelling of attention-deficit/hyperactivity disorder and conduct disorder for the Global Burden of Disease Study 2010. *Journal of Child Psychology and Psychiatry, 54*(12), 1263–1274.

Fichter, M., & Quadflieg N. (2016). Mortality in eating disorders: Results of a large prospective clinical longitudinal study. *International Journal of Eating Disorders, 49*(4), 391–401.

Fleming-Castaldy, R. (2014). Activities, occupations, and empowerment. In J. Hinojosa & M. L. Blount (Eds.), *The texture of life: Purposeful activities in the context of occupation* (4th ed., pp. 393–415). Bethesda, MD: AOTA Press.

Genetic and Rare Diseases Information Center. (2016). *Rett syndrome.* Retrieved from https://rarediseases.info.nih.gov/diseases/5696/rett-syndrome#ref_11332

Girolamo, G. D., Dagani, J., Purcell, R., Cocchi, A., & Mcgorry, P. D. (2011). Age of onset of mental disorders and use of mental health services: Needs, opportunities and obstacles. *Epidemiology and Psychiatric Sciences, 21*(1), 47–57.

Glanzman, M. M., & Sell, N. (2013). Attention deficits and hyperactivity. In M. L. Batshaw, N. J. Roizen, & G. R. Lotrecchiano (Eds.), *Children with Disabilities*, 7th ed. (pp. 369–402). Baltimore, MD: Paul H. Brookes.

Hardy, L. (2007). Attachment theory and reactive attachment disorder: Theoretical perspectives and treatment implications. *Journal of Child & Adolescent Psychiatric Nursing 20*, 27–39.

Hay, P., & Mitchison, D. (2014). The epidemiology of eating disorders: Genetic, environmental, and societal factors. *Clinical Epidemiology, 6*, 89–97.

Hilton, C. L. (2015). Interventions to promote social participation for children with mental health and behavioral disorders. In J. Case-Smith & J. C. O'Brien (Eds.), *Occupational therapy for children and adolescence* (7th ed., pp. 321-345). St Louis, MO: Elsevier.

Hyman, S. L., & Levy, S. E. (2013). Autism spectrum disorders. In M. L., Batshaw, N. J. Roizen, & G. R. Lotrecchiano (Eds.), *Children with disabilities,* (7th ed., pp. 345–367). Baltimore, MD: Paul H. Brookes.

Kaplan, J. I., & Sadock, B. J. (2007). *Synopsis of psychiatry* (10th ed.). Philadelphia: Mosby.

Lenzenweger, M., Lane, M., Loranger, A., & Kessler, R. (2007). DSM-IV personality disorders in the National Comorbidity Survey Replication. *Biological Psychiatry, 62*, 553–564.

Livneh, H., & Antonak, R. F. (1997). *Psychosocial adaptation to chronic illness and disability*. Gaithersburg, MD: Aspen Publishers.

McKenzie, K., Milton, M., Smith, G., & Ouellette-Kuntz, H. (2016). Systematic review of the prevalence and incidence of intellectual disabilities: Current trends and issues. *Current Developmental Disorders Reports, 3*, 104–115.

Medical Economics. (2007). *Physician's desk reference* (62nd ed.). Montvale, NY: Author.

Merikangas, K., He, J., Burstein, M., Swanson, S., Avenevoli, S., Cui, L., ... Swendsen, J. (2010). Lifetime prevalence of mental disorders in U.S. adolescents: Results from the National Comorbidity Survey Replication-Adolescent Supplement (NCS-A). *Journal of the American Academy of Child and Adolescent Psychiatry, 49*(10), 980–989.

Miller, L. J. (2014). *Sensational kids: Hope and help for children with sensory processing disorder (SPD)* (Revised ed.). New York, NY: G. P. Putnam & Sons.

Miller-Kuhaneck, H. (2015). Autism spectrum disorder. In J. Case-Smith & J. C. O'Brien (Eds.), *Occupational therapy for children and adolescence* (7th ed., pp. 766–792). St. Louis, MO: Elsevier.

Moreira, A., Van Meter, A. Genzlinger, J., & Youngstrom, E. (2017). Review and meta-analysis of epidemiologic studies of adult bipolar disorder. *Journal of Clinical Psychiatry, 78*, 1259–1269.

National Alliance on Mental Illness. (2017). *Bipolar disorder*. Retrieved from https://www.nami.org/Learn-More/Mental-Health-Conditions/Bipolar-Disorder

National Board Certification in Occupational Therapy. (2018). Practice analysis of the *certified occupational therapy assistant registered: Executive summary* [PDF file]. Gaithersburg, MD: Author. Retrieved from https://www.nbcot.org/-/media/NBCOT/PDFs/2017-Practice-Analysis-Executive-OTR.ashx?la=en

National Eating Disorders Association. (2018). *Statistics and research on eating disorders*. Retrieved from https://www.nationaleatingdisorders.org/statistics-research-eating-disorders

National Institute on Drug Abuse. (2018). *Sex and gender differences in substance use*. Retrieved from https://www.drugabuse.gov/publications/research-reports/substance-use-in-women/sex-gender-differences-in-substance-use

National Institute of Mental Health. (2012). *Bipolar, depression and anxiety disorders*. Retrieved July 20, 2013, from http://www.nimh.nih.gov/index.shtml

National Institute of Mental Health. (2017). *Major depression*. Retrieved from https://www.nimh.nih.gov/health/statistics/major-depression.shtml

National Institute of Mental Health. (2018). *Schizophrenia*. Retrieved from https://www.nimh.nih.gov/health/statistics/schizophrenia.shtml

Pritchett, R., Pritchett, J., Marshall, E., Davidson, C., & Minnis, H. (2013). Reactive attachment disorder in the general population: A hidden ESSENCE disorder. *Scientific World Journal*, 1–6.

Rogers, S. (2005). Common conditions that influence children's participation. In J. Case-Smith (Ed.), *Occupational therapy for children* (5th ed., pp. 160–215). St. Louis, MO: Elsevier Mosby.

Ryan, D. J., Oregan, N. A., Caoimh, R. Ó, Clare, J., Oconnor, M., Leonard, M., . . . Timmons, S. (2013). Delirium in an adult acute hospital population: Predictors, prevalence and detection. *BMJ Open, 3*(1), 1–9.

Sadock, B. J., & Sadock, V. A. (2008). *Kaplan and Sadock's concise textbook of clinical psychiatry* (3rd ed.). Philadelphia: Williams & Wilkins.

Shapiro, B. K., & Batshaw, M. L. (2013). Developmental delay and intellectual disability. In M. L. Batshaw, N. J. Rozien, & G. R. Lotrecchiano (Eds.), *Children with disabilities* (7th ed., pp. 291-306). Baltimore, MD: Paul H. Brookes.

Sheperis, C., Renfro-Michel, E., & Doggett, R. (2003). In-home treatment of reactive attachment disorder in a therapeutic foster care system: A case example. *Journal of Mental Health Counseling, 25*, 76–88.

Smink, F. R., Hoeken, D. V., & Hoek, H. W. (2012). Epidemiology of eating disorders: Incidence, prevalence and mortality rates. *Current Psychiatry Reports, 14*, 406–414.

Substance Abuse and Mental Health Services Administration. (2015, October 30). *Alcohol*. Retrieved from https://www.samhsa.gov/atod/alcohol

Swanson, S., Crow, S., Le Grange, D., Swendsen, J., & Merikangas, K. (2011). Prevalence and correlates of eating disorders in adolescents: Results from the national comorbidity survey replication adolescent supplement. *Archives of General Psychiatry, 68*, 714–723.

Volkert, J., Gablonski, T., & Rabung, S. (2018). Prevalence of personality disorders in the general adult population in Western countries: Systematic review and meta-analysis. *British Journal of Psychiatry, 213*, 709–715.

Vroman, K. (2015). Adolescent development transitioning from child to adult. In J. Case-Smith & J. C. O'Brien (Eds.), *Occupational therapy for children and adolescence* (7th ed., pp. 102–128). St. Louis, MO: Elsevier.

Review Questions

Psychiatric and Cognitive Disorders

Below are five questions about key content covered in this chapter. These questions are not inclusive of the entirety of content related to psychiatric and cognitive disorders that you must know for success on the COTA® exam. These questions are provided to help you develop the thought processes you will need to apply your studying of content to the answering of exam questions; hence they are not in the COTA® exam format. Exam items in the COTA® format that cover the depth and breadth of content you will need to know to pass the exam are provided in this text's online exams. The answers to the questions below are provided in Appendix 3.

1. You are asked to provide consultation services for an individual who lives in a group home. The resident has become dehydrated and inconsistent in taking oral medications. You interview the resident about their daily habits and routines and learn that the resident will not drink the tap water in the group home. The resident states, "The water is poisoned. They are trying to poison me. If I drink the water I will die." Identify the psychiatric symptom that is preventing this person from drinking the water. Describe an intervention approach you would use to help the resident hydrate and take prescribed medications. Explain the importance of this person staying hydrated and taking prescribed medications.

2. You meet with the occupational therapist to discuss an intervention plan for an adolescent. The adolescent has great difficulty reading the various nonverbal behaviors of others (e.g., eye contact, facial expression, gestures, and body language) that are needed to regulate social interactions. The adolescent has not been able to develop relationships with a peer group. The teen is preoccupied and intensely interested in World War II, its history, battles, and generals and talks about nothing else. The teen's bedroom is filled with World War II memorabilia and books about the war. This adolescent's cognitive, language, and communication skills, and ADL development has been age appropriate; however, the teen has not developed age-appropriate social interaction skills. Based on this information, what diagnosis is most reflective of this teen's functional status? What intervention goals would be helpful to work on with this adolescent?

3. You and the occupational therapist are conducting an evaluation of a 16-month-old toddler. The parent reports that the toddler has frequent tantrums with no clear precipitant. The parent thinks these behaviors may be the result of the toddler's frustration due to language delays. When unable to reach a toy, the toddler pulled the parent's hand toward the toy without pointing. The toddler also did not point to pictures in books. When playing with blocks or cars, the toddler lined them up, but did not spontaneously manipulate or move them. The toddler exhibited a rigid and limited repertoire of play and interaction skills. What diagnosis is most consistent with the toddler's presenting behaviors? Explain your rationale.

(Continued)

Review Questions

Psychiatric and Cognitive Disorders (*Continued*)

4. You are a home health OTA providing services to an older adult. The client's caregiver reports that the client is having trouble remembering things, sustaining attention, and making decisions. The caregiver reports the client seems mentally confused and asks whether the symptoms are indicative of dementia. As an OTA, you know that there are possible reversible causes of mental confusion. What are the reversible causes of mental confusion that you should consider during your intervention and inform the occupational therapist as needing further evaluation?

5. You observe that a very thin client in your outpatient partial hospital program has been losing weight. The individual has no medical problems. The physician supervising the program states the client is well below the normal weight for age and height. The client participates in cooking groups with peers, but will not eat whatever is prepared other than salad without dressing. When encouraged to try other foods, the client says, "I don't want to get fat, and I already need to lose a few pounds." You are concerned that the individual has anorexia nervosa. What signs of this eating disorder are being exhibited? What additional symptoms would you expect to see that would indicate this diagnosis?

11

Biomechanical Approaches: Evaluation and Intervention

COLLEEN MAHER AND RITA P. FLEMING-CASTALDY

Chapter Outline

- Biomechanical Approach, 320
- Evaluation, 320
- Intervention, 325
- References, 334
- Review Questions, 336

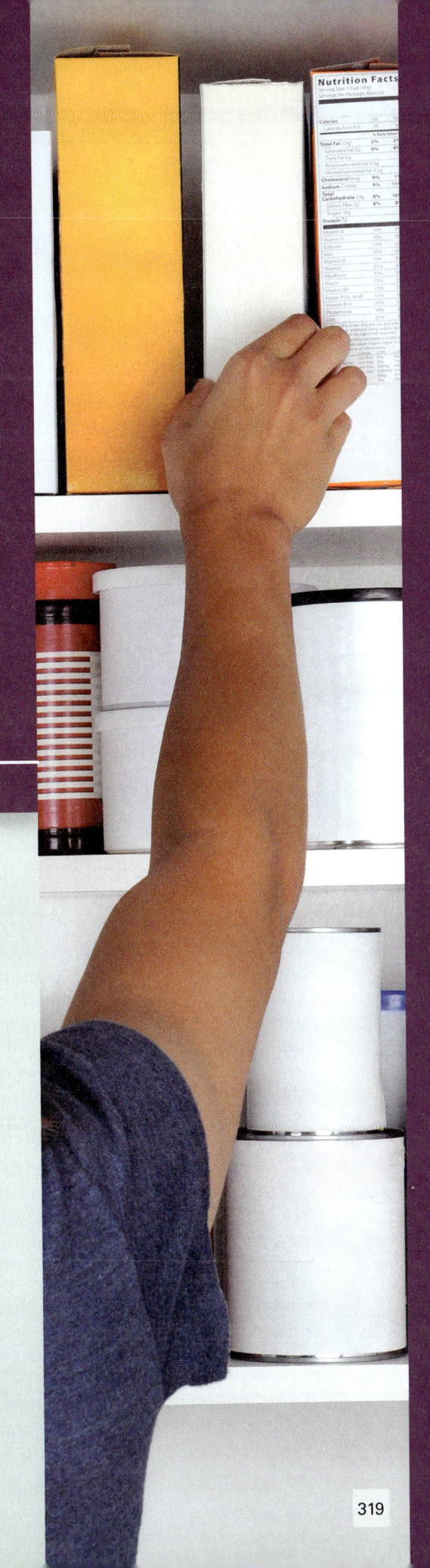

Biomechanical Approach

Overview

1. The biomechanical frame of reference is based on the works of Bird T. Baldwin (reconstruction model), Marjorie Taylor (orthopedic model), Dr. Sydney Licht, and William Dunton, Jr. (kinetic model).

   EXAM HINT: The NBCOT® exam outline for the certified occupational therapy assistant (COTA®) identifies knowledge of the "influence of theoretical approaches, models of practice, and frames of reference on information-gathering and the intervention process" (NBCOT®, 2018, p. 22) as essential for competent and safe practice. The application of knowledge about the use of biomechanical theoretical approaches will be required to correctly answer COTA® exam items about working with persons with musculoskeletal disorders.

2. The biomechanical approach focuses on the range of motion, strength, and endurance required to perform an occupation.
3. It is most commonly used to treat patients with lower motor neuron deficits and orthopedic problems.
4. The biomechanical approach is most effective when used in combination with other occupational therapy (OT) theoretical approaches, models of practice, and frames of reference that focus on the client's engagement in meaningful occupations and desired purposeful activities. See Chapter 13.
5. Settings that most commonly use the biomechanical approach:
   a. Hand clinics.
   b. Work programs.
   c. Physical medicine and rehabilitation (PM&R) departments.
   d. Ergonomic programs.

Evaluation

Role of the Occupational Therapy Assistant (OTA)

EXAM HINT: In the NBCOT® exam outline for the COTA®, Domain 01 Collaborating and Gathering Information comprises 28% of the exam and knowledge of the "purpose, advantages, limitations, and service competency needs related to the administration of commonly used standardized assessments and non-standardized screening as a means of acquiring client information" (NBCOT®, 2018, p. 21) is identified as essential for competent and safe practice. The application of knowledge about the following biomechanical assessment tools and procedures can help you correctly answer Domain 01 exam items about the evaluation of persons with musculoskeletal disorders.

1. The OTA contributes to the evaluation process.
   a. The OTA can assist with the collection of data for the evaluation once service competence has been established.
   b. The level of supervision required will be determined by the OTA's experience, established service competence, and state regulations.
   c. The OTA cannot independently evaluate or interpret evaluation results.

Range of Motion (ROM)

1. Measurement tool: goniometer consisting of an axis, stationary and movable arms.
2. Prior to assessing ROM, check prescription and chart for specific ROM orders and ROM restrictions.
3. Always begin with a ROM screen.
4. Begin in the anatomical position.
   a. There are exceptions such as the forearm for which it begins with the elbow flexed to 90° and the forearm in neutral.
5. Types of ROM.
   a. Functional ROM: ROM needed to perform functional movements (e.g., reach to top of head, small of back, etc.).
   b. AROM: active ROM (contractile structures) movement produced by one's own muscle.
   c. PROM: passive ROM (noncontractile structures) movement produced by an external force.
   d. AAROM: active assistive ROM, movement produced by one's own muscles and assisted by an external force.

e. Finger ROM: total active motion (TAM) and total passive motion (TPM).
   (1) Measures tendon excursion.
   (2) Add extension deficits and subtract from flexion measurement, e.g., for digit 2 (index finger) measurements of MCP 10°–50°, PIP 15°–75°, and DIP 0°–10°; the TAM is 110°.
   (3) An alternative method to measure finger ROM is to measure flexion of the digits to the distal palmar crease (DPC) in centimeters (cm) (Adams et al., 1992; Klein, 2014; Whelan, 2014).
6. There are precautions and contraindications to performing joint measurements.

CAUTION: The OTA should maintain close communication with the occupational therapist who will consult with the physician to identify those conditions in which ROM measurements should be restricted or are contraindicated.

   a. The following are examples of conditions that should prompt the therapist to consult with the physician prior to proceeding with ROM measurements.
      (1) Bone metastasis.
      (2) Unhealed fracture or recent dislocation.
      (3) Infection.
      (4) Postsurgery.
      (5) Myositis ossificans.
      (6) Subluxed or unstable joints.
      (7) Skin grafts.
      (8) Others as identified by the physician (Klein, 2014; Killingsworth, Pedretti, & Pendleton, 2013; Whelan, 2014).
7. Recording measurements.
   a. Neutral zero method: anatomical position is 0.
   b. Starting position/ending position (e.g., 0°–150°).
   c. Do not use negatives.
   d. Within functional limits (WFL): ROM is functional.
   e. Within normal limits (WNL): ROM achieves normal ranges (e.g., shoulder flexion 0°–180°) (Whelan, 2014; Killingsworth et al., 2013).
8. Review bony landmarks and normal ranges. Refer to Table 11-1.

Muscle Strength

1. Types of manual muscle tests (MMTs).
   a. Break test is the most common MMT.
      (1) Test position: gravity eliminated (lessened) or against gravity.
      (2) Stabilization: usually proximal to the joint the muscle crosses over. Do not hold over the muscle belly being tested.

Table 11-1

Average Normal Range of Motion (180° Method)

JOINT	ROM	ASSOCIATED GIRDLE MOTION
Cervical Spine		
Flexion	0°–45°	
Extension	0°–45°	
Lateral flexion	0°–45°	
Rotation	0°–60°	
Thoracic and Lumbar Spine		
Flexion	0°–80°	
Extension	0°–30°	
Lateral flexion	0°–40°	
Rotation	0°–45°	
Shoulder		
Flexion	0°–180°	Abduction, lateral tilt, slight elevation, slight upward rotation
Extension	0°–60°	Depression, adduction, upward tilt
Abduction	0°–180°	Upward rotation, elevation
Adduction	0°	Depression, adduction, downward rotation
Horizontal abduction	0°–40°	Adduction, reduction of lateral tilt
Horizontal adduction	0°–130°	Abduction, lateral tilt
Internal rotation		Abduction, lateral tilt
Arm in abduction	0°–70°	
Arm in adduction	0°–60°	
External rotation		Adduction, reduction of lateral tilt
Arm in abduction	0°–90°	
Arm in adduction	0°–80°	
Elbow		
Flexion	0°–135°–150°	
Extension	0°	
Forearm		
Pronation	0°–80°–90°	
Supination	0°–80°–90°	
Wrist		
Flexion	0°–80°	
Extension	0°–70°	
Ulnar deviation (adduction)	0°–30°	
Radial deviation (abduction)	0°–20°	

(Continued)

Table 11-1

Average Normal Range of Motion (180° Method) (Continued)

JOINT	ROM	ASSOCIATED GIRDLE MOTION
Thumb*		
DIP flexion	0°–80°–90°	
MP flexion	0°–50°	
Adduction, radial and palmar	0°	
Palmar abduction	0°–50°	
Radial abduction	0°–50°	
Opposition	Composite motion	
Fingers*		
MP flexion	0°–90°	
MP hyperextension	0°–15°–45°	
PIP flexion	0°–110°	
DIP flexion	0°–80°	
Abduction	0°–25°	
Hip		
Flexion	0°–120° (bent knee)	
Extension	0°–30°	
Abduction	0°–40°	
Adduction	0°–35°	
Internal rotation	0°–45°	
External rotation	0°–45°	
Knee		
Flexion	0°–145°	
Ankle and Foot		
Plantarflexion	0°–50°	
Dorsiflexion	0°–15°	
Inversion	0°–35°	
Eversion	0°–20°	

*DIP, distal interphalangeal; MP, metacarpophalangeal; PIP, proximal interphalangeal.

Data adapted from American Academy of Orthopaedic Surgeons. (1965). *Joint motion: Method of measuring and recording.* Chicago, IL: Author; Esch, D., & Lepley, M. (1974). *Evaluation of joint motion: Methods of measurement and recording.* Minneapolis, MN: University of Minnesota Press.

Killingsworth, A. P., Pedretti, L. W., & Pendleton, H. M. (2013). Joint range of motion. In H. M. Pendleton & W. Schultz-Krohn (Eds.), *Pedretti's Occupational therapy: Practice skills for physical dysfunction* (7th ed., p. 505). St. Louis, MO: Elsevier/Mosby. Reprinted with permission.

Table 11-2

Muscle Testing Grading System

GRADE	DEFINITION	DESCRIPTION
5	Normal	The part moves through full ROM against gravity and takes maximal resistance.
4	Good	The part moves through full ROM against gravity and takes moderate resistance.
4–	Good minus	The part moves through full ROM against gravity and takes less than moderate resistance.
3+	Fair plus	The part moves through full ROM against gravity and takes minimal resistance before it breaks.
3	Fair	The part moves through full ROM against gravity and is unable to take any added resistance.
3–	Fair minus	The part moves less than full range of motion against gravity.
2+	Poor plus	The part moves through full ROM in a gravity-eliminated plane and then takes minimal resistance and breaks.
2	Poor	The part moves through full range of motion in a gravity-eliminated plane with no added resistance.
2–	Poor minus	The part moves less than full ROM in a gravity-eliminated plane.
1	Trace	Tension is palpated in the muscle or tendon, but no motion occurs at the joint.
0	Zero	No tension is palpated in the muscle or tendon.

Whelan, L. R. (2014). Assessing abilities and capacities: Range of motion, strength, and endurance. In M. V. Radomski & C. A. Trombly Latham (Eds.), *Occupational therapy for physical dysfunction* (7th ed., pp. 186). Baltimore, MD: Lippincott Williams & Wilkins. Reprinted with permission.

Grip Strength

1. Measurement tool: dynamometer.
2. Position of upper extremity: shoulder adducted to side, elbow flexed to 90°, and forearm in neutral.
3. Types of grip strength tests.
   a. Dynamometer handle placed on position #2. The mean of three trials of each hand is compared to the norms.
   b. One trial in all five positions for each hand. A bell curve is observed if the individual is applying maximal effort.
   c. Sphygmomanometer cuff or vigorimeter/bulb dynamometer should be used to evaluate the grip strength of a person with arthritis. The bulb dynamometer has become a more popular alternative to the Jamar dynamometer.

(3) Resistance: applied in opposite direction of movement; should be gradual.
(4) Muscle grades. Refer to Table 11-2 (Killingsworth et al., 2013; Whelan, 2014).

Pinch Strength

1. Measurement tool: pinchmeter.
2. Position of upper extremity: shoulder adducted to side, elbow flexed to 90°, and forearm in neutral.
3. Types of pinch strength test.
   a. Key or lateral pinch: thumb pulp to the lateral aspect of the index middle phalanx.
   b. Three-jaw chuck: pulp of thumb to pulps of index and middle fingers.
   c. Tip to tip: thumb pulp to pulp of index finger.
4. Three trials on each hand are obtained for all pinch strengths. The mean of three trials on each hand is compared to the norms.

Endurance/Activity Tolerance

1. Count number of repetitions per unit of time.
2. Determine percent of maximum heart rate.
3. Measure time until fatigue.
4. Use metabolic equivalent (MET) levels. (Whelan, 2014). See Chapter 8.

Edema

1. The body's initial response to injury.
   a. It is the transfer of exudate in which the fluid from the bloodstream moves to the interstitial tissue.
   b. Edema can be localized or diffuse.
2. Types.
   a. Pitting—acute.
   b. Brawny—chronic.
3. Evaluation of circumference.
   a. Measurement tool: tape measure, recorded in centimeters.
   b. Compare extremities, document landmarks.
   c. To measure the entire hand, use the figure-of-eight method; this is the most reliable method.
4. Evaluation of hand and arm mass.
   a. Measurement tool: volumeter, recorded in millilitres (mL).
   b. Significant change in edema would be more than 10 ml. (Klein, 2014; Whelan, 2014).
      (1) The only true objective tool.

Sensation

1. Demonstrate sensory test with vision; then occlude vision for actual testing.
2. Test uninvolved side first. Apply stimulus to volar and dorsal surfaces (exceptions will be noted).

CAUTION: Standard application procedures for the progressive application of sensory testing stimuli must be followed to ensure assessment validity. These standards are based on diagnoses.
- Spinal cord injuries are tested proximal to distal following dermatome pattern.
- Neurologic disorders are tested for dermatome pattern.
- Peripheral nerve injuries are tested distal to proximal following peripheral nerves.

3. Peripheral nerve injuries assess for peripheral nerve involvement. Order of return: pain, moving touch, static light touch, and touch localization.
4. Types of sensory testing.
   a. Light touch: touch with cotton swab. Person responds "yes" or "touched" when touched. Scoring: + (intact), – (impaired), or 0 (absent).
   b. Localization: touch with cotton swab. Person responds "yes" when touched and then with vision points to area touched. Scoring +, –, 0.
   c. Pain (protective sensation): sterile safety pin or paper clip. Person responds "sharp" or "dull." Scoring: correct response indicates intact pain sensation, incorrect response indicates absent pain sensation (Cooper & Canyock, 2013). Note: a response of sharp to the dull stimulus may indicate hypersensitivity,
   d. Temperature sensation: use test tubes or thermal kit. Person responds "hot" or "cold." Scoring: +, –, 0.
   e. Stereognosis: recognition by touch of common objects. Scoring: number of correct objects.
      (1) A second set of identical common objects should be used for individuals with expressive aphasia. (Theis, 2014)
   f. Static two-point discrimination: Disk-Criminator, Boley Guage, or paper clip.
      (1) The OTA assesses the client's ability to detect one point or two points (on volar fingertips)
      (2) Person responds to the number of points they feel, i.e., one or two.
   g. Proprioception: position sense.
      (1) The OTA positions involved extremity.
      (2) Person duplicates position with contralateral extremity.
   h. Kinesthesia: movement sense.
      (1) The OTA moves segment.
      (2) Person responds up or down.
5. Refer to Figure 6-6 in Chapter 6 and Table 11-3 for dermatome distribution (Theis, 2014).

Coordination/Dexterity/Functional Assessments

1. The evaluations included in this chapter are based on the author's review of NBCOT® self-assessment tools,

Table 11-3

Dermatomes

SPINAL SEGMENT	DERMATOME LOCATION	MUSCLES FACILITATED	FUNCTION
CN V	Anterior facial region	Mastication	Ingestion
C3	Neck region	Sternocleidomastoid, upper trapezius	Head control
C4	Upper shoulder region	Trapezius (diaphragm)	Head control
C5	Lateral aspect of shoulder	Deltoid, biceps, rhomboid major and minor	Elbow flexion
C6	Thumb and radial forearm	Extensor carpi radialis, biceps	Shoulder abduction, wrist extension
C7	Middle finger	Triceps, extensors of wrist and fingers	Wrist flexion, finger extension
C8	Little finger, ulnar forearm	Flexor of wrist and fingers	C8 finger flexion
T1	Axilla and proximal medial arm	Hand intrinsics	Abduction and adduction of fingers
T2–T12	Thorax	Intercostals	Respiration
T4–T6	Nipple line	Intercostals	Respiration
T11	Midchest region, lower rib	Abdominal wall, abdominal muscles	T5–T7 superficial abdominal reflex
T10	Umbilicus	Psoas, iliacus	Leg flexion
L1–L2	Inside of thigh	Cremasteric reflex, accessory muscles	Elevation of scrotum
L2	Proximal anterior thigh	Iliopsoas, adductors of thigh	Reflex voiding
L3–L4	Anterior knee	Quadriceps, tibialis anterior, detrusor urinae	Hip flexion, extensors of knee, abductors of thigh
L5	Great toe	Lateral hamstrings	Flexion at knee, toe extension
L5–S1	Foot region	Gastrocnemius, soleus, extensor digitorum longus	Flexor withdrawal, urinary retention
S2	Narrow band of posterior thigh	Small muscles of foot (flexor digitorum, flexor hallucis)	Bladder retention

McCormack, G. (1996). The Rood approach to treatment of neuromuscular dysfunction. In L. W. Pedretti (Ed.), *Occupational therapy: Practice skills for physical dysfunction* (4th ed., p. 383). St. Louis, MO: Elsevier/Mosby.

---

major OT textbooks, and feedback obtained from OT practitioners regarding measures used in practice.
  a. As of the publication of this text, NBCOT® has not made public the names of the specific evaluation tools that may be on the exam.

> **EXAM HINT:** The COTA® exam may include the names of specific evaluation tools; therefore, a review of major commercially available coordination assessments is important for exam preparation. This can increase understanding and knowledge of common approaches in the evaluation of coordination and further strengthen the clinical reasoning skills needed to answer COTA® exam items that address the evaluation of coordination.

2. Types of coordination and dexterity assessments.
  a. Purdue Pegboard.
    (1) Test of fingertip dexterity and assembly job simulation.
    (2) Subtests.
      (a) Thirty-second test: right hand, left hand, both hands, R+, L+, both.
      (b) One-minute test: assembly.
    (3) Scoring: thirty second test is the number of pins placed in the board in 30 seconds. Assembly is the number of parts assembled during one minute.
  b. Minnesota Manual Dexterity Test.
    (1) Test of gross hand and arm movements.
    (2) Subtests.
      (a) Placing test: measures rate of hand movement (one hand only).
      (b) Turning test: measures rate of finger manipulation (bilateral).
    (3) Scoring: time to complete board. One practice trial and four scored trials.
  c. O'Connor Tweezer Test.
    (1) Test of eye-hand coordination using tweezers.
    (2) Scoring: the number of seconds to place all pins in board using tweezers.
  d. Crawford Small Parts Dexterity Test.
    (1) Test of fine motor dexterity using small tools (tweezers and screwdriver).
    (2) Scoring: time to complete assembly.
  e. Nine Hole Peg Test.
    (1) Measures finger dexterity.
    (2) Scoring: time for each hand to place nine pegs in a square board and remove them.

(3) The Purdue Pegboard is preferred over the Nine Hole Peg Test because it is unilateral and bilateral. It is also more reliable.
   f. Jebson Hand Function Test.
      (1) Test of hand function.
      (2) Seven subtests.
         (a) Writing.
         (b) Simulated page turning.
         (c) Picking up common objects.
         (d) Simulated feeding.
         (e) Stacking.
         (f) Picking up large light objects.
         (g) Picking up large heavy objects.
      (3) Scoring: time to complete each subject.
   g. Michigan Hand Outcome Questionnaire
      (1) Looks at client perceptions of unilateral (such as picking up a coin or turning a key) and bilateral (such as buttoning a shirt and tying shoes) functional activities.
      (2) Also addresses perceptions of pain level, ability to participate in household and school activities, and appearance.

3. The occupational therapist determines which coordination/dexterity assessment is best to have the OTA complete with a client. This determination is based on the client's occupational profile (i.e., a person who identified one of their roles as a jeweler should be assessed with the O'Connor tweezer test as it requires fine manipulation of small pins using a tweezer, which is a tool used by jewelers; a person who works as a machinist who assembles small parts would best be assessed using the Purdue Pegboard assembly test).
4. Informal assessment of coordination should include:
   a. Fine motor: observation of routine task performance.
      (1) Handwriting, manipulation of various-sized objects, handling money, cutting food, and buttoning are examples of daily tasks that should be observed to assess fine motor coordination.
   b. Gross motor: observation of activities that include gross motor movements.
      (1) Tossing a ball, reaching into cabinets for specific items, and dressing are examples of activities that should be observed to assess gross motor coordination.

Intervention

Role of the OTA

1. The OTA implements intervention with OT supervision.
2. The level of supervision required depends upon the OTA's experience and established service competence.
3. During the implementation of intervention, the OTA informs the supervising OT of any change in the individual's status and any other relevant information that may affect treatment.

EXAM HINT: In the NBCOT® exam outline for the COTA®, Domain 02 Selecting and Implementing Interventions comprises 55% of the exam. This domain focuses on the OTA's ability to "implement interventions under the supervision of the OTR in accordance with the intervention plan and level of service competence to support client participation in areas of occupation throughout the occupational therapy process" (NBCOT®, 2018, p. 24). The application of knowledge about the biomechanical interventions described in this chapter section can help you correctly answer NBCOT® Domain 02 exam items about the selection of interventions for persons with musculoskeletal disorders.

Increasing Range of Motion

1. Passive ROM and passive stretching.
   a. PROM is moving the joint to the desired range using an external force.
      (1) PROM can be performed by the OTA gently moving the extremity to the desired range or when resistance is felt.
   b. Passive stretching is PROM with overpressure.

CAUTION: A careful review of the physician's orders with the occupational therapist is paramount to distinguish the type of passive exercise being requested.

   c. Heat prior or other thermal agents prior to stretch increases extensibility.
   d. Joint mobilization requires special training and the establishment of service competence.
      (1) More effective if performed before passive ROM.
   e. Manual passive stretching within individual's tolerance. Also, contract/relax and hold/relax also increase ROM.
   f. Codman's exercise (pendulum exercises): common form of PROM used for postsurgical shoulder patients.
      (1) See Figure 11-1.

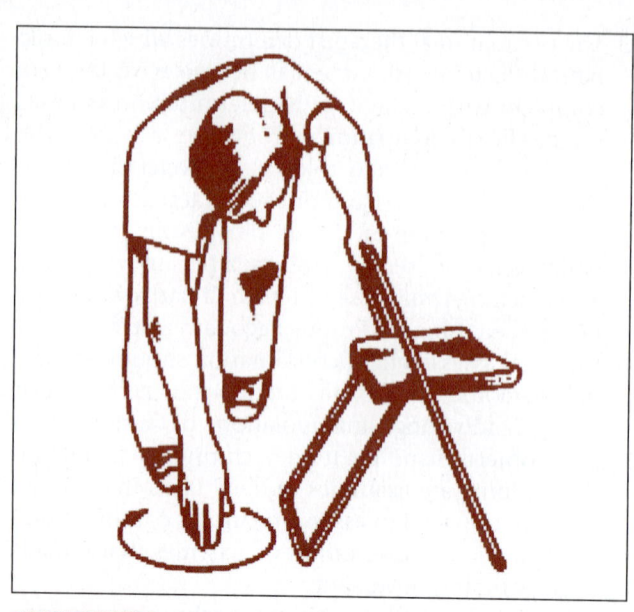

Figure 11-1 Codman's exercise.
Hawkins R. J., Bell R. H., & Lippitt S. B. (1996). *Atlas of shoulder surgery*. St Louis: Mosby. Reprinted with permission.

   c. Blocking exercises: used to isolate individual joint motion. Instruct the client to hold the end range position for 3–5 seconds.
   d. Emphasize functional use; encourage use for ADL and role activities.
   e. Preparatory methods: wall walking, AROM, table glides, cane exercises, etc.
      (1) Consider place and hold exercises when PROM is greater than AROM: assist extremity or hand to desired position and then slowly release. Ask the client to hold the position as you slowly release.
   f. Purposeful and occupation-based activities: ADL, IADL, and work activities. Incorporate the individual's leisure interests (e.g., crafts, games, sports).
   g. Emphasize active use during purposeful and occupation-based activities.

CAUTION: Heterotopic ossificans may result from overstretching (especially noted in elbow flexors).

   g. Instruction in home exercises. Stress the importance of home exercises to facilitate change in tissue length.
      (1) Postsurgical patients performing self-PROM must clearly understand the concept of passive ROM before including it as part of their home exercise program.
   h. Splinting: dynamic and serial splinting.
   i. Exercise equipment: continuous passive movement (CPM), pulleys, etc. (Breines, 2013).
2. Active ROM.
   a. Should be performed when PROM is greater than AROM.
   b. Differential tendon gliding exercises: differentiates tendon movement and increases tendon excursion.
      (1) See Figure 11-2.

The NBCOT® exam outline for the COTA® identifies knowledge of the "methods for grading various types of therapeutic exercise and conditioning programs consistent with indications and precautions for strengthening muscles, increasing endurance, improving range of motion and coordination and increasing joint flexibility in relation to task demands" (NBCOT®, 2018, p. 26) as essential for competent and safe practice. The application of knowledge about the above techniques for increasing ROM and the following approaches for improving muscle strength, endurance, and coordination can help you effectively determine the correct answers to COTA® exam items about working with persons with musculoskeletal disorders.

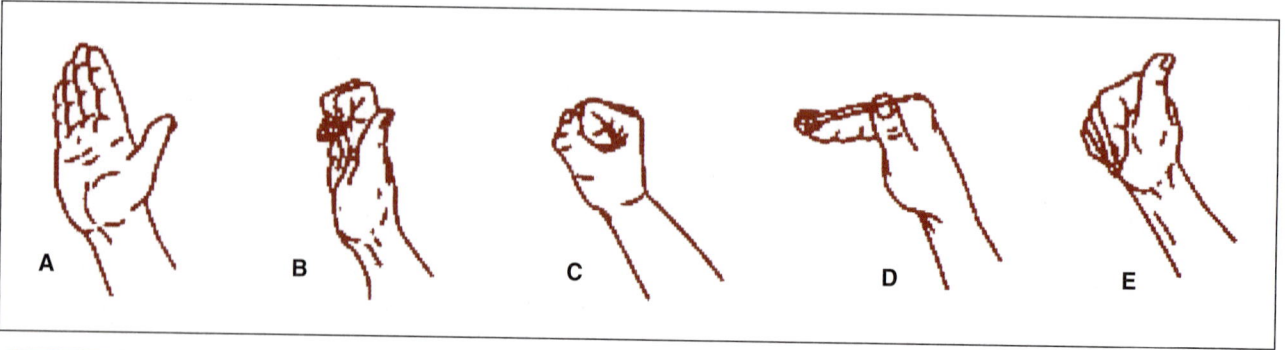

Figure 11-2 Tendon gliding exercises.
The five positions: A. Straight. B. Hook. C. Fist. D. Tabletop. E. Straight fist. Adapted with permission from Rozmaryn, L. M., Dovelle, S., Rothman, E. R., Gorman, K., Olvey, K. M., & Bartko, J. J. (1998). Nerve and tendon gliding exercises and the conservative management of carpal tunnel syndrome. *Journal of Hand Therapy*, 11, 171–179. Reprinted with permission.

Increasing Strength

1. High resistance, low repetitions.
2. Type of contractions.
   a. Isometrics: contraction without movement.
      (1) Sometimes can produce more forceful contraction.

   > **RED FLAG:** Isometrics are contraindicated for persons with hypertension and cardiovascular problems. They can increase blood pressure (BP) and heart rate (HR), so they should be avoided.

   b. Isotonic: contraction with movement.
      (1) Eccentric = lengthening contraction.
      (2) Concentric = shortening contraction.
   c. How to distinguish the type of contraction during a functional activity.
      (1) Anytime a person moves against gravity or away from the earth they are performing a concentric contraction. Also, when a person moves in a horizontal plane it is always a concentric contraction. Examples include:
         (a) Reaching into a cabinet above shoulder level would be a concentric contraction of the shoulder flexor (anterior deltoid).
         (b) Reaching over to wash the opposite axilla would be a concentric contraction of the shoulder adductor (pectoralis major).
      (2) Anytime a person moves with gravity or toward the earth it can be a concentric or an eccentric contraction. Examples include:
         (a) When the arm is used to remove a glass from an overhead cabinet and the person slowly lowers the glass to the counter (the movement is toward extension) that is an eccentric contraction of the anterior deltoid (the muscle is acting as a brake to slowly lower the arm down).
         (b) When a person lowers their arm with force, such as slamming a book down on a desk, this is a concentric contraction of the shoulder and elbow extensors.
      (3) The performance of tasks requires a combination of different types of muscle contractions. For example, lifting groceries from the trunk of a car to chest level (concentric), carrying the groceries from the car into the kitchen (isometric), and then slowly lowering the groceries onto the table (eccentric).

Increasing Endurance

1. Work at 50% of maximal resistance.
2. Increase repetitions, and duration, not resistance.
3. Use energy conservation methods.

Improving Coordination

1. Begin with gross motor activities and gradually grade up to fine motor activities.
2. Select activities in which the ROM required is within the person's reach and yet challenging.
3. Focus on accuracy and speed.
4. Begin with slow gross movements and gradually progress to faster precise movements.

Edema Reduction Techniques

1. Elevation: extremity should be placed above the heart.

   > **CAUTION:** Avoid extreme positions of elevation for individuals with right-sided heart weakness; this can cause the fluid to empty into the heart too fast.

2. Manual edema mobilization (MEM): hands-on technique that activates the lymphatic system to remove edema.
   a. This technique requires specialized training. The efficacy of MEM is supported by evidence (Artzberger, 2014).
3. Retrograde massage assists with the return of blood and lymphatic fluids to the venous system.
   a. Although this type of massage is still being used, it has limited evidence to support its efficacy; thus, it is slowly being replaced by MEM.
   b. Instructions.
      (1) Gentle stroking is applied in centripetal direction.
      (2) Massage should be performed with the extremity elevated.

   > **EXAM HINT:** In the NBCOT® exam outline for the COTA®, Domain 03 comprises 17% of the NBCOT® exam. This domain focuses on the OTA's ability to "uphold professional standards and responsibilities by . . . applying evidence-based interventions to promote quality in practice" (NBCOT®, 2018, p. 28). Because the efficacy of MEM is supported by evidence and retrograde massage is not, the correct answer to a COTA® exam item about the use of massage to reduce edema that includes MEM and retrograde massage as answer choices would likely be MEM, not retrograde massage.

4. MEM and retrograde massage are contraindicated when cardiac edema is present.
5. Compression garments prevent reaccumulation of fluids following massage. Garments should not be too tight.
   a. Common types used in OT practice.
      (1) Isotoner glove.
      (2) Tubigrip (stockinet with elastic: watch rolling).
      (3) Ace wraps.

(4) Custom-made compression garments.
(5) Coban wrap (digit is wrapped distal to proximal).
   (a) Effective for decreasing edema in a digit.
   (b) Avoid too much tension.
   (c) The individual can exercise and use their hand for ADL and role activities while wearing Coban.
6. Cold packs: most effective when combined with elevation.
   a. Monitor vascular status.
7. Contrast bath.
   a. Technique of immersing the hand in warm (temperature of bath water) and cold water.
      (1) Evidence is conflicting as to its effectiveness in reducing hand edema.
8. Other edema techniques: elastic bandage wraps, and intermittent compression pump.
   a. These techniques are not as common.

CAUTION: Heat is commonly contraindicated. However, if the use of heat is warranted in a mild case of edema, it could be cautiously used and combined with elevation.

RED FLAG: Contraindications for MEM and other edema reduction techniques.
- Do not use with people with infection, grafts, or wounds; vascular/circulation damage; blood clots; unstable fractures; congestive heart failure (CHF); or cardiac edema (Artzberger, 2014).

EXAM HINT: The NBCOT® exam outline for the COTA® identifies knowledge of "technical level techniques for implementing . . . edema reduction, and scar management programs" (NBCOT®, 2018, p. 26) as essential for competent and safe practice. The application of knowledge about the above edema reduction techniques and the following scar management approaches can help you effectively determine the correct answers to exam items about working with persons with edema and/or scars.

Scar Management

1. ROM: early mobilization programs are most effective.
2. Massage (circles and friction).
3. Compression: Coban for digits, Isotoner glove for the hand, and Tubigrip for the upper extremity.
4. Scar pad with compression, scar pads can be purchased at health supply stores.
5. Splinting: to prevent contractures resulting from scar.
6. Edema control: especially in acute phase.

Sensory Training

1. Desensitization for hypersensitivity.
   a. If postsurgery, begin in periphery of the scar and as tolerated work over the scar.
   b. Massage.
   c. Textures (graded materials and contact particles).
   d. Vibration.
   e. Desensitization kits (commercial and homemade).
   f. Fluidotherapy.
   g. Desensitization program: should be performed several times daily.

EXAM HINT: The NBCOT® exam outline for the COTA® identifies knowledge of "technical level techniques for implementing sensory . . . reeducation" (NBCOT®, 2018, p. 26) as essential for competent and safe practice. The application of knowledge about the above and following approaches can help you determine the correct answer to exam items about the implementation of OT interventions focused on sensory reeducation.

2. Sensory re-education.
   a. Same as number b through e in number 1.
   b. Loss of protective sensation at high risk for injury: must emphasize safety precautions and to avoid use of hands where vision is occluded.
   c. Impaired discriminative sensation has protective sensation, but has difficulty discriminating objects from one another or identifying an object when vision is occluded: examples of activities include identifying objects with eyes closed and picking objects out of a rice bowl (Cooper & Canyock, 2013).
   d. Review safety precautions.
3. Compensation.
   a. Avoid use of hands where vision is occluded.
   b. Observe safety precautions.

Improving Coordination

1. Begin with gross motor activities and gradually grade up to fine motor activities.
2. Select activities in which the ROM required is within the person's reach and yet challenging.
3. Focus on accuracy and speed.
4. Begin with slow gross movements and gradually progress to faster precise movements

Energy Conservation and Work Simplification Methods

1. Plan short rest periods (5–10 minutes) during daily routine.

2. Schedule tasks for the day, week, and month to alternate and balance heavy and light work tasks.
3. Organize tasks; gather all necessary items and equipment before beginning task.
4. Avoid multiple trips to obtain items by using a utility cart, a bucket, walker bag, backpack, etc., to carry all items needed in one trip.
5. Eliminate tasks that are nonessential.
6. Delegate tasks that are beyond one's capacity.
7. Combine tasks to eliminate extraneous work.
8. Sit to work at a table or use a high stool for countertop work.
9. Organize cabinets so that items are easy to reach and in convenient locations.
10. Use adaptive equipment (e.g., reachers) to avoid bending and stooping.
11. Use electrical appliances (e.g., mixers) to decrease personal effort.
12. Slide rather than lift heavy items.
13. Use lightweight equipment, tools, and utensils.
14. Rest before fatigue sets in; intermittent rest during an activity is more effective than resting after exhaustion has occurred.

> **EXAM HINT:** The NBCOT® exam outline for the COTA® identifies knowledge of the "methods for grading an activity, task, or technique based on . . . client status, response to intervention, and client needs (and). . . . adaptive and preventive interventions for optimal engagement in occupation consistent with . . . neuromotor status, and condition" (NBCOT®, 2018, p. 25) as essential for competent and safe practice. The application of knowledge about the above energy conservation and work simplification principles/methods and the following joint protection and body mechanics principles/methods can help you determine the correct answer to COTA® exam items about the implementation of adaptive and preventive interventions that enable occupational performance.

Joint Protection Principles and Methods

1. Maintain joint ROM by using maximal ROM during daily activities.
2. Maintain muscle strength by using maximal strength during daily activities.
3. Use the strongest and largest joint that is possible for task completion.
   a. Use knees and hips for lifting, not the back.
   b. Push large items that need to be moved with a full body rather than pulling.
   c. Lift objects with both hands, palms pointed upward.
   d. Carry purses and bags on the forearm rather than wrist; most preferred is use of an ergonomically designed backpack.
4. Use each joint in its most stable and functional position.
   a. Stand directly in front of item to be reached for, opened, or closed, rather than to the side.
   b. Keep wrists and fingers in proper alignment.
5. Avoid holding joints in one position or sustaining muscle contractions for extended periods of time.
   a. Use adaptive equipment to hold items for long periods of time (e.g., a book holder).
   b. Take breaks from extended activities.
6. Avoid positions of deformity and activities in the direction of deformity (e.g., ulnar drift).
   a. Perform movements in the direction opposite the potential deformity (e.g., opening a door with the left hand and closing it with the right hand to prevent ulnar drift).
   b. Use adaptive equipment that is ergonomically designed (e.g., tools and utensils with angled handles that eliminate deviations at the wrist).
7. Do not start an activity that cannot be immediately stopped if it requires capacities beyond existing capabilities.

> **CAUTION:** Recognize that some discomfort may be a reality of activity performance, but pain is a warning sign that indicates an activity should be modified or stopped (Hammond, 2014).

Body Mechanics Principles

1. Do not move items that are too heavy; ask for assistance.
2. Slide or push an object along the surface rather than lift it, if possible.
3. Directly face the object about to be lifted. Do not face the direction in which the item is going to move.
4. Keep object close to the body during lifting and carrying.
5. Hold object centered at waist level.
6. Feet should be kept flat on the floor; balancing on toes should be avoided.
7. Maintain a firm and broad base of support. Maintain the body balanced over a wide stance.
8. Bend at the knees and hips, not at the waist.
9. Keep the back as straight as possible.
10. Breathe while lifting.
11. Lift by straightening legs; do not pull upward with arms and back.
12. Move smoothly; do not jerk.
13. Do not rotate the trunk. Pick up the object completely and then pivot the entire body.
14. Lower the body to the level of work (Maher, 2014).

Splinting

EXAM HINT: The NBCOT® exam outline for the COTA® identifies knowledge of the "types and functions of immobilization, mobilization, restriction, and nonarticular orthoses for managing specific conditions" (NBCOT®, 2018, p. 26) as essential for competent and safe practice. The application of knowledge about the following splint types, purposes, and design standards and the mechanical principles of splinting will help you determine the correct answer to COTA® items about working with people who need orthoses.

1. Types of splints.
   a. Static: has no resilient components and immobilizes a joint or part.
   b. Dynamic: includes a resilient component (elastic, rubber band, or spring) that the individual moves.
      (1) Designed to increase PROM or to augment AROM.
   c. Serial static splint: a static splint or the use of casting material that is remolded to address changes in joint motion.
   d. Static progressive splint: includes a static adjustment part (e.g., turnbuckle or strap) that allows the patient or OT practitioner to make changes in the tension or angle to increase motion (Lashgari & Yasuda, 2013).
2. Purposes of splinting.
   a. Rest.
   b. Prevent deformities and contractures.
   c. Increase joint ROM.
   d. Protect bone, joint, and soft tissue.
   e. Increase functional use.
   f. Decrease pain.
   g. Restrict ROM.
3. Hand-splinting design standards.
   a. Maintain arches of the hand.
      (1) Proximal transverse arch.
      (2) Distal transverse arch.
      (3) Longitudinal arch.
   b. Do not impinge upon creases of the hand.
      (1) Distal and proximal palmar creases.
      (2) Distal and proximal wrist creases.
      (3) Thenar creases.
4. Mechanical principles of splinting.
   a. Decrease pressure: wide, long splint base is the most desirable. Round edges are needed.
   b. Use sling applied with a 90° angle of pull.
   c. Use low load to increase duration.
   d. Maintain three-point pressure versus circumference.
   e. Avoid the position of deformity.
      (1) Wrist flexion.
      (2) MCP hyperextension.
      (3) IP joints flexed.
      (4) Thumb adducted.
   f. Select the appropriate splinting position.[1]
      (1) Resting hand splint: functional position. Used to rest structures or protect structures of the hand.
         (a) Wrist 20°–30° extension.
         (b) MCPs 45°–60° flexion.
         (c) IPs 15°–30° flexion (may be referred to as slight flexion).
         (d) Thumb abducted (may be referred to as opposition).
      (2) Safe position splint (may be referred to as intrinsic-plus or antideformity splint): used to maintain the length of the collateral ligaments).
         (a) Wrist 20°–30° extension.
         (b) Several texts suggest 30°–40°. The therapist and the OTA must be cautious due to the resultant increased carpal canal pressure.
         (c) MCPs 70°–90° flexion.
         (d) IPs in extension.
         (e) Thumb palmar abduction.

CAUTION: Check the individual's skin condition before and after making any splint (Lashgari & Yasuda, 2013).

5. Education.

EXAM HINT: The NBCOT® exam outline for the COTA® identifies knowledge of the "training methods regarding the safe and effective use of orthotic... devices consistent with prioritized needs, goals, and task demands in order to optimize or enhance function" (NBCOT®, 2018, p. 26) as essential for competent and safe practice. The application of knowledge about the following education approaches can help you correctly answer exam items about the OTA's role in orthotic device training.

   a. Instruct splint wearer in procedures for splint maintenance and routine skin inspection and care.
      (1) Check skin when donning and doffing.
      (2) Provide wear and care form and instruct the person in its use and importance.
   b. Ensure individual accepts and understands the purpose(s), function(s), and limitation(s) of the splint.

---

[1] There are slight variations reported in OT and splinting textbooks in regard to the exact degrees for resting hand (functional) splints and safe (antideformity) splints. Thus, it is unlikely that the NBCOT® exam will include items that have two possible correct answers that include these subtle variations. To determine the correct answer to an exam item, you should consider the position(s) in which the joints are placed and not focus so much on the specific degrees.

c. Teach proper technique for donning and doffing splint.
d. Provide functional training in use of splint in role activities (e.g., use of tenodesis splint to do schoolwork).
e. Reevaluate the individual's use of splint at periodic intervals.
6. Occupational therapist/OTA role.
   a. The occupational therapist/OTA team must carefully assess for most appropriate splint.
   b. The occupational therapist must set splinting goals.
   c. Experienced OTAs can fabricate static splints and assist with dynamic splints upon establishment of service competence.
7. Splints for common diagnoses.

> **EXAM HINT:** The NBCOT® exam outline for the COTA® identifies knowledge of the "types and functions of immobilization, mobilization, restriction, and non-articular orthoses for managing specific conditions (NBCOT®, 2018, p. 26) as essential for competent and safe practice. The application of knowledge about the following diagnostic-specific splints and their purposes will help you determine the correct answer to items about the best orthoses for people who have these conditions.

   a. Brachial plexus injury: flail arm splint.
      (1) This splint is used for positioning.
   b. Radial nerve injury: Colditz splint or radial nerve splint to assist with partial wrist motion and finger extension (Colditz, 1987).
      (1) This splint is used for function. It assists the digits with extension to release an object.
         (a) A resting hand splint may be provided for night use to prevent flexion contractures.
   c. Median nerve injury: opponens splint, C-Bar, or thumb post splint.
      (1) The opponens splint is used to hold the thumb in opposition to use during functional activities.
      (2) Thenar webspacer is used to prevent thumb adduction contracture.
   d. Ulnar nerve injury: Anticlaw splint or lumbrical bar splint to position MCPs in flexion of digits 4 and 5.
      (1) This splint is used to prevent clawing of the fourth and fifth digits.
   e. Combined median ulnar: figure-of-eight or lumbrical bar splint to position MCPs in flexion for digits 2–5.
      (1) This splint is used to prevent the hand from assuming the intrinsic minus position.
   f. Spinal cord (C6–C7): tenodesis splint.
      (1) This splint is used to facilitate grasp and release.
   g. Carpal tunnel syndrome: wrist splint positioned in neutral.
      (1) This splint is used to decrease carpal canal pressure (especially at night).
   h. Cubital tunnel syndrome: elbow splint positions at 30° of flexion.
      (1) This splint is used to prevent elbow flexion at night, which will decrease ulnar nerve symptoms.
   i. De Quervain's: thumb splint, includes wrist, IP joint free.
      (1) This splint is used to place the first dorsal compartment (APB and EPB) at rest.
   j. Skier's thumb: (UCL) hand-based thumb splint.
      (1) This splint is used to protect the ulnar collateral ligament of the MCP joint of the thumb until it heals.
   k. CMC arthritis: hand-based thumb splint.
      (1) This splint is used to place the CMC joint of the thumb at rest until inflammation decreases.
         (a) A commercial brand is the Comfort Cool Thumb CMC orthosis.
   l. Ulnar drift: ulnar drift/deviation splint.
      (1) This splint is used to decrease pain, provide stability, and realign the MCP joints of digits 2–5 for a person with arthritic changes.
         (a) Commercial brand is a neoprene anti-ulnar deviation splint.
   m. Flexor tendon injury: dorsal protection splint.
      (1) This splint is used to protect the repair site and to allow for early controlled mobilization while wearing the splint.
   n. Swan neck: silver rings, buttonhole/hyperextension block splint or digital dorsal splint in slight PIP flexion.
      (1) This splint is used to place the PIP joint in slight flexion to prevent further development of the swan neck deformity.
   o. Boutonniere: silver rings or PIP extension splint.
      (1) This splint is used to place the PIP joint in extension to allow for the lateral bands to move dorsal to the PIP axis.
         (a) This is often combined with DIP flexion exercises while wearing the splint.
   p. Arthritis: functional splint or safe splint, depending on stage.
      (1) This splint is used to place the joints at rest until inflammation decreases.
   q. Flaccidity: resting/functional hand splint.
      (1) This splint is used to prevent joint contractures and hold the hand in a position of function until muscle return occurs.
         (a) Common wearing schedule is at night and on and off throughout the day.
   r. Spasticity: spasticity splint or cone splint.
      (1) This splint is used to prevent joint contracture.

s. Muscle weakness (amyotrophic lateral sclerosis, spinal cord injury, Guillain-Barré): balanced forearm orthosis (BFO), deltoid sling/suspension sling.
   (1) This splint/sling is used to support the proximal upper extremity to allow for use of distal extremity during activities such as eating.
   (2) Mounts to wheelchair.
   (3) Prevents loss of shoulder motions (Lashgari & Yasuda, 2013).
t. Hand burns: anti-deformity/anticontracture splints are designed based on the burn's location. See Table 6-3.
   (1) These splints are used to maintain soft tissue structures in a safe position (Cooper, 2014; Deshaies, 2013; Lashgari & Yasuda, 2013).
u. Boutonniere: silver rings or dynamic proximal interphalangeal (PIP) extension splint.
v. Arthritis: resting hand splint.
w. Flaccidity: resting splint.
x. Spasticity: spasticity splint or cone splint.
y. Muscle weakness (amyotrophic lateral sclerosis [ALS], spinal cord injury [SCI], Guillain-Barré): balanced forearm orthosis (BFO), deltoid sling/suspension sling.
   (1) Mounts to wheelchair.
   (2) Individuals must have shoulder or trunk movement.

Physical Agent Modalities (PAMs)

EXAM HINT: The NBCOT® exam outline for the COTA® identifies knowledge of "technical level indications, contraindications, precautions, and appropriate clinical application of superficial thermal agents as guided by evidence, best practice standards, scope of practice, and state licensure practice acts" (NBCOT®, 2018, p. 24) and knowledge of "technical level indications, contraindications, precautions, and appropriate clinical application of deep thermal, mechanical, and electrotherapeutic physical agent modalities as guided by evidence, best practice standards, scope of practice, and state licensure practice acts" (NBCOT®, 2018, p. 24) as essential for competent and safe practice. The application of knowledge about the following PAM information will help you correctly answer exam items about their safe, effective, and ethical use in OT practice.

1. PAMs can be used as a method in preparation for purposeful and occupation based activities.
   a. PAMs are *not* an appropriate OT intervention if they are used in isolation of purposeful activity or occupation-based activities.
   b. PAMs *are* an appropriate OT intervention if they precede, support, and/or enable the individual's ability to perform purposeful activities and meaningful occupations.
   c. PAMs are, therefore, preparatory OT intervention methods, for they add to and complement the primary OT intervention methods of purposeful activity and occupation-based activities.
   d. Many states require specialized training to use PAMs as an OT intervention.
2. Common types of PAMs used in OT practice.
   a. Superficial thermal.
      (1) Paraffin.
      (2) Hot packs.
      (3) Fluidotherapy.
   b. Superficial cooling agents.
      (1) Cold packs.
      (2) Ice massage.
   c. Mechanotherapy
      (1) Ultrasound.
      (2) Whirlpool.
   d. Electrical stimulation units.
      (1) Neuromuscular electrical stimulation (NMES).
      (2) Transcutaneous electrical nerve stimulator (TENS).
      (3) High-voltage galvanic stimulation (HVGS).
      (4) Iontophoresis.
3. Superficial thermal.
   a. Conduction (hot packs, whirlpool, and paraffin). Heats superficial structures up to 1 cm.
      (1) Convection (fluidotherapy).
      (2) Radiation (laser).
      (3) Conversion (ultrasound). Heats deeper structures up to 4–5 cm.
   b. Benefits of superficial heat therapy.
      (1) Relieves pain.
      (2) Increases tissue extensibility (increases ROM).
      (3) Assists with wound healing (increased blood flow).
      (4) Decreases muscle spasms.

RED FLAG: Contraindications for heat.
- Do not use with people with postsurgical repairs, acute injuries, impaired sensation, edema, impaired vascular supply, tumors or active cancer, multiple sclerosis, lymphedema, or deep vein thrombosis (DVT).

   c. Application of thermal heat modalities.
      (1) Hot packs.

CAUTION: Check skin prior to and after application.

         (a) Check temperature of hydrocollator; 165°F is the standard.
         (b) Place hot pack in cover and add four layers of a folded towel (one towel) in between the

patient's skin and the hot pack cover. For fragile skin, an additional towel should be considered.
- (c) Check skin after five minutes to assess for burn or any other skin issues.
- (d) Hot pack is removed after a total of 20 minutes.
- (2) Paraffin.

> **CAUTION:** Check skin prior to and after application.

- (a) Check temperature of paraffin; 125°F–130°F is the standard.
- (b) After washing and thoroughly drying the hand, dip the hand into paraffin and quickly pull out. Repeat this process 8–10 times, forming a glove of paraffin over the hand.
- (c) Following the dip method, the hand should be wrapped with cellophane and then covered with a towel for 20 minutes (Breines, 2013; Wietlisbach & Branham, 2014).
- (3) Fluidotherapy.
  - (a) Preheat the fluidotherapy machine (temperature can range between 102°F and 118°F).
  - (b) Adjust the blowers according to the person's sensitivity (if the person is hypersensitive, begin with turning the blowers down)
  - (c) Place the person's hand in the fluidotherapy via a sleeve on the machine for 20 minutes. During this time the client can exercise their hand and wrist.
  - (d) Treatment is for 20 minutes. The client's hand is slowly removed from the machine making certain no particles of ground cornhusk spill out (Wietlisbach & Branham, 2014).
- (4) Whirlpool.[2]
  - (a) To clean and débride wounds:
    - Fill the tank with water at 100°F–108°F degrees; if treating burns, water should be set at body temperature.
    - Maintain sterile technique.
    - Adjust turbine and turn it on. Check temperature again.
    - Slowly lower the extremity into the whirlpool.
  - (b) Treatment will be for 20 minutes.
4. Cryotherapy.
   a. Benefits of cryotherapy
      (1) Relieves pain.
      (2) Controls edema.
      (3) Decreases abnormal tone.
      (4) Facilitates muscle tone.
      (5) Commonly used to treat acute injuries and postsurgical repairs.

> **RED FLAG:** Contraindications for cryotherapy.
> - Do not use with people with sensory deficits (including hypersensitivity), impaired circulation, or Raynaud's disease.

   b. Application of cryotherapy.

> **CAUTION:** Check skin prior to and after application.

   (1) Ice pack.
      (a) Apply a dry or wet towel between the client's skin and the cold pack.
      (b) Check skin after three to five minutes.
      (c) Cold pack remains cold for up to 10 minutes.
   (2) Another commonly used type of cryotherapy includes ice massage (used for smaller areas; applied directly to the skin for three to five minutes) (Breines, 2013; Wietlisbach & Branham, 2014).
5. Guidelines for competent and ethical use of PAMs in OT.
   a. PAMs should be used when they can benefit the individual's treatment program.
   b. PAMs should be not be used when they will not benefit the individual's treatment program.
   c. Indications, contraindications, and precautions for use of PAMs must be adhered to strictly.

> **RED FLAG:** General contraindications for PAMs.
> - Do not use if a person is pregnant or has cancer, a pacemaker, cognitive impairment, sensory impairment, vascular impairment, or deep vein thrombophlebitis.
> - Prior to using PAMs with an individual, diagnostic and age considerations must be carefully reviewed. For example, ultrasound is never used over a growth plate.

   d. Practitioner competence must be established for any and all PAMs used in OT intervention.
   e. Refer to American Occupational Therapy Association (AOTA) Position Paper on PAMs. (AOTA, 2012).
   f. The use of physical agent modalities in OT is determined by your state practice act and the institution that you are employed.
      (1) Some state licensure laws require special training to use PAMs.
         (a) Because the NBCOT® exam is a national exam, it will not include exam items with questions about state- or facility-specific standards.
      (2) OTAs who use PAMs should have established service competence and be closely supervised by an occupational therapist when using PAMs.

---
[2] Whirlpool (WP) is not as commonly used as in the past; now used on a case-by-case basis. WP has been replaced by more advanced wound management interventions. WP requires strict cleaning and disinfecting procedures; refer to Centers for Disease Control and Prevention for recommendations.

References

Adams, L. S., Grenne, L. W., & Toppzian, E. (1992). Range of motion. In American Association of Hand Therapists (Ed.). *Clinical assessment recommendations* (2nd ed., pp. 55–70). Chicago, IL: Author.

American Occupational Therapy Association. (2012). Physical agent modalities. *American Journal of Occupational Therapy.* 66(6_Supplement): S78–S80.

American Society of Hand Therapists. (1992). *Clinical assessment recommendations*, 2nd ed. Chicago, IL: Author.

Artzberger, S. (2014). Edema reduction techniques: A biologic rationale for selection. In C. Cooper (Ed.), *Fundamentals of hand therapy: Clinical reasoning and treatment guidelines for common diagnoses of the upper extremity* (2nd ed., pp. 35–50). St. Louis, MO: Elsevier.

Breines, E. (2013). Therapeutic occupations and modalities. In H.M. Pendleton & W. Schultz-Krohn (Eds.). *Pedretti's Occupational therapy: Practice skills for physical dysfunction*, (7th ed., pp. 729–754). St. Louis, MO: Elsevier

Cameron, M. (1999). *Physical agents in rehabilitation: From research to practice.* Orlando, FL: W.B. Saunders.

Colditz, J. (1987). Splinting for radial nerve palsy. *Journal of Hand Therapy, 1*, 18–23.

Clarkson, H. M. (2000). *Musculoskeletal assessment: Joint range of motion and manual muscles strength.* (2nd ed.). Philadelphia: Lippincott Williams & Wilkins.

Cooper, C. (2007). *Fundamentals of hand therapy: Clinical reasoning and treatment guidelines for common diagnoses of the upper extremity.* Philadelphia: Elsevier.

Cooper, C. (2014). Hand impairments. In M. V. Radomski & C. A. Trombly Latham (Eds.), *Occupational therapy for physical dysfunction* (7th ed., pp. 1129–1167). Philadelphia, PA: Lippincott Williams & Wilkins.

Cooper, C. (2014). *Fundamentals of hand therapy: Clinical reasoning and treatment guidelines for common diagnoses of the upper extremity.* St. Louis, MO: Elsevier.

Cooper, C., & Canyok, D. (2013). Evaluation of sensation and intervention for sensory dysfunction. In H.M. Pendleton & W. Schultz-Krohn (Eds.). *Pedretti's occupational therapy: Practice skills for physical dysfunction* (7th ed., pp. 575–589). St. Louis, MO: Elsevier.

Deshaies, L. (2014). Burns. In C. Cooper (Ed.), *Fundamentals of hand therapy: Clinical reasoning and treatment guidelines for common diagnoses of the upper extremity.* St. Louis, MO: Elsevier.

Deshaies, L. (2013). Arthritis. In H.M. Pendleton & W. Schultz-Krohn (Eds.). *Pedretti's occupational therapy: Practice skills for physical dysfunction* (7th ed., pp. 1003–1036). St. Louis, MO: Elsevier.

Evan, R. B. (2002). Therapist's management of carpal tunnel syndrome. In E. J. Mackin, A. D. Callahan, & T. M. Skirven. (Eds.), *Rehabilitation of the hand and upper extremity.* (5th ed., pp. 660–661). St Louis, MO: Mosby.

Greene, D. P., & Roberts, S. L. (2016). *Kinesiology: Movement in the context of activity.* 3rd ed. St. Louis, MO: Mosby.

Hammond, A. (2014). Rheumatoid arthritis, osteoarthritis and fibromyalgia. In M. V. Radomski & C. A. Trombly Latham (Eds.), *Occupational therapy for physical dysfunction.* Philadelphia, PA: Lippincott Williams & Wilkins.

Jacobs, M. L., & Austin, N. M. (2014). *Orthotic intervention for the hand and upper extremity: Splinting principles and process.* Baltimore, MD: Lippincott Williams & Wilkins.

Jebsen, R. H., Taylor, N., Trieschmann, R. B., Trotter, M. J., & Howard, L. A. (1969). An objective and standardized test of hand function. *Archives of Physical Medicine and Rehabilitation, 50*, 311–319.

Kendall, F. (1995). *Muscle testing and function.* (4th ed.). Baltimore, MD: Lippincott Williams & Wilkins.

Killingsworth, A. P., Pedretti, L. W., & Pendleton, H. M. (2013). Joint range of motion. In H. M. Pendleton & W. Schultz-Krohn (Eds.), *Pedretti's occupational therapy: Practice skills for physical dysfunction* (7th ed., pp. 497–528). St. Louis, MO: Elsevier.

Klein, L. J. (2014). Evaluation of the hand and upper extremity. In C. Cooper (Ed.), *Fundamentals of hand therapy: Clinical reasoning and treatment guidelines for common diagnoses of the upper extremity* (2nd ed., pp. 67–86). St. Louis, MO: Elsevier.

Knight, K. L., & Draper, D. O. (2013). *Therapeutic modalities: The art and science.* Baltimore, MD: Lippincott Williams & Wilkins.

Lafayette Instrument. (1969). *Minnesota Manual Dexterity Test.* Lafayette, INWI: Author.

Lafayette Instrument. (1986). *O'Connor Tweezer Dexterity Test.* (1986). Menomonee Falls, WI: Smith & Nephew Roylan,

Lafayette Instrument. (2015). *Purdue Pegboard Procedure Manual.* Lafayette, IN: Author.

Lashgari, D., & Yasuda, Y. L. (2013). Orthotics. In H. M. Pendleton & W. S. Schultz-Krohn (Eds.), *Occupational therapy practice: Skills for physical dysfunction.* (7th ed., pp. 755–795). St. Louis: Mosby.

Maher, C. (2014). Orthopaedic conditions. In M. V. Radomski & C. A. Trombly Latham (Eds.), *Occupational therapy for physical dysfunction* (7th ed., 1103-1128)). Philadelphia, PA: Lippincott Williams & Wilkins.

Manning, D. C. (2000). Reflex sympathetic dystrophy, sympathetically maintained pain and complex regional pain syndrome: Diagnosis of inclusion, exclusion, or confusion? *Journal of Hand Therapy, 13*, 260–268.

Michlovitz, S. L., & Nolan T. P. (2005). M*odalities for therapeutic intervention.* (4th ed.). Philadelphia, PA: F.A. Davis.

Neer, C. (1990). *Shoulder reconstruction.* Orlando, FL: W.B. Saunders.

National Board for Certification in Occupational Therapy (NBCOT®). (2018). *Practice analysis of the certified occupational therapy assistant registered: Executive summary* [PDF file]. Gaithersburg, MD: Author. Retrieved from https://www.nbcot.org/-/media/NBCOT/PDFs/2017-Practice-Analysis-Executive-OTR.ashx?la=en

O'Connor Tweezer Dexterity Test. (1986). Smith & Nephew Roylan, Inc. Menomonee Falls, WI 53051.

Pedretti, L., Smith, R., Hammel, J., Rein, J., Anson, D., & McGuire, M. J. (1996). Use of adjunctive modalities in occupational therapy. In R. P. Cottrell (Ed.), *Perspectives on purposeful activity: Foundation and future of occupational therapy.* (pp. 451–458). Bethesda, MD: American Occupational Therapy Association.

Pendeleton, H. M., & Schultz-Krohn, W. (2013). *Pedretti's occupational therapy: Practice skills for physical dysfunction.* (7th ed.). St. Louis, MO: Mosby.

Radomski, M. V., & Trombly, C. A. (2014). *Occupational therapy for physical dysfunction.* (7th ed.). Baltimore, MD: Lippincott Williams & Wilkins.

Theis, J. L. (2014). Assessing abilities and capacities: Sensation. In M. V. Radomski & C. A. Trombly Latham (Eds.), *Occupational therapy for physical dysfunction* (7th ed., pp. 276–305). Philadelphia, PA: Lippincott Williams & Wilkins.

Sladyk, K., Jacobs, K., & MacRae, N. (2010) *Occupational therapy essentials for clinical competence.* Thorofare, NJ: Slack.

Sladyk, K., & Ryan, S. E. (2001). *Ryan's occupational therapy assistant: Principles, practices, and techniques.* (3rd ed.). Thorofare, NJ: Slack.

Weiss, S., & Falkenstein, N. (2005). *Hand rehabilitation: A quick reference guide and review.* (2nd ed.). St. Louis, MO: Elsevier Mosby.

Whelan, L. R. (2014). Assessing abilities and capacities: Range of motion, strength, and endurance. In M. V. Radomski & C. A. Trombly Latham (Eds.), *Occupational therapy for physical dysfunction* (7th ed., pp. 144–241). Philadelphia, PA: Lippincott Williams & Wilkins.

Wietlisbach, C. M., & Branham, F. D. B. (2014). Physical agent modalities and biofeedback. In M. V. Radomski & C. A. Trombly Latham (Eds.), *Occupational therapy for physical dysfunction* (7th ed., pp. 558–588). Philadelphia, PA: Lippincott Williams & Wilkins.

Review Questions

Biomechanical Approaches: Evaluation and Intervention

Following are five questions about key content covered in this chapter. These questions are not inclusive of the entirety of content related to biomechanical approaches that you must know for success on the COTA® exam. These questions are provided to help you develop the thought processes you will need to apply your studying of content to the answering of exam questions; hence, they are not in the COTA® exam format. Exam items in the COTA® format that cover the depth and breadth of content you will need to know to pass the exam are provided on this text's online exams. The answers to the questions following questions are provided in Appendix 3.

1. You work in a practice setting that serves many clients with musculoskeletal disorders. The majority of clients have decreased ROM. When collaborating with the occupational therapist to complete client evaluations, which different types of ROM should you consider during assessment? How should you document your evaluation and its results?

2. A new client is admitted into an intensive care unit with a diagnosis of a spinal cord injury. You collaborate with the occupational therapist to complete an evaluation to help the physician determine the level of injury. How would you perform a light-touch sensory test? How does this method of testing differ from the procedures used during sensory testing for other major diagnostic categories?

3. An adult client is having difficulty performing daily activities due to decreased ROM and pain in both shoulders. During an intervention planning meeting, you and the occupational therapist decide to treat the client with preparatory interventions followed by an occupation-based intervention. What interventions can you use to increase ROM and decrease pain?

4. You provide consultation services to a center for independent living that serves persons with a diversity of disabilities. You are scheduled to conduct an educational session on energy conservation and work simplification. What key principles and methods should you be sure to include in your presentation?

5. Your client is diagnosed with rotator cuff tendonitis and is experiencing severe pain. The physician has ordered the use of electrical stimulation, gentle ROM, and below shoulder level ADL. You and the occupational therapist review the client's past medical history. You learn that the person has a history of cardiac issues that required the implantation of a pacemaker. Which of the prescribed interventions should you use with this client? What are additional interventions you can use with this client to decrease pain and prepare the person for occupation-based interventions?

6. Your client is status post a below knee amputation. You assess the strength of the client's triceps in preparation for transfer training. The results of the MMT reveal that the client can take moderate resistance and then break. What muscle grade would you document the client possesses?

12

Neurological and Cognitive-Perceptual Approaches: Evaluation and Intervention

GLEN GILLEN

Chapter Outline

- Neurological Frames of Reference Related to Motor Performance, 338
- Evaluation of Motor Control Dysfunction, 344
- Orthotic/Splinting Interventions for Neuromotor Dysfunction, 345
- Oral Motor Dysfunction, 347
- Limb and Postural Control Impairments, 348
- The Ayres Sensory Integration® Approach for Sensory Processing Disorders, 349
- Cognitive-Perceptual Approaches, 351
- References, 355
- Review Questions, 357

Neurological Frames of Reference Related to Motor Performance

> **EXAM HINT:** The NBCOT® exam outline for the COTA® identifies knowledge of the "influence of theoretical approaches, models of practice, and frames of reference on information-gathering and the intervention process" (NBCOT®, 2018, p. 22) as essential for competent practice. The application of knowledge about the following neurological frames of reference will be required to correctly answer NBCOT® Domain 01 exam items about working with persons with neurological disorders.

Contemporary Task-Oriented Approaches to Motor Control Training

1. General principles/assumptions.
   a. Contemporary approaches to motor control training are based on current research and knowledge of the motor behavior.
   b. Approaches reject assumptions of the reflex-hierarchical model of motor control and of the traditional neurophysiologic therapies.
   c. Remediation of performance components and environmental modifications to improve task performance is included.
   d. Based on a systems model of motor control.
      (1) Proposes that motor control is determined by interactive systems (motor, cultural, environmental, etc.), behavioral tasks, and adaptive/anticipatory mechanisms.
   e. Movement is controlled by the integration and interaction of multiple systems including environmental influences, sensorimotor factors, musculoskeletal factors, regulatory functions, and behavioral/emotional goals.
   f. The role of the structures responsible for motor control is to tune and prepare the motor system to respond to changing environmental and task demands.
   g. Interventions are also guided by the occupational therapist's and the occupational therapy assistant's (OTA's) understanding of motor learning principles.
   h. Control is not simply over muscle actions, but over the interactions of kinematic variables.
   i. Movement dysfunction following central nervous system (CNS) damage reflects the system's best effort to accomplish task goals.

2. Principles of the Contemporary Task-Oriented Approach.
   a. Occupational performance emerges from the interaction of multiple systems, including personal and performance contexts.
   b. Personal and environmental systems, including the central nervous system, are hierarchically organized.
   c. An individual's behavioral changes reflect their attempts to compensate and to achieve functional goals.
   d. Individuals must practice with varied strategies to find optimal solutions for motor problems and develop skill in performance.
   e. Functional tasks help organize motor behavior.
   f. The occupational therapist must determine which control parameters or systems (personal, environmental, etc.) have positive or negative influences on motor behavior.
      (1) The OTA contributes to this determination with supervision from the occupational therapist.
   g. Practice opportunities are provided that are appropriate to the person's stage of learning.
   h. The therapist conducts the evaluation using a top-down approach.
      (1) The OTA contributes to the evaluation with supervision from the occupational therapist.
   i. Evaluation efforts focus initially on role performance and occupational performance tasks because they are the goals of motor behavior.
   j. After a person has identified the most important role and occupational performance limitations, the therapist and OTA use task analysis to identify which subsystem(s) of the person and/or environmental factor(s) are limiting functional performance.
   k. Interventions are focused on:
      (1) Helping individuals adjust to role and task performance limitations.
      (2) Creating an environment that utilizes the common challenges of everyday life.
      (3) Practicing functional tasks or close simulations to find effective and efficient strategies for performance.
      (4) Providing opportunities for practice outside of therapy time.
      (5) Remediating a client factor.
      (6) Minimizing inefficient or ineffective movement patterns.
      (7) Adapting the environment.

(8) Modifying the task.
(9) Using assistive technology.
3. Principles of Carr and Shepherd's Motor Relearning Program (MRP).
   a. The person is an active participant whose goal is to relearn effective strategies for performing functional movement.
   b. Postural adjustments and limb movements are linked together in the learning process.
   c. Successful task relearning has occurred when activities are performed automatically and efficiently.
   d. The learning of skills does not follow a developmental sequence.
   e. Continued practice of compensatory strategies limits functional recovery.
   f. Intervention is not focused on learning specific movements but instead on learning general strategies for solving motor problems.
   g. Obstacles to efficient movement include loss of soft tissue extensibility, balance loss, fixation patterns due to postural insecurity, and muscle weakness.
   h. Abnormal movement patterns are attributed to the repeated practice of compensatory movement strategies that become overlearned.
4. Principles of Motor Learning.
   a. Contemporary approaches to treating motor dysfunction incorporate principles of motor learning during interventions focused on remediating motor control in persons with CNS dysfunction.
   b. The ultimate goal of utilizing motor learning theory is the acquisition of functional skills that can be generalized to multiple situations and environments.
   c. Stages of motor learning.
      (1) Skill acquisition stage (cognitive stage) occurs during initial instruction and practice of a skill.
      (2) Skill retention stage (associated stage) involves 'carry-over,' as individuals are asked to demonstrate their newly acquired skill after initial practice.
      (3) Skill transfer stage (autonomous stage) involves the individual demonstrating the skill in a new context.
      (4) Refer to Table 12-1 for further description of these stages.
   d. Practice.
      (1) Random (or variable) practice involves practice of several tasks that are presented in a random order, encouraging reformulation of the solution to the presented motor problem.
      (2) Blocked practice involves repeated performance of the same motor skill.
      (3) Practice of the whole task.
      (4) Practice of parts of the task.
      (5) Variable conditions involve practice of skills in various contexts to improve transfer of learning and retention of skills.
      (6) Mental practice involves cognitive rehearsal of a skill without actually moving.
   e. Intrinsic feedback.
      (1) Information received by the learner as a result of performing the task.
      (2) Information is received from tactile, vestibular, and visual systems during and after the task.
   f. Extrinsic feedback.
      (1) Feedback provided from an outside source (i.e., the therapist, OTA, and/or a mechanical device).
      (2) Includes knowledge of performance, which is verbal feedback about the process or performance itself.
      (3) Includes knowledge of results, which is the therapist's and/or OTA's provision of feedback about the outcome or end product or results of the motor action.
   g. Factors/conditions that promote generalization of motor learning.
      (1) Capacity to generate intrinsic feedback.
      (2) High feedback regarding knowledge of performance.
      (3) Low extrinsic feedback regarding knowledge of results.
      (4) Practice conditions that are variable, random.
      (5) Whole task performance as opposed to breaking activities into contrived parts.
      (6) High contextual interference utilizes environmental conditions that increase the difficulty of learning, such as noise distractions, crowded environments.
      (7) Practice in naturalistic settings, i.e., the setting in which the skill being taught will be utilized or an environment that closely resembles the one in which the skill will be performed.
   h. Treatment sequence to promote generalization of learning.
      (1) The initial task is the first activity performed by the client.
      (2) Near transfer is an alternate form of the initial task.
      (3) Intermediate transfer has a moderate number of changes in task parameters but still has some similarities to the initial task.
      (4) Far transfer introduces an activity that is conceptually the same as, but physically different from, the initial task.
      (5) Very far transfer requires spontaneous use of the new strategy in daily functional activities.

i. Task categories.
   (1) Closed tasks are activities in which the environment is stable and predictable and methods of performance are consistent over time.
   (2) Variable motionless tasks also involve interacting with a stable and predictable environment, but specific features of the environment are likely to vary between performance trials.
   (3) Consistent motion tasks require an individual to deal with environmental conditions that are in motion during activity performance; the motion is consistent and predictable between trials.
   (4) Open tasks require people to make adaptive decisions about unpredictable events because objects within the environment are in random motion during task performance.
j. Refer to Table 12-1 for training strategies appropriate for each stage of motor learning.
5. The role of the OTA in intervention.
   a. The OTA implements intervention with OT supervision.
   b. The level of supervision required depends upon the OTA's experience and established service competency.
   c. During the implementation of intervention, the OTA informs the supervising therapist of any change in the individual's status and any other relevant information that may affect treatment.

EXAM HINT: The NBCOT® exam outline for the COTA® identifies knowledge of "technical level techniques for implementing . . . motor reeducation" (NBCOT®, 2018, p. 26) as essential for competent practice. The application of knowledge about the previously presented contemporary task-oriented approaches to motor learning and the strategies provided in Table 12-1 can help you determine the correct answer for NBCOT® Domain 02 exam items about motor reeducation.

Review of Neurophysiologic ('Traditional') Frames of Reference

1. Also known as sensorimotor or traditional approaches.
   a. They include the neurodevelopmental treatment approach (NDT), proprioceptive neuromuscular facilitation (PNF), Brunnstrom's approach, and Margaret Rood's approach.
   b. See Table 12-2 for a summary and comparison of these traditional approaches.
2. Utilized for persons with central nervous system dysfunction.
3. Approaches developed in the 1940s and 1950s based on the understanding of nervous system pathology at that time.
   a. They are outlined in this chapter only because this information is included in some of the occupational therapy textbooks that NBCOT® identifies as the references for the composition of NBCOT® exam items.
      (1) Consequently, some NBCOT® exam items may reflect these traditional perspectives.

EXAM HINT: In the NBCOT® exam outline for the COTA®, Domain 03 comprises 17% of the COTA® exam. This domain focuses on the OTA's ability to "uphold professional standards and responsibilities by . . . applying evidence-based interventions to promote quality in practice" (NBCOT®, 2018, p. 28). Because the efficacy of contemporary task-oriented approaches to motor control training is supported by evidence and traditional neurophysiologic approaches are not, the correct answer to a COTA® exam item about applying neurophysiological approaches that includes both contemporary and traditional approaches as answer choices would likely be the contemporary approach.

4. General assumptions/principles/treatment foundations.
   a. Controlled movement is preceded by stereotypic reflex responses.
   b. Sensory input regulates motor output, and sensation is necessary for movement to take place.
   c. Normal movements are governed by hierarchical centralized motor programs that determine muscle activation patterns.
      (1) The cerebral cortex controls the middle levels (basal ganglia, brain stem, etc.), which in turn control the spinal cord.
   d. Damage to higher control centers release lower level or primitive reflexes and movement patterns from inhibition.
   e. When basic movements and postures are normalized, skilled movement would occur automatically.
   f. 'Integration' of lower-level spinal and brain stem reflexes occurs by eliciting higher-level righting and equilibrium responses.
   g. Controlled sensory input applied by the practitioner can influence motor responses (i.e., a reflex model of control).
   h. The use of 'facilitation' and 'inhibition' techniques can improve motor performance.

Table 12-1

Motor Learning Stages and Training Strategies

COGNITIVE STAGE CHARACTERISTICS

- The learner develops an understanding of task; cognitive mapping assesses abilities, task demands; identifies stimuli, contacts memory; selects response; performs initial approximations of task, structures motor program; modifies initial responses
- *"What to do"* decision

TRAINING STRATEGIES

- Highlight purpose of task in functionally relevant terms
- Demonstrate ideal performance of task to establish a reference of correctness
- Have patients verbalize task components and requirements
- Point out similarities to other learned tasks
- Direct attention to critical task elements
- Select appropriate feedback
  - Emphasize intact sensory systems, intrinsic feedback systems
  - Carefully pair extrinsic feedback with intrinsic feedback
  - High dependence on vision: have patient watch movement
  - Knowledge of Performance (KP): focus on errors as they become consistent; do not cue on large number of random errors
  - Knowledge of Results (KR): focus on success of movement outcome.
- Ask learner to evaluate performance, outcomes; identify problems, solutions
- Use reinforcements (praise) for correct performance, continuing motivation
- Organize feedback schedule
  - Feedback after every trial improves performance during early treatment
  - Variable feedback (summed, fading, bandwidth designs) increases depth of cognitive processing, improves retention, may decrease performance initially
- Organize initial practice
  - Stress controlled movement to minimize errors.
  - Provide adequate rest periods (distributed practice) if task is complex, long, or energy costly or if learner fatigues easily, has short attention, poor concentration
  - Use manual guidance to assist as appropriate
  - Break complex tasks down into component parts, teach both parts as integrated whole
  - Utilize bilateral transfer as appropriate
  - Use blocked (repeated) practice of same task to improve performance
  - Use variable practice (serial or random practice order) of related skills to increase depth of cognitive processing end retention; may decrease performance initially
  - Use mental practice to improve performance end learning, reduce anxiety
- Assess, modify arousal levels as appropriate.
  - High or low arousal impairs performance and learning
  - Avoid stressors, mental fatigue
- Structure environment
  - Reduce extraneous environmental stimuli and distracters to ensure attention and concentration
  - Emphasize closed skills initially, gradually progressing to open skills

ASSOCIATED STAGE CHARACTERISTICS

- The learner practices movements, refines motor programs: spatial and temporal organization; decreases errors, extraneous movements
- Dependence on visual feedback decreases. Increases for use of proprioceptive feedback; cognitive monitoring decreases
- *"How to do"* decisions

TRAINING STRATEGIES

- Select appropriate feedback
  - Continue to provide KP; intervene when errors become consistent
  - Emphasize proprioceptive feedback, "feel of movement" to assist in establishing an internal reference of correctness
  - Continue to provide KR; stress relevance of functional outcomes
  - Assist learner to improve self-evaluation, decision-making skills
  - Facilitation techniques, guided movements may be counterproductive during this stage of learning
- Organize feedback schedule
  - Continue to provide feedback for continuing motivation; encourage patient to self-assess achievements
  - Avoid excessive augmented feedback
  - Focus on use of variable feedback (summed, fading, bandwidth) designs to improve retention
- Organize practice
  - Encourage consistency of performance
  - Focus on variable practice order (serial or random) of related skills to improve retention
- Structure environment
  - Progress toward open, changing environment
  - Prepare the learner for home, community, work environments

AUTONOMOUS STAGE CHARACTERISTICS

- The learner practices movements, continues to refine motor responses, spatial and temporal highly organized, movements are largely error-free, minimal level of cognitive monitoring
- *"How to succeed"* decision

TRAINING STRATEGIES

- Assesses need for conscious attention, automaticity of movements
- Select appropriate feedback
  - Learner demonstrates appropriate self-evaluation, decision-making skills
  - Provide occasional feedback (KP, KR) when errors evident
- Organize practice
  - Stress consistency of performance in variable environments, variations of tasks (open skills)
- High levels of practice (massed practice) are appropriate
- Structure environment
  - Vary environments to challenge learner
  - Ready the learner for home, community, work environments,
- Focus on competitive aspects of skills as appropriate, e.g., wheelchair sports

O'Sullivan, S., & Schmiz, T. (2007). *Physical rehabilitation* (5th ed.). Philadelphia: F.A. Davis Company. Reprinted with permission.

Table 12-2

Comparison of Key Treatment Strategies Used in the Traditional Sensorimotor Approaches

KEY TREATMENT STRATEGIES	ROOD APPROACH	BRUNNSTROM APPROACH (MOVEMENT THERAPY)	PROPRIOCEPTIVE NEUROMUSCULAR APPROACH	NEURODEVELOPMENTAL TREATMENT
Sensory stimulation used to evoke a motor response	YES (Uses direct application of sensory stimuli to muscles and joints)	YES (Movement occurs in response to sensory stimuli)	YES (Tactile, auditory, visual sensory stimuli promote motor responses)	YES (Abnormal muscle tone occurs, in part, because of abnormal sensory experiences)
Reflexive movement used as a precursor for volitional movement	YES (Reflexive movement achieved initially through the application of sensory stimuli)	YES (Move patient along a continuum of reflexive to volitional movement patterns)	YES (Volitional movements can be assisted by reflexive supported postures)	NO
Treatment directed toward influencing muscle tone	YES (Sensory stimuli used to inhibit or facilitate tone)	YES (Postures, sensory stimuli used to inhibit or facilitate tone)	YES (Movement patterns used to normalize tone)	YES (Handling techniques and postures can inhibit or facilitate muscle tone)
Developmental patterns/sequences used for the development of motor skills	YES (Ontogenic motor patterns used to develop motor skills)	YES (Flexion and extension synergies; proximal to distal return)	YES (Patterns used to facilitate proximal to distal motor control)	YES
Conscious attention is directed toward movement	NO	YES	YES	YES
Treatment directly emphasizes development of skilled movements for task performance	NO	NO	NO	YES

Schultz-Krohn, W., Pope-Davis, S., Jourdain, J., & McLaughlin-Gray, J. (2006). Traditional sensorimotor approaches to intervention. In W. Schultz-Krohn & H. Pendelton (Eds.), *Pedretti's occupational therapy: Practice skills for physical dysfunction*, 6th ed. (p. 733). St. Louis: Elsevier Science/Mosby. Reprinted with permission.

Neurodevelopmental Treatment (NDT)/The Bobath Technique

1. Principles/assumptions.
    a. Normalization of postural and limb tone is prerequisite to normal movement.
        (1) Tone abnormalities include flaccidity (low tone) or spasticity (high tone).
    b. Avoidance of movements and activities that increase tone.
    c. Inhibition of primitive reflexes and abnormal postural and limb movements.
    d. Development of normal patterns of posture and movement.
    e. Improvement of the quality of movement and performance of the involved side.
    f. Associated reactions (nonfunctional and involuntary changes in the uninvolved limb position and tone) should be avoided.
    g. Postural reactions are considered the basis for control of movement.
        (1) These reactions include righting, equilibrium, and protective responses.
    h. Loss of postural control results in overuse of the sound side and limits functional movements.
    i. The stereotypical patterns of the trunk and limbs observed in persons with CNS dysfunction are viewed as abnormal patterns of motor coordination.
    j. Focus is on improving the quality of movement.
        (1) Normalization of movement patterns.
        (2) Integration of both sides of the body/reestablishment of symmetry of the sides of the body to increase functional use.
        (3) Establishment of the ability to weight bear and weight shift through the limbs.
        (4) Establishment of normal righting and equilibrium patterns.
    k. Handling is the primary intervention to promote normal movement.

Proprioceptive Neuromuscular Facilitation (PNF)

1. Principles/assumptions.
   a. The response of the neuromuscular mechanisms can be hastened through stimulation of the proprioceptors.
      (1) Utilized for neurologic and orthopedic populations throughout the lifespan.
   b. Techniques are superimposed on patterns of movement (diagonals) and posture, focusing on sensory stimulation from manual contacts, visual cues, and verbal commands.
   c. Normal motor development proceeds in a cervicocaudal and proximodistal direction.
   d. Early motor behavior is dominated by reflex activity.
      (1) Mature motor behavior is supported or reinforced by postural reflexes that are integrated throughout the lifespan.
   e. Early motor behavior is characterized by spontaneous movement, which oscillates between extremes of flexion and extension.
      (1) These movements are rhythmic and reversing in character.
   f. Developing motor behavior is expressed in an orderly sequence of total patterns of movement and posture.
   g. In development, there are shifts between flexor and extensor dominance.
   h. Locomotion depends on reciprocal contraction of flexors and extensors.
   i. The maintenance of posture requires continual adjustment for nuances of imbalance.
   j. Frequency of stimulation and repetitive activity are used to promote and retain motor learning and to develop strength and endurance.
   k. Goal-directed activities coupled with techniques of facilitation are used to hasten learning of total patterns of walking and self-care activities.
   l. Goal-directed activity is made up of reversing movements.
   m. Diagonal patterns or mass movement patterns are utilized during functional activities.
      (1) All patterns cross midline and encourage rotary components to movement.
      (2) Upper-extremity patterns are identified as D1 or D2, flexion or extension.
         (a) D1 flexion.
            - Scapula: abducted and upwardly rotated.
            - Shoulder: flexed, adducted, externally rotated.
            - Elbow: slightly flexed.
            - Forearm: supinated.
            - Wrist: flexed toward radial side.
            - Fingers: flexed, adducted.
            - Thumb: flexed, adducted.
         (b) D1 extension.
            - Scapula: adducted, downwardly rotated.
            - Shoulder: extended, abducted, internally rotated.
            - Elbow: extended.
            - Forearm: pronated.
            - Wrist: extended toward ulnar side.
            - Fingers: extended, abducted.
            - Thumb: extended, abducted.
         (c) D2 flexion.
            - Scapula: adducted and upwardly rotated.
            - Shoulder: flexed, abducted, externally rotated.
            - Elbow: extended.
            - Forearm: supinated.
            - Wrist: extended toward radial side.
            - Fingers: extended, abducted.
            - Thumb: extended, abducted.
         (d) D2 extension.
            - Scapula: abducted and downwardly rotated.
            - Shoulder: extended, adducted, internally rotated.
            - Elbow: towards flexion.
            - Forearm: pronated.
            - Wrist: flexed toward ulnar side.
            - Fingers: flexed, adducted.
            - Thumb: flexed, abducted, opposed.

Brunnstrom's Movement Therapy

1. Principles/assumptions.
   a. Brunnstrom's approach focused on facilitating recovery through a specific sequence.
   b. Treatment is focused on the promotion of movement from reflexive to volitional.
      (1) Seven stages of motor recovery following the onset of hemiplegia that the individual progresses through in a stereotypical fashion were identified by Brunnstrom.
      (2) This recovery pattern includes the identification of developing synergies.

Margaret Rood's Approach

1. Principles/assumptions.
   a. Sensorimotor control is developmentally based.
      (1) Treatment must begin at the person's current level and progress sequentially.

b. Rood proposed four sequential phases of motor control.
     (1) Reciprocal inhibition/innervation.
         (a) An early mobility pattern that is primarily a reflex governed by spinal and supraspinal centers.
     (2) Cocontraction.
         (a) Defined as a simultaneous contraction of the agonist and antagonist that provides stability in a static pattern.
         (b) Utilized to hold a position or object for a long duration.
     (3) Heavy work.
         (a) Also termed 'mobility superimposed on stability.'
         (b) In these patterns, the proximal muscles contract and move and the distal segments are fixed.
     (4) Skill.
         (a) Considered the highest level of control and combines stability and mobility.
         (b) These patterns consist of a stabilized proximal segment while the distal segments move in space.
  c. Muscular responses of the agonists, antagonists, and synergists are believed to be reflexively programmed according to a purpose or plan.
  d. Rood described a sequence of motor development termed 'ontogenic motor patterns' that includes eight different patterns in sequence (i.e., supine withdrawal, rollover, prone extension, neck cocontraction, prone on elbows, quadruped, standing, walking).
  e. Rood proposed that the motor response that is achieved is dependent on the type of sensory stimulation that the therapist applies.

> **EXAM HINT:** Understanding the principles and approaches of each neurological frame of reference can help you effectively determine the correct answer to COTA® exam items about working with persons with neurological disorders according to a specific practice model. For example, a correct answer for an exam item about the use of a contemporary task-oriented approach to motor control training would include client engagement in a functional task (e.g., dressing, meal preparation) to help organize motor behavior. A correct answer for an exam item about the use of the NDT approach with a child with hypertonia would include the therapist using handling to promote normal movement and avoiding movements and activities that increase tone.

▶ Evaluation of Motor Control Dysfunction

The Role of the OTA in Evaluation

1. The OTA contributes to the evaluation process with the supervision of the occupational therapist.
2. The OTA can assist with the collection of data for the evaluation once service competency has been established.
3. The level of supervision required will be determined by the OTA's experience and established service competency.
4. The OTA cannot independently evaluate or interpret evaluation results.

> **EXAM HINT:** The evaluation of motor control is integral to the development of intervention plans for persons with neurological disorders of all ages in many OT practice settings across the continuum of care. Thus, the application of knowledge about the following motor control assessments is required to correctly answer NBCOT® Domain 01 exam items (NBCOT®, 2018).

Assessment for Components of Motor Control

1. Abnormal tone is evaluated by the elicitation of velocity-dependent stretch reflexes.
2. Reflex testing.
   a. Utilized to evaluate involuntary stereotyped responses to a particular stimulus.
   b. Responses develop during fetal life and persist through early infancy.
   c. Reflexes may be released after brain injury or not integrated during early development secondary to CNS pathology.
   d. Intensity and quality of the response is monitored.
   e. A response to stimulus is termed 'positive' and no response to stimulus is 'negative.'
   f. The therapist or the OTA notes the highest level of reflex control achieved.
   g. The therapist or the OTA must be aware of the age range that is considered normal for each reflex. Refer to Chapter 5.

h. Intervention is planned to progress individual to an age-appropriate level of reflex hierarchy.
3. Qualitative descriptions of motor control.
   a. Evaluation of motor control should include observations of the quality of movement during performance of functional tasks.
   b. Examples of motor control issues resulting in observable poor quality of movement.
      (1) Intention tremor is the worsening of action tremor as the limb approaches a target in space.
      (2) Dysmetria is the undershooting (hypometria) or overshooting (hypermetria) of a target.
      (3) Dyssynergia is a breakdown in movement resulting in joints being moved separately to reach a desired target as opposed to moving in a smooth trajectory; decomposition of movement.
      (4) Dysdiadochokinesia is impaired ability to perform rapid alternating movements.
      (5) Ataxia is loss of motor control including tremors, dysdiadochokinesia, dyssynergia, and visual nystagmus.
      (6) Resting tremor is an involuntary tremor noted in resting postures.
      (7) Rigidity is an increased resistance to passive movement throughout the range; may be cogwheel (alternative contraction/relaxation of muscles being stretched) or lead pipe (consistent contraction throughout range).
      (8) Bradykinesia is an overall slowing of movement patterns.
      (9) Akinesia is the inability to initiate movements.
      (10) Athetosis is a dyskinetic condition that includes inadequate timing, force, and accuracy of movements in the trunk/limbs; movements are writhing and worm-like.
      (11) Dystonia is an involuntary, sustained, distorted movement or posture involving contraction of groups of muscles.
      (12) Chorea consists of involuntary movements of the face and extremities, which are spasmodic and of short duration.
      (13) Hemiballismus is a unilateral chorea characterized by violent, forceful movements of the proximal muscles.

> **EXAM HINT:** Understanding how the previously mentioned qualitative motor control issues can impact function can help you correctly answer COTA® exam items about the best approach to use to enable occupational performance for persons with impaired movement. For example, it may be helpful to teach a person with dysdiadochokinesia to move slower during daily living tasks.

4. Assessment for glenohumeral joint subluxation.
   a. Allow the person's arm to dangle into gravity.
   b. Palpate the space underneath the acromion process with your index finger.
   c. Compare to the intact side and document the width of the space in terms of finger breadths.

Orthotic/Splinting Interventions for Neuromotor Dysfunction

The Role of the OTA in Intervention

1. The occupational therapist/OTA team must carefully assess for most appropriate splint.
2. The occupational therapist must set splinting goals.
3. Experienced OTAs can fabricate static splints and assist with dynamic splints upon establishment of service competency.

Purposes of Orthoses/Splints

1. Orthoses may be utilized in the population with neuromuscular dysfunction to meet the following goals.
   a. Prevent/correct deformity via prolonged stretch and proper alignment.
   b. Control spasticity by aligning joints and providing prolonged stretch to spastic muscles.
   c. Prevent/decrease/accommodate contractures of the joint or soft tissue.
   d. Correct biomechanical malalignment by external force.
   e. Position the hand in a functional posture to promote engagement in activities.
   f. Compensate for weakness to allow intact muscle groups to function.
   g. Provide proximal support.
   h. Support a painful joint.
   i. Promote distal mobility.
   j. Enhance a specific activity, e.g., fabrication of a typing or writing splint or utilization of a cock-up splint for feeding.
   k. Immobilize joints and soft tissues to promote healing.
   l. Prevent or reduce scarring via prolonged pressure and appropriate stretch.

Types of Orthoses/Splints

> **EXAM HINT:** The NBCOT® exam outline for the COTA® identifies knowledge of the "types and functions of immobilization, mobilization, restriction, and non-articular orthoses for managing specific conditions" (NBCOT®, 2018, p. 26) as essential for competent practice. The application of knowledge about the following splints and orthoses can help you determine the correct answer for COTA® exam items about the implementation of orthotic/splinting interventions.

1. Splint classification.
   a. Static (no moving parts) splints are utilized for external support, prevention of motion, stretching of contractures, aligning joints for healing, resting joints, or reducing pain.
   b. Dynamic (moving parts are included) splints have a resilient component (elastic bands or spring) and are utilized to increase passive motion, assist weak motions, or substitute for lost motion.
   c. Serial splints are utilized to achieve a slow, progressive increase in motion by progressive remolding.
2. Hand/wrist-based splints may be dorsal or volar.
   a. Cock-up splints.
      (1) Supports the wrist in 10–20 degrees of extension to prevent contracture.
      (2) Allows the digits to function (e.g., to support flaccid wrist).
   b. Resting hand splint.
      (1) Utilized for persons who need to have their wrist, digits, and thumb supported in a functional position for prolonged periods (i.e., when developing contracture of the long flexors).
   c. Opponens splints.
      (1) May be short or long.
      (2) Designed to support the thumb in a position of abduction and opposition.
      (3) Utilized during functional activities to compensate for weakness patterns.
3. Types of inhibitory/tone normalizing orthoses.
   a. Based on the neurophysiologic frames of reference.
   b. Bobath finger spreader (abduction splint).
      (1) Based on Bobath's principle of reflex inhibiting patterns.
      (2) This soft splint positions the digits and thumb in abduction in an effort to reduce tone.
   c. Rood cone.
      (1) Based on Rood's inhibitory principles of sustained deep pressure.
      (2) This cone-shaped splint is utilized to reduce flexor spasticity in the hand.
   d. Orthokinetic splints.
      (1) This type of splint utilizes tactile input (e.g., via elastic bandages) to facilitate and/or inhibit appropriate muscle groups.
   e. Spasticity reduction splint.
      (1) This splint places the spastic distal extremity on submaximal stretch to reduce spasticity.
4. Types of supportive orthoses.
   a. Overhead suspension sling.
      (1) This orthotic device incorporates an arm support that is supported by a sling and suspended by an overhead rod.
      (2) Persons presenting with proximal weakness (amyotrophic lateral sclerosis, Guillain-Barré syndrome, muscular dystrophy) with muscle grades in the 1/5 to 3/5 range are appropriate candidates.
   b. Balanced forearm orthoses (mobile arm supports or ball-bearing forearm orthoses).
      (1) Consists of an arm trough, proximal and distal arms, and a support bracket.
      (2) Allows a person with weak proximal musculature to utilize available control of the trunk and shoulder to engage in functional tasks.
   c. Shoulder slings.
      (1) Utilized to support a flaccid arm after neurologic insult for short and controlled periods of time.
      (2) Long-term use may be detrimental in terms of soft-tissue contracture, edema, and the development of pain syndromes.
   d. Supports may be utilized on a wheelchair to position a flaccid arm (e.g., lapboards, arm troughs, etc.).

> **RED FLAG:** Avoid traction injuries to a flaccid shoulder during upright activities; lack of adequate support (e.g., shoulder sling, manual support) can cause development of a painful shoulder. Avoid use of overhead pulleys in persons with poor shoulder alignment and poor shoulder function. These can cause the development of a painful shoulder.

Splinting Implementation and Training

1. Wearing schedules must be prescribed to enhance the function of the splint.
   a. Splints that are utilized to decrease spasticity or reverse contractures require longer wearing times.

2. Splints must be monitored for pressure over bony prominences.

> **RED FLAG:** The ability of persons to effectively self-monitor the use of their splints/orthoses can be hindered by diminished sensation (e.g., hypoesthesia), impaired cognitive-perceptual skills (e.g., unilateral neglect), and/or impaired neurovascular status (e.g., diabetic neuropathy).
>
> Consequently, caregiver education about the splint/orthosis wearing schedule, application, and management is required.

3. Train the individual and/or caregivers in donning/doffing procedures.
4. Instruct the person and and/or caregivers about the purposes, functions, and limitations of the splint/orthosis to ensure acceptance of the splint/orthosis and enhance its effective use during functional activities.
5. Reassess the fit, function, and construction of the splint/orthosis at periodic intervals.
6. Assess the person's habitual use of the splint/orthosis and address any issues that hinder use.
7. Teach the person and/or caregivers procedures for routine maintenance of the splint/orthosis.
8. All splint and orthotic training should be documented.
9. Refer to Chapter 11 for additional splinting information.

> **EXAM HINT:** The NBCOT® exam outline for the COTA® identifies knowledge of "training methods regarding the safe and effective use of orthotic . . . devices consistent with the client's prioritized needs, goals, and task demands in order to optimize or enhance function" (NBCOT®, 2018, p. 26) as essential for competent practice. The application of knowledge about the client and caregiver training and education described above can help you determine a correct answer to exam items about orthotic/splinting interventions.

Oral Motor Dysfunction

Presenting Characteristics

1. May result in speech impairments (dysarthria), swallowing impairments (dysphagia), or psychosocial stresses related to facial asymmetry and/or drooling.

Role of the OTA in Intervention

1. The OTA implements intervention with the supervision of the occupational therapist.
2. The level of supervision required depends upon the OTA's experience and established service competency.
3. During the implementation of intervention, the OTA informs the supervising therapist of any change in the individual's status and any other relevant information that may affect treatment.

Intervention

> **EXAM HINT:** The NBCOT® exam outline for the COTA® identifies knowledge of the "technical level intervention strategies and techniques used to facilitate oral motor skills for drinking, eating, and swallowing consistent with developmental level, client condition, caregiver interaction, and mealtime environment and context" (NBCOT®, 2018, p. 25) as essential for competent practice. The application of knowledge about the following direct and indirect oral motor interventions can help you determine the correct answer for exam items about working with persons with oral motor dysfunction.

1. Direct intervention involves techniques that utilize a bolus.
    a. Modification of consistency, amount, and pacing of solids and liquids.

b. Utilizing postural interventions to increase swallowing efficiency during meals.
      (1) Chin tuck.
      (2) Head tilt.
      (3) Head turn.
   c. Utilizing specific swallowing adaptations.
      (1) Supraglottic swallow technique to voluntarily close/protect the airway during food intake.
      (2) Mendelsohn's maneuver (voluntarily prolonging the rise of the larynx by prolonging tongue contraction).
2. Indirect intervention involves procedures that do not include use of a bolus.
   a. Thermal (cold) stimulation provides sensory input to the inferior faucial arches via a chilled dental examination mirror to elicit a swallow reflex.
   b. Reflex facilitation.
   c. Strengthening, facilitation, and coordination of oral movements.
   d. Airway adduction procedures.
   e. Positioning to maintain the trunk/head/neck in correct postures.
3. See Chapter 5 for information about oral motor development and interventions for pediatric disorders and Chapter 9 for further information on dysphagia and swallowing disorders.

Limb and Postural Control Impairments

Overview of Constraint Induced Movement Therapy (CIMT)

1. A task-oriented approach that utilizes CIMT for those who present with control of the wrist and digit can be used.
2. Current and past protocols have used the following motor control inclusion criteria for the more affected side.
   a. 20° of extension of the wrist and 10° of extension of each finger.
   b. 10° extension of the wrist, 10° abduction of the thumb, and 10° extension of any two other digits.
   c. Able to lift a washrag off a tabletop using any type of prehension and then release it.

EXAM HINT: The NBCOT® exam outline for the COTA® identifies implementing "interventions for improving . . . postural control . . . in order to support occupational performance (NBCOT®, 2018, p. 26) as an essential task for competent practice. The application of knowledge about the previously described contemporary task-oriented approaches to motor control training and the following CIMT intervention guidelines can help you determine the correct answer for NBCOT® Domain 02 exam items about intervention implementation for persons with postural control impairments.

CIMT Intervention Guidelines

1. Massed practice and shaping of the affected limb during repetitive functional activities is the main focus of therapeutic intervention.
   a. In addition, the less affected upper extremity is constrained via a splint, sling, or glove to remind the person who is undergoing the intervention to utilize the more affected side throughout the day and in therapy.
      (1) In essence, intervention is designed to "force use" of the more affected side.
2. An environment that utilizes the common challenges of everyday life is created by the therapist.
   a. In this environment, the practicing of functional tasks or close simulations that have been identified as important by participants is used to find effective and efficient strategies for performance.
3. Opportunities for practice outside of therapy time (e.g., homework assignments, circuit training, etc.) are provided.
4. Adaptations to the environment, task modifications, assistive technology, and/or a reduction in the effects of gravity are used to enhance occupational performance.
5. Contemporary motor learning principles are used to train or retrain skills. These include the following approaches.
   a. Using random and variable practice within natural contexts in treatment.
   b. Providing decreasing amounts of physical and verbal guidance.
   c. Helping the client develop problem-solving skills so that they can find their own solutions to occupational performance problems.
6. For persons with poor control of movement (e.g., incoordination, tremor, ataxia, dysmetria, etc.), the degrees of freedom are constrained to enhance performance.

The Ayres Sensory Integration® Approach for Sensory Processing Disorders[1]

Overview

1. A sensory integrative approach to view the neural organization of sensory information for an adaptive response.
2. The sensory integration frame of reference was developed by Jean A. Ayres.

> **EXAM HINT:** The NBCOT® exam outline for the COTA® identifies knowledge of the "influence of theoretical approaches, models of practice, and frames of reference on information-gathering and the intervention process" (NBCOT®, 2018, p. 22) as essential for competent practice. The application of knowledge about Ayres sensory integration approach is required to correctly answer NBCOT® Domain 01 exam items about working with persons with sensory processing disorders.

Principles/Assumptions of Ayres Sensory Integration® Approach

1. Neuroplasticity (structural changes) of the CNS allows for its modification.
2. Sensory integration occurs in a developmentally sequential manner.
3. Higher cortical-processing functions are dependent on adequate processing and organization of sensory stimuli by lower brain centers.
4. Adequate modulation of sensory stimuli must occur for an adaptive response to occur.
    a. Sensory stimuli can be either facilitatory or inhibitory, and each sensory system influences other sensory systems.
5. Adaptive responses facilitate the integration of sensory stimuli.
6. Individuals seek out sensorimotor experiences that have an organizing effect.

Evaluation of Sensory Processing Disorders

1. Role of the OTA.
    a. The OTA contributes to the evaluation process with the supervision of the occupational therapist.
    b. The OTA can assist with the collection of data for the evaluation once service competency has been established.
    c. The level of supervision required will be determined by the OTA's experience and established service competency.
    d. The OTA cannot independently evaluate or interpret evaluation results.

Intervention

1. Role of the OTA.
    a. The OTA implements intervention with supervision from the occupational therapist.
    b. The level of supervision required depends upon the OTA's experience and established service competency.
    c. During the implementation of intervention, the OTA informs the supervising therapist of any change in the individual's status and any other relevant information that may affect treatment.
2. Intervention follows the general principles of Ayres Sensory Integration Approach® theory. With the supervision of the occupational therapist, the OTA:
    a. Controls sensory input that is child-driven and play-based to improve sensory processing, facilitate sensory integration, and elicit an adaptive response.
    b. Creates an environment to facilitate active participation for the 'just right challenge.'
    c. Ensures registration of meaningful sensory input to obtain an adaptive response.
    d. Balances structure and freedom, tapping into the child's inner drive to obtain neural organization.
    e. Gradually introduces activities requiring more mature and complex patterns of behaviors.
    f. Promotes organized adaptive responses to enhance a child's general behavioral organization, including socialization.

> **EXAM HINT:** In the NBCOT® exam outline for the COTA®, knowledge of "intervention methods and activities to support optimal sensory arousal . . . for supporting engagement in occupations" (NBCOT®, 2018, p. 25) is identified as essential for competent practice. Thus, the application of the above general sensory integration intervention principles and the following deficit-specific intervention principles can help you determine the correct answer for COTA® exam items about this practice area.

---

[1] Jan Garbarini and Marge Mofffet Boyd contributed this section on Ayres Sensory Integration® approach.

3. Intervention principles for specific sensory processing deficits are followed.
   a. With the supervision of the occupational therapist, the OTA generally grades for the appropriate combination of the type of movement, rate of movement, and for the amount of proprioceptive resistance, while adhering to the precautions (e.g., autonomic nervous system responses).
      (1) Firm pressure and resistance is less threatening than light touch; see subsequent proprioceptive section.
      (2) Linear movement is less threatening than angular; see subsequent vestibular section.
      (3) Slow movement is less threatening than rapid movement; see subsequent vestibular section.
   b. A combination of stimuli must be used to elicit an adaptive response and for effective intervention.
      (1) This combination is a starting point for children with severe processing deficits.
   c. The therapist closely observes child's responses and adheres to all precautions
   d. Interventions for tactile deficits.
      (1) Tactile modulation for tactile defensiveness and hypersensitivity/overresponsivity and hyposensitivity/underresponsivity and sensory seeking.
         (a) Self-applied stimuli are more tolerable than passive application of tactile stimuli.
         (b) Provide firm pressure while making sure that the child can see the source of the stimuli that is being applied.
            - Firm pressure tends to be calming, while light touch can be perceived as aversive.
            - The face, abdomen, and palmar surfaces of the extremities are particularly sensitive to light touch.
         (c) Provide controlled sensory activities that simultaneously provide tactile and vestibular-proprioceptive information.
         (d) Begin with slow linear movements and deep touch-pressure.
         (e) Apply tactile stimuli in the direction of hair growth, which is less aversive.
         (f) Follow tactile stimuli with joint compression.
         (g) Monitor and adjust stimuli that seem to influence modulation of sensation (e.g., lighting, sound, etc.).

> **CAUTION:** Be alert and assess the child's behavioral responses up to a few hours following treatment when negative impacts may still be demonstrated.

         (h) Tactile defensiveness and sensory seeking can be reduced if the treatment approach is effective.
      (2) Tactile discrimination.
         (a) Provide deep-touch pressure to the hands as well as the body.
         (b) Deficits in tactile discrimination are rarely seen in isolation, and somatodyspraxia is typically seen; therefore, treatment for tactile discrimination is usually performed simultaneously when providing treatment for deficits in motor planning.
         (c) Provide graded activities requiring tactile discrimination using a mixture of textures and items (e.g., rice, sand).
   e. Intervention for proprioception deficits.
      (1) Deficits in modulation demonstrated by overresponsivity, underresponsivity, and sensory seeking.
         (a) Provide firm touch, pressure, joint compression or traction.
         (b) Provide resistance to active movement to help the child learn the appropriate amount of force to perform tasks.
         (c) Provide activities in various body positions combining vestibular proprioceptive information (e.g., yoga).
         (d) Provide slow linear movement, resistance, and deep pressure.
         (e) Use adaptive techniques (e.g., weighted vests).
      (2) Discrimination deficits.
         (a) Provide treatment as noted above.
         (b) Provide activities requiring the child to demonstrate the ability to grade the force or efforts of movement.
   f. Intervention for vestibular deficits.
      (1) Deficits in modulation of vestibular input include underresponsivity, overresponsivity, hypersensitivity (aversion response), sensory seeking, and gravitational insecurity (fear response).
         (a) Grade for type and rate of movement, and for the amount of resistance.
            - Precautions must be observed.
         (b) Slowly introduce linear movement with touch pressure in prone and provide resistance to active movements, especially for gravitational insecurity.
         (c) Use linear vestibular stimuli to increase awareness of spatial orientation (otolith organ).
         (d) Provide rapid rotary and angular movements with frequent starts/stops and acceleration/deceleration to increase ability to distinguish the pace of movement (semicircular canals).

4. Special advanced training and knowledge of the effects of various sensory stimuli is required.

> **CAUTION:** All occupational therapy practitioners, including OTAs, must be well aware of precautions for movements, as their impact may not be apparent for several hours. The OTA should continually ask how the child is feeling, and observe for signs involving the autonomic nervous system such as pupil dilation, sweaty palms, changes in the rate of respiration.

5. Provide interventions to develop compensatory skills (e.g., environmental adaptations, hand-writing supports).
6. Reduce environmental barriers and identify facilitators of occupational performance.
   a. Provide a safe physical and emotionally supportive environment for the child.
7. Use group treatment to develop the social interaction skills needed for improved occupational performance in a classroom with peer groups and in afterschool programs.
8. Consult with and/or educate teachers and parents.
9. Share intervention strategies to promote the child's occupational performance in the home, school, and community.

Cognitive-Perceptual Approaches

Overview of Cognitive-Perceptual Terminology and Symptoms

1. Perception.
   a. The integration/interpretation of sensory impressions received from the environment into psychologically meaningful information.
2. Cognition.
   a. The ability of the brain to process, store, retrieve, and manipulate information. It involves the skills of understanding and knowing, the ability to judge and make decisions, and an overall environmental awareness.
3. Cognitive-perceptual deficits.
   a. Occur as a result of multiple pathologies, including cerebrovascular accident (CVA), traumatic brain injury (TBI), neoplasms, acquired diseases, psychiatric disorders, etc.
4. Functional impairments.
   a. Acalculia.
      (1) The inability to perform calculations.
      (2) Example: inability to calculate change at a grocery store.
   b. Agraphia.
      (1) The inability to write.
      (2) Example: not able to sign name despite previously knowing how to write.
   c. Impaired alertness or arousal.
      (1) The person has a decreased response to environmental stimuli.
      (2) Example: the person needs tactile or verbal cues to stay awake during an evaluation.
   d. Alexia.
      (1) The inability to read.
      (2) Example: not able to read a menu despite being literate.
   e. Anomia.
      (1) Loss of the ability to name objects or retrieve names of people.
      (2) Example: the person is not able to name an apple but knows what it is and what to do with it.
   f. Anosognosia.
      (1) An unawareness of a motor deficit.
      (2) May be related to a lack of insight regarding disabilities.
      (3) Example: a person is not aware that they have hemiplegia.
   g. Aphasia
      (1) Broca's (expressive) aphasia: loss of expressive language indicated by a loss of speech production.
         (a) Example: the person presents with non-fluent speech.
      (2) Wernicke's (receptive) aphasia: a deficit in auditory comprehension that affects semantic speech performance, manifested in paraphasia or nonsensical syllables.
         (a) Example. The person is not able to comprehend verbal directions for using an adaptive device; cannot follow verbal commands.
      (3) Global aphasia: a severe loss of the ability to comprehend and express.
   h. Apraxia
      (1) Ideational apraxia: a breakdown in the knowledge of what is to be done or how to perform; a lack of knowledge regarding object use.

(a) The neuronal model about the concept of how to perform is lost, although the sensorimotor system may be intact.
(b) Examples: using a comb to brush teeth; placing butter into a cup of coffee.
(2) Motor apraxia/ideomotor apraxia: loss of access to kinesthetic memory so that purposeful movement cannot be achieved because of ineffective motor planning, although sensation, movement, and coordination are intact.
(a) The person is unable to perform a task upon request but may perform the task spontaneously.
(b) Examples: awkward grasp patterns on toothbrush making oral care ineffective; difficulty manipulating coins from the hand into a vending machine coin slot.
i. Astereognosis, also known as tactile agnosia.
(1) The inability to recognize objects, forms, shapes, and sizes by touch alone.
(2) A failure of tactile recognition although sensory testing (tactile and proprioceptive) is intact.
(3) Example: the person cannot recognize that the object in their hand is a quarter without looking at it.
j. Impaired attention.
(1) An inability to attend to or focus on specific stimuli.
(2) May result in distraction by irrelevant stimuli.
(3) Includes difficulty with sustained attention and selective attention in addition to dividing and alternating/switching attention.
(4) Example: background noise (e.g., a television) distracts the person from the task at hand; the person cannot attend to more than one task at a time.
k. Body scheme disorders.
(1) Loss of awareness of body parts, as well as the relationship of the body parts to each other and objects; includes the following.
(a) Right-left indiscrimination: inability to discriminate between the right and left sides of the body or to apply the concepts of right and left to the environment.
  • Examples: the person cannot determine which is their left arm; the person is not able to successfully use the cue "the bathroom is on the right."
(b) Somatoagnosia: a body scheme disorder that results in diminished awareness of body structure and a failure to recognize body parts as one's own.
  • Examples: the person denies ownership of a body part; the person attempts to dress the therapist's arm as if it was their own.

(c) Unilateral body neglect: failure to respond to or report unilateral stimulus presented to the body side contralateral to the lesion.
  • Examples: the person spends 75% of the time brushing the right side of their hair and 25% on the left; the person only applies shaving cream to the right side of the face.
l. Disorientation.
(1) Lack of knowledge of person, place, and time.
(2) Example. the person states that it is March 8 despite it being March 25.
m. Figure/ground dysfunction.
(1) An inability to distinguish foreground from background.
(2) Example: the person has difficulty locating a white bar of soap on a white sink; the person has difficulty finding a key in a cluttered drawer.
n. Memory loss.
(1) Long-term memory loss.
(a) Lack of storage, consolidation, and retention of information that has passed through working memory.
(b) Includes the inability to retrieve this information.
(c) Example: the person is unable to remember phone number, address, or place of birth
(2) Short-term memory loss.
(a) Lack of registration and temporary storing of information received by various sensory modalities.
(b) Includes the loss of working memory.
(c) Examples: the person is not able to remember the instructions given for a self-care routine; the person is not able to remember the therapist's name in the middle of an evaluation.
o. Impaired organization/sequencing.
(1) The inability to organize thoughts with activity steps properly sequenced.
(2) Examples: the person dons their shoes and socks before pants; the person pours laundry detergent into washing machine after rinse cycle.
p. Perseveration.
(1) The continuation or repetition of a motor act (premotor perseveration) or task (prefrontal perseveration).
(2) Example: the person continues to pull up a sock even though it is already covering the foot.
q. Impaired problem solving.
(1) The inability to manipulate a fund of knowledge and apply this information to new or unfamiliar situations.

(2) Example: the person is not able to figure out why the wheelchair keeps moving on an incline and attempts to stand.
r. Spatial relations impairment.
  (1) Difficulty relating objects to each other or to the self-secondary to a loss of spatial concepts (e.g., up/down, front/back, under/over, etc.).
  (2) Example: the person has difficulty orienting clothing to the body correctly such as putting a shirt on backwards; the person has difficulty aligning fitted sheets to the bed.
s. Topographical disorientation.
  (1) Difficulty finding one's way in space secondary to memory dysfunction or an inability to interpret sensory stimuli.
  (2) Example: the person is not able to find their hospital room after completing an OT session; after completing an errand the person tends to wander and not find their way back home.
t. Unilateral spatial neglect.
  (1) Inattention to, or neglect of, stimuli presented in the extra-personal space contralateral to the lesion. This can include near and/or far extra-personal space.
  (2) May occur independently of visual deficits.
  (3) Example: the person is not able to locate a clock on the left wall of a room; the person asks for silverware which is already placed on the left side of the plate.

EXAM HINT: Understanding how the above cognitive-perceptual deficits can impact function can help you correctly answer COTA® exam items about the best approach to use to enable occupational performance for persons with cognitive-perceptual impairments. For example, it may be helpful to train a person with unilateral spatial neglect to utilize visual scanning strategies to increase attention to the left environment.

5. Visual foundation skills.
  a. These skills must be evaluated to differentiate perceptual dysfunction and visual system deficits. For example, one cannot accurately assess figure-ground if a person's visual acuity is poor and not compensated.
    (1) Visual acuity.
      (a) The clarity of vision both near and far.
    (2) Visual fields.
      (a) The available vision to the right, left, superior, and inferior.
      (b) An example of field loss is left homonymous hemianopsia (the left temporal field and right nasal field are affected).
    (3) Oculomotor function.
      (a) Control of eye movements.
    (4) Scanning.
      (a) Ability to systematically observe and locate items in the environment.

Cognitive-Perceptual Evaluation

1. Role of the OTA.
  a. The OTA contributes to the evaluation process with the supervision of the occupational therapist.
  b. The OTA can assist with the collection of data for the evaluation once service competency has been established.
  c. The level of supervision required will be determined by the OTA's experience and established service competency.
  d. The OTA cannot independently evaluate or interpret evaluation results.

Cognitive-Perceptual Intervention

1. Role of the OTA.
  a. The OTA implements intervention with supervision of the occupational therapist.
  b. The level of supervision required depends upon the OTA's experience and established service competency.
  c. During the implementation of intervention, the OTA informs the supervising therapist of any change in the individual's status and any other relevant information that may affect treatment.

EXAM HINT: in the NBCOT® exam outline for the COTA®, Domain 02 Selecting and Implementing Intervention comprises 55% of the COTA® exam (NBCOT®, 2018). Thus, the application of knowledge about the following cognitive-perceptual intervention approaches can help you correctly answer NBCOT® Domain 02 exam items about interventions for persons with cognitive and/or perceptual deficits.

2. Remedial/restorative/transfer of training approach.
  a. Focuses on restoration of components to increase skill.
  b. Deficit specific.
  c. Targets cause of symptoms.
  d. Emphasizes performance components.
  e. Assumes improvements in performance components will result in increased skill.
  f. Assumes the cerebral cortex is malleable and can reorganize.
  g. Utilizes tabletop and computer activities such as memory drills, block designs, parquetry, etc. as treatment modalities.

3. Compensatory/adaptive/functional approach.
   a. Involves repetitive practice of functional tasks.
   b. Emphasizes modification. For example, modifying clothing with Velcro instead of buttons for those with motor apraxia.
   c. Activity choice driven by tasks the person needs, or wants, to perform.
   d. Emphasizes intact skill training.
   e. Treats symptoms, not the cause.
   f. Utilizes techniques of environmental adaptation (e.g., placing a list of morning care activities on the bathroom mirror for those with memory loss or sequencing deficit) and compensatory strategies (e.g., taping lectures in school for those with poor sustained attention).
   g. Treatment is task specific.
   h. Utilizes functional tasks (basic activities of daily living [BADL], instrumental activities of daily living [IADL], work, and leisure tasks) that the individual desires, or is required, to perform at discharge as the basis of treatment.
   i. The use of compensatory cognitive strategies requires a level of awareness of deficits.
   j. Environmental modifications may be caregiver driven.
4. Information-processing approach.
   a. Provides information on how the individual approaches the task.
   b. Investigates how performance changes with cueing.
   c. Standardized cues are given to determine their effect on performance: for example, "Try rereading the recipe" or "Try speaking the steps aloud."
   d. Cues or feedback are utilized to draw attention to relevant features of the task.
   e. Investigative questions (e.g., "Why do you think it took so long to get dressed?" or "Do you know why I had to help you balance the checking account?") are used to provide insight to the underlying deficits.
5. Dynamic interactional approach.
   a. Emphasizes transfer of information from one situation to the next.
   b. Utilizes varying treatment environments.
   c. Practice of a targeted strategy with varied tasks and situations (multicontextual).
   d. Emphasizes metacognitive skills (self-awareness of strengths and deficits) as basis of learning and generalization of learning.
   e. Transfer of learning must be taught from one situation to the next and does not occur automatically.
   f. Transfer of learning occurs through a graded series of tasks that decrease in similarity (e.g., training scanning strategies for a person with a visual neglect to find items in a refrigerator to a less similar task such as scanning to cross the street).
   g. The person's processing abilities and self-monitoring techniques are used to facilitate learning for different tasks or environments.
   h. The therapist or OTA utilizes awareness questioning (e.g., "How do you know this is right?") to help the individual detect errors, estimate task difficulty, and predict outcomes.
6. The quadraphonic approach.
   a. Based on remediation.
   b. Based on information-processing theory and teaching/learning theory.
   c. Micro-perspective includes evaluation of management of performance component subskills such as attention, memory, motor planning, postural control, and problem solving.
   d. Macro-perspective evaluation includes the use of narratives, interview, real-life occupations (shopping, cooking, etc.).
   e. Makes use of several theories.
      (1) Information processing. For example, for those that are minimally responsive after head injury, determine which type of sensory stimulus the person responds to (e.g., loud voice, painful tactile stimulus, various aromas, etc.).
      (2) Teaching/learning evaluation. For example, determining which stage of learning a person is in, determining which environment is most appropriate for treatment (i.e., quiet bedside vs. stimulating OT clinic), and or determining which cues are most effective (e.g., using more visual/gestural cues for those with aphasia).
      (3) Neurodevelopmental evaluation. For example, determining level of postural control, symmetry of movement, mobility, and stability.
      (4) Biomechanical evaluation. For example, determining amount of AROM, endurance, strength, coordination, etc.
7. Neurofunctional approach.
   a. Based on learning theory.
   b. Specifically used for individuals with acquired neurological impairments (e.g., TBI, CVA).
   c. Focuses on retraining real-world skills rather than cognitive-perceptual processes.
   d. Utilizes an overall adaptive approach but incorporates some remediation components.
   e. Treatment is focused on training specific functional skills in true contexts.
8. Cognitive disabilities model.
   a. Originally developed for use with individuals who have psychosocial dysfunction, currently also being utilized with persons with neurologic dysfunction and dementia.
   b. Describes cognitive function on a continuum from level 1 (profoundly impaired) to level 6 (normal).
   c. Each level describes the extent of a person's disability and difficulty in performing occupations.

d. After the person's level has been established, routine tasks are presented that the person can perform or that have been adapted so that they can perform them.
e. Focus is placed on adaptive approaches and strengthening residual abilities.
9. General intervention strategies for specific deficits.
   a. Impaired alertness or arousal.
      (1) Increase environmental stimuli.
      (2) Use gross motor activities.
      (3) Increase sensory stimuli.
   b. Aphasia.
      (1) Decrease external auditory stimuli.
      (2) Give the individual increased response time.
      (3) Use visual cues and gestures.
      (4) Use concise sentences.
      (5) Investigate the use of augmentative communication devices.
   c. Apraxia.
      (1) Motor/ideomotor apraxia.
      (2) Utilize general verbal cues as opposed to specific.
      (3) Decrease manipulation demands.
      (4) Provide hand over hand tactile-kinesthetic input.
      (5) Utilize visual cues.
   d. Ideational apraxia.
      (1) Provide step by step instructions.
      (2) Use hand over hand guiding techniques.
      (3) Provide opportunities for motor planning and motor execution.
   e. Body neglect.
      (1) Provide bilateral activities.
      (2) Guide the affected side through the activity.
      (3) Increase sensory stimulation to the affected side.
   f. Memory loss.
      (1) Use rehearsal strategies.
      (2) 'Chunk' information (e.g., for recalling a phone number, the person could chunk the digits into three groups: first, the area code (such as 123), then a three-digit chunk (456), and, last, a four-digit chunk (7890).
      (3) Utilize memory aids (e.g., smart phones, alarm watches, timers).
      (4) Utilize 'temporal tags,' focusing on when the event to be remembered occurred.
   g. Perseveration.
      (1) Bring perseveration to a conscious level and train the person to inhibit the behavior.
      (2) Redirect attention.
      (3) Engage the individual in tasks that require repetitive action.
   h. Sequencing and organization deficits.
      (1) Use external cues (e.g., written directions, daily planners).
      (2) Grade tasks that are increasingly complex in terms of number of steps required.
   i. Spatial neglect.
      (1) Provide graded scanning activities.
      (2) Grade activities from simple to complex.
      (3) Use anchoring techniques to compensate (e.g., a strip of red tape of placed on the left side of the sink to draw attention to the left hemifield).
      (4) Utilize manipulative tasks in conjunction with scanning activities.
      (5) Use external cues (e.g., colored markers and written directions).
   j. Spatial relations dysfunction.
      (1) Utilize activities that challenge underlying spatial skills (e.g., orienting clothing to your body during dressing, wrapping a gift, making a bed).
      (2) Utilize tasks that require discrimination of right/left (e.g., use cues such as "dress your left arm first" or "the plates are in the right lower cabinets").

> **EXAM HINT:** The NBCOT® exam outline for the COTA® identifies knowledge of "intervention methods and activities to support optimal . . . cognitive, or perceptual processing for supporting engagement in occupations" (NBCOT®, 2018, p. 25 and "compensatory and remedial interventions for managing cognitive and perceptual deficits" (NBCOT®, 2018, p. 25 as essential for competent practice (NBCOT®, 2018, p. 25). Knowing the above intervention strategies can help you determine the correct answer to NBCOT® Domain 02 exam items about intervention management for persons with cognitive-perceptual deficits.

References

American Occupational Therapy Association. (2013). Cognition, cognitive rehabilitation, and occupational performance. *American Journal of Occupational Therapy, 67,* S9–S31. doi:10.5014/ajot.2013.67S9.

Anzalone, M. E., & Lane, S. J. (2012). Sensory processing disorder. In S. J. Lane & A. C. Bundy (Eds.), *Kids can be kids: A childhood occupations approach* (pp. 437–459). Philadelphia: F.A. Davis.

Bundy, A. C., & Murray, E. A. (2002). Sensory integration: A. Jean Ayres' theory revisited. In A. C. Bundy, S. J. Lane, & E. A. Murray (Eds.), *Sensory integration: Theory and practice* (2nd ed., pp. 3–33). Philadelphia, PA: F.A. Davis.

Gillen, G. (2009). *Cognitive and perceptual rehabilitation: Optimizing function.* St. Louis, MO: Elsevier/Mosby.

Gillen, G. (Ed.). (2016). *Stroke rehabilitation: A function-based approach.* (4th ed.). St. Louis, MO: Elsevier/Mosby.

Gutman, S. A., & Schonfeld, A. B. (2009). *Screening adult neurologic populations: A step-by-step instruction manual.* (2nd ed.). Bethesda, MD: AOTA Press.

Katz, N. (2011). *Cognition, occupation, and participation across the lifespan; neuroscience, neurorehabilitation and models of intervention in occupational therapy.* (3rd ed.). Bethesda, MD: AOTA Press.

Katz, N. & Toglia, J.(2018). *Cognition, occupation and participation across the lifespan: Neuroscience, neurorehabilitation, and models for intervention in occupational therapy, 4th ed.* Bethesda, MD: AOTA Press.

Lane, S. J. (2002). Sensory modulation. In A. C. Bundy, S. J. Lane, & E. A. Murray (Eds.), *Sensory integration: Theory and Practice.* (2nd ed., pp. 101–122). Philadelphia: F.A. Davis.

Lane, S. J. (2002). Structure and function of the sensory systems. In A. C. Bundy, S. J. Lane, & E. A. Murray (Eds.), *Sensory integration: Theory and practice.* (2nd ed., pp. 35–70). Philadelphia: F.A. Davis.

Lane, S. J., Smith Roley, S., & Champagne, T. (2014). Sensory integration and processing: Theories and applications to occupational performance. In B. Schell, G. Gillen, & M. E. Scaffa (Eds.), *Willard and Spackman's occupational therapy.* (12th ed., pp. 816–868). Philadelphia: Lippincott Williams & Wilkins.

Miller, L. J. (2007). *Sensational kids hope and help for children with sensory processing disorder (SPD).* New York: G.P. Putnam's Sons.

National Board for Certification in Occupational Therapy (NBCOT®). (2018). *Practice analysis of the certified occupational therapy assistant: Executive summary.* Gaithersburg, MD: Author. Retrieved from https://www.nbcot.org/-/media/NBCOT/PDFs/2017-Practice-Analysis-Executive-COTA.ashx?la=enParham, L. D., & Mailoux, Z. (2005). Sensory integration. In J. Case-Smith (Ed.), *Occupational therapy for children.* (5th ed., pp. 356–409). St. Louis, MO: Elsevier/Mosby.

Schultz-Krohn, W., & Pendleton, H. (Eds.). (2018). *Pedretti's occupational therapy: Practice skills for physical dysfunction.* (8th ed.). St. Louis, MO: Elsevier Science/Mosby.

Shaf, R., & Lane, S. (2009). Neuroscience foundations of vestibular, proprioceptive, and tactile sensory strategies. *Occupational Therapy Practice, 14,* CE1–CE8.

Shumway-Cook, A., & Woollacott, M. H. (2017). *Motor control: Translating research into practical applications.* (5th ed.) Baltimore, MD: Lippincott Williams & Wilkins.

Vining-Radomski, M., & Trombly-Latham, C. A. (2014). *Occupational therapy for physical dysfunction.* (7th ed.). Baltimore, MD: Lippincott Williams & Wilkins.

Review Questions

Neurological and Cognitive-Perceptual Approaches: Evaluation and Intervention

Below are eight questions about key content covered in this chapter. These questions are not inclusive of the entirety of content about occupational therapy neurological and cognitive-perceptual evaluation and intervention approaches that you must know for success on the COTA® exam. These questions are provided to help you jump-start the thought processes you will need to apply your studying of content to the answering of exam questions; hence they are not in the COTA® exam format. Exam items in the COTA® format that cover the depth and breadth of content you will need to know to pass the exam are provided on this text's online exams. The answers to the questions below are provided in Appendix 3.

1. You are working with a client with hemiplegia after a brain tumor resection. The client is learning to transfer using a tub bench for the first time. Thus, the person is at the cognitive stage of learning. According to principles of motor learning, what types of interventions would be appropriate to teach this transfer skill at this stage of learning?

2. You are working with a person with a swallowing disorder. You have collaborated with the occupational therapist and determined that direct interventions using a bolus are indicated. Which approaches would you use?

3. You are observing a client with apraxia eat breakfast. What behaviors would you most likely observe?

4. Your client presents with unilateral spatial neglect and poor awareness. The client has a supportive partner. What environmental modifications will be useful to maximize performance and safety indoors?

5. Your client has left-sided body neglect. What behaviors would you expect to see during morning self-care?

6. You are working in acute care with a person with low arousal after head trauma. Describe activities that would be useful.

7. What is the purpose of applying a static orthosis (splint) to an affected body part?

8. You are working in a private practice that provides services to children with sensory processing disorders. What general principles of Ayres Sensory Integration® approach can you use to guide your interventions?

13

Psychosocial Approaches: Evaluation and Intervention

WILLIAM L. LAMBERT, RITA P. FLEMING-CASTALDY, AND JANICE L. ROMEO

Chapter Outline

- Psychosocial Frames of Reference and Models of Practice, 360
- Interdisciplinary Mental Health Practice Models, 366
- Psychosocial Assessment, 370
- Psychosocial Intervention, 371
- Special Considerations in Psychosocial Evaluation and Intervention, 376
- References, 381
- Review Questions, 383

Psychosocial Frames of Reference and Models of Practice

Overview

1. Psychosocial frames of reference and models of practice are used to address the psychosocial needs of all persons in all practice settings.
   a. Their effective use requires clinical reasoning to select assessments, identify factors that enable or limit occupational performance, develop client-centered, occupation-based intervention goals, and implement interventions.

> **EXAM HINT:** The NBCOT® exam outline for the certified occupational therapy assistant (COTA®) identifies knowledge of the "influence of theoretical approaches, models of practice, and frames of reference on information-gathering and the intervention process" (NBCOT®, 2018, p. 22) as essential for competent and safe practice. The application of knowledge about the following occupational therapy (OT) psychosocial frames of reference and models of practice can help you determine the correct answer to COTA® exam items about psychosocial OT.

Model of Human Occupation (MOHO)

1. Developed by Gary Kielhofner, based on the Occupational Behavior model of Mary Reilly[1].
2. Principles.
   a. "Occupation is dynamic and context-dependent" (Kielhofner, 2004, p. 151).
   b. Personal occupational choices and engagement in occupation shape the individual.
   c. Three elements are inherent to humans.
      (1) Volition includes thoughts and feelings that motivate people to act and is comprised of personal causation, values, and interests.
      (2) Habituation includes organized, recurrent patterns of behavior and is comprised of roles and habits.
      (3) Performance capacity includes the physical and mental skills needed for performance and the subjective experience of engaging in occupation.
   d. The environment impacts on the individual through the opportunities, demands, resources, and constraints it provides.
      (1) The environment is divided into physical and social components.
      (2) Each component is influenced by the culture(s) in which it takes place.
3. Evaluation.
   a. focuses on exploring the individual's occupational history, goals, volition, habits, and occupational performance.
   b. Many assessment tools have been designed specifically for use with the MOHO; however, any procedure or instrument that provides pertinent information about the environment and the person may be used.
4. Intervention.
   a. Focuses on occupational engagement and includes activities that are purposeful, relevant, and meaningful to people and their social context.

Person-Environment-Occupation Model

1. Developed by Charles Christiansen and Carolyn Baum.
2. Principles.
   a. Occupational performance is dynamic in nature.
   b. Occupational performance is considered the outcome of the transactional relationship between people, their occupations, and the environment.
   c. Occupational performance necessarily changes across the lifespan.
3. Evaluation.
   a. Addresses the occupational performance issues that the client identifies.
   b. Emphasizes the environment of the individual to include where they live, work, and play.
   c. Evaluation is client-centered and flexible as there are no specific evaluations.
4. Intervention.
   (1) Considers the transactional relationships of occupations with people and their environment to address occupational performance issues and goals.
   (2) Recognizes the temporal nature of occupational performance as the person, their environment, and occupations are constantly changing.
   (3) Offers many avenues for change, as practitioners can be flexible in their choice of intervention strategies.

---

[1] Note: the NBCOT® exam will not have questions about the developers and authors of frames of reference and models of practice. These names are solely provided in this chapter to give credit to their originators.

Life-Style Performance Model

1. Developed by Gail Fidler.
2. Principles.
   a. The Life-Style Performance Model seeks to identify and describe the nature and critical "doing" elements of an environment that support and foster achievement of a satisfying, productive lifestyle.
   b. It proposes a method for looking at the match between that environment and the individual's needs.
   c. Four hypotheses are proposed.
      (1) "Mastery and competence in those activities that are valued and given priority in one's society or social group have greater meaning in defining one's social efficacy than competence in activities that carry less social significance.
      (2) "A total activity and each of its elements have symbolic as well as reality-based meanings that notably affect individual experiences and motivation.
      (3) "Mastery and competence are more readily achieved, and the sense of personal pleasure and intrinsic gratification is more intense in those activities that are most closely matched to one's neurobiology and psychological structure.
      (4) "Competence and achievement are most readily seen and verified in the end-product or outcome of an activity; thus the ability to do, to overcome, and to achieve becomes obvious to self and others" (Fidler, 1996, pp. 115–116).
   d. Performance and quality of life can be enhanced by an environment that provides for 10 fundamental human needs.
      (1) Autonomy: self-determination.
      (2) Individuality: self-differentiation.
      (3) Affiliation: evidence of belonging.
      (4) Volition: the having of alternatives.
      (5) Consensual validation: acknowledgment of achievement and verification of perspectives.
      (6) Predictability: discernment and evaluation of cause and effect.
      (7) Self-efficacy: evidence of competence.
      (8) Adventure: exploration of the new and unknown.
      (9) Accommodation: freedom from physical or mental harm and compensation for limitations.
      (10) Reflection: contemplation of events and the meaning of things.
   e. Performance is measured in the quality of functioning in four domains.
      (1) Self-care and maintenance.
      (2) Intrinsic gratification.
      (3) Societal Contribution.
      (4) Reciprocal relationships.
3. Evaluation.
   a. Focuses on obtaining an activity history and a life-style performance profile related to the four skill domains.
   b. Environmental factors are explored.
4. Intervention.
   a. Addresses five main questions that identify the focus of intervention.
      (1) What does the person need to be able to do?
      (2) What is the person able to do?
      (3) What is the person unable to do?
      (4) What interventions are needed, and in what order?
      (5) What are the characteristics and patterns of activity and of the environment that will enhance the person's quality of life?
   b. Any interventions or activities that promote performance in the four domains are acceptable.

Ecology of Human Performance (EHP) Model[2]

1. Developed by Winnie Dunn and colleagues at the University of Kansas Medical Center.
2. Principles.
   a. The EHP model emphasizes the role of an individual's context (i.e., a person's cultural, physical, and social environments) and how the environment impacts a person and their task performance.
   b. This model is applicable to people across the lifespan.
   c. The four main constructs of this model include the person, tasks, context, and personal-context-task transaction.
   d. There are 11 assumptions of this model.
      (1) Ecology refers to the interaction between a person and their environment.
      (2) A person's performance is understood by looking at the relationship between the person, context, and the task.
      (3) Performance occurs when a person acts to engage in tasks within a context.
      (4) Each person is a unique individual with sensorimotor, cognitive, and psychosocial skills and abilities.
      (5) The range of a person's performance is based on the transaction between the person and the context.

---

[2] This section was written by Donna Costa, DHS, OTR/L, FAOTA.

(6) Skills that a person possess can be increased or decreased due to illness and/or stress; a person's interests and life experiences lead to continually changing variables.
(7) Contexts are dynamic rather than static; there is a reciprocal relationship between a person and their context where one influences the other.
(8) The roles that a person has in life are made up of tasks; the transactional relationship between the person, task, and context makes up occupations and roles.
(9) There is a difference between a person's performance in their natural contexts and simulated experiences.
(10) In the OT process, people are empowered by increasing their self-determination.
(11) This model defines independence as using the supports in a person's context to meet their needs and wants.

3. Evaluation.
   a. Utilizes checklists that were designed along with this model. These include checklists for the person, the environment, task analysis, and personal priorities.
   b. The Sensory Profile.
4. Intervention.
   a. Five specific strategies designed to help the person, context, task, or all three are used. These include:
      (1) Establish and restore: enhancing a person's abilities by teaching skills lost due to illness or disability or never learned.
      (2) Alter: assessing a person's context to determine which is the best match for the person's abilities.
      (3) Adapt/modify: changing the context or task in some way so that it leads the person to successful performance.
      (4) Prevent: minimizing risks that might develop so that problems in performance do not develop.
      (5) Create: assisting the person by promoting enriching and complex performances in the person's context.

Occupational Adaptation

1. Developed by Janette Schkade and Sally Schultz.
2. Principles.
   a. Occupational adaptation is concerned with the processes that the individual goes through to adapt to their environment.
   b. It consists of three elements: the person, the occupational environment, and the interaction between the two.
      (1) The person element consists of the sensorimotor, cognitive, and psychosocial components of the individual.
      (2) The occupation environment is viewed as the physical, social, and cultural systems within which work, play/leisure, and self-maintenance take place.
      (3) The outcome of the interaction between the person and the environment is referred to as the occupational response.
   c. The occupational adaptation model makes two basic assumptions.
      (1) "Occupation provides the means by which humans adapt to changing needs and conditions, and the desire to participate in occupation is the intrinsic motivational force leading to adaptation."
      (2) "Occupational adaptation is a normative process that is most pronounced in periods of transition, both large and small. The greater the adaptive transitional needs, the greater the importance of the occupational adaptation process, and the greater the likelihood that the process will be disrupted" (Schkade & Shultz, 1992a, pp. 829–830).
3. Evaluation.
   a. Focuses on occupational environment, role expectation, the individual's potential for adaptation, and the best means for adaptation to occur.
4. Intervention.
   a. Focuses on increasing the skills needed for occupational adaptation.
   b. Addresses both the individual and their environment.

Role Acquisition

1. Developed by Ann Mosey.
2. Principles.
   a. The individual employs task and social skills to meet the demands of personally desired and necessary roles.
   b. Performance is addressed through function/dysfunction continuums in seven categories.
      (1) Task skills.
      (2) Interpersonal skills.
      (3) Family interaction.
      (4) Activities of daily living.
      (5) School.
      (6) Work.
      (7) Play/leisure/recreation.
   c. Temporal adaptation addresses the individual's temporal orientation and ability to organize their use of time in a need-satisfying manner.

3. Evaluation.
   a. Focuses on gathering data indicative of function/dysfunction in the above categories.
4. Intervention.
   a. Focuses on the acquisition of the specific skills people need to function in their environment.
   b. The principles of learning are used to promote skill development. See Chapter 3's section on tools of practice
   c. General postulates for change are provided to guide the intervention process.
      (1) Long-term goals are set based on the person's expected environment.
      (2) Initially, task and interpersonal skills can be taught separately, or they can be taught within the context of the learning of social roles.
      (3) An adequate repertoire of behavior is acquired through activities that elicit the desired behavior, are interesting to the client, include socializing, and apply the principles of learning. See Chapter 3.
      (4) Intrapsychic content is shared matter-of-factly with the client, and reality testing is provided.
      (5) The OT practitioner must know very specifically what kind of behavior they wish to promote or enhance.
   d. Specific postulates are provided for each of the continuums.
   e. Any treatment activities or strategies that employ the teaching-learning principles are acceptable.

Cognitive Disabilities

1. Developed by Claudia Allen.
2. Principles.
   a. Based on the stages of cognitive development as described by Piaget and knowledge of the neurobiological sciences at the time of the model's development.
   b. Cognitive ability is determined by biological factors and the potential for improvement is dictated by those factors.
   c. Functional behavior is based on cognition.
   d. If the person's cognitive level cannot change, adapting the activity or task provides opportunities for the individual to succeed.
   e. Once the maximum level has been achieved, compensations must be made biologically, psychologically, or environmentally.
   f. Cognitive performance is placed on a continuum divided into six levels that are further divided into modes.
      (1) Automatic Actions, Level I, are characterized by automatic motor responses and changes in the autonomic nervous system. Conscious response to the external environment is minimal.
      (2) Postural Actions, Level II, are characterized by movement that are associated with comfort. There is some awareness of large objects in the environment, and the individual may assist the caregiver with simple tasks.
      (3) Manual Actions, Level III, are characterized by beginning to use hands to manipulate objects. The individual may be able to perform a limited number of tasks with long-term repetitive training.
      (4) Goal Directed Actions, Level IV, are characterized by the ability to carry simple tasks through to completion. The individual relies heavily on visual cues. They may be able to perform established routines but cannot cope with unexpected events.
      (5) Exploratory Actions, Level V, are characterized by overt trial and error problem solving. New learning occurs. This may be the usual level of functioning for 20% of the population.
      (6) Planned Actions, Level VI, are characterized by the absence of disability. The person can think of hypothetical situations and do mental trial-and-error problem solving.
3. Evaluation.

> **EXAM HINT:** The NBCOT® exam outline for the COTA® identifies knowledge of the "purpose, advantages, limitations, and service competency needs related to the administration of commonly used standardized assessments and non-standardized screening as a means of acquiring client information" (NBCOT®, 2018, p. 21) as essential for competent and safe practice. The application of knowledge about the following evaluation principles and tools can help you correctly answer Domain 01 exam items that may ask you to acquire information about persons with cognitive disorders while using the cognitive disabilities model.

   a. Focus is on identifying the individual's current cognitive abilities and their implications for performance, independence, and the need for assistance.
      (1) The potential for improvement is also considered.
   b. Observation during functional tasks is emphasized.
   c. Several evaluation tools have been developed to assist with the identification of the individual's cognitive level.
      (1) The Allen Cognitive Level Screen-5 (ACLS-5) is a structured task that allows the practitioner to observe the individual performing three increasingly complex leather lacing stitches and

make determinations about that person's cognitive skill level.
- (2) The Allen Diagnostic Manual provides craft projects that can be used for evaluation as well as treatment that can also be used to determine the individual's level of skills according to the first five levels listed above.
- (3) The Routine Task Inventory gathers data about the individual's activities of daily living (ADL) performance from an informed caregiver.
- (4) The Cognitive Performance Test was designed to assess the functional performance of individuals with Alzheimer's disease. The focus is on the identification of the effects that particular deficits have on the performance of ADL.

4. Intervention.
   a. Activities are selected based on the individual's highest cognitive level.
   b. Therapy focuses on maintaining the individual's highest level of function.
   c. Environmental changes and activity adaptations are made to compensate for deficits and allow the greatest degree of independence.
   d. The OT practitioner works with the team to develop an appropriate discharge plan.
   e. The OT practitioner should meet with the family or other caregivers to develop understanding of the individual's abilities, deficits, and care needs.

Sensory Models[3]

1. This approach in mental health is known by several different terms, including sensory integration, sensory processing, sensory motor model, sensory defensiveness, sensory modulation, and sensory based treatment.
2. Based on the work of A. Jean Ayres and originally known as sensory integration.
3. Developed by Lorna Jean King, an occupational therapist who worked with people with schizophrenia and observed that they had disturbances in posture, gait patterns, balance, and hand function.
4. Mildred Ross built upon the work of Lorna Jean King. She worked with long-term and regressed psychiatric patients and added movement patterns to the calming and alerting sensory input of King's approach.
   a. Ross' approach is known as the Five Stage Group Model because of the five different kinds of brief activities done within each group. See this chapter's section on intervention groups.
5. Pat and Julia Wilbarger developed an approach for children and adults who they observed exhibiting a specific avoidance pattern, which they termed sensory defensiveness.
   a. The Wilbargers developed a treatment protocol that is aimed at reducing these patterns of sensory defensiveness.
      (1) It includes a brushing pattern, along with a sensory diet and education.
6. Winnie Dunn developed the model of sensory processing that looked at how sensory input was processed and then responded to in one of four patterns of neurological thresholds.
   a. Sensory seeking.
   b. Sensory avoiding.
   c. Sensory sensitivity.
   d. Poor registration.
7. Tina Champagne built upon the work of all the previous work to develop her sensory modulation approach for adults.
   a. Sensory modulation approaches are used by OT practitioners to help prepare, enhance, and/or maintain the person's ability to engage actively in meaningful life roles and activities.
      (1) Approaches include the use of sensory-related assessment tools, sensorimotor activities, sensory modalities, environmental modifications, and assistance in learning how to self-regulate through the process of self-organization and positive change.
   b. The implementation of a sensory modulation program requires the use of a strengths-based, person-centered, and relationship-centered model of care.
      (1) It is essential to assist each individual in recognizing not only symptom(s) and problem areas, but also the individual's unique strengths that are utilized when following through with the exploration, practice, and integration of sensory modulation approaches into one's daily life.
8. Evaluation.
   a. Assessments used in sensory models include the Adolescent/Adult Sensory Profile and the Allen Cognitive Level Screen. The OTA can administer these evaluations with supervision.

> **EXAM HINT:** The NBCOT® exam outline for the COTA® identifies knowledge of "intervention methods and activities to support optimal sensory arousal . . . for supporting engagement in occupations based on current level of development, abilities, task characteristics, and environmental demands" (NBCOT®, 2018, p. 25) as essential for competent and safe practice. The application of knowledge about the following intervention methods can help you correctly answer NBCOT® Domain 02 exam items about using sensory models to guide the selection and implementation of intervention.

---

[3] This section was written by Donna Costa, DHS, OTR/L, FAOTA.

9. Intervention.
   a. The use of sensory-based interventions in mental health practice settings is widespread, including an alternative to the use of physical restraints. Methods include:
      (1) Snoezelen rooms, multisensory environments, and/or 'comfort rooms' to calm/alert individuals with psychiatric illness, autism, pervasive developmental disorders, and dementia.
      (2) Therapeutic weighted blankets, dolls, and stuffed animals as a modality for self-soothing.
   b. Psychoeducation to increase personal knowledge of how to self-modulate.
   c. Sensory diets including alerting/calming stimuli and heavy work patterns.

Psychodynamic/Psychoanalytic

1. An early OT frame of reference based on the work of S. Freud, A. Freud, Jung, and Sullivan.
   a. Principle developers were Gail Fidler and Ann Mosey.
   b. Due to the advances in psychiatry, temporal and financial constraints, and the nature of the population served, these approaches are rarely used today.
   c. Proper use of this approach requires further specialized training.
2. Principles.
   a. All behavior is largely determined by unconscious psychological forces and internal processes.
   b. Interaction among these forces creates behavior, thoughts, and emotions.
   c. Abnormal behavior results when these dynamic forces are in conflict, known as intrapsychic conflict.
   d. Conflicts are resolved when brought to consciousness and explored.
   e. Behavior patterns are believed to begin in early childhood.
   f. Individuals may protect themselves from anxiety through the use of defense mechanisms. Some are healthy; some are not.
   g. Understanding the function of defensive mechanisms is useful in therapeutic relationships.
   h. Defense mechanisms are grouped into a hierarchy according to the phases of maturity associated with them.
      (1) Narcissistic mechanisms.
         (a) Denial: the failure to acknowledge the existence of some aspect of reality that is apparent to others (e.g., a person who abuses alcohol is unable to acknowledge that their problems are a result of drinking).
         (b) Projection: attributing attributes or unacknowledged feelings, impulses, or thoughts to others (e.g., someone who feels guilty attributes what others say as blaming them).
         (c) Splitting: rigid separating of positive and negative thoughts and of feelings (e.g., staff members may be seen as all good or all bad when variations of behavior are anxiety-provoking).
      (2) Immature mechanisms.
         (a) Passive-aggressive: aggression toward others that is indirectly or unassertively expressed (e.g., a person is late for a treatment session when they are angry with the practitioner).
         (b) Regression: returning to an earlier stage of development to avoid the tension and conflict of the present one (e.g., an individual becomes needy and/or childlike during a period of stress or illness).
         (c) Somatization: the conversion of psychological symptoms into physical illness (e.g., a person who feels stuck in an unfulfilling job develops low back pain).
      (3) Neurotic mechanisms.
         (a) Rationalization: creating self-justifying explanations to hide the real reasons for one's own or another's behavior (e.g., a parent believes a lazy adult child is not working because the job market is poor).
         (b) Repression: blocking from consciousness painful memories and anxiety-provoking thoughts (e.g., an adult child has no memory of being mistreated by a beloved parent).
         (c) Displacement: redirecting an emotion or reaction from one object to a similar but less threatening one (e.g., a child gets angry with their parents and hits a younger sister).
         (d) Reaction formation: the switching of unacceptable impulses into its opposite (e.g., hugging someone you would like to hit).
      (4) Mature mechanisms.
         (a) Humor: using comedy to express feelings and thoughts without provoking discomfort in self and others (e.g., making fun of yourself for coming inappropriately dressed for a specific function).
         (b) Sublimation: redirecting energy from socially unacceptable impulses to socially acceptable activities (e.g., an angry individual channels their anger into aggressive sports play).
         (c) Suppression: consciously or semiconsciously avoiding thinking about disturbing problems, thoughts, or feelings (e.g., cleaning closets and drawers while waiting for the results of medical tests).

i. Appropriate individuals for therapy are nonpsychotic, with mild to moderate psychopathology, well-integrated egos, and the capacity for introspection and insight.
3. Evaluation.
    a. Historically, OT evaluations using this model included the Fidler Battery, Azima Battery, Goodman Battery, BH Battery, The Magazine Picture Collage, and the Comprehensive Assessment Process.
    b. The Magazine Picture Collage continues to be used today, for individual as well as group evaluation.
4. Intervention.
    a. Projective and functional tasks are used to promote self-awareness and the identification and exploration of intrapsychic content.
    b. By bringing unconscious conflicts to consciousness, intrapsychic content can lead to intrapsychic conflict resolution.
    c. Due to the advances in psychiatry, the use of more contemporary recovery models, temporal and financial practice-setting constraints, and the nature of the population typically served (i.e., people with serious mental illness), these approaches are infrequently used today.

CAUTION: Proper use of this approach in practice requires specialized training and education for mental health practitioners, including occupational therapists and OTAs.

Interdisciplinary Mental Health Practice Models

EXAM HINT: The NBCOT® exam outline for the COTA® identifies knowledge of the "influence of theoretical approaches, models of practice, and frames of reference on information-gathering and the intervention process" (NBCOT®, 2018, p. 22) as essential for competent and safe practice. The application of knowledge about the following interdisciplinary mental health practice models can help you determine the correct answer to NBCOT® Domain 01 exam items about psychosocial OT practice.

Cognitive Behavioral Frame of Reference/Cognitive Behavioral Therapy (CBT)

1. Relevance to occupational therapy practice.
    a. CBT is widely used in practice today.
        (1) Many of the suggested interventions in this frame of reference fall within occupational therapy's domain of practice.
    b. Research has supported CBT as an effective approach for a diversity of clinical populations.
        (1) CBT has been shown to be especially effective in the treatment of individuals with depression.
            (a) Individuals with depression tend to distort reality through dysfunctional thought processes.
            (b) CBT works to alter these individuals' negative thoughts about themselves, the world, and the future by correcting misinterpretations of life events.
        (2) CBT is also used with individuals with schizophrenia, anxiety, bipolar, panic, obsessive-compulsive, personality, somatoform, and eating disorders.

EXAM HINT: In the NBCOT® exam outline for the COTA®, Domain 03 focuses on the OTA's ability to "uphold professional standards and responsibilities by . . . applying evidence-based interventions to promote quality in practice" (NBCOT®, 2018, p. 28). Because the efficacy of CBT is supported by evidence, the application of knowledge about the following CBT principles, evaluation methods, and intervention approaches can help you determine the correct answers to COTA® exam items about working with persons with psychosocial disorders.

2. Principles.
    a. CBT combines principles of cognitive therapy and behavioral therapy.
        (1) Cognitive therapy looks at a person's thoughts and beliefs, while behavioral therapy looks at a person's actions and attempts to change maladaptive patterns of behavior.
    b. 'Cognitive restructuring' is to alter cognitions and cognitive processes in order to facilitate behavioral and emotional changes (Cara & MacRae, 2013, p. 153).
    c. The three components of cognitive therapy are didactic aspects, cognitive techniques, and behavioral techniques.
        (1) Didactic aspects involve the practitioner explaining the basic concepts and principles of CBT to the client.

(2) Cognitive techniques involve "eliciting automatic thoughts, testing automatic thoughts, identifying maladaptive underlying assumptions, and testing the validity of maladaptive assumptions" (Sadock & Sadock, 2008, p. 462).
(3) Behavioral techniques are used with cognitive techniques to test and challenge maladaptive and inaccurate cognitions.
d. A pattern of negative thinking termed the 'cognitive triad' is identified.
(1) This triad is comprised of negative self-evaluation, a pessimistic worldview, and a sense of hopelessness regarding the future.
(2) This triad underlies depression in particular and is evident in other disorders.
e. Three basic principles of cognitive therapy can help individuals with depression. These include:
(1) All moods are created by a person's thoughts and the way they look at and interprets situations and events.
(2) When people are depressed, their thoughts are pervasively negative.
(3) Research has indicated that negative thoughts that cause emotional distress usually contain distortions.
f. The development of insight is necessary for growth and change.
(1) Thinking influences behavior.
(2) Changing the way a person thinks reduces symptoms.
(3) Thinking can be self-regulated.
(4) Change occurs through clients' involvement in learning and developing skills.
3. Evaluation.
a. The Beck Depression Inventory (BDI-II) is the primary initial evaluation tool.
(1) The BDI-II is a self-completed questionnaire that assesses level of depression.
(2) No special training is required to administer this client-completed evaluation.
(a) An OTA can complete the BDI-II with the supervision of an occupational therapist.
(3) Interpretation of the results of the BDI-II must be completed by a mental health professional that has completed required training and acquired adequate knowledge about the BDI-II and CBT.
(a) An occupational therapist with this training can interpret the results of the BDI-II and is responsible for the interpretation of any assessment that is completed by an OTA.
b. The evaluation of cognition is frequently completed by OT practitioners.
c. A variety of evaluation methods and assessments are available for use by occupational therapy practitioners in many practice settings. See this chapter's section on assessments and Chapter 13.

> **EXAM HINT:** "The NBCOT® exam outline for the COTA® identifies knowledge of "intervention methods and activities to support optimal . . . cognitive, or perceptual processing for supporting engagement in occupations based on current level of development, abilities, task characteristics, and environmental demands" (NBCOT®, 2018, p. 25) as essential for competent and safe practice. The application of knowledge about the CBT principles methods previously described and the intervention methods described below can help you correctly answer NBCOT® Domain 02 exam items about using CBT to guide the selection and implementation of intervention.

4. Intervention.
a. General postulates for change are used to guide the intervention process.
(1) Dysfunctional cognitive processes produce psychological disorder.
(2) Altering a person's cognition can improve psychological health.
(3) Cognitions are the prime cause of psychopathology and therefore are the focus of intervention.
(a) Automatic thoughts cause psychological disorder, and through cognitive restructuring these thoughts are brought to awareness to be confronted and facilitate change.
b. Approaches using CBT emphasize the following.
(1) Assisting the client in the identification of current problems and potential solutions.
(2) Using active and collaborative practitioner-client interaction as an essential part of the therapeutic process.
(3) Helping the client learn how to identify distorted or unhelpful thinking patterns, recognize and change inaccurate beliefs, and relate to others in more positive ways.
(4) Gaining insight and acquiring skills that "maximize client functioning and quality of life through the development of coping skills and meaningful healthy occupational patterns" (Hemphill-Pearson, 2008, p. 68).
(5) Facilitating the client's active role in the therapeutic process by frequently providing homework and structured assignments as part of the intervention process.
(a) Intervention goals are designed to help the client monitor and refute negative thoughts about themselves.
(b) The behavioral techniques used in CBT intervention include the following:
(6) Scheduling activities.
(a) Increasing mastery and pleasure.
(b) Grading tasks to enable client success.
(7) Cognitive rehearsal.

(8) Self-reliance training.
    (a) Self-reliance can be facilitated by performing activities of daily living (e.g., making one's bed, doing personal shopping, and preparing one's own meals).
(9) Role playing.
(10) Diversion techniques and visual imagery.
(11) Engaging in physical, work, leisure/play, and/or social participation activities.
  c. Research in the area of cognitive functioning supports the importance of providing clients with meaningful tasks and therapeutic activities.
   (1) OT's focus on meaningful occupation and purposeful activities is inherently congruent with CBT.
   (2) Many of the life skills workbook activities used by OT practitioners apply cognitive therapy principles.
     (a) Activity gradation, an area of specialization for OT practitioners, is particularly useful in providing effective treatment using the CBT frame of reference.
5. Dialectical Behavior Therapy (DBT).
  a. A form of CBT.
  b. Focus of DBT.
   (1) Addresses suicidal thoughts and actions and self-injurious behaviors.
   (2) Commonly used with individuals with borderline personality disorder since a feature of this diagnosis is suicidal thinking and behavior.
   (3) Also used to treat individuals who have depression, substance abuse issues, and/or eating disorders.
  c. Evaluation.
   (1) Often begins with an accurate DSM-5™ diagnosis by the psychiatrist.
   (2) OT evaluation tools are not trait or diagnostically based.
   (3) A variety of psychological evaluations may be used, including those that address personality.
   (4) OT assessments that focus on functioning in occupational performance areas and performance contexts can provide relevant information for intervention planning.
  d. Intervention.
   (1) Programming using DBT teaches assertiveness, coping, and interpersonal skills.
     (a) OT practitioners are often involved in assisting clients develop these skills.
   (2) DBT groups address how the acquisition of skills affects occupational performance and provide opportunities to practice new skills.
   (3) A strong practitioner-client relationship is essential.
     (a) Rapport is used for validation as well as confrontation.

Recovery Model[4]

1. Relevance to OT practice.
   a. Recovery principles and approaches are highly congruent with those of OT.
   b. The active use of the recovery model throughout the OT process can help practitioners empower people by fostering the person's intrinsic motivation to redefine self and establish a sense of hope for the future.
   c. The primary focus of the recovery process is to improve quality of life and attain basic life functions through self-advocacy.
2. Principles.
   a. Conceptualizes recovery from illness as a journey of healing and transformation that enables individuals with mental health problems to live a meaningful life in a community of their choice.
   b. Individuals with mental illness can strive to meet their potential and find meaning and purpose in their lives.
   c. Major concepts that guide recovery.
     (1) Self-direction: consumers identify their own goals and their own personal track to recovery.
     (2) Individualized and person-centered: recovery is unique as dictated by each individual's personal strengths, needs, past experiences, cultural background, and desires.
     (3) Empowerment: people take control over their lives by making educated decisions that impact on their recovery.
     (4) Holistic: recovery signifies the interrelatedness of the mind, body, spirit, and community.
     (5) Nonlinear: recovery can include episodes that disrupt the track to recovery toward personal goals, including taking care of oneself to promote overall health and wellness.
     (6) Strengths-based: recovery builds on and exercises an individual's strengths.
     (7) Peer support: reciprocal relationships with others who have lived experience in supporting recovery principles are formed.
     (8) Respect: recovery is based on the premise of social acceptance of self and by others, including society, one's community, and service providers.
     (9) Responsibility: personal commitment to self in working toward personal goals, including taking care of oneself to promote overall health and wellness.
     (10) Hope: being a change agent in recovery enables the person to embrace an optimistic future.

---

[4] This section was written by Patricia Wisniewski, MS, OTR/L, CPRP.

(11) Family: members play an essential role in a person's recovery. They remain committed to supporting an individual's potential and personal strengths, despite potential setbacks.
(12) Community: supports inclusion and remains steadfast in eliminating barriers to recovery.
d. Evaluation.
(1) Objective standardized measures and qualitative structured and/or semistructured interviews are used to assess the person's self-esteem, empowerment level and capacities, living situation, ADL, work/school and leisure activities, family and social relationships, finances, legal and safety issues, general health, and overall quality of life.
(2) OTAs contribute to the evaluation process with supervision from the occupational therapist.
(3) Evaluations must be interpreted by an occupational therapist.
(4) Evaluation results can be used to develop strategies for attaining and maintaining recovery.
e. Intervention.
(1) The development and implementation of a Wellness Recovery Action Plan (WRAP) is an essential part of the recovery process.
(2) Storytelling is a means of decreasing stigma and supporting others by sharing experiential life experiences.
(3) Advocacy through the dissemination of knowledge, skill development in activism, and forming support groups to prevent discrimination and improve acceptance in society.

EXAM HINT: The NBCOT® exam outline for the COTA® identifies knowledge of the "internal and external factors influencing a client's meaningful engagement in occupation related to typical habits, roles, routines, and rituals, and the level and type of assistance required" (NBCOT®, 2018, p. 21) as essential for competent and safe practice. Because the recovery model and psychiatric rehabilitation consider the internal and external factors that influence a person's recovery from mental illness, the application of knowledge about the recovery model described above and the psychiatric rehabilitation model described in the following section can help you correctly answer NBCOT® Domain 01 exam items about working with persons with psychiatric disorders. For example, an exam item scenario can include an OTA using the recovery model to guide intervention while working with a person who is preparing for discharge from a partial hospitalization program. A correct answer to a question about the pre-discharge intervention plan would include working with the person to develop a WRAP.

Psychiatric Rehabilitation[5]

1. Relevance to OT practice.
   a. Psychiatric rehabilitation and the profession of OT both share the common goal of eliminating barriers and promoting health and wellness.
   b. Both believe recovery from physical, mental, emotional, and cognitive disabilities is possible.
      (1) Recovery is not a linear process; rather, individuals will experience challenging periods when progress may lapse.
      (2) Recovery is person specific.
   c. The goal of psychiatric rehabilitation is to help individuals develop the skills necessary to compensate for, adapt to, or control the influence symptoms have on function, including any disability caused by social or environmental barriers.
2. Principles.
   a. Individualization: any service provided to an individual is structured to support each person's unique needs.
   b. Client involvement: individuals control their recovery.
   c. Partnership with service providers: a mutual rapport between all persons involved nurtures a commitment based on respect and trust for everyone.
   d. Community-based services: all services are provided where the individual lives, works, and socializes.
   e. Strengths-focused: build on one's strengths rather than focusing on their weaknesses.
   f. Situational assessments: the focus is on collecting data while observing the individual in the environment where challenges are experienced.
   g. Holistic approach: treatment and rehabilitation services are viewed as equal and mutually dependent methods that support recovery.
   h. Continued, accessible, coordinated services: services are always available for any given period of time.
   i. Vocational focus: work is healing; a psychiatric rehabilitation professional partners with individuals (regardless of their abilities) to develop work skills, habits, and resources needed to become successful.
   j. Skills training: includes all actions or behaviors necessary to accomplish a task.
      (1) For example, writing an e-mail to a friend includes not only knowing how to organize your thoughts, but also grammar and punctuation use, knowledge of how to use a computer and the operating system, computer etiquette, and acknowledging a reply.
   k. Environmental modification: changing the environment so it supports function.

---

[5] This section was written by Patricia Wisniewski, MS, OTR/L, CPRP.

l. Partnership with family: family is viewed as a consistent source of support; thus, family education is provided to nurture healthy relationships.
m. Evaluation of outcomes: service providers are expected to monitor the services they provide for effectiveness to ensure compatibility with the individuals being served.

3. Evaluation.
   a. Assessments are based on real-life situations that will provide accurate data specific to an individual, environment, and activity at a moment in time.
   b. Evaluation of readiness for change is an essential component of the evaluation process.
      (1) Foremost, individuals with a mental disability have to make a conscious effort to address the effects of the illness on their lives.
      (2) The effort includes acknowledging one has a mental disability and overcoming stigma or other barriers that may hinder recovery.

4. Intervention.
   a. Goal is to assist individuals with a psychiatric disability to perform the physical, emotional, social, and intellectual skills needed to live and work in the community at their highest functional level with the least amount of professional support as the individual deems necessary.
   b. Assertive community treatment (ACT) uses a variety of interdisciplinary interventions aimed at restoring function and role performance in the community.
   c. Interventions take place where a person chooses to live, work, and socialize.
   d. Day programs that embed psychiatric rehabilitation principles include clubhouses where the goal is to improve quality of life by instilling self-worth and determination in its members.
      (1) Clubhouse members include individuals who have a psychiatric disability and staff who share all responsibilities in managing the clubhouse.
         (a) Common modules that support the work-ordered day at a clubhouse include outreach, transitional employment, education, meal preparation, and advocacy.
   e. Case management services strive to offer continuity of care, accessibility, accountability, and efficiency.
   f. Vocational rehabilitation is supported as a natural activity where individuals are capable of achieving success.
      (1) Supported employment affords services to the individual where they are needed: on the actual job or as a consultation.
   g. Supported education offers normalization, structure, self-determination, and fosters both hope and empowerment.
      (1) This is important because education is often interrupted when someone experiences a mental disability.

Psychosocial Assessment

EXAM HINT: The NBCOT® exam outline for the COTA® identifies knowledge of the "purposes, advantages, limitations, and service competency needs related to the administration of commonly used standardized assessments and non-standardized screening as a means of acquiring client information" (NBCOT®, 2018, p. 21) as essential for competent and safe practice. The application of knowledge about the evaluation foci and methods identified for the different OT frames of reference and models of practice previously described in this chapter and the following evaluation foci and methods will help you correctly answer NBCOT® Domain 01 exam items about working with persons with psychosocial disabilities.

Role of the OTA

1. The OTA contributes to the evaluation process in collaboration with the occupational therapist.
   a. The OTA can assist with the collection of data for the evaluation once service competency has been established.
   b. The level of supervision required will be determined by the OTA's experience and established service competency.
   c. The OTA cannot independently evaluate or interpret evaluation results.

Areas Addressed in Assessment

1. Performance skills (i.e., cognitive, perceptual, psychological, and social) and their impact on performance in areas of occupation.
2. Client factors and physical conditions or limitations that impact functional behaviors and performance in areas of occupation.
3. The impact of the individual's social, cultural, spiritual, and physical contexts.

4. Identification of the roles and behaviors that are required of the individual either by society or for the achievement of their desired self-determined goals.
5. Precautions and safety issues such as suicidal and/or aggressive behavior.
6. History of behavior patterns.
7. Individual's goals, values, interests, and attitudes.

Assessment Methods

1. Interviews—structured and unstructured.
    a. Occupational profile. See Chapter 3.
2. Standardized tests.
3. Clinical observation and rating scales.
4. Questionnaires.
5. Self-report inventories.

Psychosocial Intervention

Role of the OTA

1. The OTA implements intervention with supervision from the occupational therapist.
2. The level of supervision required depends upon the OTA's experience and established competency.
3. During the implementation of intervention, the OTA informs the supervising therapist of any change in the individual's status and any other relevant information that may affect treatment.

> **EXAM HINT:** The NBCOT® exam outline for the COTA® identifies knowledge of "methods for selecting, preparing, and adapting the intervention technique and environment to support optimal engagement in the intervention and promote goal achievement" (NBCOT®, 2018, p. 24) as essential for competent and safe practice. The application of knowledge about the intervention foci and methods identified for the different OT frames of reference and models of practice previously described in this chapter and the following intervention methods will help you correctly answer NBCOT® Domain 02 exam items about working with persons with psychosocial disabilities.

General Treatment Considerations

1. One-to-one versus group intervention.
    a. Indicators for one-to-one intervention.
        (1) Refusal to attend groups.
        (2) Inability to tolerate group interaction.
        (3) Presence of behaviors that would be disruptive to the goals of the group.
        (4) Individual is on suicide precautions or is a danger to self or others; e.g., in inpatient psychiatric settings.
        (5) The issues that must be addressed are specific to that patient/client only.

> **EXAM HINT:** The NBCOT® exam outline for the COTA® identifies knowledge of "factors related to determining the context and type of individual and group activities for effectively supporting intervention goals and objectives" (NBCOT®, 2018, p. 23) as essential for competent and safe practice. The application of knowledge about the above indicators for individual treatment and the following indicators for group intervention can help you determine the correct answers to NBCOT® Domain 01 exam items about the best approach to use to attain intervention goals.

    b. Indicators for group intervention.
        (1) More cost effective.
        (2) Effective at assisting members to learn to live in social environments.
        (3) Takes advantage of group dynamics and therapeutic milieu.
            (a) Groups that are facilitated in a therapeutic manner by an OT practitioner are inherently curative.
            (b) See Chapter 3 for a comprehensive review of therapeutic groups and Yalom's curative factors.
2. Factors that influence the effectiveness of treatment.
    a. Skillful therapeutic use of self. See Chapter 3.
    b. An understanding of the individual's cognitive abilities.
    c. Exploration of the needs and wants of the individual.
    d. The establishment of realistic goals.
    e. Skill with activity analysis.
    f. An understanding of the realities of the treatment conditions.
    g. Prioritization of the most goal-directed use of the person's time.

> **EXAM HINT:** Correct answers for COTA® exam items about psychosocial interventions will employ the above factors that positively influence the effectiveness of intervention and will apply the following principles for the design and progression of treatment activities to achieve desired goals (e.g., the skilled use of activity analysis to select interventions that match the person's capabilities to attain client-centered goals).

3. The relationship of treatment activities to desired self-determined goals.
   a. Initial treatment may need to focus on the performance skills needed for desired occupational performance.
   b. Once basic skills are in place, treatment focuses on performance of functional activities specific to the individual.
      (1) Activities that require the actual desired skills or behaviors, in their natural environment, are often the most effective (e.g., assisting the client to use a checking account to pay bills).
      (2) Activities that simulate desired behaviors in clinical setting may be less effective (e.g., using kits that simulate checking materials).
      (3) Activities that utilize the performance components of desired behaviors and rely on generalization may be the least effective (e.g., practicing arithmetic calculation).

General Considerations for Group Intervention

> **EXAM HINT:** The NBCOT® exam outline for the COTA® identifies knowledge of the "methods for facilitating individual and group participation in shared tasks or activities consistent with the type, function, format, context, goals, and stage of the group" (NBCOT®, 2018, p. 25) as essential for competent and safe practice. The application of knowledge about the general considerations for group intervention previously described and the information provided in the following sections and in Chapter 3 about the design and implementation of therapeutic groups can help you determine the correct answers to NBCOT® Domain 02 exam items about the use of groups in psychosocial practice.

1. The taxonomy of groups described by Anne Mosey provides a useful framework for designing OT intervention groups.
   a. Evaluation groups.
      (1) Designed to gather information about the individual's task and group interaction skills that can be used to establish goals and plan intervention.
         (a) Although their primary purpose is evaluation, these groups are often therapeutic through their process and/or content and can help establish rapport.
   b. Task-oriented groups.
      (1) The purpose is to assist the members in becoming aware of their needs, values, ideas, and feelings through the performance of a shared task.
   c. Developmental groups.
      (1) The purpose is to assist the members to acquire and develop group interaction skills.
      (2) Developmental groups offer five levels of interaction.
         (a) Parallel groups use individual tasks with minimal interaction required.
         (b) Project/associative groups consist of common, short-term activities requiring some interaction and cooperation.
         (c) Egocentric cooperative/basic cooperative groups require joint interaction on long-term tasks; however, completion of the task is not the focus. The members are beginning to express their needs and address those of others.
         (d) Cooperative/supportive cooperative groups learn to work together cooperatively, not specifically to complete a task, but to enjoy each other's company and meet emotional needs.
         (e) Mature groups are responsive to all members' needs and can carry out a variety of tasks. There is good balance between carrying out the task and meeting the needs of the members.
      (3) The directive leadership role of the practitioner decreases from parallel to mature.
         (a) See Chapter 3.
   d. Thematic groups are designed for the learning of specific skills.
   e. Topical groups focus on the discussion of activities and issues outside of the group that are current or anticipated.
   f. Instrumental groups are concerned with meeting health needs and maintaining function.
   g. See Chapter 3 for more detail.
2. The curative factors of groups as described by Irving Yalom support the inherent value of OT interventions that use a group format.
   a. Groups and group activities that are designed to facilitate these curative factors are most effective.
   b. See Chapter 3 for a complete descriptive listing.
3. Considerations in group planning.
   a. Member demographics including gender, age, culture, and ethnicity.

b. Individual characteristics of members.
   (1) Cognitive level.
   (2) Functional skill level.
   (3) Individual goals.
   (4) Contraindications and safety issues.
c. Logistical considerations.
   (1) Number of people in the group.
   (2) Length of sessions.
   (3) Number of sessions.
   (4) Space availability.
   (5) Environmental characteristics.
   (6) Budget and materials required.
   (7) Number of leaders.
   (8) Open group vs. closed group.
d. Frame of reference.
4. Elements of a group protocol.
   a. Title/name: reflect the purpose or goal of the group (e.g., Communication Skills Group), not the media used (e.g., Crafts Group).
   b. Purpose: a brief statement of what the group hopes to accomplish (e.g., to improve the members' ability to effectively and appropriately communicate to others their needs and feelings and to enter into satisfying interpersonal relationships).
   c. Rationale: explains the value of this group to the members and why it is important to offer this service to this population.
   d. Theoretical base/frame of reference: explains in brief and readily understandable terms the theory on which this intervention is based and the rationale for its use.
   e. Criteria for membership: explains who should/should not be included in the group, and what will indicate when the member will no longer benefit from participation.
   f. Goals/anticipated outcomes: the expectations of what the members will be able to do as a result of having attended this group.
      (1) A list of "Patient/client will . . ." statements (e.g., patient/client will be able to initiate and sustain social interactions with peers).
   g. Method/format: explains how the group will be carried out.
      (1) Includes the format, scheduling, activities, materials, procedures, etc.
      (2) Includes the information another therapist or OTA would need to lead this group.
   h. Role of the leader: the tasks of the leader in preparing for and conducting the group.
      (1) Includes such things as supplying materials, designing activities, facilitating interaction, providing a safe environment, etc.
      (2) See Chapter 3 for further discussion of leadership roles and styles.
   i. Quality assurance: explains how the need for this intervention and its effectiveness will be monitored.
   j. Outcome measures: determine whether the identified goals were met.
   k. The actual format used to write protocols varies from setting to setting.
5. Procedure for developing a group.
   a. Conduct a needs assessment to identify intervention needs. See Chapter 4 for needs assessment procedures.
   b. Develop the protocol.
   c. Present the protocol to the treatment team or program administrators.
   d. Select potential members who would benefit from the group.
   e. Meet with each potential member to explain the purpose and circumstances of the group.
   f. Hold introductory sessions of the group and revise the protocol as needed.
6. Group member leadership roles. See Chapter 3.
7. Considerations in activity selection.
   a. Degree of structure (inherent or imposed).
   b. Type(s) and degree of instruction provided.
   c. Degree of new learning required.
   d. Complexity of the activity.
   e. Length of time for completion.
   f. Nature and degree of skill required for engagement and completion.
   g. Degree of challenge to the members' skills.

Intervention Group Types

EXAM HINT: Group interventions are commonly used in psychosocial settings across the continuum of care; thus, knowing the following group types and their purposes can help you determine the correct answer for COTA® exam items about the use of group interventions in psychosocial practice settings.

1. ADL/IADL groups.
   a. Focus is on the development of ADL skills (e.g., self-care) and IADL skills (e.g., meal preparation, money management, transportation) to enable independent living.
   b. May be conducted in a modular and/or psychoeducational format.
2. Basic task skills groups.
   a. Include intervention activities designed to develop the basic cognitive skills (e.g., attention, ability to follow multistep directions, problem-solving) necessary for the completion of simple tasks.
      (1) This group uses a skill acquisition approach that differs from the psychodynamic approach used in the task-oriented group described by Fidler and Mosey.

3. Community participation/reintegration groups.
   a. Focuses on the identification and use of community resources (e.g., leisure facilities) and the development of skills (e.g., the use of public transportation) to enable full community participation.
   b. May be conducted in a modular and/or psychoeducational format.
4. Coping skills groups.
   a. Focuses on identifying and implementing the problem-solving and stress-management techniques needed to cope with life stressors.
5. Directive groups as developed by Kathy Kaplan.
   a. These are highly structured groups designed to assist persons with limited abilities in developing basic task and social skills.
   b. Each session is divided into five parts followed by a 15-minute review of the session by the leaders.
      (1) Part I consists of an orientation to the purpose and goals of the group (maximum of 5 minutes).
      (2) Part II involves a review of everyone's name and the introduction of new members (5–10 minutes).
      (3) Part III consists of warm-up activities to make members comfortable and engage them in the group (5–10 minutes).
      (4) Part IV involves one or more activities designed to address the goals of the group and the needs of its members (10–20 minutes).
      (5) Part V includes activities designed to give meaning to the activities and closure to the group (10 minutes).
6. Discharge planning groups.
   a. Focuses on activities to problem-solve potential obstacles and identify resources for successful post-discharge community reintegration.
7. Five-stage groups as developed by Mildred Ross.
   a. Expanded on the sensory integration work of Lorna Jean King, which examined the sensory distortions, postural disturbances, and vestibular stimulating activities that were observed in individuals with chronic schizophrenia.
      (1) King proposed that using noncortical, alerting, stimulating, and pleasurable activities (e.g., parachute games) would normalize movement patterns, increase strength and flexibility, and facilitate adaptive behaviors.
   b. Ross extended the use of sensorimotor approaches to other chronic populations including persons with intellectual disabilities, neurocognitive disorders, neurological impairment, etc.
   c. Each of the five stages of this group follows a clear structure to attain a specific aim.
      (1) Stage I: orientation consists of orienting the members to the session and each other.
      (2) Stage II: Movement uses a variety of vigorous gross motor activities designed to be stimulating and alerting.
      (3) Stage III: Perceptual motor uses brief (30 minutes or less) activities that utilize perceptual-motor skills designed to be calming and to increase ability to focus.
      (4) Stage IV: Cognitive includes activities to provide cognitive stimulation to promote organized thinking.
      (5) Stage V: Closure consists of brief discussions to promote a sense of satisfaction and closure.
8. Goal-setting groups.
   a. Consists of activities designed to identify personal objectives and treatment goals and the steps needed for their achievement.
9. Leisure groups.
   a. May include the identification of interests, development of activity specific skills, identification of resources, and recognition of the importance of healthy use of unstructured time for personal well-being.
10. Modular groups.
    a. The focus of each session is rotated in a way that allows an individual to join the group at any time and still cover each topic (e.g., an Independent Living Skills group that addresses nutrition the first session, money management the second, transportation the third, etc., and then begins the cycle again with a session on nutrition).
    b. This approach is similar to the 'treatment mall' approach that allows for patient choice among a variety of treatment topics.
11. Play groups.
    a. Frequently used in pediatric settings for observation, assessment, and to teach and develop a variety of skills.
    b. Play groups provide opportunities to develop play, task, and social skills at the child's developmental level and provide a developmentally appropriate outlet for children to express thoughts and feelings.
12. Pre-vocational groups.
    a. Frequently used in pediatric settings for observation, assessment, and to teach and develop a variety of skills.
    b. Play groups provide opportunities to develop play, task, and social skills at the child's developmental level and provide a developmentally appropriate outlet for children to express thoughts and feelings.
13. Psychoeducational groups.
    a. An intervention approach that uses a classroom format and the principles of learning to provide information to members and to teach skills.

b. A teacher/student relationship exists.
c. The use of homework assignments is encouraged to facilitate skill development and generalization of learning.
14. Reminiscence.
    a. Activities are designed to review past life experiences to promote the use of cognitive abilities and foster a sense of personal worth.
    b. Current memory is not necessary, nor is it facilitated.
15. Self-awareness groups.
    a. Includes such activities as values clarification; awareness of personal assets, limitations, and behaviors; and the individual's impact on others.
16. Sensory awareness groups.
    a. Includes activities to promote sensory functions and environmental awareness.
17. Social interaction groups.
    a. Include interventions to develop communication skills, socially acceptable behavior, and interpersonal relationship skills.
    b. May be conducted in a modular and/or psychoeducational format.

Managing Difficult Behaviors

EXAM HINT: The NBCOT® exam outline for the COTA® identifies knowledge of "adaptive and preventive strategies for optimal engagement in occupation" (NBCOT®, 2018, p. 25), "precautions or contraindications associated with a client condition or stage of recovery, [and] preventive measures for minimizing risk in the intervention environment" (NBCOT®, 2018, p. 29) as essential for competent and safe practice. The application of knowledge about the following methods for managing behaviors that can hinder occupational performance and/or place the client or others at risk will help you correctly answer exam items about working with persons who exhibit difficult behaviors.

1. Hallucinations.
   a. Create an environment free of distractions that trigger hallucinatory thoughts and interfere with reality-based activity.
   b. Use highly structured simple, concrete, and tangible activities that hold the individual's attention.
   c. When the person appears to be focusing on a hallucinatory experience, attempt to redirect them to reality-based thinking and actions.
2. Delusions.
   a. Do not attempt to refute the delusion.
   b. Redirect the individual's thoughts to reality-based thinking and actions.
   c. Avoid discussions and other experiences that focus on and validate or reinforce delusional material.
3. Akathisia.
   a. Allow the person to move around as needed if it can be done without causing disruption to the goals of the group.
   b. Keep in mind that participation on many levels and in many forms can be beneficial to the individual.
   c. Whenever possible, select gross motor activities over fine motor or sedentary ones.
4. Offensive behavior (physical or verbal).
   a. Set limits and immediately address the behavior during a session.
   b. Reasons that the behavior is not acceptable should be clearly presented in a manner that is not confrontational or judgmental.
   c. The consequences of continued offensive behavior should be clearly communicated.
   d. It is required that staff protects all patients from the threat of harm or abuse by another person.

CAUTION: The needs and safety of the entire unit, program, and/or group must be considered when addressing offensive behaviors.

5. Lack of initiation/participation.
   a. Together with the individual, identify the reasons for lack of participation, e.g., lack of skill, irrelevance of activity, attention deficits, embarrassment, depression.
   b. Motivational hints.
      (1) Individuals are more likely to participate in activities that address issues that are of interest or concern to them.
      (2) The more ownership people have of the activity, the more they will participate.
      (3) Success is motivating.
      (4) Fun is motivating.
      (5) Positive feedback and rewards are motivating.
      (6) Everyone has their own motivators. It is important to identify what they are.
      (7) Curiosity can be used to motivate.
      (8) Food is often motivating (as per Maslow's hierarchy of needs). See Chapter 5.
         (a) Using secondary reinforcers such as praise is usually preferable to using primary reinforcers such as food.
      (9) Offer choices.
      (10) Encourage the individual to remain in the group and participate when/if they are ready.
6. Manic or monopolizing behavior.
   a. Select or design highly structured activities that hold the individual's attention and require a shift of focus from person to person.

b. Thank the individual for their participation and redirect attention to another group member.
c. Refer to limit-setting discussed above.
7. Escalating behavior.
a. Avoid what can be perceived as challenging behavior (e.g., eye contact, standing directly in front of the person).
b. Maintain a comfortable distance.
c. Actively listen.
d. Use a calm, but not patronizing, tone.
(1) Speaking in a softer or lower tone than the individual is often effective in decreasing the volume and intensity of the escalating individual's speech.
e. Speak simply, clearly, and directly. Avoid miscommunication.
f. Do not make or communicate value judgments about the individual's thoughts, feelings, or behaviors.
g. Clearly present what you would like the person to do.

CAUTION: Avoid positions where either you or the person feels trapped.

h. Individuals most often calm in response to the above interventions. If an individual continues to escalate and is nonresponsive to interventions, additional steps are needed to ensure safety.
(1) Remove other patients from the area.
(2) Get or send for other staff.
8. Acting out behavior in children.
a. "Acting out" is the expression of thoughts and feelings through maladaptive behavior instead of verbalizing these.
b. Depending on the severity of the situation, therapeutic options include:
(1) Interpretation: a therapeutic technique where the practitioner puts words to observed behavior, enabling the child to appropriately express the feelings he or she is experiencing.
(2) Redirection: a verbal tactic that refocuses the child on the assigned or current activity that provides cues for appropriate participation.
(3) Limit setting: informing the child of what is permissible and what is unacceptable.
(4) Time-out: an intervention technique that results in behavioral changes by removing the child from a problematic situation to a specific area.
9. The effects of neurocognitive disorders.
a. Make eye contact and show that you are interested in the person.
(1) Value and validate what is said by the person.
b. Maintain a positive and friendly facial expression and tone of voice during all communications.
(1) Do not give orders.
(2) Use short, simple words and sentences.
(3) Do not argue or criticize.
c. Do not speak about the individual as if they were not there.
d. Use nonverbal communication.
e. Create a routine that uses familiar and enjoyable activities.
(1) Use activities that demonstrate and promote personal interests and independence.
(2) Do not introduce infantilizing activities.
(3) Analyze and grade activities carefully.
(4) Do not rush activities.
(a) It is the process of engaging in an activity that is important; task completion is not needed.
f. Note the effects of the time of day on behavior and activity performance.
g. Attend to safety issues at all times.

Special Considerations in Psychosocial Evaluation and Intervention

Domestic Abuse/Intimate Partner Violence[6]

1. Facts and figures.
a. In the United States, domestic abuse/intimate partner violence is a major social justice crisis and health-care concern.

EXAM HINT: The following facts and figures are provided to highlight the need for OT practitioners to be vigilant about the potential of domestic abuse/intimate partner violence during *all* interactions with *all* persons and family members, regard- less of age. Knowledge of these statistics will not be directly tested on the COTA® exam.

b. Approximately 75% of domestic abuse/intimate partner violence is committed by men against women.

---
[6] Victoria Crociata contributed to this section.

c. More than 10 million Americans experience domestic abuse/intimate partner violence annually.
d. Each day, the national domestic violence hotline receives over 20,000 calls.
e. Females between the ages of 18 and 34 are at the greatest risk for domestic/intimate partner violence.
f. Approximately 33% of female murder victims are killed by an intimate partner.
g. Approximately 30%–60% of men who abuse their partners also abuse their children.
h. Children who witness domestic violence are 74% more likely to commit assaults against others.
i. Approximately 50% of homeless women and children are homeless because of violence at home.
j. Many incidents involve alcohol and/or drug and weapon use.
k. Domestic abuse/intimate partner violence knows no boundaries. It occurs regardless of socioeconomic factors, race, culture, ethnicity, religion, or age.

2. Definition and types.
    a. Definitions vary greatly from state to state.
    b. Definitions involve violence or abuse that is used to control another member of the household.
    c. Domestic abuse can take one or more forms.
        (1) Physical abuse: hitting, kicking, punching, slapping, choking, and/or burning.
        (2) Emotional abuse: criticizing, humiliating, playing mind games, abusing or killing pets, withholding affection, isolating, and/or dominating.
        (3) Economic abuse: making the other ask for money, giving an allowance, and/or preventing the other from taking a job.
        (4) Intimidation and coercion: making the other afraid, breaking things, displaying weapons, threatening to leave or report the other for something, and/or making the other do something illegal.
        (5) Using children: making the other feel guilty about the children, using the children to relay messages, using visitation to harass the other, and/or threatening to take the children away.
        (6) Stalking: following, having followed, invading home and privacy, and/or creating fear of immediate harm.
        (7) Sexual abuse: performing and/or requiring the other to perform unwanted sexual activities through force, threats, or intimidation.
    d. Patterns of abuse.
        (1) Impulsive abuse, during which the abuser has sudden attacks of rage, which may be regular or random.
        (2) Premeditated abuse, during which the abuser is cool and calculating.

3. Signs of physical abuse.
    a. Bruises at different stages of healing or in unusual places.
    b. Burns suggestive of specific objects.
    c. Lacerations to the face or genitals.
    d. Orthopedic injuries that are inconsistent with the explanations.
    e. Internal injuries of the head and organs.
    f. Head and facial injuries suggestive of hitting, shaking, or pulling.
    g. Reluctance to talk about injuries.
    h. Abuser not wanting to leave victim alone with others.

4. Reasons for failure to report or leave an abusive relationship.
    a. Economic pressure.
    b. Religious beliefs.
    c. Feeling of love for abuser.
    d. Believing the abuse is deserved.
    e. Viewing abuse as normal due to exposure to abuse/violence as a child.
    f. Fear of increasing abuse.
    g. Fear of retaliation.
    h. Belief things will change.
    i. Concern for children.
    j. Nowhere to go.
    k. Lack of support systems.

5. Role of OT practitioners.
    a. Develop a trusting relationship.

> **EXAM HINT:** Applying the RADAR approach and the assessment and intervention approaches described below can help you correctly answer COTA® exam items about the most effective ways an OTA can screen for and respond to domestic abuse/intimate partner violence.

    b. Use the RADAR approach to screen for and respond to domestic abuse.
        (1) R = Routinely ask. Inquiring about potential abuse when interviewing all clients can be the first step in intervention; this acknowledges that abuse is not an acceptable secret.
        (2) A = Affirm and Ask. Acknowledge and support the person who discloses abuse. Ask direct questions of all clients to determine risk (e.g., Do you feel safe with your partner?).
        (3) D = Document objective findings (e.g., the person has multiple bruises) and record client statements in quotes.
        (4) A = Assess and Address the person's safety (i.e., Has abuse become more violent? Are there weapons in the home?).
        (5) R = Review options and referrals. Refer the person to domestic violence hotlines, domestic

violence shelters, and/or safe houses which have staff trained in family violence and safety planning.
- (a) The National Hotline is 800-799-7233.
- (b) The National Sexual Assault Hotline is 1-800-656-4673.
- (c) The National Teen Dating Abuse Hotline is 1-866-331-9474.

c. Areas to discuss with the person who has been/is being abused.
  (1) Stress and safety.
  (2) Fear and abuse.
  (3) Family, friends, and support network.
  (4) Emergency plan.
d. Provide information about treatment and support programs that enable empowerment of the individual.
e. Provide intervention for physical and emotional injuries and to develop skills needed to live an independent empowered life.
f. Inform supervisor and or other treatment staff.
g. Mandatory reporting is required in some states, but laws vary.

Child Abuse

1. See Chapter 5.

Elder and Vulnerable Adult Abuse

1. See Chapter 5.

Patient/Client Abuse

1. See Chapter 4.

Psychological Reaction to Disability

EXAM HINT: The following information about the psychological reactions and psychosocial adjustment to disability apply to all persons with disabilities and the parents of children with disabilities. Correct answers to COTA® exam items will be respectful of a person's or family's stage of adjustment and include intervention approaches that foster adaptation to disability.

1. Several factors influence the individual's reaction to disability.
   a. Permanency of the disability.
   b. Sudden vs. chronic onset.
   c. Appraisal of life experiences.
   d. Spiritual beliefs.
   e. Support systems.
   f. Cultural factors.
2. Adjustment.
   a. Active participation in social, vocational, and avocational pursuits.
   b. Successful negotiation of the physical environment.
   c. Awareness of remaining strengths and assets as well as functional limitations.
3. Phases of adjustment.
   a. Shock.
      (1) Initial reaction to a sudden physical or psychological trauma.
      (2) Characterized by emotional numbness, depersonalization, and reduced speech and mobility.
   b. Anxiety.
      (1) A panic-stricken reaction to awareness of the seriousness of the situation.
      (2) Characterized by restlessness, confusion, racing thoughts, and psychological symptoms associated with anxiety.
   c. Denial.
      (1) Retreat from the realization of the seriousness and implications of the situation.
      (2) Characterized by minimization, negation, aloofness, and unrealistic expectations.
   d. Depression.
      (1) Bereavement for the associated losses as the realities of those losses are identified.
      (2) Characterized by hopelessness, helplessness, isolation, and decreased self-esteem.
   e. Internalized anger.
      (1) Resentment and bitterness directed toward self.
      (2) Characterized by blaming of self for the event, the extent of the loss, or the failure to recover.
   f. Externalized anger.
      (1) An attempt to retaliate for the imposed losses, directed against those associated with the onset or rehabilitation of the situation.
      (2) Characterized by aggression, antagonism, demanding and critical attitudes, and passive-aggressive behavior.
   g. Acknowledgement.
      (1) The first step toward acceptance of the situation.
      (2) Characterized by acceptance of a new self-concept and the identification of values and goals.

h. Adjustment.
   (1) An emotional acceptance of the situation and reintegration into identified roles.
   (2) Characterized by a positive sense of self and potentialities, and achievement of meaningful goals.
4. OT intervention.
   a. Acknowledgement of the individual's losses.
   b. Identification of what the individual is able to do with emphasis on personal accomplishments.
   c. Assistance to the individual in their assumption of an active role in shaping their life.
   d. The use of person-centered approaches based on empowerment theory is critical.
   e. Reduction of limitations through changes in the physical and social environment.
   f. Development of the skills necessary to participate in valued activities and meaningful occupations.
      (1) Stress management and coping skills.
      (2) Cognitive reframing/restructuring: the process of altering cognitions and cognitive processes (usually maladaptive thoughts and thinking) to facilitate changes in emotions and behavior.
   g. Acquisition of resources and supports to enable full social participation.
   h. Development of peer supports.

Suicide[7]

1. Facts and figures.
   a. In the United States, suicide is a major social justice crisis and health care concern.

   EXAM HINT: The below facts and figures are provided to highlight the need for OTAs to be vigilant about the potential of suicide during all interactions with all clients and family members, regardless of age. These statistics will not be on the COTA® exam.

   b. In the United States, suicide is the tenth leading cause of death.
      (1) A person dies by suicide about every 12 minutes in the United States.
      (2) In 2017, suicide was the 10th-leading cause of death.
      (3) The highest suicide rate, 19.7%, is among adults between the ages of 45 and 54. The second highest suicide rate, 18.9%, is among individuals aged 85+. The third highest suicide rate, 13.15%, is among adolescents and young adults between the ages of 15 and 24.
   c. It is estimated that there are 11 nonfatal suicide attempts for every suicide death.
   d. The attempts of men and the elderly are more likely to be more fatal than those of women and youth.
      (1) Men most frequently utilize a firearm, and women most frequently use poison to attempt suicide.
      (2) The suicide rate for men is 3.4% greater than that of women due to men using firearms at a higher rate than women.
      (3) Older adults attempt suicide at twice the rate of younger adults due to the losses associated with age.
   e. The suicide rate is increasing in children and adolescents.
      (1) 13% of high school students and 2.3% of college students have written a plan.
      (2) 8% percent of high school students have attempted suicide.
2. Identification of risk.
   a. A member of the treatment team (usually a physician) will ask the individual about suicidal thinking.
   b. It is important to identify the degree of risk.
      (1) The person is usually asked, if they were to try to hurt themselves and how they would do it.
         (a) The degree of detail given indicates the seriousness of intent.
         (b) The potential for the plan to succeed also indicates the degree of risk.

   RED FLAG: The observance or knowledge of any of the following risk factors associated with suicide requires immediate action by OT practitioners to prevent suicide.

   c. Risk factors for suicide.
      (1) Previous attempt or fantasized suicide.
      (2) Anxiety, depression, exhaustion, pervasive pessimism or hopelessness.
      (3) Availability of means of suicide, e.g., firearms in the home.
      (4) Concern for the effect of suicide on family members.
      (5) Verbalized suicidal ideation, plan, or intent.
      (6) Preparation of a will.
      (7) Resignation after agitated depression.
      (8) Proximal life crisis, such as mourning, divorce, pending surgery or disciplinary or legal problems.
      (9) Family history of suicide; exposure to suicide of others.
      (10) Family violence, including physical or sexual abuse.

---

[7] Victoria Crociata contributed to this section.

(11) Clinically diagnosed depression or other mental disorder.
(12) Co-occurring mental health and/or substance abuse disorders.
(13) Incarceration.
(14) Impulsive and/or aggressive tendencies.

> **EXAM HINT:** The NBCOT® exam outline for the COTA® identifies knowledge of "precautions . . . associated with a client condition or stage of recovery. . . . [and]. . . . preventive measures for minimizing risk in the intervention environment" (NBCOT®, 2018, p. 29) as essential for competent and safe practice. The application of knowledge about the following interventions will help you correctly answer NBCOT® Domain 03 exam items about the OT practitioner's response to suicide risk and intent.

3. OT intervention.
   a. Identification of the motivation behind the suicidal intent and the identification of alternatives.
      (1) Development of a *contract for safety*, which can also be called an emergency or contingency plan, that specifies what the individual should do if experiencing suicidal ideation, plan or intent.
         (a) A contract for safety asks the individual to contract or commit to telling appropriate person/persons if they are having thoughts of suicide.
   b. Development of problem-solving skills and stress management techniques to increase the individual's resilience and ability to manage life stressors.
   c. Identification of positive goals and interests to increase motivation for recovery.
   d. Identification of positive personal attributes and support systems to increase hopefulness.
      (1) This may be facilitated by a review of past successes.
      (2) This may be difficult to facilitate in individuals with depression.
   e. Activities that produce successful outcomes, especially those with a visible end product, promote positive thinking.
   f. Activities designed for the expression and validation of feelings.
   g. Moderate physical activity elevates mood.
   h. Development of skills that increase functional performance.
   i. Activities that are future oriented, i.e., going to college, starting a new career, babysitting a grandchild, enjoying family traditions with friends and family over the holidays.
   j. Patient/client and family education including:
      (1) Managing relapse and disappointment with a plan in place for dealing with active suicidal ideations.
      (2) Developing strategies for dealing with hopelessness.
      (3) Reinforcing and supporting engagement in treatment.
      (4) Maintaining medication compliance.
      (5) Increasing family involvement.
      (6) Identifying support groups and resources.
      (7) Developing strategies to handle setbacks in recovery.
   k. National Suicide Hotline 1-800-273-TALK (8255).

Self-Harm/Self-Mutilation

1. Definition.
   a. "Deliberate destruction or alteration of one's body tissue without conscious suicidal intent" (Favazza, 1996, pp. xviii–xix).
   b. Also known as self-injurious behavior, parasuicide, self-wounding, and cutting.
2. A maladaptive coping skill for dealing with uncomfortable feelings.
3. Role of OT.
   a. Improving self-management by teaching stress, anger, and emotional regulation skills.
   b. Instructing client in the use of alternative, less destructive coping strategies (e.g., snapping a rubber band worn on the wrist instead of cutting).
   c. Implementing interventions using CBT principles.
   d. Using DBT techniques if appropriate to the client.
   e. Providing instruction in the use of sensory approaches (tactile stimulation, massage, self-soothing) to manage the feelings that lead to self-harm.
   f. Developing problem solving skills.
   g. Improving communication skills.

Adjustment to Death and Dying

> **EXAM HINT:** Understanding the below stages of adjustment to death and dying, recognizing how these may be manifested behaviorally, and knowing the most effective OT intervention for each stage of adjustment can help you determine the correct answer for COTA® exam items about working with persons with terminal conditions and their families.

1. Stages of the individual's response as described by Elisabeth Kübler-Ross.
   a. Denial.
      (1) A coping strategy that allows the individual to refuse to accept or address the reality of their illness (e.g., "There must have been a mistake with the x-rays.").

- (2) Denial may lead the individual to see many health professionals, hoping to find the one who will give a different prognosis.
- (3) Denial may be a response to the denial or discomfort experienced by others.
- (4) Denial will end when the individual is psychologically prepared to face the reality of the situation.
- (5) OT intervention includes allowing the person to ask questions and discuss the situation at their own pace.

b. Anger.
- (1) The individual becomes angry as they accept the reality of impending death (e.g., "Get out of here. You don't know what it's like.").
- (2) This anger may be projected onto anyone who is seen as healthy or in a better position.
- (3) Rages, outbursts, and hurtful behavior must be identified for the purposes they serve.
- (4) OT intervention allows the individual to vent anger while identifying its source and developing more effective coping strategies.

c. Bargaining.
- (1) In an attempt to gain control, the individual may bargain with doctors, caretakers, or God (e.g., "Just let me go to my son's graduation and then I'll be okay with this.").
- (2) Bargains are an attempt to buy time.
- (3) Bargains are often associated with guilt related to things not done or promises not kept.
- (4) The individual should not be expected to keep to these bargains.
- (5) OT intervention involves responding honestly to questions.

d. Depression.
- (1) As the individual acknowledges impending death, they begin to identify the feelings of loss and becomes depressed.
- (2) The tendency is to say goodbye to all but a few and isolate oneself as thoughts and feelings turn inward.
- (3) Physical contact or just being together replaces conversation.
- (4) OT intervention assists in providing physical and psychological comfort for both the individual and their loved ones.

e. Acceptance.
- (1) As the individual recognizes impending death, they begin to make plans and think about the future for self and family.
- (2) It may be a time of peace without fear or despair.
- (3) As time goes on, the need to communicate diminishes.
- (4) OT intervention is to provide ongoing support to the individual and family.

2. General considerations.
   a. People vary in the way they go through each stage.
   b. They may stop at any stage (e.g., some may stay in denial as their preferred coping strategy).
   c. The needs of loved ones must be considered as they are likely going through stages similar to the dying individual.
   d. Occupational therapy practitioners should assist the individual in coping with each stage without pushing for progression into the next stage.

3. OT intervention throughout each stage.
   a. Assist the individual in maintaining as much control and independence as possible.
   b. Respond honestly and at the appropriate depth to questions.
   c. Assist the individual in developing coping skills.
   d. Encourage positive life review and support the legacies the individual leaves.
      (1) Gifts and mementos can be made or selected for significant others.
   e. Assist the individual in pursuing interests and maintaining meaningful roles.
   f. Actively listen.
   g. Incorporate family and friends into the treatment process.
   h. While being realistic, the OT practitioner should not deprive the individual of hope.

References

Allen, C. K., Earhart, C. A., & Blue, T. (1992). *Occupational therapy treatment goals for the physically and cognitively disabled.* Rockville, MD: American Occupational Therapy Association.

Allen, C., Austin, S., David, S., Earhart, C., McCraith, C., & Riska-Williams, L. (2007). *Manual for the Allen Cognitive Level Screen-5 (ACLS-5) and Large Allen Cognitive Level Screen-5 (LACLS-5).* Camarillo, CA: ACLS and LACLS Committee.

American Occupational Therapy Association. (2014). Occupational therapy practice framework: Domain and process (3rd ed.). *American Journal of Occupational Therapy, 68* (Suppl. 1), S1–S48.

American Psychiatric Association. (2013). *DSM-5: Diagnostic and statistical manual of mental disorders* (5th ed.). Washington, DC: Author.

Asher, I. (2014). *Occupational therapy assessment tools: An annotated index* (3rd ed.). Bethesda, MD: AOTA Press.

Benson, A. M., & Champagne, T. (2009). *Occupational therapy using a sensory integration–based approach with adult populations.* Retrieved from http://www.aota.org/~/media/Corporate/Files/AboutOT/Professionals/WhatIsOT/MH/Facts/SI%20Fact%20Sheet%202.ashx.

Bonder, B. (1991). *Psychopathology and function.* Thorofare, NJ: Slack.

Brown, C. (2011). Cognitive skills. In C Brown & V. Stoffel (Eds.), *Occupational therapy in mental health: A vision for participation.* (pp. 241–261). Philadelphia: F.A. Davis.

Brown, C., & Nicholson, R. (2011). Sensory skills. In C. Brown & V. Stoffel (Eds.), *Occupational therapy in mental health: A vision for participation.* (pp. 280–297). Philadelphia: F.A. Davis.

Bruce, M., & Borg, B. (2002). *Psychosocial frames of reference: Core for occupation-based practice* (3rd ed.). Thorofare, NJ: Slack.

Cara, E., & MacRae, A. (Eds.). (2013). *Psychosocial occupational therapy: An evolving practice* (3rd ed.). Clifton Park, NY: Delmar Cengage Learning.

Centers for Disease Control and Prevention (CDC). (2017). *Suicide among youth.* Retrieved from https://www.cdc.gov/healthcommunication/toolstemplates/entertainmented/tips/SuicideYouth.html.

Childhood Domestic Violence Association. (2014). *10 startling statistics about children of do mestic violence.* Retrieved from https://cdv.org/2014/02/10-startling-domestic-violence-statistics-for-children/.

Cole, M., & Tufano, R. (2008). *Applied theories in occupational therapy: A practical approach.* Thorofare, NJ: Slack.

Cole, M. B. (2005). *Group dynamics in occupational therapy: The theoretical basis and practice application of group dynamics* (3rd ed.). Thorofare, NJ: Slack.

Crepeau, E., Cohn, E., & Schell. (Eds.). (2003). *Willard and Spackman's occupational therapy* (10th ed.). Philadelphia: Lippincott, Williams & Wilkins.

Drench, M., Noonan, A., Sharby, N., & Ventura, S. (2012). *Psychosocial aspects of health care* (3rd ed.). Upper Saddle River, NJ: Pearson.

Early, M. (2009). *Mental health techniques and concepts for the occupational therapy assistant.* Philadelphia: Lippincott Williams & Wilkins.

Fidler, G. S. (1996). Life-style performance: From profile to conceptual model. In R. P. Cottrell (Ed.), *Perspectives on purposeful activity: Foundation and future of occupational therapy.* (pp. 113–121). Bethesda, MD: AOTA Press.

Fleming-Castaldy, R. P. (2014). Activities, occupations, and empowerment. In J. Hinojosa & M. L. Blount (Eds.), *The texture of life: Purposeful activities in the context of occupation* (4th ed., pp. 393–415). Bethesda, MD: AOTA Press.

Getty, S.M. (2015). Implementing a mental health program using the recovery model. *OT Practice, 20*(3), CE-1–CE-8.

Greenward, B. (2001). *Death and dying.* Retrieved from www.uic.edu/orgs/convening/deathdyi.htm.

Helfrich, C. A. (2000). Domestic violence: Implications and guidelines for occupational therapy practitioners. In R. P. Cottrell (Ed.), *Proactive approaches in psychosocial occupational therapy.* (pp. 309–316). Thorofare, NJ: Slack.

Hemphill, B. J. (Ed.). (1988). *Mental health assessment in occupational therapy.* Thorofare, NJ: Slack.

Hemphill-Pearson, B. J. (Ed.). (2008). *Assessments in occupational therapy mental health: An integrative approach.* Thorofare, NJ: Slack.

Hopkins, H., & Smith, H. (Eds.). (2003). *Willard and Spackman's occupational therapy* (10th ed.). Philadelphia: Lippincott Williams & Wilkins.

Hussey, S., Sabonis-Chafee, B., & O'Brien, J. (2007). *Introduction to occupational therapy* (3rd ed.). St. Louis, MO: Elsevier Mosby.

Kaplan, J. I., & Sadock, B. J. (2007). *Synopsis of psychiatry* (10th ed.). Philadelphia: Mosby.

Kielhofner, G. (2004). *Conceptual foundations of occupational therapy* (3rd ed.). Philadelphia: F.A. Davis.

Lane, S., Scott Roley, S., & Champagne, T. (2013). Sensory integration and processing theory and application to occupational therapy. In B. A. B. Schell, G. Gillen, & M. E. Scaffa (Eds.), *Willard and Spackman's occupational therapy* (12th ed., pp. 816–868). Philadelphia: Lippincott Williams & Wilkins.

Miller, P. J., & Walker, K. F. (Eds.). (1993). *Perspectives on theory for the practice of occupational therapy.* Gaithersburg, MD: Aspen Publishers.

Mosey, A. C. (1996). *Psychosocial components of occupational therapy.* New York: Raven Press.

National Alliance to End Homelessness. (2019). *Domestic violence and homelessness.* Retrieved from https://endhomelessness.org/homelessness-in-america/what-causes-homelessness/domestic-violence/.

National Board for Certification in Occupational Therapy (NBCOT®). (2018). *Practice analysis of the occupational therapist registered: Executive summary* [PDF file]. Gaithersburg, MD: Author. Retrieved from https://www.nbcot.org/-/media/NBCOT/PDFs/2017-Practice-Analysis-Executive-OTR.ashx?la=en.

National Institute of Mental Health (NIMH). (2018). *Suicide.* Retrieved from https://www.nimh.nih.gov/health/statistics/suicide.shtml.

Pratt, C. W., Gill, K. J., Barrett, N. M., & Roberts, M. M. (2007). *Psychiatric rehabilitation* (2nd ed.). Burlington, MA: Elsevier Academic Press.

Sadock, B. J. & Sadock, V. A. (Eds.). (2008). *Kaplan & Sadock's concise textbook of clinical psychiatry.* (3rd ed.) Philadelphia: Lippincott Williams & Wilkins.

Schkade, J. K., & Schultz, S. (1992). Occupational adaptation: Toward a holistic approach for contemporary practice, part 1. *American Journal of Occupational Therapy 46,* 829–837.

Schkade, J. K., & Schultz, S. (1992). Occupational adaptation: Toward a holistic approach for contemporary practice, part 2. *American Journal of Occupational Therapy 46,* 917–925.

Sladyk, K., Jacobs, K., & MacRae, N. (2010). *Occupational therapy essentials for clinical competence.* Thorofare, NJ: Slack.

Substance Abuse and Mental Health Services Administration. (2012). *10 guiding principles of recovery* [Brochure]. Retrieved from http://store.samhsa.gov/shin/content/PEP12-RECDEF/PEP12-RECDEF.pdf.

The National Coalition Against Domestic Violence. (2015). *Facts about domestic violence and physical abuse.* Retrieved from http://www.ncadv.org.

Review Questions

Psychosocial Approaches: Evaluation and Intervention

Below are seven questions about key content covered in this chapter. These questions are not inclusive of the entirety of content related to psychosocial evaluation and intervention approaches that you must know for success on the COTA® exam. These questions are provided to help you jump-start the thought processes you will need to apply your studying of content to the answering of exam questions; hence they are not in the COTA® exam format. Exam items in the COTA® format that cover the depth and breadth of content you will need to know to pass the exam are provided on this text's online exams. The answers to the questions below are provided in Appendix 3.

1. You are working in a setting that uses cognitive behavioral therapy (CBT). What are key general postulates for change that are used in CBT to guide the intervention process? How can these be applied throughout the occupational therapy process?

2. You collaborate with an occupational therapist to determine the best method for evaluating a client's cognitive level according to the Cognitive Disabilities model. Identify three evaluation tools that can be used to assess an individual's cognitive level according to the Cognitive Disabilities model. Describe a practice situation in which each evaluation would be most effectively used.

3. You work in a setting that uses sensory models to guide treatment. Describe five current intervention approaches based on sensory models and how they can be effectively applied in occupational therapy practice.

4. You provide occupational therapy services on an acute inpatient psychiatric unit. Describe interventions that you can provide to help patients who are experiencing hallucinations and/or delusions manage their symptoms during an occupational therapy group.

(Continued)

Review Questions

Psychosocial Approaches: Evaluation and Intervention (*Continued*)

5. You work for a setting that uses the RADAR approach to screen for and respond to domestic abuse. How would you apply this approach?

6. You are conducting a group for individuals with recently acquired spinal cord injuries who now have paraplegia and need to use a wheelchair for mobility. Adjusting to this abrupt change in their lives has been difficult, and group members have developed depression. Several have anger issues as well. While participating in a group, one of the participants says to you, "You really have no idea what it's like to have to face using a wheelchair for the rest of your life, when just a month ago I ran my sixth marathon. Running has been my whole life. It was the way I relieved stress and stayed in shape. I guess that's all over now." What type of therapeutic approach should you take? What types of individual and group interventions might benefit this individual?

7. You are watching television with your roommate in the eighth-floor apartment you share. You observe a very sad, withdrawn appearance and minimal spontaneous social interaction. Lately your roommate has been drinking more than usual on social occasions and this week cancelled a scheduled weekly therapy appointment. You ask if everything is alright, and the reply is, "No, not really. I'm thinking of killing myself, I just can't take it anymore." "How do you think you would do it?" you ask. "I'm not quite sure, I think I have a couple of options here, belts, knives, I'm not sure which way I want to go, but I have to do it soon, maybe by the end of the week. Yes, definitely by the end of the week. All things considered, I think I'll jump out the window. I'm pretty sure the fall would kill me." What risk factors for suicide are you observing in your roommate, what levels of suicide lethality are present, and what should be your first intervention?

14

Evaluation and Intervention for Performance in Areas of Occupation

RITA P. FLEMING-CASTALDY

Chapter Outline

- Occupations, 386
- Evaluation of Activities of Daily Living, 387
- Activities of Daily Living Intervention, 389
- Family Participation Evaluation, 393
- Family Participation Intervention, 393
- Play/Leisure, 395
- Work Evaluation, 396
- Work Intervention, 400
- References, 404
- Review Questions, 406

Occupations

Occupations Defined

1. "Daily life activities in which people engage" (AOTA, 2014, p. S43). They are:
   a. Activities of daily living (ADL): self-care tasks such as grooming, oral hygiene, bathing/showering, toilet hygiene, dressing, eating, functional mobility, and sexual activity.
      (1) These are also termed "basic" activities of daily living (BADL) and "personal" activities of daily living (PADL).
   b. Instrumental ADL (IADL): activities that are more complex than ADL and which support community living such as home establishment and management, meal preparation, shopping, financial management; care of others (e.g., children, pets), and community mobility.
   c. Work: competitive employment for pay and other productive activities that make a societal contribution, such as volunteer work.
   d. Education: activities needed to participate in a learning environment and fulfill the role of student.
   e. Play and leisure: intrinsically motivated discretionary activities done for personal pleasure, diversion, and entertainment.
   f. Social participation: activities engaged in as a member of a community, family, and/or peer/friend group.
   g. Rest and sleep: restorative activities that support health and occupational engagement (AOTA, 2014).

Overall Evaluation Guidelines

EXAM HINT: In the NBCOT® exam outline for the COTA®, Domain 01 Collaborating and Gathering Information comprises 28% of the exam. Domain 01 exam items focus on the ability of the therapist to "acquire information regarding factors that influence occupational performance on an ongoing basis through the occupational therapy process" (NBCOT®, 2018, p. 21). The application of knowledge about the following guidelines can help you determine the correct answer for NBCOT® Domain 01 exam items about the evaluation of occupational performance.

1. The occupational therapy assistant (OTA) contributes to the evaluation process by collecting data and sharing observations.
   a. Service competency must be established to ensure data will be collected effectively and safely.
   b. The level of supervision needed for the collection of evaluation data by the OTA will depend on the OTA's experience and established service competence.
   c. The OTA cannot independently evaluate occupational performance.
2. The focus of occupational therapy (OT) evaluation must be the individual's ability to perform meaningful occupations that are needed and desired by the individual.
3. Assessments should follow a 'top-down' progression of considering the person's occupations first, rather than a 'bottom-up' approach that focuses on performance components/skills.
   a. The first step in the evaluation process is "focused on finding out what a client wants and needs to do; determining what a client can do and has done; and identifying supports and barriers to health, well-being, and participation" (AOTA, 2014, p. S13).
   b. The desired outcome of evaluation is the identification of the person's occupational performance concerns and difficulties and the establishment of the individual's priorities for performance in areas of occupation.
   c. In the OT Practice Framework, this determination is called the occupational profile. Refer to Chapter 3 and Table 3-1.
4. After the completion of a person's occupational profile, the person's client factors, performance skills, patterns, contexts, and activity demands are assessed to identify specific strengths and limitations that impact on desired and needed occupational performance.
   a. All of the factors that may influence performance in areas of occupation are considered during screening.
      (1) Based on the results of screening, aspects that are determined to warrant further evaluation are specifically assessed.
   b. In certain practice settings (e.g., acute care with a 3-day length of stay) and in certain clinical situations (e.g., there are major concerns for a client's safety) the determination of underlying problems may take precedence over the determination of an occupational profile.

c. To determine these capabilities, the evaluation process should include observation of the person's actual performance of an activity in context.
   (1) If it is pragmatically not possible during the evaluation process for the person to perform the activity in its natural context, an environment that closely simulates the natural one should be provided for the assessment (e.g., an ADL apartment on a rehabilitation unit to simulate the person's home).
d. In the OT Practice Framework, this part of the evaluation process is called an analysis of occupational performance. Refer to Chapter 3 and Table 3-1.
5. Occupational performance assessment tools include interviews, checklists, task performance, rating scales, and standardized instruments.

General Intervention Guidelines

> **EXAM HINT:** In the NBCOT® exam outline for the COTA® "Domain 02 Selecting and implementing interventions under the supervision of the OTR® in accordance with the intervention plan and level of service competence to support client participation in areas of occupation throughout the occupational therapy process" (NBCOT®, 2018, p. 18) comprises 55% of the exam. The application of knowledge about the following intervention guidelines can help you effectively determine the correct answers to Domain 02 exam items.

1. The OTA implements intervention with OT supervision.
2. Intervention should follow a 'top-down' progression of considering the person's occupation first rather than a 'bottom-up' approach that focuses initially and/or solely on performance skills and client factors.
   a. The impact of performance skill deficits and client factors on occupational performance is considered after establishing the individual's desired occupational outcome.
   b. Specific interventions to remediate, alleviate, and/or compensate for the effects of performance skill deficits and client factors on occupational performance are often required.
   c. The focus of remediation interventions for performance component/skill deficits must be related to the individual's ability to perform meaningful occupations that are needed and desired by the individual.
3. Interventions for deficits that cannot be remediated should include recommendations for adaptive strategies and/or adaptive equipment that compensate for the deficits and ease occupational performance.
   a. Strategies that can be generalized to different situations are particularly helpful (e.g., principles of energy conservation).
   b. Multiple factors should be considered when recommending adaptive strategies. See Table 14-1.
      (1) These factors are also relevant to consider when selecting adaptive equipment.
   c. Training in adaptive strategies and/or equipment used to enhance self-care performance must consider the person's privacy and dignity.
      (1) This is especially critical in interventions for the performance of BADL/PADL.

Table 14-1

Factors to Consider When Recommending Adaptive Strategies

- What is important to the individual about the task?
- Is the strategy viewed as compatible with the particular social context?
- Does the strategy enhance the individual's sense of personal control?
- Does the strategy minimize the effort?
- Does the strategy interfere with social opportunities or diminish the presentation of self?
- Is the recommended strategy temporally realistic given the context?
- Does the strategy provide for safety?

From: McCraig, M. (1994). Self-care management for adults with movement disorders. In C. Christiansen (Ed.), *Ways of living: Self-care strategies for special needs* (p. 261). Bethesda, MD: American Occupational Therapy Association. Reprinted with permission.

Evaluation of Activities of Daily Living

BADL and IADL Assessment Overview

1. BADL and IADL assessment tools include interviews, checklists, task performance, rating scales, and standardized instruments.
2. Many assessment tools used to measure BADL and IADL provide a determination of the person's level of functional performance. See Table 14-2.
3. Interpretation of BADL and IADL assessments to determine a person's functional capabilities and ability to live independently are made by the occupational therapist.

a. The OTA contributes to this determination process.
b. Due to the self-report and/or simulated nature of certain items and the limited number of items tested in many evaluation tools, interpretations must be made cautiously.

> **EXAM HINT:** The NBCOT® exam outline for the COTA® identifies knowledge of the "purpose, advantages, limitations, and service competency needs related to the administration of commonly used standardized assessments and non-standardized screening as a means of acquiring client information" (NBCOT®, 2018, p. 21) as essential for competent practice. The application of knowledge about the general BADL and IADL assessment information previously described and the following information about the evaluation of sexual expression and activity can help you correctly answer Domain 01 exam items.

Sexual Expression/Activity Evaluation

1. The ADL skill of sexual expression/activity is typically not included on commonly used ADL assessments, and it does not have a published OT assessment available for clinical use.
2. Despite this gap, the OT practitioner should assess this ADL during routine screenings and interviews, as appropriate.
3. The OTA contributes to the assessment of this ADL in collaboration with the OT supervisor.
   a. The aims of this process are to:
      (1) Determine if sexual expression/activity is valued.
      (2) Identify potential obstacles for the attainment and maintenance of safe, satisfying sexual expression/activity.
         (a) Pathophysiological changes related to disease, disability, and/or the aging process.
         (b) Psychological and/or cognitive changes related to disease, disability, and/or the aging process.
            • Judgment, impulse control, and decision-making skills must be assessed to ensure safety.
         (c) Limited partner availability due to social demographics and/or sociocultural attitudes.
      (3) Determine if a person's knowledge of their sexuality is adequate and appropriate for their age, developmental level, expected roles, and environmental contexts.
4. If an individual is reticent about discussing their sexuality during the OT evaluation, the practitioner must respect and accept this preference.

Table 14-2

Scales to Measure Functional Performance

TOTAL ASSISTANCE:
The need for 100% assistance by one or more persons to perform all physical activities and/or cognitive assistance to elicit a functional response to an external stimulation.

MAXIMUM ASSISTANCE:
The need for 75% assistance by one person to physically perform any part of a functional activity and/or cognitive assistance to perform gross motor actions in response to direction.

MODERATE ASSISTANCE:
The need for 50% assistance by one person to perform physical activities or provide cognitive assistance to sustain/complete simple, repetitive activities safely.

MINIMUM ASSISTANCE:
The need for 25% assistance by one person for physical activities and/or periodic, cognitive assistance to perform functional activities safely.

STAND-BY ASSISTANCE:
The need for supervision by one person for the patient to perform new activity procedures that were adapted by the therapist for safe and effective performance. A patient requires stand-by assistance when errors and the need for safety precautions are not always anticipated by the patient.

INDEPENDENT STATUS:
No physical or cognitive assistance is required to perform functional activities. Patients at this level are able to implement the selected courses of action, consider potential errors, and anticipate safety hazards in familiar and new situations.

Adapted from Health Care Financing Administration. (1996). *Medicare intermediary manual, Publication 13, Section 3906.4*. Washington, DC: U.S. Government Printing Office, 21–21.

a. Sexual concerns that are unexpressed during initial OT sessions are often brought forth during later sessions as a therapeutic relationship develops between the individual and their OT practitioner.
b. Sessions focused on intimate self-care issues frequently precipitate questions regarding sexuality.
c. An atmosphere of continuing permission to discuss sexual expression should be maintained throughout the person's engagement in OT.

> **CAUTION:** The potential realities of sexual abuse, assault, and exploitation must be considered during the evaluation of all individuals regardless of age. Occupational therapy practitioners are required by practice acts, protective legislation, and our professional code of ethics to report any suspected incidents of child, adult, or elder abuse or assault to the appropriate agency and/or local law enforcement.

Activities of Daily Living Intervention

Self-Care Intervention

1. Determine with the OT supervisor whether the self-care activity should be modified to enable individual performance, performance with external assistance, or eliminated.
   a. Activities that are valued, meaningful, and enjoyable to the person and related to desired role performance should be modified for individual performance, with appropriate supports provided as needed (e.g., brushing one's hair using an adapted brush to maintain one's appearance at school/work).
   b. Activities that are difficult to perform and/or are not enjoyable should be eliminated or performed with the assistance of others (e.g., dressing requires a great deal of exertion that can exhaust an individual; fasteners can be modified or eliminated, physical assistance can facilitate task).

> **EXAM HINT:** In the NBCOT® exam outline for the COTA® Domain 02 Selecting and Implementing Interventions comprises 55% of the NBCOT® exam and knowledge of "adaptive and preventive strategies for optimal engagement in occupation" (NBCOT®, 2018, p. 25) is identified as essential for competent and safe practice. The application of knowledge about the above general intervention principles and the following adaptive strategies can help you effectively determine the correct answers to exam items that address interventions to enable self-care performance.

2. Recommend adaptive strategies for self-care task performance. (See Table 14-1.)
3. Provide adaptive equipment to compensate for functional impairments during self-care activity performance.
   a. Toileting and toilet hygiene equipment.
      (1) Grab bars and/or toilet safety frame.
      (2) Bedside (three-in-one) commode or raised toilet seat.
      (3) Bowel training device, bladder control devices.
      (4) Skin inspection mirror.
      (5) Toilet paper holder.
   b. Grooming/oral hygiene adaptive equipment.
      (1) Universal cuff to hold toothbrush, razor, comb, and/or brush.
      (2) Built-up, angled, or long-handled brushes and/or razors.
      (3) Blow dryer, nail clipper, nail polish holders.
      (4) Faucet turners.
      (5) Electric toothbrush, floss holders, water flosser.
   c. Bathing/showering.
      (1) Grab bars and nonskid mat.
      (2) Tub transfer bench/shower bench.
      (3) Shower or commode chair.
      (4) Handheld shower.
      (5) Antiscald valves and/or faucets.
      (6) Built-up, angled, and/or long-handled bath sponge or bath mitt.
      (7) Soap on a rope, soap dish with suction cup.
      (8) Storage units.
   d. Dressing.
      (1) Reachers, dressing sticks/hooks, and pants dressing poles.
      (2) Built-up, angled, or long-handled shoehorn.
      (3) Pull-on clothing, Velcro-type and/or front opening closures for clothing.
      (4) Elastic shoelaces, slip-on shoes.
      (5) Button hook, zipper pull, and zipper loop or ring.
      (6) Sock/stocking aid.
   e. Feeding/eating.
      (1) Adapted nipples and bottles for infants.
      (2) Scoop dish or plate guards.
      (3) Non-slip placemat or Dycem.
      (4) Built-up, angled, weighted, or long-handled utensils, swivel utensils.
      (5) Rocker knife and/or spork.
      (6) Adapted cups and long or angled straws.
      (7) See Chapters 5, 9, and 12 for information on interventions to facilitate development of oral-motor control and feeding skills.
   f. Medication management.
      (1) Easy-open, non-child-proof medication bottles.
      (2) Pill organizers, medication minders.
   g. Refer to Table 14-3 for spinal cord injury (SCI) levels and self-care abilities.
4. Recognize the multiple dimensions of a person with a disability and the complexities of many disorders. For example, Friedreich's ataxia is characterized by tremors that may indicate the need for weighted utensils, but muscle strength is also limited so these utensils may be too heavy for functional use.
5. Train in safe use of adaptive equipment and assistive technology.
6. Practice to attain proficiency in activity performance at appropriate times and in real environments (e.g., brush teeth in the bathroom in the morning).

Table 14-3

SCI Levels and Self-Care Abilities

Level	Abilities
C1–C3	Totally dependent in all self-care but can instruct others in preferences for care. Can chew and swallow.
C4	Totally dependent in all self-care but can instruct others in preferences for care. Can drink from a glass with a long straw.
C5	Feeding requires total assist for setup; then independent with equipment. Equipment used may include: • Suspension sling or mobile arm support. • Dorsal wrist splint with universal cuff. • Dycem to prevent slippage of plate. • Scoop dish or plate guard. • Angled utensils. Dressing requires minimal to moderate assistance with upper body dressing. Dependent with lower body dressing. Bathing requires moderate to minimal assistance. Grooming requires assistance with setup; however, with splint and universal cuff can be independent with brushing teeth and combing hair. Independent using electric shaver that fits around the hand.
C6	Feeding: Independent using adaptive equipment which may include: • Universal cuff or tenodesis splint. • Rocker knife. • Scoop dish or plate guard. • Cup with large handles. Dressing: Independent in lower body dressing performed while in bed. Requires maximal assistance with socks and shoes. Independent with upper body dressing using button hook, zipper pull, Velcro fasteners. Bathing: Minimal assistance using handheld shower, tub bench, and sliding board transfer. Grooming: Independent using tenodesis grasp or splint.
C7	Feeding: Independent Dressing: Independent, but may need button hook. Bathing: Independent using handheld shower, tub bench, and depression transfers. Grooming: Same as C6.
C8–T1	Independent in all self-care; uses tub bench and handheld shower. Performs depression transfers. Can transfer from wheelchair to floor and back to chair with stand-by assist.
T6 to L4	Independent in all self-care.

7. Provide cues and assistance as needed.
    a. Verbal reminders and prompts.
    b. Nonverbal gestures, written directions, physical prompt to initiate.
    c. Physical hand-over-hand assistance through complete activity movement.
    d. Visual supervision to ensure safety with minimal or no verbal or nonverbal cues.
8. Use thematic and topical groups to develop needed skills (e.g., grooming group, medication management).
9. Teach principles and methods of energy conservation, work simplification, joint protection, and proper body mechanics. Refer to Chapter 11.
10. Educate and train caregivers to provide needed cues, physical assistance, and/or supervision.
    a. Teach organizational strategies (e.g., place clothing in proper sequence for dressing).
    b. Teach activity analysis, gradation, simplification, and adaptation skills (e.g., provide multiple small meals to decrease the amount of attention required to eat for a person with Alzheimer's disease).
11. Educate the individual with disabilities on personal care attendant training and management.
    a. Practice methods for directing self-care in the personally desired and acceptable manner.
    b. Provide assertiveness and personal advocacy training.
12. Modify the environment to maximize performance and ensure safety. Refer to Chapter 15.

Sexual Expression/Activity Intervention

1. OT intervention is provided to enable satisfying, safe sexual expression/activity regardless of disability, disease, or advanced age.
2. Myths about the sexuality of the aged and individuals with disability or disease processes must be confronted and debunked.

3. Myths include:
    a. They are asexual and have less interest in sexual expression than younger and/or healthier persons.
    b. They are physically unattractive and not desirable as a sexual partner and will be a burden to their partners.
    c. They inherently have poor judgment and cannot make safe decisions about their sexuality.
    d. Intercourse with mutual orgasm is the desired and primary means to express oneself sexually.
        (1) Intimate behaviors, such as mutual stimulation, cuddling, oral sex, and/or caressing are not adequate sexual activity.
        (2) Self-stimulation/masturbation is not an appropriate means of sexual expression.
    e. Individuals who live in shared residential settings such as nursing homes, group homes, and assisted living facilities are asexual.
        (1) They should be segregated according to gender.
        (2) Privacy for the individual is not essential and does not need to be respected.
    f. Individuals with disabilities and/or older adults who desire and/or engage in sexual activity are oversexed and inappropriate.

> **EXAM HINT:** If a COTA® exam item provides evaluation results that include a person identifying sexual expression as a desired occupation, a correct answer would include interventions that use the PLISSIT model described as follows. Because the myths about sexuality as previously described are pervasive in some practice settings, a correct answer could also include the OTA debunking these myths and advocating for the person's right to sexual expression/activities.

4. OT practitioners should use the PLISSIT model as a guide for appropriate interventions.
    a. P = permission, which requires the practitioner to create an atmosphere that gives the individual permission to raise concerns about their sexuality and sexual activity(ies).
        (1) Incorporating sexuality into the OT initial and ongoing evaluation in a matter-of-fact manner is an effective method.
        (2) An OT practitioner who is not comfortable with creating a permissive atmosphere for the discussion of sexuality due to personal, social, cultural, and/or religious reasons must honestly acknowledge this fact to the client and refer them immediately to a team member who is comfortable with addressing the individual's concerns.
        (3) It is the team's responsibility to ensure that at least one team member is comfortable with evaluating and intervening with individuals with sexual expression concerns.
        (4) Supervision and continuing professional development activities should be pursued by all to develop this needed comfort.
    b. LI = limited information that is provided by the OT practitioner to ensure that the individual has accurate knowledge about their sexual abilities and potentials.
        (1) Facts are shared (e.g., there is sex after disability), and myths are dispelled (see prior section).
    c. SS = specific suggestions that are provided by the OT practitioner to facilitate the individual's pursuit of satisfying sexual expression, either alone or with a partner.
        (1) The individual's (and partner's) goals for sexual expression and activity are identified and strategies for achieving goals are explored.
        (2) Principles of activity analysis, gradation, modification, and simplification are used to facilitate goal attainment.
        (3) Nonmedical methods to manage pain and stiffness (e.g., warm baths) are provided.
        (4) Positioning alternatives and adaptive equipment to facilitate desired sexual expression are suggested.
        (5) Energy conservation methods (e.g., timing sex for when one has the most energy and use of sexual positions that require less energy expenditures) are suggested to those with limited endurance.
        (6) Catheter care, hygiene concerns, and skin care are addressed.
        (7) Referrals to a physician for medical management of pain, impotence or other sexual dysfunctions, and hormonal treatment.
    d. IT = intensive therapy that is indicated when the individual requires intervention for long-standing relationship problems and/or enduring sexual problems.
        (1) These problems are often due to difficulties beyond the onset or presence of a disability.
        (2) Specialized training is required to provide intensive therapy, so a referral to the appropriate professional (e.g., marriage counselor, sex therapist) is indicated.
5. Methods of intervention can include one-on-one counseling sessions, therapeutic groups, and/or dissemination of printed materials.
6. Interventions for individuals with cognitive impairments (e.g., poor impulse control, limited judgment) are essential to ensure safety and to protect the individual from sexual abuse, assault, and/or exploitation.

a. Assertiveness training to increase understanding of their rights, and develop the ability, to set limits.
b. Training and practice in physical self-protection techniques.
c. Role playing to simulate potential scenarios that can challenge the individual's sexual judgment.
d. Sex education (e.g., menstrual cycle information, prevention of sexually transmitted diseases).
e. Caregiver and family education.
  (1) Socially inappropriate sexual activity is often difficult for families to understand (e.g., an older adult with a neurocognitive disorder begins to disrobe in the living room).
    (a) Recognizing that this behavior is indicative of an underlying disease process is important.
    (b) Providing strategies for effectively managing undesirable behaviors is main OT focus (e.g., eliminate clothing fasteners in the front, divert the person's attention to an activity of interest).

Home Management Intervention

1. Determine with the OT supervisor the home management expectations and demands of the individual's current and expected environment.
   a. Supportive living environments can range in expectations from requiring that a resident only clean their room (e.g., in a group home) to complete management of a home with minimal supervision (e.g., a supported apartment).
   b. Independent living environments can also have a range of expectations and demands (e.g., one spouse does the budget, the other cooks).
2. Determine with the OT supervisor and the individual whether the home management activity should be modified to enable independent performance, self-directed performance with external assistance, or eliminated.
   a. Activities that are valued, meaningful, and enjoyable to the person and related to desired role performance should be modified for individual performance, with appropriate supports provided as needed (e.g., preparing after-school snacks for children).
   b. Activities that are difficult to perform and/or are not enjoyable should be eliminated or performed with the assistance of others (e.g., cleaning a refrigerator can be delegated to another person, or a self-cleaning oven can eliminate a task).
3. Recommend adaptive strategies for home management task performance. Refer to Table 14-1.
4. Provide adaptive equipment to compensate for functional impairments during home management activity performance.
   a. Cleaning.
      (1) Suction bottom bottle and glass brushes.
      (2) Reachers.
      (3) Aerosol can holders.
      (4) Built-up, angled, or long-handled sponges, dusters, brooms, mops, dustpans.
      (5) Front-loading washers and dryers.
      (6) Electronic dishwasher, self-cleaning oven, automatic defrosting refrigerator.
   b. Cooking.
      (1) Faucet and knob turners.
      (2) Antiscald faucets and/or valves.
      (3) Jar openers, bowl holders, and saucepan stabilizers.
      (4) Nonskid pad, placemat, or Dycem.
      (5) Cutting board with a stabilizing nail and built-up edges.
      (6) Built-up or angled utensils and rocker knives.
      (7) Adapted timers.
      (8) Electric can opener.
      (9) Lightweight pots, pans, dishware.
      (10) Automatic hot water dispenser and/or hot-pots.
      (11) Strap loops to open refrigerator, cabinet, and oven doors.
      (12) Reachers and step stools.
      (13) Utility cart.
      (14) High kitchen stool.
5. Train in safe use of adaptive equipment and assistive technology.
6. Teach principles and methods of energy conservation, work simplification, joint protection, and proper body mechanics. Refer to Chapter 11.
7. Provide cues and assistance as needed.
   a. Verbal reminders and prompts.
   b. Nonverbal gestures, written directions, physical prompts to initiate.
   c. Physical hand-over-hand assistance through complete activity movement.
   d. Visual supervision to ensure safety with minimal or no verbal or nonverbal cues.
8. Practice to attain proficiency in activity performance at appropriate times and in real environments (e.g., cooking a meal in a kitchen at lunchtime).
9. Recognize and respect personal, sociocultural, and socioeconomic differences (e.g., standards of cleanliness, dietary restrictions, and preferences).
   a. Use equipment that is socioeconomically appropriate (e.g., do not use an oven to teach meal preparation if someone only uses a microwave).

10. Use thematic and topical groups to develop needed skills (e.g., cooking group, money management group).
11. Modify environment to maximize performance and ensure safety. Refer to Chapter 15.
12. Educate and train caregivers to provide needed cues, physical assistance, and/or supervision.
13. Refer to relevant social service programs (e.g., Supplemental Nutrition Assistance Program [SNAP], Home Energy Assistance Program [HEAP]).
14. Refer to the appropriate supportive living environment if independent living is not attainable (e.g., group home, halfway house, supported apartment).

EXAM HINT: In the NBCOT® exam outline for the COTA®, Domain 02 Selecting and Implementing Interventions comprises 55% of the NBCOT® exam and knowledge of "adaptive and preventive strategies for optimal engagement in occupation" (NBCOT®, 2018, p. 25) is identified as essential for competent practice. The application of knowledge about the general intervention principles and the adaptive strategies described in this section can help you effectively determine the correct answers to exam items that address interventions to enable home management performance.

Family Participation Evaluation

Overview

1. There are no specific OT published assessments that deal exclusively with family interaction.
   a. Some commonly used assessments include family participation (e.g., the Role Checklist).
2. The OTA contributes to the assessment of this occupational performance in collaboration with the OT supervisor.
3. The OTA and occupational therapist should assess this occupational performance during routine screenings and interviews. The aims of this process are to:
   a. Determine past, current, and anticipated roles, responsibilities, and expectations of family members.
   b. Identify potential obstacles for the attainment and maintenance of satisfying family interaction.

CAUTION: If the family and the OT practitioner do not share a common language, interpreters must be used to ensure the validity of information obtained.

4. The sociocultural background, values, and dynamics of the family must be considered during the evaluation process.
5. Individuals who live in shared residential settings such as nursing homes, group homes, and assisted living facilities and their families should receive intervention to assist with role transitions.
   a. Fellow residents and staff in these settings often assume the roles of surrogate family members.

Parenting/Child Care

1. Determine ability to care for child's physical needs.
2. Determine ability to care for child's emotional needs.
3. Determine knowledge of child's developmental level and its corresponding play and communication level.

Family Participation Intervention

General Intervention Guidelines

1. Collaborate with family on identifying desired goals.
   a. Provide interpreters, if necessary.
2. Determine with the OT supervisor and the individual whether the family activity should be modified to enable independent performance, self-directed performance with external assistance, or eliminated.
   a. Activities that are valued, meaningful, and enjoyable to the person and related to desired role performance should be modified for individual

performance, with appropriate supports provided as needed (e.g., reading a bedtime story to children).
   b. Activities that are difficult to perform and/or are not safe should be eliminated or performed with the assistance of others (e.g., bathing a toddler).
3. Methods of intervention can include one-on-one counseling sessions, therapeutic groups, and/or dissemination of printed materials.
4. Design interventions using activities that are meaningful to the individual's role within the family.
5. Use topical and thematic groups to develop effective family participation skills.
   a. Role-play to simulate potential scenarios that can challenge the individual's family skills (e.g., assertiveness training, anger management).
   b. Practice effective family communication.
   c. Teach principles and methods of energy conservation, work simplification, joint protection, and proper body mechanics for family activities. Refer to Chapter 11.
   d. Develop parenting skills, if needed.

Intervention for Parenting Activities

1. Teach how to care for a child's physical needs and physically practice parenting tasks (e.g., placing child into a front pack using proper body mechanics).
2. Instruct parent about typical developmental roles and tasks to ensure expectations of child/children are realistic.

> **EXAM HINT:** In the NBCOT® exam outline for the COTA®, Domain 02 Selecting and Implementing Interventions comprises 55% of the NBCOT® exam and knowledge of "adaptive and preventive strategies for optimal engagement in occupation" (NBCOT®, 2018, p. 25) is identified as essential for competent and safe practice. The application of knowledge about the previous general intervention principles and the following adaptive strategies can help you effectively determine the correct answers to exam items that address interventions to enable effective parenting.

3. Recommend adaptive strategies for home management task performance that are related to parenting (e.g., preparation of child's bag lunch for school). See Table 14-1.
4. Provide adaptive equipment to compensate for functional impairments during parenting tasks.
   a. Adapted drop-side crib, raised and/or adjustable-height crib mattress, child-resistant one-handed crib wall release mechanism.
   b. Foam rubber bathing pads for sink, portable plastic tub, and/or reclining infant seat placed in tub.
   c. Changing tables at proper height with safety straps and touch fasteners.
   d. Pillow to support breastfeeding (which physically is the easiest method to feed an infant).
   e. Lightweight and/or angled bottles.
   f. One-handed swing away release tray on highchair with safety strap.
   g. Food warmer tray.
   h. Pullover clothes, Velcro fasteners for bibs, diaper covers, clothing.
   i. Infant carriers.
5. Baby furniture and equipment should be tested and used on a trial basis to ensure it matches the parent's capabilities.
6. The family's socioeconomic status and cost of recommendations must be considered (e.g., premeasured formula and disposable diapers are convenient, energy-saving, *and* expensive options).
7. Recognize and respect personal, sociocultural, and socioeconomic differences within families.
8. Teach the child/children of a parent with a disability self-reliance at a young age.
   a. Arrange tasks so they are accessible to a child (e.g., storage for dishes and glasses next to dishwasher, not in a high cabinet).
   b. Delegate tasks that are achievable for child's/children's developmental level (e.g., even a young child can move clothes from a front-loading washer to a front-loading dryer).
9. Modify the environment to maximize parenting task performance and ensure safety of the parent and child. Refer to Chapter 15.
10. Refer family members to support groups and local and national organizations.
11. Provide caregiver/family education in verbal and written formats in family's language of choice.
12. Be aware of signs of family neglect or abuse.
    a. OT practitioners are required by practice acts, protective legislation, and our professional code of ethics to report any suspected incidents of child, adult, or elder abuse, assault, or exploitation to the appropriate agency and local law enforcement.

Play/Leisure

Evaluation Overview

1. The OTA contributes to the assessment of this occupational performance during routine screenings and interviews, in collaboration with the OT supervisor.
   a. The OTA may administer specific play/leisure assessments as determined by service competency.
2. Assessment tools for play and leisure include interviews, checklists, task performance, rating scales, and standardized instruments.
3. The aims of evaluation are to:
   a. Determine the individual's perception of the meaning of leisure and the extent the individual participates in leisure or play activities.
   b. Identify motivational and situational issues that influence leisure or play (e.g., perceived barriers to leisure/play and knowledge of leisure/play opportunities).
   c. Identify ways leisure or play activities can be modified to better meet individual needs.

CAUTION: If the family and the OT practitioner do not share a common language, interpreters must be used to ensure the validity of information obtained.

Developmental Considerations in Evaluation

1. Determine a child's or adolescent's developmental level to enable the selection of developmentally appropriate toys and play activities.
2. Assess sensory, motor, cognitive, and psychosocial skills in the context of play.
3. Determine the adequacy of a child's type of play (structured vs. spontaneous) and play environments.
   a. Family and teacher interviews and home and school observations are typically used.
4. Identify family supports and community resources for engagement in play.

Play/Leisure Intervention

1. Recognize that the acquisition of a disability often results in increased leisure time due to loss of roles.
   a. Provide support for losses, refer to support group and/or disability advocacy groups.
   b. Renew or adapt old interests.
2. Leisure activities that are valued, meaningful, and enjoyable to the person should be adapted, modified, and/or simplified to facilitate satisfying engagement.

EXAM HINT: The NBCOT® exam outline for the COTA® identifies knowledge of "interventions for supporting leisure and play-based exploration and participation consistent with client interests, needs, goals, and context" (NBCOT®, 2018, p. 25) as essential for competent practice. The application of knowledge about the previous general intervention principles and the following adaptive strategies can help you effectively determine the correct answers to exam items that address interventions to enable people's engagement in play/leisure.

3. Provide assistive technology and adaptive equipment to compensate for functional impairments during leisure activity performance.
   a. Universal cuff.
   b. Card holders.
   c. Book holders and page turners.
   d. Writing orthosis, typing aids, weighted pens.
   e. Headsticks, mouthsticks.
   f. Environmental control unit (ECU) to activate electronic equipment (e.g., CD players, TVs).
   g. Adapted computer, keyboard guards, voice-activated computer.
   h. Smartphone applications.
   i. Speaker phones.
   j. Use switches to activate toys that a child with a disability cannot operate by conventional means.
   k. Refer to Table 14-4 for a description of SCI levels and play/leisure abilities.
4. Use thematic and topical groups to develop needed skills (e.g., a parenting play group, a retirement planning group).
5. Teach principles and methods of energy conservation, work simplification, joint protection, and proper body mechanics. Refer to Chapter 11.
6. Refer to relevant community and national resources (e.g., senior centers, free concerts, parks, Compeer, Special Olympics).
7. Explore and present Internet and web-based opportunities for play and leisure participation (e.g., social networking, chat rooms, gaming sites).

Table 14-4

SCI Levels and Play/Leisure Abilities

Level	Abilities
C1–C4	Can play computer games, access the Internet and e-mail, and control radios, TVs, and other electronic devices using a mouthstick, head pointer, or voice activation. Can read using a mouthstick, head pointer, or electronic page turner to turn pages. Can paint with a mouthstick or head pointer.
C5	Can independently play computer games, turn pages for reading, play board games, do some crafts, use a speakerphone and access electronic devices, the Internet, and e-mail using a splint, universal cuff, and/or a typing splint.
C6 and C7	Can hold a phone, typing stick, and pen using a tenodesis grasp. Can independently do some crafts, turn pages for reading, use a computer, and access electronic devices, the Internet, and e-mail using a tenodesis grasp or universal cuff to hold a typing stick. Can play board games and some wheelchair sports.
C8–T1	Can do the most leisure activities due to good functional use of both upper extremities.

Developmental Considerations for Play Interventions

1. Plan with the supervising occupational therapist play interventions that consider developmental issues and the child's developmental level.
2. Provide opportunities for culturally relevant solitary play and environmental mastery.
3. Facilitate active participation in cause-and-effect learning.
4. Provide opportunities for play with siblings and/or peers.
5. Provide toys that are safe, durable, and colorful.
6. Provide toys and activities that are visually and auditory stimulating.

Work Evaluation

Prevocational Assessment Process

1. The OTA contributes to this process with supervision of the occupational therapist. The aims of this process are to:
   a. Screen to identify deficits in occupational performance areas, client factors, and/or performance skills that could impact on work abilities and potential.
   b. Determine if the individual is interested in prevocational assessment and intervention.
   c. Gather relevant work, educational, social, and medical history information.
   d. Identify prevocational interests through the use of interest inventories and/or structured interviews.
   e. Assess current level of work-related skills.
      (1) Conduct structured observations of an individual performing work tasks in a prevocational group or rehabilitation workshop (formerly called sheltered workshop) or during a job simulation.
         (a) Rating scales or checklists of prevocational skills and behaviors are used.
         (b) Refer to Table 14-5 for a listing of essential behavior skills.
      (2) Administer standardized work assessments.
         (a) Aptitude tests to determine individual's strengths and weaknesses in a variety of areas such as verbal and numerical abilities.
         (b) Behavioral and personality tests to determine personality characteristics, attitudes, motivators, and intra- and interpersonal strengths.
         (c) Manual dexterity tests to determine motor coordination skills such as speed and accuracy in performing motor tasks.
   f. Determine if the individual can return to past employment.
      (1) Identify existing abilities and supports.
      (2) Identify existing limitations and barriers.
      (3) Identify needed reasonable accommodations.
   g. Determine if prevocational and/or vocational training is indicated.
   h. Refer to Table 14-6 for an overview of the prevocational assessment process.

Table 14-5

Work Behavior Skills

PHYSICAL TOLERANCE & DEMANDS	SENSORY/PERCEPTION	MOTOR

• Work pace/rhythm
• Standing tolerance
• Sitting tolerance
• Endurance
• Performance with repetition
• Muscle strength
• Walking
• Lifting
• Carrying
• Pushing
• Pulling
• Climbing
	• Color discrimination
	• Form perception
	• Size discrimination
	• Spatial relationship
	• Ability to follow visual instruction
	• Texture discrimination
	• Digital discrimination
	• Figure-ground
	• Form constancy
	• Visual closure
	• Parts-to-whole
	• Shape discrimination
	• Kinesthesia
		• Finger dexterity
		• Manual dexterity
		• Coordination:
		  – eye-hand
		  – eye-hand-foot
		  – fine motor
		  – gross motor
		  – bimanual
		  – bilateral
		• Use of hand tools
		• ROM:
		  – stooping
		  – kneeling
		  – crouching
		  – crawling
		  – reaching
		• Balancing

DAILY LIVING SKILLS	COGNITION	AFFECTIVE

• Self-care:
  – personal hygiene
  – grooming
  – dressing
  – eating/feeding
  – object manipulation
• Mobility
  – transfers
  – travel (mode of)
  – transportation
• Communication
  – with peers
  – with supervisor
  – writing
  – dialing phone
  – talking on phone
  – typing
	• Numerical ability
	• Measuring ability
	• Safety consciousness
	• Care in handling work and tools
	• Work quality
	• Accuracy
	• Neatness
	• Attention span
	• Planning/organization
	• Ability to follow:
	  – verbal instruction
	  – written instruction
	• Retention of instruction
	• Work judgment
	• Ability to learn new task
	• Orientation
		• Attendance
		• Punctuality
		• Response to:
		  – praise
		  – criticism
		  – assistance
		  – frustrating situation
		• Relationship with
		  – evaluator
		  – coworker
		• Work flexibility
		• Attitude toward work
		• Behavior in structured setting
		• Ability to work independently
		• Initiative
		(In psychiatry you would also observe for additional pathological behavior.)

Reprinted with permission from the Occupational Therapy Assistant Program, Wayne County Community College. 1001 West Fort St. Detroit, Michigan.

Table 14-6

Occupational Therapy Prevocational Assessment Process

Gather Background information
1. Work history, education, and training background
2. Current medications and their side effects
3. History of mental and physical illnesses
4. Factors/stressors influencing symptomatology

Determine Consumer Work Interests and Support Systems
1. Available emotional support persons
2. Cultural/familial influences affecting employment
3. Skills needed for most recent employment
   a. Is that job still available?
   b. Will employer rehire?
   c. Are skills still in place?
   d. Does patient want to return to the job?

Return to Most Recent Employment
1. Identify job stressors
2. Identify accommodations needed to stay employed
3. Identify strategies needed to be practiced to return to work (e.g., relaxation techniques, medication management, cognitive therapy, etc.)
4. Which employment opportunities are considered desired by consumer?
   a. Which skills are needed for identified employment?
   b. What training is needed?
   c. Is a job analysis needed?

Assess Skill Level for Employment Opportunity
1. Determine assessments directly relating to employment tasks
   a. Work tolerance screening
   b. Functional capacity evaluation
   c. Simulated job tryout
   d. Work samples
   e. Standardized assessments for specific job tasks
2. Consider a work behavior assessment
3. Determine job interview skills

Assess for Reasonable Accommodations

Reprinted from Hemphill-Pearson, B. (Ed.). (1999). *Assessments in occupational therapy mental health: An integrative approach* (p. 113). Thorofare, NJ: Slack Incorporated. Reprinted with permission.

EXAM HINT: In the NBCOT® exam outline for the COTA®, Domain 01 Collaborating and Gathering Information comprises 28% of the exam. Domain 01 exam items focus on the ability of the OTA to "acquire information regarding factors that influence occupational performance on an ongoing basis through the occupational therapy process" (NBCOT®, 2018, p. 21). The application of knowledge about the prevocational assessment process described previously and the work assessment guidelines provided in the following section can help you determine the correct answer for NBCOT® Domain 01 exam items about the evaluation of prevocational and vocational capabilities and work performance.

Table 14-7

General Ergonomic Risk Analysis Checklist

Check the box if your answer is "yes" to the question. A "yes" response indicates that an ergonomic risk factor that requires further analysis may be present.

MANUAL MATERIAL HANDLING
- ☐ Is there lifting of loads, tools, or parts?
- ☐ Is there lowering of loads, tools, or parts?
- ☐ Is there overhead reaching for loads, tools, or parts?
- ☐ Is there bending at the waist to handle loads, tools, or parts?
- ☐ Is there twisting at the waist to handle loads, tools or parts?

PHYSICAL ENERGY DEMANDS
- ☐ Do tools and parts weigh more than 10 lbs?
- ☐ Is reaching greater than 20 inches?
- ☐ Is bending, stooping, or squatting a primary task activity?
- ☐ Is lifting or lowering loads a primary task activity?
- ☐ Is walking or carrying loads a primary task activity?
- ☐ Is stair or ladder climbing with loads a primary task activity?
- ☐ Is pushing or pulling loads a primary task activity?
- ☐ Is reaching overhead a primary task activity?
- ☐ Do any of the above tasks require five or more complete work cycles to be done within a minute?
- ☐ Do workers complain that rest breaks and fatigue allowances are insufficient?

OTHER MUSCULOSKELETAL DEMANDS
- ☐ Do manual jobs require frequent, repetitive motions?
- ☐ Do work postures require frequent bending of the neck, shoulder, elbow, wrist, or finger joints?
- ☐ For seated work, do reaches for tools and materials exceed 15 inches from the worker's position?
- ☐ Is the worker unable to change his or her position often?
- ☐ Does the work involve forceful, quick, or sudden motions?
- ☐ Does the work involve shock or rapid buildup of forces?
- ☐ Is finger-pinch gripping used?
- ☐ Do job postures involve sustained muscle contraction of any limb?

COMPUTER WORKSTATION
- ☐ Do operators use computer workstations for more than 4 hours a day?
- ☐ Are there complaints of discomfort from those working at these stations?
- ☐ Is the chair or desk nonadjustable?
- ☐ Is the display monitor, keyboard, or document holder nonadjustable?
- ☐ Does lighting cause glare or make the monitor screen hard to read?
- ☐ Is the room temperature too hot or too cold?
- ☐ Is there irritating vibration or noise?

(Continued)

Table 14-7

General Ergonomic Risk Analysis Checklist (Continued)

ENVIRONMENT
- ☐ Is the temperature too hot or too cold?
- ☐ Are the worker's hands exposed to temperatures less than 70°F?
- ☐ Is the workplace poorly lit?
- ☐ Is there glare?
- ☐ Is there excessive noise that is annoying, distracting, or producing hearing loss?
- ☐ Is there upper extremity or whole body vibration?
- ☐ Is air circulation too high or too low?

GENERAL WORKPLACE
- ☐ Are walkways uneven, slippery, or obstructed?
- ☐ Is housekeeping poor?
- ☐ Is there inadequate clearance or accessibility for performing tasks?
- ☐ Are stairs cluttered or lacking railings?
- ☐ Is proper footwear worn?

TOOLS
- ☐ Is the handle too small or too large?
- ☐ Does the handle shape cause the operator to bend the wrist in order to use the tool?
- ☐ Is the tool hard to access?
- ☐ Does the tool weigh more than 9 pounds?
- ☐ Does the tool vibrate excessively?
- ☐ Does the tool cause excessive kickback to the operator?
- ☐ Does the tool become too hot or too cold?

GLOVES
- ☐ Do the gloves require the worker to use more force when performing job tasks?
- ☐ Do the gloves provide inadequate protection?
- ☐ Do the gloves present a hazard of catch points on the tool or in the workplace?

ADMINISTRATION
- ☐ Is there little worker control over the work process?
- ☐ Is the task highly repetitive and monotonous?
- ☐ Does the job involve critical tasks with high accountability and little or no tolerance for error?
- ☐ Are work hours and breaks poorly organized?

General ergonomic risk analysis checklist. (From Cohen, A. L., et al. (1997). *Elements of ergonomics programs: A primer based on workplace evaluations of musculoskeletal disorders.* Washington, DC: US Government Printing Office.)

Work Assessment

1. The OTA contributes to this process with OT supervision.
2. If service competency is established the OTA may collect data under the supervision of the occupational therapist in the following areas:
   a. Initial screening and prevocational assessment as described previously.
   b. Functional capacity evaluation (FCE) which evaluates an individual's capabilities in relation to one of several dimensions.
      (1) The physical demands of a job, which is often termed a physical capacity evaluation, to assess the physical demands of a job according to the descriptions provided in the Dictionary of Occupational Titles (DOT) (e.g., the Smith Physical Capacity Evaluation).
      (2) The critical demands of a specific job.
      (3) The critical demands of an occupational group.
      (4) The demands of competitive employment.

3. Work capacity evaluation using real or simulated work activities to assess an individual's ability to return to work (e.g., Valpar Work Samples or BTE).
4. Job site analysis to evaluate its expectations, supports, ergonomics, essential functions of the job, the marginal functions of the job and the potential reasonable accommodations in accordance with the Americans with Disabilities Act (ADA).
   a. See Table 14-7 for assessment guidelines for determining the general ergonomic risks of work tasks and Table 14-8 for assessment guidelines for determining the ergonomic risks of computer work.
   b. Refer to Chapter 4 for ADA information.

> **EXAM HINT:** In the NBCOT® exam outline for the COTA®, Domain 01 Collaborating and Gathering Information comprises 28% of the exam and knowledge of the "administration, purpose, indications, advantages, and limitations of standardized and nonstandardized screening and assessment tools" (NBCOT®, 2018, p. 21) is identified as essential for competent practice. Thus, the application of knowledge about the nonstandardized screening and assessment methods previously described can help you correctly answer Domain 01 exam items about the evaluation of work.

Table 14-8

Risk Analysis Checklist for Computer-User Workstations

"No" responses indicate potential problem areas which should receive further investigation.

1. Does the workstation ensure proper worker posture, such as		
• horizontal thighs?	☐ Yes	☐ No
• vertical lower legs?	☐ Yes	☐ No
• feet flat on floor or footrest?	☐ Yes	☐ No
• neutral wrists?	☐ Yes	☐ No
2. Does the chair		
• adjust easily?	☐ Yes	☐ No
• have a padded seat with a rounded front?	☐ Yes	☐ No
• have an adjustable backrest?	☐ Yes	☐ No
• provide lumbar support?	☐ Yes	☐ No
• have casters?	☐ Yes	☐ No
3. Are the height and tilt of the work surface on which the keyboard is located adjustable?	☐ Yes	☐ No
4. Is the keyboard detachable?	☐ Yes	☐ No
5. Do keying actions require minimal force?	☐ Yes	☐ No
6. Is there an adjustable document holder?	☐ Yes	☐ No
7. Are arm rests provided where needed?	☐ Yes	☐ No
8. Are glare and reflections avoided?	☐ Yes	☐ No
9. Does the monitor have brightness and contrast controls?	☐ Yes	☐ No
10. Do the operators judge the distance between eyes and work to be satisfactory for their viewing needs?	☐ Yes	☐ No
11. Is there sufficient space for knees and feet?	☐ Yes	☐ No
12. Can the workstation be used for either right- or left-handed activity?	☐ Yes	☐ No
13. Are adequate rest breaks provided for task demands?	☐ Yes	☐ No
14. Are high stroke rates avoided by		
• job rotation?	☐ Yes	☐ No
• self-pacing?	☐ Yes	☐ No
• adjusting the job to the skill of the worker?	☐ Yes	☐ No
15. Are employees trained in		
• proper postures?	☐ Yes	☐ No
• proper work methods?	☐ Yes	☐ No
• when and how to adjust their workstations?	☐ Yes	☐ No
• how to seek assistance for their concerns?	☐ Yes	☐ No

Risk analysis checklist for computer-user workstations. (From Cohen, A. L., Gjessing, C. C., Fine, L. J., Bernard, B. P., & McGlothlin, J. D. (1997). *Elements of ergonomics programs: A primer based on workplace evaluations of musculoskeletal disorders*. Washington, DC: US Government Printing Office.)

Work Intervention

General Intervention Guidelines

> **EXAM HINT:** The NBCOT® exam outline for the COTA® identifies knowledge of "principles of ergonomics and universal design for identifying, recommending, and implementing reasonable accommodations and features in the workplace . . . in order to optimize accessibility and usability" (and) "processes and procedures for identifying, recommending, and implementing modifications in the workplace . . ., considering the interaction among client factors, contexts, roles, task demands, and resources" (NBCOT®, 2018, p. 27) as essential for competent and safe practice. The application of knowledge about the following intervention guidelines and approaches will be required to correctly answer COTA® exam items about OT services that enable work.

1. Evaluate the work site and adapt the environment and job tasks to enable the individual to perform essential job functions. See Figures 14-1 and 14-2.
   a. Determine with the OT supervisor the feasibility of the person's return to work.
2. Provide assistive devices, adaptive strategies, and equipment to compensate for functional impairments during work activity performance.
   a. Smartphone applications
   b. Adapted computers.
   c. Typing aids.
   d. Universal cuff, tenodesis splint.
   e. Teach principles and methods of energy conservation and work simplification. Refer to Chapter 11.
3. Practice, modify, and instruct in work activities.
4. Provide conditioning exercises and activities.
5. Educate about work safety and injury prevention.
   a. Teach principles and methods of joint protection and proper body mechanics. Refer to Chapter 11.
6. Educate employer regarding reasonable accommodations to enable performance of essential job functions. See Table 14-9 and Chapter 4.
7. Collaborate with employee assistance programs to obtain additional needed services (e.g., substance abuse counseling).

A Seated Work

- 5–10°
- 6"–12"
- 7" Minimum
- Work Surface
- 8.2"–12"
- 2–5°
- 14"–21"
- 4" ADJ.
- Footrest 25°

Optimal work surface height varies with performed:
Precision work = 31–37 inches
Reading/writing = 28–31 inches
Typing/light assembly = 21–28 inches
Seat and back rest heights should be adjustable as noted in chair requirements

B Standing Work

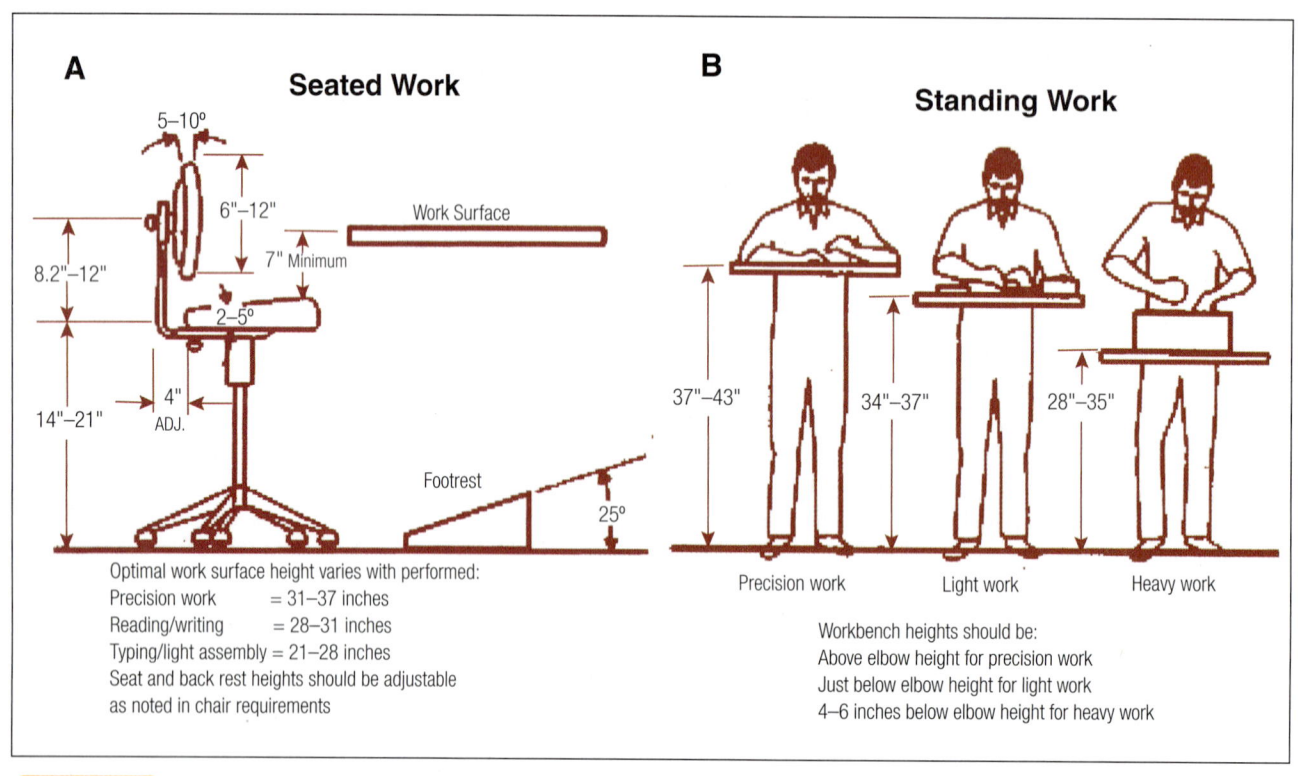

- 37"–43" Precision work
- 34"–37" Light work
- 28"–35" Heavy work

Workbench heights should be:
Above elbow height for precision work
Just below elbow height for light work
4–6 inches below elbow height for heavy work

Figure 14-1 Recommended Dimensions of Workstations
A, Seated work. **B**, Standing work. (From Cohen, A. L., Gjessing, C. C., Fine, L. J., Bernard, B. P., & McGlothlin, J. D. (1997). *Elements of ergonomics programs: A primer based on workplace evaluations of musculoskeletal disorders*. Washington, DC: US Government Printing Office.)

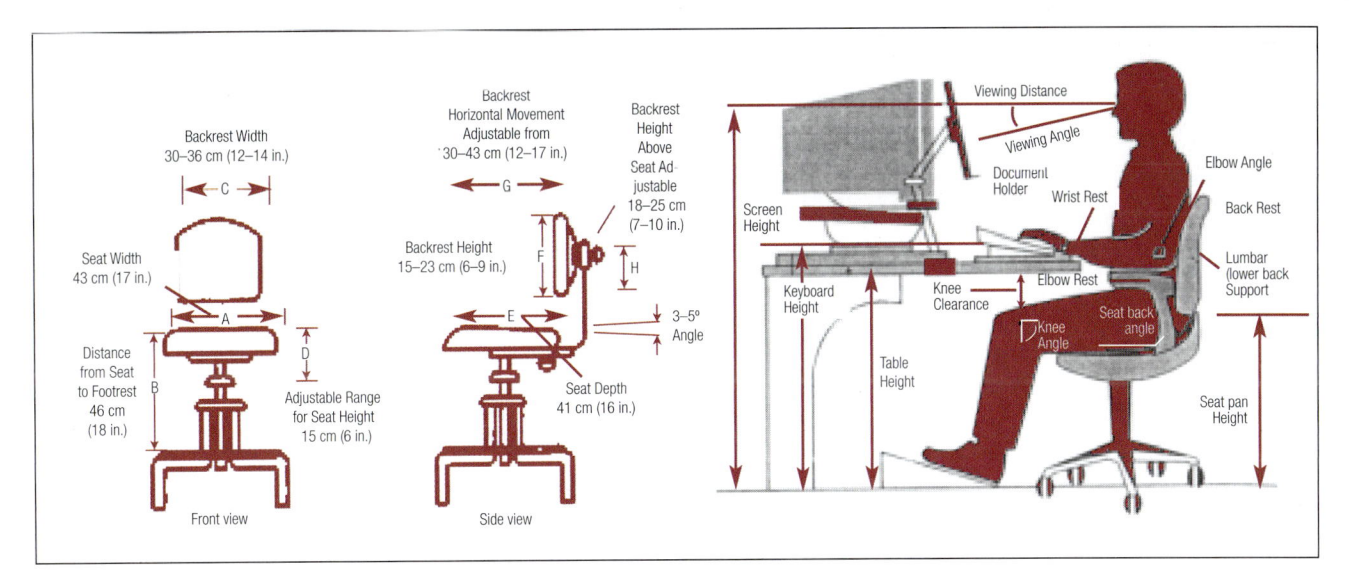

Figure 14-2 **A.** Recommended chair characteristics. Dimensions are given using both front and side views for **(A)** width, **(E)** depth, **(D)** vertical adjustability, and **(I)** angle, and for **(C)** backrest width, **(F)** height, and **(H)** vertical and **(G)** horizontal adjustability relative to the chair seat. The angle of the backrest should be adjustable horizontally from 12 to 17 inches (30–43 cm), by either a slide-adjust or a spring, and vertically from 7 to 10 inches (18–25 cm). The adjustability is needed to provide back support during different types of seated work. The seat should be adjustable within at least a six-inch (15 cm) range. The height above the floor of the chair seat with this adjustment range will be determined by the workplace, with or without a footrest.

(From Eggleton, E. [Ed.]. [1983]. *Ergonomic design for people at work* (Vol 1). New York, NY: Van Nostrand Reinhold.)

B. Proper seated position for computer user.

(From Occupational Safety and Health Administration. [1997]. *Working safely with video display terminals*. Washington, DC: US Government Printing Office. http://www.osha.gov. Publications/osha3092.pdf.)

8. Educate family members about a person's work capacities and limitations.
9. Explore alternatives to competitive work (e.g., volunteer work) if it is not an attainable goal and/or if the person is retiring.
10. Use thematic and topical groups to develop needed skills.
    a. Task skills to enable successful completion of work tasks.
    b. Social skills to facilitate effective interactions with coworkers and employer.
    c. Work behaviors to ensure a successful work experience. See Table 14-5.
11. Provide pre-retirement planning to ease transition from competitive employment.
12. Provide follow-up care, as needed (e.g., counseling, work support group, psychosocial clubhouse).
13. Refer to state offices for vocational and educational services for individuals with disabilities for further education and/or vocational training.
14. Interventions for the most common work-related injuries.
    a. Cumulative trauma such as carpal tunnel syndrome and low back pain.
       (1) Avoid static positions, repetition, awkward postures, forceful exertions, and vibration.
       (2) Design workplace and workstation to be ergonomically correct to prevent further trauma. See Figures 14-1 and 14-2.
    b. Psychosocial and cognitive deficits.
       (1) Engage person in program suitable to functional vocational abilities (e.g., vocational rehabilitation workshop, supportive or transitional employment).
       (2) Educate the person and their employer about reasonable accommodations that enable work performance. See Table 14-9.

EXAM HINT: The NBCOT® exam outline for the COTA® identifies knowledge of "prevocational, [and] vocational . . . services, options, and resources for supporting strengths, interests, employment, and lifestyle goals of the adolescent, middle-aged, and older adult client" (NBCOT®, 2018, p. 25) as essential for competent practice. The application of knowledge about the previous general intervention guidelines, and the following specific work programs can help you determine the correct answer for NBCOT® Domain 02 Selecting and Implementing Interventions exam items about prevocational and vocational services.

Table 14-9

Reasonable Accommodations for Recurrent Functional Problems Among Persons with Psychiatric Disorders

PERSONAL SELF-EFFICACY

- Reinforce or coach appropriate behaviors.
- Test for job skills on the job and avoid self-report of abilities.
- Place in job where there is a model to follow or imitate.
- Teach self-advocacy skills.
- Provide successful job experiences. Use positive feedback.
- Begin with close supervision and then cut back slowly as skills are maintained.
- Maintain similarity or consistency in work tasks.
- Encourage positive self-talk and eliminate negative self-talk.

DURATION OF CONCENTRATION[1]

- Put each work request in writing and leave in "to do" box to avoid interruptions.
- Provide ongoing consultation, mediation, problem solving, and conflict resolution.
- Provide good working conditions, such as adequate light, smoke-free environment, and reduced noise.
- Provide directive commands on a regular basis.

SCREENING OUT ENVIRONMENTAL STIMULI[1]

- Place in a separate office.
- Provide opaque room dividers between workstations.
- Allow person to work after hours or when others are not around.
- Ensure that workstation facilitates work production and organization.

MAINTAINING STAMINA THROUGHOUT THE WORKDAY[1]

- Provide additional breaks or shortened workday.
- Allow an extended day to allow for breaks or rest periods.
- Avoid work during lunch, such as answering the phone; use of an answering machine instead.
- Distribute tasks throughout the day according to energy level.
- Job-share with another employee.
- Develop work simplification techniques, such as collect all copying to be done at one time or use a wheeled cart to move supplies.
- Have a liberal leave policy for health problems, flexible hours, and back-up coverage.
- Individualize work agreements.
- Verify employees' efficacy regarding their ability to sustain effort or persist with a task.
- Teach on-the-job relaxation and stress-reduction techniques.

MANAGING TIME PRESSURE AND DEADLINES[1]

- Maintain structure through a daily time log and task schedule using hourly goals.
- Provide positive reinforcement when tasks are completed within the expected time lines.
- Arrange a separate work area to reduce noise and interruptions.
- Screen out unnecessary business.

Table 14-9

Reasonable Accommodations for Recurrent Functional Problems Among Persons with Psychiatric Disorders (Continued)

INITIATING INTERPERSONAL CONTACT[1]

- Purposely plan orientation to meet and work alongside coworkers.
- Allow sufficient time to make good, unhurried contacts.
- Make contacts during work, break, and even lunch times, adjusting the conversation to the situation.
- When standing, instead of facing each other, try standing at a 90° angle to each other.
- Allow the person to work at home.
- Have an advocate to advise and support the person.
- Communicate honestly.
- Plan supervision times and maintain them.
- Develop tolerance for and helpful responses to unusual behaviors.
- Provide awareness and advocacy training for all workers.

FOCUSING ON MULTIPLE TASKS SIMULTANEOUSLY[1]

- Eliminate the number of simultaneous tasks.
- Redistribute tasks among employees with the same responsibilities, so each can do more of one type of job task rather than a lot of different tasks.
- Establish priorities for task completion.
- Arrange for all work tasks to be put in writing with due dates or times.

RESPONDING TO NEGATIVE FEEDBACK[1]

- Have employee prepare own work appraisal to compare with supervisor's.
- Work together to establish methods employee can use to change negative behavior.
- Provide positive reinforcement for observed behavioral change.
- Provide on-site crisis intervention and counseling services to develop self-esteem, provide emotional support, and promote comfort with accommodations.
- Establish guidelines for feedback.

SYMPTOMS SECONDARY TO PRESCRIBED PSYCHOTROPIC MEDICATIONS[1]

- Provide release time to see psychiatrist or primary physician.
- Encourage employee to work with physician to establish a time schedule to take medications that are conducive to work responsibilities.
- Provide release time or changes in job tasks that match condition.

[1] From: Mancuso (1990).

From: Crist, P. A., & Stoffel, V. (1996). The Americans with Disabilities Act of 1990 and employees with mental impairments: Personal efficacy and the environment. In R. P. Cottrell (Ed.), *Perspectives on purposeful activity: Foundation and future of occupational therapy* (pp. 227–228). Bethesda, MD: American Occupational Therapy Association. Reprinted with permission.

(Continued)

Specific Work Programs

1. Work-hardening program characteristics.
   a. An interdisciplinary approach is used.
   b. Real or simulated work activities are used.
   c. A transition between acute care and return to work is provided.
   d. The issues of productivity, safety, physical tolerance, and worker behaviors are addressed.
   e. CARF accreditation is required.
2. Work-conditioning programs.
   a. One discipline is the provider of services.
   b. Real or simulated work activities are used.
   c. A transition between acute care and return to work is provided.
   d. Flexibility, strength, movement, and endurance are addressed.
   e. Accreditation is not a requirement.
3. Ergonomic program characteristics.
   a. Prevention is the main focus to fit the workplace to the human body.
   b. Types of programs.
      (1) Ergonomic survey. See Tables 14-7 and 14-8.
      (2) Specific job site analysis.
      (3) Manager and employee training.
      (4) Educational seminars.
      (5) Exercise and stretching programs.
4. Vocational rehabilitation (sheltered) workshops, supported employment programs, transitional employment programs (TEPs).
   a. A multidisciplinary or interdisciplinary approach is used.
   b. Real work activities are used.
      (1) Participants are paid at a piece-work rate in vocational rehabilitation workshops.
      (2) Participants are paid at the prevailing competitive wage for positions in TEPs and supported employment programs.
   c. Participants are considered as employees with supports provided as needed.
      (1) Job coaches are used.
      (2) Reasonable accommodations are provided. See Table 14-9.
   d. A transition between program participation and competitive employment is provided according to participant's functional level.
   e. Vocational rehabilitation (sheltered) workshops and supported employment can be the final and permanent employment goal for an individual.
   f. Accreditation is not a requirement.
      (1) Vocational rehabilitation workshops, TEPs, and supported employment programs are usually part of an accredited hospital system or a major agency (e.g., The ARC).
5. Discharge criteria from work programs.
   a. Individual exhibits limited potential for improvement.
   b. Individual has declined services.
   c. Individual is does not adhere to the program standards/nrms.
   d. Individual has met program goals.
   e. Individual has returned to work.

Rest and Sleep Evaluation

1. Given the substantial evidence supporting the importance of rest and sleep to health and occupational performance and the inclusion of rest and sleep in the AOTA Practice Framework, this area of occupation is becoming more integrated into OT evaluation and intervention.
   a. Despite this increased focus, rest and sleep are typically not included in commonly used published assessments of occupational performance.
2. Occupational therapy practitioners should always assess this area of occupation during routine screenings and interviews.
   a. Asking a person if they feel drowsy during the day is a quick and easy way to screen for problems with rest and sleep.
3. More in-depth evaluation of rest and sleep for those who report drowsiness should focus on the identification of:
   a. The person's ability to identify the need for restorative rest and sleep.
   b. Typical rest and sleep patterns and routines, intermittent or chronic insomnia.
      (1) The use of OT assessments that focus on time use and temporal adaptation (e.g., Barth Time Construction, Activities Configuration) can provide helpful information about a person's typical rest and sleep patterns.
   c. Obstacles to the attainment and maintenance of satisfying rest and sleep.
      (1) Personal issues (e.g., worrying about family [e.g., a child's illness] and/or work stressors [fear of being laid off]; being a "light" sleeper who awakens easily).
      (2) Pathophysiological changes related to disease, disability, and/or the aging process (e.g., spasticity, chronic pain, unrelenting fatigue).
      (3) Post-traumatic stress disorder resulting in hypervigilance.
      (4) Sociocultural barriers (e.g., need to work a night shift job requires sleeping during daytime hours).
4. Sleep checklists and sleep diaries can be used to obtain detailed information.

5. Persons with chronic and unrelenting insomnia should be referred to a sleep clinic/laboratory for an extensive overnight evaluation.

> **RED FLAG:** People with parasomnias (e.g., narcolepsy, restless leg syndrome, sleepwalking), those with (or at risk for) obstructive sleep apnea syndrome (OSAS), and persons with the pathophysiological changes as previously noted should be referred to a physician for a comprehensive medical evaluation to ensure that a comprehensive intervention plan is formulated to effectively address the person's primary condition(s). Because OSAS is deadly, physician referrals for persons with (or at risk for) OSAS must be completed *immediately*.

Rest and Sleep Intervention

1. Intervention must be client-centered, and focused on behavioral and environmental modifications to enable restorative rest and sleep. The therapist should help the person:
    a. Develop a daily pattern of relaxation activities (e.g., meditation, prayers, progressive muscle relaxation, visualization) and pre-sleep routines (e.g., turning off electronic devices, saying goodnight).
        (1) Pre-sleep meals should be consumed at least two hours before sleep is initiated.
        (2) Pre-sleep use of stimulants (e.g., caffeine, nicotine, alcohol) should be avoided.
    b. Establish healthy and restorative sleep-wake patterns (e.g., going to bed at a consistent time each evening).
    c. Remediate symptoms that hinder rest and sleep (e.g., using energy conservation techniques, effective pain management).
    d. Modify the rest and sleep environment (e.g., playing soothing music to relax, using room-darkening shades if daytime sleep is needed due to night-shift work, using earplugs and/or "white noise machines" to block sound).
        (1) Dark, cool, quiet environments are most conducive to sleep.
    e. Implement sleep restriction training.
        (1) Wake up at the same time every day (i.e., no sleeping in on weekends).
        (2) Avoid naps until nighttime sleeping improves.
        (3) Limit the bedroom to sleep and sexual activities (i.e., not watching TV, text messaging, or cruising the Internet).
        (4) When sleepy, go to sleep.
        (5) If sleep is not attained, get up and do an activity that is boring until sleepy again.
        (6) Allow time for sleep restriction training to work.
            (a) It typically takes 2 to 3 weeks for the body to adjust to a new sleep routine.
    f. Employ cognitive-behavioral therapy (CBT) strategies to address thought processes that cause anxiety and hinder sleep (e.g., make a list of concerns to address upon awakening and leave them outside the bedroom door). See Chapter 13.

References

Allen, C. K., Earhart, C. A., & Blue, T. (1992). *Occupational therapy treatment goals for the physically and cognitively disabled.* Bethesda, MD: American Occupational Therapy Association.

American Occupational Therapy Association. (2010). Standards of practice for occupational therapy. *American Journal of Occupational Therapy, 64*(Suppl. 6), S106–S110.

American Occupational Therapy Association. (2014). Occupational therapy practice framework: Domain and process, 3rd ed. *American Journal of Occupational Therapy, 68* (Suppl. 1), S1–S48.

Asrael, W. (1993). The PLISSIT model of sexuality counseling and education. In R. P. Cottrell (Ed.), *Psychosocial occupational therapy: Proactive approaches* (pp. 451–452). Bethesda, MD: American Occupational Therapy.

Backman, C. (1994). Assessment of self-care skills. In C. Christiansen (Ed.), *Ways of living: Self-care strategies for special needs* (pp. 51–75). Bethesda, MD: American Occupational Therapy Association.

Brown, C., & Stoffel, V. (Eds.). (2011). *Occupational therapy in mental health: A vision for participation.* Philadelphia, PA: F.A. Davis.

Christiansen, C. (1994). *Ways of living: Self-care strategies for special needs.* Bethesda, MD: American Occupational Therapy Association.

Christiansen, C. & Matuska, K. (Eds.). (2004). *Ways of living: Adaptive strategies for special needs* (3rd ed). Bethesda, MD: American Occupational Therapy Association.

Clifton, D. (2004). Workers' comp: A plethora of opportunities. *Rehab Management, 32,* 34–36.

Cohen, A., et al. (1997). *Elements of ergonomic programs: A primer based on workplace evaluations of musculoskeletal disorders.* Washington, DC: US Government Printing Office.

Crist, P. A., & Stoffel, V. C. (1996). The Americans with Disabilities Act of 1990 and employees with mental impairments: Personal efficacy and the environment. In R. P. Cottrell (Ed.), *Perspectives on purposeful* activity: Foundation and future of occupational therapy (pp. 217–228). Bethesda, MD: American Occupational Therapy Association.

Gentry, T., & Loveland, J. (2013, January 21). Sleep: Essential to living life to its fullest. *Occupational Therapy Practice, 18*, 9–14.

Gutman, S., Mortera, M., Hinojosa, J., & Kramer, P. (2007). The issue is: Revision of the occupational therapy practice framework. *American Journal of Occupational Therapy, 61*, 119–126.

Hemphill-Pearson, B. (Ed.). (1999). *Assessments in occupational therapy mental health: An integrative approach.* Thorofare, NJ: Slack.

Hinojosa, J., & Kramer, P., & Crist, P. (Eds.). (2005). *Evaluation: Obtaining and interpreting data.* (2nd ed.). Bethesda, MD: American Occupational Therapy Association.

Hussey, S., Sabonis-Chafee, B., & O'Brien, J. (2007). *Introduction to occupational therapy.* (3rd ed.). St. Louis, MO: Elsevier Mosby.

Larson, K., Stevens-Ratchford, R. G., Pedretti, L., & Crabtree, J. (1996). *ROTE: The role of occupational therapy with the elderly.* (2nd ed.). Bethesda, MD: American Occupational Therapy Association.

Pedretti, L. W., McHugh Pendleton, H., & Schultz-Krohn, W. (Eds.) (2013). *Pedretti's occupational therapy: Practice skills for physical dysfunction*, 7th ed. St. Louis, MO: Elsevier.

Mosey, A. (1996). *Psychosocial components of occupational therapy.* Philadelphia, PA: Lippincott-Raven.

Moyers, P., & Dale, L. (2007). *The guide to occupational therapy practice.* Bethesda, MD: AOTA Press.

National Board for Certification in Occupational Therapy (NBCOT®). (2018). *Practice analysis of the certified occupational therapy assistant registered: Executive summary* [PDF file]. Gaithersburg, MD: Author. Retrieved from https://www.nbcot.org/-/media/NBCOT/PDFs/2017-Practice-Analysis-Executive-OTR.ashx?la=en.

Ryan S., & Sladyk, K. (2005). *Ryan's occupational therapy assistant: Principles, practice issues, and techniques.* (4th ed.). Thorofare, NJ: Slack.

Schell, B., Gillen, G., & Scaffa, M. (Eds.). (2014). *Willard and Spackman's occupational therapy.* (12th ed.). Philadelphia, PA: Lippincott Williams & Wilkins.

Schultz-Krohn, W., & Pendleton, H. (Eds.) (2006). *Occupational therapy: Practice skills for physical dysfunction*, 6th ed. St. Louis, MO: Elsevier Science/Mosby.

Sladyk, K., Jacobs. K., MacRae, N. (2010). *Occupational therapy essentials for clinical competence.* Thorofare, NJ: Slack.

Vining-Radomski, M., & Trombly-Latham, C. A. (Eds.) (2014). *Occupational therapy for physical dysfunction*, 7th ed. Philadelphia: Lippincott Williams & Wilkins.

Review Questions

Evaluation and Intervention for Performance in Areas of Occupation

Following are five questions about key content covered in this chapter. These questions are not inclusive of the entirety of content related to evaluation and intervention for performance in areas of occupation that you must know for success on the COTA® exam. These questions are provided to help you develop the thought processes you will need to apply your studying of content to the answering of COTA® exam items. Thus, they are not in the COTA® exam format. Exam items in the COTA® format that cover the depth and breadth of content you will need to know to pass the exam are provided on this text's online exams. The answers to the questions following are provided in Appendix 3.

1. An OTA works in a hospital-based occupational therapy department that provides services to persons with medical conditions and physical disabilities. One of the OTA's primary responsibilities is to collaborate with the occupational therapist to plan patients' discharge. To ensure safety and enhance functional performance, the OTA assesses the level of assistance each client will need. What are the main categories of assistance that the OTA should use when documenting clients' functional performance? Describe each category.

2. A person with a C-7 SCI sets a goal to return to work as an accountant. The person expresses concerns about the ability to complete a morning self-care routine and job tasks. What will be realistic for the person to expect to be able to do after receiving occupational therapy services to develop self-care and work skills?

3. An OTA collaborates with an occupational therapist to ensure that the BADL of sexual activity are addressed throughout the OT process. Which model can help the OTA and supervising therapist achieve this aim? Describe the key points of this model.

4. An OTA works in a supported employment program that serves clients with cognitive limitations due to psychiatric, physical, and intellectual disabilities. What strategies should the OTA use to increase clients' ability to concentrate, manage time, and focus on multiple tasks at the same time during the workday?

5. During an occupational therapy screening, a client reports feeling tired all of the time. What should the occupational therapist and OTA address during evaluation?

15

Mastery of the Environment: Evaluation and Intervention

RITA P. FLEMING-CASTALDY, ROCHELLE J. MENDONCA, MARLENE MORGAN, AND CHRISTINA M. GAVALAS

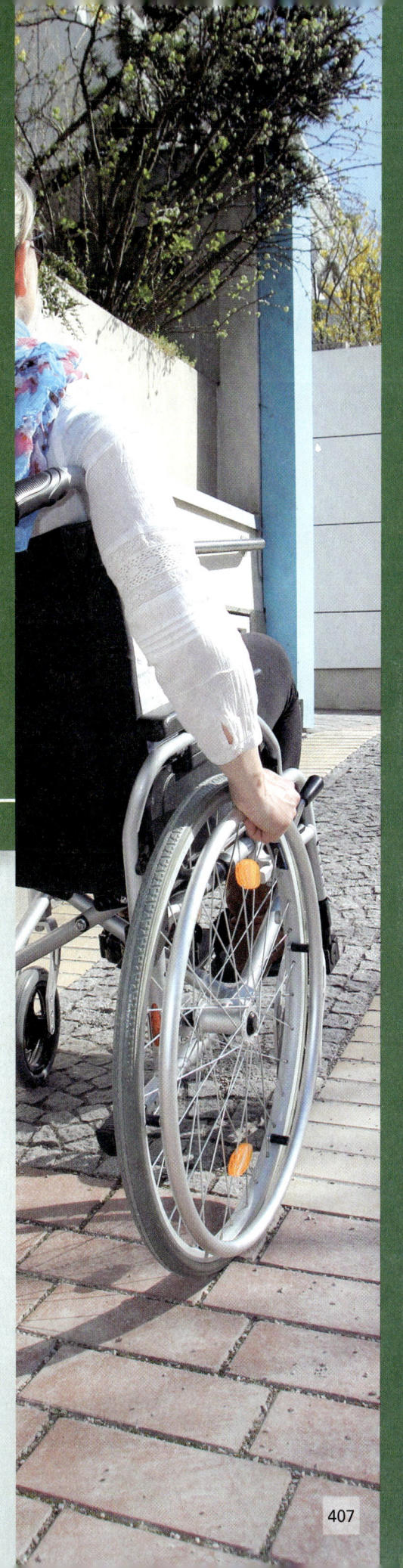

Chapter Outline

- General Environmental Considerations, 408
- Overall Environmental Evaluation, 412
- Home Evaluation, 413
- Low Vision Evaluation and Intervention, 415
- Fall Prevention and Management, 417
- Modifications for Sensorimotor Deficits and Architectural Barriers, 420
- Wheelchair Prescription, Components, and Types, 423
- Seating and Positioning Systems, 427
- Mobility Training and Mobility Aids, 429
- Transfers, 431
- Assistive Technology Devices (ATDs)/Electronic Aids to Daily Living (EADL), 432
- Community Mobility, 436
- Environmental Modifications for Cognitive and Sensory Deficits, 437
- References, 438
- Review Questions, 441

General Environmental Considerations

Definition and Major Concepts

1. The environment is "the aggregate of phenomena that surrounds the individual and influences his (her) development and existence" (Mosey, 1996, p. 171).
2. The environment in which a person lives, and the exposure to various settings, influence their development and adaptation.
3. The environment can facilitate growth because it allows for adaptation and problem-solving strategies to be developed.
4. Conversely, the environment can hinder development and adaptation if it is impoverished, inaccessible, or hostile.
5. A person's abilities, skills, limitations, problems, activities, and/or occupations cannot be fully understood without considerations of their current and expected environment.

> **EXAM HINT:** The environmental considerations described in this chapter are important for analyzing COTA® exam item scenarios and determining their correct answers. For example, the correct answer for an exam item about a COTA® collaborating with an occupational therapist to plan discharge with an older adult and family caregivers would consider the person's multiple contexts. These would include their physical (e.g., architectural barriers), sensory (e.g., home lighting), social (e.g., available social network), cultural (e.g., norms related to the care of older family members), personal (e.g., socioeconomic status and ability to pay for services and equipment not covered by Medicare), temporal (e.g., the person's and family's daily routine) and virtual (e.g., access to and ability to use assistive technology [AT]) contexts.

6. Physical/nonhuman environment (American Occupational Therapy Association [AOTA], 2014).
    a. Everything that is natural (e.g., animals, trees, sand dunes) or built (e.g., tools, devices, buildings, transportation systems).
    b. Includes the sensory qualities of the environment.
        (1) Visual: lighting, colors, clutter (e.g., dim lighting and posters covering a wall).
        (2) Auditory: sound quality and volume (e.g. loudspeaker distortion, radio static, background noise).
        (3) Tactile: room temperature and seating textures.
        (4) Olfactory: pleasant or offensive odors.
        (5) Gustatory: pleasant or offensive tastes.
7. Social-cultural/human environment.
    a. Relationships with persons, groups, or populations with whom people have contact (AOTA, 2014).
    b. Social roles: "an organized pattern of behavior that is characteristic and expected of the occupant of a defined position in a social system" (Mosey, 1996, p. 64); for example, a student, a parent, or a worker.
    c. Social network: "the web of voluntary relationships that make up an individual's social environment" (Mosey, 1996, p. 184).
    d. Cultural aspects: "the social structures, values, norms, and expectations that are accepted and shared by a group of people" (Mosey, 1996, p. 172).
    e. Psychological aspects: environmental characteristics that can affect mood and stress level (e.g., a calming, comfortable, cheerful environment versus a chaotic, uncomfortable, bare setting).
8. The AOTA practice framework has expanded the description of environment beyond the physical and social environment to include the concept of context.
    a. In the AOTA practice framework, context "refers to elements within and surrounding a client that are often less tangible than physical and social environments but nonetheless exert a strong influence on performance" (AOTA 2014, p. S9).
    b. Contexts include cultural, personal, temporal, and virtual.
        (1) The "cultural context includes customs, beliefs, activity patterns, behavioral standards, and expectations accepted by the society of which the client is a member" (AOTA 2014, p. S9).
        (2) The "personal context refers to demographic features of the individual such as age, gender, socioeconomic status, and educational level that are not part of a health condition" (AOTA 2014, p. S9).
        (3) The "temporal context includes stages of life, time of day or year, and duration or rhythm of activity, and history" (AOTA 2014, p. S9).
        (4) The "virtual context refers to interactions that occur in simulated, real-time, or near-time situations absent of physical contact" (AOTA 2014, p. S9) and may include e-mail, videoconferencing, web-based social networking, etc.

Legislation Related to the Environment

> **EXAM HINT:** The NBCOT® exam outline for the COTA® identifies the task of implementing "environmental modifications guided by . . . disability discrimination legislation . . . to support participation in occupation" (NBCOT®, 2018, p. 27) as essential for competent practice. The application of knowledge about the following laws can help you determine the correct answer for NBCOT® Domain 02 Selecting and Implementing Interventions exam items.

1. Americans with Disabilities Act (ADA) of 1990: a civil rights law with mandates to enable full participation in society for people with disabilities.
   a. Several sections mandate accessible environments for persons with disabilities.
   b. Includes policies dealing with public service, employment, transportation, and public accommodations.
2. Omnibus Budget Reconciliation Act (OBRA) of 1990: mandate that restraints cannot be used without proper justification, agreement, and documentation.
3. Individuals with Disabilities Education Act (IDEA) of 1990 and IDEA Reauthorization Acts of 1997 and 2004: mandate that children with disabilities receive education in the least restrictive and most natural environment.
   a. Inclusive models are to be used to enable the child to be taught in a general education classroom.
   b. Student-directed Individualized Education Program (IEP) goals must be developed and implemented to prepare a student for independent living, employment, and social participation.
   c. Accommodations must be provided as needed to measure the functional performance and academic achievement of all students with disabilities.
4. Assistive Technology (AT) Act of 2004: focuses on improving access to and acquisition of AT by funding direct services to support individuals with all types of disabilities and all ages, in all environments including school, work, home, and leisure.
5. Fair Housing Amendments Act of 1988: requires that all multifamily housing with an elevator and all ground-floor units of buildings without an elevator meet seven accessibility requirements. These include the following:
   a. Accessible building entrance on an accessible route.
   b. Accessible public and common use areas.
   c. Sufficiently wide, usable doors for persons using wheelchairs.
   d. Accessible routes into and through the dwelling unit.
   e. Light switches, electrical outlets, thermostats, and other environmental controls in accessible locations.
   f. Reinforced walls in bathrooms to allow installation of grab bars.
   g. Usable kitchens and bathrooms to allow a wheelchair to maneuver in the space.
6. Section 504 of the Rehabilitation Act of 1973: requires that all programs receiving federal aid make reasonable accommodations for all qualified individuals with disabilities including accessible new constructions or alterations in physical spaces.
7. The role of OT practitioners in environmental assessment and modification has increased with the implementation of previously mentioned laws.
8. Refer to Chapter 4 for additional information on these laws and other federal legislation that enables participation in a person's chosen environments.

The Role of Occupational Therapy Practitioners

1. OT practitioners should be familiar with all aspects of a person's environment (i.e., living, vocational, and leisure) whether service delivery takes place in a hospital, nursing home, school, or home environment.
2. OT practitioners can advocate for and design environments that use principles of universal design to meet the physical, sensory, sociocultural, and psychological needs of the individual.
   a. See Table 15-1.

> **EXAM HINT:** The NBCOT® exam outline for the COTA® identifies knowledge of "universal design for identifying, recommending, and implementing reasonable accommodations and features in the workplace, home, and public spaces in order to optimize accessibility and usability" (NBCOT®, 2018, p. 27) as essential for competent practice. The application of knowledge about the principles of universal design put forth in Table 15-1 can help you determine the correct answer for NBCOT® Domain 02 Selecting and Implementing Interventions exam item.

3. OT practitioners can help to identify settings and approaches to implement the ADA, OBRA, and IDEA.
4. OT practitioners can advocate for ADA, OBRA, and IDEA compliance to enable individuals to function as independently and with the least restriction possible, in their environments of choice.

Table 15-1

Principles of Universal Design

PRINCIPLE 1

Equitable Use: The design is useful and marketable to people with diverse abilities.

Guidelines:
1a. Provide the same means of use for all users; identical whenever possible; equivalent when not.
1b. Avoid segregating or stigmatizing any users.
1c. Provisions for privacy, security, and safety should be equally available to all users.
1d. Make the design appealing to all users.

PRINCIPLE 2

Flexibility in Use: The design accommodates a wide range of individual preferences and abilities.

Guidelines:
2a. Provide choice in methods of use.
2b. Accommodate right- or left-handed access and use.
2c. Facilitate the user's accuracy and precision.
2d. Provide adaptability to the user's pace.

PRINCIPLE 3

Simple and Intuitive Use: Use of the design is easy to understand, regardless of the user's experience, knowledge, language skills, or current concentration level.

Guidelines:
3a. Eliminate unnecessary complexity.
3b. Be consistent with user expectations and intuition.
3c. Accommodate a wide range of literacy and language skills.
3d. Arrange information consistent with its importance.
3e. Provide effective prompting and feedback during and after task completion.

PRINCIPLE 4

Perceptible Information: The design communicates necessary information effectively to the user, regardless of ambient conditions or the user's sensory abilities.

Guidelines:
4a. Use different modes (pictorial, verbal, tactile) for redundant presentation of essential information.
4b. Provide adequate contrast between essential information and its surroundings.
4c. Maximize "legibility" of essential information.
4d. Differentiate elements in ways that can be described (i.e., make it easy to give instructions or directions).
4e. Provide compatibility with a variety of techniques or devices used by people with sensory limitations.

PRINCIPLE 5

Tolerance for Error: The design minimizes hazards and the adverse consequences of accidental or unintended actions.

Guidelines:
5a. Arrange elements to minimize hazards and errors: most used elements, most accessible; hazardous elements eliminated, isolated, or shielded.
5b. Provide warnings of hazards and errors.
5c. Provide fail-safe features.
5d. Discourage unconscious action in tasks that require vigilance.

PRINCIPLE 6

Low Physical Effort: The design can be used efficiently and comfortably and with a minimum of fatigue.

Guidelines:
6a. Allow user to maintain a neutral body position.
6b. Use reasonable operating forces.
6c. Minimize repetitive actions.
6d. Minimize sustained physical effort.

Table 15-1

Principles of Universal Design (*Continued*)

PRINCIPLE 7

Size and Space for Approach and Use: Appropriate size and space is provided for approach, reach, manipulation, and use regardless of user's body size, posture, or mobility.

Guidelines:
7a. Provide a clear line of sight to important elements for any seated or standing user.
7b. Make reach to all components comfortable for any seated or standing user.
7c. Accommodate variations in hand and grip size.
7d. Provide adequate space for the use of assistive devices or personal assistance.

From C. Christiansen and K. Matuska. (Eds.). (2004). *Ways of living: Adaptive strategies for special needs*, (3rd ed., p. 428). Bethesda, MD: American Occupational Therapy Association. Reprinted with permission.

The Role of the Team

EXAM HINT: The NBCOT® exam outline for the COTA® identifies knowledge of the "characteristics and functions of interprofessional teams for coordinating client care and providing efficient and effective programs and services consistent with specific core competencies, expertise, unique contributions, team roles, and context of the organization" (NBCOT®, 2018, p. 22) as essential for competent practice. The application of knowledge about the following team information can help you determine the correct answer for NBCOT® Domain 01 exam items about collaborating and gathering information.

EXAM HINT: The application of knowledge about the unique contributions of each team member described in the following can help you effectively determine the correct answer to COTA® exam items about enabling performance within people's environments. For example, correct answers for an exam item about an OTA who provides home-based services to a person who is visually impaired would include the OTA collaborating with the occupational therapist to provide AT and environmental modifications, and activities of daily living (ADL), instrumental activities of daily living (IADL) and functional mobility training within the person's home; collaborating with a social worker, third-party payers, and/or case managers to obtain funding for AT and/or environmental modifications; and referring the person to a certified orientation and mobility (O&M) specialist to provide O&M training within the community.

1. OT practitioners are often part of an interprofessional team that determines the needs and abilities of an individual with a disability in a specific environment.
2. Basis for team construction.
   a. The facility in which the individual with a disability presently resides and/or participates.
   b. The individual's needs, abilities, and functional status.
   c. Geographical location.
   d. Funding available to the individual with a disability (both individually and through third-party payers and/or state offices for individuals with disabilities).
   e. Support available from caregivers.
3. The team should always include the person and caregivers, if any.
4. Professional team members may belong to the Rehabilitation Engineering and Assistive Technology Society of North America (RESNA) and/or National Registry of Rehabilitation Technology Suppliers (NRRTS).
   a. Both professional organizations help to develop standards and measuring tools to ensure proper design, fabrication, prescription, and delivery of rehabilitation technology.
5. Potential professional team members and their respective roles.
   a. Assistive technology professional (ATP): to analyze consumer needs, help select the AT that can effectively meet identified needs, and provide training in the use of the AT.
   b. Computer expert: to assist with the design and provision of efficient computer-based technology.
   c. Certified orientation and mobility specialists: to train visually impaired persons in specific skills to move independently, safely, and efficiently within the community.
      (1) Occupational therapists can receive this certification.
   d. Certified vision rehabilitation specialists or certified low vision therapists: to provide training in the use of optical devices and compensatory strategies for visually impaired persons.
      (1) The AOTA offers a program for occupational therapists to obtain a specialty certification in low vision (SCLV) credential.

e. Certified Rehabilitation and Technology Supplier® (CRTS®): for individuals who require complex and specialized rehabilitation technology that is different from standard durable medical equipment (DME).
   (1) To obtain and maintain the credential of CRTS®, practitioners must meet the registration requirements of the NRRTS.
      (a) Occupational therapists are eligible to apply for this registration.
f. Driver trainer: to provide training and/or adaptations to enable safe driving.
g. Low vision optometrists and ophthalmologists: to perform low vision eye exams, prescribe optical and nonoptical devices, prescribe low vision rehabilitation, and treat conditions/diseases of the eye that result in visual impairment.
h. Nurse: to ensure carryover of medical care and medication regimes prescribed by the doctor.
i. Occupational therapist and occupational therapy assistant: refer to previous section.
j. Physical therapist: to assess mobility difficulties an individual may encounter in the environment.
k. Physician: to authorize and assess services and purchases.
l. Psychologist: to assist with adjustment disorders, if indicated.
m. Rehabilitation counselor: to assess and advise on vocational issues.
n. Rehabilitation engineer: to design high- and low-tech AT and assist with modifications of high- and low-tech AT.
o. Seating and mobility specialist (SMS): to evaluate seating, positioning, and mobility needs and make appropriate recommendations.
p. Social worker: to assist in obtaining funding for AT and/or environmental modifications.
q. Speech language pathologist: to assess, recommend, and train in the use of augmentative communication aids.
r. Teacher: to identify students' learning needs, integrate AT into students' education, and implement modification into the school setting.
s. Third-party payer and/or their respective case manager: to approve and/or provide funding for the individual's needed AT and/or environmental modifications.
t. Vendors: to provide items requested by therapists and consumers.

Purposes of Environmental Evaluation and Intervention

1. Identify and prioritize the needs, goals, desires, and problem areas of an individual with a disability within their environments.
2. Establish the individual's abilities regarding everyday functional activities within their environment.
3. Assess functional use of devices being considered for a particular individual to facilitate mastery of the environment.
4. Determine the individual's interest in devices and their willingness to use and accept a device being considered.
5. Identify a device's availability, safety, and cost.
6. Determine a device's location and frequency of use.
7. Determine funding and financial resources for equipment and/or modifications.

CAUTION: It is of questionable ethics and not in the best interest of clients to show them devices or order top-of-the-line equipment that is not covered by their insurance, if they do not have the financial resources to self-pay for these recommendations.

8. Determine environmental constraints.
   a. For example, an individual may be living in a four-flight walk-up apartment and have to leave a device locked up in a lobby, opening it up to the risk of vandalism or theft.
9. Assess if the individual with a disability and the device will allow for reevaluation.
   a. Ensure the device will allow for possible modifications, if upon reassessment of the individual a change in status is found.

Overall Environmental Evaluation

Evaluation of Performance Skills and Client Factors

1. The role of the occupational therapy assistant (OTA).
   a. The OTA contributes to the evaluation process in collaboration with the OT supervisor.
      (1) Supervision is required.
      (2) The level of supervision required will be determined by the OTA's experience and established service competence.
   b. Service competency must be established.
   c. The OTA cannot independently evaluate or interpret evaluation results.

2. Performance skills and client factors are essential to assess when conducting an environmental evaluation, for they are the fundamental abilities that allow a person to function in their environment.
3. Upon establishment of service competency, the OTA can collect data in the following areas:
   a. Sensory functions (e.g., tactile, pain, and visual acuity) to determine if there is an impairment that could influence safety in the manipulation of devices.
   b. Visual-perceptual processing skills (e.g., unilateral neglect, figure-ground discrimination) to assess for potential difficulties with device use).
   c. Muscle functions (e.g., range of motion [ROM], strength, tone, and endurance) to assess if the person will be able to physically use the devices to optimal capability.
   d. Movement functions (e.g., reflexes, involuntary reactions, and coordination) to assess the person's ability to utilize all limbs rhythmically in mobility and environmental manipulation.
   e. Motor skills (e.g., stabilizing, reaching, and manipulating) to assess a person's ability to interact with objects and to move tasks and objects in the environment (Boyt Schell, Gillen, & Scaffa, 2014).
   f. Cognitive functions (e.g., following directions, memory, attention, and judgment) to assess if a person is aware of limitations and able to follow and recall directions regarding operation of AT and wheelchairs and the safe use of devices.
   g. Process skills (e.g., pacing, choosing, using, and initiating) to assess a person's ability to select, interact with, and use tools and materials; to carry out actions; and to modify performance when problems are encountered (Boyt Schell et al., 2014).
   h. Psychosocial skills (e.g., social support, emotional regulation) to assess if an individual with a disability can ask for assistance and obtain needed information from the right person; to assess the individual's ability to give instructions.
   i. Cardiovascular, respiratory, and voice and speech functions (e.g., stamina, endurance, and alternative vocalization) to assess a person's ability to use alternative methods to control devices.

> **EXAM HINT:** In the NBCOT® exam outline for the COTA®, Domain 01 Collaborating and Gathering Information comprises 28% of the exam and focuses on the ability of the OTA to assist the OTR in acquiring "information regarding factors that influence occupational performance on an ongoing basis through the occupational therapy process" (NBCOT®, 2018, p. 21). The application of knowledge about the evaluation of performance skills and client factors as described above and the following considerations for the evaluation of contexts can help you determine the correct answer for NBCOT® Domain 01 exam items related to a person's occupational performance environments.

Contextual Evaluation

1. The OTA contributes to the evaluation process with OT supervision.
   a. OTAs can perform home assessments and make adaptations, modifications, and recommendations to the anticipated dwelling to increase safe, independent functioning with OT supervision.
2. Areas targeted for evaluation include:
   a. Physical considerations.
      (1) Arrangement of furniture.
      (2) Accessibility of items needed for desired activities and for safety.
      (3) Ease of use.
      (4) Housing/workplace design.
      (5) Neighborhood characteristics.
         (a) Availability and use of transportation.
         (b) Overall accessibility.
   b. Sociocultural considerations.
      (1) The individual's social network: the relationships between the individual with the disability and others.
      (2) Social roles: expectations for role performance of the individual with a disability and others.
      (3) Opportunities for socialization.
      (4) Sociocultural norms, values, and expectations for independent function.
      (5) Community resources available.

Home Evaluation

General Considerations

1. OTAs can perform home assessments and make adaptations, modifications, and recommendations to the anticipated dwelling to increase safe, independent functioning with OT supervision.
2. If an individual with a disability is to be discharged to home from a facility, the on-site home evaluation should be done before the discharge date.

3. The person's current status (abilities and limitations) and potential safety risks in the home determine the need for home modifications and/or activity adaptations.

Overall Characteristics of the Home

1. Type of dwelling: private house, one-family, two-family, walk-up apartment, elevator access apartment.
2. Protection from weather/environmental changes.
3. Presence and use of a driveway.
4. Entrance to the dwelling: wheelchair access, ramp, level entrance, stairs.
   a. Number of entrances that are accessible to the individual.
   b. Some apartment buildings allow residents to use delivery entrance because it has a ramp.
5. Presence and quality of a doorbell or entrance intercom control panel.
6. Steps: the number present outside the dwelling, inside the dwelling, to the laundry room, and to the mailbox.
7. Railings: the location and number of railings when outside and facing the entrance door; the presence of secure railings for interior stairways.
   a. Interior railings should be mounted 1½" from the wall to ease grasp.
   b. Exterior railings should be waist high for those who walk 34" – 38" depending on person's height.
   c. Circular railings should be 1½" – 2" in diameter with nonskid surfaces; noncircular railings should be 4" – 6¼" in diameter, with a cross section less than 2¼".
8. Door sills/thresholds: identify where they are present (i.e., entrance to dwelling, bedroom doors, bathroom doors, kitchen doorway).
9. Consider the widths of entrance door(s), elevator doorways, and hallway entrances.
   a. For doors, measure from open door to frame, not frame to frame.
10. Direction of opening for entrance door(s) and any other doors throughout dwelling which must be opened.
    a. Space to accommodate door swing must be available.
       (1) A minimum of 18" is needed for those using wheelchairs.
11. Type(s) of door handles: lever handles are more functional than round knobs.
12. Identification of objects and/or clutter that may be obstructing doorways and/or pathways.
13. Presence of pets: they can become obstacles and/or safety concerns to those with low vision and balance problems, and those who require assistive devices.
14. Carpeting: consider location and type (i.e., wall to wall, throw rugs, and height of pile).
15. Electrical cords: placement in high- or low-traffic areas for walking, clearly visible versus hidden, and/or frayed versus intact condition.
16. Presence of a firm chair in the dwelling and its height.
17. Light switches: accessibility from various levels (standing and chair).
18. Amount and quality of natural and artificial light throughout the home:
    a. It is important to have evenly and well-lit stairways, entrances, and hallways, especially if elevation changes are present.
    b. Task-specific lighting is achieved through use of adjustable lamps. Light position and intensity should be specific for each activity, such as reading versus writing.
    c. Increasing light intensity and altering light source positions can reduce/eliminate glare.
    d. Lighting is even more essential to consider if a low vision diagnosis is present.
    e. Older individuals need six to eight times more light than people in their twenties.
       (1) Lumen refers to the amount of brightness.
       (2) Lux is the standard measure of luminescence and is defined as the amount of light from a source on a uniform surface.
          (a) There are devices to measure the amount of lux available.
19. Presence of accessible and safe storage and organization spaces that meets a person's needs.
20. Telephones: number of phones, their location and type (i.e., cordless, cell, push button or rotary), emergency numbers by telephone.
21. Presence of working smoke and carbon monoxide detectors.
22. Presence of accessible working temperature control systems for central heating system and air-conditioning systems.
23. Presence of fans, space heaters, or woodburning stoves/fireplaces.
24. Presence of an emergency call system and an emergency exit plan.
25. Overall sanitation and orderliness of the home.

Bedroom Considerations

1. Bed: size of bed, height from floor to top of mattress, type of mattress and bed, wheeled frame or not, and the position of the bed (against the wall or freestanding).
2. Side of the bed from which the individual enters/exits.

3. Ability to change bed location, if needed.
4. Accessibility of clothes and dresser drawers.
5. Sufficient room available for a bedside commode, if needed.

Bathroom Considerations

1. Number of bathrooms in the home.
2. Location of bathroom(s) relative to the bedroom, living room, kitchen, and other living spaces important to the individual.
3. Width of the bathroom doorway.
4. Type of bathing the individual performs (i.e., bath, shower, sponge bath).
5. Type of shower/tub: separate stall, glass door tub with shower, curtain-enclosed tub with shower.
6. Presence and location of grab bars (the soap dish and towel bar are not grab bars).
   a. If home is a rental, landlord's agreement to allow grab bars to be installed if needed.
7. Height of tub, sink, and toilet.
8. Presence of a nonskid mat or skid-free surface in the shower/tub.
9. Presence of a throw rug outside of the shower.
10. Availability of a handheld shower.
11. Presence of antiscald valves and/or faucets.
12. Location of toilet paper holder.

Kitchen Considerations

1. Location of meal preparation devices that the individual uses most frequently (i.e., oven, microwave, stove).
2. Presence of a countertop area between the stove and sink, between the stove and refrigerator.
3. Accessibility of food, pots, pans, dishes, and preparation materials.
4. Direction of opening for refrigerator, cabinetry, and/or pantry doors.
5. Accessibility of the sink including height and width of the sink.
6. Presence of antiscald valves and/or faucets.
7. Presence of table space and seating spaces in the kitchen that adequately accommodate the person and those with whom they live.
8. Presence of accessible and sanitary garbage cans and waste disposal.
9. Presence of a charged fire extinguisher.

Low Vision Evaluation and Intervention

Low Vision Evaluation

1. The role of the OTA.
   a. The OTA contributes to the evaluation process in collaboration with the OT supervisor.
      (1) Supervision is required.
      (2) The level of supervision required will be determined by the OTA's experience and established service competence.
   b. Service competency must be established.
      (1) When performing assessments for which service competence has been established, it is essential for the OTA to adhere to standardized test procedures (e.g., maintaining the distance between a client and the test materials, ensuring clients wear glasses, if needed) to ensure the validity and accuracy of evaluation results.
2. Evaluation focus. assess the ability of people with low vision (e.g., older adults experiencing age-related visual changes) to maintain their safety and independence within their home and community.
3. Method: assessments are administered in a well-lit clinic or home environment with no glare on the test materials.
4. Components of a comprehensive basic low vision evaluation include the following:
   a. Medical history and primary (e.g., visual acuity level at intermediate distance) and secondary diagnosis (e.g., the condition that causes primary deficits such as age-related macular degeneration [AMD], glaucoma, cataracts, cerebrovascular accident [CVA]).
   b. Other client factors that may impact function (e.g., decreased ROM, decreased strength, decreased sensation, decreased cognition, decreased hearing, decreased ambulation).
   c. Client self-report and goals.
      (1) A person's subjective complaints, use of glasses and other magnification or optical devices, and a functional gauge of materials that a person is able to read.
      (2) Goals for therapy as stated by the person.
         (a) The OT practitioner should help increase a person's awareness that a goal to fix vision may not be attainable.
         (b) The OT practitioner should collaborate with the person to establish goals focused on improving functional use of remaining

Low Vision Intervention

> **EXAM HINT:** In the NBCOT® exam outline for the COTA®, Domain 02 Selecting and Implementing Interventions comprises 55% of the COTA® exam. This domain is defined as implementing "interventions under the supervision of the OTR in accordance with the intervention plan and level of service competence to support client participation in areas of occupation throughout the occupational therapy process" (NBCOT®, 2018, p. 24). The application of knowledge about the following low vision intervention approaches can help you correctly answer NBCOT® Domain 02 exam items about intervention management for persons with low vision.

(continued from previous page)
   visual abilities and learning compensatory strategies to be safe, independent, and efficient in daily occupations.
   d. Assessment of the components of vision (e.g., eye dominance, visual acuity, contrast sensitivity).

1. Interventions address the significant impact low vision can have on a person's ability to safely, efficiently, and independently negotiate their home and community.
2. Low vision interventions are client- and environment-centered.
   a. Client-centered interventions enable people to use their remaining nonvisual capabilities and other senses more effectively. Interventions include:
      (1) Training and compensatory techniques in ADL (including mobility within the home) and IADL.
      (2) Training in the care and use of adaptive devices, including magnification devices prescribed by the medical (MD) or osteopathic doctor (OD).
      (3) Training in effective use of visual skills, including preferred retinal locus (PRL) training.
      (4) Education of the client, family, and/or caregiver.
   b. Environment-centered intervention is focused on altering the person's environment to achieve a better person-environment fit.
      (1) Educate the client in home modifications and assist with access and installation if these will increase participation and safety and are desired by the person.
3. Review the prior home evaluation section for important characteristics of a home that should be addressed in low vision rehabilitation if an evaluation determines there are concerns (e.g., poor lighting, the presence of clutter).
4. Intervention should aim to increase contrast, decrease visual clutter, and eliminate glare within the home environment.
   a. Use of solid primary colors and/or black-and-white color schemes tends to be effective in increasing contrast.
5. PRL training is an important aspect of low vision rehabilitation for clients with scotomas as a result of macular degeneration.
   a. This training teaches the client how to effectively use intact vision by looking around the scotoma ("dark spot" in vision due to macula damage) to focus on the top, bottom, left, or right of an object.
      (1) Training progresses from basic static fixation, then tracking, to consistently utilizing the PRL during saccadic eye movements.
6. Magnification is indicated for many clients with low vision.
   a. Many products are available in large print, such as books, checks, telephones, and TV remotes.
   b. Occupational therapy practitioners can provide training in the use of magnification optical devices prescribed by an MD or OD. Occupational therapy practitioners *cannot* prescribe magnification.
      (1) These devices do not cure or restore lost vision but enlarge print to increase independent and efficient completion of daily activities.
      (2) Basic devices include handheld or stand magnifiers.
         (a) Limited upper extremity (UE) ROM, weakness, or tremors may impact a client's ability to use handheld magnifiers.
      (3) Illuminated magnifiers help increase the amount of light available on a surface.
      (4) Convex lenses make objects appear larger; concave lenses make objects appear smaller.
      (5) Electronic magnification, such as closed-circuit television (CCTV), may be indicated at the level of severe visual impairment or worse.
         (a) This technology may have audio features including the option of reading text to clients.
   c. Magnification devices should only be introduced after a client has successfully learned how to use vision (PRL training) if a scotoma is present.
7. Other optical devices include prisms, which are often mounted to eyeglasses.
   a. These devices shift images by moving the nonviewing area into the viewing area.
   b. They are typically indicated after neurological injury resulting in visual field deficits.
8. Occupational therapy practitioners instruct clients in use of compensatory strategies and equipment that reduce visual demands by focusing on tactile, olfactory, and auditory senses.
   a. Adaptive equipment focused on compensating with the tactile sense may include check writing guides (typoscopes), bump dots as positional markers,

and folding different monetary denominations in different ways for organization.
   b. Adaptive equipment focused on use of the auditory sense includes talking phones, talking alarm and medication clocks, audio books, and CCTVs with audio features.
   c. Increasing contrast between rooms, elevation changes, walls and objects (i.e., grab bar, toilet paper holder), and tables and plates/utensils is a simple modification to decrease visual processing demands and increase safety.
      (1) Using bold-lined paper and 20/20 pens or a Sharpie® can help increase contrast during writing to improve task performance.
9. Removing clutter around the house can be important for preventing falls and promoting safety and ease of functional household mobility when visual impairments are present.
10. Occupational therapy practitioners can train clients and caregivers in specific sighted guide techniques to help individuals with visual impairment safely navigate their environment.
    a. Additional techniques for traveling safely within the home include "trailing" (i.e., using tactile sense) and "squaring off" (i.e., counting steps, turning 90° around corners).
11. Education regarding organizational skills and formation of patterns/routines is important for clients and caregivers.
    a. A frequently used compensatory strategy is to keep commonly used objects in the same places consistently to decrease visual demands.
       (1) Thoroughly educate caregivers so they do not change the location of frequently used objects.
    b. Be sure that any changes to daily routines are meaningful to the client.

> **EXAM HINT:** The NBCOT® exam outline for the COTA® identifies the task of selecting "assistive technology options (and) adaptive devices ... considering the client's ... physical (and functional status; prioritized needs; task demands; and context to enable participation in meaningful occupation" (NBCOT®, 2018, p. 27) as essential for competent practice. The application of knowledge about the devices previously described and the adaptive equipment and compensatory strategies described above can help you determine the correct answer for NBCOT® Domain 02 exam items about interventions for persons with low vision.

12. Certain criteria must be met for a person to qualify for low vision services.
    a. Medicare requires a minimum best corrected vision (BCV) of 20/60, which is moderate visual impairment, in the better eye to qualify for services.
    b. Orders for low vision services must be from an OD or MD.
    c. A client cannot be receiving any other occupational therapy services at the time.

Fall Prevention and Management

Falls Etiology, Prevalence, and Prognosis

1. Falls and fall injury are a major public health concern for the older adults.

> **EXAM HINT:** The facts and figures that follow are provided to highlight the reality that the incidence of falls is not rare. Knowledge of these statistics will not be directly tested on the COTA® exam. However, due to the prevalence of falls, the exam will likely include exam items that include scenarios related to falls and fall prevention.

   a. Between 30% and 50% of persons over the age of 65 fall each year. Note: percentages may be greater because data are based only on reported falls.
   b. 24% of falls result in severe soft tissue injury and fractures.
   c. Falls are the sixth-leading cause of death for the older adults; 12% of all deaths for persons aged 65 or older are caused by falls.
   d. Falls are a factor in 40% of admissions to nursing homes.
   e. Within six months of a fall, more than two-thirds of the older adults who have fallen will fall again.
2. Results of falls.
   a. Fractures: Most common fracture sites are the pelvis, hip, femur, vertebrae, and humerus head.
   b. Increased caution and fear of falling.
   c. Loss of confidence to function independently.
   d. Decreased engagement in activity and restriction of activities that can result in severe physical deconditioning and deterioration, contributing to the likelihood of reoccurrence.
   e. Increased risk of recurrent falls.

Evaluation of Risk Factors for Falls

1. The OTA contributes to the evaluation process with OT supervision.
    a. Upon establishment of service competency, the OTA can collect data about the intrinsic and extrinsic factors that contribute to falls.

> **EXAM HINT:** In the NBCOT® exam outline for the COTA®, Domain 01 Collaborating and Gathering Information comprises 28% of the exam and knowledge of the "purpose, advantages, limitations, and service competency needs related to the administration of commonly used standardized assessments and non-standardized screening as a means of acquiring client information" (NBCOT®, 2018, p. 21) is identified as essential for competent practice. The application of knowledge about the evaluation of intrinsic and extrinsic risk factors for falls described below can help you determine the correct answer for NBCOT® Domain 01 exam items about the evaluation of fall risk.

2. Intrinsic factors requiring evaluation.
    a. Age-related changes in sensory system resulting in reduced sensory capacity.
        (1) Vision.
            (a) Presbyopia (decreased acuity).
            (b) Reduced night vision means that vision in low-light situations is also reduced.
            (c) Impaired depth perception.
            (d) Decreased contrast sensitivity.
        (2) Vestibular.
            (a) Vertigo.
            (b) Postural sway combined with vision problems results is a compound risk.
    b. Age-related changes in the neuromuscular system.
        (1) Decreased number of neurons result in decreased reaction or response time.
        (2) Decreased number of muscle fibers leads to decreased strength and endurance.
        (3) Two manifestations of the combination of the previous factors include difficulties in rising from a chair and maintaining gait speed.
        (4) Improper transfer techniques can lead to falls.
    c. Comorbidities and pathological states including congestive heart failure, arrhythmias, hypotension, cerebrovascular disease, Parkinson's disease, arteriosclerosis and atherosclerosis, and diabetes mellitus.
    d. Medication side effects and/or polypharmacy.
    e. Neurocognitive disorders.
    f. Anxiety and/or depression.
    g. Cognitive deficits, decreased attention span, distractibility, impaired judgment.
    h. Prior history of falls within past year.
    i. Fear of falling can lead to decreased mobility and progressive deconditioning, which increase the risk of subsequent falls.

3. Extrinsic factors requiring evaluation: safety hazards within the environment that predispose one to slip and fall.
    a. General.
        (1) Floors: slippery or uneven, presence of throw rugs.
        (2) Trip hazards, including clutter on floors/stairs, pets, elevation changes, thresholds, throw rugs, extension cords, and high-pile carpets.
        (3) Low-lying furniture.
        (4) Stairs: excessive steepness, lack of or loose handrails.
        (5) Improper footwear.
        (6) Poor lighting or glare.
        (7) Use of furniture or other unstable objects for support.
        (8) Problems with adaptive equipment, lack of needed equipment, or excessive equipment.
    b. Bathroom.
        (1) No grab bars.
        (2) Utilization of unstable soap dish or towel bar for support.
        (3) Toilet seat too low.
        (4) Wet floor surfaces.
        (5) Utilization of wet sink surface for support.
        (6) Loose rug on floor.
    c. Kitchen.
        (1) Low cabinet doors open.
        (2) Step stool without handles.
        (3) Chairs pulled out.
        (4) Wet floor surfaces.
        (5) Loose rug on floor.
    d. Bedroom.
        (1) Bed too high or too low.
        (2) Movement of bed.
        (3) Reaching into closets.
    e. Living room.
        (1) Wires and/or clutter across floor.
        (2) Chairs too high and/or too low.
        (3) High pile or loose rugs.
        (4) Poor lighting.

Interventions to Prevent Falls

1. Intervention is based upon the determination of the individual's functional problems and the causative factors of falls as identified in evaluation.
2. The OTA implements intervention with supervision from the occupational therapist.

> **EXAM HINT:** In the NBCOT® exam outline for the COTA®, knowledge of "adaptive and preventive strategies for optimal engagement in occupation" (NBCOT®, 2018, p. 25) and "processes and procedures for identifying, recommending, and implementing modifications in the . . . home" (NBCOT®, 2018, p. 27) are identified as essential for competent practice. The application of knowledge about the following intervention approaches can help you correctly answer NBCOT® Domain 02 exam items about fall prevention.

3. Interventions are designed and implemented to:
   a. Eliminate or minimize all fall risk factors; stabilize disease states, manage medication.
   b. Improve functional mobility.
      (1) Active or resistive muscle strengthening exercises with weights and general conditioning exercises (GCEs) to improve or maintain flexibility, strength, endurance, and coordination.
      (2) Passive range of motion (PROM) stretching as indicated to increase joint ROM.
      (3) Specific coordination training.
      (4) Neuromuscular reeducation training.
      (5) Balance training.
         (a) Sit and stand positions.
         (b) Static and dynamic.
         (c) Turning, walking, stairs.
   c. Functional transfer and mobility training (i.e., bed mobility, wheelchair safety and management).
   d. Referral to physical therapy for gait/ambulation training.
4. Provide sensory compensation strategies.
   a. Ensure even lighting when moving between rooms throughout the house, so eyes do not have to adjust.
   b. Mark elevation changes (i.e., thresholds between rooms) with brightly colored tape.
   c. Refer to this chapter's section on low vision interventions for further compensatory strategies for persons with low vision.
5. Modify ADL for safety.
      (1) Order needed adaptive devices and train in safe use (e.g., reachers, long shoehorn, stocking/sock aid, leg lifter, dressing stick, walker baskets, etc.).
      (2) Allow adequate time for activities; instruct in gradual position changes.
6. Teach energy conservation techniques.
7. Communicate with family and caregivers.
8. Modify environment to reduce falls and instability; use environmental checklist.
      (1) Ensure adequate lighting.
      (2) Use contrasting colors to delineate hazardous areas.
      (3) Simplify environment, reduce clutter.
      (4) Firmly attach carpet.
      (5) Stairs.
         (a) Securely fasten handrails on both sides of stairs.
         (b) Provide light switches at top and bottom.
         (c) Install nonskid secure surface.
      (6) Bathrooms.
         (a) Install grab bars located in and out of tubs and shower and near toilets.
         (b) Provide nonskid mats and night-lights.
         (c) Use elevated toilet seat.
      (7) Bedrooms.
         (a) Install night-lights or light switch within reach of bed.
         (b) Place telephones in an easy to reach position near bed.
         (c) Replace existing mattress with one either thinner or thicker to lower or to raise bed height as needed.
         (d) Arrange furniture to ease maneuvering.
      (8) Living areas.
         (a) Ensure couches and chairs are at proper height to get in and out of easily.
         (b) Remove clutter and loose electrical cords.
         (c) Arrange furniture for easy maneuverability.
      (9) Kitchen and closet shelves.
         (a) Store items on reachable shelves (between person's eye and hip level).
      (10) Outdoors.
         (a) Fix cracked pavement or steps.
         (b) Install stable outside handrail.
         (c) Provide specific safety guidelines for the individual to follow.
            • Ask for assistance to transfer or ambulate.
         (d) Do not stand up alone; do not walk to the bathroom or kitchen alone.
            • Utilize prescribed assistive device(s) to ambulate, especially on any uneven or unfamiliar ground. Keep assistive device near at all times.
            • Use prescribed adaptive equipment.
            • Stand in place before beginning to walk to avoid dizziness from change in position and to regain balance.
            • Do not bend forward.
            • Wear supportive rubber-soled and low-heeled shoes.
            • Avoid wearing smooth-soled slippers or only socks, which makes it easier to slip.
         (e) Provide psychological support and specific interventions to deal with the fear of falling.
            • Acknowledge the validity of the individual's concerns.
            • Initiate discussions about risk factors and encourage active problem-solving.
            • Modify activities to be safe and achievable to build confidence.

- Provide activities to maintain physical conditioning to decrease risk of fear becoming a reality.
- Develop a contingency plan to use in the event of a fall to maintain safety.

Interventions for Occurrence of Falls

1. Check for fall injury.
   a. Cuts, bruises, painful swelling.

> **CAUTION:** Check for dizziness that may have preceded the fall.
> - Do not attempt to lift the individual alone, get help.

> **RED FLAG:** Serious injuries can include:
> - Head injury: loss of consciousness, mental confusion.
> - Spinal cord injury: loss of sensation or voluntary movement.
> - Hip fracture: complaints of pain in hip, especially on palpation; external rotation of leg; inability to bear weight on leg; changes in gait or weightbearing status.

2. Provide reassurance.
3. Provide first aid, call emergency services if necessary.
4. Solicit witnesses of fall event.
5. Document the incident as per setting's established procedures.
6. Refer the individual to a fall prevention intervention program to prevent reoccurrences.

Modifications for Sensorimotor Deficits and Architectural Barriers

Accessibility Standards

> **EXAM HINT:** The NBCOT® exam outline for the COTA® identifies knowledge of the "processes and procedures for identifying, recommending, and implementing modifications in the workplace, home, and public spaces, considering the interaction among client factors, contexts, roles, task demands, and resources" (NBCOT®, 2018, p. 27) as essential for competent practice. The application of knowledge about accessibility standards can help you determine the correct answers for NBCOT® Domain 02 exam items about modifying the environment for persons with sensorimotor deficits.

1. Architectural features in the home and the community that make negotiation of space difficult or impossible may require modifications to allow accessibility (e.g., steps, narrow doors).
2. Modifications should be made according to the International Code Council, Inc., Falls Church, Virginia.
3. Wheelchair dimensions and accessibility needs.
   a. Average wheelchair width is 24" – 26" rim to rim. See Figure 15-1.
      (1) Some doorways and room spaces may be too narrow, limiting clear mobility.
      (2) The minimal clearance width for doorways: 32" doorway width minimum, with ideal being 36". See Figure 15-2.
      (a) An additional 18" is needed beside the latch side of the door to allow for door swing and at least 60" of clear depth when facing the door.
      (b) Doorways can be widened or removed if necessary.

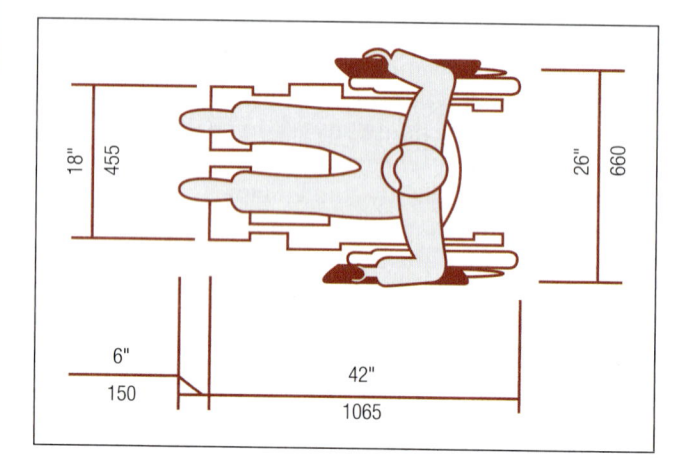

Figure 15-1 Dimensions of Standard Adult Manual Wheelchair

Width 24 to 26" from rim to rim. Length: 42 to 43". Height to push handles from floor: 36". Height to seat from floor: 19 to 19.5" (excluding cushion). Height to armrest from floor: 29 to 30". Note: Footrests may extend farther for very large people.

Copyright 2002. Falls Church, Virginia: International Code Council, Inc. Reproduced with permission. All rights reserved.

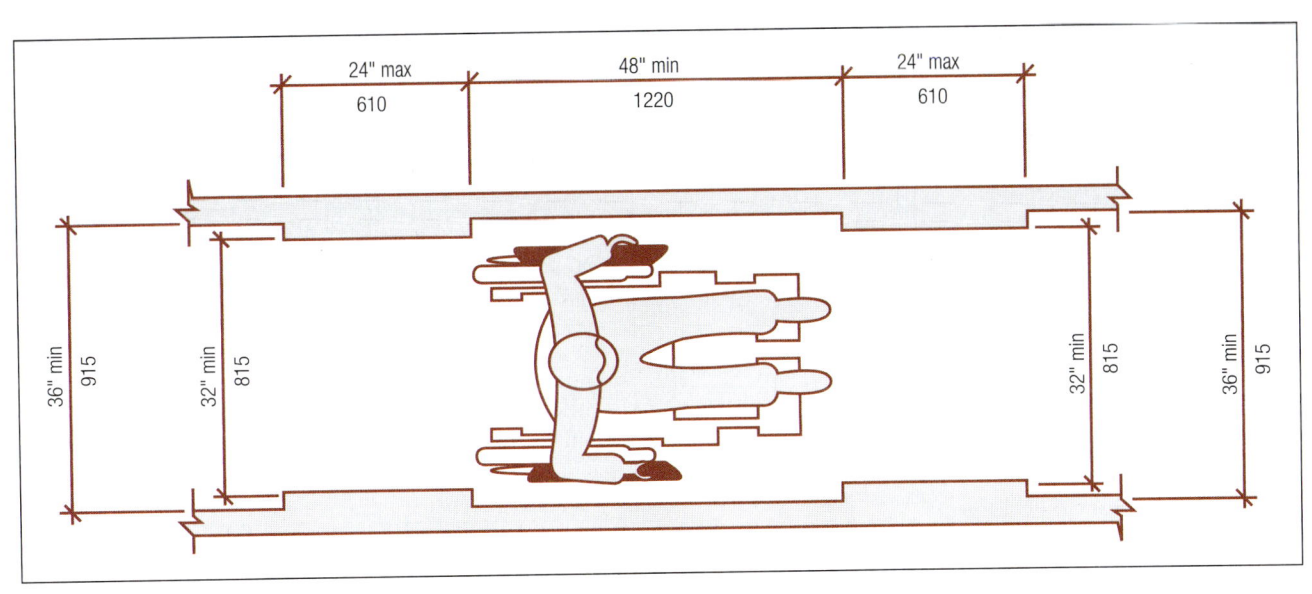

Figure 15-2 Minimum Clear Width for Doorways and Halls

A minimum of 32" of doorway width is required; the ideal is 36". Hallways should be a minimum of 36" wide to provide sufficient clearance for wheelchair passage and allow the user to propel the chair without scraping the hands.

Copyright 2002. Falls Church, Virginia: International Code Council, Inc. Reproduced with permission. All rights reserved.

- Removing doorstops can add ¾" width.
- Replacing existing hinges with offset hinges can add 1½"–2" in width.

  (c) Doorway saddles can be removed and the floor patched, or a wedge can be placed in front of the saddle, or a thin rubber mat can be placed over the saddle.

  (3) Hallways should be 36" wide. See Figure 15-2.

b. Average wheelchair length is 42"–43".

  (1) Adequate turning spaces are needed.
  (2) A 360-degree wheelchair turning space requires a clearance space of 60" × 60". See Figure 15-3.

c. The maximal height the individual can reach forward from sitting is 48", and at least 15" is needed to prevent tipping. See Figure 15-4.

d. Maximal height for reaching sideways is 54" and when an obstruction is present is 46". See Figure 15-5.

e. The maximal height for countertops should be 36".

f. Parking spaces should have an adjacent 5' aisle to allow wheelchairs to maneuver.

g. Pathways and walkways should be a minimum of 36" wide.

h. Ramps should be a minimum of 36" wide and should have a nonskid surface on upper and lower levels.

  (1) The ratio of slope to rise for a ramp is 1:12 (for every 1" of vertical rise, 12" of ramp is required). See Figure 15-6.
  (2) Railings should be between 34" and 38" high.
  (3) Curbs or edge protectors on ramps should be present to prevent a 4" wheelchair caster and walker, cane, and crutch tips from going off the ramp edge.
  (4) Level platforms must be included in the ramp design.
     (a) If the ramp is excessively long, 5' × 5' landing(s) are required to allow for rest.

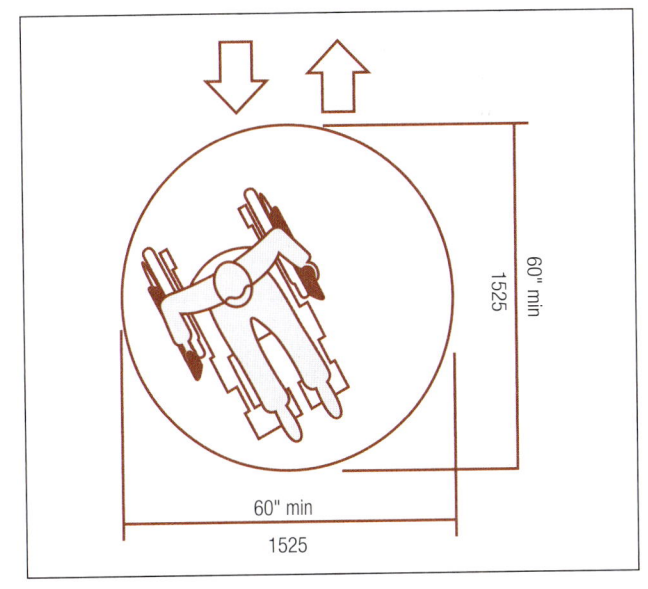

Figure 15-3 360° Wheelchair Turning Space

A 360° turn requires a clear space of 60" by 60". This space enables the individual to turn without scraping the feet or maneuvering multiple times to accomplish a full turn.

Copyright 2002. Falls Church, Virginia: International Code Council, Inc. Reproduced with permission. All rights reserved.

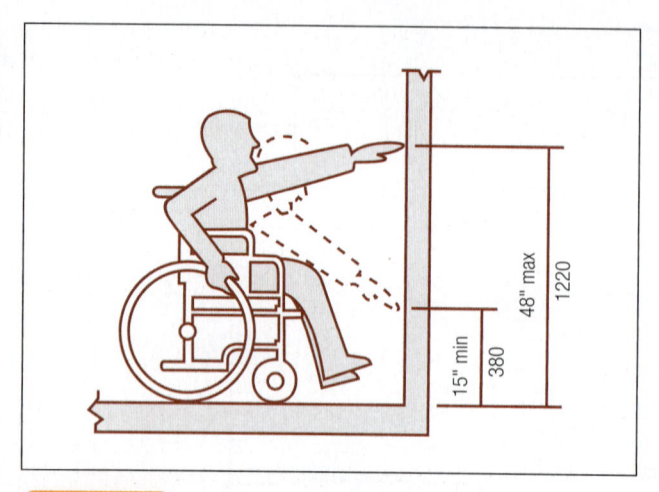

Figure 15-4 Forward Reach

The maximal height an individual can reach from a seated position is 48". Height should be at least 15" to prevent the wheelchair from tipping forward.

Copyright 2002. Falls Church, Virginia: International Code Council, Inc. Reproduced with permission. All rights reserved.

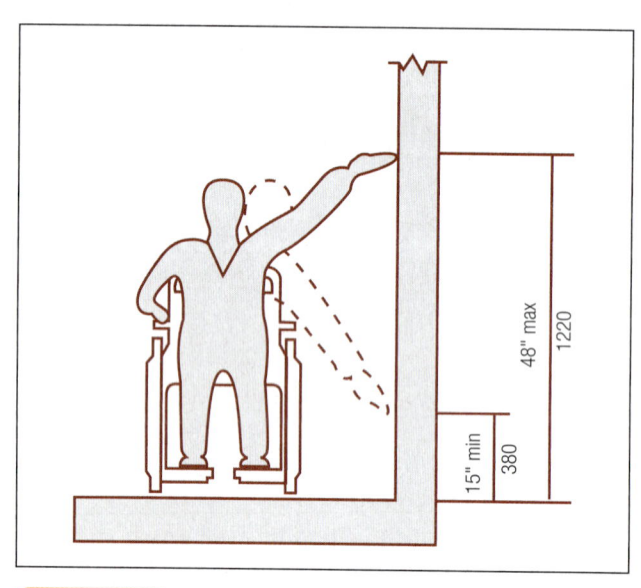

Figure 15-5 Side Reach

The maximal height for reaching from the side position without an obstruction is 48". If an obstruction such as a countertop or shelf is present the maximal height for side reach is 46".

Copyright 2002. Falls Church, Virginia: International Code Council, Inc. Reproduced with permission. All rights reserved.

Figure 15-6 Slope and Rise of Ramps

Slope	Maximum rise in	Maximum rise mm	Maximum horizontal projection ft	Maximum horizontal projection m
1:12 to 1:15	30	760	30	9
1:16 to 1:19	30	760	40	12
1:20	30	760	50	15

This diagram provides the components of a single ramp run and a sample of ramp dimensions. The slope ratio is an important consideration when designing a ramp; slope creates hazardous wheelchair propulsion conditions if it is too steep.

Copyright 2002. Falls Church, Virginia: International Code Council, Inc. Reproduced with permission. All rights reserved.

landing; a 180° turn requires a minimum 4' × 8' landing.
  (5) If the ramp leads to a door, there must be a 5' × 5' platform before the door that extends at least 12" (18" is preferred) along the side of the door to allow for door swing without backing up.
  i. Electric porch lifts and stair lifts are alternatives to ramps.

Funding for Environmental Modifications

1. State One-Stop Centers, Vocational and Educational Services for Individuals with Disabilities (VESID), Offices for Vocational Rehabilitation (OVRs), and Divisions of Vocational Rehabilitation (DVRs) will pay for home and work modifications, if the modifications enable a person to go to work or school.
2. Private companies will fund modifications to ensure ADA compliance.
3. Private insurance, Medicare, Medicaid, and workers' compensation will possibly reimburse for certain devices/adaptations.
4. Centers for Independent Living and disability rights organizations may fund modifications to enable full community participation.

  (b) If the person using the ramp has limited UE strength or decreased cardiopulmonary capacity, 5' × 5' landing(s) are required.
  (c) If there is a sharp turn in the direction of the ramp, landing(s) are required for turning space. A 90° turn requires a minimum 5' × 5'

Wheelchair Prescription, Components, and Types

Purposes of Wheelchairs and Wheelchair Seating and Positioning

1. Enable functional mobility with what means the person with a disability has available.
2. Facilitate mastery of the environment.
3. Enable occupational engagement and social participation.
4. Promote functional posture by provision of appropriate back, trunk, arm, and/or leg supports.
5. Facilitate upper limb function, that can occur with proper trunk support.
6. Promote comfort during upright ADL.
7. Provide physiological maintenance and tissue protection through prevention of shearing.
8. Promote sensory readiness through provision of proper eye and head position.
9. Decrease progression of deformity through customized seating as needed.
10. Decrease pain through provision of proper support.

General Assessment and Prescription Considerations

1. The OTA contributes to the evaluation process with the occupational therapist's supervision to:
   a. Assess the ability of the wheelchair to interact/interface with other assistive devices.
   b. Determine the individual's medical status, including prognosis (is condition temporary, stable, or progressive?) and functional level/needs.
2. Collaborate with the person, caregiver(s), and interdisciplinary team members as identified in prior section of this chapter.

Specific Assessment and Prescription Considerations

1. Upon establishment of service competency, the OTA can collect data in the following areas:
   a. Client factor and performance skill assessments.
      (1) Sensory; e.g., sensory loss places the person at risk for the development of decubiti; therefore necessitating a special seat cushion.
      (2) Neuromuscular; e.g., the individual's sitting posture can require application of seating and positioning knowledge; poor trunk control requires postural supports.
      (3) Musculoskeletal; e.g., physical limitations, such as a compromised respiratory status, may impede mobility and require a powered wheelchair prescription.
   b. For optimal seating and positioning, distinguish between flexible deformities (i.e., where the occupational therapist can manually correct the position) and fixed or abnormal postures/deformities (i.e., changes cannot occur).
   c. When assessing alignment, the pelvis should be evaluated first, and then the lower extremities (LEs), trunk, UEs, head and neck, and feet; stability is required prior to mobility and proximal control allows for better distal function.
      (1) Cognition; e.g., deficits in cognitive function may impede ability to operate powered devices.
      (2) Psychosocial; e.g., the availability of social supports to assist with transporting and transferring to the wheelchair.
   d. Personal assessment.
      (1) Age and developmental status. See subsequent section on developmental considerations.
      (2) Determine the individual's medical status, including prognosis (i.e., condition is temporary, permanent, stable, or progressive) and functional level/needs.
      (3) Education and work interests and pursuits (e.g., the need for desk arms).
      (4) Leisure interests and pursuits (e.g., a special sports chair can enable the individual to pursue past or new interests).
      (5) Daily routines and habits.
      (6) Goals and desired occupations.
      (7) Assess the ability of the wheelchair to interact/interface with other ATs and/or medical equipment used while in the wheelchair (e.g., a communication board, ventilator).
      (8) Socioeconomic status, financial assets and limitations.
   e. Contextual assessments.
      (1) Physical environment.
         (a) Areas of travel and wheelchair use.
         (b) Surfaces and terrains that will be traveled on indoors (e.g., floor surfaces) and outdoors (e.g., sidewalks).
      (2) Building characteristics of school, work, leisure, and/or worship.
         (a) Entrance accessibility.
         (b) Doorways.

(c) Hallways.
(d) Restrooms.
(e) Workspace design.
(f) Parking.
(g) Other specifics as described in the home evaluation section of this chapter.
f. Wheelchair characteristics considered in assessment.
(1) Transportability/portability.
(2) Ride quality.
(3) Types of wheelchair features available.
(a) Control mechanism (e.g., type of brakes used, use of antitippers).
(b) Propulsion method (e.g., one arm drive, use of hand rim projections, motorized, use of LEs to propel).
(c) Personalized features (e.g., use of lap tray and/or backpack to hold personal items and/or medical equipment, hard tires instead of pneumatic tires for increased durability for more active individuals, postural supports for person with poor trunk control).
g. Developmental considerations in assessment.
(1) Transportability to, from, and in school.
(2) Allowance for adjustment when growth changes are experienced.
(3) Allowance for use of other adaptive equipment (i.e., computer, augmentative communication device).
(4) Facilitation of social acceptance.

> **EXAM HINT:** The NBCOT® exam outline for the COTA® identifies knowledge of the "factors related to measuring, selecting, monitoring fit of, and recommending modifications to mobility aids" (NBCOT®, 2018, p. 27) as essential for competent practice. The application of knowledge about the previous wheelchair assessment foci and considerations and the following information about wheelchair components, measurement, and types can help you determine the correct answer for NBCOT® Domain 02 Selecting and Implementing Interventions exam items about the mobility aid of wheelchairs.

Wheelchair Components

1. Armrests.
   a. Fixed: minimal benefit but may be seen in older wheelchairs and/or in rentals.
   b. Detached: helpful for transfers.
   c. Height adjustable: allows for ease in transfers and better support of a lap tray.
   d. Desk arms: allow for moving closer to work surfaces.
   e. Full arms: allow for holding of a lap tray and possibly ease transfers.
   f. Wraparound, space saver arm rests: reduces the overall width of the chair by 1".
2. Leg rests.
   a. Fixed: minimal benefit but may be seen in older wheelchairs and/or in rentals.
   b. Swing-away: allows feet to be placed on the floor to prepare for transfers and for a front approach to wheelchair.
   c. Detachable: allows for a safe path for transfers.
   d. Elevating: allows for edema control and reduction.
   e. Limb board: supports residual limb after a LE amputation.
3. Footplates.
   a. Fixed: minimal benefit but may be seen in older wheelchairs and/or in rentals.
   b. Swing-away: allows feet to reach floor.
   c. Heel loops: prevent feet from slipping off footrest in a posterior direction.
   d. Ankle straps: prevent slipping off footrest.
4. Wheels.
   a. Wheelchair camber: the angle of the wheels in relation to the surface of the floor.
      (1) Wheels that are completely straight and perpendicular to the ground have a camber of zero.
      (2) The further the wheels angle away from the wheelchair, the greater the camber.
         (a) Increased camber provides greater lateral stability, provides a less bumpy ride, and increases the maneuverability of the wheelchair.
5. Tires
   a. Pneumatic: air-filled, requires maintenance, more cushioned ride, shock absorbent.
   b. Semipneumatic: airless foam inserts, less maintenance, good cushioning.
   c. Solid-core rubber: minimal maintenance, tires are mounted on spoked or molded wheels.
6. Casters.
   a. Smaller ones facilitate maneuverability.
   b. Pneumatic and semipneumatic types available, but solid-core are best for indoors and smooth surfaces.
   c. Caster locks can be added for increased stability during transfers.
7. Frame.
   a. Fixed: minimal benefit but may be seen in older wheelchairs or sports chairs.
   b. Folding: eases storage and facilitates mobility in community as it can fold to fit in car or van.
   c. Weight: ultra-light, active-duty lightweight, lightweight, standard, and heavy-duty frame construction are available.
      (1) The lighter the weight of the chair generally, the greater the ease of use.
      (2) The demands of the individual's expected and desired activities must be considered.

8. Additional attachments.
    a. Antitippers to prevent wheelchair from tipping backward or forward.
        (1) Can get caught on doorsills and curbs.
    b. Seatbelts for safety during mobility and functional activities.
        (1) Attach at hip level, not waist level.
        (2) Extend across hips and into lap at 45° angle.
    c. Harnesses to position a person lacking sufficient trunk control.
    d. Arm troughs to position and support a hypotonic UE and prevent edema through elevation.
    e. Lapboards can serve the same purpose as an arm trough, and they are also beneficial as a working 'tabletop' surface.
    f. Head supports allow for improved eye contact, improved communication, and feeding assistance, as the head is kept in a neutral position.
    g. Mobile arm supports allow for use of an UE with proximal weakness to engage in feeding and other activities.
    h. Brake extensions allow a person with limited range in one UE to independently manipulate the wheelchair's brakes.
    i. Hand-rim projections ease independent propulsion in persons with weak handgrip.
        (1) These increase the width of the chair and can decrease mobility through narrow doors and/or narrow spaces.
    j. Push handles allow for another individual to maneuver the wheelchair, if required.
    k. Hillholder devices (also called 'hillclimber' and 'grade aid' devices) allow the wheelchair to move forward but automatically brake when the chair goes backward by engaging a level attached to each wheel.
        (1) Useful for individuals unable to ascend a steep grade (e.g. a long ramp or hill without a rest).
    l. Seating and positioning systems (see subsequent section for details).

Wheelchair Measurement and Considerations

1. General.
    a. The size of a wheelchair should be proportional to the person. See next section for bariatric considerations.
        (1) Standard-sized chairs should be matched to a person whenever possible due to the increased expense of customized chairs.
        (2) Refer to Table 15-2.
    b. Measure on a firm surface, but also observe in a variety of positions to account for tonal influences on posture.

Table 15-2

Standard Dimensions for Wheelchairs

CHAIR STYLE	SEAT WIDTH (INCHES)	SEAT DEPTH (INCHES)	SEAT HEIGHT (INCHES)
Adult	18	16	20
Narrow Adult	16	16	20
Slim Adult	14	16	20
Hemi/low Seat			17.5
Junior	16	16	18.5
Child	14	11.5	18.75
Tiny Tot	12	11.5	19.5

    c. The cushion that will be selected for the individual needs to be considered.
2. Seat width.
    a. Measure the widest point across the hips and thighs to allow for maximal seating space and comfort, and then add 2″.
    b. This allows for clearance on the sides to prevent friction/rubbing and to allow the individual to wear heavier clothing without it being cumbersome.
    c. The bariatric client with a pear shape will have increased gluteal femoral weight distribution.
        (1) Measurement should consider the widest portion of the seated position (e.g., at the forward edge of the seated position).
        (2) Also consider room for weight-shifting maneuvers for pressure relief, and possible use of lift devices.
3. Seat depth.
    a. Measure from the posterior portion of the buttocks to the popliteal fossa and then subtract 2″ from this measurement.
    b. Measure both LEs and use the shortest length.
        (1) This prevents rubbing and potential decubiti to posterior knee region, while also allowing maximal leg swing.
4. Back height.
    a. Measurement is based on the need for postural stability, UE movements, and potential for independent wheelchair propulsion.
    b. Take measurement from seat surface (including the cushion) upward to one of the following depending on trunk control, activity level, strength, and size.
        (1) Midback under scapula: 1″–2″ below.
        (2) Midscapula or axilla.
        (3) Top of the shoulder.
    c. Lower back height can increase functional mobility as in sports chairs.
        (1) Lower back height can increase back strain.
    d. Higher back height may be needed if trunk stability is poor.

> **CAUTION:** If back height of chair is extended, potential problems must be recognized.
> - Added back height may prevent the individual from locking onto the push handle for stabilization and/or weight shifting.
> - Added back height may increase difficulty of fitting chair into car or van.

5. Seat height.
   a. Knees and ankles should be positioned at 90°; measure from distal thigh to heel.
      (1) Measure both LEs and use the shortest length if the person will be self-propelling the wheelchair using their LEs.
   b. Because footrests should have 2" clearance from the floor, add 2" to this measurement.
      (1) The wheelchair cushion selected will affect this measurement.
   c. Standard height: 20".
   d. Hemi-height: 17.5".
6. Armrest height.
   a. Shoulders should be neutral; arms positioned at the sides; elbow flexed to 90°.
   b. Measure under each elbow to cushioned seating surface.
   c. Armrests that are too low will encourage leaning forward.
   d. Armrests that are too high will cause shoulder elevation.

Types of Wheelchairs

1. Refer to Table 15-3 for descriptions of general types of wheelchairs and indications/contraindications for use.
2. Specialized wheelchairs.
   a. Reclining back: a high back reclines independently of the rest of the chair.
      (1) Used to provide pressure relief, regulate blood pressure, improve respiration, and provide support for individuals who are unable to independently maintain an upright sitting position.

Table 15-3

Types of Wheelchairs

ATTENDANT PROPELLED	MANUAL WHEELCHAIR	POWERED MOBILITY
Description	**Description**	**Description**

• Pushed by another
• Usually is manual wheelchair
• Can be a full-size chair or a stroller type chair (e.g., airplane aisle transit chairs)
	• Rigid or folding frames
	• Various frames and weights
	• Lightweight chair: 25–40 pounds
	• Standard: >50 pounds without seating.
	• Amputee frame: axle can be moved posteriorly for increased stability and accommodate for change in gravity center
	• Hemi-height chair: use nonaffected upper extremity and/or lower extremity
	• One-arm drive
	• Gurney: propel with large side wheels while prone
		• Power-base typically independent of seating system
		• Diverse four-wheel designs and three-wheel scooters
		• Add-on power units to manual chairs
		• Battery operated:
		  – deep cycle lead acid
		  – wet cell
		  – sealed cell
		• Method of operation:
		  – Microswitch
		  – proportional joystick
		  – sip and puff
		  – sensing system
		  – body part to be used

Indications/Benefits	**Indications/Benefits**	**Indications/Benefits**
• Brief or chronic disability prevents the ability to self-propel. • Transport in the community. • When powered mobility cannot be used or is being repaired. • Fit and comfort considered for all involved.	• Can independently propel and brake using upper extremities. • May use quick-release wheels (easier for cars). • Can be easily tilted to go up and down curbs.	• Cannot use hands or feet. • Energy expenditure limitations. • Arthritic upper extremities. • Prone to repetitive stress injury. • Neuromuscular injury: to prevent associated reactions. • Can change seat height or tilt. • Sturdy and useful indoors and outdoors.
Limitations	**Limitations**	**Limitations**
• Dependent on another person.	• Standard weight is heavy when considering adding seating system.	• Large/heavy to transport. • Difficult to maneuver in small places. • Cannot be tilted over curbs. • May need to use lifts.

Reference: Adapted by Colleen McCaul DeRitis from Dudgeon, B. & Deitz, J. (2008).

CAUTION: Reclining back wheelchairs extend the seat to back angle; thus, they can elicit flexor or extensor spasms and should not be prescribed to persons with spasticity.

RED FLAG: Reclining back wheelchairs should not be prescribed to persons with limited hip and/or knee ROM as the resultant reclined angles may exceed their available range.

b. Tilt-in space: Tilt-in-space: entire seat and back tilt back to maintain hip and knee angles at 90 degrees.
   (1) Used to provide pressure relief, regulate blood pressure, improve respiration, and minimize the impact of abnormal tone (e.g., severe extensor spasms that can throw a person out of the chair).
c. One arm-drive, hemi-height chair, amputee frame, and powered chairs as outlined in Table 15-3.
d. Recreational: designed with large, thick inner tube-type tires and large front casters for all-terrain use, including sand, mud, snow, and off-road surfaces.
e. Sports: specially designed for racing, cycling, basketball, and other competitive sports; typically ultra-lightweight.
f. Stander: designed to enable a person to independently change seat height and/or elevate to a standing position.
g. Stair-climbing: designed to navigate stairs while balancing on two wheels using sensors and gyroscopes.
h. Bariatric wheelchair: heavy-duty, extra-wide wheelchair designed to assist mobility for individuals who are obese. See following section.

Bariatric Wheelchairs and Prescription Considerations[1]

EXAM HINT: In the NBCOT® practice analysis, 18.1% of occupational therapists who provided services to persons across diagnostic categories indicated they provided services to bariatric clients (NBCOT®, 2018, p. 15). Due to this prevalence, the COTA® exam may have items about bariatric wheelchairs and their prescription.

1. Wheelchair users who are obese must be prescribed wheelchairs that are rated for their obesity category. Chapter 9 provides information about obesity categories and additional bariatric considerations.
   a. Selection based on client characteristics, safety, and function.
2. The bariatric client has a center of body mass that is positioned several inches forward in comparison with the nonobese person.
   a. In order to ensure wheelchair stability, the rear axle is displaced forward in comparison with the standard wheelchair.
      (1) This forward position allows for a more efficient arm push (full arm stroke with less wrist extension).
3. Bariatric wheelchairs can be ordered with special adaptations.
   a. Hard tires versus pneumatic tires for increased durability.
   b. Adjustable backrest to accommodate excessive posterior bulk.
   c. Reclining wheelchair to accommodate excessive anterior bulk, cardiorespiratory compromise (e.g., orthostatic hypotension).
   d. Power application attached to a heavy-duty wheelchair to accommodate excessive fatigue.

▶ Seating and Positioning Systems

Definition

1. The primary unit that properly positions and correctly aligns the trunk and extremities.

Goals

1. Enhance posture.
2. Provide stability, control, and comfort.
3. Promote proximal stability.
4. Allow for pressure relief and support.
5. Allow for proper positioning and correct alignment of trunk and extremities.
6. Decrease the risk of muscle contracture, deformity, and decubiti.
7. Increase sitting tolerance and energy level.
8. Allow visual readiness and use of upper extremities in ADL.
9. Increase function and enable participation.

---

[1]This section and the section on bariatric considerations for wheelchair measurement were contributed by Susan O'Sullivan.

Assessment Considerations

1. It is crucial to distinguish between flexible deformity (i.e., where the OT practitioner can manually correct the position) and fixed abnormal postures and deformities (i.e., where changes cannot occur).
2. The pelvis should be evaluated first, and then LEs, trunk, UEs, head and neck, and feet as stability is required prior to mobility and proximal control allows for better distal function.

Basic Types of Seating

1. Linear.
    a. Flat, noncontoured.
    b. Custom or factory ordered.
    c. Firm, rigid seating.
    d. Good for active individuals, those who perform independent transfers, and/or those with minimal musculoskeletal involvement.
2. Contoured and/or custom contoured.
    a. Ergonomically supports the individual.
    b. Provides excellent support.
    c. Enhances postural alignment.
    d. Provides pressure relief.
    e. May be difficult for independent transfers if decreased UE muscle strength.
    f. Good for individuals with moderate to severe central nervous system dysfunction or neurological disease.

> **EXAM HINT:** The NBCOT® exam outline for the COTA® identifies knowledge of the "factors related to measuring, selecting, monitoring fit of, and recommending modifications to seating systems" (NBCOT®, 2018, p. 27) as essential for competent practice. The application of knowledge about the basic seating styles described above and the seating system styles and accessories described below can help you determine the correct answer for NBCOT® Domain 02 Selecting and Implementing Interventions exam items about seating systems.

Major Styles and Accessories of Seating Systems

1. Solid seat insert prevents hammock effect, provides stable base of support, and is easy to remove.
2. Lumbar back support helps to give proper lumbar curve.
3. Foam cushions (of various densities) can enhance sitting posture and comfort.
4. Contoured foam cushion enhances pelvic and LE alignment.
5. Pressure relief cushions.
    a. Fluid.
        (1) Facilitates pelvic and LE alignment.
        (2) Provides pressure relief without changing support.
        (3) Good for individuals who need increased stability.
    b. Air.
        (1) Minimal postural support offered.
        (2) Provides pressure relief.
        (3) Good trunk control is needed.
    c. Viscoelastic foam.
        (1) Has memory that delays return to original shape.
        (2) Provides good envelopment and a stable base for posture.
        (3) Has good thermal properties.
    d. Flexible matrix.
        (1) Accommodates to user's body to allow pressure redistribution.
        (2) Prevents accumulation of moisture.
    e. Viscoelastic fluid.
        (1) Provides a stable base for posture.
        (2) Has good thermal and dampening properties.
    f. Alternating pressure cushions provide pressure relief while automatically changing the pressure of the cushion.
    g. Hybrid cushions.
        (1) Provides a postural support.
        (2) Has good thermal and envelopment properties.
        (3) Allows for pressure redistribution.
6. Wedge cushions or antithrust seats have a front that is higher than the back to prevent the individual from sliding out of their seat.
7. Pelvic guides inserted on the interior sides of the wheelchair at hip level keep hips stable.
8. Lateral supports extend up the side of the chair to just below person's armpits to provide trunk support.

Pediatric Seating Systems and Positioning Devices

1. Purposes.
    a. Accommodate for contractures and deformities.
    b. Enable function in home, school, and community settings.
    c. Facilitate eye contact and parent/teacher/sibling/peer interactions.
    d. Attain general positioning goals as previously stated.

EXAM HINT: The NBCOT® exam outline for the COTA® identifies knowledge of the "factors related to measuring, selecting, monitoring fit of, and recommending modifications to seating systems, [and] positioning devices" (NBCOT®, 2018, p. 27) as essential for competent practice. The application of knowledge about the purposes described above and the types of pediatric seating systems and positioning devices described below can help you determine the correct answer for COTA® exam items about the use of these interventions with children.

2. Types.
   a. Usually custom-molded created systems.
   b. Standers provide weightbearing experience that maintains hips, knees, ankles, and trunk in optimal position, facilitates formation of acetabulum and long bone development, and aids in bowel and bladder function.
      (1) Prone standers decrease effect of tonic labyrinthine reflex (TLR).
      (2) Supine standers provide more support posteriorly.
   c. Sidelyers decrease effects of TLR and put hands in visual field.
   d. Triwall construction for infants and toddlers.
   e. Abductor pads at hips decrease scissoring extensor pattern.

Mobility Training and Mobility Aids

Overview

1. Functional mobility involves "moving from one position or place to another (during performance of everyday activities), such as in-bed mobility, wheelchair mobility, and transfers (e.g., wheelchair, bed, car, tub, toilet, tub/shower, chair, floor). Includes functional ambulation and transporting objects" (AOTA, 2014, p. S19).
2. Functional mobility is prerequisite to perform ADL, IADL, work, education, leisure, and social participation tasks and activities.
3. Evaluation includes a full client factor and performance skill assessment to determine potential ability to perform mobility (including sensation, perceptual, neuromuscular, musculoskeletal, cognitive, and psychosocial areas).

Wheelchair Mobility Training

EXAM HINT: The NBCOT® exam outline identifies knowledge of "training methods and other factors influencing successful use and maintenance of commonly used . . . durable medical equipment" (NBCOT®, 2018, p. 27) as essential for competent practice. The application of knowledge about the following wheelchair mobility training considerations and approaches can help you determine the correct answer for NBCOT® Domain 02 exam items about wheelchair mobility training.

1. Assess cognition to determine the individual's ability to learn and use a wheelchair independently.
   a. Include personal care attendants and caregivers in the training, as needed.
2. Determine goals for community mobility.
3. Check wheelchair and seating system for fit and needed adjustments.
4. Instruct in proper sitting posture.
5. Instruct in pressure relief (i.e., push-ups, weight shifts leaning to one side, then the other).
6. Instruct in the purpose and use of additional devices used with the wheelchair (i.e., cushion, lap board).
   a. Provide time schedule for weight shifts.
7. Instruct in wheelchair propulsion (e.g., manual, joystick, head control, sip and puff).
   a. Use of wheelchair gloves to ease propulsion and protect hands.
   b. Compensation techniques (e.g., use of feet to assist for propulsion when UE is affected).
8. Instruct in safety concerns when operating a mobility device.
   a. Need to set/release brakes.
   b. Use of swing-away leg rests and removable armrests with transferring.
   c. Caution when using powered wheelchair.
   d. Safe ways to fall from a wheelchair and to return to wheelchair from the ground, if possible.
9. Instruct in how to manipulate basic parts of the wheelchair and break them down to ease transport (e.g., removal of parts to ease storage in a car trunk).
10. Instruct in how to maneuver wheelchair throughout the community.
    a. Practice in natural interior and exterior environments is essential.
       (1) Traverse over different surfaces (e.g., carpeted, asphalt, uneven).
       (2) Ascend and descend inclines.
       (3) Negotiate lips and curbs; how to "'pop a wheelie.'"

(4) Negotiate obstacles (e.g., garbage cans on streets, chairs in restaurants).
(5) Use car and stand lifts.
11. Train in how to transfer from wheelchair to diverse surfaces. See section on transfer training.
12. Instruct in basic maintenance of wheelchair parts.
13. Developmental considerations.
   a. Teach children early to foster independence with wheelchair mobility early to foster independence in their environment.
   b. Discourage use of strollers that prevent child from independent propulsion.

Functional Mobility Aids

EXAM HINT: The COTA® exam outline identifies knowledge of the "factors related to measuring, selecting, monitoring fit of, and recommending modifications to . . . mobility aids" (NBCOT®, 2018, p. 27) as essential for competent practice. The application of knowledge about the following functional mobility aids can help you determine the correct answer for NBCOT® Domain 02 Selecting and Implementing Interventions exam items.

1. Ambulation aids.
   a. Orthotic devices (sometimes referred to as braces) are used to prevent contractures and provide stability to joints involved.
      (1) AFO: ankle-foot orthosis.
      (2) KAFO: knee-ankle-foot orthosis.
      (3) HKAFO: hip-knee-ankle-foot orthosis.
   b. Canes.
      (1) Straight or single access: one leg.
      (2) Wide-based quad cane (WBQC): one shaft is connected to a four-pronged base to increase stability when a person is not able to balance on a straight cane.
      (3) Narrow-based quad cane (NBQC): same premise as WBQC, but prongs are situated closer together for a person who may not require as much support.
   c. Walkers.
      (1) Standard: requires the person to have fair balance and the ability to lift device with UEs to advance.
      (2) Rolling walker: for those who cannot lift a standard walker due to UE weakness or impaired balance.
      (3) Hemi-walker: for those who do not have the ability to use two hands.
         (a) May also be referred to as a hemi-cane.
      (4) Side-stepper: a walker situated on a nonaffected side of a person.
      (5) Three-wheeled walker (also known as a rollator): large pneumatic wheels, hand brakes, and a fold-down seat for those who need increased stability and/or fatigue easily.
      (6) Walker bags, trays, and baskets to assist in transporting personal items.
   d. Crutches.
      (1) Standard: situated in person's axillary region to allow ambulation.
      (2) Platform: forearms are neutral and are supported and hands are in neutral position.
      (3) Lofstrand: proximal arm has closure around it instead of support in axillary region.
   e. Slings provide support to UE, which may have fractured, and prevent poor handling of flaccid UE.
2. Wheelchairs and wheelchair training: see information previously provided in this chapter.
3. Scooters provide mobility to those who are not able to ambulate for distances.
4. Sliding boards allow independent transfers from different surfaces for those who are not able to stand-pivot.
5. UE mobility aids for task performance (e.g., mobile arm support).
6. Bariatric considerations.
   a. Selection of mobility aids are based on specific patient needs (patient safety, gait pattern, fatigue) and weight capacity.
   b. Typical gait changes include greater hip abduction and hip rotation, less knee flexion, difficulty rotating from side to side with increased girth.
   c. Extra wide walkers are used to assist with changes in elevation; e.g., sit-to-stand.
   d. Heavy duty, extra wide walkers are used to assist ambulation.

Bed Mobility

1. Rolling, bridging, sidelying, supine, and sitting.
2. Some diagnoses require special positioning in bed to:
   a. Maintain alignment of vulnerable joints.
   b. Provide variation in postures.
   c. Decrease the effect of pathological reflex activity.
   d. Provide variations in ranges of motion.
   e. Provide stretch to muscles prone to contracture.
   f. Increase comfort.
   g. Decrease risk for pressure ulcers.
   h. Include supine as well as right- and left-side positioning.
3. Specific mobility/positioning techniques.
   a. Status post-total hip replacement.
      (1) May not be permitted to roll on the nonoperated side. This may result in internal rotation of the operated hip, which may cause dislocation.
      (2) May require use of abductor pillow between LEs to prevent adduction of the operated hip.

b. Status post cerebrovascular accident (CVA).
   (1) May need education regarding proper positioning of UE to increase awareness, minimize pain, decrease swelling, and promote normalization of tone.
   (2) May also require use of pillows between knees while in sidelying position to increase comfort and promote proper positioning.
 c. Status post amputation of the LE.
   (1) May require training regarding use of pillows to prevent edema in the LE.
   (2) May also need training on how to provide passive stretching to residual limb while in bed to prevent shortening or contracture, which would make prosthetic training difficult and painful.
4. Bed mobility aids.
 a. Hospital beds, usually with bedrails and elevating head/foot surfaces to increase safety and comfort.
   (1) Bedrails can assist with rolling, positioning for sleep, and assuming to a short-sit position.
 b. Overhead trapeze frame, attached to bed to assist with rolling over and assuming to a long-sit position.
 c. Rope ladders to assist in pulling to a seated position.
 d. Hoyer lift/trans-aid, a hammock device that is attached to either hydraulic or manual lift systems to transfer individuals who are dependent.
 e. Bedpans and urinals to decrease need to leave bed.

> **EXAM HINT:** The NBCOT® exam outline for the COTA® identifies the task of implementing strategies to "support participation in activities of daily living (ADL) . . . [and] rest and sleep" NBCOT®, 2018, p. 25) as essential for competent practice. The application of knowledge about the bed mobility/positioning techniques previously described and the bed mobility aids described above can help you determine the correct answer for NBCOT® Domain 02 exam items about enabling ADL, rest, and sleep.

Transfers

Purpose

1. To move from one surface to another safely and effectively with (dependent) or without (independent) the assistance of others.

Transfer Considerations

1. Assess and identify an individual's assets and deficits, especially cognitive and physical abilities.

> **CAUTION:** The OTA should be aware of their own limitations to avoid personal or client injury.

2. Use of proper body mechanics should be strictly enforced.
 a. Use broad base of support.
 b. The OTA must know where their center of gravity is at all times.
 c. Individual to be transferred should be lifted with the OT practitioner using their LEs to lift and not their back.
3. Perform wheelchair transfers safely.
 a. Clear areas involved in transfers of any clutter.
 b. Ask for help or stand-by assist if questioning ability to transfer safely.
 c. Use transfer belts if needed.
 d. Stabilize/lock brakes.
 e. Swing away leg rests and flip up footplates.
 f. Remove armrest for a "pop-over" transfer if individual is unable to assist, is too heavy to bring to a standing position, or if the individual has a weight-bearing precaution.
4. Allow for variability of individuals and environment.
 a. Adjust transfer methods according to individual's strengths and limitations regarding performance component/skills and client factors.
 b. Be aware of different floor/ground surfaces.
 c. Be aware of the increased risk of personal injury when transferring a bariatric client.
   (1) Use good body mechanics, obtain adequate assistance during transfers, and use mechanical lifts.
5. Train in transfers to and from a variety of different surfaces (i.e., bed, wheelchair, chair, toilet, tub, and/or car).

Transfer Types

1. Stand-pivot: individual stands and turns to transfer surface.
2. Pop-over or seated sitting: a full stand position is not required; used for those with decreased endurance and/or weight-bearing precautions.

3. Sliding board transfer for those who are not able to stand to transfer (i.e., individuals with spinal cord injuries or amputations).
   a. Board is placed under individual's gluteal region during a weight shift, while the other end of board is placed on surface being transferred to.
   b. Individual then uses UEs to push buttocks up and "slide" over to transfer surface.

> **RED FLAG:** If a person who uses a tenodesis grasp or splint transfers with flattened palms, they will lengthen the digit flexors. Because this will weaken their tenodesis grasp, they should be taught to transfer by weight-bearing on clenched fists with wrists extended.

4. Dependent: caregiver is required to fully perform the transfer.
5. Mechanical lift: use of a ceiling lift, track lift, Hoyer lift, or trans-aid.
6. Use of adaptive or mobility devices.
   a. Bed transfer aids.
      (1) Trapeze.
      (2) Bedrail.
   b. Bath transfer aids.
      (1) Grab bars, potentially with a shower chair inside the shower or tub.
      (2) Transfer tub bench, to eliminate the need to step over the threshold of a tub.
      (3) Active-aid commode, a commode with small wheels to allow transfer to bathroom and shower stall when otherwise not possible.
      (4) Bedside or 3-in-1 commode.
      (5) Ambulatory devices (i.e., canes, walkers).
      (6) Wheelchairs (i.e., removable arms, swing arms, leg rests).
7. Chair lifts: chairs with power control to allow elevation from surface for individuals who may otherwise not be able to transfer independently.

> **EXAM HINT:** The NBCOT® exam blueprint identifies the task of selecting "assistive technology options, adaptive devices, mobility aids, and other durable medical equipment" (NBCOT®, 2018, p. 27) as essential for competent practice. The application of knowledge about the previously described transfer mobility aids and the adaptive and mobility devices described above can help you determine the correct answer for NBCOT® Domain 02 Selecting and Implementing Interventions exam items about wheelchair, bed, and bath transfers.

Assistive Technology Devices (ATDs)/Electronic Aids to Daily Living (EADL)

Assistive Technology Devices (ATDs)

1. Definition: "any piece of equipment or product . . . used to increase, maintain, improve functional capabilities of individuals with disabilities . . ." (Bain, 1998, p. 466).
2. An expansion of adaptive equipment.
3. Occupational therapy practitioners typically consider a range of ATs for the environment to support safety and independence at home.
   a. High tech: potentially costly devices that may require custom ordering and may require specific training to use (e.g., environmental control units [ECUs], augmentative and alternative communication [AAC] devices, computers).
      (1) "Domotics" is the integration of technology and services for a better quality of life.
         (a) Information technology and electronics that make a home become 'smart.'
         (b) Available technologies (i.e., environmental control units [ECUs]) allow people to control the electric functions of their home in a cost-effective, practical, socially relevant, and reliable manner.
   b. Mid-tech devices: inexpensive household devices that are readily available for use but tend to be electronic and may require programming/setup (i.e., personal 'talking' alarm clocks, automatic coffee pots).
   c. Low tech: inexpensive household and/or catalog items that are basic and readily available for use (e.g., jar opener, shoehorn, sock aid).
4. ATs installed in 'smart' homes support safety, access, comfort, and functional independence.
   a. Electronic aids to daily living (EADL).
   b. Assistive technology for cognition (ATC).
   c. Wireless connectivity to the community.
   d. New and rapidly developing technologies continue to appear on the market.

EXAM HINT: The NBCOT® exam outline for the COTA® identifies knowledge of the "characteristics and features of high- and low-tech assistive technology for supporting engagement in meaningful occupation" (NBCOT®, 2018, p. 27) as essential for competent practice. The application of knowledge about the types of ATs described above and the electronic aids to daily living (EADL) described below can help you determine the correct answer for NBCOT® Domain 02 exam items about AT and EADL interventions.

Electronic Aids to Daily Living (EADLs)

1. Definition: EADLs were formerly known as environmental control units (ECUs) and are a "means to purposefully manipulate and interact with the environment by alternately accessing one or more electrical devices via switch, voice activation, remote control, computer interface..." (Bain, 1998, p. 469).
2. Purposes.
   a. Enable control of devices within the environment.
   b. Compensate for functional limitations and maximize functional abilities.
   c. Increase independence in home, school, work, and other environments.
   d. Conserve energy during home management and work tasks.
3. Uses.
   a. Turn on/off lights, control appliances, open and close doors/drapes, etc.
   b. Allow use of phones, computers, and office machinery.
   c. Summon assistance.
   d. Passive occupant monitoring.
      (1) Provides communication with off-site caregiver to monitor safety.
      (2) Key consideration for many older adults, potentially with a cognitive impairment or high fall risk, and persons living with a disability.
      (3) May be accomplished with motion sensors located around the home to detect deviations from daily routines.
         (a) Allows a caregiver to monitor without the intrusion of a video camera or phone call.
4. Clients may resist having their daily activities monitored.
   a. They may see monitoring as an invasion of privacy or decrease in independence.
   b. They may fear falling victim to hackers.
   c. These concerns and fears are often legitimate and should be not be universally dismissed.

CAUTION: A backup plan for electronic support must be in place for emergency help in case of a power outage or technical malfunction.

5. Candidates for EADL.
   a. Individuals living with various conditions that limit mobility (i.e., SCI, CVA) or impaired cognition (i.e., TBI, neurocognitive disorders).
   b. Persons with a goal of transitioning from supported to independent living.
   c. Older adults who wish to age in place.
6. Considerations in device selection.
   a. Input method: selection requires knowledge of the distance of throughput/transmission.
      (1) Activation modes for input can include discrete controls, continuous controls, momentary controls, latched controls, and direct or indirect selection.
   b. Output method.
   c. Portability.
   d. Safety.
   e. Reliability.
   f. Durability.
   g. Assembly ease.
   h. Operation ease.
   i. Maintenance schedule.
   j. Current and future affordability.
   k. Person's readiness for change and ability to learn to use potentially novel technology.
7. Examples of EADL technology.
   a. Phones: large number pads, automatic dialing phones, speaker-phones, amplifiers, videophones, smartphone applications.
   b. 'Talking' pill bottles fit on most bottles; they can remind when it is time to take medication, share information with doctors, and submit orders for prescription refills.
   c. Monitoring systems allow for communication between areas.
   d. Personal emergency response system (PERS): enables a client to summon help by the push of a button or the vocalization of a command.
   e. Electronically controlled door openers and closers to promote ease of access.
      (1) These can be operated using different transmission modes, including X-10 units, infrared, radio frequency transmission, or ultrasound.
   f. Automatic lights, self-dimming bulbs, and/or motion sensor lights to facilitate adequate and even lighting throughout the home.
   g. Backsplash display screens can be used in the kitchen to allow for hands-free access to recipes or taking calls while cooking while standing supported at the counter.
   h. Smart hubs/smart home platforms (e.g., Google Home, Amazon Alexa) may control a large number

of home functions, including opening drawers, checking doors, turning on lights, activating appliances, and alerting friends or emergency responders to potential fall incidents.
  i. Computers enable individuals with disabilities to more fully participate in social, leisure, work, and productive activities. They:
    (1) Facilitate performance of multiple functional tasks (e.g., banking, shopping).
    (2) Allow for communication and socialization through e-mail and Internet support groups.
    (3) Provide the means for productive work via telecommuting.
    (4) Have alternative access modes that can compensate for a diversity of disabilities. Adaptations can include:
      (a) Alternative switch input including trackballs, paddles, joysticks, or mice.
      (b) Built-in accessibility features in computers including keylocks, sticky keys (to ease one-handed computer use for persons with hemiplegia), mouse keys, number locks, and color inversion features (to enhance contrast for persons with visual impairments).
      (c) Eye gaze for individuals with severe mobility impairments (e.g., individuals with amyotrophic lateral sclerosis).
      (d) Voice activation for individuals with severe mobility impairments with functional speech (e.g., UE contractures).
      (e) Programmable keyboards that allow for customized overlays (e.g., enlarged letters and numbers for persons with low vision; graphics and symbols for individuals with cognitive impairments).
      (f) Expanded keyboards that provide large keys for persons with visual-motor deficits (e.g., persons with residual deficits post-CVA).
      (g) Key guards for persons with limited motor accuracy and control (e.g., individuals with ataxia).
      (h) Contracted keyboards that provide smaller keys in a constrained space for persons with limited ROM and functional motor control (e.g., individuals with arthritis).
      (i) Light-touch keyboard activation systems for persons with decreased strength and/or mobility (e.g., individuals with muscular dystrophy).
      (j) Delayed touch keyboard activation systems for persons with poor motor control (e.g., individuals with athetoid movements).
      (k) Chorded keyboards that consist of a few keys which generate standard characters by pressing various combinations of keys for persons with one-handed use (e.g., individuals with hemiplegia).
      (l) Tongue-touch keypad (TTK) imbedded in an orthotic device for persons with severe motor deficits and good tongue control (e.g., an individual with a C-3 SCI).
  j. Augmentative alternative communication: methods of communication that do not require speech. Need to consider:
    (1) Speed at which message is conveyed.
    (2) Portability: easy to use in a variety of environmental settings.
    (3) Accessibility: ability of individual to independently operate.
    (4) Dependability: quality, durability, and warranty/service record.
    (5) Independence of user.
    (6) Vocabulary flexibility.
    (7) Time for repairs and maintenance.
    (8) Types range from simple communication boards or albums with a limited number of pictures to complex portable computer systems with extensive language capacity.

Evaluation and Intervention

1. The role of the OTA in evaluation.
   a. The OTA contributes to the evaluation process.
   b. The OTA can assist with the collection of data for the evaluation once service competency has been established.
   c. The level of supervision required will be determined by the OTA's experience and established service competence.
   d. The OTA cannot independently evaluate or interpret evaluation results.
2. The OTA collaborates with the OT supervisor to:
   a. Identify the activities the individual wants to engage in, the occupational roles the person wants to pursue, and potentially the home functions the individual may want to control.
   b. Determine the person's values about the use of AT.
   c. Assess the individual's abilities and deficits, including client factors and performance skills.
     (1) Stability of positioning and seating must be assessed as this will affect the person's ability to use devices.
     (2) The anatomic site at which the person demonstrates purposeful controlled movement must be determined as this will influence a device's control site (e.g., device activated by shoulder, head, elbow, hand, tongue, or eye movements).
       (a) If no physical interaction with an input is possible, the ability to use speech to use voice recognition AT should be assessed.

d. Determine the environments in which a device will be used and when it will be used.
e. Identify potential AT devices.
   (1) Consider input method: how the device will be activated (e.g., infrared, sonic, electric, touch screen, smartphone app, or radio frequency switches) and by what action (e.g., voice recognition, eye gazing, using a joystick, head pointer, mouthstick, tongue, or automated systems that do not require individual commands).
   (2) Consider the processing method: how the device will process the information from the input method.
   (3) Consider the output method: results are needed (response from input occurs).
   (4) Consider the feedback method: ensures the device is being used in the right way (could be auditory, visual, or proprioceptive).
f. The Human Activity-Assistive Technology Model (HAAT Model).
   (1) Considers the person, activity to be completed, aspects of the AT, and context in which interaction takes place.
   (2) Provides stepwise intervention to appropriately chose AT according to clients' needs. Recommends introducing one or two adaptations at a time to acclimate the use to the system prior to adding additional components.
   (3) Considers the cost of devices.

EXAM HINT: The NBCOT® exam outline for the COTA® identifies knowledge of "training methods and other factors influencing successful use and maintenance of commonly used assistive technology options" (NBCOT®, 2018, p. 27) as essential for competent practice. The application of knowledge about the evaluation considerations and HAAT Model described above and the following intervention principles can help you determine the correct answer for NBCOT® Domain 02 exam items about AT training.

3. The role of the OTA in intervention.
   a. The OTA implements intervention with the occupational therapist's supervision.
   b. The level of supervision required depends upon the OTA's experience and established service competence.
   c. During the implementation of intervention, the OTA informs the supervising occupational therapist of any change in the individual's status and any other relevant information that may affect treatment.
4. Intervention principles.
   a. Select and use several devices on a trial basis to determine what serves the individual's needs best.
   b. Determine the specific device, after reviewing and incorporating all of the team members' information.
   c. Keep devices as simple as possible.
   d. If device is stationary, ensure that it is positioned to enable ease of access.
   e. Provide multiple training sessions.
5. Documentation.
   a. Document the evaluation process.
   b. Document recommended ATD(s) selected and the rationale for each item for reimbursement justification.
      (1) Based on individual's needs and goals.
      (2) Based on functional status, abilities, and limitations.
      (3) Based on school/work/leisure status and needs.
      (4) Justify cost-effectiveness of recommended equipment.
6. Reevaluation guidelines.
   a. Assess for change in status of the individual with a disability.
   b. Determine efficiency and efficacy of use of assistive devices.
   c. Check parts of the device for durability.

Additional Considerations for ATDs and EADL

1. The appliances and electrical cords to be used with ATDs and EADL must be determined.
2. Charging instructions must be followed, as some have strict schedules.
3. The technological and computer abilities of an individual with a disability should be determined.
4. Surge protectors must be used to avoid blown circuits.
5. Backup systems for electrical high-tech devices should be established.
6. Instruction must be provided to the individual to ensure carryover when an OT practitioner and/or other supports are not present.
7. Warranty information should be obtained and the consumer educated about these terms and conditions.

Funding for ATDs and EADL

1. State Vocational and Educational Services for Individuals with Disabilities (VESID), Offices for Vocational Rehabilitation (OVRs), and Divisions of Vocational Rehabilitation (DVRs) will pay for ATDs and EADL, if they enable a person to go to work or school.
2. Private companies will fund ATDs and EADL to ensure ADA compliance.
3. Private insurance, Medicare, Medicaid, and workers' compensation may reimburse for certain devices.

Community Mobility

Overview

1. Community mobility is the ability to move around one's community to engage in desired occupations and pursue meaningful activities.
2. Community mobility includes the ability to access and use public and/or private transportation systems (i.e., buses, subways, trains, taxi cabs, or other community-based transportation systems).
   a. Transportation systems specifically developed to meet the community mobility needs of persons with disabilities are typically called 'paratransit.'
3. Community mobility also includes the ability to drive, walk, and/or bicycle.

> **EXAM HINT:** The NBCOT® exam outline for the COTA® identifies knowledge of "mobility options, vehicle adaptations, and alternative devices for supporting participation in community mobility" (NBCOT®, 2018, p. 27) as essential for competent practice. The application of knowledge about the community mobility options described above and the following information about driver rehabilitation can help you determine the correct answer for NBCOT® Domain 02 exam items about community mobility participation.

Driver Rehabilitation

1. Driving is an IADL.
2. Purposes.
   a. Provide mobility within one's community.
   b. Allow for autonomy for self-directed activity pursuit.
   c. Enable engagement in life roles including vocational, avocational, social, and familial role activities.
3. Physical, cognitive, psychiatric, and developmental disabilities can affect the ability to drive safely and effectively.
4. Driver rehabilitation requires extensive on-the-road training and behind-the-wheel driving in a diversity of driving environments.
   a. Knowledge of general state driving regulations and statutes specifically related to individuals with disabilities must be acquired prior to initiating a driver rehabilitation program.
   b. An OT practitioner who performs on-the-road driver training must become a state licensed driving instructor.
      (1) State regulations will determine OTA eligibility.
   c. Occupational therapy practitioner who practice driver rehabilitation should become certified driving rehabilitation specialists.

Evaluation of Driver Ability

1. The OTA can contribute to the evaluation process with occupational therapist supervision.
2. Upon establishment of service competency the OTA can participate in the clinical screening of performance skills, prerequisite abilities, and client factors.
   a. Visual-perceptual: intact acuity, night vision, contrast sensitivity, peripheral field, scanning, spatial relations, and depth perception are needed to access essential visual input and to accurately interpret the driving environment.
      (1) Color recognition is not a state mandated requirement as color blindness can be readily compensated for while driving.
   b. Cognitive-perceptual: intact orientation, alertness, memory, judgement, ability to shift/divide attention, problem-solving, response time, topographical orientation, sign recognition, and knowledge of 'rules of the road' are required to drive safely and appropriately for different driving conditions, and to anticipate the actions of other drivers on the road and the consequences of one's own actions.
   c. Motor: adequate ROM, strength, endurance, and motor speed are needed for basic vehicle control including accurate steering to remain in lane and make turns, and for smooth acceleration and braking.
   d. Sensory: the presence or loss of proprioception, pressure, and localization in the peripheries.
   e. Psychosocial: the presence of impulsive and/or agitated behaviors, and/or psychiatric symptoms such as suicidal intentions, delusions, and hallucinations, can affect an individual's ability to drive safely.
   f. Side effects of medications can affect motor performance, alertness, attention, judgment, and reaction time.
   g. Past driving experiences (which can range from none, to poor, to competent) can influence the individual's potential to drive with a disability.
   h. OTAs with occupational therapist supervision can perform clinical screenings for all of the previous factors that can affect driving without additional specialized training.

(1) If screening identifies areas requiring further evaluation, the occupational therapist should refer the individual to a driving rehabilitation specialist.
3. On-the-road evaluation: there are two levels of driving that must be considered when evaluating a person's abilities when they are behind the wheel and actually driving. They are:
   a. Operational: the ability to steer, brake, and turn.
   b. Tactical: the ability to respond to changes in road conditions and traffic/driving risks.
4. The ergonomics of driving should also be assessed to increase safety and prevent discomfort. Considerations include:
   (1) Seat position in relation to visibility of car's endpoints.
   (2) Positioning of seatbelt and shoulder restraint.
   (3) Access to foot pedals and/or steering column controls.
   (4) Airbag clearance of 12" between the person and the steering wheel in case of airbag deployment.
5. The person's ability to manage automotive emergencies (e.g., a breakdown) and obtain assistance should also be assessed.

Interventions for Driver Rehabilitation

1. Adaptive driving equipment can be prescribed for individuals with specific limitations.
   a. Hand controls can replace accelerators and brake foot pedals.
   b. Steering knobs for one-handed steering control can include a:
      (1) Standard round spinning knob for a person with one intact UE.
      (2) Ring to accommodate a prosthesis.
      (3) Tri-pin or cuff to accommodate absent or weak grasp.
   c. Pedal extensions can be added if feet do not reach standard foot pedals.
   d. Zero effort or reduced effort steering can accommodate for decreased range, strength, and endurance.
   e. Steering wheel positioning adjustments can place the steering wheel in atypical positions to allow for access.
2. If a person is determined to be unsafe or unable to drive, alternatives to maintain community mobility must be explored and implemented (i.e., public transportation, private car services, ride sharing, walking).
   a. Support must be provided to the individual to deal with this loss and its ramifications for the person's daily life.
   b. Interventions to ensure safety as a public transit user and/or pedestrian are required.

Funding for Driver Rehabilitation

1. State Vocational and Educational Services for Individuals with Disabilities (VESID), Offices for Vocational Rehabilitation (OVRs), and Divisions of Vocational Rehabilitation (DVRs) will pay for driver rehabilitation if it will enable a person to go to work or school.
2. Private insurance, Medicare, Medicaid, and workers' compensation will possibly reimburse for certain driver rehabilitation devices/adaptations.

Environmental Modifications for Cognitive and Sensory Deficits

General Intervention Strategies

1. The environment needs to be familiar, consistent, and predictable.
   a. Provide structure in the environment to increase orientation to time, place, person, and situation.
   b. Remove clutter to decrease extraneous stimuli when an individual is easily distracted or has limited vision.
   c. Provide visual reminders or tactile cues to decrease confusion, increase awareness, and facilitate independence (e.g., written directions, Braille labels).
   d. Keep things in the same place for consistency and ease.
2. Use contrasting colors to discriminate background from foreground or figures from background.
3. Use restraint reduction techniques if a person is confused, agitated, and/or a wanderer.
4. Educate consumer, caregiver, and family.
   a. Train caregivers for persons with memory and/or sensory impairments on effective communication techniques.
   b. Facilitate carryover of intervention techniques in the modified environment.
   c. Increase awareness of potential resources available to the individual and their families.
   d. Increase awareness of their rights to access these resources.

5. Monitor changes and adjustment after a disability to assess carryover of information.
6. Make home modifications to ensure safety as needed.
   a. Remove potential hazards such as cleaning solutions, medications, sharp objects, matches, stove knobs, and firearms if a person is confused or forgetful.
   b. Follow modifications identified earlier in this chapter for the prevention of falls.
   c. See Chapter 5 for additional modifications for age-related sensory loss.
7. Provide a personal emergency system and train in its use.

> **EXAM HINT:** The NBCOT® exam outline for the COTA® identifies knowledge of "interventions to support optimal sensory arousal, and . . . cognitive, or perceptual processing for supporting engagement in meaningful occupations consistent with developmental level, neuromotor status, mental health, cognitive level, psychosocial skills and abilities, task characteristics, context, and environmental demands" (NBCOT®, 2018, p. 25) as essential for competent practice. The application of knowledge about the intervention strategies described above and the following restraint reduction approaches can help you determine the correct answer to NBCOT® Domain 02 exam items about intervention management for persons with cognitive and/or sensory deficits.

Restraint Reduction

1. The OTA contributes to the assessment of behaviors that result in agitation, restlessness, and/or wandering with occupational therapist supervision. Areas to assess include:
   a. Pain, physical discomfort.
   b. Hunger, thirst, need for toileting.
   c. Loneliness, fear.
   d. Boredom.
   e. Unfamiliar environment.
2. The OTA implements intervention with the occupational therapist's supervision to address contributing factors and/or correct underlying problems. Interventions include:
   a. Referral to physician for medical evaluation/pain management.
   b. Proper positioning.
   c. Provision of snacks, unbreakable water bottles, or other appropriate safe source of nourishment and hydration.
   d. Adequate and client-directed toileting routine.
   e. Active listening, attention to underlying feelings and expressed concerns to promote trust.
   f. Family, peer, and/or pastoral visits.
   g. Animal-assisted or pet therapy.
   h. Social and leisure activities.
   i. Exercise and/or other outlets for restless, anxious behavior.
   j. Night-time activities.
   k. Eliminate loudspeaker and other extraneous noise, provide soothing background music.
   l. Inclusion of familiar and favorite objects in person's living space to personalize it.
   m. Provide a structured home-like environment with a set routine to promote sense of safety and security.
3. The OTA implements interventions with the occupational therapist's supervision to address agitation and/or wandering incidents. Interventions include:
   a. Approach from person's front at eye level.
   b. Communicate calmly with the use of simple statements/instructions.
   c. Distract with an activity or topic of interest to the person.
   d. Redirect back to desired location.
   e. Engage in an activity of interest or diversion.
   f. Camouflage doors, exits, and elevators with full-length mirrors, stop or no-crossing signs, wallpaper, vertical blinds.
   g. Put tape on floors or planters to mark end of hall.
   h. Install non-dead bolt locks or Velcro doors.
   i. Use door alarms, personal alarms, or monitoring devices.
   j. Make contained areas interesting and safe.
   k. Rearrange furniture to deter wandering.
   l. Provide a variety of comfortable seating and furniture, including broad-based rockers and footstools.

References

American National Standards Institute. (1992). *Accessible and usable buildings and facilities.* New York, NY: Author.

American Occupational Therapy Association. (2015). *Four ways occupational therapy makes smart homes smarter* [PDF file]. Bethesda, MD: Author. Retrieved from https://www.aota.org/Publications-News/AOTANews/2015/smart-homes-learn-technology-ot-occupational-therapy.aspx

American Occupational Therapy Association. (2014). Occupational therapy practice framework: Domain and process,

3rd edition. *American Journal of Occupational Therapy, 68*(Suppl. 1), S1-S48.

American Occupational Therapy Association. (2010). Specialized knowledge and skills in technology and environmental interventions for occupational therapy practice. *American Journal of Occupational Therapy, 64*(Suppl. 6), S44-S56.

American Occupational Therapy Association. (2010). Standards of practice for occupational therapy. *American Journal of Occupational Therapy, 64*(Suppl. 6), S106-S110.

American Occupational Therapy Association. (2010). Driving and community mobility. *American Journal of Occupational Therapy, 64*(Suppl. 6), S112-S124.

Bain, B. (1997). Evaluation. In B. Bain & D. Leger (Eds.), *Assistive technology: An interdisciplinary approach.* (pp. 17-27). New York: Churchill Livingstone.

Bain, B. (1998). Assistive technology. In G. Gillen & A. Burkhardt (Eds.), *Stroke rehabilitation: A function based approach.* (pp. 465-478). St. Louis, MO: Mosby.

Bain, B., Dooley, K., & Leger, D. (1997). Assistive technology: An interdisciplinary approach. In B. Bain & D. Leger (Eds.), *Assistive technology: An interdisciplinary approach.* (pp. 1-7). New York, NY: Churchill Livingstone.

Bausch, M. E., Mittler, J. E., Hasselbring, T. S., & Cross, D. P. (2005). The Assistive Technology Act of 2004: What does it say and what does it mean? *Physical Disabilities: Education and Related Services, 23*(2), 59-67.

Bolding, D., Adler, C., Tipton-Burton, M., & Lillie, S. (2007). Mobility. In H. McHugh Pendleton & W. Schultz-Krohn (Eds.), *Pedretti's occupational therapy: Practice skills for physical dysfunction.* (6th ed., pp. 195-247). St. Louis, MO: Mosby.

Boyt Schell, B. A., Gillen, G., & Scaffa, M. (Eds.). (2014). *Willard and Spackman's occupational therapy* (12th ed.). Philadelphia, PA: Lippincott Williams & Wilkins.

Buning, M. E. (2008). High-technology adaptations to compensate for disability. In M. V. Radomski & C. A. Trombly Latham (Eds.), *Occupational therapy for physical dysfunction.* (6th ed., pp. 510-541). Philadelphia, PA: Lippincott Williams & Wilkins.

Case-Smith, J. (Ed.). (2005). *Occupational therapy for children,* (5th ed). St. Louis, MO: Elsevier Mosby.

Cook, A., & Polgar, J. M. (2013). *Assistive technology: Principles and practices* (4th ed.). St. Louis, MO: Mosby.

Dudgeon, B., & Deitz, J. C. (2008). Wheelchair selection. In M. V. Radomski & C. A. Trombly Latham (Eds.), *Occupational therapy for physical dysfunction* (6th ed., pp. 487-509). Baltimore, MD: Williams & Wilkins.

Foti, D., & Kanazawa, L. (2006). Activities of daily living. In H. McHugh Pendleton & W. Schultz-Krohn (Eds.), *Pedretti's occupational therapy: Practice skills for physical dysfunction.* (6th ed., pp. 146-194). St. Louis, MO: Mosby.

Gentry, T. (2017, September 11). Practical, affordable, smart homes for safety and improved function. *OT Practice,* 8-13.

Giesbrecht, E. (2013). Application of the human activity assistive technology model for occupational therapy research. *Australian Journal of Occupational Therapy, 60*(3), 230-240.

Gourley, M. (2002, March 25). Driver rehabilitation. *Occupational Therapy Practice,* 15-20.

Institute for Human Centered Design. (2016). *ADA checklist for existing facilities* [PDF]. Retrieved from https://www.adachecklist.org/doc/fullchecklist/ada-checklist.pdf

Johann, C. (1998). Seating and wheeled mobility prescription. In G. Gillen & A. Burkhardt (Eds.), *Stroke rehabilitation: A function based approach.* (pp. 437-451). St. Louis, MO: Mosby.

Kane, L., & Buckley, K. (1998). Functional mobility. In G. Gillen & A. Burkhardt (Eds.), *Stroke rehabilitation: A function based approach.* (pp. 305-242). St. Louis, MO: Mosby.

Lange, M. L. (2001, July 2). Alternative keyboards. *OT Practice,* 19-20.

Lange, M. L. (2001, Aug. 6). EADLs and aging clients. *Occupational Therapy Practice,* 16-18.

Lange, M. L. (2001, Aug. 6). EADLs in the school setting. *Occupational Therapy Practice,* 17-18.

Larson, K., Stevens-Ratchford, R. G., Pedretti, L., & Crabtree, J. (1996). *ROTE: The role of occupational therapy with the elderly.* (2nd ed.). Bethesda, MD: American Occupational Therapy Association.

Mosey, A. C. (1996). *Psychosocial components of occupational therapy.* New York, NY: Raven Press.

Moyers, P., & Dale, L. (2007). *The guide to occupational therapy practice.* Bethesda, MD: American Occupational Therapy Association.

National Board for Certification in Occupational Therapy (NBCOT®). (2018). *Practice analysis of the certified occupational therapy assistant registered: Executive summary* [PDF file]. Gaithersburg, MD: Author. Retrieved from https://www.nbcot.org/-/media/NBCOT/PDFs/2017-Practice-Analysis-Executive-OTR.ashx?la=en.

National Registry of Rehabilitation Technology Suppliers (NRRTC). (2019). *About NRRTC.* Retrieved from http://www.nrrts.org/about.

Pedretti, L. (1990). Activities of daily living. In L. Pedretti & B. Zoltan (Eds.), *Occupational therapy: Practice skills for physical dysfunction.* (3rd ed., pp. 230-271). St. Louis, MO: Mosby.

Peterson, E. W., & Murphy, S. (2002). Fear of falling: Part II-Assessment and intervention. *Home and Community Health Special Interest Section Quarterly, 9*(1)-4.

Pierce, S. L. (2008). Restoring mobility. In M. V. Radomski & C. A. Trombly Latham (Eds.), *Occupational therapy for physical dysfunction.* (6th ed., pp. 817-853). Philadelphia, PA: Lippincott Williams & Wilkins.

Radomski, M. V. (2008). Assessing context: Personal, social, and cultural. In M. V. Radomski & C. A Trombly Latham (Eds.), *Occupational therapy for physical dysfunction.* (6th ed., pp. 284-309). Philadelphia, PA: Lippincott Williams & Wilkins.

Rigby, P., Lowe, M., & Stewart, D. (2008). Assessing environment, home, community, and workplace access. In M. V. Radomski & C. A. Trombly Latham (Eds.), *Occupational therapy for physical dysfunction.* (6th ed., pp. 310-337). Philadelphia, PA: Lippincott Williams & Wilkins.

Sabata, D. B., Shamberg, S., & Williams, M. (2008). Optimizing access to home, community, and work environments. In M. V. Radomski & C. A. Trombly Latham (Eds.), *Occupational therapy for physical dysfunction.* (6th ed., pp. 951-973). Philadelphia, PA: Lippincott Williams & Wilkins.

Salerno, C. (1998). Home evaluation and modification. In G. Gillen & A. Burkhardt (Eds.), *Stroke rehabilitation: A function based approach.* (pp. 452-464). St. Louis, MO: Mosby.

Schell, B., Gillen, G., & Scaffa, M. (Eds.). (2013). *Willard and Spackman's occupational therapy.* (12th ed.) Philadelphia, PA: Lippincott Williams & Wilkins.

Sladyk, K., Jacobs. K., & MacRae, N. (2010). *Occupational therapy essentials for clinical competence.* Thorofare, NJ: Slack.

Spencer, E. (1998). Functional restoration: Preliminary concepts and planning. In H. Hopkins & H. Smith (Eds.), *Willard and Spackman's occupational therapy.* (7th ed., pp. 435–460). Philadelphia, PA: Lippincott Williams & Wilkins.

Stav, W., & Kaebel, M. (2002, October). On the road again. *Rehab Management,* 26–27.

Stav, W., Pierce, S., Wheatley, C., & Schold Davis, E. (2005). Driving and community mobility. *American Journal of Occupational Therapy, 59,* 666–670.

Tinetti, M. E., Richman, D., & Powell, L. (1990). Falls efficacy as a measure of fear of falling. *Journal of Gerontology, 45*(6), 239–243.

Vandome, N. (2018). *Smart homes in easy steps: Master smart technology for your home.* Warwickshire, UK: In Easy Steps Limited.

Walls, B. S. (1999, December 6). A dangerous secret: I had a fall. *Occupational Therapy Practice,* 1–16.

West Virginia Research and Training Center. (1990). ADA—*The Americans with Disabilities Act of 1990 PL 101-336, Vol I: The Law.* Dunbar, WV: Author.

Wheatley, C. J. (2001, July 16). Shifting into drive: Evaluating potential drivers with disabilities. *Occupational Therapy Practice,* 12–15.

Review Questions

Mastery of the Environment: Evaluation and Intervention

Following are five questions about key content covered in this chapter. These questions are not inclusive of the entirety of content on occupational therapy evaluation and intervention related to mastery of the environment that you must know for success on the COTA® exam. These questions are provided to help you "jump-start" the thought processes you will need to apply your studying of content to the answering of exam questions; hence they are not in the COTA® exam format. Exam items in the COTA® format that cover the depth and breadth of content you will need to know to pass the exam are provided on this text's online exams. The answers to the following questions are provided in Appendix 3.

1. An OTA works for an environmental accessibility consultation company owned and operated by an occupational therapist. The OTA and occupational therapist meet with a group representing a number of religious organizations who want to improve the accessibility of the entrances to their buildings. All entrances currently have stairs. What should the OTA and occupational therapist recommend to allow access for persons who use mobility aids (e.g., walkers and canes) and wheelchairs?

2. An OTA provides a weekly home safety group to members of a senior center under the supervision of an occupational therapist. What strategies should the OTA recommend the group members use inside and outside their homes to prevent falls?

3. A client is status post-posterolateral hip replacement surgery. The OTA has established service competency in post-hip replacement surgery intervention protocols. What recommendations should the OTA make for bed mobility?

4. A school-based OTA collaborates with the occupational therapist to determine alternative access modes to computers for students with disabilities. What adaptations can be used to compensate for a diversity of disabilities and maximize students' independence in the school environment? Explain their use.

5. An OTA begins employment at a new skilled nursing facility (SNF). To ensure compliance with OBRA, the occupational therapy department is actively involved in the facility's restraint reduction program. What should the OTA know to be able to effectively contribute to this program?

Professional Development After Initial Certification

RITA P. FLEMING-CASTALDY

Successfully passing the NBCOT® exam for the occupational therapy assistant enables you to meet an essential criterion for initial certification as an occupational therapy assistant. The regulatory boards of all 50 states in the United States also require a passing NBCOT® exam score in order to legally practice as an occupational therapy assistant in their respective jurisdictions. Passing the NBCOT®'s COTA® exam also enables you to use the designation of certified occupational therapy assistant (COTA®) if you choose to participate in the NBCOT® certification program. Thus, your success on this high-stakes exam can mark the beginning of a rewarding and fulfilling professional career. This concept of beginning is a critical one for you to embrace. While the pursuit of the goal to become an occupational therapy assistant may end with professional licensure, it is at this point that the lifelong process of being a professional has just begun.

> Being a member of a profession requires an ongoing commitment to the attainment and maintenance of excellence. Competent practitioners value this pursuit of excellence and are personally responsible for this professional development. . . . The benefits of a life-long commitment to one's professional development are numerous. Increased personal pride and satisfaction in one's work; improved health care services for consumers and their families; enhanced professional image among policy makers, reimbursors, administrators, and the multidisciplinary team; and the prevention of burnout and professional stagnation are all viable outcomes of the continual pursuit of professional excellence (Cottrell, 2000, p. 465).

Numerous professional development resources are available to facilitate growth from entry-level novice to master practitioner. Clinical supervision, peer support, networking, professional associations, mentorships, self-study, in-services, workshops, conferences, and postprofessional education can all be used to attain and maintain professional mastery and excellence. The advent of the technological era has increased the availability and decreased the cost of many professional development activities through the use of e-mail, social networking, chat rooms, and distance learning. I strongly urge you to take advantage of both high-tech (e.g., video conferencing) and low-tech (e.g., brainstorming with a colleague about a program initiative, seeking input from a mentor about a practice dilemma,) learning opportunities early and often in your professional life. I also highly recommend that you become an active member in the American Occupational Therapy Association (AOTA) and your state association (and/or local district in a large state). These actions will immediately provide you with a network of OT practitioners who are proactive forces for professional advancement and role models for excellence. Moreover, the AOTA website at www.aota.org has countless resources available to members to ensure they provide evidence-based and occupation-based practice. See Appendix 2 for state association contact information.

As Yerxa (1966) noted, an authentic professional is one who recognizes their responsibility to be a lifelong student. I wish you well at the beginning of this journey, the journey to learn and pursue an authentic occupational therapy career. I can think of no better way to practice or live.

References

American Occupational Therapy Association Continuing Competency Task Force. (1999). *Professional development for continuing competency.* Bethesda, MD: AOTA.

Cottrell, R. P. (2000). Professional development: The attainment, maintenance and promotion of excellence. In R. P. Cottrell (Ed.), *Proactive approaches in psychosocial occupational therapy.* (pp. 465–468). Thorofare, NJ: Slack.

Yerxa, E. (1966). Authentic occupational therapy. *American Journal of Occupational Therapy, 21,* 1–9.

APPENDIX 1

Selected Prefixes and Suffixes

A working knowledge of the components of medical terminology can often help decipher the meaning of an unknown word. This can assist in question analysis and the selection of the best answer. Remember, Latin is not a dying language; it is alive and well in the language of health care. This appendix does not list all medical terms that may be on the examination, but it does provide many foundational components of medical terminology. For a complete and exhaustive presentation of medical terminology, the reader is referred to this Appendix's reference.

a-	without	-asthenia	weakness
ab-	away from	ather/o	fat
abdomin/o	abdomen	-ation	process
acous/o	hearing	audi/o	hearing
acr/o	extremity or topmost	aur/i	ear
-acusis	hearing condition	bi-	two or both
ad-	to, toward, or near	-blast	germ or bud
aden/o	gland	blast/o	germ or bud
adip/o	fat	brachi/o	arm
adren/o	adrenal gland	brady-	slow
aer/o	air or gas	bronch/o	bronchus (airway)
-algia	pain	bucc/o	cheek
alveol/o	alveolus (air sac)	carcin/o	cancer
ambi-	both	cardi/o	heart
an-	without	celi/o	abdomen
angi/o	vessel	cephal/o	head
ankyl/o	crooked or stiff	cerebell/o	cerebellum (little brain)
ante-	before	cerebr/o	brain
anti-	against or opposed to	cervic/o	neck or cervix
-arche	beginning	chondr/o	cartilage
arteri/o	artery	chrom/o	color
arthr/o	joint	circum-	around
articul/o	joint	con-	together or with
-ase	enzyme	contra-	against or opposed to

445

cost/o	rib	hist/o	tissue
crani/o	skull	histi/o	tissue
cutane/o	skin	hydr/o	water
cyan/o	blue	hyper-	above or excessive
cyst/o	bladder or sac	hypo-	below or deficient
dacry/o	tear	-ia	condition of
dactyl/o	digit (finger or toe)	-iasis	formation of or presence of
de-	from, down, or not	-iatrics	treatment
derm/o	skin	-iatry	treatment
-desis	binding	-icle	small
dextr/o	right, or on the right side	immun/o	safe
dia-	across or through	infra-	below or under
diaphor/o	profuse sweat	inter-	between
dips/o	thirst	intra-	within
dis-	separate from or apart	-ism	condition of
-dynia	pain	iso-	equal, like
dys-	painful, difficult, or faulty	-itis	inflammation
ec-	out or away	-ium	structure or tissue
-ectasis	expansion or dilation	kyph/o	humped
ecto-	outside	lacrim/o	tear
-ectomy	excision (removal)	lapar/o	abdomen
-emesis	vomiting	lei/o	smooth
-emia	blood condition	lip/o	fat
en-	within	lob/o	lobe (a portion)
encephal/o	brain	lord/o	bent
endo-	within	lumb/o	loin (lower back)
epi-	upon	lymph/o	clear fluid
erythr/o	red	-lysis	breaking down or dissolution
esthesi/o	sensation	macr/o	large or long
eu-	good or normal	-malacia	softening
ex-	out or away	meat/o	opening
exo-	outside	-megaly	enlargement
extra-	outside	meso-	middle
fasci/o	fascia (a band)	meta-	beyond, after, or change
fibr/o	fiber	-meter	instrument for measuring
gangli/o	ganglion (knot)	-metry	process of measuring
gastr/o	stomach	micro-	small
-gen	origin or production	mono-	one
glomerul/o	glomerulus (little ball)	morph/o	form
gloss/o	tongue	multi-	many
glott/o	opening	muscul/o	muscle
gluc/o	sugar	myel/o	bone marrow or spinal cord
glyc/o	sugar	myring/o	eardrum
gnos/o	knowing	narc/o	stupor
-gram	record	nas/o	nose
-graph	instrument for recording	nat/i	birth
		necr/o	death
-graphy	process of recording	neo-	new
hem/o	blood	nephr/o	kidney
hemat/o	blood	neur/o	nerve
hemi-	half	ocul/o	eye
hepat/o	liver	-oid	resembling
hepatic/o	liver	-ole	small
herni/o	hernia	olig/o	few or deficient
hidr/o	sweat	-oma	tumor

ophthalm/o	eye	sinistr/o	left, or on the left side
opt/o	eye	somat/o	body
or/o	mouth	somn/o	sleep
orth/o	straight, normal, or correct	son/o	sound
-osis	condition or increase	-spasm	involuntary contraction
oste/o	bone	sphygm/o	pulse
ot/o	ear	spin/o	spine (thorn)
pachy-	thick	spir/o	breathing
pan-	all	spondyl/o	vertebra
para-	alongside of or abnormal	squam/o	scale
-paresis	slight paralysis	-stasis	stop or stand
path/o	disease	steat/o	fat
pector/o	chest	sten/o	narrow
ped/o	child or foot	stere/o	three dimensional or solid
pelv/i	hip bone	stern/o	sternum (breastbone)
pelv/o	hip bone	steth/o	chest
-penia	abnormal reduction	stomat/o	mouth
per-	through	-stomy	creation of an opening
peri-	around	sub-	below or under
phag/o	eat or swallow	super-	above or excessive
phas/o	speech	supra-	above or excessive
-phil	attraction for	sym-	together or with
-philia	attraction for	syn-	together or with
phleb/o	vein	tachy-	fast
phob/o	exaggerated fear or sensitivity	tax/o	order or coordination
phon/o	voice or speech	ten/o	tendon (to stretch)
phot/o	light	thorac/o	chest
phren/o	diaphragm (also mind)	thromb/o	clot
plas/o	formation	-tomy	incision
-plasty	surgical repair or reconstruction	ton/o	tone or tension
		top/o	place
-plegia	paralysis	tox/o	poison
pleur/o	pleura	trache/o	trachea (windpipe)
-pnea	breathing	trans-	across or through
pneum/o	air or lung	tri-	three
pod/o	foot	-tripsy	crushing
-poiesis	formation	troph/o	nourishment or development
poly-	many	-ula, -ule	small
post-	after or behind	ultra-	beyond or excessive
pre-	before	uni-	one
presby/o	old age	ur/o	urine
pro-	before	varic/o	swollen or twisted vein
-ptosis	falling or downward displacement	vas/o	vessel
pulmon/o	lung	vertebr/o	vertebra
quadr/i	four	vesic/o	bladder or sac
re-	again or back	xanth/o	yellow
reticul/o	a net	xer/o	dry
retro-	backward or behind	-y	condition or process of
rhabd/o	rod shaped or striated (skeletal)		
-rrhage	to burst forth		
-rrhexis	rupture		
sarc/o	flesh		
scler/o	hard or sclera		
scoli/o	twisted		
semi	half		

Reference

Willis, M. C. (1996). *Medical terminology: The language of healthcare*. Philadelphia: Williams & Wilkins.

APPENDIX 2

State Occupational Therapy Regulatory Board and State OT Association Contact Information

ALABAMA

Type of Regulation: Licensure

Regulatory Authority Contact:
Alabama State Board of Occupational Therapy
770 Washington Ave., Suite 420
Montgomery, AL 36130-4510
Phone: 334-353-4466
Email: ann.cosby@ot.alabama.gov
Website: http://www.ot.alabama.gov

State Association Contact:
Alabama Occupational Therapy Association (ALOTA)
1116 20th St. South #20
Birmingham, AL 35205
Email: Secretary@alota.org
Website: https://www.alota.org

ALASKA

Type of Regulation: Licensure

Regulatory Authority Contact:
Alaska State PT & OT Board
Division of Corporations, Business, & Professional Licensing
P.O. Box 110806
Juneau, AK 99811-0806
Phone: 907-465-2580
Email: physicalandoccupationaltherapy@alaska.gov
Website: https://www.commerce.alaska.gov/web/cbpl/ProfessionalLicensing/PhysicalTherapyOccupationalTherapy.aspx

State Association Contact:
Alaska Occupational Therapy Association (AKOTA)
3705 Arctic Blvd.
PMB 1616
Anchorage, AK 99503
Email: Secretary@akota.org
Website: http://www.akota.org

ARIZONA

Type of Regulation: Licensure

Regulatory Authority Contact:
Arizona Board of Occupational Therapy Examiners
1740 W Adams St., Suite 3407
Phoenix, AZ 85007
Phone: 602-589-8352
Email: karen.whiteford@otboard.az.gov
Website: http://www.occupationaltherapyboard.az.gov/

State Association Contact:
Arizona Occupational Therapy Association (ArizOTA)
P.O. Box 11803
Glendale, AZ 85318
Phone: 623-937-0920
Email: office@arizota.org
Website: http://www.arizota.org

ARKANSAS
Type of Regulation: Licensure

Regulatory Authority Contact:
Arkansas State Occupational Therapy Examining Committee
1401 West Capitol Ave., Suite 340
Little Rock, AR 72201-2936
Phone: 501-296-1802
Email: juli.carlson@armedicalboard.org
Website: https://www.armedicalboard.org/Professionals/OccupationalTherapistandAssistant.aspx

State Association Contact:
Arkansas Occupational Therapy Association (AROTA)
P.O. Box 10674
Conway, AR 72034
Email: office@arota.org
Website: http://www.arota.org

CALIFORNIA
Type of Regulation: Licensure - OT, Certification - OTA

Regulatory Authority Contact:
California Board of Occupational Therapy
2005 Evergreen St., Suite 2250
Sacramento, CA 95815
Phone: 916-263-2294
Email: cbot@dca.ca.gov
Website: http://www.bot.ca.gov/

State Association Contact:
Occupational Therapy Association of California (OTAC)
P.O. Box 276567
Sacramento, CA 95827-6567
Phone: 916-567-7000
Email: info@otaconline.org
Website: http://www.otaconline.org/

COLORADO
Type of Regulation: Licensure

Regulatory Authority Contact:
Office of Occupational Therapy
1560 Broadway, Suite 1350
Denver, CO 80202
Phone: 303-894-7800
Email: Dora_occupationaltherapists@state.co.us
Website: https://www.colorado.gov/pacific/dora/Occupational_Therapy

State Association Contact:
OT Association of Colorado
2851 S. Parker Rd., Suite 1210
Parker, CO 80014
Email: info@otacco.org
Website: http://www.otacco.org

CONNECTICUT
Type of Regulation: Licensure

Regulatory Authority Contact:
Department of Public Health Occupational Therapy Licensure
410 Capital Ave.
P.O. Box 340308
Hartford, CT 06134-0308
Phone: 860-509-7603
Website: http://www.ct.gov/dph/cwp/view.asp?a=3121&q=389442

State Association Contact:
Connecticut Occupational Therapy Association (ConnOTA)
370 Prospect Street
Wethersfield, CT 06109
Phone: 860-257-1371
Email: info@connOTA.org
Website: http://www.connota.org/

DELAWARE
Type of Regulation: Licensure

Regulatory Authority Contact:
Board of Occupational Therapy Practice
861 Silver Lake Blvd., Suite 203
Dover, DE 19904
Phone: 302-744-4500
Email: mary.melvin@state.de.us
Website: http://dpr.delaware.gov/boards/occupationaltherapy/

State Association Contact:
Delaware Occupational Therapy Association (DOTA)
2 Sands Court
Middletown, DE, 19709
Phone: 610-506-3186
Email: Swope.kelsey@gmail.com
Website: http://www.dotaonline.org/

DISTRICT OF COLUMBIA
Type of Regulation: Licensure

Regulatory Authority Contact:
District of Columbia Board of Occupational Therapy
899 North Capitol St., NE Suite 200
Washington, DC 20002
Phone: 202-442-5955
Email: mavis.azariah@dc.gov
Website: http://doh.dc.gov/service/occupational-therapy-licensing

District of Columbia Association Contact:
1447 Corcoran St.
Washington, DC 20009-3803
Email: info@mydcota.org
Website: https://dcota.wildapricot.org

FLORIDA
Type of Regulation: Licensure

Regulatory Authority Contact:
Florida Board of Occupational Therapy
4052 Bald Cypress Way, Bin C-05
Tallahassee, FL 32399-3255
Phone: 850-245-4373
Email: MedicalQualityAssurance@flhealth.gov
Website: https://floridasoccupationaltherapy.gov

State Association Contact:
Florida Occupational Therapy Association (FOTA)
1133 Bal Harbor Blvd., Suite 1139
PMB 200
Punta Gorda, FL 33950-6574
Phone: N/A
Email: ebloch@nova.edu
Website: http://www.flota.org

GEORGIA
Type of Regulation: Licensure

Regulatory Authority Contact:
Georgia State Board of Occupational Therapy
237 Coliseum Drive
Macon, GA 31217-3858
Phone: 478-207-2440
Email: aprice@sos.state.ga.us
Website: http://www.sos.state.ga.us/plb/ot

State Association Contact:
Georgia Occupational Therapy Association (GOTA)
P.O. Box 1495
Gainesville, GA 30503
Phone: 770-435-5910
Email: info@gaota.com
Website: http://www.gaota.com

HAWAII
Type of Regulation: Licensure

Regulatory Authority Contact:
Hawaii Professional & Vocational Licensing Division
DCCA/PVL-Occupational Therapist Program
P.O. Box 3469
Honolulu, HI 6801
Phone: 808-586-2693
Website: http://hawaii.gov/dccal/pvl/programs/occupational/

State Association Contact:
Occupational Therapy Association of Hawaii (OTAH)
1544 Nehoa St.
Honolulu, HI 96822-2008
Phone: 808-544-3336
Email: OTAssociationofHawaii@gmail.com
Website: https://otassociationofhawaii.org/

IDAHO
Type of Regulation: Licensure

Regulatory Authority Contact:
Idaho Bureau of Occupational Licenses
P.O. Box 83720
Boise, ID 83720-0063
Phone: 208-334-3233
Email: oct@ibol.idaho.gov
Website: https://ibol.idaho.gov/IBOL/BoardPage.aspx?Bureau=OCT

State Association Contact:
Idaho Occupational Therapy Association (IOTA)
P.O. Box 7364
Boise, ID 83707
Phone: 208-906-8406
Email: info@id-ota.com
Website: http://www.id-ota.org/

ILLINOIS
Type of Regulation: Licensure

Regulatory Authority Contact:
Illinois Occupational Therapy Board (ILOTA)
320 West Washington St.
Springfield, IL 62786
Phone: 888-473-4858
Website: http://www.idfpr.com/profs/OccTherapy.asp

State Association Contact:
Illinois Occupational Therapy Association (ILOTA)
P.O. Box 4520
Lisle, IL 60532
Phone: 708-452-7640
Email: office@ilota.org
Website: http://ilota.org

INDIANA
Type of Regulation: Certification

Regulatory Authority Contact:
Indiana Occupational Therapy Committee
402 West Washington St., Room W072
Indianapolis, IN 46204
Phone: 317-234-8800
Email: pla14@pla.in.gov
Website: https://www.in.gov/pla/ot.htm

State Association Contact:
Indiana Occupational Therapy Association (IOTA)
P.O. Box 47803
Indianapolis, IN 46247
Phone: 317-671-4284
Email: info@inota.com
Website: http://www.inota.com

IOWA
Type of Regulation: Licensure

Regulatory Authority Contact:
Iowa Board of PT and OT Examiners
Professional Licensure
Office Lucas State Office Bldg., 5th Floor
321 East 12th Street
Des Moines, IA 50319-0075
Phone: 515-281-0254
Email: venus.vendoures-walsh@idph.iowa.gov
Website: https://idph.iowa.gov/Licensure/Iowa-Board-of-Physical-and-Occupational-Therapy

State Association Contact:
Iowa Occupational Therapy Association (IOTA)
P.O. Box 57221
Des Moines, IA 50317
Phone: 515-720-7346
Email: iowaot@gmail.com
Website: http://www.iowaot.org

KANSAS
Type of Regulation: Registration

Regulatory Authority Contact:
Kansas State Board of Healing Arts
800 SW Jackson Lower Level, Suite A
Topeka, KS 66612
Phone: 785-296-7413
Email: ksbha_alliedhealth@ks.gov
Website: http://www.ksbha.org/

State Association Contact:
Kansas Occupational Therapy Association (KOTA)
825 S. Kansas Avenue, Suite 500
Topeka, KS 66612-1253
Phone: 785-232-8044
Toll Free: 877-904-0529
Email: centraloffice@kotaonline.org
Website: http://www.kotaonline.org/

KENTUCKY
Type of Regulation: Licensure

Regulatory Authority Contact:
Kentucky Board of Licensure for Occupational Therapy
P.O. Box 1360
Frankfort, KY 40601
Phone: 502-564-3296 ext 226
Email: OT@ky.gov
Website: http://bot.ky.gov/Pages/default.aspx

State Association Contact:
Kentucky Occupational Therapy Association (KOTA)
P.O. Box 5531
Louisville, KY 40255
Phone: 502-873-5333
Email: kotaweb@kotaweb.org
Website: http://www.kotaweb.org/

LOUISIANA
Type of Regulation: Licensure

Regulatory Authority Contact:
Louisiana State Board of Medical Examiners
State Board of Medical Examiners
630 Camp Street
New Orleans, LA 70130
Phone: 504-568-6823
Email: ebarberot@lsbme.la.gov
Website: http://www.lsbme.louisiana.gov/

State Association Contact:
Louisiana Occupational Therapy Association (LOTA)
P.O. Box 14806
Baton Rouge, LA 70898
Phone: 225-291-2806
Email: lalwood@aol.com
Website: http://www.lota.org/

MAINE
Type of Regulation: Licensure

Regulatory Authority Contact:
Maine Board of Occupational Therapy Practice
Department of Professional & Financial Regulation
35 State House Station
Augusta, ME 04333-0035
Phone: 207-624-8634
Email: occ.board@maine.gov
Website: http://www.state.me.us/pfr/olr/categories/cat28.htm

State Association Contact:
Maine Occupational Therapy Association (MEOTA)
Phone: 207-453-5172
Email: amie.marzan@gmail.com
Website: https://maineot.org

MARYLAND
Type of Regulation: Licensure

Regulatory Authority Contact:
Maryland Board of Occupational Therapy Practice
55 Wade Ave. 4th Floor
Baltimore, MD 21201
Phone: 410-402-8556
Email: donna.seidel@maryland.gov
Website: http://dhmh.maryland.gov/botp/

State Association Contact:
Maryland Occupational Therapy Association
P.O. Box 131
Stevenson, MD 21153-9998
Phone: N/A
Email: all4mota@gmail.com
Website: http://www.mota.memberlodge.org/

MASSACHUSETTS
Type of Regulation: Licensure

Regulatory Authority Contact:
Massachusetts Board of Registration Allied Health Professions
Division of Professional Licensure
1000 Washington Street, Suite 710
Boston, MA 02118-6100
Phone: 617-727-0054
Email: Sonia.jordan@state.ma.us
Website: https://www.mass.gov/orgs/board-of-allied-health-professionals

State Association Contact:
Massachusetts Occupational Therapy Association (MAOTA)
57 Madison Road
Waltham, MA 02453-6718
Phone: 781-647-5556
Email: info@maot.org
Website: http://www.maot.org/

MICHIGAN
Type of Regulation: Licensure

Regulatory Authority Contact:
Michigan Board of Occupational Therapy
Ottawa Building
611 W. Ottawa
P.O. Box 30004
Lansing, MI 48909
Phone: 517-335-0918
Email: lclark@michigan.gov
Website: https://www.michigan.gov/lara/0,4601,7-154-89334_72600_72603_27529_27545---,00.html

State Association Contact:
Michigan Occupational Therapy Association (MiOTA)
124 W. Allegan, Suite 1900
Lansing, MI 48933
Phone: 517-267-3918
Email: office@miota.org
Website: https://www.miota.org

MINNESOTA
Type of Regulation: Licensure

Regulatory Authority Contact:
Minnesota Board of Occupational Therapy Practice
2829 University Ave., SE, Suite 415
St. Paul, MN 55414
Phone: 612-548-2179
Email: occupational.therapy@state.mn.us
Website: https://mn.gov/boards/occupational-therapy/

State Association Contact:
Minnesota Occupational Therapy Association (MOTA)
855 Village Center Drive, #348
St. Paul, MN 55127
Phone: 612-460-8625
Email: info@motafunctionfirst.org
Website: http://www.motafunctionfirst.org/

MISSISSIPPI
Type of Regulation: Licensure

Regulatory Authority Contact:
MSDH Professional Licensure Division
P.O. Box 1700
Jackson, MS 39215-1700
Phone: 601-364-7360
Email: Yolanda.morrow@msdh.state.ms.us
Website: https://msdh.ms.gov/msdhsite/_static/30,0,82.html

State Association Contact:
Mississippi Occupational Therapy Association (MSOTA)
P.O. Box 2188
Brandon, MS 39043
Phone: 601-853-9564
Email: MSOTA@comcast.net
Website: http://www.mississippiota.org

MISSOURI
Type of Regulation: Licensure

Regulatory Authority Contact:
Missouri State Board of Occupational Therapy
3605 Missouri Blvd.
P.O. Box 1335
Jefferson City, MO 65102-1335
Phone: 573-751-0877
Email: vanessa.beauchamp.pr.mo.gov
Website: https://pr.mo.gov/octherapy.asp

State Association Contact:
Missouri Occupational Therapy Association (MOTA)
PMB 169
Columbia, MO 65201
Email: drjjo2016@gmail.com
Website: https://www.motamo.net

MONTANA
Type of Regulation: Licensure

Regulatory Authority Contact:
Montana Board of Occupational Therapy Practice
Department of Labor and Industry
P.O. Box 200513
301 South Park, 4th Floor
Helena, MT 59620
Phone: 406-841-2385
Email: dlibsdotp@mt.gov
Website: http://boards.bsd.dli.mt.gov/otp

State Association Contact:
  Montana Occupational Therapy Association (MOTA)
  17 Bedford Rd.
  Roundup, MT 59019
  Phone: 406-208-7338
  Email: leos_r_us@msn.com
  Website: http://boards.bsd.dli.mt.gov/otp

NEBRASKA
Type of Regulation: Licensure

Regulatory Authority Contact:
  Nebraska Board of Occupational Therapy Practice
  Department of Health and Human Services Licensure Unit
  P.O. Box 94986
  Lincoln, NE 68509-4986
  Phone: (402) 471-2299
  Email: Claire.covertbybee@nebraska.gov
  Website: http://dhhs.ne.gov/publichealth/Pages/crlOccTherHome.aspx

State Association Contact:
  Nebraska Occupational Therapy Association (NOTA)
  P.O. Box 540881
  Omaha, NE 68154
  Email: notaassistant@gmail.com
  Website: http://www.notaonline.org/

NEVADA
Type of Regulation: Licensure

Regulatory Authority Contact:
  Nevada Board of Occupational therapy
  P.O. Box 34779
  Reno, NV 89533
  Phone: 603-271-8389
  Email: traci.e.weber@nh.gov
  Website: https://www.nvot.info/

State Association Contact:
  Nevada Occupational Therapy Association (NOTA)
  P.O. Box 94433
  Las Vegas, NV 89193-4433
  Email: NevadaOTA@gmail.com
  Website: http://www.nota.wildapricot.org

NEW HAMPSHIRE
Type of Regulation: Licensure

Regulatory Authority Contact:
  Occupational Therapy Governing Board
  2 Industrial Park Drive
  Concord, NH 03301
  Phone: 603-271-8389
  Email: traci.e.weber@nh.gov
  Website: https://www.oplc.nh.gov/allied-health/occupational-therapy.htm

State Association Contact:
  New Hampshire Occupational Therapy Association (NHOTA)
  1 Simons Lane, Suite 2
  Newmarket, NH 03857
  Phone: 603-868-7475
  Email: nhota@lexian.com
  Website: http://www.nhota.org/

NEW JERSEY
Type of Regulation: Licensure

Regulatory Authority Contact:
  NJ Occupational Therapy Advisory Council
  P.O. Box 45037
  Newark, NJ 07101
  Phone: 973-504-6570
  Email: askconsumeraffairs@dca.lps.state.nj.us
  Website: https://www.njconsumeraffairs.gov/ot

State Association Contact:
  New Jersey Occupational Therapy Association (NJOTA)
  P.O. Box 1415
  Toms River, NJ 08754
  Phone: 732-968-5038
  Email: management@njota.org
  Website: http://www.njota.org/

NEW MEXICO
Type of Regulation: Licensure

Regulatory Authority Contact:
  NM Board of Examiners for Occupational Therapy
  P.O. Box 25101
  Santa Fe, NM 87505
  Phone: 505-476-4940
  Email: occupationaltherapy@state.nm.us
  Website: http://www.rld.state.nm.us/boards/Occupational_Therapy.aspx

State Association Contact:
  New Mexico Occupational Therapy Association (NMOTA)
  P.O. Box 3036
  Albuquerque, NM 87190-3036
  Phone: N/A
  Email: nmota@nmota.org
  Website: http://www.nmota.org/

NEW YORK
Type of Regulation: Licensure—OT, Registration—OTA

Regulatory Authority Contact:
  New York State Board for Occupational Therapy
  89 Washington Avenue, 2nd floor
  Albany, NY 12234
  Phone: 518-474-3817 ext. 100
  Email: otbd@nysed.gov
  Website: http://www.op.nysed.gov/prof/ot

State Association Contact:
New York Occupational Therapy Association (NYSOTA)
P.O. Box 533
Chester, NY 10918
Phone: 518-301-9187
Email: nysota@gmail.com
Website: http://www.nysota.org/

NORTH CAROLINA
Type of Regulation: Licensure

Regulatory Authority Contact:
North Carolina Board of Occupational Therapy
P.O. Box 2280
Raleigh, NC 27602
Phone: 919-832-1380
Email: administrator@ncbot.org
Website: http://www.ncbot.org/

State Association Contact:
North Carolina Occupational Therapy Association (NCOTA)
P.O. Box 20432
Raleigh, NC 27619
Phone: 919-785-9700
Email: office@ncota.org
Website: http://www.ncota.org

NORTH DAKOTA
Type of Regulation: Licensure

Regulatory Authority Contact:
North Dakota State Board of OT Practice
P.O. Box 4005
Bismarck, ND 58502-4005
Phone: 701-250-0847
Email: ndotboard@aptnd.com
Website: http://www.ndotboard.com

State Association Contact:
North Dakota Occupational Therapy Association (NDOTA)
P.O. Box 14118
Grand Forks, ND 58208-4118
Phone: 701-777-1740
Email: ndotacommunications@gmail.com
Website: http://www.ndota.com

OHIO
Type of Regulation: Licensure

Regulatory Authority Contact:
Ohio Occupational Therapy, Physical Therapy and Athletic Trainers Board
77 South High Street, 16th Floor
Columbus, OH 43215-6108
Phone: 614-466-3774
Email: board@otptat.ohio.gov
Website: https://www.otptat.ohio.gov

State Association Contact:
Ohio Occupational Therapy Association (OOTA)
P.O. Box 693
Canal Winchester, OH 43110-0693
Phone: 888-231-7319
Email: webmaster@oota.org
Website: https://www.oota.org/

OKLAHOMA
Type of Regulation: Licensure

Regulatory Authority Contact:
Oklahoma State Board of Medical Licensure and Supervision
101 NE 151st St.
Oklahoma City, OK 73105-1821
Phone: 405-962-1422
Email: bsmith@okmedicalboard.org
Website: http://www.okmedicalboard.org/occupational_therapists

State Association Contact:
Oklahoma Occupational Therapy Association (OKOTA)
P.O. Box 2602
Oklahoma City, OK 73101-2602
Phone: 405-205-3942
Email: OKOTAadmassistant@gmail.com
Website: https://www.okota.org/

OREGON
Type of Regulation: Licensure

Regulatory Authority Contact:
Oregon Occupational Therapy Licensing Board
800 NE Oregon Street, Suite 407
Portland, OR 97232
Phone: 971-673-0198
Email: otlb.info@state.or.us
Website: https://www.otlb.state.or.us

State Association Contact:
Occupational Therapy Association of Oregon (OTAO)
147 SE 102nd Ave.
Portland, OR 97216
Phone: 503-253-2981
Email: info@otao.com
Website: https://www.otao.com

PENNSYLVANIA
Type of Regulation: Licensure

Regulatory Authority Contact:
Pennsylvania State Board of Occupational Therapy Education and Licensure
2601 North Third St., P.O. Box 2649
Harrisburg, PA 17105-2649
Phone: 717-783-1389
Email: ST-OCCUPATIONAL@pa.gov
Website: https://www.dos.pa.gov/Professional Licensing/BoardsCommissions/Occupational Therapy/Pages/default.aspx#.VorHzLYrKJA

State Association Contact:
Pennsylvania Occupational Therapy Association (POTA)
600 West Germantown Pike, Suite 400
Plymouth Meeting, PA 19462
Phone: 1-800-UR1-POTA
Email: help@pota.org
Website: http://www.pota.org/

RHODE ISLAND
Type of Regulation: Licensure

Regulatory Authority Contact:
Rhode Island Board of Occupational Therapy Practice Health Professions Regulation
Cannon Building 3 Capitol Hill, Room 104
Providence, RI 02908
Phone: 401-222-2828
Email: alana.rodriguez@health.ri.gov
Website: http://www.health.ri.gov/licenses/detail.php?id=234

State Association Contact:
Rhode Island Occupational Therapy Association (RIOTA)
P.O. Box 8585
Warwick, RI 02888-0599
Phone: 401-484-5207
Email: riota@riota.org
Website: http://www.riota.org/

SOUTH CAROLINA
Type of Regulation: Licensure

Regulatory Authority Contact:
South Carolina Board of Occupational Therapy
110 Centerview Drive, Suite 202
P.O. Box 11329
Columbia, SC 29210
Phone: 803-896-4300
Email: mack.williams@llr.sc.gov
Website: https://www.llr.state.sc.us/POL/OccupationalTherapy/

State Association Contact:
South Carolina Occupational Therapy Association (SCOTA)
138 Ingleoak Lane
Greer, SC 29650
Phone: 605-571-6377
Email: adminscota@gmail.com
Website: http://www.scota.net/

SOUTH DAKOTA
Type of Regulation: Licensure

Regulatory Authority Contact:
South Dakota Occupational Therapy Committee
101 N. Main Ave, Suite 301
Sioux Falls, SD 57104
Phone: 605-367-7781
Email: SDBMOE@state.sd.us
Website: http://www.sdbmoe.gov/index.php?option=com_content&view=article&id=5&Itemid=10

State Association Contact:
South Dakota Occupational Therapy Association (SDOTA)
P.O. Box 1771
Sioux Falls, SD 57101
Email: SDOTA@msn.com
Website: http://www.sdota.org

TENNESSEE
Type of Regulation: Licensure

Regulatory Authority Contact:
Tennessee Board of Occupational Therapy & Physical Therapy Examiners
665 Mainstream Drive, 2nd Floor
Nashville, TN 37243
Phone: 615-741-3807
Email: crystal.bloom@tn.gov
Website: https://www.tn.gov/health/health-program-areas/health-professional-boards/ot-board.html

State Association Contact:
Tennessee Occupational Therapy Association (TOTA)
P.O. Box 90127
Nashville, TN 37209
Phone: 888-400-3036
Email: admin@tnota.org
Website: http://www.tnota.org

TEXAS
Type of Regulation: Licensure

Regulatory Authority Contact:
Texas Executive Council of PT & OT Examiners
333 Guadalupe Street #2-510
Austin, TX 78701-3942
Phone: 512-305-6900
Email: info@ptot.texas.gov
Website: http://www.ptot.texas.gov/occupational-therapy

State Association Contact:
Texas Occupational Therapy Association (TOTA)
1106 Clayton Lane, Suite 516 W
Austin, TX 78723
Phone: 512-454-8682
Email: heather@tota.org
Website: http://www.tota.org

UTAH
Type of Regulation: Licensure

Regulatory Authority Contact:
Utah Occupational Therapy Board
1600 East 300 South St.
Salt Lake City, UT 84111
Phone: 801-530-6628
Email: jbusjahn@utah.gov
Website: https://www.dopl.utah.gov/ot/index.html

State Association Contact:
Utah Occupational Therapy Association (UOTA)
P.O. Box 58412
Salt Lake City, Utah 84158-0412
Phone: 801-585-3133
Email: president@utahassociation.org
Website: http://www.utahotassociation.org/

VERMONT
Type of Regulation: Licensure

Regulatory Authority Contact:
Vermont Occupational Therapy Advisors
89 Main Street, 3rd Floor
Montpelier, VT 05620-3402
Phone: 802-828-3228
Email: Judith.roy@sec.state.vt.us
Website: https://www.sec.state.vt.us/professional-regulation/list-of-professions/occupational-therapy.aspx

State Association Contact:
Vermont Occupational Therapy Association (VOTA)
P.O. Box 925
Richmond, VT 05477
Phone: 802-264-9671
Email: votasecretary@gmail.com
Website: https://www.sec.state.vt.us/professional-regulation/list-of-professions/occupational-therapy.aspx

VIRGINIA
Type of Regulation: Licensure

Regulatory Authority Contact:
Virginia Advisory Board on Occupational Therapy
9960 Maryland Drive, Suite 300
Henrico, VA 23233-1463
Phone: 804-367-4613
Email: Sharon.clanton@dhp.virginia.gov
Website: http://www.dhp.virginia.gov/Medicine/advisory/ot/

State Association Contact:
Virginia Occupational Therapy Association (VOTA)
6200 Lakeside Ave.
Richmond, VA 23228
Email: office@vaota.org
Website: http://www.vaota.org/

WASHINGTON
Type of Regulation: Licensure

Regulatory Authority Contact:
Washington Occupational Therapy Practice Board
P.O. Box 47852
Olympia, WA 98504
Phone: 360-236-4883
Email: Kathy.weed@doh.wa.gov
Website: https://www.doh.wa.gov/Licenses PermitsandCertificates/ProfessionsNew ReneworUpdate/OccupationalTherapist.aspx

State Association Contact:
Washington Occupational Therapy Association (WOTA)
1402 Auburn Way N, Suite 236
Auburn, WA 98002
Phone: 253-234-5809
Email: info@wota.org
Website: http://www.wota.org/

WEST VIRGINIA
Type of Regulation: Licensure

Regulatory Authority Contact:
West Virginia Board of Occupational Therapy
1063 Maple Drive, Suite 4B
Morgantown, WV 26505
Phone: 304-285-3150
Email: help@wvbot.org
Website: http://www.wvbot.org/

State Association Contact:
West Virginia Occupational Therapy Association (WVOTA)
P.O. Box 9139
Morgantown, WV 26506-9139
Phone: 681-443-7295
Website: http://www.wvota.org/

WISCONSIN
Type of Regulation: Licensure

Regulatory Authority Contact:
Bureau of Health Professions Department of Regulation and Licensing
OT Affiliated Credentialing Board
4822 Madison Yards Way
Madison, WI 53705
Phone: 608-266-2112
Email: Thomas.ryan@wisconsin.gov
Website: https://dsps.wi.gov/Pages/Professions/OccupationalTherapist/Default.aspx

State Association Contact:
Wisconsin Occupational Therapy Association (WOTA)
16 N. Carroll St., Suite 600
Madison, WI 53703
Phone: 608-819-2327
Email: wota@wota.net
Website: http://www.wota.net/

WYOMING
Type of Regulation: Licensure

Regulatory Authority Contact:
Wyoming Board of Occupational Therapy
2001 Capitol Avenue, #105
Cheyenne, WY 82002
Phone: 307-777-7764
Email: Maxie.hernandez@wyo.gov
Website: https://occupationaltherapy.wyo.gov/contact-us

State Association Contact:
Wyoming Occupational Therapy Association (WYOTA)
Casper, WY 86204
Phone: 307-251-0884
Email: wyotainfo@gmail.com
Website: http://www.wyota.org/

APPENDIX 3

Review Questions and Answers

- The Process of Occupational Therapy, 459
- Professional Standards and Responsibilities, 462
- Human Development Across the Lifespan: Considerations for Occupational Therapy Practice, 465
- Musculoskeletal System Disorders, 467
- Neurological System Disorders, 469
- Cardiovascular and Pulmonary System Disorders, 470
- Gastrointestinal, Renal-Genitourinary, Endocrine, Immunological, and Integumentary Systems Disorders, 472
- Psychiatric and Cognitive Disorders, 474
- Biomechanical Approaches: Evaluation and Intervention, 477
- Neurological and Cognitive-Perceptual Approaches: Evaluation and Intervention, 479
- Psychosocial Approaches: Evaluation and Intervention, 481
- Evaluation and Intervention for Performance in Areas of Occupation, 485
- Mastery of the Environment: Evaluation and Intervention, 487

Chapter 3 Review Questions

The Process of Occupational Therapy

1. An OTA is collaborating with an occupational therapist in preparation for the evaluation of a client. What contextual considerations should the OTA and supervising occupational therapist take into account when determining the assessments that will be appropriate to use with the client?

   > The OTA and therapist should consider the environmental contexts of the practice setting in which the assessment will be conducted (e.g., the length of stay, the setting's primary focus, legislative guidelines and restrictions, and the facility's resources of space, equipment, and supplies). In addition, the physical and sociocultural contexts of the client's current and expected environment (e.g., roles, values, norms, supports) should be taken into account by the OTA and therapist. The temporal context of the client and their disability (e.g., the client's chronological and developmental age, anticipated duration of disability, and stage of illness) should also be considered when determining which assessment tools are best to use during an evaluation.

2. An OTA provides services to preschool children with developmental, intellectual, and physical disabilities. When should the OTA use standard precautions? What policies and procedures should the OTA use to guide the use of standard precautions in this preschool practice setting?

   > Standard precautions are infection prevention practices that are applied at *all* times when working with *all* persons in *all* practice settings. They include standards for hand hygiene and the use of gloves, gown, mask, eye protection, or face shield (depending on the anticipated exposure). There are also standards for handling and caring for equipment or items in a practice setting to prevent transmission of infectious agents. The application of standard precautions during service delivery is determined by the nature of the interactions with clients and the extent of anticipated blood, body fluid, or pathogen exposure. In a pediatric preschool setting, the OTA should ensure that all staff members consistently adhere to hand hygiene and respiratory hygiene/cough etiquette standards. Signs should be posted in the facility with instructions to persons with symptoms of a respiratory infection to cover their mouths/noses when coughing or sneezing, use and dispose of tissues, and perform hand hygiene after hands have been in contact with respiratory secretions. The facility should provide tissues and no-touch receptacles (e.g., foot pedal-operated lid or open, plastic-lined waste baskets) for disposal of tissues. Resources and instructions for performing hand hygiene should be conveniently located throughout the facility. Policies and procedures for routine and targeted cleaning and disinfecting of the facility's environmental surfaces and toys used by the children must be established. Toys selected for use with the children during evaluation and intervention must be ones that can be easily cleaned and disinfected (e.g., hard plastic building blocks, not furry stuffed animals). Toys that are mouthed must be immediately cleaned, disinfected, and then rinsed with water after use. After cleaning and disinfection, toys should be stored in a designated labeled container that identifies them as clean and ready for use. Large stationary toys (e.g., climbing equipment) must be cleaned and disinfected at least weekly and whenever visibly soiled.

3. An OTA provides services in a community-based setting that offers individual and group interventions. What factors should the OTA discuss with the supervising occupational therapist when determining if it is best to use an individual intervention or a group intervention with each client?

> The level of the client's cognitive, physical, and interpersonal skills should be considered to determine if an individual or a group intervention is best to use with a client. Clients with lower capabilities and a greater need for attention and structure due to body structure and functional impairments will benefit from an individualized approach. The client's need for privacy and/or greater control over the environment also support the use of an individual intervention. Individualized interventions are indicated if the activity demands, performance skills, and performance patterns of an intervention are complex. Most important, if the client exhibits inappropriate and/or dangerous behaviors, group interventions are not appropriate. Group interventions are indicated when the intervention focus is on the development of interpersonal skills and the ability to engage socially with others. Group interventions provide the opportunity to receive feedback from people experiencing similar conditions, learn from them, place one's own condition into perspective, and become motivated by peer role models. Groups are also indicated when an intervention goal is to develop behaviors that are needed for successful performance in shared occupations (e.g., work, study, and leisure groups).

4. An OTA working in a long-term care facility is asked by the supervising occupational therapist to colead a discharge planning group with a social worker. What are the advantages to this coleadership? What issues may arise to impede effective coleadership that the OTA should discuss with the supervising occupational therapist and the social worker prior to the initiation of this group?

> Coleadership enables each leader to share their professional knowledge and skills and use their unique professional expertise to assume different leadership roles and tasks. Both leaders can provide and obtain mutual support to each other, share their observations, and model effective behaviors. Issues that may arise and must be dealt with to ensure effective coleadership include the splitting by group member(s) of one leader against the other, excessive competition among coleaders, and unequal responsibilities resulting in an unbalanced work load among coleaders.

5. An OTA provides services to a group of parents of infants and toddlers who each recently incurred a disability. The OTA collaborates with the supervising occupational therapist to plan a thematic and a topical group to address goals related to the clients' parental role. What would be appropriate foci and relevant activities for these groups?

> The purpose of a thematic group is to assist members in acquiring the knowledge, skills, and/or attitudes needed to perform a specific activity. Because the clients in this group are parents who each recently incurred a disability, this group should focus on the improvement of members' ability to engage in desired parenting activities outside of group by teaching and practicing these activities within group (e.g., how to perform child care activities using adaptive equipment and compensatory strategies; how to transfer to and from a wheelchair to the floor to enable play with a toddler). In a thematic group, simulated, clearly defined, structured activities are used for group members to practice and learn needed skills within the group (e.g., using a doll to practice diapering an infant from a wheelchair or by using a one-handed technique). The purpose of a topical group is to discuss specific activities that members are engaged in outside of group to enable them

to engage in the activities in a more effective, need-satisfying manner. Because the clients are already parents, this group would be considered a concurrent topical group. In this group, discussion would include members' current or anticipated fears and problems about parenting with a disability, potential solutions for dealing with these concerns, and coping mechanisms for increasing personal self-efficacy as a parent. The OTA would facilitate a focused group discussion on parenting activities, help members problem-solve, give feedback and support, and reinforce skill acquisition.

Chapter 4 Review Questions

Professional Standards and Responsibilities

1. You are working in a skilled nursing facility. Your supervising occupational therapist is on vacation. An administrator asks you to actively treat a new resident who is very frail with multiple medical complications. Upon admission, the occupational therapist had evaluated the resident and determined that the resident would not be able to tolerate occupational therapy services. During the evaluation, the resident had stated that chronic pain made all activities very difficult. Pain relief and rest were the only things the resident identified as personally desired. How should you respond to the administrator's request? Which principles of the AOTA Code of Ethics should you use to guide your response? Explain how these principles relate to this situation.

   You must refuse to treat the person because doing so would violate the ethical principles of beneficence, nonmaleficence, autonomy, and justice. The ethical principle of beneficence requires you to demonstrate your concern for the resident's well-being and safety. The resident has reported chronic pain that compromises health and well-being; thus, pain relief must be a priority. The ethical principle of nonmaleficence requires you to avoid doing anything that can harm or injure a person. You must use your professional judgment and avoid compromising the resident's rights or health. The administrator's request does not consider the person's current status and can cause harm. This request also violates the ethical principle of autonomy, which requires you to respect the right of the individual to self-determination and the person's right to refuse OT services. The resident has stated that pain relief and rest were the only things personally desired. According to the ethical principle of justice, you must know and apply our profession's Code of Ethics to the work setting and share them with employers when indicated to make sure that they are aware of your ethical obligations. Providing occupational therapy services to a person who is frail and too ill to participate in therapy would violate all of the above ethical principles; therefore, the administrator must be informed that you will not do this. Moreover, this arbitrary administrative directive to treat the resident in the absence of the occupational therapist must be confronted. You must remind the administrator that OT intervention decisions must be made by the supervising occupational therapist. Implementing treatment without the required supervision of the occupational therapist would violate the ethical principle of justice, which states that OT practitioners must ensure that all assigned and assumed duties match the practitioner's credentials, qualifications, experience, and scope of practice. Treating the person without OT supervision would clearly violate this ethical principle and likely also violate state laws, licensure requirements, and other regulatory mandates requirements for OTAs.

2. A large regional health care system provides occupational therapy services across the continuum of care. Settings in which occupational therapy services are provided include an acute care hospital, an outpatient clinic, a subacute rehabilitation unit, a skilled nursing facility (SNF), a palliative care unit, and a home health agency. All settings employ occupational therapists and occupational therapy assistants (OTAs). What factors should be considered when determining the level of supervision that the OTA should receive from the occupational therapist? What is a key determinant for deciding if an OTA can ethically be given more responsibility?

   The degree, amount, and pattern of supervision required in each setting will depend on the OTA's knowledge and skills (e.g., the OTA has completed advanced training in splinting); the complexities of client needs (e.g., the presence of comorbidities); and caseload characteristics and demands (e.g., focused primarily on one diagnostic category and a core intervention approach such as training clients in hip precautions pre- and post-hip replacement surgery). An OTA providing services to an acutely ill person with rapidly changing status on the inpatient unit will require a closer occupational therapist/OTA partnership than an OTA providing services to a more stable client in a long-term care setting. State laws, licensure requirements, and other regulatory mandates must also be considered when determining the level of OTA supervision required. Ethically, the OT supervisor must ensure that the type, amount, and pattern of supervision match the supervisee's level of role performance. An OTA can be given more responsibility by the occupational therapist after the OTA establishes service competency. Service competency is the ability to use a specified intervention in a safe, effective, and reliable manner. Before assigning greater responsibilities to the OTA, the occupational therapist must determine that the OTA can perform a procedure in a manner that obtains the same results as the therapist would have obtained. OTAs who establish service competency do not become independent; they continue to work with supervision from the occupational therapist.

3. An OTA is collaborating with an occupational therapist to start a private practice in OT. What procedures should the OTA and therapist implement to ensure full compliance with the Health Insurance and Portability Accountability Act (HIPAA)?

The OTA and therapist need to set standards and establish safeguards to ensure the privacy and security of health care records. Procedures must be established for informing all clients of the practice's privacy policies and obtaining clients' written acknowledgement that they received this information. Guidelines for staff members to follow if there are difficulties obtaining signed assent are needed. All staff must be advised that prior to discussing a client's status with another person, they must obtain the person's permission. Guidelines for staff members to follow if there are questions about the client's ability to give permission are needed (e.g., a client is at risk of harming self due to lack of judgment; consultation with a specialist is essential to ensure quality of care). Staff must be advised that all information used or disclosed about a person's status must be limited to the minimum needed for the immediate purpose. The OTA and therapist must set procedures to ensure patient confidentiality in oral, written, and electronic forms of communication (e.g., all conversations with clients should be conducted in private areas and in low tones; sign-in sheets should only ask for clients' names; computer monitors should have privacy screens; e-mails should be protected by encrypted passwords).

4. You are beginning a new job as an OTA for a Medicare-certified home health agency. Most of your clients will be dependent or have limited independence in basic activities of daily living. What are key Medicare guidelines for home-based occupational therapy you must consider when working with these individuals and their caregivers?

Home-based OT services for medical, physical, cognitive, and psychiatric conditions are covered if the individual is under a physician's care and needed intermittent skilled nursing care, physical therapy (PT), or speech therapy (ST) before OT began. OT services can continue after the person's need for skilled nursing, PT, or ST has ended. Services must be provided under a plan of care that was established by a physician. Care plans must be reviewed regularly by the physician. The person must be considered homebound to receive home care services. Medicare has specific criteria for determining if a person is homebound. To be considered homebound, the person is "confined" to the home and not able to easily leave the home due to a need to use an ambulatory device, the assistance of others, or special transportation. If the person leaves the home, it requires considerable effort that is taxing to the person. The person may leave their home for medical appointments (e.g., kidney dialysis) and nonmedical short-term and infrequent appointments/events (e.g., attendance at religious services). If the person receives adult day care services, they can still receive OT services in the home. Rental or purchase expenses for durable medical equipment (DME) are covered if prescribed by a physician. The DME must be considered necessary and reasonable to treat an illness or injury or to improve functioning. It must be used in the person's home and be able to withstand repeated use. To be reimbursable, the DME must be primarily and customarily used for a medical purpose (e.g., a wheelchair or walker). DME will not be reimbursed if it is useful to a person in the absence of injury or illness (e.g., self-help items such as bathtub grab bars and raised toilet seats).

5. An OTA is employed by a school system to provide direct services to students with disabilities under the supervision of an occupational therapist. The OTA's caseload includes middle and high school students. Which federal legislative mandates can help guide the OTA's interventions with these students? Describe major regulations and their relationship to the provision of school-based OT services.

The Reauthorization and Amendment of Individuals with Disabilities Education Act (IDEA) states that the education the student receives should prepare them for independent living and employment in adult life. It also clarifies that the individual education plan (IEP) can include consideration of assistive technology and behavioral interventions, strategies, and supports (an area in which OT can offer a great deal).

Transition planning for post-secondary school life must begin at the age of 14 (or younger if indicated due to the student's complex needs) to help the student plan a course of study that will lead to postschool goals. Transition services must begin at the age of 16 (or younger if indicated due to the student's complex needs) to provide the student with a coordinated set of services to attain post-secondary school goals. These services can include community participation experience, specific instruction, and/or ADL and vocational assessment and intervention—all highly relevant to OT's domain of concern. According to the IDEA, the student must be invited to attend IEP meetings that discuss their transition planning and services to allow for self-advocacy and self-determination. The Individuals with Disabilities Education Improvement Act (IDEA 2004) further emphasized that the purpose of the IDEA is to prepare children with disabilities for further education, employment, and independent living after graduation from high school. These goals are highly supportive of OT services that prepare students for post-secondary school life. IDEA 2004 requires that evaluations include relevant functional and developmental information, not just academic achievement data. It expands the IEP's annual goals to include academic and functional goals. It specifies that accommodations must be provided as needed to measure the functional performance and academic achievement of all students with disabilities. IDEA 2004 also requires that services continue to be provided to students with a disability who violate the school's code of conduct and are disciplined (e.g., suspended). These services must help the student progress toward achieving their IEP goals and include appropriate functional behavioral assessments and interventions and service modifications as needed to address the conduct violation(s). The No Child Left Behind Act (NCLB) requires schools to provide accommodations, if needed by students, for mandated tests. OT practitioners can recommend testing alternatives and/or classroom accommodations to help students with disabilities succeed on mandated middle and high school tests.

Chapter 5 Review Questions

Human Development Across the Lifespan: Considerations for Occupational Therapy Practice

1. A typically developing child with no developmental delays independently creates a building made of blocks from a mental image. Identify the child's age range and describe the skills the child would use during this play activity.

   > A child aged 3 to 4 years old would have the fine motor, balance, and coordination skills needed to build a structure using blocks and the cognitive ability to build a structure from a mental image. This activity requires the child to recognize color and shape. The child must organize the blocks by size and shape to produce a three-dimensional block structure based on a mental image.

2. You are part of an intraprofessional screening team to determine children's readiness for kindergarten. A 5-year-old child whom you and the occupational therapist are evaluating has performed at or above level on every aspect of the screening. The child has not demonstrated any fine motor, visual motor, or gross motor delays. The child has no cognitive deficits. Given the child's performance, which of Erhardt's developmental levels of prewriting skills would you expect the child to use for writing tasks? Explain your answer.

   > The information provided indicates that the child is functioning at an age-appropriate developmental level; thus, the child would be expected to use a developmentally appropriate grasp for writing tasks. Given that the child is 5 years old, the child would be expected to use a dynamic tripod posture for writing tasks. The dynamic tripod posture is observed in children ages 4½ to 6 years.

3. A 15-year-old has a group of friends who have recently become involved in experimenting with drugs, alcohol, and other risky behaviors. The teen is torn between wanting to remain friends with this group and not wanting to join them in these behaviors. The teen decides to join another group of teens who are engaged in a competitive soccer league in order to meet and become connected to a new group of friends. According to Erikson's eight stages of man, what stage of development is the teenager undergoing? Describe the characteristics of this stage.

   > According to Erikson, there are eight stages of man and each stage includes a critical personal-social crisis. When the crisis is resolved by the individual, the individual gains a sense of mastery and acquires a personality quality. Erikson identifies the crisis of the teenage years as self-identity versus role confusion. During this stage, the teenager is challenged to make choices about adult roles. The resolution of this identity crisis provides the teenager with a sense of fidelity and an integrated sense of belonging to and being a member of society.

4. A 16-month-old toddler is brought to occupational therapy for an evaluation. The parents are concerned with the frequency of the toddler's falls, which result in bangs to the head. The child demonstrates delayed motor skills. The occupational therapist and you notice that the toddler has not yet integrated primitive reflexes. Which primary primitive reflex is most likely absent in this toddler? Explain its relevance to the toddler's health status and safety, and its impact on occupational performance.

   > The toddler likely does not have a protective extension reflex. Protective extension occurs in response to a challenge to an individual's balance and it involves arm extension in the direction of the fall, protecting the head from injury. The forward protective extension reflex develops at 6 – 9 months, protective extension sideward develops at 7 months, and

465

backward protective extension develops at 9 – 10 months. This reflex persists upon development. Absence of the protective extension reflex is indicative of a neurological condition or a potential disease process. The absence of the protective extension reflex is a safety concern and may require environmental adaptations and the use of a protective helmet to allow the child to safely participate in gross motor play activities to promote normal growth and development.

5. You provide wellness and prevention services to older adults who attend a community-based senior center. What strategies to slow, reverse, and/or compensate for age-related changes to their muscular, skeletal, and neurological systems can you share with these older adults?

You can advise the older adults on ways to improve their general health (e.g., stop smoking, exercise regularly) and maintain an adequate nutritional intake (e.g., if budget is limited, use community-based food programs to supplement diet). You should stress that active engagement in functional activities and activity programs can be used to increase their levels of physical activity. Strength training can be used to increase or maintain muscle strength required for functional activity, while flexibility and range of motion exercises can be used to increase range of motion. The older adults should be advised to gradually increase the intensity of their physical activity to avoid injury. Weight-bearing (gravity-loading) exercises (e.g., walking, stair climbing, all activities performed in standing) can decrease bone loss.

You can advise the older adults to allow for increased reaction and movement times to improve accuracy of movements and to avoid long sequences of movements to allow for memory limitations. They should plan and include adequate warm-ups and cool-downs and appropriate pacing and rest periods in their routine. You can provide safety education to reduce falls.

Chapter 6 Review Questions

Musculoskeletal System Disorders

1. Your client is status post a below-knee amputation. You assess the strength of the client's triceps in preparation for transfer training. The results of the manual muscle testing (MMT) reveal that the client can extend the elbows full range against gravity. When placed in the test position the client can take moderate resistance and then break. What muscle grade would you document the client possesses?

   > A client who can extend against gravity and take moderate resistance has a 4/5 (good) muscle strength.

2. A client incurred a right Colles' fracture. One week ago, the client's cast was removed. You have worked with this client for several intervention sessions. When arriving for the current therapy session, the client is tearful and holding the right arm in a protected position. The client reports that severe pain developed over the weekend in the wrist, hand, and shoulder and that it has not gone away. The right hand is swollen and skin is shiny. On a pain scale of 0–10, the client reports a 10+. The client describes an inability (over the past 2 days) to complete exercises and basic self-care activities due to the pain. You discuss the change in client's status with the occupational therapist. What may be causing the client's increase in symptoms? How should you and the occupational therapist address the client's new presenting symptoms?

   > This client is presenting symptoms that are typical of complex regional pain syndrome (CRPS), which may follow a trauma such as a Colles' fracture. CRPS symptoms include swelling, shiny skin, pain beyond what is expected for a Colles' fracture, and difficulty using the extremity during ADL. The physician should be contacted and symptoms described. Occupational therapy intervention for CRPS include modalities to decrease pain, edema management (e.g., elevation, manual edema mobilization, compression glove), AROM to involved joints to avoid joint contractures and muscle atrophy, ADL to encourage pain-free active use, stress loading (e.g., weight-bearing and joint distraction activities, including scrubbing and carrying activities), splinting to prevent contractures, and self-management to enable the ability to engage in occupation-based activities. Interventions to avoid or to proceed with caution include passive range of motion, passive stretching, joint mobilization, dynamic splinting, and casting.

3. You begin intervention with a client with a diagnosis of de Quervain's. Upon evaluation, the client's major complaint was pain when lifting (e.g., the client's newborn child, grocery bags). Pain is reported as 8/10. What interventions should you implement?

   > De Quervain's is a tenosynovitis of the first dorsal compartment of the extensor tendons. It is characterized by pain and swelling over the radial styloid and a positive Finkelstein's Test. A forearm-based thumb splint should be fabricated to place the tendons at rest until pain decreases. The client should be instructed in ways to modify lifting and other activities without causing further trauma to the extensor tendons. Ice massage over the radial wrist and gentle AROM of wrist and thumb to prevent stiffness can be used.

4. You work with a client with a third-degree burn to the hand. The physician has prescribed a splint for the client. What is the optimal antideformity position you should use to guide your splint construction? Explain your reasoning.

   > When splinting a person with a burn to the hand, you should position the wrist in 20–30-degree extension (increases MCP flexion via tenodesis), MCP joints in 70-degree flexion (places the collateral ligaments in a lengthened position), IP joints in extension (prevents contracture of the volar plates), and thumb abducted and extended (preserves the first web space).

5. You begin intervention with a person with a diagnosis of carpal tunnel syndrome (CTS). What conservative treatment methods are indicated for this diagnosis?

    A splint that positions the wrist in neutral should be provided to the client and the client should be advised to wear the splint at night and during the day when performing repetitive activity. Median nerve gliding exercises and differential tendon gliding exercises should be used. The client should be taught how to modify activities to prevent compression of the median nerve and avoid activities with extreme positions of wrist flexion, wrist flexion with repetitive finger flexion, and wrist flexion with a static grip.

6. A child with a diagnosis of osteogenesis imperfecta receives occupational therapy services. What should be the primary foci of occupational therapy intervention? Describe the safety precautions you and the occupational therapist should integrate into the treatment of a child with osteogenesis imperfecta.

    A primary focus of occupational therapy in treating a child with osteogenesis imperfecta is the education of family members, caregivers, and educators about proper handling and positioning techniques to use with the child to avoid fractures. As the child grows, interventions must focus on revising these precautions and teaching family members and caregivers to adapt to the demands and environmental challenges encountered by the child (e.g., playground play). You and the occupational therapist should also reinforce the importance of nutrition for bone health and weight control. Occupational therapy interventions should focus on weight-bearing activities to facilitate bone growth and activities to increase muscle strength. You and the occupational therapist should also provide school-related activities and environmental modifications to enable participation. Throughout all interventions, precautions to avoid fractures must be followed. For instance, you and the occupational therapist may fabricate or order special equipment for the child to safely participate in playground or gym activities or design splints to enable the completion of desktop school activities.

Chapter 7 Review Questions

Neurological System Disorders

1. You will be working with two persons who have survived strokes. One incurred a left MCA stroke and one incurred a right MCA stroke. What symptoms might each patient present during their respective intervention session?

    > The person with a left MCA may exhibit right-sided sensory and motor loss, aphasia, apraxia, and right visual field loss. The person with a right MCA may exhibit left-sided sensory and motor loss, unilateral neglect, spatial dysfunction, and left visual field loss.

2. You are working on a spinal cord unit. You are about to evaluate a client who has injury classified as ASIA A. The injury is at the C5 level. What is the expected sensory and motor status of your client?

    > Complete loss of sensation and motor function below the lesion. No sensory or motor function is preserved in the sacral segments.

3. You have collaborated with the occupational therapist to evaluate a client who sustained a TBI two weeks ago. Your findings include that the patient was alert and in a heightened state of activity (easily overstimulated) and attempting to pull out the IV and feeding tube. The patient could not remember directions, exhibiting poor short-term memory. The patient screamed out for no reason several times during the session and was observed to be aggressive (e.g., attempting to hit you and the occupational therapist). The patient required maximum assist for BADL. Your facility requires the documentation of each TBI patient's Rancho Level of Cognitive Function. What level should be recorded for this client?

    > The behaviors described are indicative of Level IV: Confused and Agitated. Rancho Levels I–III present with very low levels of arousal and require total assistance for BADL. Persons at these levels do not respond or respond inconsistently to stimuli. Persons at Rancho Levels V and higher do not demonstrate agitation, they are not aggressive, and their ability to participate in ADL continues to improve.

4. During an occupational therapy session with a toddler, you observe that the child tends to sit or lay as placed, without moving. The parent reports that the child shows interest in toys, but never seems to reach out to them or handle them. The child is reported to be a "picky eater," who shows no interest in self-feeding. When you attempt to approach or make eye contact, the child cries. Based on this information, how would you explain the child's behaviors as related to possible underlying conditions to the parent?

    > This child exhibits signs of sensory modulation disorder, specifically sensory avoidance behaviors. These sensory avoidance behaviors were evidenced in the child's avoidance of movement, avoidance of touching and handling toys or foods, avoidance of eye contact, and nonresponse to being approached.

5. You are working with a child who suddenly has a series of seizures that occur in rapid succession and are prolonged. The parents are present, and they report that they ran out of the child's medication the day before. What type of seizure do these symptoms represent? How should you respond to this situation?

    > The child incurred status epilepticus, which can be triggered by an abrupt disruption of the child's medications. Procedures in responding to status epilepticus include remaining calm and having someone call for immediate medical attention (although rare, sudden death can occur in status epilepticus). You should remove dangerous objects from the area and protect the child from harm, without interfering with the child's movement. If the child is standing or sitting in a chair, you should gently guide the child to the floor.

Chapter 8 Review Questions

Cardiovascular and Pulmonary System Disorders

1. An adult with a diagnosis of left ventricular failure congestive heart failure (CHF) has been referred to occupational therapy for Phase I cardiac rehabilitation during an acute hospitalization. What are the primary goals of inpatient cardiac rehabilitation? What symptoms of CHF do you need to be aware of that might manifest during therapeutic activities?

    A primary focus of Phase I cardiac rehabilitation is patient and family education about the disease process and recovery. This includes teaching energy conservation and work simplification techniques and the connection between MET levels and activity. Interventions should also focus on improving the person's ability to carry out BADL, including mobility with low-level out-of-bed functional activities. Decreasing anxiety about activity performance and support for smoking cessation and dietary modification are also primary goals for Phase I cardiac rehabilitation. The ultimate goal of this phase is to discharge the patient to home and outpatient cardiac rehabilitation. During therapeutic activities, you must be aware that the patient may experience tachycardia, fatigue with activity or mobility, decreased endurance to sustain activity, and/or dyspnea.

2. What are the clinical indications that may lead you to stop an activity during a cardiac rehabilitation intervention session? How would you monitor the patient during activity for signs/symptoms of distress?

    Indications that the patient is experiencing an adverse response to treatment include a rise in diastolic blood pressure (BP) greater than or equal to 110 mmHg, a decrease in systolic BP greater than 10 mmHg, significant ventricular or atrial dysrhythmias, second- or third-degree heart block, and signs/symptoms of exercise intolerance, including angina and/or marked dyspnea. To monitor a patient for signs/symptoms of distress during activities, you should keep track of the person's vital signs. Vital signs are an important and reliable indicator of activity tolerance and response to treatment. These include heart rate, blood pressure, respiratory rate, and O2 and CO2 levels. In addition to monitoring vital signs, you should seek feedback from the patient by using angina and dyspnea rating scales, intermittent claudication rating scale, and the Borg Scale for Rating Perceived Exertion.

3. An older adult status post-myocardial infarction (S/P MI) has been referred to occupational therapy for Phase II outpatient cardiac rehabilitation. The client is able to carry out all basic ADL independently and has fair tolerance for activities that require standing and overhead movements. The client lives with a spouse and identifies being a partner, home maintainer, and gardener as primary roles. The client would like to be able to resume role-related activities. The occupational therapy prescription calls for activities beginning at MET level 3 and increasing to MET level 5 according to the patient's activity tolerance. Taking into consideration the therapy prescription, the patient's current status, desired occupational roles, and activity preferences, which treatment approaches and activities should you include in intervention?

    You should include energy conservation and work simplification techniques and IADL activities in treatment to address the patient's preferences and goals. Beginning with activities at MET level 3–4, you could include making a bed, sweeping, mopping, and gardening. As the patient tolerates these activities, the therapy program would be upgraded to MET level 4–5 activities, including changing bed linens, weeding, and raking the garden. A discussion about resuming sexual activity is also appropriate at this level.

4. You have been asked to consult with a teacher to discuss precautions for a student who has a diagnosis of cystic fibrosis. What precautions should you discuss with the teacher? Provide a rationale for your recommendations.

   > You should inform the teacher about the student's need for adequate nutrition and hydration. Nutrition and hydration are important for managing mucus production. You should advise the teacher to create an inclusive environment to promote social participation and safe participation in physical activities. You should instruct the teacher in energy conservation techniques the student can use during activities. These techniques are required to help the child work toward participating in a full school day. During physical activity, the child should be actively monitored for signs of fatigue and dehydration, which may lead to cardiac and respiratory problems.

5. You are working with a 20-month-old toddler who was diagnosed with bronchopulmonary dysplasia (BPD) shortly after birth. What are the typical deficits resulting from BPD that the child may exhibit during occupational therapy intervention sessions? Provide an explanation for your answers.

   > Delays may be observed in all areas of development, including gross motor, fine motor, visual motor, cognitive, and social-emotional development. The toddler may present with hypotonia and exhibit fatigue and a low tolerance for physical activity. Poor autonomic and sensory state regulation and poor vision may be evident. Extended time on respirators and artificial ventilation can affect vision and visual motor development and state regulation. Central nervous system problems can lead to global developmental delays. Malabsorption problems can lead to brittle bones and also to cognitive delays. Because children with BPD experience dependence on technology and lengthy hospitalizations, some children also experience attachment disorders, which may impact social emotional development and social participation.

Chapter 9 Review Questions

Gastrointestinal, Renal-Genitourinary, Endocrine, Immunological, and Integumentary Systems Disorders

1. You work with clients who have dysphagia and swallowing disorders to develop their feeding skills. What would you do if a client chokes and cannot clear their airway during the activity?

   If the person gasps for breath, but has a partial or complete airway obstruction, you should clear the obstruction and raise the bolus that has been aspirated. You can use the Heimlich maneuver as long as the person is awake and responsive. If the person loses consciousness, basic life support procedures are used to continue to try to reestablish the airway. You should seek assistance from the medical staff to ensure that the client is all right and that the oral and airway cavity have been cleared. You should document the incident in your daily notes. If requested or facility policy, you should complete an incident report/form.

2. You are working with clients who have a colostomy or a stoma due to surgery to their bowel. Some clients do not have the intact fine motor functioning to learn to manage their stoma independently. What can you do to work with these clients to develop their ability to manage their stoma care independently?

   It is best for clients with a colostomy or a stoma to have intact fine motor functioning to manage their stoma care. However, they can be taught to compensate using adaptive devices and techniques (e.g., the use of spring clasps verses twist valves). Self-care aspects of stoma care must be addressed for persons with decreased fine motor skills (e.g., individuals with peripheral neuropathy secondary to chemotherapy treatment). The OTA in collaboration with the occupational therapist can determine why a person has fine motor impairments. They can plan a course of therapy to improve the person's fine motor ability. If abilities cannot be improved, the OTA and therapist can determine the types of adaptations that could be used to substitute for lost functional mobility and train the person in their use.

3. Describe options that could be useful in providing intervention for someone who has bladder urgency with stress urinary incontinence and a diagnosis of non-insulin-dependent diabetes mellitus.

   Intervention might include using Kegel exercises to strengthen the pelvic floor and timed routines for emptying the bladder before it is full enough to cause spillage. Lifestyle adjustments to use incontinence supporting garments as a socially acceptable solution and to decrease public attention to the incontinence are also effective. Medications may be used when the physician feels the client can tolerate the side effects of drug therapy support. Electric stimulation may be used, if the client fits the parameters of recovery for the condition. For example, if the nerve damage is permanent from neuropathy, exercises may not be a useful strategy, since the muscles would not get the enervation needed to effect a change.

4. You are treating an adult client with a diagnosis of scleroderma and colon cancer who was referred to occupational therapy because soft tissue/connective tissue changes are affecting hand function. Would it be appropriate to have a restorative goal for evolving contractures? Describe your rationale.

   Yes, it can still be beneficial to try to prevent progression of the contractures using stretching, splinting, and scar management principles. By teaching the person to stretch and giving them supplies to assist the scar management, they can be taught to preserve hand function over time.

5. You work in a community-based setting that serves people with spinal cord injuries. Several of your clients report reddening of skin in their sacral regions. What should you do to work with these clients to improve their skin integrity and prevent decubiti?

> You can educate the clients about conditions that predispose them to the formation of decubitus ulcers. These include immobility or altered mobility, weight loss, edema, incontinence, sensory deficiencies, circulatory abnormalities, dehydration, inadequate nutrition, obesity, pathological conditions/multiple comorbidities, and/or changes in skin condition due to aging. You can use principles of lifestyle redesign, habit formation, and/or habit change to plan an individual course of action for behavioral change and improved self-care patterns. If there is presence of substance abuse, cognitive deficits, and/or psychological impairments that can jeopardize the individual's ability to understand and complete the required daily ulcer prevention regimen, you can alter the form of education so that a caregiver can assist with the care plan.

Chapter 10 Review Questions

Psychiatric and Cognitive Disorders

1. You are asked to provide consultation services for an individual who lives in a group home. The resident has become dehydrated and inconsistent in taking oral medications. You interview the resident about their daily habits and routines and learn that the resident will not drink the tap water in the group home. The resident states, "The water is poisoned. They are trying to poison me. If I drink the water I will die." Identify the psychiatric symptom that is preventing this person from drinking the water. Describe an intervention approach you would use to help the resident hydrate and take prescribed medications. Explain the importance of this person staying hydrated and taking prescribed medications.

   This person has a delusion. The best intervention strategy would be to ask the resident if they will agree to drink fruit juice or sealed bottles of water which they can independently open. Telling the person that the water is not being poisoned would not be an option as one must not argue with or try to refute a delusion, which by definition is a fixed, unshakeable, false belief. Working with the person to ensure consistent hydration is important because dehydration threatens the person's physical health. It is important for the resident to take prescribed medications because it stabilizes the person sufficiently so they can live in a less restrictive setting and participate in life within the group home and the community. To increase medication compliance, you can provide external structure and consistency by involving and encouraging the support of caregivers in the group home, establishing a set routine for taking medication (e.g., at a specific time of day such as right before the evening news or after a meal), using medication containers marked with the day of the week, and using calendars or daily checklists. Depending on the type of medication, the use of long-acting injections may prove useful in facilitating medication compliance.

2. You meet with the occupational therapist to discuss an intervention plan for an adolescent. The adolescent has great difficulty reading the various nonverbal behaviors of others (e.g., eye contact, facial expression, gestures and body language) that are needed to regulate social interactions. The adolescent has not been able to develop relationships with a peer group. The teen is preoccupied and intensely interested in World War II, its history, battles, and generals and talks about nothing else. The teen's bedroom is filled with World War II memorabilia and books about the war. This adolescent's cognitive, language, and communication skills, and ADL development has been age appropriate; however, the teen has not developed age-appropriate social interaction skills. Based on this information, what diagnosis is most reflective of this teen's functional status? What intervention goals would be helpful to work on with this adolescent?

   This adolescent's described behaviors are most reflective of a diagnosis of autism spectrum disorder (ASD). The teen has difficulty with social interaction, restricted interests and behaviors, adequate language skills, and misses the social interaction cues that others provide. These behaviors impair the adolescent's establishment of peer interactions and relationships. The teen's ADL, cognitive, language, and communication skills are reported as age appropriate, which is often the case for individuals with ASD. Intervention goals include increasing social interaction skills. Interventions can include the use of groups. Involvement in extracurricular activities, clubs, and sports may also broaden the adolescent's interests. Depending on the individual, addressing any milestone developmental delays may be necessary to improve age-appropriate interactions, such as impairment in sensorimotor skills. Additional intervention goals may include vocational readiness and community participation. Interventions for adolescents should also include family involvement.

3. You and the occupational therapist are conducting an evaluation of a 16-month-old toddler. The parent reports that the toddler has frequent tantrums with no clear precipitant. The parent thinks these behaviors may be the result of the toddler's frustration due to language delays. When unable to reach a toy, the toddler pulled the parent's hand toward the toy without pointing. The toddler also did not point to pictures in books. When playing with blocks or cars, the toddler lined them up, but did not spontaneously manipulate or move them. The toddler exhibited a rigid and limited repertoire of play and interaction skills. What diagnosis is most consistent with the toddler's presenting behaviors? Explain your rationale.

> The toddler's behaviors are indicative of autism spectrum disorder (ASD). Children with ASD typically have limited communication skills and language. Because pointing to express interest and/or fulfill a need is a primary means of communication, the toddler's nonuse of the pointing gesture suggests a lower level of communication skills. This also is indicative of the lack of inferred sharing that is commonly seen in children with ASD. The tantrums reported by the parent may indicate sensory-induced behavioral responses that are also common in ASD. The limited and rigid repertoire of play behaviors (as exhibited in the lining up of objects) is also consistent with the play of children with Autism Spectrum Disorder.

4. You are a home health OTA providing services to an elderly client. The client's caregiver reports that the client is having trouble remembering things, sustaining attention, and making decisions. The caregiver reports the client seems mentally confused and asks whether the symptoms are indicative of dementia. As an OTA, you know that there are possible reversible causes of mental confusion. What are the reversible causes of mental confusion that you should consider during your intervention and inform the occupational therapist as needing further evaluation?

> When working with a client who appears mentally confused, you should always consider the possible reversible causes for mental confusion. These can include sensory changes and problems caused by age-related losses in hearing, vision, and/or touch and sensory overload or deprivation. The client's need for a hearing aid or glasses (and if these prostheses are available and working properly) should also be considered. The client's environment should be assessed because it may lack cues to aid orientation (i.e., clocks and calendars). Other causes for mental confusion that you should consider and inform the occupational therapist about are depression and drug use or misuse (i.e., drug interactions, medication side effects, polymedication, and the combination of prescription and over-the-counter drugs). Urinary tract infections, viral or bacterial infections, pneumonia, or gallbladder disease are often causes of mental confusion in older adults, so these need to be ruled out. Metabolic problems such as liver or kidney disease, thyroid disorders, dehydration, and poorly controlled diabetes may also present as mental confusion and need to be further assessed by a physician.

5. You observe that a very thin client in your outpatient partial hospital program has been losing weight. The individual has no medical problems. The physician supervising the program states the client is well below the normal weight for their age and height. The client participates in cooking groups with peers, but will not eat whatever is prepared other than salad without dressing. When encouraged to try other foods, the client says "I don't want to get fat, and I already need to lose a few pounds." You are concerned that the individual has anorexia nervosa. What signs of this eating disorder are being exhibited? What additional symptoms would you expect to see that would indicate this diagnosis?

   ▶ The client refuses to maintain a body weight that is normal for age and height and has a fear of gaining weight and becoming fat, even though underweight. There is a disturbance in the way this individual perceives or experiences personal weight and appearance. Other symptoms of this disorder include the undue influence of body weight or shape on self-evaluation and denial of the seriousness of the current low body weight, even if the person were to be hospitalized or seriously ill. If the client is a postmenarcheal female, amenorrhea may occur.

Chapter 11 Review Questions

Biomechanical Approaches: Evaluation and Intervention

1. You work in a practice setting that serves many clients with musculoskeletal disorders. The majority of clients have decreased ROM. When collaborating with the occupational therapist to complete client evaluations, which different types of ROM should you consider during assessment? How should you document your evaluation and its results?

   When assessing ROM, you should consider functional ROM, which is the ROM needed to perform functional movements (e.g., reach to top of head to brush hair, reach to the small of the back to tuck a shirt into pants); active ROM (AROM), which is the movement produced by one's own muscle; passive ROM (PROM), which is movement produced by an external force; and active assistive ROM (AAROM), movement produced by one's own muscles and assisted by an external force. When recording ROM measurements, you should always record the starting position and ending position (e.g., 0–150 degrees) and not use negatives. You can use the terms within functional limits (WFL) to denote that the client's ROM is functional (e.g., the person can don socks) and within normal limits (WNL) to denote ROM that achieves established ranges (e.g., shoulder flexion 0–180 degrees).

2. A new client is admitted into an intensive care unit with a diagnosis of a spinal cord injury. You collaborate with the occupational therapist to complete an evaluation to help the physician determine the level of injury. How would you perform a light-touch sensory test? How does this method of testing differ from the procedures used during sensory testing for other major diagnostic categories?

   When determining sensation of a client diagnosed with a spinal cord injury, the test stimulus (i.e., cotton ball) is presented proximal to distal following dermatomes (beginning at cervical level and moving distal). Following the dermatome pattern will provide you with information about the client's status at each sensory level. When completing sensory testing for neurological disorders, you assess according to dermatome patterns. Peripheral nerve injuries are tested distal to proximal following peripheral nerves.

3. An adult client is having difficulty performing daily activities due to decreased ROM and pain in both shoulders. During an intervention planning meeting, you and the occupational therapist decide to treat the client with preparatory interventions followed by an occupation-based intervention. What interventions can you use to increase ROM and decrease pain?

   Applying heat and performing gentle passive ROM on the client's shoulders are preparatory interventions. The application of heat prior to stretch can increase extensibility. Manual stretching within the individual's tolerance and contract/relax and hold/relax are additional preparatory methods that can increase ROM. Working with the client to perform activities that require shoulder movements to engage in desired occupational roles (e.g., completing hair care, placing groceries on upper cabinet shelves) would be an appropriate occupation-based intervention.

3. You provide consultation services to a center for independent living that serves persons with a diversity of disabilities. You are scheduled to conduct an educational session on energy conservation and work simplification. What key principles and methods should you be sure to include in your presentation?

   You should advise presentation participants to plan short rest periods (e.g., 5 – 10 minutes) during their daily routine and to schedule daily tasks that alternate between and balance heavy and light work tasks. Tasks that are nonessential and/or those that are beyond personal capacity can be eliminated. To decrease extraneous work, tasks can be combined.

Prior to initiating a task, all necessary items and equipment should be gathered. The use of a utility cart, a bucket, walker bag, and/or backpack can be used to carry all items needed in one trip to avoid multiple trips. The participants should be advised to sit to work at a table or use a high stool for countertop work and to use lightweight equipment, tools, and utensils. Cabinets can be organized so that items are easy to reach and in convenient locations. The sliding of items across countertops is preferable to lifting them. Adaptive equipment (e.g., reachers) can be used to avoid bending and stooping, and electrical appliances (e.g., mixers) can be used to decrease personal effort. Because intermittent rest during an activity is more effective than resting after exhaustion has occurred, participants should be advised to rest before they experience fatigue.

5. Your client is diagnosed with rotator cuff tendonitis and is experiencing severe pain. The physician has ordered the use of electrical stimulation, gentle ROM, and below-shoulder-level ADL. You and the occupational therapist review the client's past medical history. You learn that the person has a history of cardiac issues that required the implantation of a pacemaker. Which of the prescribed interventions should you use with this client? What are additional interventions you can use with this client to decrease pain and prepare the person for occupation-based interventions?

▶ Gentle ROM and below-shoulder-level ADL are appropriate interventions to use with this client. The use of electrical stimulation is contraindicated and should not be used with this client. Electrical stimulation can interfere with the electrical current of the defibrillator. Additional preparatory methods to decrease pain include cryotherapy and superficial heat therapy.

6. Your client is status post a below knee amputation. You assess the strength of the client's triceps in preparation for transfer training. The results of the MMT reveal that the client can take moderate resistance and then break. What muscle grade would you document the client possesses?

▶ A client who can extend against gravity and take moderate resistance has a 4/5 (good) muscle strength.

Chapter 12 Review Questions

Neurological and Cognitive-Perceptual Approaches: Evaluation and Intervention

1. You are working with a client with hemiplegia after a brain tumor resection. The client is learning to transfer using a tub bench for the first time. Thus, the person is at the cognitive stage of learning. According to principles of motor learning, what types of interventions would be appropriate to teach this transfer skill at this stage of learning?

   > Examples of effective types of interventions include having the client demonstrate ideal performance of the task to establish a reference of correctness, verbalize the task components and requirements, point out similarities to other learned tasks (e.g., a toilet transfer), direct attention to critical task elements (e.g., lock brakes for safety, judge height of the tub), use blocked practice (i.e., repeated practice of the transfer), encourage the use of mental practice, use manual guidance to assist as appropriate (e.g., guiding legs over and into the tub), break the tasks down to component parts (e.g., wheelchair alignment and management, sit to stand).

2. You are working with a person with a swallowing disorder. You have collaborated with the occupational therapist and determined that direct interventions using a bolus are indicated. Which approaches would you use?

   > Direct interventions for swallowing disorders include the modification of the consistency, amount, and pacing of solids and liquids. Postural interventions (i.e., chin tuck, head tilt, and head turn) are used to increase swallowing efficiency during meals. Specific swallowing adaptations (e.g., the supraglottic swallow technique, Mendelsohn's maneuver) are also used when indicated.

3. You are observing a client with apraxia eat breakfast. What behaviors would you most likely observe?

   > You may see problems with tool use, such as stirring coffee with a knife or eating cereal with a fork. You would observe difficulty with the sequencing of the steps of the task such as eating cereal without pouring the milk into it. In severe cases, clients will not perform and stare blankly at the breakfast tray as they have lost the concept of the breakfast task.

4. Your client presents with unilateral spatial neglect and poor awareness. The client has a supportive partner. What environmental modifications will be useful to maximize performance and safety indoors?

   > Place perceptual anchors (e.g., brightly colored objects or strips of colored tape) in the places where the person usually engages in occupation. Place necessary grooming objects on the neglected side of the sink. Reorganize closets and dressers so that needed items are biased to the person's neglected side. Place cell phones or safety alert systems in the person's shirt pocket on the person's intact, non-neglected side.

5. Your client has left-sided body neglect. What behaviors would you expect to see during morning self-care?

   > You may observe the person spending more time combing the right side of their hair as compared to the left. The person may not shave or only partially shave the left side of the face or legs. They may not engage the left arm in the task despite having the capacity.

6. You are working in acute care with a person with low arousal after head trauma. Describe activities that would be useful.

    > The use of sensory stimulating activities would be beneficial. Examples include washing the face and upper body with a cold washcloth, using a loud and direct voice when cuing, providing visually stimulating objects, turning all lights on, opening bed curtains, sitting the person up to provide vestibular input, and playing music.

7. What is the purpose of applying a static orthosis (splint) to an affected body part?

    > Static splints are utilized for external support, prevention of motion, stretching of contractures, aligning joints for healing, resting joints, or reducing pain.

8. You are working in a private practice that provides services to children with sensory processing disorders. What general principles of Ayres Sensory Integration® approach can you use to guide your interventions?

    > According to the Ayres Sensory Integration® approach, interventions should be designed to improve sensory processing, facilitate sensory integration, and elicit an adaptive response. Interventions should provide controlled sensory input in a manner that is child-driven and play-based. Environments and activities should be designed to facilitate active participation for 'just the right challenge.' The quality of input and the type of activities used should be controlled because these will vary depending on each child's needs and the situational context. Intervention activities should balance structure and freedom and tap into each child's inner drive to obtain neural organization. Activities requiring more mature and complex patterns of behaviors should be gradually introduced.

Chapter 13 Review Questions

Psychosocial Approaches: Evaluation and Intervention

1. You are working in a setting that uses cognitive behavioral therapy (CBT). What are key general postulates for change that are used in CBT to guide the intervention process? How can these be applied throughout the occupational therapy process?

   According to CBT, dysfunctional thought processes produce or lead to the development of mental health symptoms and can result in psychological dysfunction and/or psychiatric disorders. Negative thoughts, which are considered a dysfunctional process in CBT, function as a sustaining factor for illnesses such as depression. CBT proposes that altering a person's cognition can improve psychological health. In occupational therapy, a practitioner can help the person alter dysfunctional thoughts and cognitive processes by addressing them through the use of CBT interventions. For example, using work sheets in psychoeducational groups or individual sessions can assist clients in looking at their perceptions of their problems, situations, and/or feelings. CBT interventions are also used to help clients make changes that can lead to improved emotional health.

2. You collaborate with an occupational therapist to determine the best method for evaluating a client's cognitive level according to the Cognitive Disabilities model. Identify three evaluation tools that can be used to assess an individual's cognitive level according to the Cognitive Disabilities model. Describe a practice situation in which each evaluation would be most effectively used.

   The Allen Cognitive Level Screen-5 (ACLS-5) is a structured task that allows the occupational therapy practitioner to observe the individual performing three increasingly complex leather lacing stitches. Based on these observations, the practitioner makes determinations about that person's cognitive skill level. Guidelines are available for designing other tasks that will also elicit the component skills of each level. In practice, the ACLS-5 can be used in any setting where the practitioner's observations lead them to believe that the client is experiencing cognitive dysfunction. The ACLS-5 can be effectively used, in conjunction with other evaluations, to assist in intervention and discharge planning. Clinical settings where adult individuals present with a traumatic brain injury (TBI), CVA, or mental health disorders are among the various settings where this evaluation can be used. For example, veterans' hospitals would be a current setting that may use the ACLS-5 because many returning soldiers present with TBIs. The Routine Task Inventory (RTI) gathers data about the individual's ADL performance from an informed caregiver. Practitioners in home health may use the information obtained from this evaluation to improve a patient's ADL performance by providing activity adaptations and making home modifications as indicated. Based on the RTI results, the practitioner can also provide patient and family education to enhance occupational performance and ease caregiver burden. The Cognitive Performance Test (CPT) was designed to assess the functional performance of individuals with a neurocognitive disorder. The focus is on the identification of the effects that particular deficits have on the performance of ADL. This test can be used in any clinical situation where individuals present with the symptoms of a neurocognitive disorder.

3. You work in a setting that uses sensory models to guide treatment. Describe five current intervention approaches based on sensory models and how they can be effectively applied in occupational therapy practice.

> The use of multisensory environments (e.g., Snoezelen rooms) can be effective in calming or alerting individuals with psychiatric illness, autism spectrum disorders, pervasive developmental disorders, and neurocognitive disorders. Such rooms can be used with an individual or with a group, depending upon intervention goals and objectives. The use of therapeutic weighted blankets, dolls, and stuffed animals can also be used as a modality to assist in self-soothing and as an alternative to the use of restraints in inpatient mental health settings, skilled nursing facilities, and/or any setting where individuals could benefit from interventions to decrease agitation. "Comfort rooms" are increasingly used as an alternative to restraints in mental health settings. Occupational therapy practitioners' unique knowledge in creating comfort rooms based on sensory principles can be very useful in increasing the efficacy of these rooms, particularly in acute, inpatient psychiatric settings. Occupational therapy practitioners can also use a psychoeducation approach along with sensory models during intervention. For example, after the administration of an evaluation, such as the Adolescent and Adult Sensory Profile, the practitioner can use worksheets in a group to help clients identify their reactions to sensory input and learn adaptive ways of coping with their sensory issues. Sensory diets including alerting/calming stimuli and heavy work patterns can be provided in any setting by occupational therapy practitioners and individualized to the specific sensory needs of the client. By helping clients learn how to use their sensory diets whenever sensory processing issues arise, occupational therapy practitioners can extend the effective use of occupational therapy interventions throughout the day.

4. You provide occupational therapy services on an acute inpatient psychiatric unit. Describe interventions that you can provide to help patients who are experiencing hallucinations and/or delusions manage their symptoms during an occupational therapy group.

> You can create an environment free of the distractions that trigger hallucinatory and/or delusionary thoughts and interfere with the performance of a reality-based activity for the individual. You can use highly structured simple, concrete, and tangible activities that hold the individual's attention (e.g., craft projects or meal preparation tasks) to provide reality-based experiences. These activities can be used to successfully redirect persons experiencing hallucinations and/or delusions and help move their focus away from the internal stimuli they are experiencing to refocus on their task. When a person is observed experiencing a hallucination or expressing a delusion, you can intervene with verbalizations about what the client is doing with respect to the activity and facilitate reality-based thinking and actions. A good clinical example is when clients work in a greenhouse, which provides the opportunity to engage in simple concrete tasks such as planting, pruning, and watering. Their participation in reality-based activities, the setting's consistent structure, and the group leader's positive feedback can effectively help clients manage their psychotic symptoms.

5. You work for a setting that uses the RADAR approach to screen for and respond to domestic abuse. How would you apply this approach?

> R = Routinely ask. During evaluation sessions, you should routinely ask targeted questions to screen for abuse. Inquiring about potential abuse when interviewing all clients can be the first step in intervention because this acknowledges that abuse is not an acceptable secret.
>
> A = Affirm and Ask. Acknowledge and support the person who discloses abuse at any time throughout the OT process. Ask direct questions of all clients to determine risk (e.g., Do you feel safe with your partner? Are you afraid when he/she comes home?).
>
> D = Document objective findings whenever anything that may be indicative of abuse is observed (e.g., the person has multiple bruises) and record client statements in quotes (e.g., "I am scared to go home"). This information can establish useful clinical evidence.
>
> A = Assess and Address the person's safety (i.e., has abuse become more violent? Are there weapons in the home?). This can help determine the urgency for action to help the person remain safe.
>
> R = Review options and referrals. As needed, refer the person to domestic violence hotlines, domestic violence shelters, and/or safe houses which have staff trained in family violence and safety planning. This is an essential and ethical step in preventing further domestic violence experiences. Occupational therapy practitioners should always have the contact information for these resources readily available. The public display of these resources in occupational therapy practice settings can also diminish the silence that enshrouds domestic violence.

6. You are conducting a group for individuals with recently acquired spinal cord injuries who now have paraplegia and need to use a wheelchair for mobility. Adjusting to this abrupt change in their lives has been difficult, and group members have developed depression. Several have anger issues as well. While participating in a group, one of the participants says to you, "You really have no idea what it's like to have to face using a wheelchair for the rest of your life, when just a month ago I ran my sixth marathon. Running has been my whole life. It was the way I relieved stress and stayed in shape. I guess that's all over now." What type of therapeutic approach should you take? What types of individual and group interventions might benefit this individual?

> In this case, validate this person's feelings by making statements such as, "I can only imagine what you are going through. I respect your perspective on your experience. I know and accept that this is a hard adjustment, not being able to run or walk, and that you need to use a wheelchair. I can understand why you are concerned about how to manage stress and stay active." This acknowledges the person's loss issues and may establish rapport and trust as you do not attempt to assume to know how the person feels. In providing a client-centered approach, you would next ask the group member to identify personal treatment goals. You would then collaborate with the person and the occupational therapist to develop individual and/or group interventions based on this feedback. Appropriate interventions would include addressing the person's wish to be involved in running and athletics and providing psychoeducational groups for anger management and the development of adaptive coping skills. Thematic or patient and family education to address lifestyle changes and resultant depression and to develop a plan for recovery are also appropriate.

7. You are watching television with your roommate in the eighth-floor apartment you share. You observe a very sad, withdrawn appearance and minimal spontaneous social interaction. Lately your roommate has been drinking more than usual on social occasions and this week cancelled a scheduled weekly therapy appointment. You ask if everything is alright, and the reply is "No, not really. I'm thinking of killing myself, I just can't take it anymore." "How do you think you would do it?" you ask. "I'm not quite sure, I think I have a couple of options here, belts, knives, I'm not sure which way I want to go, but I have to do it soon, maybe by the end of the week. Yes, definitely by the end of the week. All things considered, I think I'll jump out the window. I'm pretty sure the fall would kill me." What risk factors for suicide are you observing in your roommate, what levels of suicide lethality are present, and what should be your first intervention?

> The risk factors for suicide based on this scenario is a sad affect, limited interaction or social isolation and withdrawal, a mental health history, increased alcohol use, and a verbalized suicidal statement, which must be taken seriously. The roommate has suicidal ideation and a plan and intent, which presents a great potential risk for attempting suicide. Assessing this situation, your first plan of action is to stay with and not allow your roommate to be alone at any moment. You should encourage your roommate to go to the emergency room, call the doctor or therapist, and/or call the National Suicide Hotline 1-800-273-TALK (8255). If those interventions are ineffective and it can be done without leaving the individual alone, you should call 911.

Chapter 14 Review Questions

Evaluation and Intervention for Performance in Areas of Occupation

1. An OTA works in a hospital-based occupational therapy department that provides services to persons with medical conditions and physical disabilities. One of the OTA's primary responsibilities is to collaborate with the occupational therapist to plan patients' discharge. To ensure safety and enhance functional performance, the OTA assesses the level of assistance each client will need. What are the main categories of assistance that the OTA should use when documenting clients' functional performance? Describe each category.

   A person's level of functional performance is typically described along a continuum, which ranges from total assistance (i.e., the need for 100% assistance by one or more persons to perform all physical activities and/or the need for cognitive assistance to elicit a functional response to an external stimulation) to independent (i.e., no physical or cognitive assistance is required to perform functional activities). At the independent level, the person is able to implement a selected course of action, consider potential errors, and anticipate safety hazards in familiar and new situations. On this scale, maximum assistance represents the need for 75% assistance by one person to physically perform any part of a functional activity and/or cognitive assistance to perform gross motor actions in response to direction. Moderate assistance describes the need for 50% assistance by one person to help the individual perform physical activities or cognitively sustain and/or complete simple, repetitive activities safely. Minimum assistance is the need for 25% assistance by one person for physical activities and/or periodic, cognitive assistance to perform functional activities safely. Standby assistance represents the need for supervision by one person for the individual to perform new activity procedures that were adapted for safe and effective performance. A person requires stand-by assistance when errors and the need for safety precautions are not always anticipated by the individual.

2. A person with a C7 SCI sets a goal to return to work as an accountant. The person expresses concerns about the ability to complete a morning self-care routine and job tasks. What will be realistic for the person to expect to be able to do after receiving occupational therapy services to develop self-care and work skills?

   At C7, the person can use a tenodesis grasp or splint to perform many tasks. Thus, the person can expect to be independent in feeding, grooming, and dressing. A buttonhook may be used, if needed. The person will be able to transfer independently using depression transfers. For bathing, a handheld shower and a tub bench are needed. At work, the person will be able to independently hold a phone, typing stick, and pen using a tenodesis grasp or splint. Thus, the person can expect to be able to independently complete work tasks requiring the use of a calculator, computer, and telephone.

3. An OTA collaborates with an occupational therapist to ensure that the BADL of sexual activity is addressed throughout the OT process. Which model can help the OTA and supervising therapist achieve this aim? Describe the key points of this model.

   The OTA and therapist can use the PLISSIT model as a guide to address sexual activity throughout the OT process. In this model, the P stands for permission, which requires the practitioner to create an atmosphere that gives the individual permission to raise concerns about their sexuality and sexual activity(ies). This can be accomplished by incorporating sexuality into the OT initial and ongoing evaluation in a matter-of-fact manner. LI represents limited information that the practitioner can provide to ensure that the individual has accurate knowledge about their sexual abilities and potentials. The OTA and therapist can share facts (e.g., there is sex after disability) and dispel myths (e.g., people with disabilities are asexual). SS stands for specific suggestions that the OTA and therapist can provide to facilitate the individual's pursuit of satisfying sexual activities, either alone or with a partner. These can include strategies for achieving clients' goals for sexual expression (e.g., energy conservation methods, the use of nonmedical methods to manage pain and stiffness, positioning alternatives and adaptive equipment, and applying principles of activity analysis, gradation, modification, and simplification to sexual activities). In this model, IT represents intensive therapy, which is indicated when the individual requires intervention for long-standing relationship problems and/or enduring sexual problems. The application of this part of the PLISSIT model requires specialized training, so the OTA and therapist would complete a referral to the appropriate professional (e.g., couples counselor, sex therapist) if indicated.

4. An OTA works in a supported employment program that serves clients with cognitive limitations due to psychiatric, physical, and intellectual disabilities. What strategies should the OTA use to increase clients' ability to concentrate, manage time, and focus on multiple tasks at the same time during the work day?

To help the employees manage time, the employer can provide directive instructions on a regular basis and maintain structure through a daily time and task schedule using hourly goals. The provision of positive reinforcement when tasks are completed within the expected time lines is also helpful. To improve employees' concentration and management of multiple tasks, the employer can put each work request in writing and leave it in a 'to do' box to avoid interrupting the employees' work in progress. The provision of good working conditions (e.g., adequate light, reduced noise, a separate work area to reduce noise and interruptions) can also help employees concentrate. The number of tasks that need to be completed simultaneously can be decreased or eliminated, and priorities for task completion can be established. All work tasks can be put in writing with due dates or times identified. Tasks among employees with the same responsibilities can be redistributed, so that each can do more of one type of job task than a lot of different tasks.

5. During an occupational therapy screening, a client reports feeling tired all of the time. What should the occupational therapist and OTA address during evaluation?

The OTA and therapist should assess the person's ability to identify the need for restorative rest and sleep, their typical rest and sleep patterns and routines, and obstacles to the attainment and maintenance of satisfying rest and sleep. In addition, personal issues (e.g., being a light sleeper who awakens easily), pathophysiological changes related to disease, disability, and/or the aging process (e.g., chronic pain, unrelenting fatigue), and sociocultural barriers (e.g., night-shift work) should be considered. The OTA and therapist can use sleep checklists and sleep diaries to obtain detailed information.

Chapter 15 Review Questions

Mastery of the Environment: Evaluation and Intervention

1. An OTA works for an environmental accessibility consultation company owned and operated by an occupational therapist. The OTA and occupational therapist meet with a group representing a number of religious organizations who want to improve the accessibility of the entrances to their buildings. All entrances currently have stairs. What should the OTA and occupational therapist recommend to allow access for persons who use mobility aids (e.g., walkers and canes) and wheelchairs?

   > The OTA and therapist should recommend the installation of railings on the stairs and ramps as an alternative to the stairs. The exterior railings should be placed at 36 inches. This is the average of the recommended 34- to 38-inch waist height for those who walk (variance depends on people's height). The railings should be 1½ – 2 inches in diameter, with nonskid surfaces. The ramps should be built with a ratio of slope to rise of 1:12. The ramps should be a minimum of 36 inches wide, with a nonskid surface. Ramp railings should be at the average of 32 inches high. If possible, two railings (one lower and one higher) should be provided to allow for differences in people's arm reach. Curbs on the ramps should be at least 4 inches high. Level platforms should be included in the ramp design. If the ramp is excessively long, a 5′ × 5′ landing(s) are needed to allow for rest. If a sharp turn is needed in the direction of the ramp, a landing for turning space is needed. A 90-degree turn will require a minimum 5′ × 5′ landing; a 180-degree turn will require a minimum 4 foot × 8 foot landing. At the top of the ramp, a 5′ × 5′ platform is needed before the door to allow for persons in a wheelchair to swing the door without backing up. Electronic opening doors are optimal. If these are not feasible, doors should be able to be opened with a closed fist via the use of lever handles or push bars. Objects that may obstruct entrance ways should be removed (e.g., planters, garbage cans).

2. An OTA provides a weekly home safety group to members of a senior center under the supervision of an occupational therapist. What strategies should the OTA recommend the group members use inside and outside their homes to prevent falls?

   > The OTA should recommend that the members ensure that their living spaces have adequate lighting with no loose electrical cords, minimal clutter, firmly attached carpet, and furniture arranged for easy maneuverability. For homes with stairs, the OTA should recommend that members make sure that there are stair handrails securely fastened on both sides of the stairs. There should be light switches at the top and bottom of the stairs and the stairs should be covered by a nonskid secure surface. In the bathrooms, members should have grab bars located in and out of tubs and shower stalls and near toilets. The use of nonskid mats, night-lights, and an elevated toilet seat are also effective in decreasing fall risk. Good recommendations for the OTA to make to prevent falls in the bedroom are the installation of night-lights or light switches within reach of the bed, the placement of telephones in an easy-to-reach position near the bed, and the use of a mattress that is at a height that makes it easy to get in and out of bed. In the members' living areas, the OTA should advise the members to be sure their couches and chairs are at proper height to get in and out of easily. To decrease fall risk in the kitchen, the OTA should advise members to store items on reachable shelves (i.e., between the person's eye and hip level). Outside the home, members should be sure that cracked pavement or steps are fixed and stable handrails are installed if there are steps.

3. A client is status post-posterolateral hip replacement surgery. The OTA has established service competency in post-hip replacement surgery intervention protocols. What recommendations should the OTA make for bed mobility?

   ▶ The OTA should advise the person to not roll on the nonoperated side because this may result in internal rotation of the operated hip, which may cause dislocation. An abductor pillow between the lower extremities can be used to prevent adduction of the operated hip. The OTA should recommend that the person does not flex the hip beyond 90 degrees or internally rotate or pivot at the hip. The OTA should teach the person to transfer by keeping the operated hip in slight abduction and extended out in front.

4. A school-based OTA collaborates with the occupational therapist to determine alternative access modes to computers for students with disabilities. What adaptations can be used to compensate for a diversity of disabilities and maximize students' independence in the school environment? Explain their use.

   ▶ Programmable keyboards allow for customized overlays (e.g., enlarged letters and numbers for students with low vision; graphics and symbols for students with cognitive impairments). Key guards and expanded keyboards that provide large keys can be helpful for students with limited motor accuracy and control (e.g., students with ataxia). Contracted keyboards that provide smaller keys in a constrained space can be useful for students with limited range of motion and functional motor control (e.g., students with arthritis) and light-touch keyboard activation systems can be useful for students with decreased strength and/or mobility (e.g., students with muscular dystrophy). Delayed touch keyboard activation systems are helpful for students with poor motor control (e.g., students with athetoid movements) and chorded keyboards (which consist of a few keys that generate standard characters by pressing various combinations of keys) are useful for students who use only one hand (e.g., students with hemiplegia). Students with severe mobility impairments (e.g., upper extremity contractures) can use eye gaze- and voice-activated computers. Finally, students with severe motor deficits and good tongue control (e.g., a C3 SCI) can effectively use a tongue-touch keypad (TTK) embedded in an orthotic device to access a computer.

5. An OTA begins employment at a new skilled nursing facility (SNF). To ensure compliance with OBRA, the occupational therapy department is actively involved in the facility's restraint reduction program. What should the OTA know to be able to effectively contribute to this program?

   ▶ The OTA should be aware of the conditions and situations that can contribute to agitated, restless, and/or wandering behaviors. These include pain, physical discomfort, hunger, thirst, need for toileting, loneliness, fear, boredom, and an unfamiliar environment. The OTA should know interventions that can effectively address these contributing factors and correct underlying problems without the use of restraints. These can include active listening, attention to underlying feelings, and expressed concerns to promote trust, a medical evaluation for pain management, proper positioning, an adequate and client-directed toileting routine, and the provision of snacks, unbreakable water bottles, or other appropriate safe source of nourishment and hydration. Family, peer, and/or pastoral visits; animal-assisted or pet therapy; and social, leisure, and physical activities can also be helpful in decreasing agitated, restless, and/or wandering behaviors. Activities should be provided at night as well as in the day. Loudspeaker and other extraneous noise should be eliminated and replaced with soft, soothing background music. All resident rooms should include familiar and favorite objects to personalize them. A structured home-like environment with a set routine should be provided to promote a sense of safety and security. Contained areas should be interesting and safe. Furniture should be arranged to deter wandering with a variety of comfortable seating and furniture provided, including broad-based rockers and footstools.

Guidelines for Effective Use of Online Practice Examinations

EXAM HINT: To maximize the exam preparation efficacy of the three online exams that accompany this text, we strongly advise you to read the following guidelines *prior to* taking your first simulated exam.

The three online exams included with this text are purposefully designed to simulate the NBCOT® exam for the COTA®. Because you should *only* take the COTA® exam *after* the completion of a comprehensive exam preparation plan, we strongly advise you to NOT take a simulated practice exam until *after* you have reviewed the content of this text. Taking a practice exam before you have studied the information that will be tested on the COTA® exam will only reinforce what you do not know. This can negatively impact your confidence. In contrast, taking your first practice exam after you have studied can help you more effectively identify correct answers to exam items. This can boost your confidence. Learning what you know, not just what you do not know, will help you identify your specific content knowledge strengths and weaknesses. This information can then be used to develop a targeted study plan and acquire mastery of the knowledge you need to pass the COTA® exam.

Like the NBCOT® exam for the COTA®, each TherapyEd online exam contains 200 multiple choice (MC) items with three, four, or six answer options. This consistency with the COTA® exam format enables you to simulate the real exam experience and practice your timing for your actual COTA® exam administration. If you do not have an approved testing accommodation (TA) giving you extended time to complete your COTA® exam, you should take each of the three exams that accompany this text during a continuous 4-hour session. This will allow you to assess your pacing and practice implementing time management strategies to ensure that you complete the entire COTA® exam within the allotted time. The exam clock can only be stopped during the COTA® exam as a prearranged TA. Thus, if you do not have this accommodation, you should include a 15-minute break during each of your exam simulations to practice answering all exam items within 3 hours and 45 minutes. Developing the ability to complete the exam within this shortened time frame will ensure that you will be able to take a break during your exam administration without jeopardizing your ability to answer all exam items within the allotted 4 hours.

As discussed in Chapter 1, we advise you to complete each of the TherapyEd online exams during a 4-hour period. Due to the varied number of answer options you will need to consider in the exam items, the traditional recommendation to average 1 minute per exam item does not apply to all items. To allow sufficient time to complete the multi-select six-option MC items, we recommend you average approximately 45 seconds for three option exam items, 1 minute for four option exam items, and 1 minute 30 seconds for six option exam items. This will give you a 'bank' of approximately 40 minutes to answer more difficult exam items and/or take a break. During the COTA® exam, the exam clock keeps running and does not stop until you exit the exam. You can take a short break, if needed, but subtract this time from your 4-hour simulated exam session. For example, if you take a 15-minute break you need to have completed your exam in 3 hours and 45 minutes.

To further simulate your COTA® exam experience, we advise you to complete each of the TherapyEd online exams in an environment that is similar to a Prometric testing site (e.g., a study area in a library or a computer lab). This will enable you to test your ability to remain focused while taking an exam in a public place and provide you with an opportunity to practice strategies to block out distractions (e.g., not looking to see who is getting up or sitting down at the computer next to you). If you have an approved TA enabling you to take the COTA® exam in a private room, you should verify that the Prometric site at which you plan to take your exam has this capability before you schedule your exam.

Upon completing each online exam, you will receive an analysis of your exam performance. This detailed analysis will identify all of the exam items that you answered incorrectly or skipped. Extensive rationales for correct and incorrect answers are provided in this text section.

> **RED FLAG:** **DO NOT** read these rationales until *after* you have completed each respective exam in its online format.

The computer analysis of your exam performance will also provide a breakdown of your areas of strengths and weaknesses according to the content categories and critical reasoning strategies listed on the following page. After reviewing the rationales for the exam answers and the analysis of your performance on the specific content areas, you should revise your study plan using this very specific information. To help you know what to study, the content categories are labeled in accordance with this text's chapter titles. You should also reflect on the feedback provided on your critical reasoning strategies. If you had difficulty with a specific area(s) of reasoning, review the self-assessment questions and the exam preparation guidelines provided in Table 2-5 in Chapter 2.

After implementing your revised study plan and using effective exam preparation strategies, complete the second TherapyEd online exam. Use your next exam performance analysis to further revise your study plan. After implementing this revised study plan, take the third TherapyEd exam. Use the feedback provided on this exam to further revise your study plan and implement your final exam preparations before your COTA® exam. If you realize the feedback provided indicates you are particularly weak in a specific content category (e.g., musculoskeletal conditions and biomechanical approaches), the TherapyEd learning portal includes content-specific mini-exams drawn from the full exams to help you focus on specific areas. Each mini-exam is comprised of 20 exam items. Using this feature can help you further assess the efficacy of your study plan. Additional guidelines for effective exam preparation are provided in Chapter 2 of this text. It is important to understand that your performance on these practice exams is not indicative of your future performance on the COTA® exam. Many who successfully pass the COTA® exam have reported less than perfect scores on the TherapyEd exams. Remember, the exam items on these practice tests are *purposefully* designed to assist you in developing, critiquing, and revising your study plan so that you are well prepared for the COTA® exam. Therefore, if your scores on these exams are less than you anticipated, you should critically review the rationales for the answers, as well as the computerized content analysis of your performance on the exam items.

If the items you are getting wrong are scattered over a number of content areas and your errors tend to be made on the more complex and/or harder questions, it is likely that you will do well on the exam *if* you understand the item rationales upon reviewing them. If your wrong answers are clustered in a major content area, you should revise your study plan to be sure you develop the foundational knowledge of this area before you take your exam. Similarly, if most of your wrong answers indicate the persistence of a test-taking personality that is not effective for exam success (e.g., changing your answers without a good reason, reading into the question), you should practice the behavioral management strategies identified in Table 2-4 of this text before taking your exam. As previously noted, if the analysis of your exam performance identifies difficulty with a specific area of reasoning, review the self-assessment questions and the exam preparation guidelines provided in Table 2-5 in Chapter 2.

We believe that engaging in this extensive (and at times challenging) preparation based on your simulated exam performance is far better than being underprepared for the high-stakes COTA® exam. Students consistently report that the time they spend taking the TherapyEd exams, reviewing the answer rationales, and revising their study plans is well worth the effort *when they successfully pass the COTA® exam on their first attempt.*

Content Categories

C1 Human Development and Aging
C2 The Process of Occupational Therapy
C3 Musculoskeletal System Disorders and Biomechanical Approaches
C4 Neurological System and Cognitive-Perceptual Disorders and Neurological and Cognitive-Perceptual Approaches
C5 Cardiopulmonary, Gastrointestinal, Renal-Genitourinary, Immunological, Endocrine, and Integumentary System Disorders and Evaluation and Intervention Approaches
C6 Psychiatric Disorders and Psychosocial Approaches
C7 Evaluation and Intervention for Performance in Areas of Occupation
C8 Evaluation and Intervention for Environmental Mastery
C9 Professional Standards and Responsibilities

CRITICAL REASONING STRATEGIES

- Inductive Reasoning
- Inferential Reasoning
- Analytical Reasoning
- Deductive Reasoning
- Evaluative Reasoning

Exam A Answer Rationales

A1 C2

An OTA is working with an occupational therapist to develop a discharge planning group for clients being discharged within the next month from a long-term facility for adults with serious mental illness. Which initial action is best for the OTA and therapist to take when implementing this program?

Answer Choices:
A. Obtain prospective group members' occupational profile and post-discharge goals and options.
B. Identify community resources to develop a community re-integration program and enhance post-discharge participation.
C. Develop a self-medication management teaching module to increase post-discharge medication compliance.
D. Complete an evidence-based search to identify best practices in community-based mental health occupational therapy.

Correct Answer: A.

Rationale:
When developing any therapeutic group, it is imperative that the OTA and occupational therapist obtain each prospective group member's occupational profile. Completing these profiles will provide information about group members' occupational history, patterns of daily living, areas of occupation, perceived strengths and limitations, priorities, and expected outcomes. This information will influence the type, focus, structure, and activities of the group that the OTA and therapist will develop. For a discharge planning group, it is important to determine members' post-discharge goals prior to the group. A thorough occupational profile should include the identification of post-discharge goals. Before the OTA and therapist can identify community resources to develop a community re-integration program and enhance post-discharge participation, they would first need to know the group members' status and discharge goals and options. Identifying areas of occupation that the group members are successful with or having trouble with will determine if a self-medication module is necessary or not. While completing an evidence-based search can increase the OT practitioner's knowledge about best practices in community-based mental health occupational therapy, this option does not address the item's focus on developing a discharge planning group.

Type of Reasoning: Inductive
For this exam item, the test taker must determine how best to initiate a discharge planning group for adults with serious mental illness. This requires inductive reasoning skill, in which clinical knowledge is applied to therapeutic situations. In this situation, the OTA and therapist should obtain prospective group members' occupational profile and post-discharge goals and options. If answered incorrectly, review group development guidelines and standards for discharge planning. The integration of this knowledge is required to determine a correct answer. See Chapter 3.

A2 C4

An adult incurred a traumatic brain injury (TBI), which resulted in sensory and perceptual deficits that make the completion of basic activities of daily living difficult. During an intervention session focused on dressing, which will the OTA most likely observe the person have difficulty with when donning shoes?

Answer Choices:
A. Grasping and manipulating the shoelaces.
B. Sequencing the steps of tying the shoelaces.
C. Discriminating between the right and left shoe.

Correct Answer: C.

Rationale:
The sense of vision and visual perceptual skills are required to see and discriminate between the right and left shoes. A person with deficits in these areas would have difficulty with this task. According to the Practice Framework, grasping and manipulating the laces involves motor performance skills and the sequencing of steps involves mental body functions.

Type of Reasoning: Inferential
This exam item requires one to determine what is most likely to be true, given the client's deficits. This requires inferential reasoning skill. In this situation, the client is having difficulty with sensory-perceptual skills; therefore, discriminating between the right and left shoe is most likely to be difficult. If answered incorrectly, review the Practice Framework.

A3 C6

A middle school student with moderate intellectual disability does not eat lunch during the school's lunch hour. Instead the student spends the lunch period socializing with peers. A 1:1 aide is not assigned to the student. Which is the first intervention the school-based OTA should use to promote the activity of eating lunch?

Answer Choices:
A. Schedule the student's lunch to be in the classroom to limit distractions.
B. Provide positive feedback for attending to eating at 10-minute intervals.
C. Practice role playing lunch conversations in the classroom.
D. Have the student share a lunchroom table with one peer.

Correct Answer: D.

Rationale:
Persons with moderate intellectual disabilities can be distractible and have limited attention spans. Having the student share a lunchroom table with one peer will allow for socialization without too many distractors. Scheduling the student's lunch to be in the classroom can limit distractions, but this will isolate the student from peers. In addition, this action would require a staff member to be present, which would likely not be feasible. In school settings, specific staff members are typically assigned to monitor the lunchroom and/or playgrounds during students' lunchtime. These primary staff responsibilities would preclude the availability of a staff member to provide supervision in the classroom or feedback at 10-minute intervals during the student's lunch. Role-modeling is an effective learning strategy in which the participant can watch, imitate, and then practice a skill. This process can increase understanding of role expectations through active participation and feedback, rather than by verbal explanation. However, in this scenario the student has a moderate intellectual disability (ID). With moderate ID, intervention is typically focused on the individual acquiring independence in routine daily tasks and skills necessary to perform in desired occupational roles with support and structure. Therefore, working with the student in the lunchroom environment is best.

Type of Reasoning: Inductive
This exam item requires knowledge of intervention approaches for persons with intellectual disabilities in order to arrive at a correct conclusion. Specifically, the test taker must determine what would be the first appropriate intervention for the student, which is an inductive reasoning skill. In this case, the OTA have the student share a lunchroom table with one peer to encourage eating lunch while enabling socialization in an environment with limited distractions. If answered incorrectly, review intervention approaches for persons with intellectual disabilities. The application of this knowledge is required to determine a correct answer. See Chapter 10.

A4 C9

An OTA leads a community integration group for individuals with mild intellectual disabilities who reside in a group home. During a travel training session, a member of the group slips while going up the stairs of a bus. The client quickly gets up, pays the fare, sits down, and jokingly states, "Good thing I bounce well." Which action should the OTA take after assessing that the person is not injured?

Answer Choices:
A. Cancel the planned activity and return to the group home to file an occurrence report.
B. Ask the bus driver to radio for an ambulance to obtain a medical assessment of the client.
C. Continue with the planned activity and file an occurrence report upon return to the group home.
D. Continue with the activity and ask the client to report the development of any symptoms related to the fall.

Correct Answer: C.

Rationale:
Upon determination that the client has not been injured there is no need to cancel the planned activity. It is standard policy to file a report about any incidents that involve clients, but occurrence reports about minor events do not have to be done immediately. There is no information in the scenario provided to indicate a need to call an ambulance. Asking the client to report any symptoms related to the fall is appropriate, but it is not the most important action for the OTA to take.

Type of Reasoning: Evaluative
This question requires a value judgment in a situation regarding safety, which is an evaluative reasoning skill. In this situation, the most prudent procedure should be followed given the individual's status, which is to continue with the planned activity and file an occurrence report upon return to the group home. If answered incorrectly, review guidelines for reporting occurrences. See Chapter 4.

A5 C3

A restaurant employee incurred a fracture to the left humerus. After cast removal, the patient received occupational therapy and now demonstrates 3/5 strength of the left triceps and full ROM of the left elbow. To increase elbow function in order to perform work-related tasks, which activity is most effective for the OTA to next include during intervention?

Answer Choices:
A. Storing glasses on shelves at chest height.
B. Wiping off a table while standing.
C. Carrying a tray of dishes from the table to the sink.
D. Wiping off a counter at chest height.

Correct Answer: A.

Rationale:
Storing glasses at chest height is a lightly resistive activity of the triceps performed against gravity, which promotes the next level of strength (3+). This is one of the best ways to increase strength in a muscle to attain full elbow ROM. Wiping a table while standing and wiping off a counter at chest height are both isotonic gravity-assisted activities, which are a downgrade in strengthening. Carrying a tray of dishes is a high resistance activity that promotes strengthening of the elbow flexors. The focus of intervention in this exam item is strengthening the weakened triceps muscle to move against gravity.

Type of Reasoning: Inductive
One must utilize clinical knowledge and judgment to determine the functional activity that would provide resistive activity of the triceps. In this case, storing glasses on shelves at chest height is the ideal way to implement a resistive activity for the triceps. If answered incorrectly, review resistive and strengthening exercises. See Chapter 11.

A6 C7

An OTA provides occupational therapy services in an assisted living facility. The OTA meets with a new resident who expresses concern that their poor vision has made it very difficult to complete their favorite activity of embroidering tablecloths and napkins. The OTA determines that the person's low vision is age-related and not due to any pathological disorder. Which adaptation is best for the OTA to recommend to this resident use to enable engagement in these activities?

Answer Choices:
A. Concave lenses.
B. Large print instructions
C. A handheld magnifier.
D. A stand magnifier.

Correct Answer: A.

Rationale:
A magnifier can enlarge the patterns for the embroidered work and the needle and thread used to complete this work. A stand magnifier is preferable because it enables the resident's hands to be free to hold the fabric and the needle and thread. A hand-held magnifier will require the person to embroider one handed. This can be accomplished with a standing hoop. However, since a stand magnifier can effectively address the resident's concerns, there is no need to introduce another piece of equipment. The stand magnifier can also be used to enlarge directions as needed. Thus, large print instructions are not necessary. Concave lenses make objects appear smaller; convex lenses make objects appear larger.

Type of Reasoning: Inductive
One must utilize clinical knowledge and judgment to determine the recommendation that best addresses the resident's concern. This requires inductive reasoning skill. In this case, the OTA should recommend the resident use a stand magnifier enlarge their embroidery work. If answered incorrectly, review low vision interventions. See Chapter 15.

A7 C7

An individual is recovering from lumbar surgery. The patient must remain flat in bed during the initial recovery stages. The patient expresses an interest in reading from a personal collection of classic comics. Which adaptation is best for the OTA to recommend the client use for reading?

Answer Choices:
A. A page magnifier.
B. Prism glasses.
C. Audiotapes of books of interest.
D. Large print books of interest.

Correct Answer: B.

Rationale:
Prism glasses are eyeglasses that bend light by 90 degrees. This angle enables a person who is lying on their back to read anything that is resting on their lap. This recommendation enables the individual to read their collection of classic comics independently, as the client wanted. The use of audiotaped books does not meet the client's expressed interest in reading their comic collection. Large print books and a page magnifier do not address the issue that the client must remain flat on their back.

Type of Reasoning: Inductive
Clinical knowledge and judgment are the most important skills needed for answering this question, which requires inductive reasoning skill. Knowledge of the diagnosis and most appropriate equipment to address the patient's limitations are essential to arriving at a correct conclusion. In this case, the most appropriate recommendation is prism glasses, as it is the only device that addresses the individual's needs while maintaining the lumbar restrictions. If answered incorrectly, review information on the use of prism glasses and other adaptive equipment. See Chapter 14.

A8 C9

A school-based OTA is providing per diem coverage for an OTA on a disability leave. Upon reviewing the caseload, the OTA notes that ten students have had evaluations completed during the past month. Five of these students' individualized education plans (IEPs) have also been completed by the team and approved by their parents. Which is the best initial action for the OTA to take as a contract practitioner?

Answer Choices:
A. Consult with the occupational therapist, team, and students' parents to complete the IEPs for the remaining students.
B. Conduct independent evaluations of each student with the supervision of the school's occupational therapist.
C. Implement the IEPs that have been established and approved with the supervision of the school's occupational therapist.
D. Report to the supervisor of the contract agency that the school has failed to comply with IEP guidelines.

Correct Answer: A.

Rationale:
The Individuals with Disabilities Act (IDEA) mandates that an IEP be written within 30 days of evaluation. This must be done as a team effort with the professionals providing their recommendations to the team and the students' parents. Parental consent is an essential part of the IEP process and is required by IDEA. There is nothing in the scenario to indicate a need for an additional evaluation or the reporting of the school. While it is important to implement the IEPs, the first priority is to ensure that all students have an IEP within 30 days of evaluation. In addition, many aspects of the IEP can be implemented by teachers and other school personnel (e.g., resource room aides, behavioral specialists, speech-language pathologists).

Type of Reasoning: Inferential
One must infer or draw conclusions about a likely course of action, given the information presented. This is an inferential reasoning skill, where knowledge of IDEA guidelines is essential to choosing a correct solution. In this case, the OTA should consult with the occupational therapist, team, and students' parents to complete the remaining IEPs. If answered incorrectly, review IDEA guidelines for completion of IEPs. See Chapter 4.

A9 C4

An individual with a C3 spinal cord injury is participating in a community mobility group at a shopping mall. The client expresses the desire to return to the rehabilitation center due to a pounding headache. The OTA notices the client is sweating profusely. Which should the OTA do first in response to this observation and request?

Answer Choices:
A. Escort the client to outside of the mall to cool off in the fresh air.
B. Check the client's urinary catheter and collecting bag.
C. Call the rehabilitation center's transportation department to relay the client's request.
D. Immediately activate the recline feature of the patient's tilt-in-space wheelchair.

Correct Answer: B.

Rationale:
Profuse sweating and headaches are signs of autonomic dysreflexia. This is an extreme rise in blood pressure caused by a noxious stimulus, which must be treated immediately by removing the stimulus. A blocked catheter and overfilled urine bag are common precipitants to this complication and could result in a medical emergency in persons with a spinal cord injury. Other common stimuli include sitting on sharp objects, a tight abdominal binder, pressure stockings that have rolled down, or excess pressure on the buttocks. The person should remain in an upright position to help manage the rise in blood pressure.

Type of Reasoning: Evaluative
One must weigh the possible courses of action and then make a value judgment about the best course to take. This requires evaluative reasoning skill, where an understanding of what the symptoms indicate is pivotal to arriving at a correct conclusion. For this case, the symptoms indicate autonomic dysreflexia and the OTA's first action should be to check the urinary catheter and collecting bag. If answered incorrectly, review symptoms of autonomic dysreflexia and effective intervention approaches. See Chapter 7.

A10 C8

An older adult with chronic obstructive pulmonary disease and osteoarthritis is preparing for discharge from a subacute rehabilitation center. During a family training session on how to complete car transfers, a family member expresses concern about the person's ability to continue driving. The family member explains that the patient has been experiencing episodes of forgetfulness and trouble with focusing on a task. Which action is the best for the OTA to take to address the family member's concern?

Answer Choices:
A. Document and report the family member's concern to the supervising therapist.
B. Inform the family member that the episodes are likely due to typical age-related changes.
C. Administer the Standardized Mini-Mental State Exam to determine cognition status.
D. Provide intervention to optimize the client factors necessary for driving.

498   Exam A Answer Rationales

Correct Answer: A.

Rationale:
The OTA is responsible to report any changes in patient status to the supervising occupational therapist. These changes should also be documented in the person's medical record. Driver rehabilitation is an advanced practice area that requires both a clinical and on-road evaluation and intervention. While the concerns expressed by the family members may be reflective of typical age-related changes, further evaluation would be required to determine if this was accurate in this case. The OTA can contribute to evaluation and intervention processes in conjunction with an occupational therapist experienced in driver rehabilitation. An OTA can administer the Standardized Mini-Mental State Exam (SMMSE); however, interpretation of the results must be by an occupational therapist. The SMMSE results can be used as part of a comprehensive driver evaluation, but it does not generate results to address the family's concern about the person's ability to continue driving. After a comprehensive evaluation is completed, the OTA can collaborate with the occupational therapist to develop an intervention plan to improve the client factors required for driving.

Type of Reasoning: Inductive
This exam item requires one to determine a best course of action, based on knowledge of the OTA's role in responding to the expressed concerns of a family member. This requires clinical judgment, which is an inductive reasoning skill. For this scenario, the OTA is responsible to report any changes and concerns to the supervising occupational therapist for follow-up. If answered incorrectly, review the occupational therapy process and the OTA's role in driver rehabilitation. See Chapters 4 and 15.

A11   C1

An elementary school-aged child holds a pencil with a tightly held static tripod grasp and forms letters at an average rate of speed. The child demonstrates the ability to write all class and homework assignments. Which is best for the OTA to recommend this child do to improve their grasp?

Answer Choices:
A. Perform all written work with a larger pencil and jumbo crayons on a horizontal surface.
B. Take a break every 15 minutes while writing to open and close the hand several times.
C. Practice moving coins from the fingertips to the palm and then from the palm to the fingertips.
D. Write all written work on a vertical surface, such as an easel or classroom wall board.

Correct Answer: C.

Rationale:
The incorporation of finger-to-palm translation and palm-to-finger translation are in-hand manipulation skills that address the dynamic use of the fingers. These skills can assist in moving the child from the use of an immature static tripod to the use of a dynamic tripod grip. A larger pencil does not allow for the development of the dynamic movement needed for a more mature grasp. Taking writing breaks to stretch the hand can prevent or relieve cramping that may result from holding the pencil too tight, but they will not improve the dynamics of grasp. With a static tripod grasp, the child uses wrist, elbow, and shoulder movement in place of finger movement. Writing on a vertical surface encourages the use of elbow and shoulder movements instead of dynamic finger movement; this reinforces the static tripod position.

Type of Reasoning: Inductive
For this question, the test taker must utilize clinical judgment to determine a best course of action for a child with impaired grasp. Knowledge of development and expected performance when grasping a pencil is paramount to arriving at a correct conclusion. For this scenario, the OTA should recommend practice moving coins from the fingertips to the palm and then palm to fingertips. If answered incorrectly, review the development of in-hand manipulation skills. See Chapter 5.

A12 C5

An adult is hospitalized and diagnosed with mild chronic obstructive pulmonary disease (COPD). During the discharge planning session, the person identifies a desire to exercise regularly. Which of the following should the OTA recommend the client pursue?

Answer Choices:
A. The hospital wellness program's yoga group.
B. Low-impact aerobics at a local gym.
C. Weight lifting under the direction of a personal trainer.
D. Jogging with friends in a local park.

Correct Answer: A.

Rationale:
The yoga group puts the least amount of pressure on the pulmonary and cardiovascular systems. Also, the identified program is monitored by hospital personnel. All of the other activities can stress the cardiovascular and pulmonary systems too much. Also, they are not monitored by health care professionals familiar with COPD.

Type of Reasoning: Inferential
One must consider the diagnosis and needs of the client in order to choose the best exercise program for the patient. For patients with COPD, a monitored exercise program with the least amount of pressure on the pulmonary and cardiovascular systems is best. Questions that ask for a best course of action or what will best consider a patient's needs often necessitate inferential reasoning skill. If answered incorrectly, review information on exercise guidelines for patients with COPD. See Chapter 8.

A13 C3

A client is being discharged after recovery from hip replacement surgery to live at home alone. Which is the most important equipment for the OTA to review with the client prior to discharge to enable safe occupational performance in the home?

Answer Choices:
A. A rolling walker.
B. A long-handled reacher.
C. A bedside commode.
D. An emergency call system.

Correct Answer: B.

Rationale:
The client will need to observe hip precautions for several weeks. These precautions include not flexing the hip beyond 90 degrees, which can make retrieving items very difficult. A long-handled reacher can facilitate safety and independence in numerous tasks throughout the home. A rolling walker, bedside commode, and emergency call system can be helpful to many individuals with a variety of diagnoses. However, they are not necessary for an individual recovering from hip replacement surgery with no secondary diagnosis; therefore, they are not indicated in this case.

Type of Reasoning: Inferential
One must have knowledge of hip replacement and functional activities in the home setting in order to choose the most important equipment to recommend. This is an inferential reasoning skill where knowledge of the diagnosis coupled with the benefits of each of the described equipment is pivotal to choosing the correct solution. If answered incorrectly, review the benefits of a long-handled reacher and other adaptive aids for clients with post-hip replacement precautions. See Chapters 6 and 14.

A14 C2

An OTA provides occupational therapy services in a program for survivors of domestic violence. The OTA uses a client-centered approach. Which should the OTA do during intervention sessions?

Answer Choices:
A. Offer specific suggestions for more effectively dealing with confrontations.
B. Respond to self-deprecating comments with positive feedback on personal characteristics.
C. Reinforce only the consumers' neutral comments about themselves and their skills.
D. Paraphrase the consumers' statements to help clarify expressed feelings and plans.

Correct Answer: D.

Rationale:
The focus of client-centered therapy is to be directed by the consumer. A goal is to encourage self-awareness of feelings and the exploration of possible desired options for future actions. Offering specific suggestions and behavioral reinforcement are not consistent with client-centered therapy. The OTA should use techniques to encourage the consumers to generate their own ideas. In the client-centered approach, the OTA should withhold judgment on self-deprecating comments and accept the consumer unconditionally.

Type of Reasoning: Inferential
This question requires one to determine a best course of action based on the information provided, which is an inferential reasoning skill. For this situation, paraphrasing the consumers' statements to help clarify feelings and plans is best. If answered incorrectly, review information on the client-centered practice and occupational therapy for survivors of domestic violence. See Chapters 3 and 13.

A15 C7

A 19-year-old with spastic diplegia and an IQ in the range of 55–69 is graduating from a special education program. The student has been involved in transitional programming since the age of 14. The OTA collaborates with the occupational therapist and the student to complete a discharge plan to meet the student's post-secondary goals. Which of the following should the OTA recommend be included as a post-discharge referral?

Answer Choices:
A. A vocational rehabilitation workshop.
B. State vocational rehabilitation services.
C. A community college.
D. A transitional employment program.

Correct Answer: B.

Rationale:
The purpose of state vocational rehabilitation services is to provide 'one-stop' access to a multitude of vocational and educational evaluation and training programs. Since this student has been involved with transitional programming at school, a full assessment of vocational potentials and interests is warranted. Based upon this evaluation, the state vocational rehabilitation counselor can work with the individual to determine the best course of action to attain desired vocational goals. The student's IQ of 55–69 is reflective of mild intellectual disability (formerly termed mental retardation); therefore, the student's functional level is higher than the functional level appropriate for a vocational rehabilitation workshop (formerly called sheltered workshop). A transitional employment program and/or community college classes may be appropriate for the student, but a complete evaluation is needed to determine the desired intervention program. In addition, since the student has been involved in transitional services since age 14, they may have the skills necessary for competitive employment with or without reasonable accommodations or additional training.

Type of Reasoning: Inferential
One must determine the benefits of the possible referral choices, given the student's age, current status, and needs. This requires inferential reasoning, where one must draw conclusions based on the information provided. In this situation, the best recommendation is to refer the student to the state vocational rehabilitation service. If answered incorrectly, review guidelines for transition planning for students with disabilities and vocational/educational programming options across the continuum of care. The integration of this knowledge is required to determine a correct answer. See Chapters 4 and 14.

A16 C6

An OTA working on an acute psychiatric inpatient unit conducts a series of groups for clients newly admitted to the unit. Which group leadership style is most effective for the OTA to assume when leading these groups?

Answer Choices:
A. Advisory.
B. Facilitative.
C. Laissez faire.
D. Directive.

Correct Answer: D.

Rationale:
Directive leadership involves the provision of structure, clear directions, and immediate and consistent feedback. These qualities are needed in a group whose members are acutely ill with psychiatric disorders. The other choices do not provide the structure or organization needed for individuals whose symptoms often include decreased attention span, distractibility, poor social skills, and/or thought disorders.

Type of Reasoning: Inductive
Clinical knowledge and judgment are the most important skills needed for answering this question, which requires inductive reasoning skill. Knowledge of the leadership styles and the most effective style in leading groups of newly admitted clients is essential to arriving at a correct conclusion. If answered incorrectly, review directive leadership. See Chapters 3 and 13.

A17 C4

An OTA works with an 8-year-old with pervasive developmental disabilities in order to improve self-care skills. In teaching the child to brush teeth, the OTA places the toothbrush in the child's hand and guides it to the mouth. To help the child learn to complete the activity the OTA uses the somatosensory system. Which of the following is most effective for the OTA to use next during intervention with this child?

Answer Choices:
A. Tell the child to brush up and down and provide verbal prompts.
B. Provide hand-over-hand assistance to brush the child's teeth.
C. Touch the child's hand to prompt hand-to-mouth movements.
D. Instruct the child to follow a pictorial sequence card depicting toothbrushing.

Correct Answer: B.

Rationale:
In providing hand-over-hand assistance, the OTA is using tactile, proprioceptive, and movement stimuli to cue the child. The somatosensory system is inclusive of these sensory systems. Providing auditory, tactile, or visual input does not provide sufficient input for the child to learn the task.

Type of Reasoning: Inferential
One must have knowledge of somatosensory interventions for children in order to choose the best intervention approach. This is an inferential reasoning skill where one must infer or draw conclusions about a best course of action. For this case, the OTA should next provide hand-over-hand assistance to brush the child's teeth. If answered incorrectly, review sensory system terminology and interventions using a somatosensory approach. See Chapters 7 and 12.

A18 C7

An OTA completes a home evaluation for an individual with post-polio syndrome who recently moved into a rent-stabilized studio apartment. When evaluating the accessibility of the client's kitchen, the OTA notes that all appliances are freestanding with no counter space between them. Which action is best for the OTA to take in response to this observation?

Answer Choices:
A. Advise the client to purchase three stationary carts to place next to and between each appliance as a substitute for countertops.
B. Advise the client to purchase a stationary cart and a rolling cart and train the client in their safe use.
C. Refer the client to a carpenter who has expertise in the construction of accessible kitchen countertops.
D. Advise the client to seek a new rent-stabilized apartment with countertops between appliances.

Correct Answer: B.

Rationale:
The kitchen space in studio apartments is typically small. Therefore, it is best for the OTA to recommend a stationary cart and a rolling cart, rather than three stationary carts. When placed and used effectively, the two carts can enable safe meal preparation and ease the completion of other tasks typically performed in a kitchen (e.g., washing dishes). Removing hot items from a stove and oven can pose a safety hazard when there are no adjoining countertops. A stationary cart can be an affordable substitute for built-in countertops. A rolling cart can be used to transport items between the appliances, sink, and table. The client can also use the cart throughout the apartment and the apartment building (e.g., to transport mail and packages). Typically, rent-stabilized apartments are very limited in supply, so it is unlikely that the client would be able to easily obtain a new apartment. Moreover, most apartments require tenants to sign a lease, so moving is likely not feasible. Consequently, it is best to work with the client to make the existing kitchen space user-friendly and safe. While having new countertops installed is ideal, the affordability of this recommendation must be considered. Because people who qualify for rent-stabilization programs have income limits, it is likely that the client would have limited funds to renovate the apartment's kitchen. The need for accessibility recommendations to be affordable is an important reality that must be considered.

Type of Reasoning: Inductive
This exam item requires the test taker to determine a best course of action for an individual with post-polio syndrome, given the home setup. This necessitates clinical judgment, which is an inductive reasoning skill. For this case, the OTA should recommend both a stationary and rolling cart for use in the home. If answered incorrectly, review adaptive strategies for home management tasks for persons with disabilities and environmental modifications for kitchens. See Chapter 14.

A19 C8

An individual with advanced Huntington's chorea is admitted to a skilled nursing facility. The resident weighs 280 pounds and cannot independently transfer. What is the best recommendation for the OTA to make to the resident's direct care staff to ensure a safe transfer?

Answer Choices:
A. A mechanical lift transfer.
B. A two-person lift transfer.
C. A stand pivot transfer.
D. An assisted sliding board transfer.

Correct Answer: A.

Rationale:
A mechanical lift transfer is the safest for both the resident and the staff. The other transfers require motor and cognitive abilities that are beyond the capacity of an individual with advanced Huntington's chorea. Huntington's chorea, an autosomal dominant neuromuscular disease, is characterized by choreiform movements, progressive intellectual deterioration, and psychiatric disturbances. The individual's weight and movement disorder combined with potential confused and/or agitated behaviors requires the use of a mechanical lift for safe and efficient transfers.

Type of Reasoning: Inductive
This question requires one to determine the best recommendation for an individual, given an understanding of the diagnosis and limitations. This requires inductive reasoning skill, where clinical judgment is paramount to arriving at a correct conclusion. For this situation, the OTA should recommend a mechanical lift transfer for the safety of the resident and staff. If answered incorrectly, review guidelines for mechanical lift transfers and the information about the sequelae of Huntington's chorea. The integration of this knowledge is needed to determine the correct answer. See Chapters 7 and 14.

A20 C6

A client with a persistent depressive disorder and their spouse attend a discharge meeting with the OTA following the client's four day hospitalization for a major depressive episode. They express concern they have few shared activity interests and spend little time together. The client retired four months ago. The spouse continues to work full time. Which of the following should the OTA encourage this couple to do first to address this concern?

Answer Choices:
A. Immediately participate in one activity together.
B. Engage in their individual activities of interest during the week.
C. Explore activities they have enjoyed together and alone.
D. Delay planning activities until the depression is totally resolved.

Correct Answer: C.

Rationale:
Assistance with an exploration of activities is a priority given the client's recent hospitalization for depression. The client's life has changed significantly with the loss of the worker role due to retirement and the resultant change in the amount of time spent alone. It will be important for the client to explore activities they have enjoyed alone so that retirement and time separated from their spouse will be enjoyable and meaningful. Exploring activities that the couple has enjoyed together will assist both in the maintenance of their relationship and in the establishment of a new post-retirement activities pattern. Immediate participation in one activity together is premature for there has been no determination of shared interests. Involvement in their own individual activities of interest during the week may be helpful but it does not address their expressed concerns about having few shared interests and spending little time together. A delay in planning activities until the depression is totally resolved ignores the client's expressed concerns.

Type of Reasoning: Inferential
One must infer or draw conclusions about a likely course of action, given the information presented. This is an inferential reasoning skill, where knowledge of a therapeutic approach is essential to choosing a correct solution. In this case, the OTA should begin with exploration of activities that the individual and the spouse have enjoyed together and alone. If answered incorrectly, principles of client-centered practice and intervention approaches for persons with depression. The integration of this knowledge is required to select the correct answer. See Chapters 3, 10, and 13.

A21 C2

The members of a clubhouse attain a level of cohesion that enables them to perform at a cooperative/supportive cooperative level. Two members disagree with the others on the details of a group project. How should the OTA leading this group respond to this conflict?

Answer Choices:
A. Listen to all viewpoints and suggest that members vote to determine the project details.
B. Mediate only when the members have reached a deadlocked situation.
C. Encourage the members to explore alternative methods to resolve the conflict.

Correct Answer: C.

Rationale:
In a cooperative/supportive cooperative group, the OTA acts as an advisor. Group members are mutually responsible for giving feedback and meeting group needs. The OTA's interventions should facilitate group problem solving rather than direct the course of actions or decisions. Waiting until a group is deadlocked would not be beneficial to group cohesion.

Type of Reasoning: Evaluative
One must weigh the merits of the courses of action in order to arrive at a correct conclusion. This requires evaluative reasoning skill, where judgment based on values and principles is paramount to choosing the best solution. In this situation, where two members disagree in a cooperative/supportive cooperative group, the OTA should encourage the members to explore alternative methods to resolve the conflict. If answered incorrectly, review the characteristics of cooperative/supportive cooperative groups and guidelines for group conflict resolution. See Chapter 3.

A22 C3

A client with residual hemiplegia in the dominant extremity due to a prior CVA develops carpal tunnel syndrome in the non-dominant hand. The OTA constructs a splint and provides splint training to the client. Which of the following should the OTA ensure the client can do upon completion of the splint training sessions? Select the three BEST responses.

Answer Choices:
A. Understand the purposes and functions of the splint.
B. Don and doff the splint with no physical assistance.
C. Accurately state the wearing schedule after one verbal prompt.
D. Self-direct the application of pieces of moleskin to areas of the splint that leave red marks.
E. Understand that the splint should be worn at night and when performing repetitive activities.
F. Self-direct the correct application of the splint to ensure bony prominences are considered.

Correct Answers: A, E, and F.

Rationale:
If a client understands the purposes, functions, and wearing guidelines of a splint protocol they will become a collaborative partner in the intervention program. Treatment guidelines for carpal tunnel syndrome (CTS) include the wearing of a wrist splint in neutral at night and during the day when performing repetitive activities. Because the client has residual hemiplegia in the dominant extremity, the client will not be able to don or doff the splint without physical assistance. Therefore, the client will need to be able to self-direct the correct application of the splint to ensure bony prominences are considered. Even a well-constructed splint can cause harm if it is not donned properly. If a splint leaves red marks, it should be reconstructed. The application of pieces of moleskin would increase pressure on the skin; thus, this action is contraindicated. Accurately stating the wearing schedule after one verbal prompt does not ensure compliance with the recommended splint protocol. There is nothing in the scenario to indicate that the person needs verbal prompts.

Type of Reasoning: Inductive
This question requires one to determine the best approach for ensuring the client's compliance with a splinting program in order to arrive at a correct conclusion. This necessitates clinical judgment, which is an inductive reasoning skill. For this situation, the OTA should ensure the client understands the purposes, functions, and wearing guidelines of the splint. Because this client has hemiplegia, it is also important to be sure the client can self-direct the correct application of the splint to ensure bony prominences are considered. If answered incorrectly, review the splinting procedures for CTS and guidelines for improving compliance with splinting programs. See Chapters 6 and 11.

A23 C5

Several patients in a cardiovascular unit are referred to occupational therapy for rehabilitation in areas of occupation. Which diagnosis would be an inclusive criterion for participation in the home management activity group conducted in the department's simulated apartment?

Answer Choices:
A. Hypotension.
B. Unstable angina.
C. Venous thrombosis.
D. Uncontrolled atrial arrhythmia.

Correct Answer: A.

Rationale:
Persons with hypotension can be included in a rehabilitation group that includes instrumental activities of daily living. Engagement in these activities would be contraindicated for patients with the other conditions. Unstable angina is a coronary insufficiency with risk for myocardial infarction or sudden death. The person's pain is difficult to control, and it is present with low-level activity or rest. Venous thrombosis and uncontrolled atrial arrhythmia must be monitored closely, and persons with these diagnoses would be better candidates for occupational therapy services that are provided bedside.

Type of Reasoning: Deductive
This question requires the test taker to recall symptoms of cardiac dysfunction and guidelines for cardiac rehabilitation. Deductive reasoning skills are utilized, as one must recall factual information about indications and contraindications for cardiac rehabilitation programs associated with certain diagnoses. In this situation, only patients with hypotension should be included in a home management group. If answered incorrectly, review cardiac rehabilitation guidelines, especially for patients with the identified conditions. See Chapter 8.

A24 C4

An elementary school student is referred to occupational therapy to develop handwriting skills. The student complains that the dominant hand hurts when writing. The student often tears the paper because of how hard they press. The student's teacher reports that the student is frequently observed playing 'rough' with peers despite being asked to calm down. When implementing the intervention plan developed in collaboration with the occupational therapist, which activity is best for the OTA to use prior to handwriting?

Answer Choices:
A. Walking like an animal.
B. Playing hop-scotch.
C. Jumping rope.
D. Performing somersaults.

Correct Answer: A.

Rationale:
To be able to identify effective therapeutic activities for this student, the OTA must first make a link between the observed and reported behaviors and the body functions contributing to them. This is important when working with children to help explain how their behaviors relate to what sensory input they need. In this question, the OTA must make a link between the observed and reported behaviors of using too much force when writing and being 'rough' around other children to the sense of proprioception to identify relevant therapeutic activities. Proprioception involves receiving input through receptors located in the joints and muscles. Proprioceptive awareness is required in handwriting to stabilize the shoulder for controlled movements of the hand and provide adequate grasp and pencil pressure. Movement and heavy work activate the proprioceptive receptors to improve body awareness and sense of body in space. Activities that require weight bearing through the upper and lower extremities (i.e., walking like a crab, elephant, lion) will activate the proprioceptive system. This can help stabilize the joints and improve body awareness, which is an important precursor to handwriting.

Type of Reasoning: Inductive
This exam item requires the test taker to determine a best course of action based on presenting symptoms. This necessitates inductive reasoning skill, in which clinical knowledge and skills are used to draw conclusions. In this case, it is best for the child to walk like an animal prior to handwriting tasks to activate the proprioceptive system. If answered incorrectly, review the manifestations of proprioceptive processing dysfunction and intervention guidelines for children with sensory-processing deficits. See Chapters 7 and 12.

A25 C8

An OTA is implementing a community mobility group with individuals attending a traumatic brain injury day-treatment program who live in an urban area. Which activity should the OTA plan for the group members to complete during the first group session?

Answer Choices:
A. Reading bus and subway maps.
B. Taking a subway or a bus as a group.
C. Determining a desired destination.
D. Purchasing a public mass transportation fare card.

Correct Answer: C.

Rationale:
The best first group activity is to have the group members determine a desired destination. Once a destination is decided, members can review bus and subway maps to identify the public transportation route(s) that they can take to their desired destination. These maps and specific route directions are available on several websites and phone apps. Purchasing a public mass transportation fare card and taking a subway or a bus as a group would be the next community mobility activities after a route is planned.

Type of Reasoning: Inferential
One must infer or draw conclusions regarding the ideal first step in a functional task. After reviewing all of the possible choices, one must determine that one step must come before all the others in order to have a successful outcome. For this situation, determining a destination must come first in order for the remaining steps to be executed effectively. If answered incorrectly, review principles of activity analysis. See Chapter 3.

A26 C8

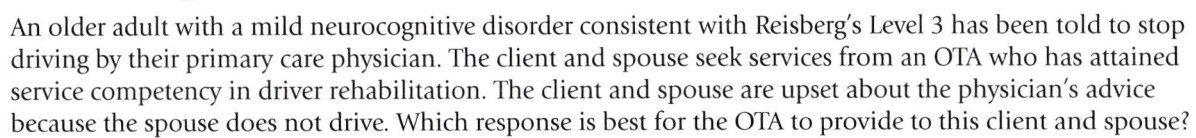

An older adult with a mild neurocognitive disorder consistent with Reisberg's Level 3 has been told to stop driving by their primary care physician. The client and spouse seek services from an OTA who has attained service competency in driver rehabilitation. The client and spouse are upset about the physician's advice because the spouse does not drive. Which response is best for the OTA to provide to this client and spouse?

Answer Choices:
A. Advise the client and spouse to seek a second opinion from a physician who specializes in neurocognitive disorders.
B. Train the spouse to use a navigation system to provide verbal directional prompts to the client.
C. Schedule the client for a full evaluation of performance skills and client factors.
D. Explore available driving alternatives to maintain community mobility and participation.

Correct Answer: D.

Rationale:
A person with a mild neurocognitive disorder that is consistent with Reisberg's Level 3 will have difficulty completing complex occupational tasks. Their participation in activities requires more concentration and time. Driving is complex and unpredictable and may require a split-second reaction time to ensure safety. Based on these activity demands and the progressive nature of neurocognitive disorders, it is best for the person to learn alternatives to driving while they are capable. At this stage, a person is independent in basic and instrumental activities of daily living, can recognize challenging situations to avoid, and utilize compensation as an adaptive mechanism. Consequently, the OTA can build on these strengths to enable community mobility.

Type of Reasoning: Inductive
This exam item requires one to determine a best course of action for an individual with a mild neurocognitive disorder. One must recall the stages of neurocognitive disorders and then determine how to best proceed with this knowledge. This necessitates clinical judgment, which is an inductive reasoning skill. In this situation, the OTA should help the couple explore driving alternatives to maintain community mobility and participation. If answered incorrectly, review the stages of neurocognitive disorders, their impact on community mobility, and community mobility alternatives to driving. The integration of this knowledge is required to determine a correct answer. See Chapters 10 and 15.

A27 C4

The parents of a 5-year-old with attention deficit with hyperactivity disorder (ADHD) express difficulty managing the child's aggressive behavior toward older siblings. Which is the most effective strategy for the OTA to recommend to the parents?

Answer Choices:
A. Allow the child to vent aggressive feelings on a stuffed animal or doll.
B. Redirect the child's energy into acceptable and safe play activities.
C. Provide consistent punishment for aggressive behaviors.

Correct Answer: B.

Rationale:
Redirecting the child's energy to activities can be an effective management of the child's aggressive behavior. It would also be effective to advise the parents to observe and record the precipitants to these behaviors to determine potential environmental modifications. This is not an option provided. Allowing the child to vent aggression onto a stuffed animal or doll would not provide the structure the child needs to learn appropriate, safe behaviors. Also, aggressive behaviors are not always coupled with aggressive feelings. Sometimes the hyperactivity of a child simply manifests itself in socially unacceptable ways, such as when a child pushes a sibling very hard in an effort to get the sibling to play 'chase.' Punishing the child does not address the child's needs. Taking punitive actions toward the child can increase feelings of resentment and promote a decrease in feelings of self-worth, which are typically already low in children with ADHD. This can fuel aggressive behavior.

Type of Reasoning: Inductive
This question requires one to determine the most effective recommendation for a child with ADHD. This requires inductive reasoning skill, where clinical judgment is paramount to arriving at a correct conclusion. For this situation, the OTA should recommend redirecting the child's energy into acceptable and safe play activities. If answered incorrectly, review treatment guidelines for children with ADHD, especially behavior management techniques. See Chapters 10 and 13.

A28 C6

An employed individual is completing an inpatient program for substance abuse. The OTA consults with the supervising occupational therapist to review the discharge plan. Which would be most beneficial for the OTA and therapist to recommend as part of the individual's discharge plan?

Answer Choices:
A. Assignment to a member of a local Narcotics Anonymous group.
B. Regular attendance at one or more Narcotics Anonymous meetings weekly.
C. Attendance at the psychosocial clubhouse for leisure skills groups.
D. Referral to the state vocational rehabilitation services.

Correct Answer: B.

Rationale:
Narcotics Anonymous (NA) is based on the same 12-step principles as AA (Alcoholics Anonymous) and has been found to be an effective resource for those in recovery. NA and AA provide critical support to maintain abstinence. NA and AA stress that the individual seek out meetings and enlist a sponsor independently. Psychosocial clubhouses provide a diversity of supportive services for persons with mental illnesses. Since the person is employed and has no secondary diagnosis of mental illness, this setting would not be an appropriate referral recommendation. Based on the information provided, one cannot assume that vocational rehabilitation is a potential goal or need for this person.

Type of Reasoning: Inferential
One must consider the information provided and make certain assumptions about that information, including what is most beneficial for the client. Judgment based on facts and assumptions utilizes inferential reasoning skill. In this case, the OTA and therapist should recommend regular attendance at NA meetings. Questions such as these can be challenging, as one may be tempted to assume information not found in the question. Therefore, be careful that conclusions drawn from questions such as these consider only the facts given. If answered incorrectly, review intervention guidelines for persons with substance abuse. See Chapter 10.

A29 C4

An individual with a spinal cord injury at the level of T1 is practicing a stand-pivot transfer in the OT department of a rehabilitation center. The patient complains of dizziness and nausea. Which action is most important for the OTA to take first?

Answer Choices:
A. Call for help according to facility procedures.
B. Return the patient to the wheelchair for a 5-minute rest break.
C. Return the person to the wheelchair and immediately recline it.
D. Return the patient to the wheelchair and transport the patient back to rest in bed.

Correct Answer: C.

Rationale:
Individuals with SCIs are at risk for orthostatic hypotension. Complaints of dizziness and nausea are indications of orthostatic hypotension and require an immediate response. Reclining the individual in their wheelchair will return blood pressure to a normal range. The other choices do not address the need for immediate remediation of this crisis.

Type of Reasoning: Evaluative
This question requires professional judgment based on knowledge of the symptoms of orthostatic hypotension and the needed response, which is an evaluative reasoning skill. Because the patient's symptoms indicate orthostatic hypotension, the OTA should return the person to the wheelchair and immediately recline it to relieve symptoms. If answered incorrectly, review guidelines effectively responding to orthostatic hypotension, especially in SCI. See Chapters 7 and 8.

A30 C8

An adolescent with myelomeningocele (spina bifida) at the C8 level wants to access a new computerized play system. Which is the best adaptation for the OTA to recommend the adolescent use to access this system?

Answer Choices:
A. A chin switch.
B. A tenodesis splint.
C. A dorsal wrist splint with a universal cuff.
D. A joystick control.

Correct Answer: D.

Rationale:
At the level of C8, the teenager can independently use a joystick control. A chin switch would be indicated for a C3/C4 level lesion, a tenodesis splint is indicated for a C6 level lesion, and a dorsal splint with a universal cuff is indicated for a C5 level lesion.

Type of Reasoning: Inductive
This question requires one to determine the best recommendation for a person with spina bifida at a C8 spinal cord level. This requires inductive reasoning skill, where clinical judgment and knowledge of the diagnosis, including functional abilities, are paramount to arriving at a correct conclusion. For this situation, the OTA should recommend a joystick control. If answered incorrectly, review the functional abilities associated with each spinal cord level, especially C8 level. See Chapters 7 and 14.

A31 C4

An OTA works with an individual recovering from a traumatic brain injury in a rehabilitation hospital. The OTA uses a transfer of training approach to help the patient develop and carry out a daily schedule of activities upon the patient's return home. Which is the most effective activity for the OTA to use during an intervention session with this client?

Answer Choices:
A. Preparation of a simple meal.
B. Organization of a list of daily activities.
C. Composition of a shopping list.
D. Completion of an interest checklist.

Correct Answer: B.

Rationale:
A transfer of training approach is a remedial/restorative approach that focuses on restoration of components to increase skill. It is deficit-specific and utilizes tabletop and computer activities as treatment modalities. According to this approach, the activity of organizing a list of daily activities will help with the ability to formulate a schedule in one's home environment. Preparing a meal, composing a shopping list, and completing an interest checklist are each discrete activities that would develop skills related to the performance of these activities, but they do not address the skills needed to schedule the multiple activities of a typical day.

Type of Reasoning: Inductive
This question requires the test taker to determine the most effective activity for a client with traumatic brain injury using a transfer of training approach. This is an inductive reasoning skill, as questions of this nature often ask one to utilize clinical judgment to determine therapeutic courses of action. For this case, the OTA should emphasize organization of a list of daily activities in treatment. If answered incorrectly, review transfer of training approach. See Chapter 12.

A32 C5

During a therapeutic feeding session, a child with spastic quadriplegic cerebral palsy demonstrates a consistent tonic bite reflex. Which technique should the OTA use to help inhibit this reflex?

Answer Choices:
A. Apply slight upward pressure of the index finger under the child's lip.
B. Press a spoon down firmly on the center of the child's tongue.
C. Place foods such soft-cooked vegetables between the gum and teeth.
D. Provide sensory input to the inferior faucial arches using a chilled dental exam mirror.

Correct Answer: B.

Rationale:
The best approach to decrease a tonic bite reflex is to press down firmly on the center of the tongue. The other answer options are techniques used for oral motor dysfunction but they are not effective for decreasing a tonic bite reflex. Applying slight upward pressure of the index finger under the child's lip facilitates lip closure. Placing food between the gum and teeth facilitates chewing. The use of chilled dental exam mirror to provide thermal (cold) stimulation to the inferior faucial arches is a technique for eliciting a swallow reflex.

Type of Reasoning: Deductive
This question requires recall of guidelines for feeding children with a consistent tonic bite reflex, which is factual knowledge. Deductive reasoning skills are utilized whenever one must recall facts to solve clinical problems. In this situation, the OTA can inhibit the tonic bite reflex by pressing down firmly on the center of the tongue. If answered incorrectly, review feeding guidelines for children oral motor control dysfunction. See Chapter 5. Chapters 9 and 12 provide additional information about oral motor dysfunction.

A33 C8

A person blinded in an accident begins an occupational therapy program for persons with vision loss. Before the accident, the person lived independently and worked as an accountant. The occupational therapist and OTA collaborate with the individual to develop an intervention plan. Which activities are best for the therapist and OTA to include in the initial intervention plan? Select the three BEST responses.

Answer Choices:
A. Exploring new vocational interests.
B. Learning alternative computer access skills.
C. Organizing the client's morning personal care routine.
D. Learning home safety and emergency procedures.
E. Adapting cooking activities to accommodate vision loss.
F. Adapting clothing care (e.g., ironing) to accommodate vision loss.

Correct Answers: B, C, and D.

Rationale:
Developing alternative computer access skills, organizing the morning routine, and learning home safety and emergency procedures are the most appropriate foci for the OTA and therapist to include in the initial intervention plan. There is no need to explore new vocational interests. The client's prior job as an accountant could be resumed with vocational training focused on how to accommodate vision loss and the provision of reasonable accommodations for essential work tasks. If the person decides that a change of careers is desired, the exploration of new vocational interests could be the focus of subsequent intervention plans. Learning alternative computer access skills (e.g., the use of voice command software) can help the client continue their social participation via social media and manage home management tasks (e.g., online banking). These new computer access skills can then be generalized to the work tasks when and if the client decides to resume work. Computers can easily be adapted for a person with vision loss and these adaptations would be considered reasonable accommodations for the client's job. Training the client in how to effectively organize a morning routine can help the person independently complete their personal activities of daily living. This can help the person feel confident and serve as a basis for organizing the rest of the person's home and work routine. Learning how to ensure personal safety in the home and how to respond to emergencies without vision is critical for independent living. While meal preparation and clothing care are important IADL, they do not need to be priorities for the initial intervention plan. The development of meal preparation skills would initially focus on non-cooked foods and meals. Typically, one of the most frightening areas for the newly-blinded person is the use of the stove because of the risk of burns and the danger of fire, so developing skills to cook hot meals would be a long-term goal. Similarly, clothing care would begin with the laundering of clothing (e.g., using tactile tags to sort clothing), not ironing. Given the risk of incurring a burn from a hot iron, the person may decide that this task will be eliminated from their clothing care routine.

Type of Reasoning: Deductive
One must infer or draw conclusions about the best initial focus for OT with a person who has experienced recent visual loss. The key to arriving at a correct conclusion is determining which approaches foster confidence and provide a starting point for future community re-entry activity. Developing alternative computer access skills, organizing the morning routine, and learning home safety and emergency procedures are the best initial approaches for achieving this goal. If answered incorrectly, review therapeutic approaches for persons with vision loss. See Chapter 15.

A34 C7

An older adult with peripheral neuropathy resulting from the effects of diabetes expresses concern over the ability to have a satisfying sexual relationship with a partner. What is the most beneficial recommendation for the OTA to make to the client?

Answer Choices:
A. Focus on intact senses and areas of intact sensation.
B. Experiment with different positions during sexual expression activities.
C. Schedule sexual expression activities after rest periods.
D. Advise the client to accept decreased abilities in sexual expression as a normal part of aging.

Correct Answer: A.

Rationale:
Peripheral neuropathy result in sensory loss; therefore, focusing on intact senses and intact areas of sensation can help the client and their partner achieve satisfying methods for sexual expression. Experimenting with different positions during sexual expression activities is an effective recommendation for individuals with neuromuscular or musculoskeletal deficits. Scheduling sexual expression activities after rest periods is effective for persons who experience fatigue that limits activity (e.g., multiple sclerosis). While the effects of aging may decrease some abilities in sexual expression, the desire to engage in sexual expression does not necessarily diminish with age. Sexual desire and interest in pursuing sexual expression activities are deeply personal and highly individualized. Advising an older adult to accept decreased abilities in sexual expression as a normal part of aging reflects an ageist bias. Moreover, in this situation the client has expressed concerns that should be directly addressed by the OTA.

Type of Reasoning: Inductive
This question requires one to determine the best recommendation for a person according to the current deficits and diagnosis. This requires inductive reasoning skill, where clinical judgment is paramount to arriving at a correct conclusion. For this situation, the OTA should recommend focusing on intact senses and areas of intact sensation. If answered incorrectly, review sexual expression guidelines for individuals with disabilities. See Chapter 14.

A35 C6

A person is recovering from a major cardiac infarct. During the initial OT session, the patient loudly and vigorously expresses plans to immediately resume a daily rigorous exercise routine. The OTA reports the individual's plan to the occupational therapist. The OTA explains that the individual appears to be in which stage of adjustment to disability?

Answer Choices:
A. Shock.
B. Denial.
C. Acting out.
D. Acceptance.

Correct Answer: B.

Rationale:
During the psychosocial adjustment to disability/illness, denial is characterized by unrealistic expectations of recovery and minimizing one's difficulties. Shock is characterized by emotional numbness, depersonalization, and reduced speech and mobility. Acceptance is reflected in the acknowledgement of the situation and the development of a new self-concept reflective of one's assets and potentialities. Acting out is a term used to describe behavior that challenges societal norms.

Type of Reasoning: Analytical
This question provides a description of a behavior, and the test taker must draw conclusions about what the behavior indicates. This is an analytical reasoning skill, as questions of this nature often ask one to analyze descriptors and symptoms in order to determine a diagnosis or draw a conclusion. In this situation the behavior indicates denial. If answered incorrectly, review the stages of adjustment to disability. See Chapter 13.

A36 C1

An OTA provides home-based services to a child with developmental delays. The child picks up and puts away toys when reminded by the parents and mimics the parents when they dry dishes and fold clothes. The family has identified a goal of including the child in home management activities. Which activity should the OTA introduce next during intervention?

Answer Choices:
A. Wiping tabletops.
B. Sorting laundry.
C. Making a bed.
D. Taking out trash.

Correct Answer: A.

Rationale:
Picking up and putting away toys when reminded and copying the parents when they do domestic chores are home management task skills that are typical of 2-year-old children. When working with a child with a developmental delay, the OTA would use a developmental frame of reference. According to the typical developmental sequence of home management tasks, wiping spills is an ability of 3-year-old children. Therefore, the next activity the OTA should work on with the child is wiping tabletops since this is consistent with typical development. The other options are too high a level at this point for this child. Sorting laundry is a 4-year-old skill; making a bed and taking out trash are 5-year-old skills.

Type of Reasoning: Deductive
One must recall the developmental sequence of home management tasks and the developmental frame of reference in order to arrive at a correct conclusion. This is factual recall of information, which necessitates deductive reasoning skill. For this situation, the OTA should introduce wiping tabletops as the next developmental activity. If answered incorrectly, review the developmental sequence of home management tasks and the developmental frame of reference. The integration of this knowledge is pivotal to answering the question correctly. See Chapter 5.

A37 C4

An OTA works with an individual recovering from traumatic brain injury who demonstrates behaviors consistent with Level VII of the Rancho Level of Cognitive Functioning Scale. The client is a resident in a transitional living program. Which is the most important focus for the OTA to include in the client's intervention plan?

Answer Choices:
A. The provision of a high degree of environmental structure to decrease confusion and ensure safety.
B. The development of strategies to accurately and safely complete IADL with minimal assistance.
C. The development of adaptive techniques to accurately and safely complete BADL with moderate assistance.
D. The provision of maximum assistance to accurately and safely complete IADL.

Correct Answer: B.

Rationale:
A person at Level VII of the Rancho Level of Cognitive Functioning Scale is able to appropriately complete highly familiar tasks such as BADL with minimal assistance. At this level, the person can learn to use strategies to accurately and safely complete IADL with minimal assistance.

Type of Reasoning: Inductive
While this question does require one to recall the Rancho Level of Cognitive Functioning Scale and the guidelines for treatment provided within these levels, one must utilize inductive reasoning skill to determine the most important focus for intervention within the individual's current abilities and limitations. This necessitates clinical judgment, which is an inductive reasoning skill. For this case, the OTA should focus on the development of strategies to accurately and safely complete IADL with minimal assistance. Review the Rancho Level of Cognitive Functioning Scale if answered incorrectly. See Chapter 7.

A38 C8

The transition plan for an 18-year-old with developmental delay includes employment in a vocational rehabilitation workshop job setting. The student has set a goal to live independent of family. Which is the best living environment for the OTA to recommend for this student?

Answer Choices:
A. An apartment in a subsidized housing project.
B. A group home with case managers available on-call.
C. A supported apartment with a roommate.
D. A group home with daily on-site supervision.

Correct Answer: D.

Rationale:
A person with developmental disabilities who meets the employment criteria for a vocational rehabilitation (formerly called sheltered) workshop will typically have cognitive deficits that require structure and supervision to successfully and safely complete tasks. A group home with on-site staff would provide this type of support. In addition, since this student has lived with family for all of their life, they may need training to develop instrumental activities of daily living (IADL) skills. Upon the attainment of IADL skills in the group home and vocational skills in the vocational rehabilitation (sheltered) workshop, the person may be able to progress to a higher level of independence in work and home management. The person would have to first develop IADL skills to live more independently in a housing project apartment, unsupervised group home, or supported apartment.

Type of Reasoning: Inductive
This question requires clinical judgment in order to determine the best living environment for an individual with developmental delay. This requires inductive reasoning skill, where knowledge of the diagnosis and ability to live independently are paramount to arriving at a correct conclusion. For this situation, the OTA should recommend a group home with daily on-site supervision. If answered incorrectly, review community living options for individuals with developmental disabilities. See Chapters 4 and 10.

A39 C4

An OTA conducts an intervention session with a client recovering from a CVA to develop transfer skills. The client has a comorbidity of epilepsy with primary generalized seizures. As the client stands to complete a transfer from the wheelchair to the bed, the client reports feeling sensations that are indicative of an aura. Which is the best immediate action for the OTA to take in response to this situation?

Answer Choices:
A. Provide reassurance and ask for guidance from the occupational therapist.
B. Return the client to a seated position in the wheelchair until the sensations pass.
C. End the session so the client can rest and inform the occupational therapist.
D. Guide the person into a side-lying position on the bed.

Correct Answer: D.

Rationale:
An aura is the brief warning stage before the tonic phase of an epileptic seizure. During an aura, changes in tactile, gustatory, olfactory, or other sensations are experienced (e.g., numbness, unexplained smells). After this brief stage, a tonic-clonic seizure will occur. The tonic phase includes a loss of consciousness, stiffening of the body, heavy and irregular breathing, drooling, skin pallor, and occasional bladder and bowel incontinence for a few seconds before the clonic phase begins. The clonic phase includes alternating rigidity and relaxation of muscles. Since a person could fall and harm themselves during a seizure, the OTA must immediately ensure the client's safety. Therefore, the best action for the OTA to take is to place the person in a side-lying position on the bed. If there are bed rails these should be raised. This will prevent the client from falling. The OTA should place pillows between the rails and the client's body so that the rails do not cause harm. Providing reassurance, having the client remain seated, and ending the session does not effectively deal with the immediate need to provide intervention for the impending seizure. The OTA does not need (nor should wait for) the input of the occupational therapist.

Type of Reasoning: Evaluative
This question requires the test taker to weigh the merits of the four courses of action presented and then determine the action that most effectively addresses the needs of the client. This requires evaluative reasoning skills. For this situation, the OTA should guide the person into a side-lying position on the bed. If answered incorrectly, review first aid guidelines for clients with seizure disorders. See Chapter 7.

A40 C2

An OTA administers a standardized cognitive-perceptual assessment to a client. The client demonstrates difficulty performing the first two tasks included in this assessment tool. Which is the next best action for the OTA to take?

Answer Choices:
A. Continue the assessment and provide additional verbal cues during task performance.
B. Continue the assessment and demonstrate each task for the client.
C. Continue the assessment according to the established administration protocol.
D. Discontinue the assessment to avoid frustrating the client.

Correct Answer: C.

Rationale:
A standardized assessment must be administered according to its established protocol to be reliable. Providing additional cues or demonstration would compromise the reliability of the assessment tool. Discontinuing the assessment would not enable the OTA to obtain needed information about the person's cognitive-perceptual status. Since most cognitive-perceptual assessments measure several skills, one cannot assume that poor performance on the first two tasks will mean poor performance on the other tasks. OTAs are able to administer standardized assessments with the supervision of the occupational therapist. For specialized evaluations, the OTA must establish service competence. The occupational therapist is responsible for the interpretation of the evaluation.

Type of Reasoning: Deductive
This question requires recall of guidelines, which is factual knowledge. Deductive reasoning skills are utilized whenever one must rely on facts to solve problems. In this situation, because the OTA is administering a standardized assessment, the established protocol must be followed. If answered incorrectly, review guidelines for administering standardized assessments. See Chapter 3.

A41 C4

A young adult incurred a left CVA, which has resulted in left visual field neglect. The occupational therapist and the OTA collaborate to develop an intervention plan based on the dynamic interaction approach. Which interventions are best for the OTA to use when working with this person to address this deficit? Select the three BEST responses.

Answer Choices:
A. Grade a series of scanning tasks that decrease in similarity to foster the transfer of learning.
B. Ask the client to describe anticipated difficulties in finding items in a closet and a strategy to use to find items.
C. Teach the person how to use a daily planner to keep track of activities that need to be completed each day.
D. Train the person in scanning strategies to locate a desired condiment in the refrigerator to put on a sandwich.
E. Work with the person on integrating both sides of the body during the completion of a morning grooming routine.
F. Provide the person with written instructions to complete instrumental activities of daily living such as laundry.

Correct Answers: A, B, and D.

Rationale:
Transfer of learning is facilitated in the dynamic interaction approach by providing a series of graded tasks that decrease in similarity (e.g., training in scanning strategies for a person to find items in a refrigerator to a less similar task such as scanning to cross the street). Asking the client to describe anticipated difficulties in finding items in a closet and a strategy to use to find items in a refrigerator are actions which uses awareness questioning. Awareness questioning is used in the dynamic interaction approach to help the individual estimate task difficulty, predict outcomes, and strategize for task success. Training a person in scanning strategies to locate items is an intervention technique for visual neglect used in the dynamic interaction approach. It is best to begin intervention by having the person locate one item in the refrigerator that is purposefully placed to the person's left. As training progresses, the complexity of the task demands can increase (e.g., locating all items to make a hot meal). A compensatory technique for visual neglect is the use of anchoring techniques (e.g., a strip of red tape of placed on the left side of the sink to draw attention to the left hemi-field). The use of external cues such as written directions and a daily planner is an intervention approach used with persons with sequencing and organizational deficits. Working with the person to integrate both sides of the body during the performance of grooming tasks would be an effective intervention for a body scheme disorder. Body scheme disorders result in a loss of awareness of body parts and the relationship of the body parts to each other and objects.

Type of Reasoning: Inductive
One must have knowledge of the dynamic interaction approach and effective intervention approaches for CVA in order to arrive at a correct conclusion. This requires clinical judgment, which is an inductive reasoning skill. For this situation, the OTA should grade scanning tasks, use awareness questioning, and train the person in scanning strategies. If answered incorrectly, review the dynamic interaction approach for cognitive disabilities. See Chapter 12.

A42 C7

An individual with obsessive-compulsive personality disorder participates in a vocational program. The client asks the OTA to speak to the supervisor of the transitional employment program (TEP). The client is concerned that compulsive behaviors are interfering with job performance and may result in the loss of a new TEP placement. Which is the OTA's best response to these expressed concerns?

Answer Choices:
A. Instruct the client to speak to the TEP supervisor about the right to receive reasonable accommodations.
B. Schedule a re-evaluation of the client's work behaviors and skills.
C. Assure the client that it is natural to have initial difficulties at a new job.
D. Schedule an appointment with the client and the TEP supervisor.

Correct Answer: D.

Rationale:
Meeting with the individual and the TEP supervisor will enable the OTA to provide support for the client's concerns. The OTA can also facilitate a dialogue about the specific difficulties the client is experiencing from both the employee and employer perspective. This will help the OTA analyze the situation and can provide a basis for making recommendations for accommodations, if needed. Instructing the client to speak directly to the work supervisor ignores the client's request for the OTA's input. In addition, knowing one's rights for reasonable accommodations as provided by the Americans with Disabilities Act (ADA) does not equate to knowing what accommodations will help with work performance. A complete evaluation of the essential functions of the job and the person's skills and abilities must be completed prior to determining the nature of accommodations. Re-evaluating the client's work behaviors and skills does not address the client's stated concerns. In addition, TEP placements are typically made after an extensive evaluation process. This information would be readily available for the OTA to review, if needed. While it is natural to have initial difficulties and concerns when one begins a new job, reassuring the client of this reality does not address the client's request for the OTA's support.

Type of Reasoning: Evaluative
This question requires professional judgment based on guiding principles, which is an evaluative reasoning skill. For this situation, the OTA should schedule an appointment with the supervisor and client in order to analyze the situation and make any needed recommendations. If answered incorrectly, review information about the ADA and transitional employment programs. See Chapter 4 and 14.

A43 C1

A 2-year-old child receives home care early intervention services. The occupational therapy intervention plan includes a goal to develop the child's pincer grasp. Which is the most appropriate activity for the OTA to work on with the child during an intervention session?

Answer Choices:
A. Finger-feeding of O-shaped cereal.
B. Picking up different sized marbles.
C. Drawing with jumbo crayons.
D. Stacking 1-inch cubes.

Correct Answer: A.

Rationale:
Picking up O-shaped cereal to finger-feed will facilitate the use of a pincer grasp. While picking up marbles also uses a pincer grasp, this activity presents a potential choking hazard, as 2-year-olds frequently put items they pick up into their mouths. Drawing with a jumbo crayon uses a gross grasp. Stacking cubes uses a radial digital grasp.

Type of Reasoning: Inductive
Clinical knowledge and judgment are the most important skills needed for answering this question, which requires inductive reasoning skill. Knowledge of the development of pincer grasp and effective strategies to facilitate it are essential to choosing the best solution. In this case, the OTA should recommend finger-feeding O-shaped cereal. If answered incorrectly, review the developmental sequence of grasp and the characteristics of different grasp patterns. See Chapter 5.

A44 C1

An older adult has lost significant functional vision over the last four years and complains of blurred vision and difficulty reading. The person frequently mistakes images directly in front, especially in bright light. When walking across a room, the person is able to locate items in the environment using peripheral vision when items are located to both sides. Based on these findings, which visual deficit should the OTA report the client is most likely exhibiting?

Answer Choices:
A. Glaucoma.
B. Presbyopia.
C. Hemianopsia.
D. Cataracts.

Correct Answer: D.

Rationale:
Cataracts are a clouding of the lens, which results in a gradual loss of vision. Central vision is lost first, then peripheral. There are increased problems with glare and a general darkening of vision with loss of acuity and distortion. Glaucoma produces the reverse symptoms: loss of peripheral vision is first (tunnel vision), then central, progressing to total blindness. Presbyopia is a visual loss in middle and older ages that is characterized by an inability to focus properly and blurred images. Hemianopsia is field defect in both eyes that often occurs following CVA.

Type of Reasoning: Analytical
In this question, symptoms are presented, and one must make a determination of the most likely diagnosis. These types of questions require analysis of the meaning of information presented, which is an analytical reasoning skill. For this situation, the symptoms are indicative of cataracts. If answered incorrectly, refer to information on visual deficits associated with aging. See Chapter 5.

A45 C2

A 3-year-old with recurring headaches and decreased gross and fine motor skills is hospitalized for a diagnostic workup. The occupational therapist completed a screening of the child and determined that the OTA should complete a standardized developmental assessment. Just prior to the scheduled OT evaluation, the parents have been told that the child has brain cancer. The parents are upset when they bring the child to OT. The OTA provides support. Which is the next best action for the OTA to take in response to this situation?

Answer Choices:
A. Cancel the evaluation session and refer the parents to their spiritual advisor or the social worker.
B. Advise the parents to speak to their spiritual advisor or the social worker after the evaluation session.
C. Ask the supervising occupational therapist to participate in the session and spend it addressing the parents' acceptance of the diagnosis.
D. Reschedule the evaluation for later in the day so that the parents can speak with their spiritual advisor or the social worker.

Correct Answer: B.

Rationale:
The best actions are to advise the family to seek a source of help and comfort and proceed with the evaluation session. The OTA can provide this advice in a supportive and empathetic manner and then complete the scheduled assessment. The child needs the occupational therapy evaluation as part of the diagnostic workup. The OTA can respond supportively to the family without direct supervision from the occupational therapist. The provision of counseling is best provided by pastoral care and/or social work practitioners. Canceling or rescheduling the evaluation session is not necessary, and in a busy hospital setting it is unlikely that make-up re-appointments would be readily available. Given the nature of the child's diagnosis, the timely completion of a developmental assessment is essential.

Type of Reasoning: Evaluative
One must weigh the possible courses of action and then make a value judgment about the best course to take. This requires evaluative reasoning skill, which often utilizes guiding principles of action in order to arrive at a correct conclusion. For this case, because the parents are obviously upset, the OTA should refer the family to their spiritual advisor or the social worker and proceed with the session. If answered incorrectly, review the role of team members and guidelines for helping individuals cope with grief. See Chapters 4 and 13.

A46 C1

A child with autism receives home care OT intervention services. The parent identifies a primary goal of developing the child's independent toileting skills. The child is completely dependent, and the parent reports not attempting toilet training for several years. The OTA collaborates with the occupational therapist to establish the first intervention goal for the child. Which behavior should this goal address?

Answer Choices:
A. The child's ability to sit on the toilet with supervision.
B. The child's ability to verbally tell someone of the need to go to the bathroom.
C. The child's ability to nonverbally indicate the need to go to the bathroom.
D. The child's ability to indicate when the diaper is wet or soiled.

Correct Answer: D.

Rationale:
The first toileting skill that must be developed is the child's recognition of being wet or soiled. This typically occurs at 12 months. Subsequent toileting skills such as sitting on the toilet with supervision and indicating the need to go to the bathroom can develop after this initial recognition of being wet or soiled.

Type of Reasoning: Inferential
One must have knowledge of the typical developmental sequence of toileting skills in order to arrive at a correct conclusion. This is an inferential reasoning skill where knowledge of guidelines and judgment based on facts are utilized to reach conclusions. In this situation, the first intervention goal would be to have the child indicate when their diaper is wet or soiled. If answered incorrectly, review the typical developmental sequence of toilet skills. See Chapter 5.

A47 C6

An individual attends a community day treatment program to assist in recovery from major depression. The client has good eye contact and responds verbally to interactions initiated by others. Cognition is intact. Which group level is best for the OTA to recommend this client attend?

Answer Choices:
A. Parallel.
B. Project/associative.
C. Cooperative/supportive cooperative.
D. Mature.

Correct Answer: B.

Rationale:
A project/associative group utilizes short-term activities that require the participation of two or more people. Tasks are shared, and the focus is on interaction rather than task completion. This level is appropriate for someone who is socially responsive to others with intact cognition. A parallel group does not require any interaction for task completion. This group is too low-level for this individual because it would not provide the opportunity to use and build existing social skills. Cooperative/supportive cooperative and mature groups require members to be self-expressive and meet socioemotional roles. These groups are too high-level for the individual at this point.

Type of Reasoning: Inductive
One must utilize clinical knowledge and judgment to determine the group level that most appropriately facilitates interaction with this individual. This requires inductive reasoning skill. In this case, a project/associative group is most appropriate to facilitate sharing and interaction. If answered incorrectly, review types of developmental groups, especially the project level group. See Chapter 3.

A48 C9

An OTA is hired to work in the occupational therapy department of an acute psychiatric unit. The OTA requests an orientation to hospital policies and procedures. Which are the most important policies and procedures for the OTA to learn during the initial orientation session?

Answer Choices:
A. Crisis intervention.
B. Reimbursement.
C. Group program scheduling.

Correct Answer: A.

Rationale:
Crises can occur at any time in any acute facility. All employees must immediately learn the policies and procedures for dealing with crises to ensure the safety of patients and staff. Reimbursement issues and group program scheduling can be reviewed during regular supervisory sessions. These issues are not immediate concerns.

Type of Reasoning: Evaluative
One must weigh the possible courses of action and then make a judgment about which focus is the most immediate need. This requires evaluative reasoning skill, which often requires one to make value judgments. For this case, the OTA should initially learn about the crisis intervention policies and procedures as they are the most critical to know in an acute psychiatric setting. The other policies and procedures are important, but they are not immediate concerns. If answered incorrectly, review information about psychiatric settings and the populations they serve. See Chapters 4 and 13.

A49 C4

An adult who incurred a CVA has difficulty dealing with increasing amounts of stimuli. This is noted in all modalities. The OTA documents these observations. Which cognitive-perceptual dysfunction should the OTA report the client is exhibiting?

Answer Choices:
A. Inability to abstract.
B. Poor organizational skills.
C. Poor semantic memory.
D. Generalized attention deficit.

Correct Answer: D.

Rationale:
Attention requires the ability to focus on a specific stimulus without being distracted by external or internal stimuli. The other options describe deficits with different manifestations. The ability to abstract requires the person to see relationships between concepts, ideas, and events. Organization is the ability to structure thoughts and actions. Semantic memory is the general knowledge shared by groups of people, such as social norms.

Type of Reasoning: Analytical
This question provides a group of symptoms and the test taker must determine the cause. This requires analytical reasoning skill where one must analyze the symptoms in order to correctly determine a diagnosis. In this situation, the symptoms indicate generalized attention deficit. If answered incorrectly, review symptoms of generalized attention deficit disorder. See Chapter 12.

A50 C7

During a clubhouse vocational support group, a client reports difficulty keeping track of the job tasks that need to be completed each day. What is the most effective recommendation for the OTA to make to the client?

Answer Choices:
A. Write down directions for each task that needs to be completed.
B. Keep a daily log of completed tasks.
C. Develop and use a checklist of tasks to be completed each day.
D. Ask the work supervisor to provide verbal cues through the workday.

Correct Answer: C.

Rationale:
Developing a daily 'to do' checklist provides a clear visual cue of what needs to be accomplished. The client can check off each job task as they complete it and immediately see what job tasks must still be accomplished. This can provide the needed organizational structure to complete all job tasks each day. There is nothing in the scenario to indicate that the person does not know how to perform their job tasks; therefore, there is no need for the person to write down directions for each task. Keeping a log of each completed job task will help the person to know what has been accomplished, but it provides no organizational cue regarding what remains to be done. There is nothing in the scenario to indicate that the person cannot independently perform their daily work tasks; therefore, there is no need for the supervisor's cueing.

Type of Reasoning: Inductive

This question requires one to determine the approach for assisting a client in keeping track of job tasks. This requires inductive reasoning skill, where clinical judgment is paramount to arriving at a correct conclusion. For this case, the OTA's most effective recommendation is to develop and use a checklist of tasks to be completed each day. If answered incorrectly, one should review vocational programs and strategies for activity adaptations. See Chapters 4 and 14.

A51 C4

An adolescent with spinal muscle atrophy shows decreased trunk balance and strength during intervention sessions. Upper extremity strength and ROM appear unchanged. When discussing these observations with the occupational therapist, which is the best recommendation for the OTA to make?

Answer Choices:
A. A re-evaluation of the client be completed.
B. The client be referred to an orthotist for a soft spinal support.
C. The client be measured for a power wheelchair.
D. A trunk strengthening program be initiated with the client.

Correct Answer: A.

Rationale:
The most important action to take after noticing a change in the functional status of a person with a progressive condition is to re-evaluate. Based on the results of the evaluation, interventions can be planned. These interventions can include orthotics, powered mobility, and/or a strengthening program; only the results of a re-evaluation can appropriately determine intervention needs. The occupational therapist would perform and/or supervise the re-evaluation.

Type of Reasoning: Inferential
One must determine the recommendation that would best address the adolescent's needs. Re-evaluation of the adolescent's capabilities and limitations is the best approach in order to determine if the decrease in trunk balance and strength will necessitate modifications to the treatment program. If answered incorrectly, review evaluation and treatment planning guidelines for patients with progressive disorders. See Chapters 7 and 12.

A52 C6

During an intervention session, a client complains of dry mouth due to prescribed medications. What is the most effective strategy for an OTA to suggest to the client to manage this side effect?

Answer Choices:
A. Suck on ice.
B. Sip water.
C. Drink iced tea.
D. Suck on hard candies.

Correct Answer: B.

Rationale:
Sipping water is the best choice to relieve dry mouth. Sucking ice and/or hard candies presents a possible choking risk. Hard candies might present a dietary risk for some clients. Iced tea contains caffeine, which can increase dehydration. Caffeinated tea can cause serious, even fatal reactions, when taken with certain medications (e.g., MAO inhibitors).

524 Exam A Answer Rationales

Type of Reasoning: Evaluative
This question requires one to evaluate the merits of the four possible choices and determine which will most effectively remedy the clients' symptoms. This requires evaluative reasoning skills. For this situation, sipping water is the best and the safest remedy for dry mouth. If answered incorrectly, review information on side effects of psychotropic medications. See Chapter 10.

A53 C5

An OTA works with the new foster parent of a 2-year-old child diagnosed with major developmental delays and severe hypotonia. The OTA advises the foster parent to position the head in midline during feeding. Which additional positioning recommendations for feeding are best for this child?

Answer Choices:
A. Sitting with hips and knees at 90 degrees of flexion, neck in neutral.
B. Sitting with hips and knees at 90 degrees of flexion, neck in extension.
C. Semi-reclined with neck in neutral.
D. Semi-reclined with neck in extension.

Correct Answer: C.

Rationale:
This semi-reclined position can be easily maintained with the use of a commercially available child seat, and it allows for correct postural alignment during the feeding activity. The support of positioning equipment is needed due to the child's severe hypotonia, which prevents the child from independently maintaining a sitting position. Although it is possible to design equipment to support a seated position, the child's severe hypotonia would require equipment that is over-restrictive (e.g., a chest restraint). Feeding in a semi-reclined position is the least restrictive and most comfortable option for the child. It is not safe to feed anyone with neck in extension because this can result in choking.

Type of Reasoning: Inductive
One must utilize clinical knowledge and judgment to determine the best position for feeding the child, given knowledge of the diagnosis. In this case, positioning the child semi-reclined with the neck in neutral is the best position for feeding. If answered incorrectly, review positioning guidelines for children with hypotonia and for feeding. The integration of this knowledge is required to answer the question correctly. See Chapters 5 and 7.

A54 C7

An individual admitted to a psychosocial day treatment program has a diagnosis of a major depressive disorder. The client reports having difficulty performing home management tasks and caring for two young children. The occupational therapist determines that the recently hired, entry-level OTA can contribute to the evaluation process. Which assessment is best for the OTA to complete with this client?

Answer Choices:
A. A cognitive evaluation.
B. A mental status exam.
C. An occupational history interview.
D. An activities of daily living evaluation.

Correct Answer: D.

Rationale:
OTAs are trained and qualified to perform ADL assessments during their entry-level education. The ability to complete a cognitive evaluation, mental status exam, and an occupational history interview requires the establishment of the OTA's service competence prior to the assignment of these assessment tasks. The establishment of service competency requires the acquisition of experience and continuing training. The OTA in this scenario has been recently hired and is an entry-level practitioner; therefore, service competency for these additional assessments may not yet have been established.

Type of Reasoning: Deductive
This question requires recall of guidelines and principles, which is factual knowledge. Deductive reasoning skills are utilized whenever one must recall facts to solve clinical problems. In this situation, the OTA can contribute to the evaluation process by performing an ADL evaluation. If answered incorrectly, review supervisory guidelines for OTAs, especially for the evaluation process. See Chapter 4.

A55 C1

An older adult expresses concern about the ability to perform daily tasks. The individual has somatosensory deficits consistent with the normal aging process. The OTA recommends adaptive equipment to assist with task performance. Which adaptive equipment should the OTA recommend the person use during meal preparation and feeding?

Answer Choices:
A. Utensils with narrow, smooth grips.
B. Utensils with wide, textured grips.
C. A rocker knife.

Correct Answer: B.

Rationale:
Wide, textured grips will provide augmented sensory feedback to the individual and will be easier to grip than narrow, smooth handles. Somatosensory changes associated with aging include decreased tactile sensation, decreased proprioception, and increased pain thresholds. A rocker knife would not address these deficits. A rocker knife is suitable for one-handed cutting.

Type of Reasoning: Inferential
One must have knowledge of somatosensory deficits and the aging process in order to arrive at a correct conclusion. This is an inferential reasoning skill where knowledge of deficits and judgment based on facts are utilized to reach conclusions. For this situation, the OTA should recommend utensils with wide, textured grips. If answered incorrectly, review somatosensory deficits in older adults and recommendations for adaptive equipment. The integration of this knowledge is required to determine the correct answer. See Chapters 5 and 14.

A56 C7

An OTA is working with a patient to develop their ability to complete dressing tasks. The patient requires assistance to pull the shirt down over the body and verbal cues to orient the shirt correctly. In documenting the patient's performance, which most accurately represents the patient's performance in upper body dressing?

526   Exam A Answer Rationales

Answer Choices:
A. Modified independence.
B. Stand-by supervision.
C. Minimal assistance.
D. Moderate assistance.

Correct Answer: C.

Rationale:
The documentation of a person's level of functional performance is typically made along a level of assistance continuum, which ranges from total assistance to independent status. According to this scale, a person who needs 25% assistance by one person to complete a physical activity and/or periodic cognitive assistance to perform functional activities safely would be reported as needing minimum assistance. Moderate assistance is the need for 50% assistance by one person to perform physical activities or cognitive assistance to sustain or complete simple, repetitive activities safely. Stand-by assistance is the need for supervision by one person for the individual to perform new activity procedures that were adapted by the practitioner for safe and effective performance. A person requires stand-by assistance when errors and the need for safety precautions are not always anticipated by the person. Modified independence means a person can independently complete a task with modifications, adaptive strategies (e.g., using a buttonhook), and/or increased time. In this case, the patient did require physical assistance and verbal cues, so modified independence is inaccurate.

Type of Reasoning: Deductive
This question requires one to recall factual information about ADL performance in order to arrive at a correct conclusion. Deductive reasoning skills are often utilized when applying scales or guidelines to determine performance levels. In this case, the performance described is that of minimal assistance. Review levels of assistance for ADL tasks if answered incorrectly. See Chapter 14.

A57 C3

An individual is status post carpal tunnel release. When the OTA conducts a sensory test for sharp/dull (pain), the person reports dull as sharp on the palmar surface of the thumb and index finger. All other responses are correct. Which is accurate for the OTA to document about the individual's sensation?

Answer Choices:
A. Impaired for pain along C5 and C6 dermatomes.
B. Hypersensitive along the ulnar nerve distribution of the palmar surface of the hand.
C. Hypersensitive along the median nerve distribution of the thumb and index fingers.
D. Absent for pain along the median nerve distribution.

Correct Answer: C.

Rationale:
The individual is so sensitive that when touched with a dull stimulus they report it as "sharp." Therefore, the sensation is not absent, but rather impaired at the median nerve distribution. Impairment at C5 and C6 would also involve the loss of sensation in the upper arm and forearm. Ulnar nerve distribution involves the ring and little fingers.

Type of Reasoning: Analytical
This question provides symptoms and the test taker must determine the likely cause for them. This is an analytical reasoning skill, as questions of this nature often ask one to analyze a group of symptoms in order to determine a diagnosis. In this situation the symptoms indicate hypersensitivity in the median nerve distribution of the thumb and index finger. If answered incorrectly, review symptoms of median nerve disorders.

A58 C6

An individual with schizophrenia begins a partial hospitalization program after a three-day hospitalization. During the initial interview, the client reports that they still experience hallucinations but that they occur less than they have in the past. Which action should the OTA take when the individual begins to actively hallucinate during an OT project/associative group?

Answer Choices:
A. Redirect the individual's attention back to the project.
B. Provide tactile reassurance to the individual.
C. Verbally reassure the individual that the hallucination is not real.
D. Use humor to divert the individual's attention away from the hallucination.

Correct Answer: A.

Rationale:
The best action to take is to redirect attention back to the project. Additional effective strategies for responding to hallucinations are to reinforce all misinterpretations of environmental noises and events, use a calm tone, avoid sarcasm, avoid arguing about the reality of the hallucinations, and help the client to find a reassuring phrase, word, and/or action to focus on reality. The client may not respond favorably to the tactile reassurance since uninvited touch between non-family members is unacceptable in some cultures and religions. Depending on the nature of the person's hallucinations, touch may also be perceived as threatening. The other choices are ineffective ways to reinforce reality for the client who is hallucinating.

Type of Reasoning: Inductive
One must determine a best course of action through clinical judgment, based on the information provided, which is an inductive reasoning skill. For this situation, the question asks about the best way to help a patient who is actively hallucinating. The best response would be to redirect the individual back to the activity at hand. If answered incorrectly, review information on the management of hallucinations. See Chapter 13.

A59 C3

An OTA conducts a standardized sensory assessment of an individual recovering from a left cerebral vascular accident. The individual has right hemiplegia and expressive aphasia. During the assessment of stereognosis, which should the OTA have the client use to identify responses to the testing stimuli?

Answer Choices:
A. Pictures of the objects.
B. A set of identical objects.
C. Cards with "1" and "2" printed on them.
D. Cards with "yes" and "no" printed on them.

Correct Answer: B.

Rationale:
Stereognosis is the ability to identify objects through touch and cognition. Having an identical set of objects from which the individual can select an object that matches the test stimulus will enable a person with expressive aphasia to participate in the assessment. The person can point to the object to indicate their response. Cards with "one" and "two" printed on them would be relevant assists for the assessment of two-point discrimination. Cards with "yes" and "no" printed on them would be relevant assists for the assessment of light touch. Presenting the person with pictures to indicate a response requires the ability to generalize the object to its symbolic representation. This ability may be compromised in an individual with a CVA. It is more accurate to have exact matches of the objects used during the assessment, for this will not require the interpretation of pictures.

Type of Reasoning: Deductive
This question requires recall of testing guidelines based on factual knowledge. This is a deductive reasoning skill, where recall of facts is essential to arriving at a correct conclusion. In this scenario, the only appropriate method for identifying the response to a stimulus in stereognosis testing is to use a set of identical objects. If answered incorrectly, review guidelines for stereognosis testing and strategies for working with people with expressive aphasia. The integration of this knowledge is required to determine the correct answer. See Chapters 11 and 12.

A60 C7

An adult diagnosed with multiple sclerosis over 10 years ago experiences an exacerbation of symptoms. The individual's principle complaint is decreased strength and endurance. The person can ambulate short distances with a cane in the home and uses a wheelchair outside of the home. The client asks for suggestions to enable independent home maintenance. Which is the best positioning recommendation for the OTA to suggest the person use during meal preparation?

Answer Choices:
A. Sitting in the wheelchair with a tray table.
B. Sitting at the kitchen table.
C. Leaning against the counter while standing.
D. Leaning against a tall stool while standing.

Correct Answer: B.

Rationale:
Multiple sclerosis is characterized by fluctuations in abilities. The best choice for an activity that will be performed frequently is to perform the activity in an adequately supported position. The avoidance of fatigue is important in the management of MS. Doing meal preparation while sitting at the kitchen table achieves these aims and uses the person's natural context. There is no need indicated in this scenario for the use of a wheelchair and a tray; the client can do meal preparation activities with readily available supports. Standing might require using too much energy and does not provide good support or stability for performing the fine motor aspects of meal preparation. Leaning against the counter or a stool requires more energy, does not provide good support or stability for performing the fine motor aspects of meal preparation, and may not be safe.

Type of Reasoning: Inductive
This question requires clinical judgment to determine which position would be optimal for a client with MS given the current status and symptoms presented. For this client, sitting at the kitchen table is best as it provides the appropriate stability and reinforces the natural context during meal preparation. If answered incorrectly, review the symptoms of MS and principles of activity adaptation. The integration of this knowledge is required to determine a correct answer. See Chapters 3 and 7.

A61 C5

A 3-year-old with severe congenital anomalies and irreparable cleft palate has a do not resuscitate (DNR) order. While being fitted for a molded seat for a wheelchair, the child stops breathing and turns blue. The OTA determines that the child has a brachial pulse. Which of the following is the first action the OTA should take in response to this situation?

Answer Choices:
A. Inform the physician about the situation and the child's DNR order.
B. Call the supervising occupational therapist to discuss the best response.
C. Implement the facility's emergency procedure.
D. Perform obstructed airway maneuver and monitor heart rate for 5 minutes.

Correct Answer: C.

Rationale:
The child is not breathing, so the OTA should initiate the facility's plan for medical emergencies and cardiac codes. It is not the decision of the OTA to withhold actions because of the DNR order. The medical team that responds to emergency procedures must make the decision. It would be desirable to inform the physician, but the current situation requires emergency attention. The OTA can call the supervising occupational therapist to advise of the event and discuss the necessary follow-up after dealing with the event, but this is not the first action. Even a minute delay is too long to wait to notify the emergency team.

Type of Reasoning: Evaluative
This question requires one to make a value judgment about a best course of action, given the information presented. This necessitates evaluative reasoning where one must weigh the merits of the possible course of action in order to make a sound decision. For this situation, the OTA should implement the facility's emergency procedure. See Chapter 8.

A62 C8

An individual cannot independently get from a supine position to a sitting position. The client has good scapular, shoulder, and elbow muscle strength. Which of the following should the OTA recommend as the most effective for the client to use to improve bed mobility?

Answer Choices:
A. A leg lifter.
B. A bed rail assist.
C. A log roll technique.
D. A rope ladder.

Correct Answer: D.

Rationale:
A rope ladder or bed loops enable the individual to loop the arm(s) into the first 'rung'/loop, and then into the next 'rung'/loop, and so on until they have achieved a sitting position. The other options do not assist with independently moving from supine to sitting. A leg lifter is used to lift a leg that cannot move independently. A bed rail assist is used to help with rising from sitting to standing. A log roll technique can be used to help a person go from supine to sitting, but this technique requires the assistance of another person. It is indicated for an individual who cannot use the rope ladder technique.

Type of Reasoning: Inductive
This question requires one to determine the most effective device to improve bed mobility in supine to sit. This requires inductive reasoning skill, where clinical judgment is paramount to arriving at a correct conclusion. For this situation, the OTA should recommend a rope ladder to assist with moving to a sitting position. If answered incorrectly, review adaptive devices for bed mobility, especially rope ladders. See Chapter 15.

A63 C6

A 17-year-old student with a diagnosis of bipolar disorder and a history of self-abusive behaviors attends a transitional school-to-work program conducted by an OTA and an occupational therapist. During the vocational skills group, the student expresses feelings of hopelessness about the future and questions the point of participating in the program. The student asks to leave the group due to being too tired to concentrate as a result of sleepless nights. The occupational therapist asks the OTA to address the student's concerns while the therapist works with the other group members. Which action is best for the OTA to take in response to the student's statements?

Answer Choices:
A. Pull the student aside from the group and ask if the student is feeling self-destructive.
B. Allow the student to leave the group after reminding the student to relay concerns to the guidance counselor.
C. Support the validity of the student's feelings and encourage the student to remain in group.
D. Remind the student that in a work setting the norm is to work even if fatigued.

Correct Answer: A.

Rationale:
All statements of hopelessness and a lack of future vision must be taken seriously, as they can indicate a suicide risk. This is especially important in this case since there is a history of self-destructive behavior. Pulling the student aside from the group allows for the maintenance of confidentiality. The student's reports of sleep disturbances, concentration difficulties, and feelings of hopelessness can reflect an increase in depression. If the student is allowed to leave the group, there is a risk that self-destructive behavior (or even suicide) may occur. Validating the student's feelings and reinforcing workplace norms do not deal safely with a potential immediate crisis.

Type of Reasoning: Evaluative
This question requires professional judgment based on guiding principles, which is an evaluative reasoning skill. Because the student is stating feelings of hopelessness and lack of a future vision, the OTA should ask the student if there are feelings of self-destructiveness. This way the OTA can determine the most appropriate course of action based on this information. If answered incorrectly, review symptoms of suicidal ideations and the role of OT practitions in suicide prevention. See Chapter 13.

A64 C5

The population of an urban homeless shelter includes individuals with histories of chronic alcohol abuse who are at risk for developing peripheral neuropathy. The OTA consulting at this shelter monitors the residents' status to ensure early detection of this problem. Which is the most important observed status change for the OTA to report to the occupational therapist?

Answer Choices:
A. Progressive deterioration in visual acuity.
B. Progressive deterioration of sensorimotor functions of the lower extremities.
C. Rapid onset of intention tremors in the upper extremities.
D. Rapid loss of sensorimotor functions of the facial and neck muscles.

Correct Answer: B.

Rationale:
Peripheral neuropathy is a syndrome of sensory, motor, reflex, and vasomotor symptoms, with symptoms exhibited according to the distribution of the affected nerve. Its etiology includes diabetes, Lyme disease, multiple sclerosis, alcoholism, and metabolic or infectious diseases. It has a slow and progressive onset and course. It does not result in a rapid loss of function, deterioration of visual acuity, or the onset of intention tremors. Treatment of the underlying systemic disorder (e.g., diabetes) can slow progression. In general, recovery takes extended time.

Type of Reasoning: Inferential
One must link knowledge of peripheral neuropathy to the symptoms presented in order to arrive at a correct conclusion. This requires inferential reasoning skills, in which one must draw conclusions based on the evidence presented. In this case, the most important status change for the OTA to report is the progressive deterioration of sensorimotor functions in the lower extremities. If answered incorrectly, review symptoms of peripheral neuropathy. See Chapter 6.

A65 C5

An adult recently diagnosed with scleroderma receives occupational therapy services to deal with the functional changes caused by this disease. Which recommendations are best for the OTA to make to this individual? Select the three BEST responses.

Answer Choices:
A. Dress in layers for neutral warmth.
B. Wear protective cotton, insulated gloves.
C. Dress in lightweight clothing for thermal comfort.
D. Use cold packs on hands when pain in hands occurs.
E. Modify activities to prevent trauma to fingers and toes.
F. Use hand splints to immobilize affected joints and promote rest.

Correct Answers: A, B, and E.

Rationale:
Scleroderma is a systemic disease of unknown etiology. Symptoms are grouped into the CREST syndrome, which includes calcinosis, Raynaud's phenomenon, esophageal dysfunction, sclerodactyly of fingers and toes, and telangiectasis or red spots covering the hands, feet, forearms, face, and hips. The systemic sclerosis of internal organs can be life threatening. A common early (and ongoing) symptom of scleroderma is poor circulation. This phenomenon usually affects the hands, and at times the feet. It is often precipitated by exposure to cold. Consequently, the use of cold packs is contraindicated. Dressing in layers can compensate for this problem. Lightweight clothing would not address the person's need for warmth. Wearing protective cotton, insulated gloves while outside or inside when getting items out of the refrigerator or freezer is also a positive compensatory approach. Because individuals with scleroderma can develop swelling of the fingers and toes and skin may become hard and thickened, normal ROM of the digits can be impacted, and joint contractures and ulcers can develop. As a result, modification of activities is needed to prevent trauma to fingers and toes. Activities that may create excess compression and shearing forces on the skin should be avoided and individuals should be advised to avoid dry, cracked skin by using lotions. Although individuals with scleroderma can benefit from splinting, immobilization is unnecessary and can further contribute to joint contractures of the hand and wrist. A splint for a person with scleroderma should protect the joints and preserve the functional position of the wrist and hand (e.g. a wrist cock-up or resting hand splint). Care should be taken to ensure the material is lightweight and appropriately padded to prevent areas of pressure and damage to the skin. Neoprene splints are an especially beneficial choice due to the material's neutral warm properties.

Type of Reasoning: Inductive
One must utilize clinical knowledge and judgment to determine the best recommendation for the patient with scleroderma. Knowledge of scleroderma and guidelines to minimize effects of the condition are critical in order to arrive at a correct conclusion. In this case, the best recommendations are for the patient to dress in layers for neutral warmth, wear protective gloves, and modify activities to prevent trauma to fingers and toes. If answered incorrectly, review characteristics of scleroderma and intervention strategies for managing this disorder and its symptoms. See Chapter 9.

A66 C4

A parent recovering from brain cancer receives home-based occupational therapy services. The client has residual problem solving deficits. Sensorimotor abilities are within functional limits. The client identifies a desire to resume the role of home maintainer. To develop the requisite problem-solving skills needed for these roles, which is best for the OTA to work on with the client during OT intervention?

Answer Choices:
A. Performing routine morning self-care.
B. Dusting the home's living room.
C. Washing the family's laundry.

Correct Answer: C.

Rationale:
Problem solving is the ability to recognize and define a problem, identify alternative plans for solving the problem, select a plan, organize steps in the plan, implement the plan, and evaluate the plan's outcome. Doing laundry can present several potential problems that must be solved (i.e., stain removal, appropriate care for different textured and/or colored fabrics). The other task choices are more structured and have less of a problem-solving component.

Type of Reasoning: Inferential
One must infer or draw conclusions about the activity that would be most difficult to perform without effective problem-solving skills. This is an inferential reasoning skill, where knowledge of an ability, such as problem solving in this situation, is essential in choosing a correct solution. In this case, the person will mostly likely require intervention for developing independence in laundry skills. If answered incorrectly, review activity analysis, problem solving skills, and instrumental ADL. The integration of this knowledge is required to answer this question correctly. See Chapters 3 and 12.

A67 C4

A client has a three-year history of multiple sclerosis. One of the client's presenting symptoms is a persistent and severe diplopia, which leaves the client frequently nauseated and unable to complete desired activities. Which of the following is best for the OTA to recommend the client discuss with an optometrist?

Answer Choices:
A. Magnifying glasses.
B. Prism glasses.
C. An eye patch.

Correct Answer: C.

Rationale:
Double vision (diplopia) can be managed by patching one eye. Patients are typically on an eye-patching schedule that alternates the eye that is patched. Loss of depth perception can be expected with eye patching, but it is not as disabling as diplopia. The other options do not correct diplopia. In some states, a physician's order is needed for this equipment. In other states, occupational therapy practitioners can make this recommendation independent of an optometrist. If allowed by a state licensure law, eye patching is an entry-level skill that can be performed by an OTA under the supervision of an occupational therapist.

Type of Reasoning: Inferential
The test taker must infer or draw conclusions about how three options will be the best remedy for the client to discuss with an optometrist. This requires knowledge of the condition of diplopia and that wearing an eye patch is the most effective choice for alleviating the condition, which is an inferential reasoning skill. For this case, the OTA should recommend that the client discuss wearing an eye patch with an optometrist. If answered incorrectly, review information about treatment of diplopia. See Chapter 5.

A68 C8

An OTA working in a skilled nursing facility observes a resident with cognitive disabilities don slippers by putting them on the wrong feet. The resident plans to go visit a friend on another floor and does not seem aware that the slippers are on the wrong feet. Which is the best action for the OTA to take in response to this situation?

Answer Choices:
A. Say nothing because this error may embarrass the resident.
B. Say nothing but follow the resident to the friend's room to ensure a safe arrival.
C. Ask the resident to look at the slippers to see if the error is noticed.
D. Supportively inform the resident of the need to reverse the slippers.

Correct Answer: D.

Rationale:
The slippers must be immediately reversed to ensure safety and prevent a fall. Poor or inappropriate use of footwear is a primary cause of falls. Letting the resident walk with slippers on the wrong feet is an unacceptable risk. Since the resident has cognitive deficits, they may not be able to notice the error and self-correct. A direct intervention done in a supportive manner is needed to ensure safety.

Type of Reasoning: Evaluative
This question requires professional judgment in a challenging situation, which is an evaluative reasoning skill. Because the resident is at risk for a fall wearing the slippers on the wrong feet, the OTA should inform the resident of the need to reverse the slippers. This can be done in a supportive and nonjudgmental manner. In judgment situations such as these, where safety is a concern, test takers should often consider the safest, most prudent response as the best one. If answered incorrectly, review safe mobility and fall prevention guidelines. See Chapter 15.

A69 C4

An individual receives OT services at a subacute rehabilitation facility. The patient's personal goal is to be independent in dressing. The patient demonstrates decreased memory, poor sequencing skills, and ideational apraxia. Which of the following is most effective for the OTA to provide when teaching one-handed dressing techniques to this patient?

Answer Choices:
A. Step-by-step verbal instructions.
B. Sequenced photographs of the steps in dressing.
C. Physical prompts to initiate the steps in dressing.
D. A full-length mirror for the client to observe self-dressing performance.

Correct Answer: C.

Rationale:
Ideational apraxia is the breakdown in the knowledge of what is to be done and how to perform specific activities. This means that one cannot perform a task either spontaneously or upon request. However, the sensorimotor aspects needed to perform the activity can be intact. Providing physical prompts to initiate dressing may be a sufficient cue for the individual to begin and then complete the task. Providing verbal instructions or sequenced photographs will not address the fundamental deficit of ideational apraxia and therefore will not enhance performance. Observing oneself dressing in front of a mirror results in a view opposite of actual performance. This can increase confusion, especially with apraxia.

Type of Reasoning: Inductive
One must utilize clinical knowledge and judgment to determine the best approach for teaching one-handed dressing techniques, given the patient's symptoms. In this case, because the patient has ideational apraxia, it is best to provide physical prompts to initiate dressing tasks. If answered incorrectly, review ideational apraxia symptoms and ADL intervention guidelines. The integration of this knowledge is required to determine the correct answer. See Chapters 12 and 14.

A70 C3

A person fell and sustained bilateral Colles' fractures. The client wore bilateral short-arm casts for 6 weeks. After cast removal, the client began OT sessions to increase endurance and strength prior to returning to work. The client tends to work hard when performing resistive exercises with both wrists. The OTA monitors the client for overexertion. Which behavior indicates overexertion?

Answer Choices:
A. Decreased respiration rate during resistive wrist flexion.
B. Increased ability to achieve full ROM of the wrist.
C. Complaints of pain in the wrist extensors.
D. Consistent strength in wrist extension activities.

Correct Answer: C.

Rationale:
Complaints of pain can be a sign of overexertion. The others are signs of adequate performance, not overexertion.

Type of Reasoning: Inferential
The test taker must reason which observation would likely indicate overexertion. Inferential reasoning skill is used as one must draw conclusions about the statements provided based upon clinical knowledge of therapeutic exercise. For this situation complaints of pain often indicate overexertion. If answered incorrectly, review exercise approaches for fracture and signs of overexertion. The integration of this knowledge is required to determine the correct answer. See Chapters 6 and 11.

A71 C2

An OTA works in a school setting with adolescents with autism spectrum disorder (ASD). The need for a social skills training group is identified. One activity that the OTA plans to use in the group is role playing. Which is the most effective way for the OTA to determine relevant scenarios for the role-play activities?

Answer Choices:
A. Survey the teachers on social difficulties displayed in class.
B. Survey parents on social difficulties they have observed in the adolescents.
C. Review literature on adolescent social skill development.
D. Ask the group members about their social concerns.

Correct Answer: D.

Rationale:
Directly asking members about their concerns will enable the OTA to identify areas of common concern that can serve as the basis of relevant role-play scenarios. This will foster Yalom's curative factor of universality. The ability to express one's concerns and needs is especially important to adolescents since their main developmental task is to separate from parents and develop their own self-identity. Surveying others provides information on their perceptions of the adolescents' needs. This may or may not be an accurate reflection of members' needs. Reviewing developmental literature can be helpful to understand adolescent concerns, but it cannot be used to plan role-play scenarios for a specific group of adolescents with unique needs.

Type of Reasoning: Inductive
This question requires one to determine the best approach for determining group members' needs. This requires inductive reasoning skill, where clinical judgment is paramount to arriving at a correct conclusion. For this situation, the OTA should ask the group members about their social concerns. If answered incorrectly, review group intervention techniques including role playing and the functional impact of ASD. The integration of this knowledge is required to answer the question correctly. See Chapters 3 and 10.

A72 C6

A school-based OTA uses behavior modification techniques to help shape the behavioral responses of students with behavioral disorders. Which action is most consistent with this intervention approach?

Answer Choices:
A. Provide frequent positive reinforcement for all desired behaviors.
B. Reprimand the students every time an undesirable behavior occurs.
C. Allow each student enough time to self-correct the undesirable behaviors.
D. Encourage the teaching staff to tell the students which behaviors are correct and which are not.

Correct Answer: A.

Rationale:
Behavioral modification is best achieved through use of positive reinforcements for all desired behaviors. Negative behaviors should be ignored. Self-correction is not a form of behavior modification.

Type of Reasoning: Deductive
For this question, the test taker utilizes knowledge and recall of behavioral modification techniques to choose the correct answer. This necessitates the factual recall of guidelines, which is a deductive reasoning skill. For this scenario, the OTA should provide frequent positive reinforcement for all desired behaviors, which is aligned with behavioral modification guidelines. If answered incorrectly, review behavioral modification guidelines. See chapter 13.

A73 C6

An individual with developmental disabilities scores a Level 4 on Allen's Cognitive Level Test. The OTA collaborates with the occupational therapist to plan intervention. Which activities should the OTA and occupational therapist include in the intervention plan to help meet the client's functional needs? Select the three BEST responses.

Answer Choices:
A. Self-care activities such as brushing teeth.
B. Home management activities such as folding socks.
C. Home management activities such as food shopping using a prepared list.
D. Leisure activities such as matching picture cards.
E. Leisure activities such as completing a 50-piece puzzle.
F. Community mobility training to develop the ability to take public transit using a map.

Correct Answers: C, E, and F.

Rationale:
An individual who scores a Level 4 on the Allen's Cognitive Level Test can perform goal directed actions. According to Allen's model, Level 4 is characterized by the ability to carry out structured tasks through to completion. The individual relies on visual cues and can perform established routines. Food shopping using a prepared list, completing a 50-piece puzzle, and using a map to access public transit are structured activities that provide visual cues to facilitate the successful completion of these activities. At level 4, the person should be able to independently perform the other listed activities. According to Allen's model, brushing teeth, folding socks, and matching picture cards would be the focus of intervention for lower levels of cognitive functioning.

Type of Reasoning: Inductive
One must utilize clinical knowledge and judgment to determine the best activities for this individual. This requires inductive reasoning skill. Because the individual is functioning at Level 4, food shopping using a prepared list, the completion of a 50-piece puzzle, and community mobility training are relevant activities to include in the intervention plan. If answered incorrectly, review Allen's cognitive disabilities model and intervention approaches for individuals functioning at Level 4. See Chapter 13.

A74 C5

A client with myasthenia gravis shows increasing difficulty with speech and oral-motor control during swallowing. Which behavior is most accurate for the OTA to document as indicative of a swallowing disorder?

Answer Choices:
A. A tendency to spit out foods of mixed textures.
B. Coughing while swallowing thin liquids.
C. Loud noises in the throat during swallowing.

Correct Answer: B.

Rationale:
Coughing and choking are signs of swallowing difficulties. It is important to determine the type and viscosity of foods that cause choking and coughing. Spitting out foods tends to reflect an oral problem such as hypersensitivity and is not a component of a swallowing dysfunction. The symptoms of a swallowing dysfunction include a gurgling quality of speech, not loud noises in the throat.

Type of Reasoning: Inferential
One must infer or draw conclusions about the symptoms that indicate swallowing dysfunction. Questions that ask what to expect from a certain diagnosis often require inferential reasoning skill. In this situation, coughing while swallowing thin liquids indicates the presence of swallowing dysfunction. If answered incorrectly, review symptoms of swallowing dysfunction. See Chapter 9.

A75 C8

An individual with left hemiplegia who is right-hand dominant receives training to resume independent driving. Which adaptation is best for the OTA to recommend the client use?

Answer Choices:
A. 'Palming' the steering wheel.
B. Hand controls for brake and gas pedals.
C. A spinner knob on the steering wheel.
D. Left-sided accelerator pedal.

Correct Answer: C.

Rationale:
A person who is right-hand dominant with left hemiplegia can drive one-handed using a spinner knob on the steering wheel. 'Palming' the steering wheel is not recommended for one-handed drivers, for it is easier to lose control of the vehicle. 'Palming' makes it difficult to maintain smooth handling and turns are made much more slowly, which can be dangerous in traffic situations. There is no functional need to change a car's existing pedal arrangement.

Type of Reasoning: Inductive
Clinical knowledge and judgment are the most important skills needed for answering this question, which requires inductive reasoning skill. Knowledge of the functional limitations and most appropriate equipment for driving is essential to choosing the best solution. In this case, a spinner knob on the steering wheel is the best recommendation. If answered incorrectly, review vehicle adaptations for one-handed drivers. See Chapter 15.

A76 C9

An OTA employed in a pediatric clinic for children with cerebral palsy participates in a performance appraisal. The OTA's supervisor identifies handling skills as an area needing improvement. Which is the most effective way for the OTA to improve handling skills?

Answer Choices:
A. Observe an experienced occupational therapist using handling techniques with a diversity of children with cerebral palsy.
B. Complete an extensive literature review of evidence-based practice for children with cerebral palsy.
C. Participate in a beginner-level experiential course on handling skills with children with cerebral palsy.
D. Attend a video teleconference on handling skills for the child with cerebral palsy.

538 Exam A Answer Rationales

Correct Answer: C.

Rationale:
Participating in an experiential handling skills course provides opportunities to interact with other occupational therapy practitioners and benefit from visual and kinesthetic learning. Observing a skill is helpful but does not offer opportunity to develop hands-on skills and obtain feedback on the application of learned techniques. A literature review and a teleconference can cover a variety of information about best practices and handling techniques for children with cerebral palsy; however, these offer little opportunity to learn handling skills, which is a hands-on competence rather than knowledge-based.

Type of Reasoning: Inferential
This question requires one to determine which course of action will be most effective for an OTA to use to improve handling skills for use with children with cerebral palsy. This requires inferential reasoning skill, as one must determine what action will have the most beneficial outcome. For this situation, the OTA should participate in a beginner-level experiential course on handling skills with children with cerebral palsy. If answered incorrectly, review information about professional development. See Chapter 4.

A77 C1

During a group session an older adult complains that everyone is mumbling. Which action should the OTA take after the group in response to these statements?

Answer Choices:
A. Notify the client's physician that the person exhibited evidence of paranoia.
B. Collaborate with the occupational therapist to remove groups from the client's intervention plan.
C. Document objective data about the complaints in the person's charts.
D. Notify the occupational therapist that the person may need an audiological evaluation.

Correct Answer: D.

Rationale:
It is common for older adults to experience hearing loss. The individual's report that people are mumbling is indicative of a potential hearing loss that warrants further evaluation. Interpreting the person's report as indicative of paranoia is subjective. Modifying the person's intervention plan to not include groups and documenting the individual's complaints does not deal directly with the issue.

Type of Reasoning: Inductive
One must utilize clinical knowledge and judgment to determine the best action to take, given the individual's complaint. This requires inductive reasoning skill. In this case, the individual's complaint warrants notifying the occupational therapist that an audiological evaluation may be needed. If answered incorrectly, review symptoms of hearing loss in adults. See Chapter 5.

A78 C7

A tool and die designer develops bilateral carpal tunnel syndrome. The local work hardening program does not have the exact equipment that the designer uses in the job setting. Which action is best for the OTA to take in response to this situation?

Answer Choices:
A. Refer the client to another work hardening program that has the equipment.
B. Inform the occupational therapist about the need for equipment to duplicate the work setting.
C. Perform some necessary aspects of rehabilitation in the client's work setting.
D. Duplicate the job task components as closely as possible.

Correct Answer: D.

Rationale:
Work hardening programs can use real or simulated tasks that duplicate, as closely as possible, the components of each client's job tasks. It is not realistic for all programs to have every possible piece of equipment related to clients' job tasks. Consequently, OT practitioners become skilled at activity analysis and adept at simulating job tasks with the equipment that they have available. An OTA who is experienced in work hardening can provide effective intervention without equipment that exactly matches the client's work. Therefore, there is no reason to refer the client to another facility. A reason to refer a client to another facility is the therapy staff's lack of experience and inability to provide effective intervention. It may be helpful to perform some aspects of rehabilitation during a site visit, but the logistics of this can be difficult. The OTA's ability to provide intensive therapy in a work environment would likely be limited. Therefore, the best answer is to duplicate the job tasks in the clinic.

Type of Reasoning: Evaluative
This question requires the test taker to weigh the merits of each possible course of action. This necessitates evaluative reasoning skill, where value judgments are paramount to arriving at a correct conclusion. In this situation, the most appropriate action is for the OTA to duplicate the job task components as closely as possible. Questions of this nature can be challenging, as value judgments often do not have clear-cut answers. If answered incorrectly, review principles of activity analysis and the aims of work hardening programs. The integration of this knowledge is required to determine the correct answer. See Chapters 3 and 14.

A79 C1

A school-based OTA receives a referral for a student who has illegible handwriting, poor attending behaviors, questionable visual skills, and problems with pencil management. After speaking with the teacher, reviewing classroom work samples, and collaborating with the occupational therapist, which action should the OTA take next?

Answer Choices:
A. Provide pencil grips and specialized paper as a trial to determine interventions.
B. Directly observe the student during a naturally occurring writing time.
C. Administer a standardized visual perceptual and visual motor assessment.
D. Administer a standardized handwriting assessment.

Correct Answer: B.

Rationale:
Skilled observation during a writing activity is an essential part of the evaluation process. Noting the student's performance in the classroom should precede standardized testing of performance components. These observations, review of the student's work and history, and the teacher interview can then be reviewed by the occupational therapist and OTA to determine the need for further evaluation and the most appropriate standardized measures to use to evaluate the child, if needed.

540   Exam A Answer Rationales

Type of Reasoning: Inductive
This question requires one to determine a best course of action, given the information provided. This requires inductive reasoning skill, where one must use clinical judgment to determine the best approach for evaluating this child. In this situation, the OTA should directly observe the student during a naturally occurring writing time. If answered incorrectly, review observational guidelines for the assessment of functional skills and the development of handwriting skills. The integration of this knowledge is required for the determination of a correct answer. See Chapters 3 and 5.

A80 C3

An older teenager with a congenital right, below-elbow amputation had never wanted a prosthesis. Now the teen wants a prosthesis "to look good at the prom and for going on dates." Which action would be most beneficial to meet the client's expressed need?

Answer Choices:
A. Recommend a prosthesis with a cosmetic passive hand.
B. Recommend a prosthesis with a voluntary opening hook.
C. Recommend a prosthesis with a myoelectrically controlled hand.
D. Recommend counseling to explore the client's sudden preoccupation with body image.

Correct Answer: C.

Rationale:
The best choice is a prosthesis that meets the teen's expressed need for a cosmetically appealing device which can also be used to perform functional, age-appropriate bilateral fine motor activities, such as text messaging or playing video games. A prosthesis with a myoelectrically controlled hand meets these goals. A prosthesis can be used for purely cosmetic reasons; however, it would be best to provide the teen with a device that they can use to increase functional performance. A passive cosmetic hand can be used for grasping large objects like a beach ball or to hold an object on a table, but has no moving parts for grasp and release; thus, it would not be the most functional choice. Although a voluntary opening hook would enable the teen to perform functional activities, recommending this would not respect the teen's expressed desire for a cosmetically appealing device. Recommending counseling based on an interpretation of the teen's request as a preoccupation with body image is judgmental. This action also violates the person's rights of autonomy.

Type of Reasoning: Inductive
This question requires the test taker to determine through clinical judgment which course of action will best address the client's request and provide optimal functioning. This requires inductive reasoning skill, where clinical judgment plus prediction of how a course of action will result in future benefit is accentuated. For this case, a prosthesis with a myoelectrically controlled hand is the best choice to facilitate function and fulfill the client's wishes. If answered incorrectly, review upper extremity prosthetic options. See Chapter 6.

A81 C2

An OTA is working with the parents of a 5-year-old child with developmental delay. This child is not self-feeding. The occupational therapist's evaluation of the child indicated that the child has potential to participate in this ADL. When talking to the parents about this possible goal, they indicate this is not a priority for them. Which action is best for the OTA to take in response to the parents' statement?

Answer Choices:
A. Ask the parents about their intervention priorities for their child.
B. Work on utensil use with the child without using food items.
C. Explain the importance of self-feeding to the child's independence.
D. Refer the parents to online sources about the typical development of feeding.

Correct Answer: A.

Rationale:
When differing values occur between occupational therapy practitioners and family members, open-ended questions should be used to help the practitioner understand the family's context. For this case, the OTA should ask the parents about their intervention priorities for their child. Based on this information, the OTA can collaborate with the occupational therapist and the parents to develop goals that honor the parents' wishes. The parents' preferences are likely founded in their personal and cultural values. Family-centered care and cultural competence are important aspects of occupational therapy service delivery. Practitioners must respect family preferences and cultural differences. The other options in this scenario ignores the parents' stated priority and do not consider cultural diversity; therefore, they are incorrect.

Type of Reasoning: Inductive
This question requires one to utilize clinical judgment in order to determine a best course of action. This necessitates inductive reasoning skill. For this scenario, it would be best for the OTA to ask the parents about their priorities for the child so effective intervention choices can be made. If answered incorrectly, review guidelines for collaborating with family members and determining person-directed intervention goals. See Chapter 3.

A82 C9

The family of an individual being discharged from a long-term care facility offers the OTA a substantial cash gift. The OTA refuses the money, but the family insists that the OTA take the cash gift. Which is the OTA's best response?

Answer Choices:
A. Donate the money to the hospital.
B. Thank the family and donate the money to charity.
C. Use the money to purchase an item on the OT department's 'wish list.'
D. Thank the family for their thoughtfulness and decline the gift.

Correct Answer: D.

Rationale:
Accepting a substantial cash gift would bring into question the ethical issue of financial gain; therefore, thanking the family for their thoughtfulness and declining the gift is the best response. If the family continues to insist on concretizing their gratitude, it might be appropriate to suggest a donation to the department or facility. It is important to note that in some cultures, it is common practice to offer small tokens of appreciation to staff. It might be considered rude and offensive to some persons to refuse a small gift. Be aware that some facilities alter their policies about accepting small token gifts in these cases.

Type of Reasoning: Evaluative
This question requires one to weigh the merits of the four possible choices and determine the most ethical response to the situation. In keeping with standard policy, the OTA should refuse the gift. Ethical questions often require evaluative reasoning skill, as there is not always a clear-cut or simple answer to the situation. If answered incorrectly, review the AOTA Code of Ethics. See Chapter 4.

A83 C2

A single parent with rheumatoid arthritis and two school-aged children reports difficulty completing a home exercise program. The parent states that multiple familial, work, and home management responsibilities fill the day and additional activities cannot fit into the day. Which is the best action for the OTA to take in response to these realities?

Answer Choices:
A. Explain and reinforce the importance of active range-of-motion exercises for remediation of dysfunction.
B. Provide interventions to improve time management skills and temporal adaptation.
C. Incorporate the parent's engagement in a diversity of role activities into the home program.
D. Increase the frequency of OT sessions to compensate for lack of follow-through on the home program.

Correct Answer: C.

Rationale:
The performance of role activities requires the individual to actively range joints, which is the purpose of an exercise program. Incorporating AROM into one's daily routines can be more easily implemented than adding a specific exercise regimen. Some people find pure rote exercise uninteresting. In addition, since activity and the pursuit of occupational roles is the foundation of OT, this choice provides the most theoretically consistent action. Reminding the individual of the importance of AROM, providing intervention to improve time management skills and temporal adaptation, and/or increasing the frequency of the OT sessions ignore the reality of a single parent's busy life. The person has reported nothing to indicate a lack of understanding of the importance of AROM, poor time management skills, or temporal dysfunction. Increasing the frequency of OT sessions would just add further demands to the parent's already busy schedule and is not indicated.

Type of Reasoning: Evaluative
This question requires a value judgment, which is an evaluative reasoning skill. In this situation, the patient has indicated that they have little time to complete a home exercise program. Therefore, the test taker should look for a solution that addresses the client's concerns, but also still provides opportunities for functional activity. The only solution that addresses both concerns is to incorporate the client's engagement in a diversity of role activities into the home program. If answered incorrectly, review principles of client-centered practice, the use of therapeutic activities, and activity adaptation. See Chapter 3.

A84 C8

A local pharmacy hires an OTA to consult on the redesign of the pharmacy's customer service area. Which height should the OTA recommend for an accessible service counter?

Answer Choices:
A. 32 inches.
B. 36 inches.
C. 34 inches.

Correct Answer: B.

Rationale:
According to established accessibility standards, the recommended maximal height for accessible service countertops is 36 inches. The other choices do not meet these accessibility standards' criteria.

Type of Reasoning: Deductive
This question requires recall of guidelines and principles, which is factual knowledge. Deductive reasoning skills are utilized whenever one must recall facts to solve novel problems. In this situation, following ADA guidelines, the counter should be no higher than 36 inches. If answered incorrectly, review standards for buildings and facilities. See Chapter 15 and the ADA Guide for Small Businesses (http://www.ada.gov/smbustxt.htm).

A85 C5

An OTA works with an acute care rehabilitation patient with diabetes and a below-knee (BK) amputation to learn how to effectively perform home management tasks while wearing a BK prosthesis. When taking laundry from a front-loading washer and placing it into a top-loading dryer, the patient reports feeling weak, dizzy, and somewhat nauseous. The OTA notices that the patient is sweating profusely and is unsteady when standing. Which is the best immediate course of action for the OTA to take in response to the patient's complaints and these observations?

Answer Choices:
A. Return the person to the unit of care due to an insulin reaction.
B. Have the patient sit and give them orange juice for developing hypoglycemia.
C. Call a nurse to administer an insulin injection for developing hyperglycemia.
D. Have the patient sit until the orthostatic hypotension resolves.

Correct Answer: B.

Rationale:
Hypoglycemia, abnormally low blood glucose, results from too much insulin (insulin reaction). It requires accurate assessment of symptoms and prompt intervention. Having the patient sit and ingest an oral sugar (e.g., orange juice) is the best immediate action for the OTA to take. Once the patient is stabilized, the physician should be notified. Profuse sweating and nausea do not usually accompany orthostatic hypotension.

Type of Reasoning: Inductive
The test taker must determine first what the cause is for the patient's symptoms and then what is the appropriate course of action. Questions such as these utilize one's clinical judgment and diagnostic thinking, which is an inductive reasoning skill. One should recognize that these symptoms are indicative of hypoglycemia and require immediate administration of sugar to relieve symptoms. If answered incorrectly, review first aid guidelines for hypoglycemia. See Chapter 9.

A86 C7

An OTA is working in an inpatient rehabilitation facility for persons with SCI. A patient sustained a C5 complete SCI following an automobile accident two weeks ago. The OTA is working with the patient to attain the patient's goal to independently self-feed. Which pieces of adaptive equipment are best for the OTA to teach the patient to use during intervention? Select the three BEST responses.

Answer Choices:
A. A rocker knife.
B. Dycem to place under plates.
C. A plate guard or scoop dish.
D. A sip-n-puff mobile arm support.
E. A dorsal wrist splint with universal cuff.
F. A drinking cup with a drinking spout.

Correct Answers: B, C and E.

Rationale:
Individuals with a C5 complete SCI have functional use of elbow flexion. They can achieve independence in feeding with the help of assistive devices, such as dycem, a universal cuff, and a plate guard or scoop dish. While persons with C5 SCIs do use suspension slings or mobile arm supports, they can use these devices with their intact upper extremity motor function. A sip-n-puff mobile arm support is needed to assist individuals with a complete C1–C4 SCI who have little or no movement of upper extremity muscles. A rocker knife is a helpful cutting adaptation for individuals who have lost function on one side of their body (e.g., hemiplegia resulting from a CVA). This outcome is not typical for a person with an SCI. A spill-proof drinking cup is used for individuals with tremors; its use requires the use of an upper extremity.

Type of Reasoning: Inductive
This question requires one to utilize knowledge of SCI, especially knowledge of intact musculature for functional use of adaptive equipment in order to arrive at a correct conclusion. This requires clinical judgment, which is an inductive reasoning skill. For this case, dycem, a plate guard or scoop dish, and universal cuff are best to teach the patient to use. If answered incorrectly, review C5 SCI musculature and effective adaptive devices. See Chapters 7 and 14.

A87 C6

An OTA is working with a teenage who is recovering from surgery to remove a brain tumor. The teen has been hospitalized for two months and exhibits a decline in cognitive functioning and muscle weakness. The client is receiving occupational therapy services to develop the skills needed to complete ADL and other desired activities. Upon evaluation, the occupational therapist determined that the client is experiencing symptoms of depression, including anhedonia, social isolation, and poor sleeping patterns. During an intervention session, the OTA learns that the client is feeling socially isolated and missing friends and family members. Which activity is best for the OTA to integrate into intervention sessions to help the client communicate with and remain connected to friends and family?

Answer Choices:
A. An online social networking service that enables users to send and read short messages of 140 characters or less.
B. An online service that allows users to post interests and explore new ones by browsing what others have posted.
C. An online networking service that enables one to call, see, and message with others in real-time by using a webcam.
D. A business-based networking service for which one creates a profile and is connected to others with similar professional interests.

Correct Answer: C.

Rationale:
Occupational therapy practitioners can use social media to help clients increase social participation and improve their outlook when they are hospitalized for long periods of time. The ability to use an online networking service, which enables the client to call, see, and chat with friends and family members in real-time by using a webcam, can help the client successfully engage in the desired roles of friend and family member. Skype is an example of a free social networking service that humanizes interactions between users through face-to-face computer screen contact with others, regardless of where they live. Advantages of this service include the ability to video chat with others and the option to download the application (i.e., 'app') for free on a smart device. An online social networking service that limits characters (e.g., Twitter) also allows the user to communicate with others; however, there is not a face-to-face interaction option. The limited allowance of 140 characters or less is not conducive to personal, heartfelt, expressive conversations. A business-based networking tool (e.g., LinkedIn) and an online 'bulletin board' that shares interests digitally (e.g., Pinterest) would not allow the teenager to communicate with friends and family members in a personal manner. The former is more relevant for a person with the current or desired role of employee, and the latter is helpful for the pursuit of leisure interests and the role of hobbyist.

Type of Reasoning: Inductive
This question requires one to utilize clinical judgment for a best course of action for a teenager who feels socially isolated from family and friends. This is an inductive reasoning skill. For this case, having the teenager use an online networking service that enables one to call, see, and message with others in real-time using a webcam will directly address the teenager's concerns.

A88 C1

An OTA provides home-based occupational therapy services. An ambulatory older adult with hemiparesis and presbycusis has recently moved in with an adult child. The child requests information from the OTA to help maintain their parent's functional ability in the home. Which is best for the OTA to recommend?

Answer Choices:
A. Remove knobs from the stove when the parent is home alone.
B. Speak directly, clearly, and slowly to the parent.
C. Add bright color strips to the edge of each stair tread.
D. Provide the parent with lists of the sequence of routine tasks.

Correct Answer: B.

Rationale:
Presbycusis is an age-related sensorineural loss that results in decreased hearing. Speaking directly, clearly, and slowly can help ensure that the parent hears what is being said. This will enable the parent to participate fully in family interactions. There is nothing in the situation to indicate the need for any of the other suggestions, as no cognitive or visual deficits are noted.

Type of Reasoning: Inferential
One must have knowledge of presbycusis and presenting symptoms in order to determine the best recommendation for this situation. This is an inferential reasoning skill where knowledge of clinical guidelines and judgment based on facts are utilized to reach conclusions. In this situation, the OTA should recommend speaking directly, clearly, and slowly to the parent. If answered incorrectly, review presbycusis and compensation approaches. See Chapter 5.

A89 C4

An adult who incurred a traumatic brain injury three months ago receives home care OT services. During meal preparation tasks, the client ignores items on the left side of the counter. Which is the best remediation approach for the OTA to use with this client to enhance performance?

Answer Choices:
A. Place a brightly colored placemat on the left side of the counter.
B. Encourage bilateral activities to promote scanning.
C. Place all items on the right side of the counter.

Correct Answer: A.

Rationale:
The placemat provides an external cue, which the client can be taught to look for during meal preparation. This anchoring technique is a basic remediation approach. The other interventions would not remediate the performance deficit caused by the client's unilateral neglect.

Type of Reasoning: Inferential
This question requires one to draw conclusions and make certain assumptions about clinical situations based on evidence, which is an inferential reasoning skill. For this scenario, placing a brightly colored placemat on the left side of the counter utilizes a remediation approach to the patient's deficit. If answered incorrectly, review information on the remediation of perceptual deficits. See Chapter 12.

A90 C6

An individual receives treatment for major depression on an inpatient psychiatric unit. The patient has received an electroconvulsive treatment (ECT) treatment at 8 am. At 2 pm, the patient walks into the occupational therapy department stating a desire to participate in the leisure skills group. Which is the OTA's best response?

Answer Choices:
A. Call nursing staff to escort the client back to the client's room.
B. Encourage the client to select one of three structured leisure activities to complete.
C. Provide the client with a leisure history questionnaire to complete.
D. Commend the client's motivation but remind the client that rest is recommended for 24 hours after ECT.

Correct Answer: B.

Rationale:
Six hours after ECT, the individual is capable of engaging in a structured task. Giving the individual a choice of structured activities to complete can increase the likelihood that the person will be interested in the selected task. There is no need to return the client to their room, and 24 hours of rest is not necessary after an ECT. However, there is some temporary memory loss after an ECT; therefore, it would not be appropriate to give the individual an activity that requires memory to complete.

Type of Reasoning: Inductive
This question requires one to determine the best response to a patient who had an ECT treatment six hours ago. This requires inductive reasoning skill, where clinical judgment is paramount to arriving at a correct conclusion. For this situation, the test taker should recall the guidelines for activity after ECT treatment. Six hours after treatment, the individual can engage in a structured task; therefore, the OTA should encourage the individual to engage in such a task. If answered incorrectly, review treatment guidelines for OT treatment post-ECT. See Chapter 10.

A91 C3

An OTA supervises a Level II fieldwork student regarding the evaluation procedures of a work hardening program. The OTA explains that some individuals attending the program magnify their symptoms to retain benefits; therefore, the validity of some evaluation measures may be compromised. Which assessment tool does the OTA identify as providing the most valid results?

Answer Choices:
A. A volumeter.
B. A dynamometer using all five positions.
C. A standardized pegboard test.
D. A total active motion (TAM) evaluation.

Correct Answer: A.

Rationale:
The volumeter is the only true objective assessment tool that occupational therapy practitioners utilize, for it is based on the displacement law of physics. It is the only tool that a person cannot manipulate in any way to lead to an invalid conclusion.

Type of Reasoning: Inferential
One must have knowledge of all the assessment tools described and proper administration in order to arrive at a correct conclusion. This is an inferential reasoning skill where knowledge of clinical guidelines and judgment based on facts are utilized to reach conclusions. In this case, the only assessment that cannot be manipulated is the volumeter. If answered incorrectly, review biomechanical assessment guidelines. See Chapter 11.

A92 C9

A patient with fibromyalgia is receiving occupational therapy to reduce pain and promote flexibility during ADL tasks. The patient expresses the intent to discontinue treatment based on information obtained during an online search that questioned the value of therapy for fibromyalgia. Which of the following actions should the OTA do first in response to the patient's statements?

Answer Choices:
A. Confront the inaccuracy of these statements and provide current evidence-based research about the benefits of therapy for persons with fibromyalgia.
B. Reassure the patient that the physician has ordered therapy; therefore, it will be beneficial.
C. Respect the patient's wishes and advise the occupational therapist that services should be discontinued.
D. Inform the patient that online information can be inaccurate and provide literature about the benefits of therapy for fibromyalgia.

Correct Answer: D.

Rationale:
It is common for patients to seek out more information about their condition. The internet can be informative and resourceful; it can also be inaccurate, incomplete, and misleading. OTAs are responsible for making sure patients have accurate information about their conditions in order to make informed decisions. In this case, the OTA should inform the patient of the inaccurate information and provide accurate information about exercise related to their condition. It is not as beneficial to directly confront the inaccuracies of this information with the latest research. This stance can be overwhelming and lead to the person feeling belittled. Reminding the patient of the physician's orders does not respect the patient's feelings or address their concerns. Discontinuing treatment overlooks the need to provide accurate information first to ensure the patient is making an informed decision.

Type of Reasoning: Evaluative

This situation requires one to consider the AOTA Code of Ethics guidelines of beneficence, nonmaleficence (do no harm), and autonomy (the right to refuse). This necessitates evaluative reasoning skill, where the test taker must determine a proper course of action that respects the rights of the patient, while doing no harm. In this situation, the OTA should inform the patient of the inaccurate information and provide accurate information about the benefits of exercise. If answered incorrectly, review the AOTA Code of Ethics, especially beneficence, nonmaleficence, and autonomy. See Chapter 4.

A93 C6

A graduate student with an anxiety disorder reports feeling confused about the future. During the OT evaluation, the client relates decreased feelings of competence for a chosen field of study and overall poor personal causation. Which is the best initial action for the OTA to take in response to the client's stated concerns?

Answer Choices:
A. Administer a vocational interest inventory.
B. Provide activities related to the client's chosen field of study.
C. Refer the client to the state office of vocational and educational services.
D. Establish short-term goals with high potential for attainment.

Correct Answer: D.

Rationale:

Decreased personal causation and feelings of incompetence are common symptoms of anxiety disorders. The establishment of short-term goals with high potential for attainment can provide the individual with the successful experiences needed to develop a sense of competence and improve personal causation. Once these skills are developed, the need for further vocational exploration and/or services can be determined.

Type of Reasoning: Inferential

One must determine the best initial action for this student, given the symptoms described. This requires inferential reasoning, where one must draw conclusions based on the evidence presented. In this situation, the OTA should establish short-term goals with high potential for achievement. If answered incorrectly, review intervention guidelines for individuals with anxiety disorders. See Chapters 10 and 13.

A94 C5

An OTA implements intervention for individuals on an inpatient cardiopulmonary rehabilitation unit. The OTA assesses a patient's heart rate during intervention sessions by palpating a peripheral pulse. Which most accurately describes the timing the OTA should use to complete this assessment?

Answer Choices:
A. 30 seconds prior to, during, and at cessation of the activity.
B. 1–2 minutes prior to, during, and at cessation of the activity and 5 minutes' post activity.
C. 1–2 minutes prior to, during, and at cessation of the activity.
D. 30 seconds prior to, during, and at cessation of the activity and 5 minutes' post activity.

Correct Answer: B.

Rationale:
On an inpatient cardiopulmonary rehabilitation unit, the OTA must monitor a patient's heart rate before, during, and immediately after an activity and a few minutes (e.g., 5 minutes) post activity. Heart rate should be assessed using palpation of peripheral pulses. The most common monitoring site is the radial artery. Individuals with normal heart rhythms require only 30 seconds of palpation. Individuals receiving treatment in an inpatient cardiopulmonary rehabilitation unit may likely have irregular heart rhythms which require 1–2 minutes of palpation.

Type of Reasoning: Deductive
This question requires recall of guidelines and principles, which is factual knowledge. In this situation, the guideline for inpatient cardiac monitoring is to monitor a patient's heart rate before, during, and immediately after an activity, plus a few minutes' post activity. If answered incorrectly, review cardiac monitoring guidelines. See Chapter 8.

A95 C3

In measuring the ROM of a client's elbow, the OTA records a flexion measurement of 145 degrees. Which is most accurate for the OTA to document based on this measurement?

Answer Choices:
A. Hypomobility.
B. Dysfunctional elbow ROM.
C. Hypermobility.
D. Normal elbow ROM.

Correct Answer: D.

Rationale:
Normal elbow ROM is 0 degrees to 135–150 degrees. Individual variation in the end range of elbow flexion is normal due to differences in muscle mass of the biceps and the forearm as they meet at the end range. Having 145 degrees of flexion is normal. ROM outside of these parameters would be atypical. Hypermobility would be evident if the person extended the elbow beyond zero and hypomobility would be indicated if the person could not flex within the normal range.

Type of Reasoning: Analytical
This question provides a functional description, and the test taker must determine the likely indicator of the description. This is an analytical reasoning skill, as questions of this nature often ask one to analyze a group of symptoms or functional indicators in order to determine a diagnosis or outcome. In this situation the description indicates typical ROM of the elbow, which should be reviewed if answered incorrectly. See Chapter 11.

A96 C7

A client in the descending phase of Guillain-Barré syndrome has bilateral shoulder strength of 2/5. The client fatigues easily. Which equipment should the OTA recommend to enhance the person's performance of activities of daily living?

Answer Choices:
A. An overhead suspension sling.
B. Long-handled utensils and tools.
C. Angled-/curved-handled utensils and tools.
D. An environmental control unit.

Correct Answer: A.

Rationale:
The overhead suspension sling is best suited for individuals presenting with proximal weakness with muscle grades in the 1/5 to 3/5 range. Long-handled and curved utensils and tools are useful for individuals with range of motion limitations. Environmental control units are used for individuals who have significant motor deficits, proximally and distally, and who cannot independently perform tasks such as controlling the switches on electronic equipment.

Type of Reasoning: Inferential
One must infer or draw conclusions about a likely course of action, given the information presented. This is an inferential reasoning skill, where knowledge of a therapeutic approach, such as providing equipment to enhance functioning, is essential to choosing a correct solution. In this case, the OTA should choose an overhead suspension sling. If answered incorrectly, review the diagnostic criteria and functional impact of Guillain-Barré syndrome and adaptive equipment for persons with proximal weakness. Integration of this knowledge is required to answer this item correctly. See Chapters 7 and 14.

A97 C2

Several adolescents with behavior problems attend a school-based after-school program. They work at an egocentric-cooperative/basic cooperative level in a group which is focused on developing the skills needed to enable successful school performance and respond effectively to peer pressure. Which of the following should the OTA focus on helping the group members do in the group to facilitate the attainment of group goals?

Answer Choices:
A. Actively take on roles such as energizer, coordinator, or opinion giver.
B. Focus on the group tasks related to the completion of a long-range activity.
C. Make decisions with minimal to no input or guidance from the group leader.
D. Perform group skills consistent with the developmental level of adolescents.

Correct Answer: B.

Rationale:
The goals of an egocentric-cooperative/basic cooperative group are to enable members to select and implement a long-range activity that requires group interaction to complete (e.g., constructing the set for a school play), develop an understanding of group goals and group interaction norms (e.g., do not interrupt others when they are speaking), and enable members to identify and meet the needs of themselves and others (e.g., safety, esteem). At this level, members do not actively assume diverse group roles and they are not able to make decisions without the group leader's input or guidance. While the clients are adolescents, an egocentric-cooperative/basic cooperative group performs at the 5- to 7-year developmental level. The age range of adolescence is from 10-19. A cooperative/supportive cooperative group is at the 9- to 12-year-old developmental level. A mature group is at the 15- to 18-year-old developmental level.

Type of Reasoning: Inferential
One must recall the typical characteristics of egocentric-cooperative/basic cooperative group members to arrive at a correct conclusion. This requires one to determine what may be true for a group of clients, which is an inferential reasoning skill. In this situation, the OTA leader can help the group members attain group goals by having them focus on the group tasks related to the completion of a long-range activity. If answered incorrectly, review egocentric-cooperative/basic cooperative level group membership characteristics. See Chapter 3.

A98 C6

The parent of two elementary school-aged children receives home care hospice services due to metastasized bone cancer. The client has pain, poor endurance, and decreased muscle strength. The client requires moderate assistance with self-care and dressing. Which is the best intervention for the OTA to incorporate into sessions with this parent?

Answer Choices:
A. Training in energy conservation techniques for self-care and dressing.
B. Training in joint protection techniques for self-care and dressing.
C. Using biofeedback to reduce the client's pain.
D. Exploring play activities for the parent to do with the children.

Correct Answer: D.

Rationale:
A major focus of hospice care is to maintain the individual's control over their life while enabling engagement in meaningful activities that are related to the person's valued roles. Although the person is dying, they are still a parent and will likely enjoy playing with their children when they are not in school. There are many play activities suitable for elementary school-aged children that can be completed by a person with decreased endurance and muscle strength. In addition, research has found that diversional activities can decrease the intensity of an individual's pain experience. There is no indication of a need to train the client in techniques for self-care or dressing. The client currently is in pain and requires moderate assistance due to functional deficits. It is likely that the client will continue to need this assistance because their cancer is at the terminal stage. Even with training in energy conservation or joint protection, the individual would still need assistance with these tasks due to the effects of advanced cancer. Biofeedback is not effective in managing pain that results from metastasized bone cancer.

Type of Reasoning: Inductive
One must utilize clinical knowledge and judgment to determine the intervention approach that best incorporates control over the patient's life. In this case, because the patient is a parent of school-aged children, the OTA should incorporate play activities to do with the children after school. If answered incorrectly, review principles of hospice care and intervention approaches for patients with terminal illness. See Chapter 13.

A99 C1

An OTA is scheduled to give a 1-hour presentation to a support group of parents of infants with a diversity of developmental disabilities. Which of the following is the most important focus for the OTA's presentation?

Answer Choices:
A. Demonstration of infant positioning techniques.
B. Discussion of typical areas of concern addressed by OT practitioners.
C. Demonstration of different types of developmental assessments.
D. Discussion of the Individual Family Service Plan (IFSP).

Correct Answer: B.

Rationale:
An overview of the domain of concern addressed by OT for infants with developmental disabilities is the most appropriate topic for a 1-hour presentation to an audience with diverse needs. Demonstration of infant positioning techniques and developmental assessments can be informative, but these techniques and assessments must be tailored to the individual child. A discussion about the IFSP can also be informative, but this information should be provided by the family's early intervention service provider.

Type of Reasoning: Evaluative
One must weigh the possible courses of action and then make a value judgment about the best course to take. This requires evaluative reasoning skill, which often utilizes guiding principles of action in order to arrive at a correct conclusion. For this case, given the audience the OTA is speaking to and the range of diagnoses of the infants, the OTA should discuss typical areas of concern addressed by OT practitioners. See Chapter 5.

A100 C9

An individual recovering from a total hip replacement is being discharged home. The individual is insured only by Medicare. For safety and independence in the bathroom, which adaptive equipment is best for the OTA to recommend?

Answer Choices:
A. A raised toilet seat.
B. Grab bars.
C. A three-in-one commode.
D. Non-skid mats.

Correct Answer: C.

Rationale:
A three-in-one commode will provide the additional height needed by the individual to maintain hip precautions. It is also the only item identified that is reimbursable by Medicare. Medicare does not cover any equipment that can be useful to individuals without a disability. Self-help items such as grab bars, raised toilet seats, and non-skid mats are not considered medically necessary and are not reimbursable since other people can use them.

Type of Reasoning: Inductive
One must utilize clinical knowledge and judgment to determine the equipment that will be reimbursed by Medicare and provide safety and independence. In this case, a three-in-one commode is the only equipment reimbursed by Medicare and provides needed safety and independence. If answered incorrectly, review Medicare guidelines for reimbursement of durable medical equipment. See Chapter 4.

A101 C3

An OTA has established service competency in completing biomechanical assessments. The OTA evaluates a person who complains of persistent wrist pain after painting a house three weeks ago. The patient demonstrates signs and symptoms consistent with de Quervain's tenosynovitis. Which assessment measure should the OTA use to confirm the diagnosis?

Answer Choices:
A. Finkelstein's test.
B. Phalen's test.
C. Froment's sign.

Correct Answer: A.

Rationale:
Finkelstein's test is specific for reproducing the pain associated with de Quervain's tenosynovitis of the abductor pollicis longus (APL) and extensor pollicis brevis (EBS). The Finkelstein's test is performed by having the patient make a fist with the thumb inside the fingers and then perform ulnar deviation. Sharp pain along the distal radius close to the wrist is a positive result. Froment's sign is used to identify ulnar nerve dysfunction. Phalen's test identifies median nerve compression in the carpal tunnel.

Type of Reasoning: Deductive
This question requires factual recall of knowledge of provocative tests for de Quervain's tenosynovitis. In this case, the appropriate test is Finkelstein's test, which reproduces the pain of the APL and EPB tendons associated with de Quervain's. If answered incorrectly, review provocative testing of the hand or wrist and de Quervain's tenosynovitis. See Chapter 6.

A102 C6

An OTA working in a skilled nursing facility conducts an inservice on validation therapy for the recently hired staff of a new psychogeriatric unit. Which fundamental principle of validation therapy is important for the OTA to include in this presentation?

Answer Choices:
A. Listen to the words the residents use to ascertain each person's underlying message.
B. Provide highly structured activities to refocus the residents on reality.
C. Provide unstructured activities to facilitate the residents' expression of feelings.
D. Listen to the words the residents use and provide reality orientation for invalid statements.

Correct Answer: A.

Rationale:
Validation therapy is an approach to working with individuals with neurocognitive disorders founded on the principle that the unspoken messages an individual conveys in their speech are more important than the actual content of the speech. Individuals with neurocognitive disorders often make statements that are not based in reality. For example, an individual introduces a daughter as their mother. In validation therapy, the factual aspects of this familial relationship are irrelevant and do not need to be addressed at all. However, the underlying message that this relationship is valued and important is worthy of comment. The use of structured or unstructured activities is not a component of validation therapy. The focus of validation therapy is to facilitate communication with persons with neurocognitive disorders in a caring, respectful, and empathetic manner.

Type of Reasoning: Inferential
This question requires one to determine the primary principle of validation therapy. This requires inferential reasoning skill, where one must infer or draw conclusions about a likely guideline or principle. For this case, the OTA should advise staff to listen to the words the residents use to ascertain each person's underlying message. If answered incorrectly, review information about intervention approaches for persons with neurocognitive disorders. See Chapters 10 and 13.

A103 C8

Occupational therapy services are provided to the clients of a psychogeriatric unit in a skilled nursing facility. An OTA presents an inservice on restraint reduction to the unit's direct care staff. Which of the following would the OTA identify as a permissible use of a restraint?

Answer Choices:
A. A bed guardrail to prevent a confused resident from wandering in the evening.
B. Prescribed medication to control a resident's agitated behavior.
C. A lapboard to enhance a resident's self-directed functional behavior.
D. A wheelchair with a lap belt to prevent a person with ataxic gait from falling.

Correct Answer: C.

Rationale:
A restraint is defined as anything that prevents access to the environment or to oneself. A restraint such as a lapboard can enhance functional performance and is permissible with a resident's informed consent. The correct answer choice states that the individual can self-direct. This indicates the person has the ability to give the required informed consent and that they can direct the staff on its removal and its desired use. The other purposes of restraints are not permissible and alternatives, such as the provision of meaningful activities, adaptive aids, and/or environmental modifications, must be actively pursued as preventative measures.

Type of Reasoning: Deductive
This question requires recall of guidelines and principles, which is factual knowledge. Deductive reasoning skills are utilized whenever one must recall facts to solve novel problems. In this situation, the use of a lapboard is the only choice that does not constitute a restraint as it does not prevent access to the environment or oneself. If answered incorrectly, review guidelines for use of restraints. See Chapter 15.

A104 C4

A patient on an acute medical unit has right homonymous hemianopsia. The OTA provides recommendations to modify the patient's room to enhance independence. What are the most effective recommendations for the OTA to make for the placement of the patient's call button and cell phone?

Answer Choices:
A. Call button on the left side and the cell phone on the left side.
B. Call button on the right side and the cell phone on the right side.
C. Call button on the right side and the cell phone on the left side.
D. Call button on the left side and the cell phone on the right side.

Correct Answer: D.

Rationale:
The call button must be placed within the person's intact visual field (which, in this case, is left) so that the person can readily access it in case of emergency. However, the cell phone can be placed outside of the person's visual field (right, in this case) to encourage the person to scan the environment. If the person initially has trouble locating the cell phone, it will not pose any danger to the client. The OTA can use the cell phone as a tool to increase scanning skills during intervention sessions. In between intervention sessions, the ringing of the phone and the other sounds that a cell phone emits when a text message, email, and other social media messages are received will provide auditory cues that can trigger scanning.

Type of Reasoning: Inductive
Clinical knowledge and judgment are the most important skills needed for answering this question, which requires inductive reasoning skill. Knowledge of the diagnosis and most appropriate clinical outcomes is essential to choose the best solution. In this case, the OTA should recommend that the call button is placed on the left and the cell phone on the right side. This best addresses the person's safety in addition to improving function in scanning the environment. If answered incorrectly review interventions for cognitive perceptual deficits. See Chapter 12.

A105 C3

An individual with rheumatoid arthritis (RA) is currently in a stage of remission. During this inactive chronic phase of this disease, the OTA works with the client to maintain range of motion (ROM) and muscle strength. Which of the following is most effective for the OTA to recommend the client include in a daily home exercise program?

Answer Choices:
A. Passive ROM.
B. Active ROM.
C. Isotonics.
D. Progressive resistance.

Correct Answer: B.

Rationale:
Activities that use active ROM are indicated for the treatment of RA both in its acute and chronic phases. Passive ROM is generally contraindicated for persons with RA. If a person is unable to perform AROM, gentle passive ROM may be used with caution. Progressive resistance is also contraindicated in the treatment of RA. The use of isotonic exercises for individuals with RA is somewhat controversial. If isotonics are considered for an intervention, the occupational therapist must establish that the individual's joints are stable and would benefit from isotonic exercises without jeopardizing other joints. The individual's response to these exercises must be monitored; therefore, isotonics are not appropriate for an unmonitored home care program.

Type of Reasoning: Inductive
One must utilize clinical judgment in order to determine the best exercise approach for a patient with RA. Questions that require one to use knowledge of a diagnosis, coupled with therapeutic approaches, often require inductive reasoning skill. For this situation, active ROM is indicated in both acute and chronic phases of RA. If answered incorrectly, review exercise guidelines for patients with RA. See Chapter 6.

A106 C6

An individual attends an outpatient parenting skills group. The person has a major depressive disorder and is taking Nardil. The client complains of recurrent headaches and difficulty focusing during the day (e.g., when helping children with their homework). Which action is best for the OTA to make in response to the client's expressed concerns?

Answer Choices:
A. Instruct the client in stress reduction techniques.
B. Ask the group for suggestions on how to deal with the parenting stress of homework.
C. Suggest that the individual consult with a nurse practitioner for headache relief strategies.
D. Tell the client you will be notifying the psychiatrist of these complaints.

556 Exam A Answer Rationales

Correct Answer: D.

Rationale:
Nardil is a monoamine oxidase inhibitor (MAOI). It has serious side effects when a person eats foods that contain the amino acid tyramine. Tyramine increases blood pressure and may lead to stroke or other cardiovascular reactions. Headache and heart palpitations are the first sign of a problem. This must be considered a serious medical situation and the physician must be contacted. To assume that the headaches are stress-related is dangerous. Suggesting that the person contact a nurse practitioner does not guarantee follow through. The individual needs to collaborate with the psychiatrist to determine if an MAOI is the best medication, given its restrictions. Chapter 10 in this text provides these restrictions.

Type of Reasoning: Evaluative
One must weigh the possible courses of action and then make a value judgment about the best course to take. This requires evaluative reasoning skill, which often utilizes guiding principles of action in order to arrive at a correct conclusion. For this case, because the patient is describing potentially serious side effects of the medication, the OTA must notify the person's psychiatrist. Questions of this nature can be challenging. Essential to arriving at a correct conclusion is concern for the person's well-being and safety.

A107 C7

Several clients participate in an outpatient daily vocational rehabilitation group. Which should the occupational therapist and OTA emphasize as the main purpose of this group?

Answer Choices:
A. Reducing costs by using an outpatient format instead of an inpatient setting.
B. Building members' trust of others to support interpersonal work relationships.
C. Enhancing members' self-esteem to build confidence to pursue work.
D. Developing essential skills required for members to pursue work.

Correct Answer: D.

Rationale:
The goal of a vocational rehabilitation group is to develop the skills needed to work. This increase in functional skills could improve clients' self-esteem in work and increase their trust of others. Reducing costs is likely achieved by the provision of services in an outpatient setting, but this is not the goal of the group treatment.

Type of Reasoning: Inferential
One must infer or draw conclusions about what is likely to be the primary purpose of a vocational rehabilitation group, which is an inferential reasoning skill. Improving work skills is the primary goal, though other secondary goals may exist, such as reducing costs or building trust. Questions of this nature may be challenging as all responses may seem correct. However, the question is ultimately asking for the main purpose of the group, rather than secondary benefits. If answered incorrectly, review the purposes of vocational rehabilitation. See Chapters 4 and 14.

A108 C7

An OTA completes an ergonomic assessment of a computer programmer and the programmer's workstation. Which is the best recommendation for the OTA to make to ensure the programmer uses ideal wrist and elbow positioning?

Answer Choices:
A. Elevate the keyboard to increase wrist flexion.
B. Use a keyboard rest to maintain a neutral wrist position.
C. Lower the keyboard to increase wrist extension.
D. Add armrests to keep the elbows away from the body.

Correct Answer: B.

Rationale:
Work involving increased wrist deviation from a neutral posture in either flexion/extension or radial/ulnar deviation has been associated with increased reports of carpal tunnel syndrome and other wrist and hand problems. Therefore, using a keyboard rest to maintain a neutral wrist position is the best recommendation for the OTA to make to ensure the programmer uses ideal wrist and elbow positioning. Rather than adding armrests to keep the elbows away from the body, the OTA should recommend the person keep their elbows close to the body during keyboarding. Elbows should be positioned at a 90 degree angle or with hands positioned slightly lower than elbows.

Type of Reasoning: Deductive
This question requires one to recall the proper ergonomic guidelines for workstation function. This is factual information, which is a deductive reasoning skill. In this scenario, it is important to prevent wrist and elbow dysfunction by facilitating neutral wrist positioning when using a keyboard. If answered incorrectly, review ergonomic workstation assessment guidelines. See Chapter 14.

A109 C7

A child with spinal muscle atrophy can no longer reach beyond 90 degrees of shoulder abduction and 90 degrees of shoulder flexion. The parents state that the child can no longer independently don or doff a T-shirt. Which is the best approach for the OTA to recommend the child use to don a T-shirt?

Answer Choices:
A. Place the T-shirt directly on the child's lap, have the child don the arms first, then don the head of the T-shirt.
B. Have the child wear front-opening shirts instead of T-shirts to eliminate the need to don shirts over the head.
C. Have the child support the elbows on a table at chest height to don the T-shirt over the arms, then don over the head.
D. Have the child lean to the right and don the right arm, repeat with the left arm, and then don the head of the T-shirt.

Correct Answer: C.

Rationale:
Spinal muscle atrophy is a progressive disorder and the OTA needs to prepare the child and family for progressive loss of skills. The best technique, as shoulder ROM decreases, is to use a table for support to don the arms then use elbow and neck flexion to don the T-shirt over the head. Wearing front-opening shirts instead of T-shirts is an effective compensatory technique to eliminate the need to don shirts over the head. However, the exam item specifically asked for an approach to help the child don a T-shirt. When the child can no longer don a T-shirt using adaptive strategies such as the use of front-opening shirts can effectively maintain the child's independence in dressing.

558 Exam A Answer Rationales

Type of Reasoning: Inductive
This question requires one to consider the best approach for completing the ADL task, given an understanding of the diagnosis and limitations. This requires inductive reasoning skill, where the test taker must utilize clinical judgment based on knowledge of the diagnosis to arrive at a correct conclusion. For this case, the OTA should have the child support the elbows on a table at chest height to don the T-shirt over the arms, then don over the head. If answered incorrectly, review information on principles of activity adaptation and adaptive dressing techniques. The integration of this knowledge is required to determine the correct answer. See Chapters 3 and 14.

A110 C9

A young adolescent with right hemiplegic cerebral palsy demonstrates a strong flexor synergy of the hand. The adolescent does not use the hand for grasp, pinch, or release, and often maintains the thumb flexed in the palm. The orthopedic hand surgeon recommends a flexor tendon release followed by several weeks of hand therapy and splinting. The parents are very anxious about the surgery and they ask the OTA what to do. Which is the OTA's best response?

Answer Choices:
A. Recommend that the parents follow the surgical recommendations presented by the doctor.
B. Suggest the parents talk to the occupational therapist about a pre-operative course of therapy.
C. Advise the family to review all of the information to make an educated decision.
D. Encourage the parents to get a second opinion from another orthopedic hand surgeon.

Correct Answer: C.

Rationale:
The OTA should offer unbiased, objective support and not give medical or other advice. The OTA does not make the decision for the parents. The surgery is an option that the parents can choose. This is an elective procedure. Any suggestion for pre-operative treatment should be first presented to the physician to be sure that it is an appropriate choice. It is not in the realm of an occupational therapy practitioner to encourage the parents to get a second opinion.

Type of Reasoning: Evaluative
One must weigh the potential course of action and determine the best response to the parent's concerns. Following guidelines for the AOTA Code of Ethics, the OTA should observe nonmaleficence, which includes doing no harm, and other duties including practicing within the parameters of the profession. The only response in this situation that does not create potential harm (physical or psychological) and follows guidelines of practice is to advise them to review all the information in order to make an educated decision. If answered incorrectly, review the AOTA Code of Ethics and principles of team communication. See Chapter 4.

A111 C3

An OTA constructs a splint for an individual with a brachial plexus injury with full arm involvement. Which orthosis would be most effective for this condition?

Answer Choices:
A. An elbow lock splint.
B. A flail arm splint.
C. A figure-of-eight splint.
D. A deltoid sling.

Correct Answer: A.

Rationale:
A flail arm splint is recommended for a brachial plexus injury resulting in whole upper extremity involvement. It provides the needed stability at both the shoulder and elbow for functional positioning of the hand. A figure-of-eight splint is used for a combined median ulnar nerve injury and to prevent MP hyperextension. A deltoid sling is used for upper extremity muscle weakness.

Type of Reasoning: Inferential
One must first determine the benefits and indications of each of the orthoses identified in the exam item in order to determine the orthosis that best addresses the patient's condition. This requires inferential reasoning, where one must draw conclusions based on the information provided. In this situation, an elbow lock splint is the ideal orthosis for a brachial plexus injury with full arm involvement. If answered incorrectly, review brachial plexus injuries and recommended orthoses. See Chapter 6.

A112 C7

A high school senior with Friedreich's ataxia is working on developing keyboarding skills in a school-to-work transition program. During the initial session, the OTA observes signs of dysmetria. Which is the most appropriate adaptation for the OTA to recommend to increase the effectiveness of the student's keyboarding?

Answer Choices:
A. An eye-gaze input system.
B. A key guard overlay.
C. A voice-activated input system.
D. A reduced size keyboard.

Correct Answer: B.

Rationale:
Dysmetria is the overshooting (hypermetria) or the undershooting (hypometria) of a target. It would be observed during a keyboarding activity as frequent misses of the desired key, either hitting keys above, below, or next to the targeted key. A key guard overlay provides raised separations between each key. This enables the individual to place their finger into the desired key space and prevents the person's finger from jumping to keys above, below, or next to the targeted key. An individual with Friedreich's ataxia has poor coordination of all muscles, including ocular muscles, rendering an eye-gaze input system ineffective. Dysarthria is also characteristic of Friedreich's ataxia, which limits the efficacy of a voice-activated system. A reduced size keyboard has smaller keys and controls. It is indicated for a person with decreased ROM and good fine motor skills.

Type of Reasoning: Inferential
One must have knowledge of Friedreich's ataxia and typical deficits in order to choose the best adaptation for keyboarding skills. This is an inferential reasoning skill where one must infer or draw conclusions based on information presented. For this case, a key guard overlay is the best recommendation to address the dysmetria during keyboarding. If answered incorrectly, review characteristics of Friedreich's ataxia and keyboarding adaptations for persons with mobility impairments. The integration of this knowledge is required to determine a correct answer. See Chapters 7 and 15.

A113 C9

A non-English-speaking family attends a discharge planning session. The assigned OTA does not share the language of the family. Which action should the OTA take first?

Answer Choices:
A. Make a referral for a home care therapist to visit the family to provide in-home education.
B. Obtain an interpreter to communicate with the family during the session.
C. Attempt to communicate with the family through nonverbal communication.
D. Consult with the occupational therapist to develop a discharge plan.

Correct Answer: B.

Rationale:
The best choice to ensure the family involvement in the discharge planning process is to seek out a way to communicate directly and verbally with the family via an interpreter. The family is not included in these processes without an interpreter. Nonverbal communication does not transcend a language barrier for abstract concepts such as incorporating the individual's needs, values, and they have already been assigned this case. The OTA can independently get an interpreter to help communicate with the family. In addition, the OTA and occupational therapist should not develop a discharge plan without the family's input.

Type of Reasoning: Evaluative
This question requires one to determine the best course of action that considers the needs of the person and most effectively facilitates delivery of services. Questions that ask the test taker to use judgment to determine a best course of action often utilize evaluative reasoning skills. In this situation, and in keeping with the AOTA Code of Ethics, the OTA should seek out an interpreter. An understanding of client-centered and culturally competent practice and the need to provide interpretation services is required to correctly answer this item. See Chapters 3 and 4.

A114 C8

A school-based OTA consults with a teacher regarding a nonspeaking student who uses a wheelchair and an augmentative communication device. The teacher reports that the student is making many errors on the communication device and is justifiably getting frustrated. The teacher reports that in the past the student did not have any difficulties using the device. Which is the most effective initial action for the OTA to take in response to the teacher's report?

Answer Choices:
A. Advise the teacher to contact the student's parents and recommend that they bring the child to a physician for an exam.
B. Recommend a re-assessment of the student's motor and communication abilities.
C. Assess the position of the student in the wheelchair and the device on the wheelchair.
D. Ask the student where they would like the device to be located and reposition it.

Correct Answer: C.

Rationale:
Even minor changes in a person's positioning can impact their access to an assistive device; therefore, the OTA's initial action must be to assess the position of the student and the device. Based upon the results of this assessment, the OTA may provide recommendations for positioning the student and/or for placement of the device. Referring the student's parents to contact a physician for a physical exam, re-assessing the student's motor and communication abilities, and repositioning the communication device are not steps indicated at this time.

Type of Reasoning: Inferential
One must determine the most likely cause for the communication difficulty, given the diagnosis and limitations of the student. This requires inferential reasoning skill, where one must draw conclusions based on the information presented. In this situation, the OTA should evaluate the position of the student in the wheelchair and the device on the wheelchair, as improper positioning can affect use of an augmentative communication device. If answered incorrectly, review information about the purposes of wheelchairs and positioning equipment. See Chapter 15.

A115 C7

Several newly homeless veterans with a post-traumatic stress disorder attend an OT community re-entry group in a shelter. Which is the best primary focus of the initial group session?

Answer Choices:
A. Development of instrumental activities of daily living skills such as meal preparation.
B. Exploration of vocational interests and employment possibilities.
C. Identification of local resources such as soup kitchens and thrift stores.

Correct Answer: C.

Rationale:
Locating basic resources is the most essential survival skill listed. Initial sessions at a homeless shelter would likely focus on basic survival and personal self-care skills prior to focusing on vocational interests, employment opportunities, or instrumental activities of daily living (IADL), such as meal preparation skills. Subsequent sessions may focus on the development of IADL and vocational skills.

Type of Reasoning: Inductive
One must consider the needs of the group and benefits of each of the four possible courses of action. This necessitates inductive reasoning skill, where the test taker must use clinical judgment to determine the merits of each of the three choices, based on client needs. In this case, location of resources is the most beneficial topic, as it is the most essential survival skill for this group.

A116 C9

An OTA working in a school system incorporates the Individuals with Disabilities Education Act (IDEA) into their daily service provision. In which location should the OTA provide intervention?

Answer Choices:
A. Regular classroom while general education classes are not in session.
B. Special education classroom specifically designed for children with disabilities.
C. Regular classroom while general education classes are in session.
D. Private occupational therapy room specifically designed for children with disabilities.

Correct Answer: C.

Rationale:
The guidelines from IDEA emphasize that children with disabilities receive services in an inclusive manner that enables each child to have full access to the general education curriculum, and full participation in a general education classroom. The other options are too restrictive and do not facilitate inclusion in general education.

Type of Reasoning: Deductive
One must recall IDEA guidelines in order to arrive at a correct conclusion. This requires deductive reasoning skill, where knowledge of protocols and guidelines are paramount to choosing the correct answer. The provision of occupational therapy services in a regular classroom while general education classes are in session is the only location that provides inclusive treatment. If answered incorrectly, review IDEA guidelines and inclusive services in the classroom. See Chapter 4.

A117 C3

An OTA works with a person who incurred full-thickness burns to both arms. Which intervention approach would be most effective for the OTA to provide to control hypertrophic scar formation?

Answer Choices:
A. Axillary splints applied in the airplane position.
B. Compression garments.
C. Wound grafting.
D. Elevation of the areas just above heart level.

Correct Answer: B.

Rationale:
Custom-made compression garments provide equal pressure over the entire area to prevent scarring. They must be worn 23 hours per day for approximately 12 months, or until the scar and wound maturation is complete. Airplane splints are used to prevent tightening of the axilla area, which would result in the inability to horizontally abduct the arm. Wound grafting is used as biological dressing to provide wound covering and pain relief. Elevation of the areas just above heart level is a technique to reduce upper extremity edema.

Type of Reasoning: Inferential
One must determine the most effective approach to control hypertrophic scar formation in order to arrive at a correct conclusion. This requires one to determine what course of action will result in the best therapeutic outcome, which is an inferential reasoning skill. For this case, compression garments are most effective. If answered incorrectly, review intervention approaches for burns. See Chapter 6.

A118 C5

During an intervention session, an individual with a spinal cord injury at C7 reports noticing redness on the ischial tuberosity during their morning self-exam with a mirror. Which action is most effective for the OTA to recommend to the client in response to the their reported observations?

Answer Choices:
A. Integrate weight shifting into daily activities.
B. Consider applying for a tilt-in-space wheelchair.
C. Use an angled foam cushion.
D. Self-direct caregivers to assist with weight shifting.

Correct Answer: A.

Rationale:
During rehabilitation, a person with a spinal cord injury must be instructed on the need to relieve pressure on a consistent basis. A person with a spinal cord injury at the level of C7 can perform depression transfers, so the ability to perform weight shifting for pressure relief is intact. The person is reporting the early signs of skin breakdown, so it is vital that the person integrates weight shifting into daily activities. This is a very effective way to prevent decubitus ulcers. Since the person is able to weight shift independently, a tilt-in-space wheelchair and self-directing caregivers to assist with weight shifting are two modifications that are at too low a level for this scenario. An angled foam cushion would position the person in a manner that would increase weight on the ischial tuberosity. This would be contraindicated.

Type of Reasoning: Inductive
One must utilize clinical knowledge and judgment to determine the recommendation that best addresses the individual's issue. This requires inductive reasoning skill. In this case, the OTA should recommend the integration of weight shifting into daily activities to prevent pressure sores. If answered incorrectly, review the functional abilities of the different levels of SCI and interventions to prevent decubiti and. The integration of this knowledge is required for a correct answer. See Chapters 7 and 9.

A119 C2

An OTA working in a skilled nursing facility conducts an initial therapeutic feeding session with an older adult with dysphagia. During the session the resident consistently expresses a desire to return home. Which is the OTA's best response?

Answer Choices:
A. Redirect the conversation to the texture and taste of the food.
B. Acknowledge the resident's desire to return home.
C. End the session and report the resident's desire.
D. Offer to contact the resident's family to convey this desire.

Correct Answer: B.

Rationale:
It is natural and normal for a new resident in a skilled nursing facility to express a desire to return home. This wish must be acknowledged and validated in order to establish therapeutic rapport. Ending the session or immediately redirecting the resident to the feeding activity ignores the validity of the resident's genuine feelings. This is counter-therapeutic. Once a person feels that they have been heard, they are often able to refocus on the activity. Because the OTA does not know the resident's relationship with their family, it is inappropriate for the OTA to offer to contact the family.

Type of Reasoning: Evaluative
One must weigh the possible courses of action and then make a value judgment about the best course to take. This requires evaluative reasoning skill, which often utilizes guiding principles of action in order to arrive at a correct conclusion. For this case, the OTA should acknowledge the resident's desire to return home. This option is consistent with principles of the therapeutic use of self. See Chapter 3.

564 Exam A Answer Rationales

A120 C4

An OTA works with a person who is recovering from the removal of a brain tumor from the cerebellum. The client has established a goal to resume the role of home maintainer. Which is most relevant for the OTA to focus on during intervention sessions focused on the development of home management skills?

Answer Choices:
A. Sensory precautions to observe when cooking and ironing.
B. Compensatory techniques for finding items in the supermarket.
C. Organizational strategies for managing the household budget.
D. The use of a wheeled cart to assist with balance while doing laundry.

Correct Answer: D.

Rationale:
The use of mobility aids such as a wheeled cart would be a helpful intervention for a person who incurred damage to the cerebellum, which would result in balance and coordination concerns. The observation of sensory precautions when cooking and ironing would be indicated for a person who has sensory loss due to parietal lobe damage. Training in compensatory techniques for finding items in the supermarket would be indicated for a person who had visual deficits resulting from occipital lobe damage. A person who had cognitive deficits from frontal lobe damage would benefit from interventions focused on the use of organizational strategies.

Type of Reasoning: Inductive
For this question, one must determine the most relevant intervention focus for a patient who has cerebellar deficits from a brain tumor. This requires clinical judgment, which is an inductive reasoning skill. For this case, the OTA should address the person's balance and coordination difficulties. If answered incorrectly, review the function of the cerebellum and intervention strategies for cerebellar deficits. The integration of this knowledge is required to correctly answer this exam item. See Chapters 7 and 12.

A121 C4

An elementary school-aged child with Duchenne's muscular dystrophy receives occupational therapy services. The family establishes a goal of maintaining the child's leisure and social participation. Which is the best activity for the OTA to recommend the family pursue with this child?

Answer Choices:
A. Electronic sports (e.g., Wii bowling).
B. Adapted little league baseball.
C. Wheelchair basketball.
D. Recreational swimming.

Correct Answer: D.

Rationale:
Recreational swimming is a social and leisure activity that the child can participate in with family members and friends. It can also be helpful in maintaining the child's functional level as long as possible. Even when the child's Duchenne's progresses, swimming can remain an activity that can be successfully pursued. The eye-hand coordination to play electronic sports games will likely be too difficult for the child with Duchenne's. Baseball and basketball also have mobility and coordination requirements that would be likely be difficult for this child. In addition, one cannot assume that an elementary school-aged child with Duchenne's is using a wheelchair.

Type of Reasoning: Inferential
In this question, one must make a link between the diagnosis, the age of the child, and the appropriate interventions. Here, swimming is appropriate because it encourages the maintenance of function for as long as possible. Questions such as these require one to draw conclusions based on evidence presented, which is an inferential skill. If answered incorrectly, review muscular dystrophy. An understanding of the progressive nature of this disorder is needed to select the correct answer. See Chapters 7.

A122 C1

A 5-year-old is referred to occupational therapy. Upon the completion of a standardized test assessment, the OTA determines that the child demonstrates age-appropriate cognitive and fine motor skills. Which activity would the child be able to complete at this developmental level?

Answer Choices:
A. Cutting long thin strips with scissors.
B. Holding and snipping with scissors.
C. Cutting simple figure shapes with scissors.

Correct Answer: C.

Rationale:
According to established developmental milestones, cutting simple figure shapes is a 4- to 6-year-old cognitive and fine motor skill. Cutting strips is a 3- to 4-year-old skill. Holding and snipping with scissors is a 2- to 3-year-old skill.

Type of Reasoning: Deductive
This question requires one to recall factual knowledge, which is a deductive reasoning skill. The question necessitates one to recall the developmental skills of a 5-year-old. In this situation, cutting simple figure shapes is a 5-year-old skill. If answered incorrectly, review the developmental sequence of scissor skills. See Chapter 5.

A123 C9

An OTA working in an outpatient clinic observes the clinic's administrative assistant leaving patient records open on the clinic's reception counter. The assistant has left the clinic to go for lunch. Which action is best for the OTA to take in response to this observation?

Answer Choices:
A. Remind the administrative assistant of the need to keep patient records private when the assistant returns from lunch.
B. Contact the administrative assistant's direct supervisor to report this observation.
C. Pick up the records and place them in a location out of public view.
D. Discuss the issue with the occupational therapist during their next scheduled supervision session.

566 Exam A Answer Rationales

Correct Answer: C.

Rationale:
The OTA must immediately act to protect patient privacy. The HIPAA Privacy Rule requires that all providers protect patient confidentiality in all forms (i.e., oral, written, and electronic). Charts and any documentation with patients' names or other identifiers must be stored out of public view and in secure locations. Reminding the administrative assistant of documentation privacy requirements when the assistant returns, contacting the administrative assistant's direct supervisor, and discussing the issue with the supervising occupational therapist do not address the immediate need for the OTA to take action that makes sure no patient record is visible to anyone in the reception area.

Type of Reasoning: Evaluative
This question requires the test taker to weigh the merits of the courses of action presented and determine the approach that will most effectively resolve the issue. This requires evaluative reasoning skill. For this situation, the OTA should pick up the records and place them in a location out of public view to protect patient privacy. If answered incorrectly, review HIPAA guidelines and the protection of patient privacy. See Chapter 4.

A124 C6

A young adult with a 10-year history of serious mental illness is being discharged home in 2 days. The client collaborates with the care coordination team to plan discharge with the client's primary family members. The team consists of a psychiatrist, a registered nurse, a social worker, an occupational therapist, and an OTA. The team conducts a pre-discharge family meeting to provide family members with information to assist them in supporting the client's recovery. What is the most relevant information for the occupational therapist and OTA to provide to the client's primary family members in this meeting?

Answer Choices:
A. Family role activity suggestions and potential adaptations.
B. The therapeutic effects and potential side effects of medications.
C. Advocacy strategies and consumer/family resources.
D. Information on family dynamics and family support groups.

Correct Answer: A.

Rationale:
The occupational therapist and OTA are the members on the identified care coordination team who are most qualified to provide information about role activities and potential activity adaptations. The ability of a client to engage in meaningful activities in the home and resume relevant role activities can facilitate positive family functioning and support recovery. The other choices are all relevant foci for discharge planning, but the other members of the team can provide this information.

Type of Reasoning: Inferential
One must determine the most relevant information for occupational therapy practitioners to provide to the family of a person with serious mental illness prior to discharge home. This requires inferential reasoning skill, where one draws conclusions based on information presented. In this situation, the most relevant information for the OT practitioner to provide to the family is role activity suggestions and potential adaptations. If answered incorrectly, review discharge planning guidelines and the recovery model for mental illness. The integration of this knowledge is required for a correct answer. See Chapters 3 and 13.

A125 C1

An OTA with established service competence completes a standardized early intervention screening of an 8-month-old child. The results indicate that the child can sit independently by propping forward on both arms. The OTA collaborates with the occupational therapist to determine the next step to take in working with this child. Which is the best action for the OTA to complete next?

Answer Choices:
A. Evaluate the child's sensorimotor skills using a standardized assessment.
B. Inform the parents that the child exhibits typical behavior.
C. Develop goals to improve sitting balance.
D. Provide play activities to develop dynamic sitting balance.

Correct Answer: A.

Rationale:
The screening indicated a sensorimotor delay, which requires further evaluation. Sitting with arms propped forward is typical of a 5- to 6-month-old. At 8 months, a child typically sits without support; therefore, further evaluation of the child's sensorimotor status is indicated. The occupational therapist and OTA cannot collaborate to set goals or prescribe activities prior to the completion of a full evaluation. OTAs are able to perform standardized assessments with the supervision of an occupational therapist.

Type of Reasoning: Inferential
One must determine the most likely next course of action for the OTA to take based on the stage of the OT process and the reported screening result. This requires inferential reasoning skill, where one must draw conclusions based on the information presented. In this situation, the next step after screening is to complete a sensorimotor evaluation since the child is demonstrating a sensorimotor delay. If answered incorrectly, review the stages of the OT process and motor development of infants, especially the 6- to 8-month range. The integration of this knowledge is required to answer this question correctly. See Chapters 3 and 5.

A126 C5

An individual with Lyme disease receives outpatient occupational therapy services. Upon evaluation, the occupational therapist and the OTA determine that the person's Lyme disease had resulted in a number of nervous system abnormalities including numbness in the hands and toes, bladder control impairments, and Bell's palsy. The person is upset that their Lyme disease is preventing them from doing things like a 'normal' person. Which intervention is best for the OTA to implement during the first intervention session?

Answer Choices:
A. Teach the person to perform Kegel exercises to improve bladder control.
B. The application of thermal heat modalities to address numbness in the hands.
C. Train person to use their fingers to prevent spillage of a bolus through the lips.

Correct Answer: C.

Rationale:
While numbness and bladder control impairments are important to address, the first intervention session should address the person's Bell's palsy. Bell's palsy is condition in which the muscles on one side of the face becomes weak or paralyzed, causing it to droop or become stiff on that side. This makes eating very difficult as the person cannot fully close their mouth or keep food in their mouth. Eating Is a basic activity of daily living (BADL) that is often completed in the presence of others. Therefore, having an open mouth with food in it and involuntarily spilling food is not consistent with established cultural norms for eating. This can contribute to embarrassment and the withdrawal from social situations. Teaching a person how to self-manage their eating can help them participate in this BADL in a more satisfying manner. Additional interventions for Bell's palsy include the fabrication of facial splint to prevent long-term asymmetry of facial muscles and supportive counselling to help a person cope with a facial deformity. Kegel exercises can strengthen the pelvic floor which can improve bladder control. This can be the focus of a subsequent intervention session. Since it takes time for these exercises to have a functional impact, the use of commercially available incontinence products can help the person engage in desired activities. The use of thermal heat modalities is contraindicated for a person with decreased sensation.

Type of Reasoning: Inferential
One must consider the person's diagnosis, presenting symptoms, and expressed concerns in order to choose the treatment activity that would be best for the OTA to include in the first intervention session. Questions that ask for a best course of action or what will best consider a person's needs often necessitate inferential reasoning skill. If answered incorrectly, review information on the interventions and approaches used to address the nervous system disorders that can result from Lyme disease. See Chapter 9.

A127 C6

An individual hospitalized for the first time due to a brief psychotic episode attends an occupational therapy group. During task performance, the OTA notices that the person is restless with hand tremors and shaking legs. Which of the following should the OTA document that the person seems to be exhibiting?

Answer Choices:
A. Akinesia.
B. Pseudo-parkinsonism.
C. Akathisia.
D. Tardive dyskinesia.

Correct Answer: C.

Rationale:
Akathisia is a side effect of antipsychotic medications that is exhibited by restlessness, hand tremors, and shaky legs. Akinesia is also a potential side effect, but this is evident by a lack of movement. Akinesia is also a negative symptom of schizophrenia. Pseudo-parkinsonism is also a side effect that appears as behaviors similar to the symptoms of advanced Parkinson's disease; that is, rigidity, pill-rolling tremors, masked face, and a shuffling gait. Tardive dyskinesia is an irreversible neurological condition caused by years of taking neuroleptic medications. It would not be evident in someone being treated for a first break with neuroleptic medications.

Type of Reasoning: Analytical
This question provides symptoms and the test taker must determine the cause for such symptoms. This is an analytical reasoning skill, as questions of this nature often ask one to analyze a group of symptoms in order to determine a diagnosis. In this situation, the symptoms indicate akathisia, which should be reviewed if answered incorrectly, along with other side effects of psychotropic medications. See Chapter 10.

A128 C5

An OTA receives a referral to provide home-based services to an older adult who lives alone in a fourth-floor walk-up apartment. Upon entering the apartment, the OTA notes the sweltering heat. The apartment has no fans or air conditioners. The client's skin is hot, dry, and red, and breathing is labored. The OTA offers the client a glass of water and places ice compresses on the arterial pressure points to help with cooling. Which is the most important action for the OTA to take next?

Answer Choices:
A. Cancel the intervention session and call for an ambulance to provide emergency medical services to the client.
B. Proceed with the planned intervention session and include documentation about the client's environmental conditions in the intervention report.
C. Contact the home health agency's occupational therapist to report the client's environmental conditions and then proceed with the planned intervention session.
D. Cancel the intervention session and advise the client to contact a doctor how to best address the impact of hot weather on personal health.

Correct Answer: A.

Rationale:
The client is exhibiting signs of heat stroke. Older adults are particularly at risk for heat-induced illnesses. Extended periods of intense heat can be life threatening to older adults and must be treated as a medical emergency. While lowering the client's body temperature with ice on the arterial pressure points is an appropriate first-aid intervention, it is not sufficient to deal with this serious situation. Immediate medical care is required.

Type of Reasoning: Evaluative
This question requires one to weigh the courses of action presented and determine the approach that will most effectively address the client's needs. This requires evaluative reasoning skill. For this case, based on the client's symptoms, the OTA should cancel the intervention session and call for an ambulance to provide emergency medical services. If answered incorrectly, review first aid approaches for heat stroke. See Chapter 9.

A129 C1

A 9-year-old girl with the diagnosis of cystic fibrosis is hospitalized in a small rural hospital. Currently, there are no other children in the hospital, and the hospital does not have a pediatric play area. The head nurse asks the OTA to suggest appropriate play activities that hospital volunteers can do with the child. Which is the most age-appropriate activity for the OTA to suggest?

Answer Choices:
A. Dressing paper dolls.
B. Coloring in coloring books.
C. Playing card games.
D. Cutting and pasting pictures onto cards.

Correct Answer: C.

Rationale:
Children aged 7–12 are developmentally able to participate in games with rules, competition, and social interaction. The other activities reflect creative play that is developed between ages 4 and 7. In addition, they are solitary activities and do not afford opportunities for competitive fun and socialization. Hospitalization can be lonely and frightening, so having volunteers play with the child can be psychologically beneficial, as well as developmentally appropriate.

Type of Reasoning: Inferential
One must determine the most appropriate play activities for a child, given knowledge of the child's age and developmental ability. This requires inferential reasoning skill, where one must infer or draw conclusions about a best course of action. In this situation, the OTA should suggest playing card games. If answered incorrectly, review information on the development of play. See Chapters 5.

A130 C6

An OTA leads an outpatient wellness program. An individual with obsessive-compulsive disorder asks for suggestions to manage symptoms that are interfering with life satisfaction. Which is the best recommendation for the OTA to make to the individual?

Answer Choices:
A. Approach activities in a nonchalant manner without high expectations.
B. Engage in concrete activities that can be broken down into simple steps.
C. Redirect thoughts and energies into meaningful activities.
D. Set limits on the number of activities done in a day.

Correct Answer: C.

Rationale:
The focus of OT in a wellness program is to help individuals attain and maintain life satisfaction through the engagement in meaningful activities. Individuals with obsessive-compulsive disorder have recurring and persistent thoughts (obsessions) and the need to engage in repetitious or ritualistic behaviors (compulsions) that interfere with functional activities. Therefore, redirecting thoughts and energy into meaningful activities can be an effective behavior management strategy. Approaching activities in a nonchalant manner without high expectations and limiting the number of activities performed during a day would not address the person's need to refocus thoughts and behaviors away from their obsessions and compulsions. Engaging in activities that can be broken down into simple steps is helpful for persons with cognitive deficits. Individuals with obsessive-compulsive disorders typically do not have cognitive deficits.

Type of Reasoning: Inductive
This question requires one to determine the most beneficial recommendation for a person with obsessive-compulsive disorder. This requires inductive reasoning skill, where clinical judgment is paramount to arriving at a correct conclusion. For this situation, the OTA should suggest redirecting thoughts and energies into meaningful occupations. If answered incorrectly, review treatment guidelines for persons with obsessive-compulsive disorder. See Chapter 10.

A131 C9

The supervisor of an acute inpatient medical unit requests that a recently hired entry-level OTA write summaries for several assessment sessions that were completed by another OTA. The evaluating OTA had to leave work unexpectedly due to a medical emergency and is not expected to return to work. Which is the best response for the OTA to make in response to this request?

Answer Choices:
A. Comply with the supervisor's request but ask for the supervisor to cosign the notes.
B. Request time to complete an independent assessment of each individual previously evaluated.
C. Report the supervisor's request to the facility's administration.
D. Suggest that the OTA's assessment results be documented by the supervisor.

Correct Answer: D.

Rationale:
It is not appropriate for a peer to document results of an assessment session in which they did not participate. It is acceptable for a supervisor to provide documentation based upon staff members' input, as long as the documentation reports that it is based upon the work of a given staff member. The supervisor must provide an accurate record of the situation (i.e., assessment completed by OTA X found that . . .). In an acute inpatient medical setting, there is insufficient time to complete another assessment. The entry-level OTA should communicate directly with their supervisor. There is nothing to report to the administration at this time.

Type of Reasoning: Evaluative
This question requires professional judgment based on guiding principles, which is an evaluative reasoning skill. In this situation, the OTA's most appropriate response is to suggest that the evaluating OTA's assessment results be documented by the supervisor. Accuracy in record keeping is important in this situation and should be used as the guiding principle in finding the best solution to this situation. If answered incorrectly, review documentation and OT supervision guidelines. See Chapter 4.

A132 C4

A patient had a brain tumor removed one month ago and exhibits residual cognitive-perceptual deficits. The OTA uses a neurofunctional approach to remediate the client's cognitive dysfunction. Which of the following are best for the OTA to include in the intervention program? Select the three BEST responses.

Answer Choices:
A. Functional activities in their real contexts.
B. Tabletop activities to practice remediation strategies.
C. Computer games to develop performance component skills.
D. Routine tasks that have been adapted so the client can perform them.
E. Client education on adaptive approaches to strengthen residual abilities.
F. Client education on strategies to remediate deficits and restore deficient abilities.

Correct Answers: A, D, and E.

Rationale:
A neurofunctional approach emphasizes functional activity performance in the actual environment. Routine tasks are presented that the person can perform or that have been adapted so that they can perform them. A neurofunctional approach places focus on adaptive approaches and strengthening residual abilities. The other options reflect a remedial/restorative/transfer of training approach.

Type of Reasoning: Deductive
One must recall factual knowledge of the neurofunctional approach to rehabilitation in order to choose the correct solution. This is a deductive reasoning skill. A typical neurofunctional approach emphasizes functional activity performance in a real-life context with adaptations provided as needed to strengthen abilities and enhance performance. If answered incorrectly, review guidelines for providing treatment under a neurofunctional approach. See Chapter 12.

A133 C4

During an intervention session focused on the development of grasp and shoulder mobility, an OTA asks a client to move numerous identical one-pound cans of vegetables from the countertop to the cabinet shelf above the counter. According to contemporary motor learning approaches, what type of practice has the OTA implemented for this client?

Answer Choices:
A. Random practice.
B. Blocked practice.
C. Planned practice.

Correct Answer: B.

Rationale:
Blocked practice involves repeated performance of the same motor skill. Since the cans are identical and weigh the same, lifting each can requires the same motor skill. If the cans were of different sizes, shapes, and/or weights, then different motor skills would be required for task performance. This would be an example of random practice, which involves the performance of several tasks in random order to encourage the reformulation of the solution to the presented motor problem. Planned practice is a contrived term.

Type of Reasoning: Analytical
This question requires one to analyze the information provided and determine the best descriptor for this functional activity. This requires analytical reasoning skill, where one must weigh all the information provided in order to arrive at a correct conclusion. For this situation, the activity presented is that of blocked practice. If answered incorrectly, review principles of motor learning, especially blocked practice. See Chapter 12.

A134 C1

A toddler attends an early intervention program as a result of developmental delay. Over the past two weeks, the toddler has successfully completed the activities the OTA has provided in order to develop a palmar grasp. Which action should the OTA take next in response to the child's progress?

Answer Choices:
A. Continue providing the child with activities to refine palmar grasp.
B. Review the initial evaluation with the occupational therapist to determine new goals.
C. Provide activities to develop a radial palmar grasp.
D. Provide activities to develop an ulnar palmar grasp.

Correct Answer: C.

Rationale:
The child has exhibited mastery of a palmar grasp. The next developmental level of grasp after a palmar grasp is a radial palmar grasp. Ulnar palmar grasp is the developmental precursor to palmar grasp. If the initial evaluation determined there was a need to work on the development of grasp, intervention can proceed to the next level without re-evaluation or the establishment of new goals.

Type of Reasoning: Deductive
One must recall the developmental guidelines for children in development of grasp patterns. This is factual knowledge, which is a deductive reasoning skill. In this case, after development of a palmar grasp, the next level is radial palmar grasp. If answered incorrectly, review development of grasp patterns in children. See Chapter 5.

Correct Answer: D.

Rationale:
It is not appropriate for a peer to document results of an assessment session in which they did not participate. It is acceptable for a supervisor to provide documentation based upon staff members' input, as long as the documentation reports that it is based upon the work of a given staff member. The supervisor must provide an accurate record of the situation (i.e., assessment completed by OTA X found that . . .). In an acute inpatient medical setting, there is insufficient time to complete another assessment. The entry-level OTA should communicate directly with their supervisor. There is nothing to report to the administration at this time.

Type of Reasoning: Evaluative
This question requires professional judgment based on guiding principles, which is an evaluative reasoning skill. In this situation, the OTA's most appropriate response is to suggest that the evaluating OTA's assessment results be documented by the supervisor. Accuracy in record keeping is important in this situation and should be used as the guiding principle in finding the best solution to this situation. If answered incorrectly, review documentation and OT supervision guidelines. See Chapter 4.

A132 C4

A patient had a brain tumor removed one month ago and exhibits residual cognitive-perceptual deficits. The OTA uses a neurofunctional approach to remediate the client's cognitive dysfunction. Which of the following are best for the OTA to include in the intervention program? Select the three BEST responses.

Answer Choices:
A. Functional activities in their real contexts.
B. Tabletop activities to practice remediation strategies.
C. Computer games to develop performance component skills.
D. Routine tasks that have been adapted so the client can perform them.
E. Client education on adaptive approaches to strengthen residual abilities.
F. Client education on strategies to remediate deficits and restore deficient abilities.

Correct Answers: A, D, and E.

Rationale:
A neurofunctional approach emphasizes functional activity performance in the actual environment. Routine tasks are presented that the person can perform or that have been adapted so that they can perform them. A neurofunctional approach places focus on adaptive approaches and strengthening residual abilities. The other options reflect a remedial/restorative/transfer of training approach.

Type of Reasoning: Deductive
One must recall factual knowledge of the neurofunctional approach to rehabilitation in order to choose the correct solution. This is a deductive reasoning skill. A typical neurofunctional approach emphasizes functional activity performance in a real-life context with adaptations provided as needed to strengthen abilities and enhance performance. If answered incorrectly, review guidelines for providing treatment under a neurofunctional approach. See Chapter 12.

572 Exam A Answer Rationales

A133 C4

During an intervention session focused on the development of grasp and shoulder mobility, an OTA asks a client to move numerous identical one-pound cans of vegetables from the countertop to the cabinet shelf above the counter. According to contemporary motor learning approaches, what type of practice has the OTA implemented for this client?

Answer Choices:
A. Random practice.
B. Blocked practice.
C. Planned practice.

Correct Answer: B.

Rationale:
Blocked practice involves repeated performance of the same motor skill. Since the cans are identical and weigh the same, lifting each can requires the same motor skill. If the cans were of different sizes, shapes, and/or weights, then different motor skills would be required for task performance. This would be an example of random practice, which involves the performance of several tasks in random order to encourage the reformulation of the solution to the presented motor problem. Planned practice is a contrived term.

Type of Reasoning: Analytical
This question requires one to analyze the information provided and determine the best descriptor for this functional activity. This requires analytical reasoning skill, where one must weigh all the information provided in order to arrive at a correct conclusion. For this situation, the activity presented is that of blocked practice. If answered incorrectly, review principles of motor learning, especially blocked practice. See Chapter 12.

A134 C1

A toddler attends an early intervention program as a result of developmental delay. Over the past two weeks, the toddler has successfully completed the activities the OTA has provided in order to develop a palmar grasp. Which action should the OTA take next in response to the child's progress?

Answer Choices:
A. Continue providing the child with activities to refine palmar grasp.
B. Review the initial evaluation with the occupational therapist to determine new goals.
C. Provide activities to develop a radial palmar grasp.
D. Provide activities to develop an ulnar palmar grasp.

Correct Answer: C.

Rationale:
The child has exhibited mastery of a palmar grasp. The next developmental level of grasp after a palmar grasp is a radial palmar grasp. Ulnar palmar grasp is the developmental precursor to palmar grasp. If the initial evaluation determined there was a need to work on the development of grasp, intervention can proceed to the next level without re-evaluation or the establishment of new goals.

Type of Reasoning: Deductive
One must recall the developmental guidelines for children in development of grasp patterns. This is factual knowledge, which is a deductive reasoning skill. In this case, after development of a palmar grasp, the next level is radial palmar grasp. If answered incorrectly, review development of grasp patterns in children. See Chapter 5.

A135 C4

A child with a tactile defensive sensory modulation disorder attends a private early intervention clinic. The OTA collaborates with the occupational therapist and the child's parents to develop strategies and guidelines to help the child handle the symptoms of this disorder at home. Which are the best recommendations for the OTA and therapist to make to the parents? Select the three BEST responses.

Answer Choices:
A. Avoid the use of swings and other moving equipment during play activities.
B. Encourage the use of swings and other moving equipment during play activities.
C. Adjust stimuli that seem to influence the child's modulation of sensation.
D. During bathing, teach the child to use firm pressure and a soft cloth to wash self.
E. Soften the child's clothing by repeated laundering and remove clothing tags.
F. Provide a variety of textures in the clothing the child wears.

Correct Answers: C, D, and E.

Rationale:
Intervention for a child with a sensory modulation disorder should follow the general principles of Ayres Sensory Integration Approach®. A fundamental intervention approach in this model is the monitoring and adjustment of stimuli that seem to influence a child's modulation of sensation (e.g., lighting, sound, etc.). Children with tactile defensive sensory modulation disorder typically find self-applied stimuli more tolerable than the application of tactile stimuli by others. Deep touch and firm pressure are also more tolerable than light touch. Therefore, teaching the child to use firm pressure and a soft cloth to wash self can make bathing more tolerable. Because stiff clothing, textured clothing, and clothing tags can be aversive to a child with a tactile defensive sensory modulation disorder, softening the child's clothing and removing clothing tags will increase the child's tolerance of clothing. The use or avoidance of swings and other moving play equipment is indicated for vestibular processing disorders.

Type of Reasoning: Inductive
This question requires one to determine the best recommendation for a child with tactile defensiveness. This requires inductive reasoning skill, where clinical judgment is paramount to arriving at a correct conclusion. In this situation, given the diagnosis of tactile defensive behaviors, the OTA and therapist should recommend the monitoring and adjustment of stimuli that seem to influence a child's modulation of sensation, teaching the child to use firm pressure and a soft cloth to wash, and softening clothing and removing clothing tags. If answered incorrectly, review treatment guidelines for children with tactile defensive behaviors. See Chapters 7 and 12.

A136 C5

An individual recovering from hepatitis, type C has decreased upper and lower extremity muscle strength and hypertension. Six months ago, the client had an angioplasty and is very fearful of having a heart attack. Which should the OTA advise the client to perform to increase muscle strength?

Answer Choices:
A. Isotonic exercises.
B. Isometric exercises.
C. Contract-relax exercise.
D. Muscle contractions and holds.

574 Exam A Answer Rationales

Correct Answer: A.

Rationale:
Isotonics are the only exercises listed that are not contraindicated for a person with hypertension or heart disease. The other choices describe isometric exercises or activities that include isometric elements and are contraindicated in this case.

Type of Reasoning: Inferential
One must determine the most appropriate exercise for an individual, given knowledge of the presenting diagnoses. This requires inferential reasoning skill, where one must infer or draw conclusions about a best course of action. In this situation, the OTA should recommend isotonic exercises, as this is the only exercise listed that is not contraindicated for individuals with hypertension or heart disease. If answered incorrectly, review exercise guidelines for individuals with hypertension and heart disease. See Chapter 8.

A137 C3

An individual has relocated to a new area and begins treatment at an outpatient OT clinic for follow-up after rotator cuff surgery. It is eight weeks' post-operation. Which is the most effective intervention for the OTA to implement at this time?

Answer Choices:
A. An isometric strengthening program.
B. Passive range of motion.
C. Active assistive range of motion.
D. An isotonic strengthening program.

Correct Answer: A.

Rationale:
At 8 weeks post-surgery, strengthening should begin with isometrics and then progress to isotonics. Passive range of motion (PROM) is the intervention for 0–6 weeks' post-operation. Active assistive ROM (AAROM) is commonly initiated from 6 to 8 weeks.

Type of Reasoning: Deductive
This question requires recall of guidelines, which is factual knowledge. Deductive reasoning skills are utilized whenever one must recall facts to solve novel problems. In this situation, a patient who is 6 weeks' post-operation for rotator cuff repair can begin an isometric strengthening program. If answered incorrectly, review treatment guidelines for post-surgical rotator cuff repair. See Chapter 6.

A138 C1

A school-based OTA is working with a child who has poor sitting posture, inefficient grasp, and excessive writing pressure into the paper. The OTA collaborates with the occupational therapist and determines that the best intervention approach requires integration of more than one intervention model. Which approaches will most effectively address all the child's deficits?

Answer Choices:
A. A combination of biomechanical and psychosocial approaches.
B. A combination of biomechanical and sensory integration approaches.
C. A combination of acquisitional and motor learning approaches.
D. A combination of psychosocial and neurodevelopmental approaches.

Correct Answer: B.

Rationale:
The task of writing is a complex process that requires sensorimotor, cognitive, language, and visual processing abilities. Occupational therapy intervention for handwriting problems often requires the integration of multiple models and frames of reference. In this case, the biomechanical frame of reference is best suited to address the areas of posture, pencil grasp, and possible compensatory strategies, including environmental and tool adaptations. The child's reported behaviors can be indicative of a sensory-processing deficit. For example, a proprioceptive-processing disorder can be evident in clumsiness, motor planning difficulties, and the use of too much force (e.g., pressing too hard on paper). Therefore, sensory integration approaches are also indicated.

Type of Reasoning: Inductive
One must determine the best intervention approaches for a child with handwriting problems and poor sitting posture in order to arrive at a correct conclusion. This requires inductive reasoning skill. For this case, the approaches that will most effectively address the child's deficits are a combination of biomechanical and sensorimotor approaches.

A139 C6

An adult with schizophrenia has been experiencing negative symptoms of restricted emotion, decreased engagement, and a lack of energy. Which group is the best for the OTA to include in the client's intervention plan?

Answer Choices:
A. An arts and crafts group in which each client works on a self-selected individual project.
B. A meal planning and preparation group in which clients works collaboratively with others.
C. A stress management group that includes biofeedback and visualization.
D. A support group for persons with schizophrenia in which all clients share their stories.

Correct Answer: A.

Rationale:
Experiencing negative symptoms associated with schizophrenia can have a significant impact on a person's ability to attain life goals, live independently, maintain a job, and nurture healthy personal and social relationships. Given the person's presenting negative symptoms of restricted emotion, decreased engagement, and a lack of energy, it is best to include the person in a group with minimal expectations to share or socialize with others. According to Mosey's developmental groups, this is called a parallel group. The use of Mosey's developmental groups can assist clients in acquiring and developing group interaction skills. An arts and crafts group in which each client works on a self-selected individual project meets the criteria of a parallel group. Enabling a client to choose an individual activity to complete will assist the client in developing a comfort level in the presence of others. Providing the client with a choice of activity and a means to express feelings through media is an effective approach to develop self-efficacy and group interaction skills. The OTA can structure a parallel group to allow graded expression and interactions with others in a safe environment as the client develops trust and comfort in the presence of others. As the client's comfort level increases in social situations, they can work collaboratively on a joint project, share life stories, and offer support to others. The concentrated focus that is required to effectively engage in biofeedback and visualization would make these approaches difficult for a person with negative symptoms.

Type of Reasoning: Inductive

This exam item requires the test taker to determine the best group for an individual experiencing the negative symptoms of schizophrenia. This requires inductive reasoning skill, in which clinical judgment is paramount to arriving at a correct conclusion. For this scenario, the OTA should choose a parallel level arts and crafts group in which the client can work on an individual project. If answered incorrectly, review negative symptoms of schizophrenia and types of therapeutic groups. The integration of this knowledge is required to determine a correct answer. See Chapters 3, 10 and 13.

A140 C8

An OTA conducts a home assessment for an individual with a complete T10-level spinal cord injury. The only entrance to the home has five steps, a total of 35 inches in height. Which ramp length is best for the OTA to recommend the family have constructed?

Answer Choices:
A. 17½ feet.
B. 35 feet.
C. 70 feet.

Correct Answer: B.

Rationale:
Accessibility guidelines state that the ramp should be constructed with 1 foot of ramp length for every 1 inch of rise. The other choices do not meet these guidelines.

Type of Reasoning: Deductive

This question requires recall of guidelines, which is factual knowledge. Deductive reasoning skills are utilized whenever one must recall facts to find ideal solutions. In this situation, accessibility guidelines indicate that for every 1 inch of rise, there should be 1 foot of ramp length. If answered incorrectly, review accessibility guidelines. See Chapter 15.

A141 C4

An OTA instructs the direct care staff of a rehabilitation unit on proper positioning techniques for a patient following the occurrence of a left CVA. In which of the following positions should the OTA recommend the patient's right affected arm be placed when the patient is sleeping in side-lying on the unaffected side?

Answer Choices:
A. In 90 degrees of humeral abduction and 15 degrees of internal rotation.
B. On the person's side, adducted and internally rotated.
C. Protracted with arm forward on a pillow and the elbow extended or slightly flexed.
D. In 90 degrees of abduction of the humerus with neutral rotation.

Correct Answer: C.

Rationale:
The best position of the upper extremities for sleeping or bed rest is to place the affected arm on a pillow in a comfortable position. Excess abduction can cause the joint capsule to loosen and reduce the stability of the humeral head in the glenoid fossa. It is important to avoid traction of the affected arm to ensure adequate positioning of the humerus with the scapula and to prevent subluxation. Correct positioning means putting the involved arm in slight abduction. Ninety degrees of abduction is excessive.

Type of Reasoning: Inferential
One must infer or draw conclusions about the optimal positioning of the affected upper extremity in side-lying. One must understand the reasons for positioning the extremity in order to prevent further problems from developing, which requires inferential reasoning skill. In this situation, positioning the extremity on a pillow in slight abduction is best. See Chapter 15.

A142 C1

A developmental evaluation has determined that an 8-month-old child with myelomeningocele at the L1 level has no developmental delays. To foster the child's continued gross motor development, which of the following activities would be best for the OTA focus on with this child during intervention?

Answer Choices:
A. Rolling from prone to supine position without assistance.
B. Increasing dynamic trunk balance when sitting without support.
C. Transitioning from sitting to supine and from supine to sitting.

Correct Answer: B.

Rationale:
The development of gross motor skills in an 8-month-old child with myelomeningocele at the L1 level with no developmental delay will parallel that of a child with no disability. Working on dynamic trunk balance while sitting without support is relevant for an 8-month-old. At this age, children develop the ability to sit unsupported and rotate the upper body while the lower body remains stationary. They are also able to play with toys in sitting position which often will require dynamic balance. Since the child has no developmental delay there is no need to focus on the ability to independently roll from prone to supine position. This ability typically develops at 5-6 months. Transitioning from sitting to supine from supine to sitting comes are gross motor skills that typically begin developing at 11 months.

Type of Reasoning: Inferential
One must infer or draw conclusions about the likely skills a typically developing child with myelomeningocele will be acquiring at 8 months of age. For this scenario, increasing dynamic trunk balance when placed in sitting is the most likely skill to be addressed for this child. If answered incorrectly, review information on typical gross motor development. See Chapter 5.

A143 C8

An OTA measures a person for a wheelchair. The widest point across the person's hips and thighs is 16 inches, and the greatest length from the person's posterior portion of the buttocks to the popliteal fossa is 18 inches. Which wheelchair seat dimensions should the OTA recommend?

Answer Choices:
A. 18 inches wide by 20 inches deep.
B. 18 inches wide by 18 inches deep.
C. 16 inches wide by 18 inches deep.
D. 18 inches wide by 16 inches deep.

Correct Answer: D.

Rationale:
To determine the width of a wheelchair seat, two inches are added to the measurement of the widest point across hips and thighs. This allows for clearance on the sides to prevent rubbing and to allow the individual to wear heavier clothing without it being restrictive. To determine the depth of a wheelchair seat, two inches are subtracted from the measurement of the length from the posterior portion of the buttocks to the popliteal fossa. This prevents rubbing and potential decubiti formation in the posterior knee region, while also allowing maximum swing length. In this case, the person's measurements were 16"W × 18"L; therefore, the resulting seat measurement is 18"W × 16"D.

Type of Reasoning: Deductive
One must recall the guidelines for wheelchair prescription. This is factual knowledge, which is a deductive reasoning skill. In this situation, because the individual's measurements were 16"W × 18"L, the seat dimensions should be 18"W × 16"D. If answered incorrectly, review wheelchair prescription guidelines. See Chapter 15.

A144 C2

A caregiver support group meets weekly at a senior center. A new member attends the group for the third time and listens intently. The person nods in agreement when others speak but does not participate verbally. Which action is most effective for the OTA to take to facilitate the individual's engagement in the group?

Answer Choices:
A. Reiterate the group's norm that active participation is expected from all group members.
B. Ask the individual several questions to encourage verbal participation.
C. Invite the individual to join in the discussion, if the person would like.
D. Refer the individual to the center's social worker for individual, non-group counseling.

Correct Answer: C.

Rationale:
Inviting the individual to join the discussion acknowledges their membership and supports attention and active listening, but it does not pressure the person to speak before ready. It can take time for an individual to feel comfortable sharing personal thoughts with a group of people who may have been just acquaintances (or even strangers) prior to this group membership. It is inappropriate to pressure for verbal participation before a person is ready. Individual counseling can be helpful, but it is no substitute for the therapeutic benefits of a group. In addition, group members can benefit from a group discussion without verbally participating. These benefits can include many of Yalom's curative factors including universality, instillation of hope, and the gaining of specific information.

Type of Reasoning: Inductive
One must utilize clinical knowledge and judgment to determine the best approach for this group situation. This requires inductive reasoning skill. In this case, because the new member has not initiated conversation, it is best to invite the member to join in the discussion if desired. If answered incorrectly, review group dynamics and methods of facilitating discussion. See Chapter 3.

A145 C3

An individual with rheumatoid arthritis has developed several boutonniere deformities. Which of the following is the most accurate description for the OTA to include in documentation of the individual's presenting signs?

Answer Choices:
A. Hyperextension of the PIP joint and flexion of the DIP joint.
B. Ulnar deviation and subluxation of the MCP joints.
C. Flexion of the PIP joint and hyperextension of the DIP joint.

Correct Answer: C.

Rationale:
A boutonniere deformity occurs when there is hyperextension of the DIP joint with flexion of the PIP joint. A swan neck deformity is evident when there is hyperextension of the PIP joint and flexion of the DIP joint. Ulnar deviation and subluxation of the MCP joints are additional deformities that can result from rheumatoid arthritis.

Type of Reasoning: Inferential
One must link the individual's diagnosis to the signs presented in order to determine which presenting signs are most representative of boutonniere deformities. This requires inferential reasoning, where one must draw conclusions about the likely presentation of a diagnosis. In this case, the diagnosis would present with flexion of the PIP joint and hyperextension of the DIP joint. If answered incorrectly, review signs and symptoms of boutonniere deformity. See Chapter 6.

A146 C2

An OTA works with an individual with chest and upper extremity burns. During the intervention session, the client expresses vague fears about personal safety at home and asks the OTA to advocate for an extension in the discharge date. According to the medical record, the client had incurred the burns during a cooking accident. Which is the OTA's best initial response to the client's stated concerns?

Answer Choices:
A. Encourage the client to speak to the occupational therapist about discharge plans.
B. Assure the client that pre-discharge fears are normal and expected.
C. Document the client's concerns and recommend an extension of the length of stay.
D. Invite the client to expand upon the nature of these concerns.

Correct Answer: D.

Rationale:
The OTA needs more information to determine the basis for the client's fears and an appropriate response. Referring the client to the occupational therapist can be helpful, but it will not address their concerns at this moment. A delay may result in the client deciding that their concerns are not worth mentioning. Many clients find it difficult to express fears, so it is important to respond immediately when they do. This is of particular importance in cases of domestic violence, which this case (and any case) can have as a contributing and complicating factor. In addition, the client's fears may be functionally based, and the OTA can address these immediately in the current intervention session. Assurance that fears are normal and expected does not address the issue at hand. A request to extend a client's length of stay requires a documented need for inpatient services. Client's stated concerns about home safety are not sufficient justification for a length of stay extension.

Type of Reasoning: Evaluative

This question requires professional judgment based on guiding principles, which is an evaluative reasoning skill. Because the OTA cannot determine the source of the client's fears, the OTA should ask for the client to elaborate on the nature of the concerns. This way the OTA can determine the best initial course of action based on further information. Without further information, clinical decision making is subject to being inaccurate or incomplete. See Chapter 3.

A147 C6

An OTA employed at a day treatment center for clients with psychiatric disorders is conducting a leisure-planning group. The members of the group decide to take a day trip to the local sculpture garden. Which side effect of psychotropic medications is most important for the OTA to discuss in terms of preventative precautions with the group?

Answer Choices:
A. Orthostatic hypotension.
B. Akathisia.
C. Photosensitivity.
D. Tremors.

Correct Answer: C.

Rationale:
Photosensitivity results in severe sunburn which can occur during an outdoor trip. The other options are potential side effects of medications, but they are not exacerbated by being outside.

Type of Reasoning: Deductive
This question requires the test taker to recall the common precautions for clients using psychotropic medications in order to arrive at a correct conclusion. This requires deductive reasoning skill, where the recall of facts is utilized to draw a correct conclusion. For this situation, the most important precaution to discuss is photosensitivity. If answered incorrectly, review psychotropic medication side effects and preventative precautions for clients taking psychotropic medications. See Chapter 10.

A148 C6

An OTA develops a task skills group for the patients of a psychiatric inpatient unit. The OTA considers several activities to use for the group's first session. Which activity is best for the OTA to present to the group members?

Answer Choices:
A. Planning a pizza party for a weekend evening.
B. Decorating Styrofoam cups and planting cuttings in them.
C. Publishing a weekly newsletter about city attractions for patients on the unit.
D. Painting a large mural to cover one wall of the day room.

Correct Answer: B.

Rationale:
Decorating cups and planting cuttings is a simple concrete task, which can be structured to ensure successful completion by individuals with acute psychiatric disorders. Because the length of stay on an acute unit is short, activities that can be completed in one session are typically best for initial treatment sessions. Publishing a weekly newsletter and painting a large mural will require multiple sessions to complete. The outcome of planning a pizza party for a weekend evening may not be implemented for several days. Given that some group members may be discharged before the weekend, this is not the best option for working on current goals.

Type of Reasoning: Inferential
One must determine the most appropriate activity for an initial group session, given knowledge of the treatment setting. This requires inferential reasoning skill, where one must infer or draw conclusions about a best course of action. In this situation, the OTA should choose decorating Styrofoam cups and planting cuttings in them as a first activity. If answered incorrectly, review the characteristics of inpatient psychiatric settings and intervention approaches used in psychosocial practice. The integration of this knowledge is required to determine the correct answer. See Chapters 4 and 13.

A149 C1

An OTA works in a school system with a child with developmental delays. One of the goals of treatment is to develop prewriting skills. The child exhibits the ability to grasp a pencil proximally with crude approximation of the thumb, index, and middle fingers and the ring and little fingers slightly flexed. The OTA collaborates with the occupational therapist to develop an intervention plan. Which grasp should be the focus for the implementation of intervention?

Answer Choices:
A. Digital pronate grasp.
B. Static tripod posture grasp.
C. Dynamic tripod grasp.
D. Palmar supinate grasp.

Correct Answer: C.

Rationale:
The grasp pattern described in the case is static tripod posture grasp. The next grasp pattern to be mastered after this grasp is the dynamic tripod grasp. The other grasp patterns are precursors to the static tripod grasp.

Type of Reasoning: Inferential
This question requires one to infer the intervention goal that will develop the next developmentally appropriate grasp for this child. This requires inferential reasoning skill, where one must draw conclusions about the described grasp pattern. For this situation, dynamic tripod grasp is the next pattern to be mastered after static tripod grasp. If answered incorrectly, review grasp patterns of the hand in children, especially dynamic tripod. See Chapter 5.

A150 C2

An OTA reviews the positioning protocol for a premature infant with severe spastic cerebral palsy with the infant's parents. The protocol is in a written format. During the review, the OTA notices that the parents do not seem able to follow along with the protocol's text. Which action is best for the OTA to take initially in response to this observation?

Answer Choices:
A. Ask the parents if they have any concerns about positioning their infant.
B. Ask the parents if they can read and understand English.
C. Include pictures of proper positioning in the protocol.
D. Demonstrate proper positioning techniques.

Correct Answer: A.

Rationale:
This is an open-ended question that enables the parents to express any concerns that they may have about positioning their infant. These concerns may be comprehension related and/or task related. The realities of caring for a premature infant with severe physical disabilities can be overwhelming. The parents' perceived difficulties in following the written protocol may be due to emotional stress, not limitations in literacy. The parents may welcome the opportunity to express their concerns. The other choices are close-ended and do not facilitate an open dialogue. If the parents have difficulty understanding English or if they could benefit from pictures and/or demonstrated positions, they can express this in response to the OTA's open invitation to express concerns.

Type of Reasoning: Evaluative
This question requires professional judgment based on guiding principles, which is an evaluative reasoning skill. Because the OTA cannot completely determine the source of the parents' difficulty, the OTA should ask if there are any concerns about positioning the infant. This way the OTA can invite the parents to share any concerns in an open-ended fashion without delineating the specific challenge. If answered incorrectly, review principles of family-centered care and client-centered practice. See Chapter 3.

A151 C3

An OTA evaluates a client's pain by asking the client which movements or activities elicit pain. Which of the following is the OTA assessing?

Answer Choices:
A. The triggers of pain.
B. The quality of pain.
C. The intensity of pain.

Correct Answer: A.

Rationale:
Pain triggers are those activities and/or movements that result in pain. The quality of pain is determined by asking the person to describe the pain. Common descriptors are sharp, throbbing, burning, tender, and shooting. The intensity of pain is measured by pain scales; a 0-to-10 scale is most commonly used.

Type of Reasoning: Analytical
This question provides a description of a functional activity and the test taker must determine the likely definition of such an activity. This is an analytical reasoning skill, as questions of this nature often ask one to analyze descriptors of functional skills to determine the overall skill involved. In this situation, the activity is assessing pain triggers, which should be reviewed if answered incorrectly. See Chapters 6 and 7.

A152 C8

An OTA evaluates the home of a person who uses a wheelchair. The OTA measures the door swing of the front door to determine if it can allow safe and independent entry into the home. The OTA determines that the door swing meets minimum accessibility standards. Which measurement should the OTA record as meeting these standards?

Answer Choices:
A. 14 inches.
B. 16 inches.
C. 18 inches.
D. 20 inches.

Correct Answer: C.

Rationale:
The minimum space to accommodate the swing of a door for a person using a wheelchair is 18 inches.

Type of Reasoning: Deductive
This question requires one to recall knowledge of the guidelines for door swing to accommodate a wheelchair. This is recall of factual knowledge, which is a deductive reasoning skill. If answered incorrectly, review door swing accessibility standards for persons who use wheelchairs. See Chapter 15.

A153 C9

An OTA leads a stress management group at a wellness center for persons recovering from substance abuse. After the group, the OTA documents a member's group participation. According to established documentation standards, which statement is best for the OTA to include in the daily progress note?

Answer Choices:
A. The client completed the checklist of stressors in the time allotted.
B. The client was able to identify three current life stressors.
C. The client appeared upset and tense throughout the session.
D. The client stated walking is a relaxing and enjoyable activity.

Correct Answer: B.

Rationale:
Documentation must be specific, measurable, and behavioral. In this scenario, it must provide information that is objective and related to the individual's performance in the group. Documenting the client's ability to identify three current life stressors effectively meets these standards and can be used to inform treatment planning. This information can be used to explore stress management strategies that do not include substance use. Timely completion of a checklist does not include sufficient information about the client's participation. More specific information would need to be provided to meet documentation standards (e.g., client became upset when discussing the stress of single parenthood). The identification of an enjoyable and relaxing activity can be relevant information to include in documentation, but this statement does not directly address the person's participation in the group. In addition, more specific information would need to be provided to meet documentation standards (e.g., client stated they go for long walks when stressed). The report of a client appearing "upset" is subjective and does not meet documentation standards.

584 Exam A Answer Rationales

Type of Reasoning: Inferential
One must determine the best statement to include in a progress note regarding a client in a stress management group. Established standards for documentation require notes to be specific, measurable, and behavioral. Therefore, the OTA should document the client's ability to identify three current life stressors. This information can be used to explore stress management strategies that do not include the use of substances. If answered incorrectly, documentation guidelines should be reviewed. See Chapter 4.

A154 C4

An adult is hospitalized in the recovery phase of Guillain-Barré syndrome. The client complains of tingling, aching, and weakness in both hands and difficulty grasping objects (e.g., grooming supplies). The client requests intervention to address these issues. Which action is best for the OTA to take to address the client's concerns?

Answer Choices:
A. Provide soft tissue massage to both hands prior to grooming activities.
B. Apply hot packs to both hands and complete stretching exercises prior to grooming activities.
C. Refer the client to a neurologist for follow-up of possible condition regression.
D. Educate the patient about sensory deficits and effective adaptive ADL strategies.

Correct Answer: D.

Rationale:
Guillain-Barré (GBS) is characterized by ascending motor weakness in the limbs, usually beginning in the hands and feet. Paresthesias and pain are also a common occurrence. The best approach for this patient is to educate the patient about the sensory deficits that are common to the condition and provide adaptive strategies for ADL so the client is successful. Soft tissue massage will not remedy the aching in the hands as the inflammation of the peripheral nerves must decrease for this to resolve. Hot packs are contraindicated in this situation due to the potential for burns from altered sensation. Referral to a neurologist is not needed as the symptoms are typical of the syndrome.

Type of Reasoning: Inductive
This question requires the test taker to understand the course of nature of Guillain-Barré syndrome in order to determine the best approach to address the patient's concerns. In this case, because the patient's symptoms will require time to improve, the OTA should educate the patient about the sensory deficits and adaptive ADL strategies. If answered incorrectly, review information on Guillain-Barré syndrome. See Chapter 7.

A155 C2

An OTA works at a community-based vocational rehabilitation program. Right before a discussion group about effective work habits is scheduled to begin, the OTA is asked to assist another OTA with this group. Which is the best action for the OTA to take?

Answer Choices:
A. Split the group in two and have each OTA work with their own group.
B. Participate as a member of the group and model desired responses.
C. Support the leader with comments and questions that keep the group on focus.
D. Act as an observer and take notes for documentation.

Correct Answer: C.

Rationale:
The role of assisting a group leader is to facilitate participation of the members and the achievement of the goals of the group. Splitting members into two groups would result in the assisting OTA having no knowledge of the group's history, process, or goals. In addition, the existing leader would receive no input from a co-leader. The benefit of receiving feedback from a co-leader is likely the precipitant for the group leader asking the OTA to participate. Participating as a member, an observer, and/or a recorder also do not provide any co-leadership benefits.

Type of Reasoning: Inductive
Clinical knowledge and judgment are the most important skills needed for answering this question, which requires inductive reasoning skill. Knowledge of the group processes and effective co-leadership are essential to choosing the best solution. In this case, the OTA should support the leader with comments and questions that keep the group on focus. If answered incorrectly, review effective group co-leadership strategies. See Chapter 3.

A156 C9

At a home care intervention planning meeting, the team discusses a client with a right CVA. The physical therapist states the individual's ambulatory status is now within functional limits. Physical therapy services will be discontinued because the person is no longer homebound. The OTA reports that the individual is frequently confused during home management task performance and becomes extremely anxious when community activities are proposed. Prior to this meeting, the OTA had discussed these concerns the occupational therapist. During the meeting, which recommendation is best for the OTA to make?

Answer Choices:
A. Refer the individual to a psychiatrist for a mental status evaluation to help inform discharge planning.
B. Continue OT services as the person should continue to be considered homebound.
C. Discontinue OT services as they are non-reimbursable because the person is no longer considered homebound.
D. Contact the physician to discuss the need for OT services on an outpatient basis and for psychosocial counseling.

Correct Answer: B.

Rationale:
The individual can be considered homebound for cognitive and psychosocial deficits. Discontinuing services can place the individual at risk because the person will not receive evaluation or intervention for their demonstrated cognitive and psychosocial deficits. There is no need for a consultation with a physician at this point. OT practitioners can continue to provide services in this scenario without physician input.

Type of Reasoning: Inductive
Clinical knowledge and judgment are the most important skills needed for answering this question, which requires inductive reasoning skill. Knowledge of the diagnosis and best courses of action is essential to choosing the best solution. In this case, because the person is considered homebound for cognitive and psychosocial deficits, the team's best approach is to continue OT services. If answered incorrectly, review home health care treatment guidelines and criteria for homebound status. See Chapter 4.

586 Exam A Answer Rationales

A157 C6

A recent high school graduate diagnosed with depression and anorexia nervosa attends an evening work adjustment group for 90 minutes each week. The client states that this group is the only activity engaged in outside of work. The OTA collaborates with the client to develop a plan to increase involvement in personally meaningful non-work activities. The client expresses interests in exercise and volunteerism and reports past roles to have included captain of the high school swim team, competitive tennis player, and volunteer in an after-school activities program for young children. Which of the following is the best resource for the OTA to recommend the client explore?

Answer Choices:
A. A local fitness center for exercise classes.
B. The town swimming pool for open swimming sessions.
C. A local community center for volunteer opportunities.
D. An area soup kitchen for volunteer opportunities.

Correct Answer: C.

Rationale:
Volunteering at a local community center can facilitate the client's stated altruistic interests while providing a diversity of potential activity pursuits. Exercise and swimming can be contraindicated for persons with anorexia nervosa because they often engage in these activities in an excessive (sometimes self-abusive) manner that is counterproductive to healthy leisure. Volunteering in a soup kitchen is altruistic, but persons recovering from eating disorders often find food-related activities difficult.

Type of Reasoning: Inductive
One must utilize clinical knowledge and judgment to determine the best avocational resource for this patient. In this case, given an understanding of the nature of anorexia, the OTA should explore the local community center for volunteer opportunities. If answered incorrectly, review the diagnostic criteria, behavioral manifestations, and intervention guidelines for eating disorders and depression. The integration of this knowledge is required to correctly answer this question. See Chapter 10.

A158 C3

An OTA works in a clinic which provides services to persons with upper extremity disorders. The OTA is constructing a dorsal forearm splint for a client. Which is the best length for this splint?

Answer Choices:
A. One-fourth of the forearm.
B. One-third of the forearm.
C. Two-thirds of the forearm.
D. One-half of the forearm.

Correct Answer: C.

Rationale:
A major splinting principle is to decrease pressure and distribute weight by having a long, wide splint base. The two-thirds length accomplishes this goal. The other measurements are too short.

Type of Reasoning: Deductive
One must recall the guidelines for construction of dorsal forearm splints, which is factual knowledge. This requires deductive reasoning skill. In this situation, a forearm-based splint should be two-thirds the length of the forearm.

A159 C9

An OTA accepts a position at an adult day care and respite program for older adults with a variety of physical and cognitive disabilities. The OTA has only clinical experience in school-based practice. Which is the most effective way for the OTA to prepare for the professional responsibilities this new position will entail?

Answer Choices:
A. Attend support group meetings for caregivers of older adults.
B. Review current literature on occupation-based and evidence-based care of older adults.
C. Review area demographic information on older adults with disabilities.
D. Confer with the program's administrative director.

Correct Answer: B.

Rationale:
The OTA must update their knowledge base about current occupation-based and evidence-based practices in the care of older adults with an emphasis on physical and cognitive disabilities. A review of the professional literature can provide relevant information about effective evaluation and intervention approaches for the setting's population. Attending a caregiver group will provide information about caregiver needs, but this is not the most important area about which the OTA should acquire knowledge for this new position. Information about demographics is too broad. The program's administrative director can provide relevant information about the setting's policies, but they would not be able to provide information on the practice of occupational therapy.

Type of Reasoning: Inductive
This question requires one to determine the most effective approach for preparing for a new job role. This requires inductive reasoning skill, where clinical judgment is paramount to arriving at a correct conclusion. For this situation, the OTA should prepare by reviewing current OT literature on occupation-based and evidence-based services for older adults. If answered incorrectly, professional development activities. See Chapter 4.

A160 C1

During an occupational therapy session, the OTA observes that a child bangs objects on a tabletop but has difficulty physically letting go of a toy upon request. The OTA documents these behaviors. Which developmental level would be most accurate for the OTA to report the child's observed behaviors indicate?

Answer Choices:
A. 9–10 months.
B. 7–8 months.
C. 3–4 months.

Correct Answer: C.

Rationale:
At 3–4 months, children are able to bang toys on a tabletop, but they do not have a voluntary release. At 7–8 months, children have a voluntary release. At 9–10 months, children can release an object into a container with a straight wrist.

Type of Reasoning: Deductive
One must recall the developmental milestones for children banging toys and release. This is factual knowledge, which is a deductive reasoning skill. The functional activity described is a skill at 3–4 months developmentally. If answered incorrectly, review developmental milestones of infants in gross motor and fine motor skills.

A161 C3

A person incurred a traumatic above-elbow amputation to the non-dominant upper extremity. The client establishes a goal to be independent in all ADL using the residual limb without a prosthesis. However, the limb is painful and very sensitive. Which should the OTA include in the OT intervention program? Select the three BEST responses.

Answer Choices:
A. Training in compensatory strategies and adaptive equipment to enable the unilateral performance of tasks.
B. Instruction in how to use the residual non-dominant upper extremity as a stabilizer during task performance.
C. Implementation of an exercise program to focus on strengthening muscles that will enable the effective use of a prosthesis.
D. Instruction in how to protectively wrap the residual limb with an elastic bandage in a circular manner to decrease pain and manage hypersensitivity.
E. Instruction in how to protectively wrap the residual limb in a figure-of-eight diagonal pattern going from a distal to proximal direction.
F. Refer the client to an amputee support group to increase acceptance of the need for a prosthesis to attain ADL independence.

Correct Answers: A, B, and E.

Rationale:
There are many techniques that the client can learn to independently perform ADL. The client can learn to use the dominant intact upper extremity to perform unilateral tasks using adaptive equipment such as a rocker knife to cut meat. Instruction on the use of the residual non-dominant upper extremity as a stabilizer and/or assist during task performance can also be very effective (e.g., stabilizing clothing to enable the fastening of closures) in attaining independence in ADL. Many unilateral amputees function independently without a prosthesis, and this is the client's stated goal. Ignoring this preference by referring the person to a support group or implementing an exercise program is a violation of the occupational therapy ethical principle of autonomy.

Wrapping a residual limb with an elastic bandage in a circular manner is a major contraindication in amputee care. This action would cause a tourniquet effect and dangerously restrict the limb's circulation. The wrapping of a residual limb should be done in a figure-of-eight diagonal pattern, going from a distal to proximal direction, with greater pressure applied at the distal end of the limb. The OTA should treat the client's pain and hypersensitivity with established intervention methods. Pain management techniques can include relaxation techniques, alternative exercise programs (e.g., aquatics, tai chi), and physical agent modalities. Methods of desensitization can include the application of diverse textures to the limb, massage, and tapping.

Type of Reasoning: Inductive
This question requires one to determine a best course of action, based on knowledge of upper extremity amputations and adaptive strategies without the use of a prosthesis. This necessitates clinical judgment, which is an inductive reasoning skill. For this case, the OTA should train the client in the use of adaptive strategies and equipment to perform ADL. To prevent harm, the OTA should also teach the client the proper method for wrapping the residual limb. If answered incorrectly, review principles of pre-prosthetic and prosthetic training for patients with upper extremity amputations. See Chapter 6.

A162 C4

An older adult who is recovering from a cerebral vascular accident attends occupational therapy two times per day. The intervention environment is highly structured and not overstimulating, yet the client's mood often changes abruptly. Within one session, the client will laugh and then become tearful with no apparent precipitant. What should the OTA document these behaviors as potential signs of in the client's daily progress note?

Answer Choices:
A. A neurocognitive disorder.
B. Anhedonia.
C. A response to auditory hallucinations.
D. Emotional lability.

Correct Answer: D.

Rationale:
Emotional lability describes abrupt changes in mood without external precipitants. It is often observed in persons recovering from CVAs. Anhedonia is the inability to experience pleasure. There is no information in the case that would substantiate a conclusion that the individual is developing a neurocognitive disorder, or is responding to the internal stimulation of hallucinations.

Type of Reasoning: Analytical
This question provides symptoms, and the test taker must determine the likely cause for them. This is an analytical reasoning skill, as questions of this nature often ask one to analyze a group of symptoms in order to determine a diagnosis. In this situation, the symptoms indicate emotional lability, which should be reviewed if answered incorrectly. See Chapter 7.

A163 C9

An OTA provides early intervention services to a 3-year-old child with left spastic hemiplegia due to cerebral palsy. During a session, the OTA observes behaviors that seem to indicate the presence of visual deficits. In discussing these observations with the occupational therapist, which recommendation should the OTA make?

Answer Choices:
A. The completion of a motor-free visual perceptual assessment.
B. The completion of a developmental vision assessment.
C. A referral of the child to an optometrist.
D. A referral of the child to an optician.

Correct Answer: C.

Rationale:
Prior to conducting a visual perceptual assessment, an anatomical visual assessment to determine visual acuity is required. Optometrists are the professionals who are qualified to perform eye exams to determine visual acuity, level of visual impairments, and damage to or disease in the visual system.

Type of Reasoning: Evaluative
One must weigh the possible courses of action and then make a value judgment about the best course to take. This requires evaluative reasoning skill, which often utilizes guiding principles of action in order to arrive at a correct conclusion. For this case, because the child demonstrates visual deficits, the OTA should discuss with the occupational therapist the need to refer the child to an optometrist. See Chapter 4.

A164 C8

An older adult lives in a second-floor apartment in a private home. The individual is experiencing sensory losses that are consistent with the aging process. All other abilities are within normal limits. Which action is best for the OTA to recommend to the client to ensure that they are able to age safely in place?

590 Exam A Answer Rationales

Answer Choices:
A. Acquire a first-floor apartment to eliminate the need to walk up stairs
B. Allow for increased time to slowly and safely walk up the stairs.
C. Install a stair glide system to eliminate the need to walk up the stairs.
D. Install light switches at the top and bottom of the stairway.

Correct Answer: D.

Rationale:
With normal aging there is decreased visual acuity (presbyopia), reduced night vision, and impaired depth perception. These sensory deficits can make ascending and descending stairs dangerous. To decrease the risk of falls, it is advisable to install light switches at both ends of a stairway so that the person can independently illuminate the stairs. The other answer options are indicated for persons with musculoskeletal and/or neurophysiological deficits. There is no information provided in this case to indicate a need for these actions.

Type of Reasoning: Inferential
One must link the individual's presenting symptoms to the recommendations presented in order to determine which recommendation is best for this individual. This requires inferential reasoning, where one must draw conclusions about the deficits in order to make a sound recommendation. In this case, the best recommendation would be the installation of light switches at the top and bottom of the stairway. If answered incorrectly, review home adaptations for sensory loss. See Chapter 15.

A165 C5

An OTA provides occupational therapy services at a homeless shelter that includes residents who are HIV positive. Which procedure should the OTA follow when conducting several therapeutic groups to develop participants' ADL and IADL skills?

Answer Choices:
A. Wash hands before and after each group session.
B. Always wear latex gloves during groups.
C. Wear latex gloves during meal preparation activities.
D. Implement transmission-based precautions.

Correct Answer: A.

Rationale:
Health professionals should use standard precautions at all times, regardless of clients' diagnoses. Washing hands is a basic precautionary step all individuals should take to prevent the spread of infections and diseases (even in their own homes). The diagnosis of HIV is irrelevant to the question's correct answer because HIV is transmitted only through the exchange of body fluids. Wearing gloves during meal preparation activities complies with health department regulations abut handling food. However, this option only addresses group sessions that involve food. One must still wash one's hands before and after glove use. In addition, due to potential latex allergies, health care environments must be latex-free. Transmission-based precautions are used when the route(s) of transmission is (are) not completely interrupted using standard precautions alone. For some diseases that have multiple routes of transmission (e.g., SARS), more than one transmission-based precaution category may be used. Transmission-based precautions have three categories: contact precautions, droplet precautions, and airborne precautions. None of these are indicated for HIV. See Chapter 9.

Type of Reasoning: Deductive
This question requires recall of guidelines and principles, which is factual knowledge. Deductive reasoning skills are utilized whenever one must recall facts to solve everyday problems. In this situation, the OTA should follow standard precautions, which include washing hands before and after each group session. If answered incorrectly, review standard and transmission-based precautions. See Chapter 3.

A166 C3

A client who incurred a nerve laceration exhibits maximum motor and sensory losses consistent with a radial nerve laceration below the supinator. Which deformity should the OTA note the client is exhibiting?

Answer Choices:
A. Claw hand.
B. Ape hand.
C. Saturday night palsy.
D. Wrist drop.

Correct Answer: D.

Rationale:
The presenting signs of a radial nerve laceration are weakness or paralysis of the extensors of the wrist, MCPs, and thumb with a characteristic wrist drop. Ape hand, which presents as a flattening of the thenar eminence, is indicative of a median nerve laceration. A claw hand is indicative of an ulnar nerve laceration. Saturday night palsy is a term used to denote a radial nerve compression that results from a position that compresses the radial nerve against the humerus.

Type of Reasoning: Inferential
One must link the diagnosis provided to the symptoms presented in order to determine which definition most accurately represents a radial nerve laceration. This requires inferential reasoning, where one must infer or draw conclusions about a diagnosis. In this case, symptoms of radial nerve laceration include weakness of the wrist, MCP, and thumb extensors. If answered incorrectly, review symptoms of radial nerve injury. See Chapter 6.

A167 C9

An OTA collaborates with an occupational therapist to develop an after-school program for adolescents with obesity who also have diabetes or who are at risk for developing diabetes. Which program development action should the therapist and the OTA take first?

Answer Choices:
A. Obtain statistical data about adolescent obesity to support the need for the program to the school administrators.
B. Collaborate with the occupational therapist to survey the adolescents about their occupational performance.
C. Collaborate with the occupational therapist to survey occupational therapy practitioners about services they provide to obese adolescents.
D. Review the professional literature about programs for obese adolescents to obtain ideas for the program's activities.

Correct Answer: B.

Rationale:
The development of new services would require a needs assessment to determine the necessity and focus of services. The information obtained from surveying potential participants is an excellent way to ensure that the program developed will meet a real unmet need. While statistics can support the rationale for a program, specific information about the target population is more relevant. In addition, prior to marketing a program, one should first determine its focus. Practitioner viewpoints and professional literature do not substantiate an unmet need that would require a program to be developed.

Type of Reasoning: Inferential
This question requires one to utilize knowledge of program development guidelines in order to determine the first approach for development of a program. This requires one to reason which action will have the most effective outcome, which is an inferential reasoning skill. For this situation, the OTA should collaborate with the occupational therapist to survey the adolescents about their occupational performance in order to determine the adolescents' needs. If answered incorrectly, review program development guidelines. See Chapter 4.

A168 C5

An OTA provides bed mobility training for an individual recovering from a left CVA. The OTA notes that the person's right calf is swollen and warm. The person complains that it is painful. Which action should the OTA take initially?

Answer Choices:
A. Elevate the leg and provide retrograde massage.
B. Advise the person to tell the physician about the symptoms during the physician's next bedside visit.
C. Continue with the training and inform the supervising occupational therapist about the symptoms after the session.
D. Contact the charge nurse immediately to report symptoms.

Correct Answer: D.

Rationale:
The signs and symptoms in this scenario are indicative of deep vein thrombosis (DVT). DVT, an inflammation of a vein in association with the formation of a thrombus, is often a complication of CVAs or the result of prolonged bed rest. DVT is a medical emergency that must be handled immediately by medical staff. While it would be appropriate to elevate the legs, massage is contraindicated. The other answers are inappropriate because they delay the acquisition of needed medical care.

Type of Reasoning: Evaluative
This question requires a value judgment in an urgent situation, which is an evaluative reasoning skill. In this situation, the symptoms indicate a DVT, which is a medical emergency. Essential to arriving at a correct conclusion in situations such as these is determining when symptoms indicate an emergency and recognizing appropriate measures to remedy the situation. For this situation, the OTA should contact the charge nurse immediately to report the symptoms. If answered incorrectly, review symptoms of DVT. See Chapter 8.

A169 C8

An individual with amyotrophic lateral sclerosis requires the use of an environmental control unit (ECU) to access electrical devices and a personal emergency response system. The individual lives alone and self-directs personal care attendants to perform activities of daily living. During instruction to the individual on the capabilities and use of the ECU, which is most important for the OTA to discuss with the client?

Answer Choices:
A. The ECU's backup power source and charging instructions.
B. Additional assistive technology available.
C. Augmentative alternative communication options.
D. Funding for assistive technology.

Correct Answer: A.

Rationale:
Backup systems for electronic devices must be specified, especially if the device is used to access emergency assistance. Batteries used as backup systems often have very strict schedules for charging (e.g., water cell batteries must be regularly checked for adequate water levels). Information about additional assistive technology, augmentative alternative communication, and funding can be helpful, but they are not the most important area for consumer education in this case.

Type of Reasoning: Inferential
One must determine the most important information to provide for an individual about an ECU. This requires inferential reasoning skill, where one must infer or draw conclusions about a best course of action. In this situation, the OTA should provide information about a backup power source and charging instructions because the device may be used to access emergency assistance. If answered incorrectly, review information on ECUs and consumer training. See Chapter 15.

A170 C3

An individual with post-polio syndrome receives an occupational therapy re-evaluation. The OTA collaborates with the occupational therapist to determine assessments to be administered during the re-evaluation process. They determine that the outcomes of an assessment of the person's sensation would help inform the development of an intervention plan. How should the OTA initiate sensory testing with this client?

Answer Choices:
A. Demonstrate the test with the individual's vision occluded.
B. Proceed proximal to distal.
C. Demonstrate the test with the client's vision not occluded.
D. Proceed distal to proximal.

Correct Answer: C.

Rationale:
Sensory testing must begin with a demonstration of the test with the client being able to visually observe the demonstration. If the client's vision is impaired, the OTA must verbally explain each step of the demonstration to ensure that the individual understands the testing process. After this demonstration is complete, the testing proceeds with vision occluded. Sensory testing for individuals with spinal cord injuries proceeds from proximal to distal. Sensory testing for individuals with peripheral nerve injuries proceeds from distal to proximal.

Type of Reasoning: Deductive
One must recall the testing guidelines for sensory testing in order to arrive at a correct conclusion. This requires deductive reasoning skill, where factual knowledge is essential to choosing the correct solution. In this case, all sensory testing must begin with demonstration of the test that the patient can visualize. If answered incorrectly, review guidelines for administration of sensory testing. See Chapter 11.

A171 C4

An OTA uses a motor learning intervention approach to develop prehension patterns with a child recovering from a brain tumor. The OTA places small toys on a table and asks the child to pick up the toys and put them into a storage box that is also on the table. The OTA uses random practice during this activity. Which types and arrangement of toys are most effective for the OTA to provide according to the motor learning approach?

Answer Choices:
A. Toys that are exactly the same shape, size, and weight in a mixed arrangement on the table.
B. Toys that are exactly the same shape, size, and weight placed in a straight line on the table.
C. Age-appropriate toys arranged in a developmental sequence according to the child's developmental age.
D. Toys of different shapes, sizes, and weights in a mixed arrangement on the table.

Correct Answer: D.

Rationale:
According to a motor learning approach, random practice involves the performance of several motor tasks in a random order to encourage the reformulation of the solution to the presented motor problem. Each time the child picks up a small toy of a different shape, size, and/or weight their grasp pattern must be different. This activity is consistent with random practice. Having the child pick up toys that are of the same shape, size, and weight involves repeated performance of the same motor skill; this activity reflects blocked practice according to the motor learning approach. The motor learning approach does not utilize a developmental sequence.

Type of Reasoning: Inductive
This question requires one to determine the best approach for arrangement of toys for prehension according to motor learning approach and utilization of random practice. This requires inductive reasoning skill, where clinical judgment is paramount to arriving at a correct conclusion. For this situation, the toys of different shapes, sizes, and weights should be placed in a mixed arrangement on the table. If answered incorrectly, review the motor learning approach, especially the principle of random practice. See Chapter 12.

A172 C5

An OTA collaborates with an occupational therapist to develop a community-based program for persons with body mass indices greater than 30. They determine that the program will use a lifestyle redesign approach to help participants address their obesity in a proactive manner. Which is best for the OTA and therapist to incorporate into the program's initial sessions?

Answer Choices:
A. Measurement of each participant's body mass index (BMI) and waist circumference.
B. Provision of devices and equipment to maximize participation in daily activities of meaning.
C. The development of personalized plans to change daily habits that contribute to obesity.
D. Nutritional classes that emphasize eating fruits, vegetables, whole grains, and lean protein.

Correct Answer: C.

Rationale:
Obesity is defined as a condition characterized by excess body fat. Occupational therapy services using a lifestyle redesign approach focus on helping clients make changes in daily habits, patterns, and routines to reduce body weight. This can include nutritional changes (e.g., emphasizing fruits, vegetables, whole grains, and lean protein for meals) and changes in activity engagement (e.g., a personalized activity-focused exercise program combining personal interests, desired participation, and self-determined goals). To help the participants address their obesity in a proactive manner, the OTA and occupational therapist should begin the program by having participants develop personalized plans to change daily habits that contribute to obesity (e.g., lack of time to devote to meal planning and preparation resulting in over-reliance on fast food, lack of time to develop and maintain a proper exercise routine resulting in a sedentary lifestyle, using food as a comfort to manage stress). Because the factors that can contribute to obesity are many, this individualization is critical to participants' success. After the development of this plan, clients can be encouraged to participate in sessions that match their identified needs (e.g., nutrition awareness, meal preparation, physical activity options, time management, and stress management). The BMI is a formula used for determining obesity. The measurement of waist circumference is used to determine distribution of body fat. These actions are diagnostic, not interventions to develop a healthy lifestyle. The provision of devices and equipment to maximize client participation in daily activities (i.e., BADL, IADL, mobility, and participation) is consistent with a compensatory approach, not a lifestyle redesign approach.

Type of Reasoning: Inductive
For this question, one must determine the best course of action based on knowledge of lifestyle redesign approaches. This necessitates clinical judgment, which is an inductive reasoning skill. For this case, the therapist and OTA should incorporate the development of personalized plans to change daily habits that contribute to obesity. If answered incorrectly, review intervention guidelines and approaches for working with persons who are obese. See Chapter 9.

A173 C4

A client recovering from a left CVA demonstrates increased flexor tone in the dominant right upper extremity while trying to re-learn to write with the left hand. Which of the following is most accurate for the OTA to state the client is exhibiting when documenting this observation?

Answer Choices:
A. An associated reaction.
B. A tonic labyrinthine reflex.
C. An asymmetrical tonic neck reflex.

Correct Answer: A.

Rationale:
Providing resisted voluntary movements to the unaffected limb facilitates an associated reaction in the affected limb. A tonic labyrinthine response results from changes in the orientation of the head, leading to bilateral flexor or extensor posturing of the arms/legs. The asymmetrical tonic neck reflex response is facilitated by rotation of the head and results in limb extension on the face side and limb flexion on the skull side.

Type of Reasoning: Analytical
This question requires the test taker to determine the functional deficit of the patient, which is an analytical reasoning skill. Questions of this nature often call upon the test taker to determine a deficit based on a functional description. Based on this information, the symptoms of the person indicate the deficit of associated reaction, which should be reviewed if answered incorrectly. See Chapter 12.

A174 C7

An intervention plan for a person with a complete lesion of the spinal cord at the C6 level has been developed by the client, occupational therapist, and OTA. Which activity should be included in this plan as a goal for the client to independently perform?

Answer Choices:
A. Typing with a mouth stick.
B. Transferring from bed to wheelchair using depression transfers.
C. Donning pants while in bed.
D. Feeding using a suspension sling or mobile arm support.

Correct Answer: C.

Rationale:
A person with a C6 spinal cord injury can independently don underwear and pants while in bed. Therefore, intervention would focus on developing the ability to don pants while lying in bed. A person with a C6 spinal cord injury uses a sliding board to transfer; depression transfers are possible at the C7 level. The client with a complete spinal cord injury at the C6 level does not need a mouth stick to type or a suspension sling/mobile arm support to complete activities. Therefore, intervention is not needed to develop these abilities.

Type of Reasoning: Deductive
This question requires factual recall of functional abilities according to spinal level lesions. Specifically, one must recall the expected outcomes of a patient with C6 complete injury. This is recall of factual information, which is a deductive reasoning skill. Donning pants while in bed is most aligned with C6 functioning. If answered incorrectly, review the functional abilities of persons with SCIs and the adaptive equipment and strategies that enable their occupational performance. See Chapters 7 and 14.

A175 C9

A young adult with diagnoses of dysthymic disorder and narcissistic personality disorder attends a vocational rehabilitation program. When the client arrives for the work adjustment group, the OTA notes that the client has an unsteady gait, slurred speech, and alcohol-smelling breath. Which is the best action for the OTA to take in response to these observations?

Answer Choices:
A. Include the topic of alcohol's effect on work performance in the scheduled group session.
B. Refer the client to the social worker to discuss treatment options for potential alcohol abuse.
C. Contact the client's parents to transport the client home.
D. Arrange for transportation to bring the client home.

Correct Answer: D.

Rationale:
The person is showing signs of being under the influence of alcohol. It is not appropriate to use the group to discuss the client's behavior and/or potential treatment needs. In the client's current state, they are impaired and cannot be a full participant in a group discussion or a one-on-one meeting with the social worker. The client is a young adult so there is no need to contact the client's parents. Doing so without the client's permission would be a violation of HIPAA.

Type of Reasoning: Evaluative
This question requires professional judgment based on guiding principles, which is an evaluative reasoning skill. Because the person is showing signs of being under the influence of alcohol, the OTA should arrange for transportation back to their home. Questions such as these are challenging to answer, as clear-cut answers may not be readily available. Essential to choosing the correct conclusion is to do what is in the best interest of the individual. This action must be compliant with the AOTA code of ethics and HIPAA. See Chapter 4.

A176 C6

An elementary school student with autism spectrum disorder is referred to occupational therapy. One of the student's goals is to self-initiate goal-directed play to decrease the frequency of self-stimulating behaviors of hand waving and rocking. The student's verbal communication is impaired, but the student compensates by using picture cards to let others know what is wanted or needed. Which of the following approaches to initiate self-play in the home environment is best for the OTA to suggest to the student's parents?

Answer Choices:
A. Provide limited play choices using picture cards, encourage choosing, and give verbal praise when the child chooses an activity.
B. Allow the child time to choose a play activity from several options and do not provide guidance to ensure self-directed decision making.
C. Provide limited choices using picture cards and only give verbal praise when the child participates in the chosen play activity.
D. Include the child in after-school programs to socialize with other children and provide role-modeling opportunities for typical play behaviors.

Correct Answer: A.

Rationale:
Autism often presents as impaired development of social interactions and communication and a limited repertoire of activities of interest. Symptoms can include repetitive movements or self-stimulating behaviors. Persons with autism may not speak. They may have a limited vocabulary and may typically not ask for help or request things. Children with autism often prefer to play alone and have difficulty sharing experiences with others. The goal of therapy is to encourage engagement in purposeful activity, self-direction, imitation, and social interaction. Using the child's form of communication of picture cards, the parents can provide a choice between a limited number of play activities at home to encourage the self-directed activity of choosing a play activity. Providing verbal praise immediately after a decision is made will reinforce a positive behavior and support continued decision making over time. As the child makes decisions more readily, verbal praise can be reduced. When decision making is difficult, providing several options to choose from can be overstimulating and cause stress. The resultant stress typically increases repetitive or self-stimulating behaviors. Including the child in after-school programs can be an option when the child is able to participate in purposeful activities and benefit from learning through imitation. At this point, an after-school program will likely be too stressful, which may result in social isolation or lost opportunity for self-directed decision making. In addition, this scenario specifically asked for an intervention strategy for the parents to use in the home environment, not within the school environment.

Type of Reasoning: Inductive
For this exam item, the test taker must determine a best course of action based on a description of the student's deficits and the identified goal. This requires clinical judgment, which is an inductive reasoning skill. In this situation, it is best to provide limited play choices using picture cards, encourage choosing, and give verbal praise when the child chooses an activity to encourage self-direction and social interaction. Review principles of activity gradation and intervention approaches for children with autism if answered incorrectly. The integration of this knowledge is required to determine a correct answer. See Chapters 3 and 10.

A177 C9

A newly hired OTA is instructed by the director of rehabilitation to supervise two hospital volunteers as they learn how to assist patients in safely completing bed to wheelchair transfers. Which is the first action the OTA should take in response to this request?

Answer Choices:
A. Recommend the hospital develop a transfer training program for volunteers.
B. Inform the occupational therapy supervisor of the director's request.
C. Supervise the volunteers during the transfers to ensure patient safety.
D. Explain to the director of rehabilitation why the request is inappropriate.

Correct Answer: D.

Rationale:
Volunteers are not trained health care professionals and they cannot perform transfers with patients. Therefore, the OTA cannot comply with the director's request to supervise volunteers in performing transfers, nor should the hospital provide transfer training to volunteers. The OTA must immediately inform the director of rehabilitation of the inappropriateness of this request. An explanation of the OTA's rationale for refusing to comply with the director's request is needed to prevent future inappropriate requests of the OTA and/or other hospital staff. After declining the director's request, the OTA should next inform the OT supervisor of this request so that the OT supervisor can follow-up with the director of rehabilitation to ensure that the director clearly understands the appropriate use of volunteers and OT staff.

Type of Reasoning: Evaluative
One must weigh the possible courses of action and then make a value judgment about the best course to take. This requires evaluative reasoning skill, which often utilizes guiding principles of action in order to arrive at a correct conclusion. For this case, because the request to supervise volunteers in transfer training is an inappropriate request, the OTA should first speak to the director to explain why the request is inappropriate. If answered incorrectly, review guidelines for supervision of personnel. See Chapter 4.

A178 C3

A carpenter recovering from injuries incurred during a fall from a ladder has decreased strength in the triceps, bilaterally. The most recent manual muscle test indicated that the triceps' muscle strength is 3. The OTA provides the client with a tabletop wood project to complete. To develop triceps' muscle strength, how should the OTA position the tabletop when the person sands the project?

Answer Choices:
A. At a 45-degree incline angled so that the individual's hands are above the elbows when the elbows are flexed.
B. At the individual's waist height so that the individual's hands and elbows are on the same plane when the elbows flex.
C. At a 45-degree incline angled so that the individual's hands are below the elbows when the elbows are flexed.

Correct Answer: A.

Rationale:
This position requires the triceps to perform movement against gravity, which is possible at a muscle strength of 3 (fair). The sanding activity will provide slight resistance, which is the next level of muscle strength (3+, fair plus). Sanding wood placed on a table at waist height, or inclined so that the hand is below the elbow when it is flexed, respectively, uses gravity-eliminated or gravity-assisted positions. These positions are too low for a person with fair muscle strength who can perform complete range of motion against gravity, and they will not increase strength.

Type of Reasoning: Inductive
One must utilize clinical knowledge and judgment to determine the exercise approach that provides gravity resisted movement. This requires inductive reasoning skill. In this case, the tabletop should be at a 45-degree inclined angle and positioned so the hands are above the elbows when the elbows are flexed. If answered incorrectly, review activity analysis principles and strengthening guidelines. The integration of this knowledge is needed to determine the correct answer. See Chapters 3 and 11.

A179 C5

A school-based OTA implements an intervention plan for an elementary school student who has cystic fibrosis. The individualized education plan (IEP) was developed during a meeting with the child's parents, teachers, and occupational therapist. The school nurse and dietitian also contributed to this plan. Which is the best primary focus for occupational therapy services for this student?

Answer Choices:
A. Ensuring that the student's school lunches and snacks provide adequate nutrition and hydration.
B. Instructing the student and teacher in the use of energy conservation techniques during activities.
C. Monitoring the student for signs of fatigue, which may lead to cardiac and respiratory problems.
D. Assessing the student for developmental delays, medical complications, and psychological status.

Correct Answer: B.

Rationale:
Cystic fibrosis is a chronic, progressive lung disease that reduces life expectancy and limits participation. Instruction in the use of energy conservation techniques during activities is the intervention that a school-based occupational therapy practitioner can uniquely provide. These techniques can help a child with cystic fibrosis participate in school activities to the fullest extent possible. Adequate nutrition and hydration are important to manage mucous production for children with cystic fibrosis. This need can be met by the school's dietician. The monitoring of signs of fatigue that may lead to cardiac and respiratory problems can be completed by the school nurse. Moreover, if the student and teacher learn how to effectively use energy conservation techniques during activities, the occurrence of fatigue should decrease. The assessment of developmental delays, medical complications, and psychological status should have been completed prior to the development of the IEP.

Type of Reasoning: Inductive
This question requires one to utilize clinical judgment to determine a best course of action for a child with cystic fibrosis. This necessitates inductive reasoning skill, where knowledge of the diagnosis and effective therapy approaches are paramount to arriving at a correct conclusion. For this situation, it is best to focus on instructing the student and teacher in the use of energy conservation techniques during activities. If answered incorrectly, review information on cystic fibrosis and intervention approaches. See Chapter 9.

A180 C4

A client has right-sided weakness and decreased motor control. The OTA uses the proprioceptive neuromuscular facilitation (PNF) approach to help the client increase use of the right upper extremity and hand. Which of the following actions should the OTA have the client do during an intervention session to apply PNF principles?

Answer Choices:
A. Reach overhead with the right hand to retrieve a dish out of a higher cabinet and set it down on the countertop in front.
B. Reach to the right side to retrieve an item out of refrigerator at hip height and place it into the left hand to set it on the countertop to the left.
C. Use both hands together to pour juice out of a heavy pitcher into a glass on a countertop.
D. Take items out of a dishwasher on the right side and reach across the body to place them in the upper cabinet on the opposite side.

Correct Answer: D.

Rationale:
Proprioceptive neuromuscular facilitation (PNF) is a technique that involves use of diagonal patterns of movement and involves rotational trunk movement. Using the right upper extremity to reach down to one side to take items out of a dishwasher and reaching across one's body (trunk rotation) to place these items into a higher cabinet on the opposite side of the body creates this diagonal pattern and encourages use of the affected side to increase motor control and volitional movement.

Type of Reasoning: Inductive
This case requires the test taker to first recall PNF guidelines and then determine the approach that will best facilitate improved functioning given the deficits. This necessitates inductive reasoning skill, where clinical judgment is paramount to arriving at a correct conclusion. For this situation, the OTA should have the patient take items out of a dishwasher on the right side and then place the items above and to the left side. If answered incorrectly, review PNF patterns and treatment guidelines, especially the D1 pattern. See Chapter 12.

A181 C2

A home care OTA seeks to enhance an older adult's active engagement in their occupational therapy intervention program. After discussing the goals of the program with the person, which intervention is most effective for the OTA to use?

Answer Choices:
A. Provide the individual with limited opportunities for practice of skills to decrease boredom.
B. Use multiple, variable instructions to ensure retention of new learning.
C. Integrate previously learned strategies into new activities to facilitate generalization.
D. Teach the family positive techniques to reinforce activity performance in the home.

Correct Answer: C.

Rationale:
The integration of previously learned strategies will increase engagement in the intervention program. This approach can foster success which can be motivating and support continued engagement. Providing the individual with limited practice of new skills can decrease engagement because they will have a smaller number of successful experiences. This can increase feelings of hopelessness. The use of multiple and variable instructions will increase the complexity of intervention. This can be difficult for the client to follow, which will be frustrating and decrease the likelihood of success during the intervention session. Discussing the person's goals with their family and providing them with methods of positive reinforcement can be helpful, but this can only be done with the individual's permission. Additionally, this does not directly address the individual who is the person that the OTA needs to engage.

Type of Reasoning: Inferential
One must determine the most effective method for enhancing compliance with a treatment program given the information provided. This requires inferential reasoning skill, where one must infer or draw conclusions about a best course of action. In this situation, the OTA should discuss the goals of the program with the person and integrate previously learned strategies into new activities to facilitate generalization. If answered incorrectly, review client-centered approaches and principles of teaching-learning. See Chapter 3.

A182 C9

An occupational therapy administrator implements a continuous quality improvement program at a large, private, hand therapy clinic. The administrator determines that the OTA staff is not completing their assigned initial standardized screenings in a timely manner, which has resulted in scheduling delays for complete functional evaluations. Which initial action is most effective for the administrator to take in response to this situation?

Answer Choices:
A. Counsel the OTAs on the need to adhere to screening schedules.
B. Examine the organizational structure of the screening process.
C. Assign the occupational therapists to complete all screenings.

Correct Answer: B.

Rationale:
A fundamental principle of continuous quality improvement (CQI) is to view problems and limitations as opportunities to explore organizational improvement needs. Blame for identified problems is not attributed to any person within the organization. Counseling the OTAs or assigning screening to the occupational therapists may not effectively address the underlying reason for the delays in screening. The administrator must first examine the organizational structure of the screening process to be able to identify the needed organizational change.

Type of Reasoning: Inductive
This question requires one to determine the most effective initial action for addressing delays in completing initial screenings. This requires inductive reasoning skill, where clinical judgment is paramount to arriving at a correct conclusion. For this situation, the administrator should examine the organizational structure of the screening process. If answered incorrectly, review CQI guidelines. See Chapter 4.

A183 C8

An OTA working in a school has been asked to recommend technological devices for a student with severe spastic quadriplegia and dysarthria. Which action should the OTA take prior to recommending specific equipment?

Answer Choices:
A. Determine access capabilities in collaboration with the speech language pathologist.
B. Identify funding source(s) in collaboration with the social worker.
C. Obtain family support in collaboration with the psychologist.
D. Determine intervention goals in collaboration with the occupational therapist.

Correct Answer: D.

Rationale:
Establishing the goals of technological interventions is essential to ensure that all equipment recommendations are meaningful and relevant to the student's needs. For example, technology can facilitate communication, functional mobility, and/or the completion of schoolwork. Determining access capabilities is an important step to take after the goal of the device is established. Funding for a device would be provided by the school in accordance with IDEA. While obtaining family support is always important and is required by IDEA, the OTA and occupational therapist must be able to explain the need and rationale for the recommended equipment to effectively obtain this support.

Type of Reasoning: Inductive
This question requires one to determine the best approach for recommending assistive technology. This requires inductive reasoning skill, where clinical judgment is paramount to arriving at a correct conclusion. For this situation, the OTA should collaborate with the occupational therapist to determine the intervention goals in order to ensure that the equipment recommendations are relevant to what the student needs.
If answered incorrectly, review assessment guidelines for assistive technology. See Chapter 15.

A184 C9

An older adult recovering from a CVA is receiving outpatient occupational therapy services. The client presents with left hemiparesis of the upper and lower extremities. The client lives with and receives care from a family caregiver. The client arrives for a therapy session, and the OTA notes multiple bruises on the client's arms and legs. When asked about the bruises, the client cannot explain how they occurred. Later in the session, the client reports that the family caregiver is under a great deal of stress and becomes angry during the provision of personal care to the client. After documenting the bruises and the client's statements, which action should the OTA take next?

Answer Choices:
A. Call the police and report the family caregiver for suspected elder abuse.
B. Report the potential abuse according to the outpatient facility's policies and procedures.
C. Recommend the family hire a home health aide to decrease caregiver burden.
D. Consult with the occupational therapist regarding an action plan for the next session.

Correct Answer: B.

Rationale:
The OTA must report the findings according to the facility's established policies and procedures, which must comply with state laws governing elder abuse and practitioner licensure acts. The AOTA Code of Ethics and most state jurisdictions obligate OT practitioners to report suspected cases of abuse involving vulnerable adults. The other choices do not meet this mandate. The OTA does not know with absolute certainty that abuse has occurred; therefore, it is inappropriate to call the police and report the caregiver as a potential suspect. Investigation into the bruises must happen to determine if abuse has occurred prior to the pursuit of a criminal investigation. Recommending the family hire a home health aide can help decrease caregiver burden; however, it does not address the immediate need to respond to the person's bruises and potential abuse. While the OTA must inform the occupational therapist of the situation, it is not appropriate to wait until the next session to act. The patient's safety must be immediately addressed. A professional skilled in abuse investigation must be notified to investigate and decide the most appropriate action to take in response to the situation.

Type of Reasoning: Evaluative
This question requires the test taker to determine the merit of the information presented and its significance to the situation at hand in order to determine the most appropriate course of action. Questions of this nature often require evaluative reasoning skill. In this situation, the unexplained bruises should prompt the OTA to report the potential abuse according to the facility's policies and procedures. If answered incorrectly, review guidelines for reporting suspected elder and vulnerable adult abuse. See Chapters 4 and 5.

A185 C7

A woman with a complete spinal cord injury at the C5 level has given birth to her first child. The client seeks suggestions on methods to facilitate independent and safe parenting. Which of the following is most beneficial for the OTA to recommend the mother use to help her independently feed her child?

Answer Choices:
A. A pillow to support the mother's arms during breast feeding.
B. Pre-measured formula to simplify the task.
C. Bottles that have molded, easy-to-grip shapes.
D. A sling to support the infant's head during breast feeding.

Correct Answer: A.

Rationale:
Providing support of the mother's upper extremities will enable her to independently breast feed her child. Breast feeding is physically the easiest method for feeding an infant, and it is the healthiest for the infant. The individual with a C5 spinal cord injury has sufficient upper extremity function to be able to support the infant's head without the use of a sling, especially since the mother's arms will be supported by a pillow to decrease fatigue. Pre-measured formula is not indicated in this case. The individual would need a splint or other piece of adaptive equipment to hold a baby's bottle.

Type of Reasoning: Inductive
Clinical knowledge and judgment are the most important skills needed for answering this question, which requires inductive reasoning skill. Knowledge of the diagnosis and most effective course of action is essential to choosing the best solution. In this case, a pillow to support the mother's arms is the best recommendation to enable independent breast feeding. If answered incorrectly, review child care adaptations for individuals with disabilities. See Chapter 14.

A186 C3

An individual with complex regional pain syndrome (CRPS), type I presents with severe pain and pitting edema in the right hand. The individual has a secondary diagnosis of degenerative joint disease (DJD). Which should the OTA initially recommend to the person to address these concerns?

Answer Choices:
A. Passive range of motion of wrist and fingers.
B. Retrograde massage from distal to proximal.
C. Elevation of the affected hand above the heart.
D. Retrograde massage from proximal to distal.

Correct Answer: C.

Rationale:
Elevation of the affected hand above the heart will promote venous and lymphatic drainage and decrease the hydrostatic pressure in the blood vessels. Retrograde massage is performed in a centripetal direction and it is not the initial treatment when severe pain is present. Passive range of motion is not advisable for persons with DJD.

Type of Reasoning: Inductive
This question requires one to determine the best recommendation for addressing the patient's symptoms. This requires inductive reasoning skill, where clinical judgment is paramount to arriving at a correct conclusion. For this situation, the OTA should initially recommend elevation of the affected hand above the heart. If answered incorrectly, review treatment guidelines for patients with CRPS type I and pitting edema. See Chapters 6 and 11.

A187 C9

An adult who incurred a severe traumatic brain injury (TBI) is entering the second week of care at a long-term TBI rehabilitation center. The patient's family visits regularly and frequently asks multiple questions of the treatment team. With the patient's permission, a team and family conference is planned to address family concerns. Which is the most important information for the team to share with the family?

Answer Choices:
A. Realistic and clear information about the individual's current status and care plan.
B. Each team member's expert opinion about the expected prognosis and discharge recommendations.
C. Reimbursement information about each professional service to help determine treatment choices.
D. Community resources for family support and respite care.

Correct Answer: A.

Rationale:
The family needs to understand the individual's current status and what is being done in treatment to facilitate recovery. This information can help the family support the team's care plan. Since the individual has been in rehabilitation for only two weeks, it is not possible for the team to know the prognosis or discharge plan. Reimbursement is always pertinent to the provision of care, but it is not the primary basis for determining intervention. Providing the family with community resources is important, but it is premature at this time. Community-based support programs are focused on individuals with TBI who have completed the acute rehabilitation phase. Most (if not all) TBI rehabilitation centers offer on-site support programs for families, which would be more relevant to this family's current needs. Respite services may or may not be needed by the family, depending upon the individual's level of recovery, and cannot be determined at this point.

Type of Reasoning: Inferential
One must consider the benefits of providing the information described in order to determine which information would be most important. This requires inferential reasoning, where one must draw conclusions of the benefits to the family based on the information provided. In this situation, providing realistic and clear information about the individual's current status and care plan is most important. If answered incorrectly, review the principles of family-centered practice and the role of family members on the intervention team. See Chapters 3 and 4.

A188 C5

An individual with an incomplete C6 spinal cord injury (SCI) has a secondary diagnosis of thromboangiitis obliterans. The OTA conducts a pre-discharge home assessment of the patient's rented apartment. Which is the most important area for the OTA to assess?

Answer Choices:
A. The apartment's electrical capacity for an environmental control unit.
B. The apartment's water temperature.
C. The apartment's electrical capacity for an emergency call system.
D. The landlord's willingness to modify the bathroom.

Correct Answer: B.

Rationale:
Thromboangiitis obliterans, also known as Buerger's disease, results in diminished temperature sense, paresthesia, pain, and cold extremities. It is most common in young men who smoke. Poor or absent temperature sense can place a person at serious risk for scalding burns. If the apartment's water temperature is higher than 102°F, an anti-scald faucet and/or valve must be installed. An individual with a C6 SCI is independent in many tasks and does not require an environmental control unit to access the environment. A special emergency call system is also not needed because this person can independently access a telephone to call 911 with minimal modifications (i.e., large push buttons, speaker phone). Structural bathroom modifications are not needed. A person with a C6 SCI can bathe with minimal assistance using a tub bench, a sliding board transfer, and a handheld shower. None of these modifications would require a landlord's permission.

Type of Reasoning: Inductive
One must utilize clinical knowledge and judgment to determine the most important area for assessment based on the individual's diagnosis. In this case, the OTA should assess the apartment's water temperature to prevent scalding burns from hot water due to the individual's diminished temperature sense. If answered incorrectly, review the symptoms of thromboangiitis obliterans and adaptations to ensure safety for patients with impaired sensory function. The integration of this knowledge is needed to determine the correct answer. See Chapters 7 and 15.

A189 C2

An individual with myasthenia gravis is being discharged home after a hospitalization for the treatment of pneumonia. The person's spouse has expressed concern about caregiving responsibilities and the client's ability to function in the home. The OTA collaborates with the occupational therapist to address the spouse's concerns and the client's needs. Which is the most beneficial recommendation for the OTA and occupational therapist to make?

Answer Choices:
A. The extension of client's length of stay to allow for caregiver training.
B. The extension of client's length of stay to provide intervention to develop ADL skills.
C. A referral for the client to an adult day care program to relieve caregiver stress and develop functional skills.
D. A referral to a home care agency for a functional evaluation and home assessment.

Correct Answer: D.

Rationale:
A functional evaluation in the client's home and an assessment of the home environment is the most beneficial choice listed to provide accurate information about the client's functional status and caregiver needs. This information will enable the home care team to collaborate with the family to develop an appropriate intervention plan to address their identified needs. An extension of length of stay is very difficult to justify because the individual was hospitalized for the medical treatment of pneumonia. Once this illness is effectively treated, discharge must occur. In addition, it is more effective to provide caregiver and ADL training in the person's home environment. A referral to adult day care may be determined based on the home care evaluation.

Type of Reasoning: Inferential
One must determine the most beneficial recommendation for this patient, given the caregiver's stated concerns. This requires inferential reasoning skill, where one must draw conclusions based upon presented evidence. In this situation, a referral to a home care agency for a functional evaluation and home assessment is the most appropriate recommendation. Review discharge planning procedures and the continuum of care. See Chapters 3 and 4.

A190 C9

An OTA applies for the position of activities program director in a skilled nursing facility (SNF). During the job interview, the OTA discusses supervisory requirements for this position with the SNF administrator. Which amount of supervision should the OTA expect from an occupational therapist?

Answer Choices:
A. Daily.
B. Weekly.
C. Monthly.
D. None.

Correct Answer: D.

Rationale:
According to AOTA standards of practice and Medicare guidelines, an OTA who works strictly as an activities program director is not providing occupational therapy. While OTAs who work as activities program directors likely use their OT knowledge (e.g., the impact of client factors on activity performance) and skills (e.g., activity analysis, adaptation, and gradation) in this position, they are not providing OT services. Rather, they are providing directorship to the SNF's activity program. Therefore, they do not require the supervision of an occupational therapist.

Type of Reasoning: Deductive
One must recall the supervisory guidelines for OTAs in the role of activities program director. This is recall of factual knowledge, which is a deductive reasoning skill. Because OTAs can perform duties as an activities director without supervision, no supervision from an occupational therapist is required. If answered incorrectly, review supervisory guidelines for OTAs and Medicare guidelines for activity program director positions in SNFs. See Chapter 4.

A191 C8

An individual with hemiplegia has inadequate ankle dorsiflexion on the affected side. Which equipment is best for the OTA to recommend the person use to compensate for this deficit and facilitate safe and effective ambulation?

Answer Choices:
A. An ankle-foot orthosis (AFO).
B. A wide-based quad cane (WBQC).
C. A narrow-based quad cane (NBQC).
D. A knee-ankle-foot orthosis (KAFO).

Correct Answer: A.

Rationale:
An AFO will provide the needed stability to the ankle joint to enable safe and effective ambulation. In this case, the knee is not involved, so a KAFO is not indicated. A WBQC and an NBQC would be indicated for an individual with poor balance. Although canes can be very helpful ambulation aids, the concern in this case was to provide equipment to compensate for the lack of ankle dorsiflexion.

Type of Reasoning: Analytical
This question provides a description of a functional device, and the test taker must determine the best device to address the patient's deficits. This is an analytical reasoning skill, as questions of this nature often ask one to analyze descriptors or equipment to determine the best match for an individual's deficits. In this situation, an AFO is the best recommendation. If answered incorrectly, review guidelines for use of AFOs. See Chapter 15.

A192 C4

An individual recovering from a head trauma exhibits a motor pattern indicative of being influenced by the symmetrical tonic neck reflex. Which is most likely for the OTA to observe the client having difficulty with during functional mobility?

Answer Choices:
A. Moving both arms to midline when supine.
B. Moving from lying supine to sitting.
C. Flexing the head from the supine position.
D. Extending the head from the prone position.

Correct Answer: B.

Rationale:
Moving from lying to sitting is initiated by flexion of the neck. The presence of a symmetrical tonic neck reflex will cause this flexion to result in increased hip extension, making it difficult to assume a sitting position. The presence of the asymmetrical tonic neck reflex can decrease the ability to bring both arms to midline when supine. Flexing the head from a supine position would be more difficult in the presence of the tonic labyrinthine supine reflex because this reflex increases extensor tone. Extending the head from a prone position would be more difficult in the presence of the tonic labyrinthine prone reflex because this reflex increases flexor tone.

Type of Reasoning: Inferential
One must have knowledge of symmetrical tonic neck reflex (STNR) and influence of the reflex on functional activity. This is an inferential reasoning skill where knowledge of clinical guidelines and judgment based on facts are utilized to reach conclusions. In this case, the presence of an STNR can affect moving from supine to sitting. If answered incorrectly, review STNR reflex. See Chapters 5 and 7.

A193 C8

An OTA providing home-based occupational therapy services implements a bed positioning plan for a person recovering from a cerebral vascular accident. The person is receiving care from family members and personal care assistants employed by a home care agency. Which action should the OTA take to ensure the accurate implementation of this plan by the client's caregivers?

Answer Choices:
A. Provide verbal step-by-step directions of the desired positions to the client's caregivers.
B. Post written step-by-step directions of the desired positions on the wall by the client's bed.
C. Post pictures of the desired positions next to the bed's headboard.
D. Require each caregiver to demonstrate the replication of the desired positions.

Correct Answer: C.

Rationale:
A visual representation of the exact positions desired can decrease any misinterpretations of a written description. Placing this picture by the bed's headboard will ensure that it is visible to all caregivers. It is the most effective method provided to ensure compliance. Providing verbal step-by-step directions for positioning is reliant on the caregiver's memory, which can be incomplete or faulty. Posting written step-by-step directions is reliant on the initiation of all caregivers to read the documented procedures and on the caregivers' accurate interpretation of the written word. These methods may also assume a knowledge base (e.g., 30 degrees of shoulder abduction) that is beyond the level of some of the client's caregivers. Requiring caregivers to demonstrate replication of the positions can be helpful, but it is highly unlikely that the OTA would be able to access every personal care assistant who will be providing direct care to this client. In addition, home care agencies often use on-call per diem staff that would not be available to participate in a demonstration session.

Type of Reasoning: Inductive
This question requires one to determine the best approach for implementing a bed positioning plan. This requires inductive reasoning skill, where clinical judgment is paramount to arriving at a correct conclusion. For this situation, posting a picture of the person in the desired bed position next to the person's bed's headboard is best to ensure effective carryover. If answered incorrectly, review bed positioning guidelines. See Chapter 15.

A194 C1

During an intervention session in a school, the OTA observes a young child turn the pages of a book. The OTA identifies this behavior as an example of an in-hand manipulation task. What task should the OTA report to the occupational therapist that the child is capable of performing?

Answer Choices:
A. Shift.
B. Simple rotation.
C. Translation.
D. Translation without stabilization.

Correct Answer: A.

Rationale:
Turning the pages of a book involves a linear movement of each page on the finger surface. This allows for repositioning of the page relative to the pads of the fingers while the thumb remains opposed. Simple rotation is not correct as this involves a turning/rolling of an object held at the finger pads with the fingers acting as a unit and the thumb in opposition (e.g., unscrewing a bottle cap). Translation is incorrect as this involves linear movement of an object from the palm to the fingers or fingers to the palm. The activity of turning pages does not use the palm with stabilization or without stabilization.

Type of Reasoning: Analytical
This question provides a description of a functional activity, and the test taker must determine the likely definition of such an activity. This is an analytical reasoning skill, as questions of this nature often ask one to analyze descriptors of functional skills to determine the overall skill involved. In this situation, the activity is that of the in-hand manipulation task of shift, which should be reviewed if answered incorrectly. See Chapter 5.

A195 C9

The residents of a halfway house plan a community leisure activity for a Saturday. Two residents state that they cannot participate in Saturday activities due to religious observances. The other residents express strong interest in the activity. Which is the OTA's best response to this situation?

Answer Choices:
A. Schedule an in-house Saturday leisure activity for the two residents.
B. Explore with the group an alternative schedule for a community leisure activity.
C. Schedule an in-house Saturday leisure activity for all residents.
D. Recommend the two members seek approval from their religious leadership to attend the Saturday activity.

Correct Answer: B.

Rationale:
All residents should be provided with the opportunity to engage in the community leisure activity. Facilitating the group's exploration of alternative schedule can result in all residents' needs being met. Engaging in an on-site activity is not congruent with the residents' statement that they could not participate in activities on Saturday. It is inappropriate to advise group members to seek the approval of their religious leadership to engage in an activity that is inconsistent with their religious beliefs. Finding an alternative schedule for a community activity that all residents can participate in does not prevent the other residents from engaging in community activities of interest on a Saturday.

Type of Reasoning: Evaluative
One must weigh the possible courses of action and then make a value judgment about the best course to take. This requires evaluative reasoning skill, which often utilizes guiding principles of action in order to arrive at a correct conclusion. Because not all residents can attend the leisure activity due to religious observances, the best recommendation in this case is for the group to explore an alternative schedule for the activity.

A196 C7

An OTA collaborates with an occupational therapist to design a program to provide occupational therapy services to inmates in a long-term forensic facility. After the completion of a needs assessment, which of the following would be the best for the therapist and the OTA to identify as the initial focus for the program?

Answer Choices:
A. Vocational planning.
B. Remedial educational.
C. Leisure management.
D. Money management.

Correct Answer: C.

Rationale:
Persons in a forensic setting have a significant amount of time that is not filled by productive or meaningful activity. A program initially focused on the development of leisure management skills would be an appropriate focus for individuals living in a long-term environment with limited leisure opportunities. Moreover, since these inmates are there for extended time periods or indefinitely, the development of skills to effectively manage leisure time would benefit them on an ongoing basis. Vocational planning and money management skills would be appropriate program foci for inmates who are preparing for their release. Remedial educational activities would be the focus of services provided by an educational professional, not by an OTA.

Type of Reasoning: Inductive
One must consider the information provided to determine the best focus for the group in this facility, which is an inductive reasoning skill. For this situation, leisure management techniques are best to address in a group within a forensic facility. If answered incorrectly, review information on the characteristics of forensic settings and the focus of OT interventions in these settings. See Chapter 4.

A197 C9

The OTA collaborates with the occupational therapist to review the use of the occupational therapy department's resources to determine medical necessity and cost efficiency. Which service management task is the OTA working on with the occupational therapist?

Answer Choices:
A. Utilization review.
B. Retrospective peer review.
C. Total quality management.
D. Risk management.

Correct Answer: A.

Rationale:
Utilization review is a plan to review the use of resources within a facility to determine medical necessity and cost efficiency. It is often a component of a continuous quality improvement (CQI) or a performance assessment and improvement (PAI) system. Total quality management is the creation of an organizational culture that enables all employees to contribute to an environment of continuous improvement. Risk management is a process that identifies, evaluates, and takes corrective action against risk, as well as plans, organizes, and controls the activities and resources of OT services to decrease actual or potential losses. Retrospective review involves the auditing of medical records by third-party payers to ensure appropriate care was rendered. Peer review is a system in which the quality of work of a group of health professionals is reviewed by their peers.

Type of Reasoning: Deductive
One must recall the definition of a utilization review for this question. This requires deductive reasoning skill, where factual knowledge is vital in choosing the correct solution. Utilization review is defined as a plan to review the use of resources in a facility, which should be reviewed if answered incorrectly. See Chapter 4.

A198 C6

A home care hospice OTA works with a client with end-stage lung cancer. The client has openly spoken to family members and friends about end-of-life issues and has completed funeral arrangements. The client expresses regret that there is "not enough time to say everything I want to everyone." Which action is best for the OTA to take in response to the client's statement?

Answer Choices:
A. Reassure the client that family members and friends will understand.
B. Remind the client that there still is time left to speak to family and friends.
C. Encourage the client to write personal letters to people who matter to the client.
D. Inform the occupational therapist that the client may be becoming depressed.

Correct Answer: C.

Rationale:
The client's concern that time is limited is very real. While there may be time to speak to some family members and friends, verbal communications can be constrained by a number of factors, for example, a lack of privacy (e.g., multiple people visiting at the same time) and fatigue (e.g., visits occurring during the time of day when the client is overtired). Encouraging the client to write personal letters will enable the client to put into words what is most important to the client. The actions of reassuring the client that family members and friends will understand the client's situation and reminding the client that there still is time left to speak to family and friends do not respect the validity of the client's feelings. There is no indication in the scenario that the client is depressed. The client's expressed desire for more time is appropriate for a person nearing the end of their life. Additional behavioral changes (e.g., withdrawal, despondency, feelings of worthlessness) would need to be observed to warrant a need to inform the occupational therapist that the client may be becoming depressed.

Type of Reasoning: Inductive
This question requires the test taker to determine a best course of action based on a client's statement regarding end-of-life issues. This requires clinical judgment, which is an inductive reasoning skill. For this situation, the OTA should encourage the client to write personal letters to those who matter to the client. If answered incorrectly, review information regarding end-of-life issues and intervention approaches in hospice care. See Chapter 13.

A199 C7

An OTA is treating an adult who sustained a radial nerve injury at work. During a therapy session, the OTA observes the client yawning excessively and having difficulty concentrating on the therapeutic activities. The client works a midnight to 7 AM shift. The client reports irregular sleep patterns due to disruptions that occur during the day when the client needs to sleep. The OTA suspects poor sleep hygiene may have been a contributing factor to the work-related injury. After discussing the client's typical sleep routine with the client, which of the following environmental approaches should the OTA recommend to the client? Select the three BEST responses.

Answer Choices:
A. Install room-darkening shades.
B. Play soothing music to relax.
C. Meditate for 30 minutes prior to bedtime.
D. Do not eat for 2 hours prior to bedtime.
E. If unable to sleep, get up and do a boring chore.
F. Use earplugs and/or white noise machines to block sound.

Correct Answers: A, B, and F.

Rationale:
Sleep is a necessary daily function for all people, and sleep hygiene is essential to health and functioning. OT practitioners are able to help people understand how their sleeping patterns impact on their overall well-being and can educate them on ways to achieve optimum sleep. The AOTA Practice Framework recognizes how one's health and wellness can be affected by behavioral, environmental, and/or psychosocial factors that impact sleep and rest. Installing room-darkening shades, playing soothing music to relax, and using earplugs and/or white noise machines to block sound are options that change the sleep environment. Meditation, limiting food intake prior to bed, and doing a less-stimulating activity if unable to sleep are all good behavioral approaches to help promote quality of sleep or falling asleep.

Type of Reasoning: Inductive
For this question, the test taker must determine the best actions to improve the sleep environment of a person with irregular sleep patterns. This requires clinical judgment to determine the most effective environmental approaches, which is an inductive reasoning skill. For this case, the OTA should recommend installing room-darkening shades, playing soothing music, and using earplugs and/or white noise machines to help improve sleep patterns. If answered incorrectly, review sleep hygiene guidelines and environmental approaches to promote sleep. See Chapter 14.

A200 C6

An OTA working on an acute psychiatric unit collaborates with the occupational therapist to expand the occupational therapy program to include a psychoeducational group based on the recovery model. Which group is best for the OTA and therapist to develop?

Answer Choices:
A. Sensory awareness.
B. Task skills.
C. Coping skills.
D. Vocational skills.

Correct Answer: C.

Rationale:
Coping skills groups focus on identifying and implementing the problem-solving and stress-management techniques needed to cope with life stressors. Because people who are admitted to acute psychiatric units are typically individuals who have experienced great stress, the development of coping skills to enable successful participation in the community post-discharge is critical. Groups that use a psychoeducational approach apply the principles of learning to provide information to members and to teach skills (e.g., how to identify common stressors and effectively manage them). The use of homework assignments is encouraged to facilitate skill development and the generalization of learning (e.g., practicing the skills learned in the coping skills groups during other intervention groups and visiting hours). A coping skills group is consistent with the recovery model. The primary focus of recovery is to improve people's ability to attain desired life goals through self-advocacy, self-direction, and individualized and person-centered services. The development of coping skills can help members attain this outcome. A sensory awareness group provides activities to promote sensory functions and environmental awareness. A task skills group includes activities designed to develop the basic cognitive skills (e.g., attention, ability to follow multistep directions, problem solving) necessary for the completion of simple tasks. Sensory awareness and task skills groups are often used in acute psychiatric settings. However, a sensory awareness group uses a sensory-processing approach and a task skills group uses a skill-acquisition approach; neither uses a psychoeducational approach or a recovery model. The development of vocational skills is an important outcome for psychiatric rehabilitation; however, this would not be a primary focus on an inpatient acute psychiatric illness.

Type of Reasoning: Inductive
This question requires one to apply guidelines for a psychoeducational approach and a recovery model in order to arrive at a correct conclusion. Questions of this nature often require inductive reasoning skill, where clinical judgment is paramount to arriving at a correct conclusion. For this case, the OTA should develop a coping skills group. If answered incorrectly, review the psychoeducational approach and the recovery model. See Chapter 13.

Exam B Answer Rationales

B1 C4

During an initial ADL evaluation, the OTA notes that a patient consistently spills food due to an inability to adjust movements while cutting food and moving the food from the plate to the mouth. When describing this behavior, which deficit should the OTA report the patient is most likely exhibiting?

Answer Choices:
A. Ideational apraxia.
B. Somatoagnosia.
C. Tactile agnosia.
D. Motor apraxia.

Correct Answer: D.

Rationale:
Motor apraxia (also known as ideomotor apraxia) is the loss of access to kinesthetic memory so that purposeful movement cannot be achieved due to ineffective motor planning, although sensation, movement, and coordination are intact. Ideational apraxia is a breakdown in the knowledge of what is to be done or how to perform an action or use an object (e.g., using a comb to brush teeth). The neuronal model about the concept of how to perform is lost, although the sensorimotor system may be intact. Somatoagnosia is a body scheme disorder that results in diminished awareness of body structure and a failure to recognize body parts as one's own. Tactile agnosia, also known as astereognosis, is the inability to recognize objects, forms, shapes, and sizes by touch alone.

Type of Reasoning: Analytical
This question requires the test taker to determine the functional deficit of the patient, which is an analytical reasoning skill. Questions of this nature often call upon the test taker to determine a diagnosis based on a functional description of deficits. Based on this information, the symptoms of the patient indicate the deficit of motor apraxia, which should be reviewed if answered incorrectly. See Chapter 12.

B2 C8

During a wheelchair evaluation, an individual with limited functional mobility expresses concern about the ability to continue volunteer work at a local church. The church's doorways are 31 inches wide. The client knows (from a recent home remodeling project) that 32 inches is the minimum width recommended for wheelchair access. After the evaluation, the OTA reviews the client's concerns with the occupational therapist and they determine the most effective way to address the client's concerns and functional mobility needs. Based on this review, what is the best recommendation for the OTA to make to the client?

Answer Choices:
A. Have the church widen its doorways to comply with ADA requirements.
B. Order a wheelchair with wrap-around armrests.
C. Have the client explore alternative volunteer activities in accessible locations.
D. Order a customized narrow adult wheelchair.

Correct Answer: B.

Rationale:
Wrap-around armrests (also called space saver armrests) reduce the overall width of a wheelchair by 1 inch. A customized chair can be very expensive. The case does not indicate the individual's measurements, so it is not possible to ascertain if a narrow wheelchair would actually fit the person. Religious organizations are exempt from ADA accessibility requirements. The individual does not need to explore alternative volunteer experiences since valued, established activities can continue with an appropriate wheelchair.

Type of Reasoning: Inductive
Clinical knowledge and judgment are the most important skills needed for answering this question, which requires inductive reasoning skill. Knowledge of available mobility equipment to remedy the issue of a narrow doorway is paramount to arriving at a correct conclusion. In this case, the most appropriate recommendation is to order a wheelchair with wrap-around armrests, which should be reviewed if answered incorrectly. See Chapter 15.

B3 C7

An OTA works with an adolescent with Duchenne's muscular dystrophy. The adolescent expresses concern that they can no longer close snaps or zip zippers on jeans. Which recommendation is best for the OTA to make to this client in response to these expressed concerns?

Answer Choices:
A. Replace snaps and zippers with Velcro.
B. Replace snaps and zippers with large buttons.
C. Use a zipper pull to zip jeans and leave the snaps unsnapped.
D. Purchase elastic waist pants to replace jeans.

Correct Answer: A.

Rationale:
Muscular dystrophy is a progressive condition. The OTA must be able to assist the person in adjusting to its progressive nature and provide options that maintain independence for as long as possible. Velcro can be more easily managed than snaps or zippers. It can also be easily sewn into the jeans and pants that the adolescent already owns. Buttoning large buttons and using a zipper pull are not the best solutions due to the progressive loss of dexterity, coordination, and strength that occurs with Duchenne's muscular dystrophy. Elastic waist pants facilitate the process of donning pants, but they do not address the identified difficulty of fastening jeans. This recommendation would not allow the adolescent to continue wearing jeans and pants in the current wardrobe. In addition, the style of elastic waist pants may not be acceptable to a teenager.

Type of Reasoning: Inductive
This question requires one to determine a best adaptation for an adolescent with Duchenne's muscular dystrophy in order to arrive at a correct conclusion. This requires clinical judgment, which is an inductive reasoning skill. For this scenario, the OTA should recommend replacing snaps and zippers with Velcro. If answered incorrectly, review self-care adaptations for persons with progressive disorders. See Chapters 7 and 14.

B4 C3

A patient is recovering from a right total hip replacement (posterolateral incision, cementless fixation). Which is the best type of bed-to-wheelchair transfer for the OTA to teach the patient to use?

Answer Choices:
A. Stand-pivot transfer to the surgical side.
B. Stand-pivot transfer to the non-surgical side.
C. Lateral slide transfer using a transfer board.

Correct Answer: B.

Rationale:
During initial healing, it is important to protect the hip from dislocation or subluxation of the prosthesis. With a posterolateral incision, excessive hip flexion, internal rotation, and adduction past neutral are contraindicated. This is minimized by transferring to the non-surgical side. Full ROM of the operated hip is also contraindicated.

Type of Reasoning: Deductive
This question requires one to recall posterolateral hip precautions and the guidelines for bed-to-wheelchair transfers of patients with total hip replacements in order to arrive at a correct conclusion. The recall of factual guidelines and information necessitates deductive reasoning skill. For this case, the OTA should perform a stand-pivot transfer to the non-surgical side. If answered incorrectly, review hip precaution and transfer guidelines. The integration of this knowledge is needed to determine the correct answer. See Chapters 6 and 15.

B5 C3

As the result of an industrial accident, an individual incurred a right transradial (below-the elbow) *amputation*. The client is right-hand dominant. The client underwent surgical revisions to their residual limb two weeks ago and now wears a limb shrinker. The client is referred to occu-pational therapy for an initial evaluation. The occupational therapist and the OTA collaborate to complete the evaluation. Which is best for them to include in the initial evaluation session?

Answer Choices:
A. Train the client in the use of adaptive strategies and equipment to perform BADL independently.
B. Measure the client's right upper extremity residual limb length, circumference, and sensitivity.
C. Assess the client's ability to protectively wrap the residual limb with an elastic bandage in a circular manner.

Correct Answer: B.

Rationale:
Measuring the client's right upper extremity residual limb length, circumference, and sensitivity can provide meaningful information that can be used to plan a relevant intervention plan. The measurement of the length and circumference of a residual limb is a fundamental component of a postamputation evaluation. These measurements are taken frequently and consistently in the same location to help determine when the client can be fitted for a prosthesis. At this early stage in the client's rehabilitation, this data is essential to obtain. Evaluating a residual limb's sensitivity is also important to determine if desensitization techniques are needed to prepare a limb for a prosthesis and/or functional use. Training the client in the use of adaptive strategies and equipment to perform BADL independently is a relevant intervention focus for a person with an amputation. However, the focus of this exam item was evaluation, not intervention. Wrapping is a preprosthetic intervention technique that is used to shape and shrink a residual limb. However, assessing the client's ability to wrap the residual limb with an elastic bandage in a circular manner violates a major contraindication for amputations. Wrapping a limb in this manner would cause a tourniquet effect and dangerously restrict the limb's circulation. When wrapping is done it must be completed in a figure-of-eight diagonal pattern going from a distal to proximal direction with greater pressure applied at the distal end of the limb.

Type of Reasoning: Inductive
This question requires one to determine a best course of action, given the information provided. This requires inductive reasoning skill, where one must use clinical judgment to determine the best approach for evaluating this person. In this situation, the OTA should measure the client's right upper extremity residual limb length, circumference, and sensitivity. If answered incorrectly, review evaluation guidelines for person with amputations. See Chapter 6.

B6 C2

In a school setting, a 6-year-old child is referred to occupational therapy for interventions to develop skills for handwriting and engagement in other fine motor activities. During an individualized education plan meeting, the OTA explains how upper extremity hypotonicity can influence handwriting and other fine motor activities. The OTA recommends having the child engage in home exercises prior to completing homework that requires handwriting. Which is the best method for the OTA to use when discussing the relationship between muscle tone and handwriting with the child's parents?

Answer Choices:
A. Use common, everyday language to explain this functional relationship.
B. Use medical terminology to emphasize the importance of the recommendations.
C. Use the Occupational Therapy Practice Framework language to support OT's focus.

Correct Answer: A.

Rationale:
Using common, everyday language to describe how home exercises (e.g., weight bearing activities such as chair push-ups) may decrease hand fatigue and improve handwriting tasks can help the parents understand this relationship. Relating the description to an observable functional outcome can lead to better comprehension and follow-through in the home. An OT practitioner cannot assume that the family is familiar with medical terminology and knows how it is related to function. The Practice Framework is a document that defines and guides the OT process. This document likely contains terms that are unfamiliar to the parents.

Type of Reasoning: Evaluative
This question requires one to weigh all the options of how to present information to parents in a meaningful way and determine the option that will have the greatest success in helping parents to understand the instructions. This is an evaluative reasoning skill. For this scenario, it would be best for the OTA to use common, everyday language to explain this functional relationship. If answered incorrectly, review guidelines for client and family centered practice. See Chapter 3.

B7 C4

An OTA works with a person who is recovering from the removal of a brain tumor from the parietal lobe. The client has established a goal to resume the role of home maintainer. Which is the most important focus for the OTA to include during intervention sessions focused on the development of home management skills?

Answer Choices:
A. Safety precautions to observe when cooking and ironing.
B. Compensatory techniques for finding items in the supermarket.
C. Organizational strategies for managing the household budget.
D. The use of a wheeled cart to assist with balance while doing laundry.

Correct Answer: A.

Rationale:
The parietal lobe of the brain is the primary sensory cortex for integration of the sensation, including touch, proprioceptive, pain, and temperature sensations. Because the person's ability to feel heat will likely be affected by a parietal lobe brain tumor, it is most important for the OTA to teach the person to use safety precautions to prevent burns while cooking (e.g., the use of oven mitts) and ironing (e.g., the use of undivided attention to the task). Training in compensatory techniques for finding items in the supermarket would be indicated for a person who had visual deficits resulting from occipital lobe damage. A person who had cognitive deficits from frontal lobe damage would benefit from interventions focused on the use of organizational strategies. The use of mobility aids such as a wheeled cart would be a helpful intervention for a person who incurred damage to the cerebellum, which would result in balance and coordination concerns.

Type of Reasoning: Inductive
For this question, one must determine the best and safest course of action for a patient who has parietal lobe deficits from a brain tumor. This requires clinical judgment, which is an inductive reasoning skill. For this case, the OTA should focus on safety precautions during cooking and ironing because of the potential for injury from sensory deficits. If answered incorrectly, review the function of the parietal lobe and intervention strategies for sensory deficits. The integration of this knowledge is required to correctly answer this exam item. See Chapters 7 and 14.

B8 C2

A child with attention deficit with hyperactivity disorder (ADHD) and conduct disorder attends an after-school program that utilizes sensory-integrative and behavioral management approaches to achieve intervention goals. Snacks are provided and occasionally used as rewards. A parent insists that a child not be given any foods containing sugar. Which is the OTA's best response to this request?

Answer Choices:
A. Discontinue providing sugary snacks but continue their use as rewards in the behavioral management program.
B. Provide the parent with recent research that refutes the link between sugar and problem behaviors.
C. Comply with the parent's request and discontinue providing sugary snacks.
D. Inform the parent that the OTA will discuss the issue with the occupational therapist to determine the best course of action.

Correct Answer: C.

Rationale:
The parent's request must be respected and honored. While an OTA may provide a parent with research information related to a child's condition, it is not the OTA's role to attempt to prove the parent wrong in their beliefs. The OTA can directly address the issue with the parent and does not need to discuss the issue with the occupational therapist prior to responding. Behavioral rewards and appropriate snacks that do not contain sugar can be used in the program. The use of non-sugar items can also be beneficial for children at risk with a secondary diagnosis of diabetes or other medical conditions.

Type of Reasoning: Evaluative
One must weigh the possible courses of action and then make a value judgment about the best course to take. This requires evaluative reasoning skill, which often utilizes guiding principles of action in order to arrive at a correct conclusion. For this case, because the parent has requested no foods containing sugar, the OTA should comply with the parent's request. This action is consistent with client-centered practice. See Chapter 3.

B9 C6

An adult with obsessive-compulsive disorder is hospitalized due to the exacerbation of symptoms. During the patient's first occupational therapy group, which is the most beneficial activity for the OTA to employ with this person?

Answer Choices:
A. Sanding a cutting board.
B. Repotting plants.
C. Stringing small beads into a necklace.
D. Lacing a wallet with the double cordovan stitch.

Correct Answer: B.

Rationale:
Persons with obsessive-compulsive disorders exhibit behaviors that are characterized by orderliness, perseverance, and driven by a pursuit for perfection. Repotting plants is the activity choice that offers an opportunity to break away from the repetitive behavioral patterns of obsessive-compulsive disorder. The other activities all have elements that could reinforce the repetitive behavioral components of the disorder; that is, sanding back and forth, stringing bead after bead, and lacing the stitch over and over. In addition, these activities could be held to a standard of perfection; that is, a perfectly smooth surface, the perfect bead pattern, a complex stitch with no twists.

Type of Reasoning: Inferential
One must determine which activity is most beneficial, given an understanding of the client's diagnosis. This requires inferential reasoning skill. In order to arrive at a correct conclusion, the test taker should infer that activities that encourage repetitive patterns of behavior and perfectionism should be avoided. Repotting plants is the only activity that does not encourage such behavior. If answered incorrectly, review the behavioral characteristics of OCD and principles of activity analysis. The integration of this knowledge is required to correctly answer this question. See Chapters 3 and 10.

B10 C7

A middle school-aged child with right upper extremity amelia attends occupational therapy to learn how to dress independently. Which of the following is most beneficial for the OTA to focus on during intervention?

Answer Choices:
A. Donning and doffing a variety of shirt types of personal preference.
B. Donning and doffing only shirts that can be donned overhead.
C. Donning and doffing shirts that button in the front.
D. Donning and doffing shirts with Velcro tabs sewn on to replace buttons.

Correct Answer: A.

Rationale:
A child with amelia, or absence of one arm, can easily learn to use a diversity of techniques to independently don and doff a variety of shirt types. This is the best way to engage a pre-adolescent and to allow the pre-adolescent to make decisions about clothing. This choice reflects incorporation of the child's developmental level, motivation level, and therapeutic use of self to work with the child's interests. There is no need to limit the child's shirt choices. Velcro tabs are appropriate for someone with decreased fine motor skills and/or strength but these adaptations are not needed in this case.

Type of Reasoning: Inductive

This requires one to understand the nature of amelia and based on this knowledge, choose the most appropriate dressing activity. This requires inductive reasoning skill, where clinical judgment is paramount to arriving at a correct conclusion. In this case, working on a variety of shirt types of personal preference is the best recommendation for this patient. See Chapter 14.

B11 C8

An OTA works in a subacute rehabilitation facility. A newly admitted patient has right hemiplegia and a right shoulder subluxation. The OTA meets with the nursing staff that will be providing primary care to the patient. The OTA recommends that the direct care staff position the patient in left side-lying. Which is the best bed position for the OTA to recommend for placement of the patient's right arm?

Answer Choices:
A. In 90 degrees of humeral abduction and internally rotated.
B. Protracted, with arm forward on a pillow and the elbow extended or slightly flexed.
C. On the person's side, adducted and internally rotated.
D. In 90 degrees of abduction of the humerus with neutral rotation.

Correct Answer: B.

Rationale:
The best position of the upper extremities for sleeping or bed rest is to place the affected arm on a pillow in a position that ensures that the shoulder is approximated and that the extremity is well supported. Excess abduction can cause the joint capsule to loosen and reduce the stability of the humeral head in the glenoid fossa. It is important to avoid traction of the affected arm to ensure adequate positioning of the humerus with the scapula and to prevent subluxation. Correct positioning means putting the involved arm in slight abduction. Ninety degrees of abduction is excessive.

Type of Reasoning: Inferential
One must infer or draw conclusions about the optimal positioning of the affected upper extremity in side-lying. One must understand the reasons for positioning the extremity in order to prevent further problems from developing, which requires inferential reasoning skill. In this situation, positioning the extremity on a pillow in slight abduction is best. See Chapters 7 and 15.

B12 C6

A person with a diagnosis of major depressive disorder is receiving treatment in an acute psychiatric inpatient unit. The patient was recently placed on suicide precautions. The OTA has scheduled 30-minute individual sessions in the patient's room to begin intervention. Which is the most beneficial activity for the first intervention session?

Answer Choices:
A. Tooling a leather wallet.
B. Writing in a personal journal.
C. Building a sand terrarium in a plastic globe.
D. Decorating cookies to contribute to the patients' lounge.

Correct Answer: D.

Rationale:
Decorating cookies is a safe, 'no-fail' project. The end product fosters the curative factor of altruism, which can be therapeutic. Also, the end product is not dangerous or potentially harmful to the patient. Tooling a wallet uses tools that can be used to harm oneself. The OTA can be careful to account for all tools but having tools available that can cause harm is an unacceptable risk on an acute inpatient psychiatric unit. While writing in a journal can be therapeutic, it may reinforce negative feelings and poor self-esteem. The globe of the sand terrarium can be broken and sharpened into an object that one can use to harm oneself.

Type of Reasoning: Inductive
One must utilize clinical judgment for a best course of action in order to arrive at a best conclusion. This requires consideration of the client's diagnosis and current status in order to choose the best activity. In this situation, decorating cookies is best as it creates the least potential for harm and is a 'no-fail' activity. If answered incorrectly, review therapeutic activities for patients with major depressive disorders, principles of activity analysis, and the characteristics of inpatient psychiatric units. The integration of this knowledge is required to determine the correct answer. See Chapters 3 and 13.

B13 C9

A mental health facility provides inpatient and outpatient services for a catchment area that encompasses five counties. The occupational therapy department meets to design a continuous quality improvement (CQI) project. The OTA will contribute to this project. Which is the best focus for this CQI project?

Answer Choices:
A. Keeping services that are rated positively on a satisfaction survey.
B. Cost reduction in specific service areas.
C. Methods to educate staff on new wellness services.
D. The follow-up process after discharge from the hospital.

Correct Answer: D.

Rationale:
Continuous quality improvement (CQI) involves a prospective analysis of specific services to improve service quality and meet the needs of a population. Since this program serves a broad geographic area, evaluating post-discharge follow-up services would be an appropriate focus for a CQI project. The determination that services be maintained should be made according to the efficacy of service outcomes in meeting the needs of a population, not based on client perspectives. Making changes in service delivery to reduce costs is a fiscal management task, not the focus of CQI. Wellness services are offered to employees as a benefit. CQI focuses on improving service quality and patient care, not on promoting employee benefits.

Type of Reasoning: Deductive
This question requires one to recall the guidelines for CQI, which is a factual (deductive) skill. Understanding the nature of CQI is key to arriving at a correct conclusion. Focusing on the follow-up process after discharge is most likely to be the focus out of all the choices provided. If answered incorrectly, review guidelines for CQI, especially in hospital settings. See Chapter 4.

B14 C7

A middle-school-aged child with osteogenesis imperfecta reports feelings of low self-esteem, social isolation, boredom, and lethargy. The OTA collaborates with the child to identify resources for after-school leisure activities to promote socialization and community participation. Which of the following activities are most beneficial for the OTA to explore with the child? Select the three BEST responses.

Answer Choices:
A. Team sports.
B. Chess clubs.
C. Computer-based gaming clubs.
D. Public park programs.
E. Adapted horseback riding.
F. Public aquatic programs.

Correct Answers: B, C, and F.

Rationale:
Osteogenesis imperfecta (OI) results in brittle bones that fracture easily. Fracture prevention through activity restrictions is a primary focus. This can result in social isolation, decreased self-efficacy, and depression. Exploring chess and computer-based gaming clubs can provide the child with a number of viable options for leisure activities that they can successfully pursue after school without risking fractures. These are age-appropriate activities which can provide opportunities for socialization with peers. Swimming is also an ideal activity for persons with OI since the water eliminates gravity and provides a safe environment in which to move and develop mastery over one's body. This can be very empowering for a child whose movements are often restricted due to safety concerns. Horseback riding is contraindicated because this movement (even if the horse is just walking) can cause fractures. Moreover, the risk of falling from a horse is too great. Team sports and public park programs typically involve more physically-based activities that would be difficult for a child with OI to safely pursue. These activities would highlight what the child is unable to do, rather than their abilities. This would be contraindicated for a child with low self-esteem. In computer-based gaming clubs, chess clubs, and aquatic programs, physical abilities are not needed because physical deficits can be readily compensated for with adaptations and modifications.

Type of Reasoning: Inferential
One must determine the most appropriate activity recommendations, given knowledge of the presenting diagnosis. This requires inferential reasoning skill, where one must infer or draw conclusions about a best course of action. In this situation, the OTA should recommend that the child explore joining a computer-based gaming club, chess club, and/or an aquatic program. If answered incorrectly, review symptoms of OI and guidelines for leisure interventions. The integration of this knowledge is required to answer this question correctly. See Chapters 6 and 14.

B15 C3

An individual is recovering from deep partial thickness burns on both upper extremities, chest, and lower neck. The OTA provides equipment to prevent positions that can result in contractures. Which are the most important positions for the OTA to prevent?

Answer Choices:
A. Positions of comfort.
B. Anti-deformity positions.
C. Positions resulting in edema.
D. Positions of discomfort and pain.

Correct Answer: A.

Rationale:
Positions of comfort are often assumed by individuals recovering from burns. These positions occur when the person assumes the protective postures of adduction and flexion of the upper extremities, flexion of the hips and knees, and plantar flexion of the ankles. These positions do decrease discomfort, but they are non-functional and can result in contractures. Anti-deformity positions are the desired positions: they are the opposite of positions of comfort. While preventing edema is important in burn rehabilitation, the question is about the prevention of contractures. Positions of pain and discomfort are unavoidable for persons recovering from deep partial-thickness burns. These burns involve the epidermis and deep portion of the dermis, hair follicles, and sweat glands, and are often very painful.

Type of Reasoning: Inductive
Clinical knowledge and judgment are the most important skills needed for answering this question, which requires inductive reasoning skill. Knowledge of the diagnosis and most appropriate positioning given the severity of the burns is essential to choosing the ideal solution. In this case, the patient should avoid positions of comfort. If answered incorrectly, review positioning guidelines for persons with burns. See Chapter 6.

B16 C4

An individual recovering from a traumatic brain injury is assessed to be at Level VI of the Rancho Level of Cognitive Functioning Scale. Which of the following should the OTA use to implement treatment?

Answer Choices:
A. Repetitive self-care tasks such as brushing hair.
B. Community re-entry activities such as taking a bus.
C. Simple meal preparation tasks such as making a sandwich.

Correct Answer: C.

Rationale:
At Level VI on the Rancho Level of Cognitive Functioning Scale the individual is appropriate and goal directed but can become confused. Cues are required. Community re-entry activities are too high level for an individual at Level VI. They are more appropriate for persons functioning at Levels VII and VIII. Repetitive self-care tasks would be appropriate for persons functioning at Level V.

Type of Reasoning: Inductive
One must utilize clinical knowledge and judgment to determine the intervention activity that would be relevant for a patient at Level VI. In this case, the OTA should implement treatment by having the individual prepare a simple meal, such as making a sandwich. If answered incorrectly, review the functional abilities and limitations of persons with TBI according to the different levels of the Rancho Level of Cognitive Functioning Scale. See Chapter 7.

B17 C8

An adolescent incurred a C4 spinal cord injury. During the initial session, the patient refuses to speak to the OTA. The OTA supportively acknowledges the client's response. Which action should the OTA take next?

Answer Choices:
A. Set up a chin-operated bedside environmental control unit (ECU).
B. Provide passive range of motion to prevent contractures.
C. Explain what OT can offer the adolescent to adjust to decreased abilities.
D. Ask the adolescent to tell nursing staff when personally ready for OT.

Correct Answer: A.

Rationale:
The individual immediately needs a method to access the environment. Being able to call staff, operate a TV and/or radio, answer the phone, turn on/off lights, and other basic ECU functions are important tasks for the adolescent to self-control. It is not necessary to explain what OT can offer. Some of the benefits of OT will likely become self-evident as the adolescent learns to use the ECU. This explanation can be expanded on as the adolescent begins to engage in intervention. Providing PROM ignores the patient's feelings. PROM can be provided by direct care staff. The individual may not be ready for quite a while to collaborate with the OTA due to the need to adjust to disability. While this is occurring, the OTA can still provide meaningful supportive interventions and work on developing a therapeutic relationship.

Type of Reasoning: Inductive
One must utilize clinical knowledge and judgment to determine the best action that addresses the adolescent's needs in the absence of their input. In this case, a chin-operated bedside ECU is the best course of action out of the choices provided, as it provides access to the environment. If answered incorrectly, review principles of client-centered practice and the therapeutic relationship and information about ECUs and electronic aids to daily living (EADL). The integration of this knowledge is required to determine the correct answer. See Chapters 3 and 15.

B18 C6

An OTA works with members of a psychosocial clubhouse who have decided to participate in the annual mental health awareness and fundraiser walk organized by the National Alliance for Mental Illness (NAMI). The NAMI walk is 5K long and circles around an urban park. Many clubhouse members express interest in training for the walk by taking extended walks four times per week. Which recommendation is most important for the OTA to make to these clients?

Answer Choices:
A. Do leg stretches before beginning each walk to prevent leg cramps.
B. Avoid sudden postural changes to prevent orthostatic hypotension.
C. Apply sunscreen to all exposed body parts to prevent sunburn.

Exam B Answer Rationales

Correct Answer: C.

Rationale:
The application of sunscreen is essential for persons on psychotropic medications, which can make the skin highly sensitive to sunlight. Photosensitivity results in a skin rash and sunburn, which can be severe. The amount of sun exposure required for a person to have a reaction varies greatly. Some individuals may develop a rash or burn after very little sun exposure. Others will have a reaction only after prolonged exposure. Because the clubhouse members are planning extended walks, the likelihood of a photosensitive reaction must be addressed. Because extended sun exposure contributes to skin cancer, the consistent use of sunscreen is an important health measure for all members, regardless of their medications. The other answer choices provide recommendations which can be helpful for preventing the outcome identified as being the focus of each choice. However, they are not as important as preventing the sunburn that can occur due to photosensitivity.

Type of Reasoning: Deductive
This question requires the test taker to recall the common precautions for clients using psychotropic medications in order to arrive at a correct conclusion. This requires deductive reasoning skill, where the recall of facts is utilized to draw a correct conclusion. For this situation, the most important precaution to discuss is photosensitivity. If answered incorrectly, review psychotropic medication side effects and preventative precautions for clients taking psychotropic medications. See Chapter 10.

B19 C4

During an occupational therapy intervention session, a client with a left CVA demonstrates extinction to the right and a tendency to ignore items on the right side. When documenting this behavior, which should the OTA report?

Answer Choices:
A. Agnosia.
B. Unilateral inattention.
C. Poor right/left discrimination.
D. Poor visual scanning.

Correct Answer: B.

Rationale:
Unilateral inattention is a situation in which the individual neglects the side of the body contralateral to the CVA site and the environment on that side. The other options describe cognitive-perceptual deficits with different manifestations. Agnosia can be the inability to identify body parts. Right/left discrimination is the differentiation of one side of the body from the other. Visual scanning is the engagement and disengagement of visual attention as the eye moves its focus from one object to another.

Type of Reasoning: Analytical
This question provides symptoms and the test taker must determine the likely cause for them. This is an analytical reasoning skill, as questions of this nature often ask one to analyze a group of symptoms in order to determine a diagnosis. In this situation the symptoms indicate unilateral inattention, which should be reviewed if answered incorrectly. See Chapter 12.

B20 C5

An OTA working in an outpatient cardiac rehabilitation center collaborates with the supervising occupational therapist to develop an intervention plan for an individual who has entered Phase 2 of cardiac recovery. Which activities would be best for them to include in the intervention plan?

Answer Choices:
A. Weeding a garden and doing low-impact aerobics.
B. Putting away groceries and keyboarding.
C. Washing dishes and playing tabletop board games.
D. Carrying groceries upstairs and playing basketball.

Correct Answer: A.

Rationale:
At Phase 2 of cardiac rehabilitation, activities should begin at a 4–5 MET level and progress to higher MET levels. Weeding a garden and doing low-impact aerobics are at this level. Putting away groceries, keyboarding, washing dishes, and playing tabletop board games are at a 1.0–2.5 MET level. These activities are appropriate for an individual in Phase I of cardiac rehabilitation. Carrying groceries upstairs and playing basketball are at a 6.0–10 MET level. These activities are not appropriate for a person just beginning Phase 2 of cardiac rehabilitation; however, they may be appropriate as the person progresses in the program.

Type of Reasoning: Inductive
One must recall the guidelines for MET level activity for patients in Phase 2 of cardiac rehabilitation. This is factual knowledge, which is a deductive reasoning skill. For this client, the intervention plan should include weeding a garden and doing low-impact aerobics. Review Phase 2 activity guidelines and MET levels if answered incorrectly. See Chapter 8.

B21 C4

A 7-year-old with complete spina bifida at the T10 level attends outpatient OT weekly. The child's parent reports that the child is losing bladder control. The OTA notes that the child shows a minimal decrease in strength of bilateral lower and upper extremities and an increase in the equinovarus position of the feet. The OTA contacts the supervising occupational therapist to report that the child's change in status may indicate which of the following?

Answer Choices:
A. Shunt malformation.
B. A recent growth spurt.
C. Arnold-Chiari formation.
D. Tethered cord.

Correct Answer: D.

Rationale:
OTAs must inform their supervising occupational therapist of any change in a client's status and any other relevant information that may affect treatment. In this case, all of the symptoms listed are indicative of tethered cord. The spinal cord of the child with spina bifida is sometimes attached to the spinal column and becomes taut as the child grows. The child requires a surgical release of the tethered cord. Shunt malformation is marked by intermittent headaches, shortened attention span, increased paralysis, decreased upper extremity strength, noticeable decrease in school performance, and increased irritability. Young children often demonstrate increased head size, nausea, and vomiting. The tethered cord presents whether the child has an even rate of growth or goes through a recent growth spurt. Arnold-Chiari formation occurs in the process of development and involves the part of the lower portion of the brain slipping or being pushed through the foramen ovale.

Exam B Answer Rationales   627

Type of Reasoning: Analytical
One must recall the signs and symptoms of tethered cord in order to arrive at a correct conclusion. Questions that provide a group of symptoms and require the test taker to determine the cause utilize analytical reasoning skills. In this case, the symptoms indicate tethered cord with spina bifida, which should be reviewed if answered incorrectly. See Chapter 7.

B22 C7

An individual with mild cognitive deficits takes medications for multiple medical conditions. The OTA works with the individual to develop the ability to safely self-administer medications. Which equipment and/or strategy should the OTA train the client to use?

Answer Choices:
A. Easy open caps on the medication bottles.
B. A chart listing medication dosages and administration times on the refrigerator.
C. A daily pill holder with time-labeled slots for each dosage.
D. Family caregiver supervision of medication administration.

Correct Answer: C.

Rationale:
The use of a pill holder with slots for each dose of medication labeled with its administration time can provide the needed structure for safe self-administration of medications. A chart on a refrigerator is not as useful because the individual cannot take the chart with them during daily activities. Easy open caps do not provide any organizational structure for the identified cognitive deficits. Family caregiver supervision could be needed if the person was not able to benefit from organizational strategies. The individual needs to be provided with the opportunity to develop abilities to self-administer medications to maintain autonomy. In addition, one cannot assume that there is a family caregiver available who would be able to provide the needed support.

Type of Reasoning: Inferential
One must determine the best recommendation for an individual with cognitive deficits. This requires inferential reasoning skill, where one must infer or draw conclusions about a best course of action. In this situation, the OTA should recommend a daily pill holder with time-labeled slots to aid in appropriate administration of medication. If answered incorrectly, review adaptive strategies for medication management. See Chapter 14.

B23 C5

An OTA advises a parent of an 18-month-old with developmental delays on techniques to facilitate feeding. The child has a reflexive bite. Which utensil is most beneficial for the OTA to recommend the parent use when feeding the child?

Answer Choices:
A. A deep-bowled soupspoon.
B. A narrow, shallow-coated spoon.
C. A plastic spork.

Correct Answer: B.

Rationale:
The use of a narrow, shallow-coated spoon will help the food slide off. Deeper spoons or a spork will make it more difficult for the food to slide off, which would not be indicated for a child with a reflexive bite. In addition, the prong edges of the spork may hurt the child as they bite.

628 Exam B Answer Rationales

Type of Reasoning: Inductive
One must have knowledge of reflexive bite in children in order to choose the best feeding utensil. This is an inductive reasoning skill where knowledge of the diagnosis coupled with an understanding of the benefits of each of the utensils is essential to arriving at a correct conclusion. In this situation the OTA should suggest a narrow, shallow-coated spoon. If answered incorrectly, review guidelines for working with persons with feeding disorders. See Chapters 5 and 9.

B24 C6

An OTA collaborates with an occupational therapist to implement a program in a domestic violence shelter. Which of the following is the most important for the OTA and therapist to do when working with the shelter residents to attain program goals?

Answer Choices:
A. Avoid asking direct questions about the residents' abuse risk factors to minimize emotional distress.
B. Support residents' beliefs that their relationships will change to sustain the hope that abuse will end.
C. Document objective findings and record resident statements in quotes to substantiate abuse history.
D. Assess and develop the skills and resources residents need to live independent empowered lives.

Correct Answer: D.

Rationale:
When working with survivors of domestic violence, occupational therapy practitioners must ensure the survivors' personal safety, promote their emotional well-being, and enable their assumption of independent empowered lives. The RADAR approach can be used to screen for and respond to domestic abuse. According to this approach, practitioners should routinely and supportively ask all clients direct questions about abuse risk factors to ensure their personal safety. Supporting residents' beliefs that their relationships will change can be dangerous because it ignores the reality that ending abuse requires a sustained commitment from the abuser to actively participate in treatment to end abusive behaviors. The documentation of objective findings and the recording of resident statements in quotes are important in a domestic violence shelter program; however, these actions do not directly help residents attain desired goals.

Type of Reasoning: Inferential
This question requires one to determine a best course of action based on the information provided, which is an inferential reasoning skill. For this situation, assessing and developing the skills and resources residents need to live independent empowered lives is best. If answered incorrectly, review information on the RADAR approach and OT approaches for survivors of domestic violence. The correct answer requires the integration of this information. See Chapter 13.

B25 C3

A client is receiving acute care occupational therapy services for an exacerbation of rheumatoid arthritis. The client presents with pain and inflammation in the wrists and fingers. The OTA and occupational therapist collaborate to plan intervention. Which approaches should they include in their initial intervention plan? Select the three BEST responses.

Answer Choices:
A. The application of hot packs to the hands.
B. Gentle stretching of the wrists and fingers.
C. Training in how to avoid positions of deformity.
D. The completion of graded isotonic exercises.
E. Education on the benefits of wearing bilateral resting hand splints.
F. Training in joint protection techniques for homemaking tasks.

Correct Answers: B, C, and E.

Rationale:
When a client who is living with rheumatoid arthritis (RA) experiences pain and inflammation, the joints are vulnerable to deformity. Training in how to avoid positions of deformity, gentle stretching, and wearing bilateral resting hand splints are interventions that are consistent with the inflammatory stage of RA. Gentle stretching will help prevent the loss of motion and prevent contractures. In the inflammatory stage, it is important to avoid positions of deformity. Patients in the acute stage of rheumatoid arthritis who have pain and inflammation in the hands can benefit from resting hand splints. The splints place the joints of the hand in an optimal position and help to manage pain, which is especially beneficial in the acute stage. Both heat and isotonic exercises are contraindicated when the wrists and hands are inflamed. While training in joint protection techniques for homemaking tasks is an appropriate focus for intervention for persons with RA, in this case it is too early in the OT process to address homemaking tasks. The person's pain and inflammation must be addressed first.

Type of Reasoning: Deductive
One must determine the most effective intervention for this client given the client's diagnosis and stage of the disease. One must recall the stages of rheumatoid arthritis and the indications and contraindications for each stage. In this case, knowledge of the intervention indications and contraindications for the inflammatory stage of RA is key to ascertaining the correct answer. This requires the use of deductive reasoning skills, in which factual knowledge is essential to choosing the correct solution. If answered incorrectly, review RA intervention guidelines. See Chapter 6.

B26 C7

An individual with bilateral proximal weakness identifies a goal of independence in self-feeding. Which equipment is most beneficial for the OTA to recommend for goal attainment?

Answer Choices:
A. An electric feeder.
B. Mobile arm supports.
C. Extended long-handled utensils.

Correct Answer: B.

Rationale:
Mobile arm supports can effectively compensate for upper extremity weakness. Extended long-handled utensils are indicated for individuals with decreased ROM. An electric feeder is indicated for individuals with no functional use of the upper extremities.

Type of Reasoning: Inductive
This question requires one to determine the most appropriate equipment for an individual based on the person's limitations. This requires inductive reasoning skill, where clinical judgment is paramount to arriving at a correct conclusion. For this situation, mobile arm supports are most effective in order to enhance self-feeding. If answered incorrectly, review indications for use of mobile arm supports. See Chapter 14.

B27 C9

A person recovering from knee replacement surgery wants to begin meal preparation. The client refuses to use the walker that was ordered by the physician. The physician is unavailable for consultation. Which is the best initial action for the OTA to take in response to this situation?

Answer Choices:
A. Work on meal preparation activities with the client sitting at a table.
B. Work on meal preparation activities with the client standing without the walker.
C. Delay working on meal preparation activities until the physician can be contacted.
D. Tell the client the walker must be used until the physician changes the order.

Correct Answer: A.

Rationale:
There are many meal preparation activities that can be done while seated, so there is no need to delay meal preparation activities. The OTA should not conduct the session without the prescribed walker or ambulatory aid until a written or verbal order is received. This is not negotiable as the client's safety is the paramount concern. Telling the client that the walker must be used violates the client's rights to self-determination.

Type of Reasoning: Evaluative
One must make a judgment call based on values and ethical principles, which is an evaluative reasoning skill. Situations such as these are challenging as one must weigh the interests of all the parties involved. The only solution that considers the safety and needs of the client is to work on meal preparation activities with the client sitting at a table. If answered incorrectly, review the AOTA code of ethics, principles of collaborating with consumers, and the role of the consumer on the team. See Chapter 4.

B28 C4

Following an acute hospitalization for the medical management of a CVA, an individual receives home-based occupational therapy services. The OTA is working on dressing skills with the patient. During one session, the OTA has the individual dress in the bedroom and during the next session the OTA has the client dress in the bathroom. During the following session, the OTA has the client don and doff a sweater and coat in the living room. Which motor learning technique is the OTA using?

Answer Choices:
A. Variable activities.
B. Variable conditions.
C. Repetition.
D. Generalization.

Correct Answer: B.

Rationale:
Variable conditions involve the practice and performance of skills in various contexts to improve the transfer of learning and retention of skills. Variable activities is not a term or approach identified in motor learning theory. Dressing during three different sessions is not repetitive. Varying the performance and practice context can facilitate the ability to generalize a skill, but generalization is not a treatment technique; rather, it is a desired outcome of intervention.

Type of Reasoning: Inferential
One must link the functional activity to the appropriate motor learning technique. This requires inferential reasoning, where one must infer or draw conclusions based on the evidence presented. In this case the technique described is that of variable conditions. If answered incorrectly, review motor learning theory and the application of variable conditions. See Chapter 12.

B29 C2

A young adult recently diagnosed with schizophrenia is referred to an OT day treatment program. Which should the OTA do first with the client?

Answer Choices:
A. Determine short-term and long-term goals for program participation.
B. Model desired behaviors during OT and therapeutic recreation groups.
C. Have the person complete an occupational interest inventory.
D. Encourage the client to maintain a daily log of medication intake.

Correct Answer: C.

Rationale:
Upon referral, the first step in the OT process is screening. The OTA can contribute to this process by having the person complete a screening tool. Determining the person's occupational interest can help identify areas requiring further evaluation. One cannot establish short-term and long-term goals with the client until an evaluation is completed. It is unknown if the client has deficits in medication management. Modeling behavior is a component of the intervention process.

Type of Reasoning: Inductive
One must draw conclusions about a best approach based on the diagnosis of the client in order to arrive at a correct conclusion. This requires inferential reasoning skill. For this case, the OTA should have the person complete an occupational interest inventory. If answered incorrectly, review client-centered approaches in psychosocial practice and the screening process. See Chapters 3 and 13.

B30 C8

An OTA provides caregiver education to the family of an individual who is dependent in all self-care. During instruction on proper wheelchair positioning, where should the OTA advise the family to place the wheelchair seatbelt?

Answer Choices:
A. At waist level.
B. Midway between waist and trunk.
C. At the widest point of the individual's midsection.
D. At hip level.

Correct Answer: D.

Rationale:
Wheelchair seatbelts are to extend across the hips and into the lap at a 45-degree angle. The other options do not meet established wheelchair positioning guidelines.

Type of Reasoning: Deductive
One must recall the proper positioning of a wheelchair seatbelt in order to arrive at a correct conclusion. This requires deductive reasoning skill, where factual knowledge is essential to choosing the correct solution. Standard practice is for the seatbelt to be placed at the hip level at a 45-degree angle. If answered incorrectly, review the use of seatbelts in wheelchairs and proper positioning. See Chapter 15.

B31 C9

An older adult with a diagnosis of moderate neurocognitive disorder was recently admitted to a skilled nursing facility (SNF). During an intervention session, the OTA observes bruises on the resident's back and upper arms. Which action is best for the OTA to initially take?

Answer Choices:
A. Talk to the resident to obtain more information.
B. Follow facility procedures for investigating resident safety.
C. Contact the resident's family to obtain more information.
D. Contact the state office for adult protective services.

Correct Answer: B.

Rationale:
Whenever there are concerns for a client's safety and well-being facility procedures for investigating the situation must be followed. Talking to the resident may not enable the OTA to obtain accurate information due to the person's diagnosis of a moderate neurocognitive disorder (formerly called dementia). At this point there is no need to contact the family. An internal investigation would determine if the family could provide helpful information or if they should be contacted by a professional who is trained in abuse investigation. The source of the bruises needs to be determined before any other action is taken. Contacting state authorities may be premature, for there may be a reasonable explanation for the bruises. Further investigation into the situation by the appropriate facility personnel according to established institutional policies is indicated. All health-care facilities have clear guidelines for investigating and reporting potential abuse.

Type of Reasoning: Evaluative
One must weigh the possible courses of action and then make a value judgment about the best course to take. This requires evaluative reasoning skill, which often utilizes guiding principles of action in order to arrive at a correct conclusion. In this case, the OTA follows facility procedures for investigating resident safety. If answered incorrectly, review guidelines for investigating potential abuse in older adults. See Chapter 5.

B32 C2

An OTA conducts a communication group in a wellness program for a large corporation. In this mature level group, what should the OTA do?

Answer Choices:
A. Help to develop the group norms of conduct.
B. Participate as a member.
C. Actively resolve group conflicts.
D. Maintain a leader role.

Correct Answer: B.

Rationale:
In a mature group, the group leader participates at the level of a member and does not act as a designated leader except in special circumstances such as a member becoming destructive to the group process. The members decide formally and informally the norms for behavior. The group leader does not usually participate in conflict resolution except to facilitate the member's participation in serious situations, such as deadlocked conflicts. The group leader functions in a variety of task, maintenance, or egocentric roles as needed to show members how these roles function in the group.

Type of Reasoning: Deductive
This question requires one to recall the guidelines for conducting a mature level group and the role of the group leader in order to arrive at a correct conclusion. This necessitates the recall of factual guidelines, which is a deductive reasoning skill. For this case, the OTA participates as a member in a mature level group. If answered incorrectly, review group levels and the role of the group leader in facilitating groups. See Chapter 3.

B33 C1

The parents of an infant born at 32 weeks' gestation are about to take the baby home after four weeks in the neonatal intensive care nursery. The OTA collaborates with the occupational therapist to provide pre-discharge family education. Which is most important for the OTA to advise the parents to avoid?

Answer Choices:
A. Placing the infant in the prone position for sleeping.
B. Placing the infant in the supine position for sleeping.
C. Using an infant swing with a head support for calming.
D. Presenting toys in the midline with the infant in the prone position for playing.

Correct Answer: A.

Rationale:
The OTA should advise the parents to avoid placing the infant in the prone position for sleeping to prevent sudden infant death syndrome (SIDS). The infant should be encouraged to sleep in supine position to prevent SIDS. An infant swing can provide slow, rhythmic vestibular input that can be calming to infants. A swing can also provide visual stimulation and proper alignment in supported sitting. Toys should be presented in midline with the infant in the prone position. This positioning provides the infant with visual stimulation and the opportunity to develop play, social, and cognitive skills. This 'tummy-time' also facilitates head control and prevents a flattened head that can occur when a child sleeps in supine.

Type of Reasoning: Inferential
One must determine contraindications for infant care. This requires inferential reasoning, in which one must determine a most important course of action. In this situation, the discharge plan should include instruction to avoid sleeping in prone position to avoid SIDS.

B34 C1

A child with congenital anomalies has significant developmental delays. The child demonstrates motor and cognitive skills at the 9-month level. Which is the best for the OTA to use during intervention to develop the child's visual and auditory awareness?

Answer Choices:
A. A handheld rattle of the child's favorite cartoon character.
B. A wrist bracelet with blinking lights that makes noise when moved.
C. A button switch that activates a CD player when the switch is pressed.
D. A communication device that offers selections of "yes" and "no."

Correct Answer: C.

Rationale:
The button switch encourages the child to begin to develop cause and effect and provides auditory stimulation as well as a visual component in focusing on the device to access it. The rattle is a tool for the child at the 3- to 6-month level. The wrist bracelet is for the child at the 3- to 6-month level. The communication device is at the level of 12 to 18 months.

Type of Reasoning: Inferential
One must infer or draw conclusions about each of the four possible choices. The key to answering this question correctly is matching an activity to the child's developmental age and current needs. For this situation, a button switch that activates a CD player helps to develop cause and effect for this child who functions at a 9-month level. If answered incorrectly, review developmental milestones and appropriate activities for a developmental level of 9 months. See Chapter 5.

B35 C8

An individual with scleroderma has limited upper extremity ROM. Coordination is within functional limits. The person wants to improve efficacy in computer inputting capabilities. Which adaptation would be most effective for this person?

Answer Choices:
A. A concept keyboard.
B. An expanded keyboard.
C. A contracted keyboard.

Correct Answer: C.

Rationale:
A contracted keyboard decreases the ROM required to strike the keys. It is indicated for someone with limited ROM. Due to smaller key size, coordination must be functional. An expanded keyboard requires increased ROM to strike the keys. A concept keyboard is used for individuals with cognitive impairments. It replaces the keyboard's letters and numbers with pictures, symbols, or words to represent the concepts that are needed by a software program.

Type of Reasoning: Inductive
One must utilize clinical knowledge and judgment to determine the keyboard adaptation that is most effective for the individual, given the diagnosis and limitations. In this case, a contracted keyboard is most appropriate. If answered incorrectly, review modifications for increasing computer accessibility and indications for issuing a contracted keyboard. See Chapter 15.

B36 C9

An OTA works in a subacute rehabilitation department. Which task is best for the supervising occupational therapist to assign to the OTA to perform independently?

Answer Choices:
A. Implementing an ADL evaluation and documenting the results.
B. Determining which information to include in the client's medical record.
C. Designing a research project to measure the efficacy of interventions.
D. Interpreting the results of a standardized assessment administered to clients.

Correct Answer: A.

Rationale:
An OTA can conduct an ADL evaluation and document the results. Depending on state licensure laws, this documentation may need to be cosigned by the supervising occupational therapist. An occupational therapist makes the decision about what to include in the medical record. An OTA can contribute to the implementation of a research project, but the occupational therapist is in charge of the design of a research protocol. An OTA can administer a standardized assessment, but an OTA cannot interpret the evaluation results. Occupational therapists are responsible for the interpretation of evaluations.

Type of Reasoning: Inferential
This question requires one to recall the standards of practice for the OTA. Inferential reasoning skills are utilized as the test taker must determine, based on knowledge of practice and supervisory guidelines, what is likely to be true. For this situation an OTA can conduct and document the results of an ADL evaluation. If answered incorrectly, review information on standards of practice and supervision guidelines for the OTA. See Chapter 4.

B37 C4

An adult with an anterior spinal cord syndrome at the C8 level is evaluated by an occupational therapist. The therapist reviews the results of the client's sensory evaluation with the OTA to plan intervention. Which sensation will not need to be included in this plan?

Answer Choices:
A. Proprioception.
B. Pain.
C. Temperature.

Correct Answer: A.

Rationale:
Proprioception is maintained with the condition of anterior spinal cord syndrome, which is caused by damage to the anterior spinal artery or anterior spinal cord. Because dorsal (posterior) columns transmit proprioceptive information, this sensation will be intact and will not require intervention. The other choices are aspects of sensation that are impaired or absent in anterior spinal cord syndrome.

Type of Reasoning: Inferential
This question provides the diagnosis, and the test taker must determine what is and is not affected by this injury. This is an inferential reasoning skill. For this case, an anterior spinal artery injury would preserve proprioception, as it is transmitted through the dorsal columns in the spine. If answered incorrectly, review symptoms of anterior spinal artery damage and other spinal tracts. See Chapter 7.

B38 C7

Several individuals participate in a work hardening program with a goal to resume working on a production line that utilizes electrical equipment and conveyor belts. The OTA collaborates with the occupational therapist to plan an intervention program. Which functional deficit should the therapist and OTA establish as a focus for intervention?

Answer Choices:
A. Poor judgment skills.
B. Incoordination.
C. Decreased task speed.
D. Visual disturbances.

Correct Answer: C.

Rationale:
Decreased task speed is the only functional deficit listed that is not a contraindication for working with electrical equipment, conveyors, or other potentially dangerous equipment. Poor judgment skills can cause serious problems in this work setting. Incoordination and/or visual disturbances can impair the clients' ability to perform the job safely or effectively.

Type of Reasoning: Inferential
One must infer or draw conclusions about which functional deficit the therapist and OTA should establish as a focus for intervention for this program. This requires consideration of the characteristics of the described work tasks. For this case, decreased task speed is the deficit that would be appropriate to work on with persons seeking to resume working on a production line that utilizes electrical equipment and conveyor belts. The other potential intervention foci raise serious concerns about safety issues. If answered incorrectly, review guidelines and goals for work conditioning and rehabilitation. See Chapter 14.

B39 C9

A coworker in the occupational therapy department complains excessively during working hours of personal problems. Which action is best for the OTA to take in response to this situation?

Answer Choices:
A. Call the employee assistance program (EAP) for the coworker.
B. Talk with the coworker using a client-centered approach.
C. Tactfully and firmly redirect the coworker to work issues.
D. Inform the supervising occupational therapist of the situation.

Correct Answer: D.

Rationale:
Informing the OT supervisor is in the best interests of the coworker, all other staff, and the facility. Resolving this issue is the supervisor's responsibility. One should not call the employee assistance program (EAP) for the coworker. A decision to contact an EAP is one that needs to be made by an employee. Coworkers are not responsible to and should not treat fellow workers. Tactfully redirecting the coworker is a common technique to avoid being drawn into the problems of others. However, this action will not address the problem in the department.

Type of Reasoning: Evaluative
One must make a decision based on ethical guidelines and value judgment, which is an evaluative reasoning skill. In this situation, the OTA should inform the supervising occupational therapist of the issue, as it is in the best interests of everyone involved. Questions of this nature can be challenging to answer as a simple solution is not often found and clear-cut guidelines are not always at hand to refer to in situations such as these. If answered incorrectly, review standards of practice and team collaboration guidelines. See Chapter 4.

B40 C4

A patient who is status-post left frontal lobe ischemia has difficulty bearing weight through the right lower extremity during reaching activities (e.g., standing at a sink during morning self-care routine). The OTA implements a Motor Relearning Program (MRP). Which is the best intervention for the OTA to provide according to this approach?

Answer Choices:
A. A stool to sit on during reaching activities.
B. Therapeutic handling to affect the central nervous system.
C. Light joint compression throughout the trunk and right lower extremity while reaching.
D. Verbal and visual feedback while practicing reaching.

Correct Answer: D.

Rationale:
An MRP approach provides verbal and visual feedback to give a person the input needed to make postural and limb adjustments. Providing a stool to sit on during reaching activities can be used for safety purposes. This is consistent with a compensatory approach. Therapeutic handling to affect the central nervous system is consistent with a neurodevelopmental therapy approach. Light joint compression throughout the trunk and right lower extremity during reaching is consistent with the Rood approach.

Type of Reasoning: Deductive
One must recall the guidelines of a Motor Relearning Program in order to arrive at a correct conclusion. This is recall of factual knowledge, which is a deductive reasoning skill. For this situation, the most appropriate intervention is verbal and visual feedback while practicing reaching. If answered incorrectly, review Motor Relearning Program guidelines. See Chapter 12.

B41 C6

A home care OTA collaborates with an occupational therapist to plan intervention for an individual with agoraphobia with panic attacks. The OTA and occupational therapist use the principles of cognitive-behavioral therapy(CBT) to guide their intervention planning. Which approach is best for the OTA and therapist to use when implementing the intervention plan?

Answer Choices:
A. A token reward system.
B. Behavioral extinction.
C. Relaxation techniques.
D. Systematic desensitization.

Correct Answer: C.

Rationale:
Panic attacks are symptoms of anxiety. A main focus of cognitive behavioral therapy (CBT) is to help people develop relaxation skills to decrease the incidence and severity of symptoms. Systematic desensitization is also a CBT approach that is used with individuals with phobias. While systematic desensitization is an effective CBT intervention, specialized training is required to effectively use this approach. There is no information in the item scenario to indicate that the OTA has completed this training. In systematic desensitization, exposure to the anxiety-producing stimulus is initially presented to the person through the use of imagery. Incremental and graded contact with the anxiety-producing stimulus is combined with reframing and relaxation until the stimulus no longer produces an anxiety response. If the scenario did indicate that the OTA had been trained in the use of systematic desensitization, relaxation techniques would still be the best approach to use in the initial intervention session. It is important to recognize that visualizing an anxiety-producing stimulus can precipitate a panic attack. Therefore, the first intervention priority is to help the client learn to manage and decrease anxiety. The use of relaxation techniques during the initial intervention session can attain this goal. A token reward system involves the granting of tokens as a reward for desired behaviors. Behavioral extinction is a technique used to decrease undesirable behaviors by ignoring them and reinforcing desirable behaviors. These are not effective techniques for agoraphobia or panic attacks because the person's anxiety must be directly treated.

Type of Reasoning: Inferential
One must infer or draw conclusions about a likely course of action, given the information presented. This is an inferential reasoning skill, where knowledge of a therapeutic approach, such as the CBT approach in this situation, is essential to choosing a correct solution. In this case, the therapist and the OTA should choose relaxation techniques. If answered incorrectly, review information about panic attacks and phobias and CBT principles and approaches. See Chapters 10 and 13.

B42 C9

An occupational therapist and an OTA establish a program for a new acute psychiatric unit in a community hospital. The OTA assists with the design of the physical layout of the occupational therapy department. Which of the following should the OTA recommend for storing arts and crafts materials?

Answer Choices:
A. A ventilated locked metal cabinet accessible only to staff.
B. Open shelving accessible to patients and staff.
C. Shelving next to a sink for easy clean up.
D. A locked closet outside of the intervention area to ensure safety.

Correct Answer: A.

Rationale:
Arts and crafts materials include flammable, hazardous materials such as paint, stain, and thinners. These must be kept in ventilated metal cabinets in accordance with fire safety guidelines. Since these supplies are also toxic and potentially dangerous, access to them must be controlled by staff; therefore, a locked storage unit is required. The other options do not meet fire safety needs.

Type of Reasoning: Inferential
One must have knowledge of safety guidelines given the clinical setting in order to arrive at a correct conclusion. This is an inferential reasoning skill where knowledge of clinical guidelines and judgment based on facts are utilized to reach conclusions. In this case, the OTA should recommend a ventilated locked metal cabinet accessible only to staff. If answered incorrectly, review safety guidelines for acute psychiatric settings. See Chapters 4 and 13.

B43 C7

During a topical work preparation group for individuals recovering from mental illness, a member expresses concern about answering questions related to personal psychiatric history during a job interview. Which action is best for the OTA to take in response to these expressed concerns?

Answer Choices:
A. Refer the client to a vocational rehabilitation counselor.
B. Encourage the other members of the group to share their interview experiences.
C. Lead a group discussion on the legal rights afforded in the interview process.
D. Support the client in not disclosing past psychiatric history.

Correct Answer: C.

Rationale:
A primary purpose of a topical group is to develop knowledge about a particular area of occupation. Since members of the group may not be aware of all of their legal rights in an interview, it is most important for the OTA to lead a discussion about this issue. The Americans with Disabilities Act (ADA) provides legal protections related to the disclosure of medical histories. This is invaluable knowledge for all members to acquire and can help them make informed decisions about disclosure. For example, if a person can perform the essential functions of a job, there is no compelling reason to disclose a past medical history. There is no need to refer the individual to a vocational rehabilitation counselor, as this area is within OT's domain of practice. While encouraging members to share experiences and supporting a client's decision are both relevant, it is more important for the OTA to share information about the ADA.

Type of Reasoning: Evaluative
This question requires a value judgment, which is an evaluative reasoning skill. By having an understanding of the ADA, the test taker should conclude that the best response in this situation is to discuss the legal rights afforded in the interview process with the group members. If answered incorrectly, review ADA regulations related to job interviewing. See Chapters 4 and 14.

B44 C6

The most complex behavior an individual is able to perform on the Allen Cognitive Level test is the running stitch while imitating an example. According to the cognitive disabilities model, this behavior is indicative of level 3 of Allen's cognitive levels. Which activities are best for the OTA to use when implementing intervention with this patient? Select the three BEST responses.

Answer Choices:
A. Sanding wooden bookends.
B. Planning a three-course meal.
C. Folding towels and washcloths.
D. Wiping the surfaces of tables and counters.
E. Exercises that require the imitation of another's posture.
F. Sorting laundry by matching the colors of clothing items.

Correct Answers: A, C, and D.

Rationale:
According to Allen's Cognitive Disability Model, people at level 3 of Allen's cognitive levels can use their hands to manipulate objects, and they are able to perform a limited number of simple tasks that are repetitive. Sanding wood, folding laundry, and wiping surfaces are activities consistent with level 3 of Allen's cognitive levels. These tasks all result in tangible outcomes (i.e., functional bookends, folded clothes, and clean tables and counters) which can facilitate the person's feelings of self-efficacy. The imitation of posture is reflective of a level 2 skill according to the cognitive disabilities model, so exercises that require postural imitation would be too low for this individual. Sorting laundry by matching clothing colors is a level 4 skill. Planning a three-course meal would require the level 5 skills of problem solving. According to Allen's Cognitive Disability Model, this level is too high for this person.

Type of Reasoning: Inductive
One must determine a functional activity that is best to implement for an individual functioning at level 3 of Allen's cognitive levels. This requires knowledge of the cognitive disability model and the functional abilities within each level. For this case, sanding wooden blocks, folding laundry, and wiping surfaces are ideal approaches because they are repetitive tasks within the capabilities of this individual. If answered incorrectly, review Allen's cognitive levels and the characteristics of level 3 functioning. See Chapter 13.

B45 C1

An OTA provides intervention to develop independent feeding skills in an 18-month-old child with significant developmental delays. The child can hold and suck on a cracker. The child has also mastered the ability to hold a spoon and bang it on the tray of the highchair. Which activity is best for the OTA to provide next during intervention?

Answer Choices:
A. Finger-feeding soft foods.
B. Scooping food and bringing it to the mouth.
C. Taking cereal from a spoon held by the OTA.
D. Bringing a filled spoon to the mouth.

Correct Answer: A.

Rationale:
The next developmental milestone after holding and banging a spoon is finger-feeding soft foods. Due to the child's developmental delay, an OTA would work on the acquisition of feeding skills according to typical developmental milestones. The typical developmental sequence of feeding is taking cereal from a spoon (5–7 months), self-feeding by sucking a cracker (6–9 months), holding and banging a spoon (6–9 months), finger-feeding soft foods (9–13 months), bringing a filled spoon to mouth (12–14 months), scooping food and bringing it to the mouth (15–18 months). In working with a child with developmental disabilities, it is the child's developmental age, not their chronological age that guides intervention.

Type of Reasoning: Deductive
One must recall the developmental guidelines for feeding infants with developmental delays. This is recall of factual knowledge, which is a deductive reasoning skill. First, the test taker must determine what developmental age the child is performing feeding at and then determine the next developmental milestone for that skill. In this case, the child is developmentally at 9 months. Finger-feeding soft foods is the next milestone for feeding. If answered incorrectly, review developmental milestones of infant feeding. See Chapter 5.

B46 C9

An OTA observes an aide having difficulty transferring a client with athetoid movements from a mat to a wheelchair. Before the OTA can cross the room to help with the transfer, the aide slides with the client to the floor. The OTA assists the aide in safely returning the client to the wheelchair. They assess that the client appears to be unharmed and return the client to the unit for a medical evaluation. Which action should the OTA take next?

Answer Choices:
A. Counsel the aide on the need to ask for assistance with difficult transfers.
B. Require the aide to attend a transfer training in-service.
C. Document the aide's unsafe actions in the personnel record.
D. Complete an occurrence report according to facility standards.

Correct Answer: D.

Rationale:
Immediately after an incident occurs, the OTA must complete documentation according to the setting's standards. Counseling an aide to ask for assistance and requiring attendance at a workshop can be appropriate aspects of risk management, but they are not the first steps. In addition, there is no information provided to clearly identify that the aide was acting unsafely. There are transfer situations that unexpectedly become beyond a person's ability to successfully complete. During those situations, the person should guide the patient to the floor in a controlled manner. This is often done by using one's own body to support the patient and can give the appearance of 'sliding'. More information is needed to determine if the aide's actions were actually unsafe.

Type of Reasoning: Inductive
This question requires one to determine the best course of action. This requires inductive reasoning skill, where clinical judgment is paramount to arriving at a correct conclusion. For this situation, after returning the client to the unit for a medical evaluation, the OTA should complete an occurrence report (often called an incident report) according to the facility standards. If answered incorrectly, review guidelines for completing facility occurrence reports. If answered incorrectly, review risk management guidelines. See Chapter 4.

B47 C5

A person with coronary artery disease (CAD) and chronic obstructive pulmonary disease (COPD) is hospitalized due to pneumonia. During a screening session, the OTA observes that the person's respiration is rapid and that they seem to be short of breath. Upon questioning, the person reports feeling light-headed, nauseous, and pain in their jaw and stomach. Which action is best for the OTA to take In response to these observations and the person's complaints?

Answer Choices:
A. End the screening and inform the person that the session will be rescheduled when they feel better.
B. Teach the person how to use pursed lip breathing to address shortness of breath.
C. Inform the occupational therapist that the screening indicates a need to administer angina and dyspnea rating scales.
D. Immediately inform the nursing staff about the person's status and complaints.

Correct Answer: D.

Rationale:
The OTA must immediately inform the nursing staff about the person's status and complaints. Rapid respiration, shortness of breath, and feeling lightheaded, nauseous, and pain are signs of a myocardial infarction (MI). Women are more likely than men to experience the symptoms of shortness of breath and feeling lightheaded, nauseous, and pain in the jaw and stomach. Men are more likely to experience severe substernal pain, which may radiate to neck, jaw, arm, and/or epigastric area. Although this exam item does not identify the person's gender, the presented cluster of MI symptoms should be taken seriously for a person with a history of CAD. Ending the screening, teaching the person to use pursed lip breathing, and informing the occupational therapist about the need to administer angina and dyspnea rating scales are actions that do not inform the medical staff about the person's symptoms. These actions place the person at grave risk.

Type of Reasoning: Evaluative
One must weigh the possible courses of action and then make a value judgment about the best course to take. This requires evaluative reasoning skill, where an understanding of what the symptoms indicate is pivotal in arriving at a correct conclusion. In this case, the symptoms indicate a possible myocardial infarction (MI) and the OTA's first action must be to immediately inform the nursing staff about the person's status and complaints. If answered incorrectly, review symptoms and management of MIs. See Chapter 8.

B48 C3

An individual is being treated in an outpatient clinic for complex regional pain syndrome, type 1. Which activity is best for the OTA to recommend the person complete at home?

Answer Choices:
A. Doing light handwork in a craft of choice.
B. Playing cards or a tabletop game.
C. Performing visualization relaxation exercises.
D. Washing a car.

Correct Answer: D.

Rationale:
Washing a car involves scrubbing and the carrying of buckets of water, which are stress-loading activities. Stress-loading is a recommended intervention for complex regional pain syndrome, type 1 (formerly known as reflex sympathetic dystrophy or RSD). Light crafts, cards, a tabletop game, and/or visualization relaxation exercises can be meaningful and relevant to the person, but they do not provide any weight bearing. Therefore, these activities are not indicated as the primary intervention approach for this disorder.

Type of Reasoning: Inferential
This question requires the test taker to recall characteristics of CRPS type I and then match this to a home program that most effectively addresses the patient's symptoms. In this situation, washing a car would provide the best approach to address the symptoms, which allows for stress-loading activity. If answered incorrectly, review treatment guidelines for CRPS, especially type I. See Chapter 6.

B49 C6

An OTA implements a group for adolescents newly admitted to an eating disorders unit. Which activity is most beneficial for the OTA to use to develop the clients' task and social skills?

Answer Choices:
A. Discussion of reasons for admission to the unit.
B. Cooking a three-course dinner to be eaten family style.
C. Watching a reality television show and discussing problem scenarios.
D. Completion of a group collage about personal interests.

Correct Answer: D.

Rationale:
A group collage is an activity that requires both task and social skills for completion. The OTA can provide interventions during this group to develop needed skills and reinforce observed skills. Discussion groups do not require task skills. A cooking and dining group does require task and social skills; however, it is not the best activity for persons with eating disorders who have established food-restricting behaviors and are just beginning treatment.

Type of Reasoning: Inferential
One must have knowledge of eating disorders and of task and social skills groups in order to arrive at a correct conclusion. This is an inferential reasoning skill where knowledge of clinical guidelines and judgment based on facts are utilized to reach conclusions. In this situation, completion of a group collage reflecting personal interests is the best choice. If answered incorrectly, review the diagnostic criteria of eating disorders and the foci of different therapeutic groups. The integration of this knowledge is required to answer this question correctly. See Chapters 10 and 13.

B50 C8

An individual prepares for discharge home following rehabilitation for a left CVA. Residual difficulties include fair dynamic balance, decreased proximal upper extremity (UE) strength, and poor dexterity. The individual's stated priority is to be able to ambulate safely to the senior center located in the client's apartment building. Which ambulatory aid would be best for the OTA to recommend to this client?

Answer Choices:
A. A hemi-walker.
B. A rolling walker.
C. A side-stepper walker.

Correct Answer: B.

Rationale:
A rolling walker is indicated for a person who cannot lift a standard walker due to impaired balance or UE weakness. A hemi-walker and side-stepper are indicated for individuals who do not have use of both hands.

Type of Reasoning: Inferential
One must determine the most appropriate ambulatory aid given knowledge of the presenting limitations. This requires inferential reasoning skill, where one must infer or draw conclusions about a best course of action. In this situation, the OTA should recommend a rolling walker. If answered incorrectly, review guidelines for use of a rolling walker and other ambulatory aids. See Chapter 15.

B51 C9

An OTA provides home care services to a person recovering from a recent CVA. The client lives alone and receives home care Medicare benefits. The OTA arrives at the client's house at the scheduled session time, but there is no response to the knocking on the door. A neighbor reports seeing the client leave with a friend. Which is the best action for the OTA to take in response to this situation?

Answer Choices:
A. Document that no one answered the door and that the appointment will be rescheduled.
B. Call the supervising occupational therapist to discuss the missed appointment.
C. Document that no one was home and that the appointment will be rescheduled.
D. Document that the client is engaged in community mobility activities and should be evaluated for discharge.

Correct Answer: A.

Rationale:
Documentation must state that no one answered the door. This is factually correct and allows the individual to continue to receive home care service reimbursement from Medicare. To receive Medicare home care reimbursement, an individual must be homebound which means they can only leave home according to specific criteria. The client may have left for a reason that would meet these criteria. It is best not to document any behaviors that may jeopardize a person's homebound status. The OTA is capable of providing this documentation and does not need to discuss the missed appointment with the occupational therapist prior to completing the documentation. The OTA can follow up directly with the individual. One missed appointment is not a basis for discharge.

Type of Reasoning: Evaluative
This question requires one to use guiding principles in order to determine a best course of action. This necessitates evaluative reasoning skill, as one must weigh the merits of the courses of action in order to arrive at a correct conclusion. For this scenario, the OTA should document that no one answered the door and that the appointment will be rescheduled. If answered incorrectly, review Medicare guidelines for homebound status. See Chapter 4.

B52 C8

Upon evaluating a client for a wheelchair, the OTA determines that a standard narrow adult wheelchair would be suitable for the individual. Which dimensions most accurately identify this chair?

Answer Choices:
A. 16 inches wide × 16 inches deep × 18.5 inches high.
B. 16 inches wide × 16 inches deep × 20 inches high.
C. 14 inches wide × 16 inches deep × 18.5 inches high.

Correct Answer: B.

Rationale:
These are the standard dimensions for a narrow adult chair. The other choices do not identify measurements consistent with standard adult wheelchairs. These measurements would reflect a customized chair. A regular adult chair has dimensions of 18 inches wide × 16 inches deep × 20 inches high. A slim adult standard chair has dimensions of 14 inches wide × 16 inches deep × 20 inches high, and a junior standard chair has dimensions of 16 inches wide × 16 inches deep × 18.5 inches high.

Type of Reasoning: Deductive
One must recall the standard measurements for a narrow adult wheelchair in order to arrive at a correct conclusion. This is factual recall of guidelines, which is a deductive reasoning skill. For this case, the standard measurements are 16 inches wide × 16 inches deep × 20 inches high. Review wheelchair guidelines if answered incorrectly. See Chapter 15.

B53 C3

An adult received daily occupational therapy after incurring severe lacerations to the extrinsic flexor tendons of the hand. The tendons were surgically repaired and have healed. As a result, the patient is being discharged. The pre-discharge evaluation found limitations of 10°–20° in active finger flexion of the MCP, PIP, and DIP joints of all fingers The occupational therapist and OTA collaborate to prepare the home program for this patient. Instructions for which intervention are most important to include in this plan?

Answer Choices:
A. Use of a resting splint.
B. Tendon gliding exercises.
C. Weight-bearing activities.
D. Home management tasks.

Correct Answer: B.

Rationale:
Tendon gliding exercises help to prevent adhesions of the tendons in the healing process. Initially after tendon repair or tendon transfer, a resting splint would be used and removed only for bathing and gentle active ROM. At the point of discharge from therapy, the client should be pursuing more active movement. A splint that allows the distal interphalangeal joints to be free for movement, or a volar splint for day use that allows active finger and thumb use, may be prescribed based on the client's needs. Weight-bearing activities help to strengthen the upper extremity, including the wrist extrinsic muscles. The focus after tendon trauma or surgery is prevention of adhesions with tendon gliding exercises and avoidance of heavy work to prevent tearing or re-injury. Home management tasks do not specifically address ROM to the flexor tendons to prevent tendon adhesions and losses in ROM. In addition, some home management tasks may be too stressful at this point of recovery.

Type of Reasoning: Analytical
One must analyze the evaluation findings and match this to the most important intervention for the patient's home program, which requires analytical reasoning skill. For this case, the findings indicate that the patient would benefit most from a home program that incorporates tendon gliding exercise to prevent adhesions of the tendons and increase ROM. If answered incorrectly, review exercise guidelines for hand tendons post-laceration. See Chapter 6.

B54 C5

An adult with schizophrenia attends a transitional employment program. The individual has a secondary diagnosis of class I heart disease. The OTA meets with the client and the client's work supervisor to discuss the work activities the client can safely complete. Which of the following most accurately describes the client's capacity for work?

Answer Choices:
A. Work with minimum limitations.
B. Work with no limitations.
C. Work with the reasonable accommodation of frequent rest breaks.
D. Work with the reasonable accommodation of no heavy lifting.

646 Exam B Answer Rationales

Correct Answer: B.

Rationale:
Class I heart disease requires no limitations on activities; therefore, no limitations or reasonable accommodations are needed.

Type of Reasoning: Deductive
One must recall the guidelines for activity and potential restrictions with class I heart disease. This is recall of factual knowledge, which is a deductive reasoning skill. For this case, the patient with class I heart disease has no limitations. If answered incorrectly, review class I heart disease activity guidelines. See Chapter 8.

B55 C5

An OTA implements a feeding program with a person who incurred a CVA two weeks ago. The OTA observes that the individual's dentures seem to slip when attempting to chew food. Which is the best action for the OTA to take in response to this situation?

Answer Choices:
A. Advise the supervising occupational therapist that a referral to a dentist is indicated.
B. Continue the intervention at a slower pace and only use soft foods.
C. Collaborate with the occupational therapist to modify the intervention plan to include compensation methods.
D. Request that nursing staff re-apply denture adhesive prior to all feeding activities.

Correct Answer: A.

Rationale:
OTAs must inform the supervising OT of any change in the individual's status and any other relevant information that may affect treatment that they observe during intervention. Dentures that slip or move can hinder the person's feeding abilities. Poorly fitting dentures must be evaluated and corrected by a dentist. It is inappropriate to continue or modify the intervention prior to ensuring that the individual's dentures are properly fitted. Re-applying denture adhesive does not address the underlying problem and can lead to additional problems if the individual chews with ill-fitting dentures (e.g., TMJ pain).

Type of Reasoning: Inferential
One must infer or draw conclusions about a likely course of action, given the information presented. This is an inferential reasoning skill, where knowledge of a therapeutic course of action is essential to choosing a correct solution. In this case, the OTA should inform the supervising therapist that the person should be referred to a dentist. Review referral guidelines for oral motor disorders in adults if answered incorrectly. See Chapters 4 and 9.

B56 C4

A 7-year-old attends an after-school program for children with sensory processing disorders. Intervention activities are designed to provide deep proprioceptive input. Which activity is most effective for the OTA to use during intervention?

Answer Choices:
A. Playing tug of war.
B. Drawing with crazy foam on a mirror.
C. Finding objects in a paper bag.

Correct Answer: A.

Rationale:
Playing tug of war is the only activity listed that has a proprioceptive component. Drawing with crazy foam on a mirror and finding objects in a paper bag are primarily tactile activities. Finding objects in a paper bag also has a strong stereognosis component.

Type of Reasoning: Inductive
One must determine the most effective intervention approach for the child given the diagnosis provided. This requires inductive reasoning skill, where one must utilize clinical judgment to draw conclusions based on the information presented. In this situation, because deep proprioceptive input is best, the OTA should choose the game of tug of war. If answered incorrectly, review proprioceptive activities for children with sensory processing disorders. See Chapter 12.

B57 C2

During an individual session with an OTA, a client states, "I don't know what I want to work on. I don't really know what my goals are." Which is the best action for the OTA to take in response to the client's concerns?

Answer Choices:
A. Defer the development of an intervention plan until the individual has self-determined goals.
B. Establish a short-term goal related to improving goal-setting skills.
C. Contact the client's psychiatrist to request a medication evaluation.
D. Initiate a discussion with the individual about what is personally important.

Correct Answer: D.

Rationale:
It is best for the OTA to employ therapeutic use of self to establish rapport with the individual and engage them in the goal-setting process by exploring personal priorities. This answer choice is client-centered and incorporates the patient's rights. Deferring the development of an intervention plan does not provide the client with the opportunity to participate in this planning process nor does it provide the opportunity for the OTA to facilitate client's ability to articulate their preferences. Setting up a short-term goal to improve goal setting skills without the input of the individual is vague and would not contribute to a client-directed intervention plan. This is a violation of the ethical principle of autonomy. There is nothing in the scenario to indicate the need for a medication evaluation.

Type of Reasoning: Evaluative
One must determine which of the four possible courses of action will best establish a therapeutic rapport and incorporate the patient's rights. This requires evaluative reasoning, where the test taker must determine which course of action is most valuable and effective. In this situation, the OTA should initiate discussion about what the client finds important. If answered incorrectly, review information on client-centered treatment planning. See Chapter 3.

B58 C6

An OTA working in a partial hospitalization program collaborates with the occupational therapist to expand the occupational therapy program to include psychoeducational groups based on the recovery model. Which groups are best for the OTA and therapist to develop? Select the three BEST responses.

Answer Choices:
A. A directive group.
B. A coping skills group.
C. A sensory motor group.
D. A self-advocacy skills group.
E. A discharge planning group.
F. A reminiscence group.

Correct Answers: B, D, and E.

Rationale:
Persons receiving services in a partial hospitalization program have psychiatric conditions that have been sufficiently stabilized to not require inpatient care; however, they still have symptoms that require active treatment. Intervention focuses on improving function in areas of occupation, remediating underlying performance skill deficits, compensating for client factors that affect functional performance, and developing skills that enable a self-directed life. A primary focus of recovery is to improve quality of life and the ability to attain desired life goals through self-advocacy and effective management of life stresses. Thus, groups focused on the development of coping and self-advocacy skills are highly appropriate. A desired outcome of partial hospitalization is the development of skills for community living and the identification of community supports for community participation. Therefore, a discharge planning group is an appropriate focus for a partial hospitalization program. Discharge planning groups provide activities focused on problem solving potential obstacles to community re-integration and identifying resources for successful post-discharge community participation. Groups that use a psychoeducational approach incorporate the principles of learning to provide information to members and to teach skills (e.g., how to use the internet to access local community resources, how to apply for social services, how to advocate for reasonable accommodations at work). The use of homework assignments is encouraged to facilitate skill development and generalization of learning (e.g., contacting a community resource supportive of a personal goal, practicing stress management techniques, advocating for services that enable participation). Directive groups are highly structured groups designed to assist persons with limited abilities in developing basic task and social skills. They are often used on inpatient psychiatric units with persons who have significant deficits in task and social skills. A directive group uses a skill acquisition approach, not a psychoeducational approach. A sensory motor group uses sensorimotor approaches with persons with serious mental illness, intellectual disabilities, neurocognitive disorders, and/or neurological impairments. Reminiscence groups are typically used with persons experiencing memory impairments. They use activities designed to help members review past life experiences, promote the use of cognitive abilities, and foster a sense of personal worth.

Type of Reasoning: Inductive
This question requires one to apply guidelines for a psychoeducational approach and a recovery model in order to arrive at a correct conclusion. Questions of this nature often require inductive reasoning skill, where clinical judgment is paramount to arriving at a correct conclusion. For this case, the OTA should develop coping skills, self-advocacy skills, and discharge planning groups. If answered incorrectly, review psychoeducational approach and the recovery model. See Chapter 13.

B59 C9

An OTA is working in a skilled nursing facility. The OTA is documenting current patient progress for the past 14 days and realizes that a required seven-day progress report to the client's insurance carrier had not been documented. Which action is best for the OTA to take in response to this omission?

Answer Choices:
A. Document the patient's status as of 14 days and backdate the note one week.
B. Write a note describing the patient's progress after seven days of treatment and sign with the current date.
C. Call the insurance company to explain the documentation was lost due to a computer failure.
D. Describe the patient's progress after seven days of treatment and backdate the note one week.

Correct Answer: B.

Rationale:
It is important to accurately document therapy progress in a timely manner. It is possible for a practitioner to inadvertently miss a documentation deadline. If this occurs, the OTA should follow the AOTA Code of Ethics for veracity and document the patient's progress for the first seven days and date it with the current date. Notes should never be backdated.

Type of Reasoning: Evaluative
This question requires one to determine a best course of action in an ethical situation. This requires evaluative reasoning skill, where one must evaluate the merits of the potential courses of action and choose the one course of action that best provides resolution while still adhering to the Code of Ethics. For this situation, the OTA should write a note that describes the patient's progress after seven days of treatment, dating the note with the current date. If answered incorrectly, review the AOTA Code of Ethics, especially veracity. See Chapter 4.

B60 C9

A rehabilitation facility is completing a utilization review. The occupational therapist and the OTA on the utilization review committee contribute to the process by submitting a detailed report about the reasons for, costs of, and outcomes of a specific aspect of occupational therapy service delivery. Which information is most relevant for the occupational therapist and the OTA to include in this utilization review report?

Answer Choices:
A. The therapeutic use of the OT department's activity of daily living apartment.
B. The splinting and adaptive equipment prescribed to clients prior to discharge.
C. The use of personal care aides to provide morning self-care assistance to clients.
D. The craft and art materials used during leisure exploration groups.

Correct Answer: A.

Rationale:
Utilization review involves the analysis of the use of the resources within a facility. It examines the medical necessity and cost efficiency of these resources. An ADL apartment would be considered a facility resource. Splints, adaptive equipment, crafts, and art materials are supplies, not facility resources. Personal care aides are personnel resources, not facility resources.

Type of Reasoning: Inferential
One must have knowledge of utilization review guidelines in order to arrive at a correct conclusion. This is an inferential reasoning skill where knowledge of guidelines and judgment based on facts are utilized to reach conclusions. In this situation, the utilization review would include therapeutic use of the OT department's ADL equipment. If answered incorrectly, review utilization review guidelines. See Chapter 4.

B61 C1

An OTA completes a developmental screening for a newly referred 1-year-old child. Afterwards, the OTA meets with the occupational therapist to discuss the screening results. They determine that a more intensive developmental evaluation is needed. Which reflex would the child have demonstrated during screening to support the need for further evaluation?

Answer Choices:
A. Quadruped tilting.
B. Labyrinthine/optical righting.
C. Tonic labyrinthine.
D. Landau.

Correct Answer: C.

Rationale:
The onset age of the tonic labyrinthine reflex (prone and supine) is at or after 37 weeks of gestation. This reflex typically integrates at six months. Thus, its persistence at one year warrants further evaluation. Quadruped tilting and labyrinthine/optical righting are normal at one year. They persist throughout the lifespan unless neurological damage occurs. The onset age of the landau reflex is 3–4 months. This reflex integrates at 12–24 months.

Type of Reasoning: Inferential
For this question, the test taker must infer or determine what is likely to be true in order to arrive at a correct conclusion. In this situation, the test taker must recall when reflexes typically integrate in order to determine the reflex that is likely to be present beyond the typical time frame. This requires inferential reasoning skill. For this case, the tonic labyrinthine reflex would most likely have been present during this screening to support the need for further evaluation. Review infant reflexes if answered incorrectly. See Chapter 5.

B62 C7

An adult has been referred to occupational therapy. The individual demonstrates decreased ROM in the dominant hand secondary to a nerve injury. Active thumb ROM for the IP and MP is within normal limits. Active ROM of the IPs of all four fingers is 0 to 60 degrees. The individual wants to be able to hold a knife, spoon, and fork. Which utensils are best for the OTA to recommend to this person?

Answer Choices:
A. Utensils held in a universal cuff.
B. Utensils with cylindrical foam handles, 1½" in diameter.
C. Utensils with custom-built handles made of low temperature thermoplastic splinting material.

Correct Answer: B.

Rationale:
The foam handle accommodates the 60-degree ROM of the IPs of the fingers to hold the utensils. Without an adapted handle, the person can use only pad-to-pad grasp, which is unstable. A custom handle is most commonly used for someone with spasticity or with more difficulty holding the utensil than mentioned in the scenario. A universal cuff is used by someone who has no functional grasp.

Type of Reasoning: Analytical
This question provides detailed information about a client's ROM in an affected hand and the test taker must determine how this information relates to functional grasp for holding utensils. This requires analytical reasoning, where the precise meaning of data must be analyzed in order to make a determination for functioning. In this situation, a cylindrical foam handle would be the best recommendation. If answered incorrectly, review adaptive feeding equipment. See Chapter 14.

B63 C1

A 6-year-old begins prosthetic training with a right below-elbow myoelectric prosthesis. To learn to operate the terminal device, the OTA implements intervention using age-appropriate play activities. Which activity is best for the OTA to first include during intervention?

Answer Choices:
A. Assembling building blocks.
B. Squeezing a squeeze toy.
C. Playing board games.
D. Stacking 1-inch blocks.

Correct Answer: A.

Rationale:
In prosthetic training, the person first learns to open and close the terminal device. Assembling building blocks provides the opportunity to develop this skill, and it is an appropriate activity for a child of this age. A squeeze toy is appropriate for a child up to 2 years of age. The pieces of board games are small and will require an advanced level of skill in operating the terminal device. Stacking blocks is appropriate for a preschool child.

Type of Reasoning: Inferential
One must determine the best activity for a 6-year-old child with a below-elbow myoelectric prosthesis. The key is to choose the activity that is age-appropriate and focuses on opening and closing the terminal device. In this situation, assembling building blocks provides opportunities to practice opening and closing the device and is age-appropriate for a 6-year-old. If answered incorrectly, review the developmental levels of play and principles of prosthetic training. The integration of this knowledge is required to determine the correct answer. See Chapters 5 and 6.

B64 C3

An occupational therapist and OTA collaborate to provide a wellness and prevention education series to the members of a community senior center. The topic of the week is joint protection. Which joint protection principles are best to include in the presentation? Select the three BEST responses.

Answer Choices:
A. Use ergonomically designed tools that eliminate deviations at the wrist.
B. Stand diagonally to the side of containers to be opened or closed to maximize torque.
C. Stand directly in front of items to be reached for, opened, or closed, rather than to the side.
D. Work through the pain experienced during activities by performing stretching exercises.
E. Preserve joint ROM and muscle strength by using the minimal effort required to perform an activity.
F. Start an activity only if it can be immediately stopped when it requires capacities beyond existing capabilities.

Correct Answers: A, C, and F.

Rationale:
Using ergonomically designed tools; standing directly in front of items to be reached for, opened, or closed; and starting an activity only if it can be immediately stopped are important joint protection principles. The other choices are counter to joint protection principles. Pain should be a warning sign indicating that an activity should be modified or stopped. ROM and muscle strength can be maintained by using maximal ROM and maximal strength during activities.

Type of Reasoning: Deductive
One must recall joint protection principles in order to arrive at a correct conclusion. This requires deductive reasoning skill, where factual knowledge is key to choosing the correct solution. For this scenario, the principles that are consistent with proper joint protection are using ergonomically designed tools; standing directly in front of items to be reached for, opened, or closed; and starting an activity only if it can be immediately stopped. Review joint protection principles if answered incorrectly. See Chapter 11.

B65 C2

An OTA works with adolescents who are survivors of child abuse. OT interventions can be provided in groups or on an individual basis. Which of the following would indicate to the OTA that an intervention should be provided to an adolescent on an individual basis rather than in a group?

Answer Choices:
A. The adolescent wants more socialization experiences.
B. The adolescent desires greater control over the environment.
C. The adolescent needs an opportunity to gain situational perspective.

Correct Answer: B.

Rationale:
The person who wants to have more control over the environment would benefit from working on an individual basis. Groups are unpredictable and effective group process requires the development of trust and the sharing of control among all members. This may be difficult for an adolescent who has survived child abuse and needs to develop a sense of personal control. Someone who wants increased socialization would benefit from group interventions. A group is also the best intervention format to put one's own personal situation into perspective.

Type of Reasoning: Inferential
One must determine the benefits of individual therapy for adolescents who are survivors of abuse in order to arrive at a correct conclusion. This requires inferential reasoning, where one must draw conclusions based on the information provided. In this situation, if the client requires greater control over the environment, individual therapy is best because a group situation can be unpredictable. If answered incorrectly, review the benefits of individual therapy versus group therapy and the characteristics of survivors of abuse. Integration of this knowledge is required for a correct answer. See Chapters 3 and 13.

B66 C4

An OTA provides pediatric home-based occupational therapy services. The parents of a school-aged child with Rett syndrome ask the OTA for activities to help their child regain lost skills. Which of the following should the OTA include in the home program?

Answer Choices:
A. Encourage the child to use pressure distribution techniques.
B. Use four-step sequencing cards to increase attention.
C. Give positive feedback for active ROM performance.
D. Perform passive ROM to prevent contractures.

Correct Answer: D.

Rationale:
Rett syndrome is a genetic progressive disorder in which motor, cognitive, social, and language skills deteriorate. If the child is school-aged, it is highly likely that the child has experienced significant functional decline. Regardless of the child's current functional level, children with this progressive condition cannot regain lost skills. Therefore, the home program must focus on maintaining function and preventing complications. Passive ROM is an activity that the parents can do to prevent contractures, which are a complication of this progressive condition. The child will not be able to respond to encouragement to use pressure distribution techniques. Since pressure relief is important to prevent the complication of skin breakdown, a more effective approach is to make sure that the parents are aware of correct positioning and the need to change positions frequently. The child in this scenario will not be able to attend to sequencing cards to increase attention or independently perform ROM.

Type of Reasoning: Inferential
One must link the child's diagnosis to the activities presented in order to determine which activity would be the most likely recommendation. This requires inferential reasoning, where one uses knowledge of a diagnosis to choose a best course of action. In this case, passive ROM is the most likely recommendation. If answered incorrectly, review symptoms of Rett syndrome. See Chapter 10.

B67 C9

During an accreditation self-study, the occupational therapy department personnel review all charts. An OTA notices that a colleague fills out the review forms without reading the charts. Which action is best for the OTA to take in response to this observation?

Answer Choices:
A. Talk to the colleague directly.
B. Report the incident to the director of medical records.
C. Report the observation to the OT supervisor.

Correct Answer: C.

Rationale:
Reporting the observation to the supervisor is the best choice since the OTA directly observed a colleague committing an act that directly violates the AOTA Code of Ethics. Any overt violation of the Code of Ethics should be reported to the direct supervisor of the practitioner. The supervisor is the person who is responsible for dealing with the situation. The OTA does not need to personally talk directly to the colleague and find out what is happening.

Type of Reasoning: Evaluative
This question requires a value judgment in an ethical situation, which is an evaluative reasoning skill. In this situation, the colleague has violated the Code of Ethics of veracity, which is to be truthful in duties. Therefore, the OTA should report the colleague's actions to the supervisor. If answered incorrectly, review the AOTA Code of Ethics, especially veracity. See Chapter 4.

B68 C9

The OTA completes an intervention session with a client in a work hardening program. As the individual is leaving, the person gives the OTA a hug and expresses much gratitude. The individual then tries to kiss the OTA on the lips. Which action is best for the OTA to take in response to this situation?

Answer Choices:
A. Forcibly push the individual away while telling the person that the behavior is inappropriate and unacceptable.
B. Say nothing but recommend the person be discharged from the work hardening program due to inappropriate behavior.
C. State that the individual's behavior oversteps professional boundaries and makes the OTA uncomfortable.
D. Tell the person the behavior is inappropriate and unacceptable and a basis for discharge from the program.

Correct Answer: C.

Rationale:
Informing the person of the boundaries of the client-therapist relationship is the appropriate action. There is no need to admonish the individual or discharge the person from the program at this point. Some individuals are more demonstrative with their affections than others and the person may be showing gratitude in a manner that in their view is socially and culturally appropriate. The OTA can respond simply by stating that this expression of affection is outside the scope of their professional relationship.

Type of Reasoning: Evaluative
This question requires a value judgment in an ethical situation, which is an evaluative reasoning skill. In this situation, the OTA's best action is to state that the behavior is outside professional boundaries and makes the OTA uncomfortable. Ethical situations such as these often rely upon the OT Code of Ethics to provide guiding principles of action. Because the behavior is outside of the acceptable realm of a professional relationship, the OTA is appropriate in stating the boundaries. See Chapter 4.

B69 C5

An individual recovering from posterolateral hip replacement surgery prepares for discharge home. The client has a secondary diagnosis of gastric esophageal reflux disease (GERD). Given the client's diagnoses, which is the best bed position for the OTA to recommend to this client?

Answer Choices:
A. Supine with flexion of the hips and the neck in neutral.
B. Side-lying on the surgical side with an abductor pillow between the lower extremities and the neck in neutral.
C. Side-lying on the non-surgical side with an abductor pillow between the lower extremities and elevation of the head.

Correct Answer: C.

Rationale:
In GERD, the stomach pyloric sphincter ineffectively closes and stomach contraction propels acid and acidic bolus back into the esophagus. Elevation of the head above the stomach when the person is reclined may decrease the upward retropulsion of the bolus from the stomach. A neutral head position is not effective for an individual with GERD. A person recovering from posterolateral hip surgery can lie in sidelying on the non-surgical side with an abductor pillow between the lower extremities to prevent adduction of the operated hip.

Type of Reasoning: Inferential
One must infer or draw conclusions about a likely course of action, given the information presented. This is an inferential reasoning skill, where knowledge of a therapeutic approach, such as the appropriate bed positioning in this situation, is essential to choosing a correct solution. In this case, the OTA should recommend sidelying on the non-surgical side with an abductor pillow between the legs and elevation of the head. If answered incorrectly, review bed positioning for individuals post-hip replacement surgery. See Chapter 15.

B70 C2

To develop the social interaction skills of adolescents with autism spectrum disorder (ASD) an occupational therapist and an OTA develop a community-based after school program. Which group is best for the therapist and the OTA to include in this program?

Answer Choices:
A. A directive group.
B. A topical group.
C. A developmental group.
D. A task-oriented group.

Correct Answer: C.

Rationale:
A developmental group's focus is to teach the social interaction skills needed for group participation in a sequential manner. It provides group structure and activities along a continuum that is consistent with how interaction skills typically develop. Individuals with ASD often have significant deficits in social interaction skills. However, they typically have normal intelligence and do not need interventions to address cognitive skills. A directive group uses a highly structured five-step approach to help low-functioning patients (e.g., persons with neurocognitive disorders or serious mental disorders) develop basic skills. A topical group is a discussion group that focuses on activities performed outside of the group (e.g., vocational planning). A task-oriented group's focus is to increase members' awareness of their values, ideas, and feelings as revealed through group activity. This emphasis on intra-psychic functioning would be inappropriate for individuals with ASD.

Type of Reasoning: Inductive
This question requires the test taker to determine the best group focus for students with ASD and the need to focus on social interaction skills. This requires clinical judgment and knowledge of ASD symptoms in order to arrive at a correct conclusion, which is an inductive reasoning skill. For this case, the OTA should use a developmental group focus. If answered incorrectly, review the foci of different groups (especially developmental groups) and the social interaction needs of individuals with ASD. The integration of this knowledge is required to determine the correct answer. See Chapters 10 and 13.

B71 C4

An OTA meets with a patient scheduled for a right hip total arthroplasty (THA) to review postsurgery hip precautions. The client has expressive aphasia resulting from a cerebral vascular accident incurred four years ago. How can the OTA most reliably determine that hip precautions will be effectively implemented postdischarge?

Answer Choices:
A. Have the patient demonstrate the techniques that have been taught.
B. Ask the family to observe the patient once home.
C Ask the patient to point to pictures of the hip precautions being used during activities.
D. Have the patient demonstrate positions that should be avoided.

Correct Answer: A.

Rationale:
Expressive aphasia interferes with the person's ability to verbally express themself. Therefore, the most effective method for assessing the individual's understanding of teaching is via demonstration. The OTA must observe the person performing the precautions during activities to ensure that the person has generalized the precautions to actually implement them during functional activities. Asking the family to observe the client may be helpful to assess carryover; however, this source can be unreliable. Family members are not trained in assessment or activity analysis and they may not accurately report details of activity performance. Pointing to pictures provides limited information. The person may recognize precautions but not use them during the performance of an activity. Therefore, the OTA still does not know for sure that the individual can perform the activity appropriately. Having the individual demonstrate positions that should be avoided is contraindicated and could cause harm.

Type of Reasoning: Inductive
One must utilize clinical knowledge and judgment to determine the educational approach that best determines effectiveness and competence. This requires inductive reasoning skill. In this case, having the client demonstrate the skills that have been taught is most reliable. If answered incorrectly, review intervention guidelines for persons with CVA and aphasia. See Chapter 12.

B72 C8

An older adult with arthritis and limited ROM and the client's caregiver are in the process of remodeling their home. They ask the OTA for recommendations to ensure aging in place. Which of the following incorporates the concepts of universal design so the client and caregiver are able to safely remain in their home and live independently for as long as possible?

Answer Choices:
A. The use of a tub bench and soap-on-a-rope.
B. The installation of lever faucet handles and rocker light switches.
C. The use of a seatbelt extender and key holder.
D. The installation of a handrail at the entrance steps.

Correct Answer: B.

Rationale:
Universal design means creating products and spaces that all people of all abilities can use. Some principles of universal design include creating products and spaces that are flexible in use and require low physical effort. Lever handles and rocker switches are easy to use by people with limited ROM and decreased strength. A tub bench, soap-on-a-rope, seatbelt extender, and key holder are considered pieces of adaptive equipment. Steps are a barrier for some people with limited ROM and decreased strength. A better option would be using a barrier-free entrance or installing two handrails to assist when entering and exiting the home.

Type of Reasoning: Inductive
This question requires one to use knowledge of universal design and aging in place to determine a best course of action for an older adult with arthritis. This necessitates inductive reasoning skill where clinical judgment is used to reach conclusions. For this situation, the OTA should recommend the installation of lever faucet handles and rocker light switches. If answered incorrectly, review universal design and aging in place guidelines. The integration of this knowledge is required to correctly answer this exam item. See Chapter 15.

B73 C6

An individual with schizophrenia is referred to a partial hospitalization program. During the intake interview, the client answers each question by consistently returning to the focus of the first question. Each time the OTA introduces a new topic to discuss in the interview, the client ignores this topic and returns to the original question. When reviewing the interview with the supervising occupational therapist, which behavior is most accurate for the OTA to report the client is demonstrating?

Answer Choices:
A. Thought blocking.
B. Perseveration.
C. Obsessive thinking.
D. Poverty of speech.

Correct Answer: B.

Rationale:
Perseveration is a persistent focus on a previous topic or behavior after a new topic or behavior is introduced. Thought blocking is the interruption of a thought process before it is carried to completion. Obsessive thinking involves the persistence of an illogical thought. Poverty of speech is speech that is limited in amount and content.

Type of Reasoning: Analytical
This item describes behaviors for which the test taker must determine the likely cause for them. This is an analytical reasoning skill, as questions of this nature often ask one to analyze a group of symptoms in order to determine a diagnosis. If answered incorrectly, review the signs and symptoms of psychiatric disorders. See Chapter 10.

B74 C2

An OTA provides community mobility training for a resident in a group home for individuals with developmental disabilities. A resident successfully completes the intervention activity the OTA had designed with the occupational therapy supervisor. The OTA needs to plan the next day's intervention session, but the supervising occupational therapist is on a two-week vacation. Which is the best action for the OTA to take in response to this situation?

Answer Choices:
A. Grade the activity that the client successfully completed to its next level of difficulty.
B. Use the same activity that the resident successfully completed during the next session.
C. Delay the next treatment session until the supervisor returns and is able to provide guidance.
D. Ask the residential program director to assign another supervisor for the duration of the current supervisor's vacation.

Correct Answer: A.

Rationale:
OTAs are trained in activity gradation and the implementation of OT intervention; therefore, the OTA can independently plan the next treatment activity. Using the same activity would not enable the resident to progress toward goal attainment. There is no need to delay the treatment session or obtain another supervisor. In this scenario, the OTA had designed the intervention activity with the supervising occupational therapist. This intervention planning would have involved collaboration between the two professionals and provided the OTA with a solid basis for designing the next level of activity needed to meet the established goals.

Type of Reasoning: Evaluative
One must weigh the possible courses of action and then make a value judgment about the best course to take. This requires evaluative reasoning skill, which often utilizes guiding principles of action in order to arrive at a correct conclusion. For this case, because the supervising therapist is on vacation, the OTA should grade the activity that the client completed to its next level of difficulty. OTAs can grade activities and implement interventions which have been developed in collaboration with the occupational therapist. See Chapters 3 and 4.

B75 C5

An OTA collaborates with an occupational therapist to develop a wellness program for persons with Stage 4 kidney disease who receive dialysis several times per week. Which is most important for the OTA and the occupational therapist to include in this program?

Answer Choices:
A. Leisure planning groups that focus on sedentary activities to prevent fatigue.
B. A diversity of activities participants can engage in while on dialysis.
C. Meal planning groups that emphasize a high protein diet to improve energy.
D. Palliative care to support participants' quality of life as their disease advances.

Correct Answer: B.

Rationale:
To counteract the boredom and isolation that typically accompanies dialysis, the program should provide a diversity of activities to facilitate participants' active engagement in activities of interest (e.g., knitting, scrapbooking, completing puzzles, gaming, journaling). Leisure planning groups should focus on promoting active leisure pursuits, not sedentary ones. When active, the body has a better ability to eliminate the lactic acid generated during dialysis; physical inactivity can result in kidney stones. Because too much protein in the diet taxes the metabolic capacity of the kidney, a high protein diet is contraindicated for persons with kidney disease. Palliative care is indicated for persons with terminal illness. While people with stage 4 kidney disease who receive dialysis have a very serious condition, they do not have a terminal one. Dialysis can extend a person's life for years and successful transplantation can give a person a normal (or close to normal) life expectancy.

Type of Reasoning: Inferential
One must determine the most effective intervention approach to include in this program, given knowledge of the presenting diagnosis and its treatment. This requires inferential reasoning skill, where one must infer or draw conclusions about a best course of action. In this situation, the therapist and OTA should ensure the program includes a diversity of activities participants can engage in while on dialysis. If answered incorrectly, review the characteristics of kidney disease and OT approaches for persons on dialysis. See Chapter 9.

B76 C5

An occupational therapist and an OTA design a dining rehabilitation program in a long-term care facility. The OTA instructs paraprofessional staff in proper feeding techniques. Which point is most important for the OTA to include in this staff training?

Answer Choices:
A. Meals should occur in a homelike environment with staff conversing with the older adults being fed.
B. Individuals with swallowing difficulties should be fed in a group so that staff can remind them to swallow at the beginning of each meal.
C. Placing three fingertips on the throat and pressing firmly will stimulate a swallow response.
D. The head should be tilted slightly backward during feeding to facilitate an assisted swallow.

Correct Answer: A.

Rationale:
Proper feeding techniques include a facilitative environment. Dining in a homelike setting with staff who are attentive to the older adults' needs and interests during feeding/mealtimes will facilitate eating and socialization during the activity. Grouping individuals with swallowing difficulties diminishes the individualized approach that is essential to quality long-term care. In addition, reminding people to swallow does not effectively deal with potential noncognitive reasons for their swallowing difficulties. If an individual does forget to swallow food, they must be reminded/cued throughout the meal to prevent aspiration or choking. Reminding/cueing only at the beginning of a meal is not sufficient. Placing three fingertips on the throat and pressing firmly does not stimulate a swallow response. Tilting the head back may facilitate aspiration and is contraindicated.

Type of Reasoning: Inferential
One must determine the most important feeding instruction to provide to staff, given knowledge of the clinical setting and oral-motor intervention guidelines. This requires inferential reasoning skill, where one must infer or draw conclusions about a best course of action. In this situation, the OTA should inform staff of the importance of meals occurring in a homelike environment with staff conversing with the older adults being fed. If answered incorrectly, review intervention guidelines for persons with oral-motor disorders. See Chapters 9 and 12.

B77 C3

A carpenter complains of tingling of the left thumb, index, and middle finger, weakened grasp, and night pain secondary to carpal tunnel syndrome. The left thenar eminence appears smaller and more flattened compared to the right thenar eminence. The OTA collaborates with the client and the occupational therapist to develop an intervention plan. Which approach is best to include in this plan?

Answer Choices:
A. Wrapping wrists with elastic bandages to provide support.
B. Modification of techniques used to hold a hammer.
C. Application of hot packs upon waking to decrease pain.

Correct Answer: B.

Rationale:
The symptoms provided are indicative of carpal tunnel syndrome (CTS). CTS includes sensory and motor deficits associated with median nerve compression, which can lead to permanent loss of motor and sensory functions. An important aspect in the treatment of CTS is modification of repetitive motions, especially those involved in everyday activities such as work. Elastic wraps are not supportive enough; soft or semi-rigid splints are helpful to allow minimal wrist movement while providing sufficient stability for day use. Sometimes positional night splints may be helpful. The administration of physical agent modalities (PAMS) such as hot packs should be done under the supervision of an occupational therapist. In occupational therapy, PAMS are used to prepare the person for functional performance of meaningful occupations.

Type of Reasoning: Inductive
One must determine the best recommendation for a carpenter with CTS, based on an understanding of the client's occupation and diagnosis. This requires inductive reasoning skill. For this situation, the best recommendation for the intervention plan is to provide modification of techniques used to hold a hammer. If answered incorrectly, review interventions for CTS. See Chapter 6.

B78 C8

A resident of a skilled nursing facility (SNF) is severely dehydrated after a viral illness. The resident is agitated and confused. The doctor has prescribed intravenous (IV) fluid infusions, but the nursing staff is concerned that the individual will pull out the infusion line. They request that the OTA provide a restraint for this resident. Which is the best action for the OTA to take in response to this request?

Answer Choices:
A. Provide soft fleeced mittens for the person to wear on their hands.
B. Provide bilateral soft elbow splints that fix the elbows at 20–30 degrees of flexion.
C. Provide a lapboard as this is the least restrictive restraint.
D. Decline the referral and explain that restraints are no longer allowed to be used in SNFs.

Correct Answer: A.

Rationale:
Wearing mittens will help prevent the individual from pulling out the IV lines. Providing mittens that are soft and fleeced can provide tactile input that is not noxious. While federal guidelines (i.e., OBRA) emphasize restraint reduction and the provision of a restraint-free environment, they also recognize the potential need to provide restraints in certain circumstances. A restraint is permissible and acceptable if it is medically necessary and temporary for lifesaving treatment. These criteria apply in this case; therefore, the OTA should not decline the request. The wearing of mittens can sufficiently deter the person from pulling out the IV line. If the person begins to rub the IV line with their hands even while wearing the mittens, the OTA may need to recommend the use of bilateral soft elbow splints that fix the elbows at 20–30 degrees of flexion. The splints would prevent the person from accessing the IV line. However, this is a more restrictive solution so it would only be allowed after the failure of less restrictive method. A lap tray would not limit the person's upper extremity mobility and thus would not be effective.

Type of Reasoning: Inductive
Clinical knowledge and judgment are the most important skills needed for answering this question, which requires inductive reasoning skill. Knowledge of the federal guidelines for use of restraints and most appropriate courses of action are essential to choosing the best solution. In this case, the OTA should provide soft fleeced mittens for the person's hands. If answered incorrectly, review restraint utilization and reduction guidelines. See Chapter 15.

B79 C3

An individual with a traumatic above-elbow (transhumeral) amputation has received a body-powered prosthesis. To train the person in the operation of the terminal device (TD), which of the following should the OTA do initially during intervention?

Answer Choices:
A. Teach the person how to control the elbow joint.
B. Combine training of TD use with training for elbow joint movement.
C. Lock the elbow in full extension and teach only TD control.
D. Lock the elbow in 90 degrees of flexion and teach only TD control.

Correct Answer: D.

Rationale:
Locking the elbow joint into flexion places the TD in a functional position for the completion of activities with the TD. Locking the elbow in extension would not place the TD in a position suitable for the completion of most functional activities. The question specifically asks about training for TD operation, not control of the elbow joint. Control of the elbow joint would occur independent of TD control training because the elbow joint must be locked for TD use in an above-elbow (transhumeral) prosthesis.

Type of Reasoning: Inductive
One must utilize clinical knowledge and judgment to determine the training approach for an individual with an above-elbow amputation (AEA). This requires inductive reasoning skill. In this case, the OTA should lock the elbow in 90 degrees of flexion and teach only TD control. If answered incorrectly, review training guidelines for individuals with AEA and body-powered prostheses. See Chapter 6.

B80 C9

A parent receiving occupational therapy services in a hand clinic asks the OTA to adjust their child's hand splint. The OTA has established service competence in splinting. The parent reports that the splint leaves red marks after being removed for 20 minutes. The child received the splint from a school therapist. Which is the best action for the OTA to take in response to this request?

Answer Choices:
A. Modify the splint using a heat gun.
B. Suggest that the parent have the child refrain from wearing the splint.
C. Have the supervising therapist in the department modify the splint.
D. Call the child's therapist and have the parent express the concern.

Correct Answer: D.

Rationale:
The best choice is to have the parent speak directly to the child's therapist. The report that the splint leaves red marks 20 minutes after removal is a concern that must be handled in a timely manner. By modifying the splint or suggesting the parents have the child refrain from wearing the splint, the OTA is providing treatment without a referral, which is not in accordance with established practice standards. Moreover, this would result in the OTA acting without having any knowledge of the diagnosis or plan of care, which would be unethical. These reasons are also why it is incorrect to have the supervising occupational therapist modify the splint. The child received a splint for a reason, and not wearing it could be detrimental to the child. However, the child's therapist must be advised of the situation so that they can plan a correct course of action.

Type of Reasoning: Evaluative
This question requires one to make a value judgment about a best course of action, which requires evaluative reasoning skill. Because the OTA is treating the parent and not the child, it is not the OTA's or the supervising therapist's place to adjust the child's splint. Thus, the OTA should have the patient contact the child's therapist for follow-up.

B81 C9

A hospital-based OTA is committed to promoting the profession to hospital staff, patients, family members, and the general public. Which is the most effective action for the OTA to take to accomplish this goal?

Answer Choices:
A. Write an article about recent accomplishments of new occupational therapy staff members in the hospital's employee newsletter.
B. Include photos of patients participating in the occupational therapy department's driver rehabilitation program in the hospital's annual report.
C. Display information sheets about major areas of occupational therapy practice on the hospital's cafeteria bulletin board.
D. Write a monthly column in a local newspaper about occupational therapy approaches for a diversity of clinical conditions.

Correct Answer: C.

Rationale:
A hospital cafeteria services hospital staff, patients, family members, and the general public, so this would be the communication venue that would be readily accessible to both audiences. Displaying information sheets about major areas of OT practice on this bulletin board is an effective method for promoting the profession. The other answer choices do include activities that can help promote OT, but they do not target all of the target populations (i.e., hospital staff, patients, family members, and the general public) identified in this exam item.

Type of Reasoning: Inferential
This question requires one to infer or draw a reasonable conclusion for a most effective course of action when promoting occupational therapy to staff and the public. Questions that ask about future benefits for a present course of action often require inferential reasoning skills. For this scenario, the OTA should display information sheets about the major areas of practice on the hospital's cafeteria bulletin board to have the most benefit. If answered incorrectly, review guidelines for the promotion of occupational therapy. See Chapter 4.

B82 C7

An occupational therapist and an OTA provide consultation services to a manufacturing company which is seeking to decrease their employees' incidence of repetitive stress disorders (RSDs). Which action is best for the therapist and OTA to take first to address this need?

Answer Choices:
A. Conduct an ergonomic risk assessment of the employees' work tasks.
B. Construct custom made ergonomic tool handles for each employee.
C. Modify the machinery used by employees to decrease vibration and force.
D. Adapt work tasks to decrease stooping, reaching, and bending.

Correct Answer: A.

Rationale:
The completion of an ergonomic risk assessment of the employees' work tasks is needed to determine the manual handling, physical energy, and other musculoskeletal demands of each task. An ergonomic risk assessment also includes the evaluation of environment in which work tasks are performed and the tools that are used. Based upon this comprehensive assessment, the therapist and OTA make recommendations and provide interventions to prevent RSD. These can include making adaptations and modifications to work activities, tools, machines, and the physical environment.

Type of Reasoning: Inductive
This question requires one to utilize clinical judgment to determine the best action in addressing the needs of employees with repetitive stress disorders. This requires inductive reasoning skill. For this case, the OTA should conduct an ergonomic risk assessment of the employees' work tasks. If answered incorrectly, review ergonomic risk assessment guidelines. See Chapter 14.

B83 C1

A resident of a skilled nursing facility has bilateral knee replacements and cataracts. The individual retains some residual vision. During intervention sessions, which is the most effective placement for the OTA to use when presenting materials to the person?

Answer Choices:
A. To the side of the person, with no direct lighting.
B. Directly in front of the person, at eye level.
C. Directly in front of the person, at tabletop level.
D. To the side of the person, with a strong light shining.

Correct Answer: A.

Rationale:
An individual with cataracts loses central vision first; therefore, presenting evaluation materials directly in front of the person will be ineffective. Peripheral vision gradually decreases with cataracts, so presenting materials to the side will enable the person to use their residual vision. Individuals with cataracts have increased difficulty with glare, so indirect lighting is indicated and strong direct lighting is contraindicated.

Type of Reasoning: Inferential
One must have knowledge of cataracts and visual limitations in order to choose the best manner of presenting evaluation materials. This is an inferential reasoning skill where knowledge of the visual disorder and presenting deficits is pivotal to choosing the correct solution. For this situation, the OTA should present materials to the side of the person, with no direct lighting. If answered incorrectly, review the functional impact of cataracts. See Chapter 5.

B84 C8

An OTA works with a child who has developmental delay and unintelligible speech to develop the child's functional communication skills using a communication board. The child has attained 100% accuracy in pointing to "yes" and "no" on the communication board in response to questions. The OTA and occupational therapist collaborate and determine that the child should be provided with the opportunity to expand communication skills. Which action would most effectively help the child attain this goal?

Answer Choices:
A. Adding two more choices such as "play" and "snack" to the communication board.
B. Reversing the positions of "yes" and "no" on the communication board to assure competence.
C. Adding the options of "play," "thirsty," "hungry," and "TV" to the communication board.

Correct Answer: A.

Rationale:
The best choice for a child with developmental delay is to maintain the consistency of the original selections and add one or two new options at a time. The best choices are to pick concrete items that the child prefers and enjoys and would therefore be interested in communicating. Reversing the position of the items will test the child's memory and ability to generalize, but this would not improve their communication skills. With a developmental delay, it is important to be consistent in intervention to retain desired behaviors. Four new options would be too many to add at this time.

Type of Reasoning: Inductive
One must determine the next step in communication after determining competency in pointing to "yes" and "no." This requires inductive reasoning, where the test taker must utilize clinical judgment to determine the next course of action. For this scenario, adding two more choices to the board is the best next step. If answered incorrectly, review the characteristics of children with developmental delays and the use of augmentative communication devices for persons with communication difficulties. The integration of this knowledge is required for the determination of a correct answer. See Chapters 5 and 15.

B85 C5

An OTA works on the development of feeding skills with a toddler. The toddler has tongue thrust which makes it difficult for the parents to effectively feed their child. Which technique is best for the OTA to teach the parents to address this difficulty?

Answer Choices:
A. Have the child suck through straws of progressively longer lengths.
B. Walk a tongue depressor from the front of the tongue to its back.
C. Press the bowl of the spoon downward and hold it onto the tongue.

Correct Answer: C.

Rationale:
Pressing the bowl of the spoon downward and holding it onto the tongue can sufficiently stop tongue thrust long enough for the child to access the food that is on the spoon. Because tongue thrust hinders the ability to close the lips, the parents should also be taught techniques to facilitate lip closure. Walking a tongue depressor from the front of the tongue to the back can desensitize a hyperactive gag reflex. Sipping straws can increase the sucking reflex; Neither of these techniques address tongue thrust.

Type of Reasoning: Inductive
This question requires one to determine the best approach for decreasing the impact of tongue thrust on feeding. This requires inductive reasoning skill, where clinical judgment is paramount to arriving at a correct conclusion. For this situation, the OTA should teach the parents to press the bowl of the spoon downward and hold it onto the tongue. If answered incorrectly, review treatment guidelines for pediatric oral motor disorders. See Chapter 5.

B86 C4

An individual who incurred a right cerebral vascular accident (CVA) has left hemiplegia and a subluxed left shoulder. Which is the most effective approach for the OTA to use to treat this subluxation?

Answer Choices:
A. Rest the person's arm on the wheelchair's lapboard throughout the day.
B. Rest the person's arm in an inclined arm trough attached to the wheelchair throughout the day.
C. Have the person wear a shoulder sling 24 hours a day to reduce stress at the shoulder joint.
D. Position the person's arm to avoid shoulder traction while in bed and in the wheelchair.

Correct Answer: D.

Rationale:
Proper positioning during the day and evening is most effective in treating subluxations. Positioning must avoid shoulder traction and weight on the shoulder. Wearing a shoulder sling 24 hours a day is contraindicated, as long-term use can result in soft-tissue contractures, edema, and the development of pain syndromes. Shoulder slings can be used to support a flaccid shoulder for short and controlled periods of time. Lapboards and arm troughs can be used for proper daytime positioning when a person is in a wheelchair; however, positioning in bed must also be considered.

Type of Reasoning: Inductive
This question requires one to determine the best approach for treating subluxation of the shoulder. This requires inductive reasoning skill, where clinical judgment is paramount to arriving at a correct conclusion. For this situation, positioning the arm to avoid shoulder traction while in bed and the wheelchair is best. If answered incorrectly, review treatment guidelines and positioning recommendations for patients with shoulder subluxation. See Chapter 12.

B87 C3

An individual recovering from myasthenia gravis has fair minus (F−) muscle strength in both upper extremities. The occupational therapist and OTA develop an intervention plan to include the goal of increasing muscle strength. According to the biomechanical approach, which should the OTA work on with the patient during intervention?

Answer Choices:
A. Complete active ROM through complete range with gravity decreased.
B. Complete active ROM through complete range against gravity.
C. Complete active ROM through 50% of range against gravity.
D. Complete active ROM against gravity and with slight resistance.

Correct Answer: B.

Rationale:
The next muscle grade after a fair minus (F−) is fair (F), which indicates the ability of the body part to actively move through its complete ROM against gravity. A F− muscle grade indicates a body part can move through its incomplete ROM (more than 50%) against gravity. An F+ muscle grade indicates a body part can move through its complete ROM against gravity and slight resistance. The ability to move a body part through complete ROM with gravity decreased is indicative of a poor (P) muscle grade.

Type of Reasoning: Deductive
This question requires recall of guidelines and principles, which is factual knowledge. Deductive reasoning skills are utilized whenever one must recall facts to solve problems. In this situation, one should recall the definition of the next grade above F− in order to arrive at a correct conclusion. If answered incorrectly, review muscle grades obtained from manual muscle testing. See Chapter 6.

B88 C4

A preschool-aged child is hypersensitive to touch. The occupational therapist and OTA plan intervention to help the child develop the ability to adequately modulate sensory stimuli. The therapist and the OTA use the sensory-integration frame of reference to guide the intervention plan. Which technique is best for the OTA to use with this child during the first intervention session?

Answer Choices:
A. Fast brushing to the child's arms in a direction opposite hair growth.
B. Lightly moving touch to the child's abdomen and extremities.
C. Firm pressure where the child can see the source of the stimuli.

Correct Answer: C.

Rationale:
Firm pressure and deep touch where the child can see the source of the stimuli is an effective approach for a child who is hypersensitive to touch. This technique tends to be more tolerable than light touch stimuli, which tend to be aversive, especially when applied to the face, abdomen, and palmar surfaces of the extremities and/or in a direction opposite hair growth. Tactile stimuli should be applied in the direction of hair growth, as this is less aversive to persons who are hypersensitive to touch.

Type of Reasoning: Inferential
One must infer or draw conclusions about a best course of action given the patient's diagnosis and presenting symptoms. For this child, firm pressure is the best initial technique as it is the most tolerated proprioceptive technique by a child with hypersensitivity to touch. Review proprioceptive techniques for hypersensitivity if answered incorrectly. See Chapter 12.

B89 C2

A 2-month-old infant with bilateral hip dislocations is being discharged home from an acute pediatric facility. The occupational therapist and OTA have developed a home program for the parents of this first-born child. Which is most important for the occupational therapist and OTA to assess before instructing the parents in the details of this home program?

Answer Choices:
A. The family's insurance reimbursement plan.
B. The parent's level of formal education.
C. The family's home environment.
D. The parent's degree of anxiety.

Correct Answer: D.

Rationale:
Prior to providing the parents with details about the home program, the occupational therapist and OTA should assess the parents' level of anxiety since excess anxiety could impact their comprehension and retention of the instructions given. This is an effective use of interactive reasoning and can help build rapport with the parents. This can contribute to increased compliance with the prescribed home program. While the other factors may also be considered, they do not represent immediate priorities for hospital-based instruction.

Type of Reasoning: Inductive
This question requires one to utilize clinical judgment in order to determine the most important item to assess before instructing the parents in a home exercise program. This requires inductive reasoning skill. In this case, it is most important to determine the parents' degree of anxiety and attention. If answered incorrectly, review guidelines for the therapeutic use of self and family-centered practice. See Chapter 3.

B90 C9

An OTA leads a transitional planning group for high school students with conduct disorders. The school fire alarm goes off five minutes before the group's scheduled termination. There have been six false alarms during the past three days at the school. Several of the students laugh and say, "There it goes again." Which is the OTA's best response to this situation?

Answer Choices:
A. Call the school's main office to determine the validity of this alarm.
B. Escort the students to the nearest fire exit.
C. Continue with the group's planned wrap-up, adding a discussion about the implications of false alarms.
D. Escort the students back to their homeroom classrooms to await directions.

Correct Answer: B.

Rationale:
All alarms must be taken seriously to ensure safety. In the event of an actual fire, any delay can be deadly. All the other choices are incorrect because they place students at potential risk.

Type of Reasoning: Evaluative
This question requires a value judgment in an emergency situation, which is an evaluative reasoning skill. In this type of situation, the safest procedure should be followed, which is to escort the students to the nearest fire exit. Questions such as these, which inquire about a course of action in a potential emergency, often require the test taker to respond in the safest, most effective manner possible.

B91 C7

An older adult is referred to occupational therapy with a diagnosis of osteoarthritis in both knees and elbows. The OTA contributes to the screening process by interviewing the patient. The OTA learns that the patient desires to return home to live alone independently in a two-level home. The OTA collaborates with the occupational therapist to determine the best response to this patient's stated goal. Which action should the therapist and OTA take next?

Answer Choices:
A. Provide suggestions for adaptations to the patient's bathroom to increase safety.
B. Train the patient in energy conservation techniques to use during IADL tasks.
C. Evaluate the patient's performance of daily activities in a simulated setting.
D. Provide the patient with a home exercise program to build strength and ROM.

Correct Answer: C.

Rationale:
The person has just been referred to occupational therapy and the screening has indicated a need for further evaluation. By observing the person perform daily activities within a simulated setting, the OTA can assess the demands of the activities the patient performs and the patient's capabilities. Because osteoarthritis is isolated to specific joints and not systemic in nature, the OTA can assess how the specific affected joints impact occupational performance. Once this information is obtained, the OTA can collaborate with the occupational therapist and use clinical reasoning to make recommendations to improve occupational performance. The resulting intervention plan may include bathroom adaptations, training in energy conservation techniques, and/or a home exercise program. However, interventions cannot be planned until after an evaluation has been completed.

Type of Reasoning: Inferential
One must determine the best action to take after a screening has been completed. This requires inferential reasoning skill, where one must infer or draw conclusions about the approach that will result in the best functional outcome. In this case, the evaluation of the patient's daily activities in a simulated setting is the best approach to learn about the patient's ability live independently in their home. See Chapters 3 and 14.

B92 C4

An OTA and occupational therapist are hired by a school system to implement an after-school sensory integration (SI) program. The therapist asks the OTA to conduct an in-service for staff to explain the indications, contraindications, and precautions for the use of a sensory integrative approach. Which precaution is most important for the OTA to review?

Answer Choices:
A. Self-abusive behavior.
B. Seizures.
C. Somatodyspraxia.
D. Hyper-responsiveness to sensory stimuli.

Correct Answer: B.

Rationale:
Individuals with seizures often have difficulty tolerating sensory input, especially brushing and vestibular input. These types of SI approaches can trigger seizures. Many children that can benefit from a sensory integration approach also have a secondary diagnosis of seizure disorders; therefore, it is important that response(s) to sensory integration interventions be carefully monitored. Since sensory integrative approaches can be inhibitory, they can be indicated for children with self-abusive behaviors or hyper-responsiveness to sensory stimuli. Somatodyspraxia is a disorder in motor planning due to poor tactile perception and proprioception, and it is an indication for SI intervention.

Type of Reasoning: Inductive
Clinical knowledge and judgment are the most important skills needed for answering this question, which requires inductive reasoning skill. Knowledge of the treatment technique and diagnoses contraindicated for the technique is essential to choosing the best solution. In this case, seizures are the most important precaution. If answered incorrectly, review precautions and contraindications for sensory integration intervention. See Chapter 12.

B93 C1

An OTA provides intervention for a 4-year-old with developmental delays characterized by the persistence of primitive postural reflexes. The child demonstrates age-appropriate cognitive skills. Which is the best play activity for the OTA to incorporate into the child's intervention?

Answer Choices:
A. Spinning on a swing.
B. Putting a puzzle together.
C. Lying on the floor and playing a game of marbles.
D. Pretending to be an explorer crawling through caves.

Correct Answer: D.

Rationale:
Pretending to crawl through caves can help facilitate the integration of primitive postural reflexes. It is also imaginative, which is appropriate play for a 4-year-old. Spinning on a swing is a fast vestibular activity indicated for treatment of sensory integration dysfunction. This activity could increase abnormal reflex activity in this child. Putting a puzzle together and playing marbles require fine motor skills and dexterity and would be too advanced for a child with the persistence of primitive postural reflexes.

Type of Reasoning: Inductive
One must utilize clinical knowledge and judgment to determine the therapeutic approach that would be best for the child. In this case, pretending to be an explorer crawling through caves is best given the child's age and limitations. If answered incorrectly, review the developmental levels of play and the impact of primitive postural reflexes on motor function. The integration of this knowledge is required to determine the correct answer. See Chapter 5.

B94 C3

A child with moderate arthrogryposis complains of profuse sweating when wearing bilateral night resting splints. When discussing this issue with the child's parents, which of the following should the OTA recommend the child wear?

Answer Choices:
A. Only one splint each night, rotating from left to right.
B. A cotton stockinet liner under the splints.
C. Bilateral volar cock-up splints instead.
D. A splint with several 1-cm perforations in the splinting material.

Correct Answer: B.

Rationale:
A stockinet liner helps to absorb sweat. It is also helpful to wash and thoroughly dry the hands prior to donning splints. Wearing only one splint each night does not address sweating and cuts wearing time in half, making splints less effective. Volar cock-up splints do not address the position of the MCPs and ICPs and can result in increased MP and IP flexion contractures. Perforations might decrease the strength and integrity of the splinting material.

Type of Reasoning: Inductive
One must utilize clinical judgment in order to determine the best recommendation for a child with sweating while wearing night splints. This requires inductive reasoning skill. For this case, the OTA should suggest wearing a cotton stockinet liner under the splints to absorb sweat. If answered incorrectly, review splinting protocols. See Chapter 11.

B95 C4

An OTA working in early intervention meets with the parents of a premature infant who cries a lot and has difficulty being soothed. The parents are concerned that they are unable to comfort their child. Which is the most effective strategy for the OTA to recommend to the parents?

Answer Choices:
A. Loosely wrap the infant in a soft blanket.
B. Provide frequent and rapid changes in movement.
C. Do nothing, as the infant's behavior is typical.
D. Tightly wrap the infant in a soft blanket.

Correct Answer: D.

Rationale:
Tightly wrapping an infant in a soft blanket can provide controlled and consistent firm pressure that is non-aversive and soothing. The crying behavior, whether typical or indicative of a difficulty, will typically respond to this strategy. Loosely wrapping the infant provides inconsistent and variable input that can increase discomfort. Frequent and rapid changes in movement are contraindicated because they can increase tone and stimulate arousal. Whether the child's behavior is considered typical or not is irrelevant; the parents are concerned and can benefit from suggestions.

Type of Reasoning: Inductive
This question requires one to determine the best approach for an infant with difficulty being soothed. This requires inductive reasoning skill, where clinical judgment is essential to arriving at a correct conclusion. For this situation, the OTA should recommend tightly wrapping the infant in a soft blanket. If answered incorrectly, review treatment guidelines for sensory processing disorders. These approaches can be effectively used to soothe infants. See Chapter 12.

B96 C6

A young adult recently diagnosed with a major depressive disorder attends a goal-setting group for persons living with depression. Which is the most helpful approach for the OTA leading this group to take with the group members?

Answer Choices:
A. Encourage the members to discuss long-range planning.
B. Say as little as possible to allow the members to do most of the talking.
C. Remain cheerful and upbeat to alleviate the members' depression.
D. Facilitate reality testing of the members' negative thinking.

Correct Answer: D.

Rationale:
People with depression often interpret events and the behaviors of themselves and others with unfounded or exaggerated negativity. Developing the group members' ability to test and correct negative thinking is an important precursor to developing the ability to set goals. This approach is consistent with cognitive behavioral therapy (CBT), which has been shown to be effective in the treatment of individuals with depression. CBT works to alter an individual's negative thoughts about themselves, the world, and the future by correcting misinterpretations of life events. Long-range planning is limited when an individual is initially adjusting to a new diagnosis. In addition, persons with depression often have difficulty with this ability. Persons with depression may also have difficulty independently initiating conversation. Cheerful, upbeat behavior may be offensive as it can highlight the members' depressed mood and appear to minimize the group members' affective state. This can bring the OTA's empathy into question.

Type of Reasoning: Inferential
One must determine the most helpful intervention approach for individuals with major depression. This requires inferential reasoning skill, where one must draw conclusions based on the information presented. In this situation, the OTA should facilitate reality testing of negative thinking. If answered incorrectly, review treatment guidelines for individuals with major depression. See Chapters 10 and 13.

B97 C5

An OTA is treating a patient with emphysema in an outpatient clinic. The patient uses two liters of supplemental oxygen and complains of shortness of breath during most functional activities. To address the patient's complaints, the OTA collaborates with the occupational therapist to develop an intervention plan to include patient education. Which is most important to include in this plan and teach the patient?

Answer Choices:
A. Methods to increase respiration rate in middle ranges of breathing.
B. Pursed-lip breathing techniques during activities of daily living.
C. Procedures for adjusting liters of oxygen during daily tasks.
D. Strategies for avoiding all strenuous activity during the day.

Correct Answer: B.

Rationale:
Pursed-lip breathing techniques are an important facet of pulmonary rehabilitation. With these techniques, the patient focuses on breathing patterns and maximizing use of the diaphragm when inhaling, rather than accessory muscles around the shoulder girdle. Pursed-lip breathing gives increased resistance to the airways on exhalation. The resistance causes increased pressure, which helps to prevent airway collapse. This is an important technique for patients with emphysema to use, especially during ADL. Encouraging increased respiratory rate of breathing in middle ranges (avoiding greater inhalation or exhalation) only encourages the typical breathing pattern present with emphysema. This is nonfunctional. A patient should not self-adjust the amount of oxygen delivered without physician approval. Changes in oxygen intake (either by increasing or decreasing levels) can have detrimental effects on the patient's well-being, which is why a physician must approve all changes. It is unrealistic for a patient to avoid all strenuous activity; therefore, the patient should learn proper breathing strategies during activities that may create strain.

Type of Reasoning: Inductive
For this question, one must have knowledge of therapeutic approaches for patients with emphysema in order to arrive at a correct conclusion. Questions of this nature often necessitate inductive reasoning skill. In this case, the OTA should teach pursed-lip breathing techniques during ADL in order to address the patient's complaints of shortness of breath. If answered incorrectly, review intervention approaches for patients with pulmonary disorders. See Chapter 8.

B98 C4

A client at the Rancho Los Amigos Level VII of automatic-appropriate is attending a vocational rehabilitation program three days a week. The client is frequently late due to difficulties with getting ready in the morning. The client asks the OTA for suggestions to address this problem. What is the most effective action for the OTA to take in response to the client's request?

Answer Choices:
A. Develop a visual chart with the client, outlining the necessary sequence of morning activities.
B. Advocate that the vocational program provides the client with a flexible start time.
C. Advise the client to call the vocational program to tell staff when running late.
D. Advise the client to wake up one hour earlier on vocational rehabilitation program days.

Correct Answer: A.

Rationale:
Individuals at Rancho Los Amigos Level VII have cognitive abilities that are automatic-appropriate. They are able to initiate and attend to highly familiar tasks (e.g., BADL) in a distraction-free environment, but have shallow recall of what has been completed. Creating a visual chart of the necessary sequence for routine morning activities will provide the person with a tool that the client can use each morning to check off their ADL task completion. This visual cueing device can also help the client refocus if they get distracted. Increasing the time available in the morning to do the daily routine is not needed. In this scenario, the client does not have any reported sensorimotor deficits that require extended time for ADL performance. In addition, having extra time can increase the potential for distractions and can decrease focus. While it is polite to call when one is going to be late, this action is not addressing the client's need to develop an organized and effective routine. Changing the vocational rehabilitation program schedule is also inappropriate for this reason.

Type of Reasoning: Inductive
One must utilize clinical knowledge and judgment to determine the most appropriate action to address the individual's unique challenge. This requires inductive reasoning skill. In this case, given the client's current level of recovery, the OTA should develop a visual chart with the individual, outlining the sequence of morning activities. If answered incorrectly, review activities for the different cognitive levels, especially activity completion for individuals at Level VII. See Chapter 7.

B99 C6

An older adult who incurred a hip fracture resides with a family caregiver. Prior to the hip fracture, the person lived independently in their own home. Upon discharge from the hospital, the person was referred to home-based occupational therapy services. During the initial home visit, the OTA observes that the individual demonstrates impaired short-term memory, disorientation to time and situation, and difficulty engaging in activities. The family caregiver expresses many concerns about the client's decreased functional capacity and reports feeling stressed. Which recommendation is best for the OTA to make first to the caregiver?

Answer Choices:
A. Explore residential placement to ensure the client's safety.
B. Contact a local office for aging to attain caregiver support.
C. Contact the local adult day treatment center to explore respite programs.
D. Make an appointment with the client's physician for a complete medical evaluation.

Correct Answer: D.

Rationale:
The client's symptoms may be due to a neurocognitive disorder or a reversible cause of mental confusion. Reversible causes of confusion include depression, polymedication, viral, bacterial, or urinary tract infections; gallbladder disease, and metabolic problems such as thyroid disorders or poorly controlled diabetes. A complete medical evaluation is needed to determine the cause(s) of the client's behavior prior to making any treatment or referral recommendations. See Chapter 10.

Type of Reasoning: Evaluative
This question requires professional judgment based on guiding principles, which is an evaluative reasoning skill. The client's symptoms warrant a medical evaluation; therefore, the OTA should recommend contacting the client's physician for an evaluation. Questions such as these can be challenging, as value judgments are often not concrete and require thoughtful reflection and professional knowledge. If answered incorrectly, review the reversible cause of mental confusion See Chapter 10.

B100 C7

A client successfully completes a work hardening program to return to work as a cable installer and repair person. The client has residual moderate impairment in temperature perception. During the discharge planning session, the OTA discusses how this impairment may impact areas of occupation and suggests activity modifications to facilitate the client's occupational performance. What is the most appropriate recommendation for the OTA to make to the client?

Answer Choices:
A. Request re-assignment to work activities that do not involve exposure to extreme temperatures.
B. Mark all potentially hot objects at home and at work with bright stickers.
C. Wear work gloves for activities involving extremes or variations in temperature.
D. Wear a protective splint during the workday and at home during home maintenance tasks.

Correct Answer: C.

Rationale:
The client should wear work gloves because of the danger of incurring a burn due to diminished temperature sensation. The work gloves can also protect the client's hands during extreme cold situations. As a cable installer and repair person, the essential functions of the client's job will frequently require them to work outdoors in all types of weather conditions. Re-assigning the client is not needed since they developed the skills needed to adequately perform all essential work tasks in the work hardening program. During the performance of work tasks, the client can easily compensate for sensory deficits by wearing work gloves. Since there is no comorbidity of a cognitive deficit, the client can be expected to be able to remember to don gloves to protect the hands when they judge a situation may involve extremes or variations in temperature. A splint would provide inadequate protection because it would not fully cover all surfaces of the hand.

Type of Reasoning: Inductive
The test taker must determine which recommendation most effectively addresses the client's current status and limitations. Because temperature perception is impaired, wearing work gloves when involved in activities that may involve extremes or variations in temperature is best to protect the client from injury. If answered incorrectly, review recommendations for sensory impairments and guidelines for adaptations of work tasks. The integration of this knowledge is required to determine the correct answer. See Chapters 5, 6, and 14.

B101 C8

A local senior center hires an OTA to consult on the re-design of the center's bathroom. Several members use wheelchairs for mobility. The center director wants to ensure that the renovations meet the needs of all active members. Which size floor space would the OTA recommend to allow members to turn a wheelchair inside of the restroom?

Answer Choices:
A. A 42-inch by 42-inch square.
B. A 48-inch circle.
C. A 60-inch by 60-inch square.

Correct Answer: C.

Rationale:
According to the American National Standards Institute (ANSI) guidelines for buildings and facilities, the recommended turning radius for a wheelchair is 60 inches by 60 inches. This dimension allows a wheelchair user to successfully execute a three-point turn. The other choices do not meet these criteria.

Type of Reasoning: Deductive
This question requires recall of the guidelines and principles, which is factual knowledge. Deductive reasoning skills are utilized when one must recall facts to solve problems. In this situation, following ANSI guidelines, the wheelchair turning radius should be no smaller than 60 inches by 60 inches to allow a wheelchair user to navigate the space using a three-point turn. If answered incorrectly, review ANSI standards for buildings and facilities. See Chapter 15.

B102 C9

An OTA employed in an outpatient pediatric clinic has been working with a child to address sensory processing deficits. After 12 treatment sessions, a denial letter for services has been received by the parents. The letter states that the diagnosis and the treatment do not meet the policy's coverage requirements. The parents want the OTA to change the child's diagnosis code in order to receive reimbursement for the billed services. What is the OTA's best respond?

Answer Choices:
A. Collaborate with the occupational therapist to plan the child's discharge from OT and develop a home sensory program for follow-up by the parents.
B. Encourage the parents to seek an alternate insurance carrier to receive improved coverage for services.
C. Explain to the parents that the current diagnosis cannot be changed in order to receive reimbursement.
D. Encourage the parents to set up a payment plan with the clinic's accounting department.

Correct Answer: C.

Rationale:
It is against the American Occupational Therapy Association (AOTA) Code of Ethics of veracity to change a diagnosis in order to receive payment from an insurance company. Changing documentation solely based on a personal request is fraudulent. If there was an error in the diagnosis when the bill was submitted for payment to the insurance company or if the OTA actually assigned an incorrect diagnosis code by mistake, then the diagnosis code could be corrected and re-submitted with a letter of explanation. However, in this scenario, there is nothing to indicate the diagnosis code was incorrect; therefore, the code cannot be changed. Discharging the child, suggesting changes in insurance carriers, and setting up a payment plan do not address the need to directly respond to the parents' request to change the diagnosis code to receive reimbursement.

Type of Reasoning: Evaluative
This question requires one to weigh the merits of the course of actions presented and determine which action effectively addresses the issue at hand. This requires judgment based on guiding principles, which is an evaluative reasoning skill. For this situation, the OTA should explain to the parents that the current diagnosis cannot be changed in order to receive reimbursement, as it violates ethical principles and is illegal. If answered incorrectly, review the AOTA Code of Ethics and established standards for documentation for reimbursement. See Chapter 4.

B103 C4

A person recently diagnosed with multiple sclerosis begins an outpatient program. During the initial intervention session, the client expresses difficulty concentrating on daily tasks due to chronic fatigue. Which should the OTA do in response to the client's stated concerns?

Answer Choices:
A. Reassure the client that these are typical symptoms of this diagnosis.
B. Inquire about the client's fatigue level during different tasks.
C. Reassure the client that medications will ease these symptoms.
D. Evaluate the client's endurance and cognition.

Correct Answer: B.

Rationale:
The OTA must obtain further information about the individual's fatigue levels and activity patterns. This information is essential to plan intervention for energy conservation and fatigue management. In addition, this action supports the validity of the client's concern and can be helpful in providing the foundation for a therapeutic relationship. Reassurance does not acknowledge the reality of the client's concern and does not deal with the stated problem. In addition, medications may not ease the client's symptoms. The client has just begun the program, so the client's abilities would have been evaluated during the admission process. There is no information provided in this exam item to indicate a need to re-evaluate the client's status at this time.

Type of Reasoning: Inferential
One must have knowledge of multiple sclerosis and typical symptoms of the disease in order to choose the best response in this situation. This is an inferential reasoning skill where one must infer or draw conclusions about the information provided. For this situation, the OTA should inquire about the patient's fatigue level during various tasks. If answered incorrectly, review symptoms of multiple sclerosis. See Chapter 7.

B104 C7

An individual with cyclothymic disorder who successfully completed a transitional employment program (TEP) is competitively employed in a busy real estate office as an administrative assistant. The person reports decreased self-efficacy and feeling overwhelmed by the number of part-time real estate agents who email work late in the afternoon and insist it be completed within one to two days. The individual contacts the OTA with whom they worked in the TEP for suggestions on dealing with this work stress. Which actions are most effective for the OTA to recommend the person take in response to this situation? Select the three BEST responses.

Answer Choices:
A. Make an appointment for a vocational skills re-evaluation to determine an intervention plan to develop needed skills.
B. Use self-advocacy skills to explain to the agents that work will be completed according to priorities set by the office manager.
C. Make an appointment with the psychiatrist for a medication evaluation to manage anxiety.
D. Employ cognitive-behavioral strategies to engage in positive self-talk and eliminate negative self-talk.
E. Meet with the office manager at the end of each day to prioritize the next day's workload.
F. Organize the next day's workload at the end of each day according to the deadlines set by each agent.

Correct Answers: B, D, and E.

Rationale:
The use of self-advocacy skills to explain to the agents that work will be completed according to priorities set by the office manager is an effective way for the client to set reasonable limits on the agents' expectations for work completion. Advocating for one's self can increase self-efficacy. The use of cognitive-behavioral strategies to engage in positive self-talk and eliminate negative self-talk can also increase self-efficacy and decrease stress. Meeting with the office manager to prioritize the next day's work can be very helpful to someone who has multiple individuals giving daily work with expectations for quick completion of this work. Speaking to the office manager will ensure that the total needs of the agency, not just the needs of individual agents, are met. Supervisory input for the prioritization of tasks can also help deal effectively with the potential interpersonal problems that can occur when all work is not completed for all the agents. Informing the agents that the manager will determine task prioritization eliminates the need for the client to personally decide which agent's work gets completed and which does not. This can decrease stress and prevent interpersonal conflicts. Organizing the next day's work according to each agent's stated priority can result in multiple expectations for work being completed at the same time. This would be difficult to fulfill and would not decrease stress. There is no information in this scenario to support a need for a vocational re-evaluation or a medication evaluation. The problem described is typical of busy offices with multiple part-time workers and can be resolved through workplace supervisory procedures. Table 14-9 in Chapter 14 provides information about reasonable workplace accommodations for persons with psychiatric and cognitive disabilities.

Type of Reasoning: Inductive
One must utilize clinical knowledge and judgment to determine the most appropriate recommendation for this individual. This requires inductive reasoning skill. In this case, the OTA should recommend that the individual use self-advocacy skills to explain to the agents how work will be prioritized, meet with the manager at the end of each work day to set these priorities, and use cognitive-behavioral strategies to decrease stress and increase self-efficacy. If answered incorrectly, review TEP guidelines and reasonable accommodation recommendations. See Chapter 14.

B105 C3

A 6-year-old child is referred to occupational therapy to improve fine motor skills. The student is having difficulty drawing simple shapes (i.e., circle, square, and triangle) and cutting a straight line with scissors. Which of the following activities is best to help develop the arches of the hand and increase hand strength to improve the student's ability to grasp a writing utensil or scissors?

Answer Choices:
A. Spelling words using 3D letter shapes.
B. Identifying simple shapes by touch with vision occluded.
C. Coloring in a coloring book while lying prone on the floor.
D. Doing chair push-ups before tabletop activities.

Correct Answer: D.

Rationale:
Weight-bearing activities, such as chair push-ups, help develop the arches of the hand and strengthen intrinsic muscles of the hand to improve fine motor activities. Using 3D letter shapes to spell words does not provide resistance to increase muscle strength. Identifying simple shapes by touch with vision occluded is stereognosis and does not address developing hand arches and muscle strength. Lying on the floor to color in a coloring book will provide weight bearing through the shoulder and increase shoulder stability, but it does not develop the arches of the hand or increase hand strength.

Type of Reasoning: Inductive
For this question, the test taker must utilize clinical judgment to determine a best course of action for developing the arches of the hand and increasing hand strength. This requires inductive reasoning skill, where clinical judgment is paramount to arriving at a correct conclusion. For this situation, the OTA should have the child perform chair push-ups before tabletop activities. If answered incorrectly, review hand development (Chapter 5), guidelines for increasing strength (Chapter 11), and principles of activity analysis (Chapter 3). The integration of this knowledge is required to determine the therapeutic activity that would be most effective to improve the child's hand strength and develop the arches of the hand.

B106 C5

An older adult recovering from a myocardial infarction is referred to occupational therapy for a home care evaluation. The referral states that the client has high blood pressure and medication-related orthostatic hypotension. Which precaution is most important for the OTA to observe with this client?

Answer Choices:
A. Avoidance of activities that require sudden postural changes.
B. Adherence to dietary restrictions during meal preparation activities.
C. Avoidance of activities that require movement against gravity.
D. Delay of the OT evaluation until the client's medications are stabilized.

Correct Answer: A.

Rationale:
Orthostatic hypotension or postural hypotension is an excessive drop in blood pressure that occurs upon assuming an upright position. All functional activities have components that are against gravity so these cannot be avoided in treatment. Adherence to dietary restrictions during meal preparation activities is important; however, the question is about an evaluation session, not an intervention session. The side effect of orthostatic hypotension may not be remediated in a timely manner and the person's need for OT evaluation cannot wait.

Type of Reasoning: Evaluative
This question requires one to weigh the merits of each of the possible courses of action, which is an evaluative reasoning skill. After weighing the person's symptoms and current status, the test taker should determine that avoidance of activities that require sudden postural changes is most important. If answered incorrectly, review activity precautions and treatment guidelines for orthostatic hypotension. See Chapter 8.

B107 C3

An individual recently had a left transfemoral amputation as a result of the complications of diabetes. The client is two years' status-post right transtibial amputation as a result of the same precipitant. The client is referred to OT for pre-prosthetic intervention. The referral notes that the complications of neuromas and phantom limb pain are present in the left residual limb. Which is best for the OTA to implement during the first intervention session?

Answer Choices:
A. Upper extremity strengthening with emphasis on the biceps.
B. Percussion to the left lower extremity's residual limb.
C. Upper extremity strengthening with emphasis on the triceps.
D. Lower extremity dressing with emphasis on donning and doffing prostheses.

Correct Answer: C.

Rationale:
Strengthening the upper extremities, especially the triceps, will facilitate independence in transfers. Neuromas are nerve endings that are adhered to scar tissue. Since neuromas can be very painful, percussion to the left residual limb and donning/doffing the left prosthesis is contraindicated at this time. Given that the right amputation is two years' status-post, it is likely that the client has achieved independence in donning and doffing the right prosthesis. This capability can be applied to the donning and doffing of the left prosthesis.

Type of Reasoning: Inferential
One must link the patient's diagnosis and current symptoms to the interventions presented in order to determine which intervention would be best to address current deficits. This requires inferential reasoning, where one must infer or draw conclusions based on facts and evidence. In this case, upper extremity strengthening, especially the triceps, is most important in order to facilitate independence in transfers. If answered incorrectly, review intervention approaches for clients with amputations. See Chapter 6.

B108 C2

An OTA conducts an initial home visit to a family with a premature infant who, at 4 months and 5 lbs. has just been discharged from the hospital. The child has multiple developmental disabilities. The occupational therapist completed an initial evaluation and collaborated with the OTA to develop an intervention plan. Which is most important for the OTA to work on with the family during this first session?

Answer Choices:
A. Communicate effectively to develop a therapeutic relationship with the family.
B. Teach the family proper body mechanics for lifting the child.
C. Teach the family assertiveness training to develop advocacy skills.
D. Determine whether adaptive aids or positioning equipment is needed.

Correct Answer: A.

Rationale:
During the first visit, it is essential that the OTA practice effective communication and work on developing a therapeutic relationship with the family. Since the child has multiple disabilities, the OTA will need to work closely and frequently with the family to address their child's needs over an extended period of time. The other choices can be addressed when and if the need evolves. In addition, one cannot assume that the family will need assertiveness training.

Type of Reasoning: Inferential
One must determine the most likely intervention approach for a child on an initial home visit. This requires inferential reasoning skill, where one must draw conclusions based on the information presented. In this situation, practicing effective communication and developing a therapeutic relationship are the primary goals. If answered incorrectly, review guidelines for family-centered practice and home health care. See Chapters 4 and 5.

B109 C6

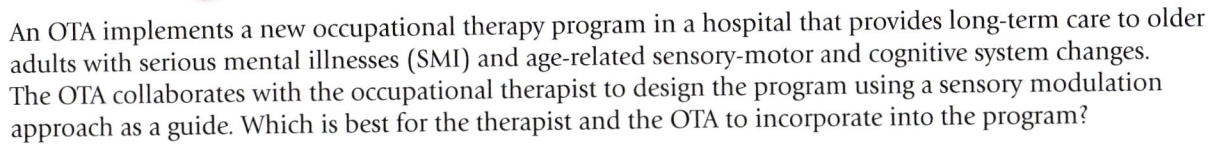

An OTA implements a new occupational therapy program in a hospital that provides long-term care to older adults with serious mental illnesses (SMI) and age-related sensory-motor and cognitive system changes. The OTA collaborates with the occupational therapist to design the program using a sensory modulation approach as a guide. Which is best for the therapist and the OTA to incorporate into the program?

Answer Choices:
A. Activities that use the clients' intact sensorimotor and cognitive capacities (e.g., dancing to music and using pictures of feet on the floor as visual cues for dance steps).
B. Activities that compensate for clients' sensorimotor and cognitive limitations (e.g. exercising along with a video of standing and seated exercises).
C. Activities that are spontaneous, fun, and do not require the client to think about the activity steps (e.g., keeping balloons afloat while music plays).
D. Activities that provide opportunities for clients to self-regulate (e.g., rocking in a rocking chair while holding and stroking a weighted stuffed cat).

Correct Answer: D.

Rationale:
According to the sensory modulation approach, sensory-based interventions should include activities that provide opportunities for clients to self-regulate. Rocking in a rocking chair while holding and stroking a weighted stuffed cat can provide vestibular, proprioceptive and tactile input that can be calming. Intervention according to a sensory modulation approach should also include psychoeducation groups and individual treatment sessions to help clients recognize their unique sensory modulation difficulties and strengths and identify personal modulation strategies that can be integrated into their daily life. In psychiatric settings, Snoezelen rooms, multisensory environments, and/or 'comfort rooms' are often provided as a resource for clients to use to calm and/or alert, as needed. Activities focused on a person's sensorimotor and/or cognitive capacities or limitations are not consistent with a sensory modulation approach. Keeping balloons afloat while music plays is consistent with the sensorimotor approach as described by King and Ross. This approach uses activities that are spontaneous, fun, 'noncortical', and do not require the individuals to think about the steps needed to complete the activity. These criteria are not consistent with a sensory modulation approach.

Type of Reasoning: Inductive
One must utilize clinical knowledge and judgment to determine which intervention approach is consistent with sensory modulation intervention principles and techniques. This requires inductive reasoning skill. In this case, providing opportunities for clients to self-regulate is the only option out of the choices provided which meets these criteria. If answered incorrectly, review sensory modulation approach for persons with SMI. See Chapter 13.

B110 C9

An OTA collaborates with a member of a psychosocial clubhouse to establish a social participation goal. The client has schizophrenia and lives alone. Which of the following short-term goals is best for the OTA to set with this client?

Answer Choices:
A. Person will independently engage in one leisure activity per week with another person within three weeks.
B. Person will consistently complete an individualized fitness routine four days per week within one month.
C. Person will independently make at least two verbal contributions to clubhouse group discussions.

Correct Answer: A.

Rationale:
Established criteria for goals include that they be occupation-based, measurable, achievable, and time-limited. Oftentimes, the mnemonic SMART (Specific, Measurable, Attainable, Relevant, and Time-limited) is used to guide goal writing. Engaging in one leisure activity per week with another person within three weeks is a SMART, realistic, functional, social participation goal. While the goal for completing an individualized fitness routine four days per week within one month does meet the SMART criteria, the activity identified in this goal does not require interactions with others. Thus, it would not facilitate social participation. Although participating verbally in a discussion group may help develop social interaction skills, the attainment of this goal would not develop social participation skills. In addition, the goal lacks a time frame.

Type of Reasoning: Inductive
This question requires one to determine the best short-term goal for an member of a clubhouse who seeks to increase their social participation. This requires clinical judgment, which is an inductive reasoning skill. For this case, setting a short-term goal of independently engaging in one leisure activity per week with another person within three weeks meets all the criteria of an ideal social participation goal for this individual. If answered incorrectly, review established standards for goals. See Chapter 4.

B111 C4

During a home visit, a client who had incurred a CVA reports difficulty finding objects during BADL and IADL. The client reports that the directions family members provide (e.g., look on the refrigerator's door, look in the medicine cabinet) are not helpful. When discussing this behavior with the occupational therapist, which cognitive-perceptual ability should the OTA report as requiring further evaluation?

Answer Choices:
A. Stereognosis.
B. Organization.
C. Spatial relations.
D. Visual closure.

Correct Answer: D.

Rationale:
This behavior may be evidence of difficulties with visual closure since the person may not be able to find an item if it is in its incomplete form (i.e., covered partially by other objects in the refrigerator or cabinet). The other options describe cognitive-perceptual deficits with different manifestations. Stereognosis is the ability to recognize objects by touch alone. Organization is the ability to structure thoughts and actions. Spatial relations are the ability to relate objects in relationship to each other or the self (e.g., up/down, front/back, under/over).

Type of Reasoning: Analytical
This question provides a description of a functional deficit, and the test taker must determine the likely cause for this deficit. This requires analysis of symptoms, which is an analytical reasoning skill. For this case, the client is reporting difficulties with visual closure. If answered incorrectly, review signs and symptoms of visual closure dysfunction and other cognitive-perceptual deficits. See Chapter 12.

B112 C9

A person with arthrogryposis undergoes serial casting with weekly cast changes of the right wrist. Upon cast removal during the fourth week, the OTA notes a small open area 1/4 cm × 1/4 cm and a red rash over the ulnar styloid. Which is the OTA's best response to these observations?

Answer Choices:
A. Pad the area and apply another cast according to the established protocol.
B. Refer the individual to the wound care team for an evaluation.
C. Fabricate a static splint that does not impede on the ulnar styloid.
D. Describe the observations to the supervising occupational therapist.

Correct Answer: D.

Rationale:
During the implementation of intervention, an OTA must inform the supervising therapist of any change in the individual's status and any other relevant information that may affect treatment. Thus, the supervising occupational therapist needs to be informed of the OTA's observations. The occupational therapist should then consult with the client's physician to determine the best course of action (i.e., whether to recast, dress the open area, refer the client to the wound care team, or fabricate a new splint).

Type of Reasoning: Evaluative
This question requires one to determine a best course of action after weighing the four possible choices. This requires evaluation of the strength and merits of the four choices, which necessitates evaluative reasoning skill. In this situation, the OTA should describe the observations to the supervising occupational therapist. If answered incorrectly review supervisory guidelines. See Chapter 4.

B113 C4

A 3-year-old child with hypotonia presents with delayed motor milestones and immature grasping patterns. The OTA begins each session with preparatory activities and positioning. This includes quadruped weight bearing and shoulder girdle compression to promote muscle activity and postural alignment. Which frame of reference is the OTA primarily using during these intervention sessions?

Answer Choices:
A. Sensory integration.
B. Neurodevelopmental.
C. Motor learning.
D. Acquisitional.

Correct Answer: B.

Rationale:
The neurodevelopmental treatment (NDT) frame of reference relies heavily on preparation and facilitation prior to active movement and task performance. Facilitation of alignment using NDT handling and facilitation techniques, key points of control, and positioning is meant to increase the potential for appropriate muscle activation.

Type of Reasoning: Analytical
This question provides a description of a functional activity and the test taker must determine the most likely frame of reference being utilized in the intervention approach. This requires analytical reasoning skill. For this scenario, the OTA is primarily using the NDT frame of reference. If answered incorrectly, review the NDT frame of reference and therapeutic approaches. See Chapter 12.

B114 C3

An individual with degenerative joint disease (DJD) incurred an injury to the right hand. The client complains of severe pain, stiffness, and extreme temperature changes in the hand. The OT referral states that the person has pitting edema and blotchy, shiny skin. The OTA collaborates with the occupational therapist to complete the patient's evaluation. Which evaluation tool should the OTA use to assess this client?

Answer Choices:
A. Vigorimeter.
B. Dynamometer.
C. Volumeter.

Correct Answer: C.

Rationale:
One of the client's major presenting problems is edema. The volumeter is an assessment tool that objectively measures edema based on the displacement law of physics. A dynamometer and vigorimeter are tools used to measure grip strength. An evaluation using these measures would be contraindicated at this time due to the client's secondary diagnosis of degenerative joint disease (DJD) and the presenting complaints of severe pain and stiffness.

Type of Reasoning: Inductive
One must have knowledge of all the assessment tools described and reasons for administration in order to arrive at a correct conclusion. This is an inductive reasoning skill where knowledge of clinical guidelines and clinical reasoning are utilized to reach conclusions. If answered incorrectly, review volumeter assessment guidelines and evaluation approaches for individuals with DJD and edema. See Chapters 6 and 11.

B115 C6

A patient with a diagnosis of borderline personality disorder attends a stress management group on an inpatient psychiatric unit. During the group, the patient's roommate states that there is a pocket knife in the patient's backpack. The patient says the roommate is exaggerating and that the item is only a keychain. Which should the OTA do in response to these statements?

Answer Choices:
A. Immediately inform the charge nurse.
B. Immediately check the patient's backpack.
C. Check the patient's backpack after the group session.
D. Inform the occupational therapist after the group session.

Correct Answer: A.

Rationale:
The possibility that there is any item on an inpatient psychiatric unit that could be used by a person to harm themselves or others presents a danger to all; therefore, the charge nurse must be immediately notified of the situation. Searching the backpack may or may not produce the item and it is not the OTA's role to conduct a room or person search. Informing the occupational therapist after the group session keeps a potentially dangerous item in a place where others could access it. This is not acceptable on an inpatient unit.

Type of Reasoning: Evaluative
One must weigh the possible courses of action and then make a value judgment about the best course to take. This requires evaluative reasoning skill, which often utilizes guiding principles of action in order to arrive at a correct conclusion. For this case, because the object could harm the patient or others, the OTA should immediately contact the charge nurse. Review safety protocols for inpatient psychiatric facilities if answered incorrectly. See Chapter 13.

B116 C5

A person recovering from a cerebral vascular accident has left-sided weakness and dysphagia. The OTA collaborates with the occupational therapist to plan intervention. Which is the most effective direct treatment approach to include in the intervention plan to help the person successfully swallow ingested food?

Answer Choices:
A. Provide pureed, thick liquids.
B. Provide thermal stimulation to the inferior faucial arches.
C. Tilt the person's head back and towards the left side.
D. Provide small, warm boluses.

Correct Answer: D.

Rationale:
Direct treatment for oral motor control involves techniques that utilize a bolus. These techniques can involve modification of bolus amount, consistency, and temperature. Providing thermal stimulation to the inferior faucial arches (e.g., using a chilled dental examination mirror) can elicit a swallow response; however, this is considered an indirect treatment method. Tilting the head back is contraindicated because it increases choking risk.

Type of Reasoning: Inferential
One must infer or draw conclusions about a likely course of action, given the information presented. This is an inferential reasoning skill, where knowledge of a therapeutic approach, such as the direct treatment to swallow food in this situation, is essential to choosing a correct solution. In this case, the OTA should provide small, warm boluses. Review direct and indirect interventions for persons with oral motor disorders if answered incorrectly. See Chapters 9 and 12.

B117 C9

An occupational therapist and OTA are conducting an outpatient post-cardiac surgery group exercise session for ten patients. The therapist is suddenly called out of the room to consult with a patient case. Which should the OTA do upon the therapist leaving the group session?

Answer Choices:
A. Stop the exercises and have the patients monitor their pulses until the therapist returns.
B. Have the patients continue with the planned exercise program until the therapist returns.
C. Have the patients switch to a less intense exercise until the therapist returns.
D. Try a new exercise with the patients that the therapist and the OTA discussed in the past.

Correct Answer: B.

Rationale:
The occupational therapist and the OTA were co-leading the exercise group. Thus, it is appropriate for the OTA to continue to conduct the group session as planned. There is no need to terminate exercise since the patients have an established exercise program. It is within an OTA's scope of practice to lead an exercise program, so there is no need to change or reduce the intensity of exercise. The OTA should not make an independent decision to try a new exercise without collaborating with the therapist about the patients' current ability to handle the new exercise.

Type of Reasoning: Evaluative
This question requires one to determine a best course of action based on knowledge of the OTA scope of practice. This necessitates evaluative reasoning skill. For this situation, the OTA should have the patients continue with the planned exercise program until the therapist returns, as this is within the OTA's scope of practice. Review OTA scope of practice if answered incorrectly. See Chapter 4.

B118 C6

An individual with peripheral neuropathy due to diabetes is scheduled for a bilateral lower extremity (transfemoral) amputation. During an OT session to develop upper extremity strength to assist with post-amputation transfers, the patient happily chats about plans to go shopping for new clothing to wear to a grandchild's wedding. Which defense mechanism should the OTA consider when working with the person to support their adaptation to disability?

Answer Choices:
A. Suppression.
B. Regression.
C. Displacement.
D. Projection.

Correct Answer: A.

Rationale:
Suppression is a defense mechanism that allows an individual to divert uncomfortable feelings (in this case, fear of an undesirable event) into socially acceptable feelings (in this case, anticipation of a desirable event) in order to avoid thinking about a disturbing issue. Regression is the returning to an earlier stage of development to avoid tension or conflict (e.g., an individual becomes needy or childlike during a period of stress). Displacement is the redirection of an emotion or reaction from one object to a similar but less threatening one (e.g., a child who is angry with parents yells at a younger sibling). Projection is the attribution of unacknowledged characteristics or thoughts to others (e.g., someone who feels guilty interprets the statements of others as blaming them).

Type of Reasoning: Analytical
This question provides symptoms and the test taker must determine the likely cause for them. This is an analytical reasoning skill, as questions of this nature often ask one to analyze a group of presenting behaviors in order to determine their meaning. In this situation the client's statements indicate the defense mechanism of suppression, which should be reviewed if answered incorrectly. See Chapter 13.

B119 C8

An individual with Charcot-Marie-Tooth disease receives services at a wheelchair clinic. The client reports difficulty keeping both feet on the wheelchair's footrests. What is the most effective action for the OTA to take to address the client's stated concerns?

Answer Choices:
A. Implement an exercise routine to strengthen lower extremities.
B. Elevate the footrests.
C. Provide heel loops on the footrests.
D. Provide ankle straps on the footrests.

Correct Answer: D.

Rationale:
Ankle straps are used to prevent feet from slipping off the footrests. Charcot-Marie-Tooth disease is a neuropathic muscular atrophy characterized by progressive weakness of the distal muscles of the arms and feet. It does not respond to strengthening exercises. Elevating footrests are indicated for edema control, LE extension contractures, and long leg casts. They do not prevent the lower extremity from slipping off the rest. In fact, the increased pull of gravity would likely exacerbate the problem. In addition, elevated footrests greatly extend the length of a wheelchair, making it very cumbersome to maneuver in the environment. Heel loops on footrests prevent the feet only from slipping posteriorly which would not be an adequate solution in this case.

Type of Reasoning: Inductive
One must utilize clinical knowledge and judgment to determine the most effective recommendation for this individual. In this case, ankle straps on the footrests is most effective to prevent the feet from slipping off the footrests. If answered incorrectly, review footrest equipment for wheelchairs. See Chapter 15.

B120 C3

An adult is referred to an outpatient hand clinic for treatment of de Quervain's syndrome. Which is the most beneficial splint for the OTA to construct for this client?

Answer Choices:
A. A dorsal wrist splint with the wrist in neutral.
B. A volar wrist splint with the wrist in 30 degrees of extension.
C. A forearm-based thumb spica splint.
D. A resting hand splint.

Correct Answer: C.

Rationale:
De Quervain's syndrome is a stenosing tenosynovitis of the abductor pollicis longus and the extensor pollicis brevis. The forearm-based thumb spica splint would immobilize the wrist and thumb CMC and MCP joints, which places the involved tendons at rest. A resting hand splint is not indicated as the entire hand does not have to be immobilized. A wrist splint, of any type or with the wrist in any position, would not immobilize the involved two tendons.

Type of Reasoning: Inductive
Clinical knowledge and judgment are the most important skills needed for answering this question, which requires inductive reasoning skill. Knowledge of the diagnosis and most beneficial splinting procedures is essential to choosing the best solution. In this case, the OTA should construct a forearm-based thumb spica splint. Review splinting procedures for de Quervain's syndrome if answered incorrectly. See Chapter 6.

B121 C5

A patient who is recovering from recent coronary artery bypass surgery is preparing for discharge. To ensure the person's safety while traveling in a car, which is best for the OTA to recommend?

Answer Choices:
A. Ride in the backseat.
B. Do not use a seatbelt.
C. Disable the airbag.
D. Resume driving in eight weeks.

Correct Answer: A.

Rationale:
Riding in the backseat of a vehicle following open heart surgery is the safest location in a car. Front seats have airbags which if deployed can harm the person. If a postcardiac surgery patient must sit in the front seat, the airbag should not be disabled. This would increase the potential for injury if an accident occurs. A seatbelt should always be used for safety. A pillow placed between the person and the seatbelt can increase comfort and safety. The patient's physician will determine when it is safe for the patient to resume driving.

Type of Reasoning: Deductive
This question requires one to determine a best recommendation when discussing traveling in a car after coronary artery bypass surgery. Knowledge of the diagnosis and postsurgical guidelines is used to draw a correct conclusion, which requires deductive reasoning skill. For this case, the OTA should recommend riding in the backseat. If answered incorrectly, review coronary bypass surgery precautions and principles of activity analysis. The integration of this knowledge is required to correctly answer this exam item. See Chapters 3 and 8.

B122 C1

An OTA is working with a preschool student who was born with congenital cytomegalovirus (CMV) infection. As a result, the child has difficulty seeing. The child enjoys playing with classmates but has difficulty when the play activity is highly dependent on vision. Which of the following are best for the OTA to recommend to the child's teacher to improve the child's play experiences with classmates? Select the three BEST responses.

Answer Choices:
A. Have the child read books in Braille aloud to the classmates.
B. Train a classmate to guide the child during play activities.
C. Incorporate three-dimensional objects into play activities.
D. Train a personal assistant to provide verbal cues during play activities.
E. Introduce tactile matching games using different shapes and textures to the class.
F. Provide the child and classmates with toy musical instruments to form a class 'band.'

Correct Answers: C, E, and F.

Rationale:
Activities which employ the use of senses other than vision (i.e., touch, hearing, smell, and taste) are effective interventions to compensate for low vision. This multi-sensory approach can enhance play for a child with limited vision and improve the child's ability to learn. Children depend on touch for learning about the world including the qualities of temperature, texture, shape, softness, sharpness, elasticity, and resilience. Incorporating three-dimensional objects into play activities and introducing tactile matching games can help a child with low vision participate in play through touch without having to rely on others for information. Providing the child and classmates with toy musical instruments to form a class 'band' can effectively use the child's intact hearing to play with peers. Having 1:1 assistance from an aide or a classmate is not a practical or effective option when the goal is to improve the child's play experiences with peers. Typically, preschoolers do not have someone to help them play with each other. Reading books in Braille aloud does not have components of active play and would not provide developmentally appropriate preschool play opportunities.

Type of Reasoning: Inductive
This question requires the test taker to determine a best course of action for a child with visual impairment. This requires inductive reasoning skill, where clinical judgment is used to reach a conclusion. For this case, considering the child's visual deficit, the OTA should incorporate three-dimensional objects into play activities, introduce tactile matching games, and provide toy musical instruments. If answered incorrectly, review principles of activity analysis and interventions for low vision. The integration of this knowledge is required to determine the therapeutic activity that would be most effective for a child with visual impairments.
See Chapters 3, 5, and 15.

B123 C4

An individual who has Parkinson's disease presents with poor trunk rotation during ambulation and while performing activities of daily living. According to neurophysiological frames of reference, which is the most effective therapeutic intervention for the OTA to use with this person?

Answer Choices:
A. Facilitation of trunk rotation using neurodevelopmental handling techniques.
B. Slow rolling with the person supine with knees and hips flexed.
C. Engagement in activities of daily living using diagonal patterns.
D. Provision of a rolling walker to compensate for limited rotation and enhance mobility.

Correct Answer: C.

Rationale:
The person is presenting with poor trunk rotation during ADL and functional mobility. This is typical in individuals with Parkinson's disease. According to neurophysiological frames of reference, the most appropriate approach is to use a technique to facilitate rotation during activity performance. PNF diagonals are the best choice because many activities (e.g., loading/unloading the dishwasher, putting away groceries) can be performed using diagonal patterns. Neurodevelopmental treatment (NDT) handling techniques and the Rood technique of slow rolling may facilitate rotation; however, they do not incorporate functional activities. Therefore, they are not the best choice. The provision of a rolling walker is a compensatory approach and does not directly address the effects of poor rotation on the person's performance of activities of daily living.

Type of Reasoning: Inferential
One must determine the most appropriate intervention approach, given knowledge of the presenting diagnosis, neurophysiological frames of reference, and incorporation of functional activity. This requires inferential reasoning skill, where one must infer or draw conclusions about a best course of action. In this situation, the OTA should choose ADL-based activities incorporating diagonal patterns. Review information on intervention approaches for Parkinson's disease and PNF intervention techniques if answered incorrectly. Answering this question correctly requires integration of this knowledge. See Chapters 7 and 12.

B124 C8

An OTA prepares to transfer an individual. The OTA cannot locate the transfer belt that the OTA had planned to use during the transfer. Which is the OTA's best course of action?

Answer Choices:
A. Locate a transfer belt and then complete the transfer.
B. Instruct the individual in a stand-pivot transfer.
C. Instruct the individual in a sliding board transfer.
D. Complete the transfer slowly and carefully.

Correct Answer: A.

Rationale:
The OTA had determined that a transfer belt was needed to complete a transfer; therefore, a transfer belt should be used. Not following the original plan would be unsafe and a liability risk. A person requiring the assistance of an OTA using a transfer belt would be an inappropriate candidate for learning to transfer independently via a stand-pivot or sliding board transfer.

Type of Reasoning: Inductive
This question requires one to determine the best course of action when considering a transfer without a transfer belt. This requires inductive reasoning skill, where clinical judgment is essential to arriving at a correct conclusion. For this situation, because safety is paramount, the OTA should locate a transfer belt and then complete the transfer. If answered incorrectly, review transfer safety procedures. See Chapter 15.

B125 C4

An OTA works in an older adult day care program. During a reminiscence group, a member removes a sweater. The OTA places the sweater on a hook for the group member. After the group, the member states the sweater is missing. The OTA shows the person where the sweater is hung. The member angrily declares that the hanging item is not a sweater. The OTA calmly takes the sweater off the hook, holds it open, and the member independently dons it. When discussing this behavior with the occupational therapist, which should the OTA state?

Answer Choices:
A. The person acted out hostilely and a referral to a psychiatrist for a medication evaluation is needed.
B. The person exhibited difficulty with form constancy and a cognitive-perceptual evaluation is warranted.
C. The person used displacement and should be referred to a counselor to help cope with age-related losses.
D. The person exhibited disorientation and confusion and a mental status examination is needed.

Correct Answer: B.

Rationale:
This behavior may reflect difficulties with form constancy. The person was unable to 'see' the sweater when it was hanging on a hook and not in a form that looked like a sweater. However, when the OTA held the sweater open for the person to don, the person was able to recognize the sweater and independently don it. This observed behavior warrants a cognitive-perceptual evaluation. The member's angry statement is not reflective of acting out, displacement, or disorientation. Acting out is the physical expression of thoughts and impulses and displacement is the redirection of an emotion or reaction from one object to a similar but less threatening one. Disorientation is a disturbance of orientation to person, place, or time; situation is sometimes used as a fourth consideration. Confusion involves inappropriate reactions to environmental stimuli, manifested by a disordered orientation in relation to person, place, and time.

Type of Reasoning: Inductive
For this question, the test taker must interpret an older adult's behavior as exhibiting a specific deficit in order to arrive at a correct conclusion. Clinical judgment and knowledge of cognitive-perceptual deficits are required, which necessitate inductive reasoning skill. For this case, the OTA should report difficulty with form constancy and recommend a cognitive-perceptual evaluation. Review cognitive-perceptual deficits, especially form constancy, if answered incorrectly. See Chapter 12.

B126 C7

An adolescent with a complete spinal cord injury at C8 is a client at an outpatient rehabilitation center. The client has met all goals for functional performance in activities of daily living. Which of the following actions should the OTA do next?

Answer Choices:
A. Provide an obstacle course activity for the client to work on functional mobility.
B. Discharge the client from OT with a referral to the local school-based OT program.
C. Establish community and social participation goals with the client.

Correct Answer: C.

Rationale:
The focus of intervention after attainment of ADL goals is community re-integration and participation. Establishing and attaining community and social participation goals can address the adolescent's physical and psychosocial adjustment to disability. Functional mobility is a component of ADL and the exam item scenario states all ADL goals have been met. Once community and social participation goals have been set, established functional mobility skills can be used during different community participation activities. This can strengthen these skills and facilitate generalization to situations that the client will encounter in their daily life. Because there are still relevant intervention goals to attain, discharge is premature.

Type of Reasoning: Inferential
One must have knowledge of intervention goals for persons with spinal cord injury in order to arrive at a correct conclusion. This is an inferential reasoning skill where knowledge of clinical guidelines and judgment based on facts are utilized to reach conclusions. For this client, after achieving goals in ADL, community and social participation would become the focus of intervention. Consequently, the OTA should initiate community and social participation activities. If answered incorrectly, review occupational performance interventions, especially those that enable leisure and community pursuits. See Chapter 14.

B127 C6

Children with a diversity of developmental disabilities participate in an after-school play group that uses a behavioral frame of reference. The play group is conducted by Level I occupational therapy assistant students who are each partnered with a child to facilitate the development of play and social interaction skills. Which should the supervising OTA advise the students to do when working with each child? Select the three BEST responses.

Answer Choices:
A. Set expectations that match and build upon each child's capabilities.
B. Speak loudly and repeat directions frequently.
C. Provide consistent directions and guidance.
D. Give detailed descriptions about the goals of each activity.
E. Provide a diversity of sensory stimulation activities.
F. Reinforce developmentally appropriate behaviors.

Correct Answers: A, C, and F.

Rationale:
According to a behavioral frame of reference, interventions should focus on the child's strengths and potential; therefore, the students should set expectations that match and build upon each child's capabilities. When using a behavioral approach, consistency and reinforcement are used to develop skills. In this scenario, there is no information provided to indicate that the children have auditory or sensory processing deficits; therefore, there is no need to speak loudly or provide sensory stimulation activities. The usefulness of detailed descriptions relies on the children's ability to process this information. This skill is often limited in children with developmental delays.

Type of Reasoning: Inductive
This question requires one to determine the best approach for conducting a group session with children who have developmental disabilities using a behavioral frame of reference. This requires inductive reasoning skill, where clinical judgment and knowledge of the behavioral frame of reference is paramount to arriving at a correct conclusion. For this situation, the OTA should advise the students to set child-centered expectations, be consistent, and reinforce developmentally appropriate behaviors. If answered incorrectly, review behavioral guidelines for working with children with developmental disabilities. See Chapters 5 and 10.

B128 C3

An OTA with established service competence in the evaluation and intervention of musculoskeletal disorders works in an outpatient orthopedic setting for persons with upper extremity impairments. A person with rheumatoid arthritis is referred by a primary care physician. The referral notes that the client has hand pain and joint deformity that includes a swan neck deformity of the index finger. Which joint positioning is the OTA likely to observe during the assessment of this client?

Answer Choices:
A. Flexion of the distal interphalangeal (DIP) joint and proximal interphalangeal (PIP) hyperextension.
B. Flexion of the metacarpophalangeal (MP) joint and DIP hyperextension.
C. Hyperextension of the DIP joint with flexion of the PIP joint.

Correct Answer: A.

Rationale:
The typical swan neck deformity presents as DIP flexion and PIP hyperextension, which results from the rupture of the lateral slips of the extensor digitorum communis or flexor digitorum superficialis tendon. Hyperextension of the DIP joint with flexion of the PIP joint is the typical presentation of a boutonniere deformity.

Type of Reasoning: Deductive
For this question, one must recall the typical positioning of a finger with swan neck deformity. This is recall of factual information, which is a deductive reasoning skill. For this case, the OTA is likely to observe flexion of the DIP joint with hyperextension of the PIP joint. If answered incorrectly, review joint deformities of the hand, especially for patients with rheumatoid arthritis. See Chapter 6.

B129 C2

An OTA implements a transitional program for a 15-year-old high school student with a history of numerous school-related failures. Which is the most important principle of intervention for the OTA to use with this student?

Answer Choices:
A. Utilize activities that are typically at the developmental level of a 12-year-old to ensure successful completion.
B. Grade an activity of interest into achievable steps to facilitate successful completion.
C. Introduce several activities during each session and change them frequently to decrease boredom.
D. Terminate the activity during a treatment session when there is difficulty with activity completion to eliminate frustration.

Correct Answer: B.

Rationale:
Grading an activity to be presented in achievable steps is the most appropriate intervention principle for a person with a history of diminished successful experiences. Employing activities appropriate for a younger child and terminating the activity when difficult will not address the teen's need for transitional services. Introducing several activities during one session can be overwhelming and decrease the ability to work in a focused manner on the attainment of transition goals.

Type of Reasoning: Inductive
Clinical knowledge and judgment are the most important skills needed for answering this question, which requires inductive reasoning skill. Knowledge of the student's limitations and most appropriate interventions to foster success is essential to choosing the correct solution. In this case, the most important principle for intervention planning is to grade the activity of interest into achievable steps to ensure successful completion. If answered incorrectly, the characteristics of transitional programs. See Chapter 4.

B130 C6

A person experiencing an acute manic episode is completing the admission process to an inpatient psychiatric unit. The intake coordinator has to unexpectedly complete an emergency admission. The admissions coordinator asks the OTA to spend some one-to-one time with this individual until the coordinator can return to complete the intake process. Which is the best way for the OTA to use this time with the client?

Answer Choices:
A. Discuss the precipitants to the hospitalization with the person.
B. Ask the person to make positive statements about them self.
C. Have the person do a craft activity requiring attention to detail.
D. Take a walk around the unit with the person to orient them.

Correct Answer: D.

Rationale:
Walking with the person can allow for some energy release, which is important for a person experiencing a manic episode. It is a non-threatening activity that can facilitate interaction. Providing the person with an orientation may decrease the stress of admission and foster rapport. Upon admission, the person may be uncomfortable discussing precipitants to hospitalization and may have difficulty making positive statements about them self. Activities requiring concentration and attention can also be difficult for a person experiencing an acute manic episode.

Type of Reasoning: Evaluative
This question requires one to determine the best response to an unexpected situation. This requires evaluative reasoning skill, where one must reach conclusions using value judgments. In this situation, the OTA should take a walk with the person around the unit to orient the person. This response is consistent with a client-centered approach. See Chapter 3.

B131 C7

An individual with a complete C6 spinal cord injury prepares for discharge. The client plans to return to work as an editor of children's books. Which adaptive equipment is best for the OTA to recommend the client use to access desktop publishing programs?

Answer Choices:
A. A wrist splint in the functional position with a slot to hold a typing stick.
B. A balanced forearm orthosis with a slot to hold a typing stick.
C. A wrist-driven flexor hinge splint with a slot to hold a typing stick.
D. A dorsal splint with a universal cuff to hold a typing stick.

Correct Answer: C.

Rationale:
A wrist-driven flexor hinge splint (also called a tenodesis splint) is indicated for a C6-level lesion. A dorsal splint with a universal cuff and a wrist splint in the functional position with a slot are very similar choices. Because they can provide the support needed due to the lack of wrist extensors and wrist flexors, they would be useful for a person with a C5 SCI. A person with a C5 SCI can perform keyboarding tasks with a typing stick inserted into a splint or universal cuff. A balanced forearm orthosis (BFO) is used to compensate for upper extremity muscle weakness. BFOs are also called deltoid aids or suspension slings. BFOs and similar equipment solely support the upper extremity and do not provide any option for holding items as a substitute for hand function.

Type of Reasoning: Inferential
One must have knowledge of C6 injury and effective adaptive devices for this level of injury in order to choose the best device to enhance participation in computer skills. This is an inferential reasoning skill where knowledge of the diagnosis coupled with knowledge of the functional ability to use devices with residual upper extremity musculature is key to choosing the correct solution. If answered incorrectly, review SCIs and the adaptive equipment that is typically prescribed for different levels of SCIs. See Chapter 14.

B132 C6

An OTA collaborates with the occupational therapist to plan individual and group activities for a child with oppositional defiant disorder. Which is most important for the OTA to address during group activities?

Answer Choices:
A. The child's willingness to take on a variety of group roles.
B. The child's ability to attend to and complete a task.
C. The child's distorted body image.
D. The child's self-regulation of energy and activity levels.

Correct Answer: B.

Rationale:
Children with oppositional defiant disorder tend to have difficulties with impulse control, attention span, and short-term memory and exhibit argumentative and resentful behaviors. These deficits often affect the ability to complete tasks and can hinder adaptive role functioning. A child does not have to be willing to take on a variety of roles to benefit from group activities. Some find security and stability in the same type of role. This stability can be healthy as long as the role contributes to productive behavior. Distorted body image is typically indicative of anorexia nervosa, bulimia nervosa, or body dysmorphia, not oppositional defiant disorder. Difficulties with energy and activity levels relate more to hyperactivity disorder than to oppositional defiant disorder.

Type of Reasoning: Inductive
This question requires one to recall the typical features of a client with oppositional defiant disorder and then to determine what would be an important skill to address in therapy. This necessitates inductive reasoning skill, where the test taker must couple knowledge of the diagnosis with clinical judgment to arrive at a correct conclusion. For this case, it is most important for the OTA to address the child's ability to attend to and complete a task. If answered incorrectly, review symptoms of oppositional defiant disorder and therapeutic approaches. See Chapter 10.

B133 C6

An OTA provides occupational therapy services in a psychiatric partial hospitalization program (PHP). During a parallel group focused on the development of basic task skills, one of the members appears restless and fidgety. The member gets up and looks out the window for a few minutes and then sits back down and quietly returns to their task. This behavior continues throughout the group. What is the OTA's best response when the group member stands again?

Answer Choices:
A. Tell the group member to remain seated or leave the group.
B. Ask the other members if the group member is bothering them.
C. Say nothing to the group member and proceed with the group.
D. Inform the group member that the observed behaviors indicate a lack of readiness for this group.

Correct Answer: C.

Rationale:
Persons receiving services in a PHP have psychiatric conditions that have been sufficiently stabilized to not require inpatient care; however, they still have symptoms that require active treatment. These symptoms and/or the side effects of medication (e.g., akathisia) can result in a person have difficulty remaining still during a group. This restlessness does not mean that the person cannot benefit from participation in a therapeutic group. Since a parallel group does not require any interaction for task completion, ignoring the person's behavior respects their stage of recovery and enables their continued participation in the group. As long as a group member's behavior is not disturbing or disruptive to the group, they should be allowed to benefit from this form of treatment.

Type of Reasoning: Evaluative
This question requires professional judgment based on guiding principles, which is an evaluative reasoning skill. Because the person is not disturbing the other group members with their behavior, the OTA should say nothing to the person. Questions such as these can be challenging. Thus, determining if the behavior is expected or typical of the person (given their diagnosis and/or its typical treatment) is essential to arriving at a correct conclusion. In a PHP, behaviors that are restless and fidgety are not unusual; therefore, no action needs to be taken. If answered incorrectly, review guidelines for responding to akathisia. See Chapter 13.

B134 C8

An OTA provides consultation services to members of a town chamber of commerce who are interested in improving their businesses' accessibility. Which is the minimum door width that the OTA should recommend to the chamber members as accessible and not requiring modification?

Answer Choices:
A. 30 inches.
B. 32 inches.
C. 34 inches.

Correct Answer: B.

Rationale:
The minimum clearance width for doorways to allow for wheelchair access is 32 inches. Measurements less than 32 inches must be modified. Measurements equal to or greater than 32 inches are acceptable and can be preferable since they allow access for persons who are using bariatric wheel chairs. The focus of this exam item was the minimum width, not the most inclusive.

Type of Reasoning: Deductive
One must recall the minimum clearance width for doorways in order to arrive at a correct conclusion. This requires deductive reasoning skill, where factual knowledge is essential to choosing the correct solution. According to established accessibility standards 32 inches is the minimum clearance for door widths. If answered incorrectly, review accessibility guidelines, especially door-width measurements. See Chapter 15.

B135 C2

In an outpatient rehabilitation clinic, an OTA is working with a high school student with a spinal cord injury at the L1 spinal cord level. The client is a competitive swimmer and is able to transfer independently from the wheelchair to the pool without an assistive device. The client's goal is to learn how to mount and ride a horse. Which is best initial action for the OTA to take to help the client attain this goal?

Answer Choices:
A. Provide transfer training to the client's family members to help them learn how to effectively assist the client in mounting a horse.
B. Develop an upper extremity exercise program for the client to complete each day to develop the strength needed for independent horse mounting.
C. Recommend the client increase their scheduled swimming sessions to include time to practice mounting large inflatable tubes in the pool.
D. Consult with an adaptive riding specialist to discuss alternative methods for persons with disabilities to use when independently mounting a horse.

Correct Answer: D.

Rationale:
Consulting with an adaptive riding specialist would be the best option initially to determine ways in which a person with a disability can mount a horse. Based upon this information, the OTA can collaborate with the client and the occupational therapist to develop an effective intervention plan. This may include interventions to improve balance and strength and/or a direct referral to an adaptive riding program. At this stage of the rehabilitation process, a person with a L1 spinal cord injury will be independent in transfers. Thus, implementing a transfer training program for the family members is not needed. It would also not be an effective approach since mounting a horse has different activity demands than transferring. Since the client is a competitive swimmer upper extremity strength is not a needed focus for intervention. The activity demands of mounting large inflatable tubes in a pool are not the same as the activity demands of mounting a horse. The ability to mount tubes in a pool would not generalize to mounting a horse.

Type of Reasoning: Inductive
For this item, one must determine the best course of action for an individual with a Li SCI. The test taker must have knowledge of the diagnosis and be able to effectively use activity analysis skills to come to a correct conclusion. For this situation, it would be best for the OTA to consult with an adaptive riding specialist to discuss alternative methods for mounting a horse. If answered incorrectly, review information on activity analysis guidelines. The application of this knowledge is required to determine the correct answer. See Chapter 3.

B136 C1

An occupational therapy assistant education program provides an after-school play program for typically developing children to help the OTA students understand development. The students observe a child who is beginning to use blunt scissors to snip paper. The child opens and closes the scissors and moves them in a controlled forward motion, but the child cannot cut circles or figure shapes. At which age are these behaviors typical?

Answer Choices:
A. 2 years old.
B. 3 years old.
C. 4 years old.
D. 5 years old.

Correct Answer: B.

Rationale:
The described activities are typical of 3-year-old children. The behaviors described in this scenario are too advanced for 2-year-old children. While older children can perform the described activities, they typically are cutting circles at 3½–4½ years and cutting simple figure shapes at 4–6 years.

Type of Reasoning: Deductive
One must recall developmental motor milestones of children in order to arrive at a correct conclusion for this question. This necessitates the recall of factual guidelines, which is a deductive reasoning skill. For this scenario, the behaviors described are typical of 3-year-old children. If answered incorrectly, review motor skills and developmental milestones of children, especially skills of 3-year-olds. See Chapter 5.

B137 C6

At the beginning of an occupational therapy activity group, a person receiving electroconvulsive therapy (ECT) treatment expresses concern that their short-term memory loss may make it too difficult to complete tasks. Which should the OTA do in response to the client's stated concerns?

Answer Choices:
A. Inform the person that directions and cues will be provided as needed during the group.
B. Immediately inform the occupational therapist of this symptom development.
C. Tell the person to immediately inform the psychiatrist of this symptom development.
D. Reassure the person that short-term memory loss is a typical response to ECT.

Correct Answer: A.

Rationale:
Short-term memory loss is typical after ECT; therefore, there is no need to immediately inform the occupational therapist or the psychiatrist. However, reassuring the person that this loss is typical does not address the person's concern about being able to complete group tasks. Informing the person that directions and cues will be provided as needed during the group directly addresses the person's expressed concern. The implementation of these interventions will help the individual effectively deal with their memory loss and enable their successful engagement in meaningful activities.

Type of Reasoning: Inductive
This question requires one to determine the best approach for assisting a person who is dealing with short-term memory loss after ECT. This requires inductive reasoning skill, where clinical judgment is paramount to arriving at a correct conclusion. For this situation, the OTA should inform the person that directions and cues will be provided as needed during the group. If answered incorrectly, review effects of ECT treatment on cognitive functioning and compensation strategies for short-term memory loss. The integration of this knowledge is required to answer this question correctly. See Chapter 12 and 13.

B138 C6

A home care hospice OTA works with a client with end-stage non-Hodgkin's lymphoma. The client is very knowledgeable about this illness and has been active in all aspects of its treatment. The client has requested activity ideas to fill the hours while family members are at work and at school. Which activity is best for the OTA to suggest to this client?

Answer Choices:
A. Complete a series of progressive resistive exercises to maintain strength and endurance.
B. Make personalized memory scrapbooks for each family member.
C. Research alternative and complementary medicine approaches on the internet.
D. Prepare an entree and dessert for the family's evening meal.

Correct Answer: B.

Rationale:
One of the main goals of hospice care is to encourage positive life review and support the sharing of the legacy that each person leaves. Creating personal memory scrapbooks can accomplish this goal and help provide a method for the family to remember and share treasured memories while the person is still living. Progressive resistance exercises are contraindicated for someone who is terminally ill and at the end-stage of the illness. These exercises can increase exhaustion. Researching alternative and complementary health care can be beneficial for a person with a terminal illness, but it does not address the need of the person in hospice for closure with significant others. In addition, the efficacy of these approaches for end-stage illness has not been demonstrated. It would be counter-therapeutic to promote an activity that could give false hope. Preparing items for an evening meal can maintain relevant role function, but this activity does not address the end-of-life issues or needs that are the primary focus of hospice care.

Type of Reasoning: Inferential
One must infer or draw conclusions about a likely course of action, given the information presented. This is an inferential reasoning skill, where knowledge of a therapeutic approach, such as activities for persons with terminal illnesses, is essential in choosing a correct solution. In this case, the OTA should suggest making memory scrapbooks for the family. If answered incorrectly, review the intervention approaches for persons in hospice care. See Chapter 13.

B139 C4

An adult with right hemisphere damage resulting from a CVA is referred to occupational therapy. The OTA contributes to the screening and evaluation process. Which deficits will the patient most likely demonstrate upon evaluation?

Answer Choices:
A. Hesitancy and cautiousness during activity performance.
B. Difficulty receiving and processing verbal auditory information.
C. Negative, self-deprecating comments and depression.
D. Difficulty attending to incoming stimuli and interpreting abstract information.

Correct Answer: D.

Rationale:
A patient with a right CVA will have difficulty attending to incoming stimuli and interpreting abstract information. Negative, self-deprecating comments and depression can be evident when a person incurs a disability; these behaviors are not necessarily indicative of a right CVA. Difficulty receiving and processing verbal auditory information are indicative of a left CVA.. The person's behaviors can appear hesitant and cautious due to the performance delays caused by perceptual or motor planning problems that are consistent with a left CVA.

Type of Reasoning: Inferential
This question requires one to draw conclusions based on the information presented, which is an inferential reasoning skill. Questions that ask about what to expect from a diagnosis are essentially asking one to infer information, even though one cannot be 100% sure. In this case, the patient would most likely have difficulty attending to incoming stimuli and interpreting abstract information.. If answered incorrectly, review the typical presentations of right versus left CVA. See Chapter 7.

B140 C8

In an outpatient rehabilitation clinic, an OTA conducts a fall prevention program for at-risk older adult clients with Parkinson's disease. The clients live alone and have had at least three falls within the past six months. Which is the most common risk factor for falls in older adults that the OTA should review with the clients?

Answer Choices:
A. Ascending and descending stairs.
B. Dressing while seated in a chair.
C. Walking with a walker with wheels.
D. Transferring out of the shower with grab bars.

Correct Answer: A.

Rationale:
Most falls occur during normal activities of daily living, including bending, getting up and down from a seated surface, turning, walking, and ascending and descending stairs. Using assistive devices such as a wheeled walker and grab bars in the correct manner reduces fall risk; completing activities of daily living while seated is a safe modification to the activity of dressing.

Type of Reasoning: Inferential
For this question, the test taker must determine the most common risk factors for falls in older adults. This necessitates inferential reasoning skill, where one determines what is likely to be true of a therapeutic situation. For this scenario, ascending and descending stairs are the most common risk factor for falls in older adults. Review fall prevention guidelines if answered incorrectly. See Chapter 15.

B141 C1

A 6-year-old child receiving OT services refuses to work on any project except an airplane model that requires multiple steps for completion. The OTA and the occupational therapist have determined that the child would be unable to complete the model. Which should the OTA do during the next intervention session?

Answer Choices:
A. Allow the child to work on the model and provide maximum assistance as the child completes the project.
B. Explore with the child why completing the model is all the child wants to do and provide alternative project choices.
C. Break the project down into accomplishable segments and instruct the child to complete one segment at a time.
D. Explain to the child several reasons why the selected model is not the best choice for the child and provide alternative project choices.

Correct Answer: C.

Rationale:
The child is in the concrete operational phase of cognitive development according to Piaget. It is best to give specific information with clear guidelines at this age. Allowing someone to do a project or activity that they cannot accomplish is inappropriate. The OTA can use their activity analysis skills to break the model down into achievable steps which allow the child to successfully engage in the activity of interest. The exploration of motivation and the rational explanation of a decision require higher cognitive abilities that are consistent with Piaget's formal operational period, from age 11 through the teen years.

Type of Reasoning: Inductive
Clinical knowledge and judgment are the most important skills needed for answering this question, which is an inductive reasoning skill. An understanding of the cognitive development of a 6-year-old is important in choosing the best solution. In this case, breaking the project down into segments the child can complete and telling the child to complete one segment at a time is the best action. If answered incorrectly, review cognitive development guidelines, especially the concrete operational phase. See Chapter 5.

B142 C7

A 5-year-old child with spina bifida at the C7 level receives home-based occupational therapy services. Which ability is most relevant for the OTA to focus on during intervention?

Answer Choices:
A. Dressing the lower body.
B. Dressing the upper body.
C. Playing tabletop games.

Correct Answer: A.

Rationale:
An individual with a spinal cord lesion at C7 has difficulty dressing the lower extremities. At age 5 years, a child is typically independent in dressing; therefore, an intervention to increase the ability to dress the lower body is age appropriate. An individual with a C7 lesion is independent in upper extremity dressing and tabletop activities; thus, no intervention is warranted.

Type of Reasoning: Inferential
One must determine the most relevant intervention approach for a child given the diagnosis provided. This requires inferential reasoning skill, where one must draw conclusions based on the information presented. In this situation, dressing the lower body is the most relevant intervention. If answered incorrectly, review levels of spinal cord injury and their corresponding functional abilities. Understanding how these capabilities would impact the ADL of children with cervical spina bifida is required to correctly answer this question. See Chapters 7 and 14.

B143 C8

Following an exacerbation of post-polio syndrome, a client is referred to occupational therapy for a wheelchair evaluation to enable independent mobility. The client wears bilateral hip-knee-ankle-foot orthoses (HKAFOs) to provide support during independent transfers and brief standing periods throughout the workday. The client's insurance is Medicare. What is the best seat-width measurement for the OTA to recommend for the client's wheelchair prescription?

Answer Choices:
A. A standard adult seat width to ensure Medicare reimbursement.
B. Two inches wider than the widest point across the individual's hips or thighs.
C. Four inches wider than the widest point across the individual's hips or thighs while wearing orthoses.
D. Two inches wider than the widest point across the individual's hips or thighs while wearing orthoses.

Correct Answer: D.

Rationale:
Two inches wider than the individual's widest measurement with the orthoses on will allow for ease of movement in and out of the chair. If the width of the orthoses is not included in the seat measurement, the chair will be too tight. A standard width adult chair would not meet this individual's needs. Four inches added to the measurement while wearing orthoses would significantly increase the width of the chair. This can complicate mobility in hallways, office spaces, and through doorways. Medicare does reimburse for wheelchairs that are prescribed based upon an individual's measurements.

Type of Reasoning: Inferential
One must have knowledge of HKAFOs and wheelchair prescription guidelines in order to arrive at a correct conclusion. This is an inferential reasoning skill where knowledge of clinical guidelines and judgment based on facts are utilized to reach conclusions. In this situation, the OTA should recommend a seat width two inches wider than the point across the person's hips or thighs while wearing the orthoses. If answered incorrectly, review wheelchair prescription guidelines. See Chapter 15.

B144 C5

An OTA provides home-based services to a neonate with significant developmental delays. Two hours before the next scheduled home visit, the child's parent informs the OTA that one of three older children has developed chickenpox. While the other children do not show signs of chickenpox, the parent expresses concern that they are contagious. Which is the OTA's best response to this situation?

Answer Choices:
A. Cancel the scheduled session and reschedule after two weeks have passed.
B. Complete the scheduled session using airborne precautions.
C. Complete the scheduled session using standard precautions.
D. Complete the scheduled session using droplet precautions.

Correct Answer: B.

Rationale:
There is no need to cancel the scheduled session. Standard precautions are used in all clinical situations. Chickenpox is a disease transmitted by airborne droplet nuclei that remain suspended in the air; therefore, airborne precautions are warranted. Wearing respiratory protection (i.e., a mask) provides sufficient protection. Droplet precautions are used with individuals known or suspected to be infected with serious illness microorganisms transmitted by large particle droplets that can be generated by the person during talking, sneezing, coughing (e.g., rubella, mumps, pertussis, influenza).

Type of Reasoning: Evaluative
One must weigh the possible courses of action and then make a value judgment about the best course to take. This requires evaluative reasoning skill, which often utilizes guiding principles of action in order to arrive at a correct conclusion. In this exam scenario there is the presence of an airborne virus; thus, the OTA should complete the session using airborne precautions. If answered incorrectly, review standard, airborne, and droplet transmission-based precautions. See Appendices 3A and 3B in Chapter 3.

Exam B Answer Rationales 701

B145 C1

A toddler attends an early intervention program as a result of developmental delay. Over the past two weeks, the toddler has successfully completed the activities the OTA has provided in order to develop a palmar grasp. Which action should the OTA take next in response to the child's progress?

Answer Choices:
A. Continue providing the child with the activities to refine palmar grasp.
B. Provide activities to develop an ulnar palmar grasp.
C. Provide activities to develop a radial palmar grasp.
D. Review the initial evaluation with the occupational therapist to determine new goals.

Correct Answer: C.

Rationale:
The child has exhibited mastery of a palmar grasp. The next developmental level of grasp after a palmar grasp is a radial palmar grasp. Ulnar palmar grasp is the developmental precursor to palmar grasp. If the initial evaluation determined there was a need to work on the development of grasp, intervention can proceed to the next level without re-evaluation or the establishment of new goals.

Type of Reasoning: Deductive
One must recall the developmental guidelines for children in development of grasp patterns. This is recall of factual knowledge, which is a deductive reasoning skill. In this case, after development of a palmar grasp, the next level is radial palmar grasp. If answered incorrectly, review development of grasp patterns in children. See Chapter 5.

B146 C2

An OTA constructs a splint for a middle-school aged child who fractured the radius and ulna. The child becomes angry and pushes the OTA as the OTA attempts to mold the splint onto the child's arm. What should the OTA initially do in response to the child's behavior?

Answer Choices:
A. Ignore the behavior and continue with the splint construction.
B. End the session and document the child's behavior.
C. End the session and notify the parents of the child's behavior.
D. Calmly remind the child of acceptable behaviors within a clinical setting.

Correct Answer: D.

Rationale:
The most appropriate initial response is for the OTA to help the child regain control so that they can receive needed services. Providing information to the child on the appropriate behavioral limits of a clinical setting enables the OTA to establish a professional relationship with the child. The child is of sufficient age to understand limit setting. Ending the session is premature because this does not provide the child with the opportunity to modify their behavior and be fitted for the needed splint. Ignoring the behavior would be inappropriate. The child's anger and loss of control must be handled in a direct, non-threatening manner.

Type of Reasoning: Evaluative
One must weigh the possible courses of action and then make a value judgment about the best course to take. This requires evaluative reasoning skill, which often utilizes guiding principles of action in order to arrive at a correct conclusion. For this case, the OTA should calmly remind the child of acceptable behaviors within the clinical setting. If answered incorrectly, review behavioral intervention guidelines and establishing a professional relationship with children. See Chapters 3 and 13.

702   Exam B Answer Rationales

B147 C1

An OTA initiates an intervention session with a child with a diagnosis of traumatic brain injury (TBI). The child presents with extension of both upper extremities and flexion of both lower extremities following a stimulus of neck extension. When informing the supervising occupational therapist of this observation, which is most accurate for the OTA to state?

Answer Choices:
A. The presence of a positive symmetrical tonic neck reflex (STNR), which is normal and not affected by the TBI.
B. The presence of a positive asymmetrical tonic neck reflex (ATNR), which is normal and not affected by the TBI.
C. The presence of positive ATNR, which is abnormal and has reappeared after the TBI.
D. The presence of a positive STNR, which is abnormal and has reappeared after the TBI.

Correct Answer: D.

Rationale:
Symmetrical tonic neck reflex (STNR) is facilitated by flexion of the neck followed by extension of the neck. The response is that flexion of the neck results in bilateral UE flexion with bilateral LE extension. Neck extension results in bilateral UE extension with bilateral LE flexion. Positive reactions are normal up to 4-12 months of age. Positive reactions after twelve months of age are indicative of delayed reflexive maturation or pathology.

Type of Reasoning: Analytical
This question provides symptoms, and the test taker must determine the likely cause for them. This is an analytical reasoning skill, as questions of this nature often ask one to analyze a group of symptoms in order to determine a diagnosis. In this situation, the symptoms indicate positive STNR, an abnormal reflexive response that has reappeared after the TBI. If answered incorrectly review the STNR. See Chapter 5.

B148 C4

An OTA is working with an older adult who is recovering from a CVA, which resulted in right side hemiparesis. Based on contemporary motor learning theory, which purposeful activity is best for the OTA to have the patient perform during intervention to improve right shoulder flexion and horizontal adduction?

Answer Choices:
A. Placing folded towels in the cabinet above the dryer.
B. Dusting the shelves, cabinets, and furniture in the clinic.
C. Playing a game of bingo with other patients with CVAs.
D. Lifting a cane overhead using both upper extremities.

Correct Answer: B.

Rationale:
Contemporary motor learning theory is based on active, repetitive practice of a functional task in order to relearn a motor skill. Dusting shelves, cabinets, and furniture requires both repetitive shoulder flexion and horizontal adduction as the patient works to produce a dust-free surface. Placing towels in an overhead cabinet primarily requires shoulder flexion and limited horizontal adduction. Tabletop tasks, such as bingo, require minimal shoulder movements. Cane exercises provide no meaningful value to a patient. A functional task promotes sustained engagement, which produces greater gains in functional ability.

Type of Reasoning: Inductive
This question requires activity analysis in order to determine the activity that best promotes right shoulder flexion and horizontal adduction and is aligned with contemporary motor learning theory. This is an inductive reasoning skill. For this situation, the OTA should have the patient dust the shelves, cabinets, and furniture in the clinic to promote these shoulder motions. If answered incorrectly, review contemporary motor learning theory guidelines. See Chapter 12.

B149 C7

An OTA and occupational therapist working in an urban school district collaborate with a high school student and the student's parents to establishing transition plan goals. The student has spina bifida. The defective closure of the student's vertebral column is at the L2 level. Which community participation activity should be included as a long-term goal for independent performance in the student's transition plan?

Answer Choices:
A. Traveling via public transportation.
B. Grocery shopping while using a wheeled walker.
C. Using a wheelchair over uneven surfaces.

Correct Answer: A.

Rationale:
A person with spina bifida at the L2 level has full upper extremity range of motion and normal strength, trunk control and balance, and may have some hip, knee, and foot movement. The person typically uses a manual wheelchair for distances and transfers independently. Walking with crutches or braces can be done, although this can be slow and challenging. The transition plan is the section of the individualized education program (IEP) that describes the services and activities needed to prepare for post-secondary life after high school graduation. The transition plan defines the student's long-term goals and outcomes related to their post-school objectives. These may include activities related to post-secondary education, vocational interests, supported employment, life skills, and community participation. While in high school, the student would have been provided transportation to and from school by the school district. Post-graduation, the student will need to be able to use public transportation to facilitate access to community services and participate in desired social activities. A person with an L2-level injury can drive a car adapted with hand controls, but driver education was not an available option in this item. In addition, many persons who live in urban areas forego the expense (e.g., monthly parking fees) and the inconvenience (e.g., scant street parking) of having a car and choose to use public transportation. Grocery shopping while using an assistive mobility device will expend too much energy with this level of spinal bifida. Because a high school student with spina bifida would have lived with this disorder since birth and have received years of therapeutic services, at this point the adolescent with this level of spina bifida would be independent in wheelchair mobility.

Type of Reasoning: Inductive
This question requires one to determine the best long-term goal for a student with spina bifida. This requires knowledge of the diagnosis and functional abilities in order to arrive at a correct conclusion, which necessitates inductive reasoning skill. For this case, traveling via public transportation should be included as part of the transition plan. If answered incorrectly, review information on spina bifida, transition planning, and community mobility. The integration of this knowledge is required to determine the correct answer. See Chapters 4, 7 and 15.

B150 C2

Several residents of a skilled nursing facility report that they are bored with their individual daily range-of-motion exercise programs. The OTA collaborates with the occupational therapist to design a group to attain the goals of the individual exercise programs. Which would be most beneficial for the OTA to recommend incorporating into the proposed group?

Answer Choices:
A. Several exercise videos with diverse exercise styles and music.
B. The residents performing gentle range of motion on each other.
C. Exercises in rhythm to a marching band video.
D. The provision of coffee and cake after the group.

Correct Answer: A.

Rationale:
Adding variety can stimulate interest and socialization. Group members can select videos that are of personal interest. Clients should not do hands-on treatment with each other. Moreover, passive range of motion is contraindicated for many diagnoses. A marching band video may be at a tempo that is too vigorous for some residents. Providing coffee and cake does not address the need to increase interest in performing daily ROM exercises.

Type of Reasoning: Inductive
One must utilize clinical knowledge and judgment to determine the exercise approach that best addresses the residents' concerns. In this case, providing several exercise videos with diverse styles and music is best. If answered incorrectly, review principles for using therapeutic activities. The application of this knowledge is needed to determine the correct answer. See Chapter 3.

B151 C3

An OTA works with a survivor of a house fire. The client has burns on both hands that limit thumb mobility. The client identifies a personal goal of being able to pick up and hold cans to enable independent shopping and meal preparation activities. The OTA collaborates with the occupational therapist to establish a long-term goal for the client. Which movement of the thumb should the goal statement include as the desired functional outcome?

Answer Choices:
A. CMC palmar abduction.
B. CMC extension.
C. MCP flexion.

Correct Answer: A.

Rationale:
CMC palmar abduction is the major movement required of the thumb to pick up cans. CMC extension places the thumb in a hitchhiking position, which makes picking up a can very difficult. MCP flexion alone will not expand the web space to pick up a can.

Type of Reasoning: Analytical
This question provides a description of a functional activity and the test taker must determine the major movement that is required in performing this functional activity. This is an analytical reasoning skill, as questions of this nature often ask one to analyze functional skills to determine the overall skill involved. In this situation, the functional activity is performed using CMC palmar abduction and this should be the focus of the long-term goal. If answered incorrectly, review movement patterns of the thumb. See Chapter 6.

B152 C4

An OTA working in a school system conducts a series of educational workshops for parents of children with attention deficit and sensory processing disorders. The series focuses on principles of sensory integration (SI). Which of the following are most beneficial for the OTA to recommend the parents provide in the home environment? Select the three BEST responses.

Answer Choices:
A. Sensory input that is child-driven, play-based, and responsive to the child's preferences.
B. A balance between structure and freedom so the child can direct their own actions.
C. Minimal auditory, visual, and tactile sensory stimuli to decrease distractibility and responsivity.
D. Adjustable lighting and sound systems to accommodate the child's ability to modulate stimuli.
E. Clear directions and structured limits to organize behavior and promote adaptive responses.
F. A wide range of auditory, visual, and tactile stimuli to increase awareness and responsivity.

Correct Answers: A, B, and D.

Rationale:
A key principle of SI theory is to structure the environment to match the child's capabilities. This 'just right' environment provides a balance between structure and freedom which enables the child to direct their own activity participation. This can then facilitate skill development. Because children with sensory processing disorders seek out sensorimotor experiences that have an organizing effect, sensory input should be child-driven and play-based. Sensory processing disorders may present along a continuum of under-responsivity (hyposensitivity) to over- responsivity (hypersensitivity) of multi-sensory processing and sensory seeking. Environments and activities must be tailored to the specific child. Therefore, lighting and sound should be adjustable to accommodate the child's ability to modulate stimuli. The design of an environment to increase awareness or to decrease distractibility is more consistent with a compensatory remediation approach. Providing structure and limits is more consistent with a behavioral approach.

Type of Reasoning: Inferential
One must have knowledge of attention deficit and sensory processing disorders and sensory integration guidelines in order to arrive at correct conclusions. This is an inferential reasoning skill where knowledge of clinical guidelines and judgment based on facts are utilized to reach conclusions. If answered incorrectly, review sensory integration treatment guidelines for children with attention deficit and sensory processing disorders. See Chapters 7 and 12.

B153 C8

The family of a two-year-old in a spica cast asks the OTA to modify the child's car seat. The child can no longer easily fit in the car seat due to the cast. Which action is best for the OTA to take in response to this request?

Answer Choices:
A. Pad the area between the car seat and the child's back with a pillow to accommodate for the lack of hip flexion.
B. Recommend the family purchase a car seat designed for a child with a spica cast.
C. Cut down the sides of the car seat to allow the cast to hang off the sides of the car seat.
D. Tell the family to use the current car seat and tighten up the straps to hold in the child.

Correct Answer: B.

Rationale:
The child needs a crash-tested car seat adapted for a child in a spica cast. A variety of specialized car seats are available. OTAs and other pediatric care providers can become trained in fitting specialized car seats. Padding the area between the child and the car seat and cutting the car seat would invalidate the warranty and is unsafe. If the child cannot fit in the car seat, it is not safe. A car seat cannot be made safer by tightening the strap.

Type of Reasoning: Inductive
The test taker must determine the safest course of action in this scenario, which requires clinical judgment; this is an inductive reasoning skill. Being able to predict what may happen as a result of such actions, the test taker should conclude that purchasing a car seat made for a child with a spica cast is the best and safest choice.

B154 C4

An OTA works in a pediatric clinic for children with sensory processing disorder. Two parents report that their child struggles every morning during dressing. While being dressed and afterwards, the child cries and fidgets. The OTA collaborates with the occupational therapist to design therapeutic activities that will decrease tactile sensitivity. Which activity is best for the OTA to have the child do during intervention sessions to decrease tactile defensive behaviors?

Answer Choices:
A. Match picture cards of clothing to the corresponding body parts.
B. Walk on uneven surfaces, such as mats, wedges, and bean bags.
C. Pop bubble wrap placed on the floor with the feet.
D. Rub different textured toys on the arms and legs.

Correct Answer: D.

Rationale:
Tactile sensitivity and defensive behaviors are commonly associated with sensory processing disorders. The feeling of clothing against skin can be aversive and uncomfortable. Activities that provide a variety of textures for the child to rub on the skin (as tolerated) will help the child gradually increase comfort level with different textures. This graded exposure can make dressing a less stressful experience. Matching cards primarily addresses cognitive skills; walking on uneven surfaces involves the vestibular system; and popping bubble wrap with the feet engages the proprioceptive system.

Type of Reasoning: Inductive
For this question, the test taker must utilize knowledge of sensory processing disorders and tactile defensiveness intervention approaches to arrive at a correct conclusion. This is an inductive reasoning skill, in which clinical judgment is used to draw conclusions. For this case, the OTA should have the child rub different textured toys on the arms and legs to decrease tactile sensitivity. If answered incorrectly, review sensory processing disorders and intervention approaches for tactile defensiveness. See Chapters 7, 12, and 13.

B155 C2

A client is admitted to a skilled nursing facility (SNF) following a fall that resulted in a concussion. Upon evaluation, the occupational therapist noted cognitive changes resulting in difficulty sequencing tasks and short-term memory impairment. The therapist and OTA decide that an analysis of the client's current activity performance based on an occupation-based approach would help guide the intervention plan. Which method is best for the OTA to use when completing this activity analysis?

Answer Choices:
A. Interview the client about how routine tasks are typically completed.
B. Assess the client's performance components using a standardized measure.
C. Provide the client with a structured task that is broken down into subtasks.
D. Observe the client complete a typical ADL morning routine in the client's room.

Correct Answer: D.

Rationale:
An occupation-based approach to activity analysis involves observing people as they complete desired occupations within their natural environment. Because it is not always possible to observe clients in their homes, OT practitioners should simulate the natural environment as close as possible. Since the client was admitted to an SNF, observing the client complete a typical morning ADL routine is acceptable, despite it not being at home. Information gathered upon completion of an occupation-based activity analysis can then be used to decide how the identified strengths can be used to support performance and how the identified limitations can be remediated through skill development, compensation, and/or modifications to the activity or its context/environment. Interviewing the client about how routine tasks are typically completed can provide helpful insights to the client's habits and routines, but it is not a method of activity analysis. Likewise, the assessment of the client's performance components using a standardized measure will provide useful information about the client's assets and deficits, but it is not a method of activity analysis. Providing the client with a structured task that is broken down into subtasks can be a helpful form of intervention, which can be based on the information gained from an occupation-based activity analysis.

Type of Reasoning: Inductive
This question requires one to apply knowledge of occupation-based approaches in order to arrive at a correct conclusion. This necessitates clinical judgment, which is an inductive reasoning skill. For this situation, the OTA should observe the client completing a typical ADL morning routine in the client's room. If answered incorrectly, review information on activity analysis and occupation-based approaches. See Chapter 3.

B156 C8

A middle school student with Duchenne muscular dystrophy is being evaluated for a power wheelchair. Which is the most important area for the occupational therapist and OTA to evaluate first to determine the student's readiness for the wheelchair?

Answer Choices:
A. Postural control.
B. Fine motor skills.
C. Cognitive skills.

Correct Answer: C.

Rationale:
Cognitive skills include alertness, spatial operations, judgment, decision making, and problem solving, which can be affected by depression. Since these abilities are needed for the safe operation of a power wheelchair, it is essential that the OTA and occupational therapist assess the student's cognitive level. Fine motor skills and postural control are likely absent due to the progression of Duchenne muscular dystrophy. Wheelchair adaptations can compensate for decreased fine motor skills and poor postural control.

708   Exam B Answer Rationales

Type of Reasoning: Inferential
One must determine the critical skills that need to be assessed prior to providing a power wheelchair. This requires inferential reasoning, where one must infer or draw conclusions based on the information provided. In this situation, the student should be assessed for cognitive skills, as this is the most important element in determining the safe and effective use of the device. If answered incorrectly, review wheelchair prescription guidelines. See Chapter 15.

B157 C2

An OTA conducts a caregiver education workshop on positioning techniques for family caregivers. At the conclusion of the class, the caregivers will be expected to utilize the skills taught. Which is the most effective method for the OTA to use when teaching these techniques?

Answer Choices:
A. OTA demonstration of general techniques followed by individualized discussion with each caregiver.
B. An oral multimedia presentation including PowerPoint slides and handouts of positioning techniques for diverse disorders.
C. OTA demonstration of techniques followed by a lab with caregivers practicing positioning on each other.
D. A question and answer session to address the specific individual positioning concerns of the caregivers.

Correct Answer: C.

Rationale:
A variety of teaching methods including demonstration, practice, and discussion has the best chance of reinforcing learning in a diverse group. Using only oral teaching methods will likely not enable the participants to develop the needed positioning skills. Psychomotor skills are best learned by practice, not lecture or question and answer. Feedback should include both knowledge of performance and knowledge of results.

Type of Reasoning: Inferential
One must infer to draw a conclusion about the best approach for educating a group of individuals. Because the group may have differing needs and abilities in learning information, one must provide a variety of approaches to delivering the information. Inferential reasoning requires one to use knowledge of therapeutic approaches to determine which approach will result in the most effective outcome. For this case, demonstration of the techniques by the OTA and the caregivers practicing the techniques on each other is most effective. If answered incorrectly, review principles of teaching-learning. See Chapter 3.

B158 C3

A child is referred to occupational therapy because of hand fatigue during handwriting and difficulty managing clothing fasteners, such as buttons and zippers. Upon evaluation, the occupational therapist determined that the child has undeveloped hand arches and a closed web space. Which activity is best for the OTA to use to facilitate an open web space?

Answer Choices:
A. Walking across the floor like a crab and a bear.
B. Playing on the monkey bars in the school playground.
C. Using both hands to roll cookie dough into snake shapes.
D. Coloring a vertically mounted picture using finger paint.

Correct Answer: B.

Rationale:
An open web space is created when the thumb opposes the index finger and creates a space between both. A child compensates for a closed web space by grasping objects harder than necessary, which leads to hand fatigue and poor hand dexterity. Grasping the round monkey bars on playground equipment inherently opens the web space while developing hand arches and strength. The other activity choices are completed using a flat palm and do not facilitate arch development.

Type of Reasoning: Analytical
This question requires one to analyze the various intervention approaches and determine the approach that will best promote an open web space of the hands and develop hand arches. This requires analytical reasoning skill. For this case, having the child play on the monkey bars on the school playground will promote these aspects. If answered incorrectly, review principles of activity analysis and hand anatomy. The integration of this knowledge is required to determine the correct answer. See Chapters 3 and 6.

B159 C2

An individual with borderline personality disorder is admitted to the hospital following a suicide attempt. After attending an OT orientation group, the patient tells the OTA, "You are the only therapist who has ever been really helpful." The patient asks to meet with the OTA privately on a regular basis instead of the assigned primary individual therapist. Which action is best for the OTA to take in response to the patient's request?

Answer Choices:
A. Refer the patient to the assigned primary individual therapist.
B. Agree to meet with the patient since a positive therapeutic connection has been expressed.
C. Tell the patient that an OTA provides only occupation-based group treatment.
D. Explain that this type of manipulative behavior is not acceptable.

Correct Answer: A.

Rationale:
The patient must be referred to the primary individual therapist assigned to their case. Although the patient has responded favorably to the initial OT group session, this does not preclude the patient's need for individual therapy. On inpatient psychiatric units, OT practitioners often serve as primary individual therapists in addition to their group therapist role. However, the assignment of caseloads is not (and cannot be) based upon patients' requests. Labeling the individual's behavior as manipulative is judgmental and can be considered antagonistic.

Type of Reasoning: Evaluative
This question requires professional judgment based on guiding principles, which is an evaluative reasoning skill. For this situation, the OTA should refer the person to the primary individual therapist for individual therapy. If answered incorrectly, review individual versus group therapy guidelines for inpatient psychiatric settings. See Chapters 3 and 13.

710 Exam B Answer Rationales

B160 C4

An OTA is instructing a patient who had a left CVA on how to lock the brakes on a wheelchair. The patient is right-handed. Their right upper extremity has partial paralysis. Based on the motor learning theory, which is the best intervention approach for the OTA to use when instructing the person to lock the right brake?

Answer Choices:
A. Practice with the left hand first and then with the right.
B. Show the person how to use an extension brake.
C. Practice the locking motions with both hands simultaneously.
D. Have the patient use the left hand to assist the right hand.

Correct Answer: A.

Rationale:
The motor learning approach acknowledges the importance of practice and repetition. When the patient practices with the left hand first and then the right, transfer of learning is promoted. Adapting the wheelchair to have an extension brake and then showing the person how to use the brake is a method used in a compensatory model of intervention. Using the left hand to assist the right hand is also a compensatory approach. These actions negate the person's ability to practice and acquire the skill, a core component of motor learning theory. Practicing with both hands simultaneously is more challenging than practicing with one hand at a time.

Type of Reasoning: Analytical
In this scenario, the test taker must identify the therapeutic approach to teaching an individual how to lock the wheelchair that follows the principles of motor learning theory. This requires analysis of the different approaches in order to determine the one approach that meets motor learning theory guidelines. For this situation, practicing with the left hand first, followed by the right hand, is most aligned with this theory. Review motor learning theory guidelines if answered incorrectly. See Chapter 12.

B161 C4

An OTA working on a trauma unit is assigned a patient with a traumatic brain injury (TBI). The patient's TBI was assessed as a 6 on the Glasgow Coma Scale (GCS), with each of the three GCS components scoring a two. Which is best for the OTA to use when initiating intervention with this person?

Answer Choices:
A. Demonstrated directions.
B. Sensory stimulation.
C. Verbal cues.
D. Hand-over-hand assistance.

Correct Answer: B.

Rationale:
The Glasgow Coma Scale rates a person's eye opening, motor responses, and verbal responses.
The scale scores range from 3 (i.e., a person in a deep coma) to 15 (i.e., a fully awake person). A total score of six on the Glasgow Coma Scale is just one level above a completely non-responsive coma. At this level, a person has severe deficits. They can open their eyes in response to pain, extend in response to pain, and make incomprehensible sounds. At this level, intervention should begin at the sensory stimulation level. The other choices are at levels that are too high for this individual.

Type of Reasoning: Inferential
One must determine the most likely intervention approach for a person, given the diagnosis provided and level of functioning. This requires inferential reasoning skill, where one must draw conclusions based on the information presented. In this situation, the OTA should begin with sensory stimulation, given the score of 6 on the Glasgow Coma Scale. If answered incorrectly, review the Glasgow Coma Scale and intervention activities for individuals with TBIs. See Chapters 7 and 12.

B162 C1

An OTA collaborates with an occupational therapist to design intervention activities for an 18-month-old toddler with multiple developmental disabilities. The child has been assessed as delayed by 6 - 8 months in all developmental parameters. Which intervention approach is most effective for developing the toddler's play skills?

Answer Choices:
A. The use of toys that encourage creative play.
B. The use of toys that are visually and auditorily stimulating.
C. Participation in a small parallel play group.
D. Engagement in activities that use sensorimotor skills prerequisite to play.

Correct Answer: B.

Rationale:
Providing toys that are visually and auditorily stimulating will help engage the child in the intervention process. As the child explores the sensory properties and characteristics of these toys, they will engage in activities that will facilitate developmentally appropriate play. Through this process, the child will develop sensorimotor and cognitive skills. Many toys that provide visual and auditory stimulation also provide opportunities to explore relationships between actions and objects (e.g., striking a colorful keyboard to produce music). The exploration of relationships between actions and consequences is typical of the cognitive development of a 10–12-month-old, which is this child's developmental age. Creative play occurs developmentally at 4–7 years, so this option is not developmentally appropriate for this child. Placing a toddler with the developmental age of a 10–12-month-old into a parallel play group is not age appropriate. Engaging the child in activities that use sensorimotor skills prerequisite to play would not achieve the stated aim of developing play skills. It is more effective to directly use play activities during intervention to develop play skills.

Type of Reasoning: Inferential
One must infer or draw conclusions about a likely course of action, given the information presented. This is an inferential reasoning skill, where knowledge of a therapeutic approach is essential in choosing a correct solution. In this case, the OTA would likely initiate intervention with toys that are visually and auditorily stimulating, given the child's diagnosis and delays. If answered incorrectly, review the developmental milestones of play. See Chapter 5.

B163 C3

An adult incurred a fracture of the right proximal humerus and is using a shoulder immobilizer for the first two weeks to aid healing and help control pain. The patient is right-hand dominant. They are referred to occupational therapy for interventions to enable independent ADL performance. Which activity will be the most difficult for the patient?

Answer Choices:
A. Putting on a pullover top.
B. Washing their hair.
C. Taking off a heavy coat.
D. Brushing their teeth.

Correct Answer: A.

Rationale:
Treatment of a proximal fracture of the humerus includes non-operative treatment using a sling or shoulder immobilizer with no shoulder mobility for the first two weeks, followed by either exercises to slowly increase the range of motion or surgery. Because there is a period of immobilization, patients need to learn how to complete ADL using modified techniques. While the person could use a one-handed technique to don a pullover top, this would put too much strain on the upper extremity and may cause increased pain. A safer alternative to dressing the upper body is to wear tops with front opening closures (i.e., zippers, buttons, or snaps). Because coats have front openings, taking off a winter coat would not pose the greatest difficulty. The patient can learn one-handed techniques to brush their teeth and wash their hair.

Type of Reasoning: Inferential
This question requires one to infer what is likely to be true of a therapeutic situation based on knowledge of the diagnosis and functional limitations. Questions of this nature require inferential reasoning skill. For this case, based on knowledge of the limitations with recent humeral fractures, donning a pullover top would present the most difficulty for this patient. If answered incorrectly, review principles of activity analysis and shoulder anatomy. The integration of this knowledge is required to determine the correct answer. See Chapters 3 and 6.

B164 C5

An adult is receiving outpatient occupational therapy for Dupuytren's disease. The client is 250 pounds overweight and seriously deconditioned. The client uses a motorized scooter for functional mobility and has recently been diagnosed with Type 2 diabetes. The OTA meets with the occupational therapist to revise the intervention plan to address the functional implications of the client's additional diagnoses. Which techniques are most important for the OTA and therapist to include as a focus for client education in a revised intervention plan?

Answer Choices:
A. Blood sugar monitoring.
B. Skin care and inspection.
C. Edema reduction.

Correct Answer: B.

Rationale:
People who have diabetes have a propensity to develop wounds. Obesity and deconditioning are also risk factors for wounds. The most effective intervention for wounds is to prevent them from developing. Thus, it is essential for the person to learn techniques for skin care and inspection. Additional relevant interventions to prevent wounds include teaching the person weight-shifting techniques. The use of a scooter cushion and a pressure-relief bed aid can also prevent wounds by distributing pressure over a larger skin surface. While it is vital for the person to learn techniques for monitoring their blood sugar, it is standard practice for these techniques to be taught upon diagnosis by medical staff. Although interventions to reduce edema are indicated for persons with Dupuytren's disease, revising the intervention plan to include these techniques is not needed in this case. In this exam item, Dupuytren's disease is identified as the original diagnosis for which the person is receiving outpatient occupational therapy. Thus, approaches to reduce edema should have been included in the initial intervention plan.

Type of Reasoning: Evaluative
This question requires one to weigh the merits of each of the possible foci for client education, which is an evaluative reasoning skill. After considering the person's diagnoses and their risk factors, the test-taker should determine that revising the intervention plan to include educating the client about techniques for skin care and inspection is most important. If answered incorrectly, review risk factors for wounds and strategies for wound prevention. See Chapter 9.

B165 C4

A sensory profile completed by a caregiver indicates that an elementary school-aged child has modulation impairments and sensation-seeking patterns. The OTA observes the child frequently wandering, bumping objects in the room, and fidgeting. The child has low muscle tone. The OTA collaborates with the occupational therapist to develop an intervention plan. Which is the best intervention approach for the OTA and therapist to use to improve this child's deficits?

Answer Choices:
A. Strategies to increase random sensory input and encourage high physical activity at home.
B. An obstacle course that requires diverse movements for varied proprioceptive and tactile input.
C. Sensory experiences that focus on body awareness and grading control during play activities.
D. A sensory diet that includes controlled sensory input integrated into the child's daily routine.

Correct Answer: D.

Rationale:
The use of skilled clinical observation is important when evaluating and planning intervention for children with sensory processing deficits. Because they create sensation for themselves, their behavior tells us what sensory input they need. Children who rock and fidget require vestibular input to help them attend and learn. Children with proprioceptive problems often rely on visual and/or verbal cues to know how to move their bodies, and they often appear clumsy or bump into objects in their environments. It is important to provide caregivers with a written sensory diet to implement on a daily basis in the child's home and school environments to facilitate carryover.

Type of Reasoning: Inductive
This question requires one to draw upon knowledge of effective therapy processes in order to determine the best approach for this child. This requires inductive reasoning skill. In this situation, the therapist and OTA should provide a sensory diet that includes controlled sensory input to integrate into the child's daily routine at home and school. If answered incorrectly, review sensory integration and sensory modulation guidelines. See Chapter 12.

B166 C8

A religious congregation obtained private funding to build a ramp so that members with disabilities can attend services. The entrance to the congregation's building has six steps with a rise of seven inches each. Which is best for the OTA consultant to recommend for construction of this ramp?

Answer Choices:
A. 42 feet long.
B. 48 feet long.
C. 42 feet long with a 5′ × 5′ landing at the ramp's midpoint.
D. 48 feet long with a 5′ × 5′ landing at the ramp's midpoint.

Correct Answer: C.

Rationale:
A ramp should provide one foot of slope for every one inch of rise. Six steps that have a rise of seven inches results in a total rise of 42 inches. A 42-foot ramp may be too long for some individuals to independently access. Therefore, a landing at the ramp's midpoint would be best to allow the opportunity to safely take a rest break. Current ADA guidelines indicate that landings must be 5' by 5' (prior guidelines set landings at 4' by 4').

Type of Reasoning: Deductive
One must recall the guidelines for ramp construction in order to choose a correct solution. This is recall of factual knowledge, which is a deductive reasoning skill. For this scenario, construction of the ramp should be 42 feet long with a 5' × 5' landing at the ramp midpoint. If answered incorrectly, review ramp construction guidelines of the International Code Council's accessibility standards. See Chapter 15.

B167 C6

An occupational therapist and an OTA provide consultation services to a parent support group for elementary school-aged children with autism spectrum disorder (ASD). The parents express concern that they have begun to limit community-based family activities due to the difficulties their children with ASD often have in public places. They are concerned that these self-imposed constraints to decrease their stress may negatively impact their child with ASD and their relationships with their siblings. Which community-based family activity is best to recommend to the parents?

Answer Choices:
A. Have dinner at a national chain restaurant which has an on-site playground.
B. Attend an outdoor musical festival which features performances for children.
C. Attend a 'sensory friendly' showing of a children's movie at a local theatre.
D. Go to a water park and have the children go on the slower 'lazy river' rides.

Correct Answer: C.

Rationale:
Children with ASD typically have difficulties with sensory processing, sensory modulation, self-regulation, and social interaction. When determining the best community-based activity to recommend to families with children with ASD, the therapist and OTA must consider the sensory and social demands of the environment and the activity. Sensory considerations relevant to the behaviors associated with ASD include the level of visual, auditory, proprioceptive, and vestibular stimulation. Social considerations include the demand for social interactions beyond the children's comfort zone and the potential for stigmatizing responses from the public, if behaviors that are deemed 'inappropriate' are displayed. 'Sensory friendly' showings of children's movies are specifically designed to accommodate children with ASD and other diagnoses which result in sensory processing deficits. During the movie, the house lights stay on and the sound is modulated to not be too loud. Over-stimulating advertisements are not played. The social environment is safe and accepting. Audience members are able to dance, twirl, walk, shout, sing, and hum. Behaviors that are often deemed unacceptable in other social settings are accepted without judgment. Each child's uniqueness is embraced. This enables all family members to enjoy a social leisure activity without environmentally-induced stress. In contrast, the other activity options have sensory and social aspects that could cause difficulties for a child with ASD. These could contribute to family stress and not enable an enjoyable family activity. Outdoor music festivals can be crowded and loud. National chain restaurants are typically brightly lit and noisy with many people coming and going in close proximity. The playgrounds in these restaurants also tend to be over-stimulating to the visual, auditory, tactile, proprioceptive, and vestibular systems. While a slow ride in a water park could be calming, the overall social environment of a waterpark can be over-stimulating. Typically, these parks require waits on lines in close proximity of others. Most important, once people are on a ride, they are on it for the ride's duration. The inability to leave if a child is having difficulty would not be conducive to decreasing family stress.

Type of Reasoning: Inductive
For this question, the test taker must determine the best community-based activity for a family with a child with autism spectrum disorder (ASD). This requires clinical judgment, which is an inductive reasoning skill. In this case, the best activity would be to attend a 'sensory friendly' children's movie at a local theatre. If answered incorrectly, review intervention guidelines for children with sensory processing disorders and ASD. See Chapters 12 and 13.

B168 C4

A client recovering from a traumatic brain injury reports frequently losing place when reading. Upon evaluation, the client exhibits difficulty with the letter cancellation task. When reviewing the evaluation results with the occupational therapist, which visual ability should the OTA report as deficient?

Answer Choices:
A. Scanning.
B. Imagery.
C. Memory.

Correct Answer: A.

Rationale:
The behaviors described relate to the ability to scan. Visual imagery is the process of making a mental picture of information so that it can be remembered. Visual memory is the retrieval and recall of information that has been stored and encoded.

Type of Reasoning: Analytical
This question provides symptoms of a deficit and the test taker must determine what these symptoms indicate. This requires analytical reasoning skill, where one must consider all of the pieces of information provided and draw conclusions about what that means as a whole. In this situation, the symptoms indicate deficits in visual scanning ability. If answered incorrectly, review the definitions of visual perceptual skills and the symptoms of visual perceptual deficits. See Chapter 12.

B169 C7

A child in fifth grade is having difficulty self-feeding and frequently spills beverages. The student has non-spastic cerebral palsy resulting in fluctuating muscle tone and poor motor control. Which is best for the OTA to recommend the student use to improve independence in self-feeding and minimize spillage?

Answer Choices:
A. A sippy cup.
B. Both hands to hold the cup.
C. A cup with a handle.
D. A straw.

Correct Answer: D.

Rationale:
Using a straw to drink from a cup is an easy and age-appropriate adaptation to prevent spills. A sippy cup is developmentally inappropriate for a 10-year-old child and should only be used if there is no age-appropriate alternative. Fluctuating muscle tone will result in the muscles relaxing and contracting involuntarily, making purposeful movements difficult to control. Using both hands to hold a cup or using a cup with a handle may not prevent spills secondary to the child's fluctuating muscle tone.

716   Exam B Answer Rationales

Type of Reasoning: Inductive
For this question, the test taker must utilize clinical judgment to determine the best feeding recommendation for a child with cerebral palsy. This requires knowledge of the diagnosis and adaptive methods in order to arrive at a correct conclusion. In this situation, it is best to recommend that the child use a straw, which will reduce the likelihood of spilling liquids when drinking. If answered incorrectly, review adaptive feeding equipment. See Chapter 14.

B170 C7

An OTA is working with a college-aged patient who incurred a complete C2 SCI. The patient has expressed a desire to resume valued life roles. During intervention, which is best for the OTA to train the patient to use to attain this stated goal?

Answer Choices:
A. Iris recognition software for computer access.
B. A mouth stick for computer operation.
C. Adaptive equipment for bathing.
D. Adaptive equipment for dressing.

Correct Answer: A.

Rationale:
People who have a C1–C3 complete SCI will have limited head and neck control depending on muscle strength. They will require complete personal assistance for all personal care tasks; thus, training in the use of adaptive equipment is not indicated. Iris recognition software will allow a patient with a complete C2 SCI to control a computer through movement of the eyes, instead of using a hand to operate a mouse. A mouth stick would be useful to a person with a C4-level SCI, as it can compensate for lack of functional elbow flexion or hand control. Training in mouth stick use can enable a person with a C4 SCI to operate a computer and turn pages of a book.

Type of Reasoning: Inductive
This question requires one to utilize clinical judgment in order to determine the best approach for a patient with a C2 SCI. This necessitates inductive reasoning skill where clinical judgment and knowledge of the diagnosis are paramount to arriving at a correct conclusion. For this scenario, the OTA should train the patient to use iris recognition software for computer access. See Chapter 14.

B171 C4

During an intervention session focused on developing home management skills, a client made a grocery list. The client grouped needed items together to make shopping easier and listed eggs separately from all of the other items. When explaining how the list was composed, the client stated, "Eggs break, they should be on top." Which of the following is the most accurate for the OTA to report that the client's approach to this task represents?

Answer Choices:
A. Diminished insight.
B. Concrete thinking.
C. Anosognosia.

Correct Answer: B.

Rationale:
The statement reflects concrete thinking which is concerned with the actual properties of things and the realities of situations, rather than abstract properties or situational potentialities. In this situation, it is a functional strength. Insight is an awareness and understanding of oneself and behavior. Anosognosia is unawareness or denial of deficits.

Type of Reasoning: Analytical
This question provides a description of a behavior and the test taker must determine the definition of the behavior displayed. This requires analytical reasoning skill where one must analyze the behavior in order to correctly determine the appropriate behavioral characteristic. In this situation, the behavior indicates concrete thinking.

B172 C4

An OTA is providing intervention for an individual recovering from a CVA who has residual body inattention. The OTA is using a deficit-specific approach to intervention. Which of the following should the OTA provide to this client during intervention sessions? Select the three BEST responses.

Answer Choices:
A. Guidance of the client's affected side through activities.
B. Increased sensory stimulation to the affected side.
C. Unilateral activities using the affected upper extremity.
D. Unilateral activities using the non-affected upper extremity.
E. Bilateral activities using both upper extremities.
F. Tasks that require right/left discrimination.

Correct Answers: A, B, and E.

Rationale:
According to a deficit-specific approach, interventions for body inattention (often called neglect) should include bilateral activities, increased sensory stimulation to the affected side, and guidance of the affected extremity during activity performance. Providing unilateral activities does not work on the identified deficits. The provision of tasks that require discrimination of right/left is indicated for spatial relations dysfunction.

Type of Reasoning: Deductive
One must recall the guidelines for use of a deficit-specific approach for body inattention. This is recall of factual knowledge, which is a deductive reasoning skill. In this situation, the most appropriate activities for the OTA to use under this approach are bilateral activities with increased sensory stimulation and guidance provided to the affected extremity. If answered incorrectly, review a deficit-specific approach to treatment of CVA. See Chapter 12.

B173 C1

An OTA is treating an 8-month-old child with mild developmental delay. The child exhibits normal cognitive development. The child has developed adequate static sitting balance but has poor dynamic sitting balance. The OTA implements intervention by positioning the child and having the child find a toy that is covered with a cloth. Which positioning and toy placement are most beneficial for the OTA to use with this child?

Answer Choices:
A. Sit the child between the OTA's extended legs and alternate placing the covered toy to the child's right and left side.
B. Sit the child in a child seat and alternate placing the covered toy to the child's right and left side.
C. Lay the child in a prone position and place the covered toy in front of the child.
D. Lay the child on their right side and place the covered toy to the left of the child.

Correct Answer: A.

Rationale:
Having the child sit between the OTA's extended legs can enable the OTA to easily provide postural support to the child as needed. Placing the covered toy to the right and then left of the seated child will facilitate the child's sideward protective extension response. Sideward protective extension in sitting is a functional, protective reaction that typically occurs at seven months and persists in normal development. Sideward protective extension is a key component to the development of dynamic sitting balance as it protects the child from a fall. This reaction also supports the body for unilateral use of the opposite arm. Sitting the child in a child seat would provide too much support and would not provide the child with the 'just-right' challenge to develop dynamic sitting balance. Laying the child in a prone position and placing the covered toy in front of the child would help facilitate a prone-on-elbows position. If the child has begun to sit, this position would have already been mastered so this intervention is not needed. Laying the child on their right side and placing the covered toy to the left of the child would facilitate rolling. If the child has begun to sit, rolling would have already been mastered so this intervention is not needed.

Type of Reasoning: Inferential
One must recall the developmental milestones of infants and infer the best choice for positioning in order to choose the correct solution. For this child, who just achieved static sitting balance, positioning that provides postural support during dynamic sitting activity with facilitation of the protective extensive response is most beneficial because this skill is essential for dynamic sitting. If answered incorrectly, review the motor developmental milestones of infants. See Chapter 5.

B174 C6

An OTA implements a sensorimotor group for six individuals with serious mental illness (SMI). According to the sensorimotor approach, which activity is best for the OTA to include in the group?

Answer Choices:
A. A discussion about favorite physical activities.
B. Relaxation activities.
C. Tai chi.
D. Parachute games.

Correct Answer: D.

Rationale:
Parachute games are consistent with the sensorimotor approach as described by King and Ross. This approach uses activities that are spontaneous, fun, 'noncortical', and do not require the individuals to think about the steps needed to complete the activity. Activities that use active, gross motor movements such as parachute games are often used. Discussion, relaxation activities, and tai chi can be relevant interventions to include in a program for persons with SMI, but they do not meet the criteria of a sensorimotor group.

Type of Reasoning: Inferential
In order to arrive at a correct conclusion, one must consider the sensorimotor needs and diagnosis of the group members, as well as the characteristics of the provided activities. This requires inferential reasoning skill, where one must draw conclusions based on evidence presented as to which activity would be the best. In this situation, a parachute game is the only activity that meets the criteria of a sensorimotor group. If answered incorrectly, review the sensorimotor approach for individuals with SMI. See Chapter 13.

B175 C9

When performing a chart audit for an on-site accreditation visit, an OTA realizes that a date of service was documented wrong. The OTA had provided this service under the direct supervision of an occupational therapist. Which actions are best for the OTA to take?

Answer Choices:
A. Use white-out to remove the incorrect date, write the correct date of service, and then initial and date the correction.
B. Write the correct date over the incorrect date and then write the supervising occupational therapist's initials.
C. Put a single line through the incorrect date, write the correct date of service, and then initial and date the correction.
D. Meet with the supervising occupational therapist to discuss the need to correct this documentation.

Correct Answer: C.

Rationale:
Medical charts are legal documents that cannot be altered without accountability. Therefore, the error found must be acknowledged with the date of correction and the initials of the person making the correction. According to established guidelines for documentation, charting errors should be corrected by drawing a single line through the error and initialing and dating the chart. The permanent removal of an error by using white-out is not acceptable nor is it acceptable to place another practitioner's initials on documentation. There is no need for the OTA to meet with the OT supervisor to discuss this situation. The OTA can make the needed correction according to established documentation standards.

Type of Reasoning: Evaluative
This question requires one to evaluate the merits of the four possible solutions in order to determine which response is consistent with documentation standards of practice. Evaluative reasoning skills are utilized whenever one must make a judgment about a best course of action. For this type of situation, drawing a single line through the incorrect information with initials and then making and dating the correction is consistent with established guidelines for OT documentation, which should be reviewed if answered incorrectly. See Chapter 4.

B176 C5

An individual with a body mass index (BMI) of 35 is joining a community-based wellness program conducted by an occupational therapist and an OTA. When formulating an individualized wellness plan, which condition should the occupational therapist and OTA take into consideration as an increased risk for this person?

Answer Choices:
A. Hypothermia during exertion.
B. Hyperthermia during exertion.
C. Rapid weight loss during the initial weeks.
D. Increased anxiety and depression.

Correct Answer: B.

Rationale:
A patient with a body mass index of 35 is considered obese and is at increased risk for hyperthermia during exertion. Weight loss will occur after the person actively engages in a wellness program that includes lifestyle redesign, a nutritional diet, and exercise over an extended period of time, not just in the initial weeks. An individualized wellness program should decrease anxiety and depression, not increase them.

Type of Reasoning: Inferential
This question requires one to infer a patient's risk factors based on the diagnosis provided. This is an inferential reasoning skill, as one must determine what may be true of a patient, although one cannot be 100% certain. In this case, the patient is likely to have hyperthermia during exertion. If answered incorrectly, review risk factors for patients with obesity. See Chapter 9.

B177 C7

A high school student is referred to occupational therapy for ADL training. The student has not received occupational therapy services for the past seven years. The student has non-spastic cerebral palsy resulting in right side hemiparesis and decreased muscle tone. The student plans to attend college and live on campus. During a transition planning meeting, the student's teacher reports the student has had several accidents during a meal preparation class (i.e., incurring cuts when using a knife and burning hands when taking items out of the oven). As part of the transition plan, the OTA will teach the student adaptive techniques used in a kitchen setting to compensate for right side weakness. Which of the following adaptations should the OTA recommend to improve the student's independence in preparing meals safely?

Answer Choices:
A. Prepare foods that do not require cutting.
B. Use a microwave oven to cook food.
C. Use a weighted knife to cut food.
D. Use oven mitts that extend to the elbows.

Correct Answer: D.

Rationale:
Non-spastic cerebral palsy will exhibit decreased or fluctuating muscle tone and can include hemiparesis, which indicates the arm and leg on one side of the body is weakened. Adaptations to an activity or the environment can prevent injuries in the kitchen and support independence during meal preparation. Using oven mitts that cover the forearms is a practical adaptation that will prevent burns when handling hot baking dishes in both the oven and microwave. The adaptation will allow the student a choice in using an oven or the microwave during meal preparation. Cutting food items regularly occurs when preparing meals. Rather than limiting meal preparation options, cutting food can be easily modified by using a cutting board with prongs to help secure the food item, using a rocker knife for one-handed cutting, or using a finger guard to prevent cutting injuries. Weighted utensils are recommended to reduce tremors, which have not been identified as a problem.

Type of Reasoning: Inductive
This question requires one to apply knowledge of adaptive techniques for individuals with cerebral palsy in order to arrive at a correct conclusion. This necessitates clinical judgment, which is an inductive reasoning skill. For this scenario, the OTA should recommend using oven mitts that extend to the elbow to prevent burns when handling hot items. If answered incorrectly, review adaptive strategies and equipment for meal preparation tasks. See Chapter 14.

B178 C4

An individual has intention tremor, dysmetria, decreased equilibrium, and nystagmus due to a cerebellar lesion. The person expresses difficulty with routine tasks. Which is best for the OTA to use during intervention with this person to improve their task performance?

Answer Choices:
A. A pegboard activity to address dysmetria while seated.
B. Quick stretch to lateral trunk muscles prior to dressing.
C. Wrist weights for the person to wear while performing meal preparation activities.
D. Upper extremity weight bearing on a sink while performing self-care activities.

Correct Answer: D.

Rationale:
The treatment goals for persons with cerebellar dysfunction are focused on strengthening proximal muscles, improving postural responses, and increasing stability. Weight bearing of the upper extremities can increase shoulder girdle stability which can ease task performance. A pegboard activity is not a functional activity and is very difficult to complete with dysmetria and intention tremor. Quick stretch to lateral trunk muscles describes a proprioceptive neuromuscular facilitation (PNF) technique that would be impractical to perform during a functional activity. Most important, the efficacy of this PNF approach is not supported by evidence. While wrist weights have traditionally been used with persons with intention tremor, their efficacy is not supported by evidence. Teaching the person to use proximal stability while performing meal preparation activities would be a more effective intervention.

Type of Reasoning: Inductive
Clinical knowledge and judgment are the most important skills needed for answering this question, which requires inductive reasoning skill. Knowledge of the diagnosis, its presenting symptoms, and the most appropriate clinical outcomes is essential to choosing the best solution. In this case, the intervention the OTA should use with this person to improve their task performance is upper extremity weight bearing on a sink while performing self-care activities. If answered incorrectly, review the functional impact of cerebellar lesions and intervention approaches for persons with motor disturbances. The integration of this knowledge is required to determine a correct answer. See Chapters 7 and 12.

B179 C6

An older adult is admitted to a skilled nursing facility following a fall that resulted in a fractured hip with open reduction, internal fixation. The resident lived alone in a second floor apartment and was unable to return home. The resident is extremely agitated over being in a nursing facility. During the first OT session, the resident angrily yells, "Leave me alone, I just want to get out of here!" Which is the OTA's best initial response?

Answer Choices:
A. Explain the benefits of active engagement in occupational therapy.
B. Console the resident by stating it is likely that this placement is temporary.
C. Calmly and supportively acknowledge the resident's feelings.
D. Advise their supervisor that the resident's mental status should be assessed.

Correct Answer: C.

Rationale:
This resident has just incurred an injury that has resulted in the loss of their home. It is natural for the resident to be angry and upset over the unanticipated placement in an institution. The OTA should not be surprised by this outburst and should respond in a calm and supportive manner to acknowledge the resident's feelings. This is an effective use of interactive reasoning and can effectively assist with building rapport. While it is important to explain the benefits of active engagement in occupational therapy, the resident's ability to adequately process this information may be diminished by their distraught state. Therefore, calmly supporting the person is the best initial response. Once rapport has been attained, the OTA can more effectively explain the OT process to the resident. Consoling the resident by stating that the skilled nursing facility placement is likely only temporary is not truthful since the OTA cannot know what the residential outcome will be for this person. Advising the OT supervisor that the resident's mental status should be assessed is not appropriate. There is no information provided in the item scenario to indicate a need for a mental status evaluation.

Type of Reasoning: Evaluative
In this type of question, one must assess the value of the four possible choices. In this scenario, the test taker should be able to determine that an agitated, newly admitted resident will require a calm and supportive approach to reduce agitation and build rapport. This type of question requires one to weigh the strength of statements, which is an evaluative reasoning skill. If answered incorrectly, review guidelines for building rapport, especially in individuals with agitation. See Chapters 3 and 13.

B180 C6

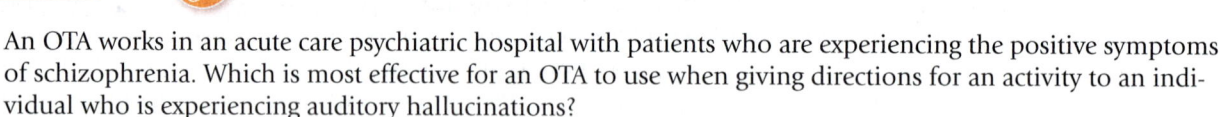

An OTA works in an acute care psychiatric hospital with patients who are experiencing the positive symptoms of schizophrenia. Which is most effective for an OTA to use when giving directions for an activity to an individual who is experiencing auditory hallucinations?

Answer Choices:
A. Written directions for making vanilla pudding.
B. Step-by-step verbal directions for making a leather link belt.
C. General verbal directions for completing a group collage.
D. Demonstrated steps and music for a popular dance.

Correct Answer: A.

Rationale:
Written directions provide concrete guidelines for the person experiencing hallucinations. Making pudding is a structured activity that has a tangible outcome; these qualities can reinforce reality. When someone is experiencing auditory hallucinations, it can be difficult to follow verbal directions. Because hallucinations can impact the ability to concentrate, an unstructured open-ended group project like a collage may be too vague and ambiguous for a person experiencing hallucinations. Demonstration can be an excellent way to provide directions, but the background music that accompanies this dance activity will provide additional auditory stimuli; this could contribute to increased hallucinations. Certain dances involve quick movements and postural changes which may be contraindicated if the person is experiencing certain medication side effects, such as orthostatic hypotension.

Type of Reasoning: Inductive
This question requires one to assess the needs of the client based upon their presenting symptoms and knowledge of the positive symptoms of schizophrenia. This necessitates clinical judgment in determining a best course of action, which is an inductive reasoning skill. For this case, the OTA should provide a structured activity with written directions to minimize the impact of auditory hallucinations on task performance. Review therapeutic approaches for patients with schizophrenia and auditory hallucinations if answered incorrectly. See Chapter 13.

B181 C9

An OTA conducts an after-school transition skills group with adolescents with a diversity of disabilities. One of the student's behavior is very different from that in prior groups (e.g., difficulty focusing when typically serving as the group initiator, making statements that are irrelevant to the topic at hand). The OTA smells a strong alcohol scent on the student's breath. Which action should the OTA take in response to this situation?

Answer Choices:
A. Directly ask the student if the student has been drinking.
B. Initiate a group discussion about the effects of substance abuse on occupational performance.
C. Proceed with the group and report suspicions of alcohol use at the next transition planning team meeting.
D. Call for a school aide to escort the student to the school's on-site health care facility.

Correct Answer: D.

Rationale:
The OTA must ensure the student's safety. The medical staff of the school's on-site health care facility can evaluate the student to determine the cause of the student's atypical behavior and alcohol-smelling breath. These symptoms can be the result of alcohol use or an indication of ketoacidosis. In either case, it is important for the student to receive a medical evaluation and the care needed to ensure the student's health and safety. The other options do not address the student's need for a medical evaluation and possible treatment. They can also be disruptive to the group process for the other group participants.

Type of Reasoning: Evaluative
This judgment question requires one to determine what will not only address the situation at hand but also ensure the student's future health and safety. The test taker must choose the answer that addresses the situation immediately and effectively. Evaluation questions are challenging in that one must evaluate the merits of each statement and conclude what will result in the best possible outcome. Decisions such as these often rely upon the OT Code of Ethics to provide guiding principles of action. Because the student's' presenting symptoms require medical attention, the therapist must act to ensure their safety. If answered incorrectly, review the AOTA Code of Ethics and the role of medical professionals on the team. See Chapter 4.

B182 C4

A patient who incurred a right CVA asks for a bottle of water to drink. The OTA gives the patient a bottle of water, but the patient is unable to open it. The OTA provides instruction on opening the bottle, but the patient remains unable to complete the task. After the intervention session, the OTA observes the patient independently open the bottle and drink from it. Which deficit is most accurate for the OTA to report to the occupational therapist as needing further evaluation?

Answer Choices:
A. Anosognosia.
B. Ideomotor apraxia.
C. Unilateral neglect.
D. Somatoagnosia.

Correct Answer: B.

Rationale:
With ideomotor apraxia, a patient cannot perform a task upon direction but can do the task when on their own. Anosognosia is a severe form of neglect that is demonstrated by a lack of awareness and denial of the severity of one's paralysis. Unilateral neglect is demonstrated by a failure to respond to or report unilateral stimulus presented to the body side contralateral to the lesion. Somatoagnosia is a body scheme disorder that results in diminished awareness of body structure and a failure to recognize body parts as one's own.

Type of Reasoning: Analytical
One must have a firm understanding of the difference between the cognitive-perceptual deficits of apraxia, neglect, and agnosia in order to arrive at the correct conclusion. Doing so requires one to assess the differences between these deficits and determine the likely reason for this deficit, which is an analytical reasoning skill. Review the definitions of these terms and other cognitive-perceptual deficits associated with CVA if answered incorrectly. See Chapters 7 and 12.

B183 C8

An OTA is working with a non-ambulatory elementary school-aged child who demonstrates moderate to severe extensor spasticity and limited head control. Which is the most beneficial positioning device for the OTA to recommend for this child to use in the classroom?

Answer Choices:
A. A wheelchair with an adductor pommel.
B. A wheelchair with a back wedge and head supports.
C. A supine stander with an abduction wedge.
D. A prone stander with an abduction wedge.

Correct Answer: B.

Rationale:
A wheelchair with a back wedge and head supports will position the child's trunk and head in slight flexion. This will help decrease the child's extensor tone and is the most beneficial positioning recommendation for this child. An abduction pommel or wedge controls scissoring of the legs, which often occurs with increased extensor tone. However, these positioning devices do not provide the head or upper trunk support that is needed for effective functioning in the school environment. In addition, supine and prone standers would not facilitate the child's ability to integrate into the classroom setting since most elementary school tasks are done at a desktop.

Type of Reasoning: Analytical
The test taker must determine which of the four possible positioning devices is most effective in addressing the child's issues. This requires knowledge of wheelchair seating and positioning and properties of spasticity in children. For this case, the OTA should recommend a wheelchair with a back wedge and head supports. If answered incorrectly, review information on seating and positioning for children with spasticity. See Chapter 15.

B184 C9

An OTA provides bedside BADL training to a patient recovering from multiple injuries incurred during a motor vehicle accident. The patient's children arrive for a visit and ask the OTA to let them look at their parent's chart while they wait outside the room for the session to conclude. Which is best for the OTA to do in response to this request?

Answer Choices:
A. Tell the family members that they must have the permission of their parent before they can look at the chart.
B. Commend the family members for their interest in their parent's status and give them the chart to read.
C. Tell the family members they cannot see the chart because they could misinterpret the information.
D. Tell the family members to ask the supervising occupational therapist for permission to look at the chart.

Correct Answer: A.

Rationale:
According to the Health Insurance Portability and Accountability Act (HIPAA), the OTA must obtain the person's permission prior to sharing any information about the person's status with family members or significant others. HIPAA does allow providers to use their clinical judgment to determine whether to discuss the person's case with others if the person cannot give permission or objects. Documentation for this decision is essential (e.g., person is at risk of harming self due to lack of judgment; consultation with a specialist is essential to ensure quality of care). All information used or disclosed about a person's status must be limited to the minimum needed for the immediate purpose. There is no need for the OTA to advise the family members to speak to the occupational therapist. The OTA can directly inform the family of the HIPAA guidelines.

Type of Reasoning: Evaluative
One must weigh the courses of action presented and determine which approach will result in the most effective outcome and follow federal guidelines for protecting patient privacy. This is an evaluative reasoning skill. For this situation, having knowledge of HIPAA guidelines, the OTA should tell the family members that they must have the permission of their parent before they can look at the chart. If answered incorrectly, review HIPAA guidelines for protecting patient privacy. See Chapter 4.

B185 C6

An OTA conducts a task-oriented activity group for adolescents recently diagnosed with anorexia nervosa. Which is the best activity for the OTA to include in the initial session of this group?

Answer Choices:
A. Making cards to send to veterans in a local hospital.
B. Baking cookies for the residents in a homeless shelter.
C. Performing low-impact aerobic exercises.
D. Composing lyrics and melody for a group song.

Correct Answer: D.

Rationale:
A task-oriented group utilizes a psychodynamic approach to increase participants' understanding of their needs, values, ideas, feelings, and behaviors. Activities are selected and designed to facilitate self-expression and the exploration of feelings, thoughts, and behaviors. Composing a song is a self-expressive activity that allows each member to contribute their thoughts and feelings. It is an activity that can be stopped to discuss behaviors, feelings, and issues that arise during the group. The other activity choices do not provide this self-expression opportunity. In addition, because persons with anorexia nervosa have a complex relationship with food that takes time to address, baking would not be an appropriate activity for an initial session. Similarly, because persons with eating disorders often engage in exercise in an excessive (sometimes self-abusive) manner, aerobic exercising is not an appropriate activity for an initial session.

726　Exam B Answer Rationales

Type of Reasoning: Inductive
Clinical knowledge and judgment are the most important skills needed for answering this question, which requires inductive reasoning skill. Knowledge of the diagnosis and most appropriate activities for a task-oriented group are essential to arriving at a correct conclusion. In this case, the most appropriate initial activity is composing lyrics and melody for a group song. If answered incorrectly, review task-oriented groups and the characteristics of anorexia nervosa. The integration of this knowledge is required to determine the correct answer. See Chapters 3 and 13.

B186　C3

A patient has extensive full-thickness burns to the dorsum of the right hand and forearm and is being fitted with a splint to support the wrists and hands in anticontracture position. In which positions should the OTA construct this splint?

Answer Choices:
A. Neutral wrist position with 70° of metacarpophalangeal (MCP) flexion, interphalangeals (IPs) in full extension, and thumb in opposition.
B. Neutral wrist position with full MCP and IP extension and thumb opposition.
C. Wrist in 30° of wrist flexion, 60° of MCP flexion, 30° of IP flexion, and thumb abduction.
D. Wrist in 5°–10° extension with full MCP and IP extension and thumb in abduction.

Correct Answer: A.

Rationale:
The anticontracture splinting position for burns to the dorsum of the wrist is neutral. The anticontracture splinting position for burns to the dorsum of the hand is 70°–90° of MCP flexion, IPs in full extension, and thumb in opposition. The other positions do not meet these criteria.

Type of Reasoning: Deductive
This question requires one to recall the protocol for anticontracture position splinting after burns, which is a deductive reasoning skill. Deductive reasoning skills are often utilized when one must recall facts to solve problems. For this case, the splint should be constructed with the wrist in the neutral position with 70° of MCP flexion, IPs in full extension, and thumb in opposition. If answered incorrectly, review anticontracture splinting guidelines for burns. See Chapter 6.

B187　C2

A school-based OTA is teaching orientation and mobility skills to an adolescent with a degenerative visual disorder. Which is the most effective motivational technique for the OTA to use with this student?

Answer Choices:
A. Provide concrete structure and frequent feedback to ensure accurate orientation and safe functional mobility.
B. Keep sessions short to allow time for emotional adjustment to orientation and mobility challenges.
C. Treat the student as an adult and incorporate the student's orientation and mobility goals into intervention sessions.
D. Limit anxiety by practicing the techniques in a quiet and self-contained environment; e.g., an empty classroom.

Correct Answer: C.

Rationale:
Adolescents prefer to be treated as adults. The most important (and most effective) motivational technique is to incorporate the student's goals into the intervention sessions. Too much structure will limit the student's trial and error learning, which is vital to learning and retaining orientation and functional mobility skills. The length of intervention sessions should be determined by the student's established goals, the methods identified to attain these goals, and the student's progress toward goal attainment. Throughout the orientation and mobility training sessions, the OTA can incorporate the therapeutic use of self to help the student emotionally adjust to the challenges of the situation and effectively deal with any anxiety they may be experiencing. Using a quiet, self-contained environment can be a helpful intervention approach when first introducing orientation and mobility techniques, but it is not a motivational strategy.

Type of Reasoning: Inductive
This question requires one to utilize clinical judgment to reach a sound conclusion, which is an inductive reasoning skill. For this question, the test taker must consider the age of the individual in order to determine the best motivational techniques. In this case, treating the patient as an adult and incorporating the patient's goals into the plan of care is best. This approach is consistent with client-centered practice. See Chapter 3.

B188 C6

An older adult is referred to home-based occupational therapy after surgery to correct a hip fracture resulting from a fall. The patient was recently diagnosed with a mild neurocognitive disorder. Which would the OTA expect the person to have the most difficulty with in the home environment?

Answer Choices:
A. Communicating personal preferences to family members.
B. Completing a morning grooming routine.
C. Choosing appropriate clothing to wear.
D. Complying with total hip precautions.

Correct Answer: D.

Rationale:
A mild neurocognitive disorder is characterized by short-term memory loss, distractibility, and difficulty learning, remembering, and using new information. Because complying with total hip precautions requires learning, remembering, and using new information, it can be expected that this will be difficult for this person. However, the person with a mild neurocognitive disorder does not have difficulty with routine tasks such as grooming and dressing. The progression of neurocognitive disorders is characterized by gradual onset and continuing cognitive decline. Difficulties with BADL would be evident at a moderately severe level of a neurocognitive disorder. Communication would not be affected until the disorder has progressed to a severe level.

Type of Reasoning: Inferential
For this situation, the test taker must utilize knowledge of deficits associated with a neurocognitive disorder to problem solve the most difficult task for the client to complete. This requires inferential reasoning skill, where one determines what is likely to be true of a situation. In this case, the older adult is most likely to have difficulty complying with total hip precautions. If answered incorrectly, review symptoms of neurocognitive disorders and their impact on function. See Chapter 10.

B189 C9

An occupational therapist and an OTA collaborate to develop a restraint reduction program. The OTA is a faculty member in an OTA education program. The OTA uses this program development experience to explain to the students the role of occupational therapy. Which is most accurate for the OTA to state restraint reduction represents?

Answer Choices:
A. Primary prevention.
B. Secondary prevention.
C. Tertiary prevention.

Correct Answer: B.

Rationale:
Secondary prevention involves the early detection of problems in a population that has diagnoses that place them at risk for the development of complicating or secondary conditions. Residents of a nursing home have preexisting medical conditions and disabilities. A restraint reduction program's aim is to prevent the development of secondary conditions, such as deconditioning. Primary prevention targets individuals with no preexisting conditions. Tertiary prevention focuses on the elimination or reduction of the impact of dysfunction on an individual (e.g., the provision of rehabilitation services to maximize community participation).

Type of Reasoning: Analytical
This question requires the test taker to determine the type of skilled service provided according to a description, which is an analytical reasoning skill. Questions of this nature often call upon the test taker to analyze an activity based on a functional description in order to draw a correct conclusion. Based on this information, the activity is that of secondary prevention, which should be reviewed if answered incorrectly. See Chapter 4.

B190 C3

An older adult experienced a fall that resulted in a Colles' fracture of the right wrist. This required external fixation to stabilize the wrist. The client had the external fixator removed 24 hours ago and is experiencing limited wrist flexion and extension. Which intervention is best for the OTA to use to facilitate the most improvement in wrist flexion and extension in the shortest amount of time?

Answer Choices:
A. Repeating wrist flexion and extension exercises.
B. Watering plants in the rehabilitation facility's greenhouse.
C. Hand washing dishes using warm soapy water.
D. Writing thank-you cards on a slanted surface.

Correct Answer: B.

Rationale:
A core premise of occupational therapy is the use of purposeful activities to attain desired goals. Studies indicate that using purposeful activities is associated with higher levels of motivation and engagement, which leads to greater improvement in movement in comparison to rote exercises devoid of any meaning. The purposeful activity of watering plants requires the most active wrist flexion and extension. Writing thank-you notes on a slanted surface requires minimal active wrist flexion and extension. Hand washing dishes is contraindicated as it will prevent proper wound healing, which is an important consideration when an external fixator is removed one day prior to a treatment session.

Type of Reasoning: Inductive

For this question, the test taker must determine a best course of action, based on knowledge of activity analysis, to determine which activity requires the most active wrist flexion and extension. This is an inductive reasoning skill. For this scenario, watering plants requires the most wrist motion and therefore would be most beneficial in improving wrist range of motion. If answered incorrectly, review activity analysis guidelines and purposeful activities to improve wrist motion. The integration of this knowledge is required to determine the correct answer. See Chapters 3 and 11.

B191 C7

A young adult with a complete C5 spinal cord injury receives occupational therapy services at a rehabilitation center. To develop skills in independent feeding, which is best for the OTA to focus on during intervention with this patient?

Answer Choices:
A. The cutting of food using a rocker knife and different consistencies of TheraPutty.
B. The use of a dorsal splint with a universal cuff to hold feeding utensils.
C. The use of a tenodesis grasp and/or tenodesis splint to hold utensils and cut food.
D. The self-direction of personal care assistants about individual preferences while eating.

Correct Answer: B.

Rationale:
A person with a C5 SCI can independently feed with the use of a dorsal splint with a universal cuff to hold feeding utensils. The ability to cut food using a rocker knife and the use of a tenodesis grasp and/or tenodesis splint to hold utensils and cut food would be an intervention focus for a person with a C6 SCI. Self-directing personal care assistants would be important for persons with a C1 to C4 SCI because these individuals would not be able to independently feed with the use of adaptive equipment.

Type of Reasoning: Inductive
This question requires one to utilize knowledge of cervical SCI to determine the best feeding approach for an individual with C5 injury. Based on knowledge of intact functioning with a complete C5 injury, the use of a universal cuff would be best to focus on to promote use of intact elbow flexion while adapting for absent composite finger flexion. If answered incorrectly, review cervical spinal cord injury intervention guidelines and the feeding capabilities of each SCI level. See Chapters 7 and 14.

B192 C2

An adolescent with Duchenne muscular dystrophy refuses to use mobile arm supports (MAS) because "they look so big and stupid." Which action should the OTA take first in response to the client's statement?

Answer Choices:
A. Collaborate with a rehabilitation engineer to design a more compact device.
B. Explore other options with the client to perform activities that do not use the MAS.
C. Provide several logical reasons for using the MAS to enhance functional performance.
D. Discharge the client and follow up with them after one month to re-assess their interest in the MAS.

Correct Answer: B.

Rationale:
The most effective first action is exploring ways the client can do activities without requiring the use of the MAS. This response is an example of therapeutic use of self and a client-centered approach. Developing a different design for a MAS is a long-term option that may not be feasible. Providing logical reasons for using the MAS is not the best initial response, as it ignores the client's feelings of frustration and is not a client-centered approach. There is no need to discharge the client from treatment. The issue needs to be addressed now, not in one month.

Type of Reasoning: Inductive
This question requires one to determine the best approach for addressing the client's concerns about using a MAS. This requires inductive reasoning skill, where clinical judgment is paramount to arriving at a correct conclusion. For this situation, the OTA should explore other options for activity performance that do not use the arm supports. This action is consistent with client-centered practice. See Chapter 3.

B193 C5

An adult with amyotrophic lateral sclerosis (ALS) receives occupational therapy services to learn adaptive strategies that can enable occupational performance within the person's capabilities. During an intervention session focused on dressing, the OTA notices a persistent area of redness over the sacrum that is still evident after the person has been upright for 30 minutes. Based on this observation, which of the following is most accurate for the OTA to report to the supervising occupational therapist as needing attention in a revised intervention plan?

Answer Choices:
A. A stage I pressure ulcer.
B. A stage II pressure ulcer.
C. A stage III pressure ulcer.
D. A stage IV pressure ulcer.

Correct Answer: A.

Rationale:
A stage I pressure ulcer is characterized by a defined area of persistent redness (as in this example). Skin is intact with visible, non-blanchable redness over a localized area, typically over a bony prominence (the sacrum in this example). See Figure 9-3. Additional changes include alterations in skin temperature (warmth or coolness), tissue consistency (firm or soft), and sensation (pain, itching). A stage II ulcer involves involves the dermis with partial thickness loss which presents as a shallow open ulcer that can be shiny or dry. A stage II ulcer can also present as a blister that is intact or open/ruptured. The wound bed is a red pink color without slough or bruising. Stages I and II are considered partial thickness ulcers. A stage III pressure ulcer involves full thickness tissue loss with subcutaneous fat possibly visible. The depth of tissue loss is not obscured if slough (i.e., dead matter/necrotic tissue) is present. Bone, tendon or muscle are not exposed or directly palpable. Stage IV involves full thickness tissue loss with bone, tendon or muscle visible or directly palpable. Osteomyelitis is possible if stage IV ulcers extend into muscle, fascia, tendon and/or the joint capsule. The National Pressure Ulcer Advisory Panel has updated the definitions and stage classifications of pressure ulcers. This revision includes the original four stages and two additional stages of deep tissue injury and unstageable pressure ulcers. While nursing staff in medical model settings typically assume the responsibility for skin and risk assessments, OT practitioners can (and should) contribute to this process. OT intervention plans should be written to address concerns related to the maintenance of skin integrity. Prevention is the most effective intervention. Effective techniques include the use of wheelchair cushions, flotation pads and pressure-relief bed aids to distribute pressure over a larger skin surface and the training of the individual and/or caregivers in positioning and weight-shifting techniques and schedules and in proper skin care.

Type of Reasoning: Analytical
This question provides a description of a condition, and the test taker must determine what the symptoms indicate. This is an analytical reasoning skill. For this case, the symptoms described indicate a stage I pressure ulcer. If answered incorrectly, review pressure ulcer stages and strategies to prevent wounds. See Chapter 9.

B194 C8

A young adult with a T10 spinal cord injury wishes to engage in sports activities. Which wheelchair features are best for the OTA to recommend to this client?

Answer Choices:
A. A heavy-duty foldable frame with a high back.
B. An ultralight foldable frame with a high back.
C. An ultralight rigid frame with a low back.
D. A heavy-duty rigid frame with a low back.

Correct Answer: C.

Rationale:
Sports competition wheelchairs are usually made with rigid construction and very strong lightweight materials. A folding wheelchair does not provide the stability needed for competition sports. A low seat back enhances the user's upper body/arm movements. A higher seat back is indicated for patients with decreased trunk control (not a factor in this example). At T10, this person has partial innervation of the abdominals (innervated T6-12) and full innervation of the upper extremities.

Type of Reasoning: Inductive
One must utilize diagnostic reasoning and clinical judgment to determine the best type of wheelchair for a person with T10 paraplegia who wishes to participate in sports. This requires inductive reasoning skill. For this case, the OTA should recommend an ultralight rigid frame with a low back. If answered incorrectly, review wheelchair types and prescription guidelines. See Chapter 15.

B195 C3

An OTA has established service competency in completing biomechanical evaluations. The OTA evaluates a person who complains of numbness and tingling of the thumb, index, middle, and radial half of the ring fingers. The person also reports dropping things more than normal. Based on this client's report, the OTA suspects that the client has carpal tunnel syndrome. Which assessment measure should the OTA use to confirm the diagnosis?

Answer Choices:
A. Finkelstein's test.
B. Phalen's test.
C. Froment's sign.

Correct Answer: B.

Rationale:
Phalen's test identifies median nerve compression in the carpal tunnel. A positive Tinel test at the wrist can also confirm the diagnosis of carpal tunnel syndrome. Finkelstein's test is specific for reproducing the pain associated with de Quervain's tenosynovitis of the abductor pollicis longus and extensor pollicis brevis. Froment's sign is used to identify ulnar nerve dysfunction.

Type of Reasoning: Deductive
This question requires factual recall of knowledge of tests used to determine hand disorders such as carpal tunnel syndrome. In this case, the appropriate test is Phalen's test. If answered incorrectly, review testing for carpal tunnel syndrome. See Chapter 6.

B196 C1

An older adult with persistent balance difficulty and a history of recent falls (two in the last three months) receives home care OT services. During the initial session, which client factors are most important for the OTA to consider?

Answer Choices:
A. Spinal musculoskeletal changes secondary to degenerative joint disease.
B. Cardiovascular endurance and level of dyspnea during IADL.
C. Mental functions of attention and orientation during functional mobility.
D. Sensory functions and sensory organization of balance.

Correct Answer: D.

Rationale:
A critical component of balance control is sensory input from somatosensory, visual, and vestibular receptors and overall sensory organization of inputs. With age, these systems undergo changes that can compromise the person's balance and safety. Therefore, these are the most important client factors for the OTA to consider during intervention. There is no information in the scenario to indicate that the person has a cognitive deficit, degenerative joint disease, or a cardiopulmonary disorder.

Type of Reasoning: Inductive
This case scenario requires the test taker to combine knowledge of the somatosensory system and possible reasons for falls in order to arrive at the correct conclusion. A key facet of this question is in the terms "initial session" and "most important." These words should cause the test taker to focus on what should come first in a sequence of intervention events and what is most important for the patient. This requires the use of clinical judgment, which is an inductive reasoning skill. For this case, sensory functions and the sensory organization of balance are most important. If answered incorrectly, review the sensorimotor changes that occur with aging and intervention approaches for balance deficits in older adults. See Chapter 5.

B197 C4

An OTA provides occupational therapy services in a patient's room. The patient has left hemiplegia and is unable to recognize the faces of family members when they enter the room to visit or the items the family members bring for the patient. The family members become upset by this behavior. Which deficit should the OTA explain to the family members as the most likely reason for the patient's behavior?

Answer Choices:
A. Ideational apraxia.
B. Anosognosia.
C. Visual agnosia.
D. Somatoagnosia.

Correct Answer: C.

Rationale:
This patient's presenting behaviors are consistent with visual agnosia, which is an inability to recognize familiar objects despite normal function of the eyes and optic tracts. The inability to recognize familiar faces, often due to occipito-temporal lobe damage, is called prosopagnosia. Patients with prosopagnosia retain the ability to recognize other things, such as objects, and can use other senses to help recognize a person. For example, hearing the sound of a familiar voice will aid in recognition of a person. Therefore, once the family members talk with the patient, they will likely be able to recognize them by their voices. Ideational apraxia is the inability to perform a purposeful motor act, either automatically or upon command. Anosognosia is the frank denial, neglect, or lack of awareness of the presence or severity of one's paralysis. Somatagnosia is an impairment in body scheme.

Type of Reasoning: Analytical
In this question, one must recall the meaning of the four choices provided and apply them to the patient's symptoms described above. This requires analytical reasoning, which often requires one to determine the meaning of symptoms or deficits. For this situation, the symptoms are indicative of visual agnosia, which should be reviewed, if answered incorrectly. See Chapter 12.

B198 C9

A six-week-old infant born prematurely is being discharged from the hospital. The infant has spastic diplegia as a result of cerebral palsy. The OTA collaborates with the occupational therapist and the family to develop a home exercise and positioning program that can be incorporated into the family's natural daily routine. The infant's parents speak limited English. Which is most important for the occupational therapist and the OTA to determine prior to discharge?

Answer Choices:
A. The parents' degree of anxiety about program implementation.
B. The parents' ability to purchase positioning equipment.
C. Characteristics and accessibility of the home environment.
D. The parents' comprehension of the instructions.

Correct Answer: D.

Rationale:
To ensure the home exercise and positioning program will be successfully implemented by the parents, the occupational therapist and the OTA must determine their comprehension of the instructions prior to discharge. Cultural competency requires occupational therapy practitioners to minimize potential barriers to service, including any language barriers. Effective communication is essential when sharing important information. Because spasticity can result in contractures, the correct implementation of a home exercise and positioning program is critical to the infant's well-being. Addressing the parents' anxiety about program implementation and determining the parents' financial resources and the characteristics and accessibility of the home should be considered in the development and implementation of a home program. However, they are not the primary pre-discharge concerns in this scenario. Any potential communication barrier needs to be addressed initially to ensure ethical practice. It is important to recognize that the positioning needs of a six weeks old infant can be met by the use of common household items (e.g., rolled towels). Expensive equipment would not be needed at this point.

Type of Reasoning: Evaluative
For this scenario, the test taker must determine a best course of action to convey home program information to parents who do not speak English well. This requires one to weigh the various courses of action presented and determine the approach that will have the best outcome. This requires evaluative reasoning skill, where one determines the merits of an approach based on information provided. For this situation, the most important determination to make is the parents' comprehension of the instructions. Review cultural considerations for therapy services if answered incorrectly. See Chapter 3.

B199 C4

A seven-year-old with spastic diplegia holds a pencil by using a tight static tripod grasp and hyperextension of the index DIP and the thumb IP. Which of the following is best for the school-based OTA to provide to improve the child's grasp on the pencil?

Answer Choices:
A. A soft built-up pencil grip.
B. Activities to relax and stretch the fingers prior to writing.
C. A plastic triangular pencil grip.

Correct Answer: A.

Rationale:
A soft pencil grip will help to inhibit the increased tone of the fingers. Relaxation and stretching activities can be helpful, but the child still needs a soft grip on the pencil. Seven-year-old children are required to hold a pencil for a great deal of time to complete school assignments, so the most effective intervention is an adaptation to the activity. A plastic grip is hard, which may increase tone.

Type of Reasoning: Inferential
One must have knowledge of spastic diplegia in children in order to choose the best recommendation. This is an inferential reasoning skill where one must draw a conclusion about a best course of action based on the information presented. In this situation, a soft built-up pencil grip is the best recommendation as it will help to inhibit the increased tone. If answered incorrectly, review adaptive techniques for writing. The integration of this knowledge is required to determine the correct answer. See Chapter 5.

B200 C8

An individual incurred a back injury while working as a stock person for a large warehouse distribution company. The individual's level of productivity is just below the warehouse minimum standards. The individual complains of pain when lifting the heaviest of boxes. The individual frequently becomes angry and verbally abusive in response to directions or feedback. What is the most important initial focus for this client's work hardening program?

Answer Choices:
A. Increasing the client's productivity to meet minimum standards.
B. Developing the client's affective work behavior skills.
C. Increasing the client's productivity to exceed minimum standards.
D. Developing the client's strength and ergonomic lifting abilities.

Correct Answer: B.

Rationale:
Affective work behavior skills include social responsiveness, attitude toward the job, and relationships with supervisors and coworkers. The individual is exhibiting significant deficits in these areas by becoming agitated and verbally abusive. These behaviors put the client at risk for not being able to maintain employment upon return to work. Increasing work productivity and developing ergonomic lifting abilities and strength can be addressed during the course of the work hardening program. The individual's ineffective work behavior skills must be immediately addressed for the individual to be able to benefit from this program.

Type of Reasoning: Inductive
This question requires one to determine the best approach for improving function for a patient in a work hardening setting. This requires inductive reasoning skill, where clinical judgment is paramount to arriving at a correct conclusion. For this situation, given the individual's behaviors, the OTA should develop affective work behavior skills. If answered incorrectly, review treatment guidelines for individuals in work hardening settings, especially work behavior skills. See Chapter 15.

Exam C Answer Rationales

C1 C4

An OTA works with an adult who incurred a spinal cord injury at the C5 level. The client's primary goal is to resume working as an accountant. The client reports that most of their work is computer-based. Which is the best piece of equipment for the OTA to teach the client to use to complete tasks on a computer?

Answer Choices:
A. A head pointer.
B. A tenodesis splint.
C. A universal cuff.
D. A mouth stick.

Correct Answer: C.

Rationale:
At the level of C5, the person can independently use a universal cuff with a pencil or typing stick inserted in it to complete computer-based tasks. A head pointer and mouth stick would be indicated for a person with a C1–C4-level lesion. A tenodesis splint is indicated for a person with a C6-level lesion.

Type of Reasoning: Inductive
This question requires the test taker to utilize knowledge of spinal cord injury levels and match that knowledge to the equipment that will enable functional independence. This is an inductive reasoning skill. For a person with spinal cord injury at the C5 level, the OTA should teach the individual to use a universal cuff to complete computer-based tasks. If answered incorrectly, review cervical spinal cord injury guidelines and equipment choices, especially C5. See Chapter 14.

C2 C3

A person who incurred a peripheral nerve injury is referred to an outpatient clinic for occupational therapy services. After the occupational therapist screens the client and determines that further evaluation is needed, the OTA completes an evaluation of the client's sensation. When administering the different types of sensory tests, which is the best protocol for the OTA to follow?

Answer Choices:
A. Test proximal to distal for all sensory tests.
B. Test distal to proximal for all sensory tests.
C. Test according to dermatome patterns for all sensory tests.

Correct Answer: B.

Rationale:
The correct procedure for administering sensory tests to a person with a peripheral nerve injury is to test distal to proximal following the peripheral nerves. Spinal cord injuries are tested proximal to distal following dermatome patterns. Neurological disorders are assessed according to dermatome patterns.

Type of Reasoning: Deductive
This question requires the test taker to recall guidelines for sensory testing. This is recall of factual information, which is a deductive reasoning skill. In this scenario, the OTA should test distal to proximal for all sensory tests. If answered incorrectly, review sensory testing guidelines. See Chapter 11.

C3 C2

An occupational therapist is supervising an OTA to establish service competence in the administration of a standardized pediatric assessment. Which of the following guidelines should the therapist highlight as important for the OTA to follow during assessment administration?

Answer Choices:
A. Review each child's referral and screening information to identify expectations for a child's assessment performance.
B. Exclude parents from the area in which the assessment is being conducted so a parent does not influence the child.
C. Adhere strictly to the planned pacing of the assessment and do not adjust timing to accommodate a child's reactions.
D. Be prepared to respond to any unexpected behavioral or physical responses a child may have during the assessment.

Correct Answer: D.

Rationale:
During a standardized pediatric assessment, a child may have unanticipated difficulties that could impede the child's performance. Thus, the OTA must be prepared to respond to any unexpected behavioral or physical responses the child may have during the assessment to maximize the child's performance. This choice is consistent with best practice in pediatrics, which uses a strengths-based approach; the other answer choices are not consistent with a strengths-based approach. The pacing of the assessment can be adjusted to accommodate the child and maximize the child's opportunity to demonstrate strengths. When reporting the assessment results, the OTA should document this accommodation. The action of reviewing each child's referral and screening information to identify assessment expectations is incorrect because all assessments should be unbiased and not based on preconceived expectations. In pediatric practice, parents should not be excluded from the area in which the assessment is being conducted. The OTA will not be familiar to the child; not having a parent present while a stranger is present could expectedly contribute to a child's anxiety. This could diminish performance.

Type of Reasoning: Inferential
For this question, one must infer or determine what is likely to be true when conducting a standardized pediatric assessment. Questions of this nature often require inferential reasoning skill, where anticipation of issues or performance is paramount to arriving at a correct conclusion. In this situation, the OTA should highlight the importance of being prepared to respond to any unexpected behavioral or physical responses a child may have during the assessment. If answered incorrectly, review assessment guidelines. See Chapters 3 and 5.

C4 C9

An OTA conducts a transition planning group for high school students with psychosocial and cognitive disorders. A major focus of the group is to increase students' awareness of community resources that are available to support the attainment of their post-secondary goals. Which resource is most relevant for the OTA to review with the students?

Answer Choices:
A. The local community college's Disability Resource Center to acquire educational supports.
B. The community's para-transit system to enable independent community mobility.
C. The local adult day care center to facilitate community-based social participation.
D. A community-based group home to develop independent living skills.

Correct Answer: A.

Rationale:
A college's Disability Resource Center (alternatively called Office for Students with Disabilities or a similar title) can work with the students to identify needed accommodations and supports that can enable full participation in post-secondary education. Many also offer specific supported education programs which provide direct interventions to develop the skills needed to succeed in post-secondary education. While independent community mobility, community-based social participation, and the development of independent living skills are relevant foci for a high school transition group, the program options identified are not appropriate for these students. Para-transit is an alternative public transit system for persons who are not capable of using available public transit (e.g., wheelchair users who require a lift to enter a bus or van). High school students with psychosocial and cognitive disorders are capable of using standard public transportation. If the students have community mobility concerns, the establishment of travel training goals would be indicated. Adult day care does offer opportunities for social participation. However, the services provided are focused on meeting the needs of adults and older adults with chronic physical and/or psychosocial impairments, and/or for individuals who are frail but semi-independent. This would not be an appropriate setting for older adolescents and young adults who are seeking community-based social participation. Group homes are residential settings for persons with developmental, medical, or psychiatric conditions that have resulted in functional deficits that impede independent living. Given that a major goal of transition planning is the development of the skills needed to live independently, these students would not be anticipated to need this level of care.

Type of Reasoning: Inductive
This question requires one to determine a best course of action, based on determination of the needs of a group. This necessitates clinical judgment, which is an inductive reasoning skill. For this case, the most relevant resource would be the local community college's Disability Resource Center to acquire educational supports. If answered incorrectly, review guidelines for transition planning. See Chapter 4.

C5 C4

An occupational therapist and OTA provide services to a small, private preschool. The OTA serves on the school committee, which plans community-based trips throughout the school year. Several students have hypersensitivity and over-responsivity to touch. Which is best for the OTA to recommend to support the participation and enjoyment of all students?

Answer Choices:
A. A children's art museum with a 'create your own masterpiece' program.
B. A beach with a designated lifeguarded children's section.
C. A zoo with large animals in their natural habitats.
D. A petting zoo with small-sized and baby animals.

Correct Answer: C.

Rationale:
Children with hypersensitivity/over-responsivity to touch demonstrate tactile defensiveness. They experience irritation and discomfort from touch sensations that others experience as ordinary. Textures such as sand, water, glue, and paint are aversive to them. Thus, the art museum and beach would not be appropriate recommendations. The museum's 'create your own masterpiece' would require the child to tactilely interact with art supplies such as paint and glue. The water and sand at a beach would not enable the enjoyment of the children who are hypersensitive/over-responsive to touch. When determining the best community-based class trip to recommend, the OTA must consider the sensory demands of the environment and the activity. Taking a trip to a zoo that has large animals in their natural habitats is the only option that will not require the child to touch or feel any potentially aversive textures. These zoos have natural barriers between visitors and the animals, so touch is not required. This differs from a petting zoo, which emphasizes tactile contact with the animals.

Type of Reasoning: Inductive
For this question, one must determine the best recommendation for children with hypersensitivity and over-responsivity to touch. This requires knowledge of tactile defensiveness and effective approaches, which necessitates inductive reasoning skill. For this case, the OTA should recommend a zoo with large animals in their natural habitats. Review information on tactile defensiveness if answered incorrectly. See Chapters 7 and 12.

C6 C1

A child with mild cerebral palsy receives OT intervention in a preschool setting. The OTA has collaborated with the occupational therapist to develop an intervention plan. This plan includes goals for developing the child's fine motor skills. Which intervention approach should the OTA employ to facilitate development of typical grasp patterns?

Answer Choices:
A. Place soft foam tubing around objects to be grasped.
B. Analyze the present components of the child's grasp.
C. Analyze the missing components of the child's grasp.
D. Grade the sizes and shapes of objects to be grasped.

Correct Answer: D.

Rationale:
Gradation of the size and shape of items to be grasped enables the OTA to begin with items that are within the child's grasp capabilities and then add different items as the child's grasp abilities progress. There is no need to add soft foam tubing at this time. Soft tubing may be used as a compensation approach if the child does not develop typical grasp patterns. Analyzing the components of grasp is part of the evaluation and re-evaluation processes, not the intervention process.

Type of Reasoning: Inductive
This question requires one to determine the most appropriate intervention for a child with mild CP. This requires inductive reasoning skill, where clinical judgment is paramount to arriving at a correct conclusion. For this situation, grading the sizes and shapes of objects to be grasped is most appropriate. If answered incorrectly, review development of grasp patterns for children. See Chapter 5.

C7 C3

An OTA works in a private practice that specializes in providing services to persons with hand injuries and disorders. The OTA contributes to the evaluation of a newly referred client by assessing their pinch strength. To complete this assessment, the OTA uses a pinch meter. To obtain the most accurate measurement, which protocol should the OTA follow?

Answer Choices:
A. Measure only the involved hand three times and calculate the mean.
B. Measure only the involved hand five times and calculate the mean.
C. Measure each hand three times and calculate the mean.
D. Measure each hand five times and calculate the mean.

Correct Answer: C.

Rationale:
The standard protocol for measuring pinch strength using a pinch meter is to obtain three measures on each hand for all pinch strengths. The mean of three trials on each hand is then compared to the norms. The three pinch strengths that are measured include key or lateral pinch (i.e., the thumb pulp to the lateral aspect of the index middle phalanx), three jaw chuck (i.e., pulp of thumb to pulps of index and middle fingers), and tip to tip. The other answer choices do not adhere to this protocol. Standard protocol must be followed for the results of the evaluation to be valid.

Type of Reasoning: Deductive
This question requires the test taker to recall the standard protocol for pinch strength testing. This requires factual recall of guidelines, which is a deductive reasoning skill. In this case, the OTA should follow the protocol of measuring each hand three times and calculating the mean. If answered incorrectly, review pinch strength testing guidelines. See Chapter 11.

C8 C8

An OTA conducts a fall prevention program at an assisted living facility for older adults. Which recommendations are best for the OTA to include in a presentation about strategies to prevent falls? Select the three BEST responses.

Answer Choices:
A. Store items on shelves that are located between the person's eye and hip level.
B. Store items on shelves that can be reached when an arm is stretched to its full length.
C. Remove high pile or loose rugs and clutter left on floors or stairs.
D. Do not use adaptive equipment such as reachers since they can affect a person's balance.
E. Install night-lights and light switches within easy reach to ensure adequate lighting.
F. Avoid resistive exercises as these can cause fatigue that can contribute to falls.

Correct Answers: A, C, and E.

Rationale:
The storing of items on shelves that are between the person's eye and hip level enables the items to be within easy reach. Overstretching to reach items can displace the person's center of gravity and throw the person off balance. High pile rugs, loose rugs, and clutter left on floors or stairs can increase the risk of falls. The use of adaptive devices (such as a reacher) while performing activities of daily living helps a person maintain stability; this decreases fall risk. Adequate lighting also decreases fall risk. Active or resistive muscle strengthening exercises and general conditioning exercises (GCE) are often used in fall prevention programs. These interventions can improve or maintain flexibility, strength, endurance, and coordination, which can decrease fall risk.

Type of Reasoning: Inductive
For this question, one must determine the best information to provide for older adults to prevent falls. This requires knowledge of fall prevention and safety guidelines, which is an inductive reasoning skill. For this scenario, the OTA should recommend that the older adults store items on shelves that are located between the person's eye and hip level, remove high pile or loose rugs and clutter left on floors or stairs, and install night-lights and light switches within easy reach. Review fall prevention guidelines if answered incorrectly. See Chapter 15.

C9 C4

An OTA is working with a child presenting with sensory-seeking behaviors and under-reactivity to touch and movement. The child has an unusually high activity level, inability to self-calm, motor impulsivity, and frequent touching and handling of items in the environment. Using Ayres' classic sensory integrative (SI) approach, which would be most effective for the OTA to use with this child to facilitate an adaptive response?

Answer Choices:
A. A pre-determined schedule of sensory activities designed by the occupational therapist.
B. The child's passive participation in a variety of vestibular and proprioceptive experiences.
C. Use of a sensory void environment to promote self-regulation.
D. Individualized therapy based on the inner drive and interest of the child.

Correct Answer: D.

Rationale:
Classic Ayres' SI treatment is based on the principles of inner drive and active involvement of the child. Sensory systems are impacted by a sensory rich environment and the balance between structure and freedom in regard to activity and participation. The OT practitioner is constantly vigilant and the interaction between the child and the practitioner is key to promoting the 'just right' challenge.

Type of Reasoning: Inductive
One must utilize clinical judgment and knowledge of therapeutic guidelines in order to determine the most effective approach for a child with sensory-seeking behaviors. This requires inductive reasoning skill. For this case, the OTA should provide individualized therapy based on the inner drive and interests of the child. If answered incorrectly, review the SI frame of reference and therapeutic approaches for sensory-seeking behaviors. See Chapter 12.

C10 C3

A welder incurred burns to the dorsal surface of the non-dominant hand. The occupational therapist and OTA collaborate to determine the best approach to prevent the contracture tendencies of this burn. Which splint will most effectively position the client in an anticontracture position?

Answer Choices:
A. A C-splint.
B. A wrist cockup splint.
C. A functional hand splint.
D. A palmar extension splint.

Correct Answer: C.

Rationale:
A burn to the dorsal surface of the hand can result in a claw hand deformity. To prevent the contractures that result in this deformity, a functional hand splint is indicated. A C-splint is indicated for burns to the web space. A wrist cockup splint is used for volar wrist burns to prevent this burn's contracture tendency of wrist flexion. A palmar extension splint is the anti-contracture splinting position for a burn to the volar surface of the hand.

Type of Reasoning: Inductive
This question requires one to utilize knowledge of splinting for hand burns in order to arrive at the best answer. This necessitates inductive reasoning skill, where clinical judgment is paramount to arriving at a correct conclusion. For this case, a functional hand splint is indicated to prevent the contractures that can result in claw hand. If answered incorrectly, review splinting guidelines for burns. See Chapter 6.

C11 C8

An elementary school-aged child with autism spectrum disorder (ASD) is non-verbal. During an individualized education program (IEP) meeting, the OTA collaborates with the speech language pathologist and assistive technology specialist to identify intervention options to help attain the child's communication goals. Which is best for this team to recommend the school purchase for inclusion in the child's IEP?

Answer Choices:
A. A contracted keyboard.
B. A programmable keyboard.
C. A voice-recognition computer.
D. A chorded keyboard.

Correct Answer: B.

Rationale:
A programmable keyboard has customized overlays, which include graphics and symbols that can be designed to help the student attain communication goals. A contracted keyboard provides smaller keys in a constrained space for persons with limited range of motion and functional motor control (e.g., individuals with arthritis). The child is non-verbal, so they would not be able to access a voice-recognition computer. A chorded keyboard consists of a few keys that generate standard characters by pressing various combinations of keys for persons with one-handed use (e.g., individuals with hemiplegia). The use of this keyboard requires an understanding of the alphabet and typical letter combinations.

Type of Reasoning: Inductive
This question requires one to determine the best intervention option for a child who is non-verbal. This requires knowledge of assistive technology options and keyboard features in order to arrive at a correct conclusion, necessitating inductive reasoning skill. For this situation, the OTA should recommend a programmable keyboard for the child. If answered incorrectly, review assistive technology options, including keyboard options. See Chapter 15.

C12 C8

An OTA works with an occupational therapist to provide consultation services to local businesses who want to improve their physical accessibility. In assessing customer access to the products displayed in a store, the OTA makes sure that there is sufficient room at the end of each aisle for customers who use wheelchairs to turn. Which dimension is best for the OTA to recommend as the turning radius?

Answer Choices:
A. 6 feet by 6 feet.
B. 5 feet by 5 feet.
C. 4 feet by 4 feet.

Correct Answer: B.

Rationale:
A 360-degree turn requires a clear space of 5 feet by 5 feet. This space enables the individual to turn without scraping the feet or maneuvering multiple times to accomplish a full turn. Providing less than 5 feet by 5 feet at the end of the aisles would require multiple turns to make a complete turn. This could increase the chance that a person in a wheelchair would collide with displays that are often at the end of store aisles. While a turning radius of 6 feet by 6 feet would ease turns, this amount of open space would limit the store's display space. Given that this space is not needed for a complete turn by a person in the wheelchair, it is not necessary.

Type of Reasoning: Deductive
This question requires the test taker to recall accessibility guidelines in order to arrive at a correct conclusion. This necessitates recall of factual guidelines, which is a deductive reasoning skill. For this case, the OTA should recommend a 5 feet by 5 feet turning radius. If answered incorrectly, review ADA accessibility guidelines. See Chapter 15.

C13 C7

An older adult with severe rheumatoid arthritis lives independently and receives occupational therapy services at an outpatient clinic. During an intervention session, the client expresses concern about the ability to assist a 3-year-old grandchild with donning and doffing clothing during a planned weekend visit. During prior visits, the client's spouse had assisted the child, but the spouse is now deceased. The client reports that the child has abilities that are typical of their age. After providing support to the client, which action is best for the OTA to take in response to these stated concerns?

Answer Choices:
A. Teach the client how to use a zipper pull to open and close the zippers on the child's clothing.
B. Teach the client how to use a button hook to open and close buttons on the child's clothing.
C. Advise the client to ask the child's parents to provide elastic waist pants and pull-on tops for the visit.
D. Advise the client to ask a friend or family member to stay over to provide assistance and ensure the child's safety.

Correct Answer: C.

Rationale:
A person with severe rheumatoid arthritis in the hands will have joint pain, stiffness, and limited range of motion. This will make the opening and closing of clothing fasteners and the use of a button hook and zipper pull difficult to impossible. Boutonniere and swan neck deformities are also associated with severe rheumatoid arthritis and further limit functional hand use. The provision of pullover shirts and elastic waist pants for the child to wear will enable the caregiver to help the child, if needed. At the age of 3, typically developing children can independently put on pullover shirts with minimal assistance, button large front buttons, and zip and unzip a jacket once on track. Assistance may be needed to remove a pullover shirt, get zippers on track, and button small buttons. Thus, it is best for the parents to provide clothing for the weekend visit that do not require the fastening of buttons or zippers. The client lives independently and there is no information in the scenario indicating that outside assistance is needed to ensure the child's safety.

Type of Reasoning: Inductive
For this question, one must determine the best recommendation for an older adult with severe rheumatoid arthritis. Additionally, this requires knowledge of modified dressing approaches, using clinical judgment, which is an inductive reasoning skill. For this case, the OTA should recommend that the client ask the child's parents to provide elastic waist pants and pull-on tops for the visit. If answered incorrectly, review principles of activity analysis and joint protection techniques. The integration of this knowledge is required to determine the correct answer. See Chapters 3 and 11.

C14 C2

An OTA and occupational therapist collaborate with a local office for the aging to design a new community-based day treatment program for individuals with neurocognitive disorders. Which groups are best for the OTA and therapist to recommend the program include?

Answer Choices:
A. Reality orientation groups.
B. Cognitive-behavioral groups.
C. Parallel groups.
D. Instrumental groups.

Correct Answer: D.

Rationale:
According to Mosey's taxonomy of groups, instrumental groups help individuals function at their highest possible level for as long as possible. They provide supportive, structured environments and activities that prevent regression, maintain function, and meet mental health needs. Activities can include reminiscence, arts and crafts, music, exercise, dance, and any other activity that is interesting and enjoyable to the members. Reality orientation groups are contraindicated for persons with neurocognitive disorders who cannot remember basic facts like dates, people, or places. Groups that focus on the use of memory can be very frustrating and countertherapeutic for persons with neurocognitive disorders. Cognitive-behavioral groups require intact cognition and are at too high a level for persons with neurocognitive disorders. Parallel groups can be indicated for individuals with neurocognitive disorders, but a schedule should not be comprised primarily of parallel groups for they are limiting in their potential for social interactions.

Type of Reasoning: Inferential
One must link the symptoms of the provided diagnosis to the type of groups presented in order to determine which group is best for individuals with neurocognitive disorders. This requires inferential reasoning, where one must draw conclusions about the features and benefits of each of the groups. In this case an instrumental group is best. If answered incorrectly, review Mosey's taxonomy of groups, especially instrumental groups. See Chapter 3.

C15 C8

An OTA and an occupational therapist provide consultation services to a home contractor who is remodeling homes to enable older adults to age in place. Which recommendation is best for the OTA and therapist to make to the builder?

Answer Choices:
A. Relocate light switches and electrical outlets so that they are accessible from various heights.
B. Replace lever door handles with round knobs to ease opening and protect joints.
C. Install handrails in all stairways on the side that matches the homeowner's dominant side.
D. Paint rooms and stairways in one neutral color to accommodate decreased vision.

Correct Answer: A.

Rationale:
Light switches and electrical outlets should be accessible from various heights. This enables their independent use while standing or sitting in a chair (including a wheelchair). Lever handles are more functional than round door knobs because they can be opened with a closed fist. To prevent falls, handrails should be securely installed on both sides of a stairway. A person's hand dominance may change due to the incurrence of a disability. Contrasting colors are needed to discriminate floors from walls, doors from walls, and steps from floors. Persons with low vision see things more clearly when there is a strong color contrast.

Type of Reasoning: Inductive
To arrive at a correct answer for this question, one must have knowledge of compensations for age-related sensorimotor changes and universal design guidelines. Questions that require one to use clinical judgment to determine best courses of action often necessitate inductive reasoning skill. For this case, the OTA should recommend relocating light switches and electrical outlets so that they are accessible from various heights. If answered incorrectly, review compensations for age-related sensorimotor changes and universal design guidelines. See Chapters 5 and 15.

C16 C8

An OTA evaluates the home of a person who uses a walker. The OTA measures the door swing of the front door to determine if it will allow safe independent entry into the home. The OTA determines that the door swing just meets minimum accessibility standards. Which measurement should the OTA record as meeting the walker accessibility standard for door swing?

Answer Choices:
A. 14 inches.
B. 18 inches.
C. 22 inches.
D. 26 inches.

Correct Answer: B.

Rationale:
The minimum space to accommodate the swing of a door for a person using a walker is 18 inches. A minimum of 26 inches is needed beside a door to accommodate its swing for persons using wheelchairs.

Type of Reasoning: Deductive
This question requires the test taker to recall factual guidelines of accessibility standards for the door swing. This necessitates deductive reasoning skill, where recall of facts is paramount to arriving at a correct conclusion. For this situation, the OTA should record the measurement as 18 inches. If answered incorrectly, review accessibility standards for the home, especially entryways. See Chapter 15.

C17 C7

An OTA collaborates with an occupational therapist and a teenager with juvenile rheumatoid arthritis (JRA) to develop a person-directed intervention plan. The teenager identifies a goal of being able to independently apply makeup. Which adaptation is best to include in the intervention plan?

Answer Choices:
A. Silver ring splints to hold makeup applicators.
B. Enlarged, soft foam handles on makeup applicators.
C. Long, thin handles on makeup applicators.

Correct Answer: B.

Rationale:
Enlarged, soft foam handles will facilitate independent grasp and increase independence in makeup application. Silver ring splints are not designed to hold objects. They are used on individual fingers to prevent boutonniere deformities that can contribute to improved functional grasp. However, there is no mention of the presence of boutonniere deformities in this item's scenario. Long, thin handles would increase the difficulty of holding applicators.

Type of Reasoning: Inductive
Clinical knowledge and judgment are the most important skills needed for answering this question, which requires inductive reasoning skill. Knowledge of the diagnosis and the most effective recommendation for the desired activity is essential to choosing the correct answer. In this case, the OTA should recommend enlarged, soft foam handles on the makeup applicators. If answered incorrectly, review self-care adaptations and adaptive devices for persons with rheumatoid arthritis. See Chapters 6 and 14.

C18 C4

An OTA works with a patient who incurred a right cerebral vascular accident (CVA) and has homonymous hemianopsia. Which is the most effective compensatory strategy for the OTA to use initially with this patient?

Answer Choices:
A. Teach the patient to turn the head to the affected left side.
B. Provide printed notes on the left side telling the patient to look to the left.
C. Place the patient's plate and eating utensils on the left side of the bed tray.
D. Rearrange the patient's room so while the patient is in bed the left side is facing the doorway.

Correct Answer: A.

Rationale:
Homonymous hemianopsia results in the loss of one-half of the visual field in each eye (nasal half of one eye and temporal half of other eye), which corresponds to the side of the sensorimotor deficit incurred by the CVA. A patient with a right CVA will have left homonymous hemianopsia. Left homonymous hemianopsia results in an inability to receive information from the left side. Initially, the patient needs to be made aware of their deficit and instructed to compensate by turning the head to the affected left side. Providing printed notes on the left side and placing the patient's eating utensils on the left side will not be effective, as these items will not be within the person's intact visual field. Initially, items should be placed on the person's right (unaffected side) so that the patient can successfully complete tasks and interact with the environment. As the person develops awareness of the deficit and additional compensatory strategies, interventions including moving items to the midline and then to the affected left side and teaching the person to scan from the right to midline to the left are appropriate.

Type of Reasoning: Analytical
For this question, the test taker must consider the best initial strategy for a patient with homonymous hemianopsia in order to arrive at a correct conclusion. This requires analytical reasoning skill, where deficits are analyzed in order to determine a most effective approach to addressing the deficits. For this case, teaching the patient to turn their head is what needs to occur first when compensating for the functional effects of homonymous hemianopsia. if answered incorrectly, review intervention approaches for visual perceptual deficits. See Chapter 12.

C19 C2

An occupational therapist and an OTA co-lead a work adjustment group. One member has become progressively more dependent on the OTA for directions, praise, and input throughout the group activities. Which action should the group leaders initially take in response to these behaviors?

Answer Choices:
A. Schedule several individual sessions with the OTA and group member to examine the issues of dependency and transference.
B. Inform the attending psychiatrist that the group member is exhibiting signs of dependency and transference.
C. Have the OTA work with the person during group sessions to develop independence in task completion.
D. Have another therapist co-lead the group with the occupational therapist and reassign the OTA to another group.

Correct Answer: C.

Rationale:
The development of dependency is not uncommon in therapeutic relationships. The best approach is to use the situation and have the OTA function as a change agent. It is not necessary to devote individual sessions to this issue. Moreover, this individualized attention could foster increased dependency. Dependency needs are best addressed in the group setting during the activities. One can notify the psychiatrist, but this does not address the potential to modify behavior in the group setting. Removing the OTA is not a good choice because the member does not have a chance to work through the dependency issues. This action does not give an opportunity for the OTA to use themselves therapeutically.

Type of Reasoning: Inductive
This question requires the test taker to problem solve a best course of action for a group member who shows dependency on the OTA. This requires inductive reasoning skill. For this case, the OTA should work with the person during group sessions to develop independence in task completion. If answered incorrectly, review group facilitation guidelines and principles of therapeutic use of self. See Chapter 3.

C20 C3

A client receives occupational therapy services following a right below elbow amputation. The client works as a carpenter and plans to return to work. The client has been fitted with a body-powered prosthesis. The current focus of prosthetic training is the development of dressing skills. What strategy is best for the OTA to teach the client for donning work pants?

Answer Choices:
A. Substitute elastic waist pants for pants with fasteners to eliminate the need to zipper and snap.
B. Use the terminal device to hold the waistband while the left hand zips the zipper and fastens the snap.
C. Use the left hand to hold the waistband while the terminal device zips the zipper and fastens the snap.
D. Dress in a supine position while in bed by rolling side to side and using the left hand to pull the pants up.

Correct Answer: B.

Rationale:
When a client utilizes a unilateral body-powered prosthesis to complete bilateral activities, the prosthesis completes the stabilizing component of the activity and the intact hand completes the fine motor component. When an individual dons pants, holding the pants in place by gripping the waist band (or belt loop) is done utilizing the prosthesis. The intact hand then completes the fine motor component of the task (in this case, zippering the zipper and fastening the snap). The client can be taught to complete the task as described in choice B. There is no need for the client to change the style of work pants to elastic waist pants. Typically, carpenters wear work pants that have multiple pockets and/or tabs to hold tools. This pant type is not typically available with an elastic waist. The fine motor skill that is required to operate a fastener is beyond the capabilities of the terminal device of a body-powered prosthesis. Dressing supine in bed while rolling side to side and pulling up the pants is not indicated in this case. This technique is utilized by clients who are not able to stand (e.g., a person living with an SCI).

Type of Reasoning: Deductive
This item requires one to recall factual knowledge about prosthetic training. This necessitates deductive reasoning skill in which facts and previous knowledge are important in drawing conclusions. Recalling that the prosthesis stabilizes while the intact side completes the fine motor component of a bilateral activity is key to determining the correct answer. If answered incorrectly, review principles of activity analysis and prosthetic training. The integration of this knowledge is required to determine the correct answer. See Chapters 3 and 6.

C21 C7

A young adult with schizophrenia is scheduled to be discharged from an inpatient setting to a halfway house and psychosocial clubhouse. The OTA is assisting the team with the discharge plan. What is the most important information for the OTA to provide to the team about this person?

Answer Choices:
A. The person's instrumental activities of daily living (IADL) skills.
B. The possible effects of medication on functional performance.
C. The person's vocational potential and opportunities.
D. The person's social interaction skills.

Correct Answer: A.

Rationale:
Knowledge of the person's level of skills for the performance of IADL is essential for the OTA to share with the team. This can provide the halfway house staff with information that can be used to determine the level of structure and support this person may need to make a successful transition. In a halfway house, residents are typically responsible for the maintenance of their rooms and personal items (e.g., laundry). They are also expected to contribute to the maintenance of the entire household (e.g., cleaning and cooking). Successful adjustment to the halfway house will require the performance of IADL, whether independently or with assistance. In addition, the IADL of community mobility will be needed to travel from the halfway house to the clubhouse. OT practitioners are the only members of the team who are able to assess the specifics of the individual's functioning in these areas. Medication management is an IADL; thus, the OTA can include the possible effects of medication on the person's functional performance in their discussion of the person's IADL skills. Since nursing staff typically report on a person's medical status, the OTA's perspectives can be a good supplement to the information reported by nursing staff about the effects of medication on the person's functional performance. While the OTA's input on the other areas identified in the answer choices can be helpful, it is not as essential as the individual's IADL status.. All team members can provide information on social skills. The individual's vocational potential and opportunities can be assessed at the clubhouse because an inherent component of the clubhouse model is vocational services.

Type of Reasoning: Inductive
This question requires one to determine the most important information to provide to the discharge planning team. This requires inductive reasoning skill, where clinical judgment is paramount to arriving at a correct conclusion. For this situation the OTA should provide information about the person's IADL skills, since the person will be transitioning to a halfway house. If answered incorrectly, review discharge planning guidelines for persons in inpatient settings and the expectations of community-based settings. Answering this question correctly requires the integration of this knowledge. See Chapter 4.

C22 C3

An OTA provides post-surgery occupational therapy services. The OTA designs a dynamic splint for an individual recovering from a tendon repair. At which angle should the OTA position the outrigger?

Answer Choices:
A. 45 degrees to the joint.
B. 90 degrees to the joint.
C. 60 degrees to the joint.
D. 110 degrees to the joint.

Correct Answer: B.

Rationale:
The most appropriate angle of pull is 90 degrees for it provides the most effective application of force. The application of a perpendicular force prevents unwanted traction on the joint and shearing stress. As the person's condition improves and mobility increases, the OTA must adjust the outrigger to maintain the 90-degree angle of pull.

Type of Reasoning: Deductive
One must recall the guidelines for dynamic splinting and angle of pull. This is recall of factual knowledge, which is a deductive reasoning skill. For this situation, 90 degrees is the appropriate angle of pull. If answered incorrectly, review splinting guidelines. See Chapter 11.

C23 C5

In a skilled nursing facility, an OTA works with a patient who incurred a CVA. The patient has insulin-dependent type I diabetes mellitus. The patient has developed hypertonicity in the right upper extremity (UE). The OTA fabricates a resting hand splint to prevent contractures and trains the patient in how to don and doff the splint independently. When providing patient education, which is most important for the OTA to review with the client as essential to complete on a daily basis?

Answer Choices:
A. Complete right UE PROM exercises to maintain mobility.
B. Position right UE within visual field to decrease visual neglect.
C. Raise right UE above the heart to decrease edema.
D. Check for red marks on the skin to prevent skin breakdown.

Correct Answer: D.

Rationale:
Pressure ulcers can be caused by too much pressure being exerted on the same area of the skin, blocking flow of blood to the skin. Wearing a resting hand splint (or any splint) can cause pressure points that can lead to skin breakdown and pressure ulcers. Daily skin inspections to identify any red spots will enable the patient to bring these pressure points to the attention of the OTA. The OTA can then modify the splint as needed to prevent skin breakdown and decrease the risk of pressure ulcers. This is particularly important in this case because the patient has diabetes. One of the most common complications associated with type 1 diabetes is delayed wound healing. If left untreated, red spots on the skin can progress to wounds that can lead to infection. Frequent monitoring of skin integrity is a key preventive technique to eliminate this complication of diabetes. Positioning the UE within the person's visual field is a technique used for left side neglect, which is not identified as a presenting symptom in this item. UE PROM exercises are not a technique used to decrease hypertonicity. UE edema is not always present in persons who have a CVA, and it is not identified as a complication in this item scenario.

Type of Reasoning: Inductive
This question requires the test taker to determine a best course of action based on the diagnosis and presenting problems. Knowledge about insulin-dependent type I diabetes mellitus and possible precautions is paramount to arriving at a correct conclusion. For this question, because of the diagnosis and likelihood for pressure ulcers from wearing a new splint, the OTA should educate the client to check for red marks on the skin to prevent skin breakdown. If answered incorrectly, review splint safety guidelines. See Chapter 11.

C24 C8

An occupational therapist and OTA are hired to implement a driver rehabilitation program for a community-based agency for older adults. Which is the first action the occupational therapist and OTA should take to develop this program?

Answer Choices:
A. Determine the cost of commercially available driving rehabilitation programs.
B. Learn their state's driving laws and requirements.
C. Develop admission criteria for program participants.
D. Develop a marketing plan to obtain program referrals.

Correct Answer: B.

Rationale:
It is essential for the occupational therapist and OTA to know their state driving laws and regulations (e.g., the mandated reporting of a person's driving ability after the incurrence of an illness or injury) prior to developing a driver rehabilitation program. Knowledge and adherence to state laws are essential to avoid potential program liability. The occupational therapist and OTA would also need to know their state laws and regulations prior to setting admission criteria or a marketing plan. While determining the cost of commercially available driving rehabilitation programs can be informative, it is not the greatest program development priority. After the occupational therapist and OTA learn their state driving laws and regulations, they will need to conduct a needs assessment. Based on this assessment they may determine that a customized program to meet their target population needs is preferable to a commercially available driving rehabilitation program.

Type of Reasoning: Inductive
Clinical knowledge and judgment are the most important skills needed for answering this question, which requires inductive reasoning skill. In this case, the occupational therapist and OTA must first learn their state's driving laws and requirements in order to proceed with the development of a driver rehabilitation program. If answered incorrectly, review program development and driver rehabilitation program guidelines. The integration of this knowledge is required to determine the correct answer. See Chapters 4 and 15.

C25 C8

An OTA provides an accessibility consultation to a business that has hired a new employee who uses a wheelchair for mobility. The only entrance to the business has four steps, each seven inches high. Which ramp length is best for the OTA to recommend the business have constructed?

Answer Choices:
A. 14 feet.
B. 28 feet.
C. 35 feet.

Correct Answer: B.

Rationale:
Accessibility guidelines state that the ramp should be constructed with one foot of ramp length for each inch of rise. The total rise for these steps is 28 inches; therefore, the ramp should be 28 feet long. The other options do not meet these guidelines.

Type of Reasoning: Deductive
This question requires recall of guidelines, which is factual knowledge. Deductive reasoning skills are utilized whenever one must recall facts to find ideal solutions. In this situation, accessibility guidelines indicate that for every one inch of rise, there should be one foot of ramp; therefore, the ramp should be 28 feet long. If answered incorrectly, review accessibility guidelines, especially ramp construction. See Chapter 15.

C26 C6

A person who is a home maintainer and parent is hospitalized for depression and prescribed Parnate to treat depressive symptoms. The patient's hobbies are gardening and jogging. Upon discussing the functional effects of medications with the patient, which is the most important precaution for the OTA to review?

Answer Choices:
A. Photosensitivity.
B. Orthostatic hypotension.
C. Amenorrhea.
D. Dietary restrictions.

Correct Answer: D.

Rationale:
Parnate is a monoamine oxidase inhibitor (MAOI). It has serious side effects when a person eats foods that contain the amino acid tyramine. Tyramine increases blood pressure and may lead to stroke or other cardiovascular reactions. Photosensitivity, orthostatic hypotension, and amenorrhea can be side effects of psychiatric medications, but they are not typically a major concern of MAOIs. These side effects are a more common concern with antipsychotic medications.

Type of Reasoning: Deductive
One must recall the precautions for psychotropic medications in order to arrive at a correct conclusion. This requires deductive reasoning skill, where factual knowledge is essential to choosing the correct solution. Dietary restrictions are critically important to consider with persons taking a MAOI, such as Parnate. Review precautions for MAOIs if answered incorrectly. See Chapter 10.

C27 C1

A 21-month-old child with severe spastic quadriplegia has major sensorimotor deficits. The child is cognitively intact and exhibits age-appropriate cognitive skills. The OTA recommends a play activity to enhance these cognitive abilities and provide the child with a fun and pleasurable experience. Which is the best object for the OTA to recommend?

Answer Choices:
A. A multicolored mobile of objects of interest placed over the child's stroller.
B. A mechanical toy with a chin-controlled on/off switch.
C. A shape sorter with foam squares, triangles, and circles.
D. A battery-controlled hammock swing.

Correct Answer: B.

Rationale:
At 21 months, a child is cognitively able to operate and control mechanical toys. The chin-controlled switch will enable this child to self-direct their play with their spastic quadriplegia. A swing and a mobile are cognitively too low for this child's abilities. They are passive activities that would not provide active engagement of the child. The ability to identify and sort shapes does occur at 21 months; however, the use of a shape sorter requires motor abilities beyond this child's capacities.

Type of Reasoning: Inductive
This question requires one to determine the best object for enhancing cognitive abilities of this child. This requires inductive reasoning skill, where clinical judgment is paramount to arriving at a correct conclusion. For this situation, a mechanical toy with a chin-controlled on/off switch is most appropriate. If answered incorrectly, review developmental levels of cognition and play. The application of this knowledge is required to answer this question correctly. See Chapter 5.

C28 C8

An entry-level OTA conducts an in-service at an outpatient wheelchair clinic for individuals with central nervous system dysfunction. According to the principles of wheelchair prescription, which of the following statements is accurate for the OTA to make during the presentation? Select the three BEST responses.

Answer Choices:
A. Firm seats are needed to provide stability.
B. Soft seats are needed to prevent decubiti.
C. Lapboards can position and support a flaccid upper extremity.
D. Back heights should be extended to facilitate weight shifting.
E. Lower back heights can increase functional mobility.
F. Seat angles should be 45 degrees to prevent falling forward.

Correct Answers: A, C, and E.

Rationale:
Firm seats provide stability and a solid base that can be used to prevent decubiti, contractures, and deformities. They can also increase sitting tolerance, proper positioning, and functional abilities. Soft seats are contraindicated as they do not provide sufficient pressure relief. Soft seats can 'collapse' under pressure and can increase the risk of decubiti. Lapboards can serve the same purpose as an arm trough to position and support a flaccid upper extremity. They can also provide a working 'tabletop' surface. Extended back heights increase the difficulty of weight shifting because the person cannot hook their arm around the push handle. Lower back heights can increase functional mobility as in sports chairs. However, a lower back height can increase back strain. The recommended seat angle ranges from 80 to 110 degrees.

Type of Reasoning: Deductive
This question requires recall of guidelines and principles, which is factual knowledge. Deductive reasoning skills are utilized whenever one must recall facts to solve everyday problems. In this situation, the OTA is accurate in stating that firm seats are needed to provide stability, lapboards can position and support a flaccid upper extremity, and lower back heights can increase functional mobility. If answered incorrectly, review wheelchair prescription guidelines. See Chapter 15.

C29 C7

An older adult with a diagnosis of osteoarthritis in both knees is referred to inpatient occupational therapy. During screening, the patient expresses a desire to return home to live alone independently. The occupational therapist and OTA collaborate to determine their next action. Which should the therapist and the OTA do next in response to the patient's stated goal?

Answer Choices:
A. Recommend adaptations to the patient's home environment to increase safety.
B. Teach the patient energy conservation techniques to use during IADL tasks.
C. Evaluate the patient's BADL and IADL using a standardized measure.
D. Train the patient in a home resistive exercise program to build strength and ROM.

Correct Answer: C.

Rationale:
The patient has just been screened for OT services, so the next step in the OT process is to evaluate the person's functional abilities. OTAs can contribute to the evaluation process using standardized measures. Osteoarthritis is isolated to specific joints and is not systemic in nature. By evaluating the patient's BADL and IADL, the OTA can collaborate with the occupational therapist to determine the activity demands of the BADL and IADL the patient performs while keeping in mind the specific joints that are affected. Once this information is obtained, then the OTA and occupational therapist can make informed recommendations based upon their observations and clinical reasoning to decrease excessive loading and repetitive use of these joints. Simple adaptations, such as moving items higher (onto counters, etc.) can be recommended and energy conservation techniques can be taught based upon the evaluation results. Resistive exercise programs are contraindicated for persons with osteoarthritis.

Type of Reasoning: Inferential
One must determine the best approach for evaluation of this patient, given their stated desires and diagnosis. This requires inferential reasoning skill, where one must infer or draw conclusions about the approach that will result in the best functional outcome. In this case, evaluation of the patient's daily activities using a standardized measure is the best approach to learn about their ability to safely return home while managing the symptoms of osteoarthritis. Review evaluation guidelines and home management assessments if answered incorrectly. Integration of this knowledge with an understanding of the impact osteoarthritis has on BADL and IADL is required to determine a correct answer. See Chapters 3, 6, and 14.

C30 C6

An OTA conducts an activity group on an acute inpatient psychiatric facility. The group members are individuals who have poor orientation to reality. Which is the best activity for the OTA to include in this group?

Answer Choices:
A. A discussion of the effects of hospitalization on occupational roles.
B. The assembly of wooden toys for a children's unit.
C. Guided imagery for stress management.
D. Structured verbalizations about personal assets and limitations.

Correct Answer: B.

Rationale:
A group on an acute inpatient psychiatric unit for persons with poor orientation to reality should include activities that are structured, easily completed in one session, and provide a concrete result to reinforce reality. Wooden toy kits meet these criteria and donating them to the children's unit facilitates Yalom's curative factor of altruism. Discussions and verbal activities are abstract, and even if presented in a structured format, they would be difficult for persons with poor orientation to reality to follow. They also involve personal issues that require time to process feelings, effective verbal skills, and an adequate level of insight. This time allotment and client capabilities are typically not available in a setting with a short length of stay. Guided imagery can be difficult for a disoriented person to focus on and can be frightening to an acutely ill person.

Type of Reasoning: Inductive
One must determine which activity best meets the needs of persons who are acutely ill and disoriented. This requires inductive reasoning skill, where the test taker must utilize clinical judgment to determine the best course of action. In this situation, the assembly of wooden toys for a children's unit is the best choice for individuals with poor orientation to reality. This option provides a structured activity that is easily completed in one session. If answered incorrectly, review Mosey's taxonomy of groups and recommended therapeutic activities for acutely ill individuals in inpatient psychiatric settings. See Chapters 3 and 13.

C31 C9

An OTA working for a home care agency provides an in-service about Medicare reimbursement guidelines for durable medical equipment (DME) to new employees. Which item is accurate for the OTA to describe as reimbursable by Medicare?

Answer Choices:
A. A raised toilet seat for a person after a hip replacement.
B. A reacher for a person with arthritis in both hips.
C. A walker for a person who cannot ambulate in the home without one.
D. Grab bars in the bathroom for a person who cannot bathe or toilet without them.

Correct Answer: C.

Rationale:
The walker is covered by Medicare. The others are not. The criteria for durable medical equipment (DME) to be reimbursable by Medicare are that the item must be necessary and reasonable to treat an illness or incidence of decreased functioning, must have a medical purpose, be used repeatedly, and not be useful in the absence of an illness.

Type of Reasoning: Deductive
This question requires one to recall Medicare reimbursement guidelines, which is factual knowledge. Deductive reasoning skills are utilized whenever one must recall concrete principles and guidelines to draw conclusions. The only item listed that is considered a medical necessity by Medicare is a walker when issued for a person who cannot ambulate in the home without one. Review Medicare guidelines for reimbursement of DME if answered incorrectly. See Chapter 4.

C32 C7

An OTA works with a parent with a complete spinal cord injury at the C7 level. The client has identified a goal of reengaging in play activities with their children aged 8 and 10. Which is the best adapted play activity for the OTA to include in the intervention plan?

Answer Choices:
A. A board game using a tenodesis grasp.
B. An arts and crafts project using a mouth stick paint brush.
C. A woodworking project using a universal cuff to hold tools.
D. A computer game using a typing stick.

Correct Answer: A.

Rationale:
An individual with a C7 SCI has a tenodesis grasp that can be effective for picking up and releasing game pieces. Board games are developmentally age-appropriate for children aged 8 and 10. The other activity adaptation options are appropriate for individuals with higher spinal cord injuries than C7.

Type of Reasoning: Inductive
One must utilize clinical knowledge and judgment to determine the best activity for a parent with a C7 injury. In this case, a board game using a tenodesis grasp is most appropriate given the person's level of injury. If answered incorrectly, review the functional abilities of persons with C7 injury. See Chapter 14.

C33 C7

An OTA screens potential members for a vocational rehabilitation group according to established inclusionary and exclusionary criteria for membership. Functional deficits in which area would exclude persons from membership in this group?

Answer Choices:
A. Problem solving.
B. Self-awareness of strengths.
C. Social skills.
D. Personal self-care.

Correct Answer: D.

Rationale:
Personal self-care skills should be developed prior to attending a vocational rehabilitation. A prevocational group would be appropriate for persons who exhibit self-care deficits. The other options can be addressed in a vocational rehabilitation group, as they are essential to success in the work setting.

Type of Reasoning: Deductive
One must recall the guidelines for membership in a vocational group in order to arrive at a correct conclusion. This is recall of factual information, which is a deductive reasoning skill. For this situation, personal self-care skills must be developed prior to attending a vocational rehabilitation group. Therefore, an individual with deficits in this area would be excluded from this group. If answered incorrectly, review vocational rehabilitation program foci. See Chapters 4 and 14.

C34 C7

An occupational therapist and an OTA provide consultation services to a manufacturing company that is seeking to decrease their employees' incidence of repetitive stress disorders (RSDs). Which action is best for the therapist and OTA to take first to address this need?

Answer Choices:
A. Conduct an ergonomic risk assessment of the employees' work tasks.
B. Construct custom-made ergonomic tool handles for each employee.
C. Modify the machinery used by employees to decrease vibration and force.
D. Adapt work tasks to decrease stooping, reaching, and bending.

Correct Answer: A.

Rationale:
The completion of an ergonomic risk assessment of the employees' work tasks is needed to determine the manual handling, physical energy, and other musculoskeletal demands of each task. An ergonomic risk assessment also includes the evaluation of environment in which work tasks are performed and the tools that are used. Based upon this comprehensive assessment, the therapist and OTA can make recommendations and provide interventions to prevent RSDs. These can include making adaptations and modifications to work activities, tools, machines, and the physical environment. See Tables 14-7 and 14-8 in Chapter 14 for more information about ergonomic risk assessment.

Type of Reasoning: Inductive
This question requires one to utilize clinical judgment to determine the best action is addressing the needs of employees with repetitive stress disorders. This requires inductive reasoning skill. For this case, the OTA should conduct an ergonomic risk assessment of the employees' work tasks. If answered incorrectly, review ergonomic assessment guidelines. See Chapter 14.

C35 C4

An OTA collaborates with the occupational therapist to complete the discharge plan for an individual with a right cerebral vascular accident (CVA) who has completed a two-week inpatient rehabilitation program. The patient is right-hand dominant. The patient exhibits residual cognitive-perceptual deficits but seems unaware of these problems. Which discharge recommendation is best for the OTA to discuss with the occupational therapist?

Answer Choices:
A. An extension of length of stay.
B. A full-time home health aide.
C. Assistance with personal care.
D. Supervision for cooking.

Correct Answer: D.

Rationale:
A right CVA results in left-sided deficits, decreased judgment, and diminished insight. The latter two deficits can pose a safety risk during cooking activities. Therefore, supervision is recommended. Since the person is right-hand dominant, the ability to perform many personal tasks will likely remain intact. In addition, it is highly likely that the individual has received intervention to increase the functional abilities of their left UE and/or to develop unilateral functional skills during their two-week rehabilitation program. Therefore, a full-time home health aide, personal care assistance, and an extension of length of stay are not warranted.

Type of Reasoning: Inductive
One must utilize clinical knowledge and judgment to determine the recommendation that best considers the person's limitations. This requires inductive reasoning skill. In this case, recommending supervision for cooking is best out of the choices provided as it poses the greatest risk to safety. If answered incorrectly, review intervention planning guidelines and IADL activity adaptations for persons with cognitive deficits. This knowledge can be used to inform discharge decisions. See Chapters 12 and 14.

C36 C4

An occupational therapist and OTA plan intervention for an individual with cognitive-perceptual deficits. In deciding whether to use a dynamic interactional approach or a deficit-specific approach, which is most important for the occupational therapist and OTA to consider?

Answer Choices:
A. The client's auditory-processing skills.
B. The availability of familial support.
C. The client's social interaction skills.
D. The client's problem-solving skills.

Correct Answer: A.

Rationale:
The dynamic interactional approach utilizes awareness questioning to help the individual detect errors, estimate task difficulty, and predict outcomes. Therefore, the occupational therapist and OTA must consider the client's level of auditory-processing skills to determine if adaptations or modifications are needed when implementing this approach. If an individual has severe auditory-processing deficits, it may indicate the need to use a deficit-specific approach for cognitive-perceptual remediation. Family support, social interaction skills, and problem-solving skills can all influence intervention, but they are not determining factors in selecting which theoretical approach to use in this case.

Type of Reasoning: Inferential
One must link the dynamic interactional approach to functional skills in order to determine which skill is most important to consider. This requires inferential reasoning, where one must consider the primary features of the dynamic interactional approach and then determine the skill that is primarily utilized. In this case, auditory processing is the most utilized skill. Review the dynamic interactional approach if answered incorrectly. See Chapter 12.

C37 C8

A 10-year-old with congenital anomalies wears bilateral ankle-foot orthoses. The parents want the child to be able to don and doff shoes independently, but the child cannot tie shoe laces. Which is the best footwear recommendation for the OTA to make for the child to wear?

Answer Choices:
A. Leather slip-on loafers.
B. Slip-on tennis shoes with no laces.
C. Running shoes with Velcro shoe closures.
D. Hi-rise sneakers with sliding adapters on the laces.

Correct Answer: C.

Rationale:
Running shoes are the best option for use with ankle-foot orthoses (AFOs). Velcro closures will help the child be independent until lace tying is learned. Leather slip-on loafers will not correctly support the AFOs. Slip-on tennis shoes that do not have laces do not have adequate support in the upper part of the foot to maintain the AFOs. The sliding adapters are a good option to replace the laces, but the hi-rise sneakers will not likely allow for placement of the AFOs on the feet.

Type of Reasoning: Inductive
Clinical knowledge and judgment are the most important skills needed for answering this question, which requires inductive reasoning skill. Knowledge of the diagnosis and most appropriate clinical outcomes is key to choosing the best solution. In this case, shoes with Velcro closures are best as they help facilitate independence while providing the needed support when wearing AFOs. See Chapter 15.

C38 C8

An OTA provides caregiver education to the spouse of a client with a moderately severe neurocognitive disorder and a secondary diagnosis of left CVA. The client is dependent upon a wheelchair for mobility. The spouse reports that the client becomes restless at mealtimes, consistently undoes the lap belt, and tries to get up from the wheelchair. The spouse reports that the need to constantly say "sit down" is personally exhausting and often increases the client's agitation. Frequently, neither eats a complete dinner. Which is the most effective recommendation for the OTA to make to the spouse?

Answer Choices:
A. Allow the spouse to get up when restless and provide dinner to the client at a later time.
B. Use a wheelchair lap tray to serve several smaller meals to the client at intervals throughout the day.
C. Hire a home care attendant to assist the client at mealtimes and provide some respite to the spouse.
D. Use a wheelchair lap tray to serve the client large meals at breakfast, lunch, and dinner.

Correct Answer: B.

Rationale:
Because a person deemed dependent upon a wheelchair for mobility has significant motor deficits, they must be considered at risk for falling if they get up without supervision. A lap tray is a permissible and reasonable restraint if it is necessary to maintain a person's safety, allows for increased function, and less-restrictive restraints have been attempted. A family member can approve the use of this device if a person is not cognitively intact. These criteria apply to this case. A lap belt has been applied, but it has not been successful. A lap tray with food on it can provide physical and sensory cues necessary to keep the client seated for a time that is sufficient for eating a small meal. It is advisable to provide small meals at frequent intervals rather than three large meals when a person has significant cognitive impairments. Hiring a home care attendant can relieve the spouse's caregiver stress, but it does not address the client's risk of falling when attempting to get up from the wheelchair. It is unlikely that this behavior would cease with the presence of a home care attendant.

Type of Reasoning: Inductive
Clinical knowledge and judgment are the most important skills needed for answering this question, which requires inductive reasoning skill. Knowledge of the diagnosis and most effective recommendations is essential to choosing the best solution. In this case, recommending use of a lap tray to serve several smaller meals throughout the day is most appropriate. If answered incorrectly, review treatment guidelines for persons with neurocognitive disorders and principles of fall prevention and restraint reduction. The integration of this knowledge is required to determine the correct answer. See Chapters 10 and 15.

C39 C4

A patient who is status-post left frontal lobe ischemia has difficulty bearing weight through the right lower extremity during reaching activities (e.g., standing at a sink during a morning self-care routine). The OTA implements a motor relearning program (MRP). Which is the best intervention for the OTA to provide according to this approach?

Answer Choices:
A. Therapeutic handling to affect the central nervous system.
B. A stool to sit on during reaching activities.
C. Joint compression to the right lower extremity during reaching activities.
D. Verbal and visual feedback while practicing reaching.

Correct Answer: D.

Rationale:
An MRP approach provides verbal and visual feedback to give a person the input needed to make postural and limb adjustments. Therapeutic handling to affect the central nervous system is consistent with a neurodevelopmental treatment (NDT) approach. Providing a stool to sit on during reaching activities can be used for safety purposes. This is consistent with a compensatory approach. Joint compression is a technique used for sensory modulation disorders (e.g., tactile defensiveness, hypersensitivity/over-responsivity, hyposensitivity/under-responsivity, and sensory seeking).

Type of Reasoning: Deductive
One must recall the guidelines of an MRP in order to arrive at a correct conclusion. This is recall of factual knowledge, which is a deductive reasoning skill. For this situation, the most appropriate intervention is verbal and visual feedback while practicing reaching. If answered incorrectly, review MRP guidelines. See Chapter 12.

C40 C4

A middle school student with learning disabilities exhibits no behavioral problems in the classroom. However, whenever the class is in a line waiting to switch classrooms, the student becomes agitated and often pushes classmates. The OTA consultant advises the teacher that this behavior may be indicative of an underlying problem. Which of the following is most accurate for the OTA to identify as a potential disorder warranting further evaluation?

Answer Choices:
A. Gravitational insecurity.
B. A conduct disorder.
C. Antisocial tendencies.
D. Tactile defensiveness.

Correct Answer: D.

Rationale:
The tactile stimuli due to closeness of peers in a line can become overwhelming to an individual with tactile defensiveness. The behavior described in the scenario is not reflective of behavior indicative of the other disorders listed.

Type of Reasoning: Analytical
This question provides symptoms and the test taker must determine the likely cause for them. This is an analytical reasoning skill, as questions of this nature often ask one to analyze a group of symptoms in order to determine a diagnosis. In this situation the symptoms indicate tactile defensiveness, which should be reviewed if answered incorrectly. See Chapters 10 and 12.

C41 C2

A cooking group meets for 1½ hours each week at a partial hospitalization program. During the group, members do not smoke, they wait for everyone to be served before eating, and they clean up after the meal. When reporting these observations, which of the following is the most accurate statement for the OTA to make?

Answer Choices:
A. The group protocol is clear.
B. Group norms are being followed.
C. Group sanctions are effective.
D. A diversity of group roles is evident.

Correct Answer: B.

Rationale:
Group norms are the expected and accepted behaviors in a group. These norms establish an atmosphere of mutual respect, safety, and support. Sanctions are implemented only in a group if members' behaviors fall outside of the group's norms and are considered deviant. The scenario does not provide sufficient information to determine members' group roles. A group protocol outlines the group's membership criteria, goals, and activities.

Type of Reasoning: Analytical
This question provides a description of a functional activity, and the test taker must determine the likely definition of such an activity. This is an analytical reasoning skill, as questions of this nature often ask one to analyze descriptors of functional skills to determine the overall skill involved. In this situation, the behaviors demonstrate that group norms are being followed. Review principles of group norms if answered incorrectly. See Chapter 3.

C42 C4

An elementary school teacher has been recently diagnosed with multiple sclerosis (MS). Which adaptation is best for the OTA to recommend the teacher use to accommodate for the effects of MS on their classroom teaching?

Answer Choices:
A. The use of anchoring techniques to compensate for scanning deficits.
B. A daily list of tasks to compensate for cognitive deficits.
C. A motorized scooter to compensate for decreased endurance.
D. A high stool to compensate for lower extremity weakness.

Correct Answer: D.

Rationale:
Lower extremity muscle weakness is common in the early stages of MS. Using a high stool will provide the teacher with an alternative to standing while maintaining visual contact with the entire classroom. In addition, the use of a stool can help minimize the effects of fatigue which is often common in all stages of MS. Visual disturbances (e.g., diplopia, partial blindness, nystagmus, eye pain) can occur during all stages of MS. However, scanning deficits are consistent with unilateral neglect which is a disorder typically associated with CVAs, not MS. Cognitive deficits are not common in the early stages of MS; thus, the composition of a daily list of tasks is likely not needed at this time. While MS can affect endurance, it is unlikely in the early stage of MS for endurance to be decreased to a level that requires the use of a mobilized scooter.

Type of Reasoning: Inferential
One must determine the most appropriate recommendation for an individual, given knowledge of the presenting diagnosis. This requires inferential reasoning skill, where one must infer or draw conclusions about a best course of action. In this situation, the therapist should recommend a high stool to compensate for lower extremity weakness, given an understanding that lower extremity muscle weakness is common in the early stages of MS. Review symptoms of MS if answered incorrectly. See Chapter 7.

C43 C8

An OTA provides caregiver training to the spouse of an individual with cerebellar cortical degeneration. The focus of the session is on community mobility using a wheelchair. The individual is dependent upon the spouse's assistance for mobility. Which of the following is most effective for the OTA to recommend the spouse do when going down a moderately graded slope?

Answer Choices:
A. Tilt the wheelchair backward to its gravitational balance point and then go down forward.
B. Go down backward, with all wheelchair wheels maintaining contact with ground surface.
C. Tilt the wheelchair backward to its gravitational balance point and then go down backward.
D. Push forward as on flat surfaces but lean body back for extra drag.

Correct Answer: B.

Rationale:
Proceeding down a moderately graded slope backward with all wheelchair wheels maintaining contact with the ground enables the spouse to use body weight to slow the chair's momentum. If the spouse tires, they can readily stop and use their body weight to hold the chair in place while putting the wheelchair brakes on. Pushing the chair in a forward position can be dangerous on a graded slope, for if the spouse loses their grip and/or tires, it could be very difficult to regain control of the situation. Maintaining the chair in a backward tilt position while going backward is an unnecessary use of energy and can greatly contribute to caregiver's physical fatigue.

Type of Reasoning: Inductive
Clinical knowledge and judgment are the most important skills needed for answering this question, which requires inductive reasoning skill. Knowledge of safety guidelines in mobility utilizing a wheelchair is essential to arriving at a correct conclusion. In this case, the OTA should recommend descending a moderately graded slope backward with all wheelchair wheels in contact with the ground. If answered incorrectly, review community wheelchair mobility guidelines. See Chapter 15.

C44 C1

An OTA leads a social skills group for children aged 10–12 years with conduct disorders. One of the children complains that the group activity is stupid and boring. Which is the most effective response for the OTA to provide in response to this complaint?

Answer Choices:
A. Encourage the child to complete the activity with the group.
B. Allow the child to leave the group since uninterested.
C. Allow the child to suggest a different group activity.
D. Tell the child the complaint will be discussed at the next family meeting.

Correct Answer: A.

Rationale:
Children between the ages of 10 and 12 are typically at the developmental age of cooperative play, which emerges at age 7 years. During this stage of development, children participate in games and learn to play according to rules in a cooperative manner. Encouraging the child to complete the activity with the group provides the child with the opportunity to develop age-appropriate social skills. Children with conduct disorders often show disregard for others and tend to violate rules; therefore, completing a planned activity with others is particularly relevant. Allowing the child to alter the group's in-progress activity does not address these issues. There is no need for the child to leave the group or for the behavior to be discussed at a family meeting.

Type of Reasoning: Inductive
This question requires one to determine the most appropriate response to a child with conduct disorder. This requires inductive reasoning skill, where clinical judgment is paramount in arriving at a correct conclusion. For this situation, the OTA should encourage the child to complete the activity with the group. If answered incorrectly, review the diagnostic criteria of conduct disorders and the typical developmental sequence of play. Integration of this knowledge is required for a correct answer. See Chapters 5 and 10.

C45 C6

An older adult diagnosed three years ago with a neurocognitive disorder has been admitted to a hospital for regulation of medication. The occupational therapist and OTA determine that the patient demonstrates diminished memory skills since the evaluation completed during a previous hospitalization. However, they determine the person is still able to live at home with support and supervision. During the discharge planning meeting, which activity should the OTA recommend family members perform for the patient?

Answer Choices:
A. Weeding the garden.
B. Sorting and folding laundry.
C. Preparing cold sandwiches.
D. Cooking hot meals.

Correct Answer: D.

Rationale:
Cooking hot meals provides the main opportunity for the person who is increasingly forgetful to be unsafe. Leaving the stove on due to memory loss can be a fire hazard. The person can continue the other activities without compromising personal safety. In addition, weeding and sorting and folding laundry are structured and repetitive activities that can facilitate the person's active engagement.

Type of Reasoning: Inductive
Knowledge of neurocognitive disorders and clinical judgment are the most important skills needed for answering this question, which requires inductive reasoning skill. In this case, because cooking independently presents the greatest risk for safety, the OTA should recommend that the patient refrain from this IADL upon return to home. If answered incorrectly, review activity guidelines for persons with neurocognitive disorders. See Chapter 10.

C46 C4

An individual with Parkinson's disease exhibits difficulty moving from sitting in a chair to standing. Which technique is best for the OTA to recommend the person use to help successfully complete this functional mobility activity?

Answer Choices:
A. Rise from the chair while sitting with buttocks against the back of the chair.
B. Extend both legs so that both feet are in front of the chair while rising.
C. Sit at the edge of the chair and rock back and forth before rising.
D. Rise while weight bearing on one foot and pushing up with both arms.

Correct Answer: C.

Rationale:
One of the most common problems that persons with Parkinson's disease have is difficulty with the initiation of movement. Rocking back and forth prior to moving from sit to stand provides the person with vestibular and proprioceptive input that can help facilitate movement. Rising from the chair while sitting with buttocks against the back of the chair increases the difficulty of the activity, so it is not effective. Rising with extended legs or while weight bearing on one foot are incorrect; both employ poor body mechanics and may be unsafe.

Type of Reasoning: Inductive
This question requires one to determine the best technique to recommend for a functional mobility activity. This requires inductive reasoning skill, where clinical judgment is paramount in arriving at a correct conclusion. For this situation, the OTA should instruct the person to sit at the edge of the chair and rock back and forth before rising. If answered incorrectly, review the functional impact of Parkinson's disease and principles of activity analysis. The integration of this knowledge is required to determine the correct answer. See Chapters 3 and 7.

C47 C3

A newborn with severe osteogenesis imperfecta (OI) is referred to occupational therapy. The occupational therapist completes an evaluation and reviews the results with the OTA. They collaboratively determine a focus for the initial family intervention session. Which is most important to include in this session?

Answer Choices:
A. Guidelines for the completion of passive range of motion to maintain mobility and prevent contractures.
B. Instruction on safe handling and positioning in gravity-eliminated positions to prevent fractures.
C. Demonstration on how to tightly swaddle the infant to soothe and provide postural support.
D. Instruction on handling techniques to encourage the infant's integration of both sides of the body.

Correct Answer: B.

Rationale:
Osteogenesis imperfecta (OI) is a disorder caused by the dysfunction of one of several genes responsible for producing collagen to strengthen bones. Severe OI results in brittle bones that fracture very easily. Therefore, it is most important to instruct the parents on how to safely handle and position their infant to prevent fractures (e.g., feed the infant in a semi-reclined gravity-eliminated position). OI does not impede joint mobility nor does it result in contractures. Therefore, passive range of motion (PROM) is not needed. Moreover, the completion of PROM would require the parents to grasp the child's extremities. This is contraindicated due to fracture risk. In addition, infants with OI are oversensitive to pressure and movement due to pain. As a result, tightly swaddling an infant with OI is contraindicated due to the pain and fracture risk it would inflict. Infants with OI do not require intervention to promote integration of both sides of the body. This focus is consistent with a neurodevelopmental treatment approach which is used for children with central nervous system dysfunction.

Type of Reasoning: Inductive
For this scenario, the test taker must have knowledge of OI and handling techniques in order to arrive at a correct conclusion. Questions of this nature often necessitate inductive reasoning skill where clinical judgment is paramount to drawing correct conclusions. For this scenario, instructions should be given on safe handling and positioning in gravity-eliminated positions to prevent fractures. If answered incorrectly, review OI presenting symptoms and OT interventions for children with OI. See Chapter 6.

C48 C1

An OTA works for a community-based program that provides wellness services to older adults. The OTA provides an in-service about the impact of activities on typical age-related body system changes. Which are best for the OTA to emphasize during this presentation? Select the three BEST responses.

Answer Choices:
A. Aerobic exercise training programs should be avoided due to their inherent cardiopulmonary risks.
B. Low-intensity strength training is most effective for increasing and/or maintaining muscle strength.
C. High-intensity strength training is most effective for increasing and/or maintaining muscle strength.
D. Increased levels of physical activity should be planned to include adequate warm-ups, cool downs, and rest periods.
E. Walking, stair climbing, and activities performed in standing should be avoided to minimize bone loss.
F. Yoga, tai-chi, and pool exercises can be used to maintain and/or increase strength and flexibility.

Correct Answers: C, D, and F.

Rationale:
Yoga, tai-chi, and pool exercises are well-tolerated by older adults. In addition to helping people maintain and/or increase strength and flexibility, they can improve cardiopulmonary function. They also can be used with persons with musculoskeletal and neurological impairments. Strength training, including isometric and progressive resistive exercise regimes, can result in significant increases in strength in older adults. Both moderate and high intensity programs have been successfully used with older adults to increase/maintain muscle strength required for functional activity. However, high intensity training programs (70-80% of one-repetition maximum) produce quicker and more predictable results than moderate ones. Older adults should be encouraged to participate in aerobic exercise training programs. These programs can significantly improve cardiopulmonary function. They help decrease heart rate, improve recovery heart rates, improve maximal oxygen uptake, decrease systolic blood pressure, reduce breathlessness, lower perceived exertion, and improve functional capacity. However, increased levels of physical activity should be planned to include adequate warm-ups, cool downs, and rest periods. Walking, stair climbing, and all activities that are performed in standing are considered weight bearing (gravity-loading) exercises. Active engagement in these activities should be encouraged because they can decrease bone loss in older adults.

Type of Reasoning: Inductive
For this question, the test taker must have knowledge of exercise and physical activity recommendations for older adults. Applying such knowledge to this exam item necessitates inductive reasoning skill. In this case, the OTA should emphasize yoga, tai-chi, and pool exercises to maintain and/or increase strength and flexibility; high-intensity strength training for increasing and/or maintaining muscle strength; and increased levels of physical activity to include adequate warm-ups, cool downs, and rest periods. If answered incorrectly, review exercise guidelines for older adults. See Chapter 5.

C49 C6

An OTA provides services to a client with depression. The client consistently makes negative comments about personal capabilities, reports feeling hopeless for the future, and has a pessimistic view of the world. The OTA collaborates with the occupational therapist and client to develop an intervention plan. Which approach is best to include in this plan?

Answer Choices:
A. The identification of unhelpful thinking patterns, changing inaccurate beliefs, acquiring coping skills, and developing self-reliance and meaningful healthy occupational patterns.
B. The provision of environmental modifications and activity adaptations to compensate for cognitive deficits, support existing abilities, and allow the greatest degree of independence.
C. The use of projective tasks to promote self-awareness, identify and explore intrapsychic content, bring unconscious conflicts to consciousness, and facilitate intrapsychic conflict resolution.

Correct Answer: A.

Rationale:
The client's pattern of negative thinking is consistent with the 'cognitive triad' identified in the cognitive behavioral frame of reference. This triad underlies depression and is comprised of negative self-evaluation, a pessimistic world view, and a sense of hopelessness regarding the future. To treat these symptoms of depression, cognitive behavioral therapy (CBT) has been shown to be effective. Because an individual with depression tends to distort reality through dysfunctional thought processes, CBT works to alter negative thoughts about oneself, the world, and the future by correcting misinterpretations of life events. It combines principles of cognitive therapy and behavioral therapy by looking at a person's thoughts, beliefs, and actions and attempting to change maladaptive patterns of behavior. Identifying unhelpful thinking patterns, changing inaccurate beliefs, acquiring coping skills, and developing self-reliance and meaningful healthy occupational patterns are consistent with CBT and are appropriate to include in the intervention plan for a person with depression. Providing environmental modifications and activity adaptations to compensate for cognitive deficits, support existing abilities, and allow the greatest degree of independence are all consistent with Allen's cognitive disabilities model. This model proposes that cognitive ability is determined by biological factors and that the person's cognitive level cannot change. Using projective tasks to promote self-awareness, identify and explore intrapsychic content, bring unconscious conflicts to consciousness, and facilitate intrapsychic conflict resolution are consistent with a psychodynamic/psychoanalytic frame of reference. The use of this approach by OT practitioners requires specialized training.

Type of Reasoning: Inductive
For this question, one must determine the best course of action based on knowledge of depression and effective intervention approaches for this disorder. This requires inductive reasoning skill, where clinical judgment is often utilized to reach conclusions. For this situation, the intervention plan should identify unhelpful thinking patterns, change inaccurate beliefs, acquire coping skills, and develop self-reliance and meaningful healthy occupational patterns. If answered incorrectly, review diagnostic information about depression and CBT intervention approaches. See Chapters 10 and 13.

C50 C3

A client has completed a one week hospitalization for an exacerbation of rheumatoid arthritis (RA). The client currently has no complaints of pain and demonstrates the ability to integrate joint protection techniques into activities. The client enjoys crafting and is a member of a club that meets regularly to share craft ideas. At discharge, the client asks the OTA for a recommendation for a craft to demonstrate at the next club meeting. Which craft is best for the OTA to recommend the client demonstrate?

Answer Choices:
A. Throwing a clay vase on a pottery wheel.
B. Knitting a scarf according to a pattern.
C. Utilizing hand tools to build a wooden birdhouse.
D. Beading a necklace using glass or wooden beads.

Correct Answer: D.

Rationale:
Beading a necklace using glass or wooden beads is the only activity that complies with joint protection principles. Joint protection is critical for a client living with RA. One of the principles of joint protection is to avoid holding joints in one position or sustaining muscle contractions for extended periods of time. Other key principles are to avoid positions of deformity and not start an activity that cannot be immediately stopped if it requires capacities beyond the client's existing capabilities. Beading a necklace is a fine motor activity that requires grasp and release to compete. To complete this activity, no sustained holding is required and no stress is placed on the joints. A beading project can be stopped at any time without compromising the final product. Conversely, an individual cannot stop shaping a clay vase without compromising the final product. Throwing a clay vase requires sustained pressure. The wrists are placed in ulnar deviation to control the shape, which is contraindicated for a person with RA.. Knitting requires holding the needles in one position for an extended period of time. Utilizing hand tools require sustaining muscle contractions. Hand tools that have not been adapted place the wrist in ulnar deviation, a position of deformity for RA.

Type of Reasoning: Deductive
One must recall the principles of joint protection and activity analysis to determine the correct answer. These principles must be used to analyze each of the activities identified in the answer options. Beading is the only activity that meets joint protection criteria. In deductive reasoning, factual knowledge is essential to choosing the correct answer. If answered incorrectly, review the principles of joint protection. See Chapter 11.

C51 C7

An OTA completes a risk analysis of computer workstations for a large corporation. Which is best for the OTA to recommend the company provide its employees to decrease ergonomic risks? Select the three BEST responses.

Answer Choices:
A. Adjustable workstations.
B. Computers with fixed keyboards.
C. Computers with detachable keyboards.
D. Moveable document holders.
E. Stationary document holders.
F. Chairs with fixed backrests.

Correct Answers: A, C, and D.

Rationale:
Workstations that allow the user to adjust their height and tilt can decrease ergonomic risk. Computers with detachable keyboards and document holders that can be moved by the user also decrease ergonomic risk. Chairs should have adjustable backrests, not fixed ones, to decrease ergonomic risk. Table 14-8 in Chapter 14 provides more information about ergonomic risk assessment for computer workstations.

Type of Reasoning: Inductive
For this question, one must utilize knowledge of ergonomic standards and risk factors in order to arrive at a correct conclusion. This necessitates clinical judgment, which is an inductive reasoning skill. For this case, the OTA should recommend adjustable workstations, detachable keyboards, and moveable document holders for the employees. Review ergonomic guidelines if answered incorrectly. See Chapter 14.

C52 C5

An OTA has accepted a position in a sub-acute facility. The OTA attends a day-long new employee orientation. The final session topic is personal safety. The instructor emphasizes that health care workers are susceptible to Hepatitis B. To address the risks presented by Hepatitis B, which precautions should the OTA use?

Answer Choices:
A. Standard precautions.
B. Airborne precautions.
C. Droplet precautions.
D. Contact precautions.

Correct Answer: A.

Rationale:
Standard precautions include a group of infection prevention practices that apply to all persons regardless of suspected or confirmed infection status. Hepatitis B is transmitted through contact with blood or body fluid. The prevention of being infected by Hepatitis B is covered under standard precautions. Airborne precautions are used to prevent infection by serious illnesses that are transmitted by airborne droplets. Droplet precautions are used to prevent infection by serious illnesses that are transmitted by large particle droplets (such as coughing). Contact precautions are used to prevent infection by serious illnesses that are transmitted by hand to hand or skin to skin contact. Hepatitis B is not transmitted by airborne, droplet, or contact means.

Type of Reasoning: Deductive
This question requires factual recall of infection control methods and precautions. This is critical information for health care workers. Specifically, it requires one to know how Hepatitis B is transmitted. Review infection control procedures if answered incorrectly. See Appendices 3A and 3B.

C53 C8

An OTA works with a client who has begun to use a wheelchair for mobility. The client expresses concern about the ability to independently prepare family meals and seeks advice on how to remodel their kitchen to allow for independent access to cooking supplies. The OTA advises the client that the maximal height for countertops should be 31 inches. Which above and below counter storage guidelines are best for the OTA to advise the client to include in the remodeled kitchen?

Answer Choices:
A. Open shelving no higher than 42" and sliding door cabinets no lower than 12".
B. Open shelving no higher than 48" and sliding door cabinets no lower than 12".
C. Open shelving no higher than 42" and sliding door cabinets no lower than 15".
D. Open shelving no higher than 48" and sliding door cabinets no lower than 15".

Correct Answer: D.

Rationale:
The maximal height an individual can reach from a seated position in a wheelchair is 48". To prevent the wheelchair from tipping forward, the minimal height to which a person should reach down is 15". See Figures 15-4 and 15-5 in Chapter 15. Open shelving and sliding cabinet doors can ease access to stored items and are typically preferable to cabinet doors or pull out drawers.

Type of Reasoning: Deductive
This question requires the test taker to apply knowledge of accessibility guidelines to a kitchen environment. This necessitates recall of factual guidelines, which is a deductive reasoning skill. In this situation, the OTA should advise the client that open shelving should be no higher than 48" and sliding door cabinets no lower than 15". Review home accessibility guidelines if answered incorrectly. See Chapter 15.

C54 C8

A client sustained a below knee (BK) amputation on the right side secondary to complications of diabetes myelitis. The client is being treated on the rehabilitation unit while waiting for their prosthesis. The occupational therapist has determined that the client will utilize a stand–pivot–sit transfer for mobility. The client is attempting to transfer independently for the first time. Which position should the OTA assume to ensure safety?

Answer Choices:
A. Stand on the client's left side.
B. Stand at the client's midline.
C. Stand on the client's right side.

Correct Answer: C.

Rationale:
Persons who have sustained a BK amputation on the right are at risk of losing balance to the right when they come to stand. When the OTA is positioned on the right, they can ensure that the client can be assisted should their balance be challenged. This position is the most effective to prevent a fall. Any other position would prevent the OTA from being able to assist the client or prevent a fall should the client's balance be compromised. Because this is the client's first time attempting the transfer, it is critical that the OTA be available to provide physical assistance if needed.

Type of Reasoning: Inferential
One must determine the best place to be positioned to ensure safety when a client is attempting any transfer independently for the first time. This requires inferential reasoning skill, where one must infer or draw conclusions about the best course of action. In this situation, the OTA must anticipate that a right BK amputation places the client at risk for falling to the right if balance is challenged. Review lower extremity amputations and the procedures for the stand–pivot–sit transfer if answered incorrectly. The integration of this knowledge is required to determine the correct answer. See Chapters 6 and 15.

C55 C3

A carpenter incurred a short below-elbow amputation. The client plans to return to work. Which components would be most important for the OTA to recommend for the client's prosthesis?

Answer Choices:
A. A fixed elbow socket and a lightweight Teflon-coated terminal device.
B. A cable-driven elbow socket and a heavy-duty serrated grip terminal device.
C. A fixed elbow socket and a heavy-duty serrated grip terminal device.
D. A cable-driven elbow socket and lightweight Teflon-coated terminal device.

Correct Answer: C.

Rationale:
An individual with a short below-elbow amputation will require a fixed elbow socket to provide stability because natural forearm rotation is not possible. A carpenter will need a heavy-duty serrated grip terminal device to hold tools and nails.

Type of Reasoning: Inferential
One must link the individual's diagnosis to the provided prosthesis options to determine which one would best meet the individual's needs. This requires inferential reasoning, where one must draw conclusions about the likely needs of an individual based on an understanding of the carpenter's occupation. In this case, a fixed elbow socket and heavy-duty serrated grip terminal device would best meet the carpenter's needs. Review prosthetic options and features for below-elbow amputations if answered incorrectly. See Chapter 6.

C56 C7

An OTA collaborates with an occupational therapist to develop a life skills group for high school students with mild intellectual disorders. The students have established the post-secondary goal of living independently. To develop the students' instrumental activities of daily living skills, which is most relevant for the OTA and therapist to include in the group?

Answer Choices:
A. Safety and emergency maintenance.
B. Employment interests and pursuits.
C. Community social participation.

Correct Answer: A.

Rationale:
Safety and emergency maintenance are key components of instrumental activities of daily living (IADL). These skills are essential for independent living. Safety and emergency maintenance includes "knowing and performing preventive procedures to maintain a safe environment; recognizing sudden, unexpected hazardous situations; and initiating emergency action to reduce the threat to health and safety; examples include ensuring safety when entering and exiting the home, identifying emergency contact numbers, and replacing batteries in smoke alarms and light bulbs" (AOTA, 2014, p. 520)[1]. Persons with a mild intellectual disorder (ID) can acquire the safety and emergency maintenance skills needed to function independently in desired occupational roles. The development of employment interests and pursuits and community social participation are appropriate for persons with mild ID, but they are not IADL skills.

Type of Reasoning: Inductive
For this question, one must determine the most relevant skills to include in a life skills group. This requires knowledge of group guidelines and the goals of this specific group, which in this case is the development of IADL skills. Therefore, safety and emergency maintenance are relevant skills to include in the group. Questions of this nature often require inductive reasoning skill, where clinical judgment is utilized to draw conclusions. If answered incorrectly, review IADL guidelines. See Chapter 14.

---

[1] American Occupational Therapy Association. (2014). Occupational therapy practice framework: Domain and process, 3rd edition American *Journal of Occupational Therapy, 68*(Supplement 1), S1-S48.

C57 C3

An individual is referred to occupational therapy for evaluation and intervention following carpal tunnel release (CTR) surgery. The client has secondary diagnoses of atherosclerosis, peripheral vascular disease (PVD), and diabetes. After the completion of a comprehensive evaluation, the therapist and OTA collaborate to determine intervention methods to use with this client. In addition to tendon gliding exercises and sensory education, which should the OTA use during treatment sessions with this client?

Answer Choices:
A. Elevation of the affected hand above the heart.
B. Manual edema mobilization to activate the lymphatic system.
C. Contrast baths in preparation for purposeful activities.
D. Passive range of motion of wrist and fingers.

Correct Answer: C.

Rationale:
In addition to tendon gliding exercises and sensory education, the post-operative treatment of CTR should include edema control, strengthening of thenar muscles, and work/activity modification. The only option for controlling edema that can be used by the OTA with this client is contrast baths. A contrast bath is a physical agent modality (PAM) that can be used as a facilitating procedure in preparation for purposeful activity. The technique is to immerse the hand in warm (i.e., the temperature of bath water) and cold water. While evidence is conflicting as to the effectiveness of contrast baths in reducing hand edema, it is the only edema reduction choice that is within the expertise of the OTA or not contraindicated for this client. Manual edema mobilization is a hands-on technique that can activate the lymphatic system to remove edema. However, this technique requires specialized training. Elevation above the heart is an effective method of controlling edema, but it is contraindicated for persons with circulation problems, such as PVD. Active range of motion is used post-CTR, not passive ROM.

Type of Reasoning: Inductive
For this question, the test taker must utilize knowledge of both carpal tunnel and circulation problems in order to determine the best intervention approach. This requires knowledge of intervention guidelines and procedures, which is an inductive reasoning skill. For this case, the OTA should include contrast baths as part of treatment in order to address the edema of the affected hand, as it is within the OTA's scope of practice and does not negatively impact circulation in the presence of an existing circulation problem. If answered incorrectly, review treatment strategies for carpal tunnel syndrome and contrast baths. See Chapter 6.

C58 C7

An adult with amyotrophic lateral sclerosis (ALS) expresses frustration that the ability to turn pages in books has been lost. The client states that their collection of classic books provides great pleasure and is saddened that reading print books is no longer an option. Which action is best for the OTA to take in response to the client's loss?

Answer Choices:
A. Provide support and refer the client to a counselor who specializes in progressive disorders.
B. Provide the client with information on resources for auditory books.
C. Teach the client to use a book holder and a head stick to turn the pages.
D. Teach the client to use a book holder with an electronic page turner.

Correct Answer: D.

Rationale:
The use of a book holder with an electronic page turner can allow the client to continue to read print books as desired. ALS is a rapidly progressive neuromuscular disorder that is fatal within 2 to 5 years. While most motor function is lost, eye movements are often spared. The electronic page turner can be configured to be activated with an eye gaze system. This would enable the client to be independent for as long as possible. A client with ALS would not retain the motor abilities to effectively use a head stick to turn pages. While auditory books can be an effective alternative to print books, in this scenario the client expressed great pleasure in reading classic print books. Thus, the best answer respects this stated interest and enables the client to continue participating in a desired activity. The client's frustration is understandable and appropriate. There is no need to refer the client to a counselor who specializes in progressive disorders based on their legitimate frustration.

Type of Reasoning: Inductive
For this question, one must determine which action will have the best outcome for a client with ALS. This requires clinical judgment, which is an inductive reasoning skill. In this case, the OTA should teach the client to use a book holder with an electronic page turner, given the diagnosis and expected progression of the disease. If answered incorrectly, review information about ALS, OT interventions for persons with progressive disorders, and types of adaptive equipment. The integration of this knowledge is required to determine the correct answer. See Chapters 7 and 14.

C59 C3

An OTA is preparing to measure the grip strength of a client using a dynamometer. The OTA places the client's elbow in 90 degrees of flexion. In which position should the OTA place the client's shoulder and forearm?

Answer Choices:
A. Shoulder abducted and forearm in pronation.
B. Shoulder adducted and forearm in supination.
C. Shoulder abducted and forearm in neutral.
D. Shoulder adducted and forearm in neutral.

Correct Answer: D.

Rationale:
The standard protocol for measuring grip strength using a dynamometer is to position the upper extremity with the shoulder adducted to the side, the elbow flexed to 90 degrees, and the forearm in neutral. The other answer choices do not adhere to this protocol. Standard protocol must be followed for the results of the evaluation to be valid.

Type of Reasoning: Deductive
This question requires the test taker to recall the proper testing guidelines for grip strength using a dynamometer. This necessitates recall of factual guidelines, which is a deductive reasoning skill. For this situation, the OTA should ensure that the arm is positioned in shoulder adduction and neutral forearm for testing. Review dynamometer testing guidelines if answered incorrectly. See Chapter 11.

C60 C4

An elementary school student experiences a grand mal seizure during an occupational therapy session. Which action should the OTA take first in response to this seizure?

Answer Choices:
A. Immediately insert a mouth guard in the student's mouth to prevent choking.
B. Place the student in the recovery side-lying position once the clonic phase of the seizure is over.
C. Implement standard rescue breathing techniques once the clonic phase of the seizure is over.
D. Immediately inform the school nurse of the seizure and the need to contact the student's parents.

Correct Answer: B.

Rationale:
Grand mal seizures are tonic-clonic seizures. They are the most common type of seizure disorder in children. Prior to the seizure, a brief warning/aura such as numbness, taste, smell, or other sensation typically occurs. The seizure's tonic phase includes a loss of consciousness, stiffening of the body, heavy and irregular breathing, drooling, skin pallor, and occasional bladder and bowel incontinence for a few seconds before the clonic phase begins. The clonic phase includes alternating rigidity and relaxation of muscles. Postictal state follows the clonic phase, and includes a period of drowsiness, disorientation, or fatigue. Once the clonus activity is over for tonic-clonic type seizures a person should be placed in the recovery position, which is side-lying. Nothing should be inserted in an individual's mouth during a seizure. Standard rescue breathing techniques are only needed if breathing actually stops. This complication is not identified in the item scenario and it is not a typical occurrence with grand mal seizures. The school nurse can be informed of the seizure after the child has recovered.

Type of Reasoning: Deductive
This question requires one to recall the guidelines for administering first aid for seizures. This is factual recall of information, which is a deductive reasoning skill. For this situation, the OTA should place the student in the recovery side-lying position once the clonic phase of the seizure is over. Review first aid for seizures if answered incorrectly. See Chapter 7.

C61 C9

A 4-year-old child with a complete myelomeningocele at the T12 level is referred for outpatient occupational and physical therapy. In setting goals with the parents, the occupational therapist established a goal to increase independence in dressing skills and the physical therapist established a goal to improve ambulation. When the OTA begins the initial intervention session, the parents state they want their child to only work on ambulation. They do not want the OTA to provide interventions to develop their child's dressing skills. Which action is best for the OTA to take first to address the family's stated preference?

Answer Choices:
A. Concur with the family that the child does not need to receive occupational therapy services.
B. Refer the family to counseling to assist them in accepting the child's functional limitations.
C. Work with the occupational therapist and parents to determine a desired focus for intervention.
D. Reinforce the importance of independence in dressing for the child to the family.

Correct Answer: C.

Rationale:
Working with the occupational therapist and parents to determine a desired focus for intervention addresses the child's and family's rights. This action allows the OTA and occupational therapist to apply therapeutic use of self. The family refuses intervention to work on the child's dressing skills and the OTA should respect their decision. The OTA can use this opportunity to collaborate with the family to help them determine a focus for occupational therapy services that meets their child's needs. A 4-year-old with a complete myelomeningocele at the T12 level will have needs in other areas of occupation besides dressing (e.g., play). There is no information provided in the item scenario to indicate that the family needs a counseling referral. Reinforcing the importance of dressing does not respect the family's stated preference.

Type of Reasoning: Evaluative
This question requires one to primarily consider the parent's needs in order to arrive at a correct conclusion. This necessitates weighing the benefits of the four possible choices, which utilizes evaluative reasoning skill. For this situation, working with the family to determine a different focus for occupational therapy best considers the parents' preferences and respects their right to refuse certain intervention approaches. This approach is consistent with client-centered practice. See Chapters 3 and 4.

C62 C4

An OTA provides home-based services to a homemaker who incurred a right CVA eight months ago. The individual and the therapist have chosen to focus on kitchen activities during the intervention session. The OTA has the client stand in front of the counter with an open dishwasher to the left. The OTA asks the client to put the clean dishes into an overhead cabinet to the right of the client using the affected UE. By setting up the activity in this manner, which proprioceptive neuromuscular facilitation (PNF) technique is the OTA using?

Answer Choices:
A. Heavy work/mobility superimposed on stability.
B. Diagonal patterns of D2 flexion/extension.
C. Diagonal patterns of D1 extension/flexion.

Correct Answer: B.

Rationale:
When person incurs a CVA, the contralateral side of their body is affected. In this exam item, the left upper extremity (LUE) would be affected because the person had a right CVA. The D1 extension pattern places the person's LUE in a position where it is down and on the same side of the body. Therefore, to grasp dishes with the affected LUE from the dishwasher on the left, the person would need to use a D1 extension pattern. A D2 extension position would place the person's LUE angled across their body toward their right hip. This position would not enable the person to grasp dishes with their affected LUE from a dishwasher that is on their left side. Using a D1 pattern would place the person's LUE on the same side as where the dishwasher is in relationship to their body. After grasping a dish, the D1 flexion would be used to reach overhead and across the body to place dishes in an above-counter cabinet on the right side. Heavy work is not a PNF technique. It is a technique used in the Rood approach. In heavy work (also termed "mobility superimposed on stability"), proximal muscles contract and move and the distal segments are fixed.

Type of Reasoning: Analytical
For this question, a description of a functional activity is provided, and the test taker must determine the functional activity that is being performed. This requires analytical reasoning skill, as questions of this nature often ask one to analyze descriptors of functional tasks to determine the overall skill involved. In this situation, the activity being performed is that of D1. flexion/extension. If answered incorrectly, review PNF patterns, especially D1. See Chapter 12.

C63 C5

An OTA working on an acute cardiopulmonary rehabilitation unit implements activities for an individual who is preparing for discharge to Phase II of cardiac rehabilitation. Which activities are best for the OTA to use during intervention sessions?

Answer Choices:
A. Clothing repair activities (e.g., sewing on a button, hemming pants).
B. Basic activities of daily living (e.g., grooming, showering).
C. Home maintenance activities (e.g., cleaning windows, vacuuming).
D. Endurance promoting leisure activities (e.g., water aerobics, vigorous calisthenics).

Correct Answer: C.

Rationale:
Patients are discharged to Phase 2 of cardiac rehabilitation when they are able to carry out activities at a MET level of 3.5. Home maintenance activities such as cleaning windows and vacuuming are at this level. Clothing repair activities such as sewing on a button and hemming pants are at a MET level of 1.3. Basic activities of daily living such as grooming and showering are at a MET level of 1.5 - 2.0. Endurance promoting leisure activities such as water aerobics and calisthenics are at a MET level of 5.5 and 8.0, respectively.

Type of Reasoning: Deductive
To correctly answer this exam item, one must remember the MET level guidelines for persons who will be discharged to Phase 2 of cardiopulmonary rehabilitation. This is recall of factual knowledge, which is a deductive reasoning skill. At this point, the person should be able to perform activities that require an energy expenditure 3.5 METs. This capability is the criteria for beginning Phase 2 of cardiac rehabilitation. If answered incorrectly, review Phase 2 recovery guidelines and activity MET levels. See Chapter 8.

C64 C1

The parents of an 18-month-old bring their child to a free community developmental screening. The child can attend to shapes and use them appropriately. However, the parents are worried because the child cannot match shapes or manipulate objects of different shapes into a shape sorter. The OTA reviews the screening results with the occupational therapist. Which action is best for the therapist and OTA to take based on the screening results and the parents' expressed concerns?

Answer Choices:
A. Advise the parents that the child is showing a typical, age-appropriate skill.
B. Complete an occupational therapy evaluation of the child's cognitive skills.
C. Refer the child to the early intervention program for developmental delay.
D. Provide the parents with activity recommendations to develop shape recognition.

Correct Answer: A.

Rationale:
The child is showing an age-appropriate skill. According to established developmental milestones, the ability to recognize shapes and manipulate differently shaped objects into a shape sorter does not typically develop until the age 21–24 months. The ability to attend to the shape of things and use them appropriately is typical of children aged 18–21 months. There is no additional information provided in the scenario to indicate a developmental delay that would warrant further evaluation of cognitive skills or intervention for developmental delay. There is no need to provide activities to reinforce shape recognition since the child is functioning at a developmentally appropriate level, and these skills can be expected to develop typically as the child ages.

Type of Reasoning: Deductive
One must recall the developmental guidelines for 18-month-old children. This is recall of factual knowledge, which is a deductive reasoning skill. Because the child is not expected to recognize shapes and manipulate differently shaped objects into a shape sorter at 18 months, the child is demonstrating age-appropriate skills. If answered incorrectly, review the major milestones of cognitive development. See Chapter 5.

C65 C2

An OTA meets with a patient with fibromyalgia who has had difficulty meeting intervention goals. The patient complains of being hurt and frustrated in attempts to resolve pain and fatigue issues. Which is the most effective technique for the OTA to use to help the patient increase insight into this situation?

Answer Choices:
A. Consult with the occupational therapist about pain management options.
B. Reflect the patient's verbal expressions back to the patient.
C. Refer the patient to a specialized pain management center.
D. Repeat the patient's exact words back to the patient.

Correct Answer: B.

Rationale:
Reflection involves expressing the feeling behind the patient's words and is an effective technique to facilitate self-reflection and develop insight. Repeating the exact words or parroting is not effective because this means merely stating the words without a focus on the emotions behind the words. Exploring options for pain treatment and a referral to a pain management center can be helpful for managing the patient's pain, but these options do not address the question's stated focus on increasing the client's insight.

Type of Reasoning: Inductive
Clinical knowledge and judgment are the most important skills needed for answering this question, which requires inductive reasoning skill. Knowledge of interpersonal skills and how to respond to a patient who expresses frustration is key to arriving at a correct conclusion. In this case, reflection is the most effective technique for the OTA to use to express the feelings behind the patient's spoken words. This approach is consistent with guideless for the therapeutic use of self and client-centered practice. See Chapter 3.

C66 C9

An OTA working for a home care agency is vacationing and sees a colleague at an all-day concert. Upon return from the vacation, the OTA notices that this colleague had billed for a full day of home visits on the day of the concert. Which action is best for the OTA to take first in response to this situation?

Answer Choices:
A. Inform the supervising occupational therapist.
B. Contact the state regulatory board.
C. Contact the National Board for Certification of Occupational Therapy.
D. Ask the colleague to clarify the situation.

Correct Answer: A.

Rationale:
The OTA must inform the supervising occupational therapist who can then investigate the employee's behavior according to the agency's guidelines. This investigation may result in the supervisor contacting the state regulatory board or NBCOT. Speaking to a colleague to clarify a situation prior to reporting it to a supervisor can often be an appropriate initial step. However, in this case, the person has committed potential fraud. This situation is very serious and must be brought immediately to the attention of a supervisor.

Type of Reasoning: Evaluative

This question requires a value judgment in an ethical situation, which is an evaluative reasoning skill. In this situation, because the OTA has witnessed unethical (and potentially illegal) behavior, the OTA should inform the supervising occupational therapist. Ethical situations such as these often rely upon the OT Code of Ethics to provide guiding principles of action. This ethical situation violates principle 6, the code of veracity, which means to be truthful and accurate in documenting services. See Chapter 4.

C67 C6

An OTA accepts a job in an after-school program. The program provides services for adolescents at risk for mental health problems due to their history of being survivors of child abuse. The OTA collaborates with the occupational therapist to plan an intervention program. They decide that an activity group to elicit the adolescents' thoughts and feelings in a safe atmosphere would be instrumental to their recovery. Which group would be most relevant for the therapist and OTA to design?

Answer Choices:
A. A task-oriented group.
B. An instrumental group.
C. A topical group.
D. A thematic group.

Correct Answer: A.

Rationale:
The purpose of a task-oriented group is to increase members' awareness of feelings, thoughts, needs, values, and behaviors through the process of choosing, planning, and implementing a group activity. Activities are selected for their expressive characteristics so that participants can project their feelings and study their behaviors. A topical group is a verbal group that focuses on the discussion of activities members are engaged in (concurrent) or will be engaged in (anticipatory) outside of the group. The purpose is to improve activity performance through problem-solving. An instrumental group is designed for individuals with chronic disabilities who are functioning at their highest level with no anticipation for improvement. The aim of this group is to provide a supportive, safe, structured environment that maintains function, prevents regression, and promotes quality of life. A thematic group assists members in acquiring the knowledge, skills, and/or attitudes to perform a specific set of skills independently.

Type of Reasoning: Analytical
This question provides a description of a group and the test taker must determine the type of group that would achieve the goals of the program. This is an analytical reasoning skill, as questions of this nature often ask one to analyze descriptors of functional activities or situations to determine the type of activity involved. In this situation the group description is that of a task-oriented group, which should be reviewed if answered incorrectly. See Chapters 3 and 13.

C68 C1

An elementary school student with hypotonic cerebral palsy receives school-based occupational therapy to improve fine motor skills. The child holds a thick marker with a static tripod grasp and holds a no. 2 pencil with a gross grasp. The OTA collaborates with the occupational therapist to revise the intervention plan based on the child's attained skills. The development of which grasp is best to include in the revised intervention plan as a short-term goal?

Answer Choices:
A. Dynamic tripod with the thick marker.
B. Lateral pinch with a thick marker.
C. Static tripod with a pencil.
D. Dynamic tripod with a pencil.

Correct Answer: C.

Rationale:
Developmentally, the best way to progressively grade the grasp is to work on static tripod with a thinner object before going to work on dynamic tripod. A lateral pinch is not an effective grasp for holding a thick marker.

Type of Reasoning: Inductive
This question requires one to determine the most appropriate modification to the intervention plan to reflect progress to the next developmental stage of grasp. This requires inductive reasoning skill, where clinical judgment is paramount in arriving at a correct conclusion. In this situation, a short-term goal of improving static tripod grasp with a pencil is the best modification to the intervention plan based on current ability. If answered incorrectly, review developmental patterns of hand grasp for writing. See Chapter 5.

C69 C2

Ten members of a community reintegration group are not working well together and show decreased levels of trust. The occupational therapist and OTA establish a goal to enhance the level of cohesiveness in the group. To begin the next group session, which is the best action for the OTA to take?

Answer Choices:
A. Read inspirational phrases to increase motivation.
B. Verbally review the goals and purposes of the group.
C. Have each person contribute a line about childhood memories to a group poem.
D. Ask each person to talk about silly mistakes to provide some levity.

Correct Answer: B.

Rationale:
The best choice is for the OTA to verbally review the goals and purpose of the group. This helps to direct the focus of the members onto the reason(s) that they are participating in the group. This reinforcement of a shared purpose can help develop cohesion. The OTA and therapist can then design and provide activities that build on this commonality. Inspirational phrases can help instill a positive attitude, but they do not address the need to develop group cohesion. Using individual members' input to compile a group poem can be an activity that could increase cohesiveness. However, some group members may have had less than wonderful childhood experiences and may be reticent to share a childhood memory with persons with whom they are not close. Consequently, this activity may be more detrimental than helpful. One way to decrease cohesiveness is to require self-disclosure in a group with decreased levels of trust. As a result, the topic of silly mistakes is also not a good group discussion focus. It is not likely to facilitate trust, openness, and willingness to share.

Type of Reasoning: Inferential
One must determine which course of action will result in improved group cohesiveness. This requires inferential reasoning where one must draw conclusions about each course of action to achieve the ultimate purpose of group cohesion. In this case, verbally reviewing the goals and purposes of the group will best enhance group cohesion. If answered incorrectly, review characteristics of cohesive groups and group facilitation techniques. See Chapter 3.

C70 C1

An OTA observes that an 18-month-old child is not able to creep more than a few steps. When the child looks up, both hips and knees flex and the child ends up W-sitting with both arms extended and propped forward. When describing this observation to the supervising occupational therapist, which is most accurate for the OTA to report the child is demonstrating?

Answer Choices:
A. Typical development of locomotion skills for an 18-month-old child.
B. The influence of the symmetrical tonic neck reflex (STNR) resulting in delayed gross motor skills.
C. An obligatory asymmetrical tonic neck reflex (ATNR) resulting in delayed gross motor skills.
D. An intact tonic labyrinthine reflex, which facilitates balance responses.

Correct Answer: B.

Rationale:
A persistent STNR would cause extension of upper extremities. The described motor behavior is not normal. An ATNR would cause the child to collapse to one side. Tonic labyrinthine reflex would cause a total body extended posture.

Type of Reasoning: Analytical
This question requires the test taker to determine if the observed motor pattern is evidence of a specific functional deficit, which is an analytical reasoning skill. Questions of this nature often call upon the test taker to determine a diagnosis based on a functional description of deficits. Based on this information, the demonstration of W-sitting with arms extended indicates influence of the STNR reflex resulting in delayed gross motor skills. Review STNR reflex pattern if answered incorrectly. See Chapter 5.

C71 C4

A patient with a left CVA and resulting contralateral hemiplegia participates in occupational therapy. When documenting the patient's performance during intervention sessions, which abilities are most likely for the OTA to describe as intact? Select the three BEST responses.

Answer Choices:
A. Temporal sequencing of a morning self-care routine.
B. Interpretation of information during a stress management group.
C. Receptive language during a leisure planning group.
D. Emotional stability during a CVA support group.
E. Spatial perception while in the ADL apartment.
F. Motor planning during a tai chi group.

Correct Answers: B, D, and E.

Rationale:
Misinterpretation of abstract information, difficulties with spatial perception, and emotional instability are typically related to a right CVA. With a left CVA, interpretation of information, emotional stability, and spatial perception would remain intact. The other options are all typically affected by a left CVA.

Type of Reasoning: Deductive

This question requires one to recall factual knowledge about expected symptoms of a patient with a right CVA. This necessitates deductive reasoning skill, where recall of facts and previous knowledge are paramount to drawing the correct conclusion. For this case, the interpretation of abstract information, spatial perception, and emotional stability are most likely to be intact. If answered incorrectly, review symptoms of CVA, especially right CVA. See Table 7-3 in Chapter 7.

C72 C6

During a therapeutic feeding session, an older adult resident with a neurocognitive disorder becomes upset and cries for their mother. Which is best for the OTA to say in response to the resident's statements?

Answer Choices:
A. "Remember that you are now in a nursing home and your mother is not here."
B. "Remember your mother passed away years ago."
C. "I will tell the nurse that you want your mother contacted."
D. "You must miss your mother, tell me about her."

Correct Answer: D.

Rationale:
This response validates the person's feelings and provides them with the opportunity to reminisce about a pleasant memory. Even a few minutes of reminiscing can provide solace to the individual, which can help calm the person. This can then enable the resident to re-engage in the feeding activity. Individuals with neurocognitive disorders generally respond well to validation therapy and reminiscence activities. Asking the individual to recall that their mother is deceased and/or not available is inappropriate, for they are asking the resident to remember something that is no longer part of their reality. Telling the person that that there is a potential for their mother to be contacted is offering an action that cannot be completed in reality. In addition, it does not address the individual's valid feelings, which need to be addressed at the moment.

Type of Reasoning: Evaluative
This question requires professional judgment based on guiding principles, which is an evaluative reasoning skill. Most important in this situation is to validate the person's feelings. This way the OTA can provide an opportunity to reminisce without asking the person to recall something that is not part of reality. Review validation strategies for persons with neurocognitive disorders if answered incorrectly. See Chapters 10 and 13.

C73 C9

An entry-level OTA with six months of experience was recently hired by an acute inpatient hospital. The OTA will be providing occupational therapy services during the direct supervisor's scheduled vacation. To maximize departmental efficacy, which level of supervision should be provided to the OTA?

Answer Choices:
A. Routine supervision from the outpatient clinic's occupational therapist.
B. Routine supervision from an on-site OTA with one year of experience.
C. Close supervision from an on-site occupational therapist.
D. Close supervision from an OTA with advanced credentialing.

Correct Answer: C.

Rationale:
The degree, amount, and pattern of supervision that an OTA requires is dependent on a number of factors. These include the OTA's established service competence, service demands, state licensure requirements, facility's procedures, and case characteristics. In this situation, the OTA is an entry-level practitioner with six months of experience and no information is provided about the OTA's established competencies. The OTA is working in an acute inpatient hospital. Patients in this setting typically have complex needs and their status can rapidly change. To ensure effective and safe service provision, the OTA should receive close (i.e., daily, direct contact at the site of work) from an occupational therapist working in the acute care hospital. Routine supervision is provided via direct contact at least every two weeks at the site of work, with interim supervision being provided by other methods (e.g., telephone, email, or written communication). Given the anticipated complexities of the OTA's caseload, the provision of this type of supervision by an off-site therapist would be insufficient. Intermediate and advanced-level OTAs who work with the supervision of an occupational therapist can provide supervision to entry-level OTAs. See Table 4-1. An OTA with a year of experience would be considered an entry-level practitioner. In this exam item, it is unknown if the OTA with advanced credentialing has the requisite experience to provide the level of supervision that is required in an acute inpatient setting. The OTA's credentialing can be in an area that does not relate to the services provided in an acute inpatient hospital (e.g., driver rehabilitation).

Type of Reasoning: Deductive
One must recall the supervisory guidelines for OTAs in acute inpatient hospitals. This is recall of factual knowledge, which is a deductive reasoning skill. Because the entry-level OTA in this case requires close supervision from an occupational therapist, another on-site occupational therapist is required to supervise the OTA in the supervisor's absence. If answered incorrectly, review supervisory guidelines for OTAs. See Chapter 4.

C74 C4

An OTA implements intervention using a contemporary neurorehabilitation approach by having a person with a neurological impairment practice an activity in different contexts. Which is the primary purpose of this approach?

Answer Choices:
A. To facilitate the generalization of learning.
B. To make it more difficult to transfer learning.
C. To foster an unstructured approach to different situations.
D. To determine if the client is easily confused.

Correct Answer: A.

Rationale:
A major principle in contemporary approaches in neurorehabilitation is the use of multiple contexts to facilitate the generalization of learning. This generalization can then make it easier for an individual to transfer their learning to new situations, which increases performance consistency, decreases confusion, and helps the person perform effectively in diverse situations.

Type of Reasoning: Inferential
One must have knowledge of neurorehabilitation and the benefits of practice in different contexts in order to draw a correct conclusion. This is an inferential reasoning skill, where the test taker must infer information in order to draw conclusions. In this situation, practice in different contexts can facilitate the generalization of learning. Review contemporary neurorehabilitation practice theories and generalization of learning if answered incorrectly. See Chapters 7 and 12.

C75 C3

A school-aged child who is right-hand dominant complains of numbness and tingling after writing for more than 15 minutes. A neurological exam shows no reason for the numbness and tingling. Which action would be most beneficial for the OTA to recommend to the child?

Answer Choices:
A. Use a custom-molded pencil grip made of splinting material.
B. Stretch the right upper extremity every 15–20 minutes during writing activities.
C. Elevate the right upper extremity at night and whenever possible during the day.

Correct Answer: B.

Rationale:
The neurological exam is negative. The best choice is to educate the child in active ROM and stretching of the upper extremity to increase circulation and to attempt to prevent numbness and tingling. A custom-molded grip is an adaptation that does not address treatment of numbness and tingling. Elevation can reduce edema and edema is not a symptom here.

Type of Reasoning: Inductive
One must determine the reason for the child's symptoms in order to determine the best recommendation for the child to alleviate the symptoms. This requires inductive reasoning skill, where clinical judgment and diagnostic thinking are central to choosing a best solution. In this situation, stretching the right upper extremity every 15–20 minutes during writing is the best recommendation to increase circulation and prevent symptoms. If answered incorrectly, review intervention approaches for paresthesias. See Chapters 6 and 11.

C76 C6

An individual with moderate intellectual disability moves into a group home. An initial goal established for this resident is the development of socially acceptable table manners. The OTA uses a behavior modification approach to achieve this goal. Which is best for the OTA to provide to the resident during dining activities?

Answer Choices:
A. Negative reinforcement for socially inappropriate behaviors.
B. Clear explanations of appropriate behaviors that are expected.
C. Clear explanations about the effects of inappropriate behaviors on others.
D. Positive reinforcement for socially appropriate behaviors.

Correct Answer: D.

Rationale:
A behavior modification program provides positive reinforcement for desired behaviors. Negative reinforcement for undesirable behaviors is not the preferred approach, because it focuses on deficits rather than skill development. While it is important to provide a person with clear explanations of behaviors, this would not be the most effective approach for the development of concrete specific skills in a behavior modification program. Because the person has moderate intellectual disability, the individual's ability to understand these expectations or the effect of the behaviors on others may be limited due to deficits in abstract thinking. As a new resident, the person may not have had sufficient time to develop meaningful relationships with other residents.

Type of Reasoning: Inferential
One must have knowledge of intellectual disabilities and behavior modification guidelines in order to arrive at a correct conclusion. This is an inferential reasoning skill where knowledge of clinical guidelines and judgment based on facts are utilized to reach conclusions. In this situation, the OTA should provide rewards for socially appropriate behaviors. If answered incorrectly, review behavior modification principles. See Chapter 13.

C77 C4

A child with tactile defensiveness is receiving intervention from an OTA who uses a sensory integrative approach. Which methods are most effective for the OTA to use when introducing tactile stimuli to the child? Select the three BEST responses.

Answer Choices:
A. Provide deep touch and firm pressure where the child can see the stimuli.
B. Apply the stimuli in the direction opposite of hair growth with vision occluded.
C. Apply the stimuli in the direction of hair growth with the child watching.
D. Apply light touch across the face and abdomen with the child watching.
E. Provide light brushing across the palmar surfaces of the extremities with the child watching.
F. Follow tactile stimuli with joint compression.

Correct Answers: A, C, and F.

Rationale:
Deep touch, firm pressure, and joint compression help to decrease tactile defensiveness. To decrease defensiveness, the child needs to see the stimuli. The self-application of stimuli can also increase tolerance. Light touch, brushing across the face and abdomen, and application of stimuli in the direction opposite of hair growth are all aversive to a person with tactile defensiveness. Stimuli should be applied in the direction of hair growth with the child watching because this is less aversive.

Type of Reasoning: Inductive
This question requires one to determine the most effective method for introducing tactile stimuli. This requires inductive reasoning skill, where clinical judgment is paramount to arriving at a correct conclusion. For this situation, the OTA should provide deep touch and firm pressure where the child can see the stimuli, apply the stimuli in the direction of hair growth with the child watching, and follow tactile stimuli with joint compression. If answered incorrectly, review approaches for sensory processing disorders. See Chapter 12.

C78 C6

An individual recently lost significant functional abilities due to post-polio syndrome. The OTA works with the individual to develop compensation skills for performing daily tasks. During a meal preparation session, the person angrily throws all of the adaptive equipment onto the floor. At the next team meeting, which defense mechanism should the OTA report that the tram members should consider when working with the person to support their adaptation to disability?

Answer Choices:
A. Acting out.
B. Passive-aggressive behavior.
C. Reaction formation.
D. Displacement.

Correct Answer: D.

Rationale:
Displacement occurs when an individual redirects an emotion from one "object" (in this case, the anger over the progression of the disease) to another "object" (i.e., the adaptive equipment). Acting out is a term used to describe behaviors that violate societal norms (e.g., sexually provocative behavior, physically assaultive behavior). Passive-aggressive behavior is characterized by indirect or unassertive aggression (e.g., being chronically late when meeting someone you had an argument with years ago). Reaction formation is the switching of an unacceptable impulse into its opposite (e.g., hugging someone you would like to hit).

Type of Reasoning: Analytical
This question provides a description of a behavior and the test taker must draw conclusions about what the behavior indicates. This is an analytical reasoning skill, as questions of this nature often ask one to analyze descriptors and symptoms in order to determine a diagnosis or draw a conclusion. In this situation the behavior indicates displacement. If answered incorrectly, review defense mechanisms. See Chapter 13.

C79 C3

A client with arthritis of both hands has ulnar drift of metacarpophalangeal joints (MPs) during finger extension and flexion and at rest. The person also has a lengthening of the central slips of the extensor digitorum communis tendons of the right index and middle fingers. Which of the following should the OTA report the person is exhibiting?

Answer Choices:
A. MP palmar subluxation-dislocations.
B. Swan-neck deformities.
C. Trigger-finger deformities.
D. Boutonniere deformities.

Correct Answer: D.

Rationale:
A boutonniere deformity is caused by a lengthening or rupture of the extensor digitorum communis tendons and is expressed by distal interphalangeal (DIP) hyperextension and proximal interphalangeal (PIP) flexion. A swan neck deformity can result from the rupture of the lateral slips of the extensor digitorum communis or flexor digitorum superficialis tendon and results in DIP flexion and PIP hyperextension. A trigger-finger deformity results from a thickening of the flexor digitorum superficialis tendon at the flexor tunnel, also called a tendon sheath. The affected joint tends to stay open upon attempt to close or fist the hand. Synovitis of the MP joints can cause damage to the MP ligaments with palmar dislocation in conjunction with, or independent of, ulnar drift.

Type of Reasoning: Analytical
This question requires the test taker to determine the likely diagnosis from a set of symptoms, which is an analytical reasoning skill. For this situation, the symptoms indicate boutonniere deformities. If answered incorrectly, review characteristics of boutonniere deformity. See Chapter 6.

C80 C4

An individual has had a brain tumor removed from the cerebellum. The occupational therapist completes a screening to determine the need for further evaluation. During the screening, the therapist identifies deficits that indicate a need for further evaluation. The therapist collaborates with the OTA to plan the evaluation session. The OTA has established service competence in the administration of standardized assessments. Which is most relevant for the OTA to evaluate based on the screening?

Answer Choices:
A. Proprioception and coordination.
B. Tactile and sensory integration.
C. Vision and visual-perception.
D. Audition and communication.

Correct Answer: A.

Rationale:
The cerebellum receives input from the proprioceptive pathways and modulates the smooth coordination of voluntary movements. Therefore, a tumor in this area would affect proprioception and coordination. These deficits would be evident upon screening. Further evaluation would be needed to determine the extent of the brain tumor's effect on these areas. Tactile and sensory integration skills would be most affected by damage to the parietal lobe. Vision and visual-perceptual skills would be most affected by damage to the occipital lobe. Audition and communication abilities would be most affected by damage to the temporal lobe.

Type of Reasoning: Inferential
One must have knowledge of the functional anatomy of the brain to arrive at a correct conclusion since tumors in a specific lobe would compromise its function. This is an inferential reasoning skill, in which knowledge of clinical guidelines and judgment based on facts are utilized to reach conclusions. In this situation, the screening will most likely indicate a need for further evaluation of proprioception and coordination skills since these are functions of the cerebellum. If answered incorrectly, review the functional anatomy of the brain. Understanding the effects of a tumor on typical neurological functioning is key to selecting the correct answer. See Chapter 7.

C81 C3

A client participates in occupational therapy for intervention following a rotator cuff injury. During an intervention session, the OTA provides progressive resistive exercises. When grading these exercises, which of the following is best for the OTA to increase?

Answer Choices:
A. The amount of resistance provided with a stronger level of therapy band.
B. The range of motion involved in completing the exercises.
C. The proximal load on the muscles the client uses during the exercises.
D. The repetitions of external rotation exercises with less distal weight.

Correct Answer: A.

Rationale:
Resistive exercises serve to increase strength of muscles from fair plus to normal through adequate ROM. Increasing the resistance level of a therapy band is the best method provided to progressively grade the resistive exercises. This approach can increase the person's strength. Increasing the ROM of an exercise helps to increase the available ROM of the muscle, but not strength. Progressively increasing strength, the focus of resistive exercise, would be helped by increasing the distal load on the muscles, not necessarily by increasing the proximal load on muscles. Increased repetitions with decreased distal weight can increase endurance, but not specifically strength.

Type of Reasoning: Inductive
One must utilize clinical knowledge and judgment to determine the exercise approach that progressively grades resistance. In this case, a stronger level of therapy band is the ideal way to foster greater resistance out of the choices provided. If answered incorrectly, review guidelines for increasing strength. See Chapter 11.

C82 C9

The supervising occupational therapist of a home care agency tells an OTA that all intervention plans will need to be submitted to clients' third-party payers prior to the implementation of treatment. By adhering to this policy, the OTA is participating in which type of review?

Answer Choices:
A. Concurrent review.
B. Utilization review.
C. Prospective review.

Correct Answer: C.

Rationale:
The evaluation and approval of proposed intervention plans by third-party payers is called prospective review. Concurrent review is the evaluation of ongoing intervention programs. Utilization review is a plan to review the use of resources within a facility to determine medical necessity and cost efficiency.

Type of Reasoning: Deductive
This question requires recall of guidelines and principles, which is factual knowledge, utilizing deductive reasoning skill. In this situation, the submission of all intervention plans to third-party payers prior to implementation of treatment is an example of a prospective review. If answered incorrectly, review characteristics of prospective payment systems and methods of program evaluation and continuous quality improvement. See Chapter 4.

C83 C6

An OTA working in a psychogeriatric unit provides services to older adults with mid-stage neurocognitive disorders. Which groups are best for the OTA to use with this population?

Answer Choices:
A. Reality orientation.
B. Sensory stimulation.
C. Reminiscence.
D. Coping skills.

Correct Answer: C.

Rationale:
Reminiscence groups are designed to review past life experiences to promote use of intact long-term memory. Current memory is not required for successful participation in reminiscence groups. Individuals with mid-stage neurocognitive disorders typically have poor recent memory but good long-term memory. Reality orientation typically involves activities that require remembering the current day, date, time, season, and activity sequence. Individuals with mid-stage neurocognitive disorders have current memory deficits that would preclude their ability to successfully participate in reality orientation activities. This lack of success can highlight deficits and increase frustration. Sensory stimulation activities are indicated for individuals with later-stage neurocognitive disorders who are at risk for sensory deprivation. Coping skills groups use activities to problem solve, apply, and critique alternative solutions that can be used to effectively manage potential life stressors/problems. These activities require cognitive abilities that are beyond the capacity of persons with mid-stage neurocognitive disorders.

Type of Reasoning: Inferential
One must determine the most likely intervention approach for a group of individuals given the treatment setting provided. This requires inferential reasoning skill, where one must draw conclusions based on the information presented. In this situation, the OTA should use groups that emphasize reminiscence. If answered incorrectly, review intervention guidelines for older adults with neurocognitive disorders. See Chapters 10 and 13.

C84 C4

A teenager with spinal muscle atrophy shows decreased trunk balance and strength. Upper extremity strength and ROM are unchanged from the last evaluation. Which is the best recommendation for the OTA to make to the supervising occupational therapist?

Answer Choices:
A. A re-evaluation of the client be completed.
B. The client be referred to an orthotist for a soft spinal support.
C. The client be measured for a power wheelchair.
D. A trunk-strengthening program be initiated with the client.

Correct Answer: A.

Rationale:
The most important action to take after noticing a change in the functional status of a person with a progressive condition is to re-evaluate. Based on the results of the evaluation, interventions can be planned. These interventions can include orthotics, adaptive equipment, powered mobility, compensation techniques, and/or a strengthening program; only the results of a re-evaluation can appropriately determine intervention needs. The physician determines the need for a soft or plastic spinal support, often called a TLSO (thoracolumbosacral orthosis). These are usually used to prevent an increase in, or to maintain, the scoliosis curve. Supports often tend to decrease trunk balance by providing fewer opportunities for trunk mobility. A power wheelchair might be indicated for a person with spinal muscle atrophy. However, indications for a prescription of a power wheelchair are decreased strength and endurance to propel a manual wheelchair, not poor trunk balance.

Type of Reasoning: Inferential
One must determine the recommendation that would best address the adolescent's needs. Re-evaluation of the adolescent's capabilities and limitations is the best approach in order to determine if the decreases in trunk balance and strength will necessitate modifications to the intervention program. If answered incorrectly, review evaluation and intervention planning guidelines for patients with progressive disorders. See Chapter 7.

C85 C1

A 4-month-old with arthrogryposis remains in position when placed and shows little spontaneous movement. The OTA implements intervention to work on rolling. Which positional changes should the OTA include in the intervention session?

Answer Choices:
A. Prone to supine.
B. Supine to side-lying.
C. Prone to side-lying.
D. Supine to prone.

Correct Answer: B.

Rationale:
When children exhibit developmental delay, the OTA should begin intervention by working on the first skill that typically occurs. Developmentally, rolling from supine to side-lying starts first. Rolling from prone to supine is the next stage; the other options occur later.

Type of Reasoning: Deductive
One must recall the developmental guidelines in mobility for infants. This is recall of factual knowledge, which is a deductive reasoning skill. Supine to side-lying is the first skill to develop; therefore, the OTA should initiate mobility with this skill first. If answered incorrectly, review developmental milestones of infants for gross motor skills. See Chapter 5.

C86 C4

A college student with post-concussion syndrome is referred to occupational therapy for cognitive rehabilitation. The occupational therapist reviews the client's evaluation results with the OTA. The therapist reports that the client has prospective memory deficits. The OTA and therapist collaborate to design interventions to address this deficit using an adaptive/functional approach. Which activity is best for the OTA to teach the client to incorporate into their daily routine?

Answer Choices:
A. The use of a step-by-step instruction sheet to enable the completion of basic activities of daily living.
B. The authorship of subject-specific index cards to help with the recall of essential course information.
C. The use of a day planner in which the student records course assignment due dates and scheduled exams.
D. Audio-taping class lectures and reviewing them after each class.

Correct Answer: C.

Rationale:
The adaptive/functional approach to cognitive rehabilitation teaches persons how to use compensatory techniques and adaptive strategies to complete desired tasks. These can include the use of step-by-step instructions, study cards, and audio-taping. However, the focus of the answer choices which include these approaches do not address prospective memory. Prospective memory is the capacity to remember to carry out actions in the future (e.g., knowing you have appointments scheduled, knowing when to pay a bill). Teaching the student to incorporate the use of a day planner in which they have recorded their course assignment due dates and scheduled exams into their daily routine is the only option that effectively addresses prospective memory deficits. Teaching the client to use a step-by-step instruction sheet to complete basic activities of daily living would be an effective compensatory strategy for procedural memory deficits. The authorship of subject-specific index cards to help with the recall of essential course information would be an effective compensatory strategy for declarative memory deficits. Audio-taping lectures is a compensatory strategy that is typically used for those with poor sustained attention.

Type of Reasoning: Inductive
This question requires one to utilize clinical judgment to determine a best course of action for a student with prospective memory deficits. This necessitates inductive reasoning skill, where knowledge of the presenting deficit and cognitive rehabilitation are paramount to arriving at a correct conclusion. For this situation, it is most effective for the OTA to address the student's prospective memory deficits by teaching them to incorporate the use of a day planner into their daily routine. If answered incorrectly, review the different types of memory and the adaptive/functional approach. The integration of this knowledge is needed to determine the correct answer. See Chapters 10 and 12.

C87 C9

An OTA with 15 years of practice and administrative experience in a community mental health day program wants to work for a school system. Which position is the best match for the OTA's qualifications?

Answer Choices:
A. A senior OTA.
B. An entry-level OTA.
C. A director of the after-school activity programs.
D. An OTA specialist in behavioral problems.

Correct Answer: B.

Rationale:
The OTA has 15 years of practice and administrative experience, but no specific experience in the school system. As a result, the OTA is only qualified to apply for a position as an entry-level OTA. The OTA must be able to develop skills in school-based practice before applying for the other positions listed. The other positions require more school-based occupational therapy experience.

Type of Reasoning: Deductive
This question requires one to recall factual guidelines and knowledge, which is a deductive reasoning skill. The question essentially tests whether one understands what constitutes experienced versus entry-level practice. Because the OTA of 15 years has never practiced in a school system, their knowledge and skill is entry-level. If answered incorrectly, review standards of practice guidelines related to experienced versus entry-level practice. See Chapter 4.

C88 C8

An individual is 5'11" and is of average weight for this height. Following a recent traumatic brain injury (TBI), the person has flaccid hemiparesis and demonstrates poor righting and equilibrium responses in standing. Which wheelchair is best for the OTA to recommend for this client?

Answer Choices:
A. A power wheelchair.
B. A reclining, hemi-height wheelchair.
C. A one-arm drive, standard-size wheelchair.
D. A lightweight, standard-size wheelchair.

Correct Answer: D.

Rationale:
A standard-size and lightweight wheelchair is the best one for this individual. It is light and therefore easy to push. It is the best size given the person's height. The client is too tall for a hemi-height wheelchair whose seat is lower to the ground to allow for propulsion with one's lower extremities. Power wheelchairs are used for persons with significant functional deficits that preclude the ability to propel a manual wheelchair (i.e., an individual with quadriparesis/quadriplegia). One-arm drive wheelchairs are difficult to learn to use effectively. This difficulty may be exacerbated by the residual deficits of the client's recent TBI.

Type of Reasoning: Inductive
One must utilize clinical knowledge and judgment to determine the wheelchair that is most appropriate for the described individual. This requires inductive reasoning skill. In this case, a lightweight, standard-size wheelchair is most appropriate. If answered incorrectly, review the functional effects of TBI and wheelchair prescription guidelines. The integration of this knowledge is required to determine the correct answer. See Chapters 7 and 15.

C89 C9

An individual recently discharged from an acute psychiatric unit interviews for a position in a transitional employment program (TEP). An OTA completes the TEP intake interview. The person answers the OTA's questions in a direct yet subdued manner and rarely looks at the OTA. Which is most accurate for the OTA to document in the summary of the interview?

Answer Choices:
A. The individual should have medications evaluated before starting the TEP.
B. The individual demonstrated limited eye contact.
C. The individual exhibited poor social interaction skills.
D. The individual appeared depressed.

Correct Answer: B.

Rationale:
The only factual answer is that the individual demonstrated limited eye contact as evidenced by rarely looking at the OTA. The other answers are based upon conjecture as to the meaning or precipitant to this decreased eye contact. Individuals from many cultures are not comfortable with direct eye contact. One cannot assume that this behavior is due to depression, poor social interaction skills, or the need for medication. The subdued answers can be due to cultural and/or personality factors.

Type of Reasoning: Analytical
This question requires the test taker to determine the functional deficit of the patient, which is an analytical reasoning skill. Questions of this nature often call upon the test taker to determine a diagnosis based on a functional description of deficits. Based on this information, the description indicates that the person exhibits limited eye contact. If answered incorrectly, review documentation guidelines. See Chapter 4.

C90 C9

An individual who is acutely psychotic has been brought to the hospital by a legal guardian. The individual neither responds to questions nor attends to visual stimuli in the room. Who should the OTA collaborate with to determine the individual's short-term goals?

Answer Choices:
A. The guardian.
B. The individual.
C. The psychiatrist.

Correct Answer: A.

Rationale:
An individual decides goals in conjunction with occupational therapy practitioners except when the person is unable to take care of self, is a danger to self or others, or is unable to participate in the process. Since the person cannot respond, it would be in the individual's best interest to have the guardian take the place of the individual. The psychiatrist is an important member of the team with whom the OTA will collaborate, but they cannot set goals for the individual. Goal setting must take into account the individual's perspective and the psychiatrist will not have this personal awareness. The guardian would be the person most informed about the individual's life situation, roles, values, needs, and desires, all of which are critical to the formulation of relevant goals.

Type of Reasoning: Evaluative
One must determine a best course of action given the information provided and the value assigned by the test taker for each of the possible courses of action. In this situation, because the patient cannot participate in goal setting, the guardian and OTA should be involved in goal setting until the individual can participate. Evaluative reasoning questions often require one to assign value to a course of action or situations in order to determine an ideal solution. If answered incorrectly, review intervention planning guidelines. See Chapters 3 and 4.

C91 C4

A home-based OTA works with a preschool child who has cerebral palsy. The occupational therapist's evaluation notes that the child has manual abilities consistent with level II of the Manual Ability Classification System (MACS) for children with cerebral palsy. Which should the OTA provide during intervention sessions to develop the child's ability to manually handle objects?

Answer Choices:
A. Hand-over-hand assistance.
B. Activity modifications.
C. Adaptive equipment.
D. Increased time.

Correct Answer: D.

Rationale:
The Manual Ability Classification System (MACS) for Children with Cerebral Palsy describes five levels of handling objects. At level II, the child can be expected to handle objects independently. However, the quality and speed of performance may be decreased; thus, increased time should be provided by the OTA.

Type of Reasoning: Deductive
This question requires one to recall the various levels of the Manual Ability Classification System in order to choose the best intervention approach. This necessitates recall of factual information, which is a deductive reasoning skill. For this case, the OTA should allow increased time during interventions based on this classification. If answered incorrectly, review Table 7-6 in Chapter 7.

C92 C2

A young adult recently diagnosed with depression and anorexia nervosa is a consumer of services at a psychosocial clubhouse. The client attends individual occupational therapy sessions once a week and several evening and weekend groups. During an individual session with the OTA, the client states, "I don't know what I want to work on. I don't really know what my goals are." Which is the most effective action for the OTA to take in response to this client's statement?

Answer Choices:
A. Advise the client to discuss these concerns with the supervising occupational therapist.
B. Establish a short-term goal related to improving the individual's goal setting skills.
C. Initiate a discussion with the individual about what is personally important.
D. Contact the individual's psychiatrist to request a medication evaluation.

Correct Answer: C.

Rationale:
It is best for the OTA to engage the person by exploring their values and priorities as soon as concerns are expressed. This choice provides the person with the opportunity to explore and articulate personal preferences. Actively engaging the person in a dialogue is client-centered, employs therapeutic use of self, and incorporates consumer rights. Advising the client to discuss concerns with the supervising occupational therapist does not provide the client with the opportunity to expand on concerns in the here and now. This could be perceived by the person as a disregard for their concerns by the OTA. The OTA can directly respond to the person's concerns, which can help establish rapport with the individual. Setting up a short-term goal to improve goal setting skills without the direct input of the individual would not contribute to a client-directed intervention plan. This is a violation of the ethical principle of autonomy. There is nothing in the scenario to indicate the need for a medication evaluation.

Type of Reasoning: Evaluative
One must determine which of the four possible courses of action will best establish a therapeutic rapport and incorporate the consumer rights. This requires evaluative reasoning, where the test taker must determine which course of action is most valuable and effective. In this situation, the OTA should initiate discussion about what the client finds important. If answered incorrectly, review information on client-centered treatment planning. See Chapter 3.

C93 C6

An individual with schizophrenia is referred to a partial hospitalization program. The referring psychiatrist notes that the individual's positive symptoms have responded well to a new medication, but negative symptoms remain. During the evaluation, what will the OTA most likely observe?

Answer Choices:
A. Inappropriate verbalizations due to delusions.
B. Limited engagement in tasks due to anergia.
C. Poor concentration and distractibility due to hallucinations.
D. Immobility due to akathisia.

Correct Answer: B.

Rationale:
Limited engagement in tasks due to anergia is the only negative symptom listed. Delusions and hallucinations are positive symptoms. Akathisia results in restlessness, not immobility.

Type of Reasoning: Inferential
This question requires one to determine the likely symptoms of a person displaying negative symptoms with schizophrenia. This requires one to infer or draw conclusions based upon the evidence provided, which is an inferential reasonning skill. In this situation, only limited engagement in tasks due to anergia is a negative symptom. If answered incorrectly, review information on negative symptoms associated with schizophrenia. See Chapter 10.

C94 C4

Two weeks after beginning kindergarten and school-based occupational therapy services, a 5-year-old with myelomeningocele develops sudden onset of headaches, vomiting, irritability, and "sunken" appearance of eyes without signs of a fever. Which action is best for the OTA to take in response to the child's presenting symptoms?

Answer Choices:
A. Bring the child to the school nurse to determine if the observed changes in the child are indicative of stomach flu.
B. Inform the parents that they should immediately have a physician examine the child for tethered cord.
C. Recommend that the supervising occupational therapist refer the child to the school psychologist for assessment of school anxiety.
D. Inform the parents that they should immediately have a physician examine the child for shunt malfunction.

Correct Answer: D.

Rationale:
The identified symptoms, along with seizures, are all indicative of shunt malfunction. Shunt malfunction is a medical emergency. The immediate evaluation of symptoms is critical because shunt malfunction can be a life-threatening condition. Stomach flu can be a possible reason for a few of these symptoms. However, given that the clustering of the symptoms is indicative of shunt malfunction, the child should be checked and immediately assessed by a physician. The signs of tethered cord include difficulties with bowel and bladder, gait disturbances, and/or foot deformities. If anxious, a child may have a tendency to complain of stomachaches and other complaints to avoid school. However, school anxiety would not include physical evidence of illness such as sunken eyes.

Type of Reasoning: Analytical
This question provides a group of symptoms, and the test taker must determine the likely diagnosis. This requires analytical reasoning, where one must determine the precise meaning of the information presented. For this case, shunt malfunction is the most likely cause and should be reported. If answered incorrectly, review the presenting signs of shunts malfunction. See Chapter 7.

C95 C5

A person is diagnosed with chronic obstructive pulmonary disease (COPD). The OTA instructs the individual on breathing exercises to use to control respiration rate during activities. The OTA tells the person to inhale as if smelling roses. How should the OTA tell the person to exhale?

Answer Choices:
A. As if blowing out 20 lit candles on a birthday cake.
B. As if blowing forcibly to relight a dying campfire.
C. As if flickering a lit candle.
D. In quick short, multiple breaths.

Correct Answer: C.

Rationale:
When one exhales to flicker a lit candle, one uses pursed lip breathing. Pursed lip breathing is a method of controlled breathing that requires the individual to purse their lips while exhaling. This slows the exhalation process and improves the carbon dioxide exchange. This decreases one's rate of breathing and prevents airway collapse. The other descriptions do not result in pursed lip breathing.

Type of Reasoning: Inductive
This question requires one to determine the best approach for performing exercises for COPD. This requires inductive reasoning skill, where clinical judgment is paramount to arriving at a correct conclusion. For this situation, the person should exhale as if flickering a lit candle. If answered incorrectly, review breathing exercises, including pursed lip breathing for persons with cardiopulmonary disorders. See Chapter 8.

C96 C4

A client with a spinal cord injury and an OTA set a goal for the client to be independent in all aspects of bowel and bladder care, including skin inspection. Which of the following is the highest or most severe level of complete spinal cord injury the client can have to be able to achieve this goal?

Answer Choices:
A. C7–8.
B. C5–6.
C. C4–5.

Correct Answer: A.

Rationale:
These skills correspond to the C7–8 level. Individuals with SCIs at the other levels do not have the fine motor control to perform the identified skills independently.

Type of Reasoning: Deductive
This question requires factual recall of functional abilities according to spinal level lesions. Specifically, one must recall the expected outcomes of a patient with a complete C7–8 injury. Therefore, a client with this level of injury could be expected to be independent in bowel and bladder care and skin inspection. If answered incorrectly, review the functional outcomes of cervical level injuries. See Chapters 7 and 14.

C97 C1

An OTA works in a school-based setting. A child with developmental delay has mastered the ability to cut simple figure shapes with scissors. Which scissor activity is best for the OTA to next introduce to the child?

Answer Choices:
A. Cutting simple geometric figures.
B. Cutting complex figure shapes.
C. Cutting multiple circles.
D. Cutting additional simple figure shapes.

Correct Answer: B.

Rationale:
The ability to use scissors to cut complex figure shapes is the next developmental task after the acquisition of the ability to cut simple figure shapes. In typically developing children, these abilities develop between the ages of 4 and 6 years. The abilities to cut circles and cut geometric shapes are earlier developmental scissors skill tasks (typically emerging between the ages of 3 and 4). In this scenario, it states that the child has mastered the specified task. Since it is typical to use a developmental frame of reference with children with developmental delays, the OTA would introduce activities that employ the next developmental skill.

Type of Reasoning: Deductive
One must recall the developmental guidelines for children in cutting figure shapes with scissors. This is recall of factual knowledge, which is a deductive reasoning skill. One must recall the next developmental ability in this situation, which is to cut out complex figure shapes. If answered incorrectly, review developmental milestones of scissor skills in children. See Chapter 5.

C98 C4

An OTA working in a skilled nursing facility overhears a resident arguing with a certified nursing assistant (CNA) that someone stole the resident's shoes. The CNA advises the resident that the shoes are in the resident's closet. The resident looks in the closet and insists the shoes are not there. The CNA states they are. The OTA sees that the resident's socks are partially covering the shoes. The OTA quietly advises the CNA to remove the socks from the shoes to help the client recognize them. In making this recommendation, which deficit is the OTA accommodating?

Answer Choices:
A. Anosognosia.
B. Astereognosis.
C. Visual closure.
D. Homonymous hemianopsia.

Correct Answer: C.

Rationale:
This resident's behavior may indicate difficulties with visual closure since the person cannot recognize the slippers in their incomplete form (i.e., covered partially by socks). By removing the socks, the resident will be able to see the shoes in their complete form, which is an accommodation for visual closure. The OTA's recommendation has no relevance to anosognosia, astereognosis, or homonymous hemianopsia. Anosognosia is an unawareness of a motor deficit. Astereognosis, also known as tactile agnosia, is the inability to recognize objects, forms, shapes, and sizes by touch alone. Homonymous hemianopsia results in the loss of half of the visual field in each eye (nasal half of one eye and temporal half of other eye). To accommodate hemianopsia, the OTA would advise the CNA to place the shoes within the person's accessible visual field.

Type of Reasoning: Inductive
For this question one must have knowledge of perceptual disorders in order to arrive at a correct conclusion. This requires clinical judgment, which is an inductive reasoning skill. In this case, the behavior exhibited by the patient indicates difficulties with visual closure. Review perceptual disorders, especially visual closure, if answered incorrectly. See Chapter 12.

C99 C4

An OTA collaborates with an occupational therapist to develop an intervention plan for a client who has decreased executive functioning following a mild cerebral vascular accident. Which are the most relevant foci for this intervention plan? Select the three BEST responses.

Answer Choices:
A. The person's initiation and planning abilities.
B. The person's decision making and problem solving skills.
C. The person's ability to switch tasks and self-correct.
D. The person's attention span and memory capabilities.
E. The person's job interests and perceived self-efficacy.
F. The person's spatial relations and praxis skills.

Correct Answers: A, B, and C.

Rationale:
Executive functions are higher-level cognitive abilities that are needed to perform unstructured, multi-step activities and role tasks. The four main components of executive functioning are volition, planning, purposeful action, and effective performance. Attention and memory are considered primary cognitive capacities that are prerequisite to higher-level cognitive abilities. The other choices do not relate to cognitive functioning.

Type of Reasoning: Inferential
One must infer or draw conclusions about a likely course of action given the information presented. This is an inferential reasoning skill, where knowledge of a therapeutic approach, such as executive functioning in this situation, is essential to choosing a correct solution. In this case, during intervention the OTA and therapist would most likely focus on the person's initiation, planning, decision making, problem solving skills, and the person's ability to switch tasks and self-correct. If answered incorrectly, review executive functions. See Chapter 12.

C100 C6

A young adult admitted to a locked inpatient psychiatric unit is referred to occupational therapy. The referral states that the client is exhibiting symptoms of bipolar disorder, manic episode, with anxiety. Which approach is best for the OTA to use to engage the client in the occupational therapy program?

Answer Choices:
A. In a scrapbooking group, encourage the client to make a page using shared decorative paper, stickers, and pens to create a unique design.
B. Ask the client to help decorate the unit for an upcoming holiday using supplies from a storage box of last year's decorations.
C. In a cooking group, have the client cut shapes to construct a gingerbread house using templates and written directions.

Correct Answer: C.

Rationale:
Choosing a structured activity with clearly defined task steps is a good choice. Because bipolar disorder interferes with executive functions of the brain, structuring the activity with directions and patterns would lessen information processing demands and lend itself to greater potential for success. Additionally, this activity can be individualized so the client works on the task alone in a parallel group or in an assembly line fashion in a project group. This action would allow for the activity to be meaningful, graded for task demands and social interaction, and organized to minimize stress. A client in a manic phase of bipolar disorder would typically approach the tasks of scrapbooking and decorating the unit in a disorganized manner. During scrapbooking, the client would likely have difficulty negotiating for shared materials and supplies, making the task difficult for other group members. The resulting psychosocial reactions would present a challenging group dynamic for the OTA to manage using therapeutic use of self. This would not be helpful to the client or group members. The task of decorating the unit has not been structured to facilitate goal attainment for this client. Instead, it can contribute to the client's mania by its lack of structure, unclear definition of roles for client participation, and laissez-faire leadership approach. The aim of inpatient hospitalization is to facilitate symptom management, so this is not an effective action.

Type of Reasoning: Inductive
This question requires one to determine the best therapeutic approach for a client to promote engagement in OT programming. This is an inductive reasoning skill, as clinical judgment is utilized in determining a therapeutic course of action. For this case, the OTA should have the client cut shapes to construct a gingerbread house using templates and written directions in a cooking group. If answered incorrectly, review principles of activity analysis and symptoms of bipolar disorder. The integration of this knowledge is required to determine the correct answer. See Chapters 3 and 10.

C101 C9

An OTA implements intervention with five patients using a group format. The OTA charges each patient's insurance provider for individual treatments. Which of the following does this action represent?

Answer Choices:
A. An example of impairment.
B. A violation of justice.
C. An established, accepted practice.
D. A correct action, if group interventions are individualized.

Correct Answer: B.

Rationale:
Justice is the principle in the AOTA Code of Ethics that requires all occupational therapy personnel to comply with the laws and regulations guiding the profession and practice of occupational therapy. This includes being truthful in charging for services and meeting legal requirements for documentation. Impairment refers to being under the influence of alcohol, drugs, or any substance that compromises judgment and abilities. It also includes personal issues, such as severe emotional distress, which impede the practitioner's abilities to fully engage in the occupational therapy process with clients. It is inappropriate and illegal to submit charges for individual treatments if the treatment was actually performed in a group.

Type of Reasoning: Evaluative
This question requires a value judgment in an ethical situation, which is an evaluative reasoning skill. Following the OT Code of Ethics, all occupational therapy practitioners should observe justice, which is to comply with all laws and rules, including being truthful in billing for services. Therefore, the billing is a potential violation of justice. If answered incorrectly, review the OT Code of Ethics, especially justice guidelines. See Chapter 4.

C102 C1

An OTA observes that a child can open a combination lock, open a lock with a key, and turn a pencil over to erase. In documenting the child's in-hand manipulation, which is most accurate for the OTA to report the child can correctly perform?

Answer Choices:
A. Finger-to-palm translation.
B. Palm-to-finger translation.
C. Shift.
D. Rotation.

Correct Answer: D.

Rationale:
The activities described involve turning or rolling. Finger-to-palm translation and palm-to-finger translation are incorrect, as no palm is involved in the performance of the described activities. Shift is incorrect because the activities do not just use a linear movement.

Type of Reasoning: Analytical
This question provides descriptions of functional activities, and the test taker must determine the likely definition of such skills. This is an analytical reasoning skill, as questions of this nature often ask one to analyze descriptors of functional skills to determine the overall skill involved. In this situation, the activities are descriptive of rotation. Review fine motor skill in children if answered incorrectly. See Chapter 5.

C103 C9

A new resident of a skilled nursing facility begins occupational therapy to improve grooming and dressing skills. The person refuses to work with the female OTA assigned to the client. The department's sole male OTA has limited experience working with individuals with traumatic brain injury (TBI). Which action is best for the supervising therapist and department OTAs to take in response to this client's stated preference?

Answer Choices:
A. Encourage the individual to work with the assigned female OTA and assure the client of the OTA's skill and competence.
B. Contract with a per diem male OTA to work with the client and provide the needed interventions.
C. Assign the male OTA to work with the individual and have the supervising therapist provide close supervision to the OTA.
D. Modify the intervention goals to include activities that the individual will feel more comfortable with when working with a female OTA.

Correct Answer: C.

Rationale:
This is the choice that respects the person's autonomy. The client's preference for working only with a male practitioner can be due to a cultural, religious, and/or personal reason(s), all of which should be honored. Therefore, this is a request that should be granted. While the male OTA has little direct experience working with persons with TBI, the evaluation and intervention of personal ADL is an area of entry-level OT practice that does not typically require specialized training. However, it would be helpful to provide the OTA with close supervision regarding the application of these fundamental skills to persons with TBI. The supervisor is responsible to help the OTA develop the skills needed for best practice. Encouraging the client to do something that is uncomfortable violates the person's rights. Modifying the goals is not appropriate, as goal modification must be based on an assessment of the client's abilities. In addition, the established goals are relevant and should be addressed.

Type of Reasoning: Evaluative
This question requires one to evaluate all of the potential courses of action and determine which one best considers the patient's needs and provides effective care. Questions that require one to weigh the merits of potential courses of action require evaluative reasoning skill. In this situation, the first action for the supervisor would be to have the male OTA work with the individual and provide supervision for the OTA. This action is consistent with client-centered practice. See Chapter 3.

C104 C7

A client with Guillain-Barré syndrome has bilateral shoulder strength of 2/5. The client fatigues easily. The OTA works with the client to develop independence in the completion of activities of daily living. During intervention sessions, which equipment is best for the OTA to train the client to use?

Answer Choices:
A. An overhead suspension sling.
B. Long-handled utensils and tools.
C. Angled/curved-handled utensils and tools.
D. An environmental control unit.

Correct Answer: A.

Rationale:
The overhead suspension sling is best suited for individuals presenting with proximal weakness with muscle grades in the 1/5 to 3/5 range. Long-handled and curved utensils and tools are useful for individuals with range-of-motion limitations. Environmental control units are used for individuals who have significant motor deficits, proximally and distally, and who cannot independently perform tasks such as controlling the switches on electronic equipment.

Type of Reasoning: Inferential
One must infer or draw conclusions about a likely course of action, given the information presented. This is an inferential reasoning skill, where knowledge of a therapeutic approach, such as providing equipment to enhance functioning in this situation, is essential to choosing a correct solution. In this case, the OTA should include training in the use of an overhead suspension sling. If answered incorrectly, review the diagnostic criteria and functional impact of Guillain-Barré syndrome and adaptive equipment for persons with proximal weakness. Integration of this knowledge is required to answer this item correctly. See Chapters 7 and 14.

C105 C1

An OTA works with an occupational therapist to provide early intervention services. The OTA completes a developmental screening for a newly referred 10-month-old infant. Afterwards, the OTA meets with the occupational therapist to discuss the screening results. They determine that a more intensive developmental evaluation is needed. Which reflex would the infant have demonstrated during screening to support the need for further evaluation?

Answer Choices:
A. Symmetric tonic neck.
B. Prone tilting.
C. Tonic labyrinthine prone.
D. Backward parachute.

Correct Answer: C.

Rationale:
The onset age of the tonic labyrinthine prone reflex is at or after 37 weeks of gestation. This reflex typically integrates at 6 months. Thus, its persistence at 10 months warrants further evaluation. The symmetric tonic neck reflex (STNR), prone tilting reflex, and backward parachute reflex are normal at 10 months. The onset age for the STNR is 4–6 months. The STNR integrates between 8 and 12 months. The onset of the prone tilting reflex is 5 months. The onset of the backward parachute reflex (also called protective extension backward) is 9–10 months. Both the prone tilting and backward parachute reflex persist throughout the lifespan unless neurological damage occurs.

Type of Reasoning: Inferential
For this question, the test taker must infer or determine what is likely to be true in order to arrive at a correct conclusion. In this situation, the test taker must recall when reflexes normally integrate in order to determine the reflex that is likely to be present beyond the normal time frame. This requires inferential reasoning skill. For this case, the tonic labyrinthine prone reflex would most likely have been present during this screening to support the need for further evaluation. Review infant reflexes if answered incorrectly. See Chapter 5.

C106 C3

A child with congenital bilateral above-elbow amputations is referred to occupational therapy to increase independence in ADL. The adolescent wants to be independent in donning and doffing shirts. The OTA and occupational therapist collaborate to determine the best action to take to help the child attain this desired goal. Which action is best to take first in response to this referral?

Answer Choices:
A. Refer the child to a prosthetist.
B. Evaluate the child's abdominal strength.
C. Evaluate child's trunk and lower extremity ROM.
D. Teach the child to use adaptive equipment to dress.

Correct Answer: C.

Rationale:
Upon receipt of a referral, the therapist and OTA must complete an evaluation. Thus, the first step in this scenario is to evaluate trunk and lower extremity ROM to determine if the adolescent can use the lower extremities to dress, as many persons with bilateral above-elbow amputations/amelia do. Hip ROM is essential to be able to don/doff shirts with the feet. After evaluating the child and determining the child's functional abilities, the next step would be to develop an intervention plan to teach the child adaptive techniques for dressing. This can include equipment such as dressing hooks. Most people who are missing both upper extremities do not use prostheses for dressing because the body jacket for the prosthetic arms prevents trunk flexion. Evaluation of abdominal strength can be informative, but it is not the first action to take in response to an initial referral.

Type of Reasoning: Inferential
One must infer or draw conclusions about the best first action to take given a patient's diagnosis and goals. Having an understanding of amelia and typical dressing strategies is pivotal to arriving at a correct conclusion. In this case, the therapist and OTA should first evaluate trunk and lower extremity ROM. If answered incorrectly, review the characteristics of amelia and adaptive dressing strategies. The integration of this information is required to determine the correct answer. See Chapters 6 and 14.

C107 C9

The parents of a child receiving occupational therapy services asks the OTA to treat their other child who does not have insurance and bill for services in the name of their child who does have insurance. Which is the OTA's best response to this request?

Answer Choices:
A. Explain why the OTA must deny the request.
B. Ask the family to get a referral from a physician.
C. Report the parents to the insurance company.
D. Refer the parents to the supervising occupational therapist.

Correct Answer: A.

Rationale:
The OTA must deny this request because complying with it would be unethical and illegal. Asking the parents to obtain a physician's referral does not directly deal with the parents' request. There is no need to report the parents since no violation of insurance law has been committed. It is a good idea to discuss the issue with the supervising occupational therapist, but this does not preclude the reality that the OTA must immediately deny this request.

Type of Reasoning: Evaluative
This question requires a value judgment in an ethical situation, which is an evaluative reasoning skill. Following the OT Code of Ethics, all occupational therapy practitioners should observe veracity, which is to be truthful in the delivery of services. Therefore, the correct response is for the OTA to explain why the request must be denied. Review the OT Code of Ethics if answered incorrectly. See Chapter 4.

C108 C3

An OTA constructs a splint for a client with a low radial nerve injury to facilitate healing and promote function. Which is the most effective splint for the OTA to fabricate for this individual?

Answer Choices:
A. A dynamic extension splint.
B. A figure-of-eight splint.
C. A dynamic flexion splint.
D. A splint to support the functional position.

Correct Answer: A.

Rationale:
The presenting signs of a low-level radial nerve injury include incomplete extension of the fingers' and thumb's MP joints. The IP joints are extended by the interossei, but the MP joints rest in about 30 degrees of flexion. A dynamic splint that provides wrist, MP, and thumb extension is indicated for radial nerve palsy to prevent overstretching of the extensor tendons during the healing phase. This splint also positions the hand for functional use. A figure-of-eight splint or a dynamic flexion splint is indicated for a combined median ulnar nerve injury. The functional position of wrist extension, MCP flexion, IP flexion, and thumb abducted is not effective in radial nerve palsy intervention.

Type of Reasoning: Analytical
This question provides a description of an injury and the test taker must determine the most appropriate splint to address the injury. This is an analytical reasoning skill, as questions of this nature often ask one to analyze information in order to determine a proper course of action. In this situation the ideal splint to fabricate is a dynamic extensor splint. If answered incorrectly, review the diagnostic characteristics of nerve injuries and splinting guidelines for nerve injuries. See Chapter 6.

C109 C4

Following medical treatment for a brain tumor, a client is referred to OT home care services. During the initial screening interview with the OTA, the client reports difficulty locating desired items. For example, at lunchtime the client could not find a can of soup in the pantry. When discussing this self-report with the occupational therapist, which functional ability should the OTA identify as needing further evaluation?

Answer Choices:
A. Visual scanning.
B. Visual acuity.
C. Spatial relations.
D. Topographical orientation.

Correct Answer: A.

Rationale:
Visual scanning is the ability to systematically observe and locate items in the environment. Visual acuity is the clarity of both near and far. Spatial relations refers to the ability to relate objects to each other (i.e., above/below). Topographical orientation is the ability to find one's way in space.

Type of Reasoning: Analytical
This question provides symptoms and the test taker must determine the likely cause for them. This is an analytical reasoning skill, as questions of this nature often ask one to analyze a group of symptoms in order to determine a diagnosis. In this situation, the symptoms indicate visual perceptual deficits, which should be reviewed if answered incorrectly. See Chapters 5 and 12.

C110 C3

The occupational therapist and OTA collaborate to plan intervention for a client with a recent diagnosis of complex regional pain syndrome (CRPS) type I. Which intervention approach is most effective to use to reduce pain and increase function?

Answer Choices:
A. Hot packs.
B. Biofeedback.
C. Paraffin.
D. Passive range of motion.

Correct Answer: B.

Rationale:
CRPS type I is a vasomotor dysfunction that causes extreme hypersensitivity to touch, edema, intense burning pain, and dramatic temperature and color changes to the affected limb. Goals for treatment include reducing pain and edema, promoting normal positioning, and increasing function. Biofeedback is a technique whereby electrodes are used to measure muscle responses and stress levels. The goal is to train the individual to release tension, which can reduce pain and prepare the individual for increased tolerance to range of motion and functional movement. Hot packs and paraffin can be too painful to tolerate in the initial stages and are contraindicated if the affected limb demonstrates elevated temperature. Passive range of motion is usually not tolerated during the initial stages of the syndrome due to the severe pain and hypersensitivity to touch.

Type of Reasoning: Inferential
One must link the individual's diagnosis to the treatment approaches provided in order to determine which treatment approach would most effectively address the individual's deficits. This requires inferential reasoning, where one must draw conclusions about the potential treatment outcomes. In this case, the occupational therapist and OTA should use biofeedback to reduce pain and promote tolerance to activity. If answered incorrectly, review treatment approaches for pain. See Chapters 6 and 7.

C111 C3

A child with juvenile rheumatoid arthritis wears bilateral nighttime resting splints with wrists in 0 degrees of extension, MPs and IPs flexed, ulnar deviation of 10 degrees, and thumbs in opposition. The child complains of pain in wrists upon awakening. No redness is noted upon removing splints. ROM measurements show ulnar deviation of 5 degrees. Which action should the OTA take in response to this complaint and these observations?

Answer Choices:
A. Modify the splints at the wrist.
B. Pad the ulnar aspect on the inside of the splints.
C. Discontinue the splints and monitor the status of pain for 2 weeks.
D. Construct volar cock-up splints for use during the day.

Correct Answer: A.

Rationale:
The splints should be adjusted by use of heat to accommodate to the current position of ulnar deviation. Padding is frequently used to attempt to modify the position of a splint, but it does not correctly allow distribution of pressure. Discontinuing the splints will serve to increase deformities and pain. The child might benefit from daytime splints, but this does not address the issue of the nighttime resting splints causing pain and being set at an incorrect angle for the child's ulnar deviation measurement.

802 Exam C Answer Rationales

Type of Reasoning: Evaluative
One must evaluate the symptoms provided and then determine a best course of action based upon this information. This utilizes evaluative reasoning skill, where the value of the information should guide one's thinking and action in clinical situations. For this case, the most effective action would be to modify the night splints at the wrist. If answered incorrectly, review splinting guidelines. See Chapter 11.

C112 C9

A patient has been discharged from a rehabilitation facility six months ago. An OTA who works at the facility sees the former patient and the occupational therapist that treated the patient in a dating situation. The occupational therapist confirms involvement in a personal relationship with the former patient. What is the OTA's best response to this situation?

Answer Choices:
A. Do nothing.
B. Advise the facility director.
C. Report the therapist to the OT supervisor.

Correct Answer: A.

Rationale:
A health care practitioner can date a former, but not a current, patient. This is no evidence that they dated while the person was a patient. The therapist is doing nothing wrong and there is no need to take any action.

Type of Reasoning: Evaluative
This question requires a value judgment in an ethical situation, which is an evaluative reasoning skill. In this situation, there is only evidence of a relationship between the therapist and patient after the patient was discharged; therefore, no action needs to be taken. Ethical situations such as these often rely upon the AOTA Code of Ethics to provide guiding principles of action. Because there is no harm involved in dating a former patient, the therapist's actions do not constitute harm. If answered incorrectly, review the AOTA Code of Ethics. See Chapter 4.

C113 C8

The parent of a newborn infant has bilateral shoulder weakness and is referred to OT for training in energy conservation techniques for the performance of parenting and home management tasks. Which adaptation(s) is/are most effective for the OTA to recommend the parent use?

Answer Choices:
A. A top-loading washer and dryer for clothing care.
B. A steamer, steamer basket, and/or crock pot for meal preparation.
C. A front pack carrier for holding the infant.
D. Cloth diapers and the use of a weekly diaper care service.

Correct Answer: B.

Rationale:
A steamer, steamer basket, and crock pot eliminate the need to move and lift heavy pans and pots, tasks which require intact bilateral upper extremity strength. A top-loading washer and dryer require more work than front-loading machines. The extra lifting required for top-loading appliances would be difficult with shoulder weakness. A front pack infant carrier has straps that cross the shoulders, so this would be contraindicated in this case. The child's weight in the carrier could contribute to shoulder strain. While a weekly diaper service can provide clean diapers each week, cloth diapers require additional care (i.e., rinsing), which can consume the client's time and energy. Lifting the week's load of wet diapers to bring to the door and picking up the week's allotment of clean diapers can be difficult with shoulder weakness.

Type of Reasoning: Inductive
This question requires one to review all of the potential recommendations and determine which one is most aligned with conserving energy, given the patient's limitations. For this situation, use of a steamer, steamer basket, or crock pot to prepare meals will best conserve energy. Inductive reasoning skills are utilized, as clinical judgment is paramount to choosing the best solution. If answered incorrectly, review energy conservation strategies for home management tasks. See Chapter 11.

C114 C3

An OTA works with an individual with cubital tunnel syndrome who reports numbness and tingling. Which of the following is the most likely location for this person's sensory symptoms?

Answer Choices:
A. The ulnar aspect of the forearm and hand.
B. Along the radial nerve distribution of the hand.
C. The medial aspect of the forearm and hand.
D. Along the ulnar nerve distribution of the hand.

Correct Answer: A.

Rationale:
Cubital tunnel syndrome is an ulnar nerve compression at the elbow. Its presenting symptoms are numbness and tingling along the ulnar aspect of the forearm and hand, pain at the elbow with extreme elbow flexion, weakness of power grip, and a positive Tinel's sign at the elbow.

Type of Reasoning: Inferential
One must have knowledge of cubital tunnel syndrome and presenting symptoms in order to arrive at a correct conclusion. This is an inferential reasoning skill where one must draw conclusions about a diagnosis. For this situation, the numbness and tingling would typically be reported along the ulnar aspect of the forearm and hand. If answered incorrectly, review symptoms of cubital tunnel syndrome. See Chapter 6.

C115 C8

After 6 months of rehabilitation for a T2 spinal cord injury, a patient is being discharged. The OTA conducts a home visit to evaluate accessibility. The individual lives with two roommates in an apartment in a private home. The doorway measurements currently range from 30 to 32 inches throughout the apartment. The patient's landlord is amenable to make changes in the apartment but has no financial resources. Which recommendation is best for the OTA to make for independent accessibility in the apartment?

Answer Choices:
A. Install offset hinges on all doors.
B. Remove doorframes of doorways less than 32 inches and install wider frames.
C. Remove all doors except for the apartment's entrance door.
D. Remove all doorframes and install 34-inch wide doorframes.

Correct Answer: A.

Rationale:
The minimal clearance width for doorways to allow for wheelchair access is 32 inches. Offset hinges can increase a doorway's width by 2 inches, which would result in all doorways meeting or exceeding minimum accessibility standards. It is not necessary to widen the doorways any further. In addition, physically removing doorframes and then installing a wider one is costly. This extra expense is not warranted. While the removal of all doors can increase accessibility, it also eliminates privacy, which may not be desirable when living with two other individuals.

Type of Reasoning: Inductive
Clinical knowledge and judgment are the most important skills needed for answering this question, which requires inductive reasoning skill. Reasoning is the most realistic and cost-effective solution to the problem at hand and is important in choosing the best solution. In this case, the best solution is to install offset hinges on all doors. If answered incorrectly, review door width accessibility standards for persons who use wheelchairs and home modification guidelines. See Chapter 15.

C116 C5

An older adult with mild chronic obstructive pulmonary disease (COPD) is hospitalized. During a session focused on the completion of home management activities, the client complains of dyspnea. Based on this response, the OTA consults with the occupational therapist to revise the client's intervention plan. To help the client engage in activities, which are best to include in the revised plan? Select the three BEST responses.

Answer Choices:
A. Methods to check respiration rate.
B. Energy conservation strategies.
C. Blood pressure monitoring.
D. Diaphragmatic breathing techniques.
E. Pursed lip breathing techniques.
F. Hyperventilation strategies.

Correct Answers: B, D, and E.

Rationale:
Dyspnea is shortness of breath or breathlessness. It is the feeling or feelings associated with impaired breathing. Clients living with COPD experience dyspnea when completing activities that most individuals would be able to complete without shortness of breath. Energy consumption is measured by the amount of oxygen that is needed to complete an activity. Energy conservation techniques are designed to reduce the level of energy required to complete an activity. Teaching the client these techniques can help prevent shortness of breath. Techniques of breath control, specifically diaphragmatic breathing and pursed lip breathing are taught to clients to help to alleviate dyspnea. While monitoring blood pressure and checking respiration rate are important in cardiopulmonary rehabilitation, they are not techniques that will support the client's ability to engage in activities. They are data collection and monitoring procedures. Hyperventilation, also known as over-breathing, is a rapid breathing pattern where the patient inhales and exhales quickly. This type of breathing pattern should not be encouraged as it does not promote the required controlled breathing for the condition of COPD. This approach only adds to shortness of breath and chaotic breathing pattern, which should be discouraged.

Type of Reasoning: Deductive
One must recall the definition of dyspnea and how dyspnea affects activity performance to arrive at a correct conclusion. This is factual knowledge, which is a deductive reasoning skill. For this situation the most appropriate interventions would be integrating energy conservation and the techniques of diaphragmatic breathing and pursed lip breathing to reduce dyspnea. If answered incorrectly, review COPD, energy conservation, dyspnea, and breathing techniques. See Chapters 8 and 11.

C117 C1

An OTA works with a 5-year-old child who has delayed motor skills. All other skills are within developmental norms. The child and the child's family have identified a goal of increasing the child's ability to complete instrumental activities of daily living (IADL) independently. Which approaches are best for the OTA to use with this child? Select the three BEST responses.

Answer Choices:
A. Provide written directions on how to prepare macaroni and cheese.
B. Demonstrate how to make a sandwich using adaptive techniques.
C. Show the child how to make a bed using adaptive strategies.
D. Develop a personalized budget to manage the child's weekly allowance.
E. Discuss with the child how to best organize the task of neatly putting toys away.
F. Discuss with the child how to best organize the task of doing laundry.

Correct Answers: B, C, and E.

Rationale:
Making a sandwich, making a bed, and neatly putting toys away are household management tasks that typically develop at the age of 5. At this age, the child is at the intuitive thought phase of the preoperational level of Piaget's levels of cognitive development. At this level, the child will imitate what they see and hear. Thus, demonstration and verbal instructions are appropriate approaches to use to teach the child to complete IADL. Children typically begin to cook simple meals and manage small amounts of money at the age of 7. The home management task of doing laundry typically develops at 10–12 years. It would be most effective to begin intervention at the child's current developmental level.

Type of Reasoning: Inductive
This question requires one to determine a best course of action based on the age and presenting deficits of a child with delayed motor skills. This requires clinical judgment, which is an inductive reasoning skill. For this scenario, the OTA should demonstrate how to make a sandwich and a bed using adaptive techniques and discuss organizational strategies for neatly putting toys away. If answered incorrectly, review developmental milestones of IADL See Chapter 5.

C118 C1

An OTA provides home-based early intervention services. The occupational therapist informs the OTA that an 18-month-old child is able to finger-feed effectively but is not able to use a spoon or suck from a straw. The OTA puts together supplies to bring to the child's home and plans activities to use during the first intervention session. When selecting objects and activities to use during this initial session, which developmental age is most important for the OTA to include?

Answer Choices:
A. 6–9 months.
B. 12–18 months.
C. 18–20 months.
D. 9–12 months.

Correct Answer: D.

Rationale:
The information that the occupational therapist provided to the OTA indicates abilities that are typical at the age of 9–12 months. Therefore, the OTA should begin intervention by using activities that are at the child's developmental age. If the child's performance in certain parameters is more or less advanced than this developmental age, the OTA can adjust interventions accordingly. Since the child cannot use a spoon or a straw, activities that are typical of the developmental ages of 12–18 months and 18–20 months may be too difficult for the child. Spoon use typically develops at 12–18 months. Straw use typically develops at about 18 months. Since the child's finger-feeding is noted to be effective, activities that are typical at 6–9 months would be too low developmentally for the child.

Type of Reasoning: Inductive
Clinical knowledge and judgment are the most important skills needed for answering this question, which requires inductive reasoning skill. Knowledge of the child's developmental age and most important activities to bring for the evaluation is essential to choosing the best solution. In this case, the OTA should bring objects and activities for the developmental age of 9–12 months. If answered incorrectly, review developmental milestones for feeding in infants. See Chapter 5.

C119 C3

A patient incurred a traumatic upper extremity amputation. During preprosthetic treatment, the OTA molds the contours of the residual limb to shrink and shape it in preparation for a prosthesis. Which method is most effective for the OTA to use?

Answer Choices:
A. Wrapping.
B. Percussion.
C. Intermittent compression therapy.
D. Massage.

Correct Answer: A.

Rationale:
Wrapping by applying an elastic bandage to the residual limb in a figure-eight pattern will reduce the volume of the residual limb and shape it for a prosthesis. Intermittent compression therapy is used for edema, but not residual limbs. Percussion and massage are used to desensitize a residual limb.

Type of Reasoning: Analytical
This question provides a description of an intervention method and the test taker must determine the likely definition of the described method. This is an analytical reasoning skill, as questions of this nature often ask one to analyze a descriptor to determine the specific method being defined. In this situation the intervention method is that of residual limb wrapping, which should be reviewed if answered incorrectly. See Chapter 6.

C120 C9

In a rehabilitation therapy clinic, a patient falls during a transfer from the wheelchair to the bed. The OTA has to complete an incident report. In addition to the names of the persons involved, which additional information is required in the report?

Answer Choices:
A. A description of the fall from both the OTA's and patient's viewpoint.
B. Witness statements and the supervising therapist's opinion as to the cause.
C. Description of the patient's injuries and the medical treatment required.
D. Facts about what occurred and witness statements.

Correct Answer: D.

Rationale:
General information on an incident report includes factual information, including names of persons involved, description of what occurred, when and where it occurred, and any witness statements. Incident reports should not include subjective interpretations such as a cause for the fall. One should not assume that all falls result in an injury or require medical intervention.

Type of Reasoning: Deductive
This question requires factual recall of guidelines in order to arrive at a correct conclusion. Deductive reasoning skills are used whenever guidelines and protocols are utilized to draw conclusions. For this situation, an incident report would require the inclusion of facts about what occurred and witness statements. If answered incorrectly, review guidelines for completion of incident reports. See Chapter 4.

C121 C7

An older adult resident of a skilled nursing facility becomes tearful during an occupational therapy session. The resident has a diagnosis of advanced osteoarthritis and states that pain is causing discomfort during sexual activities. The resident expresses fear about "losing" a valued intimate relationship and asks the OTA for advice. Which is the most beneficial action for the OTA to take in response to the resident's expressed concerns?

Answer Choices:
A. Refer the resident to social work for individual counseling.
B. Collaborate with the occupational therapist and resident to establish goals for sexual expression.
C. Refer the resident and the resident's significant other to social work for couples counseling.
D. Advise nursing staff of the resident's statements to ensure that sexual behavior is monitored.

Correct Answer: B.

Rationale:
Sexuality and sexual expression are within the practice domain of occupational therapy. It is important for the OTA to create an atmosphere that enables the person to express their concerns. Once the individual's goals for sexual expression are established, strategies to attain these goals can be explored. These strategies can include the use of activity analysis, gradation, modification and simplification, non-medical methods to manage pain and stiffness (e.g., warm baths), positioning alternatives, adaptive equipment, energy conservation methods, and/or referral(s) to other professionals. It is a violation of a person's autonomy for staff members to monitor consensual sexual expression of any individual, regardless of age or facility.

Type of Reasoning: Inductive
Clinical knowledge and judgment are the most important skills needed for answering this question, which requires inductive reasoning skill. Knowledge of OT's practice domain is essential for arriving at a correct conclusion. In this case, the OTA should collaborate with the occupational therapist to explore the resident's goals for sexual expression. If answered incorrectly, review guidelines for sexual expression. Review the PLISSIT model in Chapter 14.

C122 C5

An adolescent with a complete myelomeningocele at the T9 level is diagnosed with diabetes. The OTA meets with the adolescent and a nurse practitioner to review the impact of this new diagnosis on the teen's health and daily routines. Which is most important for the OTA to emphasize during this discussion?

Answer Choices:
A. Skin inspection performed by a parent.
B. Upper extremity strengthening.
C. Self-directed pressure relief.
D. Self-initiated pressure relief.

Correct Answer: D.

Rationale:
The person with complete myelomeningocele at the T9 level has absent sensation in the lower extremities and buttocks. Therefore, frequent pressure relief is essential to prevent skin breakdown. While it is likely that the teen has previously been taught pressure relief techniques, the new diagnosis of diabetes makes a review of the importance of consistent and routine pressure relief a priority. Skin care and inspection are important elements to include in programs for people with diabetes, especially for those with absent sensation. However, it would be unlikely that an adolescent would want to have an adult inspect the skin. Upper extremity strengthening can be helpful to provide pressure relief; however, a T9 lesion does not affect the upper extremities, so the adolescent's strength is likely within functional limitations. Consequently, the teen is capable of self-initiating pressure relief and does not have to self-direct the performance of this routine activity.

Type of Reasoning: Inferential
One must understand the nature of both myelomeningocele and diabetes in order to arrive at a correct conclusion. Inferential reasoning skills are utilized, as the test taker must infer the nature of both of these diagnoses and then determine the most important home education guidelines based on this knowledge. In this case, self-initiated pressure relief is most important to prevent skin breakdown. If answered incorrectly, review symptoms of myelomeningocele and diabetes, especially the importance of pressure relief. The integration of this knowledge is required to determine the correct answer. See Chapter 7 and 9.

C123 C3

An OTA provides outpatient services to a person status/post a Dupuytren's release of the right dominant hand. The surgical wound is healed and the physician has updated the OT referral to focus on increasing ROM and functional use. During the completion of an occupational profile, the client had identified home maintenance and meal preparation activities as valued areas of occupation. During the client's clinic-based sessions, the OTA provides purposeful and occupation-based interventions related to these interests. To enhance the client's recovery, the OTA collaborates with the occupational therapist to develop guidelines for a home program. Which activity is best for the OTA and therapist to recommend the client do as part of their home program?

Answer Choices:
A. Rake leaves.
B. Sweep the floor.
C. Peel vegetables.
D. Knead dough.

Correct Answer: D.

Rationale:
Dupuytren's is a disease of the fascia of the palm and digits in which the fascia becomes thick and contracted and cords and bands develop and extend into the digits. This results in flexion deformities of the involved digits. See Figure 6-7 in Chapter 6. Initially, intervention will focus on wound care, splinting, and ROM. With a surgeon's approval, intervention can progress to focusing on increasing strength and functional use. Occupational therapy intervention for Dupuytren's release should emphasize activities that focus on flexion (gripping) and extension (release). To knead dough, a person needs to repetitively grip and squeeze the dough and then release it. Raking leaves, sweeping a floor, and peeling vegetables require the person to maintain their grip on the rake, broom, or vegetable peeler, respectively.

Type of Reasoning: Deductive
One must recall the functional impact of Dupuytren's disease and post-surgical release intervention protocols. This is recall of factual knowledge, which is a deductive reasoning skill. For this situation, the best activity for the OTA and the therapist to recommend the client do as part of their home program activities is kneading bread. This is the only activity in the choices provided that includes finger flexion (gripping) and extension (release). If answered incorrectly, review the characteristics of and interventions for Dupuytren's disease. See Chapter 6.

C124 C2

A middle school-aged child with a sensory processing disorder participates in weekly occupational therapy sessions at a private pediatric clinic. Initial evaluation had identified the presence of symptoms consistent with a sensory-based motor disorder. The child has shown no improvement in coordination, equilibrium, and motor planning for the past two months. The parents report that the child continues to exhibit difficulties with play, learning, and social participation. Based on these observations and parental report, which is most important for the OTA to discuss with the occupational therapist?

Answer Choices:
A. Providing the parents with a home program and discharging the child from therapy.
B. Referring the child to a pediatric social worker to explore potential resistance to therapy.
C. Increasing the frequency of therapy to two sessions per week to increase the child's engagement.
D. Re-evaluating the child to determine deficit areas that are contributing to dysfunction.

Correct Answer: D.

Rationale:
The child is not making gains in occupational therapy with the current approach to address coordination, equilibrium, and motor planning, and the parents are reporting ongoing dysfunction. Therefore, the OTA should discuss the need for re-evaluation of the child with the occupational therapist. This re-evaluation by the occupational therapist would obtain information that can help revise the current intervention plan to more effectively meet the child's needs. The OTA would contribute to the re-evaluation process with supervision from the occupational therapist. Intervention focused on other performance skills and client factors may be effective and should be implemented before discharging the child. The OTA should not continue to treat the child in areas that show no progress. The child has not made gains. Increasing the frequency of occupational therapy without a revised intervention plan will not facilitate functional improvements. The identified deficits are within the domain of practice of occupational therapy, so a referral to a social worker is not necessary. There is no information provided in the scenario to indicate that the child is resistant to therapy.

Type of Reasoning: Inferential
One must infer or draw conclusions about a best course of action given the information provided. In this situation, re-evaluation of the child is ideal in order to determine a new focus of OT intervention as the current plan is not resulting in functional gains. If answered incorrectly, review treatment planning guidelines. See Chapter 3.

C125 C6

An individual is newly admitted to an acute inpatient psychiatric hospital. The OTA observes that the patient is able to follow the unit routines and construct a simple craft project by following written directions with diagrams. However, the patient is not able to complete the project if the directions are missing. According to Allen's cognitive disability frame of reference, which level is most accurate for the OTA to document as descriptive of the individual's functional level?

Answer Choices:
A. Level 2.
B. Level 3.
C. Level 4.
D. Level 5.

Correct Answer: C.

Rationale:
Individuals at level 4 require visual cues to complete tasks. Individuals functioning at level 2 and level 3, according to Allen's cognitive disabilities model, cannot follow written directions to complete a task. Individuals functioning at level 5 can complete a simple craft project without written directions.

Type of Reasoning: Deductive
One must recall Allen's cognitive levels and the behavioral descriptions for each level. This is recall of factual knowledge, which is a deductive reasoning skill. For this situation, the description of patient functioning is most representative of level 4. If answered incorrectly, review Allen's cognitive levels. See Chapter 13.

C126 C3

An individual who is scheduled for a right hip total arthroplasty (THA) is referred to occupational therapy. A posterolateral surgical approach will be used. Which should the OTA focus on during preoperative occupational therapy interventions?

Answer Choices:
A. The performance of upper and lower extremity strengthening exercises.
B. The performance of IADL tasks in a sitting rather than standing position.
C. The practice of non–weight-bearing crutch walking.
D. The use of modified techniques to perform transfers and BADL.

Correct Answer: D.

Rationale:
Intervention should cover the use of modified techniques to ensure that the person maintains correct positioning during transfers and BADL (e.g., bathing, dressing, and toileting). These essential BADL will be done daily during the postoperative rehabilitation phase. The modified techniques for the performance of BADL typically include the use of equipment (e.g., long-handled sponge/shoehorn, sock aid, three-in-one commode). There is nothing in the question scenario to indicate that the person has decreased upper extremity strength, and this answer choice does not apply to any functional outcome. Performing tasks in sitting can be more stressful on the hip joint than doing them in standing and are contraindicated. Restrictions for weight-bearing will depend on several factors (e.g., the integrity of the bone) that may not be determined until after the person's surgery. Interventions for post-surgical gait training are most effectively conducted by the physical therapist.

Type of Reasoning: Inferential
One must draw conclusions about the likely preoperative training for a patient requiring a total hip replacement. Most important in this situation is to prepare the patient for postoperative rehabilitation. Therefore, training in the use of equipment and skills needed for transfers and BADL is most important preoperatively. If answered incorrectly, review total hip replacement precautions. See Chapter 6.

C127 C4

A child with a sensory processing disorder receives occupational therapy services at a private preschool. One of the child's presenting behaviors is hyposensitivity to movement. Which is the best recommendation for the OTA to make to the parents?

Answer Choices:
A. Monitor the child's use of swings and other moving equipment during play activities.
B. Avoid the use of swings and other moving equipment during play activities.
C. Avoid play activities that involve movement in sand, grass, and/or water.
D. Provide play activities which encourage the child to use both sides of the body.

Correct Answer: A.

Rationale:
Children who are hyposensitive to movement will seek intense vestibular stimulation without complaints of feeling dizzy. They have a tendency to seek thrills without being aware of potential dangers (e.g., spinning while standing on a narrow ledge, swinging strong enough to flip a swing). Thus, it will be important for the parents to carefully monitor the child when the child uses play equipment that moves to ensure the child's safety. The avoidance of swings and other moving play equipment is indicated for children who are hypersensitive to movement. The avoidance of play activities that involve moving in sand, grass, and/or water is indicated for children with tactile defensiveness. The use of bilateral play activities is indicated for children with impaired body scheme and somatodyspraxia.

Type of Reasoning: Inductive

For this question, one must have knowledge of hyposensitivity to movement and likely behaviors associated with this in order to arrive at a correct conclusion. This requires clinical judgment, which is an inductive reasoning skill. For this scenario, the OTA should recommend monitoring the child's use of swings and other moving equipment during play activities. If answered incorrectly review guidelines for working with children with sensory processing disorders. See Chapter 12.

C128 C2

An OTA collaborates with an occupational therapist to develop the preadmission screening procedures for a supported housing program with several levels of care. The population served by this program include persons with serious mental illness who are actively engaged in their recovery. Which tool is best for the therapist and OTA to include in the recommended screening procedures?

Answer Choices:
A. A semi-structured interview.
B. An activities of daily living checklist.
C. A structured cooking task.
D. A weekly activity schedule.

Correct Answer: C.

Rationale:

The purpose of screening is to determine the need for further evaluation. A structured cooking task can be used to screen for a diversity of cognitive skills (e.g., ability to follow directions and problem solve, awareness of safety) and home management abilities (e.g., use of kitchen equipment, level of cleanliness) that can help determine the need for further evaluation. This information will be necessary to select the level of supported housing that would be most effective for each person referred to the program. A semi-structured interview can be helpful in determining interests and goals, but it is not an effective screening for functional skill level. An ADL checklist can assess knowledge of an activity/skill, but it does not assess performance; therefore, its usefulness is limited. A weekly activity schedule can provide information about time use and ability to complete a structured task, but it is a paper-and-pen task that has limited applicability to screening for housing placement recommendations.

Type of Reasoning: Inferential

One must determine the most effective screening tool, given the scenario's setting and population. This requires inferential reasoning skill, where one must draw conclusions based on the information presented. In this situation, a structured cooking task is most effective. If answered incorrectly, review screening guidelines and the characteristics of supported housing programs. The integration of this knowledge is required to determine the best answer. See Chapters 3 and 4.

C129 C5

An OTA provides intervention for an individual with a swallowing disorder. To elicit a swallow reflex, the OTA provides sensory input to the inferior faucial arches. Which should the OTA use to provide this intervention?

Answer Choices:
A. A tongue depressor.
B. A moistened cotton swab.
C. A chilled dental examination mirror.
D. A warmed metal teaspoon.

Correct Answer: C.

Rationale:
The use of cold stimulation to the inferior faucial arches via a chilled dental examination mirror will elicit a swallow reflex. The others will not.

Type of Reasoning: Inferential
One must determine the guidelines for eliciting a swallow reflex and then determine which of the listed devices is aligned with the stimulation of this reflex. This requires inferential reasoning skill. In this situation, a chilled dental examination mirror is ideal. If answered incorrectly, review elicitation of the swallow reflex. See Chapter 12.

C130 C7

An OTA provides home-based occupational therapy services. During an initial evaluation, the OTA notes that a client requires assistance from a caregiver approximately 75% of the time to dress the upper and lower extremities. Which level of independence is most accurate for the OTA to document for the activity of dressing?

Answer Choices:
A. Minimal assistance.
B. Moderate assistance.
C. Maximal assistance.

Correct Answer: C.

Rationale:
Many assessments used to measure activities of daily living provide a determination of the person's level of functional performance along a level of assistance continuum, which ranges from total assistance to independent status. According to this scale, the need for 75% assistance by one person to physically perform any part of a functional activity and/or cognitive assistance to perform gross motor actions in response to direction is classified as maximal assistance. Moderate assistance is the need for 50% assistance by one person to perform physical activities or provide cognitive assistance to sustain/complete simple, repetitive activities safely. Minimal assistance is the need for 25% assistance by one person for physical activities and/ or periodic, cognitive assistance to perform functional activities safely.

Type of Reasoning: Deductive
This question requires one to determine a level of performance based on knowledge of assessments used in activities of daily living performance. This is recall of factual information, which is a deductive reasoning skill. For this scenario, the level of performance is maximal assistance. If answered incorrectly, review guidelines for the determination of a person's level of functional performance. See Table 14-2 in Chapter 14.

814 Exam C Answer Rationales

C131 C4

A Level II fieldwork student's first assigned case is an individual with right hemiplegia. The supervising OTA reminds the student that primitive reflexes can emerge when someone incurs a CVA. The OTA demonstrates this point by rotating the client's head to the right and stating that the observed response demonstrates a subtle asymmetrical tonic neck reflex (ATNR). The OTA asks the student to describe the client's reaction that resulted in the OTA's interpretation. Which is most accurate for the student to state the client is exhibiting based on this observation?

Answer Choices:
A. Increased flexor tone of the right upper extremity.
B. Increased extensor tone of the left upper extremity.
C. Increased extensor tone of the right upper extremity.
D. Increased extensor tone in both upper extremities.

Correct Answer: C.

Rationale:
Rotating the head to one side facilitates the ATNR. When observing ATNR, one will see flexion of the upper extremity (UE) on the skull side of the body, and extension of the UE on the face side. Therefore, when assessing an adult with right hemiplegia, by turning the head to the right one would be able to observe an increase in extensor tone in the right UE and increased flexor tone in the left UE. Increased extensor tone in the left UE and increased flexor tone in the right UE would be observed if the head was moved to the left and the person had a subtle ATNR.

Type of Reasoning: Deductive
This question provides a type of reflex, and a test taker must recall the features of this reflex in order to arrive at a correct conclusion. This necessitates recall of factual guidelines, which is a deductive reasoning skill. In this situation, the OTA would observe increased extensor tone of the right UE. If answered incorrectly, review the impact of reflexes on movement and tone. See Chapters 5 and 7.

C132 C5

An OTA is collaborating with an occupational therapist to plan discharge for an adult who was hospitalized due to an acute pulmonary hypertension episode associated with the client's primary diagnosis of scleroderma. The client has lived with scleroderma for many years and has received occupational therapy services in the past. The client has expressed a current concern about going home to live alone. Previously, the client resided with an adult child, but this family member will be moving out of the client's home due to a job relocation within a week. Which is most important for the OTA and therapist to address pre-discharge?

Answer Choices:
A. Activity modifications to prevent trauma to the fingers, which are affected by sclerodactyly.
B. Clothing modifications for neutral warmth to cope with the effects of Raynaud's phenomenon.
C. The client's willingness to participate in a support group for adults with chronic illnesses.
D. The client's ability to adhere to safety procedures and respond to emergencies within the home.

Correct Answer: D.

Rationale:
Scleroderma is a rheumatic, connective tissue disease associated with an impaired immune response. Vascular components include constant recurrent constriction of small blood vessels leading to pulmonary hypertension and Raynaud's phenomenon (i.e., excessively reduced blood flow to the fingers and toes in response to cold or emotional stress). Fibrotic components include scar tissue resulting from excess collagen (protein). This causes thickness of the skin and a burning sensation in the skin. Sclerodactyly is a localized thickening and tightness of the skin of the fingers and/or toes. The use of activity and clothing modifications are effective interventions for the presenting symptoms of scleroderma. However, in this scenario, the client has lived with the diagnosis of scleroderma for years and has received occupational therapy services in the past. Therefore, it is likely that the client will have integrated these actions into daily life. While support groups can be helpful to persons living with chronic illnesses, the major change in the client's status is living alone. Thus, the client's ability to adhere to safety procedures and respond to emergencies within the home is essential to ensure the client's safety. These include (but are not limited to) routine safety measures such as the ability to safely use a stove and oven to prevent burns during meal preparation activities and the use of handrails when ascending and descending stairways to prevent falls. The client must also be able to respond to unexpected emergencies such as a fire. The client must have an emergency exit plan and be capable of dialing 9-1-1. Given that Raynaud's phenomenon and sclerodactyly can affect a person's ability to complete activities (for example in this case, turn stove burners completely on and off, close a deadbolt lock, pull and hold a fire extinguisher's trigger, and dial a phone), addressing the client's ability to be safe in the home is most important.

Type of Reasoning: Inductive
This question requires one to utilize clinical judgment to determine a best course of action for a patient with scleroderma. This requires inductive reasoning skill, which calls for knowledge of the diagnosis coupled with reasoning a best course of action. In this case, the OTA should address the client's ability to adhere to safety procedures and respond to emergencies within the home. If answered incorrectly, review safety guidelines and the discharge process. The integration of this knowledge is required to determine a correct answer.
See Chapters 9 and 14.

C133 C2

An OTA initiates a lifestyle redesign group at an assisted living facility for new residents. Which approach is best for the OTA to use during the group's initial session?

Answer Choices:
A. Encourage the members to share their feelings about moving to an assisted living facility to facilitate adaptive adjustment.
B. Review written handouts about the group's purpose, norms, and goals in an environment that minimizes auditory distractions.
C. Describe environmental modifications that can be made to the residents' apartments to compensate for low vision.
D. Provide specific recommendations for doing activities at a slower pace to accommodate for decreased reaction time.

Correct Answer: B.

Rationale:
The first session of a group should focus on orienting group members to the group's purpose, norms, and goals. Most persons who live in assisted living facilities are older adults. Therefore, it is important for the OTA to consider the impact of age-related sensory changes on the residents' ability to participate in the group orientation. Age-related sensory changes typically include hearing loss. Thus, it is best for the OTA to orient the group members by orally reviewing written handouts in an environment that minimizes auditory distractions. Providing written materials that the members can take with them can also facilitate a positive orientation to the group because the residents will have this information readily available to review as needed. Encouraging the members to share their feelings about moving to an assisted living facility is not appropriate for an initial group meeting. Revealing personal feelings about a major life change requires a cohesive group of members who trust each other. Because the members are new residents, they will likely not know each other well and may be uncomfortable with sharing personal information. Doing activities at a slower pace and modifying the environment are effective interventions for age-related sensory changes; however, they are not the most relevant focus for an initial session of a newly formed group. New members first require an orientation to the group.

Type of Reasoning: Inductive
One must have knowledge of the group process to determine the correct action. For this case, inductive reasoning skills are utilized to determine the best approach for an initial group session. In this situation, the OTA should review written handouts about the group's purpose, norms, and goals in an environment that minimizes auditory distractions. If answered incorrectly, review information about group process and the stages of group development. See Chapter 3.

C134 C7

An OTA leads a work group at a vocational rehabilitation program for persons with traumatic brain injuries. One member begins to make sexually suggestive comments to other group members. The OTA redirects the client to the work in progress, but the member continues to make sexually suggestive statements. Which is the OTA's best initial response to this situation?

Answer Choices:
A. Explain to the client that such statements are not tolerated at work and call security to have the client removed from the group.
B. Explain to the client that such statements are not tolerated at work and the client must stop or leave the group.
C. End the group before the situation escalates and reschedule the group to meet without the disruptive client.
D. Set the client up at a different workstation so the client is not in contact with other group members and cannot disrupt the group's work.

Correct Answer: B.

Rationale:
This response reinforces the norms of a work environment and gives the individual the opportunity to practice making a decision about the most effective course of action. An important aspect of vocational rehabilitation for persons with traumatic brain injuries is the development of effective social interaction skills which comply with workplace norms. Ending the group, removing the client from the group, or decreasing contact with others does not address the client's need to develop the interaction skills required for work. In addition, the role of the OTA in a vocational rehabilitation program is to act as a work supervisor, which included enforcing the expectations of a workplace. Inappropriate sexual remarks are not tolerated in a work setting. If the client cannot comply with work norms in a vocational program, they may need to be referred to a prevocational program for basic social skills and work habit training. These basic skills are not the focus of vocational rehabilitation.

Type of Reasoning: Evaluative
One must weigh the possible courses of action and then make a value judgment about the best course to take. This requires evaluative reasoning skill, which often utilizes guiding principles of action in order to arrive at a correct conclusion. For this case, the OTA should explain that the client's statements will not be tolerated; thus, the client must either stop or leave the group. If answered incorrectly, review group leadership guidelines and group norms and the development of work behaviors. The integration of this knowledge is required to determine the correct answer. See Chapters 3 and 14.

C135 C1

During an intervention session, an 8-month-old child demonstrates a positive downward parachute reflex. Which is the most accurate statement for the OTA to include in the documentation of this observed behavior?

Answer Choices:
A. The child exhibits normal reflex development.
B. The child exhibits a developmental delay.
C. The child's protective extension downward reflex needs to be evaluated by the occupational therapist.
D. The child's standing tilting reflex needs to be evaluated by the occupational therapist.

Correct Answer: A.

Rationale:
A downward parachute reflex is normal from 4 months and persists throughout one's lifetime unless neurological damage occurs. It is also called the protective extension downward reflex. The onset of the standing tilting reflex is from 12 to 21 months, so an evaluation of this reflex is premature.

Type of Reasoning: Evaluative
One must weigh the possible options and then make a value judgment about the most accurate statement to make. This requires evaluative reasoning skill, which often utilizes guiding principles of action in order to arrive at a correct conclusion. For this case, because the child is displaying normal reflex development, the OTA should document this finding as normal. Review downward parachute reflex and age of integration if answered incorrectly. See Chapter 5.

C136 C4

An older adult recovering from a right CVA has been assessed by the occupational therapist and determined to have unilateral body inattention and difficulties with body scheme. Which intervention is best for the OTA to use when working with this person to address both of these deficits?

Answer Choices:
A. Have the person point to various body parts named by the OTA.
B. Work with the person on integrating both sides of the body while dressing.
C. Train the person in scanning strategies to locate clothing in a closet.
D. Have the person construct a three-dimensional body puzzle.

Correct Answer: B.

Rationale:
Body scheme disorders result in a loss of awareness of body parts and the relationship of the body parts to each other and objects. Body scheme disorders include body inattention (often called neglect) and asomatognosia. Unilateral body neglect is the failure to respond to or report unilateral stimulation presented to the body side contralateral to the lesion. It is evident when the person does not attend to one side of the body (e.g., the person dresses one side of the body or shaves one side of the face). Asomatognosia includes a diminished awareness of body structure and a failure to recognize body parts as one's own. The best way to intervene for unilateral neglect and difficulties with body scheme is to have the person physically complete an activity that incorporates the involved limbs into the activity (in this case dressing). The activities of pointing to named body parts and completing a body puzzle only address asomatognosia, which is just one element of body scheme. Training a person in scanning strategies to locate clothing in a closet is an intervention approach for visual neglect.

Type of Reasoning: Inductive
This question requires one to determine a best intervention approach based on the person's deficits. This necessitates clinical judgment, which is an inductive reasoning skill. For this situation, the OTA should work with the person on integrating both sides of the body while dressing to best address the deficit of unilateral body neglect and difficulty with body scheme. If answered incorrectly, review unilateral neglect and intervention guidelines for this deficit. See Chapter 12.

C137 C6

An OTA is working with an individual recovering from a traumatic hand injury. The person regularly attends all outpatient intervention sessions but has little energy and is very difficult to engage. The person reports disinterest in performing the prescribed home program. Which is the best action for the OTA to take in response to this situation?

Answer Choices:
A. Advise the occupational therapist that a referral to a psychiatrist for the completion of a mental status examination should be made.
B. Tell the person that active engagement in intervention sessions and the completion of the home program is vital to recovery.
C. Inform the occupational therapist that the patient is exhibiting behaviors that indicate the need to screen for depression.
D. Defer intervention until the person's depression is evaluated and the occupational therapy intervention plan modified as needed.

Correct Answer: C.

Rationale:
The patient's observable behaviors (i.e., lethargy and disengagement) and reported disinterest can be indicative of depression. Thus, the OTA must inform the occupational therapist that the patient is exhibiting and reporting behaviors that indicate the need to screen for depression. The occupational therapist can then complete a standardized depression scale that provides objective data about the person's affective state. The therapist can also interview the person to determine contextual factors that may be impacting the person. A referral for a psychiatric evaluation would be premature at this point, as the cause of the person's behavior is not known. The person's lack of energy and non-compliance can be due to other factors that are not psychiatric in nature. For example, the individual could be providing care for a spouse and not have time for a home program and/or for adequate sleep. Explaining the importance of engaging in therapy and completing a home program does not directly deal with the issue of lack of engagement and follow through. In addition, there is nothing in the scenario to indicate that the person is not aware of the importance of compliance. Since it is not known if the person's behaviors are due to depression, it would not be effective to defer occupational therapy treatment. If the person is depressed, the treatment for depression can be provided concurrently with the treatment for the person's physical limitations.

Type of Reasoning: Analytical
This question requires one to weigh the presenting symptoms and determine the likely cause for those symptoms in order to determine the best course of action. This necessitates analytical reasoning skill, where various symptoms are weighed in order to draw a sound conclusion about the cause. For this case, the OTA should inform the occupational therapist that the patient is exhibiting behaviors that indicate the need to screen for depression. If answered incorrectly, review symptoms of depression. See Chapter 10.

C138 C1

A 4-month-old infant with developmental delay has mastered the ability to bear and shift weight on forearms when in the prone position. The OTA collaborates with the occupational therapist to plan the next session's intervention. Using a developmental approach, which would be best for the OTA to use during intervention to facilitate the infant's progression to the next gross motor skill, which typically develops in the prone position?

Answer Choices:
A. Placing a mirror within the infant's visual field and then slowly moving the mirror from right to left to encourage the infant to turn the head to the side.
B. Shaking a colorful rattle near the child's ear and then moving the rattle to midline and above the child's head to encourage the child to raise the head.
C. Touching the child's hand with a soft black and white stuffed bear and then moving the bear out of the child's reach to encourage the child to reach.
D. Placing a colorful picture within the infant's visual field and then moving the picture from left to right to encourage the child to roll from prone to side.

Correct Answer: C.

Rationale:
The ability to bear and shift weight on the forearms when in the prone position typically occurs at 0–2 months of age. Lifting the head, sustaining the head in midline, and turning the head side to side are gross motor skills that also typically develop at 0–2 months. Thus, activities that use these actions do not work on a gross motor skill that would typically develop next. The ability to shift weight on forearms and reach forward and bear and shift weight on extended arms in the prone position are the next gross motor skills that are typically developed. These milestones typically occur at 5–6 months of age. Touching the child's hand with a soft stuffed animal and then moving the animal out of the child's reach will encourage the child to reach forward while weight bearing. Rolling from the prone position to the side occurs accidentally at 3–4 months of age due to poor control of weight shift. Rolling from the supine position to the side also occurs at this age. While these gross motor skills do need to develop, they are considered rolling skills rather than gross motor skills which develop in the prone position. The latter was the focus of this exam item.

Type of Reasoning: Inductive
For this question, the test taker must use knowledge of the developmental approach and developmental motor milestones in infants in order to arrive at a correct conclusion. This requires inductive reasoning skill. For this scenario, the OTA should provide an intervention that encourages the child to reach. If answered incorrectly, review motor development in infants. See Table 5-4 in Chapter 5 for an outline of the developmental sequence of gross motor skills.

C139 C3

An OTA working in a hand clinic has established service competence in the evaluation of upper extremity disorders. During the evaluation, the therapist uses the Froment's sign. When documenting the outcome of this evaluation procedure, which is most accurate for the OTA to state was assessed?

Answer Choices:
A. Sensation of the median nerve.
B. Motor function of the median nerve.
C. Sensation of the ulnar nerve.
D. Motor function of the ulnar nerve.

Correct Answer: D.

Rationale:
The Froment's sign assesses the motor function of the adductor pollicis, which is innervated by the ulnar nerve. It involves an attempt to pinch an object firmly with the thumb. With an ulnar nerve injury, this attempt results in flexion of the distal joint of the thumb.

Type of Reasoning: Deductive
This question requires recall of guidelines and principles, which is factual knowledge. Deductive reasoning skills are utilized whenever one must recall facts to solve clinical problems. In this situation, evaluation using Froment's sign is conducted to assess the motor function of the ulnar nerve. If answered incorrectly, review ulnar nerve palsy, especially Froment's sign. See Chapter 6.

C140 C9

The occupational therapy staff of a large subacute rehabilitation facility implements a quality improvement program. They determine that the clinic's OTAs are not completing their assigned re-evaluations in a timely manner. This has resulted in scheduling delays for the completion of discharge plans. Which action is best for the OTAs to take in response to this situation?

Answer Choices:
A. Request increased supervision from occupational therapists to increase adherence to re-evaluation schedules.
B. Collaborate with the program administrator to examine the organizational structure of the re-evaluation process.
C. Request that the program's occupational therapists complete all re-evaluations to increase efficacy.
D. Provide suggestions to the program administrator to redesign the re-evaluation process to decrease its length.

Correct Answer: B.

Rationale:
Quality improvement (QI) is the systematic review and analysis of care provided to determine if this care is at an acceptable level of quality. The role of the OTA in QI is to collaborate with supervisors and administrators to contribute to the process of improving service delivery. A fundamental principle of QI is to view problems and limitations as opportunities to explore organizational improvement needs. Blame for identified problems is not attributed to any person within the organization. Increasing supervision of the OTAs and re-assigning re-evaluation to the occupational therapists may not effectively address the underlying reason for the delays in re-evaluation. To determine how best to improve the re-evaluation process, the administrator must first examine the organizational structure of the re-evaluation process to be able to identify the needed organizational change. The OTAs have direct experience with re-evaluating patients, which can be very informative to the critical evaluation and subsequent improvement of the re-evaluation process.

Type of Reasoning: Inductive
This question requires one to determine a best course of action based on knowledge of quality improvement processes. This requires clinical judgment, which is an inductive reasoning skill. For this case, the OTAs should collaborate with the program administrator to examine the organizational structure of the re-evaluation process. If answered incorrectly, review quality improvement guidelines. See Chapter 4.

C141 C8

An OTA has established service competence in driver rehabilitation. A client recovering from a left CVA is scheduled for an on-road driving evaluation. The individual is left-hand dominant and has regained all sensorimotor functions in the affected extremity. The OTA meets with the supervising occupational therapist to establish a plan for the client's evaluation. Which is most important for the OTA and therapist to include in the evaluation?

Answer Choices:
A. Tactical aspects of driving.
B. Operational aspects of driving.
C. Ergonomic aspects of driving.

Correct Answer: A.

Rationale:
The tactical aspects of driving involve the ability to respond to changes in road and traffic conditions and anticipate driving risks. Therefore, intact cognitive skills are necessary. Because a CVA can result in residual cognitive deficits, the client's tactical abilities must be assessed during an on-road evaluation. Cognitive assessments conducted during the client's rehabilitation would not have provided the real-life challenges to cognitive abilities that typically occur while driving. Operational aspects of driving involve the ability to steer, brake, and turn. Since the person in this scenario has intact dominant upper and lower extremities and functional return on their affected side, there is no reason to assess their physical driving abilities or the ergonomic aspects of driving.

Type of Reasoning: Inductive
For this question, the test taker must utilize knowledge of driver rehabilitation guidelines to arrive at a correct conclusion. This necessitates clinical judgment to determine a best course of action. For this case, the OTA and therapist should include tactical aspects of driving in the evaluation. If answered incorrectly, review driver rehabilitation guidelines. See Chapter 15.

C142 C8

An OTA provides home care services to an individual with a severe major neurocognitive disorder. The family caregiver expresses increased concern over the person's wandering behavior during late night and early morning hours. The caregiver expresses fear that the individual will leave the house while everyone is asleep. Which recommendation is best for the OTA to initially make to the caregiver in response to this potentially dangerous situation?

Answer Choices:
A. Consult with the home care case manager for an assessment for skilled nursing facility (SNF) placement.
B. Use bed guardrails to ensure that the individual remains in bed at night.
C. Install a deadbolt lock on the individual's bedroom door.
D. Use full-length mirrors or wallpaper to camouflage exit doorways.

Correct Answer: D.

Rationale:
Camouflaging the doorways is often an effective intervention to decrease wandering behavior in individuals with neurocognitive disorders or other cognitive deficits. A person cannot open a door if they do not see a door. There are many additional intervention options to explore to decrease wandering prior to placing an individual in an SNF (e.g., the use of personal alarms, Velcro doors, diversional activities, and/or the re-arrangement of furniture). The use of bed guardrails can be dangerous as the individual may attempt to climb over the rails and fall. The installation of a deadbolt lock on the person's bedroom door is very dangerous for it can prevent timely rescue in the event of a fire or accident.

Type of Reasoning: Inferential
One must link the individual's diagnosis to an effective intervention approach that considers safety and functioning. This requires inferential reasoning, where one must draw conclusions about a course of action. In this case, the OTA's best initial recommendation would be to try techniques that camouflage exit doorways. If answered incorrectly, review approaches to reduce wandering behavior in patients with neurocognitive disorders. See Chapter 15.

C143 C9

An OTA and occupational therapist have completed the evaluation of a person who has been hospitalized due to acute polyneuropathy and respiratory distress that resulted from the onset of Guillain-Barré syndrome. The OTA is scheduled to review the evaluation results and proposed intervention plan with the patient. Prior to the planned session, the OTA is informed by the patient's nurse that the patient cannot leave their room due to their medical status. The patient does not have a private room. Which action is best for the OTA to take in response to this situation?

Answer Choices:
A. Cancel the session and reschedule when the patient is medically cleared to leave their room.
B. Delay the session and meet with the occupational therapist to discuss the situation.
C. Complete the planned session in the client's room with the privacy curtain drawn.

Correct Answer: C.

Rationale:
The review of the evaluation results and the proposed intervention plan should be completed as planned. There is no need for the OTA to cancel or delay the session. The OTA can make the decision to move forward with the planned session without discussing the patient's inability to leave their room with the occupational therapist. The OTA can discretely discuss the evaluation results and proposed intervention options in the client's room with the privacy curtain drawn. This action is compliant with the Health Insurance Portability and Accountability Act (HIPAA). HIPAA does not exclude discussions with service recipients from occurring in hospital rooms, group settings, or open clinics. HIPAA does require that health care practitioners take reasonable and vigilant safeguards to protect the privacy of service recipients. To meet this requirement, discussions can be done quietly. The use of a privacy curtain, screen, or room divider is recommended.

Type of Reasoning: Evaluative
One must weigh the courses of action presented and determine which approach will result in the most effective outcome and follow HIPAA guidelines for protecting patient privacy. This is an evaluative reasoning skill. In this situation, the OTA can comply with HIPAA by completing the planned session in the client's room with the privacy curtain drawn. If answered incorrectly, review HIPAA guidelines for protecting patient privacy. See Chapter 4.

C144 C4

An OTA implements intervention in a preschool program for children who are over-responsive to touch. In the prior intervention session, the children had responded favorably when the OTA had rolled a large ball over their bodies as they lay supine on a mat. Which intervention method should the OTA use next?

Answer Choices:
A. Roll the large ball with increased pressure across the children's bodies.
B. Bounce the ball across the children's bodies.
C. Have the children jump into a pool filled with small balls.
D. Roll the large ball, as in the prior session, with the children prone.

Correct Answer: A.

Rationale:
Increasing pressure on the ball is the next gradation of the activity. Children who are over-responsive to touch (tactile defensive) respond well to firm pressure. Jumping into a pool with small balls is too large of a progression to make from comfort with a ball rolling over one's body for children who have tactile defensiveness. Bouncing a ball across their bodies can be frightening, and it does not provide the desired deep pressure input. Changing the children's position from supine to prone does not provide an activity gradation related to intervention for tactile defensiveness.

Type of Reasoning: Inferential
One must have knowledge of tactile defensiveness in children and gradation of sensory activity in order to choose the next most effective gradation of the identified activity. This is an inferential reasoning skill where knowledge of the diagnosis and progression of an activity is pivotal to choosing the correct solution. If answered incorrectly, review sensory activities for children with tactile defensiveness, especially activities that provide deep pressure. See Chapter 12.

C145 C6

A child with attention deficit disorder with hyperactivity (ADHD) receives school-based occupational therapy services. During intervention sessions, which behaviors will the OTA most likely observe the child demonstrate?

Answer Choices:
A. An excessively high energy level that can be lessened by eliminating consumption of caffeine and certain foods.
B. Symptoms of learning disabilities as evidenced by difficulties with reading and math.
C. Poor attention to school and play activities over the past three months.
D. Non-purposeful activity that interferes with the functional use of age-appropriate skills.

Correct Answer: D.

Rationale:
One of the key behavioral characteristics for the diagnosis of ADHD is the presence of non-purposeful hyperactive behavior that interferes with the functional use of age-appropriate skills in school, play, and/or social settings. In the adolescent and adult, these behaviors must also interfere with work tasks. High energy levels that are relieved by elimination of foods are more likely food allergies or sensitivities rather than ADHD. Not all children with ADHD have learning disabilities; the two conditions are separate disorders. To be considered ADHD, the behaviors must last at least six months.

Type of Reasoning: Inferential
This question essentially asks one to infer the likely behavioral characteristics of a child with ADHD, which is an inferential reasoning skill. Of all the choices, non-purposeful activity that interferes with functional use of age-appropriate skills is consistent with ADHD and is most likely to be observed. If answered incorrectly, review behavioral characteristics and diagnostic criteria of ADHD. See Chapter 10.

C146 C5

During an OT session, the OTA notes that a client who has a spinal cord injury at the C5 level is flushed and sweating excessively. The client requests that the session end early. The client reports having a pounding headache that has become impossible to ignore. Which is the best initial action for the OTA to take in response to this situation?

Answer Choices:
A. Check the client's catheter line.
B. Call the transporter to return the client to the client's room.
C. Report the client's symptoms to the client's unit head nurse.
D. Stop the session and recline the client in the wheelchair for a rest break.

Correct Answer: A.

Rationale:
The client's symptoms are indicative of autonomic dysreflexia. This is an extreme rise in blood pressure caused by a noxious stimulus. This complication is deemed a medical emergency that must be treated immediately by quickly removing the noxious stimulus that caused the problem. Common stimuli are a blocked catheter, sitting on sharp objects, a tight abdominal binder, pressure stockings that have rolled down, or excess pressure on the buttocks. Symptoms of autonomic dysreflexia include profuse sweating and a pounding headache. The other choices do not deal with this medical emergency in an effective or timely manner. The client should remain in an upright position to help manage the rise in blood pressure.

Type of Reasoning: Evaluative
One must weigh the possible courses of action and then make a value judgment about the best course to take. This requires evaluative reasoning skill, where an understanding of what the symptoms indicate is pivotal to arriving at a correct conclusion. In this case, the symptoms indicate autonomic dysreflexia, and the OTA's first action should be to check the catheter line to remove the noxious stimulus causing the dangerous rise in blood pressure. If answered incorrectly, review symptoms and management of autonomic dysreflexia. See Chapter 7.

C147 C6

A client with a diagnosis of schizophrenia is participating in an initial evaluation session at a psychiatric day treatment program. Halfway through the completion of an activities configuration, the client states the referral to this day program is inappropriate and unnecessary because it was made by an incompetent psychiatrist. The client becomes visibly upset and loud when talking about the unfounded referral and the psychiatrist's incompetence. Which is the best initial action for the OTA to take in response to the client's statements?

Answer Choices:
A. End the evaluation session and tell the client to call to reschedule when feeling better.
B. Assure the client of the referring psychiatrist's competence and advise the client to discuss concerns with the doctor.
C. Acknowledge that the client appears upset and ask if the client is able to focus on the remaining evaluation.
D. Contact the day program's occupational therapist to report the client's stated concerns about the referring psychiatrist's competence.

Correct Answer: C.

Rationale:
A simple acknowledgment of the client's concerns can validate their feelings in a non-threatening manner. Asking the person in a calm business-like manner if they can return to the task at hand can defuse the situation.. If the client states that they are not able to regain focus, the OTA can then provide the needed support. Immediately ending the evaluation does not deal with the issue of potentially escalating behavior and does not provide the individual with the opportunity to engage in a therapeutic relationship. Continuing the evaluation can allow concrete opportunities for support and reality testing. If the client's concerns are based on negative personal experiences with this psychiatrist or a delusional thought process, assuring the client of the doctor's competence could contribute to further escalation.. There is no need to report the client's concerns at this time. There is no concrete evidence of physician incompetence. The OTA should relay the client's expressed concerns at the next supervisory meeting with the occupational therapist.

Type of Reasoning: Evaluative
One must weigh the possible courses of action and then make a value judgment about the best course to take. This requires evaluative reasoning skill, which often utilizes guiding principles of action in order to arrive at a correct conclusion. In this case, the client is upset. To address the client's expressed concerns and prevent escalation, the therapist should acknowledge the client's feelings and try to redirect them to the task at hand. To address potential agitation and prevent escalation, the OTA should acknowledge the client's feelings and try to redirect them to the task at hand. If answered incorrectly, review redirection strategies for clients with escalating behavior. See Chapter 13.

C148 C8

An individual recovering from an exacerbation of multiple sclerosis is referred by a primary care physician to an outpatient OT clinic for an assessment of the person's return-to-work capabilities. The occupational therapist and the OTA collaborate to complete the evaluation. Which is best for them to include in the initial evaluation session?

Answer Choices:
A. An assessment of needed reasonable accommodations.
B. The Minnesota Manual Dexterity Test.
C. The Borg exertion scale.
D. A functional capacity evaluation

Correct Answer: D.

Rationale:
A functional capacity evaluation (FCE) evaluates an individual's capabilities for the physical demands of a specific job or for a group of occupations. Once these capabilities are determined, the OTA and therapist can determine if any reasonable accommodations are needed to enable the performance of essential job functions. The Minnesota Manual Dexterity Test is a biomechanical evaluation tool that measures gross hand and arm movements. It does not assess return-to-work capabilities. The Borg exertion scale is used in cardiopulmonary rehabilitation to measure a person's rate of perceived exertion. It is a self-report rating scale that ranges from no exertion at all (e.g., sitting or lying) to maximal exertion (e.g., hard work that is not advisable to engage in).

Type of Reasoning: Inductive
One must utilize clinical knowledge and judgment to determine the best evaluation to assess the person's return-to-work capabilities. This is an inductive reasoning skill. In this situation, a functional capacity evaluation will most effectively assess the person's return-to-work capabilities. If answered incorrectly, review evaluation guidelines for return-to-work. See Chapter 14.

C149 C6

An OTA works at a psychosocial clubhouse. The OTA is leading a closed group on stress management that has been meeting for several months. One of the members shares some concerns about personal safety at home. Which is the OTA's best response to the member's expressed concerns?

Answer Choices:
A. Tell the individual you will privately talk about the concerns after the group.
B. Immediately send the individual to see the clubhouse's occupational therapist.
C. Assure the individual that the concerns reflect normal anxieties.
D. Invite the individual to share more details about the concerns.

Correct Answer: D.

Rationale:
It can be very difficult for an individual to share concerns about personal safety. This person clearly felt safe in this group and sufficiently comfortable with the OTA and members to be able to voice these concerns. Therefore, the OTA should seize the opportunity to obtain more information about the nature of the person's concerns. Delaying the attainment of this information until after the group is not necessary and can have the risk that the person will change their mind. Even the minute delay caused by having the person go see the occupational therapist can be long enough for the person to decide that they do not want to disclose any further information. In addition, the person may have formed a positive therapeutic relationship with the OTA and the group members based on their shared experience in an ongoing closed group. It cannot be assumed that the person will have the same rapport or therapeutic relationship with the occupational therapist. Thus, the person may not be comfortable sharing personal information with the therapist. Assuring the person that these anxieties are normal minimizes their feelings and can be dangerous if the individual is truly unsafe at home.

Type of Reasoning: Evaluative
This question requires professional judgment based on guiding principles, which is an evaluative reasoning skill. The best response in this situation is to invite the individual to share more details about the concern for personal safety. This way the OTA can determine the most effective course of action based on further information. If answered incorrectly, review information on client-centered practices and the therapeutic approaches for working with survivors of domestic violence. The correct answer requires the integration of this information. See Chapters 3 and 13.

C150 C4

A person who incurred a traumatic brain injury and multiple fractures in a motor vehicle accident has been receiving hospital-based occupational therapy services for four weeks. Currently, the patient is highly distractible, forgetful, and confused, and often repeats the same questions throughout the day. The patient's family and friends visit consistently and have asked the OTA for an activity recommendation that they can do with the patient during visiting hours. Which activity is best for the OTA to recommend?

Answer Choices:
A. Playing a simple board game that is familiar from the patient's childhood.
B. Watching a TV show that the patient had enjoyed prior to the accident with the patient.
C. Reviewing the patient's memory picture book of familiar people and activities.
D. Playing a matching card game that includes pictures of the patient's past interests.

Correct Answer: C.

Rationale:
The individual's behavior is indicative of Stage V, Confused-Inappropriate on the Rancho Level of Cognitive Functioning Scale. Due to the presence of confusion and the patient's high level of distractibility, playing a board or card game or watching TV are activities that are at too high a level at this point. Reviewing the patient's memory book enables family and friends to reinforce the patient's identification of pictures that are meaningful and can serve as a precipitant to relevant focused conversation about familiar people and favorite activities. This review can help with the patient's cognitive rehabilitation as it can answer many of their repeated questions. Introducing activities that are stimulating (watching TV) or multi-step (games) may increase confusion, which can contribute to agitation.

Type of Reasoning: Inductive
One must utilize clinical knowledge and judgment to determine the best activity for this client. This is an inductive reasoning skill. In this case, reviewing the patient's memory picture book of familiar people and activities is best. If answered incorrectly, review characteristics of Stage V Rancho Level of Cognitive Functioning and effective activities for persons with cognitive impairments. See Chapter 7.

C151 C4

An individual presents with an intention tremor, dysmetria, decreased equilibrium, and nystagmus caused by a cerebellar lesion. The person expresses difficulty with routine tasks. Which intervention should the OTA provide to address the person's presenting symptoms and expressed concern?

Answer Choices:
A. A pegboard activity with wrist weights while in a seated position to control tremors.
B. Quick stretch to lateral trunk muscles during a dressing activity.
C. A power wheelchair to prevent falls during home management activities.
D. Upper extremity weight-bearing during self-care routine at a sink.

Correct Answer: D.

Rationale:
The treatment goals for persons with cerebellar dysfunction are focused on strengthening proximal muscles, improving postural responses, and increasing stability. Weight-bearing of the upper extremities can increase shoulder girdle stability. A pegboard activity does not describe a functional activity and would not generalize to activities of daily living. This activity is also very difficult to complete with dysmetria and intention tremors. Quick stretch to lateral trunk muscles describes a proprioceptive neuromuscular facilitation technique that would be impractical to perform during a dressing activity. The efficacy of this PNF approach on improving functional abilities such as dressing is not supported by evidence. The person's presenting symptoms do not indicate that a power wheelchair is needed nor will the use of a power wheelchair help the person perform home management tasks with intention tremors and dysmetria.

Type of Reasoning: Inductive

Clinical knowledge and judgment are the most important skills needed for answering this question, which requires inductive reasoning skill. Knowledge of the diagnosis, its presenting symptoms, and the most appropriate clinical outcomes is essential to choosing the best solution. In this case, the OTA should provide upper extremity weight-bearing during self-care routine at the sink. If answered incorrectly, review the functional impact of cerebellar lesions and intervention approaches for persons with motor disturbances. The integration of this knowledge is required to determine the correct answer. See Chapters 7 and 12.

C152 C8

An OTA works in a subacute rehabilitation center that is experiencing significant staffing shortages. As a result, the director of rehabilitation has temporarily suspended all pre-discharge in-home evaluations to ensure all essential direct services are provided to clients. The OTA is working with an older adult who requires a wheelchair for mobility due to hemiplegia and a lower extremity amputation. The client will be discharged to live with an adult child who will provide supportive care to the client. During an initial intervention planning meeting with the client and the family caregiver, the client and caregiver express concern that the caregiver's home is not wheelchair accessible. Which is the best action for the OTA to take in response to the client's and caregiver's expressed concerns?

Answer Choices:
A. Inform the director of rehabilitation that a home evaluation is an essential service and that the OTA will collaborate with the occupational therapist to complete a pre-discharge in-home evaluation.
B. Provide the caregiver with a home accessibility checklist and guidelines for videotaping key aspects of the home which the OTA will review with the client and caregiver during family care plan meetings.
C. Provide the caregiver with a handout describing typical areas of difficult in-home accessibility and a list of recommended modifications to make if the caregiver determines these difficulties exist.
D. Meet with the occupational therapist to discuss these concerns and recommend the client be discharged to a skilled nursing facility for supportive care due to the safety risks of living in an inaccessible home.

Correct Answer: B.

Rationale:

Providing the caregiver with a home accessibility checklist and guidelines for videotaping key aspects of the home will provide the OTA with specific information about the home's level of accessibility (e.g., width of doorways, presence and number of stairs). The completion of a written checklist will ensure all key accessibility issues are reported. The videotaping can supplement this written report in lieu of the OTA's on-site evaluation. Upon reviewing this information with the client and caregiver, the OTA can ask for additional information (if needed) and make relevant recommendations for needed accommodations (e.g., offset hinges, ramp and/or grab bar installation). These recommendations can be made prior to the client's discharge home. Informing the director of rehabilitation that a home evaluation is an essential service ignores the reality that the setting has a significant shortage of staff and that the established priority is the provision of essential direct services to clients. One cannot assume that a caregiver has knowledge of accessibility standards and how to evaluate typical areas of difficult in-home accessibility. Thus, providing the caregiver with a handout and a list of recommended modifications to be made, if the caregiver determines difficulties exist, is not the best choice. There is no need to meet with the occupational therapist and recommend the client be discharged to a skilled nursing facility for supportive care. The client and caregiver have a discharge plan for the client to live with the caregiver and the OTA should work with them to implement this plan. Accessibility problems and safety risks can be determined via the completion of the home accessibility checklist and videotaping key aspects of the home. Based on the results of this evaluation, the OTA can make recommendations to the client and caregiver to increase the home's accessibility and safety. Caregiver training can also be incorporated into pre-discharge intervention sessions to ensure the client's safety.

Type of Reasoning: Inferential
One must determine a best course of action that will have the most benefit for a patient with concerns about home accessibility. Questions of this nature often require inferential reasoning skill, where one must determine what is likely to occur based on a present course of action and the outcome of that decision. For this case, because a home evaluation is not feasible, it would be best to provide the caregiver with a home accessibility checklist and guidelines for videotaping the home in order to identify potential needs and issues. This will have the most benefit in determining home accessibility and modifications that may need to be made in preparation for discharge. If answered incorrectly, review discharge planning processes and home accessibility assessment options. The integration of this knowledge is required to determine the correct answer. See Chapters 3 and 15.

C153 C7

A person diagnosed with a mild neurocognitive disorder, is evaluated by an occupational therapist and an OTA. Although the client demonstrates attention and memory deficits, the occupational therapist and OTA determine that the person is still able to live at home with supportive structure. They collaborate with the person to identify activities to include in a structured routine that enables their continued participation. Which activity is best to recommend the client include in their daily routine?

Answer Choices:
A. Cooking dinner.
B. Doing laundry.
C. Walking with a neighbor.
D. Watching favorite television shows.

Correct Answer: C.

Rationale:
A person with a mild neurocognitive disorder can perform familiar, noncomplex ADL, IADL, leisure, and social participation activities with activity adaptations and compensation strategies. None of the answer options in this item include these therapeutic techniques. Walking with a neighbor is an activity that can be safely pursued by a person with attention and memory deficits without the use of any activity adaptations or compensatory strategies. This activity can meet the person's needs for social participation and physical exercise. Cooking is unsafe for a person with attention and memory deficits. Forgetting to turn the stove off can be a fire hazard. Inattention could result in the person accidentally touching the stove's hot surfaces or going too close to a burner's flames. Doing laundry requires remembering and attending to multiple steps that would make this task difficult to complete without adaptations or compensatory strategies. While watching television is safe for a person with cognitive deficits, it is passive activity that does not support the use of the person's intact abilities. Table 10-1 in Chapter 10 provides the Global Deterioration Scale for Assessment of Primary Degenerative Dementia which describes the capabilities and limitations of persons with neurocognitive disorders.

Type of Reasoning: Inductive
One must utilize clinical judgment in order to determine the best activity to recommend for a client with a mild neurocognitive disorder. This requires knowledge of the diagnosis and the best activity to enable participation, which necessitates inductive reasoning skill. For this situation, the occupational therapist and OTA should recommend the person include walking with a neighbor in their daily routine. If answered incorrectly, review therapeutic activity guidelines for persons with neurocognitive disorders. See Chapters 10 and 13.

C154 C8

An OTA leads a driver education group for persons recently diagnosed with diabetes who are experiencing changes in their vision. In reviewing driving safety, which action should the OTA emphasize as a concern for persons with low contrast sensitivity?

Answer Choices:
A. Buckling a seatbelt.
B. Recognizing a red light.
C. Applying the brake.
D. Driving at night.

Correct Answer: D.

Rationale:
Common vision-related changes associated with diabetes are cataracts and diabetic retinopathy; both conditions cause low contrast sensitivity. Contrast sensitivity is the ability to distinguish between objects and their background. It is especially important when light is low and the contrast between objects and their background is reduced. Therefore, driving at night would be the concern that the OTA should emphasize as needing to be assessed and addressed by persons with low contrast sensitivity. Traffic lights provide high contrast; thus, recognizing a red light would be not a major concern for persons with low contrast sensitivity. Low contrast sensitivity would not contribute to difficulties with buckling on a seatbelt or applying the brake pedal. These activities would be affected by peripheral neuropathy or a motor impairment.

Type of Reasoning: Inferential
This question requires one to determine what is likely to be true of a situation or diagnosis, which requires inferential reasoning skill. For this scenario, the test taker must determine how low contrast sensitivity may impact driving and which deficits may be expected. Driving at night is most likely to create difficulty for individuals with low contrast sensitivity. Information about low vision should be reviewed if answered incorrectly. The application of this knowledge is required to correctly answer this exam item. See Chapters 5 and 15.

C155 C5

A person is five days post-coronary artery bypass graft (CABG) surgery. The patient expresses anxiety about performing any type of activity and reports chest pain during ambulation. The cardiologist has approved activities at a MET level of 1.8–2.0. Which activity is best for the OTA to use when during an intervention session with this person?

Answer Choices:
A. .Grooming while standing.
B. Eating while sitting.
C. Showering while standing.
D. Bathing while sitting.

Correct Answer: A.

Rationale:
Grooming while standing is at a MET level of 2.0. Eating and bathing while sitting are at a 1.5 MET level. Showering while standing is at a MET level of 2.5.

Type of Reasoning: Deductive
One must recall MET level guidelines for cardiac rehabilitation. This is recall of factual knowledge, which is a deductive reasoning skill. In this situation, the only activity that falls within the range of the 1.8–2.0 MET level is grooming while standing. If answered incorrectly, review MET level guidelines. See table 8-9 in Chapter 8.

C156 C4

An adolescent incurred a spinal cord injury at the C6 level. During a family caregiver education session, the OTA instructs family members in the provision of passive range of motion (PROM) to the patient's wrist and fingers. Which method of PROM should the OTA teach the family members to perform?

Answer Choices:
A. Extend the fingers with the wrist extended.
B. Flex the fingers with the wrist flexed.
C. Flex and extend the fingers with the wrist in a neutral position.
D. Flex the fingers with wrist extension and extend the fingers with wrist flexion.

Correct Answer: D.

Rationale:
A major goal of OT for a person with an SCI at C6 is to enhance the development of a tenodesis grasp. Family caregivers can perform PROM to enhance achievement of this goal. Ranging the finger flexors with the wrist extended and the finger extensors with the wrist flexed will result in shortening of the flexor tendons without compromising joint ROM. This shortening will enhance the tenodesis grasp. The other ROM patterns do not do this.

Type of Reasoning: Deductive
One must recall the guidelines for ranging in a tenodesis pattern. This is recall of factual knowledge, which is a deductive reasoning skill. The proper ranging in this pattern is to flex the fingers with the wrist fully extended and extend the fingers with the wrist fully flexed. If answered incorrectly, review the tenodesis grasp pattern. See Chapter 7.

C157 C5

The occupational therapy staff of a large rehabilitation hospital has determined that the current inpatient cardiopulmonary rehabilitation program should be expanded to include outpatient services. The OTA contributes to the development of the program proposal that will be presented to the hospital's administrative board. Which information is most important for the OTA to acquire for inclusion in the program proposal?

Answer Choices:
A. Data on the inpatient rehabilitation program's outcomes.
B. Testimonials from patients regarding their satisfaction with the inpatient program.
C. Statistics on physician referrals to the inpatient unit and the average length of stay.
D. Literature on cardiopulmonary rehabilitation across the continuum of care.

Correct Answer: A.

Rationale:
The provision of data on the inpatient rehabilitation program's outcomes will indicate that patients are discharged when they are able to carry out activities at a 3.5 MET level. Since many IADL, work, and leisure activities are at MET levels greater than 3.5, there will be a documented need for a continuation of cardiopulmonary rehabilitation services on an outpatient basis. A needs assessment that provides information indicative of an unmet program need is the first component of a program proposal. Testimonials, statistics, and literature do not substantiate an unmet need that would require a program to be developed.

Type of Reasoning: Inferential
One must determine the most relevant information to provide to the hospital's administrative board that would best reflect the viability of a new outpatient cardiopulmonary rehabilitation program. In this situation, providing information about inpatient rehabilitation program outcomes is most relevant and beneficial for the board. Questions such as these can be challenging because one must infer or draw conclusions based upon available information and make judgments about its benefit. If answered incorrectly, review program development and cardiopulmonary rehabilitation guidelines. The integration of this knowledge is required to answer the question correctly. See Chapters 4 and 8.

C158 **C8**

A patient is recovering from a right CVA resulting in severe left hemiplegia and visuospatial deficits. The person's left lower extremity has pitting edema. Which wheelchair would be best for the OTA to recommend for this patient?

Answer Choices:
A. A powered wheelchair with a joystick control and dual elevating leg rests.
B. A lightweight active duty wheelchair with dual elevating leg rests.
C. A one-arm drive chair with an elevating leg rest on the left.
D. A hemi-chair with an elevating leg rest on the left.

Correct Answer: D.

Rationale:
A hemi-chair has a low seat height (17½ inches as compared to the standard seat height of 19½ inches) and is the best choice for this patient. The patient can propel it using both the unaffected hand and leg. An elevating leg rest for the left side is needed to address the edema in the patient's left lower extremity. There is no need for an elevating leg rest for the right lower extremity. A one-arm drive wheelchair has both drive mechanisms located on one wheel. A person can propel this type of wheelchair by using one hand. A one-arm drive wheelchair is contraindicated for patients with cognitive or perceptual deficits (as in this case) as they can be confusing to learn to propel accurately. The electric wheelchair with joystick would also be difficult for a person with visuospatial deficits. In addition, an electric wheelchair is significantly more expensive, less transportable, requires increased maintenance, and would be difficult to justify for reimbursement.

Type of Reasoning: Analytical
A number of important symptoms are described in this exam item, and the test taker must analyze all of the symptoms (not just some) in order to make the best choice in wheelchair prescription. When balancing the edema issues, hemiplegia, and visuospatial deficits, one must conclude that a hemi-chair with an elevating leg rest on the left provides the safest, most effective means of mobility and addresses all the deficits mentioned. If answered incorrectly, review wheelchair prescription guidelines and the characteristics of different types of wheelchairs. See Chapter 15.

C159 C3

An OTA provides home-based services to a client with a history of falls. The client has osteoarthritis and reports joint pain and fatigue during meal preparation activities. Which intervention approach is best for the OTA to implement with this client?

Answer Choices:
A. Completing meal preparation using supplies located in high and low cupboards to promote active range of motion.
B. Using progressive resistive exercises to develop strength for independent task performance.
C. Training in the use of a trigger handle reacher to safely obtain items needed for meal preparation.
D. Training in the use of joint protection and energy conservation techniques during meal preparation.

Correct Answer: D.

Rationale:
Training in joint protection can help the person safely and effectively complete meal preparation activities without causing harm to the joints. Learning how to use energy conservation techniques can help decrease the client's fatigue. Having the client retrieve items from high and low areas can increase fall risk. Given the client's history of falls, this would not be safe. To decrease fall risk, items should be stored on shelves between eye and hip level. Progressive resistive exercises are contraindicated for persons with osteoarthritis. While the use of adaptive equipment can ease task performance, the use of a trigger handle is contraindicated for a person with arthritis.

Type of Reasoning: Inductive
This question requires the test taker to determine the best intervention approach for a client with osteoarthritis. This necessitates clinical judgment, which is an inductive reasoning skill. For this case, the OTA should implement training in the use of joint protection and energy conservation techniques during meal preparation. If answered incorrectly, review intervention activities for individuals with arthritis, including joint protection and energy conservation guidelines. See Chapter 11.

C160 C6

An OTA completes an evaluation with a client who recently was accepted into a home care agency's hospice program. The client is single and lives alone. The client's home is adorned with objects obtained during trips throughout the world for work and leisure. During the psychosocial portion of the evaluation, the client describes a full life working as an engineer who completed many international projects. Besides international travel, the client's leisure interests are hiking, gardening, reading, and staying in contact with family members and friends via the internet. The client expresses sadness that previously enjoyed physical activities are not possible due to pain and fatigue. The client reports boredom since "you can't read all day" and "I never watched TV." Which action is best for the OTA to take in response to the client's reported concerns?

Answer Choices:
A. Train the client in energy conservation techniques and pain management strategies that can be used to continue engaging in the leisure activity of gardening.
B. Inform the client about a local park that has short and level nature trails where the client can walk as an alternative to the leisure activity of hiking.
C. Provide the client with a list of television shows which focus on activities that the client has previously enjoyed (i.e., gardening, hiking, and travel).
D. Have the client take pictures of treasured objects to send electronically to family members and friends along with the story of each object.

Correct Answer: D.

Rationale:
A major goal of hospice care is to encourage positive life review and support the sharing of the legacy that each person leaves. This client has reported a life that has been enriched by international travel. The OTA has observed that the client has collected many objects over the years that are clearly valued given their display throughout the client's home. Having the client take pictures of treasured objects to send electronically to family members and friends along with the story of each object will provide the client with the opportunity to share cherished memories. The initiation of this correspondence can foster an ongoing dialogue between the client and family members and friends about the value of the client's life. Having the client begin a conversation about their life can be very helpful to individuals who have difficulty knowing what to say to a loved one who is dying. The process of reflecting on the history and personal meaning of treasured objects can also help the client determine to whom they would like to bequeath each item. Training the client in energy conservation techniques and pain management strategies, informing the client about local walking trails, and providing a list of potentially interesting television shows do not address the terminal nature of the client's condition. To receive hospice services, a person must have an illness with a life expectancy of 6 months or less.

Type of Reasoning: Inductive
This question requires one to determine a best course of action based on the presenting information about the client. This necessitates clinical judgment, which requires inductive reasoning skill. For this situation, the OTA should have the client take pictures of treasured objects to send to family members, as it encourages positive life review. If answered incorrectly, review intervention approaches for individuals receiving hospice care. See Chapter 13.

C161 C9

A recently credentialed entry-level OTA is asked by the supervising occupational therapist to contribute to the evaluation of newly admitted clients with traumatic brain injury. Which is best for the OTA to evaluate given the OTA's established level of competence?

Answer Choices:
A. Cognitive-perceptual skills.
B. Visuomotor skills.
C. Activities of daily living.

Correct Answer: C.

Rationale:
Entry-level OTA education includes the development of the knowledge and skills needed to competently complete an evaluation of activities of daily living. Given that the OTA has been recently credentialed, it is unknown if the OTA has developed the competencies needed to effectively evaluate cognitive-perceptual or visuomotor skills. Before the OTA assumes responsibility for the evaluation of these performance skills, the supervising occupational therapist will should establish the OTA's service competence.

Type of Reasoning: Evaluative
For this question, the test taker must weigh the options presented and determine what is best for an entry-level OTA in terms of knowledge and skills needed to contribute to an evaluation. Questions of this nature often require evaluative reasoning skill. Because the OTA is recently credentialed, it is best for the OTA to evaluate activities of daily living. If answered incorrectly, review service competency guidelines. See Chapter 4.

C162 C6

An OTA works in a halfway house with a new resident who takes antipsychotic medications to manage symptoms. The resident wants to become actively involved with maintaining the home's vegetable and flower gardens. After reviewing the precautions for the side effect of photosensitivity with the resident, which potential medication side effect should the OTA review next with the resident?

Answer Choices:
A. Akathisia.
B. Orthostatic hypotension.
C. Akinesia.
D. Tardive dyskinesia.

Correct Answer: B.

Rationale:
Antipsychotic medications can result in all of the side effects or conditions listed. However, the side effects of photosensitivity and orthostatic hypotension would be of the greatest concern in this case given the resident's stated interest in working in the home's gardens. A person who takes psychotropic medications can incur severe sunburns if the precautions of wearing sunscreen, hats, and/or long-sleeved shirts are not taken while in the sun. While this is the most important side effect for the OTA to review with the resident, the resident should also be made aware of the risk for orthostatic hypotension. Orthostatic hypotension or postural hypotension is a form of low blood pressure that happens when a person stands up very quickly from sitting, crouching, and/or lying down. It can make a person feel dizzy or lightheaded and fainting may occur. Typically, when people garden, they sit, kneel, or crouch to reach the garden beds. Thus, the person should be advised to move slowly when standing up to avoid this side effect. There are no precautions to prevent akathisia or akinesia other than medication adjustments by a physician. Tardive dyskinesia is not a medication side effect. It is an irreversible neurological condition caused by prolonged use of neuroleptic medications.

Type of Reasoning: Deductive
This question requires one to recall the common side effects of antipsychotic medications in order to arrive at a correct conclusion. Questions of this nature necessitate recall of facts and guidelines, which is a deductive reasoning skill. For this case, the OTA should review the medication side effect of orthostatic hypotension. If answered incorrectly, review side effects of antipsychotic medications. See Chapter 10.

C163 C1

A school-based occupational therapist and OTA consult with the director of an elementary after-school program to increase the participation of students with disabilities. The current program provides two groups. One group provides activities for children in kindergarten to first grade and the other provides activities for children in grades two to four. Which activities are best for the therapist and OTA to modify for members of the younger grade group to enable the students with disabilities to participate more actively with their peers?

Answer Choices:
A. Building with blocks.
B. Creative art projects.
C. Board games.
D. Video games.

Correct Answer: B.

Rationale:
According to the developmental milestones of play, children in grades kindergarten to first grade (ages 4–7 years) typically enjoy creative play. Thus, it is most relevant for the therapist and the OTA to provide modifications to creative art activities (e.g., the use of large crayons and markers and alternative ways to grasp paintbrushes, crayons, and markers). Because children in grades two to four are typically 8–10 years old, they are at the developmental level of participating in play activities with rules, competition, and social interaction. Therefore, the adaptation of board and video games are most relevant for the older group of students. Building with blocks is a play activity most typically associated with children who are 36 to 48 months old. This activity would be appropriate to adapt for a prekindergarten group of students.

Type of Reasoning: Inductive
This question requires one to determine a best course of action based on knowledge of developmental milestones. This requires clinical judgment, which is an inductive reasoning skill. For this scenario, the OTA should modify creative art projects for the younger grade group. If answered incorrectly, review developmental milestones of play for school-age children. See Chapter 5.

C164 C9

An OTA employed by a large regional rehabilitation facility has excellent evaluation and intervention skills in most areas of physical rehabilitation. The OTA has been re-assigned to the facility's work-hardening program. The OTA has limited skills in the evaluation of body mechanics and intervention for work-related disorders. Which is the best action for the OTA to take in response to this re-assignment?

Answer Choices:
A. Develop an action plan with the supervising occupational therapist to acquire service competence in the evaluation of body mechanics and intervention for work-related disorders.
B. Decline the re-assignment to the work-hardening program until service competence in the evaluation of body mechanics and intervention for work-related disorders is established.
C. Complete evaluations of clients' body mechanics and implement interventions for work-related disorders with routine supervision of the occupational therapist.
D. Complete a continuing education course in body mechanics and work-related disorders to increase knowledge about this area of practice.

Correct Answer: A.

Rationale:
To ensure clients receive competent service delivery and to assure no harm, the OTA must demonstrate service competence. Thus, the OTA must develop a plan with the supervising occupational therapist to develop the skills needed to competently assess body mechanics and provide interventions for work-related disorders. There is no need for the OTA to decline the re-assignment as long as the OTA's service provision is under the supervision of an occupational therapist. In this exam item scenario, it is stated that the OTA has established service competence in most areas of physical rehabilitation evaluation. In addition to evaluating body mechanics, persons with work-related disorders typically require standard physical assessments (e.g., ROM, MMT). Therefore, the OTA can complete these evaluations while developing service competence in the assessment of body mechanics. Similarly, many physical rehabilitation approaches (e.g., joint protection, strengthening) can be beneficial to persons with work-related injuries. In this scenario, it is stated that the OTA has established service competence in most areas of intervention. Thus, the OTA can provide these interventions while developing skills specific to work-related disorders. An OTA without established service competence cannot evaluate with routine supervision since this level of supervision requires limited (minimum of every two weeks) direct contact between the supervisor and supervisee. A continuing education course can help increase the OTA's knowledge, but improved knowledge does not ensure competence in the actual performance of an evaluation or the implementation of an intervention.

Type of Reasoning: Inductive
This question requires the test taker to determine a best course of action based on knowledge of OTA supervision and service competency guidelines. This necessitates clinical judgment, which is an inductive reasoning skill. In this situation, the OTA should develop an action plan with the supervisor to acquire service competence. If answered incorrectly, review service competency guidelines. See Chapter 4.

C165 C3

A client has been evaluated as having fair muscle strength. In planning intervention activities with the occupational therapist, which level of functional performance should the OTA expect the person to be capable of performing?

Answer Choices:
A. Move through full range of motion against gravity and be able to take moderate resistance.
B. Move through full range of motion against gravity and be able to take minimal resistance.
C. Move through full range of motion against gravity and not be able to take any resistance.
D. Move through full range of motion with gravity eliminated and with no resistance.

Correct Answer: C.

Rationale:
A muscle grade of fair will enable the client to move through full range of motion against gravity without any additional resistance. The ability to move through full range of motion against gravity and take moderate resistance is indicative of a muscle strength grade of good, while moving through full range of motion against gravity and being able to take minimal resistance is indicative of fair plus muscle strength. A poor grade of muscle strength is evident when the person can move through full range of motion with gravity eliminated but can take no resistance.

Type of Reasoning: Deductive
For this question, one must recall the muscle strength grading scale and expected performance in order to arrive at a correct conclusion. This requires recall of factual guidelines, which is a deductive reasoning skill. According to the muscle testing grading system, the expectation of performance for fair muscle strength is to move through full range of motion against gravity and not tolerate any resistance. If answered incorrectly, review muscle testing guidelines and Table 11-2 in Chapter 11.

C166 C1

During an initial evaluation session, an OTA completes a standardized assessment with an older adult to determine the person's functional abilities. The assessment includes multiple timed subtests. The client successfully completes several components of the first subtest but runs out of time to complete the remaining subtest tasks. Which action is best for the OTA to take in response to the client's performance?

Answer Choices:
A. Record the client's performance and proceed to the next timed subtest according to the established protocol.
B. Record the client's performance and end the evaluation session because the assessment is too difficult.
C. Ask the client to complete the remaining subtest's tasks and continue the assessment in an untimed manner.
D. End the evaluation session and collaborate with the occupational therapist to determine an alternative assessment.

Correct Answer: C.

Rationale:
Because the reaction time of older adults is typically diminished, it can be expected that an older adult would run out of time during the completion of a timed task. The norms for most timed tests are established with younger adults. Adhering to the timing of tasks makes it more difficult for older adults to demonstrate their functional capabilities. Since the aim of the OTA's evaluation is to determine the person's functional abilities, it would be best for the OTA to continue the assessment in an untimed manner. Allowing the older adult to complete the assessment subtests at their own speed will provide an accurate representation of the person's functional level. In documenting the results of the evaluation, the OTA should note that the timed aspects of the assessment were not followed. While this will make it impossible to compare the client's performance with established norms, the information that is acquired about the person's functional level can help inform intervention planning. There is no need to end the evaluation session as the desired outcome of this evaluation session is attainable.

Type of Reasoning: Evaluative

This question requires one to weigh various courses of action and determine the action that will have the best therapeutic outcome. This requires evaluative reasoning skill. For this scenario, the OTA should ask the client to complete the remaining subtest's tasks and continue the assessment in an untimed manner. If answered incorrectly, review standardized testing guidelines and the body system changes that occur with aging. The integration of this information is required to answer exam items about the completion of evaluation tools with older adults. See Chapters 3 and 5.

C167 C7

An OTA works with a person who is recovering from the removal of a brain tumor from the occipital lobe. The client expresses a strong desire to return to the hobby of woodworking. Which compensation technique is best for the OTA to teach the client to facilitate the ability to successfully complete woodworking projects?

Answer Choices:
A. The use of proximal stability to stabilize upper extremities.
B. The use of stereognosis to distinguish the pieces of a wood project.
C. The use of goggles to protect the eyes from wood chips.
D. The use of a hot glue gun as an alternative to a hammer and nail.

Correct Answer: B.

Rationale:
Stereognosis is the ability to recognize objects, forms, shapes, and sizes by touch alone. The use of stereognosis is a very effective compensation technique for visual impairments, which is a likely outcome of occipital lobe damage. The use of proximal stability would be a helpful intervention for a person who incurred damage to the cerebellum, which would result in coordination concerns. It is not relevant in this case. The use of goggles is a safety procedure typically used by woodworkers; therefore, it is likely the person has established this habit. Moreover, protective eye gear is not a compensation for decreased vision. The use of a hot gun can pose the danger of burns because the person will not be able to use stereognosis to compensate for decreased vision. It would be safer and more effective for the OTA to teach the client how to adapt established woodworking skills (e.g., the use of a vise) and use stereognosis to safely join items using a nail gun.

Type of Reasoning: Inductive

For this question, one must determine the best and safest course of action for a patient who has decreased vision from a tumor of the occipital lobe. This requires clinical judgment, which is an inductive reasoning skill. For this case, the OTA should teach the client to use stereognosis to distinguish between pieces of a wood project in order to compensate for the vision loss. If answered incorrectly, review compensatory strategies for vision loss. See Chapters 5 and 15.

C168 C1

An OTA provides home-based early intervention services to a 3-year-old child with developmental delay. The child has an established intervention goal to develop grasp and release skills. Cognitively, the child is at the level of a 22-month-old. Which play activity is best for the OTA to include during an intervention session?

Answer Choices:
A. Building a tower with blocks.
B. Pushing a train on a track.
C. Rolling a ball across the floor.
D. Placing shapes into a shape sorter.

Correct Answer: D.

Rationale:
Placing shapes into a shape sorter is the best activity given the child's cognitive level. A child at a cognitive level of 22 months can match circles, squares, and triangles and manipulate objects into small openings. This capability will enable the child to successfully engage in the play activity of placing shapes into a shape sorter. This activity can be graded to begin with large textured shapes, which are easier to grasp than smaller, smoother shapes. Pushing a train and rolling a ball are consistent with the cognitive developmental level of 9–12 months. This is below this child's cognitive level. Moreover, these activities do not have components that would allow the OTA to grade the activity to develop grasp and release skills. Building a block tower can be easily graded to develop grasp and release skill; however, this activity is consistent with a cognitive developmental level of 36 months. Thus, it is beyond the child's current cognitive capabilities.

Type of Reasoning: Inductive
One must use knowledge of developmental milestones in order to determine the best play activity for a child with cognitive delays. This requires inductive reasoning skill. For this situation, the OTA should choose placing shapes into a shape sorter for this child, as it is appropriate for the child's cognitive level. If answered incorrectly, review the developmental milestones of cognitive skills in children and developmental theory. The integration of this knowledge is required to correctly answer this exam item. See Chapter 5.

C169 C8

An OTA provides home health services to a middle-aged adult with amyotrophic lateral sclerosis (ALS). The client's parents are responsible for assisting the client with all basic activities of daily living. The client's ALS has progressed to a level at which the client can no longer actively assist with transfers. Which is best for the OTA to recommend the client and parents use to complete safe transfers?

Answer Choices:
A. A mechanical lift.
B. A sliding board.
C. A transfer belt.
D. A bed trapeze.

Correct Answer: A.

Rationale:
ALS is a progressive motor neuron disease with no cure. If the client can no longer assist with transfers, the client will not be able to regain this ability. Given that the client is middle-aged, their parents will likely be experiencing age-related changes to their motor systems. Thus, they would likely not have the physical strength to transfer the client using a sliding board, transfer belt, or bed trapeze. All of these transfer aids require the client to participate in the transfer, and in this case the client is completely dependent. Consequently, the use of a mechanical lift (e.g., a Hoyer lift/trans-aid) to assist with transfers is indicated to ensure the safety of the client and the client's parents.

Type of Reasoning: Inductive
One must utilize clinical judgment in order to determine a best course of action for a middle-aged client with ALS. Questions of this nature often require inductive reasoning skill. For this scenario, it would be best for the OTA to recommend a mechanical lift for the client. If answered incorrectly, review intervention guidelines for the development of transfer skills and the progression of ALS. The integration of this knowledge is required to correctly answer this exam item. See Chapters 7 and 15.

C170 C4

An OTA provides pre-discharge education to a caregiver of a person with ideational apraxia. In explaining the functional effects of this cognitive-perceptual deficit to the caregiver, which is most accurate for the OTA to state the patient will have difficulty doing?

Answer Choices:
A. Correctly using objects such as a toothbrush to complete daily grooming.
B. Completing bilateral activities such as folding a sheet and pillowcase.
C. Crossing the midline to complete activities such as putting on a shirt.
D. Completing two tasks, such as making tea and toast at the same time.

Correct Answer: A.

Rationale:
Ideational apraxia is evident when a person uses objects incorrectly (e.g., using a hairbrush as a toothbrush and vice versa). Ideational apraxia is also observed when a person cannot sequence the steps of an activity (e.g., meal preparation) and when the person does not engage in a task at all. Difficulty with the completion of bilateral activities such as making a bed can be a result of motor/ideomotor apraxia. When motor/ideomotor apraxia is evident, the person will also appear clumsy and have difficulties crossing the midline (e.g., to dress) and with bilateral activities (e.g., folding laundry). Difficulty completing two tasks at the same time (e.g., making tea and toast) is evident when a person has difficulties with divided attention.

Type of Reasoning: Deductive
This question requires one to recall the functional deficits related to ideational apraxia in order to arrive at a correct conclusion. This necessitates recall of facts, which is a deductive reasoning skill. For this case, the patient would have difficulty correctly using objects with ideational apraxia. If answered incorrectly, review features of apraxia, especially ideational apraxia. See Chapter 12.

C171 C3

A school-based OTA works with an elementary school-age child who has juvenile rheumatoid arthritis. The child's teacher expresses concern that the child does not engage in play activities with other children during recess. The teacher asks the OTA for recess activity suggestions that could be offered to foster the child's participation in play activities with peers. Which activity is best for the OTA to recommend?

Answer Choices:
A. Balloon volleyball.
B. Jumping rope.
C. Finger painting.
D. Basketball.

Correct Answer: A.

Rationale:
Rheumatoid arthritis (RA) is a systemic disorder which affects many joints. It most commonly attacks the small joints of the hands. Balloon volleyball is an interactive game that does not place any undue stress or force on the joints of the hand. It is a game that can be played outdoors or indoors during inclement weather. RA can make gripping items such as a jump rope difficult. Although finger painting does not require grasp nor does it place a lot of force on the joints, it is a solitary or parallel task that would not foster interaction with peers. Basketball is a game during which balls are thrown with force. Catching a ball thrown forcefully is contraindicated for a person with RA.

Type of Reasoning: Inductive
This question requires one to choose a best activity for a child with juvenile arthritis based on knowledge of the condition and functional limitations. This necessitates clinical judgment, which is an inductive reasoning skill. For this scenario, the OTA should recommend balloon volleyball to foster play with peers without placing undue stress on the joints of the hand. If answered incorrectly, review juvenile rheumatoid arthritis information and the development of play. The integration of this knowledge is required to correctly answer this exam item. See Chapters 5 and 6.

C172 C7

An OTA reviews the results of a role checklist with an adult who has rheumatoid arthritis. The client describes active and present engagement in the valued roles of parent, spouse, older adult caregiver, friend, home maintainer, and gardener. The client identifies difficulties completing daily activities due to joint pain during engagement in daily tasks and difficulty falling asleep at night due to the inability to not think about tasks that need to be completed the next day. Which behavioral approaches are best for the OTA to recommend to the client to facilitate restful sleep? Select the three BEST responses.

Answer Choices:
A. Modification of desired activities to incorporate joint protection and work simplification techniques to ease task performance.
B. Provision of adaptive equipment, such as ergonomically designed garden tools, to decrease the force exerted on joints.
C. Implementation of cognitive behavior management strategies (e.g., making a to-do list and then letting it go) into a pre-sleep routine.
D. Development and use of a daily pattern of relaxation activities (e.g. meditation, progressive muscle relaxation, visualization) before going to bed.
E. Establishment of pre-sleep routines (e.g., turning off electronic devices, saying goodnight, not eating too late).
F. Modification of the sleep environment by using room-darkening shades to block light and a white noise machine to block noise.

842   Exam C Answer Rationales

Correct Answers: C, D, and E.

Rationale:
Sleep can be affected by behavioral, environmental, and/or psychosocial factors. The client's reported difficulty in being able to sleep due to pre-occupation with the next day's tasks is best addressed with a behavioral approach. Training the client in cognitive behavior management strategies, such as making a to-do list and then letting it go, can help the client develop a healthy pre-sleep routine. The development and use of a daily pattern of relaxation activities before going to bed and the establishment of relaxing pre-sleep routines are also effective behavioral strategies to facilitate a more restful sleep. The use of room-darkening shades to block light and the use of a white noise machine or earplugs to block noise can help a person sleep, but these are environmental adaptations. The client did not report any difficulties with the sleep environment. Working with the client to modify activity performance by incorporating joint protection techniques, training in work simplification techniques, and providing the client with adaptive equipment to decrease the force exerted on joints can help prevention and management of pain. This was not the stated focus of this exam item.

Type of Reasoning: Inductive
For this question, one must determine a best course of action based on the client's presenting deficits. This requires clinical judgment in order to reach a correct conclusion, which is an inductive reasoning skill. In this case, the OTA should train the client in cognitive-behavior management strategies to improve difficulty in falling asleep. Review cognitive-behavior management techniques and the area of occupation of rest and sleep, if answered incorrectly. The integration of this knowledge is required to correctly answer this exam item. See Chapter 14.

C173 C3

An OTA constructs a volar hand splint to allow 90 degrees of MCP flexion. In constructing this splint, which crease should the OTA ensure the splint does not extend beyond?

Answer Choices:
A. Thenar crease.
B. Distal palmar crease.
C. Distal interphalangeal (DIP).
D. Proximal interphalangeal (PIP).

Correct Answer: B.

Rationale:
If the splint impinges on the distal palmar crease, then the person will not be able to flex the MCPs to 90 degrees. Impinging on the thenar crease will impede thumb opposition. Impinging on the distal interphalangeal crease would impede DIP flexion and impinging on the proximal interphalangeal crease would impede PIP flexion. Typically, volar hand splints do not extend beyond the distal palmar crease.

Type of Reasoning: Deductive
This question requires one to recall splinting guidelines in order to arrive at a correct conclusion. Questions that necessitate the recall of facts and guidelines often require deductive reasoning skill. For this scenario, the OTA should ensure the splint does not extend beyond the distal palmar crease so MCP flexion is not restricted. Review splinting guidelines if answered incorrectly. See Chapter 11.

C174 C3

An individual with carpal tunnel syndrome (CTS) is referred to occupational therapy. The client's physician has decided to treat the CTS conservatively. The physician has requested a wrist splint be constructed for the client to wear during the night and when performing repetitive activities during the day. Which splint is best for the OTA to construct?

Answer Choices:
A. An MCP flexion splint.
B. A thumb spica split.
C. A wrist splint with the wrist in neutral position.
D. A wrist splint with the wrist in 30 degrees of extension.

Correct Answer: C.

Rationale:
The conservative treatment of carpal tunnel syndrome (CTS) includes the wearing of a splint that positions the wrist in a neutral position during the night and when performing repetitive activities during the day. An MCP flexion splint is used for cubital tunnel syndrome if clawing is noted. A thumb spica split is used for persons with de Quervain's.

Type of Reasoning: Deductive
One must recall splinting guidelines for individuals with carpal tunnel syndrome in order to arrive at a correct conclusion. This requires recall of factual guidelines, which is a deductive reasoning skill. For this case, the OTA should construct the splint with the wrist in a neutral position. If answered incorrectly, review splinting guidelines, especially for CTS. See Chapters 6 and 11.

C175 C4

An OTA works with a client who has motor apraxia. The OTA applies a compensatory, adaptive approach to increase the person's ability to independently complete functional tasks. Which intervention is best for the OTA to use with this client?

Answer Choices:
A. Place a list of morning grooming tasks on the bathroom mirror.
B. Replace buttons and/or zippers on clothing with Velcro.
C. Provide cues to draw attention to the steps required to prepare a meal.
D. Demonstrate each step required to wash and dry clothing.

Correct Answer: B.

Rationale:
Motor apraxia is the loss of access to kinesthetic memory. Because of defective motor planning and sequencing, purposeful movement cannot be achieved. Persons with motor apraxia have difficulty with manipulation activities; therefore, modifying clothing closures by using Velcro to replace buttons and/or zippers is an effective compensation. Placing a list of morning care activities on the bathroom mirror is an effective strategy for persons with memory loss or sequencing impairments. Providing cues to draw attention to relevant features of a task is an intervention technique used in the information processing approach to cognitive disabilities. Demonstrating the steps of an activity can be an effective intervention approach for aphasia; it does not work for motor apraxia.

Type of Reasoning: Inductive
One must utilize knowledge of motor apraxia in order to determine a best intervention approach for this client. This necessitates clinical judgment, which is an inductive reasoning skill. For this scenario, the OTA should replace buttons and/or zippers with Velcro in order to promote independence in functional tasks. If answered incorrectly, review the effects of motor apraxia and compensatory and adaptive strategies for functional tasks. The integration of this knowledge is required to correctly answer this exam item. See Chapters 3, 7 and 14.

C176 C4

An OTA works with an elementary school-aged child who has a sensory processing disorder. The OTA observes that the child moves awkwardly, stomps while walking, and often breaks objects unintentionally. When describing these observations to the occupational therapist, which is most accurate for the OTA to report the child is exhibiting?

Answer Choices:
A. Tactile defensiveness.
B. Gravitational insecurity.
C. Proprioceptive processing deficits.
D. Hyposensitivity to movement.

Correct Answer: C.

Rationale:
The manifestations of a proprioceptive processing disorder include clumsiness, awkwardness, poor motor planning, and the use of too much or too little force. In this exam item, these deficits are evident in the child's awkward movements, stomping when walking, and breaking objects unintentionally. Tactile defensiveness is over-responsiveness to ordinary touch sensations, which will be demonstrated as irritation and discomfort from a variety of textures such as clothing, sand, grass, glue, water, paint, and/or food. Gravitational insecurity is characterized by excessive fear during typical activities, especially when the individual's feet are off the ground, when moving backward or upward in space, walking on uneven terrain, jumping, and using any playground equipment involving movement. Hyposensitivity to movement is evident when the individual seeks intense vestibular stimulation without complaints of feeling dizzy.

Type of Reasoning: Analytical
This question provides manifestations of a child with a sensory processing disorder, and the test taker must determine the most accurate description for the manifestations. This requires analysis of different pieces of information in order to draw conclusions, which is an analytical reasoning skill. In this scenario, the child is exhibiting proprioceptive processing deficits. If answered incorrectly, review sensory processing disorder and proprioceptive processing deficits. See Chapters 7 and 12.

C177 C6

An older adult diagnosed with panic disorder and agoraphobia receives home-based occupational therapy services. The client reports that the panic attacks worsen when the client drives to work and to complete home management errands. The client states "I just want to be normal again." Which approach is best for the OTA to use during intervention sessions with the client?

Answer Choices:
A. Instruct the client on the use of online shopping and banking.
B. Teach the client to use public transportation independently.
C. Advocate for the client to be able to telecommute to work.
D. Train the client to use cognitive-behavioral techniques prior to driving.

Correct Answer: D.

Rationale:
Agoraphobia is anxiety about being in places or situations from which escape may be difficult or embarrassing or in which help may not be available if needed. As a result, situations are avoided or endured with anxiety about having a panic attack. Cognitive-behavioral therapy (CBT) can help people examine their thoughts, beliefs, and actions and learn to change maladaptive patterns of behavior. CBT techniques are used to help the person identify current problems and potential solutions and challenge maladaptive and inaccurate cognitions. The client's active role in the therapeutic process is facilitated by the OTA frequently providing homework and structured graded assignments (e.g., driving around the block to mail a letter) as part of the intervention process. Diversion techniques (e.g., listening to a book on tape while driving) and visual imagery (e.g., imagining a peaceful country road) are used to decrease anxiety. Advocating that the client telecommute to work and teaching the client to use online shopping, online banking, and public transportation do not address the client's expressed desire to address the agoraphobia.

Type of Reasoning: Inductive
For this question, one must determine a best intervention approach for a patient with panic disorder and agoraphobia. The client's statement of wanting to be "normal" again guides one's thinking about how to approach the problem at hand, using inductive reasoning skill. For this case, the OTA should train the client to use cognitive-behavioral techniques prior to driving. If answered incorrectly, review intervention techniques for individuals with agoraphobia and panic disorder and cognitive-behavioral techniques. The integration of this knowledge is required to correctly answer this exam item. See Chapters 10 and 13.

C178 C3

An OTA working in a hand clinic has established service competence in the evaluation of upper extremity disorders. During the evaluation, the therapist uses the Froment's sign. When documenting the outcome of this evaluation procedure, which is most accurate for the OTA to state was assessed?

Answer Choices:
A. Sensation of the median nerve.
B. Motor function of the median nerve.
C. Sensation of the ulnar nerve.
D. Motor function of the ulnar nerve.

Correct Answer: D.

Rationale:
The Froment's sign assesses the motor function of the adductor pollicis, which is innervated by the ulnar nerve. It involves an attempt to pinch an object firmly with the thumb. With an ulnar nerve injury, this attempt results in flexion of the distal joint of the thumb.

Type of Reasoning: Deductive
This question requires recall of guidelines and principles, which is factual knowledge. Deductive reasoning skills are utilized whenever one must recall facts to solve clinical problems. In this situation, evaluation using Froment's sign is conducted to assess the motor function of the ulnar nerve. If answered incorrectly, review ulnar nerve palsy, especially Froment's sign. See Chapter 6.

C179 C3

A 6-month-old child with osteogenesis imperfecta does not have sufficient trunk control to maintain a seated position. The parents are concerned that their child is not receiving enough intellectual stimulation. Which recommendation is best for the OTA to make to the parents?

Answer Choices:
A. Place the child in an infant swing to watch a colorful mobile hung from the swing's frame.
B. Place the child in a semi-reclining seat with an attached tray to enable the child to place different shapes into a shape sorter.
C. Place the child in a semi-reclining seat with an attached tray containing toys covered by a cloth for the child to find and hide again.
D. Prop the child up with pillows to maintain a seated position and enable the child to bang on a toy drum.

Correct Answer: C.

Rationale:
Osteogenesis imperfecta (OI) is a disorder caused by dysfunction to one of the genes responsible for producing collagen to strengthen bones. As a result, the child born with OI will have brittle bones that fracture easily. Thus, the positioning and activity recommendations the OTA makes must decrease the risk of fractures. OI does not cause cognitive deficits so the activity suggestion should be developmentally appropriate. Placing the child in a swing or in a semi-reclining seat will provide the child with appropriate support. However, watching a mobile is a passive activity that is beneath the child's cognitive level. At 6 months, a child with intact cognition will explore the characteristics of objects and actively interact with objects (e.g., banging, pulling, turning, finding hidden objects). Providing the child with access to a tray containing toys covered by a cloth will enable the child to engage in a developmentally appropriate activity of finding and hiding objects. The ability to sort objects by shape and use a shape sorter develops at the age of 21 to 24 months, which is too high for the child's current developmental level. Propping the child up with pillows to maintain a seated position is contraindicated because spinal and pelvic fractures might result. Banging a toy drum is also contraindicated because this activity could cause fractures of the hand and wrist.

Type of Reasoning: Inductive
This question requires one to determine a best course of action for a child with OI. This necessitates clinical judgment, which is an inductive reasoning skill. For this scenario, the OTA should place the child in a semi-reclining seat with an attached tray containing toys covered by a cloth for the child to find and hide again. This approach will promote intellectual stimulation. If answered incorrectly, review information about the development of cognition and play and the effects of OI. The integration of this knowledge is required to correctly answer this exam item. See Chapters 5 and 6.

C180 C7

An adolescent with a complete C4 spinal cord injury receives inpatient occupational therapy services. To foster independence in basic activities of daily living (BADL), which is the best intervention activity for the OTA to use with this patient?

Answer Choices:
A. Brushing teeth by holding a toothbrush in a universal cuff.
B. Using a suspension sling to feed self independently.
C. Completing personal grooming using a tenodesis splint.
D. Role-playing how to self-direct personal care assistants.

Correct Answer: D.

Rationale:
A person with a C4 SCI is dependent in self-care and will require the help of personal care assistants to complete BADL. However, this person can independently self-direct how this care is provided. Therefore, training in the self-direction of personal assistance services is the most effective intervention focus. It is important to remember that independence does not mean only independent performance. Rather, independence is the ability to live one's life as one desires. Brushing teeth with a universal cuff and feeding using a suspension sling are capabilities that are present with a C5 SCI. A tenodesis splint can be effectively used by persons with a C6 SCI.

Type of Reasoning: Inductive
One must determine the best intervention activity for an adolescent with C4 SCI in order to arrive at a correct conclusion. This requires knowledge of functional ability with C4 injury, necessitating inductive reasoning skill. For this situation, the OTA should use role-playing for how to self-direct personal care assistants with the patient. If answered incorrectly, review cervical SCI guidelines and functional expectations for C4 injury. See Chapters 7 and 14.

C181 C6

An adult with hereditary ataxia receives home care occupational therapy services. Recently, the client has become more withdrawn and the client's spouse has become more verbal about caregiver strain. During an intervention session, the OTA works with the client on attaining the goal of dressing independently. The OTA notices and comments on several large bruises on the middle section of the client's back. The client tearfully states that a bad fall that morning had caused these and that the progression of the ataxia is becoming too difficult to handle. Which action is best for the OTA to take in response to the observed bruises and the client's statements?

Answer Choices:
A. Provide reassurance and support of the client's legitimate feelings of loss.
B. Conduct an evaluation of the home to remove items that can contribute to falls.
C. Report the incident to the local domestic violence hotline.
D. Supportively question the client about the incident.

Correct Answer: D.

Rationale:
While persons with ataxia often do fall, resulting in bruises, it would require a very unusual fall to incur bruises in the middle of the back. The possibility that the injuries were the result of an incident of domestic violence must be seriously considered given the location of the injury and the increasing evidence of caregiver strain. The client may respond to the OTA's supportive questioning and share concerns. Due to the serious nature of domestic violence, the OTA must provide the client with this opportunity to disclose. Providing reassurance and conducting a home evaluation may be relevant to the case, but they do not assess the immediate need to determine if the individual is experiencing domestic violence. Contacting the domestic violence hotline when a client has not disclosed this as a problem is premature since a shelter can only work with persons who self-disclose. This action could increase the client's fear of disclosure and escalate the situation.

Type of Reasoning: Evaluative
This question requires a value judgment in an ethical situation, which is an evaluative reasoning skill. In this situation, there is evidence of injury, which could be caused by abuse rather than a fall. Ethical situations often rely upon guiding principles of action to choose best courses of action. Because the potential for abuse exists, the OTA's best course of action is to supportively question the client about the incident. If answered incorrectly, review guidelines for addressing and following up on suspected abuse. See Chapters 4 and 13.

C182 C2

A 5-year-old child with cerebral palsy has right side upper extremity weakness. As a result, the child predominantly uses the left upper extremity during all functional tasks. The OTA collaborates with the occupational therapist to design intervention activities that will facilitate the child's use of both upper extremities and improve the child's fine and gross motor coordination. Which of the following activities is the best for the OTA to use during intervention to promote symmetrical bilateral integration?

Answer Choices:
A. Walking, wheelbarrow walking, walking like a crab, and walking like a bear.
B. Cutting, stringing beads, tracing stencils, and getting dressed.
C. Popping beads, rolling clay or dough, clapping, and catching a beach ball.
D. Typing, making a tie-dyed T-shirt, playing poker, and lifting weights.

Correct Answer: C.

Rationale:
Bilateral integration is the ability to use both sides of the body together in a coordinated manner. Fine and gross motor coordination is necessary to facilitate independence in ADL and IADL. Symmetrical bilateral integration occurs when both sides of the body perform the same action. Popping beads, rolling clay, clapping, and catching a beach ball are all age-appropriate symmetrical bilateral activities that address both fine and gross motor coordination. Walking, wheelbarrow walking, walking like a crab, and walking like a bear are reciprocal bilateral activities. Cutting, stringing beads, tracing stencils, and getting dressed are asymmetrical bilateral activities. Typing, making a tie-dyed T-shirt, playing poker, and lifting weights are not age-appropriate activities for a 5-year-old child.

Type of Reasoning: Inductive
This question requires the test taker to determine a best course of action for a child with cerebral palsy. Symmetrical bilateral integration are important key words in choosing the best course of action, and one must use clinical judgment to arrive at a correct conclusion. For this case, the OTA should use popping beads, rolling clay or dough, clapping, and catching a beach ball to promote symmetrical bilateral integration. Review principles of activity analysis, if answered incorrectly. The integration of this knowledge is required to correctly answer this exam item. See Chapter 3.

C183 C8

An older adult with arthritis and limited ROM and the client's caregiver are in the process of remodeling their home. They ask the OTA for recommendations to ensure aging in place. Which of the following incorporates the concepts of universal design so the client and caregiver are able to safely remain in their home and live independently for as long as possible?

Answer Choices:
A. The use of a tub bench and soap-on-a-rope.
B. The installation of lever faucet handles and rocker light switches.
C. The use of a seatbelt extender and key holder.
D. The installation of a handrail at the entrance steps.

Correct Answer: B.

Rationale:
Universal design means creating products and spaces that all people of all abilities can use. Some principles of universal design include creating products and spaces that are flexible in use and require low physical effort. Lever handles and rocker switches are easy to use by people with limited ROM and decreased strength. A tub bench, soap-on-a-rope, seatbelt extender, and key holder are considered pieces of adaptive equipment. Steps are a barrier for some people with limited ROM and decreased strength. A better option would be using a barrier-free entrance or installing two handrails to assist when entering and exiting the home.

Type of Reasoning: Inductive
This question requires one to use knowledge of universal design and aging in place to determine a best course of action for an older adult with arthritis. This necessitates inductive reasoning skill where clinical judgment is used to reach conclusions. For this situation, the OTA should recommend the installation of lever faucet handles and rocker light switches. If answered incorrectly, review universal design and aging in place guidelines. The integration of this knowledge is required to correctly answer this exam item. See Chapters 5 and 15.

C184 C9

An OTA works in a subacute rehabilitation facility with an older adult who incurred a Colles' fracture and a hip fracture during a fall. The patient has osteoarthritis, age-related sensory changes, and cognitive deficits consistent with a mild neurocognitive disorder. The patient's adult child has been given durable power of attorney by the patient. During a treatment session, the patient states all therapy must stop because it is too painful. After ending the treatment session in response to the patient's reported pain, which action is best for the OTA to take next?

Answer Choices:
A. Contact the patient's adult child to request permission to continue with the established intervention plan and procedures.
B. Revise the intervention plan to include the application of hot packs to painful areas to reduce pain during intervention.
C. Collaborate with the patient to modify the intervention plan to meet the patient's goals in a pain-free manner.
D. Collaborate with the occupational therapist to determine the most effective ways to meet the patient's goals in a pain-free manner.

Correct Answer: D.

Rationale:
The client is complaining of pain during therapy; therefore, the OTA has an ethical responsibility to collaborate with the occupational therapist to determine the most effective ways to meet the patient's goals in a pain-free manner. Although the patient has given durable power of attorney to an adult child, it would be unethical to request permission to continue services that are causing distress to the individual. Hot packs can effectively decrease pain. However, the client in this scenario is recovering from acute injuries and has age-related sensory changes; thus, the use of a hot pack is contraindicated. The ability to collaborate with the patient to modify the intervention plan will be constrained by the patient's reported cognitive deficits.

Type of Reasoning: Evaluative
This question requires one to weigh the potential courses of action for this case and determine the action that will most effectively address the problem at hand. This requires evaluative reasoning skill. For this case, the OTA should collaborate with the occupational therapist to determine the most effective ways to meet the patient's goals in a pain-free manner. Review the AOTA Code of Ethics, the OT process, and OT/OTA collaboration if answered incorrectly. See Chapters 3 and 4.

850 Exam C Answer Rationales

C185 C8

An older adult recovering from quadruple bypass surgery was recently admitted to an inpatient rehabilitation facility for cardiac conditioning. The client has been living with Parkinson's disease for the past three years. The client's family expresses concern about the client resuming driving upon discharge. The family reports that the client has had increased difficulty walking and is more confused since being diagnosed with Parkinson's disease. Which action is best for the OTA to take to address the family's concerns about the client's safe driving?

Answer Choices:
A. Complete an on-road driving assessment to determine the client's physical and mental capacities to drive safely.
B. Educate the client and family about Parkinson's disease and how motor skills and cognition can affect driving ability.
C. Contact the client's primary care physician and advise the physician that actions should be taken to rescind the client's driver's license.
D. Inform the supervising occupational therapist of the family's concern related to the client resuming driving post-discharge.

Correct Answer: D.

Rationale:
Occupational therapy practitioners have an ethical responsibility to address driving and community mobility. It is not an occupational therapy practitioner's responsibility to determine if driving privileges need to be rescinded. The physician determines the client's ability to safely drive and informs the department of transportation, if indicated. The OTA's supervisor can direct a plan of action to address the family's concern, which may include additional assessments, intervention, and communicating findings with the client's physician. Parkinson's disease may eventually result in a decline in motor skills and cognition. Education is important after initially informing the OTA's supervisor. An OT practitioner with specialty certification in driving and community mobility or a certified driving rehabilitation specialist are the only practitioners with the qualifications to safely complete an on-road driving assessment.

Type of Reasoning: Evaluative
For this question, one must weigh the options provided to determine the course of action that will be best for an individual with recent cardiac surgery and Parkinson's disease. Evaluative reasoning skills are often used when one must determine the merits of the options presented to determine an approach that will have the most positive outcome. Due to the nature of the family's concern, it is best for the OTA to inform the supervising occupational therapist of the family's concerns. If answered incorrectly, review driving and community mobility guidelines. See Chapter 15.

C186 C4

An adult who incurred a CVA has been evaluated by the occupational therapist and determined to have poor cognitive skills. During an intervention session focused on feeding, the OTA observes the person having difficulty eating due to these cognitive deficits. In reporting this observation to the therapist, which of the following tasks is most likely for the OTA to state the client had trouble doing?

Answer Choices:
A. Choosing a knife to cut food.
B. Holding a fork and a knife.
C. Asking for help to cut their food.
D. Lifting the fork to the mouth.

Correct Answer: A.

Rationale:
According to the AOTA Practice Framework, selecting appropriate tools for a task is a cognitive performance skill. Holding and lifting eating utensils are motor performance skills. Asking for assistance is a communication and social interaction performance skill.

Type of Reasoning: Inferential
This question requires one to determine what is likely to be true of a situation, which requires inferential reasoning skill. In this case, cognitive deficits related to a CVA would most likely result in impairments in choosing a knife to cut food. If answered incorrectly, review the descriptions of cognitive deficits. The application of this knowledge is required to correctly answer this exam item. See Chapter 12.

C187 C3

An individual is recovering from posterolateral total hip replacement surgery. An OTA provides training to teach the client how to safely complete daily tasks while observing post-surgery hip precautions. Which piece of adaptive equipment is best for the OTA to teach the client to use to bathe independently and safely?

Answer Choices:
A. Walk-in shower.
B. Long-handled sponge.
C. Non-skid bath mat.

Correct Answer: B.

Rationale:
Adaptive equipment refers to tools designed to help people become more independent by compensating for impairments caused by an illness, injury, or a decline in function. Following total hip replacement surgery, an individual will need to adhere to total hip precautions. Posterolateral precautions include not flexing the hip beyond 90 degrees, not adducting or crossing the legs, not internally rotating the hip, and not pivoting at the hip. The person should sit only on a raised chair and raised toilet seat and transfer from sitting to standing by keeping the operated hip in slight abduction and extended out in front. A long-handled bath sponge will prevent an individual from bending beyond 90 degrees of hip flexion when washing their lower extremities. A walk-in shower and non-skid bath mat are not pieces of adaptive equipment; instead, they incorporate the concept of universal design, which will increase a patient's independence and safety when bathing. A non-skid bath mat is important for safety while getting in and out of a tub, but the person should only bathe using a shower chair.

Type of Reasoning: Inductive
This question requires one to determine the best adaptive equipment for someone who had a total hip replacement (posterolateral approach). Knowledge of the diagnosis and precautions help one arrive at a correct conclusion using inductive reasoning skill. For this case, the OTA should teach the client to use a long-handled sponge. If answered incorrectly, review hip precaution guidelines and adaptive equipment for individuals with total hip replacement. The integration of this knowledge is required to determine the correct answer. See Chapters 6 and 14.

C188 C3

An occupational therapist and OTA complete an evaluation of a client with rotator cuff tendonitis. The client is experiencing severe pain and has a history of cardiac dysfunction that required the implantation of a pacemaker. The occupational and the OTA collaborate to develop an intervention plan. The OTA has established service competence in the use of physical agent modalities (PAMs). Which preparatory intervention method is best for the therapist and OTA to include in this plan before the initiation of occupation-based intervention?

Answer Choices:
A. Cryotherapy.
B. Whirlpool.
C. Neuromuscular electrical stimulation (NMES).
D. Transcutaneous electrical nerve stimulator (TENs).

Correct Answer: A.

Rationale:
Cryotherapy is the use of superficial cooling agents (e.g., cold packs, ice massage). It is a PAM that can safely relieve the patient's pain. Most important, because it is a superficial thermal agent it is not contraindicated for persons with cardiac pacemakers. Conversely, the use of electrical stimulation is contraindicated for persons with cardiac pacemakers. Whirlpool is a PAM that is used to clean and débride wounds, not relieve pain.

Type of Reasoning: Inductive
One must utilize clinical knowledge and judgment to determine the best recommendation for a patient with pain and a cardiac pacemaker. Knowledge of PAMs and their indications and contraindications are critical to arrive at a correct conclusion. In this case, it is best for the therapist and OTA to include cryotherapy as a preparatory intervention method before the initiation of occupation-based intervention. If answered incorrectly, review the indications and contraindications of PAMs. See Chapter 11.

C189 C6

An OTA works in a psychosocial clubhouse. The OTA collaborates with the clubhouse members and the occupational therapist to develop a group that integrates core occupational therapy approaches with the recovery model. Which group is best for the OTA and therapist to develop?

Answer Choices:
A. An evaluation group.
B. A task-oriented group.
C. An instrumental group.
D. A community participation group.

Correct Answer: D.

Rationale:
Community participation groups focus on the identification and use of community resources (e.g., leisure facilities) and the development of skills (e.g., the use of public transportation) to enable full community participation, IADL skills (e.g., meal preparation, money management, transportation), and ultimately independent living. They are highly congruent with a psychoeducational approach, the recovery model, and a clubhouse setting, all of which emphasize the development of life skills to enable a self-directed life of choice. Evaluation groups are designed to gather information about the individual's task and group interaction skills that can be used to establish goals and plan intervention. Their primary purpose is evaluation, not the intervention. Task-oriented groups are designed to assist members in becoming aware of their needs, values, ideas, and feelings through the performance of a shared task. Instrumental groups are concerned with meeting health needs and helping members function at their highest level for as long as possible.

Type of Reasoning: Inductive
For this question, one must have knowledge of the psychoeducational approach and the recovery model, coupled with knowledge of a clubhouse setting in order to arrive at a correct conclusion. This requires inductive reasoning skill. For this situation, the OTA should develop a community participation group. If answered incorrectly, review the psychoeducational approach and the recovery model. See Chapter 13.

C190 C4

An OTA is working with a client who incurred a left CVA that resulted in right hemiplegia. Initially, the client was unable to initiate any movement with the affected upper extremity. After several intervention sessions, the OTA observes that the client is now able to initiate movements; however, performance is inconsistent. Which action is best for the OTA to take next?

Answer Choices:
A. Recommend activity adaptations and environmental modifications to enable the unilateral performance of desired tasks.
B. Incorporate verbal, visual, and kinesthetic cues during the performance of functional tasks to help organize motor behavior.
C. Provide encouragement to motivate the client to engage in tasks and positive feedback after active engagement in a task.
D. Meet with the supervising occupational therapist to plan discontinuation of treatment and determine discharge recommendations.

Correct Answer: B.

Rationale:
According to contemporary approaches to motor control training, varied strategies are used to find optimal solutions for motor problems and develop skill in performance. Occupational performance emerges from the interaction of multiple systems including personal and performance contexts. Thus, the use of multi-sensory cues during the performance of functional tasks can help organize the motor behavior needed to initiate movement. The use of activity adaptations and environmental modifications to enable the unilateral performance of desired tasks is consistent with a compensatory approach. This approach is used when recovery is not anticipated (e.g., a person several years after the incurrence of a CVA) or not possible (e.g., person has a progressive disorder such as amyotrophic lateral sclerosis). According to contemporary motor learning theory, the use of compensatory strategies can limit functional recovery. Providing encouragement and positive feedback can help motivate a person to engage in a task, but these actions do not directly address the client's ability to initiate movement, which is the focus of this exam item. In this scenario, the person has only had several intervention sessions. There is nothing to indicate that the person is not capable of making progress; therefore, there is no need to meet with the supervising occupational therapist to plan discontinuation of treatment and discharge.

Type of Reasoning: Evaluative
This question requires the test taker to weigh all the courses of action in order to determine the action that has the most positive outcome for a patient with a CVA. This requires evaluative reasoning skill. In this situation, the OTA should incorporate verbal, visual, and kinesthetic cues during functional tasks to help organize motor behavior. If answered incorrectly, review the functional limitations typical of a left CVA and intervention approaches for individuals with neurophysiological disorders. The integration of this knowledge is required to correctly answer this exam item. See Chapters 7 and 12.

854 Exam C Answer Rationales

C191 C8

An OTA is working with a client who incurred a disability that will require the client to use a wheelchair for functional mobility. The client's insurance will only pay for a wheelchair with a standard non-removable armrest. The OTA plans to include transfer training during client and family education sessions before discharge. Which transfer is best for the OTA to include in a training session?

Answer Choices:
A. A sliding board transfer.
B. A pop-over transfer.
C. A stand-pivot transfer.
D. A mechanical lift transfer.

Correct Answer: C.

Rationale:
A stand-pivot transfer does not require the removal of wheelchair armrests. During this transfer, the individual stands and turns to the transfer surface. The armrests can be used to support the sit-to-stand movement. If needed, a caregiver can provide assistance ranging from standby to maximum assistance during the transfer. A pop-over or seated sitting transfer and a sliding board transfer require wheelchair armrests to be removed as the person moves laterally from the wheelchair to the transfer surface. A mechanical lift transfer can be done with fixed armrests; however, a mechanical lift transfer requires the use of a ceiling lift, track lift, Hoyer lift, or trans-aid. These are cumbersome and expensive. There is no information in the item scenario to indicate the need for this type of equipment.

Type of Reasoning: Inductive
For this question, one must determine which transfer approach will be best for an individual using a wheelchair with fixed armrests. This requires knowledge of transfer approaches to arrive at a correct conclusion for a successful transfer with armrests remaining in place. This requires inductive reasoning skill. For this case, the OTA should include training in stand-pivot transfers. If answered incorrectly, review types of transfers with the use of a wheelchair. See Chapter 15.

C192 C3

An OTA assesses the sensation of a person who had incurred a right CVA. During the sensory test, the OTA positions the person's left elbow in 90 degrees of flexion and asks the client to duplicate this position with the right elbow. The person cannot replicate this position. When documenting the results of this evaluation, which is most accurate for the OTA to report?

Answer Choices:
A. The person has limited range of motion.
B. The person has poor muscle strength.
C. The person has impaired proprioception.
D. The person has impaired kinesthesia.

Correct Answer: C.

Rationale:
Proprioception is the sense of the position of body parts. This sense is tested by positioning the involved extremity and asking the person to duplicate the position with the contralateral extremity. Range of motion, which is measured with a goniometer, and muscle strength, which is measured by manual muscle testing, are not sensations. Kinesthesia is tested by moving the body segment (e.g., the forearm) and asking the person to identify the direction of the movement (e.g., up or down).

Type of Reasoning: Analytical
This question requires the test taker to determine the type of sensory testing that is being conducted and documented based on a description of the activity. This requires analysis of the information to draw a conclusion, which is an analytical reasoning skill. For this case, the description is that of proprioceptive testing and the person has impaired proprioception. If answered incorrectly, review sensory-testing guidelines, especially proprioception. See Chapter 6.

C193 C7

An OTA provides occupational therapy services at an assisted living facility. A new resident with Parkinson's disease expresses a desire to maintain the role of home maintainer. The resident also reports difficulty performing home management tasks due to tremors. Which action is best for the OTA to take in response to the client's stated goal?

Answer Choices:
A. Assure the resident that the facility's staff members will assist with home management tasks on a daily basis.
B. Train the client in the use of compensatory approaches and adaptive techniques during home maintenance tasks.
C. Train the client in the use of energy conservation and joint protection techniques during home maintenance tasks.
D. Advise the occupational therapist that the client is experiencing symptoms that may require an evaluation by a physician.

Correct Answer: B.

Rationale:
The client can be trained to use compensatory approaches (e.g., proximal stability) and adaptive techniques (e.g., heavy pots and pans) during home maintenance tasks. Assuring the resident that the facility's staff members will assist with home management tasks does not address the client's expressed desire to maintain a home maintainer role. Energy conservation techniques are most effective for persons with decreased endurance (e.g., multiple sclerosis). Joint protection techniques are most effective for persons at risk for joint deformities (e.g., rheumatoid arthritis). These approaches do not address the client's stated difficulty with tremors. It is typical for a person with Parkinson's disease to have tremors; thus, a physician's referral is not indicated.

Type of Reasoning: Inductive
For this question, one must determine the approach that will be best for an individual with Parkinson's disease. This requires inductive reasoning skill. Given the resident's desire to maintain the role of a home maintainer, the OTA should choose to train the client in compensatory approaches and adaptive techniques in home maintenance tasks. If answered incorrectly, review the functional impact of Parkinson's disease and compensatory intervention approaches. The integration of this knowledge is required to correctly answer this exam item. See Chapters 7 and 14.

C194 C7

An OTA is conducting an educational group in a rehabilitation facility with individuals who recently sustained a complete spinal cord injury at the T1 level. The group's goal is to develop members' ability to attain and maintain maximum independence in their BADL. Which of the following home modification and adaptive equipment recommendations are best for the OTA to make to help members attain this goal?

Answer Choices:
A. Non-slip kitchen cookware and plates, built-up handles, rocker knife, and a knife guard.
B. Long-handled duster, lightweight vacuum cleaner, and bedrails to prevent falling out of bed.
C. Clutter-free floors, low clothing racks, tub bench, and long-handled shower head.

Correct Answer: C.

Rationale:
A complete T1 spinal cord injury (SCI) typically affects the muscles of the trunk and legs, resulting in paraplegia. Clutter-free floors, low clothing racks, a tub bench, and a long-handled shower head will improve a person's independence and confidence in completing the ADL of functional mobility, dressing, and bathing. The other choices relate to the IADL of home management. An individual with a complete T1 SCI will have full function of the upper extremities and will not require adaptive equipment for poor grasp or decreased hand strength.

Type of Reasoning: Inductive
This question requires one to determine activities that will most likely develop and maintain independence in ADL. This necessitates knowledge of spinal cord injury (SCI) and ADL intervention approaches, which is an inductive reasoning skill. For this scenario, recommending clutter-free floors, low clothing racks, a tub bench, and a long-handled shower head would best develop independence in ADL. If answered incorrectly, review functional expectations for individuals with thoracic level SCI. See Chapters 7 and 14.

C195 **C3**

An OTA develops an intervention plan with the occupational therapist for a client with fibromyalgia syndrome. Which is most important for the therapist and OTA to include in the intervention plan?

Answer Choices:
A. Pain management.
B. Endurance training.
C. Muscle strengthening.
D. Sensory compensation.

Correct Answer: A.

Rationale:
Fibromyalgia syndrome (FMS) is a non-articular rheumatic disease characterized by musculoskeletal pain and fatigue that can vary in intensity. Widespread pain is accompanied by tenderness of muscles and adjacent soft tissues. Thus, interventions to decrease and/or manage pain must be the intervention priority.

Type of Reasoning: Inductive
This question requires one to determine the best intervention approach for an individual with FMS. Knowledge of the diagnosis and common intervention approaches is paramount to arriving at a correct conclusion. This requires inductive reasoning skill. In this situation, the OTA should include pain management techniques, given pain is a common symptom for individuals with FMS. If answered incorrectly, review FMS and intervention approaches. See Chapter 9.

C196 C3

An OTA constructs a splint for a person who has incurred burns to the volar surface of the hand. Which splint is best for the OTA to construct for this client?

Answer Choices:
A. A safe position splint.
B. A palmar extension splint.
C. A resting hand splint.
D. A PIP extension splint.

Correct Answer: B.

Rationale:
A palmar extension splint places the wrist in 0 to 30 degrees of extension, the MCP joints in neutral to slight extension and abduction, the IP joints in full extension, and the thumb in abduction and extension. This is the anti-deformity splinting position for a burn to the volar surface of the hand. A safe position splint (may be referred to as intrinsic-plus or anti-deformity splint) places the wrist in 20 to 30 degrees of extension, the MCPs in 70 to 90 degrees of flexion, the IPs in extension, and the thumb abducted and extended. A resting hand splint places the wrist in 20 to 30 degrees of extension, the MCP joints in 30 to 45 degrees of flexion, the IP joints in 0 to 20 degrees of flexion, and the thumb in abduction. While several components of the safe position and resting hand splint will cause no harm to a person with a volar burn, flexion of the MCP and IP joints is contraindicated for a volar burn to the hands. A PIP extension splint (also called a silver ring splint) is used for a boutonniere deformity.

Type of Reasoning: Inductive
This question requires one to utilize knowledge of splinting for hand burns in order to arrive at a correct conclusion. This necessitates inductive reasoning skill, where clinical judgment is paramount to arriving at a correct conclusion. For this case, the OTA should construct a palmar extension splint to promote proper positioning for the affected hand. If answered incorrectly, review splinting guidelines for burns. See Chapter 6.

C197 C4

An OTA is interviewing a patient with a recent right CVA. The patient exhibits flaccidity of the left side of the body. The patient states that the left arm and leg are "just sleeping" and that the ability to move and walk will return once the limbs "wake up." In documenting the results of this interview, which deficit is most accurate for the OTA to use to describe the patient's symptoms?

Answer Choices:
A. Somatoagnosia.
B. Spatial relations disorder.
C. Unilateral inattention.
D. Anosognosia.

Correct Answer: D.

Rationale:
Anosognosia is a perceptual disorder that is characterized by denial, neglect, and lack of awareness of the presence or severity of one's paralysis. This patient is exhibiting symptoms consistent with this disorder. Somatoagnosia is a perceptual disorder characterized by an impairment in body scheme (i.e., a lack of awareness of body structure and the relationship of body parts of oneself or of others). Spatial relations disorders encompass a constellation of impairments characterized by difficulty in perceiving the relationship between self and two or more objects. Unilateral inattention is a perceptual disorder characterized by an inability to register and integrate visual stimuli and perceptions from one side of the environment.

Type of Reasoning: Analytical
This question requires the test taker to determine the deficit represented by a group of signs and symptoms. This necessitates analytical reasoning skill, where clusters of information are weighed in order to determine their value and relevance. In this case, the symptoms describe that of anosognosia. If answered incorrectly, review perceptual disorders, especially anosognosia. See Chapter 12.

C198 C9

An OTA works for a private occupational therapy practice that provides consultative services to several corporations. The OTA presents an in-service about interviewing and hiring job applicants with disabilities to members of the corporations' human resources departments. During the in-service, which should the OTA state is acceptable to ask of all job applicants?

Answer Choices:
A. Medical history and need for time off for medical appointments.
B. Ability to complete a computer-based job orientation module.
C. Accommodations needed to successfully perform assigned work tasks.
D. Ability to perform the job functions listed as essential on a job description.

Correct Answer: D.

Rationale:
The OTA should include information in the in-service about how the members of the human resources departments must be compliant with the Americans with Disabilities Act (ADA). Title I of the ADA prohibits discrimination against qualified persons with disabilities in employment in any aspect or phase of employment, including recruitment, hiring, working conditions, hours, promotion, training opportunities, termination, social activities, and other privileges of employment. It legally protects job applicants by prohibiting any questions about medical history and/or the nature of an individual's disability. However, an employer can legally ask if a person can perform the job functions listed as essential on a job description. Essential functions are the tasks which are fundamental to the position. These must be outlined for all jobs and include the different skills required to perform the job (e.g., the ability to interact with customers; keyboard documents; stand for 1 hour; and bend, pick up, and transport items weighing up to 30 pounds). An employer can deny someone employment if the individual cannot perform the essential functions of the job with or without reasonable accommodations. Reasonable accommodations must be provided by businesses with 15 or more employees to persons with disabilities to enable them to perform essential job functions unless such accommodations would impose an undue hardship on the business. Reasonable accommodations can include modifications or adjustments to training materials; therefore, it is not necessary to determine if the person can perform the computer-based job orientation module upon initial interview. If the person is qualified for the job and hired, the method of providing an orientation to the job can then be determined.

Type of Reasoning: Deductive
This question requires one to recall factual information about ADA and Title I guidelines in order to arrive at a correct conclusion. Deductive reasoning skills are often utilized when applying factual guidelines to everyday decision-making. In this case, the OTA should state that it is acceptable to ask about one's ability to perform the job functions listed as essential on a job description. If answered incorrectly, review ADA guidelines, especially Title I. See Chapter 4.

Exam C Answer Rationales 859

C199 C7

An OTA is teaching joint protection techniques to persons with arthritis. The OTA emphasizes methods to prevent stress on the joints in the hand that can lead to deformities. Which is the best method for the OTA to teach the clients to use to open a jar?

Answer Choices:
A. Stabilize the jar in the right hand and twist using the left hand.
B. Stabilize the jar in the left hand and twist using the right hand.
C. Stabilize the jar in an under-the-counter jar opener and use both hands.

Correct Answer: C.

Rationale:
Joint protection guidelines include the use of adaptive equipment to prevent deformity and decrease stress on small joints and the avoidance of gripping and twisting motions which can contribute to deformities. Thus, the use of an under-the-counter jar opener is the best method for the OTA to teach persons with arthritis. The OTA should instruct the individuals to use both hands with the wrists aligned in neutral and remove the lid by using flexion and extension of the wrists, elbows, and shoulders. Stabilizing the jar in the left hand and twisting with the right hand contributes to radial deviation of the wrist. Stabilizing the jar in the right hand and twisting with the left hand encourages ulnar translation of the flexor/extensor tendons which leads to ulnar drift. Ulnar drift is a result of multiple factors including innate MCP anatomy, normal hand use, ulnar translation of the flexor tendons, and proximal joint disease (e.g., radial deviation of the wrist). Disruption of stabilizing ligaments at the MCP joint also leads to palmar subluxation of the proximal phalanx and permanent flexion deformities. Just fact-checking that radial deviation of the wrist can contribute to ulnar drift. It seems opposite to me, but I may just not know the specifics.

Type of Reasoning: Inductive
This question requires one to utilize knowledge of joint protection techniques in order to arrive at a correct conclusion. This necessitates clinical judgment, which is an inductive reasoning skill. For this scenario, the OTA should teach the clients to stabilize the jar in an under-the-counter jar opener and use both hands. If answered incorrectly, review joint protection techniques. See Chapter 11.

C200 C9

A premature infant is scheduled to be discharged from the hospital. The infant has spastic diplegia as a result of cerebral palsy. The OTA collaborates with the occupational therapist and the family to develop a home exercise and positioning program that can be incorporated into the family's daily routine. The infant's parents speak limited English. Which strategy is best for the OTA to use when providing instructions to the parents about the home program?

Answer Choices:
A. Use of a tablet personal computer program to verbally translate the program guidelines.
B. Use of a family member fluent in English to verbally translate the program guidelines.
C. Use of the hospital's interpreter service to verbally translate the program guidelines.
D. Use of gestures and demonstration of the home program to convey the program guidelines.

Correct Answer: C.

Rationale:
The hospital translation service is the best choice because certified interpreters are used. They can ensure that the information the OTA provides is conveyed accurately to the parents. Hospital translation services are provided in a variety of languages to help with both verbal and written translations of important information. While a family member fluent in English could be used to translate basic introductions and supportive statements, the OTA cannot assume that the family member will be able to accurately translate medical terms (e.g., abduction). A computer-based translation program could provide verbal information; however, the accuracy of the translation is not guaranteed. Moreover, this program may limit the parents' ability to ask questions. A certified interpreter employed by a hospital is familiar with medical terminology, and this will ensure accuracy in the translation. A trained interpreter will also be able to ensure that the family understands the information via follow-up questions. Using gestures and demonstrations will not ensure that the parents understand the guidelines. Most important, non-verbal communication will not be adequate to convey abstract information such as the development of contractures when proper positioning is not used.

Type of Reasoning: Evaluative
For this question, the test taker must evaluate each potential course of action and determine which strategy will most effectively address the issue at hand. This requires evaluative reasoning skill, where one determines the merits of various courses of action. For this case, the OTA should use the hospital's interpreter service to verbally translate the program guidelines for the parents. If answered incorrectly, review guidelines for collaboration with family members and cultural competency guidelines. See Chapters 3 and 9.

Index

Note: *b* indicates box; *f*, figure; and *t*, table.

A

Abuse and neglect
  child, 138–140
  domestic, 376–378
  of older adults, 151–152
  patient/client, 67–68
ACA. *See* Patient Protection and Affordable Care Act (ACA)
Acalculia, 351
Accessibility standards, 420–422
Accommodations, testing, 5–6, 7*t*
Accreditation, 80–81
Accreditation Council for Services for Mentally Retarded and Other Developmentally Disabled Persons (AC-MRDD), 80
Acquired immunodeficiency syndrome (AIDS), 267–268
Acting out, 285
Active assistive ROM, 320
Active ROM, 320, 326, 326*f*
Activities, purposeful, 45–46
Activities of daily living (ADL), 242
  evaluation of, 387–388, 388*t*
  interventions for, 389–393, 390*t*
Activity groups, 50–56, 52*t*
Activity tolerance, 242, 243*t*, 323
Acute care hospitals, 99
Acute distress disorder, 301
Acute pain, 211
ADA. *See* Americans with Disabilities Act (ADA) of 1990
ADA Amendments Act (ADAAA) of 2008, 94–95
Addictive disorders, 294–295
ADHD. *See* Attention-deficit/hyperactivity disorders (ADHD)
Adhesive capsulitis, 168
Adiadochokinesia, 285
Adjustment disorders, 301
Adult day care, 104–105
Affect, disturbances of, 284
Age, 116
Age Discrimination in Employment Act, 98
Age-related macular degeneration (AMD), 144
Aggression, 285
Aging
  cardiopulmonary system changes and adaptations in, 148–149

cognitive changes and adaptations in, 147–148
demographics, mortality, and morbidity in, 141
gastrointestinal system changes and adaptations in, 149–150
general concepts and definitions in, 140–141
legislation related to, 98
muscular system changes and adaptations in, 141–142
neurological system changes and adaptations in, 143–144
other systems changes and adaptations in, 149–150
sensory system changes and adaptations in, 144–147
skeletal system changes and adaptations in, 142–143
Agnosia, 285
Agoraphobia, 296
Agraphia, 351
Airborne precautions, 60
Akathisia, 285
Alertness or arousal, impaired, 351, 355
Alexia, 351
Allen Cognitive Level Screen-5 (ACLS-5), 363–364
Allen Diagnostic Manual, 364
ALS. *See* Amyotrophic lateral sclerosis (ALS)
Alternative practitioners, 76
Ambulation aids, 430
American Association on Intellectual and Developmental Disabilities, 312
American Occupational Therapy Association (AOTA), 64, 68
Americans with Disabilities Act (ADA) of 1990, 93–94, 409
Amnesia, 285
Amputations
  classifications/levels of, 175–176, 176*t*
  classifications of, 175–176
  complications of, 176
  etiology of, 175
  preprosthetic treatment for, 178
  prosthetic terminal devices (TDs) for, 176, 177*t*
  prosthetic treatment of, 178, 178*t*
  treatment for lower extremity (LE), 178
Amyotrophic lateral sclerosis (ALS), 206
Analytical reasoning, 25–26

Anatomy
  cardiovascular system, 224
  musculoskeletal system, 158–160*f*, 158–162, 162*f*
  neurological system, 188–189*f*, 188–192, 190–191*t*, 192*f*
  pulmonary system, 235
Angina pectoris, 228, 240*t*
Anomia, 351
Anorexia nervosa, 305
Anosognosia, 351
Anticonvulsants, 291
Antideformity positions following burn injury, 181*t*
Antidepressants, 292, 296, 311
Antipsychotics, 289, 291
Antisocial personality disorder, 297
Anxiety disorders, 284, 296–297
Anxiolytic medications, 296, 311
AOTA. *See* American Occupational Therapy Association (AOTA)
Ape hand, 166, 167*f*
Aphasia, 286, 351
Application process, Certification Examination, 4–5
Apraxia, 285, 351–352, 355
Architectural barriers, 420–422, 420–422*f*
Arms. *See* Upper extremities
Arterial disease, 232
Arteries, 226, 226*f*
Arthritis, 169–171, 170*f*
Arthrogryposis multiplex congenita, 204
ASD. *See* Autism spectrum disorders (ASDs)
Asperger's disorder. *See* Social (pragmatic) communication disorder (SCD)
Aspiration pneumonia, 236
Assessment
  activities of daily living/instrumental activities of daily living, 242, 387–388, 388*t*
  activity tolerance, 242, 243*t*
  angina, 240, 240*t*
  arthritis, 170–171
  assistive technology, 434–435
  biomechanics, 320–325, 321*t*, 322*t*, 324*t*
  burns, 179–180
  cardiopulmonary system, 239–244, 240–243*t*
  chronic pain, 212–213
  cognition, 242
  cognitive-perceptual, 353

861

Assessment (Cont)
  condition of extremities, 241–242, 242t
  coordination/dexterity/functional, 323–325
  developmental considerations in, 37–38
  driver ability, 436–437
  edema, 323
  endurance/activity tolerance, 323
  environmental, 244, 412–413
  fall risk factors, 418
  family participation, 393
  grip strength, 322
  hip fractures, 173
  home evaluation, 413–415
  low vision, 415–416
  mental health, 313–314
  mobility, 242
  motor control dysfunction, 344–345
  muscle strength, 321–322, 322t
  neurological system disorders, 209–211
  occupations, 386–387
  osteogenesis imperfecta (OI), 172
  pain, 182
  pediatric pulmonary disorders, 253
  pinch strength, 323
  play/leisure, 395
  psychosocial, 242, 244, 370–371, 376–381
  range of motion (ROM), 320–321, 321t, 322t
  rest and sleep, 403–404
  review and re-evaluation, 43–44
  role of occupational therapy assistant in, 137–138
  seating and positioning systems, 428
  sensation, 323, 324t
  sensory processing disorders, 215–216
  sexual expression/activity, 388
  total hip replacement (THR)/total hip arthroplasty, 174
  vital signs, 240–241, 241t
  for wheelchairs, 423–424
  work, 396–399, 397–399t
Assessment tools, occupational therapy (OT), 35
Assistive Technology (AT) Act of 2004, 95
Assistive technology devices (ATDs), 432–433. *See also* Electronic aids to daily living (EADLs); Mobility; Wheelchairs
Astereognosis, 285, 352
Asthma, 238
Asymmetric tonic neck reflex, 118t, 119f
Ataxia, 285
ATDs. *See* Assistive technology devices (ATDs)
Atelectasis, 239
Atherosclerosis, 228
Athletic trainers, 76
Attention, disturbances of, 284, 352
Attention-deficit/hyperactivity disorders (ADHD), 310–312
Atypical antidepressants, 292
Audiologists, 76
Auditory system, age-related changes in, 146–147
Augmentative alternative communication, 434
Autism spectrum disorders (ASDs), 308–309, 309t

Autonomy, 65
Avoidant personality disorder, 297
Avoidant/restrictive food intake disorder, 306
Ayers Sensory Integration model, 213
Ayres sensory integration approach, 349–351

B

Backward parachute (protective extension backward) reflex, 120t, 121f
Bacterial pneumonia, 235–236
Bariatric issues, 272–273
Bariatric wheelchairs, 427
Baroreceptors, 227
Basal ganglia, 189
Basic activities of daily living (BADL), 386–388, 388t
Basic life support (BLS), 249, 250t
Bathroom evaluation, 415
Beck Depression Inventory (BDI-II), 367
Becker's muscular dystrophy, 204
Bed mobility, 430–431
Bedroom evaluation, 414–415
Bell's palsy, 274
Benediction sign, 166, 167f
Beneficence, 64
Beneficiary, 81
Binge-eating disorder, 305
Biomechanics
  body mechanics principles and, 329
  coordination/dexterity/functional assessments, 323–325
  coordination improvement exercises, 327, 328
  edema, 323, 327–328
  endurance/activity tolerance, 323, 327
  energy conservation and work simplification methods and, 328–329
  evaluation of, 320–325, 321t, 322t, 324t
  intervention, 325–333, 326f
  joint protection principles and methods and, 329
  muscle strength, 321–322, 322t
  overview of, 320
  physical agent modalities (PAMs) and, 332–333
  pinch strength, 323
  range of motion (ROM), 320–321, 321t, 322t, 325–326, 326f
  scar management, 328
  sensation, 323, 324t
  sensory training and, 328
  splinting and, 330–332
  strength increasing exercises, 327
Biomedical engineers, 76
Bipolar and related disorders
  diagnostic criteria for specific mood disorders, 290
  hypomanic episode, 293
  major depressive episode, 291–293
  manic episode, 290–291
  onset, prevalence, and prognosis for, 290
  overview of, 290
Bleeding, first aid for, 249–251
Blood pressure (BP), 241

BLS. *See* Basic life support (BLS)
Bobath Technique, 342
Body dysmorphic disorder, 298
Body mass index (BMI), 272
Body mechanics principles, 329
Body neglect, 355
Body-operated prostheses, 176
Body righting (on body) (BOB) reflex, 118t, 119f
Body scheme disorders, 352
Borderline personality disorder, 297
Boutonniere deformity, 170, 170f
BP. *See* Blood pressure (BP)
BPD. *See* Bronchopulmonary dysplasia (BPD)
Brachial plexus disorder, 206–207
Brain, 188–189, 188f
  anatomy of, 188–189, 188f
  hemispheric specialization, 193t
  traumatic brain injury (TBI), 194–195, 195t, 196–197t
Brief psychotic disorder, 289
Broca's aphasia, 351
Bronchitis, chronic, 237
Bronchopulmonary dysplasia (BPD), 252–253
Brunnstrom's movement therapy, 343
Bulimia nervosa, 305
Burns
  antideformity positions following, 181t
  classification of, 179, 179f
  hand splints for, 180
  hypertrophic scar from, 180

C

CAD. *See* Coronary artery disease (CAD)
Cancer, 264–266
Canes, 430
Capillaries, 226
Capitation, 81
CAPTA. *See* Child Abuse Prevention and Treatment Act (CAPTA)
Cardiac cycle, 225
Cardiopulmonary rehabilitation
  basic life support and cardiopulmonary resuscitation, 249, 250t
  first aid, 249–251
  for lymphatic disease, 247–249
  phase 1: inpatient rehabilitation/hospitalization stage (acute), 244–246, 246–247b
  phase 2: outpatient rehabilitation/convalescence stage (subacute), 246–247
  phase 3: maintenance/training stage (community exercise program), 247, 248t
Cardiopulmonary resuscitation (CPR), 249, 250t
Cardiopulmonary system. *See also* Cardiovascular system; Pulmonary system
  age-related changes in, 148–149
  assessment of, 239–244, 240–243t
  pediatric pulmonary system disorders, 251–253

rehabilitation, 244–251, 246–247b, 248t, 249f, 250t
Cardiovascular system
   anatomy and physiology of, 224
   disorders of, 228–234, 230t, 233t, 234t
   function of, 224
   heart and circulation in, 224–226, 225f
   neurohumoral influences, 227–228
   peripheral circulation, 226–227, 226–227f
CARF. *See* Commission on Accreditation of Rehabilitation Facilities (CARF)
Carpal fractures, 164
Carpal tunnel syndrome (CTS), 165–166
Case management programs, 106
Cataracts, 145
Catatonia, 285
CBT. *See* Cognitive behavioral therapy (CBT)
Centers for Medicare and Medicaid Services (CMS), 80
Cerebellar/spinocerebellar disorders, 205
Cerebellum, 189
Cerebral hemispheres, 188
Cerebral palsy (CP), 199–200, 200t
Cerebral vascular accident (CVA). *See* Stroke
Certification Examination
   administration and scheduling of, 6–7
   after the, 12–15
   application process for, 4–5
   background information on, 2–3
   complaints regarding, 12–13
   completion of, 11–12
   content of, 3
   critical reasoning and, 23–28, 28t
   eligibility requirements for, 4
   examination day, 8–12
   format of, 3–4
   implications of not passing, 14
   levels of exam questions, 18, 18–19t
   pre-preparation plans for, 8
   procedures of, 4–7, 7t
   psychological outlook and, 19–20, 20t
   retaking of, 14–15
   scoring and reporting of, 13
   test center procedures, 8–10
   testing accommodations for, 5–6, 7t
   test-taking strategies, 10–11, 11t
   time and time keeping, 10
   waiting for and receiving results of, 13–14
Certified Occupational Therapy Assistant (COTA), 2
   documentation guidelines for, 86–87
   practitioner role, 70–71
   supervisory guidelines for, 72–74, 73t
Certified orthotists, 76
Certified prosthetists, 76
CF. *See* Cystic fibrosis (CF)
Change process interventions, 39
Charcot-Marie-Tooth disease, 205
Child abuse, 138–140
Child Abuse Prevention and Treatment Act (CAPTA), 95–96
Children and youth, legislation specific to, 95–98
Chiropractors, 76
Chronic obstructive pulmonary disease (COPD), 237–238
Chronic pain, 211
   assessment of, 212–213

Chronic restrictive diseases, 238–239
Chronic venous insufficiency, 234
CIMT. *See* Constraint induced movement therapy (CIMT)
Circulation
   heart and, 224–226, 225f
   peripheral, 226–227, 226–227f
Circumstantiality, 286
Clinical/critical pathway, 81
Clinical nutritionist, 77
Clinical reasoning, 48–49
Clubhouse programs, 104
CMS. *See* Centers for Medicare and Medicaid Services (CMS)
Code of Ethics, AOTA, 64
Codman's exercise, 325, 326f
Cognition assessment, 242
Cognitive behavioral frame of reference, 366–368
Cognitive behavioral therapy (CBT), 366–368
Cognitive development
   aging and, 147–148
   Jean Piaget on, 128–129
   major milestones in, 129–130
Cognitive disabilities. *See also* Psychiatric and cognitive disorders
   environmental modifications for, 437–438
   frames of reference on, 363–364
Cognitive-perceptual approaches, 351–355
Cognitive Performance Test, 364
Cognitive restructuring, 366
Cognitive triad, 367
Coinsurance, 81
Cold therapy, 332–333
Colles' fracture, 164
Commission on Accreditation of Rehabilitation Facilities (CARF), 80
Common law, 69–70
Communication difficulties, 49
Community-based practice settings, 101–106
Community exercise programs, 247, 248t
Community mobility, 436–437
Community model, 99
Compensatory/adaptive/functional approach, 354
Complex regional pain syndrome (CRPS), 163, 211
Computers, 434
Computer-user workstations risk analysis checklist, 399t
Conditional reasoning, 49
Conduct disorder, 297, 307
Confusion, reversible causes of mental, 284, 304t
Congenital myasthenia gravis, 205
Consciousness, disturbances of, 284
Constraint induced movement therapy (CIMT), 348
Contact precautions, 60
Contextual evaluation of environment, 413
Coordination
   assessment of, 323–325
   improvement of, 327, 328
COPD. *See* Chronic obstructive pulmonary disease (COPD)

Coronary artery disease (CAD)
   atherosclerosis, 228
   definition of, 228
   heart failure, 229–231, 230t
   main clinical syndromes of, 228–230
   medical and surgical management/ relevant pharmacology, 231–232
   peripheral vascular disease (PVD), 232–234, 233t, 234t
COTA. *See* Certified Occupational Therapy Assistant (COTA)
Cough etiquette, 58
Countertransference, 50
CP. *See* Cerebral palsy (CP)
CPR. *See* Cardiopulmonary resuscitation (CPR)
Cranial nerves, 192
Craniofacial pain, 212
Crawford Small Parts Dexterity Test, 324
Credentialing agencies, 2
Critical reasoning
   analytical reasoning or analysis in, 25–26
   deductive reasoning in, 25
   developing skills in, 27–28, 28t
   evaluative reasoning or evaluation in, 26–27
   five subskills of, 24
   inductive reasoning in, 24–25
   inferential reasoning in, 26
   overview of, 23–24
   relationship to the NBCOT exam, 24
CRPS. *See* Complex regional pain syndrome (CRPS)
Crutches, 430
Cryotherapy, 333
CTD. *See* Cumulative trauma disorders (CTD)
CTS. *See* Carpal tunnel syndrome (CTS)
Cubital tunnel syndrome, 166
Cumulative trauma disorders (CTD), 164–165, 165f
CVA. *See* Stroke/cerebral vascular accident (CVA)
Cylindrical grasp, 125t
Cystic fibrosis (CF), 251–252

D

DBT. *See* Dialectical behavior therapy (DBT)
Death and dying, adjustment to, 380–381
Decision-making, ethical, 68
Declarative memory, 285
Decubitus ulcers, 274–277, 275b, 275f
Deductive reasoning, 25
Deep vein thrombosis (DVT), 234
Defense mechanisms, 365–366
Delirium, 284, 301–302
Delusional disorder, 288
Dementia, 304t
Demyelinating disease, 209
Department of Health and Human Services (HHS), 80
Dependent personality disorder, 297
Depersonalization, 285
Depressive disorders, 293
de Quervain's syndrome, 165, 165f
Dermatomes, 162f, 323, 324t

863

Index

Development
- aging and (*See* Aging)
- child abuse and (*See* Child abuse)
- cognitive, 128–130
- definition of, 116
- fetal sensorimotor, 116, 117*t*
- lifespan and occupational therapy developmental theorists and, 135–138
- motor, 121–127, 122–125*t*, 124*f*, 126*f*
- of play, 131
- psychosocial, 127–128
- reflex, 117, 118*t*, 119*f*, 120–121*f*, 120*t*
- self-care, 131–132, 133–135*t*
- sensorimotor, 116–127
- sensorimotor integration, 116–117

Developmental considerations
- in intervention, 43
- in occupational therapy (OT) evaluation, 37–38
- role of the occupational therapy assistant in pediatric evaluation and, 137–138
- role of the occupational therapy assistant in pediatric intervention, 138

Dexterity assessment, 323–325
Diabetes, 270–272
Diabetic angiopathy, 233
Diabetic retinopathy, 144–145
Diagnostic and Statistical Manual of Mental Disorders, 5th edition (DSM-5), 287
Diagnostic related groups (DRGs), 81
Dialectical behavior therapy (DBT), 368
Dietitian, 77
Disability
- legislation related to, 93–95
- psychological reaction to, 378–379

Discharge planning, 44
Disciplinary actions for ethical violations and professional misconduct, 69
Disinhibited social engagement disorder, 300
Dislocations, shoulder, 169
Disorientation, 284, 352
Disruptive mood dysregulation disorder, 293
Disruptive, impulse-control, and conduct disorders, 307
Dissociation, 285
Dissociative identity disorder, 285
Distal phalanx fracture, 164
Documentation
- content of, 87–88
- COTA/OTA guidelines for, 86–87
- general standards for, 87
- for Medicare reimbursement, 90–91
- purpose of, 86
- for reimbursement, 89–90
- specific formats for, 88–89

Domestic abuse, 376–378
Downward parachute (protective extension downward) reflex, 120*t*
Dressing skills, 134*t*
Driver ability evaluation, 436–437
Driver rehabilitation, 436–437
Droplet precautions, 60
Duchenne's muscular dystrophy, 204
Dupuytren's disease, 162–163, 163*f*
DVT. *See* Deep vein thrombosis (DVT)
Dynamic interactional approach to cognitive-perceptual disorders, 354
Dynamometer, 322
Dysphagia and swallowing disorders, 258–260, 258*f*, 260*f*
Dyspnea, 240*t*

E

EADL. *See* Electronic aids to daily living (EADL)
Early Intervention and Education Acts, 96
Early intervention programs, 101
Eating. *See* feeding
ECFs. *See* Extended Care Facilities
Echopraxia, 285
Ecology of human performance (EHP) model, 361–362
Edema, 323
- reduction techniques for, 327–328

Education, fieldwork, 110
Education model, 99
Elbow
- anatomy of, 161
- fracture of, 164

Elder abuse, 151–152
Elderly, the. *See* Aging
Electroconvulsive therapy (ECT), 292
Electronic aids to daily living (EADL), 433–435
Emotion, 284
Emphysema, 237–238
Endocrine and metabolic system disorders
- diabetes, 270–272
- Lyme disease, 273–274
- obesity and bariatric issues, 272–273

End-of-life care. *See* Hospice
Endurance/activity tolerance, 242, 243*t*, 323, 327
Energy conservation, 328–329
Environment
- assessment of, 244, 412–413
- contextual evaluation of, 413
- general considerations related to, 408–412, 410–411*t*
- home evaluation, 413–415
- legislation related to, 409
- modifications for cognitive and sensory deficits, 437–438
- modifications for sensorimotor deficits and architectural barriers, 420–422, 420–422*f*
- occupational therapy role in mastery of, 409, 410–411*t*
- purposes of evaluation of and intervention in, 412
- role of the team in addressing, 411–412

Episodic memory, 285
Erb's palsy, 207
Erikson, Erik, 127–128
Ergonomic Risk Analysis Checklist, 398*t*
Erikson, Erik, 127–128
ESSA. *See* Every Student Succeeds Act (ESSA)
Ethics. *See* Professional ethics
Evaluation, 32, 34–35, 36*t*. *See also* Assessment
Evaluative reasoning, 26–27
Every Student Succeeds Act (ESSA), 97–98
Expressive aphasia, 286
Expressive/creative arts therapists, 77
Extended care facilities (ECFs), 100

F

Facioscapulohumeral muscular dystrophy, 204
Fair Housing Act, 93
Fall prevention and management, 417–420
Family members as team members, 75–76
Family participation, 393–394
Federal legislation
- disability rights-related, 93–95
- Health Insurance Portability and Accountability Act (HIPAA), 92–93
- overview of, 91
- Patient Protection and Affordable Care Act (ACA), 79, 92
- related to the environment, 409
- specific to children and youth, 95–98
- specific to older adults, 98
- specific to technology, 95
- Substance Use-Disorder Prevention that Promotes Optimal Recovery and Treatment (SUPPORT) for Patients and Communities Act, 93

Feeding and eating disorders, 305–306
Feeding skills, 131–132, 133*t*
Fetal sensorimotor development, 116, 117*t*
Fibromyalgia syndrome (FMS), 181
Fieldwork education, 110
Fine motor assessment, 325
Finger ROM, 321
First aid, 249–251
Folstein Mini-Mental, 287
Forearm, anatomy of, 160–161
Forensic settings, 100–101
Forward parachute (protective extension forward) reflex, 120*f*, 120*t*
Fractures
- hand/upper extremity, 163–164
- hip, 173

Freedom to Work Act, 98
Frozen shoulder, 168
Functional assessment, 323–325
Functional mobility aids, 430
Funding
- for ATDs and EADL, 435
- for driver rehabilitation, 437
- for environmental modifications, 422

G

Galant reflex, 118*t*
Gambling disorder, 295
Gamekeeper's thumb, 163
GAS. *See* Goal attainment scaling (GAS)
Gastric esophageal reflux disease (GERD), 261
Gastrointestinal system
- age-related changes in, 149–150
- dysphagia and swallowing disorders, 258–260, 258*f*, 260*f*
- gastric esophageal reflux disease (GERD), 261
- renal-genitourinary system disorders, 261–264, 262*b*

Generalized anxiety disorder, 296
GERD. *See* Gastric esophageal reflux disease (GERD)

864

Glasgow Coma Scale, 195t
Glaucoma, 145
Global aphasia, 286, 351
Goal attainment scaling (GAS), 35
Grants, 86
Grasping patterns, 121t
Grasping skills, 117, 119–121
Grief, stages of, 380–381
Grip strength, 322
Gross motor assessment, 325
Gross motor skills, 118–120t
Group intervention, 372–375
  individual *versus*, 43t
Group processes, 50–56, 52t
Guillain-Barré syndrome, 207–208
Gustatory and olfactory system, age-related changes in, 147

H

Hand
  anatomy of, 158–160, 158f
  disorders and injuries of, 162–169, 163f, 165f, 167–168f
  fractures of, 163–164
  nerve and tendon repairs, 168
  peripheral nerve injuries, 165–167, 167–168f
Hand hygiene, 57
Hand splints, 180, 330–332
Havighurst theories of development, 135–136
Headache, 212
Healthcare Facilities Accreditation Program, 80
Health-care system, U.S., 79–81
Health insurance marketplace, 81. *See also* Payment, occupational therapy services
Health Insurance Portability and Accountability Act (HIPAA), 92–93
Health maintenance organization (HMO), 81
Health needs interventions, 38–39
Hearing, age-related changes in, 146–147
Heart and circulation, 224–226, 225f
Heart failure (HF), 229–231, 230t
Heart rate, 241
  Lyme disease and, 274
Heat syndromes, 277–278
Heat therapy, 332–333
Heimlich maneuver, 259, 260f
Hemispheric specialization, 193t
Hepatitis, 268
HF. *See* Heart failure (HF)
HHS. *See* Department of Health and Human Services (HHS)
Hierarchy of basic human needs, 128
Hip
  fractures of, 173
  total hip replacement (THR)/total hip arthroplasty of, 174–175, 174f
HIPAA. *See* Health Insurance Portability and Accountability Act (HIPAA)
Histrionic personality disorder, 297
HIV/AIDS, 267–268
Hoarding disorder, 299
Home evaluation, 413–415

Home health aides (HHAs), 76
Home health care, 105
Home/household management tasks, developmental sequence for, 134–135t
  interventions for, 392–393
Hospice, 105–106, 266
Hot/cold therapy. *See* Physical agent modalities (PAMs)
Human development. *See* Development
Humerus fractures, 164
Huntington's chorea, 205
Hyperactivity, 285
Hyperthermia, 277–278
Hypertrophic scars from burns, 180
Hypnotic medications, 296
Hypomanic episode, 293

I

IDEA. *See* Individuals with Disabilities Education Act (IDEA)
Ideational apraxia, 355
Ideomotor apraxia, 352
Immunological system disorders
  acquired immunodeficiency syndrome (AIDS), 267–268
  cancer, 264–266
  hepatitis, 268
  methicillin-resistant staphylococcus aureus (MRSA), 269
  rehabilitation for, 269–270
  scleroderma, 266–267
  tuberculosis (TB), 236–237
Impulse-control disorder, 307
Individuals with Disabilities Education Act (IDEA), 96–97, 409
Individual *vs.* group intervention, 40, 43t
Inductive reasoning, 24–25
Inferential reasoning, 26
Information processing approach to cognitive-perceptual disorders, 354
Inpatient rehabilitation, 244–246, 246–247b
Institutional practice settings, 99–101
Instrumental activities of daily living (IADL), 242, 387–388
Insula (brain), 188
Integumentary system
  age-related changes in, 149
  wounds and pressure/decubitus ulcers, 274–277, 275b, 275f
Intellectual disorders, 312–313
Interactive reasoning, 48
Intermediate-care facilities (ICFs), 99
Intermittent claudication, 240t
Interprofessional teams, 75
Intervention. *See also* Rehabilitation
  activities of daily living, 389–393, 390t
  arthritis, 171
  assistive technology, 434–435
  biomechanics, 325–333, 326f
  burns, 179–180
  change process, 39
  cognitive-perceptual, 353–355
  developmental considerations in, 43
  environmental modifications for cognitive and sensory deficits, 437–438
  fall prevention, 418–420
  family participation, 393–394

general guidelines for occupations, 387, 387t
health needs, 38–39
hip fractures, 173
home management, 392–393
implementation of, 40–43, 41–42t
individual *vs.* group, 40, 43t
low vision, 416–417
maintenance, 39
management, 39
mental health, 314–315
neurological system disorders, 209–211
nutrition for older adults, 151
oral motor dysfunction, 347–348
orthotic/splinting, for neuromotor dysfunction, 345–347
osteogenesis imperfecta (OI), 172
pain, 182, 213
pediatric pulmonary disorders, 253
planning for, 39–40
play/leisure, 395–396, 396t
prevention, 38
psychosocial, 371–376
range of motion (ROM), 325–326, 326f
re-evaluation/review of, 43–44
rest and sleep, 404
role of the occupational therapy assistant in musculoskeletal system, 169
role of the occupational therapy assistant in pediatric intervention, 138
seizure disorders, 218
self-care, 389–390, 390t
sensory processing disorders, 216
sexual expression/activity, 390–392
total hip replacement (THR)/total hip arthroplasty, 175
types of, 38–39
work, 400–401f, 400–404, 402t
Interviewing guidelines for occupational therapy (OT), 35, 37
Intimate partner violence, 376–378
Intradisciplinary teams, 75

J

Jebson Hand Function Test, 325
Job coaches, 77
Joint Commission (JCAHO), 80
Joint protection principles and methods, 329

K

Kidney disease, 261–264, 262b
Kitchen environment, 415
Klumpke's palsy, 207
Known genetic condition, 310
Kohlberg, Lawrence, 128

L

Labyrinthine/optical (head) righting reflex, 120t
Landau reaction, 118t, 119f
Language difficulties, 49
Lateral and medial epicondylitis, 165

Index

Lay team members, 75–76
Legislation. *See* Federal legislation
Legs. *See* Lower extremities
Leisure, 395–396, 396t
Lifespan and occupational therapy developmental theorists
   Anne Mosey on, 136–137
   Havighurst on, 135–136
   Lela Llorens on, 136
   overview of, 135
Life-style performance model, 361
Limb and postural control impairments, 348
Limb-girdle muscular dystrophy, 204
Limbic system, 189
Llorens, Lela, 136
Long-term acute care hospitals (LTAC), 100
Long-term goals, 40
Long-term hospitals, 100
Low back pain, 181
Lower extremities, amputations of, 178
Lower motor neuron (LMN) syndromes, 191, 191t
Low vision evaluation and intervention, 415–417
Lyme disease, 273–274
Lymphatic system, 226–227, 227f
   rehabilitation guidelines for, 247–249
Lymphedema, 234, 234t

M

Maintenance interventions, 39
Major depressive episode, 291–293
Major neurocognitive disorder, 301, 302t
Malpractice, 69–70
Managed care, 81, 82
Management
   fieldwork education, 110
   management principles, functions, and strategies in, 107
   personnel management in, 108
   professional development, 110–111
   program development in, 107–108
   program evaluation and quality improvement in, 108–110
Management interventions, 39
Mandatory reporting, 140, 152
Manic episode, 290–291
Manual muscle tests (MMTs), 321–322, 322t
MAOIs. *See* Monoamine oxidase inhibitors (MAOIs)
Maslow, Abraham, 128
Median nerve laceration, 166–167, 167f
Medicaid, 85–86
Medical model, 99
Medicare, 82–85
   coverage of durable medical equipment, prostheses, and orthoses by, 85
   criteria for group leadership, 52t
   disability rights and, 93
   documentation for reimbursement by, 90–91
   indicators for group membership, 52t
Memory, disturbances of, 284–285, 352, 355
Meningitis, 274

Mental health practice models
   cognitive behavioral frame of reference/cognitive behavioral therapy (CBT), 366–368
   psychiatric rehabilitation, 369–370
   recovery model, 368–369
Mental status examination, 287
Metacarpal fractures, 164
Methicillin-resistant staphylococcus aureus (MRSA), 269
MI. *See* Myocardial infarction (MI)
Michigan Hand Outcome Questionnaire, 325
Middle phalanx fractures, 164
Mild neurocognitive disorder, 301, 302t
Mini-Mental State Examination, 287
Minnesota Manual Dexterity Test, 324
Mobility and mobility aids
   assessment of, 242
   bed, 430–431
   community, 436–437
   functional, 430
   transfers, 431–432
Mobility training, wheelchair, 429–430
Model of human occupation (MOHO), 360
Models of practice, 98–99
Modifications for sensorimotor deficits and architectural barriers, 420–422, 420–422f
Monoamine oxidase inhibitors (MAOIs), 292
Mood, disturbances of, 284
Mood disorders, 290
Mood-stabilizing medications, 291
Moral development stages, 128
Moro reflex, 118t
Mosey, Anne, 136–137
Motor apraxia, 352
Motor behavior, disturbances of, 285
Motor control
   development of, 121–127, 122–125t, 124f, 126f
   evaluation of dysfunction in, 344–345
   orthotic/splinting interventions for neuromotor dysfunction and, 345–347
   proprioceptive neuromuscular facilitation (PNF), 343
Movement disorders
   cerebellar/spinocerebellar disorders, 205
   classification of symptoms in, 201
   Huntington's chorea, 205
   limb and postural control, 348
   muscular dystrophies/atrophies, 203–205
   Parkinson's disease, 201–202
   progressive supranuclear palsy, 205
   spina bifida, 202–203
   spinocerebellar degenerations, 206
   structural cerebellar lesions, 205
MRSA. *See* Methicillin-resistant staphylococcus aureus (MRSA)
MS. *See* Multiple sclerosis (MS)
Multidisciplinary teams, 75
Multiple sclerosis (MS), 209
Muscle strength, 321–322, 322t
Muscular dystrophies/atrophies, 203–205
Musculoskeletal system
   age-related changes in, 141–142
   amputations, 175–178, 176f, 177t, 178f
   anatomy of, 158–160f, 158–162, 162f
   arthritis, 169–171, 170f

   burns, 179–180, 179f, 181t
   dermatome distribution, 162f
   elbow, 161
   forearm, 160–161
   hand, 158–160, 158f
   hip fractures, 173
   osteogenesis imperfecta (OI), 171–172
   pain, 181–182
   scapula, 161–162
   shoulder, 161
   total hip replacement (THR)/total hip arthroplasty, 174–175, 174f
   wrist, 159–160f, 160
Myasthenia gravis, 208
Myocardial infarction (MI), 229
Myoelectric prostheses, 176
Myofascial pain, 181

N

Narcissistic personality disorder, 297
Narrative reasoning, 48
National Board for Certification in Occupational Therapy (NBCOT), 2, 4, 24. *See also* Certification Examination
   in ethical jurisdiction of occupational therapy, 69
NBCOT. *See* National Board for Certification in Occupational Therapy (NBCOT)
NDT. *See* Neurodevelopmental treatment (NDT)
Neck righting (on body) (NOB) reflex, 118t, 119f
Negligence, 70
Neonatal period sensorimotor integration development, 116–117
Nerve and tendon repairs, 168
Nervous system. *See* Neurological system
Neurocognitive disorders, 301–303, 302–303t, 304t
   cognitive-perceptual approaches to, 351–355
Neurodevelopmental disorders
   attention-deficit/hyperactivity disorders, 310–312
   autism spectrum disorders (ASDs), 308–309, 309t
   intellectual disorders, 312–313
   known genetic condition, 310
   social (pragmatic) communication disorder (SCD), 310
Neurodevelopmental treatment (NDT), 342
Neurogenic bowel, 261
Neurohumoral influences on cardiovascular system, 227–228
Neuroleptic-induced Parkinsonism, 289
Neuroleptic malignant syndrome, 289
Neurological frames of reference in motor performance
   Brunnstrom's movement therapy, 343
   contemporary task-oriented approaches to motor control training and, 338–340, 341t
   Margaret Rood's approach, 343–344
   neurodevelopmental treatment (NDT)/Bobath technique, 342
   neurophysiologic ('traditional'), 340, 342t
   proprioceptive neuromuscular facilitation (PNF), 343

Neurological system
  age-related changes in, 143–144
  anatomy and physiology, 188–189f, 188–192, 190–191t, 192f
  brain, 188–189, 188f
  neurons, 191, 191t
  peripheral nervous system, 192, 192f
  spinal cord, 189–191, 189f, 190t
Neurological system disorders
  demyelinating disease, 209
  evaluation and intervention for, 209–211
  movement/neuromuscular diseases, 201–206
  pain, 211–213
  peripheral nervous system/neuromuscular, 206–208
  seizure disorders, 216–218
  sensory processing, 213–216
  stroke/cerebral vascular accident (CVA), 192–194, 193t
  traumatic, 194–200, 195t, 196–197t, 200t
Neuromuscular diseases
  movement disorders, 201–206
  peripheral nervous system, 206–208
Neurons, 191, 191t
Neuropathic pain, 211–212
New York Heart Association (NYHA) Functional Classification, 230–231
Nine Hole Peg Test, 324–325
Nominal aphasia, 286
Nonmaleficence, 64–65
Nonspontaneous speech, 286
NOS. See Personality disorders not otherwise specified
Nurse practitioners (NP), 77
Nutrition in older adults, 150–151
Nutritionists, 77

O

OA. See Osteoarthritis (OA)
Obesity, 272–273
  wheelchairs for, 427
OBRA. See Omnibus Budget Reconciliation Act (OBRA) of 1981
Observation skills in occupational therapy (OT), 35
Obsessive-compulsive and related disorders, 298–299
Obsessive-compulsive personality disorder, 297
Occipital lobe, 188
Occupational Safety and Health Administration (OSHA), 80
Occupational Therapists, Registered (OTR), 2
  supervisory guidelines for, 72
Occupational therapy (OT)
  assessment tools in, 35
  developmental considerations in evaluation in, 37–38
  discharge planning, 44
  documentation guidelines in, 86–91
  ethical jurisdiction of, 68–70
  evaluation in, 32, 34–35, 36t
  federal legislation related to, 91–98
  intervention in, 38–43, 41–42t, 43t
  interviewing guidelines for, 35, 37
  observation skills in, 35
  overview of, 32, 33t
  payment for, 81–86
  practice framework, the OT process, 33t
  practitioner roles, 70–71
  referral for, 32
  role in addressing child abuse, 140
  role in addressing elder abuse, 152
  screening in, 32
  service delivery models and practice settings in, 98–106
  service management in, 107–111
  supervisory guidelines for, 71–74, 73t
  team roles and principles of collaboration in, 74–79
  tools of practice, 44–56
  in the U.S. health-care system, 79–81
Occupational therapy aides, 71
Occupational therapy assistants (OTA)
  certification of, 2–15
  documentation guidelines for, 86–87
  professional ethics of, 67
  role in evaluation (See Evaluation)
  role in intervention (See Intervention)
  roles of, 70–71
  supervisory guidelines for, 72–74, 73t
Occupational Therapy Code of Ethics, 64–66
O'Connor Tweezer Test, 324
OI. See Osteogenesis imperfecta (OI)
Older adults. See Aging
Omnibus Budget Reconciliation Act (OBRA) of 1981, 93
Omnibus Budget Reconciliation Act (OBRA) of 1990, 98, 409
Oppositional defiant disorder (ODD), 307
Optometrists/vision specialists, 77
Oral motor dysfunction, 347–348
Organization/sequencing impairments, 352
Orthotic/splinting interventions for neuromotor dysfunction, 345–347
Orthotists, 76
Osteoarthritis (OA), 170
Osteogenesis imperfecta (OI), 171–172
OT. See Occupational therapy (OT)
OTA. See Occupational therapy assistant (OTA)
OTR. See Occupational Therapists, Registered (OTR)
Outpatient/ambulatory care, 101, 105
Outpatient rehabilitation, 246–247
Overuse syndromes, 164–165

P

Pain, 211–213
  Lyme disease, 274
  musculoskeletal, 181–182
  neurological, 211–213
Palliative care for cancer, 266
Palmar grasp reflex, 118t, 119f
PAMs. See Physical agent modalities (PAMs)
Panic attacks, 296
Panic disorder, 296
Paraffin, 333
Paranoid personality disorder, 297
Parenting/child care, 393–394
Parietal lobe, 188
Parkinson's disease, 201–202

Partial hospitalization/day hospital programs, 104
Passive ROM, 320, 325–326
Pastoral care, 77
Patient-care equipment and instruments/devices, 59
Patient/client abuse and neglect, 67–68
Patient placement, 58–59
Patient Protection and Affordable Care Act (ACA), 79, 92
Payment, occupational therapy services
  key terms in, 81–82
  Medicaid, 85–86
  Medicare, 82–85
  Medicare coverage of durable medical equipment, prostheses, and orthoses, 85
  personal payment, 'pro bono,' philanthropic care, and grants, 86
  private insurance and managed care plans, 82
  worker's compensation, 86
PCP. See Pneumocystis pneumonia (PCP)
Perception, disturbances of, 285
Per diem, 81
Peripheral circulation, 226–227, 226–227f
Peripheral nerve injuries, 165–167, 167–168f
Peripheral nervous system, 192, 192f
  disorders of, 206–208
Peripheral neuropathies, 207
Peripheral vascular disease (PVD), 232–234, 233t, 234t
Perseveration, 286, 352, 355
  in speech, 286
Persistent depressive disorder, 293
Personal activities of daily living, 386
Personal care assistants (PCAs), 76
Personal emergency response systems (PERS), 433
Personalities of test takers, 22, 22t
Personality disorders, 297–298
Personality disorders not otherwise specified (NOS), 298
Personal payment, 86
Personal protective equipment (PPE), 57–58
Person-environment-occupation model, 360
Personnel management, 108
Phantom limb pain, 212
Pharmacology
  coronary artery disease (CAD), 231–232
  major depressive episode, 292
  schizophrenia spectrum and other psychotic disorders, 289
Philanthropic care, 86
Physiatrists, 77
Physical agent modalities (PAMs), 332–333
Physical therapists, 77–78
Physical therapy assistant (PTA), 78
Physician's assistant, 78
Piaget, Jean, 128–129
Pica, 305
Pinch strength, 323
Planning, intervention, 39–40
Plantar grasp reflex, 118t
Play, 395–396, 396t
  development of, 131
Pleural effusion, 239

Index

Pneumocystis pneumonia (PCP), 236
Pneumonia, 235–236
PNF. See Proprioceptive neuromuscular facilitation (PNF)
Positioning and seating systems, 427–429
Postconcussion syndrome, 195
Post-polio syndrome (PPS), 208
Post-traumatic stress disorder (PTSD), 301
Poverty of content in speech, 286
PPS. See Post-polio syndrome (PPS)
Practice settings. See Service delivery models and practice settings
Pragmatic reasoning, 48–49
Premenstrual dysphoric disorder, 293
Prenatal period sensorimotor integration development, 116
Pressured speech, 285
Pressure ulcers, 274–277, 275b, 275f
Prevocational assessment process, 396, 397–398t
Prevocational programs, 103
Primary care physicians (PCP), 78
Primary prevention, 38
Private/independent practice, 106
Private insurance, 82
Private payment, 81
Problem solving, impaired, 352–353
'Pro bono' services, 86
Procedural memory, 285
Procedure codes, 81
Professional development, 110–111
Professional ethics
  American Occupational Therapy Association (AOTA) and, 68
  Code of Ethics overview, 64
  common law related to, 69–70
  disciplinary actions for violations of, 69
  in ethical decision-making, 68
  ethical jurisdiction of occupational therapy and, 68–70
  National Board for Certification in Occupational Therapy (NBCOT) and, 69
  Occupational Therapy Code of Ethics, 64–66
  patient/client abuse and neglect and, 67–68
  in practice, 67
  practitioner roles and, 70–71
  state regulatory boards and, 69
Program evaluation, 108–110
Progressive supranuclear palsy, 205
Prone tilting reflex, 120t
Proprioceptive neuromuscular facilitation (PNF), 343
Prospective memory, 285
Prospective payment system (PPS), 82
Prosthetic terminal devices (TDs), 176, 177t
Prosthetists, 76
Proximal phalanx fractures, 164
Psychiatric and cognitive disorders
  anxiety disorders, 296–297
  bipolar and related disorders, 290–293
  depressive disorders, 293
  diagnosis of, 286–287
  disruptive, impulse-control, and conduct disorders, 307
  feeding and eating disorders, 305–306
  interventions, 314–315
  neurocognitive disorders, 301–303, 302–303t, 304t
  neurodevelopmental disorders, 308–313, 309t
  obsessive-compulsive and related disorders, 298–299
  occupational therapy mental health evaluation for, 313–314
  occupational therapy mental health intervention for, 310–311
  personality disorders, 297–298
  reasonable accommodations for persons with, 402t
  schizophrenia spectrum and other psychotic disorders, 288–290
  signs and symptoms of, 284–286
  substance-related and addictive disorders, 294–295
  trauma- and stressor-related disorders, 300–301
Psychiatric rehabilitation, 369–370
Psychiatrists, 78, 286
Psychodynamic/psychoanalytic frames of reference, 365–366
Psychologists, 78
Psychology of successful test taking, 19–20, 20t
Psychomotor agitation, 285
Psychomotor retardation, 285
Psychosocial assessment, 242, 244, 370–371
Psychosocial development
  Abraham Maslow on, 128
  Erik Erikson on, 127–128
  Lawrence Kohlberg on, 128
  overview of, 127
  Ryan and Deci on, 128
Psychosocial frames of reference and models of practice
  cognitive disabilities, 363–364
  ecology of human performance (EHP) model, 361–362
  life-style performance model, 361
  model of human occupation (MOHO), 360
  occupational adaptation, 362
  overview of, 360
  person-environment-occupation model, 360
  psychodynamic/psychoanalytic, 365–366
  role acquisition, 362–363
  sensory models, 364–365
Psychosocial intervention
  general treatment considerations, 371–372
  group, 372–373
  group types, 373–375
  for managing difficult behaviors, 375–376
  role of OTA in, 371
  special considerations in, 376–381
Psychosomatic pain, 212
Psychotic disorders, 288–289
  diagnostic-specific considerations for occupational therapy, 290
  impact on function, 289
  symptom management in, 289
PTSD. See Post-traumatic stress disorder (PTSD)

Pulmonary disorders, pediatric
  bronchopulmonary dysplasia (BPD), 252–253
  cystic fibrosis (CF), 251–252
  respiratory distress syndrome (RDS), 252
Pulmonary edema, 239
Pulmonary emboli, 239
Pulmonary system, 235
Pulmonary system dysfunction
  acute diseases and, 235–236
  chronic obstructive diseases and, 237–238
  chronic restrictive diseases and, 238–239
  other conditions and, 239
  tuberculosis (TB) and, 236–237
Pulse, 241, 242t
Purdue Pegboard, 324, 325
Purposeful activities, 45–46
PVD. See Peripheral vascular disease (PVD)

Q

Quadraphonic approach to cognitive perceptual disorders, 354
Quadruped tilting reflex, 120t
Quality improvement, 108–110

R

RA. See Rheumatoid arthritis (RA)
Radial nerve injury, 167, 168f
Radial nerve palsy, 166
Rancho Los Amigos Levels of Cognitive Functioning Scale, 196–197t
Range of motion (ROM), 320–321, 321t, 322t
  interventions, 325–326, 326f
Raynaud's phenomenon, 233, 267
RDS. See Respiratory distress syndrome (RDS)
Reactive attachment disorder (RAD) of infancy or early childhood, 300
Reasonable accommodations, 94, 402t
Reauthorization and Amendment of Individuals with Disabilities Education Act (IDEA), 96
Receptive aphasia, 286
Recovery model, 368–369
Recreational therapists, 78
Re-evaluation/intervention review, 43–44
Referral for occupational therapy (OT), 32
Referred pain, 212
Reflex development and integration, 117, 118t, 119f
  persisting throughout life, 120t
Registered nurses (RP), 77
Regulations, health care, 80
Rehabilitation. See also Intervention
  cancer, 266
  cardiopulmonary, 244–251, 246–247b, 248t, 249f, 250t
  driver, 436–437
  immunological system disorders, 269–270
  psychiatric, 369–370
Rehabilitation Act of 1973, 93
Rehabilitation hospitals, 100
Reimbursement, documentation for, 89–90

Remedial/restorative/transfer of training approach to cognitive-perceptual disorders, 353
Remote memory, 285
Renal-genitourinary system disorders
　kidney disease, 261–264, 262b
　neurogenic bladder/UTI, 264
　stress incontinence, 264
Repetitive strain disorders (RSIs), 164–165
Residential program, 103–104
Respiration rate and depth, 241
Respiratory distress syndrome (RDS), 252
Respiratory hygiene, 58
Respiratory therapy technicians, certified, 78
Rest and sleep
　evaluation of, 403–404
　intervention for, 404
Restraint reduction, 438
Retrograde amnesia, 285
Rett's syndrome. See Known genetic condition
Reversible causes of mental confusion, 304t
Rheumatoid arthritis (RA), 169–171, 170f
Right-left indiscrimination, 352
Role acquisition, 362–363
ROM. See Range of motion (ROM)
Rood, Margaret, 343–344
Roofing reflex, 118t
Rotator cuff tendonitis, 168
Routine Task Inventory, 364
RSI. See Repetitive strain disorders (RSIs)
Rule of nines, 179, 179f
Rumination disorder, 306

S

Safe injection practices, 59
SARS (severe acute respiratory syndrome), 236
Scapula, 161–162
Scar
　hypertrophic, 180
　management of, 128
SCD. See Social (pragmatic) communication disorder (SCD)
Schizoaffective disorder, 288
Schizoid personality disorder, 298
Schizophrenia, 288–290
Schizophreniform disorder, 288
Schizotypal personality disorder, 298
Schools as practice settings, 101–102
SCI. See Spinal cord injury (SCI)
Scissor skills, 127
Scleroderma, 266–267
Scooters, 430
Screening in occupational therapy (OT), 32
Seating and positioning systems, 427–429
Secondary prevention, 38
Seizure disorders
　diagnostic criteria for, 217
　etiology of, 216
　impact on occupational performance, 217
　intervention for, 218
　medical management of, 217–218
　prevalence of, 216
　specific classifications and presenting signs and symptoms of, 216–217
Selective mutism, 296

Selective norepinephrine or serotonin and norepinephrine inhibitors (SNRIs), 292
Self, therapeutic use of, 49–50
Self-care development
　dressing, 134t
　feeding, 131–132, 133t
　home management tasks, 134–135t
　toileting skills, 134t
Self-care intervention, 389–390, 390t
Self-determination theory, 128
Self-harm, 380
Self-mutilation, 380
Self-reliance training, 368
Semantic memory, 285
Sensation, 323, 324t
Sensorimotor deficits, modifications for, 420–422, 420–422f
Sensorimotor development
　development of sensorimotor integration in, 116–117
　fetal, 116, 117t
　motor development, 121–127, 122–125t, 124f, 126f
　reflexes, 117, 118t, 119f, 120–121f, 120t
　sensory integration, 116–117
Sensory models, 364–365
Sensory-processing nosology, 214
Sensory processing disorders
　Ayres sensory integration approach for, 349–351
　environmental modifications for, 437–438
　etiology of, 213
　evaluation of, 215–216
　interventions for, 216
　medical management of, 215
　presenting signs and symptoms in, 214–215
　symptom classification in, 213–214
Sensory systems, age-related changes in, 144–147
Sensory training, 328
Separation anxiety disorder, 296
Service delivery models and practice settings
　community-based, 101–106
　institutional, 99–101
　models of practice, 98–99
　overview of, 98
　private/independent practice, 106
Service management. See Management
Severe neurocognitive disorder, 303t
Sexual expression/activity
　evaluation of, 388
　intervention for, 390–392
Shingles, 212
Shock, first aid for, 251
Short Portable Mental, 287
Short-term goals, 40
Shoulder
　adhesive capsulitis, 168
　anatomy of, 161
　dislocations of, 169
　rotator cuff tendonitis, 168
Sideward parachute (protective extension sideward) reflex, 120f, 120t
Skeletal system, age-related changes in, 142–143. See also Musculoskeletal system
Skier's thumb, 163
Skilled nursing facilities (SNFs), 100

Skin assessment, 241–242, 242t
Sleep, 403–404
Sliding boards, 430, 432
Small bowel obstruction, 261
Smart hubs/smart home platforms, 433–434
SNRIs. See Selective norepinephrine or serotonin and norepinephrine inhibitors (SNRIs)
Social (pragmatic) communication disorder (SCD), 310
Social phobia, 296
Social workers, 78–79
Somatoagnosia, 352
Spatial neglect, 355
Spatial relations dysfunction, 355
Spatial relations impairment, 353
Special educators/teachers, 79
Specific phobia, 296
Speech impairments, 285–286, 347–348
Speech-language pathologists (SLP), 79
Speech therapists (ST), 79
Sphygmomanometer, 322
Spina bifida, 202–203
Spinal cord, 189–191, 189f, 190t
Spinal cord injury (SCI), 198–199
Spinal muscular atrophy, 204–205
Spinocerebellar degenerations, 206
Spiritual care, 77
Splinting, 330–332
　in interventions for neuromotor dysfunction, 345–347
Splints, hand, 180
SRBs. See State regulatory boards (SRBs)
Standard Precautions, 57–59
Standing tilting reflex, 120t
State regulatory boards (SRBs), 2
　in ethical jurisdiction of occupational therapy, 69
Stereotypy, 285
Stimulants, 311
Strength increasing exercises, 327
Stress incontinence, 264
Stroke/cerebral vascular accident (CVA), 192–194, 193t
Structural cerebellar lesions, 205
Sub-acute care, 99
Substance abuse counselors, 79
Substance-related and addictive disorders, 294–295
Substance Use-Disorder Prevention that Promotes Optimal Recovery and Treatment (SUPPORT) for Patients and Communities Act, 93
Suck-swallow reflex, 118t
Suicide, 379–380
Sundowner syndrome, 284
Superficial vein thrombophlebitis, 234
Supervision, occupational therapy personnel, 71–74, 73t
　continuum of, 72
　general supervision information, 71
　methods of, 72
　specific roles and guidelines for, 72–74, 73t
Supine tilting and sitting tilting reflexes, 120t
Supported education programs, 102–103
Surgery, coronary artery disease (CAD) and, 231–232

869

Swallowing disorders, 258–260, 258f, 260f
Swan neck deformity, 170, 170f
Symmetric tonic neck reflex, 118t

T

Tangentiality, 286
Tardive dyskinesia, 289
Task/activity analysis and synthesis, 46
Task management strategy index items used by caregivers of persons living with dementia, 304t
Task-oriented approaches to motor control training, 338–340, 341–342t
TB. *See* Tuberculosis (TB)
TBI. *See* Traumatic brain injury (TBI)
TDs. *See* Prosthetic terminal devices (TDs)
Teaching-learning process, 46–48
Team roles and collaboration
   in addressing the environment, 411–412
   lay team members, 75–76
   overview of, 74
   paraprofessional team members, 76
   principles in, 74–75
   professional team members, 76–79
   types of teams and, 75
Technology, assistive, 432–435
Technology-related legislation, 95
Telehealth model, 99
Temporal lobe, 188
Tendon gliding exercises, 326f
Tertiary prevention, 38
Test center procedures for Certification Examination, 8–10
Testing accommodations, 5–6, 7t
Test-taking strategies for Certification Examination, 10–11, 11t
Textiles and laundry, 59
Thalamic pain, 211
Therapeutic groups, 50–56, 52t
Therapeutic recreation specialists, 78
Therapeutic use of self, 49–50
Thermal therapies, 332–333
Third-party payers, 82
Thought, disturbances of, 286
Thought blocking, 286
THR. *See* Total hip replacement (THR)
Thromboangiitis obliterans, 232–233
Ticket to Work and Work Incentives Improvement Act (TWIIA), 95
Toileting skills development, 134t
Tonic labyrinthine-prone reflex, 118t, 119f

Tonic labyrinthine-supine reflex, 118t, 119f
Tools of practice, occupational therapy (OT), 44–56
   clinical reasoning, 48–49
   definition, 44
   group process, therapeutic groups, and activity groups, 50–56, 52t
   occupation, 44–45
   purposeful activities, 45–46
   task/activity analysis and synthesis, 46
   teaching-learning process, 46–48
   therapeutic use of self, 49–50
Topographical disorientation, 353
Total hip arthroplasty, 174–175, 174f
Total hip replacement (THR), 174–175, 174f
Traction reflex, 118t
Transdisciplinary teams, 75
Transference, 49
Transfers, 431–432
Transient ischemic attack (TIA), 192
Transmission-based precautions, 60
Trauma, neurological
   cerebral palsy (CP), 199–200, 200t
   postconcussion syndrome, 195
   spinal cord injury (SCI), 198–199
   traumatic brain injury (TBI), 194–195, 195t, 196–197t
Trauma- and stressor-related disorders, 300–301
Traumatic brain injury (TBI), 194–195, 195t, 196–197t
Treatment authorization requests (TAR), 82
Tricyclics, 292
Trigger finger, 165
Tuberculosis (TB), 236–237

U

Ulcers, pressure/decubitus, 274–277, 275b, 275f
Ulnar nerve laceration, 167
Unilateral spatial neglect, 353
Universal design, 410–411t
Upper extremities
   amputations of, 175–178, 176f, 177t
   anatomy of, 158–160f, 158–161
   disorders and injuries of, 162–169, 163f, 165f, 167–168f
Upper motor neuron (UMN) syndromes, 191, 191t
Usual and customary rate (UCR), 82

V

Veins, 226, 227f
Vendors/suppliers, 82
Venous disease, 234
Veracity, 66
Viral pneumonia, 236
Vision, low
   evaluation of, 415–416
   intervention for, 416–417
Visual foundation skills, 353
Visual system, age-related changes in, 144–146
Vital signs, 240–241, 241t
Vocational programs, 103
Vocational rehabilitation counselors, 79
Voluntary accreditation, 80

W

Walkers, 430
Wellness and prevention programs, 106
Wernicke's aphasia, 351
Wheelchairs
   bariatric, 427
   components of, 424–425
   general assessment and prescription considerations for, 423
   measurements of, 425–426, 426t
   mobility training, 429–430
   purposes of, 423
   seating and positioning on, 423
   specific assessment and prescription considerations for, 423–424
   types of, 426–427, 426t
Whole body system disorders, 277–278
Work. *See also* Occupations
   assessment of, 398–399, 399t
   interventions for, 400–401f, 400–404, 402t
   prevocational assessment process for, 396, 397–398t
   specific programs for, 403
Worker safety, 59
Worker's compensation, 86
Work Investment Act (WIA), 95
Work simplification, 328–329
Wounds and pressure/decubitus ulcers, 274–277, 275b, 275f
Wrist
   anatomy of, 159–160f, 160
   peripheral nerve injuries of, 165–167, 167–168f
Wrist drop, 167, 168f